THIRD EDITION

The Art of M&A

A Merger/
Acquisition/
Buyout Guide

Stanley Foster Reed

Alexandra Reed Lajoux

McGraw-Hill

New York San Francisco Washington, D.C. Auckland Bogotá
Caracas Lisbon London Madrid Mexico City Milan
Montreal New Delhi San Juan Singapore
Sydney Tokyo Toronto

Library of Congress Cataloging-in-Publication Data

Reed, Stanley Foster.
     The art of M&A : a merger/acquisition/buyout guide / Stanley
  Foster Reed, Alexandra Reed Lajoux . — 3rd ed.
        p.   cm.
     Includes biographical references and index.
     ISBN 0-07-052660-5
     1. Consolidation and merger of corporations.   I. Lajoux,
  Alexandra Reed.   II. Title.   III. Title:
  Art of M and A.   V. Title: Art of M & A.
  HD2746.5.R44   1998
  658.1´6—dc21   98-45524

McGraw-Hill

*A Division of The **McGraw·Hill** Companies*

6 7 8 9 0 DOC/DOC 0 3 2

ISBN 0-07-052660-5

The sponsoring editor for this book was *Kelli Christiansen,* the editing supervisor was *John M. Morriss,* and the production supervisor was *Suzanne W. B. Rapcavage.* It was set in Times Roman by *Judy Brown.*

Printed and bound by R. R. Donnelley & Sons Company.

CONTENTS

PREFACE   vii

Chapter 1   **Getting Started in Mergers and Acquisitions   1**

Introduction. Basic Terms. Concluding Comments.

Chapter 2   **Planning and Finding   11**

Introduction. Strategic Planning for Operating Companies. In-House Search. Brokers and Finders. Using Intermediaries. Role of Investment and Commercial Banks in M&A. General Regulatory Considerations for Buyers. Antitrust Considerations for Acquisitions. Hart-Scott-Rodino. Concluding Comments. *Appendix 2A—Revision to the Horizontal Merger Guidelines Issued by the U.S. Department of Justice and the Federal Trade Commission.*

Chapter 3   **Valuation and Pricing   79**

Introduction. Valuation Fundamentals. Pricing Issues. Expressing the Purchase Price in the Acquisition Agreement. Concluding Comments. *Exhibit 3-1, Estimating the Cost of Capital.*

Chapter 4   **Financing and Refinancing   139**

Introduction. Highly Leveraged Transactions. Minimizing Borrowing. Pros and Cons of Preserving Debt and Lease Obligations. Determining Financing Structure. Senior Debt. Sale-Leasebacks. The Bank Book and Commitment Letter. Fraudulent Conveyance and Other Litigation Concerns. Other Principal Issues in Senior Loan Agreements. Insurance Company Financing. Junk Bonds. Bridge Loans. Equity Investment Funds. Seller Takeback Financing. Registration Rights. Intercreditor Issues. Subordination Issues. Intercreditor Agreements. Refinancing Issues. Concluding Comments. *Appendix 4A—Typical Subordination Provisions of Publicly Issued Notes. Appendix 4B—Typical Subordination Provisions of Privately Placed Institutional Notes. Appendix 4C—Typical Subordination Provisions of Seller Notes. Exhibit 4-1, Installment Sale Models.*

Chapter 5   Structuring M/A/B Transactions:
           General, Tax, and Accounting Considerations   255

Introduction. General Considerations. Tax Considerations. Accounting
Considerations. Concluding Comments. Transaction Diagrams.
*Figure 5-1, Stock Purchase. Figure 5-2, Asset Purchase. Figure 5-3,
Taxable Forward Merger. Figure 5-4, Taxable Reverse Merger.
Figure 5-5, Taxable Forward Subsidiary Merger. Figure 5-6, Tax-Free
Forward Merger (A Reorganization). Figure 5-7, Tax-Free Forward
Triangular Merger [Hybrid A Reorganization—Section 368 (a)(2)(D)].
Figure 5-8, Tax-Free Acquisition of Stock for Voting Stock (B Reorganization).
Figure 5-9, Acquisition of Property for Voting Stock (C Reorganization).
Figure 5-10, Acquisition of Property for Voting Stock (D Reorganization).
Figure 5-11, National Starch Transaction (Section 351 Acquisition).*

Chapter 6   The Due Diligence Inquiry   347

Introduction. Getting Started. Litigation Analysis. Environmental
Exposure Analysis. Emerging Legal Issues. Do-It-Yourself Due
Diligence. Assessing Information. Duration of Due Diligence.
Concluding Comments. *Appendix 6A—Due Diligence Checklist.
Appendix 6B—Sample Confidentiality Agreement.*

Chapter 7   Pension, Labor, and Compensation Concerns   387

Introduction. Compensation Basics. Employee Benefit Plans. Determining
Plan Assets and Liabilities and Their Effect on Company Books. Plan
Split-Ups and Partial Terminations. Underfunded and Overfunded
Plans. Employee Stock Ownership Plans. ESOP Securities Issues. Using
Non-ESOP Stock Plans. Plans Holding Stock. Effect of Corporate Structure.
Problems in Acquisitions of Unionized Companies. Concluding Comments.

Chapter 8   Negotiating the Letter of Intent and the Acquisition Agreement   445

Introduction. The Letter of Intent. The Acquisition Agreement.
Components of the Agreement. Introductory Material. Representations and
Warranties. Covenants. Conditions to Closing. The Indemnity Section.
Termination Procedures. Auctions. Acquisitions from an Affiliated
Group. Transactions Involving Public Companies. Negotiating and
Documenting an MBO. Employment Agreements. Stockholders'
Agreements. Concluding Comments. About the Appendices.
*Appendix 8A—Sample Letter of Intent.   Appendix 8B—Typical Merger
Agreement and Commentary.*

Chapter 9 Closing 611

Introduction. The Basics of Closing. Pre-Closing. Closing. Wire Transfers. Post-Closing. Planning Aids. Closing Memorandum. Concluding Comments. *Appendix 9A—Merger of Target Acquisition Corp. into Target Co. Inc. Closing Memorandum.*

Chapter 10 Postmerger Integration 643

Introduction. Postmerger Performance: The Basics. Integration Elements in the Acquisition Agreement. The Integration Plan. The Role of Outsiders in Planning M&A Integration. Communicating the Integration Plan. Integrating Human Resources. Integrating Assets (on Paper and in Reality). Integrating Commitments to Employees. Concluding Comments. *Appendix 10A— Principles for Business: The Caux Round Table. Appendix 10B—A Master Checklist for Postmerger Integration.*

Chapter 11 Workouts and Bankruptcies 697

Introduction. Workouts. Bankruptcies. Prepackaged Bankruptcies. State Insolvency Procedures. Investment Opportunities. Bankruptcy Information Sources. Concluding Comments.

Chapter 12 Special Issues for M&A in Public Companies 723

Introduction. Legal and Business Considerations. Tender Offer Basics. Proxy Solicitation Disclosures. Merger Disclosure Issues. Director Responsibilities in Responding to Unsolicited Bids. Insider Trading. Financing the Public Transaction. Considerations Applicable to Hostile Acquisitions. Antitrust Defenses. Restructuring Defenses. Poison Pills. Charter and Bylaw Amendments. Defensive Sales or Acquisitions. Defensive Payments. Related State Laws. Concluding Comments.

Chapter 13 M&A in Family Businesses, Partnerships, Franchises, and Nonprofits 799

Introduction. Family Businesses. Partnerships. Franchises. Nonprofits. Concluding Comments.

Chapter 14 Beyond M&A: Spin-Offs and Strategic Alliances 817

Introduction. Spin-Offs. Strategic Alliances. Concluding Comments. *Appendix 14A—The AT&T Spin-Offs. Appendix 14B—The Joint Venture Agreement: A Checklist from the Regional and Economic Development Services of Saskatchewan, Canada. Appendix 14C—Diagrams. Exhibit 14-1, Spin-Offs. Exhibit 14-2, Split-Offs. Exhibit 14-3, Split-Ups.*

Chapter 15   Special Issues for Transactions with International Aspects   839

Introduction. Nontax Issues Regarding Foreign Investment in the United
States (Inbound). Nontax Issues Regarding U.S. Investment Abroad
(Outbound). International Tax and Disclosure Considerations. Tax
Considerations in Inbound Acquisitions. Tax Considerations in Outbound
Acquisitions. Concluding Comments.

Epilogue   M&A in the New Millennium   903

Introduction. The Megamerger Wave. The "Merger Wave" Concept.
Problems with the Merger Wave Concept. The First Wave (Crest: 1890s).
The Second Wave (Crest: 1920s). The Third Wave (Crest: 1960s). The
Fourth Wave (Crest: 1980s). The Fifth Wave (Crest: 1990s). The Sixth
Wave. M&A: The Ultimate Entrepreneurship.

Case   A WOFC Case Study: J.T. Smith Consultants   927

The Case. The WOFC Sessions. Discussion and Observations. Growth
Variables. Marketing-Related Variables. Operations. The Market
Intensification Mode. The Vertical Integration Mode. The Diversification
Mode. *Exhibit Case-1, Schedule for J.T. Smith Strategic Planning Meeting.*
Exhibit Case-2, Strength Analysis (Fit Chart Supplement). Exhibit Case-3,
Weakness Analysis (Fit Chart Complement). Exhibit Case-4, Description of
Potential Variables. Exhibit Case-5, Opportunity Description. Exhibit
Case-6, Stanley Foster Reed's Systems Approach to Corporate Growth.
Exhibit Case-7, Instant Delphi Tally Sheet for Fit Chart. Exhibit Case-8,
Fit Chart: J.T. Smith Consultants. Exhibit Case-9, A Wheel of Opportunity
for J.T. Smith Consultants.

TABLE OF CASES   969

LANDMARK LEGAL CASE SUMMARIES   973

INDEX   995

PREFACE

Early on in Homer's *Odyssey,* Athena, the goddess of wisdom, urges young Telemachus to "question old King Nestor" about an important matter, but the young man hesitates. "Someone my age might feel shy . . . interrogating an older man," he explains.[1]

If you sometimes feel the same way about approaching a seasoned merger/acquisitions/buyout specialist, you are not alone.

Telemachus's attitude lives on in the arena of M&A and buyouts, where even the most inexperienced executives and professionals are expected to know it all before they begin their journey.

The same principle operates across business and professional lines. Whether the subject is SBUs, S corporations, or swaps, everyone—newcomer and old hand alike—is expected to nod knowingly. Few have the courage to ask "What does that mean?" or "How does that work?"

This is unfortunate, because only good questions, given good answers, foster true learning. That is why this 1999 edition of our M&A "classic" preserves the question-and-answer format used in the original text.

What is a good question? What is a good answer? These change almost daily in the fast-paced M&A field.

The Art of M&A: A Merger/Acquisition/Buyout Guide, third edition, attempts to provide accurate and practical answers to over 1,000 questions you are likely to confront now or in the near future as a principal or an advisor when you buy or sell companies, whether public or private, domestic or foreign.

What is your burning question of the moment? It may be as basic as "What is a merger?" Or it may be as arcane as "Who is liable for tax on the sale of stock in a Section 338 election?" In either case, you need correct and current answers. Fortunately, you can find them here.

This book began at the height of the 1980s merger boom as the "joint effort of an entrepreneur and a law firm," as the first edition noted. The entrepreneur was Stanley Foster Reed and the law firm was Lane and Edson, P.C. Alexandra Reed Lajoux served as project manager. This new edition, with

Reed as principal author and Lajoux as coauthor, contains many of the gems contributed in that first effort. Although Lane and Edson no longer exists as a law firm, the original contributions of its many brilliant principals—acknowledged in the first edition—continue to shine through in these pages. To these attorneys and the professionals cited below, the authors express enduring thanks.

Chapter 1, Getting Started in Mergers and Acquisitions, and *Chapter 2, Planning and Finding,* still contain wisdom from Dr. Robert H. Rock, President, MLR Holdings, Philadelphia, and Charles E. Fiero, Co-Chairman, MLR Holdings; Robert F. Burgess, Jr., Growth Strategies, Ltd., Alexandria, Virginia; Edward A. Weihman, Wasserstein Perella, New York City; Malcolm Pfunder of Hopkins, Sutter, Hamel & Park, Washington, D.C.; Gerald Wetlaufer, Professor of Business Law, Indiana University, Bloomington; Clive Chajet, Chairman, Lippincott and Margulies, New York City; and Mark Feldman, Partner, PricewaterhouseCoopers (formed from two predecessor firms). In addition, these chapters benefit from research conducted by the authors and referenced in the endnotes. Also, recent conversations with Bob Bates, an independent broker in Falls Church, Virginia, added valuably to the Chapter 2 section on finders and brokers. Whitney Adams, principal, Madison Financial Group, Washington, D.C., provided commentary and information on the subject of business and economic research. The authors also gratefully acknowledge the guidance of Martin Sikora, Editor, *Mergers & Acquisitions;* Thomas West, publisher, *M&A Today;* and Russell Robb, Editor, *M&A Today,* and Vice President, O'Conor, Wright, Wyman, Inc.

Chapter 3, Valuation and Pricing, still benefits from the expertise of Al Rappaport, Principal, The LEK/Alcar Consulting Group, La Jolla, California; and various partners at Wesray Capital Corporation, New York City. This chapter has been revised extensively, however. It features models developed by the principal author, Stanley Foster Reed.

Chapter 4, Financing and Refinancing, still contains the canny expertise of Lane and Edson attorneys credited in the first edition. Coverage here is updated and expanded—with extensive discussion on lease-based financing from Robert Neal, Managing Director, Newcourt Capital, Brookfield, Connecticut, a subsidiary of the Toronto-based Newcourt Credit Group.

Chapter 5, Structuring M/A/B Transactions: General, Tax, and Accounting Situations, remains heavily indebted to E. Burke Ross, Jr., Principal, Wesray Capital Corporation, and Harold Nidetz, Partner, Ernst &

Young, Chicago. New guidance in this third edition has come from several attorneys at the law firm of Jones, Day, Reavis & Pogue, whose detailed guide to the Taxpayer Relief Act of 1997 (cited in the endnotes) was very helpful in highlighting and interpreting the most important sections of this extremely complex law. The authors would also like to acknowledge the expert guidance of Martin D. Ginsberg, Professor of Law, Georgetown University Law Center, Washington, D.C., and Jack S. Levin, Lecturer, University of Chicago Law School—and by extension their affiliated law firms. (Professor Ginsberg's professional firm is of counsel to the law firm of Fried, Frank, Harris, Shriver & Jacobson; and Professor Levin, through his professional firm, is a senior partner with the law firm of Kirkland & Ellis.) In updating this chapter, the authors relied heavily on the most recent edition of their two-volume, biannual reference work, *Mergers, Acquisitions, and Buyouts: A Transactional Analysis of the Governing Tax, Legal, and Accounting Considerations* (New York: Aspen Law & Business, 1998).

Chapter 6, The Due Diligence Inquiry, contains a checklist with elements suggested by Dan L. Goldwasser, an attorney based in New York City, and expanded by the authors.

Chapter 7, Pension, Labor, and Compensation Concerns, contains extensive discussion of employee stock ownership plans. As in the past, this discussion features information and insights provided by Corey Rosen of the National Center for Employee Ownership in Oakland, California. In this third edition, this chapter contains additional guidance from Dickson C. Buxton, Cofounder of Private Capital Corporation and former Chairman of Kelso and Company. It also includes materials from the coauthor's new book, *The Art of M&A Integration: A Guide to Merging Resources, Processes, and Responsibilities* (New York: McGraw-Hill, 1998). The chapter benefited from the compensation experts consulted for that book, including Edwin Lewis, President, Lewis Consulting International, Westport, Connecticut; Alan Johnson, Managing Partner, Johnson Associates, Inc., New York City; and Aaron Berg, President, Pentech Corporation, Parsippany, New Jersey. The accounting aspects of postmerger compensation were provided by Scott Hakala and Travis Keath, of Business Valuation Services in Houston, Texas; Andrew Malec of Plante & Moran in Southfield, Michigan; and Dr. Robert Stobaugh, Emeritus Professor of the Harvard Business School.

Chapter 8, Negotiating the Letter of Intent and the Acquisition Agreement, and *Chapter 9, Closing,* still contain much from the Lane and Edson principals credited in the first edition.

Chapter 10, Postmerger Integration, is adapted from *The Art of M&A Integration,* cited above as a source for Chapter 7. As such, Chapter 10 owes a debt to many of the 50 postmerger experts consulted for that book. J. Fred Weston, Cordner Professor of Money and Financial Markets at the Graduate School of Management, University of California at Los Angeles, provided guidance in financial performance research. Planning expertise was provided by George A. Steiner, Kunin Professor of Management Emeritus at UCLA. Comments on the role of third parties in postmerger planning were provided by William J. Altier, CMC, President, Princeton Associates, Buckingham, Pennsylvania. Mark J. Feldman, an advisor to Chapter 1, imparted wisdom and experience on the importance of position statements in postmerger planning. Observations on the typical merger agreement came from Gabor Garai, of Epstein, Becker & Green, Boston. Eugene Grossman, Chairman, Anspach Grossman Enterprise, New York City, provided the "Audience/Media Communications Matrix." Information on noncompete agreements came from Lawrence F. Carnevale, Litigation Partner, Carter, Ledyard & Milburn, New York City. Guidance on integrated financial statements came from Kermit D. Larson, Arthur Andersen & Co. Alumni Professor of Accounting at the University of Texas at Austin. Valuation materials in this chapter were provided by Hakala, Keith, and Malec, cited earlier as sources for Chapter 7.

Chapter 11, Workouts and Bankruptcies, retains some of the information originally provided by Michael P. Marsalese, Esq., Adjunct Professor at Wayne State University in Detroit, and an attorney in private practice in Troy, Michigan.

Chapter 12, Special Issues for M&A in Public Companies, contains answers provided by Robert D. Ferris, President, Ruder & Finn Investor Relations, New York City; and James J. Hanks, Jr., partner, Ballard Spahr Andrews & Ingersoll, Baltimore.

Chapter 13, M&A in Family Businesses, Partnerships, Franchises, and Nonprofits, and *Chapter 14, Beyond M&A: Spin-Offs and Strategic Alliances,* are new to this edition. The authors wish to extend special thanks to J. Fred Weston (cited above in the credits for Chapter 10) for his contributions to Chapter 14.

Chapter 15, Special Issues for Transactions with International Aspects, includes materials originally provided by Van Kirk Reeves, Partner, Porter and Reeves, Paris, France, and Riccardo R. Trigona, a former Lane and Edson associate now in private practice in Rome, Italy. For this edition, we have consulted other international attorneys as well. They are credited in the endnotes. The authors also wish to thank the principals of Capital Management, Tokyo, Japan, for general guidance on international M&A. Capital Management is a joint venture of Deloitte Touche Tohmatsu and IntellAsset.

Our *Epilogue, M&A in the New Millennium,* is based on extensive readings and, but owes its greatest debt to the classic work of the late, great historian Ralph Nelson and to Bruce Wasserstein, Chairman and CEO, Wasserstein Perella & Co., author of *Big Deal,* cited herein. The *WOFC Case Study: J. T. Consultants* is a composite case based on consulting work by the principal author.

The *Table of Cases* and *Landmark Legal Case Summaries* concluding this book expand upon the prior work of Michael Marsalese, mentioned above. Information on the *Healthco* case came from Mark W. Parry, Esq., Partner, Moses & Singer, L.L.P., and Robert Stobaugh, cited in the credits to Chapter 7.

The authors also wish to extend thanks to Misty Grooms and Travis Piazza of Reed Associates, and Mary Graham and Braulio Agnese of Alexis & Co. Their skills all made a vital difference. Last but not least, the authors wish to thank the fine professionals at McGraw-Hill for their encouragement and expertise—especially Kelli Christiansen, our top-notch sponsoring editor; Judy Duguid, our fine-handed copy editor; Judy Brown, our miracle-working typesetter; Edwin Durbin, our thorough indexer; and to John Morriss, editorial supervisor *par excellence.* Thanks also to publisher Jeffrey Krames for his continuing commitment to the "big book."

TRENDS

This third edition comes during a time of rapid consolidation in many major industries, with parallel activities in the fields of deal advisors. In the past 10 years (from January 1988 through December 1997) the world has seen 124,598 completed deals, worth almost $6 trillion. During this time, the overall trend has been upward—in both deals and dollars. Big deals are getting bigger as corporations test new heights in scale. Meanwhile, small deals continue to proliferate.

In 1997, AT&T stunned the financial world when it announced that it was in merger discussions (soon canceled) with SBC Communications Corp. The combined firm would have been worth $50 billion—a staggering amount at the time. Yet now as we go to press in late 1998, this figure no longer seems gargantuan—considering 1998 announcements of mergers between BankAmerica and NationsBank (worth $60 billion) and between Citicorp and Travelers Group Inc. (worth $83 billion). The value of announced deals involving U.S. companies during the first half of 1998 was over $1 trillion—an all-time record—boosted by *dozens* of multibillion-dollar transactions. Advisors aren't flinching because they too are involved in massive consolidations—notably within major accounting, consulting, and law firms.

But megadeals are still only a small percentage of the transactions that go on day in and day out in the heartlands of countries around the world. According to Securities Data Company of Newark, New Jersey (courtesy of Richard Peterson and Carrie Smith), the total number of M&A transactions completed worldwide in 1997 was 15,891, valued at $1,011,638 million (or just over $1 trillion). That gives us an average deal value (not counting transactions worth less than $5 million) of only $63.7 million—hardly beyond the grasp of most major companies.

Whether crafted in times of M&A boom or bust, whether valued at many billions or a few million, each deal must be planned, valued, financed, and structured. Each one must be checked out through due diligence, described in a written agreement, and formally closed. All these phases are described here—and augmented through special-issue chapters. This edition includes newly expanded guidance on buying troubled companies. It also features for the first time a chapter on postmerger integration, as well as one treating issues "beyond M&A" in the realms of spin-offs and strategic alliances. New to this edition also is guidance on issues faced by family businesses, franchises, partnerships, and nonprofits. The concluding chapter of this book is a big-picture review of M&A movements past and future.

In this new edition, we have spared few fine points and have provided much fine print in an attempt to teach the most important mechanics of the dealmaking process. We hope they get you where you need to go, whether you are just beginning your M&A journey or are already well on your way.

If you wish to contact Stanley Foster Reed, please feel free at: reeds@cofc.edu. If you wish to contact Alexandra Reed Lajoux, please feel free at: arlajoux@aol.com. We look forward to hearing from you.

E N D N O T E S

1. Quoted from Homer, *The Odyssey,* translated by Robert Fagles (New York: Penguin, 1997), p. 108.

CHAPTER 1

Getting Started in Mergers and Acquisitions

A little learning is a dangerous thing.
Drink deep or taste not the Pierian spring.
There shallow draughts intoxicate the brain,
And drinking largely sobers us again.

—Alexander Pope

INTRODUCTION

Perhaps nowhere else does Pope's maxim prove more true than in the merger/acquisition/buyout (m/a/b) area. The purchase or sale of a business enterprise is one of the most complex transactions a person or a firm can undertake. It has proved to be a make-or-break decision for leaders of many major corporations. And for many small business owners, the sale of a business is a once-in-a-lifetime thing. They must know what they are doing.

In the fall of 1965, the principal author of this book launched the first issue of *Mergers & Acquisitions* (*M&A*) magazine, prefacing it as follows:

Dedicated to the Ever-Renewing Corporate Society
As we take part in this third great wave of merger and acquisition activity in America, we are struck by the rate of economic growth, and by the speed with which corporations are merging and being formed. Research indicates that at present rates one out of every three corporations will either merge or be acquired

1

during the next ten years. This makes change the condition by which we grow and develop.

Each day here in the United States one thousand new businesses are born. Some drive for the heights like a great Fourth of July rocket and end in a burst of color—a hasty life, beautiful but short. . . . A few, carried on a quick tide of youthful energy and special knowledge, will grow great and strong and eventually wise and will become a shelter for the less strong and the less wise.

This is the ever-renewing corporate society.[1]

As this prologue shows, *M&A* magazine was founded with one clear goal in mind: to show buyers and sellers of companies how to create strategies—and shelter—for continued growth in a world of constant change.

The authors had this same purpose in mind when they teamed up with the law firm of Lane and Edson, P.C., to produce the first edition of this guidebook at the height of the leveraged buyout movement in the mid-1980s.

However, as deals structures changed under the weight of hundreds of legal precedents and new accounting rules, a major revision in the basic text proved necessary, and the second edition followed in the mid-1990s.

And now, at the fin de siècle, this third edition is born, again reflecting hundreds of changes in the economic and regulatory life of the M&A movement, which now seems to know no bounds—of either space or time. Deals that seemed big yesterday seem small today—and transactions that once took months of courtship are now sealed in a day. And as the months go by, so do the deals—at an ever-increasing pace.

The year 1997 closed with over 15,891 deals completed worldwide, valued at over $1 trillion, according to Securities Data Company in Newark, New Jersey. And, contrary to previous years, most of the deals were "strategic." That is, they involved synergies: deals where there was some economic relationship (either actual or potential) between the buyer and seller, or between the mergees, that would enhance the bottom line—whether the products involved were pharmaceuticals, movies, digital communications, or computer chips.

This present merger movement is different from recent movements in that many of its deals are done with equity interests, driven by the highest stock prices in terms of earnings multiples in over 60 years.

In spite of the euphoria that many of us involved with the M&A phenomenon feel when we see the unfolding of what the principal author predicted 33 years ago, we can't emphasize enough how complex and dangerous the merger process can be.

As in all past merger movements, there are always some major disasters. The "urge to merge" motivates many successful CEOs, who suffer "the winners' curse" whenever they overpay, or worse, overleverage themselves to fund a major entry.

Just as there are fashions and fads in clothes, toys, and computer games, so there are fashions and fads in the M&A field. Intrigued by the management buyout of Macy's, and without waiting to discover how that famous deal would work out, Canadian shopping center genius-king Robert Campeau, who never made mistakes, and never me-tooed anyone before, paid $612 million in lawyer, accounting, investment, and commercial banking fees to take over Allied Department Stores, which included high-glamour names like Brooks Brothers and Ann Taylor, paying $4.1 billion and loading himself with debt at mind-numbing interest rates. Later he bought Federated Department Stores, which owned New York's famed Bloomingdale's and Boston's Filene's. In time, he added Miami's Burdine's and Los Angeles's Bullock's, and all of this on mountains of borrowed money. Bankruptcy followed like a shadow—because Campeau had a blind spot: He didn't know merchandising. Meanwhile, Macy's went into bankruptcy because its top merchandiser, Ed Finkelstein, who honchoed the buyout, didn't know finance; he knew even less about management, and complicated the deal by excessive "greed, ambition, and folly."[2]

So, reader, remember, it's not all sweetness and light out there. There's a Jurassic Park of flesh-eating monsters waiting to pounce on the fad-following M&A enthusiast.

One dramatic case in point is old-line Quaker Oats, which, basking in the glow of many years of profits from its long-ago acquisition of Gatorade, in late 1994 paid $1.7 billion for high-flying Snapple, the king of the new and sexy "alternate beverages business." But Quaker, to its horror, discovered that melding Snapple with Gatorade was a no-no with their distributors! With annual sales at only the $550 million level, Snapple lost so much money that Quaker, in desperation, sold it off in early 1997 for only $300 million, the biggest deal disaster since Novell bought WordPerfect for nearly $1 billion and sold it off for one-fifth the price a few years later. Deal-addicted CEOs act like the Energizer Bunny and just keep going and going until they make the Big Mistake!

And there are always problems for the tyro acquisitor. The accounting rules have always been a problem because the accounting profession writes special rules when it comes to mergers and acquisitions. For instance, the accounting profession insists that when a noncash merger or acquisition takes place, the transaction be booked using the quoted price for the stock on a particular day. But many things can affect the price on that particular day. It can sell one day for $10 during negotiations, and in two weeks, at the closing, have a market price of $20. The books, by accounting fiat, must reflect the $20 price—and that $20 price must be maintained for decades even though, the day after closing, the stock went back to $10 (which was evidently all it was really worth). In the M&A world, the real problem is that buyers and sellers alike begin to believe that stock is equivalent to cash because the accountants told them to record it that way. Reality accounting is called for in M&A analysis. Although you are stuck with the rules in keeping the books, you are not stuck with them in pricing out an acquisition.

In this new environment, acquirers and sellers large and small must drink at the ever-renewing spring of M&A knowledge. To drink deep, they must recognize first that there is something called an acquisition process going on, with many crucial stages and many key players. To carry out any one stage well requires solid grounding in the entire process. In the spirit of Pope's caveat, this book sets forth the basic elements of the acquisition process as it is conducted today, reflecting the technical requirements, the negotiating points, the language, and the objectives of those who actually do these deals or help others to do them.

Each of the players plays a different role, and so we have tried to reflect the differing perspectives of buyer and seller and the contrasting views of two main types of buyer: (1) the operator-buyer, who makes what are called "strategic" acquisitions supplementing or complementing existing operations, and (2) the investor-buyer, who makes "financial" acquisitions in order to operate the acquired company as an independent, nonintegrated entity in order to repay acquisition debt and eventually resell it or take it public.

BASIC TERMS

Following are some general definitions for those without a background in the basics.

What is a merger?

The word *merger* has a strictly legal meaning and has nothing to do with how the combined companies are to be operated in the future.

A merger occurs when one corporation is combined with and disappears into another corporation. For instance, the Missouri Corporation, just like the river, merges and disappears corporately into the Mississippi Corporation. Missouri Corporation stock certificates are turned in and exchanged for Mississippi stock certificates. Holes are punched in the Missouri certificates, and they are all stuck in the vault. The Missouri Corporation has ceased to exist. Missouri is referred to as the *decedent,* while the Mississippi Corporation is known as the *survivor.*

All mergers are *statutory* mergers, since all mergers occur as specific formal transactions in accordance with the laws, or *statutes,* of the states where they are incorporated. The Missouri Corporation must follow Missouri law, and the Mississippi Corporation, Mississippi law. However, there are rarely major differences between states. (Overseas it's different.)

The post-deal manner of operating or controlling a company has no bearing on whether or not a merger has occurred. It is misleading for a prospective acquirer to state to a prospective seller, "We don't do acquisitions. We only do mergers," implying that the two groups will go skipping hand-in-hand into the future as equal partners in enterprise, when in fact, and by statute law, one corporation is owned and (without an agreement by the stockholders to the contrary) is controlled by another.

A corporate consolidation is a special legal form of merger. It's like the Monongahela and the Allegheny Rivers, which meet at Pittsburgh to form the Ohio River. Monongahela and Allegheny shares are turned in for shares in the Ohio Corporation, which was formed for the specific purpose of receiving them. The Monongahela and Allegheny Corporations cease to exist after the consolidation. In that case, rather than survivor, the Ohio Corporation is usually called the successor. (Do not confuse the legal word *consolidation* with the operating word *consolidation,* which has recently gained currency to describe the process of making a series of acquisitions in one industry—like buying up golf courses one after another—and "consolidating" the operations.)

What is a corporate acquisition?

A *corporate acquisition* is the process by which the stock or assets of a corporation come to be owned by a buyer. The transaction may take the form of a purchase of stock or a purchase of assets.

What's the difference between a merger and an acquisition?

Acquisition is the generic term used to describe a transfer of ownership. *Merger* is a narrow, technical term for a particular legal procedure that may or may not follow an acquisition. For example, Mississippi and Missouri shareholders agree to merge, and the merger is effected by Mississippi calling in Missouri stock in exchange for Mississippi stock or cash.

Much more common is an acquisition in which no subsequent merger occurs. For example, Mississippi acquires a significant amount of Missouri stock, even enough for a merger, but Mississippi decides that the Missouri Corp. should remain permanently as a separate, corporate subsidiary of the Mississippi Corp., although no one may know it except the lawyers. Or Mississippi acquires all or most of Missouri's assets, paying for them with cash or Mississippi shares, leaving Missouri as a shell corporation with no operations and its stockholders unchanged. It has one principal asset: Mississippi shares.

In a merger, which gets to be the survivor? Is it always the larger company?

No. For tax and other reasons, sometimes big Mississippi Corporation might be merged into little Missouri Corporation with Missouri the survivor. Size of operations, net worth, number of employees, who winds up as chairman, even the name selected, have nothing to do with which company is the corporate survivor.

What is a short-form merger?

When all or substantially all the stock of one corporation is owned by another corporation, a simplified, *short-form merger* is generally permitted under state law without a vote of stockholders. Other than short-form mergers, all mergers require an affirmative vote of stockholders of both corporations, and all sales of all or substantially all the assets of a corporation require the affirmative vote of the selling but not necessarily of the buying corporation's stockholders.

What is an amalgamation?

This is not a term of art in the United States. Any group of entities can associate together, or amalgamate, operationally with no corporate ownership in common.

What is a leveraged buyout?

A *leveraged buyout* (LBO) is a transaction in which a company's capital stock or its assets are purchased with borrowed money, causing the company's new capital structure to be primarily debt. An acquisition of all the selling corporation's stock, usually by a new corporation created by the buyer for that sole purpose, will be immediately followed by a merger of the buyer's new corporation and the acquired company, so that the assets of the acquired corporation become available to the buyer-borrower to secure debt.

There are several types of leveraged buyouts:

- Management buyouts (MBOs), in which a key ingredient is bringing in the existing management team as shareholders
- Employee buyouts (EBOs), in which the employees, using funds from an employee stock ownership plan (ESOP), most of which will have been borrowed, buy out the company's owners
- Restructurings, in which a major part of the acquired assets is subsequently sold off to retire the debt that financed the transaction

What is a recapitalization?

This is not an acquisition, but it can make a company look as if it had just gone through an LBO. In a *recapitalization,* or *recap,* a public company, principally for takeover defense, reconfigures the right side of its balance sheet, adding more debt and reducing its equity through a buyback of its shares. It is an extremely effective maneuver for cash-rich or creditworthy companies to discourage prospective acquirers who have counted on using target company cash and credit to finance their deal.

What is a hostile acquisition?

A *hostile acquisition,* also called a *hostile takeover* or an *unsolicited bid,* is an offer to buy shares in a public company's stock that is initially rejected by the board of the target company or target.

What is a target?

The term *target* has two meanings—one narrow and one broad. In its narrow meaning, consistent with the use of the term target in a military or sporting sense, a target is the object of a hostile acquisition. In its broad sense, a target is any company that may be, is being, or has been acquired by another company.

Acquirers tend to use the term *target* for all types of transactions. By contrast, sellers avoid this word because of its hostile (and even demeaning) overtones. In this book, we will not say "target" unless we mean the object of a hostile acquisition. The one exception to our rule will be in the appendix to Chapter 8, presenting a typical acquisition agreement. Because most acquisition agreements use the term *target* in a broad sense, we will too.

What are friendly transactions?

Friendly transactions are negotiated deals struck voluntarily by both buyers and sellers. The vast majority of acquisitions today are of this kind. They are based on mutual accommodation of the interests of two or more parties who believe they will be better off together than apart if they can just work things out.

Will this book cover both takeovers and friendly transactions?

Yes, but it will concentrate on friendly deals. The objective of this book is to acquaint the specialist and the nonspecialist alike with the basics of the friendly negotiated acquisition, including the financial, legal, accounting, and business practices and rules that govern deals done today. It is also intended to give the reader some feel for the way that today's deals are being negotiated.

How is this book organized?

The chapters of the book follow the basic sequence of the acquisition process, from planning, finding, and pricing through financing, structuring, investigation, and negotiation of acquisition agreements right up to the closing. Much of the content of these chapters is advanced and sophisticated material; it wouldn't be very useful if it were not.

Working things out involves exploring the answers to many serious questions. Is there a fit between our operations? Exactly what does each party bring to the table? How much should we pay? What kind of financing can be obtained? How much control will a financing third party want? Should we do a forward or a reverse merger? What sort of investigation should we make of each other? What should the obligations of the parties be under the acquisition agreement? How do we bring all the parties to a closing?

We chose the question-and-answer format for the book for one reason: As Socrates said, asking the right question is as important as getting the right answer. There is much myth surrounding the M&A process. The authors have worked very hard to dispel those myths as they and various specialists ask and answer the down-to-earth, difficult questions. At the same time, this book is designed to be read straight through for those who are involved in or intrigued by the m/a/b process in which, annually, many billions of dollars change hands—in the purchase of not only huge companies or of major interests in them, but the tens of thousands of smaller companies that are bought and sold from Peoria to Paris.

To find a particular piece of information in this book, use the index. If you have a name for the specific point—if you want to know about "fraudulent conveyance" or the "Herfindahl-Hirschmann Index," for example—look it up directly in the index. If the point has a number but not a name—for example, "Section 338" or "Rule 10b-5"—look it up under "Section" or "Rule" in the index noting the source. (For example, both the U.S. tax code and U.S. securities law have well-known "sections.") If you want to review a broad area of the acquisition process—for example, "financing"—look up that area in the index and there you will find the book's entire coverage of that area, organized alphabetically by each aspect of financing that appears in the book.

Throughout the book, where legal cases contribute important precedent, we have provided brief descriptions in the text. Cases not only appear in the index but are listed in alphabetical order in the table of legal cases in the back of this book. The most important cases in the m/a/b area are fully described in the landmark case summaries, also found in the back of this book.

CONCLUDING COMMENTS

This book aims to be comprehensive, but it cannot claim to be exhaustive in all areas. After all, there are not that many universalities or even commonalities to the merger process—especially those that involve the growing and constantly changing field of transnational agreements and financings.

What we have accomplished, however, is to create a sourcebook in readable form where the entrepreneur and the professional alike can find not only the answers to a myriad of M&A-related questions, but, more important, the questions that must (or at least should) be asked about the M&A process when one gets involved in its complexities.

It's the latter that makes the M&A process an art and not a science.

Drink deep!

E N D N O T E S

1. Stanley Foster Reed, "Dedicated to the Ever-Renewing Corporate Society," *Mergers & Acquisitions* Fall 1965, p. 3.
2. Jeffrey A. Trachtenberg, *The Rain on Macy's Parade: How Greed, Ambition, and Folly Ruined Americas Greatest Store* (New York: Random House, 1996).

CHAPTER 2

Planning and Finding

INTRODUCTION

This chapter addresses the first two stages in the merger/acquisition/buyout process—deciding what to buy and then finding it. In the first stage, the potential buyer determines the characteristics that it wants in a company. In the second stage, it seeks to identify specific companies that meet or approximate its criteria.

But there are two kinds of buyers: those looking to buy something to operate as part of a larger whole and those looking strictly for a stand-alone investment.

The typical buyer of the first kind is already an operating company with at least one core business or perhaps several. This "strategic" buyer wants to direct its acquisition efforts to strengthen, extend, and build up its existing operations. Most of its analysis will be directed at selecting a company that offers reinforcing relationships with its own current lines of business.

In the second case, the typical buyer is a "financial" acquirer—usually an investor group—that may not care at all about interrelationships with its other holdings. Its primary concern is whether the company will generate enough cash flow to repay the purchase price and permit it to turn a profit on the transaction. In some cases the profit may be derived through dividends. In others it may be gained through resale in whole or in parts to another buyer or buyers, or to the public in a stock offering. In most cases this buyer will want to minimize the interrelations of the companies it owns so that each can be refinanced or disposed of without affecting the others.

These two types of buyers might be differentiated as "opportunity makers" versus "opportunity takers." Buyers in the first category are primarily plan-driven; they're looking for "strategic investments," things that "fit." Buyers in the second category are deal-driven; they're looking for value, things that can be financed.

This chapter will be of most interest to the first type, the operator-buyer that, most likely, has institutionalized the strategic planning process. The deal-driven buyer, on the other hand, will be impatient to move on to Chapters 3 and 4. Such a buyer is likely to have a much narrower field of concern: price and its best friends, cash flow and financeability. The deal-driven buyer can buy and make good use of just about any company if the price is right and the funds can be borrowed.

The portions of this chapter relating to finders and brokers and searching for specific acquisition candidates should be of use to both the plan-driven and the deal-driven buyer. In fact, the deal-driven buyer can probably benefit from a review of strategic planning considerations. After all, it's difficult to price out an acquisition without some kind of plan. If one can't see the company's plan, the buyer must make one—especially if the buyer has investors backing it. A plan is part of the so-called due diligence process for both types of buyers (see Chapter 6).

This chapter also addresses general government regulatory issues affecting acquisitions. Review of any potential restrictions on acquisition decision making, particularly those relating to antitrust, should be performed as a part of the initial planning process. It makes no sense for either a plan-driven or a deal-driven buyer to evaluate and search out a candidate unless it can legally acquire that company and operate it afterward without regulatory hassles.

Finally, the last section of this chapter covers post-acquisition planning. For the plan-driven buyer, how much integration should take place? And if the deal-driven buyer has bought management along with the company, managers who don't agree with the buyer's plans for the company may cause trouble.

STRATEGIC PLANNING FOR OPERATING COMPANIES

How can strategic planning help the corporate merger/acquisition/buyout process?

Strategic planning, for operating companies, is the process of identifying and quantifying strengths and weaknesses. The M&A process should target only those industries and companies in which an entry will both exploit strengths and shore up weaknesses. In the process, the M&A staff becomes an opportunity maker, but it pursues only those opportunities that will fit with its chosen strategy.

Planning of this sort greatly reduces the cost of analyzing randomly submitted opportunities. Do they fit at all? If so, how well do they fit? A truly sophisticated strategic plan will measure quantitatively how well or how poorly potential opportunities fit into it, and given a number of competing opportunities, it will rank-order them against each other by degree of desirability. This ranking is another way of defining "risk" and will be a factor in pricing.[1]

For many years, under the banner of "diversification," many systems of analysis were developed to generate workable strategies. Some prepackaged strategic planning systems segmented a company's operations into market-share/market-growth categories and yielded such classifications as *star* for high-growth/high-share units, *dog* for low-growth/low-share units, *cash cow* for high-share/low-growth units, and *wildcat* for low-share/high-growth units. The "strategy" was to redeploy revenues from cash cows to wildcats. (Many other such matrix approaches to diversification were also popular—especially General Electric's nine-element construct.) These concepts, originally developed and successfully promulgated worldwide in the late 1960s and early 1970s by Boston Consulting Group's M&A guru Bruce Henderson, were widely taught and widely used. Why? Because they were certainly better than the random processes that had gone on in previous decades, during which many deals were made for noneconomic reasons—out of fads, friendship, or family ties.

But now, as we approach the year 2000 surrounded by seas of software, these simple four-element and nine-element matrixes have been supplanted by multivariate analyses easily handled by even the simplest of desktop computers. Rather than four or nine, there are literally hundreds of variables that may be considered when contemplating a growth-by-acquisition strategy. Only the systems approach to strategic planning can encompass them all, isolate the key variables, and use them to develop strategic plans that will work.

One of the principal benefits of having a strategy for acquisitions in place is to prevent disastrous decisions made with random "whyncha" processes. ("Whyncha" is what "why don't you" sounds like when said real fast.) For example, the CEO of a cash-rich manufacturing company making filing cabinets sits by chance next to an M&A broker on a plane and mentions that his company is looking for "growth" acquisitions. His seatmate says, "Fish farming. That's the ticket! It's hot stuff. Catfish, crayfish, shrimp—they're even growing *lobsters* in tanks! *Whyncha* get into fish farming? It just so happens that I know of a fish farm for sale!"

Well, our CEO, bored by 30 years of pounding out filing cabinets, is soon hooked on fish farming, and in short order the company's managers forget about buying a company that can use their manufacturing know-how and their file cabinet sales and distribution system and instead start looking at cat-fish-growing operations. They wind up paying top dollar for a large, money-losing farm at the peak of the catfish-farming boom, and it's trouble, trouble, trouble from there on out in Catfish City. They don't know anything about fish farming, and while they're learning it, their file cabinet business goes to hell in a handbasket.

Such poor decisions simply do not happen in companies where strategic thinking is ingrained in the board of directors and in the executive team that has made the strategic plan. Before deciding to enter a new area of business, strategic thinkers will make industry forecasts and study the fit of the proposed acquisition with their present operations. Further, because strategic planning requires choices, any "opportunity," no matter how "hot," should always be forced to stand trial against other potential entries. So a formal inventory of opportunities and methods for comparing them is a practical necessity.

The plan resulting from strategic thinking, once installed, acts as a disciplining force on everyone at the decision-making level. Instead of hundreds of in-house and out-of-house ideas and acquisition suggestions coming up for detailed evaluation at great expense, any proposed area of entry can simply be matched against pre-agreed criteria that describe the company's strategy. If it doesn't meet the majority of those criteria, it is turned down forthwith with little executive time diverted from day-to-day business.

Strategic planning can also help in the divestiture process. In any multiprofit-center operation, strategic planning that does not automatically produce candidates for sell-off or shutoff is probably not truly strategic. It is necessary in any strategy to weigh what you *are* doing against what you *could* be doing with your resources. If the potential is greater in new areas of opportunity, the old lines of business should be converted to cash by selling them off, possibly at a premium to a firm where they fit, and the cash should be redeployed to new lines through internal or external development. Controlling this continuous redeployment process is what strategic planning is all about.

Are there various levels of strategy?

Yes. As mentioned, strategic planning revolves around the reallocation and redeployment of cash flows from lower-yielding to higher-yielding investments. This process takes place at many different levels in any large company and even in small companies. Strategic planning may be (and probably should always be) different at these different levels.

What are the typical strategic planning levels?

The "six-level approach," developed at Hay Group (today Hay Management Consultants) in the early 1980s, is probably most suitable for the largest companies; it can be reduced to four or even three levels, but probably not below that even for the smallest companies. (See Exhibit Case-6 on pp. 962ff.)

Enterprise strategy generally is developed at the board-of-directors level. It asks the questions "Why are we in this business (or these core businesses) anyway?" and "Is there something out there that can better utilize our cash flows?" Thus a strategy might develop at the enterprise level to *expand* the enterprise by making a major horizontal acquisition—acquiring a major competitor of about the same size or bigger. Alternatively, the board may opt to temporarily *contract* the enterprise by selling off major lines and later reallocating cash flows into entirely new and higher-yielding lines unrelated to historic lines. Two dramatic examples of this latter strategy in America are the transformation of Grace Lines—a 100-year-old shipping and fertilizer company—to a 100-division conglomerate under the leadership of the late Peter Grace, and the conversion of the venerable American Can Company from a manufacturer of cans and paper cups into a major financial services company under the guidance of Jerry Tsai and Sanford Weill—now sharing leadership of Citigroup, heir to this evolution. Other examples are Primark, a former Detroit-based utilities holding company that has converted itself to an information services company based in McLean, Virginia, and the old American Tobacco Company, which changed to American Brands and then to Fortune Brands, Inc., in a move away from its roots.[2]

Corporate strategy calls for putting together under common management several groups of strategic business units (SBUs) that have some common operating elements—technology, marketing, geographic location, and so on. These "megagroups" are formed via the *group strategy* described below. Cash flows from the group members are reallocated internally to maximize long-term return. The group is also constantly seeking new investment opportunities that fit with the group's commonalities. In some enlightened companies, the group may administer its own M&A activity independent of headquarters.

Sector or group strategy calls for assembling, under one corporate or operating group, SBUs that have some commonality to them. Then, as in the corporate strategy, cash flows are allocated and reallocated back out to the individual business units or into new internal or external investments.

Business unit strategy deals with assembling under common management those product lines that have some commonalities—most often manufacturing or marketing. Cash flows are reinvested into the most promising of the units after comparing the potential return that could be realized from the acquisition of new product lines or start-ups.

Product-line strategy deals with product life cycles—supplementing or replacing mature or aging products with new products.

Functional strategy deals with alternative methods of manufacture—changing from aluminum die casting to plastic injection molding, for instance, or switching from wood to fiberglass or aluminum for a line of boats. It should also include plant relocation—looking for lower labor rates, cheaper rents, more employee amenities, proximity to raw materials, and so forth.

How should a company begin to plan strategically?

Planning begins with the board of directors, which sets the tone. Directors should ensure that managers make M&A decisions only in accordance with a plan, and should impose discipline on the implementation of that plan. Without that discipline, managers might spend only a few months and $25,000 for pre-acquisition "studies" of a $25 million manufacturing operation in Spain that appears to be a bargain but does not fit the company's long-term strategy. At best, if the company decides not to buy the firm, it will lose $25,000. At worst, if it takes the plunge, it could lose millions.

To begin the planning process, the board might appoint a *corporate strategy policy group,* whose first job should be the preparation and issuance of a *corporate strategy procedures guide.*

The guide should specify who is responsible for what in the corporate planning hierarchy, outlining the responsibilities of each person involved. It should define at what level M&A search-and-screen activity is to take place, what kinds of reports are to be filed, and where structuring, financing, pricing, and post-acquisition operating decisions will be made. The guide will normally expand the subheadings from generic to specific for "Strategic Skills and Behaviors," as shown in Exhibit Case-6 on pp. 962ff.

The guide should also emphasize that, in general, any investment in an acquisition must be rated against the cost of getting the same results from an *internal* development program—that is, creating the same operation *de novo.* Such analyses should be part of the due diligence procedures. In other words, why spend money for something you can do yourself and perhaps at less capital cost?

However, it should be noted that most internal entries fail such analyses because of three things: The buyer does not eliminate the proposed acquiree as a competitor, and market shares are thus lower; there are no earnings during the buildup period; and the discount rate that is applied to the future earnings stream must be higher because of the added risk that must be accorded to *de novo* entries, which seem to have a higher failure rate than do M&A entries (though statistical support for this last statement is lacking). Furthermore, some acquisitions can almost "pay for themselves." (In some retail store acquisitions, the entire cost of acquiring a company in a horizontal integration can be recovered in a year or two because of the efficiencies created by inventory reduction and the elimination of duplications in staff and management.)

The reader will note that the flow chart in Exhibit 16-6 has three basic components: the internal development program, the external development program, and the organization design and development program. The last program is necessary to ensure that the organization will be able to manage the fruits of its external and internal development programs as they are brought on-line.

Can a company achieve profitable growth by a series of acquisitions in its own industry?

Certainly. Nondiversifying growth by acquisition is quite common and often successful in many industries, particularly *fractionated* or *fragmented* industries in which there are many independent operators, as in home health care, plumbing, software, and trucking. Synonyms for this type of growth include *bundling, leveraged buildup, progressive buildup, serial consolidation,* and *rollup.* Another type of industry where buying competitors has become common is the financial services industry. Attorney and merger guru Edward D. Herlihy, in his comprehensive analysis of M&A activity by banks, rightly called this activity *consolidation.*[3] As mentioned in Chapter 1, this term may refer to a type of merger (a *corporate consolidation*). More important, however, it can become a fighting word (*industry consolidation*) for antitrust lawyers, with implications for restraint of trade. Although Herlihy wrote his study before passage of the Interstate Banking and Efficiency Act of 1994 (Public Law No. 103-328, 108 Stat. 2341), his basic description of the bank merger process continues to hold true in the new environment.[4]

How does an acquirer achieve growth in this mode?

By buying one company at a time. After a buyer has bought one firm, it uses it as a base for building a much larger business through acquisition add-ons in the same or a related industry. Effecting concentration through *serial consolidation* like this in a fractionated industry can be rewarding—automobile retail outlets, real estate agencies, and breweries are three examples in which huge businesses that benefit from national advertising have been built by the coalescence of many smaller units. In other cases technological change has created opportunities. For instance, the advent of Federal Express (and other overnight delivery firms, such as UPS) has changed the way that many distribution companies locate and operate their warehouses. In one case, the potential to use nationwide overnight delivery made it possible to consolidate the activities of 19 medical supply warehouses into one with tremendous savings in costs.

Many such firms that have been created by serial consolidation are privately owned, and numbers are difficult to come by. But there are exceptions. For example, U.S. Office Products is a publicly owned firm. In 1996, this office supply firm bought 52 small companies, as reported by *Mergers & Acquisitions* magazine (in the April/May 1997 issue). In 1998, after acquiring another 53 small firms (and divesting a few due to pooling quibbles), the company made headlines by splitting into five separate firms.[5]

Some former conglomerates that used to buy anything and (almost) everything, such as Alco Standard, have finally concentrated on one highly profitable field—in Alco's case, the distribution of paper and paper products. Alco, renamed Ikon Office Solutions in January 1997, is still an active acquirer. Having made well over 100 acquisitions worldwide in the past five years, it has doubled its sales to over $10 billion in this niche.

The new company, headed by John E. Stuart, took a cue from the motto of his predecessor Tinkham Veale II—"corporate partnership." Headquarters gives acquirees not only cash for their companies but continuing encouragement along with decision-making independence. The company has fostered the exchange of information between subsidiary presidents, forestalling duplicative errors. It has also encouraged innovation, installing bar code-driven inventory controls for copier parts.

Why is it important to have a business development program?

Every business should have a development program, and that program should remain open to all modes of growth, ranging from internal development to joint ventures to acquisitions. Because these modes of development are similar and complementary, to do any one of them well requires an understanding of the others. In other words, even if a company does not plan to do acquisitions, it should have a business development program that includes M&A perspectives.[6]

A business development program may be necessary to support the price for entry into a new industry in which financial benchmarks are lacking. In any event, it is incumbent upon management to make a plan for any enterprise or for any subsidiary group, subsidiary, unit, product line, product group, or even factory that is to be acquired. Failure to do so might result in charges, if the acquisition loses money, that management had failed to use due diligence in protecting the stockholders' interests. Even if it's a bad plan, management (in the U.S.) is protected by the "business judgment rule." But plan they must.

Any business development program should have a *net present value* (NPV) calculation for each unit. Without this, it is difficult to evaluate any unit for sell-off, retention, or expansion purposes. And regardless of what a public stock might sell for in the marketplace, every public company should have some idea of the net present value of its future earnings stream or streams to discover if the market is properly pricing its shares.

For operating companies looking for synergies, the best way to evaluate a proposed acquisition is the present value of the future earnings stream to be developed under a business development plan that includes the proposed new acquisition. If more than one candidate is under consideration and a choice must be made, they should be compared with each other. The present value of a plan for A is rated against the present value of the plan for B. This classical process, when applied to the purchase of capital goods such as machine tools, is called making an "alternative capital investment decision."

What is the wheel of opportunity/fit chart approach to strategic planning?

One of the major problems in corporate planning is the strange notion that the vice president of corporate planning is supposed to make a plan. That way lies disaster, for the planner has no way to carry it out. The job of the planner is to see that a plan is made. Plans should be formulated by the same people who are to carry them out! The principal problem facing corporate planners is the lack of a structure into which to cast up a plan.

The wheel of opportunity/fit chart (WOFC) construct supplies the structure in a step-by-step method for creating a strategic plan. It accomplishes this by asking and answering these fundamental questions:

- What are our strengths and weaknesses?
- What are our alternative opportunities for acquisitions?
- What are our priorities for building on strengths and correcting weaknesses?
- How do our opportunities fit with our priorities?

Before going on, the reader is asked to look at Exhibit Case-6, in which a sample WOFC appears. An extensive exposition of the WOFC construct appeared in *Mergers & Acquisitions* magazine (see note 1). It was the result of several hundred WOFC exercises conducted for companies all over the world, and is far too long to be reproduced here. However, its principal parts are described herein. A reader who wants to do a WOFC should get a copy of the referenced article, follow the text in this book, and refer to Exhibit Case-6.

What are the general phases involved in the WOFC?

The WOFC process begins after the board of directors, the chief executive officer (CEO), and the person in charge of planning make a basic commitment to the strategic planning process in general and to the WOFC process in particular.

Having decided to construct a WOFC, they then ask the unit, group, company, or profit center performing the analysis to assemble its top people to create a business development plan by consensus. This group should include the line chiefs because they are responsible for profit and loss. For example, for an enterprise-level WOFC, the CEO, chief operating officer (COO), and any executive vice president with profit and loss responsibilities would certainly be expected to attend, in addition to the vice president of finance, the comptroller, the vice president of marketing, and the regional (or sector) main operating heads. The number of participants is important. If there are more than 12, the process seems to drag out. If there are less than seven people, however, not enough differentiation in viewpoints comes through. Nine or ten has proved optimum. The vice president of planning or, if there is none, someone designated as "facilitator" coordinates the program and then writes up the findings as the definitive business development plan.

Once the group is formed, it goes through three phases. First, from files of "opportunities" that have been assembled for evaluation, candidates are entered on the "wheel of opportunity." Next, the group develops a set of criteria for selecting between these and future alternative acquisition opportunities using the strength and weakness analysis developed by the fit chart. Finally, the group differentially rates the alternative acquisitions on the wheel against each other using the scoring criteria developed in the fit chart, and then prioritizes the search process.

Previous to the first formal meeting, each of the participants has been given pads of blank "strength analysis," "weakness analysis," and "wheel of opportunity" sheets, as shown in Exhibits Case-2, Case-3, and Case-9.

The WOFC sessions start with an informal review of the opportunities in terms of focus industries, and sometimes particular candidates in the industry. Many opportunities of both types are discarded outright because of lack of definition, previous unhappy experiences, obvious bars to entry such as antitrust considerations, and so on. But the group should strive to consider *all* reasonable candidates at this stage. This is a very sensitive area; some contributors may have spent *years* developing a concept and will be hurt if the opportunity is summarily dismissed without going through the fit chart process.

After all opportunities have been identified, those of the same or a similar nature are combined. Then a final list is typed up and redistributed to the group as a package. All submittals should be preserved and made part of the permanent file. No attempt should be made to rate any proposed entry or relate any entry directly to any specific potential corporate acquisition move at this stage. The purpose of this first informal review is to make sure that the group understands each proposed entry. Only the most harebrained schemes or suggestions should be discarded at this point.

How does the wheel of opportunity work?

The wheel helps managers and advisors visualize with the help of a model (see Exhibit Case-6) the universe of acquisition opportunities surrounding any enterprise or any subunit.

A wheel of opportunity has six areas grouped into three modes. Each area sets forth a different type of acquisition to be considered. In general, the wheel of opportunity and fit chart use terms that are common in the academic discipline referred to as *industrial organization*.[7]

What are the basic types of strategies described in the wheel of opportunity?

There are three basic strategic modes: horizontal integration, vertical integration, and diversification. (The coauthor calls the third one "diagonal integration," to complete the geometry.)

What is market intensification?

This strategy might be called the "shoemaker" strategy. Derived from that sage advice, "Shoemaker, stick to your last," it dictates that you should expand in the businesses that you know. It says that before considering any other external growth opportunities you should weigh the advantages to be realized by buying out a head-to-head competitor and integrating its operations with yours; this is called a *horizontal integration*.

An example of the power of this particular mode can be illustrated with the case of the retail camera industry. Every major metropolitan area has developed at least one and in some areas two or three multilocation camera store chains usually built by serial consolidation. In the Washington, D.C., area their creation wiped out hundreds of small camera shops. Why? Advertising cost is one reason. The price of a display ad in the *Washington Post* at, say, $30,000 would be impossible for a single stand-alone store to pay for. But if Ritz Camera has 50 stores in the D.C. metropolitan area covered by the *Washington Post,* the cost to each individual store for that full-page ad will be only $600.

Next, the market intensification strategy dictates that you also "extend" your operations into new geographical territories by targeting companies in your line of business in a geographical area you do not now serve; this is called a *market extension.* Here again the entire cost of a market extension entry may be returned in the increased efficiencies realized from operations especially in the costs of supplies and purchased services such as advertising. For Ritz Camera—which consolidated not only locally but nationally—a full-page ad in a national camera magazine costing $50,000 can be spread out to Ritz's 500 stores nationwide, and that cost would be only $100 per store. (Whether Ritz or its competitor chains were built by buying up individual camera shops or by establishing stores *de novo* is immaterial for strategic purposes—those are tactical and logistical considerations, not strategic.)

Avis Rent-A-Car was built by Warren Avis from the ground up—literally, as he traveled across the country putting a national chain together from hundreds of small, independent car-rental firms—most of them former livery stables. Ryder Systems, the giant truck-rental firm, was built in much the same way.

What is vertical integration?

Vertical integration is a strategy mode used to achieve economies in purchasing, sales, and distribution. It is composed of two subcomponents: *vertical backward integration* and *vertical forward integration.* Henry Ford was the world's first major vertical integrator. His company had its own iron mines and steel mills and the railroads that connected them. Ford even grew its own rubber for its tires. Today, Ford-type vertical integration is frowned on as a strategy except under special circumstances—for example, the aforementioned boom in M&A and strategic alliance activity in digital communications.

What is vertical backward integration?

Vertical backward integration is buying a current or potential supplier. If combined with the strategy of effecting one or a series of horizontal integration or market extension moves, it can mean increased sales for the acquired supplier entity and increased profits as the company rides down the experience curve. The primary disadvantage is the loss in the efficiencies generated from competitive bidding.

What is vertical forward integration?

Vertical forward integration is buying a current or potential customer. Owning your own distribution network is important in many industries in which preventive "freeze-outs" are common, such as electronic entertainment.

What are the advantages of the vertical integration strategy?

Quality control is one of the prime advantages of a vertical integration strategy, whether buying up or down the supply line. Where there is a high level of technology, especially in emerging fields, vertical integration can pay off in an increasingly better product produced at increasingly lower cost because parts and materials can be produced to exact tolerances—neither overengineered, which cuts into profit margins, nor underengineered, which creates assembly and service problems.

Product planning, research and development, product engineering, and in some cases distribution and service functions are all aided by vertical integration. Inventory control in times of tight money, just-in-time (JIT) deliveries, and reduction in sales costs are other positive results of vertical integration. And in times of shortages, owning a supplier has saved many a company from failure.

A vertical return on investment (ROI) analysis can help decision making as to which way to move—backward, forward, or both.

A classic example of a company using vertical ROI analysis is Sherwin-Williams. This century-old paint manufacturer—producer of Dutch Boy, KemTone, and so on—was having trouble making money manufacturing paint. But its customers—distributors and retailers—were doing well. In the house paint industry there are five levels of activity: raw material extracting, processing, manufacturing, distributing, and retailing. Sherwin-Williams discovered that for the household paint industry, there were profits in the extraction stage—mining titanium dioxide—and at the distribution and retail level; but because competitive conditions in the industry forced it to make intensified investment in plant and facilities, it received little return at the manufacturing level. In response to these findings, 30 years ago Sherwin-Williams converted itself from a manufacturer of paint to a manufacturer, distributor, *and* retailer of household paint and the equipment to apply it. Today the company has 2,000-odd retail paint stores with sales in the $4 billion area.

However, there are dangers in this mode. The transfer-pricing of goods from a subsidiary to a parent is an invitation to accounting trickery in "protecting" an acquisition from the reality of proper costing processes. That is why activity-based costing (ABC) is a near necessity in long-term support of this acquisition strategy.

What is the diversification mode?

The *diversification mode* is composed of two kinds of activity: *product* (or *service*) *extension* and *free-form diversification.*

What is product (or service) extension?

It is adding a product or service that can be sold in your present geographic areas, generally to your present customers.

One company that used the product extension process very successfully was the Hewlett-Packard Company (HP). In the early 1950s HP brought out a voltmeter with a very large dial that made it much easier to read than the old Ballantine voltmeters that were standard for voltage measurement in a laboratory setting. One satisfied customer, Reed Research, Inc. (RR), a scientific research company founded by the principal author, retired all its Ballantine voltmeters and replaced them with HP models. In a typical product extension move, HP soon added a signal generator to go along with its voltmeter, and RR retired its Cambridge signal generators and bought HP. Then came more and more instruments that set Hewlett Packard up as the principal supplier of electronic laboratory instruments in the country. RR bought them all.

What is free-form diversification?

It is an entry in a field of activity and in a geographic area where the acquirer has no present operations. This is the highest-risk category in the M&A field. It is the land of the "whynchas." It is the manufacturer of file cabinets in Wisconsin buying a catfish farm in Alabama.

The primary purpose of the classification scheme is to make it possible to discover, through the device of the fit chart, not only which of the six particular kinds of entries score the highest, but which modes hold the most potential.

How do you fill in the wheel?

This discovery process occurs in a series of steps:

Step 1. *Horizontal integration.* Enter on the opportunity wheel the principal market (geographical) areas served by present product lines or services, and list your principal competitors and their market shares, if known. Note also growth in the market area if known.

Step 2. *Market extension.* Enter all potential new geographical markets for your present principal line or lines by logical geographical break-downs. If known, enter growth rates for sales of your products or services in each potential new geographical market.

Step 3. *Vertical backward integration.* Enter your suppliers by industry and by name, lumping your purchases.

Step 4. *Vertical forward integration.* Enter the names of your principal customers by industry and individually, lumping their purchases from you and others.

Step 5. *Product or service extension.* List all the possible products or services that you might add to your present lines that can be sold in your present geographical areas. (Here it is very important to discover what your current customers buy that you might supply.)

Step 6. *Free-form.* Here enter the best of the opportunities that you have discovered that cannot be categorized in any of the other forms.

(Try not to anticipate the fit chart. As mentioned, try not to reject too many ideas at this stage. It is best to leave rejection to the controlled and dis-passionate process of the fit chart. The utility of the fit chart construct will be demonstrated when a few "whynchas" are injected and subsequently rejected when the entries are quantified.)

An opportunity wheel can be constructed in this manner for any company or operation doing anything anywhere. Next comes the fit chart, which will show how efficient these potential entries might be relative to each other.

How does the fit chart work?

There are three stages in developing and using a fit chart:

- The first step is to identify the kinds of actions that can be taken to benefit the company. If these offset its weaknesses, we call them *complements.* If they exploit or reinforce its strengths, we call them *supplements.*
- The second step is to select the principal complements and supplements and weight them according to their relative importance.
- The third is to rank acquisition opportunities by their ability to maximize the desired complementary and supplementary effects.

Note: It is always easy to discover potential opportunities that are heavily complementary or supplementary. The trick is to discover opportunities that have values on *both* sides. Entries that complement your weaknesses and at the same time supplement your strengths are the key to successful growth by the M&A process.

What is synergy?

Synergy literally means the process of working together. It is the 2-plus-2-equals-5 effect. It is the thing that drives most M&A activity—or at least it should! The term *synergy* is used most often in the case of complement-driven mergers in which candidates give each other some previously "missing" element. But synergy also happens in supplement-driven mergers. In the horizontal integration area, the merging of two hardware stores in the same block, or two Ford retailers in the same small town, has lots of synergy—the probability is high that the total inventories necessary to carry the same total level of sales can be reduced substantially.

The purpose of a fit chart is to quantify the *relative* synergies of the opportunities inventory, to quantitatively differentiate the fit and thus the profit potential offered by various competing entries.

Should the process start with supplements or complements?

It can be done either way. Some managers and many planners tend to be concerned solely with complements ("We should get into something new"), and others tend to be concerned solely with supplements ("Where else can we apply our special technology?"). Not surprisingly, many programs of diversification take either one approach or the other, depending on the psyche of those making the plan. Complements seem to draw attention first, however. It has been the principal author's experience that the human psyche in the business environment dotes on strengths and tends to ignore weaknesses. In the long run, concentrating solely on one or the other is a recipe for failure.

The basic concept of the fit chart is to form a strategy that answers two basic questions: What do we lack that can be supplied by the acquisition? What strengths or assets, human and physical, do we have that are transferable to the acquisition? Anyone can find industry entries heavily weighted on one side or the other. But, as mentioned, the trick is to find entries *with high values on both sides*. With work, they can always be found—and that's where the money is.

What are some examples of complements and supplements?

There are hundreds of generally applicable strengths and weaknesses and perhaps thousands that are industry- or company-specific. The article referenced in note 1 contains long lists of potential complements and supplements taken from hundreds of real-life situations, to stimulate your thinking. During a downturn in the economy, a primary complement for manufacturers might be "a company that can utilize present vacant plant and underutilized capital equipment." Another might be "a firm that produces something our salesforce can add to present lines that aren't selling." Both of these are complements. On the supplement side there may be entries such as "What industries can use our proprietary technology in high-temperature hard coatings?" and "What can we buy that can use our famous trademark to boost its sales?"

Are there any general rules to guide the creation of fit chart variables?

Yes. Here are a few guidelines taken from hundreds of WOFC programs run by the principal author:

- Don't overdo it with technology. Raising the level of technology will not automatically raise the return on capital, as many mistakenly believe.

- Don't overdo it with financial variables. The classic equation $S/C \times P/S = ROI$ (where S is sales, C is capital, and P is profit) will suffice for this stage of the planning process. One of the major decisions facing acquirers is to discover where profits come from in present operations. Is it from turning capital (S/C) *or* from generating high-margin sales (P/S)? A business can make money either way, but it is rare to make it both ways. Operations are usually either *turns-driven* or *margin-driven*. A turns-driven buyer should probably stay in businesses where profits are turns-driven, and a margin-driven operator should stay in margin-driven operations. Other financial variables, such as above-market returns based on patent protections, are generally impounded in the purchase price as part of the deal's NPV.

- Financial variables often cause trouble because some people believe that certain kinds of businesses are inherently more profitable than others. This is simply not true over time. High-margin mining businesses at 65 percent gross profit go broke while the chain grocer gets rich at 5 percent. The difference is in the risk profile: One is high, the other low. When a low-margin operator acquires a high-margin operator or vice versa, there's usually trouble because they won't have an operating fit.

- Labor variables also pose problems. The principal author has known many executives who went on the record in the first few hours of a fit chart session about "getting away from the union" as a complement. They believed that their unionized operations were a weakness. But often, after much discussion, these same managers would decide that, because they knew how to get along with labor, how to forestall a strike, or how to take one comfortably, they could bid for and buy companies in labor-sensitive industries at bargain prices. Their perceived weakness turned out to be a strength!

- Management variables are also troublesome. Only after days of honest introspection do managers begin to see that many of their past acquisition failures were caused by poor management fit between acquirer and acquiree. Research at Hay Management Consultants has shown that there is more to fear along the production axis than along the marketing axis. It is probably easier to teach an engineer marketing than to teach a salesperson engineering.

■ Look for seasonal supplements. "In the winter, when the marine
park closes, the staff teaches skiing at our ski resort." "We're
cash-poor all summer while we make Christmas tree light strings.
Now we make garden light strings." These kinds of entries can
make money for years.

■ Be careful of transitory benefits. In tax-driven deals, when the
short-term benefits run out, what's left may be a long-term loser.
Many an LBO or MBO uses post-acquisition asset sales to show a
profit. But when those are gone, owners must fall back on operations for earnings and cash flows to pay off debt—and some don't
make it. Without permanent operating synergies, most acquisitions
are bound to fail.

How do you weigh the relative importance of complements and supplements and narrow the list to the most important?

The WOFC uses the Delphi process, introduced some 40 years ago as a method
of forecasting the future. The theory behind it is that the collective, intuitive
judgments of a group of experts in an area with many unknowns (such as technological change) are probably superior to quantitative extrapolations of
known trends.

How does the Delphi process work?

In the Delphi process,[8] a series of questions formulated by monitors are put to a
panel of experts. The monitors study the answers, group them into four
quartiles of opinion, and send back anonymous abstracts of the upper and
lower quartiles to the panel of experts. The experts all read the abstractions and
respond again, modifying their opinions, it is hoped, in accordance with the
group wisdom. These answers are again abstracted and grouped, the upper and
lower quartiles are again distributed (still without identification of contributors), and the new, usually modified opinions or estimates are fed back to the
experts. The process goes on until some kind of a consensus is reached.

In the fit chart process, in order to discover the potential "profit drivers,"
we use the principal author's "instant Delphi" process. Each participant is
given 1,000 points to distribute out to a set of variables—complements and

supplements (see Exhibit Case-6). The anonymous allocations of each participant to each of the variables are tallied and summed. These averages are then made known to the group. The persons giving the lowest and highest scores to each variable are now identified from the tally sheets as either high or low without giving their actual ratings, and each attendee must defend his or her position. These decisive players may be joined by others in the low or the high quartile depending on how structured the inquiry system is. Each variable is discussed in an adversarial fashion.

The chairman: "I think that 'management fit' is for the birds. The bottom line is what counts. That's why I gave it zero." In opposition, the president, who spent 300 precious points on it, says, "But, Hal, the last three companies we bought were run by people that you wouldn't even have to dinner—and we sold them all off at a loss! Management fit is extremely important."

It is not at all uncommon in the Delphi process to uncover vast differences in opinion about basic operating and strategic philosophies right at the very top of the organization—major differences that have never been discussed, much less resolved.

If the lows wish to caucus and bring out a joint position, they are allowed to. The highs can do likewise. Middle-value people are not allowed to participate in the discussion because, in effect, they've not taken a position and have entered "chicken values." They soon learn that if they want to participate, they'd better take a stand. The lows and the highs battle it out verbally until debate is cut off by the facilitator. Thus, each variable is treated in discussion, after which the participants again spread their points. Variables not scoring an average of some minimum number of points (e.g., 25) are dropped from consideration.

The process continues for as many as five rounds. Experience shows that it is seldom necessary to go beyond the third round before consensus is reached. At the last round, a final cutoff figure for dropping variables is set (it might drop to 20 points), the points dropped are proportionately reallocated, and the final, average number per variable, a true consensus in numerical form, is then posted on the fit chart for all to see, as shown in Exhibit Case-7.

Exactly how is each opportunity ranked?

The easiest thing about the WOFC process is distributing the values to the acquisition opportunities. The final value ascribed to each variable represents the maximum score that any of the acquisitions being considered can achieve for that variable. (Most acquisitions would presumably achieve lower scores.) Say that candidates promising to "reduce shop overhead," a quite common complementary goal for manufacturers in tough times, wound up with a consensus value of 200 points. Say that the acquisition opportunities can use 100, 50, 25, and 0 percent of the acquirer's excess shop capacity. The opportunity scoring 100 would get the full 200 points, the one scoring 50 would get 100 points, the one scoring 25 would get 50 points, and the one scoring zero would get zero points.

When all the values have been distributed, they are summed across and rank-ordered (see Exhibit Case-8).

Can the WOFC process be used to identify sell-offs?

Yes, most certainly. The converse of the foregoing analysis is the sell-off decision, which can also be made using the WOFC. All present and potential product (or service) lines are put in their proper sector and, in effect, rated against each other. If the WOFC process has been institutionalized, present operations are rated against potential acquisitions. The lower-rated operations are sold off and the funds reallocated to the acquisition of new, higher-ranking candidates.

After completing the WOFC, what's next?

All the information generated in the WOFC process, including all the voting sheets, should be bound in a report and the final results summarized into a strategic statement, which is the first page of the strategic plan or the business development plan. This serves as a guide for the search-and-screen process that follows and prevents future waste of time and money in considering nonfitting "whynchas" over and over.

IN-HOUSE SEARCH

When does a search-and-screen program begin?

The search-and-screen program begins once the acquiring company has completed its strategic self-evaluation and has developed its acquisition strategy. It is now ready to start some search activity and begins by identifying *focus in-*

dustries and isolating specific *focus companies* (also known as *candidates* or *prospects*) that might meet the fit chart criteria. (Other terms used in this context are target industry and target company, but as mentioned earlier we prefer to avoid this terminology.)

How should it be organized?

There are two primary ways to go about making acquisitions: to *centralize* leadership of the company's entire acquisition program at corporate headquarters, or to *decentralize* leadership of the phases of the process at different levels of the organization. For example, strategy may be developed at headquarters—the enterprise or corporate level—while search and screen may take place at a lower level, with pricing, legal, and negotiation controlled at the corporate level. Whichever approach is taken, as mentioned, plans must be developed by the people who must make them work. Acquisitions dreamed up at corporate headquarters and dumped onto the subsidiaries have a good chance of failure.

How long does a search-and-screen program last?

For strategic acquisitions it depends on the scope of the program and how much in-house data are available on the subject. Normally, to produce a few viable candidates, a search-and-screen program takes a minimum of six months. At the end of six months, some negotiations should be under way. However, don't be surprised if the process takes longer, since many candidates will not always be ready to sell at first. If the buyer is interested in only a few companies and those companies are not immediately available, it could take years for the seeds its inquiries planted to grow into bona fide negotiations.

What are the primary steps in completing a full search-and-screen program?

- Define focus industries as derived from the fit chart program.
- Conduct a literature search.
  - Which publications are dedicated to the focus industries?
  - Which publications report on M&A activity in those specific industries?

- Identify the trade associations in those industries.
  - Do they publish any numbers? Sales? Margins? Profits?
  - Do they have local chapters?
  - Do they report on M&A activity?
  - Do they or others sponsor trade shows? Domestic? International?
- Start building specific focus company files.
- Screen candidates using fit chart data.
- Contact principals.
- Begin developing preliminary post-acquisition integration plans.
- Obtain a price expression from any potential sellers.
- Get Dun & Bradstreet (D&B) and credit reports if candidates are stand-alones.
- Begin the negotiation process. Get expressions of preliminary price and terms.
- Engage in the due diligence process and make a business plan for the candidates.
- Move toward closing your chosen transactions, while remaining open to alternatives.

What are the primary means of a search-and-screen program?

As mentioned in the introduction to this chapter, there are two main types of buyers—opportunity takers and opportunity makers.

Opportunity takers, which tend to be investment companies, are looking for investments at a favorable price. Their main line of defense against making an imprudent purchase is the care and completeness of their pricing and financing analysis. (See Chapters 3 and 4.) Their main enemy is impatience. Unless they are constrained by the need to borrow the purchase price against the acquired company's assets and cash flows, they often develop a determination to buy something—anything—and they do, sometimes to their sorrow.

Opportunity makers, on the other hand, which tend to be operating companies, care about operating fit and synergies. They tend to narrow the scope of their search. They examine their own strengths and weaknesses and then target opportunities that offset those weaknesses and/or exploit those strengths.

However, they too often get caught up in the imperative to buy something. And they often do so without considering true fit.

How does an opportunity taker work?

As mentioned earlier, for the opportunity taker, the deals are finance-driven rather than operations-driven. The opportunity taker establishes a network of brokers, financial intermediaries, investment bankers, finders, and the like to pinpoint companies—such as corporate spin-off fire sales—that appear to be bargains. The opportunity-taker approach tends to be random, unstructured, and unplanned; yet it is this very flexibility that allows opportunity takers to seize an opportunity when it presents itself. If they have cash or can raise it, they can move quickly and sometimes can pick up really good deals. Sometimes a large company with immediate cash-flow problems will sell off its *best* operation because it can be done quickly.

How does an opportunity maker operate?

Unlike the opportunity taker, the opportunity maker is probably searching for an acquisition with particular operational characteristics in one or two specific industries. This practitioner seeks to cherry-pick the proper industry player that best complements or supplements current operations and overall long-range plans. The structure is important.

For example, if the opportunity maker's core business is the distribution of industrial laboratory supplies, it may make strategic sense to integrate vertically backward into self-manufacturing of high-profit-margin items that the company currently purchases from suppliers and then distributes. (In the telecommunications field it is this strategy that is currently driving some megamergers.)

The opportunity maker will typically develop acquisition criteria through the fit chart process or a similar tool, so it knows what it's looking for. Now it's just a matter of finding it. Most companies, including subsidiaries of large companies, are listed in many different databases. Most are classified by Standard Industrial Classification (SIC) code or the new North American Industrial Classification (NAIC) code and are easily identified. Some are classified by sales, net profit, and net worth ranges to fit some preset criteria. Standard & Poor's (Compustat) and D&B both offer excellent databases for this purpose.

As part of this approach, the opportunity maker would be wise to sift through the literature—both published and nonpublished technical databases and news reports—for data to confirm or add to the results. The U.S. government, for example the Internal Revenue Service (IRS), has an abundance of free or low-cost data about industries and even about specific companies.

How should an effective literature search be conducted?

Each acquirer will want to develop its own procedure. In the experience of the principal author, however, the following seven steps are mandatory for the vigilant researcher:

- First, develop an *industry situation analysis.* This analysis determines an industry's pricing and current profitability structure, growth, maturity, cyclicality, seasonality, and other economic indicators.
- Second, develop a clear *nomenclature* so that everyone involved is communicating properly.
- Third, assemble a list of *industry players.* These are the companies that are movers and shakers in the field.
- Fourth, assemble a list of *industry gurus.* These are the people who know everything worth knowing about an industry sector. Without tipping your hand, you might want to contact industry specialists who belong to associations such as the Association for Corporate Growth (ACG), the Institute of Management Consultants (IMC), and International Merger and Acquisition Professionals (IMAP). Operating managers—for example, purchasing agents, plant managers, or engineers—are also ideal contacts. For larger deals, every major investment bank has specialists who track specific industries.
- Fifth, begin to collect *industry and deal data* by contacting the industry trade associations, independent research firms that publish reports on specific industries, product/market segments and companies, and published databases. Use your public and nearest university library. Tap into databases such as Dialog and Nexus. And don't neglect the booming bulletin boards of the on-line ser-

vices, such as America OnLine/CompuServe, GEnie, Prodigy, and hundreds of specialized bulletin boards. Don't forget government sources. The Internal Revenue Service and the Department of Commerce publish economic and industry data.

- Sixth, start calling contacts identified in steps three through five. Develop contact lists to conduct one-on-one telephone interviews with the leading players. Send out direct-mail questionnaires.

- Seventh, attend industry trade shows. You can physically see the target products/services and talk directly with potential acquisition candidates in some cases. Also, most trade shows attract industry gurus. They seem to know before management when something is going to be sold off. If you're interested in expansion by serial consolidation, trade shows are the place to start. Many a management buyout, leveraged or not, has been started right on the exhibit floor.

What are some good Internet sites for dealmaking information?

Good question. This could be the topic for an entire book—in fact we know of an Internet dealmaker (rbrauns@tiac.net) who is working on one. It can also be the basis for a business—we know of a pair of Web sites entirely devoted to doing business deals on the Internet (fourleaf.com and boldfund.com).

It is difficult to come up with a short list of top sites. If you ask any Internet search engine to find you sites relating to mergers, you are likely to be flooded with answers. For example, at press time (October 1998), a search on NetFind via Excite for sites pertaining to "mergers" produced 32,777 hits and the search phrase "mergers or acquisitions" produced 83,337 hits! That's sort of like finding a stretch of land that contains gold—but where, exactly?

Some merger sites carry nothing more than commentaries on specific mergers or mergers in general. Of interest, but not the gold we are looking for. And some are advertisements for advisory firms, such as accountants, brokers, lawyers, and management consultants specializing in M&A. Also good, but not glittering. Many, however, do contain the precious materials that dealmakers seek—hard data on deals and deal contacts. Here are just a few of the *scores* of "golden" sites out there—including links to others:

www.bizbuysell.com (general M&A site aimed at brokers and finders) www.bizlist.com (links to firms that offer services to companies wishing to sell; also has list of professional corporate buyers)

www.cbex.com (site for info exchange on middle market M&A opportunities, including bulletin board)

www.egroups.com (bulletin boards at "mergers")

www.firstlist.com (national listing of acquisition, merger, financing, joint venture, and licensing opportunities)

www.hazlewoods.co.uk/malinks.html (links to other M&A networks worldwide)

www.madaily.com (reports on M&A activity)

www.maol.com (free data base used to post companies for sale)

www.masource.org (directory of members of the International Business Brokers Association representing M&A intermediaries for the middle market and indexed by state/region)

www.mergernetwork.com (discussion groups and M&A classifieds including buyers, sellers, and advisors)

www.mergers.net (annotated directory of international firms specializing in M&A organized by country)

www.nvst.com (links to professionals, publications, and associations such as ACG and IMAP, mentioned above)

www.onelist.com (technical discussion group with listings)

www.riggsallen.com (M&A resources including *Riggs/Allen Report,* a bimonthly newsletter with M&A classified for both buyers and sellers)

www.worldm-anetwork.com (M&A classified including buyers and sellers, organized by industry)

Some sites specialize in industries, for example:

www.fourleaf.com (acquisition, alliances, and investments in internet-related businesses)

Other sites specialize in countries or regions, for example:

www.innostar.com (for deals and financing in China)

www.niemi.no (Eurodeals—particularly in energy)

Also some links focus on financing, for example:

www.datamerge.com (worldwide funding sources of debt and equity capital)

www.snlnet.com (links to the financial services industry)

Some regions have local networking groups for M&A, for example:

www.netpreneur.org (for the greater Washington, D.C. area)

Also, the principal author is developing a bibliographic Web site to be called www.mergercentral.com, with both print and electronic sources.

Do you have any general advice on Internet searches?

Think big! The World Wide Web is a vast sea of ever-changing information. There is no single way to explore it.

For example, *don't just use one search engine,* such as Yahoo! (even though it is great). After all, there are hundreds! To gain access to several engines, get onto a Web site that provides such access. The Web site 14u.net, for example, gives instant access to Excite, InfoSeek, Lycos, WebCrawler, and Yahoo! To find other points of access, merely type the "search engines" as your search phrase on any engine. You will be amazed at the multitude of search engine choices.

Also, *don't be satisfied with just one search per engine* on a particular phrase. The word "merger" searched on Excite one day might yield 24,367 hits. The identical search conducted two months later might produce over 35,000! This is because the search engines are continually mining the Web for new information. The converse is also true: sometimes search engines reduce the number of sites they offer for particular search terms. You might find some great M&A sites in a particular industry one day using one search engine, and return to the same search engine the next day and find that it no longer directs searchers to those sites. So if you find sites you like, *jot down addresses* for direct access.

Another tip: *go with the flow.* When you find a good site with multiple links, use those links to branch out to other sites with new sets of links. When you are doing this kind of exploration, *create a paper trail* of your research, maintaining a record of where you have gone and how you got there.

How does the researcher compile a list of industry players?

It takes a combination of sources, in print and on the telephone.

- First, contact the focus industry's trade association(s) and obtain the membership directories. (This is not as difficult as it seems. Trade association officials will help a potential entrant to enter with the quid pro quo that it will continue its membership if it makes an entry or will join if it buys a member.) The executive secretary of the trade association (or any other top staff member who is accessible) usually knows where all the treasure is buried and may lead a potential acquirer directly and immediately to a potential candidate. This is particularly true where an operating division of a larger parent might be covertly for sale. The executive of the association is often privy to such normally confidential information.

- Second, use reference books such as *Thomas Register* and trade periodical buyer's guides. These reference books normally group companies by the product or service sold. For example, the researcher looking for companies that manufacture fluid-bed dryers should start by referencing fluid-bed dryers in *Thomas Register.* If you want to be more specific and discover those manufacturers that produce fluid-bed dryers for the pharmaceutical industry, you would look under fluid-bed dryers in *Pharmaceutical Technology's Annual Buyer's Guide.*

- Third, study special industry research reports by independent research firms, such as Frost & Sullivan (www.frost.com). Prospectuses for these studies are listed and indexed by subject in *Findex* (www.findex.com) and are also on the Dialog database. These prospectuses contain the study's table of contents, which usually discloses the names of key industry players. Also, both trade association and industry/company reports are invaluable information centers for industry data. These normally cover an entire industry's structure or a particular product/market segment's structure. Some industry reports can be expensive—sometimes in the $25,000 range. But the publisher will usually send you a précis that in itself can be very valuable. Another good but expensive source—accessible, free through public and university libraries—is Predicasts, a vast proprietary database.

- Fourth, if you are considering publicly held targets, don't overlook the reports of securities research firms. There are nearly 800 such firms worldwide, many of them major brokerage houses. They are listed annually in *Nelson's Directory of Investment Research.* The *Wall Street Transcript* reprints thousands of company reports written by analysts for the bigger investment banking firms. Other sources for public companies include the *Value Line Investment Survey,* annual reports, Securities and Exchange Commission (SEC) filings (10Ks, 10Qs, prospectuses, and proxies), press releases, product literature, catalogues, company case studies, and executive speeches. Standard & Poor's (S&P) publications (*Register, Corporation Records, Industry Survey,* and *Stock Guide*), *Directory of Corporate Affiliations—Who Owns Whom* (published by National Register Publishing Company, a division of Reed Elsevier, Inc., in New Providence, New Jersey, and various Moody's publications (industrial manuals and *Handbook of Common Stocks*) will also serve.

How can a buyer find information on private companies?

At least four U.S. directory publishers provide such information:

- D&B lists 160,000 U.S. public and private companies, service and manufacturing, with sales of $25 million and over in its multivolume *Million Dollar Directory.* D&B's online database (www.dnb.com/mdd) lists 1 million U.S. companies of all descriptions with sales over $1 million. D&B also has products covering international firms.

- Harris Infosource (www.harrisinfo.com), based in Cleveland, is the leading source of information about U.S. manufacturing companies. Its directories cover 48 states, and its database all 50 states. It has data on 360,000 manufacturers, public and private.

- Hoover's *Handbook of Private Companies* lists 600 major private companies, from Ace Hardware, with 1995 sales of $2.4 billion, to the Yucaipa Companies, with sales of $4.3 billion.

- Standard & Poor's *Register,* published by McGraw-Hill (www.mcgraw-hill.com), lists details on 75,000 public and private companies.

Some states compile extensive company information through their chambers of commerce or economic development programs. Washington Researchers (www.researchers.com), based in Rockville, Maryland, is expert in accessing such data. To find similar resources, contact the Society of Competitive Intelligence Professionals (www.scip.org) in Alexandria, Virginia.

Usually, private companies do not give out financial information such as balance sheet and profit and loss numbers. Even when they have done it for credit purposes, many do not keep it up to date. Even smaller public companies fail to update. Gross sales information is often four to five years old. Normally D&B will give some numbers, such as the number of employees. Thus, to get a ballpark figure for a potential target's annual sales volume, the buyer can generate a sales-per-employee ratio and apply it. Service company information is harder to come by than manufacturers' because service-industry trade associations, if they exist, often do not collect hard numbers.

How does the researcher develop a contact list of industry gurus?

One can pick up their names at trade shows and meetings of technical societies. Many are at universities, and many more are independent consultants. Most such gurus publish articles about their specialties in technical journals and the trade press. For books, the largest collection is, of course, at the Amazon Web site (www.amazon.com), which lists 3 million titles accessible by subject. (By the way, previous editions of the book you are reading have been Amazon's number one best-seller in the M&A category.) For articles, the best place to start is with the *Business Periodicals Index* (*BPI*), which lists tens of thousands of technical and nontechnical articles arranged by industry. Lexis/Nexis also offers an in-depth service for searching articles by subject matter—actually counting the number of times a given word or phrase (for example, "iron and coal") appears. In many cases, a trade association maintains a list of consultants who specialize in their industry. Also, list brokers, such as Info U.S.A. (www.info/usa.com), of Omaha, Nebraska, may have industry contact lists. As with research on industry players, don't stop at the printed word. Developing a contact list requires a great deal of hard-slogging telephone work.

Could you give a checklist of research sources?

Here is a checklist of these and other sources listed above:

- Annual reports and 10Ks filed with the SEC

- Bibliographies (e.g., *BPI*)
- Census of manufacturers, retail trade, and mineral industries
- Credit raters (e.g., D&B)
- Directory publishers
- Government sources
- Libraries
- List brokers
- Local newspapers
- Online researchers
- Stock brokerage firms and independent researchers
- Trade associations
- Trade periodicals
- Last but not least, the wonderful World Wide Web

When conducting focus industry surveys, what is the best approach?

Superior results come from talking to "users" over the telephone and going over a questionnaire with them. A user is someone who makes decisions to buy, or use, a product or a service. Talking to these users is especially helpful. Many a good lead has been developed this way, as a major user might help you target a company and might even be interested in helping you finance the deal! Such conversations are easily started: "Who there buys high-capacity filter presses?" You should talk to both the end user and the purchasing person.

One caveat: The direct approach works well *once you know the industry.* If you don't know what a filter press looks like, do some research. When you place that call, you may have more up-to-date information than the industry player. You can trade information in a telephone call. Key personnel generally open up and talk about their own company if they have learned something new about the industry from you.

Another word of warning: It may take many hours and even days before one gains a sense of the industry. So never start with the candidate company even if you have one. Learn the industry on the peripherals. Always talk to customers first and discover what they are looking for.

What does a proper survey cost?

Telephone charges, travel, computer time, and basic office personnel expenditures for any kind of a proper search and identification program can run from the low-to-middle six figures to several million dollars. As a rule of thumb, it costs a minimum of from $75,000 to $200,000 to bring a group of modest-sized focus companies—$10 million to $300 million in sales—to the point where a preliminary offer can be made for one of them. Megadeal searches—over $300 million—start at the $200,000 level and can run into the low seven figures.[9]

What information should be accumulated in a focus company's file?

After completing basic research, the potential acquirer needs to decide whether or not moving into this industry is desirable. If that decision is positive, the buyer puts together a target profile on each of the acquisition candidates. This may entail a technology and manufacturing audit to make sure the acquired company's process will survive in the future. A marketing audit may be highly revealing and may support a premium price for the company. These audits are the very beginning of the buyer's "due diligence." (See Chapter 6.)

Other information that goes in the focus company's file includes annual reports, 10Ks, D&B credit reports, company fact books and product catalogues, press releases, print advertisements, published articles and executive speeches, and director and officer profiles. *Business Week, Forbes, Fortune,* the *Wall Street Journal,* and many other publications—some available online (e.g., *Business Week*)—do summary articles on industries. These articles and others can be found through *BPI* as previously mentioned. Go back at least five years and copy the *BPI* abstracts. Then find the articles, read them, and copy the best into the focus company's file if specifically about the candidate, or into the industry file if about the industry in general. If data are offered giving market shares by geographical breakdown, that's important information. It is also important to itemize how each candidate's product is differentiated in any way from the competition's and whether it enjoys any special niche advantages—by geographic location, by age groups, and so on.

At this time the potential buyer must rank-order candidates. What is the best way to do this?

If the buyer's team is using the fit chart or a similar approach, it should now run specific candidates through the fit chart and rate them against the buyer's specific weaknesses and strengths (as complements and supplements). The first company evaluated may have a strong marketing force and weak technology, whereas the fifth in line may have the opposite attributes. That might lead a strong marketer to the decision to buy number five, believing that it can be integrated into its own strong marketing and distribution channels.

Who should be contacted at the focus company?

Callers should start at the top. The principals contacted may include the CEO, the CFO, or the COO. In a wide-ranging search, the focus company's directors, outside counsel, accountants, and bankers—both commercial and investment—can also be contacted. Contacting a candidate's outside counsel is usually unproductive. First, attorneys, because of attorney-client confidentiality, are not supposed to give out any information; and second, *they* have their own fish to fry. They may want to initiate the deal so that they will continue to be retained, and will try to discourage you. The same thing, to a lesser extent, applies to the candidate's accounting firm.

Try to structure any conversation with a principal officer or owner so as to avoid a direct turndown. One technique that has been honed to a fine art by executive headhunters is to call desired candidates and ask if they know of an executive who might be available. The candidates might then offer themselves. It works the same way in an acquisition search. Tell prospects that you are considering making an entry in the industry by either a *de novo* entry (a start-up) *or* an acquisition and ask if they know any company for sale. That is sure to get their attention; their response might just be, "Well, if the price were right, *we* might be for sale."

If the acquisition proposal involves a relatively small subsidiary of any relatively large company, the contact person should be the senior vice president of corporate planning or corporate development—but don't call the division head unless it's public knowledge that the unit is on the block. And even then it's best to deal with planning at either the corporate, sector, or business unit level rather than with the executives who might be intimately affected by a sale, and may, in fact, be trying to buy the operation themselves.

What should the caller say—and not say?

The focus company's nonowner management will be impressed with any expertise demonstrated by the caller. The focus company profile will give the buyer more "information leverage" because the focus company will often know very little about the buyer. To set the management more at ease, the buyer (or its agent) should provide some useful information about itself.

The ultimate goal of the initial conversation is to set up a meeting to discuss "working together" or "teaming up" through a possible "business venture." The business relationship could be a merger, acquisition, or joint venture, or a customer-supplier relationship. The more broadly you define it, the better—but avoid out-and-out misrepresentation. No mention of price should be made at this stage of the process.

Where should buyer and candidate representatives meet at this early stage?

The parties have to agree on a mutually satisfactory meeting place. Visiting the focus company may start the rumor mill, and that can hurt a deal. On the other hand, the buyer can get a better feel for the candidate's operations and personnel if they are at least eyeballed. But the usual practice of a large group of "suits" descending on a candidate should be discouraged.

An alternative would be a meeting at the offices of an investment banker or law firm, or in neutral territory, such as a conference room at a hotel. Try not to meet in airline clubs, hotel lobbies, coffee shops, or other public places—it starts the rumor mill going and can create competition.

Once you have decided on a meeting place, try to obtain the focus company's latest financial statements.

Once a meeting place has been decided, it will benefit the buyer to obtain the focus company's financials prior to the meeting. (We assume you already have all the sales literature, D&B reports, and, if it's a public company, the 10Ks.) The company may ask you to sign a *confidentiality agree-*

ment at this point. By all means do so, but make sure you are protected. (See Chapter 8.)

With such information in hand, an agenda for the meeting can be easily set—and it's important to have a written agenda at least for your side so that all the important subjects will be covered.

Also important is to recast the candidate's historical financials into a more easily read form such as common-size, trended, and industry comparisons. When these are done, it is easy to compile a list of questions identifying the financial and operating anomalies for discussion.

What are common-size, trended, and industry comparisons?

These are invaluable techniques for identifying problems and isolating areas for potential profit improvement. As such, they can be an important tool in the negotiation process and can influence price.

Instead of looking at absolute numbers, common-size and trended analyses uncover hard-to-detect anomalies that may exist in a company's balance sheet or income statement. Common-size financial statements utilize a common denominator such as net worth for balance sheets; all the components are entered as percentages and are easily compared year to year. The operating statements use net sales as a base and the cost components as percentages of that base. Trended analyses use an appropriately selected base year or period that represents 100 for all items of the balance sheet and income statement. All dollar amounts for each item on the balance sheet and income statement in years subsequent to the base year are expressed as a percentage of the base-year amounts. The anomalies become immediately apparent as areas for further investigation and become part of the negotiating process because they must be explained.

For example, if accounts receivable and inventory combined accounted for 50 percent of total assets during the first year and increased to 62 percent the second year while sales only increased a meager 2 percent, the company may be boosting sales by serving poorer-quality customers creditwise. As a result, the buyer will want to double-check the collection period for accounts receivable by interviewing customers and suppliers. Although this is a point of stress for sellers—especially the customer interviews—and generally can take place only at advanced stages in the negotiation, the buyer should let the seller know that it is something that is expected.

What else can be accomplished at the first meeting with an acquisition candidate?

The meeting should give the buyer a sense of the company and its operations, whether there are any skeletons in the seller's closets that may preclude a deal, and whether the chemistry is right if there are to be any continuing management relationships. The meeting should give the prospective seller a sense of the buyer and the benefits to managers if they are to stay and to owners if they are to continue to own.

There must be *reasons* for combining companies corporately and operationally. In most cases these are discussed in the early meetings, unless the buyer deems the plans confidential. If the potential seller is a public company, this is a sensitive area; both disclosure and nondisclosure of future plans involve complicated legal niceties.

For public companies, it is good to have copies of any financial write-ups issued by investment bankers—even if issued by a regional house. Also, ask the sellers if they ever had a management consultant in to run a survey. If they did, ask to see the report, no matter how old it may be. And ask to see the outside auditors' management letters or reports. Find out if the company has changed auditors within the past five years, and if so, get permission to talk to the old auditors.

What happens next?

If the parties' objectives and personalities seem to mesh, and more meetings take place, a deal is likely. It is important to follow up by telephone or letters to keep the candidate's interest alive. Further, many deals wind up in court, and the side that builds the most complete record has a better chance to win. Some of the principal causes of litigation are verbal assertions or representations—usually made by sellers or their representatives—that later prove untrue, and buyers sue. But those suits are hard to win. *Caveat emptor* certainly applies in the M&A field.

Remember, most sellers (and many buyers) somewhere along the line get cold feet. So keep the deal moving. It may not jell for months—or even years. But if it's right, it's right. So never give up on it. Never.

BROKERS AND FINDERS

Much of the foregoing describes in-house search processes, but many companies seeking to expand by the M&A route—especially the opportunity makers—use finders and/or brokers.

What's the difference between a broker and a finder?

A *broker* is an agent and a legal fiduciary with all the responsibilities and restrictions that those terms imply in law. Brokers may represent only one side in a transaction. The rules governing their behavior have been established over the past five centuries by the common law. Many M&A matchmakers have lost their fees because they were ignorant of these rules. Generally, brokers represent sellers and as fiduciaries must try to get a top price for a company. Any cheating and it's a civil suit, and in some cases criminal if the broker favors buyers over sellers in a transaction or secretly takes money from a buyer to knock down the price.

Finders, as opposed to brokers, are not agents of or for anyone. They are not fiduciaries. Unlike brokers, they represent the *deal* rather than one of the parties. Finders can be paid by both parties or by either party, even without the knowledge of the other. Finders, however, must be careful not to negotiate, for it is the act of negotiation that takes them out of the finder class, creates an act of agency, places them squarely in the broker category, and creates fiduciary responsibilities for them. The act of *negotiation* can also create a licensing obligation. Depending on the locale, a *business opportunity* or *business chance* broker's license may be required. These licenses are supposed to have (and probably should have) regulatory impact, but often serve as mere revenue-generators. Finders are generally excepted from this licensing requirement.

How is *negotiation* defined for the purposes of a broker/finder distinction?

Generally, if the finder merely introduces the prospective purchasers and otherwise acts only to maintain contact between the parties to make the introduction effective, no negotiation will be deemed to have taken place. If, however, the finder gets involved in determining the purchase price and stands in the place of the buyer or seller, a court may decide that he or she negotiated. In a few states, the courts have stated that they cannot see how a finder can operate without negotiating, and automatically lump finders in the brokers category.

What is an intermediary?

People who are foggy about the distinction between brokers and finders try to solve their dilemma by billing themselves as *intermediaries*. This straddling category can be risky because intermediaries are supposed to negotiate, and a *negotiating intermediary* is an agent of one party or the other in a contemplated transaction unless both sides have agreed—usually in writing—that the negotiation is in their common interest. Such an agreement is not a recommended practice because, depending on the language of the agreement, it may relieve the intermediary of his or her fiduciary duties as a broker.

Are business brokers, finders, and intermediaries regulated, and if so, by whom?

In general, the act of the brokering, finding, and negotiating between businesses is not regulated, which is why it is so important to prequalify them. The fact that some investment bankers or stockbrokers have passed exams run by the National Association of Securities Dealers (NASD) or that they are "regulated" by the SEC is of no moment to the business of finding and brokering the sale and purchase of businesses—even very large businesses.

What does matter is regulation by state and local authorities, including local real estate boards, of acts of "business brokerage." This includes the licensing and regulation of business opportunity and business chance brokers. Generally, such brokers deal with the sale of bars and taverns, car washes, dry-cleaning shops, gas stations, taxi licenses, and other service-oriented businesses.

Many states have passed laws regulating the activity of such brokers, or allow cities and counties to enact local ordinances to regulate their activity. Often state regulation is combined with the regulation of real estate brokerage activity, usually through the acts of examination, licensing, inspection of the broker's premises, and so on. Lawyers, contrary to popular belief, are seldom exempted from the requirement to be licensed as business opportunity brokers if they negotiate the sale of a business and collect a *success fee* as a result.

No state has yet regulated the activity of the nonnegotiating finder, with the possible exception of New York. In a long series of tortured court decisions and supporting legislation, New York law has said, in effect, that no finder can perform the act of finding without negotiating. Finders are, therefore, ipso facto agents and brokers involved in the transfer of property, and in order to comply with a specific provision of New York's statute of frauds, anyone (including investment banking firms) dealing in the transfer of "property" must have an agreement in writing to collect a finder's or a broker's fee. But guess what? Lawyers are excepted from this requirement.

Other states have similar statutes of fraud but do not bar collection under general concepts of contract law, such as *quantum meruit,* in which the services of the finder, even in the absence of a written contract, must be valued and paid for so as not to unjustly enrich a buyer or seller from the services provided. In New York State, however, *quantum meruit* recovery not supported by a written contract is strictly barred. As a result, many frauds have been perpetrated on unknowing finders and brokers. Even major investment banking houses have been cheated out of legitimately earned fees for failure to have a verbal fee agreement reduced to writing. One major Chicago house put two banks together in a large transaction and lost its fee because it had not registered as a business broker in the city of Chicago. Finders in Miami, Florida, have faced similar problems, but the courts there have recessed and allowed offenders to go downstairs, pay $15 for a license, come back to court, and get judgments for their fees—and those fees can be in the six figures!

Many states try to regulate finders and brokers if real estate is involved in the transaction—even if the real assets, which include leases, are only a tiny fraction of the assets transferred. Prodded by real estate brokers, many suits result. Most are lost by the state and the brokers, but once in a while one slips through—especially when an out-of-state finder or broker does deals across a state line. In this case it is extremely important that the finder or broker not perform any act that a court could consider to be negotiation, and make sure that the principals do all the negotiating and acknowledge it in writing. An excellent discussion of these problems can be found in the 1998 edition of the *Business Reference Guide,* which also has a state-by-state review of business brokerage laws, describes some interesting legal cases, and lists the addresses of those states (and in Canada those provinces) that regulate business brokerage activity.[10]

What about fees for brokers, finders, and intermediaries?

Fees are not regulated by anyone. They are what the market will bear. In the 1920s the investment bankers were happy to get straight commissions for the shares exchanged. But when the conglomerate merger boom began in the 1950s, Lehman Brothers dreamed up the *Lehman scale,* also known as the *M&A formula,* or the *Wall Street rule.* This is a sliding scale—generally the 5-4-3-2-1 formula: 5 percent of the first $1 million of the price of the transaction, 4 percent of the second, 3 percent of the third, 2 percent of the fourth, and 1 percent of the balance.

In the 1950s and early 1960s perhaps 75 percent of the fees were computed in this manner. Thus a $5 million deal would call for a fee of $150,000, a $25 million deal would call for a fee of $350,000, and a $50 million deal $600,000. In larger transactions, the final 1 percent might drop down to 0.5 percent at the $50 million to $100 million level, or $850,000 for a $100 million deal. As the deals got larger, sometimes a cap was put on the fee by agreement, such as "no fee to exceed $2 million." Generally, in transactions above $100 million, the fee was and is negotiated. An $800 million transaction might call for a base fee in the $2 million to $5 million range rather than a fee of $8.1 million dictated by the straight 5-4-3-2-1 Lehman scale.

Many finders who build themselves up as "investment bankers," though they have only a phone number and an office, try to get Lehman scale for their services, but they usually are forced to settle for a flat fee or to sue. Some have successfully sued and collected very large fees using the Lehman scale. The principal author has acted as an expert witness in many such cases.

Fees are sometimes modified by the type of deal. If it is a hostile deal, the bankers might be involved for many months or even years. Hostile deals carry much larger fees than friendly deals, especially when they are successful. If the deal is complicated, as were many of the leveraged buyouts of the 1980s, the fees would be higher. Now, at the turn of the century, many of the deals are done with an exchange of securities. These deals are much less complicated and call for reduced fees. In hostile deals, however, in the heat of battle, many a tendering corporation has failed to reach a final fee agreement with the bankers, lawyers, consultants, accountants, and others that may be involved until after the deal is closed, and then there are problems, which sometimes wind up in court with a judge or jury making the fee decisions. Juries are particularly tough on finder's and broker's fees that are legally due; they find it hard to believe that the simple act of introducing a potential seller to a potential buyer is worth a large sum.

The fee payment often depends on the final price paid in the deal. But determining the final "price" in a complicated, highly leveraged deal with equity kickers such as detachable warrants and rights, simultaneous spin-offs or spin-outs, or sales of subsidiaries can be very difficult and can lead to disagreements about the price of the transaction. As a result, more and more fees are negotiated ahead of time in round numbers. "If we do the deal you get $3 million" might be the language that one hears today for a prospective $400 million deal. That works out to 0.75 percent. In such an arrangement, whether the buyer pays $300 million or $500 million, the finder or broker gets a $3 million fee for initiating the transaction.

Whenever a bidding war develops, investment bankers stand to gain millions, as in the battle for control of Paramount Communications, Inc., in 1993. At the height of that battle, it was reported that Smith Barney Shearson, Viacoms advisor, would walk away with $20 million; Lazard Frères, Paramount's advisor, with $10 million to $12 million; and Allen & Company, QVC's advisor, with $10 million to $20 million.[11] Not every hostile tender offer generates so many big fees, but there is no doubt that advising such deals can be much more lucrative to advisors than advising friendly transactions.[12]

The average advisory fee in 1993, based on the 210 deals with advisors disclosing fees that year, was only about $2 million, according to *Mergers & Acquisitions* magazine's *Almanac* issue for that year. Although the average fees paid to advisors have risen in recent years—some $7 million in 1997, for example—these single-digit amounts are still lower than the fees paid in hostile deals, where work often involves round-the-clock teamwork.

During the 1980s, when the LBO/MBO movement was on, it was common practice for the finder or broker, as part of or in addition to the fee, to make a *bargain purchase* of some of the original stock—say, 1 percent of the equity—as an added inducement to bring a deal to a successful closing. As we move into the next millennium, we may see a recurrence of this practice as consolidation in advisory firms (such as investment banks) leads to layoffs. As former employees become entrepreneurs, we could see a boom in the independent finder/broker population—and a consequent rise in such creative fee making.

Are investment bankers different from other brokers and finders?

Yes. First of all, some investment bankers act as stockbrokers by retailing stocks and bonds. Many also act as finders and brokers and are retained to locate entire businesses to buy. They also represent stockholder groups wanting to sell a company or one or more of its divisions, generally by a practice known as an *auction*. (But it is nothing like the usual auction; it usually winds up in an extensive negotiation with multiple bidders on price and terms.) And as "bankers," they may do much more. They may render a *fairness opinion* to help raise the funds to finance the deal. Some investment bankers even help finance deals themselves, for example, through funding "bridge loans." As a result they stand to receive a series of fees—finder's, broker's, opinion, consulting, origination, and underwriting fees, and, if the securities are exchanged through their offices, a *security broker's fee*. Together these fees are called *investment banking fees*. In times of heavy merger activity these fees bring in as much revenue as retail stock brokerage, and in some years considerably more.

Is it true that large firms (major accounting firms and banks) shun small deals, leaving these to brokers and finders?

No. Although each investment bank has a minimum size, the floor is getting lower for many enterprising accounting firms and Wall Street houses. It used to be that larger companies would take $10 million-plus deals (maybe), and anything below that went to the small shops, who were eager for any business. Today, however, this dividing line is crossed from both directions. There are large accounting firms and banks (commercial and investment) that are willing to take on smaller deals because of the cross-selling opportunities they provide. Conversely, some busy small shops will not take deals below $50 million. So never assume that your deal is too small or too big for the firm you want. Find out who's the best in your business, and go from there.

What is an arbitrageur?

An "arb" gambles with the investment bank's money that there will be a bidding contest for a company that has been put "in play" by someone making an offer for it, as in the famed Paramount contest with Viacom and QVC duking it out. With the stock selling initially in the $50 area, Viacom's friendly offer in the $60 area eventually wound up in the $100 area and the arbs made money—lots of it. Ideally, arbitrageurs sit on the sidelines, making bets on a reality they do not control. In the real world, some can succumb to the temptation to make things happen in their favor. The famous (and, for some, infamous) arbitrageur, Ivan Boesky, went to jail for insider trading in support of his art. (See Chapter 12.) Equally famous, though, is arbitrageur Guy Weiser-Pratt, who could practically be canonized for his impeccable conduct in a career spanning four decades.

Do investment banking firms pay fees to finders for bringing them prospective deals?

Yes. Most investment banking firms will pay a finder's fee to someone who brings them a deal. Some firms, like Goldman, Sachs, accept such leads but publicly claim they have never paid for them. But most successful firms are happy to pay in the area of 10 percent of their fees for a successful lead.

What is a mere volunteer?

Volunteers usually cannot collect finder's or broker's fees. A so-called telephone book finder, for instance, one who sends out thousands of letters suggesting acquisition opportunities to major corporations and does little or nothing more, is considered a "mere volunteer" and cannot collect a fee when one of the companies is actually acquired, for lack of proof that the volunteer was, in fact, the "procuring cause" of the transaction. Many legitimately earned fees have been defeated using the "mere volunteer" defense—especially in the oil business. Some degree or sign of invitation or consent is necessary to establish a compensable finder or broker relationship.

As a buyer, how can you protect yourself against claims for payment of unwarranted finder's or broker's fees?

There are several ways:

- Keep a log of inquiries and correspondence.

- Answer every unsolicited letter by rejecting offers of companies, and keep copies of all such correspondence. But be truthful. Don't say you're not interested if you are. It can cost you dearly.
- Keep your contacts up to date. Finder A refers your company to a business. Then you drop the deal for six months until Finder B "revives" your interest and you acquire. You may owe fees to both Finder A and Finder B.
- Find out whether your state regulates business opportunity brokers. If the broker is not licensed, you can defeat an illegitimate claim for a fee if the broker negotiates. But you must prove that he or she negotiated, and that is often hard to do.
- Find out if the state you're in has a statute of frauds. If so, the broker or finder may need a written agreement to collect a fee.
- Be aware that you may invite a possible Racketeer Influenced and Corrupt Organizations Act (RICO) claim and triple damages if you try to defraud the broker or finder of a legitimately earned fee. Also, a broker or finder may be able to obtain punitive damages if you conspire to defraud him or her of a legitimate fee.

As a finder or broker, how do I ensure that I will be paid if I do a deal?

Get some early writings on the record that you expect to be paid, that you are not a mere volunteer or doing it out of friendship. The retired president of Joy Manufacturing worked for a year and a half and brought about the sale of his best friend's coal-mining business for $275 million. He had two filing cases of correspondence in support of his efforts. But the "best friend" testified that the finder had never told him he expected to be paid and there was nothing in all those filing cabinets that stated that he expected to be paid. Always get a written agreement that includes specific language on the fee schedule.

- Keep a log of conversations—especially telephone conversations. If you are out of the office when a client calls, make sure that whoever answers the phone makes a *written record of the call* and make sure the date, time, and message are recorded and are *readable*. Transcribe any message tapes into a file *and save the tapes*. Such "message logs" can be powerful evidence in some courts.

- Get your client to agree (in writing if possible) that the deal won't close unless you get paid. At least send a letter requesting this.
- Insist on participating in all meetings of the principals. If you are acting as a finder, be sure to clearly announce that you are there as a facilitator and not a negotiator. If possible, get a letter from the other side that you did not negotiate. Again, get a letter to that effect in the mail.
- Get some paper on the record. The more the better. Judges like to read letters from you to the buyer or seller. So do juries. They both want you to work for a living since they do. Many juries and some judges have trouble approving fees in the million dollar area in payment for the simple act of introducing two parties. But such fees are paid all the time. Be sure to save your telephone bills, train and plane tickets, hotel receipts, and so on. The principal author was an expert witness in a finder's case where the judge based his decision, at least in part, on the fact that the finder could prove that he had paid for a series of lunches with the buyer's representative. (That person, in turn, had billed his company for that same expense. The judge didn't care for that!)
- Sue the second you're not paid. Don't wait. In another case in which the principal author was the expert witness, the buyer had set up his old college roommate as the finder and claimed that the roommate had originated the deal. He then paid him a $300,000 fee and cited that payment in court as a defense. It didn't work. He lost. Fortunately, our side had proof of who the real finder was. Be sure to get a lawyer with some experience in finders and brokers cases, an area in which many lawyers have little or no experience.

USING INTERMEDIARIES

If a broker advises a buyer about an opportunity that another broker closes, which broker should be paid?

Such contingencies should be spelled out in the broker/finder agreement. If they are not so defined, however, the second, successful intermediary should be paid—either the entire fee or at least half.

For example, suppose the XYZ Waxworks is for sale and investment banker A tells potential buyer John Smith about it. The seller wants $50 million in cash. Smith offers him $40 million, is turned down, and goes away.

Two weeks later another investment banker talks to Smith and says, "By the way, the XYZ Waxworks is for sale." Smith says, "I know that. I was out there. The guy wants $50 million. I offered him $40 million and he turned me down." However, investment banker B says, "Yes, but why don't you offer him $40 million plus a royalty of 2 percent of sales for the next 10 years, tax deductible to you? On $1 billion of sales over the next 10 years, it looks like another $20 million to the seller, who can brag about it. But the present value cost to you is only about $3 million." Smith makes the offer and XYZ Waxworks accepts it. Who is entitled to the fee?

The second banker. The first investment banker, who originally showed XYZ Waxworks to Mr. Smith, does not collect a fee because it's not the same deal. Somebody came along with a new idea about how this could be accomplished; therefore, the second broker earned the fee.

There's an old common law principle cited in many court decisions in the real estate area that states: "It isn't the person who points out the tree that gets the apples; it's the person who shakes the tree."

Suppose the same situation occurs, but with a twist. An investment banker proposes a deal to Mr. Smith, who makes the $40 million offer, and the seller turns it down. Another broker comes along six months later. He brings Mr. Smith to the same company, and Smith just reiterates his old offer. But this time the offer is accepted. This time the first investment banker *does* collect a fee in the absence of any agreement to the contrary, because it is the same deal. However, Smith (the buyer) should arrange that the fee be split.

ROLE OF INVESTMENT AND COMMERCIAL BANKS IN M&A

What is the difference between the M&A services offered by an investment bank and those offered by a commercial bank?

In today's increasingly competitive market for financial services, the differences in M&A services offered by investment banks and at least some commercial banks have narrowed considerably. As commercial banks' lending margins shrank in the 1980s, the banks became more aggressive in their search for other kinds of income. Many targeted the M&A advisory business as an extension of their work in financing LBOs, MBOs, and other kinds of highly leveraged transactions (HLTs). In the process many banks developed capabilities that rivaled those of the most prestigious investment banking houses.

The commercial banks' capabilities include developing strategies for their clients with respect to acquisitions, recapitalizations, and LBOs and acting as dealer-manager in tender offers, as well as rendering fairness opinions, something that the investment bankers are not always very good at (as proved by the myriad of overpriced deals that have taken place in the past).

The Glass-Steagall Act, however, despite repeal efforts by members of Congress sympathetic to commercial banks, prohibits commercial banks from underwriting corporate securities. Although subsidiaries of commercial banks may engage in underwriting activities, the involvement of commercial banks is restricted by heavy "Chinese walls" or "fire walls" preventing information exchange.

Investment banks, meanwhile, began to invade some of the commercial banks' traditional territories by offering to commit their capital in the form of bridge loans to their M&A clients to underwrite at least a portion of the cost of an acquisition, something that commercial banks may not do.

Although they compete against each other, commercial and investment banks often need each other. It is not unusual for them to share clients. For example, a Wall Street investment banker might act as an advisor to a company doing an acquisition. The Wall Street firm might then take its deal to a commercial bank to obtain an acquisition bridge loan plus the long-term senior bank debt needed to refinance existing senior debt, later refinancing some or all of the bank debt with a private placement and/or an underwriting of senior or subordinated public debt. (See Chapter 4.)

Because commercial banks have not been that involved with stock market operations, they have been spared the temptations faced by investment bankers to engage in illegal activity.

The insider trading scandals of the mid-to-late 1980s, Salomon Brothers' rigging of the Treasury bond market, Prudential Securities' problems with illegal sales of partnerships, and trading irregularities at Kidder Peabody have hurt the investment banking industry and its image. Illegal acts by rogue brokers and traders continue to dog the industry: Complaints that have gone to arbitration through the NASD have risen almost every year since. As a result, many acquisition planners prefer to deal with commercial banks that can provide the same services.

Is it illegal for a bank to fund one offeror for a company and to advise another, competing offeror?

No, it is not illegal. But many commercial and investment banks avoid such situations for fear of offending one or the other client or creating the impression of a conflict of interest. Commercial banks may offer financing for more than one offeror; if an advisory role is involved, the bank will attempt to erect fire walls between the different areas involved to avoid the possibility of a breach of confidentiality. "Tie-in" deals, where a client is given a loan only if the client also buys the bank's advisory services, are illegal. However, some clients prefer a bank as an advisor if it is also willing to commit its capital in the form of a loan to facilitate the acquisition. Documentation of such an arrangement should explain that it is not quid pro quo.

What is merchant banking?

Merchant banking describes a combination of advisory and investment banking services under which the commercial or investment bank uses its capital to assist the client in achieving its financial objectives. The term often applies to services offered to new ventures and recapitalized companies. Most banks in the world operate as merchant banks, take active equity positions in their customer universe, and play a decision-making role. (See Chapter 4.)

Are U.S. commercial banks involved in merchant banking?

Yes, but still in only a limited way. Many commercial banks have subsidiary venture capital groups that invest in both the equity and mezzanine securities in promising ventures, including start-up companies and leveraged buyouts. Commercial banks, in their role as investment bankers, are also increasingly becoming partners with their clients by purchasing both the equity and mezzanine securities of companies to whom they also provide senior debt.

GENERAL REGULATORY CONSIDERATIONS FOR BUYERS

What sorts of legal issues can be raised by an acquisition?

Depending on the facts and nature of the transaction, an acquisition may require compliance with federal, state, or local statutes or regulations in a variety of areas, including laws with respect to antitrust, securities, employee benefits, bulk sales, foreign ownership, and the transfer of title to stock or assets. Some of these laws require only routine acts to achieve compliance, which can be attended to relatively late in the acquisition process. Other laws pose potential regulatory barriers that must be considered before proceeding with a given acquisition plan.

How does the purchaser determine what regulatory barriers may exist for a proposed transaction?

Unless the purchaser is a veteran in the relevant field of business it plans to enter, the purchaser must engage legal counsel familiar with the field and/or skilled in the legal complexities of acquisitions.

Can the failure to identify and satisfy all regulatory requirements in a timely manner delay or kill the deal?

Yes. In some cases, one or both parties must obtain the consent or approval of the responsible agency or agencies before the transaction can be consummated. Failure to do so can result in penalties or even rescission of the contract covering the transaction.

What regulatory hurdles must be surmounted in consummating an acquisition?

Each industry has its own regulatory maze, but some general areas can be identified.

> *Antitrust.* Certain business combinations require filings and clearances with the Department of Justice (DOJ) or the Federal Trade Commission (FTC) under the Hart-Scott-Rodino Act.

Disclosure. Public companies have a myriad of rules to consider, including filings to the SEC. These rules are discussed in Chapter 12.

Environmental concerns. Corporate acquisitions can trigger state law requirements relating to cleanup of sites contaminated by hazardous wastes. A buyer can also be hit under both federal and state law with cleanup costs even if it had no involvement in or knowledge of the pollution. The Environmental Protection Agency (EPA) is now vigorously enforcing 1990 amendments to the Clean Air Act of 1977 that contain nearly 200 separate regulations—all of which can affect acquirers in environmentally sensitive industries.[13] Commercial banks acting as trustees are also exposed. (See Chapter 6.) Also, certain federal or state laws preclude the transfer by one party to another of environmental operating permits issued in the name of the first party.

Foreign ownership of U.S. assets. Federal law requires reporting of or prohibits ownership of certain industrial or commercial assets by non-U.S. citizens or entities, including U.S. flag-registered vessels and aircraft, telecommunications facilities, newspapers, nuclear power plants, and certain defense industries. (See Chapter 15.)

Industry concerns. The transfer of title to certain types of industrial or commercial assets may be subject to approval by one or more regulating agencies.

- Airlines (the Department of Transportation)
- Banks and other financial services institutions [the Controller of the Currency, the Federal Reserve Board, the Federal Deposit Insurance Corporation (FDIC), the Office of Thrift Supervision (OTS), and various state agencies]
- Insurance companies (state regulatory agencies)
- Public utilities (the Federal Energy Regulatory Commission, the Nuclear Regulatory Commission, and state public utilities commissions)
- Shipping (Maritime Administration)
- Telecommunications facilities (Federal Communications Commission)

U.S. ownership of foreign assets. Many foreign governments closely regulate the ownership by noncitizens of domestic corporations or assets and reserve the right to refuse transfer of any such property to a noncitizen.

Some of those restrictions may apply to only a portion of the transaction. For example, where there are real property assets in several states, only one of which regulates the transfer of contaminated real property, the parties can structure the transaction to close on the unaffected assets in a timely manner, leaving the affected asset for subsequent transfer upon compliance with applicable law, or excluding it from the acquisition. Alternatively, if the principal purchaser cannot obtain regulatory consents for certain assets, the seller may consider selling those assets to another purchaser.

How can the parties assess the significance of regulatory barriers at the planning stage of an acquisition?

Interested parties should determine early on how likely it is that they will obtain the necessary consents, how long this will take, and how difficult and expensive it will be. When the criteria and the procedures for obtaining consents are well defined, this regulatory "audit" can be performed relatively quickly and reliably. Avoid flexible or discretionary criteria and procedures for approvals, as these can extend the time and increase the uncertainty of obtaining approvals in a timely fashion.

Remain informed of major regulatory and deregulatory developments in your industry and in focus industries of interest to you as a potential acquirer. Regulatory and deregulatory developments can change the business climate dramatically.

In the telecommunications arena, many an acquirer still faces regulatory hurdles because of the consent decree issued after AT&T's breakup in 1982.

Conversely, in defense, a deregulatory movement promises change. In April 1994 a panel of officials from the DOJ, the FTC, and the Department of Defense announced an agreement to develop and apply special standards to defense acquisitions to facilitate mergers that would be in the nation's defense interests. After development of the new standards, approval for defense mergers came more swiftly. Noticeable examples are the mergers between Northrop Corp. and Grumman in 1994, Lockheed Martin and Martin Marietta in 1995, Boeing Co. and McDonnell Douglas in 1997, and Raytheon and Hughes Aircraft in 1998. In July 1998, Lockheed Martin announced that it was dropping plans to acquire Northrop-Grumman, citing antitrust challenges. This may signal a reversal of the pro-merger trend in this industry.

In general, and especially where third-party financing is involved, it may be not only imprudent but impossible to proceed with the affected part of the transaction prior to obtaining the necessary approval. Therefore, potential buyers and sellers should be sure at the initial planning stages to provide adequate time and resources for the regulatory compliance effort.

ANTITRUST CONSIDERATIONS FOR ACQUISITIONS

What general antitrust considerations should acquisition planners consider when contemplating an acquisition?

Antitrust practitioners divide corporate acquisitions into three types:

- *Vertical acquisitions*—acquisition of suppliers or customers—which may foreclose markets to competitors
- *Horizontal acquisitions*—between competitors—which may give "monopoly" power or cause overconcentration
- *Conglomerate acquisitions*—between firms in different fields— which might remove potential competition or discourage competition by others because of the financial or marketing strength of the resulting firm

Section 7 of the Clayton Act prohibits a corporation from acquiring stock or assets of another corporation if the acquisition might "substantially lessen competition or tend to create a monopoly" in any line of commerce in any section of the country. A violation of Section 7 may give rise to a court-ordered injunction against the acquisition, an order compelling divestiture of the property or other interests, or other remedies. Section 7 is enforced by the Antitrust Division of the DOJ and by the FTC. In November 1990 Congress passed the Interlocking Directorate Act of 1990 amending Section 8 of the Clayton Act to state that "no person shall, at any time, serve as a director or officer in any two corporations (other than banks, banking associations and trust companies) that are: A) engaged in whole or in part in commerce; and B) by virtue of their business and location of operation competitors." The provision does not apply if both companies are small (with capital and surplus and undivided profits under $10 million) or if the competitive sales involved are low (less than 4 percent market share for each or less than 2 percent for either). Individual and corporate fines were increased under the law to $350,000 and $1 million, respectively.

In conjunction with the federal laws, there are state laws that can restrict mergers. Under federal law (the McCarran-Ferguson Act, 15 U.S.C. 1011f) states are given broad authority to regulate mergers involving insurance companies. States have similar authority in certain other areas in which the states have special regulatory jurisdiction, such as the alcoholic beverages industry.

Mergers of companies with foreign operations or subsidiaries sometimes require review and approval by foreign governments. In addition, some foreign countries (most notably, Canada) have their own premerger notification programs that may have to be complied with.

HART-SCOTT-RODINO

How does the government gather information about proposed mergers and acquisitions?

The Hart-Scott-Rodino Antitrust Improvements Act of 1976 (the HSR Act) requires the parties to a proposed acquisition transaction to furnish certain information about themselves and the deal to the FTC and the Antitrust Division of the DOJ before the merger is allowed to go forward. The information supplied is used by these governmental agencies to determine whether the proposed transaction would have any anticompetitive effects after completion. If so, in general, they must be cured prior to closing. A mandatory waiting period follows the agencies' receipt of the HSR filings.

What mergers or acquisitions require premerger notification under the HSR Act?

Generally, all mergers and acquisitions that meet the following three criteria must be reported under the HSR Act and the related premerger notification rules:

- The transaction is between two persons with minimum sizes of $100 million and $10 million, respectively, in gross assets or, for manufacturing companies, in annual sales.
- As a result of the transaction, the acquiring person will own either (a) more than $15 million of the acquired person's voting securities or assets or (b) 50 percent or more of the voting securities of a company that has consolidated annual sales or gross assets of $25 million or more.

- One of the persons involved is engaged in U.S. commerce or in an activity affecting U.S. commerce.

The "persons" involved include not only the corporations involved, but also any other corporation that is under common control. "Control," for purposes of the HSR Act, is defined as ownership of 50 percent or more of a company's voting securities or having the contractual power to designate a majority of a company's board of directors. Special control rules apply to partnerships and other unincorporated entities.

What information is required to be included in the HSR premerger notification form?

The form requires a description of the parties and the proposed merger or acquisition, certain current financial information about the parties, and a breakdown of revenues of the parties according to industry codes, currently changing from the old Standard Industrial Classification codes to the new North American Industrial Classification codes (SIC and NAIC, as abbreviated earlier). This breakdown of revenues is used by the DOJ and the FTC to determine whether the proposed combination of the businesses would result in anticompetitive effects. The information filed is exempt from disclosure under the Freedom of Information Act, and no such information may be made public except pursuant to administrative or judicial proceedings.

After the premerger notification form has been filed, how long must the parties wait before the merger or acquisition may be consummated?

Where the acquisition is being made by a cash tender offer, the parties must wait 15 days before the purchaser may accept shares for payment. In all other cases, the parties must wait 30 days before the transaction may be completed. If the acquisition raises antitrust concerns, the government may extend the waiting period by requesting additional information from the parties. In that case, the waiting period is extended for 20 days (10 days in the case of a cash tender offer) past the time when the additional information is provided.

The parties may request early termination of the waiting period. Where the acquisition raises no antitrust concerns, the government may grant the request at its discretion.

Are certain mergers and acquisitions exempt from the HSR Act?

Yes. Acquisitions made through newly formed corporate acquisition vehicles are frequently exempt from the reporting requirements of the HSR Act because the vehicle does not meet the "size-of-person" test; that is, it does not have $10 million in gross assets or sales prior to the transaction. This is true, however, only where no other person having $10 million in gross assets or annual sales owns 50 percent or more of the voting stock of the vehicle or has the contractual power to designate a majority of the vehicle's directors. If the vehicle is not controlled by another person, it will be the only company matched against the $10 million size-of-person test. If another company or person does control the vehicle, through either a 50 percent stock ownership or a contractual power to appoint a majority of its directors, that controlling person will be matched against this test. Special rules apply in determining control of partnerships and other unincorporated acquisition vehicles.

Special rules are also used to determine the "size" of a newly formed corporation, and care must be taken to avoid making contractual commitments for additional capital contributions or for guarantees of the new corporation's obligations until after the formation has been completed.

The assets of a newly formed acquisition vehicle that is not controlled by another person do not include the funds contributed to the vehicle or borrowed by the vehicle at the closing to complete the acquisition.

The HSR Act and FTC rules also provide numerous exemptions for special situations.

How can you tell whether a particular horizontal merger is likely to be challenged by the federal government?

Current administration policy is set forth in the Horizontal Merger Guidelines, revised as recently as April 1997. (See Appendix 2A.) The basic text of these guidelines was issued in April 1992 by the DOJ and the FTC. The 1992 guidelines, the first comprehensive joint statement ever issued by the two agencies, update those issued by the FTC in 1982 and the DOJ in 1984.

As in previous guidelines, horizontal mergers are assessed according to a sliding scale of permissiveness. Thus, the less concentrated the industry, the larger is the permissible merger. The index used to measure concentration, the Herfindahl-Hirschmann Index (referred to as the HHI), sums the squares of the individual companies' market shares to measure both postmerger share and the growth in market share resulting from the transaction. The 1992 guidelines retain the HHI scoring system introduced in the 1984 guidelines: "unconcentrated" (under 1,000), "moderately concentrated" (between 1,000 and 1,800), and "highly concentrated" (over 1,800). As in the 1984 guidelines, a score is only one factor to be considered. It is not enough by itself to make or break a charge of market concentration.

What might be an example of a merger that would create a "highly concentrated" industry?

Suppose an industry of five firms having market shares of 30 percent, 25 percent, 20 percent, 15 percent, and 10 percent, respectively, has an HHI score of $30^2 + 25^2 + 20^2 + 15^2 + 10^2$, or 2,250. If the third and fifth firms merge, the resulting score is $30^2 + 25^2 + 30^2 + 15^2$, or 2,650, and the increase in the score would be 400.

Is the HHI analysis conducted on the acquirer's industry only?

No. An HHI analysis must be performed for each distinct "relevant market" in which *both* of the merging companies operate.

How likely is it that any given merger will be challenged as being in a highly concentrated industry?

Given basic business demographics, chances are relatively low. In unconcentrated industries (with an HHI below 1,000) the largest four firms have 50 percent or less of the market. Historically, this description fits about 60 percent of U.S. industries. In such unconcentrated industries, the DOJ is unlikely to challenge any merger. In moderately concentrated industries (where the HHI falls in the range of 1,000 to 1,800) the four largest firms normally account for between 50 percent and 70 percent of the market. This is the case with approximately 25 percent of U.S. companies. Within this range the DOJ will review other factors bearing upon the likelihood of predatory practices. Generally, within this range only mergers that increase the HHI by more than 100 points are likely to be challenged. Thus, for example, the over-100 prohibited zone would be reached in such an industry by a merger of two firms each with a 7.1 percent market share, a 10 percent firm with a 5 percent firm, a 25 percent firm with a 2 percent firm, and a 50 percent firm with a 1 percent firm.[14]

In highly concentrated industries (where the HHI exceeds 1,800) the four-firm concentration ratio will exceed 70 percent. This is true of only about 15 percent of U.S. companies. Even here, only a merger increasing the HHI by more than 50 points is likely to be challenged. If the merger increases the HHI by between 50 and 100 points, the merger may or may not be challenged. If the increase is above the 100-point threshold, a challenge is relatively likely.

What factors would the DOJ and FTC consider beyond the HHI?

The 1992 guidelines express an intent to scrutinize mergers that can in some circumstances confer market power on a single firm, even if that firm does not have a sizable market share. If, for example, the two merging firms had previously sold products that were perceived by a substantial number of customers to be close substitutes for one another, the merged firms could raise prices on one product line and risk only some diversion of sales to its other product line.

Whatever the level of concentration, regulators will challenge any merger that is likely to create or enhance one-firm domination of a market. Thus a leading firm that accounts for 35 percent of the market and that is twice the size of its next largest competitor will normally not be allowed to acquire any firm accounting for even 1 percent of that market.

In addition, analysis of horizontal mergers is no longer governed by the single-minded focus on market concentration that has, in theory, been the rule since the Supreme Court's 1963 *Philadelphia National Bank* case. It considers instead other real-market factors, including the following:

- Ease of entry into the market (the 1992 guidelines make it clear that the easier it is for new firms to enter the market, the less likelihood there is of challenge).
- The availability of out-of-market substitutes (the more readily available, the less prospect of collusion).
- The degree to which the merging firms confront one another within the relevant market (if they occupy separate sectors of the market, the merger is less a cause of concern than if they are head-to-head in the same corner).

- The level of product homogeneity (the more homogeneous the product, the easier to collude).
- The pace of technological change (the slower the rate of change is, the greater the likelihood of collusion is).
- The importance of nonprice terms (the more important they are, the harder it is to collude).
- The degree to which firms have access to information concerning their competitors' transactions (the more information available, the greater the likelihood of collusion).
- The size and frequency of orders (the smaller and more frequent, the greater the likelihood of collusion).
- Whether the industry is characterized either by a history of collusion or by patterns of pricing conduct that make collusion more likely (if it is, the likelihood of a challenge increases).
- Historical evidence of noncompetitive performance (challenge is more likely).

What about vertical or conglomerate mergers?

The 1984 DOJ guidelines addressed acquisitions involving vertical mergers, but the new guidelines made no new waves in this arena. Vertical and conglomerate mergers have been relatively free from challenge for the past 15 years.

What about foreign competition?

The 1992 guidelines state that "market shares will be assigned for foreign competitors in the same way in which they are assigned to domestic competitors." These shares may have to be calculated over a longer period of time to account for exchange rate fluctuations. They may also have to be adjusted to account for import quotas. Finally, market shares may have to be combined if foreign firms appear to be acting in a coordinated or collusive way.

You mentioned 1997 revisions to the 1992 guidelines. What did the revisions say?

The revisions, which are reprinted as Appendix 2A, addressed the subject of efficiency. The FTC and DOJ noted that mergers can increase efficiency, even if they reduce competition.

If the FTC and the DOJ either do not investigate a reportable transaction or allow it to proceed after investigation, can the transaction still be challenged afterward?

The government can challenge any merger or acquisition at any time—theoretically, General Motors could be broken up piece by piece back to its beginnings in the early part of the 20th century. But the chances are vanishingly small. And challenges are almost unheard of where HSR filings have been made and the waiting period has been allowed to expire or has been terminated.

Does that mean that after the HSR waiting period the parties can be assured of being able to close their transaction?

In recent years mergers and acquisitions have occasionally been challenged by state attorneys general and by private parties. The law is unsettled about whether, and under what circumstances, such challenges may be brought, but injunctions have been granted in private antitrust suits by targets of hostile takeovers and by competitors of one or both of the merging companies. Such an injunction was granted, in April 1988 in California, despite a DOJ consent decree permitting the acquisition (*Beazer PLC*). These suits fail because the challenging party cannot show that it will suffer "antitrust injury," but they can be disruptive nevertheless.

In addition, state attorneys general continue to be active in reviewing proposed mergers that may affect consumers within their states.

CONCLUDING COMMENTS

Planning and finding are only the beginning of the merger process—just two of many stages to come. Up ahead are structuring, due diligence, negotiating, closing, and integration—not to mention all the perfecting that must be done in areas like pension, labor, and compensation. But although planning and finding might take up only 20 percent of the M&A process, they require fully 80 percent of the energy.

In fact, this phase is a perfect example of the "80/20" law—named after economist Vilfredo Pareto. Buyers, you have to get this part right or nothing else will matter. It's worth putting 80 percent of your energy into this important phase. So do your strategic planning. Set up your in-house search. Hire your brokers or finders and advisors. And last but not least, study the regulatory angle. All this preparation will pay off in success down the road.

A P P E N D I X   2 A

Section 4 of the Horizontal Merger Guidelines Issued by the U.S. Department of Justice and the U.S. Federal Trade Commission

(Reprinted verbatim from www.findlaw.com)

April 8, 1997

Efficiencies

Competition usually spurs firms to achieve efficiencies internally. Nevertheless, mergers have the potential to generate significant efficiencies by permitting a better utilization of existing assets, enabling the combined firm to achieve lower costs in producing a given quantity and quality than either firm could have achieved without the proposed transaction. Indeed, the primary benefit of mergers to the economy is their potential to generate such efficiencies.[1]

Efficiencies generated through merger can enhance the merged firm's ability and incentive to compete, which may result in lower prices, improved quality, enhanced service, or new products. For example, merger-generated efficiencies may enhance competition by permitting two ineffective (e.g., high cost) competitors to become one effective (e.g., lower cost) competitor. In a coordinated interaction context (see Section 2.1), marginal cost reductions may make coordination less likely or effective by enhancing the incentive of a maverick to lower price or by creating a new maverick firm. In a unilateral effects context (see Section 2.2), marginal cost reductions may reduce the merged firm's incentive to elevate price.

Efficiencies also may result in benefits in the form of new or improved products, and efficiencies may result in benefits even when price is not immediately and directly affected. Even when efficiencies generated through merger enhance a firm's ability to compete, however, a merger may have other effects that may lessen competition and ultimately may make the merger anticompetitive.

The Agency [DOT] will consider only those efficiencies likely to be accomplished with the proposed merger and unlikely to be accomplished in the absence of either the proposed merger or another means having comparable anticompetitive effects. These are termed merger-specific efficiencies. Only alternatives that are practical in the business situation faced by the merging firms will be considered in making this determination; the Agency will not insist upon a less restrictive alternative that is merely theoretical.

Efficiencies are difficult to verify and quantify, in part because much of the information relating to efficiencies is uniquely in the possession of the merging firms. Moreover, efficiencies projected reasonably and in good faith by the merging firms may not be realized.

Therefore, the merging firms must substantiate efficiency claims so that the Agency can verify by reasonable means the likelihood and magnitude of each asserted efficiency, how and when each would be achieved (and any costs of doing so), how each would enhance the merged firm's ability and incentive to compete, and why each would be merger-specific. Efficiency claims will not be considered if they are vague or speculative or otherwise cannot be verified by reasonable means.

Cognizable efficiencies are merger-specific efficiencies that have been verified and do not arise from anticompetitive reductions in output or service. Cognizable efficiencies are assessed net of costs produced by the merger or incurred in achieving those efficiencies.

The Agency will not challenge a merger if cognizable efficiencies are of a character and magnitude such that the merger is not likely to be anticompetitive in any relevant market.[2] To make the requisite determination, the Agency considers whether cognizable efficiencies likely would be sufficient to reverse the merger's potential to harm consumers in the relevant market, e.g., by preventing price increases in that market.

In conducting this analysis,[3] the Agency will not simply compare the magnitude of the cognizable efficiencies with the magnitude of the likely harm to competition absent the efficiencies. The greater the potential adverse competitive effect of a merger—as indicated by the increase in the HHI and post-merger HHI from Section 1, the analysis of potential adverse competitive effects from Section 2, and the timeliness, likelihood, and sufficiency of entry from Section 3—the greater must be cognizable efficiencies in order for the Agency to conclude that the merger will not have an anticompetitive effect in the relevant market. When the potential adverse competitive effect of a merger is likely to be particularly large, extraordinarily great cognizable efficiencies would be necessary to prevent the merger from being anticompetitive.

In the Agency's experience, efficiencies are most likely to make a difference in merger analysis when the likely adverse competitive effects, absent the efficiencies, are not great. Efficiencies almost never justify a merger to monopoly or near-monopoly.

The Agency has found that certain types of efficiencies are more likely to be cognizable and substantial than others. For example, efficiencies resulting from shifting production among facilities formerly owned separately, which enable the merging firms to reduce the marginal cost of production, are more likely to be susceptible to verification, merger-specific, and substantial, and are less likely to result from anticompetitive reductions in output.

Other efficiencies, such as those relating to research and development, are potentially substantial but are generally less susceptible to verification and may be the result of anticompetitive output reductions. Yet others, such as those relating to procurement, management, or capital cost, are less likely to be merger-specific or substantial, or may not be cognizable for other reasons.

ENDNOTES TO THE APPENDIX

1. The Agency will not deem efficiencies to be merger-specific if they could be preserved by practical alternatives that mitigate competitive concerns, such as divestiture or licensing. If a merger affects not whether but only when an efficiency would be achieved, only the timing advantage is a merger-specific efficiency.

2. Section 7 of the Clayton Act prohibits mergers that may substantially lessen competition "in any line of commerce . . . in any section of the country." Accordingly, the Agency normally assesses competition in each relevant market affected by a merger independently and normally will challenge

the merger if it is likely to be anticompetitive in any relevant market. In some cases, however, the Agency in its prosecutorial discretion will consider efficiencies not strictly in the relevant market, but so inextricably linked with it that a partial divestiture or other remedy could not feasibly eliminate the anticompetitive effect in the relevant market without sacrificing the efficiencies in the other market(s). Inextricably linked efficiencies rarely are a significant factor in the Agency's determination not to challenge a merger. They are most likely to make a difference when they are great and the likely anticompetitive effect in the relevant market(s) is small.

3. The result of this analysis over the short term will determine the Agency's enforcement decision in most cases. The Agency also will consider the effects of cognizable efficiencies with no short-term, direct effect on prices in the relevant market. Delayed benefits from efficiencies (due to delay in the achievement of, or the realization of consumer benefits from, the efficiencies) will be given less weight because they are less proximate and more difficult to predict.

E N D N O T E S

1. The principal author of this book described such a system two decades ago. See Stanley Foster Reed, "Corporate Growth by Strategic Planning," *Mergers & Acquisitions* 12, Nos. 2, 3, and 4, 1977.

2. Fortune Brands receives prominent mention in Robert A. G. Monks's *The Emperor's Nightingale: Restoring the Integrity of the Corporation* (Oxford: Capstone, 1998), a book applying the findings of the complexity movement in science to corporate governance. Monks cites Fortune as an example of metamorphosis, a trait of complex adaptive systems. "Rarely has a company that was so prominent in one industry voluntarily turned itself inside out to assume an utterly different form," writes Monks (p. 99).

3. *Source:* "Bank Mergers and Acquisitions—1993: A Year of Increasing Franchise Consolidation," New York, Wachtell, Lipton, Rosen & Katz.

4. The Interstate Banking and Efficiency Act became effective June 1, 1997. Although this law left considerable room for states to impose limitations on acquisitions across state borders, it did open up the doors to a new wave of bank acquisitions and alliances in the late 1990s.

5. *Source:* "Ledecky's U.S. Office Products to Split in 5," *Washington Post,* January 14, 1998, p. D-9.

6. This is the well-supported conclusion of strategists Philippe C. of INSEAD in Fontainebleau, France, and David B. Jemison of the University of Texas at Austin, who wrote up the results of their eight-year study of 20 multinational acquirers in *Managing Acquisitions: Creating Value through Corporate Renewal* (New York: Free Press, 1990). We cannot resist quoting an important passage from this book at length:

"Although there are no clear a priori prescriptions for deciding on the role of acquisitions in renewal, one message that flows from our research is that the various renewal modes (*e.g.* acquisitions, joint ventures, license agreements, technology-sharing arrangements) are not only conceptually similar but highly complementary. They are similar in that in each type of renewal, capabilities are transferred to improve competitive advantage. They are complementary in the sense that most internal development relies on some acquisition of capabilities. By the same token even the acquisition of a complete business position needs to be made in [an internal] developmental perspective if it is to create the most value—the acquisition's price is the first installment on a future investment program." (pp. 246–247)

7. Industrial organization is an academic discipline that is involved with the relationships among actual and potential suppliers, customers, and competitors within an industry. All antitrust activity uses the terms that have been developed in the industrial organization field. The wheel of opportunity/fit chart construct described in the next section has adopted this standard language.

8. Harold A. Linstone and Murray Turoff, *The Delphi Method* (Reading, MA: Addison-Wesley, 1975).

9. This is based on annual reports published in *Mergers & Acquisitions* in a feature called "M&A Services," which presents lists of advisory firms by value of deals by firm, number of deals by firm, and total advisory fees by firm, among other statistics. For the most recent trends, see the March–April 1998 issue, pp. 61–63.

10. *Business Reference Guide—1998* (Concord, MA: Business Brokerage Press, 1998).

11. "Prudential Securities' Reserves for Suits over Partnerships near $500 Million," *The Wall Street Journal*, March 4, 1993.

12. It is no mere coincidence that the firms that advise tender offers tend to be the firms that report higher M&A fees. See, for example, the "M&A Services" lists in *Mergers & Acquisitions* (March/April 1998), pp. 61 ff.

13. Douglas F. Rohrman, "Meeting the Clean Air Challenge in an Acquisition," *Mergers & Acquisitions,* July–August 1993, pp. 26–32.

14. This discussion of the HHI is based on client memos from Hogan & Hartson (Washington, D.C.). For a financial point of view on HHI, see J. Fred Weston, Kwang S. Chung, and Juan A. Siu, *Takeovers, Restructuring, and Corporate Governance* (Upper Saddle River, NJ: Prentice Hall, 1998), pp. 31ff.

Valuation and Pricing

CHAPTER 3

Valuation and Pricing

INTRODUCTION

No factor counts more than price in closing a transaction. Yet very few operating executives know the worth of their own company, much less anyone else's. They may know the prices at which their competitors' securities are traded (whether on a stock exchange or through market makers in an over-the-counter market), and they may be able to calculate the premiums paid for those securities. Those prices, however, are only one indicator of value—and not always the best one.

Even assuming that a reported price paid for a security is a proxy for "value," the first problem is to decide which quoted price to use—as there are several possibilities. Should one use the current closing price or the average price over the past year, month, week, or day? In the M&A area the "20-day" figure—the average of the closing prices of the security over the past 20 trading days—is often used. Why, no one knows.

Furthermore, few people consider the other factors that have affected the price of a company's securities. Are takeover rumors inflating the price? Are there "overhanging blocks" that have depressed the price? What is the "trading supply"? Has an investment banker—or worse yet, a deal principal—been "front-running" on the stock? These things not only *can* happen—they *do*.[1]

In the case of a privately held company the problems are even more complex because many transfers of shares in a closely held company are made for noneconomic purposes. In each case it is the set of circumstances behind the sale that must be divined and its effect on the price assessed.

The first thing a buyer should do is discover why the company is for sale. Sellers should also have their reasons well thought out. Yet some buyers seem reluctant to begin a negotiation with the question, "Why is the company for sale?"

Although most entrepreneurs know how to start businesses and run them profitably by watching costs, many fail to bring that same circumspection to the acquisition process. As buyers, entrepreneurs often overpay. Further, in selling their businesses, many owners have little idea how to price them. In general, however, buyers are far more skilled at buying than sellers are at selling. Why? Because most buyers buy many times and most sellers sell only once or twice.

Any company under consideration for sale merits competent, objective valuation, whether its stock is privately owned by one individual, closely held by several individuals (as in many family-owned companies), or publicly traded on one or more of the major exchanges or in the over-the-counter market. An entity also deserves careful valuation when it has no stock per se, but is part of a larger whole—whether as an operating division or simply a product line. All these situations demand and deserve proper valuation.

Many valuations are poorly done and are challenged in court—sometimes years later. The principal author has found in such cases that whenever a family-owned or family-controlled company has an investment banker involved with the buying group, undervaluations are quite common. In other cases, overvaluations by sellers result from factual distortions and deliberate misstatements, and by failure to reveal significant negative facts. There is even outright fraud from time to time in setting prices for nonpublic companies. The principal author has been an expert witness in many valuation cases where the value was based on distortion of historic numbers. We are not talking about a few thousand dollars or a few percentage points; we're talking about millions of dollars and valuations off by 300 percent.

Professional help in setting values is not only a practical necessity; it is required for the proper discharge of "due diligence" requirements, and that means employing a professional appraiser. Truly "professional" appraisals should not be confused with so-called fairness opinions issued by investment bankers. Such opinions are not objective when the bankers have a stake in the outcome of the transaction.

The appraiser's job is to come up with *fair market value*. That value is one arrived at between a willing buyer and a willing seller, both being adequately informed of the relevant facts, and neither being under any compulsion to buy or to sell.

To help readers get a grip on this key area, this chapter first focuses on various valuation methods, and then develops the details of a typical discounted cash flow (DCF) analysis to discover the NPV of the focus company. This method has emerged in recent decades as the method of choice in valuation, beginning with the World Bank's adoption of the method in the late 1960s.[2] The second part of the chapter applies DCF in a practical way to explain how leveraged buyouts (LBOs) are priced. Once the price is determined, it must be expressed in the pricing clauses of the acquisition agreements. The final portion of this chapter gives guidance in this area.

VALUATION FUNDAMENTALS

Why bother with valuation? Why not turn it over completely to the experts?

Valuation is a highly specialized process. For this reason, it requires the knowledge and experience of specialists. At the same time, however, valuation requires oversight—and good common sense—from the buying and selling management teams. The principal author has spent many days in court as an expert witness testifying about the value of companies and parts of them. He has been astonished at the range of values that the representatives of top-ranking investment banking, accounting, consulting, and in some cases professional appraisal firms can come up with in valuing the same entity. Under these circumstances judges and in some cases juries have a tough job making decisions—especially in cases where representatives of two of Wall Street's top investment banking firms have testified to widely differing values—say, as much as 50 percent on seven-, eight-, or even nine-figure values.

Most valuations should be operations-based. When investment bankers get involved in valuations, the valuations are often flawed: Investment bankers tend to set asset-based values because they understand assets but not operations. Estimates from owners, especially owner-managers, are also frequently seriously flawed because their providers either are overenthusiastic about their prospects or are consciously distorting the numbers. In either case these insiders' projections are easily attacked in court. That is why values in any major merger/acquisition transaction must be backed up by the opinions of professional appraisers, whose primary business is appraising the value of operating companies and their subsidiaries.

Specialists abound in the valuation of going businesses. There are consultants and firms that value only printing companies, supermarket chains, knitting and weaving mills, paper mills, mining properties, shipping companies, or railroads. Other firms value only engineering consulting firms, accounting firms, or law practices. Banks, insurance companies, and even investment banking firms and "stockbrokers" have their valuation specialists with a similarly narrow scope.

Business brokers value and sell smaller businesses or "stores"—bar/taverns, car washes, dry-cleaning establishments, grocery stores, restaurants, and all kinds of franchised operations depending heavily on goodwill value—well into eight figures. And they may be worth it.

It's a tricky business because many stores underreport sales and earnings by substantial amounts. When they are put up for sale, the tax returns don't agree with the projected revenues. This same thesis may also apply to subsidiary units of larger companies that may not have kept an accurate set of books and may not have been audited by an outside independent auditor for many years.

This gives many buyers the idea that it is okay to pay much more than the going multiple of book for such enterprises. They don't always realize that stores that are part of national chains, which report store sales and profits accurately, may not be such a steal. Many inexperienced buyers coming from middle management and loaded with mid-six-figure cash settlements from their severance deal—very often a buyout of their postemployment benefits—think they're dealing with one of those "stores" and often overpay. Buyers should remember that by law the broker represents the *seller* and is out to maximize the price received. While it *is* possible to cut a deal with a broker to represent a buyer rather than a seller and buy at the lowest price, such brokers are hard to find in the business brokerage area.

High-technology companies in the health field can see overnight swings in valuation as investors alternately embrace or flee stocks as they learn the results from scientific testing or regulatory approval. In the United States, approval by the Food and Drug Administration can save or savage a pharmaceutical company's stock, particularly for a smaller company with a small product range. In the biotechnology arena, companies can attract capital for years without earnings or even revenue. But the same gleam-in-the-eye companies that can attract $40 million or $50 million in an initial public offering (IPO) and $100 million in a secondary offering can have a poor clinical result and then lose hundreds of millions in a single day. When the IPO market shies away from these losers, they are forced into other modes of survival, and "what would have been IPOs . . . become M&A transactions."[3]

Even conservative investors in conservative industries such as banking can get swept away. That happened with J.P. Morgan & Co. when it raised $1 billion to invest in undercapitalized banks (named "Corsair Partners" after J.P.'s fabulous yacht, which foundered off Acapulco in the late 1920s). By the time the fund was completed, most U.S. banks had refinanced themselves and didn't need Morgan's money. Roberto Mendoza, Morgan's chief M&A honcho, rushed an investment of $162 million into Spain's Banco Español de Credito, "Banesto," which everyone knew was badly managed. The investment, and Mendoza's advice as a board member, couldn't cure the problems and within a year the Bank of Spain had tossed out Banesto's board—including Mendoza.[4]

Are rules of thumb helpful in valuation?

These are tempting, but they can be treacherous. For example, a few years ago, supposedly knowledgeable people said "Any good tech-based company is worth its annual sales," or "Never pay more than 80 percent of net worth." These numbers would be too conservative in the current market, despite corrections. (Consider the high multiples being paid for Internet-based companies.) Conversely, it may be too generous in any market to say that, "The average company listed on the New York Stock Exchange is worth at least 50 percent more than the current public value," another common rule of thumb. All these statements are often wrong because they are based on past numbers and transitory trends of only a few deals on a local or industry basis.

What role does risk play in valuation?

Risk, like beauty, is in the eye of the beholder. To a firm with very substantial funds either on hand or easily available to it, money is worth considerably less than it is to a cash-short firm. Financial economists call this the *utility function*.

Its proof is found in the observable fact that being cash-short makes one risk-averse. Neither rational individuals nor firms run by them will risk their entire net worth on a double-or-nothing flip of a coin. They might risk a third or even half of their net worth, but would most likely require a disproportionate return—one higher than the mathematics of the risk would dictate—and find no takers.

Very wealthy individuals and cash-rich firms give disproportionate odds the other way. They become risk-loving. That is why many cash-rich companies constantly overpay for acquisitions, as Japanese acquirers did in the 1980s for Manhattan skyscrapers, California golf courses, and Hawaiian hotels—they had too much cash.[5] In one overly generous deal gone bad, Mitsubishi Bank's $360 million loan on the Hyatt Waikola was sold for only $52 million.[6] Today, Japanese acquirers are unlikely to repeat such fiascos. Not only are they more sophisticated in the art of M&A—as the coauthor detected in a 1998 trip to Tokyo—but they are also more constrained financially.

Risk is an important factor in many valuation methods, particularly in DCF analysis discussed below. In some cases it takes a great deal of sophistication to discover, pre-acquisition, just what is and is not considered truly "cash" in order to perform a discounted cash flow analysis and quantify the risk.[7] Where historical cash flow numbers are lacking, buyers in "hot" areas—such as software and genetic engineering—seem to look at companies as "commodities." What others paid per employee seems to have developed as a proxy for risk.

Impounded in the utility function is a long string of indeterminates. They outline a buyer's or seller's response to any of hundreds of risk factors that are revealed as part of the due diligence process. Risk factors include the past history of similar deals, both in the buying company and in the industry; the future expected inflation rate, including the expected risk-free interest rate; the present and possible future costs of capital to the buyer; the possibility of noncyclical downturns in the economy; the loss of key people; technical and market obsolescence factors; the possibilities of "Bhopal-type" disasters; and so on. In order to lower risk, more buyers are willing to pay a premium to an owner who agrees to stay and manage the company for a minimum of two years.[8]

For public companies—those trading on an exchange—the capital asset pricing model (CAPM) divides risk into two categories: *systematic risk,* risk that cannot be diversified away because it is inherent in the ups and downs of the securities markets, and *specific risk,* risk inherent in the operation of the company itself. Many investors assume that systematic risk can be estimated by the firm's "beta," a number that describes its volatility—how closely the stock follows the ups and downs of the public stock markets. A firm's "alpha," as opposed to its "beta," is its specific rather than its systematic risk. It derives from how efficiently the firm is managed as compared with others of the same kind.

Most betas use the Standard & Poor's S&P Index, a measurement of the average movements of prices of 500 widely held common stocks times the number of shares issued. The S&P 500 is considered a measurement of average stock market performance because the shares represent over 70 percent of the total "value" of all the common stocks traded in the public markets (400 industrial, 20 transportation, 40 public utility, and 40 financial companies of the several thousand publicly traded companies in the public market).

A firm with a beta of 1.0 follows the market exactly. For years the beta of IBM was held to be 1.0 by some who tracked stock prices and compiled and sold beta information. They said that the price of IBM stock followed the market exactly, and thus inferred that the systematic risk for investment in IBM stock was zero. IBM holders who believed in betas could then relax and think only of the future of the computer industry and IBM's place in it and forget about market risk because there was little or nothing they could do about it. In contrast to IBM, another stock had a beta of 1.5. It moved faster than the market in both up and down markets and was therefore considered (by those who believe that a stock's beta is a proxy for market risk) to be half again as risky as old 1.0-beta IBM.

In pricing out nonpublic companies—that is, companies whose stock is not traded publicly—some appraisers, trying to use CAPM methodologies, tried to find "comparables," public companies that "looked" like the candidate operationally. They then "borrowed the betas" of those companies in assessing the systematic risk component of total risk.

There are five things wrong with this. First, true operational comparables between traded and nontraded companies are difficult to find, although it is possible to develop averages of betas of operationally similar public companies. Second, selecting the particular beta to be used is a very real problem because five or six different beta series are published, all based on timing differences. Third, if a high beta represents high risk, it should also correlate with high return. Yet it seldom does, even with manipulation of timing differences. Fourth, some analysts say flatly that both betas and standard deviations penalize funds and firms for variations in upside performance.[9] Fifth, betas change.

IBM's beta increased in the early-to-mid-1990s when the market deemed many large companies "dinosaurs," triggering rapid declines in their stock prices during a time of relative market calm.

It is the principal author's firm conviction that betas should not be used in assessing risk. A beta is simply a descriptor of the volatility of a particular stock over some arbitrary time period in relation to the volatility of the market itself and does not properly describe systematic risk except for very short and usually unusable time periods. As with IBM's beta, betas for many stocks change with time. Anyone who uses a beta as a proxy or a major component of risk in setting a purchase or selling price is taking a major risk of being wrong.

Mutual funds are constantly searching for ways to measure risk. The Securities and Exchange Commission (SEC) is concerned about the subject. Some funds use betas modified by the time it takes for the fund to "recover." Others use the standard deviation, which measures the probable variation in a fund's expected return based on its past fluctuations. The standard deviation is descriptive, not predictive.

What is discounting?

In the sixth or seventh grade your teacher taught you that a $1 investment, when compounded at 6 percent interest, will have a *future value* of $2 in 12.4 years, as that original $1 has earned and added $1 in interest. What the teacher did not teach was the reciprocal corollary: that $2 to be paid out 12.4 years from now, when *discounted* at 6 percent, has a *present value* of only $1 today. Most M&A investments revolve around projecting how much the investment will yield over some pre-set time horizon and factoring the uncertainties into the discount rate. The business of estimating *M&A investment risk* involves including in the discount rate the certainties and uncertainties of receiving a future stream of earnings or cash flows from your M&A investment. The lower the certainty, the higher the discount rate; the higher the certainty, the lower the discount rate.

What are hurdle rates?

A hurdle rate is the discount rate usually set by the board of directors or other major powers in a corporation that must be applied to a projected earnings stream that must be met or exceeded before an investment will be approved.

Most companies set the hurdle rate as equivalent to their own cost of capital. (See the calculation in Exhibit 3-1.) Special situations then call for documented reasons to add points to the discount rate either for inexperience in the field, for high deviation rates on historical earnings for the company or its industry, or for other risk-related reasons.

In dealing with Scott Paper's planners many years back, the principal author discovered that Scott had developed different hurdle rates for entries into different industries that coincided with the comfort level of the executive corps' personal "feelings" about the industry, which, upon investigation, turned out to coincide with their familiarity with the industry. This approach appears rational but is not at all a proper proxy for risk because those assessing the risk were not necessarily the ones who would be managing the acquisition. As a result, Scott Paper at that time was notorious for making bad acquisitions.

Are historical figures useful in assessing risk?

Generally not. However, if the industry is well defined and the acquisition candidate has good numbers comparing itself with its competitors, historical figures can be useful. One measure of risk is the variability (standard deviation) of past comparative reported earnings of the prospect: low deviation, low risk; high deviation, high risk. However, for some acquirers, unexplained variabilities in sales, cash flows, and executive or customer turnover might be far more important than variability in accounting-based earnings in assessing the risk of entry. In general, though, the higher the deviation of historical financial variables, such as pretax earnings, the higher the risk, and the higher the discount rate that will be applied to projected earnings.

But remember: *Financial history doesn't just happen; it is created by the people who write about it.* The legally permissible variations in accounting methodologies available to corporations in the United States are legion. Moreover, they often depend on the personal proclivities and experience of the corporate comptroller and his or her staff, and may or may not have been consistently applied over past periods. Any earnings history is only as good as the accounting processes that created the record. *Consistency, uniformity,* and *comparability* are the watchwords of good accounting practices. Only the establishment of a sophisticated audit trail will reveal the effect of accounting changes on the accuracy of historical reporting of accounting-based earnings. Activity-based costing can also help buyers and sellers alike perceive value accurately.

What is activity-based costing?

Activity-based costing (ABC) is one of the audit tools used to uncover hidden values in a company. Some of the discoveries are dramatic since much accounting seems designed to cover up rather than uncover the real costs associated with the production of goods and services. Judging from a fairly recent survey by the Cost Management Group of the Institute of Management Accounting, nearly half of all companies are now using this method.[10]

Normal accounting methodologies have few if any negative inputs. They do not quantify and cost out glitches. Such factors as parts reworks, unplanned scrap, and systems that impede the flow of work are not assessed their proper negative costs, as is done in ABC. One company, after implementing ABC, was soon found to be "basking in operating margins that are roughly four times the industry's average."[11] Sophisticated ABC accounting can also generate large cash windfalls, because it allows companies to reverse arbitrary rulings by the Internal Revenue Service (IRS) on M&A-generated taxes.[12]

What is capital rationing?

Few if any companies have unlimited funds. Therefore they must "ration" their capital. This is sometimes accomplished by including funds for M&A in the capital budget. But for "go-go" companies that make acquisitions using their stock and debt rather than budgeted cash flows from earnings and depreciation, capital rationing becomes very complicated. This, in fact, is the reason for the growth in importance of the job of chief financial officer (CFO) in the modern corporation and his or her elevation to board status.

Companies wanting to ration their capital usually perform what the principal author calls *differential diagnosis*—which acquisition will best "fit" the buyer, that is, best complement its weaknesses and best exploit its strengths. A similar but simpler textbook process known as the *alternate investment decision* process is used to purchase things like machine tools but can be used for making acquisitions—one acquisition candidate is compared with several others using basic financial criteria, and the best is chosen. These kinds of analyses, if institutionalized, force an acquirer to do the analysis that is so often skipped in the rush to close a deal.

But no matter what kind of analysis you employ, never buy a company unless you compare it with at least two other potential acquisitions. And further, always estimate the costs of entering the business *de novo,* as explained below.

What about time horizons?

Any analysis requires the selection of a time horizon, also known as the "forecast period." Most companies have standardized at 10 years. However, in the fashion industry, or any industry that depends on styles or fads, such as toys or clothing, five to seven years is much more common. Public utilities traditionally spun their forecasts out for 20 years, but have lately turned to much shorter time horizons as patterns of energy production, consumption, and conservation have changed, along with the regulatory climate. In Europe, now approaching conversion to a common currency, and in Asia, now laboring to prevent a financial meltdown, traditional planning horizons no longer make sense. Tomorrow is charted on a deal-by-deal basis. This is where a few financial skills can really help a dealmaker. One of the benefits of "sensitivity analysis" is to discover the effects of different time horizons on a target company's net present value (NPV).

Unfortunately, there is a trend toward shortening the time horizon or forecast period under conditions of uncertainty that are not random. This shortening is a poor substitute for factoring in quantifiable risk. In many cases, with a little work, the uncertainties can be converted to probabilities that can be described in numbers without creating a jumble of forecast periods. You don't have to be a financial economist yourself to get this work done. Any accredited business school is likely to have a team of them ready, willing, and able to help—at an affordable price, or even pro bono.

What is M&A leverage?

M&A leverage is the ability to borrow money to finance an acquisition. Borrowing adds to the risk of the transaction because interest payments must be "earned" by operations before dividends can be paid. In bad times the cash available for dividends is reduced or even eliminated. In good times there is an excess of cash. Together, they amplify reported earnings results and tend to produce a "yo-yo" earnings record that tends to discourage investors and depress the value of the company. This is especially true of companies whose stock is publicly traded.

What is the commodity theory of M&A pricing?

Generally, commodities are *fungible,* alike in character—one kernel of wheat or one soybean or one dollar bill is pretty much like another. But there is a futures market in ships' bottoms—the ability to move goods over water at a locked-in price at some future shipper's contract date. Certainly they are not as fungible as pork bellies or fuel oil, but there is still a futures market for them. Supply and demand affect the present and future prices of all commodities. At any one time, in commodities markets, there are oversupplies and undersupplies of corn, wheat, pork bellies, frozen orange juice, and so on.

The same economics laws that apply to commodities that are traded on commodity exchanges *may* apply to businesses for sale. This has been made possible through the concept of the strategic business unit (SBU). Many of them are remarkably alike—especially in franchised businesses, many of which are sold over and over. A McDonald's franchise is really a commodity.

Further evidence that SBUs are commodities is found in the fact that there is a kind of futures market developing in biotech companies as capital is raised with IPOs based on the promise to investors that the principal object of starting the business is to build it up and then sell it off at some later date to one of the larger pharmaceutical manufacturers for a huge profit—just like planting a crop of corn or soybeans that may or may not survive drought and flood.

Techniques for the founding and the building of businesses, generally incorporated in the term *entrepreneurship,* are being taught at more and more academic institutions. Just as the soybean futures market sells soybeans before they are even planted, much less harvested, demand is so great for SBUs in the desktop software, biotech, and Internet-related areas that it is possible to sell shares or even the whole company before it has made its first dollar of sales, much less a profit.

Right now, the hunger for SBUs seems insatiable. The recent mass restructuring of much of business in the United States and the resultant reduction in the white-collar workforce of middle-management executives has generated the start-up of tens of thousands of new businesses, many of them surprisingly successful. High prices are being paid for some of these start-ups—especially those that are, in reality, spin-offs from larger companies as part of their downsizing programs. Some are even financed by a seller that has induced a group of its own executives to buy out one of their own in-house suppliers.

Another similar trend moving the SBU market is the tens of thousands of nonintegrated stand-alone SBUs being sold off by larger companies. These firms are streamlining as they learn that technological and market change are difficult enough to track in one or two fields, much less dozens.

The growing trading market for SBUs is not confined to the United States; it is happening worldwide. With the global shift from socialism to "privatism," there is developing a worldwide market in SBUs, and there are highly localized shortages and surfeits in that marketplace and various sectors within it.

In the international markets, the offer for sale of tens of thousands of state-owned companies in the "privatization" process in semisocialized countries in Europe, Latin America, and Africa has been enthusiastically received, yet the market appears far from glutted. In Russia, only half the largest firms have been privatized. The Asian financial crisis of the late 1990s has caused government leaders in that region to consider more privatization and more foreign investment in general.[13] Still to come to market are an equal number from the other members of the former Soviet Union, some 50,000 SBUs from Eastern Bloc countries, and several hundred thousand each from India and China. It appears that the privatization market's production of SBUs will be active for several more decades.

Will there eventually be an "SBU crash"? Yes. Too many new companies will be founded, especially in popular fields, and there will be minicrashes in software, genetic engineering, fast foods, carbonated beverages, electronic games, Internet-related companies, and so on. The reader is advised to be careful in paying premiums for entry into such popular fields. It is almost certain that there will be a market glut of such companies sometime in the future, just as there always is in corn and pork bellies and soybeans. The big SBU crash worldwide, across many industries, may not come along for several decades. But it will come, sooner or later. So be careful out there!

What are some of the specific methods used for pricing a company, an operating division, or a product line?

There is a long list. Just counting valuation methods used by institutional investors to analyze public companies, there are at least 17. That's the number of methods used by expert John J. Lewis of Valuation Technologies, LLC, Berkeley, California.[14] Our own list is a little more basic—and includes methods used for privately held companies. Let's begin with the simplest and work toward the more complex. (Sample calculations for each of the methods are shown in Exhibit 3-1.)

1. *The replacement value method.* The replacement value method is the simplest but the most tedious of the valuation processes. Given an operation to analyze, the buyer sets out to discover the cash costs to create from scratch an exact duplicate of the company in all its perspectives. It includes both hard and soft assets. Hard assets include land, buildings and machinery, inventories, work in process, and so forth. Soft assets include the costs of recruitment and training of people, the creation of markets and protective devices such as copyrights and trademarks, the development of a customer base, and so on. This estimate is compared with the asking price for the company or is used as the basis for an offer and the subsequent negotiation. Properly done, it is the best of the valuation methods because it asks and answers the simple question "What will it cost the buyer to duplicate the company right now?" without the complications of factoring in past or future accounting-based earnings that may or may not represent reality.

Such a formal estimate of replacement value can be used in internal negotiations within the buying company since it can be used to support the argument that it is often "cheaper to buy than to build."

One major advantage in the replacement value approach is that professional appraisal firms are highly skilled in generating the basic numbers. These numbers will usually stand up in court should there be a challenge. Its disadvantage is the difficulty getting enough accurate information about the focus company and its industry to generate the costs to duplicate.

In an acquisition, the buyer will not have to compete with the seller. With a replacement value calculation for *de novo* entry, continued competition must be factored in. The replacement value method seems to give a potential buyer a negotiating edge over a seller. Computing out replacement value can also be a factor in fulfilling due diligence requirements.

2. *The investment, or average rate of return, method.* The investment, or average rate of return, method has been the most common method used to value acquisitions. It is an accounting-based method that compares the projected average return with the projected average investment in the project. The projected average required return is sometimes called a *hurdle rate,* which is most often the buyer's cost of capital. This, as mentioned above, is modified at will to reflect entry risk, as the rate will be lowered for businesses with which the buyer is more familiar.

In practice, in the M&A field, this valuation analysis begins with the up-front sum to be paid for the company being acquired or, in an installment purchase, for the down payment. This figure is modified through the years as additional capital is invested or capital is recovered. It is especially useful if an installment purchase is to be made or when major assets are to be sold off or acquired. Its advantage is in its simplicity. Its usual disadvantage is in its failure to properly take into account the time value of money.

3. *The payback method.* This is one of the time-honored methods used for the evaluation of an acquisition. Borrowed from the capital budgeting area, payback has been and is still used for the purchase of major machine tools and other capital items. In the payback method, the corporate powers that be arbitrarily decide that their capital investments should be recovered or "paid back" in some set period of time. Typically, the purchase of a large computer-controlled machine tool or a bank of such tools must pay back its purchase price including the costs of freight, installation, operator training, and so on in three to five years or the investment will not be made. Risk factors of technological obsolescence, downturns in sales, labor strikes, and other catastrophes are all taken into account by shortening the payback period, while projected positive events will lengthen it.

Payback is a simple method that can be understood by people who are not trained in finance, and it is easy to incorporate in simple budgeting and marketing programs. For many years it was used (and still is) for the purchase of competitors in the service industries. Like the investment method, its advantage is in its simplicity; its disadvantage is that it does not properly take into account the time value of money. It is recommended for use only in the simplest of transactions where the operating parameters are well known and are easily budgeted and controlled.

4. *The internal rate of return (IRR) method.* For many, many years the larger companies that had access to computers or ranks of junior accountants used the IRR method to value investments, and some still do. In this method, the object is to discover what discount rate is needed to make the present value of the future cash flows of an investment equal the cost of the investment. When the net present values of cash outflows and cash inflows equal zero, the rate of discount being used is the IRR. To be acceptable, it must equal or exceed the hurdle rate.

The IRR method, unless fully understood by the analyst, is badly flawed. First, mathematically, there are always at least two solutions to an IRR calculation and sometimes, when there are several income reversals projected, many more. Second, the calculations take time even on the fastest computers since they are done by a long series of successive approximations. Third, varying the inputs in performing sensitivity analyses to produce the NPV, compared with the DCF method, is tiresome; computational errors are frequent, and results can be misleading and are not easily defended in court. The IRR method of valuation is "old hat" and is not recommended.

5. *The market value method.* The market value method, used primarily for the acquisition of publicly traded companies, requires a search for "comparables" in the publicly traded markets. It assumes that the public markets are "efficient"; that is, all the information about the comparables is available to buyers and sellers and is being used to set the prices for their securities. Still used today, and required by the due diligence process in the case of the purchase of controlling interests in publicly traded companies, the market value method uses the published price/earnings (or P/E) multiples of publicly traded comparable companies to establish a price or a range of prices.

In many cases the problem of comparability is difficult to solve. There are simply no truly comparable companies anywhere, and the valuator then must average the figures for a group of close comparables. For some sellers it is a dangerous method, as an experienced buyer can cherry-pick the comparables.

Also, one might argue that the market is not always efficient. In past markets, many stocks were undervalued by the public, and it was not unusual for a buyer to pay a 50 percent premium over the publicly traded stock price *after* a DCF or other analytical method indicated that a premium price was in order. In those cases, it was assumed that the market was "*in*efficient."

Accounting variables are also challenging here. For instance, one can average the prices and the P/E ratios of several dozen property/casualty (P/C) insurance companies and use the resulting number to negotiate a purchase price. But insurance accounting is not uniform from company to company, and historically accurate numbers are difficult to come by since they were never kept product by product. Allocating the surpluses to the product lines that produced them is a near impossibility, and figuring the marginal incremental costs of fixed and working capital to add $1 of premium inflow on a product-by-product valuation is nearly impossible. The only way to properly price out a purchase of a P/C company is by direct examination of the risks that the particular insurer has exposed itself to product by product; and when this is run against projected revenues and totaled, it will generally yield an entirely different number than the average of the P/E multiple-derived prices of a group of "comparable" insurances. (In 1990 Aetna Life & Casualty split itself into 15 SBUs that report profits independently within the company. The strategy is considered a strategic success.[15])

Although the differences are dramatic in the insurance industry, lack of accounting standards and their consistent application makes historical earnings figures difficult to rely on in many industries. But many, many investors still rely on the "efficient market theory" that says that the investing public sees through the accounting facade and properly values most securities, even those where there are attempts at price manipulation in anticipation of a sale. The market value method has been for many years the method of choice in the M&A area until the advent of the DCF method, which has largely displaced it in generating NPVs. (As mentioned earlier, however, due diligence for public company acquisitions requires a review of the market values of comparables based on P/Es.)

6. The comparable net worth to market value method. A method of valuation developed by the principal author, which is now one of the approved methods of valuation in the state of Pennsylvania after a long litigative history, is the *comparable net worth to market value method.* This method is a way of estimating future sales and profits in the absence of information. It is usually employed in unfriendly situations such as "squeeze-outs" where a majority control group is squeezing out the minority holders, and refuses to give information on future sales and profits.

Net worth is not a good measure of the present value of anything unless it's all in cash and can be immediately withdrawn, which is never the case. In most cases, only lip service has been paid to the requirements for consistency, uniformity, and comparability in generating operating figures that have produced earned surpluses. Thus, a net worth progression is difficult to use as a proxy for predicting future profits. *Where* and *when* the surpluses arose is of great importance in understanding past performance in order to predict future performance.

Comparing net worth to market value involves several steps. First, 5 to 10 comparable publicly traded companies are identified. Their accounting practices are carefully analyzed; various adjustments, especially to accounting treatments of inventories, cash, and receivables, are made to increase the comparability; and any excesses (or shortages) of cash, cash equivalents, and other nonworking assets are computed. The resulting adjusted net worths are then compared with the price at which their stocks are being traded. In the Pennsylvania case it was discovered that the average price of a share of common stock of the 10 "comparables" was selling for exactly twice the average adjusted net worth at the time of the squeeze-out with a very low standard deviation in the sample group. This method, approved by the court, yielded a figure more than double the valuation made by a major Wall Street investment banking house using the market value method, and resulted in a multimillion dollar recovery for the minority stockholders.

The method's major advantage is that it uses only publicly available information in computing values. Its disadvantage is that it requires a great deal of sophistication to remake the balance sheets, and in some cases the operating statements, of the sample group of public companies to make them comparable to the company being valued.

7. The discounted cash flow method. The *discounted cash flow* method, also called the *discounted future earnings* method, is the only proper way to value a going company. It basically estimates the net present value of its future cash flows or earnings, discounted to reflect risk. (We will return to the topic of cash flow later when discussing financial buyers. The point here is to *discount* the cash flow.)

Before explaining *how* DCF can be calculated, it may be important to explain why DCF *should* be calculated—and heeded. In the long run, a company is worth what someone is willing to pay for it in cash or cash equivalents. History provides indisputable evidence of what people have been willing to pay. However, accounting rules are so variable—company by company, industry by industry, and country by country—that accounting numbers based on past earnings can rarely be used as a basis for negotiating a price. Thus, numbers must be converted to a future value. Aside from those who might pay twice what a company is worth because "the stars are right" (and that happens), the final price should depend on what the buyer believes the net *cash flows* will be in the future.

The seller can maximize the price received by having a plan for the future with rational reasons for predicting future cash flows and explaining anomalies in past cash flows. Those plans are usually secret and not disclosed to the public. Even stockholders are not privy to the plans. As a result, the NPV might well differ from the value the public has in the stock market. When this happens it is difficult to close a deal, and due diligence requires that if the NPV is at a substantial premium over the "market cap," that is, the total value of the shares of the company, and is paid out, that price must be justified. That is sometimes very hard to do.

Many maintain that support for outlandish prices can be purchased from investment bankers simply by paying premium prices for premium valuations, but the principal author disagrees that this is common practice. It is true that the investment banking profession has only in the past few years adopted sophisticated financial analysis as an essential tool, but it has done so for its own good, as trading for its own account provides more and more of its net revenues, and this has rubbed off—to the advantage of its M&A clientele.

Fortunately, factoring in the future, which before the advent of the desktop computer required laborious calculations by hand, has become relatively simple. Buyers and sellers alike can choose from a plethora of software packages containing DCF programs to produce a number that is the net present value of a projected cash stream. A buyer can easily negotiate with a seller by varying the financial elements that go into the computation of the NPV.

It is thus that many if not most negotiations on price today are held in front of a computer screen, or should be. For all these reasons, the discounted cash flow method has displaced all other methods in yielding NPVs that serve at least as the takeoff point for bargaining out the price of a company or a subsidiary operation for sale. In its simplest form, the DCF process proceeds as follows:

Step 1. Set aside the value of all assets—current and fixed—not used in the business to produce the estimated future earnings stream that is to be discounted.

Step 2. Estimate future sales year by year over a preselected time horizon.

Step 3. Estimate the gross margins year by year including depreciation expenses.

Step 4. Estimate earnings before interest and taxes (EBIT) year by year.

Step 5. Subtract interest and estimated taxes year by year.

Step 6. Compute and subtract the average marginal incremental working capital costs required to put on each additional dollar of sales year by year (reverse for any downsizing).

Step 7. Compute and subtract the average marginal incremental fixed capital costs of putting on each additional dollar of sales year by year (reverse for any major asset sales).

Step 8. Add back depreciation (reverse for recaptures).

Step 9. Compute the residual value of the company after the end of the horizon period by capitalizing the last year's projected earnings at the reciprocal of the selected discount rate.

Step 10. Discount all values, including residual value to present value, using a risk-adjusted cost of capital for the discount rate.

Step 11. Add back all set-aside values (Step 1) for current and fixed assets not used to produce revenues. The total will be the NPV of the business.

Do managers always know the NPVs of their companies?

Often, but not always. Why? To compute NPV by the DCF method requires long-term time horizons and some long-term educated guesses about the future, which managers are often reluctant to make for fear of being wrong. Outsiders, however, are not so reluctant, which is one reason why premiums are often paid over market values for going companies. Acquirers are far more willing to make the analyses with a minimum of information than the managers are with a maximum! This is how prospective buyers uncover values that long-term managers have never considered.

Isn't this because the sum of the breakup values of parts of an operation is often greater than the market value?

Precisely. There is all too often no economic rationale for a conglomerate—notwithstanding the prefix *con,* connoting some commonality of market or production or distribution methods. Most are *ag*glomerates—an assortment of disparate operations, each paying a fee for what often proves to be headquarters hindrance rather than headquarters help. The benefits of association, synergies such as the smoothing of cash flows effected by joining countercyclical operations, are often more than offset by headquarters stultification of the entrepreneurial process so necessary to successful growth. The agglomerators are discovering that their disparate operations will generally do better as stand-alones if they cannot be integrated with similar operations.

PRICING ISSUES

The previous discussion was about value; we now move to price, the practical manifestation of value for a buyer and a seller. As explained in Chapter 2, there are two basic types of buyer—*strategic* and *financial*. Very different prices may be offered for the same business by these two types of buyer.

What are the characteristics of a strategic buyer?

Typically, the strategic buyer has accumulated cash for the acquisition program and is considering where to spend it. Alternatively if it has been profitable and is publicly traded, the strategic buyer may use its own stock, which can be used to effect a tax-free exchange and/or a pooling, structures that have a great appeal to many sellers and selling groups. Strategic acquirers tend to avoid the heavy use of borrowed cash.

The time horizon of the strategic buyer is probably relatively long term, 5 to 10 years (although an important exception will arise if the acquisition is being considered as a defensive maneuver against a hostile takeover). Moreover, the strategic buyer is probably operating in an institutional, corporate framework in which full strategic planning is part of the corporate culture. As such, the typical strategic buyer will impound into its price the potential long-term synergies of combining operations.

What are the characteristics of a typical financial buyer?

The typical financial buyer is usually a group (though it can be a single individual), perhaps organized in the form of a leveraged buyout (LBO) fund, that intends to finance the purchase price primarily through maximizing borrowing against the assets and future cash flows of the acquired company and minimizing its provision of equity. The LBO buyer typically plans to pay down the debt through pumping up operating cash flows by sharply reducing expenses and by selling off surplus or underutilized assets.

Once the debt is substantially reduced or eliminated, LBO buyers will reap the benefits of their investment through dividends, through taking the company public with an IPO or by sale of the company to another buyer—typically a strategic buyer—or to the company's employee stock ownership plan (ESOP). LBO buyers usually rely on the existing management of the acquired company to operate it without major changes in structure or personnel and may include key managers in the ownership group. They may be simultaneously investing in other companies, but they don't look for synergies among all these investments; rather, their philosophy is "each tub on its own bottom." They prefer to keep their companies independent so that each can be operated and disposed of without affecting the others.

How does the LBO buyer price a potential acquisition?

Most experienced LBO buyers try to determine how much they must pay for a company and then analyze whether the deal will work on this basis. In so doing, they look at a number of standard ratios that focus principally on the relationship of the gross unleveraged price to operating cash flow, operating income, or unleveraged book value. The ratios really perform only a support function. However, the business of finding, pursuing, negotiating, consummating, and overseeing LBOs is a practical business and, more than anything else, a people business. There is little reliance on theoretical financial models.

That seems to be a backward approach. Why is it done this way?

A key element of success in structuring and completing LBOs is creativity. If an LBO buyer tries to value a company in a vacuum, using the standard valuation techniques—earnings, cash flow, book value multiples, and DCF analyses—the buyer will probably overlook the unusual elements that separate the truly successful LBOs from all others. If, however, the buyer has a target price that must be reached, the buyer will tend to push hard and be more creative in order to reach that target. It is basic human nature: People will perform better when they have a specific goal. One of the great things about LBOs is that if the deal works, it does not matter what conventions have been broken.

How do you decide if a deal works at a certain price?

That depends on the answer to two fundamental questions.

- Can the deal be financed, given that only limited amounts of senior debt, subordinated debt, and equity are available for any company?
- Can the company service the debt and still provide an attractive return to the equity holders?

Who typically holds equity in an LBO and what do they want?

Typically, the equity holders in an LBO will include two or three different types of investors, often with differing goals and objectives. They have differing risk/return objectives and thus differing investment decision-making criteria.

The management team of the company not only is an equity investor but is also devoting its full time to running the business. Its equity stake, and the appreciation of the value of that stake, is an integral part of management's compensation. The potential value of that stake, when added to management's current compensation, must be competitive with other opportunities available to the individuals who form the management team.

The LBO buyer who leads the deal—often called the *sponsor*— also has several objectives. This sponsor must analyze an acquisition in terms of the opportunity cost of the time expended in pursuing, negotiating, closing, and subsequently overseeing the company. Regardless of the return on hard dollars invested, the sponsor must see a potential total dollar return that justifies the time investment. An LBO investment firm must also carefully consider risk. A successful LBO firm must look at every deal knowing that there is a lot more at risk than just its time and equity dollars. If the buyout eventually fails and a lender suffers a loss, it will adversely affect the firm's ability to attract and finance acquisitions in the future.

Finally, there are the institutional equity investors. These are institutional investors who invest in LBO funds or who are given the right to buy equity as part of an agreement to lend senior or subordinated debt to the company. Institutional investors in LBO funds, which many of the major LBO firms use to finance deals, are looking for a pure financial return on their high-risk dollars. During the 1980s, their target was 40 percent or more, and many LBO firms delivered returns significantly higher than that. Lenders also frequently sought equity participation in order to boost their blended returns to the middle to high teens in the case of senior lenders (typically banks) or the high teens or twenties in the case of subordinated lenders (usually insurance companies or junk bond buyers).

How do you decide whether a deal can be financed?

We will discuss financing at greater length in Chapter 4, but because the valuation and pricing of LBOs is so closely linked to financing, we will preview some financing material here.

Financing LBOs is certainly more an art than a science, but there are some useful guidelines. The first step is to gather some basic information about the company in order to begin formulating a financing plan. The financing requirement is based, first, on the purchase price and the need to refinance any existing debt and, second, on the company's ability to repay the loan out of its projected cash flow. (See Chapter 4.)

You mentioned earlier that it is important to *discount* cash flow. Could you give some more advice on how to *project* cash flow in the first place?

The figures used in our earlier explanation of DCF are a good beginning, but they can benefit from additional "street smarts."Projecting cash flow requires addressing a myriad of questions, including the following:

- What are the company's projections?
- Are they reasonable?
- Has the company been able to meet its projections in the past?
- What are the industry's prospects?
- How secure is the company's competitive position?
- Is it a cyclical business?
- Do the projections properly take this into account?
- What are the company's growth or expansion plans?
- What are the working capital and fixed-asset requirements attendant to these plans?
- Is the business seasonal?
- What are the seasonal working capital needs?
- What events (such as strikes, currency fluctuations, foreign competition, loss of suppliers, and so on) could affect the projected results?
- Does the company have any excess assets or divisions that can or should be sold?
- How long would it take to make these sales, and how much money would they generate?
- Are there any other potential sources of cash?

- What can go wrong in all this, and does the company have any contingency plans?

This list is far from exhaustive, and it can take anywhere from a few hours to several weeks or months of due diligence to get a good feel for the cash flow. Once this has been done, the LBO buyer will be able to estimate reasonably the total financing needed at the closing date and prospectively for a 5- to 10-year period thereafter.

What do you do with all this information?

Armed with these data, the buyer can begin to map out a financing plan. The 1980s boom in LBOs spawned a variety of debt instruments and financing sources, but generally all LBO debt can be classified as either senior debt or subordinated debt.

Most senior debt in LBOs has traditionally come from banks and is either secured, meaning that specific assets or stocks are legally pledged to secure the loan, or unsecured. Because senior debt is the cheapest source of financing, an acquirer should try to obtain the greatest amount of senior debt possible.

How does a senior lender decide how much to lend in an acquisition?

That depends on a number of factors, including the type of loan being obtained. Senior loans to LBOs generally defy strict classification, but they can usually be divided into three groups: asset-based loans, cash flow loans, and bridge or interim loans.

In an asset-based loan, the bank is lending against specific assets or pools of assets and will decide how much to lend against each type of asset (the advance rate). For example, a bank may lend 80 percent against the book value of current accounts receivable, 60 percent against the book value of inventory in a warehouse, 30 percent against the book value of inventory in a retail store, and 50 to 75 percent against the fair market value of property, plant, and equipment.

In a cash flow loan, the bank is lending based on the company's ability to consistently generate cash flow from operations. On a cash flow loan, a bank will typically look for interest coverage (operating income divided by total interest expense) in the first year of at least 1.3 to 1.5 times and total repayment of the bank loan within 5 to 7 years. An important factor in determining an acceptable coverage ratio is the degree of certainty of the projections. A lender may prefer 1:1 coverage with a 95 percent probability to 1:5 coverage with a 50 percent probability of achieving the projections.

A bridge or interim loan often contains elements of both asset-based and cash flow loans. Typically, it is used to finance the purchase of assets or discrete businesses marked for sale in the acquisition and usually amounts to a percentage, between 50 and 100, of the estimated net proceeds. The advance rate depends on the timing and certainty of the disposition and on the bank's degree of comfort with the value and marketability of the subsidiaries or assets to be divested. The loans are generally secured by the stock of subsidiaries or the assets of the operations for sale. Loans that bridge to future subordinated debt financing—so-called junk bond bridge loans—are a different matter and are described in Chapter 4.

How do you decide which type of senior loan to take out?

It depends on several factors, including the acquirer's plans for the company, the nature of its key businesses, and the composition of its assets. The primary goal, again, is to maximize the dollar amount of senior loans. A secondary goal is to obtain the lowest cost of funds. Certain types of companies, such as basic manufacturing companies and retailers, are rich in fixed assets, inventory, and receivables. If these assets are not already pledged back to existing debt, an asset-based loan may yield the larger amount.

On the other hand, many businesses tend not to have large amounts of hard or tangible assets. This group usually includes companies in the fields of communications and high technology and most service industries. For acquisitions of these types of companies, a cash flow loan will tend to yield the greater amount.

In LBOs where the acquirer anticipates realizing significant proceeds from the sale of assets or entire businesses within a relatively short period (up to two years) after the acquisition date, the acquirer should attempt to obtain a portion of the senior bank debt in the form of an interim or bridge loan tied to the realization of those proceeds.

What is the typical payment term of an LBO loan?

Bridge or interim facilities, which will be repaid upon the occurrence of specified events, can have a maturity in the range of six months to two years, depending on the expected timing of those events.

Revolver and term loans usually have terms of three to seven years. Revolver loans are often "evergreen" facilities, with no repayment schedule until final maturity, or sometimes one or two mandatory reductions over the life of the loan. Term loans generally mandate repayment schedules beginning immediately or certainly within one year of the acquisition closing date and specify a repayment schedule tied to the company's projections. Often, term loan repayment schedules are prorated over the life of the loan. Term loans may require both scheduled repayments and additional payments out of excess cash flow.

What is the role of junk bonds in an LBO?

Junk bonds, which are subordinated debt usually sold to institutional investors, have played an integral role in LBO financing. Subordinated debt bridges the gap between what banks are willing to "pay" for companies and the equity that investors can and will contribute (again, see Chapter 4).

The junk bond debt market is a relatively new market. More than any other factor, its tremendous growth in the 1980s fueled much of the LBO boom by allowing companies to be acquired for relatively small amounts of equity.

Compared with the market for senior debt, the junk bond market is less developed and much more volatile. In fact, after the stock market crash on October 19, 1987, the market for new junk bonds virtually dried up for two to three months and led to a temporary, but dramatic, slowdown in large LBO activity. The crash of October 13, 1989, also had a depressing effect on junk bond financing of LBOs. However, junk bonds have survived into the late 1990s and seem to have become a permanent fixture in acquisition financing.

How do issuers of junk bonds decide how much to lend?

Junk bond lenders generally bear a significant portion of the risk in an LBO and are looking for a return to compensate them for their risk. Generally, the amount and terms of a subordinated loan or debt offering will reflect the risk/return relationship. Depending on the perceived riskiness of an acquisition, a junk bond lender will seek a return anywhere from a straight interest yield of 11 to 12 percent to a combined IRR, factoring in equity participation, in the range of 25 to 30 percent. If risk is excessive, the lender will be unwilling to lend at any return.

In evaluating risk, junk bond buyers look to see (1) if the breakup value of the company exceeds the aggregate amount of senior and subordinated debt and (2) whether cash flow from operations and asset sales is sufficient to meet senior and subordinated debt payment requirements.

How much equity should be invested in an LBO?

The amount of equity in an LBO is really a "plugged" number—there should be enough equity to get the deal done and provide assurance for the company's success. Equity must fill the gap between the total debt financing obtained and the total funds required to consummate the acquisition. A minimum amount of equity contribution is necessary to ensure solvency of the company (see Chapter 4); how much a lender will require depends on the lender's confidence in the company and the general business cycle.

Typically there is a complex interplay between the senior lenders, subordinated lenders, and equity investors in the financing of an LBO. The senior lenders seek to maximize the amounts of subordinated debt and equity; the subordinated lenders aim to maximize the amount of equity; and the equity investors try to minimize the amount of equity, maximize the senior debt, and bridge the gap with subordinated debt. It is occasionally said that 10 percent equity is a common starting point in the analysis, although deals have gone down with as little as 3 to 5 percent equity.

Every deal eventually comes down to the moment when the equity principal sets down all the facts (or his or her best estimate of the facts)—the terms and amounts of senior and subordinated debt and the required amount of equity—and decides whether the potential returns to the equity justify the investment in time and dollars, and the risk.

In other words, you do your financial plan for an LBO before you price?

Exactly. Pricing is a function of financeability. The price will be equal to what the LBO buyer is able to borrow against the assets and cash flow of the company being acquired, plus a marginal amount of equity. The process is interactive. The buyer tries to ascertain what he or she must pay and to design a financial structure based on that price. As a result of these activities, the buyer discovers whether he or she can meet the seller's price, or at what level he or she can bid for the company.

How is this method of pricing consistent with the DCF analysis earlier in this chapter?

It is entirely consistent; in fact, it directly applies DCF concepts. The LBO buyer simply sets out to accomplish in fact what the DCF analyst does in theory: to extract in cash, through borrowings or equity investments, the present value of the acquired company on a DCF basis, and use the proceeds to buy the company. The returns required by senior lenders, subordinated lenders, and equity investors, when blended, represent the required discount rate. The LBO buyer looks at the price and the amounts and costs of available financing. This allows the buyer to determine what return remains for the equity investment. If it is sufficient to justify the risk, the deal works.

What is the role of the various financial ratios in valuing companies?

The financial ratios are important tools used to address the fundamental issues of financeability and return to the equity investors. The ratios provide quick ways to value businesses and to quantify prices and values in terms of easily understood figures. The ratios also facilitate easy comparisons of different divisions within a company, different companies within an industry, and different industries.

What is the most commonly used ratio?

The most common measurement of price or value relates the price paid, free of debt, to the free cash flow available to service debt. The exact calculation can vary depending on the nature of the company or industry. The numerator is the gross unleveraged purchase price, which is the price paid for the equity, plus any debt assumed, plus the fees and expenses of the acquisition. The denominator is the company's "free cash flow," that is, operating cash flow (operating income before deducting taxes, interest, and depreciation) less the amount of capital expenditures required to maintain the company's current level of operations (the maintenance level).

For many manufacturing or industrial companies, the maintenance level of capital expenditures is approximately equal to depreciation, and operating income is therefore a good proxy for free cash flow. On the other hand, many service businesses—broadcasting, publishing, cable television, and others—require minimal amounts of maintenance-level capital expenditures. For these companies, operating cash flow is a good proxy for free cash flow. Obviously, 1:1 is a floor for this ratio, with 1.5:1 a more normal coverage benchmark.

Which year's financial statements should be used to calculate the free cash flow multiple?

Theoretically, you should be looking at free cash flow for the 12-month period beginning on the acquisition closing date. This number will obviously be a forecast and should be viewed in light of historical results. Investors, being relatively aggressive and optimistic people, will always look for the best numbers—generally tend to look at last year's numbers during difficult or depressed economic times and at next year's numbers during buoyant times.

The picture changes when a company is going through a major transition at the time the acquisition is closed, or will go through a major transition as a result of the acquisition. For example, suppose that a company is undergoing a major restructuring involving dramatic overhead reductions, the sale of an unprofitable business, and the absorption of a recently completed acquisition. Once the restructuring is completed, operating profit is expected to jump dramatically, giving rise to what is called a "hockey stick" projection: The line of the graph goes down a little, then turns and goes way up. Assume that actual and projected profits are as follows:

Year	Profits (in millions)
1999	$15
2000	$10
2001	$5
2002	$10
2003	$20

If acquirers anticipate such a pattern, they should warn their lenders. That way, when the difficult years come, lenders won't panic and call their loans early.

How do you apply the free cash flow ratio to acquisitions where several divestitures are envisioned?

In situations where an acquirer plans to divest one or more businesses, both the numerator and the denominator of the ratio must be adjusted. The gross purchase price should be reduced by the sum of the estimated net after-tax proceeds of the divestiture, plus any debt to be assumed by buyers of divested operations. Operating income should be adjusted to reflect the *pro forma* operating income of the remaining operations.

What are the limitations of the free cash flow ratio?

The ratio fails to take into account a number of factors, including cyclicality and growth.

Cyclical companies tend not to make attractive LBO candidates because of the unpredictability of cash flow. When analyzing a cyclical business, it is important to determine the company's current stage in the economic cycle and factor the likelihood of an economic shift (for example, a downturn) in the company's projections. Because of the volatility of earnings over the cycle, a free cash flow ratio based on just one year can be misleading, whereas a projection encompassing the entire business cycle will adjust cash flows properly. For further discussion of the kinds of companies suitable for LBOs, see Chapter 4.

The free cash flow multiple does not adjust in any way for the growth of a company. Obviously, a company with $10 million of operating income growing at 20 percent per year is worth more than a company with the same earnings growing at 5 percent per year. A pure multiple, whether of free cash flow, earnings, or any other financial statistic, does not indicate growth or the ultimate value of the company.

Growth prospects may, however, be reflected in the price to be paid for the company expressed as a multiple of free cash flow.

What rules of thumb does a lender use in considering how long a loan will be outstanding?

Lenders, particularly banks, like to see their loans retired and coverage improve reasonably rapidly. One common test is to see how much of the loan is projected to be paid off in five years. If most or all of the loan can be paid off in this time, the company has a good chance of getting through the early high-debt danger period successfully.

Another test is to see how soon the target 1.5:1 coverage ratio can be reached between annual earnings and interest payments. Lenders can feel substantial confidence if this 50 percent cushion is projected to be achieved in two to three years, which is a period of time short enough to be somewhat reliably predictable by management. If projections don't indicate this point will be reached until the fifth year or beyond, lenders may be much more reluctant to lend.

At what prices have LBOs been done historically, expressed as a multiple of free cash flow?

Since 1980, prices have generally been increasing for free-standing investments. In the early 1980s, companies could be bought at three to four times free cash flow. By the late 1980s, as competition for deals increased, transactions were being priced at up to six or seven times free cash flow.

Such higher prices were made possible, in part, by a rising stock market and the higher prices the public was willing to pay for equity in IPOs of LBO companies, and by the greater availability of cash from subordinated debt and from junk bond sales.

The LBO "going public" movement has also sparked an increase in so-called shell transactions, where an LBO goes public not by merging into a public company or by launching an IPO, but by "backing into" an inactive public corporation with an exchange of shares, and a deal with an investment banking firm or firms to immediately "make a market" in the shares. It's quick, it's inexpensive, and it no longer has the stigma it once had.

What effect do these price/cash flow multiples have on debt payout?

At three to four times free cash flow, a company can withstand a decline in operating cash flow and retire its debt within seven years. At four to five times free cash flow, a company can go a number of years with flat earnings and the equity will still appreciate in value. But at six to seven times free cash flow and higher, the company must have solid prospects of earnings increases for the deal to make sense.

What is the utility of a debt-equity ratio?

A lot of people focus too much on capitalization ratios, such as the ratio of debt to equity. LBOs sometimes exhibit dramatic ratios of 100:1 or more, and these are taken as demonstrations that the company is overleveraged and will be in trouble after the closing. However, the ratio of debt to purchase price is not the real test. Much more important are the ratios of (1) debt to market value, which indicates the public's perception of the degree of solvency of the company, and (2) operating income to interest and principal payments, which measures the company's ability to service its debt.

For example, suppose you contract to purchase a broadcast company for $100 million—10 times cash flow—and then, before closing, negotiate a deal to pre-sell half of its stations for $65 million—13 times their total cash flow—thereby effectively obtaining the remaining stations for 7 times cash flow, substantially below the prevailing market price. Your purchase price for the remaining stations was, in effect, $35 million, on which you borrowed $34 million and put up $1 million in equity. The stations are worth $50 million on closing day. It is more accurate to say that your debt-equity ratio is 34:16 ($50 million – $34 million = $16 million) rather than 34:1.

Similarly, if the buyer is overpaying, a good debt-equity ratio won't make the deal successful. Suppose the acquired company's cash flow will support $40 million of debt, and it has been purchased for $60 million, of which $45 million is debt and $15 million is equity from a too-eager buyout fund. The capitalization ratio is a reasonable 3:1, but trouble is sure to come. Capitalization ratios work when the total value can be clearly determined by a smoothly functioning market, which is reflected in the purchase price of the target rather than from go-go bankers. The valuation of companies in go-go markets is too complex and the market too imperfect to apply rule-of-thumb capitalization ratios as go/no-go criteria.

How useful are company projections in evaluating future cash flow prospects?

They are extremely important. Where the LBO buyer is doing a management buyout and pre-acquisition management will remain in place after the buyout, managers stand to gain either as stockholders or with increased salaries if the company prospers. After all, they know the business better than the buyer does—at least in the early stages—and it is to their advantage to make accurate projections.

It is generally advisable for the buyer to begin by asking managers to share their business plan projections of future economic performance, and then ask for their past projections and compare them with how they actually did. Any major differences must be explained.

Generally speaking, the management team that can present a solid business plan and can give a crisp, precise, well-thought-out set of projections will be a winner. Losers are found in the team that fumbles around and says "Gee, we don't do projections," or "We only do them once a year," or "We did them six months ago; we have to bring them up to date."

How do you avoid undue optimism in projections?

Classic planning systems use *best, most likely,* and *worst* cases for projections. Another way to plan ahead is to project the *base case* and a *reasonably worst case.* The base case assumes a 100 percent likelihood of meeting targets, and the reasonably worst case assumes a 90 percent chance of meeting them. The buyer's decision to pursue a deal and the amount of money the buyer plans to borrow will depend on that 90 percent case. If the buyer relies on the reasonably-worst-case projection, everything need not fall exactly into place for the acquired company to meet its debt obligations.

If base-case projections are far more optimistic than the reasonably worst case, be cautious. The company may have too high a level of volatility in its earnings to be a good LBO candidate.

When studying projections, as mentioned earlier, the buyer should be sure to ask selling management why the company or division is for sale—is there something out there in the future that will cause this business not to earn as much money as it has been earning?

Buyers should also focus on what effect the post-LBO company's leverage ratio will have on its operations—for example, in obtaining trade credit.

EXPRESSING THE PURCHASE PRICE IN THE ACQUISITION AGREEMENT

Once the parties agree on the price, they must express it properly and concern themselves with the effect on the price, if any, of any significant change in profits and losses between the signing and closing.

Once the purchase price is arrived at by buyer and seller, how is it set forth in the acquisition agreement?

The buyer and seller can agree that the price is a fixed amount or an amount determined by a formula. A fixed amount is specified as a total dollar amount, which may be payable in cash or a combination of cash and securities. The noncash portion of the price will normally be in the form of subordinated promissory notes, preferred stock, or, if the buyer is a publicly held company, common stock of the buyer. It is less common for the seller to retain a common stock interest in the acquired company.

Where the price is determined by a formula, it is commonly based on book value, or stockholders' equity from a balance sheet prepared as of the closing date, plus or minus a dollar amount.

Under another variation, a fixed price is established, and the buyer receives a credit against the price for any excess earnings or is required to pay an increased amount equal to any losses realized by the business after a specified date. This can be expressed as an adjustment for changes in working capital, that is, the difference between cash and other current assets versus current liabilities of the company on the closing date.

How is a book value formula price implemented?

Typically, the acquisition agreement provides that the buyer will purchase the company by paying the estimated book value at closing, plus or minus x, and that an adjustment will be made after the closing when a precise book value figure has been determined.

How do these provisions work?

The seller typically delivers an estimated closing balance sheet five business days prior to the closing together with supporting documentation. The parties agree on, and close on the basis of, the estimated balance sheet. After the closing, the seller prepares the balance sheet as of the closing date, which is usually the end of an accounting period. The actual balance sheet (ABS) at closing is compared with the estimated balance sheet (EBS) at closing. If the closing ABS shows a higher book value than the closing EBS, the buyer pays the seller the difference. If this value is lower, the seller pays the buyer.

Are accountants used in this process?

Absolutely. The seller's accounting firm will often audit the closing balance sheet. The buyer's accountants then review the audit. If the parties and the accountants differ on the correct presentation of the balance sheet, buyer and seller (or their accountants) may turn to a third accounting firm to resolve any differences.

Such review procedures vary from the simple to the exceedingly complex. The agreement often provides that if the final balance sheet varies by more than a specified percentage (often 10 percent), then the challenging parties' fees are paid. If they do not vary materially, the challenger may be required to pay the fees of the prevailing party.

Because of the different results that can be obtained while complying with generally accepted accounting principles (GAAP), some agreements provide that the net effect of any challenge to the seller's balance sheet presentation must be more than a specified dollar amount to require an adjustment.

What other issues arise in such provisions?

In addition to specifying that balance sheets must be prepared in accordance with GAAP, the parties should specify which method of inventory valuation should be used. Taxes may also be important in determining book value. It is also wise to state that the balance sheet should not reflect any liability that arises solely from the sale of the business.

What other arrangements are used in pricing?

Some deals provide that the acquisition be effective on a specific date. After that date, the profits and losses of the business are for the buyer's account. This period is sometimes called the *interim* or *stub period*. Typically, gains decrease and losses increase a fixed purchase price. As with adjustments to book value, rather than waiting for the final results, closings are often made on the basis of an estimate and adjusted when the actual results are determined.

Many things can happen between agreement and closing. A buyer's best protection is to put someone on the site or sites monitoring operations. Even so, the usual provisions that the business shall be operated in the ordinary course of events should be incorporated in the agreement. Some buyers have been surprised at the amount of time consumed in getting from agreement to closing.

To measure profit and loss, the parties must define precisely what they intend. For example, "net income" may be calculated without deduction for administrative charges and interest expense. Net income should not be reduced by nonrecurring expenses incurred in connection with the transaction, such as legal and accounting fees, or separation payments (so-called "golden parachutes").

Sophisticated sellers may credit the buyer with the stub period earnings but may try to build up offsets against them such as interest at a fixed rate (for instance, 10 percent) on the purchase price during the interim period.

When is it appropriate to use a formula rather than a fixed-price provision in the acquisition agreement?

If a substantial period of time is to pass between signing the acquisition agreement and closing, the buyer will want protection against changes in the value of the company during the interim. While most of the value is impounded in the earnings stream, changes in operations may not show up in operating losses for many years and are difficult to guard against. However, one kind of protection is to set forth a "book value" formula. Generally this will detect any sales of assets or other major changes in operations from the ordinary course of business. (Files on intangibles, such as patents and trademarks, should be sequestered so as not to be encumbered by either intent or error.)

The variant method of setting a fixed price and then providing a working capital or earnings adjustment to the closing price may have the advantage for both buyer and seller of reducing the amount of variation possible between estimated and final price, and focusing more sharply on those aspects of company performance that the adjustment is intended to cover.

The variant method thus reduces the difficulty of that critical moment in the process that arises when the seller presents the buyer, on the eve of the closing, with the estimated balance sheet book value number. Significant differences between estimates and actuals serve as an opening for further negotiations, not only on price but also on other issues that both parties have been identifying as loose ends since the acquisition agreement was signed. A seller nervous about closing would prefer that any closing price differences be as large as possible in order to stall the deal, while the buyer who is anxious to get into operations wants it as small as possible so the seller can't.

What issues arise where the price is determined by reference to the seller's or buyer's stock price?

The parties could agree that the value of a share is equal to the market price on the day the deal is struck no matter what happens to the stock after the news gets out. However, because the market price can be higher or lower on the closing date, sometimes substantially so, the parties may instead agree to use the market price on the closing date. Another alternative is to use the average price at closing for the 20 days prior to the closing. Another method is to look at the price of the stock over the past year and, while using the price on the day of closing, place a maximum and minimum (a *collar*) on the stock price independent of the trading price on closing day. The parties will have set limits, or a collar, on the total consideration. For example, if a stock's average price is $30 prior to signing, the parties may agree that, regardless of the actual average before closing, the price per share will be no lower than $25 or higher than $32. The collar can also regulate the maximum and minimum number of the buyer's shares that the buyer must deliver to selling stockholders.

How can locked-in buyers protect themselves against stock price drops?

An underwriting agreement is, in effect, a "firm" commitment to buy the company's stock at a set price regardless of whether or not the underwriter can resell it. The precise firmness of the agreement is set by the number and the terms of the "market outs" negotiated by the parties. One typical market out states that the underwriter does not have to go through with the contract if there is a 25 percent drop in the S&P 500, or if the United States gets into a war, or if other adverse market conditions exist. Sellers can also request market outs, but they rarely do so because they don't want the underwriter to trade them off for a new set of market outs.

With what form of consideration should one pay—stock, cash, notes, or a combination?

The form of the consideration to be paid can be almost as important to the buyer and seller as the amount that will be paid because of the tax treatment accorded the deal. This is discussed in depth in Chapter 5, on structuring.

In transactions involving public companies, how can buyers use a combination of cash and securities?

Some transactions are structured, usually for tax reasons, to provide for fixed percentages of cash and stock. For example, the buyer might offer $20 million in cash and 2 million shares of buyer's stock to holders of the 2 million shares of the company it is acquiring. The agreement can allocate such cash and securities proportionally—$10 in cash and 1 share for each share of the company. Alternatively, stockholders of the company being acquired may be given the option to elect between all cash and all securities or any combination. If too many stockholders elect cash, they may be forced to take some stock as well. Such provisions are often referred to as a *cramdown* because of their coercive nature. As an alternative, to avoid a cramdown, certain large insider stockholders may agree separately to take a combination of cash and securities so that other, smaller holders can elect to be paid all cash. (See Chapter 12.)

What is an earnout?

An *earnout* is a method of compensating a seller based on the future earnings of a company. It is the contingent portion of the purchase price. A common type of earnout provides for additional payments to a seller if the earnings exceed agreed-upon levels. Another type of earnout may provide that certain debt given to the seller as part of the acquisition price is "anticipated" and will be paid early out of earnings exceeding agreed-upon levels.

Earnouts require consideration of various factors: the type of contingent payment (cash or stock), the measurement of performance (operating income, cash flow, net income, or other), the measurement period, maximum limits (if any), and the timing of payments.

Why would the parties use an earnout?

The parties may disagree on the value of the business because they have different opinions about the projected profit stream. Often the buyer is relying on the seller's projections of future cash flow in setting the price. The buyer and seller may disagree on the seller's ability to realize the projected results. A buyer will be willing to pay a higher price for greater cash flow if, and only if, the projected cash flow is realized. An earnout permits the buyer to pay a reasonable price plus a premium when and if the cash flow is realized. It also allows the seller to realize the full value of the business if it is as profitable as represented.

Why are earnouts difficult to administer?

A typical earnout might provide that the seller will receive an additional payment of a certain amount in each of the early (say, three) years after the sale, provided that in each of those years the acquired company realizes operating income at or above a target—say, $1 million or more.

Although simple in concept, earnouts raise a number of definitional problems. The buyer and seller must agree on the definition of operating income. The buyer will want to be sure that such income comes from continuing operations and not extraordinary or nonrecurring events. Furthermore, the earnout may require that the acquired company be operated separately and consistently with past practice. If the buyer wants to combine certain of its operations or modify them, such changes will be difficult to factor into the levels of earnings to be achieved, particularly if they are not decided upon until after the sale.

What concerns will the seller have in an earnout?

The seller will be interested in ensuring that changes in the operation of the company after the sale do not affect the company's ability to attain the targeted earnings. The seller may thus seek agreements that goodwill will be ignored in making the calculations and that the company will continue to be operated in a fashion consistent with past practice and will not be charged with new administrative overhead expenses. The seller may also focus on depreciation, interest charges, and intercompany transactions with the buyer's company.

The seller will want to receive credit for post-acquisition results, even if the $1 million level in the example is not achieved. If in the first three years the company earns, respectively, $800,000, $1 million, and $1.2 million, the seller will feel entitled to receive the total contingent payment, even though operating income did not exceed $1 million in the first year. The parties may agree on a sliding scale or averaging approach and a maximum payment.

The seller will also focus on when it receives a contingent payment—after each year or at the end of the agreed-on period (in our example, three years). The buyer must now consider whether this will trigger any obligation to refund a payment for year one if the results in years two and three are substandard.

Ultimately, no legal agreement can provide complete protection for both parties in earnout agreements; there are far too many variables. Buyer and seller must rely either on the provisions expressed in terms of the intent or good faith of the parties or on their reasonable business judgments. By the time buyer and seller have gone through a turbulent acquisition closing with each other, they may find little comfort in such arrangements. Many painfully negotiated earnout agreements are bought out as the closing approaches.

Are there tax and accounting considerations with earnouts?

Earnouts can spread out income in taxable transactions for sellers with resulting tax benefits. To have a tax-free reorganization, contingent shares must be issued within five years of the closing. The buyer may also obtain a tax deduction where the earnout is paid as compensation under an employment agreement. However, the payments may be ordinary income to the recipient.

Why are earnouts not more common?

The principal author has negotiated many earnouts but has always been surprised at the number that are bought out at or very near closing. It comes from the difficulty of policing of costs with the buyer now in command. The buyer could overspend on research and development (R&D), advertising, and so on, and reap benefits in the future but avoid paying on an earnout now by reducing reported earnings. If the seller is still running the business, the reverse is true: The seller reduces essential expense and thus ensures the earnout.

There are also earnout challenges when the acquired company has been part of a conglomerate where units have not undergone regular audits, and where direct and indirect transfer costs have not been properly charged. No one knows, from the record, whether it is currently profitable or not, and audits won't help because the records are missing or miskept. In such a case, buyer and seller alike may be reluctant to arrange an earnout. (Ironically, however, this is precisely a time to encourage an earnout—to discover whether or not it is profitable, and if so, how profitable.)

In other cases, where an earnout might look feasible, the buyer may need to own all the upside potential to interest investors or lenders and doesn't want to share the upside potential with the seller. Very often, the buyer may be lucky: All the seller wants is to get out and go on to something else. The last thing it wants to do is ride herd on decisions about what are and are not direct expenses, the essence of the proper administration of an earnout.

Are there alternatives to the earnout concept?

Yes. A buyer may offer additional or "makeup" stock in the event of above-target performance. This is used especially when stock has been used as the purchase medium. The problem with this is dramatized by one Detroit seller that got a guarantee on stock price, with makeup shares as the compensating vehicle. The seller wound up in control of a major buyer when the buyer's stock price plummeted. Other types of contingent consideration are preferred stock and warrants.

What are solvency opinions, who generally requests them, and who issues them?

Solvency opinions, also known as *comfort letters,* are written opinions about solvency designed to meet the needs of lenders and investment bankers, particularly in highly leveraged transactions. The purpose of the solvency opinion is to help the lender or banker document solvency and enable it to rebut potential fraudulent conveyance claims in case the borrower encounters financial difficulties. Solvency opinions are issued by appraisers and valuation consultants.

Can outside accountants issue solvency opinions?

No. Although an accounting firm may certify that a company meets one or more of the definitions of solvency under GAAP (see Chapter 4), it may not provide any assurance that an entity (1) is not insolvent at the time debt is incurred or will not be rendered insolvent thereby, (2) does not have unreasonably small capital, or (3) will have the ability to pay its debts as they mature. These matters are business and legal concepts subject to varying interpretations that are not clearly defined for financial reporting purposes.[16]

What services may an outside accountant provide to assist in solvency determinations?

Although outside accountants may not and do not give any direct assurance about solvency, they do provide services that may be useful to a company seeking financing. Such services include examination and review of historical information, examination and review of pro forma financial information, and examination and compilation of prospective financial information. Restricted use reports (that is, agreed-upon procedure reports pursuant to auditing attestation, or prospective financial information standards) may be provided in connection with a financing, but may not address the issue of solvency.

What are comfort letters, who requests them, and who issues them?

Under federal securities laws, an underwriter is responsible for carrying out a "reasonable investigation" of financial and nonfinancial data included in registration statements filed with the SEC under the Securities Act of 1933. As part of this reasonable investigation, underwriters typically request letters of assurance regarding financial data ("comfort letters") from outside accountants in connection with an underwritten offering of securities under the 1933 law. Comfort letters may also be requested by underwriters in conjunction with securities offerings not subject to the 1933 law.

In issuing comfort letters, accountants generally apply selected procedures to financial data not otherwise reported on by the accountant, such as (1) unaudited financial statements, condensed interim financial statements, capsule information, and pro forma financial information; (2) changes in selected financial statement items (such as capital stock, long-term debt, net current assets or net assets, net sales, and the total or per-share amounts of net income) during a period subsequent to the date and period of the latest financial statements included in the registration statement; and (3) tables, statistics, and other financial information.

What comfort does such a letter provide underwriters?

The assurance outside accountants provide underwriters by way of comfort letters is subject to limitations. First, any procedures performed short of an audit, such as the agreed-upon procedures contemplated in a comfort letter, provide the outside accountants with a basis for expressing, at most, negative assurance (that is, that nothing came to their attention that indicated that something was wrong). Second, the outside accountants can properly comment in their professional capacity only on matters to which their professional expertise is relevant (for example, the outside accountant's ability to measure does not make it appropriate for them to give comfort on the square footage of a plant).

In addition, what constitutes a "reasonable investigation" sufficient for an underwriter's purposes has never been authoritatively established. As a result, the underwriter, not the outside accountant, is responsible for the sufficiency of the comfort letter procedures for the underwriter's purposes.

CONCLUDING COMMENTS

To be effective as a buyer or a seller, you don't need to be a valuation expert—in fact, thinking you have enough knowledge can be (to quote Alexander Pope again) a "dangerous thing." Valuation is such a complex art, and there are so many good specialists to consult, that this is one area where pride can be counterproductive. At the same time, to avoid overpaying for a company (or getting underpaid as a seller) you do need to know valuation fundamentals, and how to express them in an acquisition agreement. In closing, then, let us reflect on the words of the Chinese philosopher Confucius, writing some 2,500 years ago: "When you know a thing, to hold that you know it; and when you do not know a thing, to allow that you do not know it—this is knowledge." The valuation stage is a good time to develop and strengthen these twin virtues of confidence and humility.

E X H I B I T 3-1

Estimating the Cost of Capital

Any for-profit operation is worth the present value of its future earnings stream taken out to infinity and discounted back to today at a rate that approximates the risk. Most valuators use the company's cost of capital as a proxy for the discount rate or to compute the "opportunity cost" of an acquisition. The *historical* cost of capital, which may include sunk costs, may be quite different from the *marginal* cost of capital—the rate that would be used to compute the NPV of the earnings stream of a contemplated acquisition. We will deal here only with the marginal rate, weighted for the percentage used to effect the acquisition.

	Weight (%)	Cost (%)	Risk premium (%)	Weighted cost (%)
Cost of debt	30	7.5	2.5	3.00
Cost of preferred	20	10.0	—	2.00
Cost of equity	50	20.0	—	10.00
Net pretax cost of capital				15.00

Notes:
- This model uses a risk-free rate of 7.5 percent.
- Most cost-of-capital rates are after-tax models, but this one is pretax since the analytical methods described in the text lump and deduct all interest payments whether short or long term.
- The risk premium is derived from market expectations, which are driven by two factors: (1) supply and demand for similar funds in the marketplace and (2) financial risk, which factors in increased risk associated with post-acquisition increased debt-to-equity ratios.
- The use of retained earnings has been lumped with equity, although its cost is usually 5 to 10 percent less than the cost of new equity, reflecting the saved costs of marketing and underwriting.

PRICING OUT

The Replacement Value Method (RVM)

If a target appears to be profitable but information about the components that produce the profit is lacking, the only valid method of pricing is replacement cost. Once replacement cost has been established, the buyer's cost of capital is used to discover what kinds of earnings or cash flows must be achieved to justify the investment using the IRR or DCF methods described below.

The Investment, or Average Rate of Return, Method

Let us assume that you are offered your choice of two different franchised restaurants in a shopping center that is to be torn down in six years. Which should you buy?

E X H I B I T   3-1 (Continued)

Cash price	Store A—$60,000		Store B—$72,000	
Year	After-tax profit	Sales	After-tax profit	Sales
1	$10,000	$20,000	$33,000	$45,000
2	10,000	20,000	10,000	22,000
3	10,000	20,000	8,000	20,000
4	10,000	20,000	1,000	13,000
5	10,000	20,000	1,000	13,000
6	10,000	20,000	1,000	13,000
Average	$10,000	$20,000	$9,000	$21,000

The averaging process assumes that straight-line depreciation is used over the six-year life of each store, and no salvage value is taken at the end. Dividing the initial investment by 2 gives the *average* investment. For Project A, that is $30,000; for Project B, $36,000. The average rate of return for Project A is thus 33.33 percent ($10,000/$30,000), while that for Project B is only 25 percent ($9,000/$36,000). Store A is obviously a better investment than Store B.

A variation on the above is to use the original investment rather than the average investment. The average rates of return for Store A and Store B would then be 16.67 and 12.50 percent, respectively; again, the Store A deal looks better.

The Payback Method

In the above example, the original investment in Store A would be "paid back" in exactly three years ($20,000 × 3 = $60,000). Store B presents some problems in analysis as it is based on what is known as a *mixed stream* of returns. At the end of the third year, $87,000 will have been "paid back." This is more than required if the firm has established a three-year payback hurdle for such acquisitions. The payback period is therefore 2.25 years. For many managers this would be a better buy because the payback period to fully recover the original investment is significantly shorter. For many, this means less risk and is preferred even though the return on investment (ROI) is lower than it is for Store A.

The Internal Rate of Return (IRR) Method

The ABC Warehousing Company is considering buying out a competing warehousing firm and would like to fully recover its investment in four years when it expects to get $120,000 for it when the firm merges into a larger company. The hurdle rate on all investments has been established at 10 percent. It has projected that it will have after-tax profits of $7,000, $8,000, and $8,000 on the acquisition. Will this investment meet its objectives? The answer is yes. The IRR for the investment is 10.29 percent.

The Market Value Method

	Price	Earnings per share	P/E
Comparable A	$40.00	$2.00	20
Comparable B	62.50	2.50	25
Comparable C	45.00	3.00	15
Comparable D	20.00	1.00	20
Comparable E	30.00	1.50	20
Average			20

This kind of analysis has been the standard for investment bankers for many years and is still required in a due diligence inquiry. It is more indicative than determinative as it has been displaced by the discounted cash flow-derived NPV method.

The Comparable Net Worth to Market Value Method

	Adjusted book	Price	Multiple
Comparable A	$40	80	2.0
Comparable B	20	30	1.5
Comparable C	30	75	2.5
Comparable D	30	45	1.5
Comparable E	20	50	2.5
Average			2.0

If the adjusted net worth or book value of the target is $15 per share, then the proper value or price will be $30.

The Discounted Cash Flow Method

Following is an example of a relatively sophisticated computerized program to yield NPV for a target company. The program is sold by the Alcar Group Inc., 5215 Old Orchard Road, Suite 600, Skokie, IL 60077.

Please note that the printout is only for the most likely scenario. The most optimistic and the most pessimistic scenarios, normally an integral part of an Alcar analysis, do not appear.

E X H I B I T 3-1 (Continued)

Income Statement for Sample Company: Most Likely Scenario

($ in Millions)	1999	2000	2001	2002	2003	2004	2005
Sales	$1,934.5	$2,032.0	$2,235.2	$2,414.0	$2,558.9	$2,712.4	$2,875.1
Cost of Goods Sold	1,435.2	1,529.9	1,698.8	1,834.7	1,842.4	1,844.4	1,955.1
Gross Profit	499.3	502.1	536.4	579.4	716.5	868.0	920.0
Salary Expense	156.2	169.3	109.5	118.3	125.4	132.9	140.9
Selling Expense	54.3	57.8	55.9	60.4	64.0	67.8	71.9
Administrative Expenses	87.2	93.5	148.2	125.2	251.0	365.7	377.8
Total SG & A Expense	297.7	320.6	313.6	303.8	440.4	566.4	590.6
Other Operating Income	0.5	1.2	0.9	0.9	0.9	0.9	0.9
Depreciation Expense	49.3	55.1	57.5	61.0	64.0	66.1	68.1
Operating Profit	$152.8	$127.6	$166.3	$215.4	$213.1	$236.3	$262.3
Interest Income	0.0	0.0	8.7	20.5	33.0	47.4	64.2
Interest Expense: Sched. Debt	N/A	N/A	16.0	16.0	16.0	16.0	16.0
Total Interest Expense	15.4	17.6	16.0	16.0	16.0	16.0	16.0
Less: Interest Capitalized	3.0	3.0	3.0	3.0	3.0	3.0	3.0
Interest Expense	12.4	14.6	13.0	13.0	13.0	13.0	13.0
Gain on Sale of Assets	6.5	7.3	0.0	0.0	0.0	0.0	0.0
Other Non-Operating Income	32.4	36.3	40.2	43.1	45.0	45.0	45.0
Earnings Before Taxes	$179.3	$156.6	$202.2	$266.1	$278.0	$315.7	358.5
Provision for Income Taxes	67.1	23.4	70.2	92.9	91.8	102.5	114.4
Extraordinary Items	0.0	(2.8)	0.0	0.0	0.0	0.0	0.0
Net Income	$112.2	$130.4	$131.9	$173.2	$186.3	$213.3	$244.1
Preferred Dividends	4.1	4.3	4.5	4.7	5.1	5.1	5.1
Income Available for Common	$108.1	$126.1	$127.4	$168.5	$181.2	$208.2	$239.0
Common Dividends	$12.5	$13.4	$14.1	$57.2	$61.5	$70.4	$80.6

Balance Sheet for Sample Company: Most Likely Scenario

($ in Millions)	1999	2000	2001	2002	2003	2004	2005
Cash	$4.3	$17.8	$24.3	$30.0	$34.7	$39.6	$44.8
Marketable Securities	4.1	70.9	166.9	268.2	385.3	522.3	673.1
Accounts Receivable	357.9	397.6	420.4	440.4	456.6	473.8	492.0
Raw Materials	73.0	75.7	78.3	80.7	82.5	84.5	86.7
Work in Progress	182.6	189.2	200.2	209.8	217.7	225.9	234.7
Finished Goods	109.5	113.4	120.5	126.7	131.7	137.1	142.7
Total Inventories	365.1	378.3	399.0	417.2	431.9	447.6	464.1
Other Current Assets	43.7	43.7	43.7	43.7	43.7	43.7	43.7
Total Current Assets	$775.1	$908.3	$1,054.3	$1,199.5	$1,352.2	$1,527.0	$1,717.7
Gross PP & E excl. Int. Cap.	769.8	798.1	844.2	882.7	910.4	934.9	955.6
Cum. Forecast Interest Cap.	N/A	N/A	3.0	5.8	8.4	10.8	13.0
Less: Accum. Depreciation	276.5	269.9	293.7	312.3	329.2	341.2	341.3
Net Property, Plant & Equip.	493.3	528.2	553.5	576.1	589.5	604.5	627.4
Goodwill	52.9	46.5	46.5	46.5	46.5	46.5	46.5
Other Intangibles	4.5	3.3	3.3	3.3	3.3	3.3	3.3
Other Assets	22.6	42.3	42.3	42.3	42.3	42.3	42.3
Total Assets	$1,348.4	$1,528.6	$1,699.9	$1,867.7	$2,033.9	$2,223.5	2,437.2
Accounts Payable	$145.9	$192.7	$221.1	$246.2	$266.5	$288.0	$310.7
Current Portion L-T Debt	12.4	11.8	24.9	25.2	25.9	26.6	27.4
Income Taxes Payable	17.3	17.5	16.4	21.7	21.5	24.0	26.8
Other Current Liabilities	71.6	71.6	71.6	71.6	71.6	71.6	71.6
Total Current Liabilities	$247.2	$293.6	$334.0	$364.7	$385.4	$410.2	$436.5
Total L-T Debt	323.7	335.9	340.0	350.0	360.0	370.0	380.0
Deferred Income Taxes	87.3	98.2	108.9	122.7	136.4	151.5	168.4
Other Liabilities	22.6	14.2	15.0	15.0	15.0	15.0	15.0
Total Liabilities	$680.8	$741.9	$797.9	$852.4	$896.8	$946.7	$999.9
Preferred Stock	37.9	39.4	41.4	43.4	45.4	47.4	49.4
Common Stock and Paid-In Cap	612.4	620.3	620.3	620.3	620.3	620.3	620.3
Retained Earnings	17.3	127.0	240.3	351.7	471.4	609.1	767.6
Total Liabilities and Equity	$1,348.4	$1,528.6	$1,699.9	$1,867.7	$2,033.9	$2,223.5	$2,437.2
Unused Debt Capacity (UDC)	$35.3	$98.6	$153.1	$213.2	$278.3	$355.1	$445.4
UDC plus Mkt. Securities	$39.4	$169.5	$320.1	$481.4	$663.6	$877.4	$1,118.4

E X H I B I T 3-1 (Continued)

Funds Flow Statement for Sample Company: Most Likely Scenario

($ in Millions)	2000	2001	2002	2003	2004	2005
Net Income	$130.4	$131.9	$173.2	$186.3	$213.3	$244.1
Depr. Exp. excl. Int. Cap.	55.1	57.5	60.8	63.6	65.5	67.3
Depr. Exp. on Cum. Int. Cap.	N/A	N/A	0.2	0.4	0.6	0.8
Less: Interest Capitalized	3.0	3.0	3.0	3.0	3.0	3.0
Incr. in Deferred Inc. Taxes	10.9	10.7	13.8	13.7	15.2	16.8
Incr. in Other Liabilities	(8.4)	0.8	0.0	0.0	0.0	0.0
Incr. in Debt: Scheduled	12.2	4.1	10.0	10.0	10.0	10.0
Net Bk. Value of Ret. Assets	8.1	20.9	18.3	20.0	20.2	14.0
Incr. in Accounts Payable	46.8	28.4	25.0	20.3	21.5	22.8
Incr. in Curr. Port. L-T Debt	(0.6)	13.1	0.3	0.7	0.7	0.7
Incr. in Income Tax Payable	0.2	(1.1)	5.3	(0.3)	2.5	2.8
Proceeds from Sale of Common	7.9	0.0	0.0	0.0	0.0	0.0
Proceeds from Sale of Pf. Stk.	1.5	2.0	2.0	2.0	2.0	2.0
Total Sources of Funds	**$261.1**	**$265.3**	**$306.0**	**$313.7**	**$348.5**	**$378.4**
Fixed Capital Investment	$98.1	$100.7	$98.9	$94.4	$98.2	$102.0
Additions to Goodwill	(6.4)	0.0	0.0	0.0	0.0	0.0
Additions to Intangibles	(1.2)	0.0	0.0	0.0	0.0	0.0
Incr. in Other Assets	19.7	0.0	0.0	0.0	0.0	0.0
Incr. in Cash	13.5	6.5	5.7	4.6	4.9	5.2
Incr. in Mkt. Securities	66.8	96.0	101.3	117.1	137.0	150.7
Incr. in Accts. Receivable	39.7	22.8	20.0	16.2	17.2	18.2
Incr. in Raw Materials	2.7	2.6	2.3	1.9	2.0	2.1
Incr. in Work in Progress	6.6	11.0	9.7	7.8	8.3	8.8
Incr. in Finished Goods	3.9	7.1	6.2	5.0	5.3	5.7
Total Incr. in Inventories	13.2	20.7	18.2	14.7	15.6	16.6
Preferred Dividends	4.3	4.5	4.7	5.1	5.1	5.1
Common Dividends	13.4	14.1	57.2	61.5	70.4	80.6
Total Uses of Funds	**$261.1**	**$265.3**	**$306.0**	**$313.7**	**$348.5**	**$378.4**

Cash Flow Statement for Sample Company: Most Likely Scenario

($ in Millions)	2000	2001	2002	2003	2004	2005
Sales	$2,032.0	$2,235.2	$2,414.0	$2,558.9	$2,712.4	$2,875.1
Cost of Goods Sold	1,529.9	1,698.8	1,834.7	1842.4	1,844.4	1,955.1
Gross Profit	502.1	536.4	579.4	716.5	868.0	920.0
Salary Expense	169.3	109.5	118.3	125.4	132.9	140.9
Selling Expense	57.8	55.9	60.4	64.0	67.8	71.9
Administrative Expenses	93.5	148.2	125.2	251.0	365.7	377.8
Total SG & A Expense	320.6	313.6	303.8	440.4	566.4	590.6
Other Operating Income	1.2	0.9	0.9	0.9	0.9	0.9
Depreciation Expense	55.1	57.5	61.0	64.0	66.1	68.1
Operating Profit	127.6	166.3	215.4	213.1	236.3	262.3
Depr. Exp. excl. Int. Cap.	55.1	57.5	60.8	63.6	65.5	67.3
Depr. Exp. on Cum. Int. Cap.	N/A	N/A	0.2	0.4	0.6	0.8
Funds from Opers. before Tax	182.7	223.7	276.4	277.0	302.4	330.4
Cash Income Taxes	19.5	65.8	85.3	84.3	93.5	103.8
Funds from Opers. after Tax	$163.2	$157.9	$191.2	$192.7	$208.9	$226.6
Increm. Working Cap. Invest.	19.4	22.6	13.6	15.6	13.7	14.4
Fixed Capital Investment	98.1	100.7	98.9	94.4	98.2	102.0
Additions to Goodwill	(6.4)	0.0	0.0	0.0	0.0	0.0
Additions to Intangibles	(1.2)	0.0	0.0	0.0	0.0	0.0
Proceeds (af. tax) Asset Sale	15.4	20.9	18.3	20.0	20.2	14.0
Cash Flow from Operations	$68.7	$55.5	$97.0	$102.7	$117.1	$124.2
Cash Flow from Operations	$68.7	$55.5	$97.0	$102.7	$117.1	$124.2
Interest Expense: Sched. Debt	N/A	16.0	16.0	16.0	16.0	16.0
Total Interest Expense	17.6	16.0	16.0	16.0	16.0	16.0
Interest Expense after Tax	10.6	9.8	9.8	9.8	9.8	9.8
Non-Operating Inc. after tax	33.5	48.9	63.6	78.0	92.4	109.2
Non-Operating Sources	(8.4)	0.8	0.0	0.0	0.0	0.0
Non-Operating Uses	19.7	0.0	0.0	0.0	0.0	0.0
Proceeds from Sale of Common	7.9	0.0	0.0	0.0	0.0	0.0
Preferred Dividends	4.3	4.5	4.7	5.1	5.1	5.1
Net Cash Provided	$67.1	$91.0	$146.1	$165.8	$194.7	$218.5
Common Dividends	13.4	14.1	57.2	61.5	70.4	80.6
Funding Surplus/(Deficit)	$53.7	$76.9	$89.0	$104.4	$124.3	$138.0
Funding Surplus/(Deficit)	$53.7	$76.9	$89.0	$104.4	$124.3	$138.0
Incr. in Curr. Port. L-T Debt	(0.6)	13.1	0.3	0.7	0.7	0.7
Incr. in Debt: Scheduled	12.2	4.1	10.0	10.0	10.0	10.0

E X H I B I T 3-1 (Continued)

Cash Analysis Statement for Sample Company: Most Likely Scenario

($ in Millions)	2000	2001	2002	2003	2004	2005
Net Income	$130.4	$131.9	$173.2	$186.3	$213.3	$244.1
Plus: Depr. Exp. excl. Int. Cap.	55.1	57.5	60.8	63.6	65.5	67.3
Depr. Exp. on Cum. Int. Cap.	N/A	N/A	0.2	0.4	0.6	0.8
Extraordinary Items	(2.8)	0.0	0.0	0.0	0.0	0.0
Interest Expense	14.6	13.0	13.0	13.0	13.0	13.0
Provision for Income Taxes	23.4	70.2	92.9	91.8	102.5	114.4
Less: Non-Operating Profit	36.3	48.9	63.6	78.0	92.4	109.2
Gain on Sale of Assets	7.3	0.0	0.0	0.0	0.0	0.0
Cash Income Taxes	19.5	64.8	85.3	84.3	93.5	103.8
Funds from Opers. after Tax	$163.2	$157.9	$191.2	$192.7	$208.9	$226.6
Plus: Incr. in Accounts Payable	46.8	28.4	25.0	20.3	21.5	22.8
Incr. in Income Tax Payable	0.2	(1.1)	5.3	(0.3)	2.5	2.8
Less: Incr. in Cash	13.5	6.5	5.7	4.6	4.9	5.2
Incr. in Accts Receivable	39.7	22.8	20.0	16.2	17.2	18.2
Incr. in Raw Materials	2.7	2.6	2.3	1.9	2.0	2.1
Incr. in Work in Progress	6.6	11.0	9.7	7.8	8.3	8.8
Incr. in Finished Goods	3.9	7.1	6.2	5.0	5.3	5.7
Total Incr. in Inventories	13.2	20.7	18.2	14.7	15.6	16.6
Cash from Operating Cycle	$143.8	$135.4	$177.5	$177.1	$195.2	$212.1
Less: Fixed Capital Investment	98.1	100.7	98.9	94.4	98.2	102.0
Additions to Goodwill	(6.4)	0.0	0.0	0.0	0.0	0.0
Additions to Intangibles	(1.2)	0.0	0.0	0.0	0.0	0.0
Plus: Proceeds (af. tax) Asset Sale	15.4	20.9	18.3	20.0	20.2	14.0
Cash Flow from Operations	$68.7	$55.5	$97.0	$102.7	$117.1	$124.2
Less: Non-Operating Uses	19.7	0.0	0.0	0.0	0.0	0.0
Plus: Non-Operating Sources	(8.4)	0.8	0.0	0.0	0.0	0.0
Non-Operating Inc. (af. tax)	33.5	48.9	63.6	78.0	92.4	109.2
Cash bef. Fin. Cost & Ext. Fin.	$74.1	$105.2	$160.6	$180.7	$209.5	$233.4
Less: Interest Expense (After Tax)	10.6	9.8	9.8	9.8	9.8	9.8
Preferred Dividends	4.3	4.5	4.7	5.1	5.1	5.1
Common Dividends	13.4	14.1	57.2	61.5	70.4	80.6
Cash bef. External Financing	$45.8	$76.9	$89.0	$104.4	$124.3	$138.0
Plus: incr. in Curr. Port. L-T Debt	(0.6)	13.1	0.3	0.7	0.7	0.7
Incr. in Debt: Scheduled	12.2	4.1	10.0	10.0	10.0	10.0
Proceeds from Sale of Pf. Stk.	1.5	2.0	2.0	2.0	2.0	2.0
Proceeds from Sale of Common	7.9	0.0	0.0	0.0	0.0	0.0
Incr. in Mkt. Securities	$66.8	$96.0	$101.3	$117.1	$137.0	$150.7
Proceeds from Sale of Pf. Stk.	1.5	2.0	2.0	2.0	2.0	2.0
Incr. in Mkt. Securities	$66.8	$96.0	$101.3	$117.1	$137.0	$150.7

Financial Ratios for Sample Company: Most Likely Scenario

	1999	2000	2001	2002	2003	2004	2005
Profit Performance Ratios							
Gross Profit Margin (%)	25.810	24.710	24.000	24.000	28.000	32.000	32.000
Change in Net Income (%)	N/A	16.221	1.153	31.317	7.538	14.497	14.467
Return on Sales (%)	5.800	6.417	5.901	7.175	7.279	7.863	8.491
Return on Equity (%)	17.818	17.449	15.327	17.821	17.063	17.347	17.589
Return on Assets or Inv. (%)	9.022	9.407	8.334	9.796	9.638	10.030	10.417
Return on Net Assets (%)	11.047	11.643	10.372	12.173	11.892	12.299	12.690
Leverage Ratios							
Debt/Equity Ratio (%)	59.393	51.800	47.206	43.064	39.509	36.117	32.911
Debt/Total Capital (%)	37.262	34.124	32.068	30.101	28.320	26.534	24.762
Equity Ratio (%)	46.700	48.888	50.626	52.040	53.674	55.292	56.948
Times Interest Earned	12.448	9.727	13.447	17.442	18.190	20.546	23.221
Activity Ratios							
Days in Receivables	N/A	67.854	66.785	65.072	63.974	62.602	61. 307
Days in Payables	N/A	40.391	44.460	46.487	50.781	54.858	55.886
Inventory Turnover	N/A	4.116	4.371	4.496	4.339	4.194	4.289
Fixed Asset Turnover	N/A	3.847	4.038	4.190	4.340	4.487	4.583
Total Asset Turnover	N/A	1.329	1.315	1.292	1.258	1.220	1.180
Liquidity Ratios							
Quick Ratio	1.482	1.656	1.831	2.025	2.274	2.525	2.772
Current Ratio	3.136	3.094	3.156	3.289	3.508	3.723	3.935
Per-Share Data							
Earnings Per Share	8.07	9.41	9.51	12.58	13.52	15.54	17.84
Change in EPS(%)	N/A	16.65	1.03	32.27	7.51	14.91	14.82
Primary EPS	8.07	9.41	9.51	12.58	13.52	15.54	17.84
Fully Diluted EPS	8.07	9.41	9.51	12.58	13.52	15.54	17.84
Dividends Per Share	0.93	1.00	1.05	4.27	4.59	5.25	6.01
Cash Flow Per Share	N/A	5.13	4.14	7.24	7.66	8.74	9.27
Book Value Per Share	47.70	56.61	65.20	73.63	82.70	93.14	105.14

E X H I B I T   3-1 (Continued)

Financial Ratios for Sample Company: Most Likely Scenario (Continued)

	1999	2000	2001	2002	2003	2004	2005
Valuation Ratios							
Change in Share. Val./Share	N/A	N/A	7.93	10.12	(0.86)	3.66	3.33
Share. Value Per Share (PV)	N/A	N/A	40.11	50.23	49.37	53.03	56.36
Oper. Profit Margin (%)	7.899	6.280	7.439	8.924	8.326	8.712	9.123
Threshold Margin (%)	N/A	7.664	6.325	7.278	8.695	8.118	8.472
Threshold Spread (%)	N/A	(1.384)	1.115	1.646	(0.369)	0.594	0.650
Incremental Profit Margin (%)	N/A	(25.846)	19.035	27.486	(1.638)	15.139	15.971
Increm. Threshold Margin (%)	N/A	2.999	6.774	5.270	4.881	4.639	4.482
Increm. Threshold Spread (%)	N/A	(28.846)	12.261	22.216	(6.519)	10.500	11.490
Value Drivers							
Sales Growth Rate (%)	N/A	5.04	10.00	8.00	6.00	6.00	6.00
Oper. Profit Margin (%)	7.90	6.28	7.44	8.92	8.33	8.71	9.12
Inc. Fixed Cap. Inv. (%)	N/A	44.10	21.30	21.30	21.30	21.30	21.30
Inc. Work. Cap. Inv. (%)	N/A	19.90	11.10	7.62	10.76	8.95	8.86
Cash Inc. Tax Rate (%)	N/A	15.29	39.58	39.58	39.58	39.58	39.58
Discount Rates							
Average Cost of Capital (%)	15.30						
Long-Term Cost of Capital	15.30						
Internal Rate of Return (%)	32.05						

Memo: Average cost of capital and internal rate of return (IRR) based on forecast data. IRR uses pre-strategy residual value as investment ($433.673 million).

Reconciliation for Sample Company—2002
Most Likely Scenario ($ in Millions)

	Earnings	Adjustments	Cash Flows
Sales	$2,414.0		
Less: Incr. in Accts Receivable		20.0	
Cash Receipts			$2,394.0
Cost of Goods Sold	1,834.7		
Less: Incr. in Accounts Payable		25.0	
Plus: Total Incr. in Inventories		18.2	
Cash COGS	_____		1,827.8
Gross Profit	$579.4		
Total SG&A Expense	303.8		
Plus: Incr. in Cash		5.7	
Less: Incr. in Income Tax Payable		5.3	
Cash SG &A Expense		_____	304.3
Increm. Working Cap. Invest.		$13.6	
Other Operating Income	0.9		0.9
Depreciation Expense	61.0		
Plus: Depreciation Expense: Funds		61.0	
Depreciation in Other Items			0.0
Fixed Capital Investment	_____	98.9	98.9
Operating Profit	$215.4		
Interest Income	20.5		
Interest Expense	13.0		
Other Non-Operating Income	43.1		
Earnings Before Taxes	$266.1		
Provision for Income Taxes	92.9		
Less: Incr. in Deferred Inc. Taxes		13.8	
Cash Income Taxes			85.3
Proceeds (af. tax) Asset Sale			18.3
Cash Flow from Operations			97.0
Net Income	$173.2		

E X H I B I T   3-1 (Concluded)

Cash Flows and Shareholder Value for Sample Company
Most Likely Scenario
(Average Cost of Capital (%)=15.3%)
($ in Millions)

Year	Cash Flow	Pres. Value Cash Flow	Cum. PV Cash Flow	Pres. Value Residual Value	Cum PV CF+ PV Residual Value	Increase in Value
2001	$55.5	$48.2	$48.2	$490.1	$538.3	$104.6
2002	97.0	72.9	121.1	550.8	671.8	133.5
2003	102.7	67.0	188.1	472.4	660.5	(11.3)
2004	117.1	66.3	254.4	454.4	708.8	48.3
2005	124.2	60.9	315.3	437.5	752.8	44.0
						319.1

Marketable Securities	70.9
Corporate Value	$823.7
Less: Mkt. Val. of Debt	63.0
Less: Unfunded Pension Liabs.	16.7
Shareholder Value (PV)	$744.0
Share. Value per Share (PV)	$56.36
Current Stock Price	$49.50
Prem./Disc. Over/Under Mkt. (%)	13.86

Profit Margins for Sample Company
Most Likely Scenario

Year	Operating Profit Margin	Threshold Margin	Threshold Spread	Incremental Profit Margin	Incremental Threshold Margin	Incremental Threshold Spread
2001	7.439%	6.325%	1.115%	19.035%	6.774%	12.261%
2002	8.924%	7.278%	1.646%	27.486%	5.270%	22.216%
2003	8.326%	8.695%	(0.369)	(1.638)	4.881%	(6.519)
2004	8.712%	8.118%	0.594%	15.139%	4.639%	10.500%
2005	9.123%	8.472%	0.650%	15.971%	4.482%	11.490%

Valuation Summary for Sample Company
Most Likely Scenario
Five-Year Forecast ($ in Millions)

Cumulative PV Cash Flows	$315.3
Present Value of Res. Value	437.5
Marketable Securities	70.9
Corporate Value	$823.7
Less: Mkt. Val. of Debt	63.0
Less: Unfunded Pension Liabs.	16.7
Shareholder Value (PV)	$744.0
Less: Pre-Strat. Share. Value	424.9
Value Contrib. by Strategy	$319.1
Share. Value per Share (PV)	$56.36
Current Stock Price	$49.50
Prem./Disc. Over/Under Mkt. (%)	13.86
Value ROI (%)	180.62
Value ROSE (%)	55.79

Relative Impact of Key Variables on Shareholder Value for Sample Company
Most Likely Scenario
($ in Millions)

A 1% Increase In:	Increases Shareholder Value by:	% Increase
Sales Growth Rate	$0.4	0.054
Operating Profit Margin	8.7	1.163
Increm. Fixed Capital Investment	(1.2)	(0.164)
Increm. Working Capital Investment	(0.5)	(0.074)
Cash Income Tax Rate	(2.8)	(0.377)
Residual Value Income Tax Rate	(4.0)	(0.543)
Cost of Capital	(4.2)	(0.560)

E N D N O T E S

1. As for takeover rumors, John R. Dorfman, in his column "Heard on the Street," says that takeover rumors can add as much as 30 percent to a stock price. In Viacom's famous late-1993 run at Paramount Industries, which after six long months resulted in a March 1994 merger, Viacom chairman Sumner M. Redstone (and Redstone-controlled WMS Industries) bought significant numbers of Viacom shares before, during, and after the contest started, and continued purchases even as he was negotiating supporting investments in Viacom from Nynex and Blockbuster Entertainment. Certainly those actions bolstered the price of Viacom shares.

2. George B. Baldwin, "Discounted Cash Flow," *Finance & Development,* September 1969.

3. The eloquence of Mark N. Schwarz, of Wertheim, Schroder & Co., in an investment banker roundtable called "On the Threshold of an Upbeat in M&A Dealmaking," *Mergers & Acquisitions,* September/October 1993, p. 20.

4. "Mendoza Led Morgan to Buy Banesto Stake," *The Wall Street Journal,* January 6, 1994.

5. "Japanese Purchases of U.S. Real Estate Fall on Hard Times: Office Buildings and Resorts Weigh Heavily on Owners, Who Sometimes Overpaid," *The Wall Street Journal,* February 21, 1992.

6. "A Sushi Special for Bottom-Fishers," *Business Week,* December 27, 1993.

7. James McNeill Stancill, "When Is There Cash in Cash Flow?" *Harvard Business Review,* March–April 1987.

8. "Sellers Find That It Pays to Stick Around after a Deal: Buyers of Businesses Reward Former Owners Who Help Reduce the Risks," *The Wall Street Journal,* November 9, 1993.

9. "Grasping the Slippery Idea of Risk," *The New York Times,* December 12, 1993.

10. "Corporate Controller Survey Reveals Progress on Ethics Codes, Performance Measurement," *Director's Monthly,* May 1994, p. 8.

11. "A Bean-Counter's Best Friend," *Business Week,* Special Issue, "Managing for Quality," 1991.

12. "When Tax Audits Might Mean Windfalls to Companies," *The New York Times,* April 16, 1991.

13. *Source:* Ronald Chung, Treasury Management Association, Bethesda, MD, interviewed February 11, 1998.

14. *Source:* William F. Mahoney, editor, *Valuation Issues,* West Chester, PA, interviewed February 15, 1998. John Lewis can be reached at jjlewis@valtechs.com.

15. "Aetna Mulls Another Revamping amid Sluggish Profits: Big Insurer May Unload Businesses and Lay off More Workers," *The Wall Street Journal,* January 14, 1994.

16. Note, such opinions, typically issued without an accompanying audit, were given from time to time in the past to provide reassurance to lenders. After adverse outcomes on some such opinions, in early 1988 the American Institute of Certified Public Accountants (AICPA) prohibited all accounting firms from rendering solvency letters.

CHAPTER 4

Financing and Refinancing

INTRODUCTION

Of all aspects of the merger/acquisition/buyout process, perhaps none is as critical as financing. There is no such thing as a free merger: It takes money to buy a company, and the money must come from somewhere. At the simplest level, all transactions are paid for in the form of cash, stock, and/or notes, but these three basic modes of payment exist within a complex universe of funding sources and issues.

If the deal is funded by *stock,* will the stock come from existing shares, an initial public offering, or a private placement? Will a venture capital firm be involved in the deal, and if so, will it want control over the company's operations going forward? If the deal is funded from *cash,* will the cash be generated internally from profits, or will it be borrowed? If it is borrowed, will it come from a traditional commercial bank or from a less traditional source, such as a commercial finance company, a leasing company, or a life insurance company? How many lenders will be involved and under what terms? Will the terms of any loan agreements or notes unduly restrict plans the acquirer has to pay back the lender or seller?

Although the full range of these questions lies beyond the horizons of this chapter, we hope to give a glimpse of them as we discuss a common source of deal funding: *borrowed cash.* (For more on equity financing, see Chapter 12.) This chapter, as in previous editions of this book, will focus on highly leveraged transactions (HLTs), with an emphasis on leveraged buyouts (LBOs)—that is, taking publicly held companies or units private using borrowed cash.[1] Some of the principles described here are also applicable to the less-leveraged acquisitions, but we will not take pains to point out such broad applications.

Herein lies the dynamic terrain of financial dealmaking—where what matters most is not so much where the money will come from as how it will be structured. In this highly creative field, much depends on written agreements between buyers, seller, and various third parties (including, but not limited to, commercial bankers), all of whom are betting on the future. Creativity, negotiating skills, and a keen eye for detail can make the difference between success and failure here.

This arena is a bit like the fable in which a clever traveler gets himself invited into his host's kitchen by promising to feed him "stone soup." The most important ingredient, of course, is the stone, which the traveler provides. But the traveler needs a pinch of this and a bit of that. The result is superb—and the host never even realizes that little by little he has provided all the soup's edible ingredients. In such a way, the leveraged financier brings little to the table aside from expertise. If he or she is good at the trade, however, all the needed ingredients will come forth.

Leveraged deals fall in and out of fashion,[2] but in any environment, company executives and their advisors need to ask "How much debt financing is enough? How little is too little?" The main objective of the leverage maestro is, was, and ever shall be to finance as large a part of the cost of an acquisition as possible by borrowing against the assets and the future cash flows of the acquired company. Through aggressive structuring of financing, leveraged buyers have been able in some cases to reduce their equity investment to as little as 5 percent or less of the acquisition price. This chapter will provide a variety of strategies that dealmakers can use to achieve such results.

HIGHLY LEVERAGED TRANSACTIONS

How can a buyer finance the acquisition with the acquired company's assets and revenues?

As this question implies, LBOs seem to defy conventional buy-sell wisdom. How, one may ask, can the buyer borrow against the assets of the acquired company when it is a different entity and needs the money as a precondition to the acquisition? If a person wants to buy stock in IBM, IBM won't finance it; why is a leveraged buyout different?

The typical leveraged acquisition is not simply a stock purchase, although it often starts as one. A key structuring objective is to cause the assets and revenues of the acquired company to be located in the buyer-borrower. This can be achieved in three different ways:

- The buyer can acquire the assets and business of the company.
- The buyer can acquire the stock of the company and immediately thereafter merge with it (the question of which entity survives the merger is important for tax, and occasionally other reasons; it is dealt with in Chapter 5).
- Skipping the stock acquisition stage, the buyer and the company can simply merge directly.

If the buyer and company merge, a problem of timing arises at the closing: Payment for the stock purchased by the buyer must be made *before* the merger places the assets of the acquired company in the buyer's hands, but the loan to the buyer cannot be funded until *after* the merger is consummated. To resolve this problem, the parties to the closing agree that all transactions will be treated as occurring *simultaneously* or, for the sticklers, that the seller of the stock will get a promissory note, which is repaid minutes later when the merger documents are filed. Sometimes lenders prefer to have both the seller and the buyer named as the borrowers on the acquisition loan. Tax or contract compliance questions may be raised by these timing issues (see Chapter 5), and they should be thought through carefully.

Why would a buyer want to do a highly leveraged buyout? Doesn't this leave the acquired business in a very exposed position?

Certainly it does—this was the great lesson of the 1980s, the era of overleverage. According to *Fortune* writer Gregory Smith, roughly half of the magazine's "Deals of the Year" from 1985 to 1990 were experiencing financial troubles by 1991—with some in bankruptcy. Prudently undertaken, however, a high level of debt need not harm postmerger performance. Indeed, there is some evidence that debt-driven mergers do as well as or better than stock-driven mergers.[3] Furthermore, as a mode of payment, debt is an equalizer. Few have the cash or stock already in hand to buy a company, but many can borrow; debt financing enables a buyer with limited resources—in particular, a management group—to own a company. It also gives an investor a chance to reap an enormous return on equity. The Gibson Greeting Cards LBO, which returned several *thousand* percent to its equity suppliers, is a classic example. Other LBO successes include the many successful small and midsized investments by Forstmann Little.[4]

But for every example of easy success there is one of precarious struggle. Some investors have experienced both. Investor Donald P. Kelly, who joined with KKR to buy Beatrice Cos. in 1986 with other shareholders, made $3 billion in profits by breaking it up and selling off many of its parts. But another Kelly LBO investment, the 1989 purchase of Envirodyne Industries Inc., has not gone as well. The company, which went public again in 1994, and today (since September 1998) is called Viskase Companies, Inc., has had some difficult times. Kohlberg Kravis & Roberts (KKR) had solid success with Duracell Inc., Owens-Illinois Inc., and Safeway Stores Inc., but trouble with its blockbuster $25 billion RJR Nabisco deal.

What is the verdict, then, on heavy leverage? Good or bad?

The jury is still out, and the evidence is mixed. The conventional business wisdom that looked with alarm at the prospect of imposing large amounts of debt upon a company was challenged in the mid-to-late 1980s, when underpriced companies could be bought with borrowed money that was to be paid off by selling assets and pumping up cash flows. But by the decade's end, the old anti-leverage school seemed to be vindicated when the inevitable failures came.

Pro-leverage forces point to the successes and say that having a large amount of debt on the balance sheet provides "survival" incentive for managers to perform efficiently. Management, say these LBO boosters, will focus on making the core business profitable, minimizing the use of capital and maximizing cash flow, rather than on building personal empires. As the first edition of this book pointed out, with the burden of debt came an advantage: a real outside check on the leveraged buyer's economic analysis.

The anti-leverage philosophers would disagree. Heavy debt servicing competes against operating excellence as dollars once marked for needed research and development or plant and equipment go to interest payments, often with dire consequences for the acquired company and eventually its community. This was the dominant view of the nearly 50 witnesses testifying in Senate and House hearings on leveraged buyouts and mergers held in January and February 1989, and it has been echoed in the decade since.

Both sides agree, however, on one point: If the buyer plans to impose heavy financial leverage on a company, the buyer must be sure that the company can bear the interest and paydown burdens and must minimize operating risks. LBOs are *not* recommended for those who feel uncomfortable with substantial amounts of financial exposure for their companies. (We are not even contemplating here the personal exposure of individual buyers through guarantees, which presents an even higher level of risk.)

But isn't it true that the higher the leverage in a buyout, the greater the risk that the new owner may become insolvent?

True enough, but remember: Leverage is not static—it drops as the owners repay their loans.

What kinds of businesses lend themselves to financial leverage?

Look for businesses that generate cash flow on a steady basis. High growth potential is not necessarily a prerequisite; more probably, suitable candidates will show only moderate growth and will be easier to buy. Leveraged buyout candidates should be on the opposite end of the spectrum from venture capital operations, which tend to be predominantly equity-financed. Producers of basic products or services in stable markets are the best LBO candidates. Start-ups and highly cyclical companies should be avoided. So should companies whose success is highly dependent on forces beyond the control of management. Oil and gas deals that depend on fuel prices are thus not suitable for highly leveraged deals, in contrast to oil pipeline or trucking companies, which receive a steady, stable payment for transportation charges and do not speculate on oil prices.

Trucking companies, by the way, are good candidates for leveraged *buildups* or *rollups,* an industry-focused strategy based on buying a series of small companies in the same industry. Other industries good for leveraged buildups include companies and partnerships involved in cable TV, collections, document management, financial services, health care (physicians groups, home health care), publishing, radio, resort properties, storage, telemarketing, and temporary help firms.[5]

In any industry, stable management offers an important element of reassurance. A team that works well together and has been through several business cycles can be better relied upon to provide the stable, conservative projections necessary to evaluate whether the debt can be paid off.

MINIMIZING BORROWING

How can a buyer minimize borrowing?

A buyer's first thought in financial planning should be a very simple one: The less I have to lay out at closing, the less I have to borrow.

The financing needs to be met at the closing can be calculated as follows:

- The purchase price of the stock or assets of the acquired company
- Plus any existing debt that must be refinanced at closing
- Plus any working capital needs of the acquired company (These amounts need not actually be borrowed, but the credit line must be large enough to cover them.)
- Plus administrative costs to effect the acquisition
- Plus post-acquisition payments that may be necessary because of settlement of litigation
- Less cash or cash equivalents of the acquired company
- Less any proceeds from partial divestitures of the acquired business

(Seller takeback financing also reduces the closing payment but is analyzed here as part of the borrowing program because of the many interconnections between it and other financing layers.)

The next step in our analysis is thus to explore how to minimize each of the cost elements and minimize the closing payment.

How can the buyer minimize the purchase price?

A buyer need not necessarily offer the highest price in order to gain the contract. It should also offer the seller noncash incentives for the deal, such as the following:

- "We can close faster."
- "We have a good track record in obtaining financing and closing similar transactions."

- "We can offer a substantial deposit on signing the acquisition agreement."
- "We can work well with you and your management."

Close relations with and incentives for management are likely to be an important part of the financial plan; management may be receiving shares in the company, favorable employment contracts, profit-sharing plans, and the like. If the seller is interested in ensuring that the departing management is well treated, these arrangements may favorably dispose a seller toward a particular buyer.

One of the most delicate questions of buying (or buying out) a company is whether to obtain a lower price by assuming substantially greater risks or to accept significant defects in the candidate. Such risks or defects can loom very large in the eyes of the acquisition lenders, and the timing of negotiations does not always permit them to be checked out with a lender before signing the contract. Here is a cardinal rule: Negotiate and sign *fast* when the price is right. Some of the most spectacularly successful deals have been achieved when a buyer has been able to discern that management and a lender could live with something the seller thought was a major problem primarily because it had stymied other deals.

Another way to lower the purchase price is to buy only some of the assets or divisions of a company.

When planning post-deal sell-offs, how easy is it for an acquirer to pick and choose among acquired assets?

It is desirable—but often difficult—for a buyer to be selective about what it acquires. The seller may be packaging some "dogs" together with some strong operations; therefore, the buyer should consider "gaming" the offer out from the seller's point of view and making a counterproposal. Crucial for such selection is knowing the seller's business better than it does—not impossible if the seller is a large conglomerate shedding only a fraction of itself, and management is the buyer or is already on the buyer's side. The offer of sale may include several businesses, some of which are easier to finance than others, or assets used in part by each of several business operations. The buyer may have a choice, for example, between buying a building or a computer system or merely renting it.

Sometimes a deal can be changed to the buyer's advantage after the main price and other negotiations have been completed. The seller may then be re-

ceptive to either including or excluding what appear to be minor ancillary facilities as a last step to signing. To encourage the seller, the buyer may guarantee the resale price of unwanted assets or share any losses realized on their
disposal. Taking or not taking these "minor" assets may become the key to
cash flow in the critical first three years after the buyout.

Can a buyer always finance all or part of a transaction through partial divestments or spin-offs?

Not necessarily. This is possible only when the business acquired consists of
separate components or has excess real estate or other assets. The buyer must
balance financial and operational considerations; there should always be a
good business reason for the divestment. Consider selling off those portions of
the business that are separable from the part you are most interested in. As indicated earlier, not all businesses generate the cash flow or have the stability necessary for highly leveraged transactions, yet many cash-rich buyers are available for such businesses. A solid domestic smokestack business with valuable
assets, itself highly suitable for leveraged financing, may have a subsidiary
with foreign manufacturing and distribution operations, a separate retail division, and a large timberland holding—all candidates for divestiture. The foreign operations are accessible to a whole new set of possible buyers; the retail
division would function better as part of another company's nationwide chain;
and the timberland does not generate cash flow.

Many buyout transactions are undertaken in order to divest assets at a
profit. These transactions are better called restructurings or breakups. For example, the acquisition of Beatrice Foods by KKR resulted in the disbanding of
its senior management and the sale of most of its assets. This is an entirely different kind of transaction from a management buyout (MBO), where the core
business is highly leveraged, but preserved, and management takes an ownership interest and stays on as a team.[6]

There is a question of timing here; it is never too early to start beating the
bushes for a purchaser of the Buggy Whip Division—as long as you have a
signed contract for the purchase of General Buggies Company as a whole. Ensuring that the sale closes in a timely fashion can be crucial. It is not uncommon
to have an escrow closing of the divestiture in advance of the closing to minimize the risk of last-minute holdups. Even if the deal does not close simultaneously with the main acquisition, the presence of the divestiture agreement of
such "pre-sold assets" may make it possible to take out a bridge loan at closing.

Don't forget: Identify and take into account the cash and cash equivalents held by the acquired company. You need not borrow the dollar you spend to buy cash.

What cash can a buyer find in the company?

Cash can be found on the balance sheet, as well as in more unusual places. Does the acquired company have a lawsuit pending against a third party that can be settled quickly and profitably? Does it have excess funded reserves? Is its employee benefit plan overfunded, and if so, can it be terminated or restructured? Can its pension plan acquire any of the company assets? Typically, pension plans can invest a portion of their assets in real estate of a diversified nature, including real estate acquired from the company. Has the company been acquiring marketable stock or debt of unrelated companies? Does it have a valuable art collection that can be cashed in at the next Sotheby's auction?

Keep track of changes in the company's cash position between signing the acquisition agreement and closing. The terms of the acquisition agreement can ensure either that the buyer retains cash at the closing or that all cash goes to the seller. (See Chapters 3 and 9.)

PROS AND CONS OF PRESERVING DEBT AND LEASE OBLIGATIONS

What are the pros and cons of keeping existing debt in place?

Review carefully the existing debt of the target and determine whether prepayment may be necessary or advisable. In some cases, the acquisition may entitle the lender to prepayment, perhaps at a premium. In other cases, even where prepayment is not required, it might be a good idea to repay existing debt because of high interest rates or burdensome covenants in leases, loan agreements, or indentures.

Restrictive covenants in leases or loan agreements may prohibit a sale of assets without the lessor's or lender's consent, a condition that could hamper postmerger restructuring or spin-offs. Restrictions on the sale of assets provide important protection to a lessor or lender that otherwise cannot prevent major changes in the structure or operations of its lessee or debtor, and courts have interpreted them liberally in favor of lessors and lenders. Although many covenants use the language "all or substantially all" in describing this restriction, even modest asset sales may be challenged. Any sale of more than 25 percent of the assets raises questions, particularly if the assets being sold constitute the major revenue-producing operations of the historical core business.

Indentures for unsecured borrowings also typically contain covenants prohibiting the imposition of liens on assets of the lessor or debtor and may prohibit more than one class of debt. Such financing must be done on an unsecured basis and without recourse to some of the techniques for layering of debt discussed later in this chapter.

Debt of this kind is deceptively simple. It may first appear that the lack of elaborate and specific covenants, such as those contained in the typical secured loan, offers many opportunities to substantially restructure the company without lenders' consents. It is likely to turn out, however, as the buyer analyzes the loan agreements, that the broad prohibitions on sale or encumbrance of assets and on the making of dividend payments or similar payments defeat most financing plans. Just as the technically tight, detailed loan agreement encourages and legitimizes the use of loopholes based on technicalities, so the broadly written loan agreement makes lawyers and other technicians less willing to rely on highly refined justifications for arrangements that may violate the spirit of the existing debt agreement.

In addition to restrictions on sales of assets or liens on assets, the selling company may also be subject to preexisting covenants prohibiting a change of control of the lessee or debtor. In such cases, preservation of existing debt may require changing the structure of the acquisition. A common legal issue that arises in such cases is whether the merger of the lessee or debtor into another corporation constitutes a transfer of ownership requiring the lessor's or lender's consent. In most cases it is possible to conclude that the merger is not a transfer to another entity, because the original lessee or debtor continues as part of the surviving entity, although the conclusion varies according to state law.

How common is it for an acquired company to have many leases, and how important are they?

In recent decades, leasing has increased as a source of financing, as companies (particularly smaller ones) lease their equipment, vehicles, and other valuable property, in order to leverage their cash and equity. As mentioned earlier, in a recent survey of small businesses, 16 percent said they had used leasing as a source of capital.[7] Conversely, these lessors have found a ready market: A full 80 percent of companies lease the equipment they use.[8] Although such lease obligations are not material to the overall balance sheet position of large companies, they can greatly affect the value of small and midsized firms.

Suppose an acquirer wants to buy a company that has many valuable leases, but the leases contain a lot of fine print about cancellation in the event of a change of control. How serious is such fine print?

The seriousness of the fine print, as with everything in M&A life, depends first and foremost on the size and nature of the entities involved and the past relationship between them. Beyond this general rule, the situation will vary according to whether the company being acquired is a heavy *lessee,* a *lessor,* or both.

What advice do you have for the acquirer of a heavy lessee (i.e., a company with major lease payables)?

If the company being acquired has signed one or more important lease agreements as a lessee, the first decision to be made will be whether or not the acquirer will be assuming the lessee's obligations. This is usually what happens. Note, though, that the original lessee will almost always need to get approval from the lessor before it can assign its lease obligations or sublease to a new owner.

Therefore, the first order of business for any acquirer will be to contact the lessor and inform it of the pending transaction. The lessee should also contact the lessor. The importance of this contact cannot be overemphasized. Almost every lease includes a requirement that the funding source must be notified if there is a change in ownership. (This is to enable the lessor to look at the credit history and creditworthiness of any new owners before allowing the previous ownership to assign its obligations over to them.) On almost any lease, *nonnotification of change in ownership or location of the equipment is generally considered a technical default of the terms of the lease.* If the new and old owners are in technical default, the funding source may call the remaining payments due.

If the company that is leasing survives, and is as strong as it was before the merger, the funding source will welcome the change in ownership and will not call the payments due.[9] At the end of the day it isn't as much the change in ownership but the change in credit risk that is of concern. Generally (it is hoped) the credit of the acquiring company is better than that of the existing entity, and so the acquirer can decide on its own whether or not to assume the lease, renegotiate it, or pay it off.

But in cases where the lease must be assigned and the credit of the acquiring company is not sufficient, then there is a chance that the original lessee, especially in small privately held companies, will be required to remain as a guarantor of the lease or find some structure to comfort the funding source that it will continue to receive timely and complete payments.

In LBOs the financial ratios of the company generally change dramatically, so the creditworthiness of the new entity may not be sufficient for the original funding source. In this case, the obligations to the funding source may have to be fulfilled through a prepayment of the lease with monies raised in the LBO, or some sort of additional collateral may need to be pledged in order to give the funding source sufficient comfort (from a credit perspective) in what it may see as a new transaction.

Differing funding/lending sources have different tolerances and/or policies for rewrites, buyouts, and refinancing. What is important to understand on any substantive lease is what the options for early termination are and whether the funding source plans to sell or discount its paper and/or maintain the servicing of the lease after the inception.

What advice do you have for the acquirer of a heavy lessor (i.e., a company with major lease receivables)?

Buying a company with major lease receivables raises a different set of issues. Many companies have contracts with customers whereby those customers agree to pay for their equipment in a lease or lease-style acquisition, structured as an installment contract. Some companies that sell as well as rent equipment may bundle their lease papers with purchases, in order to tie their customers to them over time. In these types of companies, an acquirer will find accounts receivable from installment contracts or bundled lease papers. Also, companies that manufacture capital equipment may offer a lease alternative to customers that can't afford to pay up-front cash. In such a company, acquirers will also find significant lease receivables carried on the balance sheet.

In either case prospective acquirers should perform a due diligence on the portfolio of leases. On the upside, there may be options to discount the leases to third parties, generating a possible premium—or at least a vehicle to reevaluate the asset values of the receivables given by the company being acquired. On the downside, leases may not be included in the lessor's delinquency, days sales outstanding, or bad debt accounts, thus giving a higher level of performance of the overall company than they should. For example, some capital equipment leases are really sales that the lessor would not take for credit or documentation reasons—so they may not be a liquid asset.

Companies account for leases in various ways, and how a company "books" its leases may not give a true picture of the company's balance sheet or revenue stream. For instance, say the company being acquired is a subsidiary of a large entity with a low cost of capital, and that this subsidiary historically wrote contracts with its customers as leases at current market rates, but booked the deals by discounting the stream at its (much lower) cost of funds. Since the company books these transactions by discounting the paper, the booked sales amounts or present value amounts may in fact be higher than the actual sales price.

One company that looked great as an acquisition candidate turned out to be a dud after the deal because of such a practice. This company leased internally about 15 percent of its capital sales, and then discounted the stream up front at the corporate cost of funds. This elevated the company's reported revenues by 110 percent! The company's good-looking revenues didn't take into account a differing cost of funds. Revenues dropped after the acquisition since the new entity couldn't borrow at the same rates and/or discount the deals below market.

What is working capital debt? Should an acquirer leave it in place or refinance it?

Working capital debt of a company being acquired is likely to appear in any of at least four forms:

- A secured revolving credit loan from an outside lender
- A parent's intercompany transfers, either with or without interest
- Bank letters of credit or guarantees to secure purchases from suppliers, principally for foreign sourcing
- More or less generous payment terms from suppliers

The first two kinds of debt will almost certainly have to be refinanced at the acquisition closing. A secured revolver, or even an unsecured one, will inevitably tie up assets and stand in the way of any plans for secured acquisition financing, and the parent/seller will not want to retain what are probably short-term, rather informal financial arrangements of an in-house nature. There may, however, be some room for a buyer to argue for at least some short-term financing through a seller takeback of existing intercompany loans.

Refinancing the third type of debt is also common, but risky for all parties. A senior revolving credit acquisition lender often provides letter of credit financing after the acquisition and will probably insist upon doing this financing as part of the deal. Sometimes this can be trouble, because while the new acquisition lender is learning the ropes, there can be awkward slip-ups in a sensitive area. One possible solution is to invite the existing letter of credit lender to join the lending group.

As for the fourth type of debt, it usually should not be a problem to retain existing relationships and favorable terms with suppliers. They will probably be relieved to find that the buyer doesn't plan to close the business or move it elsewhere. In some cases, suppliers may be looking for the continuing presence of a deep-pocket parent company as added security. In other cases, suppliers may focus on the unit. In such cases, it is possible to structure the acquisition to give the new subsidiary a better debt-to-equity ratio than its new parent, so that the subsidiary and can retain favorable trade terms.

What should be done if existing debt includes tax-exempt industrial development bonds?

Tax-exempt industrial development bonds give the borrower the advantage of low interest rates but also carry disadvantages: They encumber assets better used to support new borrowings, and they may carry with them old parent company guarantees that must be lifted as a condition of the acquisition. Often these bonds can be "defeased" under the terms of their trust indentures; that is, high-quality obligations (usually issued or guaranteed by the U.S. government) can be deposited with the trustee bank for the bond issue in an amount high enough to retire the bonds over their term through scheduled payments on the obligations. If the interest rate on the bonds is low enough, the amount of obligations required to defease them may be less than their face amount; and once the bonds are defeased, their covenants and liens cease to have any effect. Note, however, that the defeasance of high-interest-rate bonds is expensive, and the defeasance of variable-rate bonds is impossible because they lack a predictable interest rate for which a sufficient sum certain can be set aside. In addition, tax problems can arise: Are the earnings on the defeasance fund taxable, and does the defeasance give rise to discharge of indebtedness income for the borrower?

Tax-exempt bond issues are likely to be complex, and any transactions involving them may require special attention from the bank serving as bond trustee and the issuer's original bond counsel. Such issues involve a two-step process: The funds are borrowed by a governmental body and are then reloaned to the company to build a facility or are used to construct a facility that is leased to the company, normally but not necessarily on terms that permit a purchase for a nominal price at the end of the lease term. Check with a tax or leasing expert for hidden problems.

Suppose that an acquisition candidate is leasing a facility under terms that guarantee purchase for a nominal price at the end of the lease (say, under a tax-exempt bond deal). How easy is it for an acquirer to assume the lease and get the same purchase rights?

This is very hard to answer as a general rule. Most leases issued under tax-exempt funding involve very large sums of money; and as with all large transactions, each lease tends to have some unique terms and conditions. A few points of advice may be in order here nonetheless.

First, it should be noted that the nominal end-of-term price generally does not matter as much as the original structure and reason for issuing the tax-exempt funds. Changes in ownership more often than not signal changes in the conditions of the lessee—the primary reason tax-exempt funding was available. Remember, just because an entity is tax-exempt does not always mean that it is qualified to receive tax-exempt leasing or funding. For these reasons, under the terms of most agreements, the issuing authority must be notified of any changes in the status of the lessor.

In general, both the lessor and the lessee will hope for continuation of a lease of this type. Although tax exemption was given originally to the lessee, it winds up (through the economics of leasing) being enjoyed by the lessor. Tax-exempt leases enable the lessor to offer a lower cost of funds to the lessee, since the lessor does not have to pay tax on the profit from the interest charges within the lease.

What issues arise in leases extended to tax-exempt organizations?

When a company leases a piece of equipment, it must pay taxes including personal property tax, sales tax, and/or use tax. Many different tax authorities may require that the tax be paid up front, and some require the tax to be paid on the payments over the term of the lease. In tax-exempt situations where an entity is exempt from items such as sales and use taxes, this exemption may also be in effect on its current leases. If a company is acquired by an entity that does not qualify for tax-exempt status, the leasing company can't always be relied upon to recognize this during the transfer of the lease from one entity to another. Furthermore, although leases usually specify that the leasing entity is liable to collect and submit any taxes owed, some leases state that the lessee is also liable. Thus the acquiring entity needs to raise the issue of possible changes in its tax-exempt status and tax-payment obligations to the leasing company.

Such concerns should be incorporated into the assignment of obligations in the acquisition agreement—and possibly in the deal's payment structure as well.

DETERMINING FINANCING STRUCTURE

After the need to borrow is minimized, the next step is to organize and orchestrate the borrowing program. The art of structuring a financing is to allocate the revenues and assets of the acquired company to lenders in a manner that does the following:

- Maximizes the amount loaned by the most senior and highly secured and thus lowest-interest-rate lenders
- Leaves sufficient cash flow to support, if needed, a layer of subordinated, higher-interest-rate "mezzanine" debt, as well as any seller takeback financing
- Provides for adequate working capital and is consistent with seasonal variations and foreseeable one-time bulges or dips in cash flow
- Permits the separate leveraging of distinct assets that can be more advantageously set aside for specialized lenders, such as sale-leasebacks of office buildings or manufacturing facilities

- Accommodates both good news and bad—that is, permits debt prepayment without penalty if revenues are sufficient and permits non-payment and nonenforcement of subordinated debt if revenues are insufficient
- Avoids and, where necessary, resolves conflicts between lenders

Customarily, these results are achieved through layering of debt.

What types of debt are typically used in an LBO?

Although sometimes only one secured lender is needed (or in the case of a very simple business with strong cash flow, only a single unsecured lender), multiple tiers of lenders are normally necessary for large transactions. The multilender LBO may include several or all of the following layers of debt, in rough order of seniority:

- *Senior revolving debt,* secured by a first lien on current assets (inventory and accounts receivable), a first or second lien on fixed assets (property, plant, and equipment, or PPE), liens on intangibles, and perhaps a pledge of stock of the acquired company or its subsidiaries. This debt typically provides a part of the acquisition financing and working capital, including letter of credit financing, and is generally provided by commercial banks or similar institutional lenders. It is often referred to as *commercial paper.*[10]
- *Senior term debt,* secured by a first lien on fixed assets, a first or second lien on current assets, and liens on intangibles and stock of the company and subsidiaries, to provide acquisition financing. Sometimes—but not very frequently—this debt is subordinated to the senior revolving debt. It is normally provided by commercial banks in conjunction with senior revolving debt, or by similar commercial lenders or insurance companies.
- *Senior subordinated debt,* known as mezzanine debt (or in its less secure manifestations, junk bonds), unsecured or secured by junior liens on the assets securing the senior debt used for acquisition financing. It is mainly placed by investment bankers, the principal purchasers being insurance companies, pension and investment funds, and financial institutions.

- *Sale-leasebacks or other special financing arrangements* for specific facilities or equipment. These arrangements may range from installment purchases of the acquired company's office copiers or computers, to sales of the company's real estate to an independent investment partnership, which then "net-leases" such real estate back to the company.
- *Seller's subordinated note,* secured or unsecured, perhaps convertible to stock.
- *Seller's preferred stock,* perhaps exchangeable for a subordinated note, usually appearing as an alternative to the previous item.
- *Preferred or common stock sold to an independent third party,* perhaps to an LBO investment fund or to one of the lenders.
- *Common stock sold to the buyer* or its principals, key managers, and employees.
- *Warrants or options* to acquire common stock granted to any of the parties providing financing or to the seller. These do not provide financing directly but provide inducements to financing participants.

We will discuss senior debt from both banking and insurance companies, junk bonds, LBO investment funds, and seller takeback financing in greater detail later in this chapter. First, however, we should consider how much debt can be obtained at each of these layers.

How are the amounts of the different layers of debt determined?

The initial decision is, of course, the lender's. As discussed in Chapter 3, the lender for each layer of the financing will indicate to the buyer a range or approximation of the amount it is prepared to lend. The lender's decision (or if there are several lenders, each lender's decision) will be based not only on amount, interest rate, and payback period, but also on ability to perform. A basic objective is to maximize senior debt, which bears the lowest interest rate. At the same time, senior debt also requires relatively favorable coverage ratios; therefore, there will be excess cash flow left over after servicing senior debt to support junk bonds or other mezzanine debt. After mezzanine debt is covered, something should still remain to persuade the seller that its takeback financing has a reasonable chance of payment.

The process is not exact. Each lender evaluates the cash flow and assets of the target differently, and uses a different formula for setting the loan amount. The term lender may be willing to lend more if the revolving lender lends less, but the buyer may be reluctant to explore that possibility for fear that the term lender had not previously focused on the exact amount being loaned by the revolving lender, and a second review by the term lender's credit committee could result in a decision not to make the loan at all.

When resources and time permit, the best course of action for a buyer will probably be to obtain bids from several lenders on each layer, and then to select, at the moment when lenders' commitment letters are about to be signed, the optimum combination and present it to each approved lender as a fait accompli, burning no bridges to the unsuccessful lenders until the package has been accepted by all the intended players. In this way, commitments can be entered into with the optimum combination of lenders. The competitive nature of the process will discourage objections by the lender fortunate enough to be selected. In addition, lenders tend to leave to the later stages of the closing a full investigation of the other lenders' terms, by which time they may be less likely to rethink the terms of their loan.

How does a senior lender decide how much to lend in an acquisition?

A number of considerations are key to a bank's lending decision:

- Liquidation value of the collateral
- Credibility of the borrower's financial projections
- Whether the borrower's projections show enough cash flow to service the debt (including junior debt)
- Whether proposed asset liquidations are likely to take place in time and in sufficient amount to amortize the term debt (or reduce the revolver commitment)
- Potential company profitability and industry prospects
- The amount of junior debt (and capacity of the junior creditor to assist the borrower with additional funds in a workout scenario)
- The amount of equity the bank will or might receive
- The amount of the fees the bank will receive

SENIOR DEBT

When should the senior lender in a transaction enter the picture?

Ideally, the senior lender should be brought into the transaction as early as possible, and thus one of the first steps a buyer takes is to prepare its presentation of the deal to lenders. Many lenders are reluctant to review a proposed acquisition unless they already have a formal or informal agreement to go through with the transaction, or at least to cover their costs and, perhaps, a fee. Thus, the presentation is quickly followed by a commitment letter.

The senior lender's loan will usually represent the single largest portion of the cash to be raised for the transaction. If the senior lender is not willing to finance, the deal cannot be done. For that reason, the buyer must be sure to make a correct judgment about the financeability of the transaction before incurring the considerable expense of negotiating an acquisition agreement.

What form does senior debt take?

Typically, senior debt is part term loan and part revolving loan, with the term loan used to finance the purchase price and the revolving loan used to provide working capital (although a portion of the revolving loan is often used to finance the purchase price as well). Usually, senior debt is provided by banks or their affiliates, and thus we often use the term *bank* to refer to a senior lender.

What is demand lending?

It is becoming more and more common for senior debt to be provided by banks in a demanding—or so-called *demand*—format quite different from traditional local bank financing, which relied primarily on the personal guarantees of the business owner, had a fixed term and limited covenants, and kept its nose out of the borrower's business. By contrast, demand lending gives the initial impression to a borrower of being intrusive and one-sided: The bank may have the right to call the loan at any time, make revolving loan advances only at its discretion, require all business receipts to be applied immediately to repayment, and have a bristling array of protective covenants that require bank consent for almost any action not in the ordinary course of business. The appropriate trade-offs for these provisions are absence of personal guarantees and a willingness to lend relatively large amounts.

Because this style of lending is unfamiliar to many borrowers and lenders, the logic of the trade-offs may not be observed: The bank may require a demand loan and guarantees as well, or the borrower may seek a high loan limit but refuse to consider demand repayment. Borrower and bank need to clearly understand their relationship from the start. Success depends on both players recognizing that it will be an intimate one involving cooperation and mutual dependency.

Can lenders be arbitrary?

No. A borrower can take considerable comfort in the principle of "commercial reasonableness" that binds lenders and should thus understand that many of the rights the bank obtains on paper it cannot exercise in practice. A number of cases have held that if a bank makes a loan on terms that give it extensive power over a company's financial affairs, it cannot use that power arbitrarily and may in fact be liable for consequential damages if the company is put out of business or otherwise damaged because of an unreasonable refusal to lend. (See the summary of the *Irving Trust* case cited in the landmark legal case summaries in the back of the book.)

What guidelines do banks use to judge the quality of a loan made in a leveraged transaction?

Banks follow guidelines issued by bank regulators, adding, of course, their own experience. By regulatory definition, with certain exceptions, highly leveraged transactions (HLTs) are loan-financed transactions in which the borrower would end with a debt-to-equity ratio of 75 percent or higher. These HLTs must be identified as such in bank disclosure documents. Regulators also encourage banks and bank regulators to discourage other HLTs, and they have published guidelines for this purpose.[11]

SALE-LEASEBACKS

What are sale-leasebacks, and what are the pros and cons of using them?

A sale-leaseback involves the sale of the seller's real estate or equipment to a third party, which then net-leases the real estate or equipment back to the company. In essence, a company takes out a mortgage on a property in the form of a sale-leaseback. The ownership remains with the original entity, yet the lender is taking a lien on the assets of the surviving company as collateral on the loan. This type of financing is ideal for LBOs, where companies are often looking for ways to replace expensive unsecured debt or equity debt with less expensive secured debt as a means of raising cash or controlling capital debt structure.

A sale-leaseback may be structured as an installment contract, an operating lease, or a finance lease. These distinctions have important tax and accounting ramifications and should always be kept in mind.[12] When a leaseback is structured as a *finance* lease, which is considered a type of *capital* lease under U.S. accounting rules, the acquirer as lessee can make a case as the owner of the asset for tax and accounting purposes. The lending source (lessor) generally retains title and takes a perfected first security interest in the equipment. The lessee raises cash from the sale-leaseback.

Acquirers should note several points:

- Price can be negotiable. If the value of the leaseback is expressed as a percentage of the equipment price, beware. The lessor will most likely want to value the equipment only at its liquidation value, which may be significantly different from any remaining depreciation or book value of the equipment.
- If the title is in the lessee's name, in a true sale-leaseback the title must now pass to the leasing company, so applicable sales taxes must be accounted for.
- A finance lease acts the same as a loan against the asset. Thus the obligation and the yield of the transaction might be greater than the borrower's incremental borrowing rate at its primary bank. The acquiring entity must weigh the benefits of leasing (conservation of capital and credit lines for unsecured lending, etc.) as a way to manage the cost of funds or available capital instead of pledging the same assets in other forms of borrowing.
- In any leaseback scenario, there are tax and accounting implications. These must be reviewed—and structured for maximum benefit.

Some sale-leasebacks offer an option to buy. How does this type of transaction affect an acquirer?

In this type of leaseback, the leasing company is purchasing the equipment at a fixed amount, then leasing back to the entity. In this type of deal, the stream of payments may or may not equal the value of the equipment and interest charged over the term. In this instance there is a residual position in the equipment on behalf of the leasing company (the lease is not a full-payout lease). Thus at the end of the term of the lease, the leasing company is looking for one of two things to happen:

1. For the original entity to make it whole on its residual position
2. For the original entity to return the equipment so the leasing company can remarket the equipment to another user, thus recapturing its residual position

Why would an acquirer want to do a leaseback?

Let's say an acquirer has bought a company that has assets suitable for a sale-leaseback, and has found a leasing company that is willing to take a residual position on the equipment. Let's also assume that the acquirer is able to sell the equipment for 100 percent of its value to the leasing company, and promises a stream of payments, not including the end purchase option, that equals only 90 percent of the transaction. At the end of the lease, the lessee must either exercise its purchase option or return the equipment. If the lessee elects to return the equipment (in effect using the leasing company as a remarketing agent as well as a funding source), it has raised relatively inexpensive capital by only paying the stream rate versus the full yield of the transaction (stream plus residual). Here is the math for a three-year sale-leaseback with a 10 percent purchase option (written as a finance lease):

Asset value at time of sale-leaseback	$100,000.00
Residual position at three years taken by leasing company	$ 10,000.00
All-in yield required by leasing company including residual	12%
Payment terms	
36 payments @	$ 3,089.28
Purchase option	$ 10,000.00
Total payments made if lessee does not exercise purchase option*	$111,214.08
Thus effective interest rate paid by lessee would be	7.9%
Total payments if lessee exercises purchase option	$121,214.08
Thus effective interest rate paid by lessee would be	12.00%

*Leasing company remarkets the equipment looking for at least its residual position plus remarketing expenses.

What paperwork is involved in a sale-leaseback?

To prepare for a sale-leaseback, a detailed appraisal, an as-built survey, and title insurance for the real estate must be ordered, preferably at least six weeks in advance of closing. The other loan documents must be drafted to permit the sale-leaseback. The sale-leaseback may be financed by a mortgage loan. The lease and the mortgage loan documents must clarify that the borrower/tenant continues to own, and the senior lender continues to enjoy a first and prior lien upon, all equipment and fixtures used in the borrower's/tenant's business.

THE BANK BOOK AND COMMITMENT LETTER

How is an LBO transaction presented to prospective lenders?

The normal medium of the LBO transaction is the so-called *bank book,* a brief narrative description of the proposed transaction and the target company. The bank book indicates what financing structure is contemplated and includes projections of earnings sufficient to cover working capital needs and to amortize debt, along with a balance sheet setting forth the pledgeable assets. (Since the balance sheet will typically value assets based on generally accepted accounting practices or GAAP, an appraisal of actual market and/or liquidation value, if available, may be attached or referenced.)

What happens after the bank book is presented to a lender?

If the loan officer believes that the bank may be willing to make a loan that meets the dollar amount and general terms requested by the buyer, he or she will seek to obtain as much information as possible about the company from the buyer. This information will include proxy statements, 10-Ks and 10-Qs if the target is a public company, and audited financials or tax returns if it is not. The loan officer will also send out a team of reviewers to visit the company's facilities and interview its management and will obtain an internal or outside appraisal of the assets. This review can take from half a week to a month or more. Banks are aware that they are in a competitive business and generally move quickly, particularly if the loan is being simultaneously considered by several of them.

The loan officer will then prepare a write-up recommending the proposed loan and will present it to the bank's credit committee. The committee may endorse the recommendation as made, approve it with changes (presumably acceptable to the buyer), or turn it down. If the proposal is approved, the bank will prepare a commitment letter (sometimes with the assistance of its counsel, but often not) setting forth the bank's binding commitment to make the loan. This letter thereafter becomes the bank officer's governing document in future negotiations.

What does the commitment letter contain?

Apart from the bare essentials (the amount of the loan, how much will be term and how much revolver, the maturity of the term loan and amortization provisions, and interest rates), the commitment letter will also set forth the bank's proposals on the following:

- Fees to be paid to the bank
- Voluntary prepayment rights and penalties under the term loan
- What collateral is required, whether any other lender may take a junior lien on any collateral on which the bank has a senior lien, and whether the bank is to receive a junior lien on any other collateral subject to another lender's senior lien
- How the funds are to be used
- The amount of subordinated debt and equity that may be required as a condition to the making of the senior loan
- Payment of the bank's expenses

The commitment may also set forth in some detail lists of covenants, default triggers, reporting requirements, and conditions to closing, including legal opinions to be furnished by counsel to the borrowers; it also usually contemplates additional closing conditions and covenants that may be imposed by the bank as the closing process evolves. The commitment letter will also contain an expiration date, typically a very early one. For example, it may provide that the offer to make the loan will expire in 24 hours if not accepted in writing by the borrower, or it may allow as much as two weeks.

The commitment letter, if it provides for a revolving line of credit (usually called a *revolver*), will generally state both the maximum amount that may be borrowed under the line (the *cap*) and a potentially lower amount that the bank would actually lend, sometimes expressed as a percentage of the value of the collateral pledged to secure the revolver. This lower amount is called the *borrowing base*. The difference between the amount actually borrowed on the revolver at any time and the amount that could be borrowed (i.e., the lower of the cap or the borrowing base) is called *availability*.

How is the borrowing base determined?

If receivables are pledged, the commitment letter may distinguish between "eligible receivables" and other "receivables." Both are subject to the bank's lien, but only the former may be used to enhance the amount of availability; that is, they may constitute assets against which borrowings may be made.

In a typical situation, eligible receivables will be those that are not more than 90 days old or past due, have been created in the normal course of business, arise from bona fide sales of goods or services to financially sound parties unrelated to the borrower or its affiliates, and are not subject to offset, counterclaim, or other dispute. The bank will lend up to a specified percentage (typically 70 to 90 percent) of eligible receivables. This percentage is known as the *advance rate*. Thus, notwithstanding the maximum amount of the line theoretically available to the borrower, revolving loans outstanding may not at any time exceed that stated percentage of eligible receivables, determined monthly or even weekly.

Inventory is also usually used as collateral. To be eligible, inventory will generally have to be of the kind normally sold by the borrower (if the borrower is in the business of selling goods) and will be limited to finished goods boxed and ready for sale, not located in the hands of a retail store or in transit. In such circumstances an advance rate of 50 percent is not uncommon. In addition, in some circumstances banks will lend against work in process or raw materials. However, a rather low advance rate—perhaps 15 percent—will be applied against such unfinished goods because of the problem a bank would experience in attempting to liquidate such collateral. The bank may also impose an "inventory sublimit"—an absolute dollar ceiling on the amount of inventory-based loans.

What does this method of determining the amount of the loan imply for company operations?

It is important to have accurately calculated the need for working capital at the time the loan is committed for and then to operate within the ceiling and borrowing formulas imposed by the revolving loan. A heavy penalty falls on the manager who allows inventory to build up, and a lesser but still significant penalty falls on the one who fails to collect receivables promptly. Only 50 or 60 cents can be borrowed for every dollar tied up in finished inventory, and every dollar of uncollected receivables costs the company 10 to 30 cents of inaccessible revenues. Financing practices of the pre-acquisition company may have been much looser, particularly if it was part of a well-heeled conglomerate or run as a family business, and untried financial managers can get in trouble very quickly after the closing if they don't understand the business implications of their loan terms.

Are the terms of the commitment letter negotiable?

Yes, but the best, and often the only, time to negotiate is when early drafts of the commitment letter are circulated or when the loan officer sends the buyer an initial proposal letter before credit committee approval. Buyers should be careful to involve their lawyers and other advisors at that stage, and not wait until later to get into details. The proposal letter may be the only opportunity to negotiate a document in advance; sometimes commitment letters appear only after the credit committee has met. Afterward, expectations of the lender become set, and the loan officer will find it awkward to resubmit the proposed loan to the credit committee. The borrower typically does not know how much latitude the loan officer has to modify the commitment without returning to the credit committee. Because time is of the essence in the typical LBO, and a new credit action can result in delay, it is also frequently not in the interest of the borrower to return to the credit committee.

Once the commitment letter is signed, how long will the commitment remain open?

The lender's commitment to make a loan will typically provide that definitive documentation must be negotiated, prepared, and signed by a certain date. Sometimes the time allowed is quite short: 30 or 45 days. Sometimes closing on the LBO will be protracted because of the need to obtain administrative consents, such as Federal Communications Commission (FCC) consents to change of ownership of television stations. In such cases, the termination date of the commitment must be pushed back to allow reasonable time to accomplish all the actions necessary to effect the closing of the acquisition.

FRAUDULENT CONVEYANCE AND OTHER LITIGATION CONCERNS

Lenders worry about fraudulent conveyances in LBOs. Why?

Leveraged acquisitions and buyouts have an unfortunate tendency to attract lawsuits. When buyouts are successful, parties may sue to get a larger share of success; when unsuccessful, parties may sue to reduce their exposure to the failure. Parties suing or sued may include bondholders (senior and junior), shareholders (majority and minority),[13] underwriters, and, of course, lenders. A bank that lends money to finance the acquisition of a business needs to be assured that, in the event of a bankruptcy of that business, its lien on the assets will secure the loan and the note given by the acquired company will be enforceable. However, if the pledge of assets and the giving of the note are determined to be "fraudulent conveyances or transfers" under the Federal Bankruptcy Code or under comparable state law (either the Uniform Fraudulent Conveyance Act or its successor, the Uniform Fraudulent Transfer Act), the lien will be set aside and voided, and even the note can be rendered worthless.

Shareholders in LBOs are also at risk: If a transaction is judged to be a fraudulent conveyance, they may have to return the proceeds received from selling their shares.[14]

Can a pledge of collateral or a note or guaranty be a fraudulent conveyance even though there is no intent to defraud anyone?

Yes. Both the Bankruptcy Code and comparable provisions of state law permit the voiding of a lien or obligation as "fraudulent" without the requirement of malign intent. These laws may, in effect, be used to protect the interests of general creditors of acquired companies where the transactions financed by the banks have the effect of depriving the acquired company of the means to pay its debts to its general creditors, whether those transactions are actually intended to do so or not.

Is there a special risk of creating an unintended fraudulent conveyance in an LBO loan as opposed to an ordinary corporate loan?

Yes. Under Section 548 of the Bankruptcy Code and comparable provisions of state law, a lien given by the acquired company on its assets, or the note secured by that lien, will be deemed "fraudulent" if the company receives less than "reasonably equivalent value" in exchange and one of the following three conditions exists: (1) The company was "insolvent" at the time of such transfer or became "insolvent" as a result of the transfer; (2) the company was left with "unreasonably small capital" as a result of the transfer; or (3) the company incurred or intended to incur debts beyond its ability to pay.

In an LBO loan, no matter how the transaction is structured (whether as a cash merger, stock purchase, or asset purchase), most of what the bank lends winds up not in the hands of the acquired company, but in the pockets of the sellers. On the date after closing, the acquired company is, by definition, "highly leveraged." It has a great deal of new debt, and liens on all its assets, but a large portion of the money raised by such debt (which the company is required to repay) has gone to the previous stockholders. It is not hard to see why an unsecured creditor of the company, viewing the new debt obligations of the company and the encumbrance of its assets, would complain that the company (as opposed to its former owners) did not receive "reasonably equivalent value" in the transaction.

Assuming that the lack of reasonably equivalent value may be a problem in all LBO loans, can't the problem be solved by showing that none of the other three conditions that would trigger a fraudulent conveyance exists?

It can if each of the three conditions can be shown not to exist, but that is not always easy to do in the typical LBO. Of the three conditions—(1) "insolvency," (2) "unreasonably small capital," and (3) "ability to pay debts"—the last two are the easiest to overcome. To the extent that the company and the bank can demonstrate, through well-crafted, reasonable projections, that the company will have sufficient revenues and borrowing capacity to meet its reasonably anticipated obligations (including servicing the acquisition debt), it should be possible to establish that the company's capital, although small, is adequate, and that the company will be able to pay its debts. Solvency, however, is another matter.

Why is it difficult to show that an acquired company is solvent for fraudulent conveyance purposes?

Because the definition of solvency as used in the Bankruptcy Code and state counterpart legislation is different from that used under GAAP. Solvency under GAAP can mean having sufficient assets to pay debts as they mature, or having book assets that are greater than book liabilities. In the typical LBO, at least one of the tests for GAAP solvency can usually be met. But for fraudulent conveyance purposes, a company is solvent only if the "fair, salable value" of its assets is greater than its probable liabilities. In valuing assets, the approach should be conservative—using liquidation value rather than book value or other measures. Probable liabilities are not limited to GAAP balance sheet liabilities. All liabilities, contingent as well as direct, must be considered. This is a tall order, given the current regulatory push toward disclosure of such contingencies. [Consider, for example, the 1993 Staff Accounting Bulletin No. 92 of the Securities and Exchange Commission (SEC) on reporting and accounting for environmental loss exposure.]

Why is the "fair, salable value" test a problem for LBO loans?

In the early days of LBOs, companies were generally sold at prices that reflected the actual cash value of hard collateral—plant, machinery, and equipment—rather than a relatively high multiple of earnings. As the LBO field became more crowded and stock market multipliers increased as well, prices were bid up, with the result that pro forma balance sheets for acquired companies began to reflect more and more goodwill. In addition, companies with relatively little in the way of hard assets, such as advertising agencies, came into play.

While such deals could be financed on the basis of their cash flow performance and projections, they would typically flunk the GAAP balance sheet test for solvency with the acquisition debt loaded on. Although they might be able to meet an alternative GAAP test based on capacity to service debt, they would inevitably lack hard assets having "fair, salable value" at least equal to their direct and contingent liabilities.

Is the "fraudulent conveyance" problem inescapable for all LBOs?

Each sophisticated lender that is willing to make an LBO loan has made a bottom-line decision that it can live with the risk of unclear law in this area. The classic case on the subject, *Gleneagles,* actually involved intentional misconduct, although the court's reasoning in that case cast a cloud over innocent LBOs as well. A number of commentators in the late 1980s, supported by some court decisions (*Kupetz, Credit Managers*), argued that the fraudulent conveyance doctrine should not be employed as a blunt instrument against LBOs. Courts in the 1990s have also shown a range of opinions in the matter. The Massachusetts Bankruptcy Court used fraudulent conveyance laws to subordinate claims of a lender in *In re O'Day Corporation*. In *Crowthers McCall Pattern Inc. v. Lewis et al.,* the court refused to dismiss most of the causes of action brought by a creditor's committee against the equity investors, lenders, and directors. On the other hand, in *Kaiser Steel Corporation v. Pearl Brewing Co.,* the U.S. Court of Appeals for the 10th Circuit held that a debtor in possession or trustee cannot recover payments, even if made as a fraudulent conveyance to stockholders in an LBO.[15]

Although it is not possible yet to say how the law will develop in the 21st century, a reasonable compromise might be that creditors who predate the acquisition and did not consent to it have a right to exact realistic standards for solvency at the time of the acquisition, while subsequent creditors who knew or could have known of the terms of the acquisition loan and its security arrangements should not be entitled to the benefit of fraudulent conveyance laws.

Are there structural arrangements in LBOs that can trigger fraudulent conveyance problems?

Yes. In addition to the issue of lack of "reasonably equivalent value" to the company, lenders and borrowers can get into trouble in transactions involving multicompany groups. These problems are not unique to LBOs, but they can occur in such transactions. Typically they occur when collateral is provided by a subsidiary to secure a borrowing by its parent (upstreaming) or when collateral is provided by one subsidiary to secure a borrowing by a sister subsidiary (cross-streaming). Similarly, upstream and cross-stream guaranties can run afoul of the fraudulent conveyance prohibitions. By contrast, guaranties and pledges by a parent to support a borrowing by its subsidiary (downstreaming) do not present fraudulent conveyance problems.

Why are upstreaming and cross-streaming bad?

Because the donor entity—the one providing the collateral or the guaranty—is not getting "reasonably equivalent value," which is going instead to its affiliate. Thus, one of the triggers (although not the only one) for fraudulent conveyance is tripped. In addition, each subsidiary is typically asked to guarantee all the senior debt of its parent, and yet the assets of the subsidiary represent only a fraction of the total acquisition. The result is that each subsidiary, taken by itself, cannot repay the full acquisition debt and may be rendered insolvent if the guarantee is called against it alone. This illogical result would be avoided if the test of solvency took into account that all the subsidiaries would share in meeting the guarantee obligation. Some cases give support for this conclusion, but the law is unfortunately not clear enough to eliminate the risk.

Are there ways to solve upstreaming and cross-streaming problems?

Yes. If the transaction passes each of the three additional tests:

- No insolvency
- Not unreasonably small capital, and
- Ability to pay debts—there is no fraudulent conveyance.

However, to guard against the risk of flunking one of the tests, two kinds of additional solutions can be explored:

- Merging the entity providing the collateral or guaranty with the borrower before the acquisition is consummated
- Dividing up the loan into two or more distinct credit facilities, each collateralized by (and commensurate with) the collateral provided by each borrower.

Care should be taken, if the latter course is used, to avoid having the loan proceeds simply pass through one of the borrowers into the hands of another borrower or affiliated entity. The loan proceeds can be used to pay off bona fide intercorporate debt, but if the cash flow among the borrowing entities indicates that the separate loans are shams, the transaction runs the risk of being "collapsed" in a bankruptcy proceeding. In such a case, the liens and guaranties could be voided.

Are upstream or cross-stream guaranties that are limited to the net worth of the guarantor fraudulent conveyances?

No. Indeed, limiting the guaranty (and the lien collateralizing it) to the amount of the guarantor's net worth at the time of delivery of the guaranty can provide an ingenious way to ensure that the guarantor is not rendered insolvent by delivery of the guaranty and consequently should eliminate any fraudulent conveyance problem. However, the guarantor must have the requisite "net worth" in the bankruptcy sense, and not just GAAP net worth, in addition to being able to pay its debts and not having unreasonably small capital. Net worth guaranties have yet to be fully tested in a bankruptcy proceeding; dealmakers should ask their attorneys to keep a lookout on this evolving area.

Will law firms give opinions that fraudulent conveyance laws have not been violated?

Almost never. Law firms generally refuse to give fraudulent conveyance opinions, largely because they cannot evaluate the question of solvency, and because lawyers have traditionally refused to predict what actions a bankruptcy court may take under a set of unforeseeable circumstances. Lenders usually understand and accept this reluctance, although sometimes some skirmishing occurs at the closing on this point.

What are some other types of litigation that inappropriate financing can spur?

Shareholder suits can certainly advance fraudulent conveyance-type arguments. These suits may be derivative or class-action suits.

OTHER PRINCIPAL ISSUES IN SENIOR LOAN AGREEMENTS

What fees are typically charged by banks?

Bank fees for lending services tend to be as varied as the ingenuity of lenders can devise and as high as borrowers can accept. In some cases, the lender may charge a fee upon the delivery of the commitment letter signed by the bank (the *commitment letter fee*) and a second commitment letter fee upon its execution by the borrower. Both such fees will probably be nonrefundable, but they may be credited against a third due from the borrower at closing on the loan (the *closing fee*).[16]

If the loan has been syndicated, the lead bank may charge an agency or management fee for its services in putting together the syndicate. This will typically be an ongoing fee (as opposed to the one-time commitment letter and closing fees), payable quarterly or monthly as a percentage of the total facility (0.25 percent per annum is not uncommon).

The total amount of fees charged by a bank at the closing ranges between 1 and 2.5 percent. The percentage depends on the speed demanded of the bank, the complexity of the transaction, the size of the banking group (the more lenders there are, the more expensive it is), and the degree of risk. A short-term bridge loan will probably involve a higher front-end fee than a long-term facility, since the bank has less opportunity to earn profit by way of interest over the life of the loan. Usually, the New York money center banks charge fees at the higher end of this range. In addition to the front-end fees, there will usually be a commitment fee or facility fee (typically a fraction of a percent) on the amount from time to time undrawn and available under the revolver.

If the borrower will need letters of credit, the bank will typically assess a letter of credit fee (typically 1 to 1.5 percent per annum) on the amount committed under a standby or commercial letter of credit.

Finally, the bank will often seek early termination fees on the unpaid balance of the term portion of the financing. These are intended to compensate the bank for economic losses it may suffer if the borrower terminates the term loan prior to its maturity because of a cheaper financing source, thus depriving the bank of the anticipated profit on the loan for the balance of the term. These fees may step down in amount the longer the term loan is outstanding. It is usually possible to get the bank to drop these termination fees or at least limit them to terminations occurring in the first year or two. This is worth spending some bargaining chips to achieve. If the company does well, the buyer will probably want to refinance the senior loan as quickly as possible to escape a whole panoply of burdensome covenants, and these fees are likely to be a problem.

What bank expenses is the borrower required to pay?

Typically, whether the loan is made or not, the commitment letter will require that the borrower be liable for all the lender's out-of-pocket expenses and obligations for fees and disbursements of the bank's outside counsel. This provision is not negotiable; banks never expect to pay their own counsel for work done in connection with a loan. Such fees are always assessed against the borrower or, if the loan does not close, the intended borrower.

What interest rates do banks charge for LBO loans?

Typically, a bank will charge 1.5 to 2 percent over the prime rate or base rate. Contrary to popular belief, *prime* does not necessarily mean the lowest rate a bank charges its customers, as the loan agreement will often admit. Rather, the prime or base rate will be whatever the lending bank from time to time says it is.

Are reference rates other than prime ever used in floating-rate loans?

Yes, and the loan agreement may permit the borrower to switch back and forth. A common alternative is the London InterBank Offered Rate (LIBOR). This rate, which used to be called the Eurodollar rate before the advent of the euro, is typically calculated as the rate the lender would have realized on deposits in dollars with a "first-class" bank in the London interbank market (see Chapter 15). Another reference rate frequently used is the federal funds effective rate. This rate may be based on the weighted average of rates on overnight federal funds transactions with members of the Federal Reserve System arranged by federal funds brokers, as published by the Federal Reserve Bank of New York, or as an average of quotes from a specified number of federal funds brokers "of recognized standing" selected by the bank.

The amount of the premium charged by the bank above the reference rate will depend on which reference rate is used, and the present and anticipated differentials between the bank's own "prime" and the alternative third-party reference rate or rates; premiums are generally about 100 basis points greater for Eurodollar rate loans than they are for prime rate loans. This is largely, but not completely, offset by the fact that LIBOR is usually a lower rate than prime; the net effect of selecting LIBOR is probably to increase rates about 25 to 50 basis points. LIBOR is more responsive to interest rate changes and will move more quickly. A change in prime represents a significant political decision for a bank, and thus changes in prime come less frequently and in bigger steps.

How can more than one lender participate in a loan? What are some problems this raises?

Frequently LBO loans are made by groups of banks, or *syndicates.* In some cases, the banks involved in making the loan will all be parties to the loan agreement, with one of their number designated as the agent bank. In other cases, only one bank will sign the loan agreement, but it will sell off participation interests to other banks. Even when no formal syndicates are involved, loans may be structured with layers of debt, as mentioned earlier.

The practical implications of having to deal with multiple lenders can be serious and troublesome. Because of the high degree of leverage involved, LBO lenders tend to limit their risks by imposing an intrusive array of covenants—negative and affirmative, financial and operational—upon the borrower. These covenants are designed to ensure that the business will be conducted as represented to the bankers and in accordance with the financial projections submitted to the bankers by the borrower. Any deviation, any change in the manner of operation of the business, or any bad financial development is likely to trigger a default. Because it is not always possible for a buyer to foresee all future developments in the way the business will be conducted, it is generally not possible, even in the absence of bad financial news, to operate at all times within the requirements imposed by the loan covenants. Hence, the borrower will generally find it necessary, from time to time, to go back to the lenders to have certain covenants waived or amended. If only one lender is involved, the process can be relatively simple. If the consent of a dozen or more is involved, the process can be expensive, time-consuming, and painful.

Do all the members of a lending group have to approve every waiver and amendment?

Generally, no. But the provisions that relate to interbank matters, such as the percentage of lenders needed to grant waivers, are generally contained in a document (sometimes called the *participation agreement*) to which the borrower is not a party, and, frequently, that it may not even be allowed to see. Although lender approval arrangements vary, it is not unusual for them to provide that certain changes in the loan (such as changes in interest rates, due date, and principal amount) are so fundamental that all lenders must consent, whereas other changes can be approved by banks holding at least a 51 percent interest (or in some cases a 66.6 percent interest) in all loans outstanding or in lending commitments.

Can junior lenders ever be paid back before senior lenders?

Not generally. Under a long-standing principle in bankruptcy law called the *absolute priority rule,* junior creditors may not go ahead of senior creditors.

There are exceptions—such as the "new capital" exception for junior lenders who invest—but the rule generally prevails.[17]

What is a negative pledge covenant, and why do lenders seek it?

A negative pledge is an undertaking by the borrower not to pledge to someone else assets that may be subject to the bank's lien or to no lien. It generally is used to bar junior liens on collateral that is subject to the bank's senior lien. Although in theory the rights of a junior loanholder should not impinge on the senior lender's rights in the collateral, in practice lenders strongly prefer not to be accountable to a second loanholder with regard to their stewardship over the collateral on which they have a first lien. A junior loanholder is, in the eyes of a senior lender, someone who can second-guess your actions in realizing upon the collateral and sue you if you slip up, or even if you don't.

What kinds of problems are most likely to be encountered in attempting to perfect liens on the collateral?

- Prior unsatisfied liens may be discovered. For this reason, as well as for general due diligence considerations (see Chapter 6), it is prudent to begin a lien search as promptly as possible in all jurisdictions in which record filings may have been made affecting the collateral.

- Liens on patents, trademarks and trade names, and copyright assignments require special federal filings, which may be time-consuming and require the services of specialized counsel.

- Collateral assignments of government contracts and receivables from the U.S. government may require federal approval, which involves a potentially time-consuming process.

- Uniform Commercial Code (UCC) filings giving notice to the world of security interests must be made at state and, sometimes, local government offices where the target and its assets are located. Filing requirements in Puerto Rico and Louisiana, the two non-UCC jurisdictions in the United States, are markedly different from, as well as more elaborate than, filing requirements in other U.S. jurisdictions. Local counsel should be contacted early and will play key roles.

- Security interests in real estate and fixtures require separate documentation and recordation in the localities and states in which they are located. Lenders will often require title insurance and surveys, both of which involve considerable lead time.

- Lenders will often want local counsel opinions on perfection and priority of liens, and obtaining these can be a major logistical task (see Chapter 9).

For interest rate and fee calculations, bankers typically treat the year as having only 360 days. Why?

Because it produces a slight increase in yield over the stipulated rate or fee. This practice has acquired the status of a convention and is not generally subject to negotiation.

What are default rates?

Loan agreements typically provide for an increase in interest rates in the event of default, or at the time of acceleration of the loan. A premium of 2 or 3 percentage points above the rate normally in effect is not uncommon. A borrower should try to have a default rate go into effect only after the lender makes a formal declaration of default, since minor technical defaults are all too easy to stumble into and should not be a source of profit to the lender.

Why are mandatory prepayment obligations imposed by lenders?

Reasons for mandatory prepayment requirements vary depending on the bank's perception of the transaction. In some transactions, the lender is anxious to recoup and redeploy its money as swiftly as possible. This desire, and the anticipated availability of cash derived from cash flow projections, will tend to drive in the direction of an aggressive amortization schedule on term debt. (In some cases borrowers may also be asked to "amortize" revolving lines of credit as well by accepting scheduled reductions in availability over a period of time and making any principal payments required by such reductions.)

In addition, a bank may schedule amortization payments to match the buyer's plans for selling off assets or terminating pension plans, in effect forcing the buyer to honor its promise to follow through on the promised sell-offs or terminations. Finally, lenders may require that all or a portion of excess cash flow be paid down to reduce senior term debt.

The bank may permit distributions of dividends to stockholders of an S corporation (one of many corporate forms under U.S. tax law, as explained in Chapter 5) for the purpose of paying federal, state, and local income taxes on income of the company and retaining some earnings for capital expenditures. On the other hand it may also require that the buyer use everything left over after paying off junior debt to pay off any outstanding balance on the term loan.

Why do banks insist on applying prepayments first to the last installments due (in inverse order) rather than the other way around?

Banks reverse the order of LBO loan payments in order to keep the flow of cash coming into the bank and to get the loan paid off as swiftly as possible. If borrowers could prepay the next payments due, they would, in effect, be buying themselves a payment holiday. Sometimes prepayments may result from sale of income-producing assets (or the bank's application of casualty insurance proceeds to prepay principal in lieu of making such proceeds available to the borrower), because such events can reduce the subsequent capacity of the borrower to pay debt service. In such cases, the loan should be recast to lower proportionately the combined total of subsequent interest and principal payments.

Can a letter of credit facility be combined with an LBO loan?

Yes. If the business uses letters of credit in its ongoing operations (for purposes such as assuring payment for raw materials or foreign-sourced goods), it can generally obtain a commitment from the lenders to provide such letters of credit up to a stipulated aggregate amount. The letter of credit facility will typically be carved out of the revolving line of credit, will be collateralized by the same collateral that secures the revolver, and will have the effect of limiting availability under the revolver to the extent of the aggregate letter of credit commitment. Draws on letters of credit will be treated, in such circumstances, as draws on the revolver. Separate fees (frequently ranging from 1 to 1.5 percent per year) will be charged from time to time by the lenders for outstanding standby letters of credit.

Sometimes companies have a practice of issuing a large letter of credit for all shipments in a certain period and then securing specific orders as they arise. In such cases, it may be possible to limit availability by the amount of claims that can be or have been made against the letter of credit for specific orders, and not by the larger unused balance of the letter of credit.

LBO loan agreements typically contain a lengthy list of conditions to closing. Are there any that are likely to be particularly troublesome?

Although points of sharpest contention vary from transaction to transaction, there are some that crop up regularly. They include the following:

- *Requirements regarding perfection and priority of security interests in collateral.* If, for example, first liens are to be given to the lenders on inventory in various jurisdictions, certain events must occur: First, lien searches have to be completed and reports received and reviewed (there are professional companies that can be hired to conduct computerized searches of liens on record in any state or county office); second, documents terminating old liens have to be prepared, signed, and sent for filing; and third, documents perfecting new liens have to be prepared, signed, and sent for filing.
- *Related filing schedules.* Once all that has been done, filing must be coordinated in each of the jurisdictions so that it occurs contemporaneously with the funding of the new loan and the payoff of the old loan. In a complex, multijurisdictional transaction, such coordination, if it is to be done successfully, requires a combination of monumental effort and plain old good luck. Not infrequently, lenders have some flexibility about the filing of termination statements in connection with the old loan being discharged and will allow a reasonable period after closing for this to be accomplished.
- *Counsel opinions.* Few deals crater over the failure of counsel for the borrower to deliver required opinions, but it is not unheard of for a closing to be delayed while final points in the opinions are negotiated between counsel for the bank and the borrower. Problems typically occur in local counsel opinions and relate to the validity of the

bank's lien in a particular jurisdiction. There is no magic solution, but early involvement of local counsel for the borrower is always a good idea.

- *Auditors' opinions.* Ever since the American Institute of Certified Public Accountants (AICPA) banned them from issuing insolvency opinions in 1988, auditors have been reluctant to express any views whatsoever on the solvency of borrowers despite continuing requests from banks wanting to limit their fraudulent conveyance risk. Similarly, auditors may be reluctant to address the reliability of financial projections provided by the borrower to the bank. Banks need to determine at an early stage what the auditors will, and will not, agree to say in writing at the closing.

- *Governmental consents and approvals.* In certain transactions, approval of a governmental entity is a central element in the transaction. For example, a sale of a television station cannot be effected without requisite approvals from the FCC. The timing of such approvals, even if they are reasonably assured, is outside the power of the parties, and the failure of a governmental agency to act when expected can wreak havoc on the schedule for closing an LBO.

- *Material litigation and adverse changes affecting the company.* Some loan agreements give the buyer and/or lender the right to back out if the target gets hit by a major lawsuit that, if successful, could seriously harm the company's business. If this contingency does occur, the burden is on the seller's counsel to persuade both the buyer and the bank that the suit is unlikely to succeed or, if successful, would not be material to the company or its operations. Similarly, bad economic news can cause either the buyer or the bank to halt the process, resulting in either a negotiated price reduction or a termination.

Are there continuing conditions that apply to subsequent draws on the revolving line of credit?

Yes. In most loan agreements, the bank's obligation to honor subsequent draws upon the revolver is subject to a variety of conditions. Chief among them is reaffirmation by the borrower that the original warranties and representations made in the loan agreement are still true (including those stating that there have been no material adverse changes in the business since a date generally preceding the closing date) and a requirement that no covenant default exists. If the foregoing conditions are not met, the bank is not required to lend.

What purposes do the representations and warranties in the loan agreement serve?

The representations and warranties are intended to corroborate and complete the acquired company information upon which the lender based its credit decision. They constitute, in effect, a checklist of potential problem areas for which the borrower is required to state that no problem exists, or to spell out (by way of exceptions or exhibits) what the problem is. Thus, typical warranties will state that:

- The financial statements of the borrower that have been submitted to the bank are correct. (Although it is comforting to have this conclusion backed by an auditor's certification, usually the auditor's report is laced with qualifications.)
- There are no liens on the borrower's assets, except as disclosed to the bank or permitted pursuant to the loan agreement.
- The transactions contemplated will not conflict with laws or any contracts to which the borrower is a party or by which it is bound (the so-called noncontravention representation).
- There are no lawsuits pending or threatened against the borrower that are likely to have a material adverse effect on it if decided against the borrower, except as disclosed to the bank.
- The loan will not violate the "margin rules."
- The borrower has no exposure under the Employee Retirement Income Security Act (ERISA).
- The borrower is not a regulated public utility holding company or investment company (since if it were, various governmental orders would be required).
- The borrower is "solvent" (so as to mitigate concerns about fraudulent conveyance risks).
- The borrower's assets (and principal office) are located in the places specified. (This information is needed to ensure that perfection of security interests in the collateral is effected by filing notices in the correct jurisdictions.)

What happens if a representation is wrong?

A breached representation can have two practical consequences for a borrower: (1) If such a breach occurs, the bank may refuse to make a requested advance, either at or after the closing, and (2) breach of a representation or warranty can trigger a default under the loan agreement.

The first consequence—bank refusal to fund—should not be surprising. The truth and accuracy of the representations is typically a condition to the initial loan made at the time the loan agreement is signed and also to any subsequent draws on the revolving line of credit. If, for example, the borrower has warranted in the loan agreement that it has no significant environmental problems, and subsequently it is discovered that it has been guilty of illegal dumping of hazardous wastes, the bank will probably have the right under the loan agreement to shut off further draws on the line of credit. Such a decision could be catastrophic for a company precluded from financing itself from cash flow because its loan agreement also provides for the "lock boxing" of revenues and mandatory paydown—that is, a requirement that they be deposited in a lock box under the lender's control and used to pay off bank debt.

The second consequence—a default under the loan agreement—triggers the remedies a lender generally has under a loan agreement, one of which is the right to "accelerate" the loan, that is, to declare all moneys loaned immediately due and payable, even though the amounts due under the term portion may not be otherwise due for several years and the revolver may not expire until the end of the current year.

The right to accelerate is, in a practical sense, the right to trigger the bankruptcy of the borrower and for that reason is unlikely to be exercised except in those cases where a lender determines that its interests will be better protected by putting the borrower into bankruptcy than through other means. Since bankruptcy is viewed by most secured lenders as risky, slow, and a last resort (and potentially liability-producing for the bank), a breached warranty is generally unlikely to bring the house down. But unless the breach is waived by the lender, its existence in effect turns what was originally conceived of as a term loan into a demand loan, callable by the bank at any time. Frequently, highly leveraged transactions result in the bank having a demand loan even in the absence of a default, so going into default does not make matters much worse; also, some lenders and their counsel try to negotiate loan agreements that are so tight that the company is arguably in default from the moment the agreement is entered into. Banks also impose default rates of interest in some cases, so that the cost of borrowing can go up on a warranty breach. This is a more effective sanction for the bank, provided that the borrower's fiscal health is not endangered.

Covenants in LBO loan agreements frequently appear more intrusive than those in most commercial loan agreements. Why?

Because in a typical leveraged acquisition the lenders are significantly more at risk than they are in a normal business loan. Both from a balance sheet standpoint (because of the absence of a substantial equity "pad" under the senior debt) and an operating standpoint (because of the burden that debt service will place on the borrower's cash flow), the lender is likely to view itself as significantly exposed. Lenders attempt to address this problem by imposing covenants on the borrower to achieve the following five results: first, to obligate the borrower, by express contractual provision, to operate the acquired business in accordance with the business plan submitted to and approved by the bank; second, to provide early warning of divergence from the business plan or of economic bad news; third, to protect the collateral; fourth, to prevent the leakage of money and property out of the borrower, whether as "management fees" or other payments to related parties, costs of new acquisitions, capital expenditures, or simply as dividends; and fifth, to enable the bank to exercise its remedies at as early a stage as possible if things go awry by exercising its right to declare a default as a result of a covenant breach.

What are the covenants a borrower is most likely to be confronted with?

When borrowing funds in a leveraged transaction, the buyer is often asked to sign off on promises that it will comply with the business plan, provide early warning of potential economic trouble, protect collateral, and control expenditures.

How can a seller in a contingency payment deal make sure the buyer will comply with the business plan?

The buyer is typically asked to promise to:

- Use the proceeds of the loan only for the stipulated purposes.

- Engage only in the kinds of business contemplated by the lenders.
- Refrain from merging or selling all or substantially all its assets, or any portion thereof in excess of a specified value, without the bank's consent.
- Limit capital expenditures, lease payments, borrowings, and investments in affiliates and third parties to agreed amounts.
- Prevent change in ownership or control of the borrower without the lenders' consent.
- Bar acquisitions of other businesses.
- Make changes in the acquisition agreement, subordinated debt instruments, or other material documents.

What about covenants designed to give early warning of economic trouble?

The seller typically asks the buyer to promise to:

- Remain in compliance with financial covenants (discussed below).
- Provide periodic (monthly, quarterly, annual) financial reports, with annual reports to be audited.
- Give prompt notice of any material adverse development affecting the operations of the business.
- Provide revised and updated projections, on at least an annual basis, prior to the commencement of each new fiscal year.
- Permit visits and inspections by bank representatives.

How can the seller protect its collateral?

The buyer must typically promise to:

- Keep the business and property adequately insured.
- Limit sales of property to merchandise sold in the ordinary course of business.
- Require property to be kept free of liens (a "negative pledge").
- Bar leases of property by the borrower.
- Provide key-man life insurance for principal executives of the borrower.

What loan agreement covenants can discourage financial leakage out of the borrower?

Lenders will often ask the borrower to agree to:

- Cap executive compensation and management fees.
- Limit, or often prohibit (at least for a specific time period, or until specified financial tests are satisfied), dividends and other distributions to equity holders.
- Prohibit transactions with affiliates, except as expressly agreed upon and except for those provided on an "arm's-length" basis for services definitely required by the borrower.
- Lend money or guarantee the obligations of other parties.

What kinds of financial covenants are likely to be imposed?

The financial covenants that lenders are most concerned with relate to the company's cash generation and cash distribution. Lenders are vitally concerned about monitoring the company's ability to service current and future obligations to the lender. Thus, in general, they want to limit "unnecessary" cash outflows such as dividends, excessive capital expenditures, and future payment obligations (that is, additional debt) until their claims are satisfied. In addition, lenders want sufficient advance information about the company's cash inflow relative to debt service requirements. If this ratio starts to deteriorate and approach default levels, the lender will increase monitoring activity and notify management of relevant default consequences. Therefore, the borrower may be required to maintain stipulated ratios for:

- Interest coverage (earnings before interest and taxes to interest expense)
- Debt to net worth
- Current assets to current liabilities
- Fixed charges to net income (or cash flow)

In addition, the borrower may be required to attain stipulated minimum goals for:

- Net worth
- Cash flow

The borrower may also be required not to exceed stipulated maximum limits for:

- Capital expenditures
- Total debt

How do lenders determine financial covenant levels?

Lenders use information provided by the borrower and their own lending experience combined with regulatory guidelines to set financial covenant levels. The projected financial statements serve as the basic data for establishing covenant levels. Since financial covenants are usually designed as early warning devices, lenders want covenants that are good indicators of debt service capability. Contrary to popular belief, lenders do not want financial covenants as high as possible. What they try to achieve is an effective filter system, identifying problem loans that merit special attention. If covenants are too high, the lender may waste valuable administrative time on a relatively low-risk situation.

For example, assume a senior lender provides $2 million at 12 percent fixed interest to be paid over five years. The company's projected cash flow and debt service requirements appear in Table 4-1.

The projected coverage ratio is calculated by dividing projected cash flow by total debt service.

T A B L E   4-1

Sample Company's Projected Cash Flow and Debt Service Requirements (in thousands of dollars)

Year	1	2	3	4	5
Loan balance at 1/1	2,000	1,700	1,250	800	350
Interest	240	204	150	96	42
Principal payments	300	450	450	450	350
Total debt service	540	654	600	546	392
Projected cash flow	1,000	1,200	1,400	1,600	1,800
Projected coverage ratio	1.85	1.83	2.33	2.93	4.59

Given these data, the lender will make a judgment about the projected volatility of the company's cash flow. Assuming the company's prospects satisfy the senior lender's loan committee, a projected coverage ratio covenant must be determined. The level selected will probably be a simple discount on expected performance that still provides the lender with reasonable security. Once the company is out of the woods, the lender should be comfortable and should not keep increasing the level of required performance even if the projections indicate that it can be achieved.

The covenant level will probably rise over time to reflect the lender's desire to see the company's cash flow continue to increase. A sample covenant and the resulting minimum cash flow to prevent default appear in Table 4-2. The covenant levels shown in this table require the company in effect to increase cash flow each year until the last, when the lender's risk has been significantly reduced.

Borrowers are faced with an interesting dilemma when presenting a prospective lender with the projected financial performance of the acquisition candidate. A borrower may be motivated to make the acquired company's future performance look good in order to obtain the loan. However, these same projections will form the basis for the lender's financial covenants. If the projected performance was inflated, the company could continually be in default on the loan agreement. On the other hand, if the borrower downplays the future performance of the company to avoid this possibility, the borrower runs the risk of making the loan relatively unattractive to the lender. Ultimately, both sides benefit the most when forecasts are submitted that genuinely reflect the buyer's expectations for the company.

T A B L E 4-2

Sample Covenant (in thousands of dollars)

Year	1	2	3	4	5
Covenant ratio	1.4	1.4	1.8	2.1	2.5
Minimum cash flow (covenant ratio × debt service)	756.0	915.6	1,080.0	1,146.6	980.0

When are financial covenants usually negotiated?

Very late in the process, usually just before closing. The typical buyer prefers to get the commitment for the loan before negotiating these provisions in detail. Often the most reliable financial projections become available only at the last moment, and they provide the base for the covenants. Sometimes, the bank sets the covenants too tightly at the closing, and the negotiating process continues through the initial months of the loan in the form of waivers. This should be avoided if possible.

What events typically trigger default?

- Breach of one or more of the covenants described above (sometimes subject to a right to cure certain breaches within a specified cure period and/or to the qualification that the breach be "material" or have a "material adverse effect" on the borrower).
- Payment defaults (failure to pay interest, principal, or fees when due or, in the case of interest and fees, sometimes within a stipulated grace period—see below).
- Breach of a representation or warranty (sometimes subject to the qualification that the breach be material—see below).
- Cross-default (default in the loan agreement triggered by a default in another loan document, such as a security agreement, or in another unrelated but material agreement to which the borrower is a party, such as a subordinated debt instrument). Typically, for a cross-default to be triggered, the default in the other instrument must be "mature"; that is, all cure periods must have expired and the other lender must have the right to accelerate. In addition, defaults on other debts below a specified dollar threshold may be expressly exempted from a loan agreement's cross-default provisions.
- Insolvency or voluntary bankruptcy, or involuntary bankruptcy if not discharged by the borrower within a stipulated period (typically 60 days).
- An adverse final court judgment above a stipulated dollar amount that is not discharged or stayed on appeal within a prescribed period.
- The imposition of a lien (other than a lien permitted pursuant to the loan agreement) on assets of the borrower.

- The occurrence of an event triggering ERISA liability in excess of a stipulated amount.
- The death of the chief executive officer or an individual guarantor or other termination of the employment of certain specified managerial employees.

What techniques can be used to take some of the bite out of default provisions?

There are basically two default softeners: the use of *grace* or *cure* provisions and the concept of *materiality*.

A *grace period* is a period of time, following the due date for the making of a payment, during which payment may be made and default avoided. It is rare, but not without precedent, for a grace period to be accorded to a principal repayment obligation. More common are grace periods for interest payments or fees. Five days' grace beyond the due date is not uncommon; sometimes 10 or even 15 days may be granted.

Cure periods are extended deadlines for defaults triggered by covenant breaches. Generally, the lender will attempt to limit their application to those covenants that are manifestly susceptible of cure such as the duty to submit financial reports at specified dates but deny them for covenants designed to provide early warning of trouble such as breach of financial ratios. Sometimes, the cure period will not begin to run until the lender has given the borrower notice of a failure to perform; in other cases, the cure period will begin to run when the borrower should have performed, whether the lender knew of the borrower's failure or not. Cure periods vary greatly from transaction to transaction and from provision to provision. However, 5-day, 10-day, and 30-day cure periods are seen from time to time, and sometimes the concept of counting only "business days" is used to extend the period by excluding Saturdays, Sundays, and nationally recognized holidays.

The concept of materiality is more commonly applied in the case of defaults triggered by warranty breaches. The borrower will assert that default should not be triggered if a representation turns out to be untrue, but the effect of such inaccuracy is not materially adverse to the borrower or the collateral, or to the lender's position. The concept of a cure right for misrepresentations is not at all common but is not illogical in many cases. In some cases, where the loan agreement does not afford the borrower the right to cure a breached covenant, it is sometimes provided that such a breach will nevertheless not trigger a default if the effect is not material and adverse.

So far, we have been talking about commercial bank loans. What other major sources of loans are there?

In addition to commercial banks, leveraged acquirers can turn to *insurance companies* (for loans), *underwriters* (to do *junk bond issues* or to make *bridge loans*), and *equity investment funds* or other funds, all discussed below. Another emerging source—but an approved one for m/a/b purposes—is the *nonbank banks*.

What is a nonbank bank?

A nonbank bank—also called a limited-service bank—is one that provides depository services or lending but not both. Such banks are exempt from the Glass-Steagall Act "wall" forbidding bank ownership by industrial companies. In the 1980s, hundreds of industrial companies applied to the Federal Reserve Banking System to establish nonbank banks. In 1987 the Competitive Equality in Banking Act limited growth of such banks to 7 percent in most states.[18]

INSURANCE COMPANY FINANCING

For many years, insurance companies have provided senior fixed-term financing—both secured and unsecured—for terms of up to 10, 12, or 15 years through "private placements." If a company's capital requirements are sufficiently great, one or more additional insurance companies may participate in the transaction as co-lenders. Frequently these groups are assembled by investment bankers. Because the behavior and practices of insurance company lenders differ somewhat from those of banks, they deserve special attention.

What kind of financing is usually available from insurance companies?

Loans may be secured, unsecured, or a combination of each. All, or any portion, may be senior debt, the remainder being subordinated debt generally bearing a higher rate of interest. Rates are usually fixed for the term of these financings.

Does it make a difference which insurance companies are solicited?

It may, for several reasons. Although lending terms tend to be somewhat standardized, certain companies will lend into a riskier credit, with a rate premium and perhaps a somewhat more onerous set of covenants, although most won't. In addition, over the years, several life insurance companies and their counsel have devised and perfected lengthy, onerous forms of note purchase agreements (essentially the equivalent of loan agreements), with which many borrowers became disenchanted, taking their business elsewhere. Since then, in an effort to regain the lost business, at least one company has developed a new, streamlined, and more readable form of agreement that is definitely preferable to its predecessors, from the borrower's point of view. It may be appropriate to agree in advance of documentation that a streamlined form of agreement will be utilized.

How long does it take to obtain insurance company funding?

Insurance companies are generally more bureaucratic than banks, and decision making often seems to take longer. In-house counsel to insurance firms can, in some cases, march to a different drummer, delaying legal responses, but their input is required notwithstanding the presence of an outside law firm.

Although substantial acquisitions have been closed with insurance company funds, these closings did not break any records for speed. Often, if time is of the essence, it is prudent to arrange for a bridge lender to fund initially and be taken out within a period of several months by an insurance company private placement. The bridge lender can even be the bank providing the revolving financing. Even this solution can be difficult to achieve, however, since the principal terms of the takeout financing must be negotiated in advance with the insurance company, and often between it and a senior lender, to be sure the takeout financing can be closed in the future.

How are insurance company private placements generally negotiated?

The deal is negotiated and, frequently, put in the form of a "term sheet" that is "circled" (approved) by each insurance company; or commitment letters may be issued, particularly if sufficient pressure is placed on the lenders by the borrower or its counsel.

Once a term sheet or commitment letter is agreed to, the lead lender (usually the insurance company taking the largest percentage of the total loan) will have its outside counsel prepare a first draft of the note purchase agreement. The lead lender's counsel generally acts for the entire lending group, although with varying degrees of authority and effectiveness. The other participants (and their in-house counsel) will generally review this draft before it is forwarded to the borrower and its counsel. The content of this agreement has the potential to change significantly for the worse—from the borrower's perspective—as it progresses through successive drafts, as in-house counsel for each participant gets additional bites at the apple. A strong lead lender, however, can often prevent this from occurring.

How should the borrower or its counsel respond if, during the negotiation of a note purchase agreement, a representative of the insurance company refuses to strike an objectionable covenant, saying that the borrower can request a waiver at a later date if necessary?

These agreements should be negotiated as fully as possible prior to closing. Although subsequent waivers are obtainable, a borrower should not be surprised if some payment is required in connection with the waiver, particularly if interest rates have risen significantly since the funding of the transaction. Even when rates have not risen, some companies have been known to impose fees when waiver requests are made, frequently in order to compensate for their staff time spent in evaluating the requests; of course, the cost of any outside counsel will be the responsibility of the borrower. Furthermore, waivers are generally more readily obtainable from banks, less so from insurance companies. One should act accordingly in negotiating the initial insurance company documentation.

Is it possible to provide for optional prepayments without incurring significant prepayment premiums?

Yes. Generally, prepayment provisions in note purchase agreements have followed a formula that allows for optional annual prepayments in any year in the amount of any specified annual mandatory prepayments, without additional charge. If, however, the loan is to be prepaid in any given year by an amount in excess of this permitted optional prepayment, a percentage premium (typically around 9.5 percent) would be applied to this excess, with the amount of this percentage declining annually, reaching zero within a year before maturity. The applicable percentage would then be multiplied by the amount prepaid in excess of any permitted optional prepayment; the resulting product is the dollar amount that must be paid, in addition to the outstanding principal balance, in order to prepay the principal indebtedness evidenced by the note purchase agreement or an appropriate portion.

Recently, many life insurance companies have become gun-shy of the fixed-premium method for prepayments and are moving toward what is known as a *make-whole* arrangement. This consists of a formula that pays to the lender the net present value of the lost return during each year that the notes issued under the note purchase agreement would have been outstanding, compared with a theoretical reinvestment at an agreed formula rate.

Are other prohibitions on prepayment typically found in insurance company financings?

Yes. Prepayment is usually prohibited if the source of funds for such prepayment is borrowings, or proceeds from the sale of preferred stock, having a lower after-tax interest cost to the company than the company's after-tax cost of interest at the rate payable under the insurance company's notes.

Is there any way to structure the borrowing in order to reduce the amount of prepayment premiums?

Yes. If a portion of the amount borrowed is at a variable rate tied to prime or Eurodollar rates, prepayment premiums on that portion can be avoided.

Do insurance companies provide revolving loans, takeout commitments, or other forms of guarantees?

Insurance companies don't do revolving loans; they are not organized for the continuous financial monitoring required for revolving lending. For this reason, they are not suitable for working capital lending. Also, unless operating as a surety, insurance companies do not give guarantees. They may not make a loan unless it would be prudent at the time made. Thus, they may not give enforceable commitments to take out or back another lender if the borrower gets into trouble.

What material covenants would you expect to find in a more streamlined insurance company note purchase agreement?

- Typical financial reporting covenants, including requirements for a statement of the principal financial officer of the company setting forth computations pertaining to compliance with financial covenants (including long-term and short-term debt incurrence, secured debt incurrence, and the making of restricted payments)
- Maintenance of corporate existence, payment of taxes and compliance with statutes, regulations and orders of governmental bodies pertaining to environmental and occupational safety and health standards, or even broader governmental statutes and regulations with a materiality standard
- Maintenance of specified types of insurance
- Restrictions on debt incurrence (including limits on short-term debt and long-term debt, each of which may be restricted to specified dollar amounts or by formulas relating to consolidated tangible net worth and consolidated net earnings available for fixed charges)
- Restrictions on encumbrances, sale and leasebacks, and payment of restricted payments
- Maintenance of financial condition—minimum amount of consolidated tangible net worth, minimum ratio of consolidated net tangible assets to consolidated debt, minimum current ratio, maximum long-term rentals, restriction on subsidiary stock dispositions, and issuance of shares by subsidiaries
- Limitations on amounts of annual capital expenditures
- Restrictions on mergers and consolidations affecting the company and subsidiaries, and disposition of company or subsidiary assets

JUNK BONDS

What are junk bonds?

Junk bonds are medium-term to long-term obligations of the target that (1) are subordinated to its senior debt, (2) are normally unsecured, and (3) bear high interest rates. Their rather inelegant name, reportedly coined by Michael

Milken in a conversation with Rik Riklis,[19] comes from the fact that they are riskier than senior debt: They get a below-investment-grade rating from one or more of the bond rating services.[20] They generally deserve a better label, however, and are thus called by some underwriters *high-yield securities*. Indeed, the term *junk* arguably had the effect of discounting the price, which helped some purchasers realize enormous returns, to the detriment of issuers. Junk bonds are normally not prepayable for an initial period (three to five years), and thereafter only prepayable at a premium.

The main purpose of junk bonds is to provide mezzanine financing for acquisition transactions, filling in the gap between senior secured debt, which pays a lower interest rate, and the seller's takeback financing or the buyer's equity financing, which is the last to be paid back. There is sometimes more than one layer of junk debt—one being senior subordinated and the other junior subordinated debt.

In 1997, $120 billion in new junk bond issues came to market—an all time record. As we go to press in 1998, current trends promise another record-breaking year.[21]

To whom and how are junk bonds sold?

They are commonly sold to large financial institutions—insurance companies, pension funds, and mutual funds, including overseas investors—usually in blocks of $500,000 or more—and are primarily for the sophisticated investor. Funds that invest in junk bonds often attract supersophisticated money managers, who are known to go in and out of the junk bond market rapidly, causing volatility in prices.[22] Often, but not necessarily, the offerings are registered under the federal securities laws to increase their marketability and are sold in a package with warrants to acquire common stock in the target. If they are privately placed, they often carry registration rights that will enable the holders to require the borrower to register the debt for sale in a public offering. (See the discussion of registration rights below.)

How do the warrants relate to the junk bonds?

The junk bonds offer some of the same high-risk/high-reward characteristics of equity, and it is a natural combination to offer them together with an "equity kicker" in the form of warrants. Warrants are rights to buy stock from the company at a specified price for a future period of time. Frequently, the institutions buying the bonds sell the warrants (sometimes back to the underwriter), thereby obtaining the junk bonds at a discount.

What is a bond indenture?

The indenture is the basic agreement setting forth the terms of the junk bonds and is entered into between the borrower and a bank, acting as trustee for the bondholders. It serves the same function as the credit or loan agreement executed with the senior secured lender and the note purchase agreement executed with an institutional mezzanine lender. The indenture contains the covenants, events of default, and other material terms of the transaction, including the various responsibilities and rights of the issuer, trustee, and bondholders. If the bonds are issued or subsequently sold pursuant to a public offering, the indenture must qualify under the Trust Indenture Act of 1939. Much of the boilerplate in the indenture is derived from requirements under that law.

The principal objectives of the indenture's covenants are:

- To prevent disposition of the assets of the borrower (unless the sale proceeds are reinvested in assets used in the same business by the borrower or used to pay off the junk bonds or senior debt)
- To ensure that if any merger, consolidation, or change of the borrower occurs, the successor entity is obligated to repay the bonds on the same terms and is in as strong a financial position after the transaction as before
- To limit the creation of additional debt and liens (particularly secured debt senior to the bonds)
- To limit payments of dividends and distributions to stockholders ("restricted payments")
- To restrict transactions with affiliates

What covenants do junk bonds normally contain?

Compared with senior debt agreements, unsecured junk bond indentures are simpler, fitting the classic bond indenture mold. Unlike senior debt instruments, which provide for total information flow to lenders, hair-trigger default provisions, and, in theory, extensive second-guessing and approval of management decisions, junk bond indentures tend to rely more on the borrower's good judgment and the value of the company as a going concern and limit themselves to protecting against major restructurings or asset transfers or increases in amounts of senior or secured debt. This difference in approach reflects the longer-term nature of such debt and the impracticality of obtaining consents from a large, diverse group of public bondholders. In the very rare case that the junk bonds are secured, however, a more elaborate set of covenants relating to the protection of collateral will be included.

Generally, borrowers should try to limit the financial covenants in junk bond issues to "incurrence" tests rather than "maintenance" tests. In other words, the covenants should not require that any specified level of financial health be maintained and should be breachable only by a voluntary act, such as (these are the four normal circumstances) paying a prohibited dividend, incurring prohibited debt, merging or combining with another company or selling assets unless certain tests are met, or dealing with affiliates other than at arm's length. These covenants will often closely restrict operating subsidiaries of the borrower to ensure that all debt is incurred on the same corporate level.

In many transactions the covenants go much further. They may include detailed financial maintenance covenants relating to net worth, current ratios, interest coverage and the like, limitations on investments, and application of asset sale proceeds.

Which bond covenants are particularly subject to negotiation?

The following key issues should be covered in the indenture:

- *Restrictions on mergers and asset sales.* There are a variety of such restrictions. The most onerous require that the surviving entity in the merger or the purchaser of all or substantially all the assets have a net worth not lower than the borrower had before the merger and that the fixed charge coverage ratios [generally the ratio of debt payments to cash flow (pre-debt service)] equal a certain percentage of the ratio that pertained before the merger. The effect of this type of provision is to preclude a sale of the business in an LBO that will cause a material increase in total debt of the company after the merger. The borrower thus has fewer means available for disposing of the business.

  Some indentures require the borrower to offer to prepay junior debt from asset sale proceeds that are not used to prepay senior debt. (It must be an "offer" because the debt is usually not prepayable without the consent of the lender.) Senior lenders object to this provision because they believe that it may be necessary for the proceeds to be left in the business, particularly if there is trouble and the asset sale was used to gain needed liquidity for the business. The dispute can usually be solved by allowing, until the senior lender is paid in full, a limited amount of such proceeds to be left in the business before a prepayment offer must be made.

A borrower should always check in advance to learn what the investment banker's standard format is (best done by reviewing indentures from previous transactions). Once you've locked in with an investment banker, you'll hear over and over again that it can't market the debt without the restrictions it is used to. Be prepared with examples of other junk debt with less onerous provisions. If you have any specific plans to sell off assets, be sure they don't violate this provision.

- *Debt incurrence.* Many junk bond indentures have very tight restrictions on debt incurrence by the issuer. The simplest form of restriction is that the issuer cannot issue "sandwich debt" or "interlayered debt," that is, debt subordinated to the senior debt but senior to the junk debt. This restriction allows the issuer to borrow as much senior debt or debt junior to the junk debt as the lenders are willing to lend. The holders of the junk debt are relying on the limitations senior lenders will place on the amount of senior debt that can be incurred.

  Other types of restrictions limit the incurrence of debt to a percentage of the original amount of debt or require the achievement of certain financial ratios before incurring additional debt. The ratios, and any particular provisions necessary for a particular business plan, are all subject to negotiation with the lender. The senior lender will want the borrower to be able to incur new senior debt somewhat in excess of the unpaid amount of the existing senior debt in order to permit minor workout arrangements and to finance some expansion.

- *Restrictions on prepayments.* Most junk bonds preclude prepayments for several (often five) years and thereafter may permit prepayments only on payment of substantial premiums. This restriction is not as troublesome if the covenants in respect of mergers and debt incurrence are not too strict. A long nonprepayment period means that the issuer can't rid itself of the debt except through defeasance of the bonds, if the covenants become too burdensome.

- *Subordination provisions.* See below under the heading "Subordination Issues."

- *Restricted payments.* These restrictions prohibit dividends and other distributions as well as stock redemptions unless specified conditions are satisfied. The conditions usually prevent payments until a specified minimum net worth level has been attained; thereafter, payments may not exceed a certain percentage (25 to 50 percent) of accumulated net income.

    Be careful of this provision; it may have the effect of precluding a sale of the company through an LBO unless the junk bonds are also prepaid. Such a buyout normally requires the borrower, or a successor obligor under the junk bond indenture, to borrow the acquisition debt and pay the proceeds to the target's shareholders. Such payments probably constitute a restricted payment that may not be made unless the tests are satisfied (and in most such cases they won't be). Even if all the other tests for the merger are satisfied (such as net worth and coverage ratios), this test may present another and often insurmountable hurdle.

But won't it be possible to just waive these covenants if they prove to be too restrictive?

No. Prepaying the junk bonds will likely be either impossible or very expensive because of prepayment restrictions and penalties. In addition, unlike the case of senior lenders, it is often impossible, or at the least very difficult, to obtain waivers of covenants from a multitude of public bondholders. Therefore, the restrictions contained in the junk bond indenture should be something the borrower can live with for a long time. Special care must be taken to ensure that the covenants fit the long-term plans of the company with respect to acquisitions, dispositions of assets, expansions, and so on. Once the covenants are in place, you'll have to live with them pretty much unmodified.

From the point of view of bondholders, how have junk bonds been performing?

The junk bond market took off in the mid-to-late 1980s, dropped precipitously in the very late 1980s and early 1990s, and have been headed toward a middle course in the 1990s.[23] Interest rates also play a part in junk bond demand: Low rates increase the appeal of junk bonds' high potential return.[24] Within these general trends, individual junk bond issues respond to specific company events or rumors, and these in turn cause variations in the market for junk bonds.

What about default rates for junk bonds?

It varies over time, with a very *low chance* of default for a year or so, then a *higher likelihood* in years three and four, and then a *decreasing chance* after four years.[25]

What is a quasi-junk bond?

A bond that gets a split rating—where one credit rating service gives it a second-tier rating and another grades it at the third tier.[26]

What recourse do bondholders have in the event of poor bond performance?

Creditor lawsuits against parties involved in failed LBOs have targeted numerous parties, including issuers of junk bonds. Many of these cases are filed under state fraudulent conveyance laws. Few are brought to trial. Many are settled out of court.[27] Junk bondholders often have a say in restructuring or changes of control.[28]

Is there ever insider trading in junk bonds?

Some investors believe there is widespread insider trading—trading based on material nonpublic information—in various debt securities including junk bonds, municipal bonds, government securities, commodities, and futures. A common symptom of such trading, often seen in junk bonds, is a sharp increase in price prior to a positive announcement. Investigation, pursuit, and punishment of such trading has been limited to date, though, because the federal agency with explicit authority to go after insider trading in securities—the SEC—fears that it may not have jurisdiction to pursue such cases. There are also detection problems. Junk bond trading, done only over the counter, is more difficult to track than equity trades, which occur on the major stock exchanges.

BRIDGE LOANS

Underwriters will sometimes offer a buyer immediate short-term financing for an acquisition in exchange for the right to replace that financing with a later junk bond issue. Junk bond bridge lending began as a marketing device for underwriters trying to break into the market dominated by Drexel. Drexel's practice had been to issue "highly confident" letters stating that it had reviewed a transaction and was sure that it could place the financing. Bridge loan financing gained popularity initially in 1986, during the year-end rush to beat the new tax law deadline, and thereafter, prior to the October 1987 stock market drop, because it met the needs of buyers for immediate funding in situations in which a rapid private placement of junk bond debt was not possible and there was not time before the acquisition closing for the lengthy process of registering the bonds for public sale.

The risk in bridge lending is that the market will go sour before the loan is repaid and the bonds are sold, which in fact happened in October 1987. For a three-month period following the crash, interest rates rose to over 17 percent, and many deals could not be financed. A similar pattern of events occurred in late 1989.[29] Nevertheless, the market recovered thereafter, and despite subsequent market downturns (as recently as late 1998), bridge loans are still being made.

What should the interest rate on the bridge loan be?

The interest rate on the bridge loan, being short-term financing, should initially be 5 to 8 points over the Treasury or federal funds rate, lower than the expected rate on the junk bonds that will be sold to repay the bridge loan. This rate should rise by 0.5 percent or more per annum if the underwriter cannot refinance the bridge loan in a three- to six-month period. The increasing interest rate compensates the underwriter for the bridge financing risk, as does a warrant for a small amount (normally 3 to 5 percent) of the common stock of the target. The underwriter will also receive substantial fees: commonly 2 percent—1 percent upon execution of a commitment letter for the bridge loan and another 1 percent or more when the loan is funded.

What issues arise in the negotiation of a bridge loan/junk bond financing?

The bridge lender is most concerned about ensuring that it will be able to market the refinancing debt, that is, the junk debt that will be used to repay its loan. Thus, it will seek to clarify in advance any potential issue that could arise with the borrower or with other lenders. The bridge lender will also seek utmost flexibility in the terms of the refinancing debt that it can offer (for example, interest rate and equity kickers such as warrants) and will further require that the borrower use its best efforts to get the offering done as soon as possible. The bridge lender's prime concern is to get its debt refinanced, and it will seek to build into the contract strong incentives to motivate the borrower toward that end.

The borrower, on the other hand, wants to be sure, if possible, that its permanent mezzanine debt is borrowed on terms it can repay. The borrower should seek to place limits on the terms of the refinancing debt and also to ensure that the bridge lender's debt will roll over into longer-term debt if the refinancing debt can't be placed.

These general concerns are reflected in the following specific points of negotiation:

- *The term of the bridge loan.* In many cases, the bridge loan falls due at the end of a fixed period, usually three to nine months. If the refinancing debt is not placed by then, the bridge loan is in default. The senior lenders are often unwilling to accept this risk, and the borrower should be concerned as well. The refinancing debt may not be marketable on reasonable terms even though the company is doing extremely well; the problem may simply be a temporary downturn of the markets or in the marketing efforts of the bridge lender. The other parties will have made financial commitments based on the confidence level of the investment banker that the refinancing debt would be available.

  For the foregoing reasons, the bridge lender can often be persuaded (particularly in a competitive environment) to commit to a longer-term investment if the refinancing debt doesn't get placed. This often takes the form of a "rollover" provision where the terms of the note change after the maturity date and it becomes long-term subordinated debt with covenants and other provisions, similar to subordinated junk debt. Another technique is to cast the original bridge note as a long-term note that the borrower is obligated to prepay with the proceeds of the refinancing debt or other cash proceeds such as equity offerings. In either case, the extended bridge note will have higher than normal, or increasing, interest rates to encourage refinancing of the bridge debt at the earliest possible time.

- *The terms of the refinancing debt.* The borrower should obtain reasonable limits on the terms of the refinancing debt that it will be obligated to accept. The usual formulation is something like "at prevailing market rates and terms," subject to limitations on the interest rate, the term, scheduled principal payments, and the amount of equity that the purchasers of the refinancing debt will be entitled to receive. The borrower may seek a limitation on the amount of cash interest payable annually or, alternatively, on the average yield on the instrument, although it is difficult to bar access of the bridge lender to takeout financing, even if there has been a major interest rate move in the market. The senior lender also will be interested in ensuring that the terms of the refinancing debt don't violate its expectations about coverage ratios and limits on other indebtedness.

- *The covenants and events of default of the bridge loan.* The senior lender and the borrower will generally try to make the bridge loan covenants, events of default, and subordination provisions similar to the refinancing debt that will take out the bridge loan. They resist, often successfully, attempts by the bridge lender to make the bridge loan agreement a tighter, restrictive document or to have the bridge lender ride on the covenants of the senior lender. Avoidance of overly tight default triggers is especially important where the obligation of the bridge lender to sell the refinancing debt is conditioned on absence of a default under the bridge note. The tighter the covenants, the greater the risk of a default that could prevent the rollover into the longer-term note and thus could put the company into a financial crisis soon after the acquisition.

EQUITY INVESTMENT FUNDS

What is an equity investment fund?

An *equity investment* fund is a type of financing vehicle often used to provide the mezzanine level of financing in a management buyout or business recapitalization. The fund raises equity capital from private investors and uses the capital to make equity and subordinated debt investments in a portfolio of companies. In return for their capital, investors in an investment fund typically receive income from the debt the fund provides to its portfolio and the potential for capital appreciation from the fund's equity investments.

The dominant players have been Forstmann Little and Kohlberg Kravis Roberts (KKR), but there have been others—notably Adler & Shaykin, Blackstone Group, Clayton & Dubelier, Fieldston Investors, Foreman Associates, Hicks Muse Tate & Furst, Kelso & Co., and Warburg Pincus Investors. Other funds may be organized for specific deals.[30] Also, many brokerage firms, Merrill Lynch, Morgan Stanley, and brokerage units of Citigroup, have organized funds.

How are investment funds structured?

Generally, investment funds are organized as limited partnerships.[31] The interests in the partnerships are considered securities under federal and state securities laws and, consequently, are offered and sold in a registered public offering or in reliance on an exemption from the registration requirements.

Most commonly, the investment funds have been marketed to a limited number of sophisticated, wealthy individuals; financial institutions; and public and private pension funds in a private placement offering.[32] Investors typically pay millions (or even 10s of millions) to participate. Proceeds of the offering are used by the investment fund to acquire common equity, preferred stock, and subordinated debt in a series of management buyouts.

Do investment funds generally make majority investments?

They have done so traditionally, but in the early 1990s, following a drop in available bank financing, many began to take on minority investments.[33]

How do the fund investors share in the benefits of the investment?

Fund investors do not directly own any stock or other interests in the company to be acquired. Instead, each participant, or investor, in an investment fund contributes capital to each acquisition vehicle formed and will become a limited partner in the acquisition vehicle, receiving a return on investment in accordance with the partnership agreement. For example, in two private funds sponsored by Forstmann Little & Co. and KKR, respectively, the general partner receives 20 percent of the realized profits from the investments made by the fund, and the remaining balance is distributed to the limited partners. In certain public funds, income and gain may be distributed 99 percent to the limited partners and 1 percent to the general partner until the limited partners have received distributions of an amount equal to a 10 percent cumulative annual return on their capital contributions. Thereafter, the general partner is permitted to take a larger share of the profits.

Are the acquisitions in which the fund will invest identified in advance?

No. Investment funds are typically structured as "blind pools," meaning that the portfolio of companies in which a fund will invest will not be identified or known at the time each investor purchases an interest in the fund. The general partner of the fund will have complete discretion in selecting the companies in which the fund will invest. Generally, the funds do not invest in companies where management is opposed to the acquisition.

What kind of time frame and returns can an investor in an equity fund expect?

Private investment funds are often structured so that each investor enters into a commitment—for an average period of five to six years—to make a capital contribution upon the request of the general partner. Investors have control over and use of their capital until it is actually invested in a particular acquisition vehicle upon request of the general partner.

Returns on equity fund investments vary, especially between equity and debt investors.[34]

What other investments do funds make besides mezzanine and equity financing?

Occasionally, an investment fund will provide bridge financing rather than mezzanine financing. Bridge financing is provided for a short term, typically nine months or less, to supply funds during the interim period before permanent financing is arranged. After the bridge loan is repaid, the fund remains with an equity interest in the acquired company and can roll the loan proceeds over into another acquisition.

In addition, investment funds may be structured to allow the fund to use its capital to finance a friendly tender offer for stock of a publicly held company whereby 51 percent of the stock is acquired in the tender offer and the remaining stock is acquired in a cash merger. This structure permits leveraged purchases of public companies, despite the margin requirements that prohibit acquisition financing secured by more than 50 percent of the value of the securities acquired. The initial 51 percent of the stock acquired in the tender offer is financed half by borrowings and half by equity from the fund. When the cash merger occurs, the additional financing can be supported by the assets of the target, and all or a part of the initial equity investment can be repaid.

What regulatory controls are imposed on investment funds?

The principal regulatory control is the Investment Company Act of 1940, a particularly complex statute that is for experts only. It is likely to apply to any investment fund that raises money from the public and uses the proceeds primarily to acquire securities of other companies, other than operating subsidiaries held and managed in a classic holding company manner. The law prohibits dealing with affiliates, requires a primarily equity-based capital structure, and imposes various public reporting and fiduciary obligations on the fund's principals. To avoid the effect of the law, most leveraged buyout funds raise their capital from private placements.

Equity funds that are structured as limited partnerships are subject to a growing body of state and federal law governing these structures.[35]

A word of warning: Anyone who is in the business of buying companies, holding them for a short term (particularly less than two years), and selling them, all without actively engaging in their day-to-day management, should check to be sure he or she is not subject to regulation under the Investment Company Act. Problems can arise even if no investment fund is involved, especially if the buyer uses the proceeds of publicly held junk bonds for financing.

What about direct investment from state pension funds or other state sources?

This is rare. Pension funds usually invest in the financial transactions listed above. In some cases, however, funds do make direct investments in transactions that could benefit their states. The Kansas Public Employees Retirement System state pension fund is known to make such investments. The state of Minnesota loaned Northwest Airlines $740 million for expansion in late 1991, boosting the fortunes of Northwest's parent company, NWA Inc., which had gone private in 1989.

How do small business investment corporations work?

These usually make investments in start-ups and are not a major source of m/a/b financing. Small Business Investment Companies (SBICs), a creation of the Small Business Administration, have been compared with savings and loan institutions because of their high rate of failure.[36]

SELLER TAKEBACK FINANCING

Many leveraged acquisitions involve some by the seller of debt or stock. This is particularly likely to occur if the seller is a major corporation divesting a minor operation. If debt is taken back, it may be structured as a simple installment sale (see Exhibit 4-1 later in this chapter), or it may involve accompanying warrants. In either case, the claims of the seller are generally junior to those of other creditors, such as the senior lenders to the buyer. A seller takeback is not always possible. In particular, it may be necessary to pay stockholders of publicly held companies the acquisition price entirely in cash because of the delays and disclosures involved in offering them debt or other securities that require a prospectus registered under federal securities laws.

Why do sellers consider takeback financing, including junior class financing?

Sellers are generally reluctant to take back stock or debt that is junior to all other debt. Still, a seller benefits from such subordinated financing by receiving an increased purchase price, at least nominally, and obtaining an equity kicker or its equivalent. The seller may well be aware, and should be prepared to face the fact, that the note or stock will realize full value only if the acquired company prospers, and that there is a real risk that this part of the purchase price will never be paid.

By the same token, however, the upside potential that the seller can realize if the transaction is successful can be much greater than it could receive if no part of its purchase price were contingent or exposed. There may also be cosmetic advantages to both buyer and seller in achieving a higher nominal price for the target company, even though a portion of that price is paid in a note or preferred stock with a market value and a book value below face. Thus, for example, if a seller has announced that it will not let its company go for less than $100 million, but has overestimated its value, the seller may eventually be pleased to settle for $60 million cash and a $40 million 10-year subordinated note at 4 percent interest. The note will go onto the seller's books at a substantial discount. (The amount of the discount will be useful for the buyer to know in case it wants to negotiate prepayment of the note in connection with a restructuring or a workout.)

What are the relative advantages of subordinated debt and preferred stock?

Preferred stock has the advantage of increasing the equity line on the balance sheet and thus helps protect the highly leveraged company from insolvency and makes it more attractive to senior and junk bond lenders. Remember that an insolvent corporation cannot transfer its property to anyone else without receiving full consideration. To do otherwise would be to defraud its creditors—that is, to deprive them of access to its assets. Thus, if solvency is an issue, the seller and lenders may feel more comfortable in including some preferred stock on the balance sheet.

Subordinated debt offers considerable advantages to the seller, however. Payments are due whether or not there are corporate earnings, unless otherwise restricted by subordination provisions. Negotiators may have been told to sever completely the seller's connection with the company. Taking back a note bespeaks a greater degree of separation and greater apparent certainty that the amounts due will be paid. The seller may intend to sell the paper it takes back and can get more for a note than it could get for preferred stock. The seller may be able to obtain security interests in the acquired company's assets, junior of course to the liens of the acquisition lenders, but no such security interest accompanies preferred stock.

From the buyer's point of view, a note has the major advantage of generating deductible interest payments rather than nondeductible dividends. Preferred stock has the important disadvantage of preventing a buyer from electing pass-through tax status as an S corporation. For both reasons, be sure that if a note does emerge, it is not subject to reclassification as equity by the Internal Revenue Service (IRS). Seller preferred stock can also have other adverse tax consequences (see Chapter 5).

Absent unusual circumstances, if the buyer can persuade the senior and junk bond lenders to accept a seller's subordinated note rather than preferred stock, the seller should have no objections. If not, the lenders and seller may accept preferred stock convertible into a note at the buyer's option once the company achieves a certain net worth or cash flow level. As a last resort, the buyer may persuade the seller, six months or a year after closing when debt has been somewhat reduced, to convert the preferred stock into a note.

E X H I B I T 4-1

Installment Sale Models
Cash Requirements for 10-Year Payout (in thousands), Purchase Price = $1.0 Million[a]

Year	1	2	3	4	5	6	7	8	9	10	Cum.
No depreciation											
Gross earnings	$145	$165	$189	$214	$244	$276	$308	$350	$395	$447	$2,733
Interest	53	47	42	37	32	26	21	16	11	5	289
Pre-tax earnings	93	118	147	177	213	250	287	334	385	442	2,444
Tax 38%	35	45	56	67	81	95	109	127	146	168	929
After-tax earnings	57	73	91	110	132	155	178	207	238	274	1,515
Amount retired	75	75	75	75	75	75	75	75	75	75	750
Net cash flow	**(18)**	**(2)**	**16**	**35**	**57**	**80**	**103**	**132**	**163**	**199**	**765**
Cumulative cash flow	(18)	(20)	(4)	31	88	168	271	403	567	765	
With depreciation[b,c]											
Pre-tax earnings	$93	$118	$147	$177	$213	$250	$287	$334	$385	$442	$2,444
Depreciation (10% per year)	69	69	69	69	69	69	69	69	69	69	690
Net earnings	24	49	78	108	144	181	218	265	316	373	1,754
Tax 38%	9	19	30	41	55	69	83	101	120	142	667
After-tax earnings	15	30	48	67	89	112	135	164	196	231	1,088
Amount retired (net of depreciation)	6	6	6	6	6	6	6	6	6	6	60
Net cash flow	**9**	**24**	**42**	**61**	**83**	**106**	**129**	**158**	**190**	**225**	**1,028**
Cumulative cash flow	9	33	75	136	219	325	454	613	803	1,028	

[a] Assumes down payment of $250,000, plus balance in 10 annual installments of $75,000 plus interest of 7% on the unpaid balance. Down payment covered by $300,000 cash and securities held in current assets. Tax rates vary. See Chapter 5.
[b] Assumes depreciation of $690,000 value of copyrights over 10-year period of contract.
[c] Net worth is $310,000.

Cash Requirements for Five-Year Payout (in thousands), Purchase Price=$1.0 Million[a]

Year	1	2	3	4	5	6	7	8	9	10	Cum.
No depreciation											
Gross earnings	$145	$165	$189	$214	$244	$276	$308	$350	$395	$447	$2,733
Interest	53	42	32	21	11						159
Pre-tax earnings	93	123	157	193	233	276	308	350	395	447	2,575
Tax 38%	35	47	60	73	89	105	117	133	150	170	978
After-tax earnings	57	76	97	120	144	171	191	217	245	277	1,596
Amount retired	150	150	150	150	150						750
Net cash flow	**(93)**	**(74)**	**(53)**	**(30)**	**(6)**	**171**	**191**	**217**	**245**	**277**	**846**
Cumulative cash flow	(93)	(166)	(219)	(249)	(255)	(84)	107	324	569	846	
With depreciation[b,c]											
Pre-tax earnings	$93	$123	$157	$193	$233	$276	$308	$350	$395	$447	$2,575
Depreciation (10% per year)	69	69	69	69	69	69	69	69	69	69	690
Net earnings	24	54	88	124	164	207	239	281	326	378	1,885
Tax 38%	9	21	33	47	62	79	91	107	124	144	716
After-tax earnings	15	33	55	77	102	128	148	174	202	234	1,168
Amount retired (net of depreciation)	81	81	81	81	81						405
Net cash flow	**(66)**	**(48)**	**(26)**	**(4)**	**21**	**128**	**148**	**174**	**202**	**234**	**763**
Cumulative cash flow	(66)	(114)	(140)	(145)	(124)	5	153	327	529	763	

[a] Assumes down payment of $250,000, plus balance in 5 annual installments of $150,000 plus interest of 7% on the unpaid balance. Down payment covered by $300,000 cash and securities held in current assets. Tax rates vary. See Chapter 5.
[b] Assumes depreciation of $690,000 value of copyrights over 10-year period of contract.
[c] Net worth is $310,000.

How can a seller obtain an equity kicker in the company it is selling?

Sometimes, as mentioned before, a takeback note has the same effect as an equity kicker because it serves to inflate the sales price beyond the company's real present worth, and it can only be paid if the company has good future earnings. It is also quite possible for the seller simply to retain common stock in the acquired company. In the alternative, the seller can obtain participating preferred stock, in which dividend payments are determined as a percentage of earnings or as a percentage of dividend payments made to common stockholders, and in which the redemption price of the preferred rises with the value of the company. Some of these choices have tax significance (see Chapter 5).

What is the role of warrants in seller takeback financing?

One increasingly popular alternative to preferred or common stock is a warrant to acquire common stock at some time in the future. This has the double advantage for the buyer of not making the seller a common stockholder entitled to receive information and participate in stockholders' meetings during the immediate post-acquisition period, and of not adversely affecting the company's eligibility for S corporation status. S corporations may not have more than 75 stockholders; and—with some exceptions, such as married couples—all stockholders must be individuals. A corporate seller cannot remain as a stockholder of an S corporation, but it can remain as a warrant holder. It is important, however, that the warrants not be immediately exercisable, since their exercise will cause a loss of S corporation status. Thus, certain "triggers" are established as preconditions to their exercise. These are basically events that entitle the stockholder investors to extract value from their stock: a public sale of stock, a sale of substantially all the stock or assets, or a change of control of the target. Once one of these events occurs, S corporation status is likely to be lost anyway, and it is logical to let the warrant holder cash in and get the benefit of equity ownership.

What are the key terms generally found in warrants?

Key provisions will address how many shares can be acquired upon exercise of the warrant; the amount of the "exercise price" (the amount to be paid to acquire the shares); the period of time during which exercise may occur (which, to prevent interference with any future sale of the company, should not extend beyond the date of any such sale); any restrictions on transfer of the warrant; and any rights, discussed more extensively below, when the warrant holder may have to register shares or participate in registrations by the company for a public stock offering under the securities laws. There are also lengthy and technical provisions providing for adjustment in the number of shares for which the warrant can be exercised to prevent dilution if there are stock splits or dividends or if shares are sold to others at less than full value.

Does the seller ever receive security as a subordinated lender?

Occasionally, but not typically. The seller may take a subordinated note either on an unsecured basis or with security. Security interests strengthen a seller's bargaining power with senior lenders in the event of bankruptcy or refinancing. The collateral gives the seller a right to foreclose as well as a seat at the bankruptcy table, even if under the subordination provisions the seller has no immediate right to payment. Possession of a security interest also gives the subordinated lender leverage to initiate and influence a refinancing.

REGISTRATION RIGHTS

What are registration rights?

Registration rights are rights given to an owner of debt or equity securities to require the issuer of the securities to register the securities for public sale under federal and state securities laws, or to participate in any such public sale initiated by the issuer or another securityholder. They are key provisions of warrants, preferred stock, and privately placed subordinated debt issues and thus deserve special attention here. They also appear in stockholders' agreements and agreements with management. (See relevant portions of Chapter 5 on structuring transactions.)

Why do securityholders want registration rights?

Registration rights give securityholders more liquidity.[37] Absent such rights, debt or equity privately placed in connection with an acquisition usually cannot be resold freely to the public. Any such resale either must be made by another private placement or otherwise pursuant to an exemption from the applicable registration provisions of federal and state securities laws or must comply with the holding period and other limitations of Rule 144a of the Securities Act of 1933 (Securities Act), which restricts the amount of "control," the amounts of restricted or unregistered securities that can be sold at any one time, and the manner in which those securities may be sold.[38]

These restrictions are more than just an administrative nuisance and, because of the decrease in the liquidity of the investment represented by such securities, may reduce substantially their market value. In order to minimize the effect of these restrictions, holders of acquisition debt or equity, particularly holders of privately placed junk bonds, preferred stock, warrants for common stock, or common stock, are usually interested in obtaining from the buyer a promise to include the securities in a registration statement under the Securities Act at the securityholders' request.

Note that registration is not an all-or-nothing process: Each registration statement relates only to a particular, specified number of shares or amount of debt obligations of a particular type, and thus some securities of a company may be freely available for sale while others, even if otherwise identical, may still be restricted.

Why wouldn't the buyer automatically grant registration rights?

There are considerable costs to the company in granting registration rights. The registration process involves substantial expense for preparation of the registration statement, including the fees of accountants, attorneys, and financial printers. These costs usually amount to several hundred thousand dollars. In addition, the registration process is an arduous one for the issuing company and its officers and directors, and it requires company employees to spend a significant amount of time and attention that would otherwise be focused on management of the company and its business.

Perhaps most important of all, the buyer wants to control when and if the company goes public. The exercise of registration rights may cause the company to become a "reporting company" under the Securities Act, necessitating the filing of periodic reporting documents with the SEC and resulting in additional expenses. Through the registration process, the target subjects itself to various potential liabilities as well as a host of regulations under federal and state securities laws. If the registration rights relate to common or preferred stock, the buyer will, furthermore, not want to go to the public market until its acquisition debt has been paid down and it is sure that the offering will be a success.

What are demand registration rights?

Demand registration rights entitle a holder of securities of a company to cause the company to register all or a part of such securities for resale by the securityholder. Usually, the company is required to effect such registration promptly upon demand of the securityholder, or within some other reasonable time frame.

What are piggyback registration rights?

Piggyback registration rights entitle a securityholder to cause the company to include all or a part of its securities in a registration of the same or other classes of securities of the company undertaken at the request of a third party, such as a lender. Piggyback registration rights might allow a lender holding warrants, for example, to have the shares of common stock for which the warrants can be exercised included in a registration of common stock or subordinated debt of the company that was undertaken by the company with a view toward raising additional capital.[39] Piggyback registration rights generally are not exercisable, however, in the issuance of securities in connection with an acquisition or exchange offer, or pursuant to employee benefit plans, including employee stock ownership plans (ESOPs).[40] For more on ESOPs, see Chapter 7.

How many times should securityholders be entitled to exercise their registration rights?

Generally, the number of registration rights that securityholders receive is a function of the relative bargaining powers of the buyer-borrower and its securityholders. It is fairly common for lenders with common stock warrants or privately placed junk bonds to receive one or two demand registration rights. It is often the case, however, that for demand registration rights beyond the first demand, certain terms and conditions of the original registration rights—such as payment of expenses and limitations on the number of shares allowed to be included—become more restrictive with respect to the securityholder and more favorable to the borrower.

A greater or unlimited number of piggyback registration rights are often granted to securityholders, with the primary limitations being the time during which such rights are exercisable and the amount of securities that the securityholder can include in the registration.

What time restrictions usually apply to demand registration rights?

The company's desire for a period of stability after the acquisition must be balanced against the selling securityholder's desire for liquidity. Therefore, demand registration rights usually will not be exercisable for some fixed period of time, often several years, after the acquisition. In addition, demand registration rights are often not exercisable until after the company has conducted its own initial public offering of its common stock. In this manner the company can control the key decision whether and when to go public. Sometimes, if the company has not gone public before a certain extended deadline, perhaps the date on which warrants will expire, the securityholder can compel registration.

Registration rights should not be exercisable during a stated period, usually six to nine months, following a prior registration of securities by the company. This helps prevent an "overhang" problem—marketing of the prior offering can be hurt if a large block of additional securities is entitled to go to market in the near future.

Securities are sometimes registered by a company for a sale to take place at a future time, but the exact date and terms of the sale are not yet determined. Such a registration, allowed under Section 415 of the Securities Act, is referred to as a *shelf registration* because the securities are put on the shelf for sale up to two years later, with most of the work on the registration process already done. Demand registration rights usually do not entitle a securityholder to demand registration of its securities in a shelf registration until after the company has already effected such a shelf registration of its own securities, if at all.

What about timing for piggyback registration rights?

Piggyback registration rights raise additional timing issues, since they may be exercisable upon a registration by the company of securities of a type other than the securities to which the rights attach. A holder of common stock, for example, could require inclusion of some or all of its shares in a registration statement that covers debt securities of the company. In the acquisition context, in which the company's ability to sell debt securities during the first months or years after the acquisition may be crucial, care must be taken that piggyback rights do not create competition for the company's own offering. It is thus normal for piggyback registration rights to be restricted only to registrations of equity securities for several years after the acquisition.

When do registration rights terminate?

The exact termination date for registration rights is a matter for negotiation, but it is common for such rights to terminate under any of the following conditions: when the securities of the issuing company are widely held; when the securityholders could otherwise make use of the existing market for such securities to sell their shares without significant limitations; or when a securityholder has sold, or has had the opportunity through piggyback rights to sell, a specified percentage of securities held.

What benefits can accrue from registration rights agreements?

Registration rights agreements usually provide that the holders of a certain percentage, often as high as a majority, of the securities must join together in order to exercise their demand registration rights. The agreements may also provide that a threshold dollar amount must be reached before the offering will be large enough to be marketed efficiently by underwriters. Demand registration rights are usually not exercisable unless the aggregate offering price (or market price, if a market exists for such securities) of the securities to be registered exceeds a certain amount, which may be $5 million or more.

Without such agreements in place, the company could be forced to undertake the expensive and time-consuming process of registration for relatively small amounts of securities. Conversely, even with such agreements in place, the company can forestall an offering by persuading a substantial number of securityholders that an offering would be inadvisable at any particular time.

What amount of securities may each securityholder include on a demand or piggyback basis in any particular registration statement?

This issue arises when the number of securities sought to be included in the registration is so great that the underwriter cannot place such a large number of securities at a suitable price. Registration rights agreements usually provide that the underwriter is the final arbiter of the question of just how many securities may be included in the registration statement. In such a case, an orderly system for priorities with respect to inclusion of securities in the registration statement must be spelled out in the registration rights agreement. If the registration is being carried out pursuant to a demand registration right, those making the demand usually have priority. Securityholders with piggyback registration rights often have the next priority, the includable shares being allocated among them on a pro rata basis, depending on the relative bargaining positions of the securityholders. In demand registrations, the company is often the last one that is able to participate and thus may be unable to sell for its own account.

These priorities usually change, however, with respect to registrations of securities initiated by the company in which securityholders are exercising piggyback rights. If the registration involves an underwritten distribution of securities, then the priorities will generally be as follows: first, securities that the company proposes to sell for its own account (this is important in order to permit the company to raise needed capital), and, second, shares of selling securityholders, who may be either members of the investor/management control group or outside securityholders exercising piggyback registration rights. Such selling shareholders will generally participate pro rata according to the relative numbers of shares held by them or the relative number of shares sought to be included in the registration statement by them, although it is a matter of negotiation between the control group and those with piggyback rights as to which group gets priority.

Who selects the underwriter and pays the expenses of registration—the company or its security holders?

The company generally selects the underwriter and pays the expenses of registering securities. This is true at least with respect to the first demand registration right exercised by a securityholder. These expenses include SEC filing fees, accountants' and attorneys' fees, and expenses of financial printers. The securityholders that include securities in the registration statement will, if such shares are sold by an underwriter, have to pay underwriters' and broker-dealers' commissions from the sale of their shares, as well as applicable stock transfer fees. An open item for negotiation is the payment of any applicable fees and expenses relating to the sale of securities under various state securities laws ("blue sky" fees). Responsibility for payment of expenses of registering securities pursuant to exercises of demand registration rights (other than the first such exercise) is often the subject of negotiation. Expenses may be payable in whole or in part by the securityholder demanding registration, in order to put some limitation on the exercise of such subsequent demand rights. Sometimes state blue sky commissioners will insist that selling stockholders pay a pro rata share of expenses, particularly if they feel that insiders would otherwise get a free ride; such a possibility should be provided for in the registration rights provision.

Expenses incurred in registering securities included in a registration pursuant to the exercise of piggyback rights are usually relatively small and, except for underwriters' and brokers' commissions, are typically paid by the company.

What indemnification will a securityholder seek in negotiating a registration rights agreement?

Registration rights agreements, because of the potential liabilities involved under federal and state securities laws, generally provide that the company will indemnify the securityholders, including their shares in a registration statement, against liabilities arising through any misstatement or omission of a material fact in the registration statement and the prospectus. This indemnification should not, however, include statements supplied by the selling securityholders themselves for inclusion in the registration statement or prospectus.

A mirror image of this indemnification should be included in the registration rights agreement to provide for indemnification of the company by the securityholders including securities in the registration statement with respect to the information provided by them. The SEC and several court decisions have maintained that indemnification against liabilities under federal and state securities laws is against public policy and therefore unenforceable. In the event that such indemnification is unenforceable, "contribution" (that is, a right to require pro rata sharing of liabilities) between the company and the securityholders may be allowed, however, and is customarily included in the registration rights agreement as an alternative to indemnification.

What special problems arise with respect to registration rights of debt securities and preferred stock?

The company and the debt holders may have planned from the start to sell the debt publicly, in which case the initial placement is really a bridge loan pending the registration, and the registration rights provisions serve to lay out the next stage in the proposed financing sequence. In the alternative, the debt holders may plan to continue to hold the debt, but with a shelf registration in place so as to be able to sell publicly at any time. Under either circumstance, the registration rights provision presents no problems, and the subordinated debt should be issued from the start in a publicly held junk bond format with appropriate covenants and other indenture provisions.

Sometimes, however, the mezzanine debt has been structured to be privately held. The covenants may be tight, so that the company knows that it can operate only on the basis of repeated requests for waivers. This is particularly likely to occur if the subordinated debt holder has also taken a substantial equity position in the company and plans to operate effectively as a business partner of the company. Under such circumstances, the loan agreement with the subordinated debt holder must be completely rewritten before a public registration can occur. It will be necessary either to negotiate in advance and include an entire alternate indenture in the registration rights provisions or to have a brief, more informal, understanding that registration of the debt can occur only under certain conditions—for example, only if the loan covenants are adjusted to a conventional format for a public issue and/or the company has otherwise issued some class of publicly held securities.

Preferred stock raises some of the same issues, since a private placement of preferred stock may contain provisions, such as special exchange or redemption rights, not suitable for publicly held preferred. In addition, demand or piggyback registration rights create marketing problems when they compel the simultaneous offering of different classes of securities, particularly at the time of an initial public offering of common stock. The company should consider offering the preferred stockholder a right to redeem preferred stock from a specified percentage of the proceeds of the common stock offering in lieu of granting preferred stock registration rights. In the alternative, a demand preferred stock registration should not be permitted until a reasonable time (120 to 180 days) following an initial public offering of common stock, and no piggyback rights should arise on such initial public offering or thereafter without the approval of the common stock underwriter.

INTERCREDITOR ISSUES

What are intercreditor issues?

Intercreditor issues are legal and business conflicts arising between lenders. The major areas of difference relate to (1) subordination provisions and (2) rights to collateral.

Do not underestimate the importance of these issues. Intercreditor issues can give rise to serious negotiating problems and can even imperil the deal itself. Unlike buyers and sellers, both of which usually have a strong stake in achieving a closing and therefore considerable negotiating flexibility, lenders may feel less impelled to close the deal and may condition their participation on compliance with a rather narrow and specific set of security and return criteria.

Once misunderstandings or conflicts arise about which lender is to get what collateral or how subordinated the junior debt will be, they are often very difficult to resolve. For example, if two lenders' negotiators have sold the deal to their loan committees on mutually inconsistent bases, misunderstandings can take weeks to straighten out. Competitor banks or insurance companies, rather than focusing on closing the deal, may try to settle old scores, to prove their negotiating skills, to win points with their superiors, or to meet the not-always-appropriate standards of their lending manuals. Nothing can be more alarming and frustrating for buyer and seller than watching lenders' loan officers or counsel come to loggerheads over major or even minor points where neither lender has much incentive or institutional flexibility to accommodate or withdraw gracefully. The situation becomes worse when each lender is not a single entity but a syndicate of banks or insurance companies. For these reasons, transactions should be structured and planned to minimize and resolve intercreditor conflicts as rapidly and as early as possible.

Why doesn't the buyer simply make clear to each lender from the start which security rights and priorities each will have?

Most intercreditor problems arise when two creditors are negotiating subordination rights or rights over collateral and encounter an issue that has not been raised and resolved as part of their respective loan commitments. Consequently, solution number one is to identify as fully as possible at the commitment stage which priorities, assets, or kinds of assets will be allocated to each lender. Some areas are clear and well accepted: Revolving lenders get a first lien on current assets; term lenders get a first position in property, plant, and equipment. Less clear is which lender gets the first position in intangibles, other than those (such as patents) necessary to use a particular piece of equipment, or licenses necessary to sell inventory, which go with the tangible assets to which they relate.

The buyer may, however, choose to keep this point unclear as a matter of negotiating tactics—the buyer may not want to deprive one lender of a particular piece of collateral unless it is sure that another lender will insist on getting it. The lender may be more easily persuaded to get along without the additional collateral once its loan officers are fully involved and appraisals and due diligence have been satisfactorily completed. The buyer may also be trying to keep some assets unencumbered.

Or the buyer may simply miss the point. There is likely to be a lot of time pressure while loan commitments are being negotiated; the buyer may have landed the target by promising to close in two weeks. Furthermore, even if all the major terms can be worked out between the parties, the commitment letter won't cover minor issues, such as how much time the term lender will give the revolving credit lender to complete processing of or to remove the inventory (revolving credit collateral) from the premises before being free to close down and sell the plant (term lender collateral). Even these questions can be troublesome sources of delay or conflict at the late hours of the closing.

How can such intercreditor problems be avoided?

There are two cardinal rules for borrowers to follow in minimizing intercreditor issues. (1) Try to resolve the major issues in advance while there is still competition between potential lenders and before substantial commitment fees are paid. (2) Try for as long as possible to negotiate the issues via "shuttle diplomacy" between the lenders, forestalling direct negotiation between them.

How do you identify and solve intercreditor issues early in the process?

Prior to signing the commitment letter, the borrower should seek to obtain from each potential lender copies of its most recent executed (as opposed to draft) intercreditor documents. The executed documents will reflect concessions that the drafts will not. The documents should be compared to see which senior and junior lender has the most reasonable provisions, and these should be used as the basis for negotiating with all the lenders. A comparison of the junior and senior documents will reveal the areas most likely to create material conflicts, that is, those that could imperil the deal, as opposed to those that are susceptible to easy resolution in the course of negotiations.

If the borrower has decided which junior lender it will use and is choosing among competing senior lenders, it is often useful to present the typical language that the junior lender has agreed to with respect to the major intercreditor issues for review by the potential senior lenders. Before the commitment is made final, the borrower should seek senior lender approval of the most important parts of the typical junior lender language. The same process works in reverse if the senior lender has been chosen and there are several potential junior lenders.

Once the conflict areas are identified, the borrower must make a judgment about whether the differences are so great that the issues must be resolved at this stage of the negotiation. This would be the case, for example, where one lender requires provisions that are novel or likely to be provocative. Where subordinated debt is to be sold in a public offering, investment bankers will often insist on subordination provisions that, they assert, the market expects and demands. If the investment banker is making a bridge loan that depends for its takeout upon having easily marketable junk debt, it will be particularly insistent on the inclusion of these basic provisions in the junk debt. If the senior lender expects substantially different provisions, you as a borrower are in for big problems. Iron them out at this stage, while you still have time to get a new lender if necessary.

Nothing helps more on such a negotiation than having an in-depth knowledge of the current practices in the marketplace. It's always easier to decide to postpone resolving an issue if you know you can make the argument later to your senior lender that all or most other lenders give in on this point.

Remember that you are engaged in a balancing act between the desire to resolve intercreditor issues early and the other more crucial economic terms of the loan, such as interest rate, fees, term, and prepayment schedule. It is foolish to press hard unnecessarily on intercreditor issues before you have commitments on basic terms, when the result could be adverse trade-offs on material terms. On the other hand, great economic terms are meaningful only if the deal actually closes.

Shouldn't lenders work out intercreditor questions between themselves?

Typically, no—at least not in the initial stages of negotiation. Especially early on, the buyer should try to avoid having the lenders communicate directly with each other about these issues. The buyer will have much more control over the negotiating process if, like Henry Kissinger or Madeleine Albright shuttling between Cairo, Damascus, and Jerusalem, the buyer filters the proposals of each party. More important, there is a much better chance of reaching agreement if the buyer can formulate a compromise position and sell it to each party. This is especially true because the intercreditor meetings can involve a "cast of thousands"—each tier of lenders, the borrower, and sometimes trustees and their respective counsel, each of whom brings its own group of partners and associates. It is far harder to achieve major concessions in such a crowded environment with everyone's ego on display. If you're forced to agree to direct intercreditor negotiation, try to minimize the size of the meeting.

By the late stages of negotiating the loan agreements and the intercreditor agreement the lenders are more likely to come into direct contact; and if the transaction is well advanced and the personalities and relationships of the lenders are suitable, the final minor issues can often be resolved most efficiently directly between them. Even then, however, the buyer should be ready to continue the shuttle diplomacy process right up to the end if any of the lenders or their counsel is difficult or the negotiating atmosphere is tense.

The one exception to the no-early-direct-negotiations rule can arise when the lenders involved have worked together successfully in prior deals and agreed precedents exist between them for resolving intercreditor issues. If one lender says, when you mention the identity of the other, "Oh, is Jim doing it? Then we'll use the Amalgamated Co. format," you can relax a little. But still keep a close eye on them.

SUBORDINATION ISSUES

What are subordination provisions?

Subordination provisions are loan agreement clauses that say which of the lenders gets paid first if the borrower can't pay all the lenders. The subordinated lender (often referred to as the *junior lender*) is the one that gets paid after the lender to which it is subordinated (the *senior lender*). A distinction is commonly made between "substantive" subordination (which subordinated lender gets paid first in the event of trouble) and "procedural" subordination (when and how the subordinated lender can proceed against the borrower if there is a default in the subordinated loan). Priority of payment under subordination provisions is different from lien priority, which relates only to the question of which lender has first access to proceeds of sale or foreclosure on the particular asset covered by the lien.

What are the principal subordination provisions?

- *In the event of any insolvency or bankruptcy proceeding, the junior lender agrees that the senior lender will be paid in full before the junior lender receives any payment.*

- *Payment of the junior debt is prohibited if the senior debt is in default.* Sometimes only defaults in payment (or certain major financial covenants of senior debt) will block payments of junior debt, or blockage will only occur, in certain types of default, for a limited period. Since any major default in the senior debt can lead to an acceleration of the debt, in theory the senior lender can convert any major covenant default into a payment default, if necessary, to prevent payment of junior debt. Senior lenders do not want, however, to be forced into taking the extreme step of acceleration, which can quickly lead to bankruptcy. Much negotiation of subordination provisions arises from the senior lender's desire to keep the junior lender from (1) being paid even if the senior debt is not accelerated and (2) being able to force the senior lender to accelerate.

- *The junior lender agrees to hold in trust for, and pay over to, the senior lender any amount received by the junior lender not in accordance with the subordination provisions.* This clause, known as a "hold and pay" provision, gives the senior lender a direct right to recover from the junior lender without going through the borrower.

What issues arise in negotiating substantive subordination provisions?

- *Principal payments on junior debt.* The financing is almost always arranged so that no principal payments are scheduled to be made on junior debt until after the final maturity date on the senior debt. The senior loan agreement normally prohibits payments of junior debt ahead of schedule. A common exception to this rule is that senior lenders will often permit prepayment of junior debt with the proceeds of equity offerings or other junior debt. Also, the borrower is often allowed to prepay the junior debt to the extent it could otherwise make dividend or similar payments to shareholders. Where there are notes to the seller, the parties are sometimes able to negotiate financial tests that, if satisfied, will permit principal payments on the notes. This is especially true where the note involves contingent payments to the seller.

- *Priority of ancillary obligations to the senior lender.* The senior lender will often seek (and get) the right to have all its penalties, fees, and expenses of collection paid before the junior lender gets any payments. If there is conflict with the junior lender over this point, it can usually be resolved by setting a cap on the fees.

- *Priority of refinancings of senior debt.* A very important clause for the borrower in a typical subordination agreement is one that provides that the junior lender continue to be junior to any refinancing or refunding of the acquisition debt. Refinancing eventually occurs in at least half of all LBOs, and borrowers want to be sure they can replace a senior lender with another one on more favorable terms. They don't want such a transaction to become an opportunity for the seller or any other junior lender to make trouble. This provision is more often an issue with sellers in seller takeback financings than it is with junior institutional lenders, which tend to accept rather broad definitions of senior debt. Senior debt is usually defined in junk bond subordination provisions as any debt for borrowed money that is not expressly made subordinate to the junior loan. Seller subordinated debt is more likely to define senior debt in terms of specific debt instruments and any refinancings or refundings thereof. Sellers sometimes exclude from the definition of senior debt any debt owed to the buyer or its shareholders. Both seller and junk bond subordination provisions often will limit the amount of debt to which the junior loan is subordinated to a fixed amount, say 125 to 150 percent of the senior debt on the original date of borrowing. This limitation is designed to prevent the junior lender from being buried under a growing burden of senior debt that could substantially reduce its chances of getting paid.

- *Priority of trade debt.* This issue, again, is particularly likely to arise with sellers. Trade debt is particularly important in buyouts because in a typical LBO the buyer is purchasing a company that has been under the credit umbrella of its parent. Company management has never worried about its trade credit security because everybody knew that it was a subsidiary of a great big parent with all the money in the world, and now it has become a separate, heavily leveraged company on its own. All parties should consider at an early stage the impact that the acquisition will have on all the target's suppliers. It may be necessary in order to preserve supplier relationships that the seller be willing to remain below the suppliers in loan priority. The senior lender may insist on this feature in order to ensure that the company can retain its suppliers if financial storm clouds start to gather.

What issues arise in negotiating procedural subordination provisions?

These tend to be particularly difficult. They can best be divided into *blockage* and *suspension* provisions.

What is blockage?

The blockage provisions are those parts of the subordination agreement that prevent the borrower from making payments to the junior lenders under certain circumstances. Seller subordinated notes frequently provide that if there is any default of any kind to a senior lender, no payments may be made on the seller note. In the case of institutional and junk bond lenders, payments on the junior debt are usually barred indefinitely when there is a payment default on the senior loan, and for a limited period of time (anywhere from 90 to 270 days, but usually around 180 days) when a nonpayment default exists, unless the senior lender accelerates its debt, in which case the blockage continues. Such periods of blockage are often available only once each year.

The fact that a payment is blocked does *not* mean that there is no default under the junior loan. The blockage provisions do not by themselves prevent the junior lender from declaring a default, accelerating its loan, and, if appropriate, forcing an involuntary bankruptcy on the borrower, although the "suspension" provisions discussed below may prevent this. Such provisions are merely an agreement between the lenders and the company that no matter what action the junior lender takes, during the blockage period the company may not make the proscribed payments. Because a blocked payment will constitute a default on the junior debt and entitle the junior lender to accelerate the loan, unless prevented by the suspension provisions, a senior lender is likely to waive its right to blockage unless the company is in serious trouble.

What are the suspension provisions?

These are the parts of the subordination agreement that limit a junior lender's rights to take enforcement actions if there is a default on the junior loan. These provisions are prevalent in privately placed subordinated debt. Enforcement actions include suing the borrower, accelerating the loan, and declaring the entire amount due or putting the borrower into bankruptcy. Depending upon the type of loan, these rights may be severely restricted until the senior debt is paid in full or for a significant length of time, or they may be subject to few or no restrictions.

The suspension provisions are also important where both lenders have security interests in the same collateral (that is, a senior and junior lien on fixed assets). In such a case it is not uncommon for the junior lender to be required to refrain from taking any action against the collateral until the earliest to occur of (1) the expiration of a fixed period of time, (2) acceleration of the loan by the senior lender, or (3) the full payment of the senior lender.

What rights do the senior and junior lenders want to have if the borrower defaults?

The senior lender wants to be as certain as possible that its superior position is meaningful in a practical sense. It wants no money leaving the corporation if there is any default on its loan, and it wants to control the timing, pace, and final resolution of any workout including possible asset sales or restructuring of the business. For that reason it wants to restrict the junior lender to relatively few events of default (generally only those that are a signal of substantial financial difficulties, such as a payment default on the junior loan or acceleration of other significant debt) so that the junior lender will have fewer opportunities to force the borrower into a workout, or worse, bankruptcy. If there are fewer possible events of default under the junior loan, a senior lender may be able to keep the junior lender on the sidelines by keeping the interest payments on the junior debt current while it arranges a workout with the borrower. Once there is actually a default on the junior loan, the senior lender seeks the suspension provisions to forestall efforts by the junior lender to sue the borrower, accelerate the maturity of the junior loan, or throw the borrower into bankruptcy. The effect of all these provisions is to reduce the negotiating leverage of the junior lender.

The junior lender wants to minimize the time it is not participating in the workout and the ability of the senior lender to work out matters with the borrower without its consent or, at least, participation. It basically wants a "seat at the table" of any workout as soon as possible. It also wishes to keep the blockage periods as short as possible and minimize suspension provisions so that it can pressure the senior lender not to block payments on the junior debt. To gain negotiating leverage, the junior lender will also seek to structure the subordination provisions so that once there is a default it can threaten to accelerate its loan and bring down the financial house of cards. In actuality, however, the junior lender is unlikely to accelerate, since it would probably have more to lose than the senior lender in a bankruptcy.

What default provisions should the borrower seek?

The typical borrower is trapped in the middle. It is mainly concerned with not letting default issues kill the deal. It also wants to avoid a situation where there will be little or no time or leverage to work out problems with the senior lenders before financial Armageddon arrives. The borrower does not favor an unrestrained senior lender that can sell off all the assets and close down the business to pay its own loan off rather than live with an extended workout that offers a better chance for ultimate survival of the borrower. And it particularly wants to be sure that the seller will be tied down without the ability to compel action by the institutional lenders, both senior and junk bonds. A deeply subordinated seller is more likely to accept 10 cents on the dollar and go away—often a key step in a workout if the borrower's stockholders are to have any incentive to make the additional effort and investment necessary to save the company.

What does the senior lender require with respect to defaults on the junior loan?

A basic objective of the senior lender is to eliminate or at least minimize opportunities for the junior lender to declare a default. Thus, the senior lender will be likely to strongly oppose a "cross-default" provision in favor of the junior lender, that is, that any default under the senior loan is a default under the junior loan. If such a provision is given, it should at least be narrowed to certain specific senior loan defaults and should provide that any waiver by the senior lender or cure of the default terminates the default and rescinds any resulting acceleration on the junior loan as well. The senior lender will also wish to be sure that any default on the junior loan is a default on the senior loan; that is, the senior lender will have a cross-default provision running in its favor, so that the junior lender is never in a position to take enforcement action against the borrower at a time when the senior lender cannot. The senior lender should not object, however, to a "cross-acceleration" clause permitting the junior lender to declare a default and accelerate its loan if the senior lender accelerates the senior loan.

Are subordination provisions generally the same for all junior loans?

Definitely not. First, the subordination provisions and all other intercreditor issues are the subject of negotiation and rarely are two deals exactly the same. Second, the subordination provisions vary greatly depending upon the type of junior lender, and whether the junior debt is privately placed or sold in a public offering. The range of junior debt subordination includes (from most deeply subordinated to least) seller's notes, institutional mezzanine lenders and other privately placed funded debt, and public junk bonds.

Typical provisions for public junk debt, for privately placed institutional debt, and for seller paper are set forth in an appendix at the end of this chapter. Note that there are almost no suspension provisions in the case of public debt and very extensive ones for seller debt.

The public debt provisions are worth special note because of their prevalence in today's transactions. In almost all cases you will end up with provisions close to these. If a senior lender has plans to deviate from the current norms for blockage periods or other customary provisions, you will run into serious problems in getting a bridge loan from an investment banker. The areas where negotiations do occur are typically (1) the number of days in a blockage period (120 to 180 days has been customary) and the number of blockage periods that can occur in any 365-day period; (2) notice periods before the junior loan can be accelerated; and (3) rescission of acceleration by the junior lender resulting from cross-acceleration provisions if the other lender has rescinded its acceleration.

For how long is the subordinated debt subordinated?

Usually the junior debt is subordinated throughout its term or until the senior debt, including refinancings, is paid in full.

Is preferred stock subordinate to all debt?

Preferred stock is subordinated in liquidation to all debt. But preferred stock is a creature of contract between the company and its preferred stockholders; and if it is to be subject to payment restrictions imposed by lenders, the company's articles of incorporation should specifically say so.

In what agreement do subordination terms appear?

Very often, subordination provisions are found in the junior debt instrument itself, but in many cases the lenders prefer to have a separate subordination agreement. This is especially true when the junior lender doesn't want some or all of the subordination provisions to apply after the particular senior loan has been repaid. The borrower must be careful here because if the subordination provisions fall away, the borrower may have a hard time refinancing its senior loan. As discussed above, it is customary to expect and get continuing subordination of some kind on the part of the junior lenders.

How are subordination issues affected by corporate structure?

Corporate structure has a powerful effect on relative rights and priorities of lenders, and sometimes is deliberately taken advantage of to keep intercreditor relationships, and thus problems, to a minimum, or to enhance one lender's position against another's. An oversimplified example will illustrate how this works. Suppose a group wants to buy a retail company in the form of a parent corporation with a principal operating subsidiary. The revolving credit and term lender could lend to the operating subsidiary, secured by its current and fixed assets, except the stores. The stores could be financed through loans to a separate partnership that owns them and leases them to the subsidiary. The subsidiary can obtain its working capital by selling certain categories of its accounts receivable to a separate corporation, which would finance the purchase with notes secured by the accounts. The mezzanine debt could be loaned to the parent corporation, as shown in Figure 4-1, which follows.

Because each lender lends to a different entity, there is minimal contact between lenders and their security rights, and relative priorities are determined by the assets and corporate structure of their respective borrowers. The revolving credit and term lender to Corporation B is in the senior position, except that its rights do not extend to the stores, which are owned by Partnership D, or accounts receivable, which are sold to Corporation C. Proceeds from the sale of accounts receivable are used to pay down both the revolving and term loan and to pay rent on the stores; after these needs are met, the proceeds can be paid out as dividends to Corporation A, which then can pay the mezzanine debt.

Lending at different levels can also present state tax problems. Some states do not permit consolidation of parent and subsidiary tax returns. Consequently, in those states, the deductions derived by Corporation A from interest payments on the mezzanine debt cannot be netted against the operating income received by Corporation B. In addition, care must be taken to be sure that loan agreements and corporate laws permit the necessary dividends to be paid so

F I G U R E   4-1

Subordination and Corporate Structure

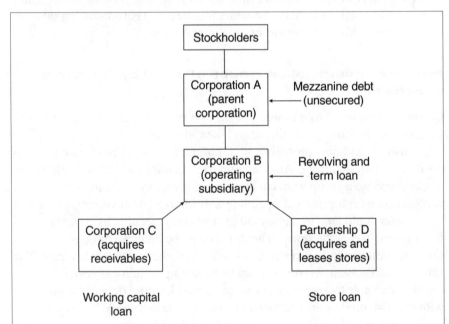

that funds can flow as required between the different corporations. (See also Chapter 5.)

INTERCREDITOR AGREEMENTS

What is an intercreditor agreement?

This is an agreement among lenders to a particular borrower to which the borrower may or may not be a party. It governs, among other things, the priority rights of lenders in collateral and proceeds of collateral and sets forth which lender or group of lenders shall have the right to make decisions about collateral. It is normally drafted by the most senior lender.

What issues are most likely to come up in negotiations of an intercreditor agreement?

- *Issues of equal or fair treatment.* When one lender has a first priority in some assets and another lender in other assets, each should have parallel rights as to priority, initiation of foreclosure proceedings, exercise of other remedies, payment for related expenses, and the like. A senior lender may seek to write in overbearing provisions with respect to junior liens. It may, for example, try to grant itself the right to foreclose on or sell collateral whether or not at market price. Such provisions should be avoided because they are probably not enforceable and raise the hackles of junior lenders.

  Preserving the form of equal treatment between lenders can be very important. In one situation where the term and revolving lenders had been at each other's throats and the intercreditor agreement was expected to be very difficult to negotiate, no problem arose because despite great differences in the quality and amount of the collateral, the lawyer for the senior lender was careful to keep the clauses of the intercreditor agreement in strict parallel—for every grant of a right to the revolving lender there was a similar (if less valuable) grant for the term lender.

- *Rights of one lender to amend its loan agreement without the consent of another lender.* It is not uncommon for a junior lender to be barred from shortening amortization schedules or the weighted average life of a financing, since senior lenders will not want subordinated lenders paid off while senior debt is still outstanding. Nor will one lender permit another lender to increase interest rates or rate formulas without its consent, because these terms may affect the company's ability to service all its debt. However, a borrower should be able to agree with any one lender to ease terms of payment or to amend covenants or waive defaults without involving other lenders. Subordinated lenders frequently require that the borrower not enter into amendments to its loan agreement that could "materially and adversely affect" the junior lender. This is a vague provision that will tend to make the senior lender cautious but leaves leeway for the run-of-the-mill adjustments and corrections that normally are needed in a loan agreement after the closing. It often provides a reasonable compromise.

- *Changes in status between lenders.* Sometimes one lender is prepared to take a lower priority against another only for a limited period of time or until some external event occurs. If one lender ceases to be secured, another lender may also be willing to release its security. If a senior lender agrees to extend the term of its loan past a certain date, the subordinate lender may demand the right to gain equal seniority, that is, to become *pari passu.*

- *Allocation of shared rights over collateral.* If an intangible right, such as a patent or copyright, is needed for realization of value for assets pledged to two different lenders, or if exercise of its rights by one lender blocks another lender's rights (as, for example, if the term lender's right to foreclose on a factory building blocks the revolving lender's right to remove or complete processing of inventory), these matters should be covered.

- *Voting rights of creditors and other rights in bankruptcy.* Senior lenders try very hard to have control of creditors' committees in bankruptcy. Although such rights may not be enforceable, they may seek to require junior creditors to waive contests of bankruptcy plans, marshaling questions and issues of interpretation of the intercreditor agreement.

REFINANCING ISSUES

Just as financing fueled the 1980s, *re*financing has sustained the 1990s. Strategies to meet creditor obligations and/or maintain creditor relations include:

- Renegotiating loan terms
- Changing or adding lenders
- Selling or restructuring assets, debt, or stock to gain cash
- Combinations of the above

Although each of these can be employed up front as a way to find initial financing, they are often used after an acquisition or buyout to pay that financing back.

How does one go about renegotiating loan terms? A deal's a deal, isn't it?

Yes, a deal is a deal when it comes to leveraged transactions, as in others, but the higher the loan amount and the more sophisticated the lender, the more likely it is that the terms of a loan can be changed, despite the numerous technical provisions discussed earlier in this chapter. (For ample evidence of the flexibility of creditors when they are hard-pressed, see Chapter 11.) On the other hand, lenders, too, may wish to renegotiate loan terms, particularly during periods of falling interest rates.

What about changing lenders?

Some m/a/b heirs do change or add on banks, but this is not the only way to "switch horses in midstream." In considering a change or expansion of lenders, refinancing teams should not forget corporate sources, including potential future acquirers that might be willing to loan funds or take over loans in exchange for an option to acquire.

How can leveraged buyers sell off assets? Doesn't this violate covenants protecting lender collateral?

Many leveraged acquirers include specific asset sales in their strategic plans approved by lenders. As long as such sales do not come as a surprise and are priced well, they generally meet with lender approval. On the other hand, the kind of wholesale dismantling of going concerns for mere cash flow purposes has fallen into disfavor even at the planning stage. One way to preserve company integrity and still generate cash from assets is to pursue sale-leasebacks. As discussed earlier, in a sale-leaseback, the owner of an asset sells it and then leases it from the buyer. A common practice in small company loans, this has also been employed in major refinancings.

Another way to raise additional capital postmerger is to issue corporate paper. (For more on commercial paper, see note 10.)

How can selling debt—corporate paper—help to pay back other debt? Isn't it just another leverage burden?

If a company can sell its paper, this can be preferable from the point of view of interest obligation. As of August 1998, for example, 90-day AA commercial paper was paying interest rates of 5.5 percent (according to the Federal Reserve Board), while the equivalent LIBOR, which is a baseline for much bank lending, was at 5.758 percent [according to Federal National Mortgage Association (Fannie Mae)].

So high-grade commercial paper issuers can get away with paying low interest rates. What's the catch? Why don't all companies use this approach?

First, not every company can achieve and sustain a high credit rating from the credit rating agencies. Second, the paper is issued with short maturities, ranging from 14 to 270 days. Issuers must find new buyers or convince present buyers to roll over their investments. This is why many companies take out standby lines of credit from banks to back up their paper in the event that they have trouble in rolling over their commercial paper lines.

What are some ways companies can restructure the debt they issue?

With so many types of corporate debt finding their way to market, opportunities to restructure obligations are limited only by an issuer's imagination—and the quality of underlying company values. Some strategies include:

- Offering to buy back debt from holders at less than its original price
- Offering to trade debt for new issues that mature later
- Asking bondholders to trade their holdings for equity

What are the chief benefits and drawbacks of issuing new stock as a means of refinancing if a company is already a public company?

On the upside, there is financial flexibility. When a company issues stock, it receives cash for it but incurs no obligation. It can seem like free money. On the downside, stock sales may decrease:

- Control of the original owners
- Earnings per share (if the "shares" denominator increases without a corresponding increase in the "earnings" numerator, EPS declines—a problem referred to as *dilution*)
- Market value (when management sells, the market may, too)

If a company is privately owned as a result of an LBO, what are the pros and cons of going public again (reverse LBOs)?

The burdens, risks, and rewards of being a public company are treated exhaustively in other sources, but the best teacher is experience. To get a good sense of the private versus public trade-off, study the fortunes of the public companies that went private and then returned to public markets. Classic examples from both Big Board and smaller exchanges include Ann Taylor Stores, Burlington Industries, Coltec Holdings Inc., Duff & Phelps, Duracell International Inc., Enquirer/Star, Forstmann & Co., Equity Coleman Co., Gulfstream Aerospace Corp., Haemonetics, Holopark Technologies Inc., Hospital Corporation of America (later merged with Columbia), International Specialty, Owens-Illinois, Perrigo, Reliance Electric Co., R. P. Scherer, Scotts Co., Stop & Shop, Toastmaster Inc., Warnaco, and York International Corp.[41]

Do refinancing methods differ by industry?

Yes. For example, in the financial services industry there are several creative refinancing techniques that are relatively foreign to other industries. Some commercial banks use a *good bank, bad bank* technique. This involves placing nonperforming and other lower-quality assets into a *collecting bank,* or liquidating trust, that is sold or spun off to shareholders. Insurance companies sometimes employ *securitization,* the sale of several chunks, or *tranches,* of securities backed by the mortgages or junk bonds held by the insurance company. Insurance companies and savings and loans can raise capital by converting from depositor-owned mutual organizations to stockholder-owned structures, in a process called *stocking* a mutual. A major insurance example in 1998 was the stocking of Prudential Insurance Co. of America. All these practices have come under regulatory scrutiny in recent years.[42]

What are some recent innovations in refinancing?

One new stock-based refinancing method used in private placements is called preferred equity redemption cumulative stock (*percs*), a security designed by Morgan Stanley. Percs offer a higher dividend than would be received in the underlying common stock. They are automatically convertible on a share-for-share basis but are subject to the issuer's earlier call.

CONCLUDING COMMENTS

Financing is truly an art—particularly when the buyer wants to put as little money down as possible. In a leveraged transaction, it takes a rare combination of ingenuity and prudence to determine the right financing structure, to pick the right lender—be it a bank, insurance company, equity investment fund, or other source—and to resolve sensitive issues such as registration rights, intercreditor agreements, and refinancing. Once again, buyers and sellers alike are advised to engage expert advisors—and to take full advantage of them by learning as much as possible themselves about this crucial aspect of M&A life.

A P P E N D I X   4A

Typical Subordination Provisions of Publicly Issued Notes

Section 1.1. Agreement to Subordinate. The Company agrees, and the holders of the Subordinated Notes by accepting the Subordinated Notes agree, that the Indebtedness evidenced by the Subordinated Notes is subordinated in right of payment, to the extent and in the manner provided in this Article, to the prior payment in full of all Senior Debt of the Company and that the subordination is for the benefit of the holders of Senior Debt of the Company, but the Subordinated Notes shall in all respects rank *pari passu* with all other Subordinated Debt of the Company.

Section 1.2. Default on Senior Debt of the Company. No direct or indirect payment by the Company of principal of or interest on the Subordinated Notes whether pursuant to the terms of the Subordinated Notes or upon acceleration or otherwise shall be made if, at the time of such payment, there exists a default in the payment of all or any portion of principal of or interest on any Senior Debt of the Company (and the Trustee has received written notice thereof), and such default shall not have been cured or waived. In addition, during the continuance of any other event of default with respect to such Senior Debt pursuant to which the maturity thereof may be accelerated, upon the receipt by the Trustee of written notice from the holders of Senior Debt, no such payment may be made by the Company upon or in respect of the Subordinated Notes for a period of [180] days from the date of receipt of such notice; provided, however, that the holders of Senior Debt may give only [one] such notice in any 360-day period, and provided, further, that this provision shall not prevent the payment of an installment of principal of or interest on the Subordinated Notes for more than [180] days.

Section 1.3. Liquidation, Dissolution, Bankruptcy. Upon any distribution of the assets of the Company in any dissolution, winding up, liquidation, or reorganization of the Company (whether voluntary or involuntary and whether in bankruptcy, insolvency, or receivership proceeding or upon an assignment for the benefit of creditors or any marshaling of the assets and liabilities of the Company or otherwise):

1. Holders of Senior Debt of the Company shall be entitled to receive payment in full on the Senior Debt of the Company before the holders of the Subordinated Notes shall be entitled to receive any payment of principal of, or premium, if any, or interest on the Subordinated Notes; and

2. Until the Senior Debt of the Company is paid in full, any distribution to which the holders of the Subordinated Notes would be entitled but for this Article shall be made to holders of Senior

Debt of the Company as their interests may appear. Consolidation or merger of the Company with the sale, conveyance, or lease of all or substantially all of its property to another corporation upon the terms and conditions otherwise permitted in this Agreement shall not be deemed a dissolution, winding up, liquidation, or reorganization for purposes of this Article.

Section 1.4. When Distribution Must Be Paid Over. If distributions are made to the holders of the Subordinated Notes that because of this Article should not have been made, the holders of the Subordinated Notes who received the distribution shall hold it in trust for the benefit of the holders of Senior Debt of the Company and pay it over to them as their interests may appear.

Section 1.5. Subrogation. After all Senior Debt of the Company is paid in full and until the Subordinated Notes are paid in full, the holders of the Subordinated Notes shall be subrogated to the rights of holders of Senior Debt of the Company to receive distributions applicable to Senior Debt of the Company. A distribution made under this Article to holders of Senior Debt of the Company that otherwise would have been made to the holders of the Subordinated Notes is not, as between the Company and the holder of the Subordinated Notes, a payment by the Company on Senior Debt of the Company.

Section 1.6. Relative Rights. This Article defines the relative rights of the holders of the Subordinated Notes and holders of Senior Debt of the Company. Nothing in this Agreement shall:

1. Impair, as between the Company and the holders of the Subordinated Notes, the obligation of the Company, which is absolute and unconditional, to pay principal of, premium, if any, and interest on the Subordinated Notes in accordance with their terms; or

2. Prevent the holders of the Subordinated Note from exercising their available remedies upon a Default, subject to the rights of holders of Senior Debt of the Company to receive any distribution otherwise payable to the holder of the Subordinated Notes.

Section 1.7. Subordination May Not Be Impaired by Company. No right of any holder of Senior Debt of the Company to enforce the subordination of the Subordinated Notes shall be impaired by any act or failure to act on the part of the Company or its failure to comply with this Agreement.

Section 1.8. Modification of Terms of Senior Debt. Any renewal or extension of the time of payment of any Senior Debt or the exercise by the holders of Senior Debt of any of their rights under any instrument creating or evidencing Senior Debt, including without limitation the waiver of any default thereunder, may be made or done without notice to or assent from the holders of Subordinated Notes or the Trustee.

No compromise, alteration, amendment, modification, extension, renewal, or other change of, or waiver, consent, or other action in respect of, any liability or obligation under or in respect of any Senior Debt or of any of the terms, covenants, or conditions of any indenture or other instrument under which any Senior Debt is outstanding, shall in any way alter or affect any of the provisions of this Article or of the Subordinated Notes relating to the subordination thereof.

Section 1.9. Reliance by Holders of Senior Debt on Subordination Provisions. The holders of the Subordinated Notes by accepting the Subordinated Notes acknowledge and agree that the foregoing subordination provisions are, and are intended to be, an inducement and a consideration to each holder of any Senior Debt, whether such Senior Debt was created or acquired before or after the issuance of the Subordinated Notes, to acquire and continue to hold, or to continue to hold, such Senior Debt and such holder of Senior Debt shall be deemed conclusively to have relied on such subordination provisions in acquiring and continuing to hold, or in continuing to hold, such Senior Debt.

Section 1.10. This Article Not to Prevent Events of Default. The failure to make a payment pursuant to the Subordinated Notes by reason of any provision in this Article shall not be construed as preventing the occurrence of a Default or an Event of Default. Nothing in this Article shall have any effect on the right of the holders of the Subordinated Notes to accelerate the maturity of the Subordinated Notes.

Section 1.11. Definition of Senior Debt. "Senior Debt" means the principal of, premium, if any, and interest on (1) all indebtedness incurred, assumed, or guaranteed by the Company, either before or after the date hereof, which is evidenced by an instrument of indebtedness or reflected on the accounting records of the Company as a payable (excluding any debt that by the terms of the instrument creating or evidencing the same is not superior in right of payment to the Subordinated Notes) including as Senior Debt (a) any amount payable with respect to any lease, conditional sale, or installment sale agreement or other financing instrument, or agreement that in accordance with generally accepted accounting principles is, at the date hereof or at the time the lease, conditional sale, or installment sale agreement, or other financing instrument or agreement is entered into, assumed, or guaranteed by the Company, required to be reflected as a liability on the face of the balance sheet of the Company; (b) all borrowings under any lines of credit, revolving credit agreements, or promissory notes from a bank or other financial renewals or extensions of any of the foregoing; (c) any amounts payable in respect of any interest rate exchange agreement, currency exchange agreement, or similar agreement; and (d) any subordinated indebtedness of a corporation merged with or into or acquired by the Company and (2) any renewals or extensions or refunding of any such Senior Debt or evidences of indebtedness issued in exchange for such Senior Debt.

A P P E N D I X   4B

Typical Subordination Provisions of Privately Placed Institutional Notes

Section 1.1. Agreement to Subordinate. The Subordinated Notes shall be subordinated to Senior Debt to the extent set forth in this Article, and the Subordinated Notes shall not be subordinated to any debt of the Company other than Senior Debt.

Section 1.2. Default on Senior Debt of the Company. In the event of a default in any payment of interest or principal in respect of any Senior Debt, whether at the stated maturity, by acceleration or otherwise, then no payment shall be made on account of principal of or interest or premium, if any, on the Subordinated Notes until such default shall have been cured or waived.

Section 1.3. Liquidation, Dissolution, Bankruptcy. In the event of (i) any insolvency, bankruptcy, liquidation, reorganization, or other similar proceedings or any receivership proceedings in connection therewith, relative to the Company or its assets, or (ii) any proceedings for voluntary liquidation, dissolution, or other winding up of the Company, whether or not involving insolvency or bankruptcy proceedings, then all principal of and interest (including postpetition interest), fees (commitment or other), expenses, and premium, if any, then due and payable on all Senior Debt shall first be paid in full, or such payment shall have been duly provided for in the manner set forth in the proviso to the next sentence, before any further payment on account of principal or interest, or premium, if any, is made upon the Subordinated Notes. In any of the proceedings referred to above, any payment or distribution of any kind or character, whether in cash, property, stock, or obligations, which may be payable or deliverable in respect of the Subordinated Notes shall be paid or delivered directly to the holders of the Senior Debt (or to a banking institution selected by the court or Person making the payment or delivery as designated by any holder of Senior Debt) for application in payment thereof, unless and until all Senior Debt shall have been paid in full, provided, however, that in the event that payment or delivery of such cash, property, stock, or obligations to the holders of the Subordinated Notes is authorized by a final non-appealable order or decree which takes into account the subordination of the Subordinated Notes to Senior Debt, and made by a court of competent jurisdiction in a reorganization proceedings under any applicable bankruptcy or reorganization law, no payment or delivery of such cash, property, stock, or obligations payable or deliverable with respect to the Subordinated Notes shall be made to the holders of Senior Debt. Anything in this Article to the contrary notwithstanding, no payment or delivery shall be made to holders of stock or obligations which are issued pursuant to reorganization, dissolution, or liquidation proceedings, or upon any merger, consolidation, sale, lease, transfer, or other disposal not prohibited by the provisions of this Agreement, by the Company, as reorganized, or by the corporation succeeding to the Company or acquiring its property and assets, if such stock or obligations are subordinate and junior at least to the extent provided in this Article to the payment of all Senior Debt then outstanding and to payment of any stock or obligations which are issued in exchange or substitution for any Senior Debt then outstanding.

Section 1.4. When Distribution Must Be Paid Over. In the event that the holder of any Subordinated Note shall receive any payment, property, stock, or obligations in respect of such Subordinated Note which such holder is not entitled to receive under the provisions of this Article, such holder will hold any amount so received in trust for the holders of Senior Debt and will forthwith turn over such payment to the holders of Senior Debt in the form received to be applied on Senior Debt. In the event of any liquidation, dissolution, or other winding up of the Company, or in the event of any receivership, insolvency, bankruptcy, assignment for the benefit of creditors, reorganization or arrangement with creditors, whether or not pursuant to bankruptcy laws, sale of all or substantially all of the assets, or any other marshaling of the assets and liabilities of the Company, holders of Subordinated Notes will at the request of holders of Senior Debt file any claim or other instrument of similar character necessary to enforce the obligations of the Company in respect of the Subordinated Notes.

Section 1.5. Subrogation. Upon payment in full of all Senior Debt the holders of the Subordinated Notes shall be subrogated to the rights of the holders of Senior Debt to receive payments of distributions of assets of the Company applicable to Senior Debt until the principal of the premium, if any, and interest on the Subordinated Notes shall have been paid in full, and, for the purposes of such subrogation, no payments to the holders of Senior Debt of any cash, property, stock, or obligations which the holders of Subordinated Debt would be entitled to receive except for the provisions of this Article shall, as between the Company and its creditors (other than the holders of Senior Debt) and the holders of the Subordinated Notes, be deemed to be a payment by the Company to or on account of Senior Debt.

Section 1.6. Relative Rights. The provisions of this Article are for the purpose of defining the relative rights of the holders of Senior Debt on the one hand, and the holders of the Subordinated Notes on the other hand, against the Company and its property; and nothing herein shall impair, as between the Company and the holders of the Subordinated Notes, the obligation of the Company, which is unconditional and absolute, to pay to the holders thereof the full amount of the principal thereof, and premium, if any, and interest thereon, in accordance with the terms thereof and the provisions hereof, and to comply with all of its covenants and agreements contained herein; nor shall anything herein prevent the holder of any Subordinated Notes from exercising all remedies otherwise permitted by applicable law or hereunder upon Default hereunder or under any Subordinated Note, subject to the rights, if any, under this Article of holders of Senior Debt to receive cash, property, stock, or obligations otherwise payable or deliverable to the holders of the Subordinated Notes and subject to the limitations on remedies contained in sections 1.5 and 1.9.

Section 1.7. Subordination May Not Be Impaired by the Company.
No present or future holder of any Senior Debt shall be prejudiced in the right to enforce the subordination of the Subordinated Notes by any act or failure to act on the part of the Company.

Section 1.8. Modification of Terms of Senior Debt.   Each holder of Subordinated Notes consents that, without the necessity of any reservation of rights against such holder of Subordinated Notes, and without notice to or further assent by such holder of Subordinated Notes, (a) any demand for payment of any Senior Debt may be rescinded in whole or in part and any Senior Debt may be continued, and the Senior Debt, or the liability of the Company or any other Person upon or for any part thereof, or any collateral security or guaranty therefor or right of offset with respect thereto, and any Senior Debt, may, from time to time, in whole or in part, be renewed, extended, modified, accelerated, compromised, waived, surrendered, or released and (b) any document or instrument evidencing or governing the terms of any Senior Debt or any collateral security documents or guaranties or documents in connection therewith may be amended, modified, supplemented, or terminated, in whole or part, as the holders of Senior Debt may deem advisable from time to time, and any collateral security at any time held by such holder or any collateral agent for the benefit of such holders for the payment of any of the Senior Debt may be sold, exchanged, waived, surrendered, or released, in each case all without notice to or further assent by the holders of Subordinated Notes which will remain bound under this Agreement, and all without impairing, abridging, releasing, or affecting the subordination provided for herein, notwithstanding any such renewal, extension, modification, acceleration, compromise, amendment, supplement, termination, sale, exchange, waiver, surrender, or release. Each holder of Subordinated Notes waives any and all notice of the creating, renewal, extension, or accrual of any of the Senior Debt and notice of or proof of reliance by any holders of Senior Debt upon this Agreement, and the Senior Debt shall conclusively be deemed to have been created, contracted, or incurred in reliance upon this Agreement, and all dealings between the Company and the holders of Senior Debt shall be deemed to have been consummated in reliance upon this Agreement. Each holder of Subordinated Notes acknowledges and agrees that the lenders in any refinancing have relied upon the subordination provided for herein in entering into such refinancing and in making funds available to the Company thereunder. Each holder of Subordinated Notes waives notice of or proof of reliance on this Agreement and protest, demand for payment, and notice of default.

Section 1.9. Limitations on Rights of Subordinated Noteholders to Accelerate. The right of the holders of Subordinated Notes to declare the Subordinated Notes to be immediately due and payable pursuant to this Agreement upon the occurrence and continuance of an Event of Default under this Agreement shall be subject to the following:

1. If such Event of Default shall arise solely out of a default in specified financial covenants, then such holders may only so declare the Subordinated Notes due and payable if the holder of any Senior Debt shall have declared to be due and payable any obligations of the Company in respect of Senior Debt by reason of a default in respect thereof;

2. If such Event of Default shall arise out of a failure to make payments on the senior debt then such holder may not so declare the Subordinated Notes due and payable until the earliest to occur of (a) the continuance of such Event of Default for 180 consecutive days, (b) the day upon which the next payment is actually made of principal of or interest on any Senior Debt, or (c) the day upon which holders of Senior Debt declare to be due and payable before its normal maturity any obligations of the Company in respect of Senior Debt.

Section 1.10. Definition of Senior Debt. "Senior Debt" means Debt which is not by its terms expressly subordinated in right of payment to other Debt.

"Debt" of any Person means (i) all indebtedness of such Person for borrowed money or for the deferred purchase price of property, (ii) all obligations under leases which shall have been or should be, in accordance with generally accepted accounting principles (GAAP, as defined herein), recorded as capital leases in respect of which such Person is liable as lessee, (iii) all indebtedness referred to in clause (i) or (ii) above secured by (or for which the holder of such indebtedness has an existing right, contingent or otherwise, to be secured by) any lien, security interest or other charge or encumbrance upon or in property (including, without limitation, accounts and contract rights) owned by such Person, (iv) all indebtedness referred to in clause (i) or (ii) above guaranteed directly or indirectly in any manner by such Person, or in effect guaranteed directly or indirectly by such Person through an agreement to pay or purchase such indebtedness or to advance or supply funds for the payment or purchase of such indebtedness, or to otherwise assure a creditor against loss, and (v) liabilities in respect of unfunded vested benefits under Plans and withdrawal liability incurred under ERISA by such Person or by such Person as a member of the Controlled Group to any Multiemployer Plan, provided that Debt shall not include trade and other accounts payable in the ordinary course of business in accordance with customary trade terms and which are not overdue for a period of more than 60 days, or, if overdue for a period of more than 60 days, as to which a dispute exists and adequate reserves in accordance with GAAP have been established on the books of such Person.

A P P E N D I X 4C

Typical Subordination Provisions of Seller Notes

Section 1.1. Agreement to Subordinate. The obligations of the Company in respect of the principal of and interest on the Subordinated Notes shall be subordinate and junior in right of payment, to the extent and in the manner set forth in this Article, to any indebtedness of the Company in respect of Senior Debt.

Section 1.2. Default on Senior Debt of the Company. No payment of principal of or interest or distribution of any kind on the Subordinated Notes shall be made at any time when a default has occurred and is continuing under any Senior Debt, and, if any such payment or distribution is made, then the holder of the Subordinated Notes will hold the same in trust and pay it over to the holders of the Senior Debt.

Section 1.3. Liquidation, Dissolution, Bankruptcy. (a) In the event of any insolvency or bankruptcy proceedings, and any receivership, liquidation, reorganization, arrangement, readjustment, composition, or other similar proceedings in connection therewith, relative to the Company or to its creditors, as such, or to its property, or in the event of any proceedings for voluntary liquidation, dissolution, or other winding up of the Company, whether or not involving insolvency or bankruptcy, or in the event of any assignment by the Company for the benefit of creditors or in the event of any other marshaling of the assets of the Company, then the holders of Senior Debt shall be entitled to receive payment in full of all principal, premium, interest, fees, and charges on all Senior Debt (including interest thereon accruing after the commencement of any such proceedings) before the holder of the Subordinated Notes is entitled to receive any payment on account of principal or interest upon the Subordinated Notes, and to that end the holders of Senior Debt shall be entitled to receive for application in payment thereof any payment or distribution of any kind or character, whether in cash or property or securities, which may be payable or deliverable in any such proceedings in respect of the Subordinated Notes.

(b) In the event that the Subordinated Notes are declared due and payable before their expressed maturity because of the occurrence of an Event of Default (under circumstances when the provisions of the foregoing clause (a) shall not be applicable), the holders of the Senior Debt outstanding at the time the Subordinated Notes so become due and payable because of such occurrence of such Event of Default shall be entitled to receive payment in full of all principal of, and premium, interest, fees, and charges on, all Senior Debt before the holder of the Subordinated Notes is entitled to receive any payment on account of the principal of, or the interest on, the Subordinated Notes.

Section 1.4. Relative Rights and Subrogation. The provisions of this Article shall not alter or affect, as between the Company and the holder of the Subordinated Notes, the obligations of the Company to pay in full the principal of and interest on the Subordinated Notes, which obligations are absolute and unconditional. In the event that by virtue of this Article any amounts paid or payable to the holder of the Subordinated Notes in respect of the Subordinated Notes shall instead be paid to the holders of Senior Debt, the holder of the Subordinated Notes shall to this extent be subrogated to the rights of such holders; provided, however, that no such rights of subrogation shall be asserted against the Company until the Senior Debt has been paid in full.

Section 1.5. Subordination May Not Be Impaired by the Company.
No present or future holder of Senior Debt shall be prejudiced in his right to enforce the subordination of the Subordinated Notes by any act or failure to act on the part of the Company. This subordination of the Subordinated Notes, and the rights of the holders of Senior Debt with respect thereto, shall not be affected by any amendment or other modification of any Senior Debt or any exercise or nonexercise of any right, power, or remedy with respect thereto.

Section 1.6. Modification of Terms of Senior Debt. The holders of Senior Debt may, at any time, in their discretion, renew or extend the time of payment of Senior Debt so held or exercise any of their rights under the Senior Debt including, without limitation, the waiver of defaults thereunder and the amendment of any of the terms or provisions thereof (or any notice evidencing or creating the same), all without notice to or assent from the holder of the Subordinated Notes. No compromise, alteration, amendment, modification, extension, renewal, or other change of, or waiver, consent, or other action in respect of any liability or obligation under or in respect of, any terms, covenants, or conditions of the Senior Debt (or any instrument evidencing or creating the same) and no release of property subject to the lien of the Senior Debt (or any instrument evidencing or creating the same), whether or not such release is in accordance with the provisions of the Senior Debt (or any instrument evidencing or creating the same), shall in any way alter or affect any of the provisions of the Subordinated Notes.

Section 1.7. Restrictions on Holders of Subordinated Notes. (a) The terms of the Subordinated Notes shall not be modified without the prior written consent of the holders of the Senior Debt.

(b) The holder of the Subordinated Notes shall not take any action against the Company with respect to any Event of Default until and unless (i) any event described in Section 1.3(a) has occurred, or (ii) a holder of Senior Debt shall have accelerated payment of any Senior Debt obligation of the Company, or (iii) the Senior Debt shall have been paid in full.

(c) The holder of the Subordinated Notes shall provide to the Company, at any time and from time to time, at the Company's request and at no expense to the holder of the Subordinated Notes, a written acknowledgment by the holder of the Subordinated Notes addressed to any holder of Senior Debt to the effect that such holder is a holder of Senior Debt, provided that prior to furnishing such acknowledgment, the holder of the Subordinated Notes shall have received from the Company such information as the holder of the Subordinated Notes shall reasonably request demonstrating to the holder of Subordinated Notes reasonable satisfaction that such holder is a holder of Senior Debt.

Section 1.8. Definition of Senior Debt. "Senior Debt" means (i) any indebtedness of the Company in respect of a certain Revolving Credit and Security Agreement between the Company and [the specific Lender], including any advances or readvances under refunding or refinancings with the same or other lenders of the aforementioned loan agreement, (ii) [specific existing long-term indebtedness of the Company], and (iii) all trade debt of the Company.

E N D N O T E S

1. Borrowed cash obtained from commercial banks is only one of many sources of financing. In a 1997 survey of 953 of its members, Small Business United found the following sources of financing for small businesses: commercial bank loans (38 percent), credit cards (34 percent), vendor credit (20 percent), personal and home equity loans (16 percent), leasing (16 percent), private loans (16 percent), asset-based loans or selling/pledging accounts receivable (8 percent), Small Business Administration loans (4 percent), private placement or stock (3 percent), and venture capital (2 percent). (Answers add up to more than 100 because multiple answers were allowed.) At the other end of the spectrum, large public companies will be more likely to use bank loans, commercial paper, or equity as sources of financing. This chapter's emphasis on LBO financing began early. The original edition of this book (1989) was coauthored with the law firm of Lane and Edson, P.C., whose partners provided much of the genius behind some of the most successful leveraged buyouts of the 1980s—notably Gibson Greeting Cards.

2. The 1980s merger boom was so debt-fueled that a mere rumor of pending congressional action on this front sparked an M&A freeze and a stock market minicrash (remember Black Monday in October 1987?). In the volatile but still bullish market of the 1990s, equity financing seems to have greater pull. The 1998 "Almanac" issue of *Mergers & Acquisitions* magazine (March/April 1998) reported that of all deals disclosing payment terms in 1997, 51 percent of all deals were all cash, 33 percent were all stock, and 17 percent were a combination. Ten years before, the *M&A* Almanac issue reported that 67 percent of all deals disclosing payment terms were all cash, 12 percent were all stock, and 21 percent were a combination.

3. Tim Loughran and Anand M. Vijh, "Do Long-Term Shareholders Benefit from Corporate Acquisitions?" *The Journal of Finance,* Winter 1997.

4. Of the first 18 companies Forstmann Little acquired since its founding in 1978, it sold 11. By the mid-1990s, the $2.67 billion it invested in these companies achieved average annual returns of 32.2 percent to investors in debt and 86.4 percent to investors in equity. Goldman Sachs's $25 million stake in the 1989 buyout of Hospital Corporation of America (now part of Columbia HCA) was valued at $162.5 million by December 1991, when it did a partial "reverse buyout" by selling shares to the public. Another success was AFG Industries. In 1988, 30 investors paid $13 million to buy 41 percent of AFG. In 1992, they made over 10 times that amount—$150 million—by selling to Asahi Glass Co.

5. For a good article on roll-ups featuring dealmaker Howard D. Ross of Arthur Andersen LLP, see "Howard Ross Wants You," the cover story in the

February/March 1998 issue of *Your Company: The Magazine for Small Business* (an American Express publication), pp. 26ff.

6. As discussed in Chapter 5, successful MBOs often include large interest deductions, aggressive write-ups, and accelerated depreciation of asset values, and sometimes the adoption of an employee stock ownership plan. In his classic study of 27 early MBOs, Louis Lowenstein found some or all of these elements present in all the buyouts studied.

7. See note 1 above.

8. *Source:* Robert Neal, Vice President, Corporate Development Group, Newcourt Financial, Parsippany, New Jersey, a subsidiary of the Toronto-based Newcourt Credit Group, the expert consulted for all leasing material in this chapter.

9. Note, however, that if the original lease is secured by the company owner's personal wealth, the lessor may be more likely to make such a call.

10. Commercial paper sometimes appears as a part of a buyout, but only as an element of working capital financing. Commercial paper refers to very short-term (usually six months or less) low-interest-rate notes, or paper, sold to large corporations and institutions. It needs to be highly secure and thus is usually backed by a takeout commitment from the senior lender and can be thought of as part of the revolving credit financing. Sales of commercial paper are usually transacted under securities registration requirements stipulating that the proceeds be used for working capital.

11. See, for example, the 12-page "Examining Circular on Highly Leveraged Transactions," distributed by the Controller of the Currency to its key personnel (Executive Communication 245, December 14, 1988), and subsequent updates.

12. The rules for the accounting treatment of leases are covered by Financial Accounting Statement No. 13 (U.S.), which distinguishes between an operating lease, which can be treated off balance sheet, and a capital lease, which should be treated as an on balance sheet transaction. Both finance leases and installment contracts are forms of capital leases.

13. For example, in November 1991 Salomon Brothers agreed to pay $29.7 million to buyers of securities used to finance the buyout of Revco D. S. Inc. Litigants claimed that Salomon did not review the buyout properly and did not disclose fully the troubles it did see. After suing that same year, minority shareholders in Brooks Group Ltd. settled out of court with the firm for a merger that had increased debt and wiped out net worth.

14. For a thorough discussion of these liability issues, see Peter Weil, *Troubled Leveraged Buyouts* (New York: Practicing Law Institute, 1990).

15. These 1991 fraudulent conveyance case descriptions are based on client memos written by attorneys at Wachtell, Lipton, Rosen & Katz in New York. More recent case descriptions came from the Findlaw Internet site (credited in the Table of Cases in the back of this book).

16. Borrowers should pay fees only to reputable institutions. Advance-fee loan rackets have proliferated in recent years. Complaints about such scams make up a significant percentage of complaints to local Better Business Bureau offices in a typical year.

17. The U.S. Court of Appeals for the Fourth Circuit recently refused to uphold a "new capital exception" ruling by a U.S. district court. The appeals court refused to grant priority to a limited partnership that had defaulted on a mortgage loan granted by Travelers Insurance Co., the senior lender. The partnership had submitted an impressive plan to bankruptcy court, but the appellate panel said the group had "carried their opportunity for self dealing too far." See James Lyons, "A Creditor's Comeback," *Fortune,* June 8, 1992.

18. The only exception was Utah.

19. "Mike" Milken, of course, is the financier who rediscovered and popularized junk bonds in the 1980s. Through him, his employer Drexel Burnham Lambert became famous—and then notorious. Rik Riklis is CEO of Rapid American Corp. Their story is chronicled in Connie Bruck's *The Predators' Ball* (New York: Penguin Books, 1989).

20. The major bond rating services—Duff & Phelps, Fitch Investor's Service, Moody's Investors Services, and Standard & Poor's—use different symbols and sometimes arrive at different conclusions. The most well-known rating system is S&P, which is, from the top, as follows: AAA, AA, A, BBB for investment grade; and BB down through D for non-investment grade. In July 1994, S&P added an "r" rating for bonds of any grade that carry a relatively high risk factor.

21. "Junk Bonds Have Grown Up," *Business Week,* May 18, 1998.

22. Ibid.

23. Even in the early 1990s, there were signs of a junk bond market recovery. According to Lipper Analytical Services (LAS), mutual funds investing in "high-current-yield" bonds funds realized a 36.36 percent return on investment in 1991, much of it in the second half of the year, when the market was rebounding.

24. A January 8, 1992, *New York Times* article, "Junk Bond and Mark Funds Excel," by Leslie Wayne, states that according to LAS principal A. Michael Lipper, "high yield funds benefited from lower interest rates, which allowed many issuers to refinance their balance sheets, and from the scarcity of new issues of junk debt, limiting the available supply and raising the prices of some bonds."

25. The latest scholarship shows a bell curve for annualized cumulative default rates of non-investment-grade bonds rated BB, B, and CCC, in descending order of quality. Studies issued in 1992 by Merrill Lynch, Moody's Investor Service, and Bond Investors Association support the bell curve idea.

26. For example, a company might get a Baa rating from Moody's and a CCC rating from Standard & Poor's.

27. In mid-1992, Merrill Lynch & Co. was faced with a newly formed "litigation trust" made up of bondholders in a failed $800 million LBO of Insilco. Burned holders of $400 million in bonds were reportedly planning to sue Merrill Lynch on the grounds that the prospectus for Insilco's junk bonds didn't disclose all the risks associated with the buyout.

28. For example, when Six Flags was contemplating a 1991 bid by Time Warner and two investment groups, the arrangement had to be approved by holders of Six Flags junk bonds issued in connection with a $600 million LBO by Wesray Capital Corp. in 1987.

29. For example, Shearson Lehman Brothers, then a unit of American Express Corp., was not able to refinance a $500 million bridge loan to J. H. Whitney & Co., the venture capital partnership that acquired Prime Computers Inc. in a 1989 buyout. The junk bond market collapsed shortly after the deal was closed, so shareholders could not refinance the loan.

30. For example, Green Equity Investors Fund bought Carr-Gollstein Inc. for $300 million in 1990. Trefil Investments, which specializes in troubled companies, made a $100 million investment in L.A. Gear in 1991.

31. Another type of fund increasingly—although still rarely—used for investment is a tax-exempt money market or mutual fund. The Federal Tax Code and the Investment Company Act of 1940 require mutual funds to be at least 75 percent diversified, but up to 25 percent of the fund may be invested in a single company, leaving the door open for control-seeking investments.

32. For a good overview of private placement funds, see Marc H. Morgenstern, "Private Guidelines—A Lawyer's Letter to a First-Time Issuer," *Business Lawyer,* November 1992. Traditionally, public pension funds avoided speculative control-oriented investments such as LBOs, but in the 1980s, as reported by Sarah Barlett in *The Money Machine: How KKR Manufactured Power and Profits* (New York: Warner Books, 1991), KKR broke the barrier and other funds followed.

33. Classic examples include Blackstone Group's 35 percent offer to Six Flags, Forstmann Little & Co.'s 33 percent stake in Whittle Communications L.P., and Kohlberg Kravis Roberts's offer to buy 17 percent of Fleet/Norstar Financial Group Inc.

34. For example, *equity* investors in Forstmann Little & Co.'s 1985 investment in the buyout of FL Industries (formerly American Electric) had made a 50 percent annualized return on their investment by the time Forstmann sold its stake to Thomas & Bets in 1991. This was in part because of a large dividend. During the same period, *debt* investors made an annualized return of about 21 percent, according to Forstmann Little executives. For an overall picture of Forstmann Little on this score, see note 4.

35. For more on limited partnerships, see Chapter 12.

36. For a sobering look, see *The Small Business Administration's Small Business Investment Company Program: A Review of Selected Issues,* a report of the Committee on Small Business, United States Senate, July 1991.

37. The benefits of investor liquidity can be seen in the case of ICF International Inc. of Fairfax, Virginia. During an equity offering in mid-1991, seven insurance companies that were ICF investors announced their intention to convert warrants to stock and then sell the stock to underwriters, who would then sell to the public.

38. In October 1992, the SEC expanded the range of companies qualified to participate in the shelf-registration process. This meant that an additional 2,000 companies, including some over-the-counter issuers, may register their offerings with the SEC and then offer their securities for the next two years without obtaining additional approval.

39. Banks should note, however, that when they provide both lending and underwriting services, they may be sued for violation of the Bank Holding Company Act. Under that law, regulators and bank customers may sue banks on these grounds.

40. ESOPs in and of themselves can be used to finance a deal. For thorough guidance on structuring an ESOP-financed transaction, see the National Center for Employee Ownership, *Leveraged ESOPS and Employee Buyouts* (Oakland, CA: The National Center for Employee Ownership, 1998). For a useful guide to ESOP-based financing from the founder-owners's perspective, see Dickson C. Buxton, *You've Built a Successful Business—Now What? A Guide to Perpetuating Your Business* (Glendale, CA: Griffin Publishing, 1996).

41. For a financial analysis of reverse LBOs, see François Degeorge and Richard Zeckhauser, "The Reverse LBO Decision and Firm Performance: Theory and Evidence," *Journal of Finance,* Vol. 48, No. 4, September 1993, pp. 1323ff.

For a technical guide to the IPO phase of reverse LBOs, see Jack S. Levin, *Structuring Venture Capital, Private Equity, and Entrepreneurial Transactions* (New York: Aspen Law and Business, 1998), pp. 319ff.

42. For a detailed guide to this subject, see Michael D. Wagner and Bradford W. Rich, *Corporate Governance of Mutual Insurers and Reciprocal Insurance Exchanges* (Washington, DC: The National Association of Corporate Directors, 1998).

CHAPTER 5

Structuring M/A/B Transactions: General, Tax, and Accounting Considerations

INTRODUCTION

The structuring of the merger/acquisition/buyout transaction—the determination of what form it will take—is often the most challenging aspect of any deal. The range of available forms (asset sales, stock transfers, mergers of a variety of types, tender offers, and so on) and the variety of relevant factors (legal, tax, accounting, and so on) provide fertile ground for the imaginative planning needed to respond to the many and often conflicting goals of buyers, sellers, investors, and lenders. This chapter can help managers determine the most efficient and desirable form of each transaction coming before them. It will be particularly helpful in structuring friendly transactions involving privately owned companies. (Issues unique to change of control in public companies, particularly hostile tender offers and proxy contests, are covered in Chapter 12.)

Although the first part of this chapter will discuss general structuring factors, it is important to recognize that in most cases where the parties have a choice about the structure, tax and accounting considerations will be paramount. Structuring a transaction as an asset sale can enable a buyer to avoid assuming the liabilities of the seller and any disputes about them. Further, tax problems dealing with undervaluation of inventories are the seller's problem and not the buyer's. Accounting considerations can also be crucial. Using "purchase" accounting often results in a stronger-looking acquisition balance sheet relative to the historical financial information, and a weaker-looking income statement in the future. Using "pooling" accounting can result in opposite effects. These two accounting methods are discussed in the section of this chapter on accounting considerations.

Do not skip this chapter's sections on taxes and accounting simply out of fear that they may be arcane or complex. They are designed to accommodate both the neophyte and the old hand.

This chapter concludes with a discussion of structuring matters unique to management buyouts, including special tax considerations affecting management compensation and special considerations for employee benefits and stock ownership.

One caveat: All tax laws and accounting principles are subject to change. In some areas, the pace of change is glacial. In others, it can happen with lightning speed. Keep an eye out for all major changes in the tax law—they almost always affect merger taxation. And *always* consult with qualified m/a/b tax and accounting professionals. (If dealing with a major law firm, remember that nearly every local office has an M&A specialist and sometimes a special department at headquarters. This also applies to accounting firms. Make sure your legal and accounting advisors have recent experience in the M&A area.)

GENERAL CONSIDERATIONS

What are the various forms that a transaction can take?

Three general forms are used for the acquisition of a business: (1) a purchase of the assets of the business, (2) a purchase of the stock of the business owning the assets, and (3) a statutory merger of the buyer (or an affiliate) with the business. It is possible to combine several forms so that, for example, some assets of the business are purchased separately from the stock of the company that owns the rest of the assets, and a merger occurs immediately thereafter between the buyer and the acquired company. Or a transaction may involve the purchase of assets of one corporation and the stock of another, where both corporations are owned by the same seller.

ASSET TRANSACTIONS

What happens in an asset transaction?

The acquired company transfers all the assets used in the business that is the subject of the sale. These include real estate, equipment, and inventory, as well as "intangible" assets such as contract rights, leases, patents, trademarks, and so on. These may be all or only part of the assets owned by the selling company. The acquired company executes the specific kinds of documents needed to transfer the specific assets, such as deeds, bills of sale, and assignments.

When is an asset transaction necessary or desirable?

Many times, the choice of an asset transaction is dictated by the fact that the sale involves only part of the business owned by the selling corporation. Asset sales are the only way to go in the sale of a product line that has not been run as a subsidiary corporation with its own set of books and records.

In other cases, an asset deal is not necessary but is chosen because of its special advantages.

- Where the seller will realize taxable gain from the sale (that is, where the tax basis of the assets in the acquired company is lower than the selling price), the buyer generally will obtain significant tax savings from structuring the transaction as an asset deal, thus stepping up the asset basis to the purchase price. Conversely, if the seller will realize a tax loss, the buyer is generally better off inheriting the tax history of the business by doing a stock transaction, and thus keeping the old high basis. What is best for the buyer may not be best for the seller, who may lose tax advantages by structuring the deal in favor of the buyer. This conflict can and should give rise to lively negotiations—and even an adjustment of price in favor of the conceding party.
- As mentioned, in an asset sale, as a legal matter, the buyer generally assumes only the liabilities that it specifically agrees to assume.

In an asset purchase, will the buyer be able to avoid all liabilities that it doesn't expressly assume?

The general rule is yes, but there are several exceptions.

- In certain jurisdictions, most notably California, the courts have required the buyer of a manufacturing business to assume the tort liabilities for faulty products manufactured by the seller when it controlled the business.
- There is also the bulk sales law, explained in greater detail below. This is found in the Uniform Commercial Code, and it is applicable

in one form or another in all jurisdictions in the United States (except Louisiana). If the parties fail to comply with that law, and there is no available exemption, the buyer can be held responsible for certain liabilities of the seller.

- Under certain state statutes, if the transaction constitutes what is known as a "fraudulent conveyance," the assets acquired by the buyer can be reached by creditors of the seller. Such statutes do not require actual fraud but can be applicable where the purchase price is not deemed fair consideration and the seller is left insolvent or without sufficient capital to finance operations and to meet its debts as they come due.

- In certain jurisdictions, if a buyer buys an entire business and the shareholders of the seller become the shareholders of the buyer, some courts may apply a doctrine known as the *de facto merger doctrine* that treats the transaction as a merger. In a merger transaction, the buyer takes on all the seller's liabilities. The de facto merger doctrine is generally not applicable in Delaware, the state where many corporations are incorporated.

- Buyers cannot usually terminate a collective bargaining contract by doing an asset sale and then refusing to honor the liabilities under the contract.

What are the disadvantages of an asset sale?

- First and foremost is its potentially high tax cost. All asset transactions are taxable, whereas some stock transactions (e.g., a tax-free exchange of stock) are not taxable.

- Second, an asset transaction is usually more time-consuming and significantly more costly than the alternatives because of legal, accounting, and regulatory complications. An asset transaction requires a legal transfer of each asset. For instance, in wholesale distribution, the agreements with manufacturers may not survive an asset-based reorganization. There might be hundreds of exclusive distribution agreements extant. The cost of preparation of a large number of new contracts is prohibitive. Real estate transfers are often subject to significant state and local transfer and recordation taxes. Such transfers may also motivate local tax assessors to increase the assessment of the property and thereby significantly increase the real estate tax burden on the company. If the property is spread over numerous jurisdictions, different forms may be required for each jurisdiction.

- Third, many intangible assets and leases may not be assignable without the consent of the other party to the transaction. Assuming the other party is willing to consent (and it isn't always willing), you can expect the other party to exact a price for its consent. This can be especially true where the seller has leases providing rent below the then-prevailing rental rates. It is possible that consent may then be obtained only by agreeing to significant rent increases. The same is true of other types of contracts with terms that are favorable for the acquired company. The loan agreements of the acquired company must also be carefully reviewed to ensure that the asset transaction will not trigger default provisions.

- Fourth, many businesses have local licenses needed to operate their business, and a change of ownership may involve lengthy hearings or other administrative delays as well as a risk of losing the license. Similarly, many businesses are grandfathered, and thus exempt, from requirements mandating costly improvements to their property under local fire codes or rules relating to access for the handicapped. The asset transfer route can require the implementation of costly improvement programs to conform to such rules.

- Finally, the asset transaction may require compliance with the bulk sales law, described further below.

For these reasons, before plunging into an asset transfer, be sure to conduct an in-depth review of all the legal arrangements of the business to determine whether such a deal is feasible. If problems are discovered, the parties must negotiate to decide which should bear the costs, such as the costs of obtaining consents. Usually, it is the buyer's responsibility because the purchase price has been premised upon certain cash flows that may be impaired without the consents. Increasing rents or other fees can lower the value of the company and may require renegotiation of the purchase price.

What is the bulk sales law, and what effect does it have on asset transactions?

The bulk sales law, subject to variations among states, requires the purchaser of a major part of the material, supplies, merchandise, or other inventory of a seller whose principal business is bulk sales—the sale of merchandise from inventory—to give at least 10 days' advance notice of the sale to each creditor of the seller. The notice must identify the seller and the buyer and state whether or not the debts of the seller will be paid as they fall due. If orderly payment will not be made, further information must be disclosed. In addition, many states require the buyer to ensure that the seller use proceeds from the sale to satisfy existing debts, and to hold in escrow an amount sufficient to pay any disputed debts.

Although the requirements of the law are straightforward, its applicability to particular sellers and to particular transactions is ambiguous, so acquirers should consult qualified legal counsel to ensure compliance when and if necessary.

Are any stockholder approvals required for an asset transaction?

Yes. Under Delaware law, for example, a sale of all or substantially all the assets of a company requires the approval of a majority (more than 50 percent) of common stockholders.

Does an asset transaction always involve a cash payment to the seller?

No. Payment for the assets can be made in any form acceptable to the seller, including the stock of the buyer.

STOCK TRANSACTIONS

What happens in a stock transaction?

The seller transfers its shares in the acquired corporation to the buyer in exchange for an agreed-upon payment. Although the buyer occasionally will buy less than all the stock in a public company (through a tender offer), this occurs rarely in purchases of private corporations—typically only when some previous stockholder who will be active as a manager of the post-acquisition company retains a stock interest.

When is a stock transaction appropriate?

A stock transaction is appropriate whenever the tax costs or other problems of doing an asset transaction make the asset transaction undesirable. Asset transfers simply produce too onerous a tax cost in any major transaction. Apart from tax considerations, a stock deal may be necessary if the transfer of assets would require unobtainable or costly third-party consents, or where the size of the company makes an asset deal too inconvenient, time-consuming, or costly.

The sellers frequently prefer a stock deal because the buyer will take the corporation's business subject to all its liabilities. This often is not as big an advantage as it appears, because the buyer will usually seek to be indemnified against any undisclosed liabilities.

Will a stock deal always avoid the problem of obtaining third-party consents that often arise in an asset transaction?

No. The pertinent documents must be carefully reviewed for "change of control" provisions. Many recently drafted leases, for example, require consent if there is a change in the control of the tenant. Other contracts or local permits or leases may have similar requirements.

What are the disadvantages of a stock deal?

There are two major ones:

- First, it may be more difficult to consummate the transaction if there are a number of stockholders. Assuming that the buyer wants to acquire 100 percent of the company, it must enter into a contract with each of the selling stockholders, and any one of them might refuse to enter into the transaction or might refuse to close. The entire deal may hinge on one stockholder. As will be shown below, the parties can achieve the same result as a stock transfer through a merger transaction and avoid the need for 100 percent agreement among the stockholders.

- The stock transaction may result in postacquisition tax disadvantages that can be avoided only by choosing an asset transaction. Under Section 338 of the Internal Revenue Code (the Code), however, it is possible to have most stock transactions treated as asset acquisitions for federal income tax purposes. Under a so-called Section 338 election, the tax benefits can be achieved while avoiding the nontax pitfalls of an asset transaction.

MERGER TRANSACTIONS

What happens in a merger transaction, and what are the differences between a reverse merger, a forward merger, and a subsidiary merger?

A merger is a transaction in which one corporation is legally absorbed into another, and the surviving corporation succeeds to all the assets or liabilities of the absorbed corporation. There are no separate transfers for the assets or liabilities; the entire transfer occurs by operation of law when the certificate of merger is filed with the appropriate authorities of the state.

In a *reverse merger* the acquirer is absorbed by the acquiree. The shareholders of the buyer get stock in the acquired corporation, and the shareholders of the acquired corporation receive the consideration agreed to. For example, in an all-cash deal, the shareholders of the acquired corporation will exchange their shares in the corporation for cash. At the end of the day, the old shareholders of the acquired corporation are no longer shareholders, and the shareholders of the buyer own both acquirer and acquiree—now combined. For federal tax purposes, a reverse merger is often treated essentially like a stock deal.

In a *forward merger* the acquiree merges into the acquirer, and the shareholders of the acquired company exchange their stock for the agreed-upon purchase price. When the dust settles, the buyer has succeeded to all the assets and liabilities of the acquired company. For federal income tax purposes, such a transaction is treated as if the acquired company sold its assets for the purchase price and liquidated and distributed the sales proceeds to its shareholders as a liquidation distribution.

Although both forms of merger convey the assets in the same simple manner, in the forward merger, assets end up in another corporate shell. In certain jurisdictions, this may violate lease and other contract restrictions the same way a direct asset transfer does. Similarly, in some jurisdictions, recordation taxes may be due after a forward merger when the buyer seeks to record the deeds in its name to reflect the merger.

A *subsidiary merger* is simply a merger where the buyer corporation incorporates an acquisition subsidiary that merges with the acquired company. In a reverse subsidiary merger, the acquisition subsidiary merges into the company; in a forward subsidiary merger, the company is merged into the acquisition subsidiary.

The reverse subsidiary merger offers the special advantage of simplicity. Since the advent of the Section 338 election for tax purposes (discussed in greater detail below), using a reverse merger to avoid asset transfer problems will not preclude taking advantage of the tax benefits of an asset deal. If certain conditions are met, the Internal Revenue Code allows the taxpayer that uses a reverse merger to elect to treat the transaction as an asset deal.

Various forms of reverse, forward, and subsidiary mergers are presented in figures at the end of this chapter.

What steps must be taken to effect a merger?

Generally, the board of directors of each corporation that is a party to the merger must adopt a resolution approving an agreement of merger. Shareholders owning a majority of the stock must also approve the transaction. In some cases the corporate charter may require a higher percentage for shareholder approval. The merger becomes effective upon the filing of a certificate of merger. Under Delaware law the approval of the surviving corporation's stockholders is necessary only if its certificate of incorporation will be amended by the merger and if the shares of the survivor issued to the sellers comprise less than 20 percent of the outstanding shares of the survivor.

The agreement between buyer and seller in the case of a merger is essentially the same as in a stock or asset deal, except that the means of transferring the business will be the statutory merger as opposed to a stock or asset transfer. (See Chapter 8.)

What are the advantages of using a merger?

The merger method has many of the advantages of a stock deal: It is simple and will generally avoid the problems of an asset transaction.

Yet a merger agreement, unlike a stock deal, is executed only with the acquired company. Although it generally must be approved by a majority or some specified higher percentage of the stockholders, it does not depend upon reaching an agreement with each individual stockholder. The stockholders who dissent from the transaction are forced to go along as a matter of law, subject to certain statutory protections for minority investors, or "dissenters rights."

In addition, mergers are the best format from the secured lender's point of view in a leveraged buyout. In this format, the lender lends to the surviving corporation (either directly or to a holding company that owns it) and obtains a security interest in the assets of that corporation; the loan proceeds are used to satisfy the obligation to pay off the stockholders of the acquired company.

Under what circumstances is a stock acquisition combined with a merger?

In certain cases a stock deal is combined with a merger transaction. The first step is an acquisition of part of the stock (usually at least a statutorily sufficient majority) of the company, and the second step is a merger with the company.

Two-step transactions are useful if the buyers wish to pay a majority stockholder a premium for its control block, a premium that generally is permissible under most state laws. The buyer would buy that stock separately and then in a second-step vote the majority stock to approve a merger transaction. The balance of the stock owned by the selling shareholders would be exchanged in the merger for a lesser purchase price that reflects the absence of a control premium. (Federal law may prevent this for the acquisition of publicly held companies. See Chapter 12.)

Another use for two-step transactions arises where part of the consideration consists of notes or preferred stock in the survivor and there is a desire to limit the persons to whom the noncash payments are to be made. The first step would consist of a stock deal with certain of the stockholders where the consideration includes noncash payments. The second step would be an all-cash merger.

This may be important, for example, if there are many individual shareholders and the distribution of the securities to all of them would constitute a public offering that would require the filing of a registration statement under the securities laws. This also may be useful where some of the sellers want to encourage a positive vote of the stockholders by absorbing the risk of holding notes or equity in the acquired company and allowing the other stockholders to receive the full purchase price in cash.

Two-step transactions are very common in public company acquisitions where the first step is the acquisition of a control block through a tender offer and the second step is a merger in which the minority is bought out. (See Chapter 12.)

What are the benefits of a subsidiary merger?

One benefit is time. Generally speaking, mergers must be approved by the stockholders of each corporation that is a party to the merger, but this requirement does not apply to a merger of a subsidiary into its 90 percent or more parent. Only the board of directors, and not the shareholders, of the acquiring entity must approve the transaction on behalf of the acquiring entity.

Another benefit is accounting clarity. After a subsidiary merger, the buyer owns the newly acquired business in a subsidiary. This has the effect of keeping the businesses legally separate and not subjecting the assets of the parent to the liabilities of the acquired business. The shareholders of the acquired company must, of course, consent to the merger.

What is the most typical form for an LBO?

The buyer usually creates an acquisition corporation solely for the purpose of merging with the company it is acquiring, typically through a reverse merger. If the buyer wants a holding company structure—that is, if it wants the company it is buying to be a subsidiary of a holding company after the transaction is complete—it forms a holding company with an acquisition corporation subsidiary. After the merger, the holding company will own all the stock of the acquired company (now merged into the acquisition corporation), and the buyer will own all the stock of the holding company.

When do senior lenders prefer lending to a holding company, and how does this work?

Senior lenders may have this preference when the real value of the company lies in a sale of the business as a going concern rather than in a piecemeal transaction. This is true where the business depends upon a valuable license, or where there are relatively few assets producing substantial earnings. The company being acquired may own a number of operating subsidiaries and may wish to keep litigation or other potential liabilities of each subsidiary separated. With separate subsidiaries, an extraordinary loss by one subsidiary generally won't taint the operations of the others.

In such cases the senior lender may prefer to have a transaction structured in a holding company arrangement. In such a structure, the senior lender lends to a corporation (the holding company) that acquires the stock of the company being acquired. The senior lender obtains a senior security interest in the stock of the newly acquired subsidiary; and if there are loan defaults, the lender can foreclose and sell the stock to pay off the debt. For this structure to succeed, all the layers of financing must be made at the holding company level.

In addition, the senior lender in a holding company structure will often ask for a secured guarantee from the newly acquired subsidiary, notwithstanding the fraudulent conveyance risks. Junior lenders often ask for a backup guarantee in such a case. This adds a layer of complexity to the intercreditor negotiations and to the structure of financing and refinancing.

What is the role of federal and state securities laws in acquisition structuring?

The state securities laws tend to have their greatest impact when the acquired company is a public company. But these laws also affect the structure of corporate acquisitions of private companies. When a buyer issues consideration other than cash—say, notes, stock, and/or warrants—or when the merger agreement provides that the stockholders of the acquired company will receive noncash payment in exchange for their stock, the noncash consideration will almost certainly be classifiable as a security for federal and state securities law purposes.

When the sellers receive securities in connection with a merger or a sale of assets requiring approval of stockholders (because securities will be distributed to them), Rule 145 under the Securities Act of 1933 provides that the transaction is an offer to sell the securities. If the offer constitutes a "public offering," the transaction may not take place unless there is a registration statement that has been declared effective under the Securities Act. These rules would apply, for example,

- Where a buyer uses a reverse merger and where the acquired company survives as a subsidiary of the buyer, and the stockholders get notes or preferred stock or warrants of the acquired company or of the buyer (if the buyer is a corporation)
- Where the buyer sets up a corporation that buys the stock of the company being acquired in exchange for cash and notes or other securities of the corporation[1]

What is a private placement?

A *private placement* is a transaction in which securities are offered and sold in reliance on an exemption from the registration requirements under federal and state securities laws. Typically, the entity selling its securities (the "issuer") will rely on the exemption from registration provided by Rules 504 to 508 of Regulation D of the Securities Act of 1933. The registration procedure requires the preparation and filing of documents that provide detailed information about the issuer, the offering, and the securities being sold.

In a private placement, a brief notice of sale on federal Form D must be filed with the SEC for informational purposes. There is, however, no federal review or comment process for a Regulation D private placement.

Recent changes to Regulation D broadened the availability of the exemption from registration by permitting up to 35 nonaccredited investors to participate in a Regulation D private placement and an unlimited number of "accredited investors." An "accredited investor" is defined under Regulation D, Rule 501(a), to include wealthy individuals, entities with substantial net worth, certain institutional investors, and executive officers and directors of the issuer. Anyone who does not fit within the definition of "accredited" is considered nonaccredited.

TAX CONSIDERATIONS

What are the principal goals of tax planning for a merger, acquisition, or divestiture?

From the purchaser's point of view, the principal goal of tax planning is to minimize, on a present value basis, the total tax costs of not only acquiring but also operating, and even selling, the acquired corporation or its assets. In addition, effective tax planning provides various safeguards to protect the parties from the risks of potential changes in circumstance or the tax laws. Moreover, the purchaser should attempt to minimize the tax costs of the transaction to the seller in order to gain advantage as a bidder.

From the seller's point of view, the principal goal of tax planning is to maximize, on a present value basis, the after-tax proceeds from the sale of the corporation or its assets. This tax planning includes, among other things, changing the company's structure prior to its acquisition, developing techniques to provide tax benefits to a potential buyer at little or no tax cost to the seller, and structuring the receipt of tax-deferred consideration from the buyer.

Are the tax planning goals of the buyer generally consistent with those of the seller?

No. More often than not, the most advantageous tax plan for the buyer is the least advantageous plan for the seller. For example, the tax benefit of a high basis in the assets of the acquired corporation may be available to the purchaser only at a significant tax cost to the seller. But buyers rarely if ever pursue tax benefits at the seller's expense, because the immediate and prospective tax costs of a transaction are likely to affect the price. Generally, the parties will structure the transaction to minimize the aggregate tax costs of the seller and buyer, and allocate the tax burden between them through an adjustment in price.

What tax issues typically arise in an acquisition or divestiture?

There is no definitive checklist of tax issues that may arise in every acquisition or divestiture. The specific tax considerations for a transaction depend upon the facts and circumstances of that particular deal. Certain tax terms and issues, however, many of which are interrelated, are far more common than others:

- To engage in useful discussion of tax matters, participants in a transaction must grasp certain terms, such as *earnings and profits* or *distribution.* The next section of this chapter will define these terms.

- A primary issue is the *basic structure of the transaction:* whether the transfer is effected as a stock acquisition or as an asset acquisition. The optimal structure is generally that which maximizes the aggregate tax benefits and minimizes the aggregate tax costs of the transaction to the acquired corporation, the seller, and the buyer.

- Another initial question to be resolved in many acquisitions is the *choice of entity* issue: whether the operating entity will be a C corporation, an S corporation, or a general or limited partnership.

- The tax implications of the *financing arrangement* must also be analyzed. Two key issues are the debt-equity distinction and the effect of the original issue discount rules.

- The issue of *management participation and compensation* should also be addressed. Top-level managers of the company being acquired may be invited to purchase stock, or they may be granted stock options, stock appreciation rights, bonuses, or some other form of incentive compensation. Different structures of management participation may create vastly different tax results.

- In addition, tax advisors should examine the *tax effects* that the proposed structure will have on the post-acquisition operations of the company. Consideration should generally be given to, for example, net operating loss, credit carrybacks and carryforwards, amortization of goodwill, the alternative minimum tax, planned asset dispositions, elections of taxable year and accounting methods, integration of the company's accounting methods into the buyer's existing operations, foreign tax credits, and the interrelationships among the differing tax systems of the countries in which the combining companies do business.

- Tax advisors should also give attention to other matters, including the *effects of state tax laws,* the tax consequences of future *distributions* of the acquired company's earnings, and the ultimate *disposition* of the acquired company or its assets.

These issues should be analyzed with an eye on pending and recent m/a/b-related tax legislation, keeping retroactivity in mind.

Does the IRS play a direct role in business acquisitions?

Generally speaking, no. Unlike certain transactions regulated by federal agencies, such as the Federal Communications Commission or the Federal Trade Commission, one is not required to obtain advance approval from the IRS before consummating an acquisition, divestiture, or reorganization. Ordinarily, the IRS will not have occasion to review a transaction unless and until an agent audits the tax return of one of the participants.

An important and often useful exception to this rule is that the parties to a transaction can frequently obtain a private letter ruling issued by the national office of the IRS. Such a ruling states the agency's position with respect to the issues raised and is generally binding upon the IRS. Requesting such a ruling is a serious business and should never be undertaken without expert legal help.

BASIC TAX CONCEPTS AND DEFINITIONS

What are earnings and profits?

The term *earnings and profits* is a term of art in the Internal Revenue Code. For financial reporting purposes, the amount of a corporation's earnings and profits is roughly equivalent to a corporation's net income and retained earnings as distinguished from current or accumulated taxable income. The primary purpose of the earnings and profits concept is to measure the capacity of a corporation to distribute a taxable dividend. If the IRS believes that a corporation, by virtue of its current and accumulated earnings and profits, *can* pay a taxable dividend, it may view certain "nonliquidating distributions" as dividends and tax them as such.

What is a distribution?

A *corporate distribution* means an actual or constructive transfer of cash or other property (with certain exceptions) by a corporation to a shareholder acting in the capacity of a shareholder. For tax purposes, a transfer of property to a shareholder acting in the capacity of an employee or lender, for example, is not a corporate distribution.

What is a liquidation?

Corporate liquidation occurs when a corporation ceases to be a going concern. At this point, its actions are limited to winding up its affairs, paying its debts, and distributing its remaining assets to its shareholders. A liquidation for tax purposes may be completed prior to the actual dissolution of the corporation under state law.

What is a liquidating distribution?

A *liquidating distribution* is generally a distribution (or one of a series of distributions) made by a liquidating corporation in accordance with a plan of complete liquidation.

What is a nonliquidating distribution?

A *nonliquidating distribution* is any distribution by a corporation to a shareholder that is not a liquidating distribution. A nonliquidating distribution is generally either a dividend or a distribution in redemption of some (but not all) of the corporation's outstanding stock.

What are the tax consequences to corporations of distributions of property to their shareholders?

The taxation of corporate distributions involves myriad complex rules, many with exceptions and qualifications. In general, however, the tax consequences to corporations of distributions of property depend upon three factors: (1)

whether the property distributed is cash or property other than cash, (2) whether the recipient shareholder is an affiliated corporation, and (3) whether the distribution is a liquidating or nonliquidating distribution.

Distributions of cash, both liquidating and nonliquidating, generally have no tax consequences to the distributing corporation, except that the amount distributed reduces the corporation's earnings and profits.

Distributions of appreciated property, both liquidating and nonliquidating, generally trigger the recognition of gain to the distributing corporation to the extent of the appreciation in the asset.

What is an affiliated group of corporations?

An *affiliated group of corporations* consists of two or more "member" corporations where the "parent" corporation controls, directly or indirectly, the stock of each of the "subsidiary" corporations. More precisely, the parent corporation must generally own a certain percentage (usually 80 percent) of the voting power and equity value of at least one of the subsidiary corporations. Other members of the group have similar ownership levels in the other subsidiaries. Certain corporations, such as foreign corporations, are not permitted to be members of an affiliated group.

What is a consolidated federal income tax return?

It is a single federal income tax return made by an affiliated group of corporations in lieu of a separate return for each member of the group.

What are the advantages of filing consolidated federal income tax returns?

The principal advantages of a consolidated return are as follows:

- Losses incurred by one member of the group may be used to offset the taxable income of another member.
- The tax consequences of many intragroup transactions are either deferred or wholly eliminated.
- Earnings of the subsidiary corporations are reflected in the parent's basis in the stock of the subsidiary, so that such earnings are not taxed again on the sale of such stock by the parent.

Is there such a thing as a consolidated state income tax return?

Yes, but not all states allow an affiliated group of corporations to file a combined (consolidated) tax return. Some states do not allow combined returns at all; others allow them only in limited circumstacnces.

What is a tax year?

Every entity and individual that is required to file a tax return must do so on the basis of an annual accounting period. For individuals the annual accounting period is almost always the calendar year. For other entities, however, the tax accounting period may be either a calendar year or a fiscal year ending on the last day of a month other than December. An entity's tax year need not coincide with its fiscal year for purposes of financial accounting. Extensive rules govern the selection of tax years other than calendar years by C corporations, S corporations, partnerships, and trusts.

What is the current U.S. federal income tax rate structure?

The Taxpayer Relief Act of 1997 preserved corporate tax rates. These are still 34 percent for businesses with taxable income of up to $10 million, and 35 percent for larger companies (plus a surtax on taxable income above $15 million). Capital gains may still be taxable at 28 percent, with exceptions in both directions.[2]

Is the distinction between capital gains and ordinary income still relevant in tax planning?

Yes. In its most recent tax bills, Congress retained the myriad rules and complexities in the Internal Revenue Code pertaining to capital gains and losses. More important for tax planning is that the Code retains various limitations on the use of capital losses to offset ordinary income. So m/a/b planners must still pay attention to the characterization of income or loss as capital or ordinary.

What is the significance of the relationship between the corporate and individual tax rates?

Corporations can be used to accumulate profits when the tax rate on the income of corporations is less than the tax rate on the income of individuals. (Offsetting this benefit is the "double tax" on corporate earnings—paid once by the company and then by the stockholders receiving the company's dividends.) Conversely, noncorporate "pass-through" entities can be used to store profits when the tax rate on the income of corporations is greater than the tax rate on the income of individuals.

How does capital gains tax fit in?

A shareholder's tax on the sale or liquidation of his or her interest in the corporation is determined at preferential capital gains rates.

How does the double tax on corporate earnings work?

The Code sets forth a dual system of taxation with respect to the earnings of corporations. Under this system, a corporation is taxed as a separate entity, unaffected by the tax characteristics of its shareholders. The corporation's shareholders are subject to tax on their income from the corporation, if and when corporate earnings are distributed to them in any form.

What are the practical consequences of the dual system of corporate taxation?

The primary consequence of the dual system of taxation is that corporate earnings are generally taxed twice—first at the corporate level and again at the shareholder level. The shareholder-level tax may be deferred but not eliminated where the corporation retains its earnings rather than paying it out in dividends. The shareholders will pay a second level of tax when they sell their interests in the corporation.

How can leverage reduce the effects of double taxation?

A leveraged company's capital structure is tilted toward debt instead of equity. Leverage reduces or eliminates the negative effect of double taxation of corporations in two ways. First, unlike dividend payments to shareholders, which are generally taxable,[3] debt repayments to lenders are not generally taxable to the recipient. Second, in most cases, interest payments are tax-deductible to the corporation making them.[4]

It is very important to remember, however, that the IRS may take the position that a purported debt is actually equity, thus eliminating the benefit of leverage.

What is the alternative minimum tax, or AMT?

The alternative minimum tax was enacted in 1969 to curb exploitation of deductions and preferences by certain high-income individuals and corporations. In later tax legislation, Congress amended the minimum tax provisions and created a rather severe regime of alternative minimum tax, particularly for corporations. The *alternative minimum tax* for both individuals and corporations is determined by computing taxable income under the regular method (with certain adjustments) and then adding back certain deductions or "preferences" to obtain alternative minimum taxable income. To this amount is applied the alternative minimum tax rate for individuals or for corporations. The taxpayer is required to pay the greater of the regular tax or the alternative minimum tax. The 1997 tax law repealed the alternative minimum tax for small businesses for taxable years beginning after December 31, 1997.[5] For the purpose of the new law, a small business is a corporation that had average annual income of less than $5 million in its first taxable year after December 31, 1996, and less than $7.5 million for taxable years thereafter.[6]

What is the General Utilities rule?

Under the dual system of taxation, corporate earnings from the sale of appreciated property are taxed twice, first to the corporation when the sale occurs and then to the shareholders upon the distribution of the net proceeds. A long-standing exception to this system was the so-called General Utilities rule. Named after a 1935 Supreme Court decision, this rule permitted nonrecognition of gain to corporations upon certain distributions to shareholders of appreciated property.

The breadth of the General Utilities rule was narrowed over the years, both statutorily and judicially. In the Tax Reform Act of 1986, Congress repealed the rule entirely, with certain temporary exceptions (now expired) for small corporations.

What is the significance of the repeal of the General Utilities rule?

The repeal of the General Utilities rule increased the tax costs, or reduced the tax benefits allowed under prior law, of acquiring and disposing of appreciated corporate assets. Specifically, the change in law has substantially narrowed the circumstances in which an acquisition or divestiture will be structured as an asset purchase, and will increase the prevalence of stock transactions. Additionally, the repeal of the General Utilities rule placed greater emphasis upon the use of "pass-through entities" wherever possible, as discussed below.

BASIC STRUCTURE

How does an asset acquisition differ from a stock acquisition?

The primary distinction between an *asset acquisition* and a *stock acquisition* concerns the purchaser's basis in the assets acquired. When a purchaser directly acquires the assets of a corporation, and the acquired corporation is subject to tax on the sale or exchange of the assets, the basis of the assets to the purchaser is their cost. This is called *cost basis*. When a purchaser indirectly acquires the assets of a corporation through the acquisition of stock, the basis of the assets in the possession of the corporation is generally not affected. This is called *carryover basis* because the basis of an asset in the acquired corporation "carries over" on the change of stock ownership.

With the exception of a stock acquisition governed by the provisions of Section 338 of the Code, the acquisition of all or part of the stock of a corporation does not alter the bases of the assets owned by the corporation. And with the exception of an asset acquisition governed by the Code's tax-free reorganization provisions, the acquisition of the assets of a corporation will produce a cost basis to the purchaser.

A cost basis transaction is, therefore, often referred to as an "asset acquisition," and a carryover basis transaction is often referred to as a "stock acquisition." Neither of these terms necessarily reflects the actual structure of the transaction.

What is basis?

A taxpayer's *basis* in an asset is the value at which the taxpayer carries the asset on its tax balance sheet. An asset's basis is initially its historical cost to the taxpayer. This *initial basis* is subsequently increased by capital expenditures and decreased by depreciation, amortization, and other charges, becoming the taxpayer's *adjusted basis* in the asset. Upon the sale or exchange of the asset, gain or loss for tax purposes is measured by the difference between the amount realized for the asset and its adjusted basis.

The basis of the asset represents, in effect, the amount at which the cost of the asset may be recovered free of tax through depreciation deductions and adjustments to gain or loss upon disposition.

Are there any other significant tax differences between a cost basis, or "asset," transaction and a carryover basis, or "stock," transaction?

Yes. In carryover basis transactions, the purchaser acquires (or the acquired corporation retains), by operation of law, the corporation's tax attributes—net operating loss carryovers, business credit carryovers, earnings and profits, accounting methods, and others—each of which may be either beneficial or detrimental to the purchaser. The most beneficial tax attributes, however, are generally subject to various limitations that are triggered upon a significant change of stock ownership of the acquired corporation. In all cost basis transactions, the purchaser acquires a corporation's assets but not its tax attributes.

What types of transactions are carryover basis, or "stock," transactions?

As a general rule, a carryover basis, or stock, transaction includes any transaction where the stock or assets of a corporation are acquired by the purchaser, and the bases of the assets are not increased or decreased on the change of ownership. There are several types of stock or carryover basis transactions. The direct purchase of the acquired corporation stock in exchange for cash and debt is the most straightforward stock acquisition. Another transaction that is treated as a sale of stock for tax purposes is the merger of the acquiring corporation into the acquired corporation—a reverse merger—where the shareholders of the acquired corporation relinquish their shares in exchange for cash or debt in a fully taxable transaction. Another common stock transaction is the acquisition of the stock or assets of a corporation in a transaction free of tax to its exchanging shareholders.

What types of transactions are cost basis, or "asset," transactions?

As a general rule, a cost basis, or asset, transaction includes any transaction where the pre-acquisition gains and losses inherent in the assets acquired are triggered and recognized by the acquired corporation. There are several types of cost basis transactions. The direct purchase of the assets from the acquired corporation in exchange for cash or indebtedness is the quintessential asset acquisition. Another common asset transaction is the statutory merger of the acquired corporation into an acquiring corporation—a forward cash merger—where the shareholders of the acquired corporation exchange their shares for cash or other property in a fully taxable transaction. In certain circumstances, a corporation may acquire the stock of another corporation and elect under Section 338 of the Code to treat the stock acquisition, for tax purposes, as an asset acquisition.

What is the significance to the buyer of the basis of the assets in the acquired corporation?

The basis of the assets in an acquired corporation may have a significant and continuing effect on the tax liabilities and, therefore, the cash flow of either the acquirer or the acquiree. The basis of an asset represents the extent to which the asset may be depreciated or amortized (if at all), thereby generating noncash reductions of taxable income. Basis also represents the extent to which the consideration received in a taxable sale or exchange of an asset may be received by the seller free of tax.

What is the prospective cost basis of an asset to the purchaser?

The prospective cost basis of an asset to the purchaser is the price that it will pay for the asset, directly or indirectly, which is presumed to be its fair market value.

What is the prospective carryover basis of an asset to the purchaser?

The prospective carryover basis of an asset to the purchaser is simply the "adjusted basis" of the asset in the possession of the acquired corporation prior its acquisition. As explained above, the adjusted basis of an asset is general its historical or initial cost, reduced or "adjusted" by subsequent deprecia or amortization deductions.

What is meant by "stepped-up basis"?

Where the basis of an asset is increased from the acquired corporation's initial basis (or adjusted basis, if different) to a basis determined by chaser's cost or fair market value, the basis of the asset is said to ha "stepped up." The term may refer, however, to any transaction in which the basis of an asset is increased. In most asset, or cost basis, transactions, the basis of the assets of the acquired corporation is stepped up to the purchaser's cost. An acquisition in which the basis of the assets of the acquired corporation is increased is referred to as a "step-up" transaction.

Who benefits from a step-up?

Generally, the buyer. High tax basis in an asset is always more beneficial to its owner than low basis. The higher the basis, the greater the depreciation or amortization deductions (if allowable), and the less the gain (or the greater the loss) on the subsequent disposition of the asset. An increase in these deductions and losses will reduce the tax liabilities of the purchaser or the acquired corporation during the holding period of the assets, thereby increasing after-tax cash flow. For the same reasons, a high basis in the acquired corporation's assets will enhance their value to a potential carryover basis purchaser.

The acquisition of an acquired corporation should generally be structured to maximize the basis of the assets of the acquired corporation. If a purchaser's prospective cost basis in the assets of the acquired corporation exceeds its prospective carryover basis, an asset acquisition or step-up transaction is generally more beneficial to the purchaser than a stock acquisition. If a purchaser's prospective carryover basis exceeds its prospective cost in the assets of the acquired corporation, a stock acquisition is generally beneficial to the purchaser than an asset, or cost basis, acquisition.

The primary exception to this general rule is the situation where (1) in a basis transaction the purchaser would acquire beneficial tax attributes operating losses, tax credits, or accounting methods—and (2) the such tax attributes to the purchaser exceeds the value of the basis in the acquired corporation's assets that would have obtained transaction.

aser's cost basis in an asset generally be its carryover basis?

has appreciated in value, or where the economic deprecia- than the depreciation or amortization deductions allowed rchaser's prospective cost basis in the asset will exceed ver basis. The depreciation and amortization deductions allowed for tax purposes for most types of property are designed to exceed the actual economic depreciation of the property. As a result, the fair market value of most assets, which represents the prospective cost basis of the asset to a purchaser, generally exceeds the adjusted tax basis. The aggregate difference between the purchaser's prospective cost and carryover bases of the acquired corporation's assets is often substantial.

Will a purchaser generally receive greater tax benefits by acquiring an acquired corporation through a cost basis transaction than through a carryover basis transaction?

Yes. A purchaser will generally acquire a higher basis in the assets of the acquired corporation through a cost basis transaction than through a carryover basis transaction because the cost or fair market value of the acquired corporation's assets is generally greater than the adjusted basis of the assets prior to the acquisition. In that circumstance, a cost basis transaction will "step up" the basis of the assets of the acquired corporation. The amount of the increase in basis—the excess of cost basis over carryover basis—is referred to as the *step-up amount.*

Do all asset, or cost basis, transactions step up the bases of the acquired corporation's assets?

No. Where the purchase price of the assets of the acquired corporation, which is presumed to equal their fair market value, is less than the carryover basis of the assets, a cost basis, or asset, transaction will result in a net reduction of basis. In such cases, the transaction should generally be structured as a carryover basis, or stock, acquisition.

In what circumstances are carryover basis transactions more beneficial to a purchaser, from a tax standpoint, than cost basis transactions?

There are two situations where a carryover basis, or stock, transaction may be more beneficial to the purchaser than a cost basis, or asset, acquisition. The first is where the carryover basis of the acquired corporation's assets to the purchaser exceeds their cost basis. This excess represents potential tax benefits to the purchaser—noncash depreciation deductions or taxable losses—without a corresponding economic loss. That is, the tax deductions or losses from owning the assets may exceed the price paid for such assets. The second is where the acquired corporation possesses valuable tax attributes—net operating loss carryovers, business tax credit carryovers, or accounting methods, for example—that would inure to the benefit of the purchaser. Situations where carryover basis transactions are preferable to the purchaser over cost basis transactions, however, are more the exception than the rule.

What are loss carryovers and carrybacks?

If a taxpayer has an excess of tax deductions over its taxable income in a given year, this excess becomes a net operating loss of that taxpayer. Section 172 of the Code allows that taxpayer to use its net operating loss (NOL) to offset taxable income in subsequent years (a carryover or carryforward) or to offset taxable income in earlier years (a carryback). For most taxpayers an NOL may be carried back for up to two taxable years and may be carried forward for up to 20 years.[7]

Under other provisions of the Code, certain tax losses or tax credits that are unusable in a given year may be carried forward or carried back to other tax years. Examples of such deductions or credits are capital losses, excess foreign tax credits, and investment credits. Generally, Code provisions for a company's ability to utilize NOL carryovers apply as well to these other items. For purposes of simplicity, all these items tend to be grouped together with loss carryovers. This is a practice that we will follow in the discussion here.

Generally speaking, each state has its own NOL carryback and carryforward rules, which may not necessarily match the federal rules. Therefore, an acquired corporation may have different amounts of available federal and state NOLs.

What role do loss carryovers play in mergers and acquisitions?

As stated earlier, a potential advantage in carryover basis acquisitions—both taxable stock purchases and tax-free reorganizations—is the carryover of basis and of favorable tax attributes in the hands of the buyer. To the extent that a buyer can acquire an acquired corporation and retain favorable NOL carryovers, it can increase the after-tax cash flow generated by the activities of the acquired corporation and, to some extent, utilize those losses to offset tax liability generated by the buyer's own operations.

Over the course of many years, Congress and the IRS have imposed various limitations on the use of loss carryovers by persons other than those who owned the entity at the time that the loss was generated. For example, after a substantial ownership change, an acquiring corporation can deduct only the NOLs of the acquired corporation up to a certain limit, called a "Section 382 limitation," and must meet a *continuity of interest* test. *Continuity of interest* means the continuation of a significant business of the acquired corporation or the continued use of a significant portion of the corporation's business assets. These rules have achieved a level of complexity that is extreme even by the standard of the tax laws generally.

What happens when corporations having loss carryovers acquire other corporations that generate taxable gains?

This is covered in Code Section 384, which imposes limitations upon a loss corporation's ability to offset its losses against taxable gains recognized by subsidiaries that it acquires and with which it files a consolidated tax return. These limitations apply as well where the loss corporation acquires the gain assets from another corporation in a tax-free reorganization or liquidation that results in a carryover of basis. Loss carryovers of the acquiring corporation include unrealized built-in losses.

How do *accounting authorities* treat net operating losses? Is there some flexibility here?

Financial Accounting Statement No. 109 of the Financial Accounting Standards Board (FAS No. 109) mandates recognition of the tax consequences of a transaction or an event in the same period that the transaction or event is recognized in the enterprise's financial statements. Under FAS No. 109, FASB adopted a liability approach to comprehensive tax allocation, consistent with the approach used under its predecessor standard FAS No. 96, but changed its conclusion in asset recognition and adopted the "one-event" approach. The Board decided that the critical event for recognition purposes is the event that gives rise to the deductible temporary difference or tax credit or NOL carryforward. Once that event occurs, those tax benefits should be recognized subject to an impairment challenge.

Under FAS No. 109,

- Deferred tax liabilities are recognized for future taxable amounts, deferred tax assets are recognized for future deductions and operating loss and tax credit carryforwards, and the liabilities and assets are then measured using the applicable tax rate.
- A valuation allowance is recognized to reduce deferred tax assets to the amounts that are "more likely than not" to be realized, and the amount of the allowance is based on available evidence about the future.
- Deferred tax expense or benefit is computed as the difference between the beginning and ending balance of the net deferred tax asset or liability for the period.
- Generally, deferred tax assets and liabilities are classified as current or noncurrent in accordance with the classification of the related asset or liability for financial reporting purposes.
- The effects of changes in rates or laws are recognized at the date of enactment.

There are two particularly important issues to consider upon application of FAS No. 109:

- *Operating loss and tax credit carryforwards and carrybacks.* Enterprises must identify the availability of NOL and tax credit carryforwards, their expiration dates, and limitations on their use, for each taxing jurisdiction. FAS No. 109 presumes that the enterprise will be able to use these benefits, subject to an impairment challenge. Under either of the predecessor standards, tax credit carryforwards that could not be used to reduce recorded deferred tax liabilities were not recognized but were disclosed in the notes to the financial statements.
- *Valuation allowance.* A key concept underlying the measurement of net deferred assets is that the amount to be recognized is the amount of deferred tax benefit expected to be realized. In its deliberation, the FASB considered how high the recognition threshold should be. The Board concluded that if it allowed asset recognition only when realization was ensured beyond a reasonable doubt, some assets would not be recognized even though they were expected to be realized. This led to the conclusion that a lower threshold—recognition if realization is more likely than not—would be preferable.

Realization of tax benefits is dependent on whether there will be sufficient future taxable income of the appropriate character in the period during which deductible temporary differences reverse, or within the carryforward period established under the tax law. If, on the basis of available evidence, it is more likely than not that all or a portion of the deferred tax asset will not be realized, the asset must be reduced by a valuation allowance.

What are the tax consequences of a cost basis, or asset, acquisition to the acquired corporation?

The general rule is that the basis of an asset in the possession of an acquired corporation may not be stepped up to cost or fair market value without the recognition of taxable gain to the corporation. In a cost basis transaction, the acquired corporation will generally be subject to an immediate tax on an amount equal to the aggregate step-up in the bases of the assets. In addition, the sale or exchange of an asset may trigger the recapture of investment or business tax credits previously taken by the acquired corporation on the acquisition of the asset.

What are the tax consequences of a cost basis, or asset, acquisition to the shareholders of the acquired corporation?

The shareholders of the acquired corporation will be subject to tax upon the receipt of the asset sales proceeds (net of the corporate-level tax) from the acquired corporation, whether the proceeds are distributed in the form of a dividend, in redemption of the shareholder's acquired corporation stock, or in complete liquidation of the acquired corporation. If the asset sales proceeds are retained by the acquired corporation, then the value of those proceeds is indirectly taxed to the shareholders upon the sale or exchange of the stock of the acquired corporation.

In what circumstances will an acquired corporation and its shareholders be subject to double tax on a cost basis, or asset, acquisition?

The acquired corporation and its shareholders will typically be subject to double tax where (1) the acquired corporation sells, or is deemed for tax purposes to sell, its assets to the purchaser in a taxable transaction; (2) the shareholders of the acquired corporation will ultimately receive the proceeds of the sale, either directly or indirectly through the sale of their stock in the acquired corporation; and (3) the receipt of the proceeds by the shareholders of the acquired corporation will be taxable to them. The cost basis transaction in these circumstances causes the proceeds of the sale to be taxed twice, first to the acquired corporation and again to its shareholders. There are several significant exceptions to this general rule.

The most common exception is those situations where a selling shareholder of the acquired corporation stock is a C corporation: The proceeds from the sale of the acquired corporation's stock by a corporate shareholder will likely be taxed again upon their ultimate distribution to noncorporate shareholders.

On balance, which type of structure is preferable?

Generally, a stock acquisition is preferable to an asset acquisition. The immediate tax cost to the acquired corporation and its shareholders on the basis step-up amount of asset acquisition is generally greater than the present value of the tax benefits to the purchaser.

What are the circumstances in which a cost basis, or asset, acquisition transaction is justifiable for tax purposes?

An asset, or cost basis, transaction is generally advisable for tax purposes in situations where the double-tax burden to the seller can be partially or wholly avoided and in situations where double tax is inevitable regardless of the structure.

Can a seller avoid the double tax by converting the acquired corporation to a pass-through entity immediately prior to a sale?

No. The principal pass-through benefits to members of a consolidated return group, to shareholders of an S corporation, and to the partners of a partnership are achieved only on a going forward basis. A corporation, for example, can convert to a partnership only by undergoing a taxable liquidation. Where an acquired C corporation converts to S corporation status, a special corporate-level tax will be imposed upon the sale or exchange of the assets of the acquired corporation to the extent of the built-in gain in its assets as of the time of the conversion.

How can a seller reduce tax costs?

The simplest way to reduce the seller's tax bill is to postpone the recognition of gain. This may be accomplished in a tax-free or partially tax-free acquisition or via the installment sale route.

What is an installment sale?

An *installment sale*, to recap and extend our discussion in Chapter 4, is a disposition of property (by a person who is not a "dealer" in such property) where at least one payment is to be received after the close of the taxable year in which the sale occurs. Basically, an installment sale is a sale or exchange for a promissory note or other debt instrument of the buyer. In the case of an installment sale, the gain on the sale is recognized, pro rata, whenever principal payments on the note are received, or if earlier, upon a disposition of the installment obligation. For example, if A sells property to B for a note with a principal amount of $100 and A's basis in the property was $60, A realizes a gain of $40. Since the ratio of the gain recognized ($40) to the total amount realized ($100) is 0.40, this percentage of each principal payment received by A will be treated as taxable gain. The other $60 will be treated as a nontaxable return of capital.

Installment treatment is available only with respect to a debt obligation of the buyer itself, as opposed to even a related third-party issuer. An obligation of the buyer will not qualify if it is payable on demand, or, generally, if it is in registered form and/or designed to be publicly traded. Note, however, that an installment obligation may be guaranteed by a third party and may even be secured by a standby letter of credit. In contrast, installment obligations secured by cash or cash equivalents, such as certificates of deposit or U.S. Treasury instruments, do not qualify.

What kinds of transactions are eligible for installment sale treatment?

The installment method is generally available for sales of any property other than installment obligations held by a seller, and other than inventory and property sold by dealers in the subject property. Subject to certain exceptions, installment treatment is generally available to a shareholder who sells his or her stock or to a corporation or other entity that sells its assets. Installment treatment is not available for sales of stock or securities that are traded on an established securities market.

What are the tax consequences of a typical tax-free reorganization?

In the classic tax-free acquisition, Al Smith (Smith) owns all the stock of Mom and Pop Grocery, Inc. (Grocery), which is acquired by Supermarkets, Inc. (Supermarkets). In the transaction, Smith surrenders to Supermarkets all his stock in Grocery solely in exchange for voting stock of Supermarkets. This is a fully tax-free B reorganization, in which Smith recognizes no immediate gain or loss.

The corollaries to tax-free treatment here as elsewhere are carryover and substituted basis and holding period. In other words, Smith obtains a basis in his Supermarkets stock equal to his basis in the Grocery stock surrendered (substituted basis) and continues his old holding period in the stock. Similarly, Supermarkets takes a basis in the Grocery stock acquired equal to Smith's basis (carryover basis) and also picks up Smith's holding period.

What are the advantages of tax-free transactions to sellers and buyers?

By participating in a tax-free transaction, the seller is provided the opportunity to exchange stock in the acquired corporation for stock of the buyer without the immediate recognition of gain. Because the seller will have a basis in the buyer's stock that is the same as the seller's old basis in the acquired corporation's stock (a "substituted basis"), tax is only deferred until the acquired corporation's stock is ultimately sold. Where the acquired corporation is closely held and the buyer is publicly held, the seller may obtain greatly enhanced liquidity without a current tax.

Additionally, although death and taxes are both said to be inevitable, a seller participating in a tax-free transaction may utilize the former to avoid the latter. Under a long-standing but controversial rule in the Code, an individual's estate and beneficiaries may take a new, fair market value basis in the decedent's properties at his or her death. Thus, a seller may avoid the payment of any tax on the buyer's stock received in exchange for the old acquired corporation stock by holding this new stock until the seller's death.

For the buyer, there are two principal advantages to a tax-free acquisition. First, if it can use its stock in the transaction, it may not incur significant debt. Where equity financing in general is attractive from a buyer's point of view, it will often make sense to do so in a business acquisition. Second, although subject to certain limitations, the acquired corporation's tax attributes (including net operating loss carryovers) will remain usable after the acquisition.

What kinds of transactions may qualify for tax-free treatment?

Every transaction involving an exchange of property is taxable unless otherwise specified in the Code. Thus, corporate acquisitions are generally taxable to the seller of stock or assets. However, several types of acquisition transactions may be tax-free to the seller, but only to the extent the seller receives stock in the acquiring corporation (or in certain corporations closely affiliated with the acquiring corporation).

In general, tax-free acquisitions fall into three categories: statutory mergers, exchanges of stock for stock, and exchanges of assets for stock. Except for the Section 351 transaction discussed later, all the available tax-free acquisition transactions are provided under Section 368 of the Code. In all, considering the various permutations of its provisions, Section 368 ultimately sets forth more than a dozen different varieties of acquisition reorganizations. The most commonly used forms of reorganizations are the A, B, C, and D reorganizations. (Others are F and G reorganizations and various hybrids.)

What is an A reorganization?

An *A reorganization* (named after its alphabetic place in Section 368) is very simply "a statutory merger or consolidation."[8] This type of reorganization has other, more complex names—such as a *reorganization not solely for voting stock,* as distinct from a *B reorganization,* which *is* solely for voting stock (see below). It is also referred to as a *tax-free forward merger,* as opposed to the taxable forward merger and taxable reverse merger forms discussed earlier (there is no tax-free reverse merger).

What is a B reorganization?

A *B reorganization* is a stock-for-stock exchange in which one company buys the stock of another company using only ("solely") its own stock.

What is a C reorganization?

A *C reorganization* is a transaction in which one company buys the assets of another company using only its own stock.

What is a D reorganization?

A *D reorganization* is a transaction in which a company transfers its assets down into a subsidiary. This kind of transaction would disqualify a company from meeting the requirements of Section 355, although there are still some complicated loopholes here.

How does Section 368 define tax-free transactions?

To qualify as tax-free reorganizations under Section 368, all acquisition reorganizations must meet three nonstatutory requirements. First, the reorganization must have a *business purpose*. Second, the acquiring corporation must satisfy the *continuity of business enterprise* requirement. As mentioned earlier, continuity of business enterprise means the continuation of a significant business of the acquired corporation or the continued use of a significant portion of the corporation's business assets. The third requirement, probably the most burdensome, is the *continuity of interest* requirement.

What is the continuity of interest requirement?

As noted above, tax-free treatment is generally only available to an acquired corporation's stockholders to the extent they either retain their stock or exchange it for stock in the acquiring entity or group. Continuity of interest requires that this qualifying stock consideration constitute a substantial portion of the total consideration received by the acquired corporation's shareholders in the overall transaction. For this purpose, a substantial portion is at least 40 percent; if a private ruling from the IRS is desired, the stock consideration must be at least 50 percent of the total.

What is a Section 351 transaction?

Section 351 of the Code provides nonrecognition treatment on the transfer of property to a corporation by one or more parties in exchange for stock or stock and securities of the transferee corporation, provided the transferors possess 80 percent control of the transferee corporation immediately after the transaction. Although designed for the initial incorporation of a previously unincorporated business, Section 351 can be used as an alternative to the reorganization provisions in order to allow nonrecognition of gain to some of the acquired corporation shareholders.

What is a National Starch transaction?

A so-called *National Starch transaction* (named after an acquisition technique first employed by that company) is a type of Section 351 transaction. (This should not be confused with the later *National Starch* case discussed at the end of this chapter.) It involves the joint transfer of cash by the buyer and acquired corporation stock by one or more acquired corporation shareholders to a newly formed corporation under Section 351, in exchange for acquired corporation common and preferred stock, respectively. The new corporation then utilizes the cash to purchase the remaining acquired corporation stock in the company being acquired. Because the initial transfer of acquired corporation stock and cash to the new entity qualifies under Section 351, no gain is recognized to the acquired corporation shareholders on the receipt of the new company's preferred stock. A diagram of this transaction appears at the end of this chapter.

What is the difference between a Section 351 transaction and a recapitalization?

In a recapitalization, the stockholders in the acquired corporation will end up holding minority interests in the acquired corporation itself, whereas in the Section 351 transaction a newly formed holding company that makes the acquisition will be issuing the preferred stock or minority stock to the acquired corporation shareholders.

What is a tax-free spin-off?

The tax law provides for a corporation to "spin off" the stock of a corporate subsidiary to its shareholders in a tax-free transaction under Section 355 of the

Code. This transaction is illustrated in a figure at the end of this chapter. For more on spin-offs, see Chapter 14.

CHOICE OF ENTITY

What types of entities may operate the business of an acquired company?

Four types of entities may be used to acquire and operate the business of the acquired corporation: (1) C corporations, (2) S corporations, (3) partnerships, either general or limited, and (4) the limited liability company (LLC). This LLC is a new kind of hybrid entity authorized in 1988 by the IRS. It offers the legal insulation of a corporation and the preferred tax treatment of a limited partnership. Today, all 50 states and the District of Columbia permit LLCs.

What are the primary differences among the four types of business entities?

A regular, or C, corporation is a separate taxpaying entity. Therefore, its earnings are taxed to the corporation when earned and again to its shareholders upon distribution. Partnerships and S corporations (and presumably LLCs), in contrast, are generally not separate taxpaying entities.

The earnings of partnerships and S corporations are taxed directly to the partners or shareholders, whether or not distributed or otherwise made available to such persons. Moreover, partnerships and S corporations may generally distribute their earnings to the equity owners free of tax. Because S corporations and partnerships are generally exempt from tax, but pass the tax liability with respect to such earnings directly through to their owners, these entities are commonly referred to as *pass-through entities.*

What are pass-through entities?

Pass-through entities are structures that permit a single—rather than double—tax. There are three types of pass-through entities: (1) a partnership, both general and limited, (2) an S corporation, and (3) a C corporation that files a consolidated income tax return with its corporate "parent." The earnings of all C corporations are subject to double tax, but the consolidated return provisions generally permit the earnings of subsidiary members of the consolidated return group to be taxed to the ultimate parent only. The earnings of an S corporation, with certain exceptions, are subject to taxation only at the shareholder level. The earnings of a partnership are also subject to a single tax, but only to the extent that such earnings are allocated to noncorporate partners (unless the partner is an S corporation). Partnership earnings that are allocated to corporate partners are subject to double taxation, just as though the income were earned directly by the corporations.

What is a C corporation?

A *C corporation* is defined in the Internal Revenue Code as any corporation that is not an S corporation. The term *C corporation* as used in this chapter, however, excludes corporations granted special tax status under the Code, such as life insurance corporations, regulated investment companies (mutual funds), or corporations qualifying as real estate investment trusts (REITs).

What is an S corporation?

An *S corporation* is simply a regular corporation that meets certain requirements and elects to be taxed under Subchapter S of the Code. Originally called a "small business corporation," the S corporation was designed to permit small, closely held businesses to be conducted in corporate form, while continuing to be taxed generally as if operated as a partnership or an aggregation of individuals. As it happens, the eligibility requirements under Subchapter S, keyed to the criterion of simplicity, impose no limitation on the actual size of the business enterprise.

Briefly, an S corporation may not (1) have more than 75 shareholders, (2) have as a shareholder any person (other than an estate and a very limited class of trust) who is not an individual, (3) have a nonresident alien as a shareholder, (4) have more than one class of stock, (5) be a member of an affiliated group with other corporations, or (6) be a bank, thrift, insurance company, or certain other types of business entity.

It should be noted that not all states recognize the S corporation. For those that do not, the corporation pays state income taxes as if it were a C corporation. For those states that do recognize S corporations, both resident and nonresident shareholders of the state where the corporation does business must file returns and pay taxes to that state. In such cases, a shareholder's state of residence will usually (but not always) provide a credit against its own tax.

What is a partnership for tax purposes?

Except under rare circumstances, a *partnership for tax purposes* must be a bona fide general or limited partnership under applicable state law.

How are LLC mergers treated?

Under most state laws, an LLC may merge with or into a stock corporation, limited partnership, business trust, or another LLC. All members of the LLC must approve the merger unless they agree otherwise. Filing of articles and the effective date operate the same as for corporate mergers.

What is the most tax-efficient structure for acquiring and operating a business?

If practicable, not even a single level of corporate tax should be paid on income generated by the business. For this reason, a pass-through entity owned by individuals (as discussed below) should be the structure wherever possible. With respect to an acquisition of assets by individuals, this means that the acquisition vehicle would be either a partnership (presumably limited) or an S corporation. In the case of a stock acquisition by individuals, the acquired corporation generally should be operated as an S corporation.

Where the buyer is a C corporation, the acquired business, whether acquired through an asset or stock purchase, should be operated as a division of the buyer or through a separate company included in the buyer's consolidated return. In either case, the income of the business will be subject to only one level of corporate tax prior to dividend distributions from the buyer to its shareholders.

Under what circumstances may a consolidated return be filed?

In order for two or more corporations to file a consolidated return, they must constitute an "affiliated group" for tax purposes. Although subject to numerous qualifications and complications, an affiliated group is essentially a chain of corporations in which a common parent owns at least 80 percent of the voting power and at least 80 percent of the value of the stock of the other members of the group. In the case of the parent's ownership of at least one first-tier subsidiary, this 80 percent stock ownership must be direct; as to all other members of the group, the 80 percent ownership may be through combined holdings of other members of the corporate group.

Nonvoting preferred stock that does not share in corporate growth and that does not have a significant discounted issue price relative to its liquidation value—so-called pure preferred—is not taken into account as stock for purposes of the affiliation rules. Thus, ordinarily, a parent may file a consolidated return with a subsidiary in which it owns at least 80 percent of the common stock, even though one or more series of pure preferred stock may be held by third parties.

When should an S corporation be considered?

Typically, an S corporation should be considered where the acquired corporation is, or can become, a freestanding domestic operating corporation owned by 75 or fewer U.S. individual shareholders. Because the S corporation requirements are designed to ensure that such entities will have relatively simple structures, they are not inherently user-friendly vehicles for larger, complex operations. Nevertheless, because there is no limit on the size of the business that may be conducted in an S corporation, it is often possible to plan around obstacles to qualification under Subchapter S and to use this favorable tax entity.

When should a partnership be considered?

The partnership is an alternative to the S corporation, with several notable advantages. First, it is always available without restriction on the structure or composition of the acquired corporation's ownership; therefore, it can be used when the S corporation is unavailable for technical reasons. In addition, the partnership is unique in enabling the partners to receive distributions of loan proceeds free of tax. Finally, if the acquired corporation is expected to generate tax losses, a partnership is better suited than an S corporation to pass these losses through to the owners. The last two advantages result from the fact that partners, unlike S corporation shareholders, may generally include liabilities of the partnership in their basis in the partnership.

In addition to the choice of entity, what major structural issue should be considered?

From a tax standpoint, probably the most important issue is whether the buyer should seek to obtain a cost basis or a carryover basis in the assets of the acquired corporation. Because of the potential for obtaining either of these re-sults regardless of whether assets or stock is actually acquired, the determina-tions of the tax goal and the actual structure may initially be made on a separate basis.

What are the mechanics of achieving a cost or carryover basis?

In a taxable acquisition, carryover basis can be achieved only through a stock acquisition. For federal tax purposes, however, stock may be acquired in two ways: first, through a direct purchase of seller's stock and, second, through a reverse cash merger.

As indicated earlier, a cost basis can be achieved by purchasing either as-sets or stock from the seller. As in the case of a stock purchase, the tax law per-mits an asset purchase to be effected in two ways: first, through a direct pur-chase of the seller's assets and, second, through a forward cash merger. In the context of a stock acquisition, a cost basis can be achieved by making an elec-tion under Section 338 of the Code.

Is it possible to obtain a cost basis in some of the assets of the acquired corporation and a carryover basis in other assets?

Generally, this is a result that Congress and the IRS have sought to prevent, and at this effort they have been for the most part successful. Thus, Section 338 of the Code provides that where a buyer makes a qualified stock purchase of more than one corporation affiliated with the acquired corporation, it may not make a Section 338 election with respect to one of those corporations without auto-matically making a Section 338 election with respect to all of them. This rule is commonly called the *stock consistency rule* under Section 338.

What is Section 304 of the Code?

Section 304 of the Code was enacted many years ago to address a tax avoid-ance technique involving the sale of stock in one related corporation to another related corporation, in which a common shareholder could withdraw cash or property from his or her corporations while retaining undiminished owner-ship. The classic case involves individual A who owns all the stock of Corporations X and Y, and who sells some or all of his X stock to Y for cash. In such a case, Section 304 recharacterizes the transaction and treats it as a dividend from Y accompanied by a nontaxable contribution of X stock to Y, instead of merely a sale of X stock that would qualify as capital gain.

The reach of Section 304 goes far beyond the above example. It encompasses any situation in which there is direct or indirect "control" by the selling shareholder of the stock of both the buying corporation and the acquired corporation. Control is defined here as 50 percent of the voting power or 50 percent of the value of a corporation's stock (including pure preferred). Control of the buyer acquired in the transaction itself is included.

Section 304 transactions became popular during the leveraged buyout era of the late 1980s. When a corporation is acquired in a leveraged buyout, and the value of the common stock of both the acquired corporation and the newly formed purchasing corporation, on a book value basis, is fairly negligible, even a relatively small amount of preferred stock in the purchasing corporation issued to the seller may cause its ownership of the buyer to exceed the 50 percent mark in terms of value. In such a case, Section 304 would come into play.

How may preferred stock be issued to the seller without falling under Section 304?

One way of avoiding these problems is to issue the seller a subordinated debenture or other long-term debt instrument rather than stock. In such a case, unless the debt has peculiar features involving a high risk of recharacterization as equity, Section 304 and the 80 percent affiliation problems can be clearly avoided.

Where financing for a transaction requires that the seller receive equity rather than debt, an alternative approach may be in order. In such a case, it might be worthwhile to seek out a third-party preferred stock investor, whose interest could be superior to that of the seller. By thus increasing the amount of stock value not held by the seller, Section 304 can be avoided.

How can Section 351 prevent a qualified stock purchase?

Section 351 of the Code is designed to provide nonrecognition treatment to one or more persons who transfer property (including cash) to a corporation in exchange for substantially all the corporation's stock. Where the purchasing corporation is a newly formed entity, there is some risk that everyone who receives stock in the entity in connection with transactions that were firmly contemplated at the time of its incorporation will be treated as a transferor receiving nonrecognition treatment under Section 351.

The facts in this regard can vary significantly. On the one hand, where a group of investors forms a corporation to negotiate for and ultimately acquire another corporation, and the purchasing corporation has been fully capitalized prior to the commencement of negotiations with the acquired corporation and its shareholders, any stock ultimately received by the shareholders should probably not be treated in connection with the initial incorporation of the purchaser. On the other hand, where a group of individuals contemplating an acquisition negotiates with the shareholders of the acquired corporation prior to the incorporation or even the capitalization of the purchasing corporation, the risk that stock in the purchaser ultimately issued to the acquired corporation shareholders will be treated under Section 351 is very high.

As was the case with Section 304, where more than 20 percent of the stock of the acquired corporation is received, or is treated as received, by the purchasing corporation in a Section 351 transaction, the qualified stock purchase under Section 338 will fail.

After a Section 338 acquisition, must the purchaser retain the acquired corporation as a subsidiary?

The purchasing corporation is permitted to liquidate the acquired corporation in a tax-free liquidation as soon after the qualified stock purchase as it wishes. Such a liquidation may be effected by way of a statutory merger.

How are purchase price allocations made for tax purposes?

Although businesses are usually bought and sold on a lump-sum basis, for tax purposes each such transaction is broken down into a purchase and sale of the individual assets, both tangible and intangible. There is no specific requirement under the tax laws that a buyer and seller allocate the lump-sum purchase price in the same manner. Because each party has tended to take positions most favorable to it, allocation issues have been litigated by the IRS fairly often over the years. At the same time, courts and, to a lesser extent, the IRS have tended to defer to allocations of purchase price that have been agreed upon in writing between a buyer and seller in an arm's-length transaction.

Are there any rules governing the allocation of purchase price?

Yes. If the seller transfers assets constituting a business and determines its basis as the consideration (for example, purchase price) paid for the assets, then this transfer is considered a Section 1060(c) "applicable asset" acquisition. Both buyer and seller in such a transaction must use the "residual method" to allocate the purchase price received in determining the buyer's basis or the seller's gain or loss. This method, which is the same as the one used for a stock purchase, requires that the price of the assets acquired be reduced by cash and cashlike items; the balance must be allocated to tangible assets, followed by intangibles, and finally by goodwill and going concern value. IRS regulations state that both buyer and seller are bound by the allocations set forth in the acquisition agreement.

What about amortization of intangibles following an acquisition?

Until the passage of the Omnibus Reconciliation Act of 1993, acquirers found it impossible to amortize intangibles at anything close to their economic obsolescence due to arbitrary standards set forth in Accounting Principles Board No. 17 (APB No. 17), which set a 40-year maximum for amortization of goodwill. Although some write-offs were mandated at shorter periods, the burden was on the company to justify shorter periods not explicitly covered by the mandates. The 1993 tax law proposed a new Code section (Section 197) that sets a uniform standard of 15 years for amortization of intangibles at a rate of 100 percent.[9]

Exceptions to the 15-year rule include the following:

- Land
- Financial interests
- Certain computer software
- Certain interests or rights acquired separately
- Interests under leases and debt instruments
- Sports franchises
- Mortgage services
- Transaction costs

These are treated with either longer periods (e.g., land) or shorter periods (e.g., computer software). All other forms of goodwill and other intangibles are amortizable at 15 years (with certain restrictions meant to discourage purchase of intangibles-rich companies for tax reasons).

In general, Code Section 197 benefits acquirers of companies that have intangibles with a long life that normally would have to be amortized over a longer period. In general, businesses like to write off intangibles as quickly as possible, as this creates cash in hand from tax savings and rids the company of a drag on profits—so the 15-year rule is a great improvement over the old 40-year standard.

Didn't this change in the law open up an acquisition floodgate?

Congress thought of that and inserted protective language that effectively prevents acquisition of intangibles-rich companies for mere tax avoidance purposes.[10]

Can equity in an S corporation be offered to corporate investors?

As we have said, a corporation will be disqualified under Subchapter S if it either has more than one class of stock or has any shareholder that is a corporation, partnership, or other nonqualifying entity. In a world where lenders and institutional investors are increasingly insistent upon receiving some kind of equity kicker in addition to a more conventional, albeit generous, fixed return, it is necessary to adapt the S corporation to equity participation by nonindividuals. This can be accomplished through the issuance of warrants, other options, or convertible debt. These must be carefully constructed to avoid the appearance or reality of de facto corporate equity holders.

There are in fact numerous tax issues that are unique to the financing of partnership operations, many of which directly affect the partners in the partnership rather than the lenders. These concerns relate to the determination of the partners' basis in the partnership as well as to the allocation and utilization of deductions. Careful tax planning, in light of the partners' objectives, should be able to mitigate these concerns. One example of such a concern is where tax planners seek to ensure that the particular form of the indebtedness of a limited partnership allows the limited partners to allocate their pro rata share of basis attributable to such debt. This will often involve simply making sure that the loan documents indicate that the lender will not have recourse to the assets of the general partner, but only to the assets of the limited partnership itself. If the loan were guaranteed by any partner, or were made by a party related to a partner in the partnership, special problems would arise.

What is the main difference between a partnership and an S corporation as far as their pass-through status goes?

The partnership is a more complete pass-through entity. With respect to issuance of stock or debt, the S corporation is treated in exactly the same way as a C corporation: Such events are not taxable transactions to it. Likewise, no taxable event is recognized to an S corporation when its warrants are issued or exercised. In contrast, most transactions undertaken by a partnership are viewed for tax purposes as if they were undertaken by the partners themselves. If one treats the partnership solely as an entity apart from its partners, the business arrangement will be undermined. Thus, the issuance and exercise of a warrant to buy a stated percentage of the outstanding stock of a corporation becomes a far more complex transaction to structure when it involves an interest in a partnership.

TAX CONCERNS IN FINANCING THE ACQUISITION

What tax issues should be analyzed in structuring straight debt financing?

Generally, straight debt is an unconditional obligation to repay principal and interest, has a fixed maturity date not too far removed, is not convertible, and has no attached warrants, options, or stock. A straight debt instrument ordinarily does not include interest that is contingent on profits or other factors, but it may provide for a reasonable variable interest rate. It will not have a principal that is subject to contingencies.

In short, straight debt is an instrument without significant equity features. Straight debt instruments are generally classified as debt for tax purposes. Accrued interest on a straight debt instrument is deductible by the borrower and taxable to the lender. As a practical matter, the only tax issue in straight debt financing is the computation of the accrued interest.

The Code and proposed regulations contain an extremely complex set of comprehensive rules regarding interest accruals. These rules generally require that interest must accrue whether or not a payment of interest is made. Thus, interest may be taxed, or deducted, before or after interest is paid.

How is debt distinguished from equity for tax purposes?

U.S. federal tax law offers no specific, objective criteria to determine whether a given instrument should be treated as debt or equity. State tax law, which generally applies federal criteria, offers more exemptions than rules. The debt-equity characterization issue has produced an abundance of tax litigation, with a resulting body of case law in which there are very few common principles. The judicial response in defining debt and equity has much in common with its response in defining an obscenity under the First Amendment; that is, judges have been unable to enunciate a complete definition, but they know it when they see it.

In 1969 Congress enacted Section 385 of the Code authorizing the IRS to issue regulations regarding the debt-versus-equity issue. Eleven years later, the IRS promulgated the first version of the Section 385 regulations. These regulations were rewritten twice and were finally withdrawn in 1983.

Since the failure of the Section 385 approach, tax advisors have dealt with the issue by consulting a number of resources, including the defunct Section 385 regulations, related Code Sections 163 and 279 (on interest deductibility), court cases, and IRS rulings. They look for rulings to see the criteria that are most often and prominently cited, the fact patterns that are most commonly associated with recharacterization, and the arrangements that have received the most acquiescent treatment by the IRS. Finally, they best keep track of what most other tax advisors—through blind faith or otherwise—are recommending.

What does the debt-equity issue boil down to then?

A few useful generalizations can be made. Virtually all the litigation and activity by the IRS has been in the recharacterization of purported debt as equity, and not the other way around. Therefore, it is quite safe to say that recharacterization is not a problem when one is dealing with a purported equity instrument.

In examining a purported debt instrument, the courts look for objective indicia that the parties intended a true debtor-creditor relationship. In particular, they have placed great weight on whether the instrument represents an unconditional promise to pay a certain sum at a definite time. Other significant factors that are considered include whether the loan was made by shareholders of the borrower, what the borrower's debt-to-equity ratio is, whether the loan is subordinated to third-party creditors, and whether it has a market rate of interest.

What about debt issued to third-party investors?

Until the IRS signals a newly aggressive stance, the view of most tax advisors is that debt issued to third-party investors for cash is not likely to be recharacterized as equity, even though the debt may be subordinated to senior debt, convertible into common stock, or part of a capital structure involving a high ratio of debt to equity. This will at least be true where the instrument contains the common indicia of indebtedness, that is, a certain maturity date that is neither unduly remote nor contingent, a reasonable interest rate, and creditor's rights upon default. Note, however, that even if the above criteria are met, the IRS is likely to argue for equity characterization if the conversion features of the instrument are such as to make it economically inevitable from inception that the instrument will be converted into stock. This was how the IRS characterized certain adjustable-rate convertible notes that were issued in the early 1980s.

What are the tax consequences if debt with equity features is recharacterized as equity?

The tax consequences of recharacterization of purported debt into equity may be quite severe. *First,* interest payments with respect to recharacterized debt will be treated not as interest but as distributions to a shareholder and, therefore, will not be deductible. Repayment of debt principal is tax-free to the debt holder, but if treated as a redemption of stock, it may be taxed as a dividend.

Second, the recharacterization may destroy the pass-through status of the issuer. When debt is recharacterized as equity, it is ordinarily expected to be treated as a kind of preferred stock. Because an S corporation may not have two classes of stock, a recharacterization of debt into equity can create a second class of stock, invalidating the S election and causing a corporate-level tax. If the issuer is a member of a consolidated group, the recharacterized debt will most likely be treated as preferred stock that is not "pure preferred" stock. As such, the company may be disaffiliated from the consolidated group if, after taking into account the newly recharacterized stock, the members of the consolidated group own less than 80 percent of the company's stock.[11]

Third, a recharacterization of debt into equity may completely change the structure of the deal. For example, the recharacterization may invalidate a Section 338 election, because for a valid election the buyer and the acquired corporation must be affiliated at the time of the election. If the recharacterization of a purported debt into equity disaffiliates the buyer and the acquired corporation, the election is invalid. In the case of purchase money notes, the conversion of debt into stock consideration may convert a taxable acquisition into a tax-free reorganization.

Finally, a recharacterization of debt held by foreign investors may be an especially difficult event. It is relatively easy to structure a debt to allow a foreign investor to receive interest free of U.S. tax. If the debt is recharacterized, however, a payment of purported interest will be treated as a dividend. Dividends received by foreign taxpayers are subject to U.S. tax either at the 30 percent regular withholding rate or at a lower withholding rate provided for in a treaty. Where a foreign investor asks for and obtains an indemnification for U.S. taxes, the incidence of tax will fall on the issuer and, indirectly, its shareholders. (For more on this subject, see Chapter 15.)

What if the acquired operations are to be held in an affiliated group of corporations filing a consolidated federal income tax return?

In such a case, the acquisition debt will often be issued by the parent. Therefore, for federal income tax purposes, the group is treated as a single taxpayer, in which the parent's interest deductions offset the operating income of the subsidiaries. But from the point of view of the various states in which the subsidiaries do business, there is no consolidation with the parent; therefore, the parent's interest payments, even though funded by cash flow from the subsidiary, will not reduce the subsidiary's state income tax liability.

In such cases, it will ordinarily be important, where feasible, to pass the parent's interest deductions directly down to the subsidiaries by their assuming portions of the parent's indebtedness directly, or indirectly via bona fide intercorporate indebtedness owed to the parent by the respective subsidiaries. Great care must be taken to avoid adverse tax treatment to the parent in its own state of residency or under the federal tax laws as a result of such restructuring.

You mentioned Code Sections 163 and 279. What do they say?

Section 163(e)(5) says interest payments on loans may not be deducted if the debt bears a rate of interest higher than the federal rate plus five percentage points, among other features. Section 163(j) disallows deductions on interest payments made to nonprofits.

Section 279 of the Code disallows interest deductions in excess of $5 million a year on debt that is used to finance an acquisition, to the extent that the company's interest deductions are attributable to "corporate acquisition indebtedness."

Corporate acquisition indebtedness is a type of debt incurred by a corporation to acquire either stock in another corporation or at least two-thirds of the assets of another corporation. To avoid being characterized as Section 279 debt, this debt must meet certain specific subordination tests and must not be convertible into stock or issued as part of an investment unit. The issuing corporation must have a low debt-to-equity ratio as specifically set forth in the statute and regulations.

From a tax standpoint, when might preferred stock be more advantageous than subordinated debt?

When an issuer is not in need of additional interest deductions (for example, when it expects to generate or otherwise have available net operating losses), there may be no tax imperative to use debt, and preferred stock may be a sensible alternative.

The most common tax reason for using preferred stock over debt is to enable an acquisition to qualify as a tax-free reorganization. As discussed earlier, shareholders can obtain tax-free treatment on the receipt of nonvoting, redeemable preferred stock, and such stock will qualify in satisfying the continuity of interest requirement. More generally, preferred stock can be used to provide tax-free treatment to an acquired company's shareholders, while still effectively converting their interest to that of a passive investor or lender. Preferred stock can be sold to corporate investors that can take advantage of the dividends received deduction. Although dividends are not deductible to the issuer, the corporate holder may exclude from its taxable income 70 percent of the dividends received.

What role can special-class, or "alphabet," stock play in tax planning?

Special-class, or alphabet, stock financing is a device that tax planners have thought about a good deal in the past few years but have rarely acted upon. Special-class stock is a variation upon series-class stocks that have been used by mutual funds for many years, but was first used for a standard business organization when General Motors acquired Electronic Data Systems Corporation in 1984. GM again used the device a year later when it acquired Hughes Aircraft Company (subsequently sold to Raytheon Co., in 1998). In those two acquisitions, GM issued a new class E and class H stock, respectively. Holders of these stocks have the same basic rights under state and federal law as common shareholders, but they receive dividends that are more sensitive to the fortunes of their unit. Because these stocks are listed in an exchange and actively traded, they can be valued for tax purposes.

Can an ESOP be used to provide favorable financing in a leveraged buyout?

As described in Chapter 7, an employee stock ownership plan (ESOP) is a type of qualified employee benefit plan that invests primarily in stock of the employer. In order to encourage the use of ESOPs, Congress has provided a variety of special tax benefits both to stockholders who sell their stock to an ESOP and to lenders providing financing for so-called leveraged ESOPs. Shareholders who sell their stock to an ESOP may qualify for tax-free rollover treatment under Section 1042 of the Code. That section permits the shareholder to defer the payment of a capital gain tax upon the sale of stock, provided he or she reinvests the sale proceeds in stock of another active business corporation within one year after the sale. Additionally, where the selling shareholder is an estate, or other entity holding the employer's stock at the time of the decedent's death, as much as one-half of the proceeds of the sale of the stock to an ESOP may be deducted from the gross estate for federal estate tax purposes.

Two tax benefits are provided to a company that sets up a leveraged ESOP. First, all payments of both interest and principal on loans incurred by an ESOP to purchase employer stock are deductible to the company. Additionally, qualified lenders on ESOP loans are permitted to exclude 50 percent of the interest received on such loans. Such a tax exclusion for the lender may be expected to provide a strong incentive to make loans available for ESOP financing on favorable terms.

With such clear tax incentives, the ESOP should be considered in many contexts in mergers and acquisitions. Provided an investor group is willing to share the ultimate economic benefits of an acquisition with the employees of the acquired company, at least to the extent required by the tax laws, the leveraged ESOP may be a viable alternative to other means of financing a leveraged buyout.

MANAGEMENT BUYOUT TAX BASICS

What is a management buyout?

A *management buyout* (MBO) is a transaction in which a company, or subsidiary or division, is acquired by a new company in which management of the acquired business holds a significant, if not controlling, equity stake. The purchaser is typically privately held and has not been an operating company or a subsidiary of one. Its funds typically consist of borrowed money, so most MBOs are also LBOs.[12]

How is an MBO typically structured?

In brief, management, together with any financial partner, typically forms a new company to acquire its employer. As mentioned earlier in our discussion of LBOs, the acquiring company may acquire all the assets of the company or all stock of the company, or it may merge with the company. Often management forms a holding company and engages in a forward or reverse merger with the company. If management owns stock, it can either have the acquiring company repurchase its existing shares or contribute its equity in the business to the acquiring company. These methods have different tax consequences, discussed below.

Should an MBO be structured as a merger, a stock purchase, or an asset purchase?

A stock purchase via a tender offer is the fastest method to purchase a majority of any public company's stock. However, tender offers have certain disadvantages. Tender offers may require a good deal of up-front money before ever gaining access to the cash flow of the company being acquired, and without any assurance of ever tapping it. The margin rules of the Federal Reserve Board (Regulations G and U) restrict a purchaser from borrowing more than half of the purchase price against the pledge of publicly traded securities. Because the margin rules complicate financing, acquisitions of public companies are often done as mergers or use unsecured financing.

The MBO transaction is usually structured as a merger. A merger usually requires approval of the stockholders of both corporations in noncash transactions and of the nonsurviving corporation in cash transactions. A merger transaction involving a public company will require the filing of proxy materials with the SEC and a registration statement complying with federal and state securities laws where securities are to be issued. A stock purchase can be done where ownership of the stock is concentrated in the hands of a few persons, but it typically must be consummated contemporaneously with a merger to obtain the required financing.

Can an MBO involve management employees as owners?

Yes—it can be structured as an ESOP. In an ESOP buyout, the ESOP is the sole or a principal purchaser of its company's stock. Senior management can own stock in addition to the stock owned through the ESOP. The ESOP purchase of the stock is financed by a loan, either directly to the ESOP or through the company. The loan is almost always backed by the company's assets. Interest payments to the ESOP lender are given favorable tax treatment and therefore can be obtained at below market rates, lowering the company's interest expense. Loan repayments are treated for tax purposes as contributions to a pension plan and are deductible in full, in effect making principal repayments deductible as well as interest. Thus, the ESOP is a powerful and efficient financing tool. However, because the ESOP is a tax-qualified pension plan subject to tax law and the Employee Retirement Income Security Act of 1974 (ERISA), there are limits on the size of the ESOP and the extent to which it may benefit senior management. (An ESOP's advantages, disadvantages, structure, and legal constraints are discussed in detail in Chapter 7.)

What special tax issues ordinarily arise in an MBO?

For the most part, an MBO raises the same tax issues as any other LBO. In addition, a few categories of issues pertain specifically to acquisitions with equity participation by management. These issues relate primarily to the manner in which management's investment will be paid for or financed and generally involve questions of whether significant amounts of compensation income will be deemed to be received by management. Where members of management already own stock or stock rights in a company they are trying to buy, special care must be taken in structuring the transaction to allow a tax-free conversion of these existing equity rights.

A discussion of management equity participation in a buyout inevitably leads to a broader discussion of executive compensation. Here, we will focus primarily on management's direct equity participation in an acquisition. It is worth noting, however, that to the extent management does obtain a direct ownership interest in the company, many of the conventional devices employed by large companies to motivate and reward management, such as bonus plans and stock option plans, may become less important.

An MBO will likely require a greater cash investment than most of the management participants will have available from personal resources. Unless the management pays for the stock, in cash, at fair market value, there may be taxable income to the employee when he or she obtains stock. The employee and the corporation will have some control over when the taxable income is treated as being received. Their interests may differ. The tax consequences of the alternative ways of making this investment are governed by the basic rules under Section 83 of the Code.

What is the basic rule for taxation of an employee who receives or purchases stock in an MBO?

As a general rule, under Section 83 an employee receives taxable compensation to the extent that the value of any property received from the employer exceeds the amount the employee pays for that property. To the extent that the employee has taxable income, the employer is entitled to a deduction and is required to withhold tax on the same basis as if regular salary were paid. These rules apply whether the employee is receiving stock or other kinds of property. If an employee has not paid full value for the stock and is thus taxed on the receipt of the stock, the employee will obtain a basis in the stock equal to the amount actually paid for it, plus the amount of taxable income recognized. If an employee has paid full value for the stock, the employee will have a basis in the stock equal to his or her cost and will have no compensation income. In either case, when the employee later sells the stock, the employee will have capital gain or loss measured by the difference between the sale proceeds and the basis in the stock.

There is an important exception to the general rule. If the stock is not substantially vested in the employee, there is no tax to the employee and no deduction to the employer until such time as the stock does become substantially vested. Stock is substantially vested if it either is not subject to a "substantial risk of forfeiture" or is transferable by the employee. When the risk of forfeiture or the restriction on transferability lapses, rendering the property substantially vested, the employee will be required to pay tax on the excess of the stock's value at the time the property vests over the amount paid for the stock. This rule will apply even if the employee originally paid full value for the stock and cannot be avoided unless the employee otherwise elects under Section 83(b).

Here is how it works. Assume that a management employee will acquire 100 shares of company stock from the company in the MBO. The employee buys the stock for $100, which is the full fair market value of the stock. If the stock is then fully vested and transferable, the employee recognizes no taxable income. If, two years later, the stock is worth $150, there will be no impact on the employee; only if the stock is actually sold for $150 will the employee have $50 in long-term capital gain. The company will have no deduction. But if the employee acquires the stock subject to a substantial risk of forfeiture that does not lapse for a two-year period, the result is different. There is still no income at the outset. Two years later, when the stock is worth $150, the risk of forfeiture lapses. The employee must then recognize taxable income of $50 (which is the difference between the $150 fair market value of the stock at that time and the $100 paid for the stock two years earlier), even if the employee has not sold the stock and has no cash proceeds to pay the tax. At that time, the company is entitled to a $50 deduction.

Are there circumstances that might impel an employee to forfeit his or her stock?

Yes. Many typical "golden handcuff" techniques create a substantial risk of forfeiture and can therefore undermine the tax plans. The receipt of stock may be subject to forfeiture if the employee will be required to return the stock upon the happening of a particular event or the failure to satisfy some condition. The typical example of a provision creating a substantial risk of forfeiture is one requiring that the employee return the stock to the company in the event that the employee terminates his or her employment with the company within a certain period after the receipt of the stock. A requirement that the employee return the stock unless certain earnings goals are met also creates a substantial risk of forfeiture.

There is not, however, a substantial risk of forfeiture where the company is required to pay the employee full value for the stock upon a termination of employment. Also, where the event that will produce a forfeiture is peculiarly within the control of the employee, such as being dismissed for cause or taking a job with a competitor of the company, there will not be a substantial risk of forfeiture.

Will receipt of stock by a management investor always be treated as receipt of stock by an employee?

Technically, Section 83 applies to the receipt of stock or other property by an employee only if he or she receives it in connection with the performance of services. This includes past, present, and future services. In some circumstances, a reasonably strong case can be made that the employees are not receiving stock in connection with the performance of services but are receiving stock on the same basis and in the same context as other members of an investor group. In spite of this commonsense analysis, most tax advisors recommend that planning in this area proceed on the assumption that the IRS will apply Section 83 in determining the tax consequences to members of an investor group who are employees of the company.

May employees elect to recognize any taxable income currently?

If an employee receives stock that is substantially nonvested, the employee may elect under Section 83(b) to take any gain into income at the time of receipt of the stock. The employee will recognize compensation income in the amount of the excess, if any, of the stock's value over the amount paid for it. The employer receives a deduction at that time, equal to any compensation income recognized. The election must be made no later than 30 days after the receipt of the stock by filing a form with the IRS Service Center at which the employee files his or her tax returns. The employee must also file a copy of the election with his or her tax return. The IRS is quite strict in applying the 30-day filing deadline, and one should not expect any flexibility on this point. Additionally, once such an election is made, it may not be revoked.

Note that a Section 83(b) election may be made even where the effect of making the election will be to recognize no income because at the time the stock was issued there was no spread between its value and the amount paid. Thus, such an election can be useful for an employee who does pay full value at a time when the prospects for subsequent appreciation in the stock are significant. The employee described above, with $100 in forfeitable stock, could have filed an 83(b) election, recognized a gain of zero, and avoided the $50 gain when the risk of forfeiture lapsed.

Where management is purchasing stock in an acquiring entity or in a company that is the subject of an LBO at or before the acquisition closing and at the same price as other investors, it can usually be comfortably argued that the amount paid for the stock at the inception of the transaction is equal to its fair market value. In such a case, there will be no compensation income to the management participants under Section 83, provided that either the stock is substantially vested or the management participants file Section 83(b) elections.

If the employee's stock purchase is financed with a note, is Section 83 income avoided?

Management rarely has enough cash to buy as large an equity interest as it would like. The stock acquisition of management is usually financed by the company, the investor partner, or a third party. A promissory note from the employee will be treated as a bona fide payment for the stock in an amount equal to the face amount of the note, provided it meets two important requirements. First, the note should provide for adequate stated interest at least equal to the applicable federal rate. Second, the note should be with recourse to the employee.

When should the employee be treated as receiving income?

The employee's principal objective is to make sure that whatever event will trigger income to the employee will also cause the employee to have converted the stock investment into cash. Suppose an employee buys 100 shares of company stock for $100, which is its fair market value at that time. To ensure that the employee will not later be taxed on appreciation in the stock on the basis of a claim that the interest has not yet vested, he or she files a Section 83(b) election. Thereafter, the employee sells the stock for $500. Traditionally, the main planning goal would be to ensure that the $400 of appreciation would be taxed at favorable capital gains rates. If the employee is in a low tax bracket, however, he or she will be largely indifferent to whether the $400 gain is taxed as capital gain or as ordinary compensation income, so long as the employee is not taxed until he or she sells the stock. It appears that the employee's objective has been achieved.

On the other hand, the company's tax planning objectives may not have been well served. There is no benefit to the company as a result of the employee's recognition of $400 of capital gain upon the sale of the stock. Where, however, the employee is able to defer the triggering of Section 83 until he or she sells the stock, the company will obtain a deduction in the amount of $400. The value of this deduction will be very significant for any company that is a C corporation. The employee is taxed at the capital gains tax rate (currently 20 percent); the employer deducts at the corporate income tax rate (currently 34 percent or higher).

In some cases, the tax problem can be solved by a company commitment to pay the employee a bonus sufficient to cover the employee's tax. The bonus is deductible to the company, of course, at rates currently higher than those paid by the employee. The combination of tax bonus plus Section 83 deduction may be better for the employer than the employer's making an 83(b) election, and the employee will be indifferent since the tax is paid by the employer.

Are there additional adverse consequences to an employee who purchases stock with a nonrecourse note when the employer is a partnership?

As explained above, where the employee purchases stock with a nonrecourse note secured solely by the stock, he or she will be treated as holding only a nonqualified option to buy stock. As such, the employee is not treated as owning any of the stock for tax purposes. This will have a dramatic effect where the company is a pass-through entity, such as a partnership. For each tax year before the note is paid, all the income or loss of the entity will be passed through to all other partners, excluding the employee. The resulting distortions will be permanent and will almost always work to the disadvantage of the employee. This used to be true of S corporations, too, but the Taxpayer Relief Act of 1997 changed the rules.

Assume that an employee has purchased with a note and is therefore treated as having an option to purchase 10 percent of the stock of a partnership for $100. In each of the next two years, the company generates aggregate taxable income of $1,000 and distributes $350 to the shareholders (including the employee) to reimburse them for federal and state income taxes. At the end of year two, the employee completes the purchase and sells the stock for $300. Because the employee's basis is $100, he or she recognizes a short-term capital gain of $200. If the employee had been treated as a stockholder in the company, his or her basis in the company stock would have been increased by $65 (10 percent of the company's undistributed taxable income) for each taxable year in which the company stock was held. Upon the sale of the company stock for $300 after year two, the employee would have recognized only $70 long-term capital gain, that is, $300 proceeds realized, less $230 basis. This adverse consequence is somewhat offset by the fact that the employee was not taxed on the company income during prior years.

What happens when management borrows from third-party investors rather than from the company itself?

Where stock of the company or a nonrecourse loan to buy stock in the company is made available to an employee from a party that is a shareholder in the company, the Section 83 rules make it clear that the employee will suffer the identical income tax results as if the stock or loan were made available directly from the company itself. As to the shareholder who makes the stock or loan available to the employee, any value transferred to the employee thereby is treated as having been contributed to the company by the shareholder on a tax-free basis. The only benefit obtained by the shareholder will be an increase in the basis in his or her stock of the company.

Can some of the employee's assets be protected from the recourse loan?

Typically, even in the most highly leveraged transactions, the amount of money required for management to purchase its shares cannot be repaid if the buyout does not succeed, without having a fairly severe impact on the lifestyle of the employee. Given a high level of confidence in the venture, and a relatively low stock purchase price, a management participant should be willing to risk his or her capital in a meaningful way, albeit not with personal bankruptcy as the consequence. In such cases, it might be worthwhile to consider a loan that gives the lender recourse to the borrowing employee, but specifically excludes recourse with respect to certain assets—for example, a house.

Although there is no authority on this question, one would have to stretch the Section 83 regulations substantially to treat such partially nonrecourse loans as nonqualified options. As long as the debt, and the personal liability of the employee thereon, is bona fide and real, it should probably be respected as such for tax purposes.

What other techniques provide management with full equity rights at a lower cost than the cost to third-party investors?

The most direct and effective means of reducing the cost of management stock relative to that purchased by other investors is through some multiclass arrangement. There are numerous variations on this theme. Here is an example of the most straightforward: Assume that an LBO is to be capitalized with $5 million in common equity, and that third-party investors are willing to put up this entire sum. The third-party investors could be given a preferred stock with a liquidation preference of $5 million and some reasonable preferred dividend rights. For a relatively nominal sum, both the third-party investors and management would purchase all the common shares of the company.

By providing the third-party investors with preferential rights equal to virtually the entire shareholders' equity of the corporation, the book value, and arguably the fair market value of the common stock, will be nominal.

There are two problems with this arrangement. First, the IRS can argue that the preferred stock was in fact worth less than $5 million, and that in any event the common stock was worth more than the nominal value ascribed to it because of the very low risk-to-reward ratio of the investment. Second, having more than one class of stock will prevent the company from electing to be an S corporation. Where S corporation status is desired, the purchase price of the common stock can be reduced by having third-party investors purchase deeply subordinated debt instruments in addition to their common stock.

If management already owns stock, how can management convert its existing stock ownership into stock in the buyer on a tax-free basis?

There are several tax-free ways in which management (as well as other shareholders) of an acquired corporation may exchange existing equity in the acquired corporation for a participating interest in the acquiring company in an LBO. Depending upon the other structural goals and requirements, a tax-free rollover may occur in the context of a recapitalization of the acquired company, some other tax-free reorganization, or a "Section 351 National Starch" transaction (again, no relation to the *National Starch* case discussed later).

Achieving a tax-free rollover of management's equity can adversely affect other aspects of the tax structuring of the transaction. Most notably, if the MBO is intended to be treated for tax purposes as a cost basis asset acquisition, overlapping ownership between the acquired company and the buyer may thwart such a characterization.

If cash is received as part of the exchange, how is it treated?

Because LBOs involve a significant reduction in the value of the acquired corporation's equity through increased debt financing, shareholders in a company being acquired who wish to keep their stock will either realize a significant increase in their percentage ownership of the outstanding stock or receive cash or other nonequity consideration in addition to the stock. In the latter case, management's tax advisors must analyze the facts to ensure that the receipt of nonstock consideration will be treated as capital gain rather than a dividend to the participant. One key difference between a dividend and capital gain is that under the latter characterization the shareholder will be permitted to reduce taxable income by his or her basis in the stock.

Do the same rules apply where management owns nonqualified options or substantially nonvested stock?

No. In the case of both nonqualified options and restricted stock subject to a substantial risk of forfeiture for which a Section 83(b) election has not been made, the exchange of the option or stock for stock in the buyer that is not subject to a substantial risk of forfeiture will give rise to compensation income under Section 83 in an amount equal to the value of the acquired corporation stock involved. If the employee holds restricted stock for which he or she has made a Section 83(b) election, the employee will be eligible for tax-free treatment.

POST-ACQUISITION TAX ISSUES

What is the principal tax planning goal in post-deal asset dispositions?

Post-deal asset disposition, if structured properly, can reduce or eliminate taxable gain.

It will be helpful to illustrate this point with a simple factual scenario. Purchaser corporation P wishes to acquire target T from selling corporation S in an LBO for $100. (In this example, we will bow to common usage and speak of a "target.") The operations of T consist of two divisions, T1 and T2. The purchase price for the T stock has been financed largely through borrowed funds. S has a tax basis in its T stock of $20, and T has a tax basis in the T1 and T2 assets of $0. To pay down acquisition debt, P must dispose of the T2 division to a third party shortly after the acquisition of T. Although the two divisions of T are of approximately equal value, P believes that it will be able to sell the T2 division alone for $60.

Proposition: If P has purchased all of T for $100, it should be able to dispose of all of T immediately thereafter for $100 and recognize no taxable gain. What should follow is that if P disposes of the T2 division, constituting one-half of the value of T, for $50, then no gain should be recognized there as well.

As a general matter, whether or not this proposition will be true depends upon whether P has purchased the assets of T or the stock of T. As explained earlier, where P, directly or through a subsidiary, purchases the assets of T for $100 or makes a Section 338 election, it will obtain a cost basis in all of the T assets and will recognize no gain if it disposes of some or all of those assets for an amount equal to their cost. However, where P purchases the stock of T and no Section 338 election is made, T retains a carryover basis in its assets and P will have to incur a tax on T's $50 of "built-in gain" upon a disposition of the T2 division.

The general rule is that the assets of T may not be disposed of by T without the recognition of a tax on the appreciation in those assets, notwithstanding that a buyer may have obtained a cost basis in the stock of T. The most direct and sure means of eliminating a second tax on built-in gain inside a target will be to obtain a cost basis in the target's assets through a direct asset acquisition, forward cash merger, or Section 338 transaction.

What restrictions are there on stock sales following an acquisition?

As a general matter, where a spin-off is followed by a sale by the shareholder of the stock of either the distributing corporation or the spun-off subsidiary, the spin-off is likely to violate the requirements of Section 355. One important exception to this rule is that a corporation is permitted to spin off a subsidiary to its own shareholders before combining with another company in a Section 368 tax-free reorganization, with some restrictions on cash payments.

OTHER TAX ISSUES

What role do state and local taxes play in structuring mergers and acquisitions?

State and local taxes generally play a secondary role in planning acquisitions and divestitures. First, most state income tax systems are based largely on the federal system, particularly in terms of what is taxable, to whom, when, and in what amount. Second, where an acquired corporation operates in a number of states, it can be inordinately difficult to assess the interaction of the various state tax systems. On the other hand, serious and embarrassing mistakes have been made by tax planners who ignored a transaction's state tax consequences. Although a detailed discussion of state income tax consequences deserves a book on its own, several extremely important state tax issues will be mentioned throughout the following discussion.

First and foremost, there are income taxes. These vary from state to state and may affect companies located outside the state.[13]

Beyond income taxes, there are numerous taxes imposed by states and localities that may affect an acquisition. Although these rarely amount to structural prohibitions or incentives, they often increase cost. For example, where real estate is being transferred, there will often be unavoidable real property gain, transfer, or deed recordation taxes. Perhaps the most notorious of the real property gain and transfer taxes worth mentioning specifically are those imposed by New York State and New York City, respectively, upon certain sales of real estate and of controlling interests in entities holding real estate.

Purchases of assets may not be exempt from a state's sales tax. Many states offer exemptions, but this should not be taken for granted. Check it out.

Certain types of state and local taxes that one would not associate directly with an acquisition can be significantly affected by an acquisition or by the particular structure of the acquisition. For example, a state's real property and personal property taxes are based upon an assessment of the value of the property owned by a taxpayer. Often, a transfer of ownership of the property will trigger a reassessment of the value of the property.

Are takeover expenses tax-deductible?

In 1992 the Supreme Court decided a case involving the deduction or capitalization of expenses incurred by a company (*National Starch*) in connection with a friendly takeover by another company (*Indopco*). The expenses included investment banking fees, legal fees, and other acquisition-related expenses.

The High Court affirmed the decision of the U.S. Court of Appeals for the Third Circuit in holding that the expenses do not qualify as current deductions since deductions are exceptions to the norm of capitalization, and they are allowed only if there is clear provision for them in the Tax Code. The burden of proof is on the taxpayer to show its right to the current deduction, and this burden was not met in the *National Starch* case.

The Court specifically rejected the taxpayer's interpretation of a previous Supreme Court decision that the expenditure had to be capitalized only if it created or enhanced a separate or distinct asset. An important factor in determining whether the appropriate tax treatment is an immediate deduction or capitalization of the expenditures is the taxpayer's expectation of benefits beyond the year in which the expenditures are incurred. The Court found that those future benefits did in fact exist and, consequently, that capitalization was appropriate.

On the other hand, in a 1992 bankruptcy court case involving the unsuccessful effort by Federated Department Stores and Allied Stores to prevent their being taken over by Campeau, fees paid by Federated and Allied to potential "white knights" (Edward DeBartolo and Macy's) were held to be deductible. Testimony elicited at the hearing indicated that such fees are ordinary and customary provisions demanded by potential "white knights" to compensate them for all the cost and expenses they have incurred in a hostile takeover situation.

The bankruptcy court in *Federated* had little difficulty distinguishing this case from *National Starch*. It pointed out that both the courts and the IRS had historically allowed deductions for costs related to abandoned business transactions. The bankruptcy court noted that here, unlike *National Starch*, the merger expenditures of the abandoned "white knight" conferred no possible benefits in the corporations taken over, since the outcome resulted in the exact opposite of any possible long-term future benefit.

ACCOUNTING CONSIDERATIONS

What are the principal authoritative accounting pronouncements covering the accounting for mergers and acquisitions?

The principal authoritative accounting pronouncement covering the subject of accounting for mergers and acquisitions (business combinations) is Accounting Principles Board Opinion No. 16, "Accounting for Business Combinations" (APB No. 16). Since its issuance in 1970, APB No. 16 has been the subject of formal interpretations by the SEC, the American Institute of Certified Public Accountants (AICPA), and the FASB, including the Emerging Issues Task Force.

What are the accepted methods of accounting for business combinations and how do they differ?

Two acceptable methods of accounting for business combinations are described in APB No. 16: the purchase method, and the pooling of interests method. In general, the purchase method accounts for a business combination as the acquisition of one company by another. The purchase price and costs of the acquisition are allocated to all the identified assets acquired and liabilities assumed, based on their fair values. If the purchase price exceeds the fair value of the purchased company's net assets, the excess is recorded as goodwill. Earnings or losses of the purchased company are included in the acquiring company's financial statements from the closing date of the acquisition.

The pooling of interests method accounts for a business combination as a uniting of ownership interests of two companies by the exchange of voting equity securities. No acquisition is recognized because the combination is accomplished without disbursing resources of the constituents. In pooling accounting, the assets, liabilities, and retained earnings of each company are carried forward at their previous carrying amounts. Operating results of both companies are combined for all periods prior to the closing date, and previously issued financial statements are restated as though the companies had always been combined.[14]

Are these methods alternatives in accounting for the same business combination?

No. In APB No. 16, the Accounting Principles Board concluded that both the purchase method and the pooling of interests method are acceptable in accounting for business combinations, but not as alternatives in accounting for the same business combination. The structure of the business combination transaction (as more fully described below) dictates which accounting method must be used. Also described below are the potential advantages and disadvantages of using each.

What are the advantages of using the pooling of interests method?

- Pooling of interests accounting is often preferred if the focus subsequent to the transaction is on the income statement. Income statements for periods subsequent to a pooling of interests are not burdened with additional depreciation, goodwill amortization, and other charges attributable to a purchase price in excess of book value. The higher reportable future income that usually results from application of pooling versus purchase accounting may be of added importance if the objective is a future sale of stock where the sales price is expected to be based on a multiple of reported earnings.

- There are no uncertainties or issues regarding purchase price determination and valuation.

- Prior years' financial statements are restated to reflect the business combination; thus, financial statement year-to-year comparability is not lost.

What are the disadvantages of using the pooling of interests method?

- Assets of the acquired company are not written up to fair value; return on assets and other financial performance measurements may not be comparable with other companies in the same industry.

- A trend of prior increases in earnings may be reversed because of restatement of prior years' results to include the combining company.

- The combining company may not have been audited, and performance of the audit work necessary to restate the financial statements may not be possible or, if possible, may be costly. Further, if audited, any exception in the reporting company's auditor's report may affect the report of the combined company.

When must the pooling of interests method be used to account for a business combination?

If a business combination meets 12 specific criteria outlined in APB No. 16, it must be accounted for as a pooling of interests. These criteria are broadly classified as pertaining to (1) the attributes of the combining companies, (2) the manner in which the companies are combined, and (3) the absence of planned transactions. All 12 criteria must be met if pooling accounting is to be used. If any one of the criteria is not met, the purchase method of accounting must be used. Pooling criteria include attributes of the combining companies:

- Neither company can be a subsidiary or division of another company within two years before the plan of combination is initiated.
- Each of the combining companies must be independent of the other combining companies: Intercorporate investments in a combining company cannot exceed 10 percent of outstanding voting common stock.

A business corporation wherein these conditions are met indicates that independent ownership interests are combined entirely to continue previously separate corporations. This avoids combinations of selected assets, operations, or ownership interests, which are more like purchases than sharings of risks and rights.

Pooling criteria also include the manner in which the companies are combined:

- The combination must be effected in a single transaction or completed in accordance with a specific plan within one year after the plan is initiated.
- A corporation must offer and issue only common stock with rights identical to those of the majority of its outstanding voting common stock (the class of stock with voting control) in exchange for substantially all of the voting common stock interest of the other company at the date the plan of combination is consummated ("substantially all" means a minimum of 90 percent).
- None of the combining companies may change the equity interest of the voting common stock in contemplation of the combination, either within two years before the plan of combination is initiated or between the dates the combination is initiated and consummated; changes in contemplation of the combination may include distributions to stockholders, additional issuances, exchanges, and retirements of securities.
- If either of the combining companies has acquired shares of the other's voting common stock (treasury stock), this must be for a purpose other than business combination, and no combining com-

pany may acquire more than a normal number of shares between the initiation date and the consummation date. Treasury stock acquired for purposes other than business combinations includes shares for stock option and compensation plans and other recurring distributions, provided a systematic pattern of reacquisitions is established at least two years before the plan of combination is initiated.

- The ratio of the interest of an individual common stockholder to that of other common stockholders in a combining company must remain the same as a result of the exchange of stock to effect the combination.
- The voting rights to which the common stock owners in the resulting combined company are entitled must be exercisable by the stockholders; the stockholders may be neither deprived of nor restricted in exercising those rights for any period. The issued shares may not be transferred, for example, to a voting trust.
- The combination must be resolved at the consummation date, and no provisions of the plan relating to the issue of securities or other conditions may be pending. This precludes the contingent issuance of additional shares.

The essence of a pooling of interests, or "pooling," is that separate shareholder interests lose their identity and all share mutually in the combined rights and risks of the combined entity. Mutual sharing is incompatible with alterations of relative voting rights, preferential claims to profits or assets for some shareholder groups, preservation of minority shareholder groups, acquisitions of common stock for assets or debt, and acquisitions of stock for the purpose of exchanging it.

These conditions prohibit the inclusion in the negotiations, either explicitly or by intent, of certain types of transactions after consummation of the transaction. These are prohibited because they are inconsistent with the concept of combining entire shareholder interests.

- The combined company may not agree directly or indirectly to retire or acquire all or part of the common stock issued to effect the combination.
- The combined company may not enter into other financial arrangements for the benefit of the former stockholders of a combining company—such as the guarantee of loans secured by stock issued in the combination—that in effect negate the exchange of equity securities.

- The combined company may not intend or plan to dispose of a significant portion of the assets of the combining companies within two years after combination, other than disposals in the ordinary course of business of the formerly separate companies or disposals in elimination of duplicate facilities or excess capacity.

The SEC generally requires that, in order to qualify for pooling accounting, the combining company must be an operating entity with "significant operations" (that is, something other than nominal). In one case, the SEC stated that a company with little operating activity, but with a substantial asset base (principally natural resource assets whose book values were significantly below fair market values), could not be party to a pooling of interests. The concept is that, in order to qualify for pooling accounting, there must be a combination of operating businesses. The SEC has not defined "little operating activity"; this must be determined on a case-by-case basis.

What are some reasons that preclude a business combination from being accounted for as a pooling of interests?

Literally hundreds of reasons preclude a business combination from being accounted for as a pooling of interests. Here are some of the more common ones:

- Sale of significant assets by the combining companies, either prior to consummation of the business combination or subsequent to the business combination. Dispositions occurring within three months prior to the business combination are presumed to be in contemplation of the pooling (and, accordingly, violate the pooling rules). Dispositions between three and six months prior to the business combination are also presumed to be in contemplation of the pooling if a company cannot substantiate that they were not. Between six months and two years prior to consummation, a disposition is presumed not to be in contemplation of the pooling if a company will represent that fact. The measure of "significance" for this purpose has generally been construed to be the same that is used for a reportable segment in FAS No. 14, "Financial Reporting for Segments of a Business Enterprise," that is, 10 percent of operating profits, assets, or sales.
- Combination with a new company formed by spinning off a subsidiary, or a new company formed to acquire the spun-off subsidiary.

Although it is generally understood that the acquisition of a company through an LBO will not qualify for pooling accounting, the autonomy criterion may also prevent the acquired business from subsequently qualifying for pooling accounting. For example, if the LBO group's investment vehicle is one of several subsidiaries of an LBO fund or holding company, an acquired business would fail to satisfy the autonomy criterion. If, however, the LBO is structured so that the acquired company is not controlled by another operating entity, that is, it is not a subsidiary following the LBO, it can qualify for pooling of interests accounting after two years, provided that all the other criteria are met.

- Acquisitions of "material amounts" of Treasury shares in relation to the planned combination. Treasury shares are material if they exceed 10 percent of the shares to be issued in the business combination.

- A contingency arrangement that is based on earnings levels, book values, or stock market prices subsequent to the consummation date. A contingency arrangement that relates to conditions existing at the consummation date, however, would not preclude pooling accounting (for example, an escrow related to tax returns not yet examined by the IRS).

Does the existence of a standstill agreement preclude a business combination from being accounted for as a pooling of interests?

The FASB's Emerging Issues Task Force has addressed this issue in connection with standstill agreements that prohibit a more than 10 percent shareholder from acquiring additional shares for a specified period. The Task Force reached a consensus that pooling accounting would not be precluded if the standstill agreement was not made in contemplation of the combination and was with a less than majority shareholder. A standstill agreement made in contemplation of a particular business combination with a more than 10 percent shareholder, however, would preclude pooling accounting. Pooling accounting would also be precluded if a standstill agreement with a 10 percent or less shareholder was in contemplation of the combination, if that shareholder and other dissenters aggregated more than 10 percent of the shares issued in the combination.

Does the granting or exercise of a lockup option preclude pooling accounting for a subsequent merger between the parties?

Lockup arrangements take many forms, but most have the same basic structure: an agreement that Company A will acquire all or a specific part of Company B, and that Company A will realize an economic gain if another company buys Company B or the specified part of Company B.

A lockup structured as an option agreement does not preclude pooling accounting, provided that no consideration is issued or received for the option and the option is not exercised. If the lockup is structured as a sale of stock, pooling accounting becomes more questionable.

If a buyer is required to account for a business combination using the pooling of interests method, how will this affect the combining companies' financial statements?

In a pooling, the carrying amounts of the assets and liabilities of the constituent companies remain unchanged. The carrying amounts of assets and liabilities of the separate companies are added together to become the assets and liabilities of the combined corporation. (For more on this subject, see Chapter 10.)

At what date should a buyer that applies the pooling of interests method report combined results?

A buyer that applies the pooling of interests method of accounting for a combination should report results of operations for the fiscal period in which the combination occurs as though the companies had been combined as of the beginning of the period. Results of operations for that fiscal period thus comprise those of the separate companies combined from the beginning of the period to the date the combination is consummated and those of the combined operations from that date to the end of the period. Previously issued financial statements are restated as though the companies had always been combined.

What accounting is required for expenses related to a pooling?

All costs incurred to effect a pooling transaction should be recognized as expenses of the combined corporation in determining net income. Such expenses include SEC filing fees; investment banking fees; legal, accounting, and consultant fees; and costs incurred in combining and integrating the operations of the previously separate companies, including implementation of efficiencies.

What are the advantages of the purchase method?

- Purchase accounting is often preferred if the acquirer's focus after the transaction will be on the balance sheet. Assets and liabilities are recognized at their fair values instead of at the acquired company's historical costs. Thus, the post-combination balance sheet appears healthier under purchase accounting than under pooling accounting. This may be of added importance if the post-combination balance sheet is a key factor in a lender's decision to finance the acquisition.

- No restatements of prior years' financial statements are required, so reported sales and earnings trends may show an improvement.

What are the disadvantages of the purchase method?

- Accounting income is exposed to the write-off of additional depreciation, goodwill amortization, and other charges that may adversely affect reported earnings trends.

- Uncertainties regarding purchase price determination and valuation exist.

- Prior years' financial statements are not restated and, therefore, are not comparable.

When must the purchase method be used to account for a business combination?

The purchase method of accounting must be used for any business combination that does not meet all the conditions for pooling of interests treatment.

How is the recorded purchase price of a transaction determined under the purchase method?

The purchase method follows principles normally applicable under historical cost accounting for acquisitions of assets and issuances of stock. The principles applied depend on the nature of the transaction:

- If the company is acquired by exchanging cash or other assets, the purchase price is the amount of cash disbursed or fair value of other assets distributed.
- If the company is acquired by incurring liabilities, the purchase price is the present value of the amounts to be paid.
- If the company is acquired by issuing shares of stock, the value assigned to the stock is the fair value of the consideration received. As a practical matter, in most business combinations it is easier to value the stock exchanged, and this is normally done for convenience.

Cash paid, liabilities incurred, and securities issued constitute the major portion of the purchase price of most acquisitions. Numerous other items, however, must be considered for inclusion in the purchase price. Here are some of them:

- Direct expenses, such as finder's and directly related professional fees (legal, investment banking, accounting, appraisal, and environmental consulting)
- Premium or discount on a debt security issued or assumed, with the imputed liability adjusted to present value based on current interest rates, if stated rates differ significantly from current market rates
- A negotiated adjustment to the purchase price related to assumption of a contingent liability such as a lawsuit or tax examination

Under the purchase method, how should the buyer's cost be allocated to the assets acquired and liabilities assumed?

Under APB No. 16, the buyer's cost is allocated to individual assets and liabilities at their fair market values at the time of acquisition. Independent appraisals may be used in determining the fair value of some assets and liabilities. Subsequent sales of assets may also provide evidence of values.

The following are general guidelines for assigning amounts to individual assets acquired and liabilities assumed:

- Present value, determined at appropriate current interest rates, of receivables (net of estimated allowances for uncollectibility and collection costs, if necessary); accounts and notes payable, long-term debt, and other claims payable; and other liabilities, such as warranty, vacation pay, deferred compensation, unfavorable leases, contracts and commitments, and plant closing expenses incident to the acquisition

- Current replacement cost of raw materials inventories and plant and equipment, adjusted to remaining economic lives
- Net realizable value of marketable securities and property and equipment to be sold or to be used temporarily
- Appraised value of identifiable intangibles and other assets
- Finished goods and merchandise at estimated selling prices less the sum of (1) the cost of disposal and (2) a reasonable profit allowance for the selling effort of the acquiring corporation
- Work-in-process inventory at estimated selling prices of finished goods less the sum of (1) the cost to complete, (2) the cost of disposal, and (3) a reasonable profit allowance for the completing and selling effort of the acquiring corporation based on profit for similar finished goods

Previously recorded goodwill of the acquired company is not recognized in the purchase price allocation. If the acquired company sponsors a single-employer defined benefit pension plan, the assignment of the purchase price to the individual assets acquired and liabilities assumed shall include a liability for the projected benefit obligation in excess of plan assets, or an asset for plan assets in excess of the projected benefit obligation.

The following example illustrates the above principles. Assume that Corporation A acquires Corporation B in a business combination accounted for as a purchase on September 30, 1998. The purchase price is $750,000 cash and 50,000 shares of Corporation A common stock. Transaction costs are $200,000 (unrelated to stock issuance).

The historical carrying amounts and fair values of Corporation B's assets and liabilities on September 30, 1998, are as shown in Table 5-1. The purchase price allocation to the acquired assets would have been as shown in Table 5-2. If the fair value of Corporation A common stock on September 30, 1998, was $20 per share, the purchase price would have been computed as follows in Table 5-2. The purchase price allocation based on $30 per share value would have been as shown in Table 5-3.

T A B L E 5-1

Corporation B Balance Sheet, September 30, 1998

	Carrying Amount (in thousands)	Fair Value
Assets		
Cash	$100	$100
Accounts receivable, net	300	300
Inventories	600	680
Short-term prepayments	120	100
Land	500	650
Other plant assets, net	1,000	1,250
Patent	80	100
Total assets	$2,700	$3,180
Liabilities and Stockholder's Equity		
Current liabilities	$700	$700
Long-term debt	500	480
Capital stock, $5 par	600	
Paid-in capital in excess of par	400	
Retained earnings	500	
Net assets acquired		2,000
Total liabilities and stockholder's equity	$2,700	$3,180

How should the difference in the value of the acquired net assets versus cost be accounted for? Suppose this is negative?

If the sum of the market or appraised values of identifiable assets acquired less liabilities assumed exceeds the cost of the acquired company, the values otherwise assignable to noncurrent assets acquired (except long-term investments and marketable securities) should be reduced by a proportionate amount of the excess to determine the assigned values. If the values of noncurrent assets are reduced to zero, then a deferred credit is recorded on the buyer's balance sheet for the excess of the aggregate assigned value of identifiable assets over cost

T A B L E   5-2*

Purchase Price Allocation Based on $20 Per Share

	Fair Value	Purchase Price Allocation
	(in thousands)	
Cash	$100	$100
Accounts receivable, net	300	300
Inventories	680	680
Short-term prepayments	100	100
Land	650	634[a]
Other plant assets, net	1,250	1,219[a]
Patent	100	97[a]
Total assets	$3,180	$3,130

[a]Discount ($50) was allocated pro rata to noncurrent assets.

T A B L E   5-3*

Purchase Price Allocation Based on $30 Per Share

	Fair Value	Purchase Price Allocation
	(in thousands)	
Cash	$100	$100
Accounts receivable, net	300	300
Inventories	680	680
Short-term prepayments	100	100
Land	650	650
Other plant assets, net	1,250	1,250
Patent		
Goodwill	100	550
Total assets	$3,180	$3,630

*In both transactions, the purchase price was computed as cash of $750, out-of-pocket costs of $200, assumed liabilities of $1,180, plus 50,000 shares of stock. If the stock is valued at $20 per share, the asset value is $50 more than the purchase price of $3,130,000. If the stock is valued at $30 per share, the asset value is $450,000 less than the purchase price (additional goodwill).

(sometimes called "negative goodwill") of an acquired company. Negative goodwill is considered a deferred credit rather than an intangible (such as "positive goodwill"), and it should not be netted against positive goodwill when reporting those amounts in the financial statements. Negative goodwill is amortized systematically as an increase in reported income. The list of factors discussed above for amortizing goodwill should be considered in determining the amortization period for negative goodwill.

How are the differences between the market or appraised values of specific assets and liabilities and the income tax bases of those assets accounted for?

FAS No. 96, "Accounting for Income Taxes," requires, as a general rule, that a deferred tax liability or asset be recognized for the tax consequences of differences between the assigned fair values and the tax bases of assets and liabilities recognized in a business combination. A deferred tax liability or asset is not recognized for a difference between the assigned amount and the tax basis of goodwill, unallocated "negative" goodwill, and leveraged leases. FAS No. 96 contains complexities that could affect the accounting for business combinations. The facts and circumstances of each transaction need to be evaluated.

How much time does a buyer have to complete the accounting under the purchase method?

The so-called allocation period, during which the buyer identifies and values the assets acquired and the liabilities assumed, ends when the acquiring enterprise is no longer waiting for information that it has arranged to obtain and that is known to be available or obtainable. Although the time required varies with circumstances, the allocation period should usually not exceed one year from the consummation of a business combination. The existence of a pre-acquisition contingency for which an asset, a liability, or an impairment of an asset cannot be estimated does not, of itself, extend the allocation period.

What are pre-acquisition contingencies, and how should they be considered in the allocation of purchase price?

A contingency is an existing condition, situation, or set of circumstances involving uncertainty about possible gain or loss to an enterprise that will ultimately be resolved when one or more future events occur or fail to occur. A pre-acquisition contingency is a contingency of the acquired enterprise that is in existence before consummation of a business combination; it can be a contingent asset, a contingent liability, or a contingent impairment of an asset. Examples of pre-acquisition contingencies include pending or threatened litigation, obligations relating to product warranties and product defects, and actual or possible claims or assessments. These include income tax examinations, assessments by environmental agencies, guarantees of indebtedness of others, and impairment of the carrying amount of productive assets used in the business.

A pre-acquisition contingency is included in the allocation of the purchase price based on an amount determined as follows:

- If the fair value of the pre-acquisition contingency *can* be determined during the allocation period, that pre-acquisition contingency is included in the allocation of the purchase price based on that fair value.

- If the fair value *cannot* be determined during the allocation period, that pre-acquisition contingency shall be included in the allocation of the purchase price only if information available prior to the end of the allocation period indicates that it is probable that a contingent asset existed, a contingent liability had been incurred, or an existing asset might be impaired at the consummation of the business combination. Implicit in this condition is that it must be probable that one or more future events will occur confirming the contingency, and that amount of the asset or liability can be reasonably estimated.

Contingencies that arise from the acquisition and that did not exist prior to the acquisition are the buyer's contingencies rather than pre-acquisition contingencies of the acquired company.

At what date should a buyer who has applied the purchase method report combined results?

The acquisition date of a company ordinarily is the date assets are received and other assets are given or securities are issued. The reported income of the buyer includes operations of the acquired company beginning with the date of acquisition. In a purchase business combination, there is no restatement of prior-period financial statements. In certain situations, however, the acquisition date may be "as of" a date earlier than the closing date. These include, for example, situations in which the parties intend to fix a determinable price as of a specified date other than the closing date or to develop a formula whereby changes in earnings or market price between the specified date and the closing date will be considered in the final purchase price. If a date earlier than the closing date is considered appropriate, the following conditions should be met in order for the earlier date to be used as the date on which the buyer includes the results of operations of the acquired company:

- The parties reach a firm purchase agreement that includes specifying the date of acquisition other than the closing date. Effective control of the acquired company (including the risks and rewards of ownership) transfers to the acquiring company as of the specified date.
- The time period between the specified date and the closing date is relatively short.

What are typical forms of contingent consideration in an acquisition, and how should such consideration be included in determining the cost of an acquired company?

A business combination may provide for the issuance of stock or the transfer of cash or other consideration contingent on specified transactions or events in the future. Agreements often provide that a portion of the consideration be placed in escrow and distributed or returned when the specified event has occurred. In general, to the extent that the contingent consideration can be determined at the time of the acquisition, such amount shall be included in determining the cost of the acquired company.

As is often the case, however, the amount of the contingent consideration may not be known at the time of the acquisition. As an example, additional consideration may be contingent on maintaining or achieving specified earnings levels in the future. When the contingency is resolved or resolution is probable and additional consideration is payable, the acquiring company shall record the current fair value of the consideration paid as an additional cost of the acquired company. This subsequent recognition of additional cost requires an adjustment to the initial amounts recorded at the date of acquisition. Generally, the amount of goodwill is adjusted for the amount of additional consideration paid.

What accounting is required for expenses related to a purchase?

Direct acquisition costs incurred by an acquiring company effecting a business combination accounted for under the purchase method are included as part of the purchase price of the acquired company. Direct acquisition costs incurred by an acquired company, or its major or controlling shareholders, should generally not be included as part of the cost of the acquired company. Acquisition costs incurred by the acquired company are presumed to be taken into account indirectly by the acquiring company in setting the purchase price. If, however, the acquiring company agrees to reimburse the acquired company's major or controlling shareholders for acquisition costs incurred by them, these costs should be included as part of the purchase price of the acquired company. Direct acquisition costs include fees paid to investment bankers, legal fees, accounting fees, appraisal fees, and other consulting fees.

Fees paid to an investment banker in connection with a business combination accounted for as a purchase when the investment banker is also providing interim financing or debt underwriting services must be allocated between direct costs of the acquisition and debt issue costs.

What are the disclosure requirements for business combinations?

The disclosures required for a business combination accounted for by either the purchase or pooling of interests method are governed by APB No. 16, as amended, and the rules and regulations of the SEC.

For a *purchase* business combination, the following disclosures are required in the notes to the financial statements of both public and nonpublic enterprises:

- Name and a brief description of the acquired enterprise
- Method of accounting for the combination—that is, by the purchase method
- Period for which results of operations of the acquired enterprise are included in the income statement of the acquiring enterprise
- Cost of the acquired enterprise and, if applicable, the number of shares of stock issued or issuable and the amount assigned to the issued and issuable shares

- Description of the plan for amortization of acquired goodwill, the amortization method, and the amortization period
- Contingent payments, options, or commitments specified in the acquisition agreement and their proposed accounting treatment

In addition, notes to the financial statements of the acquiring enterprise for the period in which a purchase business combination occurs should include as supplemental information the following pro forma information (public companies only):

- Results of operations for the current period as though the enterprises had combined at the beginning of the period
- Results of operations for the immediately preceding period as though the enterprises had combined at the beginning of that period, if comparative financial statements are presented

The supplemental pro forma information should, at a minimum, disclose revenue, income before extraordinary items, net income, and earnings per share. To present pro forma information, income taxes, interest expense, preferred stock dividends, depreciation, and amortization of assets, including goodwill, should be adjusted to their accounting bases recognized in recording the combination. Pro forma presentation of results of operations of periods prior to the combination transaction should be limited to the immediately preceding period.

For a *pooling* of interests, the following disclosures are required in the notes to the financial statements:

- Name and brief description of the enterprises combined, except an enterprise whose name is carried forward to the combined enterprise
- Method of accounting for the combination—that is, by the pooling of interests method
- Description and number of shares of stock issued in the business combination
- Details of the results of operations of the previously separate enterprises for the period before the combination is consummated that are included in the current combined net income (The details should include revenue, extraordinary items, net income, other changes in stockholders' equity, and amount of and manner of accounting for intercompany transactions.)

- Description of the nature of adjustments to the net assets of the combined enterprises to adopt the same accounting practices
- Description of the effects of the changes on net income previously reported by the separate enterprises and now presented in comparative financial statements
- Details of an increase or decrease in retained earnings attributable to a change of the fiscal year of a combining enterprise (The details should include revenue, expenses, extraordinary items, net income, and other changes in stockholders' equity for the period excluded from the reported results of operations.)
- Reconciliation of revenue and earnings previously reported by the enterprise that issues the stock to effect the combination with the combined amounts currently presented in financial statements and summaries (The new enterprise formed to effect a combination may instead disclose the earnings of the separate enterprises that constitute combined earnings for prior periods.)

In addition, the notes to the financial statements should disclose details of the effects of a pooling business combination consummated before the financial statements are issued, but that are either incomplete as of the date of the financial statements or initiated after that date. The details should include revenue, net income, earnings per share, and the effects of expected changes in accounting methods as if the combination had been consummated at the date of the financial statements.

What is pro forma financial information?

Pro forma financial information reflects the impact on historical financial statements of a particular business combination and its financing as if the transaction had been consummated at an earlier date. Pro forma information ordinarily includes (1) a description of the transaction, the entities involved, and the periods for which the pro forma information is presented, and (2) a columnar presentation of historical condensed balance sheet and income statements, pro forma adjustments, and pro forma results.

Pro forma adjustments to the income statement are computed assuming that the transaction was consummated at the beginning of the fiscal year and include adjustments that give effect to events that are (1) directly attributable to the transaction, (2) expected to have a continuing impact on the registrant, and (3) factually supportable.

How should the fair value or carrying amount of preferred stock issued in business combinations be determined?

The distinctive attributes of preferred stock make some preferred issues similar to debt securities, whereas others are more similar to common stock, with many variations between the extremes. Determining the appropriate carrying value to assign to preferred stock issued in a business combination will be affected by its characteristics.

Even though the principle of recording the fair value of consideration received for stock issued applies to all equity securities, preferred as well as common, the carrying value of preferred securities may be determined in practice on the same basis as debt securities. For example, the carrying value of a nonvoting, nonconvertible preferred stock that lacks characteristics of common stock may be determined by comparing the specified dividend and redemption terms with debt securities that have similar terms and market risks.

What is pushdown accounting?

Pushdown accounting refers to the establishment of a new accounting and reporting basis in an acquired company's separate financial statements, resulting from the purchase and substantial change of ownership of its outstanding voting equity securities. The buyers purchase price is "pushed down" to the acquired company and used to restate the carrying value of its assets and liabilities. For example, if all the voting equity securities of a company are purchased, the assets and liabilities of the company are restated using fair market values so that the excess of the restated amounts of the assets over the restated amounts of the liabilities equals the buyer's purchase price.

In what circumstances should pushdown accounting be applied?

The SEC requires the use of pushdown accounting by public enterprises with respect to corporations that are substantially or wholly owned. The SEC stated that when the form of ownership is within the control of the buyer, the basis of accounting for purchased assets and liabilities should be the same regardless of whether the entity continues to exist or is merged into the buyer. The SEC recognized, however, that the existence of outstanding public debt, preferred stock, or a significant minority interest in a subsidiary might affect the buyer's ability to control the form of ownership. As a result, the SEC, although encouraging its use, generally does not insist on the application of pushdown accounting in these circumstances. Pushdown accounting is optional for the separate financial statements of a nonpublic company.

CONCLUDING COMMENTS

Deal structuring stands with financing at the vital center of any transaction. Occurring after the wide-ranging adventures of planning and finding, and before the narrower pursuits of due diligence and closing, structuring (along with financing) lies at the heart of the M&A process. Using the basic categories of U.S. tax law, this chapter has shown some of the many ways a merger or acquisition can be accomplished to achieve the best tax and accounting results for both buyer and seller. Parallel challenges await dealmakers venturing into other countries. As always, specialists are needed, but dealmakers who seek to understand the basic concepts in this area will reap rich rewards. Whether you are a buyer, a seller, or an advisor, you are sure to benefit not only financially but professionally as you carry the lessons of structuring from one deal into the next one (and the next . . .).

TRANSACTION DIAGRAMS

The following diagrams (Figures 5-1 to 5-11) illustrate graphically many of the transactions discussed in this book. In each diagram, an SH represents a shareholder, a square is a corporation, and a circle represents corporate assets. Vertical and diagonal lines indicate the ownership of stock or assets, and arrows represent the flow of cash, assets, stock, and so on.

F I G U R E 5-1

Stock Purchase

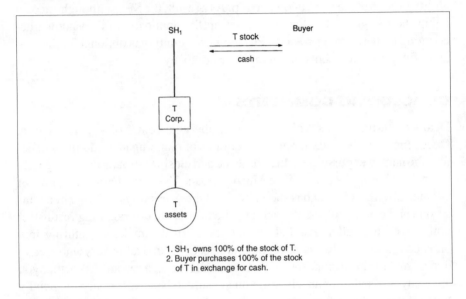

1. SH₁ owns 100% of the stock of T.
2. Buyer purchases 100% of the stock of T in exchange for cash.

F I G U R E 5-2

Asset Purchase

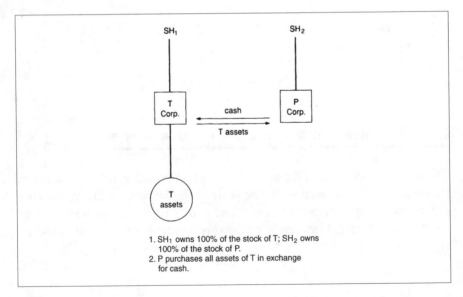

1. SH₁ owns 100% of the stock of T; SH₂ owns 100% of the stock of P.
2. P purchases all assets of T in exchange for cash.

F I G U R E 5-3

Taxable Forward Merger

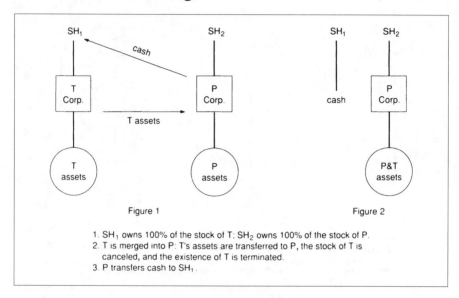

Figure 1   Figure 2

1. SH$_1$ owns 100% of the stock of T; SH$_2$ owns 100% of the stock of P.
2. T is merged into P: T's assets are transferred to P, the stock of T is canceled, and the existence of T is terminated.
3. P transfers cash to SH$_1$.

F I G U R E 5-4

Taxable Reverse Merger

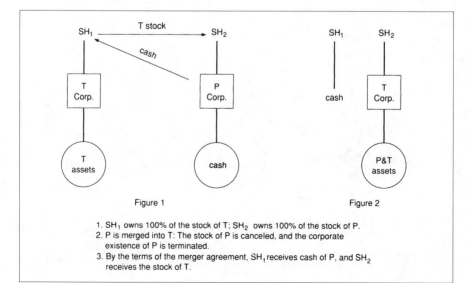

Figure 1   Figure 2

1. SH$_1$ owns 100% of the stock of T; SH$_2$ owns 100% of the stock of P.
2. P is merged into T: The stock of P is canceled, and the corporate existence of P is terminated.
3. By the terms of the merger agreement, SH$_1$ receives cash of P, and SH$_2$ receives the stock of T.

F I G U R E   5-5

F I G U R E   5-5

Taxable Forward Subsidiary Merger

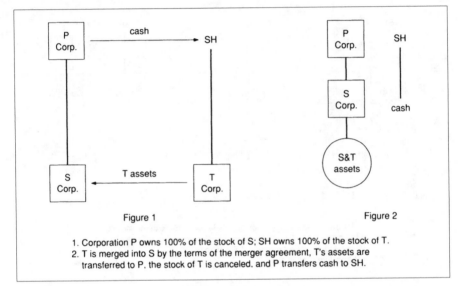

Figure 1

Figure 2

1. Corporation P owns 100% of the stock of S; SH owns 100% of the stock of T.
2. T is merged into S by the terms of the merger agreement, T's assets are
   transferred to P, the stock of T is canceled, and P transfers cash to SH.

F I G U R E   5-6

Tax-Free Forward Merger (A Reorganization)

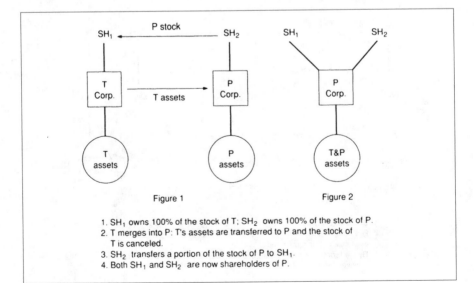

Figure 1

Figure 2

1. SH_1 owns 100% of the stock of T; SH_2 owns 100% of the stock of P.
2. T merges into P: T's assets are transferred to P and the stock of
   T is canceled.
3. SH_2 transfers a portion of the stock of P to SH_1.
4. Both SH_1 and SH_2 are now shareholders of P.

Tax-Free Forward Triangular Merger
[Hybrid A Reorganization–Section 368 (a)(2)(D)]

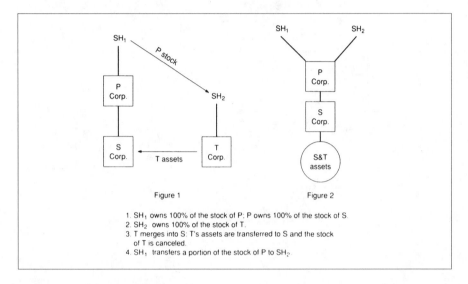

Figure 1   Figure 2

1. SH₁ owns 100% of the stock of P; P owns 100% of the stock of S.
2. SH₂ owns 100% of the stock of T.
3. T merges into S: T's assets are transferred to S and the stock of T is canceled.
4. SH₁ transfers a portion of the stock of P to SH₂.

Tax-Free Acquisition of Stock for Voting Stock
(B Reorganization)

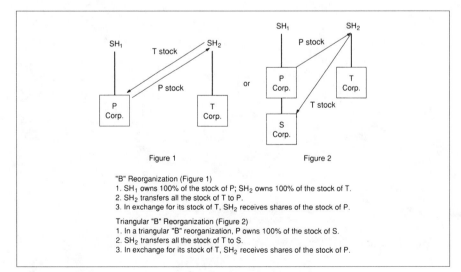

Figure 1   Figure 2

"B" Reorganization (Figure 1)
1. SH₁ owns 100% of the stock of P; SH₂ owns 100% of the stock of T.
2. SH₂ transfers all the stock of T to P.
3. In exchange for its stock of T, SH₂ receives shares of the stock of P.

Triangular "B" Reorganization (Figure 2)
1. In a triangular "B" reorganization, P owns 100% of the stock of S.
2. SH₂ transfers all the stock of T to S.
3. In exchange for its stock of T, SH₂ receives shares of the stock of P.

F I G U R E 5-9

Acquisition of Property for Voting Stock (C Reorganization)

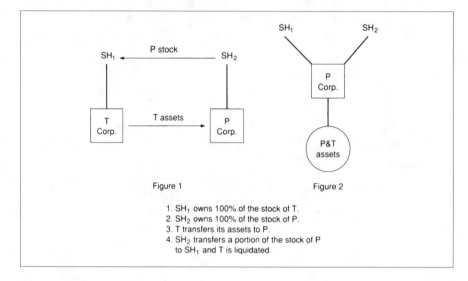

Figure 1   Figure 2

1. SH_1 owns 100% of the stock of T.
2. SH_2 owns 100% of the stock of P.
3. T transfers its assets to P.
4. SH_2 transfers a portion of the stock of P to SH_1 and T is liquidated.

F I G U R E 5-10

Acquisition of Property for Voting Stock (D Reorganization)

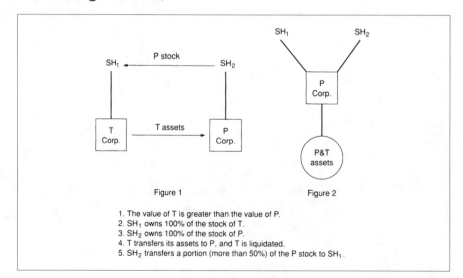

Figure 1   Figure 2

1. The value of T is greater than the value of P.
2. SH_1 owns 100% of the stock of T.
3. SH_2 owns 100% of the stock of P.
4. T transfers its assets to P, and T is liquidated.
5. SH_2 transfers a portion (more than 50%) of the P stock to SH_1.

F I G U R E   5-11

National Starch Transaction (Section 351 Acquisition)

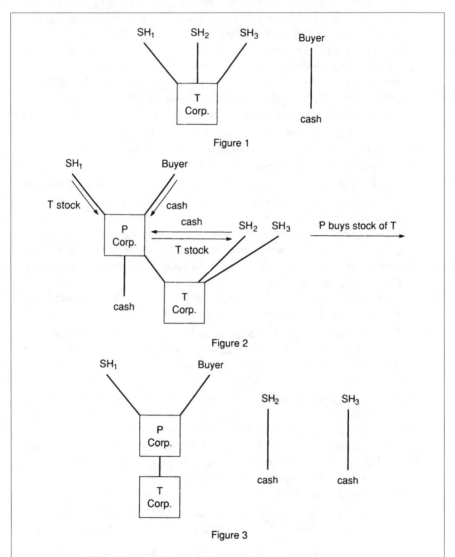

Figure 1

Figure 2

P buys stock of T

Figure 3

1. SH_1, SH_2, and SH_3 together own 100% of the stock of T.
2. Buyer and SH_1 incorporate P: Buyer transfers cash to P;
   SH_1 transfers its stock of T. Buyer and SH_1 receive the stock of P.
3. P buys the stock of T from SH_2 and SH_3 in exchange for cash.

E N D N O T E S

1. Rule 145 of the Securities Act of 1933, concerning "Reclassification of Securities, Mergers, Consolidations and Acquisition of Assets," defines transactions within the rule as including "an 'offer,' 'offer to sell,' 'offer for sale,' or 'sale.'" These fall under the rule when "there is submitted for the vote or consent of such security-holders a plan or agreement for: reclassifications . . . mergers or consolidations . . . or transfers of assets." *Securities Act Rules, Volume 1, Rules 100 through 236: General Rules and Regulations under the Securities Act of 1933,* September 15, 1998 (New York: Bowne & Co., 1998).

2. Gain from the sale of assets may be taxed at 8, 10, 14, 15, 18, 20, 25, 28, 31, 36, or 39.6 percent, depending on the holding period, date sold, type of asset, and the amount of other income.

3. Shareholders may not have to pay taxes on their dividends if they hold their stock for a certain period of time. This "dividends received deduction" is available to shareholders who have held the stock (and been at economic risk from it) for more than 45 days—or more than 90 in some cases (such as preferred stock). The Taxpayer Relief Act of 1997, in Section 1015, preserved this deduction but made it more stringent by setting forth some more complex buy/sell time frame requirements, and by stipulating that the dividends received deduction will only be available to shareholders that meet the holding period requirement with respect to each dividend received.

4. Under current law, an issuer of debt can deduct the interest that it pays, but an issuer of equity may not deduct dividend payments it makes. The interest/dividend distinction became somewhat complicated after the Taxpayer Relief Act of 1997, which stated that no deduction will be allowed for interest on an instrument that is payable in stock of the issuer or a related party. This raises the issue of treatment of convertible debt, but Kenneth R. Goldberg of Jones, Day, Reavis & Pogue (New York) assures clients that "it is not anticipated that the new rule will apply to convertible debt if the conversion price is significantly higher than the price of the issuer's stock at the time the debt is issued." *Source: 1997 Tax Reform: Summaries of Selected Provisions Affecting Corporations, Other Entities, and Business Executives,* August 1997, p. 31.

5. See Section 401 of the Taxpayer Relief Act of 1997, effective for years beginning after December 31, 1997, and for property placed in service after December 31, 1998.

6. The actual wording is as follows: "The tentative minimum tax for a corporation shall be zero for any taxable year if—(A) such corporation met the $5,000,000 gross receipts text . . . for its first taxable year beginning after December 31, 1996, and (B) such corporation would meet such test for the

taxable year and all prior taxable years beginning after such first taxable year if such test were applied by substituting '$7,500,000' for '$5,000,000.'"

7. See Section 1082 of the Taxpayer Relief Act of 1997. Prior to August 5, 1997 (the effective date of this provision), the carryback period was up to three years and the carryforward period was up to 20 years. The new tax law preserved the three-year carryback for losses incurred by farmers and small businesses in presidentially declared disaster areas. The 1997 changes do not apply to special carryback rules relating to real estate investment trusts, specified liability losses, excess interest losses, or NOLs arising from casualty losses of individual taxpayers.

8. Code Section 368 (a) 1 (A). The regulation specifies that the merger or consolidation must be "effected pursuant to the corporation laws of the United States or a State or Territory or the District of Columbia." Reg. Section 368-2(b) 1 cited in Martin D. Ginsberg and Jack S. Levin, *Mergers, Acquisitions, and Buyouts: A Transactional Analysis of the Governing Tax, Legal, and Accounting Considerations* (New York: Aspen Law and Business, March 1998), Section 801. 1. Ginsberg and Levin are the main source for our definitions of A, B, C, and D reorganizations.

9. Except for transactions closed before July 25, 1991, the OBRA '93's treatment of intangibles rendered moot (at least for now) a 1991 Supreme Court decision that broadened the definition of intangibles to include goodwill. In *Newark Morning Ledger Co. v. U.S.,* the U.S. Supreme Court said that if the value of an acquired asset can be measured and will diminish over time, this value can be depreciated over time. Assets covered under the *Newark* decision were any identifiable asset the value of which obviously depends on the continued and voluntary patronage of customers." These will now all fall under OBRA's 15-year, 100 percent treatment, as none were excepted. In 1998, proposed regulations treat Section 197 intangibles as Section 1245 property and thus subject to "recapture" as ordinary income. See Ginsberg and Levin (op. cit., note 8). Section 403.4.4.2.

10. '93, Section 13261, reads in part at Subsection F (9) as follows: "The term 'amortizable section 197 intangibles' shall not include any Section 197 intangibles . . . for which depreciation or amortization would not have been allowable but for this section . . . and which is acquired by the taxpayer after the date of the enactment of this section under certain conditions." Further, Section 197 treatment will not apply to an intangible "acquired by the taxpayer . . . to recognize gain on the disposition of the intangible and to pay a tax on such a gain" under certain conditions.

11. A recharacterization of debt into equity raises a somewhat different concern in the case of the debt of a partnership. Debts of a limited partnership for which no general or limited partner is personally liable (nonrecourse debts) increase

the basis of the limited partners in the partnership. A recharacterization will not convert a partnership into a taxpaying entity. Rather, the lender will become a partner, and the entire amount of the recharacterized debt will be allocated to increase the lender's basis. Other partners' bases will shrink, causing them to encounter unexpected tax results. For example, cash distributions in excess of their recharacterized bases will produce income, and if the partnership generates a taxable loss, some or all of the loss may have to be allocated to the lender-partner.

12. Conflicts of interest have become a common theme in court-ordered studies of bankrupt MBOs. One such study is a 369-page report on the buyout of Best Products Inc., released in August 1992. Written by Joel Plassick, a partner in the Atlanta law firm of Kilpatrick & Cody, this study alleges a number of problems with the buyout, including apparent conflicts of interest, and finds grounds to sue several parties. For an early critique of the conflicts of interest raised in MBOs, see Louis Lowenstein, "Management Buyouts," *Columbia Law Review,* May 1985. The issue of parent company liability arises frequently in litigation following leveraged buyouts. In August 1992, bankruptcy court judge Alexander Pashay cleared such a post-LBO case for trial. In this decision, *In re: Hillsborough Holdings Corp. et al. U.S. Bankruptcy Court, Tampa, Florida, Division 89-9715-8p1,* Judge Pashay questioned whether certain post-buyout divestitures by Walter Industries (which themselves were structured as buyouts) "were done for legitimate business purposes or . . . solely for the purpose of denuding [the acquired company] Celotex of assets."

13. One of the laws limiting the reach of state income taxes was broadened in early 1992 when the U.S. Supreme Court declared a "de minimis" exception to a 1959 law establishing a federal limitation on state income taxes. This exception, set forth in *Wisconsin Department of Revenue v. William Wrigley, Jr., Co.,* found that certain activities were "not entirely ancillary to requests for purchases" and therefore not exempt from state income tax.

14. In June 1997, the FASB issued a report warning about problems with the current pooling-versus-purchase distinctions. Although the FASB has taken no major formal action on this front, it is worth noting the 34-page report, by L. Todd Johnson and Bryan D. Yokley, *Issues Associated with the FASB Project on Business Combinations.* This report is No. 174-A in the Financial Accounting Series of the FASB, a subscription service published monthly by FASB's parent, The Financial Accounting Foundation, in Norwalk, Connecticut. For a discussion of this report and a related FASB project, see Martin Sikora, "Do Acquirers Face a Goodwill Squeeze?: Accounting Board Weights Fast Goodwill Write-Offs and Elimination of Pooling," *Mergers & Acquisitions,* May/June 1998, pp. 6ff.

CHAPTER 6

The Due Diligence Inquiry

INTRODUCTION

The basic function of due diligence, using the term in the context of mergers and acquisitions, is to assess the benefits and the liabilities of a proposed acquisition by inquiring into all relevant aspects of the past, present, and predictable future of the business to be purchased. The term is also used, in securities law, to describe the duty of care and review to be exercised by officers, directors, underwriters, and others in connection with public offerings of securities.

Due diligence plays a critical role in the m/a/b process. Lack of good M&A due diligence is a leading cause of poor postmerger financial performance and a major reason for postmerger lawsuits against officers and directors. Ongoing research by Mercer Management Consulting shows that half of mergers decrease shareholder wealth, and that a leading cause of this decline in value is "inadequate due diligence." Annual surveys of directors and officers (D&O) liability insurance conducted by Watson Wyatt Worldwide of Chicago consistently show that companies involved in mergers are more likely than others to be sued, and that a leading cause of lawsuits arises from poor due diligence.[1] Clearly, then, the due diligence phase of any acquisition will be critical to the future of the new company and its owners.

GETTING STARTED

When does the due diligence process begin?

The due diligence process begins from the moment a buyer senses a possible acquisition opportunity. The buyer then starts to examine the information about the company that is readily available at this early time. For public companies, this information is usually derived from public documents, ranging from broadly disseminated press reports about the company to the company's recent filings with the SEC, to an offering memorandum the company or its bankers might have prepared for the consideration of potential buyers.

The initial stage of due diligence review is really the search and screen, valuation, and financing process described in Chapters 2, 3, and 4. This review (which may be conducted by the acquirer or a qualified independent professional) seeks to answer three basic questions:

- Is it in our stockholders' interest to own and operate this company?
- How much is it worth?
- Can we afford it?

To discover the answers, the early focus is on the firm's operations and its assets: What does it do for a living, and how efficiently does it employ its assets?

What assets should be appraised?

Appraisal of salable assets used in the business, such as machinery, real property, or inventories, is mandatory. Such appraisals can be key for lenders that base the amount of their loans on the market value of the assets available as security. Appraisal of assets not used in the business—such as unused real property, marketable securities, excess raw material, investments in nonintegrated subsidiary operations, and reserves in the extracting industries—is not mandatory but is still very important. Appraisals can also be made of the company's operations and of intangibles such as patents or trademarks that support an earnings stream.

How can I find a good business appraiser—preferably one who is certified?

As yet, no state or governmental body, to our collective knowledge, has yet regulated appraisers or has set up an examination/certification/licensing/sanctions process like the ones imposed on accountants, doctors, engineers, and lawyers—to name only a few certified professions. However, there are four trade associations whose members perform various appraisal functions who do "certify" their own members:

- American Institute of Certified Public Accountants in New York City (aicpa.org, 1-212-596-6200), which is planning to start a certification program for business appraisers who are also CPAs.
- American Society of Appraisers in Herndon, Virginia (appraisers.org, 1-800-ASA-VALU)
- Institute of Business Appraisers in Boynton Beach, Florida (instbusapp.org, 1-561-732-4304)
- National Association of Certified Valuation Analysts, Salt Lake City, Utah (cacva.com, 1-800-486-0600)

After the appraiser helps determine the value of the acquisition candidate, what is next?

At the stage where a sufficient investigation has occurred to arrive at a tentative value for the deal and to tentatively decide to proceed, the buyer should engage attorneys and accountants to conduct a more thorough study of the company to be acquired. Buyers can never start this "dirty linen" phase of the due diligence inquiry—discovering what's wrong with the company—too early. This phase is often neglected because, for one thing, buyers do not want to offend sellers and, for another, the natural euphoria that accompanies deal-doing displaces natural caution.

What public records should be checked?

To take a complete look at a company's past and current standing, the due diligence process should check out the present and previous corporate names and all trade names, service marks, and trade dress registrations. Any potential infringements by the acquisition candidate should be noted. (Readers should note that the famous Bell Telephone mark, due to a fluke, was never registered.)

The next concern to be satisfied in the due diligence search is basic: The buyer must confirm that the corporation was legally formed and continues to exist. To do so, the buyer will establish the jurisdiction of the company's incorporation and document the company's organization by finding and examining the articles of incorporation, including any amendments such as name changes.

Articles of incorporation are public documents that may be obtained (in the form of certified copies) from the secretary of state of the jurisdiction of incorporation. There should also be obtained, from the same office, evidence of the corporation's continuing status in good standing in the eyes of the state of incorporation. It is also necessary to review carefully the relevant state statutes and corporate minute books to establish that the articles and amendments have been properly adopted and that no action has been taken to dissolve the corporation. An examination of the minute book should also ascertain that it is up to date and that the election or appointment of the corporation's directors and officers is duly reflected therein.

Having established that the corporation was indeed duly formed, the buyer then examines the company's qualifications to do business in jurisdictions other than its state of incorporation—in other words, in whatever other states or countries it may conduct business. To be thorough in wrapping up this initial due diligence stage, the buyer must seek out good-standing certificates and tax certificates from each of the states and foreign jurisdictions in which it operates.

Once corporate formation, qualification, and good standing are established, a search should be made for liens, encumbrances, and judgments that may exist against the company or any of its assets. Sources to be searched in uncovering liens, encumbrances, and judgments include the following:

- The offices of the secretary of state of the state where the company's principal office is located and of other relevant states and, sometimes, county clerk offices where filings disclose creditors' interests in assets under the Uniform Commercial Code (UCC)
- All relevant recorder of deeds offices
- All relevant courts, including federal, state, and local
- Any special filing jurisdictions for:
  - Patents and trademarks
  - Copyrights
  - Bankruptcy
  - Maritime/aviation assets

Beyond checking basics such as corporate formation and liens, how extensive should the due diligence process be?

How far a buyer wishes to go in the due diligence process depends in part on how much time the buyer has and how much money there is for the investigation. This will depend to some extent on the status of the seller in the community, the years it has been in business, whether it has been audited by a major firm for some years, whether executive turnover is low, and other factors that would establish the basic stability of the firm, such as long-term customer retention. If the operation has been a subsidiary of another firm that is itself the product of an LBO or MBO, there is need for extreme caution.

Of particular importance are intracompany transactions—especially subcontracts and transfers of assets including cash and credits. Such transfer payments might not have been audited internally *or* externally for years. Of interest might be the percentage that purchased parts play in the cost of goods sold. At 85 percent, it calls for lots of attention; at 10 percent, very little. It is good to bear in mind that although most due diligence inquiries are conducted under the color of law, seeking out misstatements of fact, they can also uncover unexpected sources of future revenue and even unbooked raw assets. A buyer should also bear in mind that in any acquisition that will require a public offering, the underwriters and their counsel will also perform a due diligence study the extent of which will depend on the size of the offering and the history of the company's previous security registrations. In publicly financed acquisitions all parties are interested in uncovering problems early, as post-deal problems that *could* or *should* have been uncovered can be very expensive to solve.

What staffing does the due diligence effort typically require?

The acquirer typically draws from sources of expertise available both in-house and from retained consultants and advisors. At a minimum, the due diligence team will include financial/accounting and legal personnel. It may also bring in economic consultants, engineers, environmental experts, and a host of other professional talent.

The thoroughness of due diligence also depends to some extent on what information the seller is willing to give in the form of the representations and warranties to be included in the purchase agreement. Beware the seller that wants to get out clean with a quick deal and will make no representations or warranties. Such deals are high-risk transactions and are rarely the bargains they appear to be. If stockholders' money is involved, the business judgment rule may not protect the quick dealer on either side if things go wrong later. Many sellers discourage heavy due diligence effort and in negotiating reductions in the representations and warranties will insist that the buyer visit the plant. (By all means, buyers, do so, but do not let such "eyeballing" and "tire-kicking" relieve the seller of any possibility of misrepresentation.)

Even if the buyer decides to rely on the seller's representations and warranties, it must nevertheless still conduct at least enough due diligence to be assured that there will be a solvent seller to back the representations and warranties. If there is any doubt about post-deal solvency of the seller, cash reserves must be established.

Due diligence is also greatly affected by whether or not the acquisition candidate is a publicly reporting company. If it has outstanding 10Ks and 10Qs on file with the SEC, the buyer not only should obtain copies, but should examine in detail the agreements, contracts, and other significant company documents that may be filed with them as exhibits.

How can the buyer conduct proper due diligence without harming its relationship with the seller?

The ground rules for due diligence are negotiated by the buyer and seller in the *letter of intent* or, if there is no letter of intent, in the *acquisition agreement.* The letter of intent will state the time available for due diligence. The buyer will want a covenant from the seller promising the buyer adequate opportunity to conduct the due diligence inquiry and will guarantee it access to its personnel, sites, and files. (Refer to the sample letter of intent in Chapter 8.)

The seller, on the other hand, will be concerned about confidentiality and will often require the prospective buyer to enter into a separate *confidentiality agreement.* (A sample confidentiality agreement is found in Appendix 6B at the end of this chapter.) The buyer and seller will discuss at length the way in which the seller's disclosures and documents will be handled, the degree of confidentiality that will be given to them, and the disposition of those documents if the deal falls through, often agreeing to a "burn or return" provision in the letter of intent or the confidentiality agreement.

Any representations and warranties made by the seller in any of these documents should appear on a master *due diligence checklist.* The due diligence checklist provided in Appendix 6A is extremely detailed in some areas and more general in others. It is provided as a sample, not a model.

How can an acquirer create a thorough due diligence checklist?

In drafting a workable checklist, acquirers should concentrate on areas of particular relevance to the transaction at hand. For example, inquiries regarding the frequency and extent of customer complaints and returned goods would be more relevant to a consumer goods retail business than to a management consulting business, while questions regarding environmental violations are obviously more critical in making an acquisition in a smokestack industry than in buying a bank.

Depending on the size of the acquisition, the checklist may or may not reflect a threshold of materiality. For example, a checklist may include only those capital expenditures above $50,000 or may say that in some categories the seller has to produce documents from the past five years only (and no earlier). Acquirers should agree to limits of this kind carefully, bearing in mind that any ground given at this point is likely to limit the scope of the seller's representations and warranties in the acquisition agreement.

Remember, the seller's attitude will not be improved if the buyer asks for information that requires the seller to create new documentation. Thus, to the extent feasible, the checklist should require the seller to produce only documents already in existence. The purchaser should attempt to obtain other data through interviews with the seller's officers or by other peaceful means.

LITIGATION ANALYSIS

Litigation analysis of acquisition candidates requires a special procedure, usually conducted by trained litigation analysts. Management or its counsel can ask an attorney who specializes in commercial/corporate litigation and is familiar with the seller's industry to determine the validity of and exposure on existing claims.

How does one begin to analyze existing or potential litigation against an acquisition candidate?

The individual primarily responsible for the litigation risk review must first determine the parameters of the review and identify the litigation or administrative actions that warrant particular scrutiny. The primary reviewer must obtain a schedule of all litigation, pending and threatened, and must arrange to receive copies of all relevant pleadings.

Before reviewing specific cases, the primary reviewer should ascertain what cases the seller believes are covered by liability insurance and then determine what cases, if any, are in fact covered. Because the two do not always coincide, it is critical to review all insurance policies. The individual responsible for the litigation analysis must have a working knowledge of both the structure of the transaction—for example, whether it is to be a stock or asset purchase—

and the corporate and tort law rules concerning successor liability for debts and torts, especially with regard to compensatory and punitive damages. These are then applied case by case.

What general rules govern the buyer's potential liability for the seller's debts and torts?

The traditional rule is that where one company sells or otherwise transfers all its assets to another company, the successor is not liable for the debts and tort liabilities of the predecessor. The successor may be liable, however, under the following circumstances:

- If it has expressly or implicitly agreed to assume liability
- If there is a merger or consolidation
- If the successor is a "mere continuation" of the predecessor
- If the transaction was fraudulently designed to escape liability

A further exception exists for labor contracts. If the successor buys the predecessor's assets and keeps its employees, the successor will probably also be bound to recognize and bargain with unions recognized by the predecessor, and to maintain existing employment terms. Existing contracts may also create successorship problems. State law may vary with respect to assumption of debts and liabilities, so the reviewer must be cognizant of the specific statutory or case law that will govern the transaction.

Courts are increasingly likely to find successor liability, particularly with respect to product liability claims, under the "continuity of product line" or "continuity of enterprise" exceptions to the general rule of nonliability. The first of these exceptions applies where the successor acquires a manufacturer in the same product line. The second exception applies where the successor continues the predecessor's business. Faced with an increasingly aggressive plaintiffs bar in search of ever-deeper pockets, with the public and the courts searching for *someone* to blame, *someone* to shoulder the costs of injury to plaintiffs with no other course for recovery, the courts are increasingly looking to corporate successors for product liability damage awards, including in some instances punitive damages. This trend is particularly egregious in the case of asbestos manufacturers, whose long struggle to achieve a class settlement continues to this day after nearly two decades. Accordingly, the due diligence reviewer must be aware of the current state of the law concerning successor liability for both compensatory and punitive damages.

What about insurance policies and cases being handled by insurance companies?

Each and every insurance policy must be reviewed to ensure that pending claims for compensatory damages will be covered. What is the deductible? What are the liability limits per occurrence and in total? Are punitive damages excluded by the policy or by state law? Does the policy contain "regulatory" or other exclusions? For large companies, there may be overlapping policies; all policies must be reviewed in light of these questions. (The job of finding out this information can be subcontracted to firms specializing in the area of insurance-based "risk analysis," *provided* that the firms are reviewed for their "deal-killing potential" before being retained.)

Another consideration when reviewing insurance policies is whether the policies are for "claims incurred" or for "claims made." Coverage under a claims-incurred policy continues after the cancellation or termination of the policy and includes claims that arose during the period of insurance coverage, whether or not those claims are reported to the insurance company during that period. Claims-made policies cover only those claims actually made to the insurance company during the term of the policy. In addition, under some policies, coverage will continue only if a "tail" is purchased. A "tail" is a special policy purchased to continue coverage that would otherwise be terminated. It is important that the reviewer identify the nature of the seller's policies and determine any potential problems that may result from a failure to give the insurance company notice of claims during the policy period or from a failure to purchase a tail.

Also, cases being handled by insurance companies should be scrutinized. The reviewer should determine if the insurer has undertaken the representation under a "reservation of rights" (that is, where the insurer agrees to pay for or provide legal representation, without prejudice to its right to later deny coverage), if the insurer has preliminarily denied coverage, or if the damages claimed include punitive or treble damages, which may not be covered.[2]

How does counsel determine whether particular litigation is material to the acquiring company in the due diligence context?

Before gathering information through a due diligence request, counsel must determine what litigation is "material." The materiality determination for litigation, as for other aspects of due diligence, will be relative. A $5 million lawsuit, even if it has merit, may have little significance in the context of a $1 billion deal. On the other hand, even a case with little financial exposure may jeopardize a $20 million deal if the buyer and seller cannot agree on how to handle that case.

When evaluating litigation pending against a midsized company, a materiality cutoff point of $250,000 might be reasonable. In addition, certain types of cases might merit close attention, whatever the financial exposure. For example, a product liability case that looks like it might be the first of many should receive close attention, even if the financial exposure on that one case is insignificant.

In assessing the cost of potential litigation, companies should consider the option of settling out of court. Lately, more and more companies have discovered that much litigation is wrongly created and stubbornly maintained by their executive staff, internal and external legal advisors, and even some corporate directors. Many firms, such as Motorola, have set up special groups to reduce litigation costs and are exploring the possibilities of alternative dispute resolution (ADR), a fast-growing field of law where minitrials that bypass or "supplement" the courts are held to quickly resolve disputes at a fraction of the usual legal costs. The mainstay of this movement is arbitration, but other techniques growing in importance are mediation, fact-finding, minitrials, and partnering.[3]

The ADR process may yield hidden income as many companies maintain expensive legal actions that can be replaced by inexpensive ADR processes and cases are easily, quickly, and inexpensively settled. Attorneys serving as outside counsel have traditionally opposed ADR processes, which can reduce their litigation revenues. In recent years, however, some leading firms have opted to join (and even lead) the ADR movement rather than fight it. In examining offers of current counsel to undertake ADR work, client companies should determine how committed counsel is to this alternative. Begin by asking about counsel's ADR track record. (For more information on this topic, refer to Chapter 8.)

What material information should the litigator review?

In the due diligence request, counsel should seek a summary of all pending or threatened actions that satisfy the materiality standard that has been established. The summaries should include the following:

- Names and addresses of all parties
- The nature of the proceedings
- The date of commencement
- Status, relief sought, and settlements offered

- Sunk costs and estimated future costs
- Insurance coverage, if any
- Any legal opinions rendered concerning those actions

A summary should also be provided for the following:

- All civil suits by private individuals or entities
- Suits or investigations by governmental bodies
- Criminal actions involving the target or any of its significant employees
- Tax claims (federal, state, and local)
- Administrative actions
- All investigations

In addition, counsel should request copies of all material correspondence during the past five years with government agencies such as the Department of Justice, Federal Trade Commission, Equal Employment Opportunity Commission, Environmental Protection Agency, Internal Revenue Service, Occupational Safety and Health Administration, Department of Labor, and any other regulatory agency (city, county, state, or federal) to which the seller is subject. If subject to the rules of quasi-regulatory bodies such as the New York Stock Exchange or any other exchanges, all material correspondence should be gathered. If the target itself has subsidiaries, all relevant information should be requested for the subsidiaries as well.

After all this information has been gathered, how is the litigation analysis conducted?

Before the actual analysis begins, the individual in charge of the review must determine who will analyze which claims. Highly specialized claims should be assigned for review to attorneys with the most knowledge of the area involved.

The individual reviewer must arrange to receive pleadings and documents concerning any additional relevant claims and to have access to the attorneys representing the seller in those matters. Even in an acquisition characterized by cooperation, obtaining all the relevant pleadings may be difficult. This is particularly true if the seller is represented by more than one law firm.

The individuals responsible for this aspect of the litigation analysis must establish a particularly good working relationship with the attorneys representing the seller. In some instances, communications with outside counsel should be handled gingerly because that firm may see some portion of its legal work disappearing as a result of the acquisition. More often, with larger selling companies, litigation is being handled by several firms around the country; all those firms will have to be consulted.

In some cases, it will be sufficient to review the case file and consult briefly with the seller's outside counsel. In other cases, outside counsel will have to become more involved in the analytic process. The reviewer should be particularly cautious accepting the representations made by the seller's outside counsel currently handling the case; those representatives may be overly optimistic.

Finally, each pending material case should be systematically evaluated and some number assigned to the pending liability or recovery and should include the costs of executives' time. For litigation being handled on the seller's behalf by outside law firms, the reviewer should evaluate whether the case is being capably handled. Even a meritless case can create significant exposure if handled by an inexperienced or incompetent firm or practitioner.

The reviewer should concentrate on cases that could have a negative "ripple effect" on postmerger operations. The investigation should consider not only cases where the company being acquired is a defendant, but also major cases involving other companies in the same industry. For example, suppose a court decides that a business practice of one company in the industry constitutes a deceptive trade practice or other violation of law. If the company being acquired is in the same industry and engages or might engage in the same practice, this can have a significant impact on the future business of the acquired company, even if it is not a party to the litigation in question.

Any reviewer should have at hand the latest trends on D&O litigation. A leading source for this information is Watson Wyatt Worldwide, based in Chicago, which has tracked this information annually for 20 years.

Who might be suing (or planning to sue) a company, and what are some of the issues that give rise to lawsuits against companies?

- *Customers*—as well as competitors, suppliers, and other contractors—might sue over:

  Contract disputes

  Cost/quality of product or service

  Debt collection, including foreclosure

  Deceptive trade practices

Dishonesty/fraud

Extension/refusal of credit

Lender liability

Other customer/client issues

Restraint of trade

- *Employees*—including current, past, or prospective employees or unions—might sue over:

Breach of employment contract

Defamation

Discrimination

Employment conditions

Harassment/humiliation

Pension, welfare, or other employee benefits (e.g., unfunded pension benefits)

Wrongful termination

- *Regulators* might sue over:

Antitrust (in suits brought by government)

Environmental law

Health and safety law

- *Shareholders* might sue over:

Contract disputes (with shareholders)

Divestitures or spin-offs

Dividend declaration or change

Duties to minority shareholders

Executive compensation (such as golden parachutes)

Financial performance/bankruptcy

Financial transactions (such as derivatives)

Fraudulent conveyance

General breach of fiduciary duty

Inadequate disclosure

Insider trading

Investment or loan decisions

M&A scenarios (target, bidder)

Proxy contents

  Recapitalization
  Share repurchase
  Stock offerings
- *Suppliers* might sue over:
  Antitrust (in suits brought by suppliers)
  Business interference
  Contract disputes
  Copyright/patent infringement
  Deceptive trade practices

Of all these specific areas, which one is the biggest magnet for lawsuits?

According to Watson Wyatt, the most active area in recent years, accounting for more than 1 out of 10 suits, is wrongful termination. Severance agreements also rank high among potential litigation sources. Landmark cases in the field have held that severance plans are "employee welfare benefit plans" and that such plans are subject to the disclosure, reporting, and fiduciary requirements imposed by the Employee Retirement Income Security Act of 1974 (ERISA). For instance, in *Adcock v. Firestone Tire & Rubber Co.* (1987), a Tennessee district court held that employees had a contractual right under federal common law to severance benefits established by their employer. This holding is important in the context of mergers and acquisitions because, in at least one case, a court has held that an employer that sells a division or part of its operations as an ongoing business may remain liable under the seller's severance plans to former employees who continue employment in the division after the sale. For more on this topic, see Chapter 7.

ENVIRONMENTAL EXPOSURE ANALYSIS

How worried should acquirers be over environmental suits?

The pace of government lawsuits in this area has slowed. Today only about 1 in 100 lawsuits is filed over environmental matters. Settlement amounts can be very high, however, especially in major disasters, so it is worth keeping an eye on this area.

In assessing a company's potential exposure to environmental liability, where should an acquirer start?

Before getting into details, an acquirer should conduct a broad environmental exposure analysis under federal and state environmental laws. The primary federal law governing this area is the Comprehensive Environmental Response, Compensation, and Liability Act (CERCLA), also known as "Superfund." Some states, taking their cue from the federal government, have enacted environmental protection statutes that create a "superlien" on property of those persons liable for pollution. Generally speaking, there are two kinds of environmental problems to be feared in a proposed acquisition: those that adversely affect the balance sheet and those that adversely affect the financial projections. Either kind can destroy the economic benefits the buyer hopes to achieve.

What is the difference between a balance sheet environmental problem and a projection environmental problem?

Balance sheet problems result from liabilities, either disclosed or undisclosed, that the buyer becomes subject to as a result of acquiring the business. Such liabilities typically include the cost of cleaning up a mess caused by the seller or one of the seller's predecessors. The costs can include charges for removing contaminated soil or purifying tainted groundwater and can cover not only the site purchased by the buyer but also adjoining properties or remote locations on which hazardous substances generated by the business were dumped. Moreover, under Superfund, officers, directors, and even stockholders can be personally liable for cleanup costs, and the liability of companies that contributed to the pollution of a common dump site are jointly and severally liable for such cleanup costs. Finally, even secured lenders that wind up operating or controlling the contaminated property can be liable for such cleanup costs. As a result, the buyers must approach these problems not just from their own point of view; they must also consider how the lender will react. In addition to cleanup costs, a company can be liable to third parties who have become ill or died as a result of drinking contaminated groundwater, or whose property has been contaminated by pollution emanating from the company's facilities.

Projection problems adversely affect the company's ability to achieve its projected cash flow and earnings goals. They typically arise in situations in which the acquired company has a history of noncompliance with applicable air or water emissions standards. Where the due diligence process discloses such a history of operating problems, the prospective purchaser needs to calculate the cost of bringing the company into compliance and keeping it in compliance. This may involve significant unbudgeted capital costs (to procure needed emissions control equipment) or operating costs higher than anticipated (to ensure that the offending equipment is operated in conformity with applicable environmental standards) or both. In extreme cases, the buyer's diligence may disclose that the company (or a particular plant) cannot be economically operated in compliance with environmental law.

What kinds of acquisitions are most likely to present significant environmental problems?

The classic asset-based LBO, involving a smokestack industry, is the one most likely to present environmental concerns. However, environmental problems are by no means limited to the manufacturing sector. Warehouses, retail businesses, and service companies may own structures that contain asbestos in wall insulation or pipe wrapping; electrical transformers filled with polychlorinated biphenyls (PCBs) are found in many types of facilities; and underground motor fuel tanks can exist in any business that operates or has operated a fleet of trucks or cars. Eventually they *all* leak. All these situations are common environmental troublemakers, making environmental problems a common "skeleton in the closet" for many acquirers.

What are the principal environmental trouble spots to look for in an acquired company?

Any diligent buyer should work from a comprehensive environmental checklist in performing due diligence on a company or retain an environmental consultant to do it. But be sure to do a thorough background check on the consultant. Due diligence requires the buyer or its representative to be sensitive to certain key areas of potential concern:

- Were any toxic or hazardous substances used or generated by the target business? The ones most commonly encountered are PCBs, used in electrical transformers and commercial solvents such as those found in paint thinner and degreasing agents, which are potent carcinogens and which migrate readily into groundwater if spilled.

Also considered toxic or hazardous are heavy metals (such as lead, arsenic, and cadmium) from various industrial processes and paints.

- Were any hazardous wastes shipped off-site for disposal?
- Are there lagoons or settling ponds that may contain toxic wastes?
- Are there underground tanks that may have leaked and discharged their contents (heating oil, gasoline) into the groundwater?
- Is asbestos present in any structure (as insulation in walls, pipe wrapping, or other application)?

Why should the buyer worry about hazardous wastes shipped off the premises?

Because if they were shipped to a dump that has been or may be declared a federal Superfund site, the buyer might inherit a potential liability that could be substantial. This liability may flow through to the purchaser even if he or she purchases assets rather than stock. Moreover, even if the purchaser expressly does not assume the liability, the purchaser may still be liable if in fact it intends to continue the same business as the predecessor.

What special problems are posed by superfund liability?

First, Superfund can pierce the corporate veil. Officers, directors, and even shareholders can be held personally liable. Second, cleanup costs can be enormous—well beyond the value of the assets purchased. Third, liabilities of companies that generated wastes dumped in a common site are joint as well as several: Every contributor of hazardous waste to that site is theoretically liable for the whole cleanup. And fourth, it can take years before liability is finally determined.

Is "joint and several liability" common in environmental cases?

Yes. But the problem extends far beyond Superfund. "Joint and several liability" is a major problem in tort law generally. For example, it has been the bane of defendants in securities litigation, although in that sector there have been reforms (notably the Private Securities Litigation Reform Act of 1995). However, in other areas such as environmental law, the injustice of joint and several liability persists.

What can the buyer do to protect itself?

Due diligence requires that an acquirer hire an environmental consulting firm to do an environmental liability audit of the target company. Lenders are tending increasingly to require delivery of such an audit report, showing an essentially clean bill of health, as a condition to lending. Although the EPA has relaxed lender liability under Superfund, lenders still remain cautious.

The buyer should make sure that the seller's warranties are broad enough to cover (1) environmental liabilities arising as a result of on-site or off-site pollution and (2) all actions causing pollution, whether or not at the time such actions were taken they were in violation of any law or standard. The latter point is critical because Superfund liability can reach back to actions taken before the adoption of modern environmental protection laws, when the shipment of such wastes by unlicensed carriers to unlicensed sites was not illegal.

Also, the buyer needs to check all environmental warranties and any escrows or offset rights. These should survive as long as possible. It may take years before the pollution is discovered and traced back to the company.

Are environmental clearances typically required?

Yes. Federal, state, and local permits and consent decrees relating to water quality, air emissions, and hazardous wastes should be checked carefully to make sure they remain effective after closing. In addition, in at least one state (New Jersey), state approval of a cleanup plan or any cleanup process must be granted or formally waived in connection with the transfer of virtually any kind of industrial or commercial facility in order for the seller to pass an effective title to the buyer.

EMERGING LEGAL ISSUES

What are some of the emerging legal issues to be concerned about in a due diligence investigation—ones that a buyer might never think of but that could hurt the company later?

Such issues crop up constantly as courts around the country offer legal theories, set new precedents, and abolish old ones. No list of such new legal theories could be complete, but here are a few to consider:

- To what extent can the head of a company be held accountable for the wrongful acts of subordinates? This "agency" theory is constantly being tested.

- To what extent can advisors rely on the word of management? To what extent can management rely on advisors? The nature of attorney-client privilege is changing rapidly, with courts demanding more skepticism on both sides.

- How many times can a company be sued for the same action? Is there a limit to the number of plaintiffs who can ask for punitive damages? So far, no court has set a limit, despite the obvious unfairness of this multiple jeopardy practice, unsuccessfully challenged most recently in *Dunn v. Hovic* (1993).

- What areas are the trial lawyers targeting? At any given time, the Association of Trial Lawyers has scores of special groups studying hot legal areas. Could your "target" (candidate) company also be one of *their* targets?

- Is the candidate CEO's compensation reasonable? If not, the IRS and shareholders could sue.

DO-IT-YOURSELF DUE DILIGENCE

Suppose the seller refuses to produce the requested documentation but offers access to its files?

If the buyer is faced with a do-it-yourself due diligence process, it must organize an on-site document review effort. This will typically entail traveling to the entity's corporate headquarters and, depending on the number of sites involved and the nature of the business conducted at each site, other sites as well.

The seller in these circumstances should be willing to direct the buyer to employees with knowledge of each subject of inquiry detailed on the checklist or, at least, to the relevant files. In this event, the buyer should ask the seller to make a representation that it has been given access to all relevant files for requested information. The buyer should also ask the seller to provide sufficient personnel and photocopying facilities to make copies of all significant documents produced by the review effort. If the seller refuses to cooperate, the buyer may have to rent photocopying machines and hire temporary help. Should it come to a court contest, such a refusal will not go well with the seller.

As a courtesy to the seller and to avoid confusion between or among documents, which can vary in format from company to company, the buyer can make two copies, one of which will be retained by the seller. In any event, some identification system involving numbering should be devised to keep track of the documents produced, especially of those that are copied.

Throughout the process, the buyer should be sensitive to the stress on its own personnel and on its relationship with the seller. The due diligence effort is a disruption of the ordinary business routine and may be viewed by the seller as a sign of unwarranted suspicion by the buyer and disregard for the seller's interests. The seller may fear adverse consequences for the conduct of its business and its future sale to others if the contemplated deal does not close. Indeed, many potential transactions do fall through because of the rigors of the due diligence process, which alienates the seller, the buyer, or both. This has been especially true in recent years where environmental concerns have exacerbated closing problems.

Thorough due diligence can substantially increase pre-transaction costs and can absorb the attention of key employees who have other jobs to do. Nonetheless, it is unavoidable. Without timely and proper due diligence, even transactions that seem to be "made in heaven" can fall apart on earth.

ASSESSING INFORMATION

What guidelines should a buyer follow when assessing a seller's assets?

The buyer's examination of the seller's assets occurs both on-site (tire-kicking) and off-site (record-hunting). On-site inquiries may involve discussions with officers and employees as well as inspections of real property, machinery, equipment, and inventory. In conducting interviews with key executives and employees, the investigator seeks to fill in the gaps in the documentation and to ascertain whether there may be areas of potential concern or liability (or definable assets) not identified in the due diligence checklist. Good interview notes will include the following:

- Time and place of the interview
- Name and title of the person interviewed
- Scope of the interview
- Significant disclosures made during the interview

Depending on the size and structure of the transaction and the importance of the specific assets, the buyer may wish to use a real estate appraiser to value any owned real property involved, an engineer to inspect plant and equipment, and an accounting team to review inventory. The accountants should also review the seller's financial statements with respect to these items.

Off-site investigations may include the search of public records listed above and discussions with parties with whom the acquisition target has significant relationships. These include customers and suppliers, private lenders, and former key employees such as directors and officers. Key people to interview are those who have filed major suits against the target—especially former employees and stockholders. Another good interview candidate is any former outside auditor. Interviewers should ask why the auditor resigned or lost the account.

Special care must be taken when discussing the seller's business with third parties. Such discussions may, if correctly conducted, be the source of valuable information. They may also give rise to tensions between buyer and seller if the seller believes that the discussions may be impairing its ability to carry on its business or the buyer will use the information when and if it buys a competitor. However, this should have been taken care of in the letter of intent. Discussions with the buyer's lenders may be particularly sensitive in this regard.

Another delicate area is that of standing agreements. If the buyer begins negotiating with parties to existing supplier or customer agreements, requiring that they be assigned to the buyer when and if it acquires the business, the supplier or customer might refuse. This may be the basis for a cause of action as an "adverse change" in the affairs of the business between the execution of the acquisition agreement and the closing.

How much information can a buyer get about an acquisition candidate that is a corporate subsidiary or division?

It depends on whether the company is private or public and if public, what percentage of its revenues comes from the subsidiary.

Private corporations may not have to make any public disclosure of subsidiary or divisional performance, depending on their states of incorporation (some states do require the filing of such data). Public corporations must make such disclosure (as "line of business" reports) for units generating 5 percent or more of corporate revenues.

Some companies, private and public, make voluntary public disclosure of all subsidiary and divisional financials, however, and all well-managed companies report such results on an internal basis.

DURATION OF DUE DILIGENCE

How long should the due diligence process take?

The due diligence process occurs throughout the acquisition process, which lasts from a few weeks to a year or more. Surprisingly, the due diligence process does not slow the pace of the acquisition negotiation in most cases; sometimes the buyer accelerates the process by doing extensive investigation before making the first offer. At the other extreme, management buyers, who believe they know their own company, may willingly dispense with extensive due diligence inquiry, sometimes to their regret. If the parties are eager to deal, they may substitute extensive warranties for the due diligence process.

When buyers do initiate formal, organized due diligence investigations, they should not let it drag out. The greatest benefit of speedy due diligence is minimal disruption to ongoing business activities and the minimization of out-of-pocket costs to both parties. Another benefit can be smoother relations between the parties. Finally, the most valuable result of fast-track due diligence is timely information to the buyer, who can quickly determine whether the acquisition is of interest and, if so, on what terms and conditions.

The buyer can then focus attention on determining the appropriate structure for the transaction; the basis for calculation of the purchase price; what representations, warranties, and covenants should be negotiated into the contract; and what conditions to closing need to be imposed. (In fact, the earlier the draft of the schedule "Conditions Precedent to Closing" is generated, the better. Somehow, with that document on the table and under constant revision as the due diligence proceeds, confidence that the deal will close seems to improve.)

When does the due diligence process properly end?

As important as it is for due diligence to be completed rapidly, the due diligence effort really should extend up to, through, and beyond closing. The discipline imposed by the process—dealing with the realities of the complications of business—should never be abandoned, and it is a rare deal that does not have, on closing day, a revision to the acquisition agreement covering unfinished items of due diligence inquiry. This "bring-down" list can be extensive and makes both buyers and sellers nervous as it provides for a subsequent effective closing. Many prefer to wait until everything is completed and the purchase agreement can be executed simultaneously with closing the deal.

Does diligence continue to be significant after closing?

Yes. The post-closing significance of the due diligence effort is twofold.

First, individuals who had hands-on involvement in the due diligence process will have a particularly good insight into the operational areas they studied, and they may be called upon during the initial post-acquisition "re-start-up" period under new ownership to answer questions or provide guidance. There are *always* items of unfinished business that grow out of the due diligence process that must be resolved after closing. They should be listed and assigned to people to solve with completion dates attached, and someone should be assigned to follow up. (The principal author of this book learned this lesson the hard way. He sold one of his periodicals. The law firm handling the deal was supposed to record a lien on a piece of property that backed up the notes issued in payment. The law firm broke up in a bitter battle, and the lien was never filed. The property was subsequently sold illegally, but a subsequent bankruptcy wiped out the assets of the malefactor note maker and no recovery was possible for the fraud. The author found it impossible to find a law firm willing to sue the individual lawyers who failed to file the lien.)

Second, if the buyer sues the seller (and/or vice versa), the claim may go back to a due diligence issue—that is, whether one party disclosed or made available to the other the documents or pertinent facts. If the acquisition agreement fails to identify the information the defendant is supposed to know, the court (or ADR agent) will look at the due diligence process to determine where liability lies. For this reason, it is absolutely essential to maintain complete written reports on due diligence processes and results.

CONCLUDING COMMENTS

In the bright world of merger beginnings, the due diligence process can seem somber indeed—a negative presence spoiling the love fest. This is understandable. In their search for harmony, buyers and sellers naturally want to see the best in each other, not the worst. Due diligence, the search to discover hidden defects and risks, restrains that desire—and it should. To ensure a lasting union, due diligence—"the Shadow"—must arrive on the scene early and linger long, getting behind the reflected surface of things, looking for signs of trouble, asking always "What if?" Without such deep, dark searching, there can be no true light—clarity that can help all parties move with mutual confidence from premerger idea to postmerger reality.

APPENDIX 6A

Due Diligence Checklist[4]

DOCUMENTS

Corporate Documents

Certificate of Incorporation (CI) Including All Amendments, Name Changes, Mergers The CI is particularly helpful in determining what name to search for title to real estate. Special care should be taken not to overlook name variations, for example, "Rocket Airlines Inc.," "Rocket Air Lines, Inc.," and "Rocket Airlines Corp." These are quite likely to be very separate legal entities. The date and state of incorporation are also critical. There may be different companies with identical names incorporated in different states.

Bylaws Look for change of control provisions. Many bylaws contain "poison pill" provisions designed to place restrictions on changes in control, or to make such changes very expensive to the potential acquirer.

Minutes Look in particular for information on past acquisitions or mergers and other transactions affecting capital; this will help trace ownership of assets and equity. Make certain the election and appointment of current directors and officers is duly reflected, and that the issuance of all outstanding stock has been properly authorized.

Financial Statements

Develop breakdowns, by location, of assets (land, buildings, equipment, inventory, vehicles, and, if not billed out of a central office, receivables). Consider whether those provided are adequate for use in possible SEC filings and whether pro forma financials are needed. Examine footnotes as a source of information for more detailed inquiries into existing debt, leases, pensions, related party arrangements, and contingent liabilities. Especially in leveraged acquisitions, consider the target's debt.

Engineering Reports

Try to find "as-built" drawings, especially if surveys are not available. Review for environmental problems or other concerns that might require major capital expenditures.

Market Studies/Reports On Company's Product

These may be written in-house or by outside consultants. In the case of public companies, if findings are material, they may be mentioned in the company's "management discussion and analysis" section of its annual report. Check the 10Ks and proxies, too. Note that marketing is a land mine of potential liability concerns.

Key Intangibles

Patents, Trademarks, Trade Names, and Copyrights   These items generally involve "registered" or "filed" rights that can be searched for at the U.S. Patent and Trademark Office and, for copyrights, at the Library of Congress, Washington, D.C. However, such rights may not have been filed for. Also, corporations frequently have other key intangibles that are not filed for anywhere, such as trade secrets. This is especially true of companies that deal in high technology, software, and the like. Due diligence would call for inquiry into the status of and the methods of protection for these items. Review all related trade secrets, know-how, and license agreements.

Licenses   Whether granted by the government or by a private third party, licenses may be absolutely essential to the ability of a corporation to continue legally to conduct its business. The buyer should ensure that all such necessary licenses are current and in good order and that these licenses will be readily transferable, or remain valid, in the context of the acquisition transaction. It is generally useful to obtain the advice of special counsel or experts in the particular field (for example, FCC counsel in the case of broadcasting licenses).

Key Tangibles

Mortgages   If these are significant, request a closing binder. Look for notes or other evidence of indebtedness. In the case of International Development Bank (IDB) or other quasi-public financing, request the closing binder, and be sure to review indenture, etc.

Title Documents to Real Estate and Personal Property   Review title policies and documents creating any encumbrance upon the title and deeds/bills of sale by which the company acquired assets. If assets were acquired by stock purchase or merger, find evidence of filing of appropriate corporate documents in jurisdiction(s) where the assets are located as well as in state(s) of incorporation.

Real Property and Assets Identification   Ask the seller to give the complete address (including county) of every facility or piece of real estate owned or leased by the company, and describe each such facility using the following list of categories (indicate more than one category if appropriate):

- Corporate offices
- Production, manufacturing, or processing facilities
- Warehouses, depots, or storage facilities
- Distribution facilities
- Sales offices
- Repair/warranty work facilities
- Apartments or other residential real property
- Undeveloped real property
- Any other facilities

If *owned,* the seller should indicate as "O" and provide the full legal name in which the title is recorded. If *leased,* the seller should indicate as "L" and provide the full name of the lessor. The seller should indicate whether there is any *inventory* at any such facility by "I."

The seller should indicate whether any goods/products/materials at any such facility are there on consignment from a supplier, as "Supp C." Ask the seller to provide the complete address (including county) of every site not described above where any of the company's assets are located, including every facility of any customer/processor at which the company has raw materials/goods/products/inventory on consignment, and the name of the party in possession of such assets, including any such customer/processor.

Compare actual documents with title insurance. Look for encumbrances, easements, rights of third parties, and personal property encumbrances appearing on UCC records that should be checked. When in doubt, send someone to the site. (Remember Cascade International, Inc., whose founder, Victor G. Incendy, disappeared in 1991 following the discovery that the company had overstated not only its sales and profits but the number of stores and cosmetic counters it owned. By comparing financial records with state tax records and with industry rules of thumb, outside sources were able to determine that the exaggeration was at least 300 percent. Later investigation found that this was a conservative estimate.)

Contracts

Supply and Sales Agreements Do these meet the company's future business requirements? Review as to assignability, term, and expenditures required. (Some long-time distribution contracts will survive a merger but not an acquisition of assets.)

Employment and Consulting Agreements These relate both to the current key employees the acquirer wishes to retain to ensure that the terms are good enough to hold them and to exposure to claims of past employees or those the acquirer does not wish to retain. They should also be reviewed to discover if they restrict the retaining of proprietary information such as customer lists.

Leases Get legal descriptions. Have particular concern about term and expiration dates and renewal rights, rent, and special provisions concerning assignment that may include change of corporate ownership.

License and Franchise Agreements Look for correspondence concerning extension, expansion, disputes, and estoppels. Franchise relationships are likely to be stormy. Is there a franchise organization? Note assignment clauses and clauses creating a landlord's lien. Are any prior consents required? Are these sufficient for the business's requirements?

Loan Agreements Review terms, intention, and assignability provisions as to any need to refinance or to obtain consents to an acquisition from lenders. Schedules/exhibits should be reviewed to glean useful information regarding the company's assets and structure.

Shareholder Agreements Review provisions and their effect on proposed transaction and, if the agreement will survive, its effect on future transactions, that is, registration rights and antidilution or dissenters' rights.

Sponsorship Agreements Are these tax-deductible to the giver and tax-free to the receiver? (In December 1991, the IRS said no to both questions, disappointing organizers and sponsors of the Mobil Cotton and John Hancock Bowls.)

Agreements with Labor Obtain and study all agreements for unusual provisions that would unduly constrain management's options. Review benefits, severance, and plant closing provisions.

- Will the agreements terminate at sale, or are they binding on the buyer?
- Are the agreements binding on the buyer?
- Do the agreements have provisions that restrict the buyer?
- Is the company presently in compliance with the agreements? Does the agreement expire soon? Will the buyer want it to be reopened? (Notice may be required.) Is a strike likely?
- Are there any grievances that raise general issues of contract interpretation?

Agreements with Management

- Are there golden parachutes?
- Is there excessive compensation? (Compare with current compensation studies by executive search firms such as Korn/Ferry Interna-

tional and executive compensation firms such as Hay Group or William L. Mercer.)

Security Agreements or Other Agreements Giving Other Parties the Right to Acquire Assets of the Company Review financing statements or other evidence of perfected security interests. Lien searches conducted by professional services engaged in this business are usually the most efficient way of uncovering UCC financing statements of record, but it is also sometimes necessary to check for third-party interests recorded against particular assets of the seller, rather than against the name of the seller itself. For example, security interests in assets such as vessels or aircraft are recorded in special registries (outside the scope of the usual UCC lien search) against the particular vessel or aircraft itself, rather than against the owning company.

Sales and Product Warranty Agreements Review for provisions that vary from the description or understanding of such documents that are provided or held by management. Review for provisions that may be illegal and/or unenforceable. Review for indemnity obligations of the company.

Selected Correspondence This is a useful means of uncovering past problems that may recur.

Acquisition Agreements Review prior acquisition agreements concerning surviving provisions, that is, noncompete clauses and indemnification obligations.

Pension and Profit-Sharing Plans Check out the fine print in all plans and trust documents and review the personnel handbook and any policy manual.

- Form 5500
- Summary plan description
- Actuarial valuation
- Auditor's report and accompanying management reports
- Investment manager agreements
- Fiduciary insurance and bonds
- Investment contracts
- Investment policy

- Accrued, unfunded liabilities
- Fringe benefits

Welfare Benefit Plans   Be aware that potential liabilities in this area can be substantial and that valuation of plans requires expert guidance. Check out fiduciary insurance and bonds.

Multiemployer Plans   As shown in Chapter 7, these can be a major problem.

Deferred Compensation Plan and Stock Option Plans   SEC-registered companies must disclose details about such plans in their proxy statements under Regulation S-K.

Supplemental or Excess Pension Plan

- Is the plan exempt from ERISA?
- Will future law affect costs/benefits?
- Are large claims anticipated?
- Are reserves on company books adequate?
- Can the plan be terminated or amended?
- Are there any benefits in pay status?
- Are the benefits in effect funded with insurance?

Insurance Policies

Review all policies and ask at least these questions:

- Do policies cover the areas of risk exposure? (Consider a risk analysis consultant to review this very technical area.)
- What is the deductible?
- What are the liability limits per occurrence? In total?
- Are punitive or treble damages excluded by the policy or by state law?
- Are policies written for "claims incurred" or "claims made"?
- Must a "tail" be purchased to extend coverage?
- Is there a "reservation of rights" clause?
- Is there a regulatory exemption clause?

- What about coverage for director and officer liability?
- What about environmental liability?

KEY INFORMATION FROM THE COMPANY'S MANAGEMENT

Financial and Ownership Information

Financial Information   Perform an analysis of the company's past operating and financial performance. Document any planned substantive changes. In conducting such an analysis keep in mind the latest tax and accounting changes. For example, companies may report their projections of how current losses may offset future gains, even if it is not certain the losses will trigger an offsetting tax benefit. (See also Chapter 5.)

Relative Profitability of the Company's Various Classes of Products and Business Segments   Compare with companies of similar size in the industry.

Ownership of Company's Securities   Trace the title of the present owners of the corporation (if privately held). Review for existing pledges/liens that must be released to permit transaction.

Litigation Matters

Potential Defaults under Existing Contracts or Potential Litigation
Identify as many as possible and obtain waivers, consents, and so on. Ask for a summary of all pending or threatened legal actions that are material:

- Names and addresses of all parties
- The nature of the proceedings
- The date of commencement
- Current status
- Relief sought
- Estimated actual cost
- Insurance coverage, if any
- Any legal opinions rendered concerning those actions

Summaries should also be provided for the following:

- All civil suits by private individuals or entities
- Suits or investigations by governmental bodies
- Criminal actions involving the target or any of its significant employees
- Tax claims (federal, state, and local)
- Administrative actions
- All investigations
- All threatened litigation

Ask for copies of all material correspondence during the past five years with government agencies. In rough order of likely importance, these include the following:

- Department of Justice
- Internal Revenue Service
- Securities and Exchange Commission
- Environmental Protection Agency
- Department of Labor
- Federal Trade Commission
- Occupational Safety and Health Administration
- Equal Employment Opportunity Commission
- Public Utility Commission/s
- Federal Energy Regulatory Commission

Recent or Pending Changes in Laws or Regulations That Might Affect the Company's Business Evaluate risk and potential existing noncompliance. Don't forget state laws, particularly tax laws. These can carry surprises for new owners. (Consider Proposition 13, a 1978 amendment to the California constitution. It set property taxes at 1 percent of assessed valuation, rolled back assessments to 1975 levels, and limited increases to 2 percent per year. But when property is under new ownership, it is reassessed and the buyer pays taxes based on the purchase price.)

Product Backlogs, Purchasing, Inventory, and Pricing Policies Is the company accurately tracking the flow of goods in a company? Falsification of records can abet fraudulent schemes of massive proportions. Cases in point include Crazy Eddie Stores, where founder Eddie Antar created a "giant bubble" of a company according to the U.S. attorney in Newark, and Miniscribe Corp., where managers shipped bricks to distributors and booked them as sales.[5]

Pending Negotiations for the Purchase or Disposition of Assets or Liens The buyer may want to drop real property that it is planning to dispose of into another entity (such as an affiliated partnership) to avoid gain recognition or provide for means of early investment return to acquiring persons.

Charitable Contributions Claimed Are valuations accurate? If not, this can lead to IRS challenges.

KEY INFORMATION FROM OUTSIDE SOURCES

Market and Capital Information

Market and Product Studies Whether or not the company has conducted market and product studies, it's always a good idea to consult independent research. (See Chapter 2.) Try also to obtain product test data from regulatory agencies. Contact major customers to determine their level of satisfaction and copies of test programs they have run.

Capital Confirmation Confirm outstanding capitalization from the company's stock transfer agent.

Lien Search

Acquirers will want to confirm the absence of liens or judgments via searches of public records. Note that names of debtors to be searched are often difficult to determine.

- Prior names—four-month rule regarding after-acquired collateral—cannot rely on creditor
- Fictitious names or other false information
- Continuation statements

Sometimes a search must be conducted at the state or local level. In such cases it may be necessary to do the following:

- Coordinate between the search firm and title company (sometimes not done).
- Consult the Uniform Commercial Code (UCC, as mentioned) to determine if state(s) at issue has additional or unusual search requirements.
- Obtain the lender's/borrower's approval.

Ordering a Search   Send a letter to the search firm/title company listing names, location, cost, and deadline, and request copies of all liens found. Send a copy to the client and lender's/borrower's counsel.

Reviewing a Search   What is your client buying, selling, liening, or loaning against? Are certain equipment, goods, and intangibles supposed to be free and clear? Are they vital to the business? To the closing? If so, watch for liens against those items.

- If certain secured debt is to remain in place, one would expect related UCC-1 forms to show up on the search report.
- If secured debt is to be paid off at closing, the seller must produce UCC-3 or other required forms of releases from the relevant parties.
- What does the appraisal say? What does the commitment/finance package say?

Check the report for names and jurisdictions. Review the UCC-1s sent.

- Debtor
- Secured party
- Date (five-year rule)
- Description of collateral

Compare against schedules to be incorporated into loan documents, contracts, and bills of sale. Often, local counsel will need copies of lien searches in order to deliver a priority opinion.

Bring-Down of Search   A search bring-down is a telegram or telephone update of lien searches and of corporate good-standing certificates. It is often difficult to get closer than a few days before closing, but every effort should be made to close on the basis of the most recent bring-downs possible.

Creditor Check

Assumption of Debt   If secured debt is not to be paid off, get security documents to see if the following are permitted:

- Incurring of acquisition debt
- Imposition of related liens
- Merger
- Change of control
- Sale of assets

Are there burdensome covenants? Is prepayment permitted, with or without penalty? (See Chapter 4.)
Confirm the absence of defaults from the principal lenders.
Confirm the absence of defaults from lessors (landlords).
Look for the unusual or the potential problem.

- Is the affiliate of the seller named as the secured party?
- Is the debtor using multiple names to hide bad credit?

Other Searches

Patent and trademark searches for possible infringement of products or product names
Certificates of good standing for all corporate subsidiaries whether active or inactive
Title search/acquisition of title insurance
Appraisals of company-owned real property and improvements
Any equipment appraisals made by or for insurance companies

A P P E N D I X   6B

Sample Confidentiality Agreement

STRICTLY PRIVATE AND CONFIDENTIAL

[Date]

Acquisition, Inc.
Corporate Office Towers
New York, New York

To the Board of Directors:

In connection with your consideration of a possible transaction with Seller, Inc. (the "Company") or its stockholders, you have requested information concerning the Company so that you may make an evaluation of the Company to undertake negotiations for the purchase of the Company. As a condition to your being furnished such information, you agree to treat any information (including all data, reports, interpretations, forecasts and records) concerning the Company which is furnished to you by or on behalf of the Company and analyses, compilations, studies or other documents, whether prepared by you or others, which contain or reflect such information (herein collectively referred to as the "Evaluation Material") in accordance with the provisions of this letter. The term "Evaluation Material" does not include information which (i) was or becomes generally available to the public other than as a result of a disclosure by you or your directors, officers, employees, agents or advisors, or (ii) was or becomes available to you on a nonconfidential basis from a source other than the Company or their advisors provided that such source is not bound by a confidentiality agreement with the Company, or (iii) was within your possession prior to its being furnished to you by or on behalf of the Company, provided that the source of such information was not bound by a confidentiality agreement with the Company in respect thereof, or (iv) was independently acquired by you as a result of work carried out by an employee of yours to whom no disclosure of such information has been made directly or indirectly.

Y ou hereby agree that the Evaluation Material will not be used by you in any way detrimental to the Company. You also agree that the Evaluation Material will be used solely for the purpose set forth above, and that such information will be kept confidential by you and your advisors for five (5) years provided, however, that (i) any such information may be disclosed to your directors, officers and employees, and representatives of your advisors who need to know such information for the purpose of evaluating any such possible transactions between the Company and you (it being understood that such directors, officers, employees and representatives shall be informed by you of the confidential nature of such information and shall be directed by you to treat such information confidentially and shall assume the same obligations as you under this agreement), and (ii) any disclosure of such information may be made to which the Company consents in writing. You shall be responsible for any breach of this agreement by your agents or employees.

In addition, without the prior written consent of the Company, you will not, and will direct such directors, officers, employees and representatives not to disclose to any person either the fact that discussions or negotiations are taking place concerning one or more possible transactions between either the Company or its stockholders, on the one hand, and you, on the other hand, or any of the terms, conditions or other facts with respect to any such possible transactions, including the status thereof. The term "person" as used in this letter shall be broadly interpreted to include without limitation any corporation, company, group, partnership or individual.

In addition, you hereby acknowledge that you are aware, and that you will advise your directors, officers, employees, agents and advisors who are informed as to the matters which are the subject of this letter, that the United States securities laws prohibit any person who has material, nonpublic information concerning the matters which are the subject of this letter from purchasing or selling securities of a company which may be a party to a transaction of a type contemplated by this letter or from communicating such information to any other person under circumstances in which it is reasonably foreseeable that such person is likely to purchase or sell such securities. You consent that you will not, and you will cause each of the aforementioned persons to not, violate any provisions of the aforementioned laws or the analogous laws of any State.

You hereby acknowledge that the Evaluation Material is being furnished to you in consideration of your agreement (i) that neither you nor any of your affiliates nor related persons under your control will for a period of three (3) years from the date of this letter make any public announcement with respect to or submit any proposal for a transaction between you (or any of your affiliates) and the Company or any of its securityholders unless the Company shall have consented in writing in advance to the submission of such proposal, nor will you, directly or indirectly, by purchase or otherwise, through your affiliates or otherwise, alone or with others, acquire, offer to acquire, or agree to acquire, any voting securities or direct or indirect rights or options to acquire any voting securities of the Company, for a period of three (3) years from the date of this letter without such permission, and (ii) that you will indemnify any director, officer, employee or agent of the Company and any "controlling person" thereof as such term is defined in the Securities Act of 1933, for any liability, damage or expense arising under federal and state securities laws from an actual or alleged breach of this agreement by you or your directors, officers, employees, representatives or affiliates. You also agree that the Company shall be entitled to equitable relief, including an injunction, in the event of any breach of the provisions of this paragraph.

In the event that you do not proceed with the transaction which is the subject of this letter within a reasonable time, you shall promptly redeliver to the Company all written material containing or reflecting any information contained in the Evaluation Material (whether prepared by the Company or otherwise) and will not retain any copies, extracts or other reproductions in whole or in part of such written material. All documents, memoranda, notes and other writings whatsoever, prepared by you or your advisors based on the information contained in the Evaluation Material, shall be destroyed, and such destruction shall be certified in writing to the companies by an authorized officer supervising such destruction.

Although we have endeavored to include in the Evaluation Material information known to us which we believe to be relevant for the purpose of your investigation, you understand that we do not make any representation or warranty as to the accuracy or completeness of the Evaluation Material. You agree that you shall assume full responsibility for all conclusions you derive from the Evaluation Material and that neither the Company nor its representatives shall have any liability to you or any of your representatives resulting from the use of the Evaluation Material supplied by us or our representatives.

In the event you are required by legal process to disclose any of the Evaluation Material, you shall provide us with prompt notice of such requirement so that we may seek a protective order or other appropriate remedy or waive compliance with the provisions of this agreement. In the event that a protective order or other remedy is obtained, you shall use all reasonable efforts to ensure that all Evaluation Material disclosed will be covered by such order or other remedy. Whether such protective order or other remedy is obtained or we waive compliance with the provisions of this agreement, you will disclose only that portion of the Evaluation Material which you are legally required to disclose.

This agreement shall be governed by and construed and enforced in accordance with the laws of the State of New York, U.S.A.

Any assignment of this agreement by you without our prior written consent shall be void.

It is further understood and agreed that no failure or delay by the Company in exercising any right, power or privilege hereunder shall operate as a waiver thereof nor shall any single or partial exercise thereof preclude any other or further exercise of any right, power or privilege.

If you are in agreement with the foregoing, please so indicate by signing and returning one copy of this letter, whereupon this letter will constitute our agreement with respect to the subject matter hereof.

Very truly yours,

SELLER, INC.

By: Its:

Confirmed and Agreed to:
ACQUISITION, INC.

By: Its:
Date:

ENDNOTES

1. For more on these sources, see Alexandra Reed Lajoux, *The Art of M&A Integration: A Guide to Merging Resources, Processes, and Responsibilities* (New York: McGraw-Hill, 1998), pp. 8 and 289.

2. For an expert guide to this subject, see Ty Sagalow, *D&O Liability Insurance: A Guide for Directors and Officers,* Second Edition (Washington, DC: National Association of Corporate Directors, 1999) (forthcoming).

3. For readers wishing to learn more about ADR, the best place to begin is the American Arbitration Association, based in Washington, DC (Web site: adr.org). Founded in 1922, this organization now has 38 offices in the United States and links to 51 organizations worldwide.

4. For checklists useful in appraising this and other areas of liability exposure, see handbooks published by Aspen Law and Business, Clark Boardman Callaghan, Matthew Bender, Prentice-Hall, and other legal publishers.

5. The publications of the Institute of Internal Auditors (IIA), based in Altamont Springs, Florida, provide excellent guidance in the detection of fraud. To find out more about the IIA, or to request a catalog, contact www.iia.org. For a current guide to fraud detection, see also the *Report of the NACD Best Practices Council: Coping with Fraud and Other Illegal Activity* (Washington, DC: National Association of Corporate Directors, 1998).

CHAPTER 7

Pension, Labor, and Compensation Concerns

INTRODUCTION

Sooner or later in every m/a/b transaction, the subject of compensation comes up. The buyer may want to resist making any promises, since it will naturally want as much freedom as possible to determine postmerger compensation. Such freedom is rarely granted, however, as seller expectations and even legal constraints will almost always force buyers to make new commitments or confirm preexisting ones. Sellers will have a natural interest in what lies ahead for the managers and employees of the company being sold—especially in MBOs and in transactions involving closely held companies, where the sellers and the managers are often one and the same. In companies with employee stock ownership plans and/or a unionized labor force, rank and file employees will also have a say in postmerger pay.

The best time for going to the table on pay will be right in the middle of the "brass tacks" phase of the deal, when the due diligence phase is gearing up and the legal team is hard at work preparing the acquisition agreement. This chapter is a general guide to the myriad issues that may arise at this phase.

This chapter is offered as a mere introduction to the subject. First, we introduce the reader to some compensation basics. Then, we zero in on employee benefit plans,[1] paying particular attention to the employee stock ownership plan (ESOP) because of its importance as a financing device. In closing, we cover some of the principal issues that arise in acquiring a unionized company.

Our goal is not to turn you, our reader, into an expert. Rather, it is to help you appreciate the need for guidance in this complex domain.

COMPENSATION BASICS

What are the basic elements of compensation?

There are basically four pay elements:

1. *Base pay,* otherwise known as *salary,* is a fixed amount of cash. It is typically determined annually and paid on a weekly or (in small companies) monthly basis. For most employees, this is the dominant portion of pay (though to large-company senior executives it is of minor importance).[2]

2. *Bonus pay* is a lump-sum award in cash and/or stock paid to an employee for past performance. Bonus pay is typically determined and paid on an annual basis. Some companies call their bonuses *incentive pay,* but compensation purists reserve the latter term for pay that is awarded according to a predetermined plan, not after the fact.

3. *Incentive pay* is compensation awarded to employees because they (or their team, division, or company) have met a predetermined performance target. This pay, which may be in cash and/or stock (either outright grants or options), is truly variable; it may not be paid at all. It may be awarded annually and/or "long term," with the term defined by the company. Incentive pay is often awarded as *deferred compensation.* Funds are usually put into an escrow account that appreciates according to a standard interest rate (such as Treasury bills).

4. *Benefits* include plans for pensions, health care, employment security, and, at the board level, liability insurance. There are also extras, or *perquisites,* such as use of a company car.

In addition, there is a potentially infinite universe of *special pay arrangements* that can come up during or after a merger:

1. Through *noncompete agreements,* companies can take the first of many steps in keeping key executives and preventing them from competing against the new company.

2. Through *signing bonuses* (called *golden handshakes*), companies can increase the motivation of executives they wish to hire.

3. Through *severance agreements,* a company promises to compensate employees in the event of job loss. Moreover, through change-of-control plans (offered in addition to plain-vanilla severance agreements), a company agrees to pay employees in the event of job loss following a merger or acquisition. At the senior level, these M&A-related severance packages are called *golden parachutes.* At lower levels, they are called *tin parachutes.*[3]

4. Finally, through *retention agreements* (also called *golden handcuffs*) companies promise rewards if an employee stays a stated length of time.

The sum total of all basic pay elements and all special compensation arrangements is generally referred to as *total compensation.* Most consultants today offer services in *total compensation planning.*

What liabilities arise when one is acquiring or merging with a company that has medical plans?

Medical plans fall into two basic types, funded and unfunded. If a funded plan is in place, it is funded through a trust and that trust must be terminated or transferred. In these cases, because of strict deductibility rules under Internal Revenue Code Section 419A, the buyer should demand representations that the contributions to the plan are deductible.

If the plan is not funded through a trust, then it is either an insured plan or a self-insured plan (also called an *administrative-services-only,* or ASO, plan). However, the term *insured* can be a bit misleading in that most modern insured plans contain features, such as retrospective rating programs, minimum premium adjustments, or reserves, that essentially adjust the premium cost of the policy to the claim experience under the policy. These features may create unexpected benefits or costs for a buyer.

With medical plans of any type, it is critical to determine exactly what benefits are covered, as of what time, and what will happen if the policy is terminated. If a stand-alone company is purchased, it is probably possible simply to assume the policy. At that point, it is important to determine whether the policy has an excess reserve built up or whether a large retrospective premium assessment is due, and whether buyer or seller is to get the advantage or disadvantage of that reserve or retrospective rating buildup. Another key question is whether the premium rates are based on the acquired operations or on the seller's entire workforce. If the rates are based on the latter, a smaller group may be more costly—as will be a higher-risk group (older, more hazardous occupation, and so on).

If the operations sold are not a stand-alone company, then it is important to understand how benefits of persons who are severed from the policy will be treated. It is critical to have a clear understanding in the agreement about who will cover the preexisting conditions, whether the seller will cover all claims incurred up to the closing or only claims filed up to the closing, and who will cover persons who are on sick leave or disability or retired at the time of the closing.

What other hidden liabilities should be avoided in medical plans?

Another area of great concern is benefits for retired employees. The general rule is that retiree medical benefits cannot be modified or eliminated unless the company has clearly stated that those benefits are subject to modification or elimination. In most cases, a court will probably be able to find some ambiguity in the promise made to the employees. Retiree medical costs are footnoted in the financial statements but are not booked, although the Financial Accounting Standards Board (FASB) may change this. The estimates of these costs are variable, subject to health-care cost inflation and to problems such as occupational disease in a particular workforce. The buyer of an entity that offers retiree medical benefits either should attempt to have the seller retain the retiree medical costs or should factor the cost into the price paid for the company.

Does a severance agreement or policy create potential liability?

Definitely. Sellers of divisions and subsidiaries who have signed severance agreements may have severance obligations after a sale even if the employees continue their employment with the purchasing entity.

Severance obligations are most likely to be triggered if the benefit or salary programs of the buyer are less extensive than those of the seller. However, this is not a necessary precondition to a holding that the seller is liable. Purchase agreements can also contain seemingly innocuous provisions that actually transfer severance liability to buyers (for example, by requiring buyers to assume all obligations under benefits plans).

Severance plans are employee benefit plans subject to the Employee Retirement Income Security Act of 1974 (ERISA). They should be written up and disclosed to participants. In *Blau v. Del Monte Corp.* (1984), the seller claimed that its plan did not provide for post-acquisition severance payments, but the Ninth Circuit Court of Appeals disagreed, declaring that the denial of benefits violated ERISA and that the seller was responsible for paying the benefits. When there is self-interest on the part of the company, courts will often call a severance decision "arbitrary and capricious," and thus illegal.

When two companies merge, to what extent should they merge their compensation plans?

It depends on whether or not the new companies will be integrated or managed separately. If the acquirer has only a financial (as opposed to strategic) reason for buying a company, it may choose to keep its pay plans separate. And even if an acquirer has a strategic reason to buy a company and does plan to integrate resources and systems, it may still decide to keep some aspects of pay separate (especially if it is venturing outside its core industry).

Given all these factors, the burden of compensation design is generally shared between the acquirer parent company and its units.[4] In a typical situation:

- The parent company will determine a policy for how much of senior management pay will be in stock (for example, five times salary) and how managers will receive it (by award or purchase, and, if the latter, whether the purchase will be mandatory or voluntary). The division will encourage and enforce compliance with the parent's target ownership plan (often called a *TOP*).[5]

- The parent company will determine the desired competitiveness of base pay (below market, at market, above market), while the unit will identify the labor market in which it will be competing (local, regional, national).

- The parent company will decide on a policy for bonuses, while the unit will decide who will receive them.

- The parent company will set targets for incentive pay (accounting measures, stock price, qualitative factors, and/or discretionary factors) and valuation methodology for performance measurement (traditional accounting ratios, economic value added, cash flow return on investment, or other model), while the unit will select whether to award the incentive pay based on team or individual performance. The parent is also responsible for ensuring that pay plans do not incentivize short-term performance at the expense of ethical behavior.[6]

- The parent company will decide on a benefits policy, while the unit will administer the policy, making occasional exceptions as necessary by contract or law.

Note, however, that even when parents have the power to set policies and targets, they may use their power to meet differing unit needs, if not delegate their power outright.

Why would a newly combined company want to have different pay plans for its units?

Because the units may have very different pay environments:

- Base pay may differ from region to region and industry to industry for similar jobs. Also, a company in a mature industry will have a greater percentage of pay in base pay as opposed to variable pay from bonuses or incentives.

- Bonus pay may be hard to align following a merger between a firm with huge bonuses and one with none. Any acquirer of a Wall Street investment bank or brokerage firm knows that trying to moderate year-end bonuses in these cultures can be difficult if not impossible. (Even Warren Buffet, widely revered and successful chairman of Berkshire Hathaway, failed to do this as outside chairman of Salomon Brothers in the early 1990s.)

- Incentive pay targets for early-stage high-growth companies should be linked to sales growth, market share, and product development, not short-term profit performance, whereas the opposite would apply for a mature company. Or to use an industry example, consider the differences between a mutual fund, which lives and dies on stock prices, and the mutual insurance industry, which depends more heavily on long-term relations with policyholders. Incentive plans in such companies are likely to be different and should remain so in a merger. Finally, incentive plans may reflect differences in managerial philosophy, valuing the formal versus informal, and quantitative versus qualitative.[7]

- Benefits are another area where postmerger disparity may be necessary. Suppose that in the negotiation phase, the acquirer agreed to let the selling company's senior management keep certain perquisites, knowing full well that it would not extend these same perks to its own senior team. If that was the deal, the acquirer has no choice but to live with it and to explain this "grandfather clause" to the envious. In any event, sometimes the pay-planning team has no choice in the matter. A deal may have come with strings attached in the form of special pay arrangements for acquired company executives. There may also be regulatory restrictions on merging certain benefits, such as retirement plans.[8]

These differences can add up, resulting in sharp contrasts between companies and, once merged, units.[9] For example, a mature, centralized business with heavy capital investments, stable profit margins, little technological change, and few competitors should strive for the following:

- Senior management depth
- Predominantly fixed compensation
- Moderate incentives
- Moderate equity participation

At the other end of the spectrum, a changing, decentralized business with low capital investments, pressured profit margins, significant technological change, and many competitors should strive for the following:

- Little senior management depth
- Predominantly variable compensation
- Heavy incentives
- Heavy equity participation

Are you saying there is no role for pay-plan integration, that each unit should have its own?

No, to the contrary. To be fair to all employees, pay plans should be as uniform as possible—within the limits of what makes sense for each business unit. Few mergers will involve companies as diverse as the two described above. (Indeed, mergers between such opposites face immense barriers to success, partly because of the incompatibility of their pay cultures!) The important thing is to recognize and value differences, not ignore them. At the same time, pay planners should work holistically. A pay plan—whether for an entire company or a single unit—must be a true plan, not a patchwork quilt.

Aren't there some *general* principles of compensation that apply in *any* type of company? If so, what are they?

Yes, there are universal principles for good pay planning. The first one is that if it works, it is good. Compensation theory is continually testing itself against the reality of experience. That blend of theory and proven practice appears continually in articles and books written by compensation experts.

Take, for example, the principle of equity ownership. The basic idea of linking management and ownership is good, but there are challenges, such as the volatility of stock prices. In recent years, a number of innovations have emerged to solve this problem; for example, linking pay to share price might be done through an indexed option plan.[10] Will this become common practice? If it works, it will.

Moreover, compensation experts have put a greater emphasis on stock-based pay in the high-tech, high-growth arena and have not promoted this trait in pay plans of companies in lower-tech, mature industries. But in a telling profile of Tyco Industries' phenomenal growth by mergers, *Business Week* noted that one of the keys to Tyco's success has been heavy equity participation by acquired managers.[11]

As a diversified manufacturer of fire-prevention equipment, Tyco does not exactly fit the mold of the high-tech, early-growth company, but it is paying like one—and lo, it is growing like one. And its loyal executive ranks include not only U.S. managers used to a high degree of risk but foreign managers as well. What is the lesson in this for compensation theory? Stock-based pay, if properly structured, is for all companies everywhere. Watch for more on this in years to come.

Meanwhile, here is a list of principles already widely accepted in corporate and compensation circles.

DO:
- Encourage real share ownership at all levels.

- Link pay to performance.
- Reward executives for both shareholder value and quality of products/services.[12]
- Make sure that pay is competitive in local markets.
- Communicate in words as well as through pay.

DON'T:

- Award excessive, repriceable stock options to senior management.
- Keep increasing pay no matter what.
- Restrict performance targets to accounting factors.
- Blindly follow national or international benchmarks.
- Let pay do all the talking.

What generally happens to senior management pay levels after a merger and why?

Pay levels per employee tend to go up following a merger. This is not surprising, since mergers make companies bigger, and bigger companies tend to pay their top managers more than smaller companies do. Size is not the only factor, though. Companies that have expanded by takeover have "systematically higher" top-management pay growth than same-size peers that are expanding by internal growth.[13]

There are two reasons for postmerger pay inflation. First, postmerger equality is easier to achieve through pay raises than pay cuts. If senior executives from Company A and Company B are doing similar work, but Company A executives are getting paid more, it is more likely that B executives will be raised to A levels than the other way around.[14]

Second, there are the special M&A compensation arrangements mentioned earlier, such as golden handshakes, golden parachutes, and golden handcuffs. Total costs for these elements, if paid, can run in the tens of millions.

Speaking of golden parachutes, aren't they discouraged by law?

Yes and no. Ironically, the law that was passed to discourage parachutes may have actually *encouraged* them.

The 1984 Deficit Reduction Act set fines against companies that pay them and executives who receive them. Triggered by public outrage over the $5 million golden parachute William Agee got after the Bendix-Allied Signal merger in 1983, the law added two new sections to the tax code, which exist to this day. Section 280G to the Internal Revenue Code defines an "excess parachute payment" as one that equals or exceeds three times the executive's average W-2 compensation over the previous five years. Section 4999 imposes in such cases a 20 percent excise tax on the amount exceeding average annual compensation and denies the company a tax deduction for that amount.

But the government maximum quickly became an industry norm. Many companies began to raise their levels of parachutes to 2.99 times average annual compensation—just in time for the merger boom of the mid-1980s (and in plenty of time for the boom of the mid-1990s). Parachutes proliferated. At the time of the golden parachute laws, only about one-third of major companies had parachutes. Today, the figure is over two-thirds. And nearly half of all companies *offer to pay taxes* on amounts in excess of the 2.99 norm! Fortunately (given the way the private sector responds to government limits) lawmakers refrained from raising this bar in the Taxpayer Relief Act of 1997, which left this area of law alone.

You mentioned golden handshakes. Could you give an example of one?

Ted Turner, the well-known chairman of Turner Broadcasting, was promised 1.3 million options in Time Warner stock—worth about $10 million—as an incentive to work at the new company.[15] This is relatively high for a signing bonus.[16]

If an acquirer gives golden handshakes to acquired company managers, what prevents the managers from walking away with the gold the very next day?

An acquirer can prevent a golden handshake from becoming a golden escape hatch by adding either a *back-end* provision or a *takeback* provision to the manager's contract. In a back-end provision, a company defers part of the promised sums, making them payable late in the contract period. In the takeback provision, an acquirer states in the manager's employment agreement that he or she will have to repay all or part of the bonus in the event of departure prior to contract expiration. This second strategy can be layered, with heavier penalties for earlier departure. For example, a four-year contract might set the following penalties for repayment of a $4 million signing bonus:

Year 1: $4 million repayment
Year 2: $3 million repayment
Year 3: $2 million repayment
Year 4: $1 million repayment

These retention provisions are often referred to as *golden handcuffs.* Another type of golden handcuff is the noncompete agreement, discussed earlier.

Could you give some examples of particularly generous golden parachute agreements?

Sure. When Pacific Telesis Group agreed in mid-1996 to merge with SBC Communications, Inc., the top seven officers of PacTel signed employment agreements that promised them severance payments in the event of an "involuntary" termination, including "constructive" termination within three years of the merger. The agreement for the $24 billion deal defined constructive termination as "a material reduction in salary or benefits, a material change in responsibilities," or a relocation requirement. The total value of the agreements for all seven executives was $25 million, with the highest-paid executive (PacTel's chairman and CEO) standing to gain $7.9 million. The severance payments would be offered in addition to regular separation compensation.

A similar deal brought a measure of job security to senior executives with Turner Broadcasting in their late-1996 merger agreement with Time Warner. Under those agreements, Turner's top eight executives (not including the chairman) will qualify for a combined $28.3 million.

Assuming that two companies want to combine their pay systems, how should they do this?

A newly combined company must reconcile the individual and the collective, the past and the future. As individuals, employees will naturally want a pay package comparable to or better than what they had in the past. But pay planners must also look ahead, designing a pay system that makes sense for the long-term future.

One very simple way is to chart the basic elements of compensation (base pay, bonus pay, incentive pay, and benefits) against the past approaches of each of the merging companies and the future needs of the combined enterprise in the view of senior management. By weighing these, planners can come up with a bridging strategy that takes both into account (see Table 7-1).

When designing new compensation plans (or adjusting old ones), what general principles should compensation planners keep in mind?

First, reach out. Consult some of the many guides available on this topic. Ask for expert advice. Most leading compensation firms offer services in "total compensation planning," and many have expertise in the postmerger arena.

Of course, there are many things a company can do on its own. The important thing is to strive for viability—financial, emotional, and technical.

How can a planner ensure the financial viability of a new pay plan?

Planners need to carefully consider the financial condition of the newly combined company. Although this condition will be based in part on the previous condition of the two merging companies, the new entity will have its own financial dynamics.

Aside from the merger price tag and related charges (which can be substantial), the new company's condition will naturally be affected by the way the deal is financed.

There are four common ways to finance a merger. In order of frequency, these are cash, stock, a combination of cash and stock, and a combination of notes and cash and/or stock.[17] Each of these payment strategies can have an impact on the financial condition of the new company—and therefore on the new company's compensation system.

1. *Pay after an all-cash deal.* If the acquirer uses its own cash to finance the deal, depending on the amount of cash used, the impact on compensation planning may be slight, especially if the cash used came from a full treasury. In such a case, planners have a clean slate for their creations. If the acquirer borrows cash to finance the transaction, the deal may be a "heavily leveraged transaction," or

T A B L E 7-1

Sample "Sketchpad" for Compensation Planning

	Past Approach of Company A	Past Approach of Company B	Future Needs of Company AB	Bridging Strategy
Compensation Elements				
Base Pay	Below market	At market	At market	Raise A's salaries. Keep B's on course.
Bonus Pay	None	Generous	Minimal	Finish out yr. status quo. Then start modest awards for all, based on B's system, but reduced.
Incentive Pay	None	None	Generous	Design pay-for-performance. Employees: Additional 20 percent on base if meet goals for unit profits. Sr. management: Additional 30 percent on base if meet goals for company ROA.
Benefits	Average hlth. and ret. (cafeteria). No perks.	Below av. in h&r. Lavish perks.	Average h&r. Modest style.	Extend B's health and retirement plans. Cut A's perks. Upgrade health coverage.
Special	1-year sev.	6-mo. sev.	1-year sev.	Extend B's sev.

Note: This is a sample, not a paradigm. Planners should use their own terminology and make their own choices. Reprinted from Alexandra R. Lajoux, *The Art of M&A Integration: A Guide to Merging Resources, Processes, and Responsibilities* (New York: McGraw-Hill, 1998), p. 225.

HLT. As mentioned earlier (in Chapter 4), regulators have defined an HLT as a deal that leaves the borrower with a debt-to-equity ratio of 75 percent or more. Pay packages following HLTs should not be cash-heavy, since the company will need cash to pay debt. Incentive pay should be paid in stock or stock options and based on improvements in cash flow.

2. *Pay after an all-stock deal.* If the acquirer finances the deal through an exchange of stock using newly issued shares, the transaction may cause dilution. In such a scenario, pay planners should be conservative about granting more stock or stock options to managers, unless the company can buy back its own stock (which is difficult following a pooling of interests). Companies facing potential dilution by using stock-based pay might consider "phantom" stock grants (payments based on stock performance).

3. *Pay after cash-and-stock deal.* If the acquirer combines cash and stock in the payment, the impact on postmerger compensation may be nil, unless the cash is borrowed (in which case, the HLT caveats may apply) or the stock is generous (in which case, beware of dilution).

4. *Pay after a contingency deal.* If the acquirer offered notes to the seller, promising additional payments or "earnouts" based on contingencies (such as 20 percent sales growth), postmerger compensation should be structured to give managers a chance to make good on those targets.[18] Managers who were owners of the merged company (and therefore noteholders after the merger) will be most concerned about being given the authority, autonomy, and resources they need to meet performance targets. Obviously, the performance targets in pay-for-performance plans should be in sync with the targets set in the earnout notes.

How can planners make sure that a new compensation plan will be, as you say, "emotionally" viable?

Mergers bring up many negative emotions: loss, anxiety, jealousy. Planners need to make sure their pay plans signify the opposite: gain, security, fairness. One of the best ways to do this is to strive for *positive comparability*. Employees of the newly merged firm may not get the same compensation they got before, but it should be *similar or better*.

Consider employees of Company AB (shown in Table 7-1). The employees who worked for old Company A will rue the decline in their benefits, and employees in old Company B will dread the phase-out of their bonuses, even though both groups stand to benefit from other, positive adjustments in the total pay package. For example, in this scenario, A employees have a lot to gain: raises, bonuses, and additional incentive pay. B employees gain in the areas of incentive pay and benefits.

It is up to management to help employees focus on the positives, not the negatives. In this example (and in the case of any postmerger pay plan worth its salt), the message is this: "Your pay package is not the same as it was in the past, but it is comparable, and in some ways it is better." (In other words, don't just practice your compensation philosophy, preach it!)

In addition to comparability, another byword in the emotional realm is *patience*. It is widely believed that employees resist change, hence the burgeoning field of "change management." Certainly new compensation plans meet with resistance. According to one pay consultant, it takes three years for a new plan to take hold. The first year is for trial and error, the second for progress, the third for noticeable impact.[19]

Of course, change doesn't end with a new plan. As time goes on, managers will want to continually adjust their pay practices to meet changing realities. A word of advice, though: Compensation is a very expensive way to tell employees they are valued. Pay can do only so much to attract, retain, and motivate people. Meaningful work, a sense of worth, and a chance to advance must also come into play. If these are absent, no amount of raises, bonuses, incentives, benefits, and special deals can take their place. The best and brightest will take their talents elsewhere.

Finally, how can planners make sure a new pay plan is technically viable?

Compensation rules change frequently. Every day, some new rule or some new interpretation of a rule appears to change the technical nuances of a pay plan. Therefore, compensation planners should rely on specialized experts inside and, often, outside their companies to find out the latest appropriate changes in accounting and legal treatment of base, bonus, incentive, and benefits pay.

Benefit pay is particularly complex, so much so that many employers use outside vendors to keep records for their benefit programs.[20] But outsourcing does not free an employer of its obligations, whether long-standing or newly acquired. Buyers and sellers alike often fail to realize how many different kinds of benefits there are—and what obligations each entails.

What are the main kinds of employee benefit plans?

There are three primary employee benefits: *pension* plans, *health* plans, and *employment/advisory security* plans. The rest of benefits can be considered perquisites limited only by the human imagination.

What are the different types of pension plans?

There are two types of pension plans: *qualified* (meaning that they meet certain federal standards and qualify for tax-favorable treatment) and *nonqualified.* Furthermore, there are two types of qualified pension plans: a *defined benefit plan* and a *defined contribution plan.* (In this context, the term *defined* is synonymous with qualified.)

A *defined benefit* plan is a pension plan that determines the total value of benefits by a formula and requires the employer to meet certain actuarially determined standards in making contributions to the plan. Contributions must be enough to pay obligations when they fall due.

A *defined contribution plan* is a pension plan with shorter-term requirements. Minimum contributions are required year by year for each year in which the plan is in existence. These plans can take the form of profit-sharing plans with or without salary deferral [the well-known 401(k) plan] and usually have variable contribution levels.

Both of these qualified, defined plans are subject to a compensation cap under recent tax law.[21] More broadly, they are subject to rules set forth under the Internal Revenue Code and ERISA, administered by the Department of Labor (DOL). *Nonqualified plans*—generally plans for senior executives—are often funded through a compensation deferral mechanism called a *rabbi trust.*[22]

If a buyer and seller both have defined contribution plans, how can these be merged?

This is a complex area best understood on a plan-by-plan basis.[23] Let's take the example of the most common defined contribution plan, the 401(k). It depends on whether the acquirer bought the stock of the acquired company or its assets. In an asset acquisition, plans must remain separate, and the acquired company plan must be managed by the seller. In stock acquisition, three approaches are possible: maintaining separate plans, terminating the acquired plan, or merging the two plans.

- To maintain separate plans, the acquirer simply has to make sure that each group files its own forms (Form 5500) and satisfies federal requirements for nature and extent of coverage. One benefit of maintaining separate plans is that there is no break in coverage, as both plans continue to exist. If plan years are the same, the acquirer can take a full calendar year to come into compliance. (If plan years are different, the acquirer should check on its timetable; it may be shorter.)

- Terminating the seller's plan requires a one-year waiting period. The IRS's "successor plan rule" says that an acquired company's plan will be disqualified if more than 2 percent of its employees participate in another defined contribution plan (except for an employee stock ownership plan) within one year of the acquisition. And even if an employer respects the 2 percent limit, it must pay sanctions to prevent those employees from being taxed.

Merging the two plans can save administrative expense,[24] but it also has its complications. All "valuable benefits" in both plans must be preserved in both plans, complicating plan administration. Furthermore, if a company with a 401(k) plan is acquired by a nonprofit, procedures become extremely complex.[25]

What health plans do most major U.S. public companies today offer?

Most offer one of two types.[26] The *indemnity plan* is a fee-for-service plan. The *managed care plan,* which has become more prevalent in recent years,[27] falls into three categories, ranging from most restrictive to least restrictive. All three types of managed care plans are offered by major health-care insurers such as Prudential, Aetna, and CIGNA, as well as some 50 other organizations of varying size and quality. Also, some corporations act as self-insurers for their plans.

On the most restrictive end of the managed care spectrum you will find *health maintenance organizations* (HMOs). These plans rely on a tight network of health-care providers (physicians and hospitals) and require participants to use a primary care physician as a gatekeeper. HMOs can keep their costs down by obtaining contracted rates from participating providers for specific services during a set time frame. These plans have the strongest cost controls and quality oversight and therefore tend to be on the low end of the cost spectrum.

On the least restrictive end of the spectrum you will find *preferred provider organizations* (PPOs). These plans rely on a loose network of providers that have agreed to provide medical services at a discount to PPO plan participants. These plans do not require the use of a physician-gatekeeper; participants can go directly to specialists and still be covered under the plans. Because of their flexibility, these plans tend to be on the high end of the cost spectrum.

Between these two extremes are *point of service plans* (POSs), a relatively new hybrid product. POSs feature the physician-gatekeeper and tight provider network of the HMO, thus offering relatively low costs. On the other hand, they enable participants to opt for providers outside the network at lower rates of reimbursement, as long as the care is accessed through the gatekeeper.

In addition to managed care plans, many companies offer additional health benefits. These include not only dental, vision, long-term disability, dependent care, accidental death or disability (business travel, accident), and of course traditional life insurance, but also sick leave and various "wellness" benefits—often linked at no cost or low cost with local health-care providers. These can be single health-care events such as "flu shot day" or "spring health fair," or they can be ongoing wellness programs such as employee assistance programs (EAPs), which provide ongoing treatment referral for substance abuse or mental health problems.

What usually happens when a company with one type of health-care provider network buys a company with another type? What should happen?

Many acquirers phase out their affiliations with the networks of acquired firms and put the firm's employees on their own network. For example, if the acquirer has an HMO and the acquired company has a PPO, the acquirer will cancel the PPO and put everyone on the HMO.

But this may not always be the best course of action. Companies often make their selections based on the conditions prevailing in their *geographical region*. In one area, an HMO may be the best choice, while in another area, a PPO will be the best choice.[28]

Therefore, the best strategy is to reexamine the needs of the new company and maintain (or switch to) one or more network types according to need. Even if a company uses multiple networks, it can still use a single insurance carrier. This will require extra work on the part of the company and the insurer, but it is worth the effort. By using one carrier for all networks, the company can enjoy economies of scale and spread risk. It can also accomplish efficient price structuring.

EMPLOYEE BENEFIT PLANS

What are the concerns of a buyer with respect to employee benefit plans?

A buyer will have several basic concerns:

- What am I buying? What benefits does each plan provide? What does each benefit cost? What will it cost in future years? What ongoing liabilities does it involve? Can it be terminated or changed? Does it have assets, and do they exceed or fail to cover its liabilities—that is, is it overfunded or underfunded? Will contemplated company changes, or law changes, alter its costs?
- Does the price I am paying for the company properly reflect the costs and benefits of these plans?
- Can employee benefit plans help in financing the acquisition?
- What benefits structure do I intend to have in the post-acquisition company, and what constraints and opportunities do I have in adapting to this goal the benefits structure I am acquiring?
- How will the purchased benefit plans affect the rest of my family of companies?
- Am I organized to take over the seller's administrative obligations under the plans?

In addition, the buyer will want to be familiar with the seller concerns outlined below.

What are the concerns of a seller?

A seller will want to know about the above-mentioned buyer concerns in order to empathize with the buyer. In addition, the seller will need to know the following:

- To what extent will I be responsible for plan or personnel changes made by the buyer?
- Am I protecting the selling company's employees against adverse impacts from the acquisition?
- Do I have continuing liabilities or administrative burdens under any of the plans?
- Does the price I am receiving properly reflect the costs and benefits of the plans?

How do these concerns interrelate?

To a certain extent, buyer and seller share complementary concerns that boil down, like many of the issues between them discussed in Chapter 8, to an appropriate allocation of costs or risk between them. The expense of maintaining an elaborate benefit structure, and the increased productivity it may generate, affects the cash flow and thus the value of the company and logically should be weighed as part of the price calculation (see Chapter 3). For that reason, a seller may decide to include information about the costs of plans in the financial information initially provided the buyer, so that thereafter when the buyer protests the high costs, the seller can say that these were already factored into the price. Often, however, as discussed below, ongoing plan liabilities are not reflected in financial statements or are based on unstated assumptions that are not examined until a later stage.

An important question in negotiating the allocation of plan responsibilities is whether the price is based on a continuation of the seller's past employment practices or assumes that the buyer will carry out significant layoffs or reductions in benefits. The buyer may argue that the target's workforce or benefit structure is a problem for which the seller must take responsibility as a condition of sale, and thus that severance obligations should be borne by the seller or the price should be lowered because the buyer is willing to assume these obligations or the political heat and unpleasantness associated with layoffs. The seller's response to this argument is that it will be blamed for layoffs regardless of who does them, and that the buyer will be enjoying the enhanced profits of subsequent operations with reduced labor costs and thus should bear the cost of layoffs.

Unless the company is obviously overstaffed, the seller, both out of loyalty to its former employees and to minimize its possible future obligations to them as a result of the buyer's actions after the acquisition, will often require that the benefit structure be preserved or at least not degraded for some period of time after the closing, and that the buyer must assume severance obligations. Under such circumstances, the buyer must fully calculate the costs of these requirements and the degree of adaptability of the acquired plans to its present benefit structure.

What is a multiemployer plan?

In a unionized workforce, the employer and other unionized employers often contribute to a multiemployer pension or welfare plan jointly maintained by the union and an employers' association. If pension plans, the plans are usually defined benefit plans (DBPs). An acquisition can trigger substantial additional liability to these plans for the seller, and/or can transfer liability to the buyer. If the buyer plans facility closings or layoffs, it may trigger very large liabilities. In addition, the terms and administration of these plans are typically out of the control of buyer and seller, and information about them can be difficult to obtain. For these reasons they often present problems in an acquisition.

What are current trends in designing employee benefit programs?

In recent years, DBPs have been on the wane—with only hundreds being set up while thousands are being retired. DBPs give rise to fixed and fairly inflexible costs. Their benefit structure is geared to the full-career employee—a creature who seems to have disappeared. Every year, new legislation increases the complexity and costs of these plans. As a result, employees and employers have become more interested in defined contribution plans (DCPs). With a DCP, plan contributions can be flexible and can be tied to company performance. Benefits are more portable and more easily understood. The DOL's Pension Benefits Guaranty Corporation (PBGC) has no regulatory role; no actuary is needed. For these reasons, a buyer who values flexibility and ease of administration will usually prefer the DCP. However, in some workforces, especially older or unionized workforces, employees may insist on a DBP, or a DBP may be needed to attract skilled employees.

Sometimes an acquisition represents a major shake-up and belt tighten-
ing for a company whose benefit programs have grown excessively generous
over the years. Major savings can sometimes be achieved in the fringe benefit
area. Here the buyer may be able to maintain the basic benefit program and
make economizing changes that appear somewhat ancillary. For example,
costs of medical plans can be cut (or increases stemmed) with self-insured or
minimum premium policies, higher deductibles, second opinion programs,
preferred provider options, and employee contributions. The buyer may also
wish to convert to a flexible benefit program known as a *Section 125 plan,*
which permits employees to select their own mix of benefits.

In many cases, the lower-paid employees can receive DCP benefits
through matching employer contributions that are (or approximate) benefits
under a DBP, while higher-paid employees can receive supplemental benefits
through nonqualified programs.

DETERMINING PLAN ASSETS AND LIABILITIES AND THEIR EFFECT ON COMPANY BOOKS

How can a buyer determine the amount of a plan's assets and liabilities?

For defined benefit plans, the best source of information is the latest actuarial
valuation of the plan. This document will show the assets and liabilities of the
plan and its annual costs (which will probably be different from its accounting
expense). The valuation will also show whether assets would exceed liabilities
if the plan were terminated. Most important, the valuation will show the assumptions used to calculate these liabilities.

Another source of information about plan value is the "employee benefits"
notes to the company's financial statements. These notes will reflect assumptions made by the plan actuaries. The company financials will also show historical and current pension costs. Financial Accounting Statement (FAS) No. 106 of
the FASB requires companies to recognize the future cost of retiree benefits.

Plan assets and liabilities are extremely sensitive to interest and other actuarial assumptions. The interest assumption determines the rate at which plan assets will appreciate; thus, the higher the assumed interest rate, the more adequate
present assets are to meet projected liabilities. If the interest rate is even 1 percent off, adequacy of funding can be affected dramatically: A 1 percent change
in interest rates can result in a 6 percent change in liabilities. An actuary or an

actuarially knowledgeable lawyer may be needed to help extract the true cost and funded status from the valuation, by adjusting the assumptions to the market reality or buyer's intentions, and it is a good idea to get the actuary started early.

If the plan is expected to be ongoing, a conservative interest rate may be appropriate. If the buyer intends to terminate the plan, the current rate would be more appropriate. If the rate deemed appropriate by the buyer is higher than the rate used in the plan valuation, from the buyer's point of view the valuation overstates funding obligations. Conversely, the seller may have used relatively high interest rate assumptions, thereby concluding that the plan is overfunded and enabling the seller to minimize funding obligations. In such a case, supposed plan surpluses may be inflated above the amount that could actually be recovered, or may even be nonexistent, and the buyer should resist the seller's request for a purchase price increase or other benefit based on the supposed overfunding. Other assumptions can also be very important, including rates of increase in amounts of medical claims, frequency of such claims, changes in the size and age of the employee workforce, and the like.

For defined contribution plans, issues of overfunding and underfunding do not arise. Assets of a DCP will always equal liabilities, by definition, because liabilities are simply the balance of accounts. The buyer should be aware of any contribution commitment imposed by the plan.

Multiemployer plan liabilities are extremely difficult to determine, unless the seller has a trustee on the plan's board of trustees. The seller should be asked to provide its contribution history to the plan and to obtain a withdrawal liability estimate from the plan. Not all plans have this information readily available, and the seller may be reluctant to alert the plan, or the public, to a proposed transaction. A rough estimate can be made from Schedule B to Form 5500 (filed annually with the IRS and the DOL). Some plan valuations now routinely include withdrawal liability information. Copies of Form 5500 and valuation can sometimes be obtained from the DOL, but these are usually not very current.

How are plan assets and liabilities reflected on the corporate books?

As mentioned above, the FASB requires recognition of plan liabilities as well as assets. This recognition must appear in the financial statement of an employer rather than in a footnote to the financial statements. One important financial accounting statement on this subject was FAS No. 106, which requires companies to disclose the future cost of retiree benefits.

Under FAS No. 87, a base liability or asset is recognized equal to cumulative expense less amounts funded. An additional liability for unfunded accumulated benefits is required to be recognized and is generally offset by an intangible asset. Uniform actuarial cost methods and assumptions are required, and assumptions are required to be "explicit," meaning individually set forth and determined. Multiemployer plan liabilities do not need to be recognized unless withdrawal liability is "probable." FAS No. 87 also contains elaborate transitional rules that may affect the accounting for a specific plan.

Except in an acquisition, as discussed in the next question, companies with overfunded plans are not permitted by FAS No. 87 to book the excess assets directly on their balance sheet. Even in the absence of an acquisition, however, the excess may be indirectly recognized on the books in some cases because the treatment of pension expense may actually result in a decrease in pension expense or even in pension income if a plan is overfunded.

How are book liabilities for a plan affected by the acquisition of the company?

If an acquisition occurs, the buyer is required to recognize an acquisition asset (or liability) equal to the difference between the acquired projected benefit obligations and the fair value of plan assets. The projected benefit obligation takes into account future salary progression and is thus typically a higher liability amount than the unfunded accumulated benefits required to be booked when an acquisition is not involved. In all cases an actuary or accountant should be consulted to determine the impact of any proposed transaction on the financial statements of the company.

FAS No. 88 covers employers' accounting for "settlements" and "curtailments" of defined benefit pension plans and for termination benefits, a circumstance that may arise in the mergers and acquisitions situation. FAS No. 88 permits recognition of a gain when there is an irrevocable transfer of liabilities from the employer to another party, for example, by a plan spin-off. The seller may thus be able to recognize a gain by transferring assets and liabilities to the buyer.

Can the seller's other plans (those the buyer isn't acquiring) create liabilities for the buyer?

If the purchased operation is a part of a controlled group of corporations, under Code Sections 414(b) and (c) and 1563, the buyer must consider the possibility that it will be liable for unfunded benefits and defaulted contribution to plans maintained for parts of the controlled group not being acquired. All members of a controlled group are jointly and severally liable for unfunded DBP liabilities and for unpaid DBP contributions under ERISA Section 4062 and Code Section 412. ERISA Section 4064 may be interpreted to continue that liability for a period of five years after the sale of a member of the controlled group, although this theory is relatively untested. In addition, ERISA Section 4069 provides that if a "principal purpose" of any person entering into any transaction is to evade liability to the PBGC, that transaction is treated as null and void. Thus, under these rules, a sale could be ignored and the acquired company could continue to be liable for plan obligations of other members of its former controlled group as if the sale had not taken place.

What IRS requirements are imposed on a controlled group basis?

The Internal Revenue Code coverage, participation, and benefits tests all operate on a controlled group basis, so any pension or fringe benefit plan must be tested on such a basis. The control group rules incorporate Code Section 1563. Essentially, these are the 80 percent parent-sub or brother-sister tests with attribution among corporate family members and principal shareholders of corporations.

There is an exception for collectively bargained plans. There is also a separate line of business exception that may allow treatment of benefits differently among the different companies for some purposes. However, the legislative history of the Tax Reform Act of 1986 makes it very clear that a headquarters cannot be a "separate line of business." The parent organization may not have significantly better benefits than the bulk of the controlled organizations. Similarly, a buyer accepting a defined benefit plan for a newly acquired division could find that it must extend that defined benefit plan to all other parts of the operation. A one-year transitional rule permits companies to take at least a year to rationalize their benefits programs when there has been a merger or acquisition.

How does the structure of the acquisition affect the buyer's obligations under the selling company's employee benefit plans?

When purchasing a company, the buyer will normally acquire as part of the transaction all the assets and liabilities of its employee benefit plans, unless other provisions are made in the acquisition agreement. An asset purchase, by contrast, often does not involve the explicit assumption of benefit plan assets and liabilities, although in the benefit area the purity of an asset purchase is frequently eroded by collective bargaining agreements, successorship concepts, and statutory and regulatory definitions of the "employer" liable for benefit costs. Thus the buyer should take great care if it intends not to assume seller's plan obligations.

An example of how a buyer can inadvertently subject itself to the terms of a seller's plan is provided by the *Accord* case, later reversed on appeal. In that case, by agreeing to assume the seller's plans, the buyer was held to have assumed the seller's interpretation of those plans as well and could not interpret them by reference to its own benefit programs in an ambiguous situation. The seller was IBM, and the court took judicial notice of IBM's policy of extremely generous benefits to apply a generous interpretation of the buyer's assumed plan.

The acquisition structure is very important if the seller contributes to a multiemployer pension plan. A stock sale will not trigger withdrawal liability for the seller but will transfer it to the buyer in the event that the buyer later ceases contributions to the plan. (Withdrawal liability is calculated as a share of the unfunded vested benefits of the plan—ERISA Section 4201, 29 U.S.C. Section 1381.) An asset purchase, unless special agreements are made which meet statutory exceptions (ERISA Section 4204, 29 U.S.C. Section 1384), will trigger withdrawal liability for the seller but will permit the buyer to start with a clean slate. Purchase of stock in the seller's subsidiary may appear more like an asset purchase in some circumstances.

If the purchase involves only a part of a company, it will be necessary to divide plan assets and liabilities in some negotiated manner. This process provides many opportunities for a buyer to increase the amount of assets transferred to it and for a seller to transfer liabilities to the buyer.

PLAN SPLIT-UPS AND PARTIAL TERMINATIONS

If a defined benefit plan covers more than the purchased operations, what techniques can be used to separate the benefit programs?

Unless the seller's entire company is being purchased, the plan will frequently cover employees for more of the seller's operations than those being purchased. Under such circumstances, the buyer and seller have a number of choices.

The buyer or the acquired company could simply hire the employees and place them in whatever benefit programs the buyer has in place. The seller would likely, but not necessarily, incur a "partial termination" in the seller's pension plan, vesting all the transferred participants [Code Section 411(d)]. The IRS's position is that for a DBP, there would not be separation of service for the participants, so that the plan may not immediately distribute benefits to the separated participants. [A 401(k) plan may distribute benefits.] Any surplus assets (or liabilities) will be retained by the seller, which has the obligation at the time the employees retire to pay them benefits attributable to their service during the pre-acquisition period. The employees will receive, on retirement, benefits from both the seller's plan (for their pre-acquisition service) and the buyer's plan (for their post-acquisition service). The buyer may demand compensation for the loss of any excess assets retained by the seller.

If the buyer and seller do not wish to take the partial termination approach, the plan can be split up and assets and liabilities transferred to the buyer, to the extent attributable to the operations being purchased by the buyer. In a plan split-up there is a great deal of flexibility in the amount of assets and liabilities to be allocated to each party, subject to the restrictions of Section 414(l) of the Code. Obviously, if the plan has excess assets, a key question is who gets the excess and how much of it.

It is very important to consult an actuary and to establish clearly in the acquisition document the assumptions that will be used to divide the plan. It is also very important to establish the treatment of contribution obligations to the plan for periods prior to the closing that may not have been paid to the plan, so these are not double-counted. The liabilities transferred are extremely sensitive to the actuarial assumptions used for the computations, and to the basis on which the allocation is made (such as termination basis, ongoing basis, projected benefits obligation basis), so that seemingly minor differences can have a major impact. For that reason, the party who gets to select the actuary has a major advantage. Also, the allocation technique should protect the buyer and seller from adverse market performance in the time between the signing of the agreement and the closing or, if later, the transfer of plan assets.

If the buyer is not going to accept a plan spin-off but has no existing plan, it will have to decide what types of benefit programs, if any, to put in place for the employees. For example, if the buyer decides to set up a new defined benefit plan and provide benefits to the employees under that plan, it must decide whether to credit service prior to the acquisition. If the buyer is beginning the defined benefit plan accruals from the date of closing, and the plan is a salary-based plan, the employees will end up with fewer benefits than if the plan had been based on the employees' initial service dates. In order to avoid a reduction in employee benefits, the buyer can give credit for service from the employee's initial date of employment with the seller, and offset against the benefits any benefits paid out of the seller's plan. By so doing, however, the buyer is assuming liability for projected benefits based on service that was accrued for the prior employer.

Must buyers provide past service credits for the purposes of eligibility and vesting?

The IRS has stated that under Section 414, an acquisition of assets or stock will create a successorship situation requiring the buyer to provide past service credits (for service with the seller) for purposes of eligibility and vesting.

What practical difficulties arise in a transfer of plan assets?

Acquirers need to be very clear about who will get what plan paperwork when. Unless assets are transferred to an existing plan, a new trust will be required. During the transitional period, unless a new trustee is appointed, the existing trustee will have to serve for two separate plans. The trustee—new or old—will be reluctant to collectively invest two different trust accounts, for reasons involving Comptroller of Currency regulations. Valuation poses another serious challenge, especially in a volatile market. It's important to provide that the transferee plan has the right to review the outgoing trustee's allocation of assets and administrative fees in order to ensure a fair allocation.

Another practical question is whether and at what rate interest should be paid between the valuation date and the actual transfer date. If plan assets are to be liquidated, the trustee would normally request a fairly lengthy period of time to liquidate so as to avoid temporary market dips or to keep from having to dump securities on the market. During this time, the assets should be held in some kind of interest-bearing account. The transferee plan may be willing to accept assets in kind, rather than cash, but the details of this concept can become very complex.

In some situations, the buyer may not be in a position to accept the plan initially. This can create an unusual type of plan, the "multiple employer plan," subject to special application of the Code (and not the same as a "multiemployer plan" discussed above). It is important to begin planning for the plan transfer at the earliest possible date and to have it occur as quickly as possible on or after closing. This goal is frequently not met in practice.

What problems are posed by an acquisition requiring the division of a defined contribution plan?

The main question with a defined contribution plan is whether to terminate the plan (or part of the plan) and vest and distribute accounts to participants, or to transfer accounts in a trust-to-trust transfer to a new defined contribution plan maintained by the buyer.

The seller could hold the participant accounts, but this is usually inconvenient administratively. If the buyer is willing to accept participant accounts, a trust-to-trust transfer is probably the most practical and the most beneficial from the point of view of the participants, because it preserves the tax treatment of the accounts in the plan rather than forcing them into an IRA tax treatment (resulting in loss of income averaging). However, the transfer of defined contribution accounts could cause problems for the new plan if the old plan is required to have a joint and survivor benefit and the new plan does not. If the accounts in the seller's plan contain considerable employee contributions, recovery of basis rules will come into play. In such cases, it may be better for employees not to merge the seller's plan with a buyer's plan that does not contain employees' contributions, since the blending of different accounts can trigger taxation of benefits based on employee contributions when received under the basis recovery rules.

Other practical problems arise with the valuation of accounts and time lags in accrual of interest on accounts. At some point, accounts need to be liquidated if they are to be transferred, and this may raise valuation issues, particularly in a volatile market. Defined contribution plans will also involve extensive record-keeping questions, and unless a third-party record keeper is used and the contract can be easily transferred, the buyer may face high start-up administrative costs.

If the plan is a salary deferral or employee contribution plan, another problem is a smooth changeover of the employee contributions. On a given day, the buyer will have to cut the paychecks and process a deduction from paychecks for deposit to the plan. The buyer will need to be prepared to implement these deductions.

What fiduciary concerns arise in an acquisition of employee benefit plans?

All plans subject to ERISA have been created and are operated for the benefit of the employees who participate in them, and both buyer and seller must recognize that they assume fiduciary obligations to employees in any transaction involving benefit plans. As discussed below, a quasi-fiduciary level of review is imposed by courts in plan terminations, spin-offs, and other situations in which the employer is believed to have a conflict of interest. Particular conflicts of interest can arise inadvertently: For example, an acquisition could turn out to be a prohibited transaction under Code Section 4975 if the acquired plan has been invested in securities of the buyer.

Naturally, the implementation of the plan transfer, spin-off, or termination will also be subject to fiduciary standards. The buyer should probably obtain fiduciary insurance even before the plan is actually in the buyer's hands, and the acquisition contract should clearly specify who has the fiduciary obligations during the transitional period. The practitioner should review the cofiduciary provisions of ERISA in drafting these provisions. Note also that "small" companies (as variously defined under federal law) may lose their pension law exemptions when they grow through acquisition.[29]

What reporting obligations to government agencies will be created by the transaction itself?

It is important that the agreement specify who will undertake reporting obligations of the plans arising out of the transaction. Typically, a change in employer is an event that must be reported to the IRS, pursuant to Section 6057 of the Code. However, this event is generally reported on Form 5500 filed annually with the IRS, DOL, and PBGC. The obligation to file this form will usually be assumed by the post-acquisition company as sponsor of the plan at the time that the form is due; however, because the plan will address prior periods, it may make sense to require the seller to file the form for all periods prior to the closing. It is helpful to demand that the seller cooperate by providing necessary data for the filings. In addition, if the plan is underfunded, a reportable event notice may need to be filed with the PBGC when the plan changes hands.

If the plan assets are to be transferred, then Form 5310 will have to be filed by both recipient and transferring plan, prior to the actual transfer. If there is a plan termination, the plan as terminated is qualified through Form 5310.

Any new plan adopted by the buyer should be qualified with the IRS by the buyer's filing the appropriate Form 5300, 5301, or 5302.

All filings with the IRS require extensive notification to the plan participants. If the plan is actually terminated, and if it is a defined benefit plan, there are required filings with the PBGC. In the case of partial termination, there will be no IRS filings, except that if the plan should be amended to vest all participants subject to the partial termination, this amendment should be qualified with the IRS. Also, if there is a sufficient drop in participants, a partial termination can create a reportable event to the PBGC. Withdrawal of a substantial employer (10 or more employees) from a multiple or multiemployer plan can also trigger some reporting obligations.

UNDERFUNDED AND OVERFUNDED PLANS

How are liabilities in underfunded benefit plans divided between buyer and seller?

Underfunding is a problem, as we have mentioned, in DBPs, but not in DCPs, in which benefits equal assets by definition. There are two degrees of underfunding in DBPs. In the worst case, the plan does not have assets sufficient to meet liabilities even if terminated at the measurement date. In the less severe, and in fact normal, case, the plan is underfunded on an ongoing basis and thus has continuing pension costs but would have assets sufficient to meet liabilities if the plan were terminated.

If a plan is underfunded on a termination basis, under current law it cannot be terminated without funding all benefit commitments, unless the plan sponsor and all members of the sponsor's controlled group are in extreme financial distress. In practice, if the plan is purchased from a seller in distress, the buyer, which is presumably not in extreme financial distress, cannot terminate the plan unless it pays the unfunded benefits. Any plan termination underfunding is a real liability shown on the company books and should be factored into the value of the acquired entity. The buyer should review carefully with an actuary or an accountant the financial assumptions underlying the booking of the underfunding, because this may differ from the actuarial amount and may not truly reflect the anticipated costs of the plan.

If the plan is fully funded on a termination basis, the buyer can transfer or keep the plan without immediate adverse financial consequences. However, from the buyer's point of view, the future cost of an ongoing plan is not the termination liability, but the difference between the projected future benefit obligations and the assets of the plan. Even a plan with sufficient assets on a termination basis will probably create a long-term liability for the buyer and may create a book liability.

To terminate or continue the plan are not the only options. It may be possible to freeze the plan and thereby curtail future increases in plan liabilities, if this can be done without serious detriment to employee relations. Benefits can be cut prospectively or perhaps replaced to some extent by a DCP. It may also be possible for the buyer or the seller to merge the plan into another, better-funded plan, thereby eliminating the underfunding of the plan. In such a case, the merged plan could be continued, frozen, or terminated.

Generally, if a plan is funded on a termination basis but not on a projected benefits obligations basis, it is considered in good condition. The seller might even seek to get a little additional consideration based on any funding in excess of the termination liabilities. The buyer should be aware of the future costs of the plan and should consider whether the acquisition provides a good opportunity to shift from a defined benefits to a defined contribution structure.

If the company has a defined benefit plan that is overfunded, in what ways can buyer or seller obtain the benefits of the overfunding?

Any assets of a plan in excess of plan liabilities on a termination basis are corporate assets, but ones that it may be difficult for buyer and seller to get their hands on. Under present law, the owner of such an asset may convert it to cash in one of two ways:

- Decrease future funding, which will recover the excess assets over a period of years.

- Terminate the plan and take a reversion of the excess; a reversion is subject to an excise tax unless it is transferred to an ESOP.

Flexibility to change funding was curtailed by the Omnibus Budget Reconciliation Act of 1987 (OBRA), which imposed a standard range of interest assumptions for funding purposes. OBRA also precludes termination and reversion unless the plan is new or has permitted a reversion for at least five years.

The assets can also be realized, but not in cash, through recognition of the excess on the corporate books. Although recognition of the excess assets directly is not permitted under FAS No. 87, recognition may be possible through application of purchase accounting rules or through the "settlement" of benefit liabilities in the plan by the purchase of annuities by the plan.

A less tangible benefit can be realized by passing the excess through to employees in the form of cost-of-living adjustments or improvements to the benefit formula. It may be possible to place the surplus assets in an ESOP, using the ESOP as a source of financing and avoiding the 10 percent tax on a reversion. (ESOPs are discussed further below.) Plan assets can also be used to purchase employer stock or property. This technique is available whether or not there are excess assets. With DOL approval, plan assets, whether they are excess or not, can also be loaned to the employer. The seller can in effect realize plan assets by selling them to the buyer. The value of those assets will be a matter of debate—and the seller may have to pay excise tax if the IRS concludes that the purchase price reflects such excess assets.

How can plan funding requirements be adjusted to recover a surplus?

The plan funding requirements are determined by the plan actuary based on a set of assumptions about interest, inflation, and plan turnover (Code Section 412). Often the actuary is willing to vary these assumptions so that future contribution obligations are lessened, particularly if the plan is fully funded. Of course, the actuary is required to certify that the assumptions are reasonable in the aggregate and so will not have unlimited flexibility. Sometimes decreased future funding assumptions can be obtained by changing the actuarial method used to calculate funding obligations or even by converting from a smoothing average asset valuation method to a market valuation method.

The actuary might also be able to use an alternative funding method under Code Section 412, which decreases short-term funding costs by amortizing unfunded liabilities within a five-year period. Another possibility may be to apply to the IRS for a funding waiver under Code Section 412(f). However, a funding waiver may be obtained only upon a showing of substantial business hardship for the entire control group and would not be appropriate for all situations.

What are the tax consequences to the seller in a sale of an overfunded plan?

Code Section 4980 imposes an excise tax on any indirect or direct reversion. IRS officials have informally suggested that the IRS may issue regulations saying that the sale of a company with an overfunded plan creates a taxable indirect reversion that imposes the excise tax on the seller. The IRS apparently believes that the sale price includes a payment for the surplus, and the seller has thus received a reversion. Section 4980 contains an exception for a surplus placed in an ESOP investing in common stock [as defined in Code Section 409(e)] of the employer.

Why might a buyer prefer not to terminate the plan and receive a reversion of the surplus?

The termination/reversion technique can be cumbersome, complex, and expensive. Several governmental approvals are required. Typically, a new plan, either defined benefit or defined contribution, will be put in place, which is also expensive and obviously entails future pension costs. The lengthy process exacerbates the risk of adverse congressional action (Congress is considering restricting plan reversions in a number of different ways) and also places the surplus at risk in the market. However, market risk can be minimized by hedging techniques.

Recovery of the surplus through a reversion will be undercut by a nondeductible excise tax and by income tax on the surplus. In addition, if the plan had employee contributions, employees are awarded a part of the surplus under PBGC regulations pursuant to ERISA Section 404(d)(2).

What are the potential legal restraints on plan termination?

Under ERISA and the Internal Revenue Code, when a plan terminates, surplus assets may revert to the employer only if the plan so provides. As mentioned, the 1987 tax law required the plan provision to have been in place for five years or, if less, the life of the plan. Thus the first potential restraint may be that the plan does not adequately provide for termination and/or a reversion, or did not do so at all relevant times. Even if the plan does provide for termination, there could be legal impediments to terminating the plan if the language is ambiguous and plan descriptions provided to regulators and/or distributed to participants suggest that the plan will not be terminated.[30] Such language ambiguities have been used successfully to block terminations in a number of cases brought by unions and employees, who do not like terminations.

Recently, courts have begun to attack plan termination in somewhat obtuse ways. The *Blessit* case permitted a plan to terminate but calculated the benefits obligations so that all the surplus had to be applied to benefit payments, and the benefit of the reversion to the employer was virtually eroded. Similarly, the *Tilley* case interpreted accrued benefits in such a way that the plan termination created accelerated benefits for participants.

Another possible restraint on plan termination is a collective bargaining agreement. If the agreement can be interpreted to require the employer to continue the plan, it may prevent a termination. Notice must be given to any unions and to employees in the case of an anticipated plan termination. If the union then protests to the PBGC that the termination is precluded by a collective bargaining agreement, the PBGC will halt or reject the planned termination. In short, unions have a strong weapon for enforcing what they believe to be the provisions of a collectively bargained agreement.

A termination decision may also be invalidated if it is shown to be "arbitrary and capricious." Recent case law interpretation of the arbitrary and capricious standard provides a heightened level of fiduciary scrutiny for plan terminations when the employer has an interest in the decision involved. Courts seem unwilling to go so far as to make a decision such as whether to terminate a plan or a fiduciary decision, but they are likely to read some stiff requirements into the arbitrary and capricious standard when there is a substantial plan reversion at stake.

EMPLOYEE STOCK OWNERSHIP PLANS

What is an ESOP, and what is its main purpose?

An ESOP (employee stock ownership plan, as explained earlier) is a type of DCP designed to permit the plan to invest in certain employer securities on a leveraged basis. According to the National Center for Employee Ownership in Oakland, California, an ESOP can help a company:

- Sell all or part of the company to its employees
- Divest a subsidiary, division, or product line through an ESOP buyout

- Repurchase shares from the (public equity) market using pretax dollars

- Restructure existing benefit plans by replacing them with an ESOP

- Acquire capital by having the company borrow through the ESOP and repay the loan with pretax dollars[31]

In addition to these common uses, an ESOP can be used to defend a company against a hostile takeover, by concentrating its stock in friendly hands.

What are the benefits and drawbacks of ESOPs?

Aside from the obvious "psychic" benefit that accrues from ownership, ESOPs offer four main tax benefits:[32]

- An ESOP is eligible to be a shareholder in an S corporation (discussed further below).

- The acquired company can generally deduct its contributions to the ESOP to the extent that they can be used to pay the principal of the ESOP's loan and the interest on the loan.

- The acquired company may deduct the amount of cash dividends paid with respect to its own stock held by the ESOP if such dividends are paid in cash to ESOP participants, allotted to the ESOP participants' accounts, or used to make principal or interest payments on the ESOP's loan (with certain restrictions).

- A shareholder (other than a C corporation) in an acquired corporation who sells stock to the ESOP may elect under Code Section 1042 not to pay long-term capital gain tax under certain conditions. This is referred to as the selling shareholder's *rollover*. In this type of transaction, the buyout can proceed in stages. For example, an LBO for half the company may be repaid over five years, followed by a second leveraged transaction for the rest.

But for these tax benefits there is a price to be paid: Companies that have ESOPs must satisfy the plan trustee, who is an independent fiduciary. They also must repurchase the stock under certain circumstances, among other obligations.

Could you give some regulatory background on ESOPs?

ESOPs work in different ways in different countries. In the United States, they are governed by ERISA. An ESOP is only one type of plan that may own employer securities under ERISA: Any plan can acquire and hold up to 10 percent of its assets in employer stock or real property if certain conditions of ERISA are met (ERISA Section 406). Plans that qualify as "eligible individual account" plans, under ERISA Section 407(d), may exceed the 10 percent limit: These are simply plans that are profit-sharing, stock bonus, thrift, savings, ESOP, or pre-ERISA money purchase plans that explicitly provide for the holding of employer stock [ERISA Section 407(d)(3)] and that provide for an individual account for each participant with benefits equal to the account plus or minus earnings, losses, and so on.

Each type of plan has its own set of ERISA and Code rules. An ESOP is a type of individual account plan, called a qualified stock bonus plan, that meets the Code and ERISA ESOP requirements and may therefore enter into an ESOP loan and take advantage of other special ESOP provisions such as higher deductions, higher benefit limits, and special stock transfer and estate tax rules, as well as interest deductions and income exclusions for the lender, all described more fully below. (Two other forms of stock ownership plans, TRASOPs and PAYSOPs, are no longer popular because the tax credits formerly available to them have expired.)

How common are ESOPs?

According to the National Center for Employee Ownership (see note 31), there are some 10,000 U.S. companies with ESOPs, covering almost 9 million participants.

What is the basic structure of an ESOP buyout?

A leveraged ESOP is an ESOP that borrows cash to purchase the stock of the acquired company. The ESOP is the only qualified plan that can do this. The shareholders of the acquired company sell all or a portion of their stock to the ESOP, which finances the purchase with a loan from an outside lender or, more commonly, from the acquired company itself (which has borrowed the money from an outside lender in a back-to-back loan). The loan is then repaid over time out of contributions to the plan and perhaps out of dividends and stock appreciation. The securities need not be securities of the plan sponsor, but could be securities of any control group member. The loan, if not made by the seller, is typically guaranteed by it, and secured by the stock or other assets of the company to be sold. Because of special tax benefits obtainable from an ESOP buyout, the loans may be, in some cases, obtained at lower than market rates.

How much stock must be held by the ESOP?

There is no required stock holding. However, at least 30 percent of each class of stock of the company to be sold, or 30 percent of the total value of the company's stock, must have been sold in the aggregate by all selling stockholders if the selling stockholders are to receive all the "rollover" tax benefits mentioned above. In addition, the ESOP must be "primarily," that is, at least 50 percent, invested in stock of the company sold.

What is the tax benefit to the selling stockholder?

No gain is recognized by the selling stockholder on the sale of closely held stock, provided that the 30 percent ESOP stock ownership test is met and that, within one year of the sale, the stockholder reinvests in "qualified replacement property" (Code Section 1042). The replacement property is basically a rollover investment: It must consist of securities of operating companies, cannot be a government security, may have no more than 25 percent passive income, and must be issued by an entity independent of the ESOP sponsor. The replacement property retains the basis of the stock sold to the ESOP, which is usually low, and tax is paid on the deferred gains upon sale of the replacement property. However, there is always the possibility that the next disposition will also be exempt from tax on gain as a result of a gift to a charity, the estate tax rules, another Section 1042 transaction, or a Section 368 reorganization in which the Section 1042 shareholder does not control the replacement property issuer.

The selling stockholders must elect tax-exempt treatment on a timely return and must advise the IRS of the qualified replacement property. There are some strings attached: The acquired company to be sold will be subject to a 10 percent excise tax if the stock is sold by the ESOP within three years and the ESOP owns less stock than before the nontaxed sale to the ESOP, or owns less than 30 percent of the total value of stock, unless the ESOP has disposed of the stock due to plan distributions. Another tax, of 50 percent, applies to any "prohibited allocation" of awards attributed to the transaction, which is an allocation of ESOP benefits to the taxpayer, the taxpayer's relatives, or any 25 percent shareholder other than a de minimis allocation. The seller must provide a written consent to both of these taxes. (A prohibited allocation also disqualifies the plan with respect to the recipients.)

Are there any kinds of stockholders who will not receive tax-free rollover benefits?

Yes. As mentioned, stockholders that are C corporations are ineligible. Also, the tax-free treatment is not available for publicly traded stock. This has the effect of limiting the full tax benefits of ESOP buyouts to situations in which the acquired company is not publicly traded and a substantial amount of its stock is held by individuals, trusts, or S corporations. In publicly traded situations, the ESOP will still benefit from the other tax advantages and the favorably priced loans.

What are the tax benefits to a lender?

Under very narrow conditions (such as refinancing of certain types of tax-qualified loans), institutional lenders (banks, insurance companies, investment companies, and the like) can exclude from income taxation 50 percent of the interest earnings on an ESOP loan. Prior to passage of the Small Business Job Protection Act of 1996, which repealed most of Code Section 133, this tax deduction was much broader.

In any event, from the lender's point of view, a loan to the company is preferable to a loan to the ESOP, because the lender is then not treated as a fiduciary to the plan and may treat the loan as an ordinary commercial loan. The lender may also be able to impose obligations on the company that cannot be imposed in a direct loan to the ESOP.

What tax benefits does the selling company enjoy?

The selling company can repay the loan through its contributions to the ESOP. Such contributions are deductible in their entirety, unless they exceed the limits set forth in Code Sections 404 and 415. Consequently, the selling company can in effect deduct not only interest, but also principal repayments on the ESOP acquisition loan.

Code Section 404 limits ESOP contributions to a certain percentage of total compensation. The current percentage is 25 percent (up from 15 percent for non-ESOPs) counting only the first $150,000 from each participating employee subject to cost-of-living adjustment. Code Section 415 limits contributions to DCPs allocable to employees to $30,000 per year per employee or, if less, 25 percent of compensation. If no more than one-third of the allocations are made to highly compensated employees, only amounts used to repay the principal on the loan are counted toward the contribution limits. For any ESOP, the value of the allocation is based on the contribution allocated, not on the value of the securities released to the employee's account [Treas. Reg. Section 1.415(6)(g)(5); Code Section 415(c)(6)(A)]. As a result of these rules, an ESOP can be "richer" than a non-ESOP. Dividends on the securities may also be used to pay the loan. The sale of securities, however, can be used in only very limited circumstances for this purpose.

Do these limits tend to make certain types of acquisition candidates more suitable for ESOPs?

Yes. Basically, an ESOP buyout is most effective for buying a manufacturing, service, or retail business that has substantial numbers of employees and has a relatively high ratio of payroll to acquisition cost. Also, shareholders of closely held companies receive the maximum tax benefits.

Why did Congress treat ESOPs so generously?

ESOPs are frequently touted as an "employee motivational technique." Indeed, this is the basis for Congress's continued favorable treatment of ESOPs. The General Accounting Office (GAO) and the National Center for Employee Ownership have both found that when ESOPs are supported by participative management programs (work teams, cross-functional teams, employee empowerment programs, and the like), companies perform substantially better.

What are the drawbacks of a leveraged ESOP?

An ESOP is a plan subject to ERISA's fiduciary standards. As a result, all transactions between the company and the ESOP are subject to fiduciary rules. The valuation of the stock contributed to the ESOP is a fiduciary issue. All valuations of employers' securities acquired after December 31, 1986, unless readily tradable on an established market, must be made by an independent appraiser unless the company's stock is publicly traded. These fiduciary constraints may limit the flexibility in structuring a deal, especially if the ESOP terms are different from those given to other investors. In several cases the DOL has torpedoed ESOP deals or forced changes in them because it viewed the transaction as unfair to the ESOP in relation to the other investors. Blue Bell (which was ultimately successful) and Scott Fetzer are two well-known examples. To allay DOL concerns, independent legal and financial advisors are a practical necessity, even if not a legal prerequisite.

The ESOP can restrain or complicate later transactions. For example, the sale of non-ESOP stock at an increased price may call into question the ESOP value of stock allocated to the ESOP. Also, all nonunion employees must be eligible to participate, and stock must be allocated on a nondiscriminatory basis. In addition, there are limits on benefits for highly compensated employees.

What is the effect of ESOP ownership on voting control by management?

ESOPs necessarily involve a certain sacrifice of control. Shares owned by the ESOP are in hands probably friendly to management, but they are not controlled by management. Nonallocated securities are controlled by a trustee, who is imbued with a fiduciary mandate to act in the sole interests of plan participants. In some cases, the employer will retain voting and investment control, but in these cases the employer assumes the duty to act for the sole benefit of the plan participants. Even if the employer has taken control, the trustee will not be relieved of responsibility and is required to ignore the employer's directions if they are not in the sole interest of plan participants. DOL advisory letters make it clear that ESOP fiduciaries must obtain (and follow) independent legal and financial advice.

Once securities have been allocated to a participant's account, the participant must be permitted to vote the securities. In closely held companies, voting is required only on certain major issues, such as liquidation, merger, and sale. Employees can be given full voting rights, such as the right to vote for board members, but companies are not legally required to do so. In public companies full voting rights must be passed through.

There are also issues about how securities must be voted when the participant does not respond to the pass-through voting ballot or, more significantly, for unallocated shares, which are the large majorities in the early stages of an ESOP.

How much voting discretion does the trustee have? Should he or she vote the securities in accordance with the majority rule of the participant votes as directed by the employer, or make an independent voting decision?

Should the trustee vote the securities in accordance with the majority rule of the participant votes, may the trustee be subject to direction by the employer, or must the trustee have an independent voting decision? At present, the DOL says the trustee should use independent judgment in voting unallocated and undirected shares. Many ESOP experts contend that trustees can vote these shares proportionately to directed shares. (The issue is now being tested in court.) Clearly these issues are the more significant the larger the ESOP holding and can be especially critical when the employer is sold, although they have rarely presented difficulties when sales have taken place.

What happens when the ESOP company is sold?

Fiduciary questions can be especially cumbersome when the company with the ESOP is sold. It is advisable to retain an independent trustee, of which there is now a good supply. The trustee, being independent, may not be willing to go along with the deal that has been worked out between buyer and seller and may have the voting power to block the sale if he or she does not consider it to be in the interests of plan participants.

With a leveraged ESOP, on subsequent sale, the Section 415 limits on plan additions and benefits can restrict the termination of the plan and the allocation of securities to the employee accounts. This may require that the securities be sold by the plan trustee, with attendant fiduciary considerations, and that any net proceeds after the loan is paid be distributed to the employees, perhaps over time. A reversion from an ESOP is not favored by the IRS (based on informal discussions), and therefore all ESOP assets will have to be distributed to employees.

What types of companies are suitable for ESOPs?

An ESOP is not right for every company. Tax deductions are only of value to a company with taxable income. ESOP debt, like any other debt, can be burdensome. Unless the shares are publicly traded, the ESOP must permit employees to put securities acquired from the ESOP back to the company. This can cause a debilitating cash drain in later years.

The company compensation levels must be large enough to support the ESOP contributions, or deductions will be lost.

Finally, if the company does not offer other benefit plans, employees must be willing to accept ESOP benefits in lieu of investments in more diversified and thus safer vehicles. Employees may be reluctant to stake their retirement benefits on company performance, especially if the ESOP replaces a plan with fiduciary controls on plan asset investments.

Does the ESOP impose repurchase obligations on the company?

There are two rules that can impose repurchase obligations on the company. First, an ESOP must provide a put option for any company securities distributed to a participant, unless the shares are readily tradable on an established market [Code Section 409(h)]. The put option cannot be terminated even if the loan or the plan is terminated. No other put, call, or buy/sell is permitted; this rule can impinge on typical corporate control techniques for smaller companies. Another rule that can impinge on control is that an ESOP cannot be required to acquire stock "from a particular security holder at an indefinite time determined upon the happening of an event such as the death of the holder" [Treas. Reg. Section 54.4975-11(a)(7)(i)].

However, if the securities are not publicly traded, a right of first refusal is allowed [Treas. Reg. Section 54.4975-7(b)(9)]. Note that stock not publicly traded may be used in the ESOP only if there is no publicly traded stock or if the securities are preferred stock, convertible to traded stock [Code Section 409(l)]. For new rules applicable to S corporations in 1998 and beyond, see the end of this chapter.

Second, TRA '86 added a requirement that a participant who is age 55 and has 10 years of service be permitted to elect "diversification" of his or her account in each of the following five years. The participant can elect to direct the plan to diversify up to 25 percent of the account (50 percent in the last year). The plan must offer three investment options. The plan may distribute the amount to be diversified, thus triggering the put, or may substitute employer securities equal to the diversification with other investments, which may require dispositions of the securities [Code Section 401(a)(28)(B)]. For new regulations pertaining to ESOPs in S corporations in 1998 and beyond, see the end of this chapter.

What is the accounting treatment of an ESOP?

The American Institute of Certified Public Accountants, in Statement of Position 76-3, with the surprising title of "Accounting Practices for Certain Employee Stock Ownership Plans," made several recommendations to the FASB that have now been adopted. The recommendations were (1) that the employer record a liability equal to the ESOP obligations, but not include ESOP assets, as long as the employer guarantees the obligation or has a commitment to fund the debt; (2) that the offsetting debt be recorded as a reduction in shareholders' equity; (3) that the liability and reduction of equity are reduced as the ESOP pays down the loan; (4) that ESOP contributions are reported as interest and compensation, with dividends charged to retained earnings; and (5) that ESOP-held shares are treated as outstanding for determining earnings per share.

ESOP SECURITIES ISSUES

What is the securities treatment of ESOP stock?

The company stock sold to an ESOP is a security subject to the federal securities laws and to state securities laws. In addition, an ESOP interest may itself be a security if participation in the plan is voluntary or if the participant has a choice whether to invest his or her own funds in addition to employer funds. If the ESOP interest is a security, the plan must be registered unless an exception applies.

The SEC takes the view that a stock contribution to a plan is not a sale and therefore registration is not required under the Securities Act. Similarly, the distribution of stock to ESOP participants is not a registerable event because it is not a sale. Registration is required only if employees make voluntary purchases of stock, something they almost never are allowed to do. The company is almost always exempt from registration under the Exchange Act, under Rule 12h-1(a), 12g-2(H), or 12g-1, at least until significant distributions have been made. Under these rules, the following are exempt: an interest held in trust and issued in connection with a qualified plan; an interest in stock bonus or purchase plans that are not transferable except on death, or accompanying an interest issued solely to fund such plans; and any issuers whose assets are less than $3 million. Section 12(g) requires registration for issuers with assets in excess of $1 million and securities held by more than 500 persons. For this test, all shares held by one trust are treated as held by one person.

The antifraud provisions of the Exchange Act do apply to ESOPs with certain special rules. For example, Rule 10b-13, prohibiting purchases by the offeree during a tender offer, does not apply to ESOP trustee purchases. Similarly, Rule 10b-6, which prohibits purchases of a security that is the object of a distribution, does not apply to purchases by an independent ESOP trustee.

ESOP participants in public companies who have pass-through voting rights are entitled to proxies and annual reports under Section 14 of the Exchange Act.

Can ESOP participants encounter insider trading problems?

Although extremely rare, it is still possible that ESOPs can create problems under Section 16(b), which imposes penalties on short-swing trading profits—buying and selling or selling and buying for a profit within a six-month period—by controlling persons. Vested ESOP rights create beneficial earnings ownership for purposes of the Section 16(a) requirement that beneficial ownership of more than 10 percent be disclosed. In some cases, ESOPs may be exempt under Rule 16a-8(b), which applies if less than 20 percent of the trust is owned by officers and directors, or the employer and beneficiary have no right to control ownership, acquisition, or disposition of the securities. An ESOP will not necessarily meet this last test. If an ESOP owns more than 10 percent of a security, the ESOP itself is considered a controlling person [Rule 16a-8(c)].

The short-swing trading rules of Section 16(b) specifically exclude many transactions typical of an ESOP. Rule 16b-3 sets forth specific rules for plans that will be exempt from Code Section 6166, including shareholder approval, disinterested administration, and limits on awards to officers and directors. Although shareholder approval may be desirable for Section 16(b) purposes, it may also be an impediment to plan changes, including plan termination, in the future.

USING NON-ESOP STOCK PLANS

Can a nonleveraged ESOP or other stock plan be used to help with acquisition funding?

A nonleveraged stock plan can invest in any qualifying employer security rather than being limited to Code Section 409(e) common stock. A nonleveraged stock plan can invest in notes, debt, bonds, debentures, preferred stock, or any other marketable securities (ERISA Section 408). As a result, it may be a more flexible funding technique than an ESOP if there are substantial assets in the plan.

Can a plan own employer stock or real property?

Yes. Up to 10 percent of plan assets may be placed in qualifying employer securities and qualifying employer real property. Qualifying employer securities include debt as well as common stock or preferred stock (ERISA Section 408). Qualifying employer real property is property owned by the plan and leased to the employer plan sponsor or an affiliate. The property must meet detailed and rigid ERISA requirements: It must be dispersed geographically, suitable for more than one use, and purchased at fair market value; and the acquisition must otherwise be consistent with ERISA prudence and diversification standards.

A defined contribution plan that permits participants to select investment options for their own accounts can permit employees to select company securities as an investment. Some plans encourage the stock investment by, for example, an offer to double the employer's matching contribution if the employee elects to take the match in employer stock. A plan can be structured as an individual account plan that permits participants to invest in employer stock as one of several options, in which case (if DOL rules are met) the employer is relieved from fiduciary concerns as to the investment decision, but obviously loses control over the amount of stock in the ESOP.

PLANS HOLDING STOCK

What problems arise when a plan assumed by a buyer holds stock of the selling entity?

A plan could hold employer stock in at least two ways. A plan that is invested by a plan trustee may have invested in employer securities. Unless the trustee finds that these securities are not a prudent investment (which is unlikely, because that was a requirement for the investment in the first place), there will probably be no objection to the plan's continuing to hold these securities. If the company is being taken private, and the stock is stock of the acquired company, then the plan trustee will be treated like any other shareholder in that transaction. The seller, however, should be alert to the possibility of fiduciary problems or prohibited transaction problems and would probably want to have an independent trustee, or at least an independent appraisal of the transaction, before taking any action. In most cases, the plan would be a minority holder and will be forced out by the going private transaction.

Company stock could also be held in an individual account plan in which each employee has been permitted to invest in employer stock. Again, unless the entity is being taken private, the buying entity may have no objection to permitting the employees to continue to hold the employer stock. If the stock is not stock of the sold entity, the selling entity may wish to recover the stock. Because the stock is held in individual accounts, individual employees may have the right to make their own decisions (such as whether or not to accept an exchange offer) unless the stock is forced out or the plan is terminated and liquidated. Under DOL regulations under Section 404 of ERISA, the fiduciary problems should be much less difficult for an individual account plan.

In the case of ESOPs, the sale of the employer stock will destroy the treatment of the plan as an ESOP. This would also be true in a stock bonus plan. More elaborate steps must be taken to remove the stock feature from these plans if that is desired. In the case of an ESOP, the stock ownership must be reduced from the levels acceptable for an ESOP, because the ESOP exception will no longer apply, and the plan will be subjected to the basic prudence and diversification requirements. The ESOP will have to be converted into a profit-sharing or defined contribution plan and the stock holdings reduced. If the stock is held in an ESOP suspense account pending payment of a loan secured by the stock, the ESOP trustee will have to make a fiduciary decision about whether or not to sell or tender the stock.

Also, ERISA's maximum benefit and contribution limits will apply if the stock is distributed to the participant. The stock may have to be sold, the proceeds used to pay the loan, and then the excess distributed to participants. This is clearly another area where qualified legal counsel should be consulted.

What happens if the entity being purchased has granted stock options to its employees?

An existing stock option plan must be examined to see whether it can be terminated and whether outstanding options are affected by a change in control of the company. In some cases, plans will provide for acceleration of options in the event of a change in control. Persons who wish to exercise their options will thus have stock that will be subject to whatever terms are generally applicable under the purchase agreement and will have rights of vote and dissent, if applicable.

If the company is taken private, there may be problems in settling out existing stock options. If the options are incentive stock options (ISOs), care must be taken in modifying them for fear of losing the incentive stock option treatment. Under the Code, a disqualifying disposition of an ISO (a disposition not in accord with Code Section 422A) will create income in the year of the disqualifying disposition. Therefore, if an incentive stock option is cashed out, it will be taxed in the year of the cash-out. Although it will be taxed at ordinary tax rates, so long as these are the same as capital gains rates, there will be no negative impact on the employee.

In some cases, employers desire to replace the stock option program with a stock appreciation rights plan so as to eliminate equity ownership by employees. This is feasible; a stock appreciation rights plan does create a charge against earnings, unlike stock option plans.

At times, subsidiary employees have been granted stock rights to parent stock. These may well continue to exist after the sale of the subsidiary, and the seller may wish to reach some agreed-upon resolution of this problem before the closing.

EFFECT OF CORPORATE STRUCTURE

What effect will corporate structure have on employee benefits?

The Deficit Reduction Act of 1982 basically eliminated the benefits differences between partnerships, S corporations, and C corporations. However, there are still a few areas where corporate structure can affect employee benefits.

An S corporation may have no more than 75 shareholders, and none of those shareholders may be a trust. Therefore, an S corporation cannot place its stock in a pension plan and typically cannot provide equity rights to employees beyond the first 75. It might be possible to create future option rights that would mature only when the S corporation becomes a C corporation.

Under Section 1372 of the Code, S corporation shareholders holding more than 2 percent of the corporation's stock are treated as partners in a partnership. A partner may not take loans from a plan under Section 4975 of the Code. A cafeteria plan may be provided only to employees, not to partners. Other benefits that may be provided only to employees include the exclusion of up to $50,000 of group term life insurance under Section 79 of the Code, the exclusion for accident and health payments under Section 105 of the Code, the exclusion for employer payments to an accident or health plan under Section 106, and the exclusion for meals and lodging furnished for an employer's convenience. However, to the extent a partner functions and is compensated as an employee, the partner may be treated as an employee.

Factors in determining whether a person is receiving benefits as a partner or as an employee include whether the payment is subject to significant entrepreneurial risk, whether the partner status is transitory or continuing, whether the distribution closely follows in time the performance of service, whether the recipient became a partner primarily for tax benefits, and whether the partner's interest in the partnership is small in relation to the allocation.

What new twists did the 1997 tax law add to the status of ESOPs in S corporations?

The Taxpayer Relief Act of 1997 (in Section 1506) changed the rules with respect to three areas: interests held by ESOPs in an S corporation, general distribution rules, and transactions between ESOPs and shareholder-employees.

- Under previous law, the interest of an ESOP in an S corporation was treated as interest in an "unrelated business" and was taxable to the ESOP. Also, any gain or loss incurred by the ESOP in trading the stock of an S corporation was counted as taxable income. The 1997 tax law repealed both of these rules, reducing the tax burden of subchapter S ownership by ESOPs.
- Federal pension laws place various conditions on the way ESOP participants receive their distributions. For example, participants can require that distributions be made in the form of stock, and that the stock be distributed under a fair valuation formula. The new law extended to any ESOP maintained by an S corporation.
- Finally, the new tax law lifted prohibitions on certain transactions between shareholder-employees and S ESOPs.

The rules are effective for tax years beginning after December 31, 1997.

PROBLEMS IN ACQUISITIONS OF UNIONIZED COMPANIES

What complications can unionization bring to an acquisition?

If there is a union in place or a collective bargaining agreement, the buyer must examine whether successorship rules under the labor laws will require the buyer to assume the union, that is, recognize it, or to assume the collective bargaining agreement. In a stock purchase or merger, with the operations continuing, all obligations are assumed, including the obligation to recognize the union and any union contract.

However, if there has been a hiatus in operations, the National Labor Relations Board (NLRB) may find that the buyer is a new entity. In an asset transaction, if a "representative complement" of the union workforce is hired, the employer is required to recognize the union and bargain with it. In that circumstance, the employer may be required to keep the terms and conditions of employment static while negotiating a new agreement. Some cases have gone further: In *Fall River Dyeing* the Supreme Court found successorship in an asset sale despite the fact that the buyer acquired only one of the seller's three plants, and only after a seven-month shutdown.

In both asset and stock transactions, the labor agreement may contain successorship language that requires the seller to require that the buyer agree to assume the union agreement. Technically, of course, if the buyer does not assume the agreement, the seller is the only person liable under the collective bargaining agreement. This nicety can, however, be all too easily eroded in the purchase agreement through general allocations of liability.

What restraints can be caused by the collective bargaining agreement?

As discussed above, the collective bargaining agreement may have to be assumed by a buyer. If so, the agreement will obviously dictate the buyer's compensation programs for union employees. However, it may also restrain the buyer from introducing new technology, from instituting layoffs, from consolidating workforces, from instituting incentive bonuses and productivity plans, and from changing pension and benefit programs, including, as mentioned above, terminating plans, changing their nature, and taking a reversion of surplus assets. Moreover, under Code Section 89, if any union employee is eligible for a particular plan or a plan of the same type, Section 89 discrimination rules apply with respect to both union and nonunion employees, and the terms of the collective bargaining agreement may thus affect the employer's other benefit programs, as other benefits are changed to meet the Section 89 tests.

Does the presence of a union restrain changes in the workforce even if no bargaining agreement exists?

Yes—if the buyer assumes an obligation to recognize and bargain with the union. In practice, this means that the buyer cannot change the economic terms of employment until either an agreement is reached with the union or an impasse is reached. At impasse, the employer may implement its last offer. A change in the economic terms during bargaining would be construed by the NLRB as an interference with bargaining.

Are employees entitled to notice of a sale of the company?

Employees represented by unions are entitled to notice of a plant closing, a move, a subcontracting change, or other major change. They have no right to bargain about the change itself, but they must be given sufficient notice to enable them to bargain effectively about the effects of the change. Federal law and several state statutes now require prior notice of plant closing to employees.

Absent such a major change or a contractual provision, there is no requirement that unions be notified of a company sale. The federal law passed in 1988 requires 60 days' notice to employees of mass layoffs or plant closings and applies to employers of over 100 people. Notice to a union can cause confidentiality problems. In some cases, employee morale may be best served by the earliest notification of a plant change, or the employer may find that the employees have bolted prematurely. There may be a duty to notify the union if bargaining negotiations which would be affected by the sale are in progress.

Can a merger or acquisition create an unfair labor practice?

If a merger or acquisition is found to be designed to avoid recognition, bargaining, or contractual obligations, it can be an unfair labor practice. This is the so-called runaway shop. The test is whether the action was motivated by anti-union feeling.

If a merger or acquisition will require layoffs, how can the buyer minimize the potential for litigation?

- First, buyer and seller should negotiate to reach an agreed severance program and allocate the financial responsibility for the costs of severance.
- Second, the buyer should establish as neutral a layoff ranking as possible. Seniority is a well-accepted ranking system. If a division, line, or operation is discontinued, that can also provide an objective ranking. If possible, give employees bid rights into remaining jobs.
- Third, be prepared to give each employee a clear statement of termination benefits. Be sure to include continued medical coverage and accrued vacation, pension, and severance benefits. Pay earned benefits immediately (except pension).
- Fourth, review the proposed terminations for trouble spots—that is, concentrations of protected groups such as minorities, women, persons age 40 and over, veterans, and persons with disabilities. Also beware of "whistle-blowers"—state law is becoming increasingly protective of employees, and the "at-will" employment doctrine has been significantly eroded.

What is the employee role in changing benefit plans?

Any plan required to be maintained by a collective bargaining agreement cannot be eliminated without union consent. Many times, however, the union agreement is quite vague, and in these cases it may be possible to change benefits without breach of contract. ERISA now requires that unions and employees be given notice of a plan termination. Unions and employees are also entitled to notice of every application to the IRS for a ruling on the plan's qualified status.

Union or no, employees may claim a vested right to continued pension or welfare benefits. Most such cases involve medical benefits for retirees. However, any employee who can show a contractual promise of continued benefits, and reliance on that promise, has a potential claim. Thus a buyer should exercise caution in planning benefit changes.

CONCLUDING COMMENTS

It is tempting to see pension, labor, and compensation issues as a tangle of complex rules and requirements that should be referred to the experts and otherwise disregarded. Don't treat it this way. These issues—from salt-of-the-earth payouts to sumptuous perquisites—have such a great impact on operations, take up so much of the company budget, and present so many opportunities and pitfalls for both buyer and seller that they cannot be safely ignored in acquisition planning and structuring. Many a merger has failed because the most influential executives delegated this important area entirely to their advisors.

Don't get us wrong. This is by no means a "do-it-yourself" domain. No other area faced by executives is as complex or changing as the world of pension, labor, and compensation issues. Once again, we will preach the moral of this book. These issues absolutely require live professional guidance, which is generally worth every penny paid for it.

E N D N O T E S

1. Some purists say "employee benefits plans," but most experts use the simpler term "employee benefit plans." In this edition, we are adopting the simpler usage.

2. Among the top 200 U.S. industrial and service firms (based on the first 100 to file proxies in 1998), only 11.3 percent of the CEO's total pay on average came from salary. A full 53 percent came from stock options, 20.7 percent in incentive pay, 8.1 percent in restricted stock, and 6.8 percent in long-term incentive plans. *Source:* Pearl Meyer & Partners' ongoing 1998 study of CEO compensation (based on an interview with Ed Archer, August 24, 1998).

3. For example, Mellon Bank, considered a positive model for compensation planning, has both golden and tin parachutes. The tin parachutes award severance equal to continued salary and benefits for 12 months, plus payout of all accrued retirement benefits, to any full-time corporate staff member who loses his or her job without cause within three years of a change of control. *Source: Change of Control: Triggers & Parachutes* (Fairfax Station, VA: 1996), cited in Carol Bowie and Judy Fischer, "Have Parachutes Become More Than a Security Blanket?" *Mergers & Acquisitions,* November–December 1996, pp. 17ff. All data on golden parachutes in this section are based on this article.

4. For more on the topic of parent/unit sharing, see Walter I. Jacobs, "Combining Compensation Programs," in Milton L. Rock, Robert H. Rock, and Martin Sikora (eds.), *The Mergers & Acquisitions Handbook* (New York: McGraw-Hill, 1994), pp. 431ff. See also Eric P. Marquardt, "Consolidating Compensation Plans Following Mergers or Acquisitions," *Executive Topic* 6, no. 1 (first quarter 1996), p. 2. *ET* is a client newsletter published by Compensation Resource Group in Pasadena, California.

5. Target ownership plans are becoming more common. John Moyer, a partner with Ernst & Young LLP based in Atlanta, who has designed TOPs for several leading U.S. public companies, estimates that over 200 now have TOPs. The TOP universe appears to be concentrated in large, widely held companies. Pearl Meyer & Partners has estimated that half of the largest 200 U.S. companies offer TOPs, noting that where such plans are disclosed, the range is typically from two to eight times salary. For a pioneering article on the subject, see Robert Salwen, "Stock Ownership Guides for Corporate Executives," *Corporate Governance Advisor,* September/October 1994, pp. 4ff.

6. In *Internal Control—Integrated Framework* (Jersey City, NJ: The American Institute of Certified Public Accountants, 1992), p. 135, the Committee of Sponsoring Organizations of the Treadway Commission warns against "pressure to meet unrealistic performance targets—particularly short-term results," and against any program that includes "extreme incentives . . . that can unnecessarily and unfairly test people's adherence to ethical values."

7. The Quaker Oats case is instructive: "When Quaker Oats acquired Chiari & Forti, an Italian grocery products company, it had formal incentives based on quantitative factors, while C&F had informal incentives based on qualitative factors. . . . Today, C&F participates in Quaker's worldwide management incentive plan. Funds for incentive payment are based on a combination of the value added performance of C&F and Quaker. However, C&F retains substantial discretion in allocating incentive funds to individuals, typically deviating from formula awards by plus or minimum 20 percent." *Source:* Marquardt, op. cit., note 4.

8. If an acquisition is structured as a subsidiary, and if the parent company tries to extend rabbi trust to the subsidiary, it may run afoul of IRS guidelines in this area. See "Rabbi Trust Modification: IRS Revokes Private Ruling for Mobil Stock Set-Aside," *Pensions and Investments,* May 27, 1996, p. 38. A rabbi trust is a separate pool of money set up as a vehicle to defer compensation—typically employee retirement or health benefits. These trusts are "nonqualified," meaning that they do not conform to certain federal government guidelines for tax-favorable treatment.

9. This example comes from Alan Johnson and Sarah Sumner, "Using Compensation to Reinforce Cultural Change," a talk delivered at the American Management Association Human Resources Conference, May 1, 1996. Alan Johnson is managing director of Johnson Associates, Inc., in New York. Sarah Sumner is vice president of worldwide compensation at Digital Equipment Corporation.

10. This idea was first advanced by Ira M. Millstein, senior partner, Weil, Gotshal & Manges, New York, and by Paul W. McAvoy of the Yale School of Management, New Haven, Connecticut, in a letter mailed to the members of the National Association of Corporate Directors on April 11, 1996.

11. "Tyco's Deal-of-the-Month Man," *Business Week,* January 13, 1997 (retrieved from the Internet—no pages given). In this article, shareholder activist Robert A. G. Monks, a former Tyco director, hails Tyco as "one of the great American companies."

12. For example, links to quality can be offered through a variety of means, including customer satisfaction survey results, rate of returned merchandise, defect rate, and other quantitative measures. It may seem difficult to use more than one measure, but this is a fundamental principle of the "balanced scorecard" approach that is sweeping management consulting circles.

13. *Source:* The U.K's National Institute of Economic and Social Research Source, 1996.

14. Eric P. Marquardt, of the Compensation Resources Group (op. cit., note 4), puts it well: "Rarely is consolidation accomplished by lowering the pay levels of the higher paying organization. Rather, it is quite the opposite."

15. "Turner Executives Eligible for Big Severance Pay," *The Wall Street Journal,* September 9, 1996, p. B-10. (In this article, Alan Johnson, of New York–based Johnson Associates, Inc., calls the $1.3 million options a "signing bonus.")

16. Judging from a recent overview of signing bonuses based on data from Executive Compensation Reports of Fairfax Station, Virginia, most are in the $1 million to $5 million range (with one notable $20 million exception).

17. For recent trends in M&A payment modes, see *Mergers & Acquisitions,* March/April 1998.

18. For a look at earnouts in a high-technology environment, see Spencer Feldman, "The Use of Performance (Not Economic) Earn-Outs in Computer Company Acquisitions," *Insights: The Securities Law Advisor,* August 1996, pp. 12ff.

19. *Source:* Johnson and Sumner, op. cit., note 9.

20. More than 8 out of 10 benefit managers surveyed by Merrill Lynch in 1996 reported that they outsourced benefit administration.

21. The Revenue Reconciliation Act of 1993 imposed a $150,000 cap on the amount of compensation that can be held in a qualified plan [amending Internal Revenue Code Section 401(a)17] as well as a $1 million cap on the deductibility of compensation [adding IRC Section 162(m)]. The latter cap

may be waived for plans that include performance incentives approved by an independent committee of the company's board of directors.

22. For an excellent article on regulatory aspects of nonqualified benefits in the merger context, see Pamela Baker, "Executive Compensation in Mergers & Acquisitions," *The Practical Lawyer,* June 1993, pp. 75ff. Part 2 of this article, which appeared in the July 1993 issue of the same publication, is a more general discussion of equity-based pay, which is also very helpful.

23. For a useful overview, see Kenneth P. Shapiro and Michael Carter, "Merging Benefit Plans," in Milton L. Rock, Robert H. Rock, and Martin Sikora (eds.), *The Mergers & Acquisitions Handbook* (New York: McGraw Hill, 1994), pp. 419ff.

24. A notable example from the defined benefits world was the 1996 plan consolidation at RTC America Inc., a unit of The RTC Corporation, PLC, a London-based mining company. RTC America, which owns Kennecott Corp., Luzenac America Inc., and U.S. Borax, used to run their defined benefit plans separately. Prior to the consolidation, RTC was using 20 money managers to manage the plans' assets. After the consolidation, it terminated its relations with thirteen of the firms and hired four in their place, thus cutting the number of money managers dedicated to these plans in half. *Source:* "RTC Creates 1 Plan from 3 Subsidiaries," *Pensions & Investments,* April 1, 1996, p. 46. By contrast, when AT&T took over NCR in a $7.5 billion hostile deal in 1991, the two companies decided to maintain separate pension plans. Five years later, when AT&T spun off NCR, it was the unit, not the parent, that was responsible for funding the plans.

25. See Rebecca Hallowell, "Consolidations, Mergers, and Acquisitions: Maximizing Retirement Plan Design," *Horizons: Fidelity's News Magazine for Non-Profits,* 7, Spring 1996, pp. 8ff.

26. For a discussion of these steps as they apply to smaller companies, see Dick Dobkin, "How to Evaluate Your Company's Insurance Needs," *Tampa Bay Business Journal,* March 10, 1996, p. 10.

27. In 1996, for the first time ever, managed care plans covered more workers than traditional fee-for-service plans, reported KPMG Peat Marwick in a survey of 1,100 major employers. In 1996, only 57 percent of employees had the option of choosing traditional insurance, compared with 63 percent in 1995 and almost 90 percent in 1988. *Source:* "Employers' Health Costs Are Stabilizing," *The Wall Street Journal,* October 7, 1997, p. A-2. And even more significantly, 71 percent of Americans in 1995 with employer-sponsored health-care plans were in managed care programs, compared with only 10 percent a decade before. *Source:* "Aetna to Purchase Fast-Growing HMO," *The Washington Post,* April 2, 1996, p. A-1.

28. For a good discussion of this point, see Aaron Berg, "Cost Effective Health Care Plans for Merging Firms," *Mergers & Acquisitions* 30, no. 1 (July/August 1995), pp. 20–24.

29. One striking example is the small company exemption contained in the Family and Medical Leave Act of 1993, signed into law on February 5, 1993 (Public Law 103-3).

30. Employers are required to prepare and furnish summary plan descriptions to participants and beneficiaries of employees, and to furnish these descriptions to the secretary of the DOL upon request. (Prior to passage of the 1997 tax law, filings were mandatory.)

31. This list came from the National Center for Employee Ownership, *Leveraged ESOPS and Employee Buyouts* (Oakland, CA: The National Center for Employee Ownership, 1998), cited in Chapter 4, note 40. See also Dickson C. Buxton, *You've Built a Successful Business—Now What? A Guide to Perpetuating Your Business* (Glendale, CA: Griffin Publishing, 1996).

32. The main source for this answer was Martin D. Ginsberg and Jack S. Levin, *Mergers, Acquisitions, and Buyouts: A Transactional Analysis of the Governing Tax, Legal, and Accounting Considerations* (New York: Aspen Law & Business, March 1998), Sections 1102.2.1 and 1319.1. The first benefit mentioned is relatively new, being effective for tax years starting after December 31, 1997. For more on the strategic aspects of this issue, see Virginia Bartlett and Duncan Harwood, "Employee Stock Ownership Plans at S Corporations: A New Venue for Tax Savings," *HR Director: The Arthur Andersen Guide to Human Capital* (New York: Profile Pursuit, 1998), pp. 178ff.

Negotiating the Letter of Intent and the Acquisition Agreement

INTRODUCTION

The legal centerpiece of any acquisition transaction is the acquisition agreement. It is difficult—if not impossible—to comprehend the negotiation of any acquisition without understanding the rationale underlying the typical provisions of the agreement that makes it possible. Although negotiations begin earlier with the crafting of the letter of intent, it is the acquisition agreement that is most likely to make or break a deal.

This is not to downplay the importance of the letter of intent. Although some lawyers dislike letters of intent and will insist on going directly to the final agreement, this is the exception and not the rule. Therefore, this chapter begins with a discussion of the purpose and uses of that vital document as it is employed in the acquisition context, and Appendix 8A contains a sample letter of intent. The major portion of this chapter, however, is devoted to the acquisition agreement and the most basic negotiation issues it raises. Appendix 8B contains the principal provisions of a typical merger agreement (in smaller print), together with commentary explaining them and highlights the alternatives available to the buyer and the seller (in larger print).

Numerous issues must be negotiated in connection with this complex agreement, many of which are purely legal issues. Most of the legal points discussed in this chapter are those that lawyers bring to their clients as "business" issues—the type of issues that lawyers normally do not and should not be asked or expected to resolve. This chapter is not intended to review every conceivable issue that may confront the parties in the negotiation of a merger agreement; instead, it is to serve as a guide to the major themes of negotiation. It is thus designed to facilitate an understanding of the key points of a negotiation.

The form of agreement analyzed in this chapter is one that would be prepared by a buyer; it is comprehensive and contains many provisions that favor a buyer. Accordingly, many of these provisions may not appear in a document prepared by a seller. Indeed, unless the seller is represented by a total incompetent, there is no way the buyer should expect to get everything contained in this form into the final contract. But from a buyer's perspective, it is a good starting point. In addition, a document used for the acquisition of a public company is likely to be quite different from the form set forth in this chapter. Those differences will be noted, both in the general discussion and, where appropriate, in the context of the agreement itself. Before proceeding further, it would be a good idea to review the table of contents of the form agreement at the end of this chapter to become familiar with key provisions of a typical merger agreement.

THE LETTER OF INTENT

What is a letter of intent?

A *letter of intent* is a precontractual written instrument that defines the respective preliminary understandings of the parties about to engage in contractual negotiations. In most cases, such a letter is not intended to be binding except under very unusual circumstances, and then only for certain limited provisions. The terms of a typical letter of intent are set forth in Appendix 8A. Every acqusition is different, so letters of intent vary. This said, however, Appendix 8A can serve as a checklist of items that usually appear in letters of intent.

What is the purpose of the letter of intent?

The letter of intent crystallizes in writing the basic terms of the transaction, which up to that point have been the subject of oral negotiations between the parties. The letter will set forth the proposed structure of the transaction, the price and how it will be paid, the terms of notes or stock to be conveyed as part of the price, and other important, but general, features of the transaction such as special accounting or tax considerations (for example, will it be a tax-free reorganization or a taxable transaction?).

The letter of intent also sets forth the preconditions to consummating the transaction, including, among others, the need for regulatory approvals and, most importantly, the completion of due diligence and the execution of a mutually satisfactory acquisition agreement.

Does the letter of intent create a binding legal obligation to close?

Not necessarily. Most letters of intent specifically state that the letter does not create a binding obligation to close the transaction. But simply declaring that the letter is nonbinding in a given area may not be enough to make it nonbinding. The legal test for the binding character of an agreement is the intent of the parties as determined from all the circumstances. For this reason, all parties involved in a transaction should take pains to treat the letter, in all possible respects, as a nonbinding memorandum of the terms of a proposed transaction. Note, however, that the letter of intent is usually intended to create binding obligations with respect to confidentiality, the bearing of expenses, and any "no-shop" agreement the parties may have reached (see discussion below).

If the letter of intent is not binding, is it really needed? Why not proceed directly to the contract itself?

Except in rare cases, use of a letter of intent is recommended. First, the letter contains certain binding provisions that can give both parties a clearer understanding about the basic terms of the deal. For example, experienced buyers do not want to spin their wheels while the seller shops an offer around to other potential buyers. Thus, the buyer may wish to obtain a no-shop agreement from the seller, a provision requiring the seller to refrain from negotiating with other parties for a specified period of time. The letter of intent offers a way to obtain such an agreement early in the negotiations.

Second, the parties will have to expend a considerable amount of time and money to complete due diligence and negotiate and draw up a contract. To do so without a clear understanding of the basic terms of the transaction may prove to be a costly error. Thus, the parties may enter into a letter of intent agreement before incurring the expense of negotiating an acquisition agreement in an attempt to provide an additional level of assurance that negotiations will be successful.

Third, although the document is technically not a binding agreement, the execution of the letter often has the effect of creating a moral commitment to use good-faith best efforts to consummate the transaction in accordance with the outlined terms. The parties, particularly if they are part of large organizations, become emotionally and, more importantly, bureaucratically committed to getting the deal done. After announcing the execution of the letter of intent, neither party wants to be the one to walk without a very good reason. A carefully drafted letter can be used repeatedly by a party in negotiations to establish initial positions and to rebuff the opposing party's efforts to retake lost ground. The document discourages attempts to "re-trade" long-settled terms, which can lead to ill will between the parties even before they begin business. For all these reasons, it is the principal author's position that a letter of intent helps to make the deal go.

Some rare exceptions to this rule should be noted, however. If negotiations will be difficult and time-consuming, the parties may want to negotiate only once. Also, if the agreement can be struck quickly, why waste time negotiating a separate letter of intent?

When should the letter of intent be executed?

It usually is executed after the acquirer has completed its basic financial due diligence but before it embarks on its major legal due diligence. This timing reduces the likelihood of incurring substantial expenses before the parties have reached an agreement in principle about basic business terms.

Many times the buyer and seller will have reached an agreement and set it down in a letter of intent but will make signing the actual agreement conditional on the occurrence of an external event, such as obtaining financing.

What can happen if buyer and seller have different expectations regarding the letter of intent?

The *Texaco v. Pennzoil* (1988) decision highlights the magnitude of problems that can result when buyer and seller have a different understanding of their respective obligations arising from the letter of intent. The primary question before the court in the *Pennzoil* case, which rendered a $10.2 billion judgment against Texaco for tortious (wrongful and illegal) interference, was whether Pennzoil's agreement with Getty Oil via Gordon Getty, a major shareholder in Getty Oil, was a binding contract.

How can negotiators avoid the Pennzoil problem?

When writing the letter of intent, the parties should define the terms under which it is and is not acceptable to withdraw from negotiations and, in the case of an unacceptable withdrawal, the amount of the liquidated damages, if any. The parties should also agree in advance on their freedom to undertake parallel negotiations, defining the contract as exclusive or nonexclusive. Inclusion of such clauses in the letter of intent may help to avert legal (tort) liability, as they support the conclusion that the parties did not intend the letter to be a binding agreement in respect of the terms of their transaction.

THE ACQUISITION AGREEMENT

Who usually drafts the agreement?

Customarily, the buyer controls the drafting of the agreement, and it is in the buyer's interest to safeguard this prerogative. It is a grave mistake to assume that control of the drafting of the document is not significant. The drafter sets the initial framework of discussions and can regulate the pace of negotiations by controlling the pace of drafting. No matter how many agreements one has worked on, it is always difficult to be certain that an agreement prepared by an opposing party isn't missing some crucial provision or that it doesn't contain the seeds of subsequent legal destruction.

As a buyer, do not be surprised if the seller tries to wrest control of the document from you and put it on its own word processing system. The explanation can sound convincing: "We respect your normal prerogative as the buyer to draft the document, but our business is so complex and we anticipate such substantial changes that it just seems to make more sense to put it on our machines."

Do not fall for this argument, however well-meaning the seller may be. It is very important for the buyer to protect its customary right to control the drafting of the documents, and the attorneys for the buyer should not be shy about pressing the point and forestalling attempts to usurp control. It is the shortsighted buyer who tries to save legal fees by letting the "other guys" do the drafting. First, the savings in fees are illusory because substantial redrafting will be necessary to make the agreement work from the buyer's perspective if the sellers are allowed to do the drafting. Moreover, the change in the tone of the negotiation, along with the loss of control over its pace, is likely to cost the buyer more in the long run. Every time new sections of the agreement are negotiated, the buyer is left to the less than tender mercies of the seller's attorney to draft the changes. Even well-intentioned lawyers may have a hard time shedding their adversarial instincts to include things that will protect the buyer's interests.

Notwithstanding the usual rule, when a company is sold in an auction procedure, it is customary for the seller to submit the first draft of the contract for comment by the buyer. The buyer submits a bid for the company together with its comments on the draft.

What is the purpose of the acquisition agreement?

The agreement, of course, will set forth almost all the legal understandings of the buyer and seller about the transaction. Ideally, it accomplishes four basic goals:

1. It sets forth the structure and terms of the transaction.
2. It discloses all the important legal and financial aspects of the company being acquired, as well as pertinent information about the buyer and seller.
3. It obligates both parties to do their best to complete the transaction and obligates the seller not to change the company in any significant way before the deal closes.
4. It governs what happens if, before or after the closing, the parties discover problems that should have been disclosed either in the agreement or before the closing but were not properly disclosed.

Unlike the typical letter of intent, an acquisition agreement is a legally binding agreement. Once it is signed, a party that fails to consummate the transaction without a legally acceptable excuse can be liable for damages.

The negotiation of the agreement is, in large part, an effort by the parties to allocate the risk of economic loss attributable to legal (and certain financial) defects in the company being acquired that may surface after the closing. A question might arise, for example, if the parties discover legal problems after the contract is signed (such as a major lawsuit against the company being acquired, or identification of the main plant site of the company as a toxic waste dump): Will the buyer still be required to close the transaction and thus bear the risk of loss, or will the seller suffer the loss because the buyer is not required to close?

The same question can be asked if the bright financial prospects of the acquisition candidate are suddenly dimmed by a new ruling on import quotas affecting the company's entire industry. Similarly, if after the closing the buyer discovers a liability that existed at the time of the closing but that was not properly disclosed in the agreement, will the buyer suffer the loss, or will it be able to recover damages from the seller? To understand the risks addressed in a typical acquisition agreement, we suggest that the reader review the representations and warranties section of the sample agreement found at the end of this chapter. This is extremely important as much post-deal litigation revolves around the representations and warranties made by the seller.

This all sounds beguilingly simple. It is in fact quite complex. This (and not the lawyer's need to bill time) is why acquisition agreements take days, weeks, or even months of negotiation and much redrafting.

What are the buyer and seller really concerned about when negotiating the acquisition document?

Once the parties agree to the key substantive aspects of the transaction (price and terms), the seller wants to be as certain as possible of at least two things: (1) that the closing will occur as soon as possible after the agreement is signed, and (2) that no post-closing events will require a refund of any of the purchase price.

The buyer's concerns are the converse of the seller's. The buyer would like flexibility to abandon the transaction in the event that it discovers any legal, financial, or business defects in the company it hopes to acquire. After paying the seller at the closing what the buyer feels is a fair price, the buyer would like to know that it will be compensated penny for penny for any economic loss resulting from legal or financial problems that it didn't expect to assume. This is not to be confused with the business risk of operating the company after the closing. General economic downturns, new competition, and failures of management after the closing are pure business risks that any sensible buyer knows it is assuming when it buys a business. But the buyer will seek to protect itself against hidden flaws in the business of the company such as pending litigation, undisclosed liabilities, and environmental problems—to name only a few—that existed at the time of the closing and that cause the company to be worth less than the buyer agreed to pay for it.

It is the extraordinary case where the buyer or the seller is entirely satisfied with respect to these basic points. Without fail, the buyer will try to increase its flexibility to withdraw from the transaction before the closing. However, with such flexibility, the contract is simply an option to acquire the company and not a contract that legally binds the buyer to acquire the company. If the buyer really wants to buy the company, it should be willing to be legally obligated, within reason, to do so.

On the other hand, the seller can never be certain that the transaction will close, simply because there are too many conditions beyond the control of both buyer and seller that must be satisfied before any transaction can close. (These conditions are discussed in greater detail below.) Moreover, although the seller invariably would like to sell the company on an as-is basis, affording the buyer little or no protection after the closing, the vast majority of private companies are not sold on this basis. Thus, the seller will grudgingly give the buyer a modicum of protection in the event that the company is not what the seller represented it to be.

In this process of risk allocation, is there one correct answer? Who should bear the risk of loss associated with undisclosed legal defects in the acquired company discovered after the closing—the buyer, the seller, or both?

At the outset, it is important to understand the basic themes for the negotiation. The smart seller will say,

> Look, before you sign anything, we'll show you everything we have. Talk to our management, our accountants, and our lawyers. Kick the tires to your heart's content. If you discover problems, we'll negotiate a mutually fair resolution in the agreement. Then tell us how much you'll pay on the assumption that any unknown problems are simply your risk of buying and owning the business. Once we close, the business and the risk are yours.

The canny buyer's answer will be as follows:

Our contractual arrangements should be structured to provide both of us with strong incentives to unearth problems before the closing. You will have a strong incentive to uncover all the issues only if you share some or all of the risk of undisclosed problems. Anyway, if after our mutual diligent efforts the company we buy suffers a dollar loss attributable to undiscovered problems, and if we bear the entire risk of loss, we will, in effect, be paying an additional purchase price. In the end we may be paying more than the company is worth. Our price is premised upon your assurance that your company does not have any material undisclosed problems. We're willing to do our share of tire-kicking, but we can't do it all—and we can't see the future. You, the seller, should share the risk of hidden problems, too.

The real issue is, what is a fair price for the company? The answer hinges on the assumptions of the parties when the transaction was agreed to. The buyer can either:

- Determine a price based upon assuming the risk (that is, an as-is deal, which presumably would be less than the price that would be paid if the seller retains some or all of the risks)

or

- Determine a higher price premised on the seller's retention of some part of the risk.

The first alternative is more of a riverboat gamble, but it may be acceptable to a buyer comfortable with its knowledge of the company it is acquiring, especially if the company is in a low-risk industry.

If custom is the equivalent of truth, then the second alternative is the "right" answer. It is the rule in most sales of private companies that the seller will bear a significant portion of the risk of defects in the company being sold, and the deal is priced accordingly. The seller, however, does have legitimate concerns about being pestered incessantly about relatively insignificant items that prove not to be true about the company. Everyone knows going into an acquisition that no company is perfect and that in due course blemishes on its legal and financial record will undoubtedly surface. Accordingly, although seller accountability is the general rule, the seller's accountability is usually reduced by limiting the time during which it can be held liable and by requiring the buyer to limit its claims to significant problems. (See the discussion of the indemnity section and Article XII in the model acquisition agreement at the end of this chapter.)

What are the advantages of having the seller assume some of the risk of postmerger problems stemming from pre-deal conditions?

There are three good reasons for this customary practice. First, an as-is transaction may force the buyer to reduce the purchase price even though the likelihood of a claim is not substantial. A seller ought to evaluate whether its concern about post-closing hassles is sufficient to justify the trade-off in price that may result from forcing a buyer to price the deal on an as-is basis. Second, a sharing of the risk between buyer and seller will provide both with a strong incentive to try to discover problems before the agreement is signed or the deal is closed. Thorough investigation by both parties who have a stake in the outcome reduces the likelihood that a claim will arise. Third, if the problem were discovered before the closing, it probably would result in a price adjustment, even to an as-is deal. Logically, the result should not be different because the problem arises after closing.

Does this mean that every seller should cave in on this issue?

No. In certain circumstances the seller may just prefer taking a lower price to avoid the risk of post-closing adversities. Nor should one assume that the pricing will necessarily reflect the risk of an as-is approach. In the case of a deal-hungry buyer, or a buyer that has confidence in its assessment of the risk of loss attributable to breaches of representations and warranties, the seller may get the best of both worlds—a high price with little or no post-closing risk. This is especially true in a competitive bidding situation. In the end, the allocation of risk will depend more on the bargaining power and negotiating skills of the parties than the niceties of pricing theories.

COMPONENTS OF THE AGREEMENT

What are the major parts of an acquisition agreement?

The major segments of a typical agreement are as follows:

- Introductory material
- The price and mechanics of the transfer

- Representations and warranties of the buyer and seller
- Covenants of the buyer and seller
- Conditions to closing
- Indemnification
- Termination procedures and remedies
- Legal miscellany

How are the general concerns of the buyer and seller reflected in the acquisition agreement?

The major concerns of the parties are focused on in two sections of the agreement: the *conditions* section and the *indemnity* section. The conditions section lists the conditions that must be satisfied before the parties become obligated to close the transaction, and thus controls whether the buyer or seller can "walk" from the deal with impunity. The indemnity section establishes the liability, if any, of each party to the other for problems relating to the target that are discovered after the closing. Both sections are generally keyed to two earlier parts of the agreement: the *representations and warranties* and the *covenants*.

In the representations and warranties section, the parties make statements as of the date of the signing about the legal and financial state of affairs of the target, the seller, and the buyer, including the legal and financial ability of each party to enter into and consummate the transaction. The covenants section contains the parties' agreement to take no action that would change the state of affairs described in the representations and warranties section. Of course, both changes resulting from the ordinary operation of business actions that are necessary to complete the transaction (such as seeking government approvals and other third-party consents) and changes that are contemplated by the acquisition agreement (such as certain corporate reorganizations) are permitted under the covenants.

The most significant conditions to closing are that the representations and warranties are true on the closing date and that the parties have not breached the covenants. Liabilities under the indemnity section, in turn, arise from breaches of representations, warranties, and covenants.

The fewer the representations, warranties, and covenants of the seller, the less the risk that a closing condition will not be satisfied, and the less the exposure to post-closing indemnity liabilities.

Conversely, with broad and detailed representations, warranties, and covenants, there is a greater likelihood of a breach that will allow the buyer to "walk," and a greater degree of protection afforded the buyer by the indemnity section.

The effect of this structure on the negotiation is to divide the process into two discrete parts. In the first part, the parties thrust and parry about how much the seller will say in the representations and warranties section and how much it will agree to do (or not to do) in the covenants section. This is an important process because the risk of loss from any areas not covered by the seller's statements or covenants falls on the buyer. In the second stage, the parties agree on the consequences if the representations and warranties the seller agrees to make, and the covenants it undertakes, turn out to be untrue or breached before or after the closing.

INTRODUCTORY MATERIAL

What is covered in the first two sections on introductory material and pricing mechanics?

It has become customary to introduce the agreement with a series of "recitals" that set forth the purpose of, and parties to, the agreement. The legal significance of the introductory material is usually not great, but it can be useful in any contract to describe the intentions of each of the parties. If set out in the agreement, the parties' intentions may aid in interpreting the agreement in the event of a dispute.

The next sections of the agreement set forth the most significant substantive business points of the agreement, the price, and the mechanics of transfer. This section identifies the structure of the transaction as a stock disposition, an asset disposition, or a merger and describes the mechanics to be utilized to transfer the property from seller to buyer. The parties may also provide in this section the requirement for a deposit by the buyer, or other security for the buyer's obligations to close.

In the case of an asset acquisition, this section identifies exactly which assets are to be conveyed to the buyer and, often more importantly, which liabilities of the seller will be assumed by the buyer. In the case of a merger, these sections contain the consideration per share to be received by the exchanging shareholders, as well as all the other terms of the merger, including the identity of the surviving corporation, the articles of incorporation and bylaws governing the surviving corporation, the composition of its board of directors, and the names of its officers. For both asset purchases and mergers, this section will, of course, also identify the nature of the consideration to be received by the seller as well as the timing of its payment.

Frequently this section will contain provisions regarding intercompany liabilities, and how they must be satisfied by the surviving company or forgiven by the seller and capitalized as additional equity in the transaction. For a detailed discussion of issues relating to pricing, see Chapter 3.

As a part of the purchase price provisions, should the seller require a deposit of some kind?

The value of the seller's right to sue the buyer if the buyer wrongfully fails to close the contract will depend upon the financial responsibility of the buyer. Both strategic buyers and investment buyers usually effect the deal through a "shell" company with no assets, set up specifically and solely for the purpose of the acquisition. Thus, although the seller will have recourse against the shell company, the seller may have no economically meaningful remedy in the event the buyer breaches the agreement. The seller may win the lawsuit but won't be able to collect damages.

In such circumstances, sellers often insist upon a cash deposit, a cash escrow, or a letter of credit that can serve as security for the buyer's obligations. It is hard for most buyers to argue their way out of such a requirement. This is particularly true where the seller has several creditworthy suitors for the company and where signing with the buyer will cause those potential buyers to lose interest in the deal. However, even if the acquisition company is a shell company, where the buyer has a proven track record of closing deals, and the price is right, it is often possible to avoid the need for a deposit or to delay posting the deposit until some period of time after the signing. For example, a deposit may have to be posted only if the deal hasn't closed by a specified date or if the buyer hasn't obtained financing commitments by a certain date.

At the very least, a seller should make a strong effort to get a deposit sufficient to cover all its expenses and to limit the time given to close the contract so that the company is not off the market too long. Also, if the seller has limited remedies against the buyer, the seller should be expected to try to have similar limitations on its potential liability for its own failure to close on the contract. But there should be financial sanctions against parties that walk from near-completed deals without substantial cause.

REPRESENTATIONS AND WARRANTIES

What is the purpose of the representations and warranties section of the agreement?

In this section of the agreement, the seller makes detailed statements about the legal and financial condition of the company being sold, the property to be conveyed, and the ability of the seller to consummate the transaction. The representations and warranties reflect the situation as of the date of the signing of the agreement and, together with the exhibits or schedules (see the discussion of exhibits and schedules below), are intended to disclose all material legal, and many material financial, aspects of the business to the buyer. The seller also gives assurances that the transaction itself will not have adverse effects upon the property to be conveyed. Some of the representations and warranties are not related to the legal condition of the company but serve to provide the buyer with information. For example, the seller might represent that it has attached a list of all the major contracts of the company. The buyer makes similar representations and warranties about its legal and financial ability to consummate the transaction and certain other limited representations and warranties.

The buyer should be aware that lenders providing acquisition financing will require the buyer to make extensive representations and warranties about the company as a condition to funding. To the extent that the acquisition agreement does not contain comparable representations from the seller, with appropriate recourse in the event of a breach, the buyer will take on the dual risk of a loan default and any direct loss as a result of the seller's breach. In some cases, it may be more difficult to obtain adequate financing if there are insufficient representations and warranties about the business. The buyer should make every effort to anticipate the representations and warranties that the lenders will require, and should attempt to include language in the acquisition agreement to obtain coverage for these areas.

What is the role of exhibits or disclosure schedules?

The exhibits commonly used in the sale of nonpublic companies form an integral part of the representations and warranties. Each exhibit is usually keyed to a specific representation or warranty and sets forth any exceptions to the statements made in the representation. For example, a representation might provide that there are no undisclosed liabilities of the company "except as set forth on

Exhibit A," or state that there is no litigation that might have an adverse effect "except as set forth on Exhibit B." Another representation might state that "except as set forth on Schedule C," the company is not bound by any contracts of a "material nature," or there are no contracts involving amounts in excess of a fixed sum, say $100,000. Schedule C would contain a list of all the contracts that meet the criteria in the representation, that is, contracts that either are material or involve dollar amounts above the threshold.

The use of exceptions to create exhibits might seem odd, but it is merely a practical drafting device. The alternative would be to incorporate all relevant documents in the acquisition agreement, which would make the agreement unwieldy. Separating matters into two parts makes good sense, because the contract is about terms (*how* the parties are buying/selling) and the exhibits are about the company (*what* the parties are buying/selling).

The agreement should state that the information in the exhibits is part of the representations and warranties. If the buyer incurs losses attributable to conditions disclosed on an exhibit, the responsibility for those losses falls on the buyer alone, unless the parties specifically agree otherwise. For this reason, the exhibits and all the documents or matters they cover must be reviewed carefully by attorneys and businesspeople who are knowledgeable about the matters covered (not the most junior person on the project!). Each litigation matter should be checked and each contract reviewed, and if necessary, backup documents must be provided. Because the review is time-consuming, it should not be left to the day before signing.

The exhibits provide a succinct legal and business synopsis of the company, so they make a good "short list" of things to check during the due diligence review.

What if the seller tries to limit the representations and warranties it will make?

Good question. The seller often tries to limit the scope of the representations and warranties because of the time involved. When the seller has prepared the agreement, it often skips representations and warranties completely. When the buyer submits proposed changes, including significant "beefing up" of the representations and warranties, the seller will say:

> This is going to hold us up. We'll have to recirculate questionnaires to everybody in the company's corporate group (often scattered around the world) and

review all the pertinent documents again (and, of course, there are hundreds) to make sure we don't violate these tighter representations and warranties. And we'll have to redo all the exhibits.

When everybody is in a hurry to sign quickly, this tactic pressures the buyer's lawyers, whose client will ask, "Are we really asking for a lot of unnecessary garbage?" First, the lawyer should be aware of applicable time pressures in preparing the representations and warranties. Having done so, he or she must be ready to defend the relative importance of the various requests. One way to deal with the problem is to sign the contract but give the seller additional time to prepare the exhibits. The buyer can reserve the right to abandon the deal if the revised exhibits reveal any material problems. A word of caution—don't leave too much time or you'll be getting revised schedules the night before the closing.

Should exhibits be used if the company being acquired is, or will become, a public company?

No. If the company is a public company, or the buyer has intentions to take the company public, the buyer should use a disclosure statement as opposed to an exhibit or disclosure schedule in order to avoid the public disclosure of information about the company. A disclosure statement is a separate document that sets forth all the items that would otherwise be listed in exhibits or schedules to the acquisition agreement. However, since the disclosure statement is a separate document from the acquisition agreement, it may not have to be filed with the SEC.

Just how important are the representations and warranties in an acquisition agreement?

Very important. A buyer or seller will be able to back out of the agreement if it discovers that the representations or warranties of the other party are untrue to any material extent. Thus, the fewer the items represented to, the less the risk that the other party will be able to back out of the agreement. Also, the seller must indemnify the buyer for problems that surface after the closing only if the seller breached a representation or warranty in the agreement. Again, the fewer the representations and warranties and the narrower their scope, the less the exposure to the seller. For these reasons, a great deal of the negotiation of the agreement centers on the scope of the representations and warranties.

How can a seller narrow the scope of its representations and warranties?

There are several ways in which the seller can attempt to reduce its exposure attributable to representations and warranties. First, the seller may steadfastly refuse to make any representation or warranty about specific items, for example, accounts receivable or the financial condition or liabilities of certain subsidiaries.

Second, the seller may refuse to make representations and warranties about matters not "material" to the transaction or the company being acquired, or may attempt to make representations and warranties only to the "best of its knowledge." To protect itself, the seller can seek to insert the word *material,* or phrases with the same effect, in every place in the representations that it can. For example, it can state that it is disclosing only "material liabilities," or "material litigation," or that it knows of no violations of law by the company that will have a "material adverse effect" on the company.

What does the term *material* mean when it appears in representations and warranties?

It is often said that materiality is in the eyes of the beholder. Although the courts have defined material information in specific cases (see Chapter 12), the concept remains vague. Generally, the case law holds that *material* means important to a normal, prudent investor in determining whether to make a given investment. In many contracts the parties agree that a "material" fact must be material to the business of the target and any subsidiaries taken as a whole. The purpose of the emphasized language is to ensure that the importance of the fact relates to the entire enterprise acquired and not solely to the parent corporation or to a single subsidiary.

In order to reduce the opportunity for disagreement, the parties often set a dollar threshold that defines materiality in particular circumstances. For example, rather than asking for representations about "material contracts," the buyer will substitute a request for disclosure about all contracts involving payments above a specified dollar amount. Similarly, the buyer may request disclosure of all liabilities greater than a certain sum. Use of numbers tends to fine-tune the disclosures and in many ways provides protection for the seller as well. If there is a dollar threshold of, say, $100,000 for liabilities, the seller can be assured that a $95,000 undisclosed liability will not be deemed "material" in a later dispute.

How and to what degree can the buyer resist the narrowing of the scope of the representations and warranties?

Generally speaking, it is in the buyer's interest to have the broadest possible representations and warranties. However, unreasonable requests for disclosure can threaten a deal. Pressuring the seller of a large, complex company to make comprehensive disclosures may cause the seller to fear that it will inadvertently fail to disclose minor matters, jeopardizing the transaction or leading to unfair liabilities after the closing.

Moreover, anyone buying a business must recognize that no business is more perfect than the human beings who conduct it. Therefore, there are bound to be a variety of problems in connection with the operation or ownership of the business, including litigation, liabilities, or violations of law, which the buyer must accept as part of the package of owning the business. As a result, in most transactions the buyer will permit the seller to limit the scope of the matters that are being represented to those things that are material, individually or in the aggregate, but where appropriate will negotiate over dollar threshold amounts to require more, rather than less, disclosure.

What different motivations might a seller have for narrowing representations and warranties?

For negotiation purposes it is important for the buyer to understand the seller's real concerns. The seller may be concerned simply about the time and expense necessary to uncover a lot of detailed information that in its view shouldn't matter to a buyer or that, under the time pressure of the deal, just can't be obtained. Or the seller may be far more concerned about making representations and warranties that will increase the risk that the buyer will be able to back out of the transaction. Alternatively, the seller's most significant concern may be with post-closing liabilities for breaches of representations, warranties, and covenants in the agreement.

How can a buyer address these different motivations?

Concern about time and expense is legitimate only to the extent that the buyer is asking for truly inconsequential or irrelevant representations or warranties. Remember that the seller's negotiator on these points is likely to be an in-house lawyer or technician more worried about being imprecise than about the broad scope of the deal. Where time is truly a critical factor (as opposed to a negotiating point for the parties), the buyer's lawyer should exercise care and use good judgment to pare down the more burdensome, yet noncritical, representations and warranties.

The buyer should, however, address the more legitimate concerns of the seller. The buyer can address the risks of deal cancellation or of post-closing liability while still including very broad representations and warranties with low dollar thresholds. The buyer can explain to the seller that it wants very broad, in-depth disclosure of items so that the buyer can determine on its own what is material. Most buyers prefer to determine the materiality of information themselves rather than leaving it up to the lawyers or officers of the seller, whose idea of materiality may differ from the buyer's, and who may not be aware of the buyer's specific concerns about certain legal or financial aspects of the company or the assets to be acquired.

The seller should be assured that extensive disclosures will not increase the risk of a terminated transaction or post-closing liability. The buyer may provide the requisite assurance by agreeing that it will not terminate the transaction, and that the seller need not indemnify the buyer, except in the event of material breaches of representations, warranties, or covenants. In summation, the buyer must look through the stated position of the seller, determine its real interests, and deal creatively with those concerns, rather than simply viewing negotiations as an argument over whether or not the word *material* is going to modify a particular representation or warranty.

What is the purpose of the phrases *ordinary course of business* and *best of knowledge* often found in representations and warranties?

These phrases are simply other ways in which the parties can agree to narrow the scope of the representations and warranties required of the seller. The phrase *ordinary course of business* is usually found in representations and warranties to exclude certain things from the representations. For example, the seller may not be required to disclose supply contracts entered into in the ordinary course of business, or may not be required to disclose liabilities accrued in the ordinary course of business. The definition of *ordinary course of business* will depend upon the normal practice of the specific business being acquired and the industry of which it is a part, including the normal character and size of routine transactions. It can be generally defined not to include business activities that the seller does not engage in on a regular and consistent basis. For greater clarification, the parties could enumerate in the acquisition agreement the seller's ordinary practices. An important point is that any transactions that are extraordinary in nature, price, or size will be included in such representations and warranties.

The phrase *best of knowledge* serves a similar function. A seller may ask that its representation as to litigation be limited to the litigation about which it has knowledge, so that it will not be required to represent and warrant absolutely that there is no material litigation. The seller often argues that the phrase should modify other representations and warranties.

At each juncture the buyer should ask, Is the "best of knowledge" modification appropriate? Usually it is not, but it is often agreed to in respect to the existence of threatened litigation and infringements by third parties of copyrights and patents. Beyond those few customary areas, the buyer should vigorously resist efforts to base the representations on the knowledge of the seller. Because such a representation and warranty tells the buyer only that the seller is unaware of any problems, it protects the buyer only if problems known to the seller are not disclosed. Thus, "best of knowledge" representations have the effect of allocating to the buyer all the risk of defects no one knows about.

From a philosophical perspective, the knowledge of the seller is not pertinent to the key question of the buyer: "Am I getting what I am paying for?" The fact that the seller didn't know that the buyer was overpaying is of little comfort to a buyer who discovers significant defects in its acquisition. Thus, the "knowledge" caveat should be used sparingly unless the buyer is willing to accept a substantial risk in connection with breaches of representations and warranties.

"Best of knowledge" qualifiers may be presented as a compromise to a seller who adamantly refuses to indemnify the buyer for breaches discovered after closing. At the very least, an indemnity should be forthcoming in respect to problems the seller knew about but didn't disclose.

There are other issues in connection with the phrase *best of knowledge.* First, whose knowledge are we talking about? Careful sellers will attempt to limit the knowledge to a narrow group of people, such as the executive officers of the company they are selling (sometimes themselves, in the case of a smaller, closely held firm). The argument will go something like this: "We don't want to be held responsible if the company has some problems that we don't know about and couldn't easily learn. Suppose some trucking platform loader takes a bribe a continent away. How could we know?" Aside from the fact that any proposition reduced to that level can become absurd, there is some merit to the idea that a large organization ought to be careful about making representations about what "the corporation" knows. Consequently, a buyer accepting a "best of knowledge" representation will often permit the seller to limit the persons whose knowledge will be tested. The buyer ought to be certain that everyone who has material information about the company is included in the selected circle of officers. In any event, listing such people will cause them to be more forthcoming about what they know.

Another issue is whether the phrase *best of knowledge* implies any obligation of the seller to conduct its own due diligence on the matters covered. That is, does it assume that the knowledge is based upon a reasonable effort to ascertain the existence of any problems? In most cases, the seller's inquiry is limited to information already in the seller's possession. A buyer wishing to impose a further duty on the seller to make reasonable investigations into the matters represented to the buyer should augment the "best of knowledge" phrase with the words "after due inquiry."

What if the seller claims to have no knowledge, or ability to get knowledge, about an area that is the subject of a representation or warranty?

Good question. In this era of rapidly changing ownership, it is not unusual to hear the seller say, "I really don't know that much about this company, so I don't want to take much risk on these representations and warranties. I don't want to make representations about too many matters or in too much detail."

This may be reasonable from the perspective of the seller, but the buyer should not give the argument much weight. As noted above, if a future loss due to a breach is absorbed by the buyer, the buyer will have paid an increased purchase price. The buyer has a right to push forward on this point.

An appropriate response to the seller might be the following:

> We certainly understand your concern, but we have even less of a basis for intimate knowledge of the company's operations. The real issue is, who should absorb the risk in the event that there are undisclosed material defects in the business? We have different views, of course, of who should bear the risk, but let's

really talk about what matters, not about what each of us knows about the company right now. The agreement between us ought to be structured to provide incentives for both of us to do the best job possible to unearth problems and to increase our knowledge of the company now, before we close, rather than wait for problems to surface afterward. Then, if something does surface later, either after we sign or after we close, we need to decide where the risk should reside.

This response addresses the real interest of the parties and will prevent digressions into who knows most about the company or who can know the most about the company.

Sometimes the seller is leery of making legally important statements without being absolutely certain of their truth. It is important for both sides to recognize that the representations and warranties are not a test of the integrity of the parties making them. A party cannot properly be accused of dishonesty if it makes a representation about which it is not certain (provided, of course, that it has no knowledge that the representation is in fact untrue). In order to reduce legal exposure, it makes sense to try to verify the accuracy of the representations and warranties as much as possible. There will always be, however, some degree of uncertainty. But if the parties recognize that the representations are not a test of integrity but a legal device for allocating risk, the process becomes more manageable and less subject to emotional decision making.

Does the seller always know more than the buyer about the company being sold?

In some rare cases the seller will be in a position to argue persuasively that the buyer has much more knowledge about the company and should be more willing to accept the risk associated with the sale. For example, in an MBO, where the buying group includes the management that has operated the company for several years, it is very possible that management could be persuaded to accept the risk of inaccuracy in the representations and warranties because management is in the best position to assess that risk and make a business decision based upon it.

But even here, the shift of the risk to management is not necessarily fair or logical. If a latent problem causes a loss, the management buyers absorbing the loss are paying an additional purchase price, as mentioned earlier.

Moreover, this line of reasoning will not apply in most MBOs because a promoter, investment bank, or the lenders, and not the management group, typically end up owning the majority of the equity. They, unlike management, have no basis for certainty with respect to the accuracy of the representations and warranties, and they should be much less willing to accept the risk that management inadvertently neglected to properly assess the accuracy of the representations and warranties.

Are some representations and warranties more important than others?

Yes. The most important representations regard financial statements, litigation, taxes, and undisclosed liabilities, particularly in the environmental area, despite the Supreme Court's recent finding in *Bestfoods*. A buyer should, at a minimum, argue hard for solid representations and warranties on these points. Protection for breaches of the representations on financials should be the last point the buyer concedes.

COVENANTS

What is the major purpose of the covenants?

The covenants section of the agreement defines the obligations of the parties in respect to their conduct during the period between the signing and the closing. For negotiation purposes, the most significant covenant relates to the obligation of the seller to conduct the business in the ordinary course with such exceptions as are agreed upon by the parties between the time of signing and closing. In the representations and warranties, the seller assures the buyer of the legal characteristics of the company being sold as of the date of the signing of the agreement; in the covenants section, the seller in essence agrees not to do anything to change that picture in any material way, except as necessary in the normal operations of the business.

Any changes other than those that are specifically allowed by the agreement can be made only with the consent of the buyer. Under appropriate circumstances it is often necessary to limit the restrictions by requiring the buyer not to "withhold consent unreasonably." This limitation should be used sparingly so as to ensure that it achieves its limited purpose; that is, in narrow circumstances the seller may be required to take certain actions in order to preserve the business, and the buyer should not be allowed to prevent them unless such actions have a material impact on the transaction.

Many attorneys feel that this limitation is never appropriate because as long as the conditions to closing are fulfilled, the buyer is obligated to purchase the company. The buyer should therefore have control over any extraordinary actions pending closing. That position, however, must be tempered with the following consideration: If there is a specific area of business conduct about which the seller has a great deal of concern, liberalizing the restriction may be the only way to close the gap between the parties. If the phrase *reasonable consent* is troublesome, it is often possible to craft language that more carefully defines the circumstances under which the seller should be permitted to do things not otherwise permitted by the agreement. If the seller is willing to spend the time to come up with a list of such circumstances, these can be included as exceptions to the consent process.

CONDITIONS TO CLOSING

What role do the conditions to closing play in the acquisition agreement?

The form agreement appearing as Appendix 8B at the end of this chapter contains the typical conditions that must be satisfied before the buyer or the seller is obligated to close.

The agreement typically sets forth separate conditions for each of the parties. If a condition to the buyer's obligation to close is not satisfied, the buyer will have the right to terminate the agreement without being liable for damages to the seller. Similarly, if one of the seller's conditions is not satisfied, the seller will not be obligated to close. Under appropriate circumstances a condition might be established that applies to both parties, but that is the unusual case. One mutual condition might be the receipt of certain key governmental consents; another is the absence of litigation or any administrative ruling that precludes the closing. Either party may waive a condition and proceed to close the acquisition notwithstanding the failure of the other party to satisfy each condition.

How do the conditions to closing affect the key concerns of the buyer and seller?

The conditions to closing section is the first part of the agreement that addresses one of the two major concerns of the parties. The conditions section sets forth the ability of each party to terminate the contract with legal impunity. For example, if any condition is not met by the company being acquired or the seller, the buyer will be free to terminate the contract.

The most significant condition is the so-called *bring-down* condition, which makes the buyer's obligation to close contingent upon two factors: The buyer will not be required to close if (1) the seller has breached any of its covenants or (2) any of the representations and warranties in the acquisition agreement were not true when made or are not true on the closing date, or as if made on the closing date. This condition provides an escape for the buyer if the representations and warranties were true on the date of signing but are no longer true as of the closing date, either because of events that occurred after the signing or because of breaches that were discovered after the signing.

The following example illustrates the process. On the signing date the seller represents that there is no material litigation involving the company it is selling. As a condition to closing, the buyer says that the representations and warranties must be true when made. This means the buyer can abandon the transaction if it discovers that material litigation existed on the signing date. But what about a lawsuit arising after the signing and before the closing? Since the representation was true when made, there is no breach of the litigation representation as a result of the post-signing events. The bring-down condition obligates the seller to make the same representation as of the closing date. Therefore, the buyer will be able to terminate the agreement if interim events such as new litigation, liabilities, or other post-signing occurrences have reduced the value or viability of the company it is buying.

The bring-down assures the buyer that, on the closing date, the company it is buying will be the same company, from a legal and financial perspective, that it bargained for in the contract. The buyer is not required to close the transaction if any bring-down condition is not satisfied, which gives the buyer leverage to renegotiate a lower price reflecting the changes.

The form agreement requires a corporate officer to certify that the representations and warranties are accurate in all material respects as of the closing date. This certificate must be provided as a condition of closing, but it has another very important effect: It is a restatement of all the representations and warranties as of the closing date.

If the certificate is not accurate, the inaccuracy will constitute a breach of a representation or warranty and may give rise to liability from buyer to seller under the indemnity section of the agreement. In the absence of an officer's certificate, a buyer might be unprotected against certain adverse events occurring between signing and closing. For example, if a material liability arises and is discovered before closing, a closing condition will be unsatisfied, and the buyer can walk from the deal. But if it is not discovered, the parties may close because to their knowledge each closing condition—including the condition that the representation and warranty about undisclosed liabilities is true—was satisfied. Clearly, the buyer needs more than a condition to closing to fully insulate it from undiscovered problems. Requiring the seller to represent that the closing condition is satisfied allows the buyer to treat the seller's failure to satisfy the condition as a breach of the representations. If the buyer is indemnified for losses attributable to such breaches, the buyer, by virtue of the certificate, will be protected against losses resulting from undiscovered problems.

As an aside, it is important that the officer's certificate be made solely on behalf of the corporation and that it not constitute a personal affidavit. Otherwise, the corporate officer might be personally liable to the buyer if the certificate is proved untrue, irrespective of whether the corporate officer is at fault.

The usual bring-down clause also states that representations and warranties that apply as of a specific date in the past need not be restated as of the closing date. But be careful! Certain representations are always limited to a specific date. And occasionally a seller will attempt to limit the applicability of a representation (for example, an assurance that it is not currently involved in material litigation) by adding language like "As of the date hereof. . . ." Such a qualifier, combined with the standard bring-down clause, would deprive the buyer of the right to claim breach of promise and walk from the deal. (See the discussion of the importance of controlling the drafting of the agreement at the beginning of this chapter.)

What is a *financing out condition,* and when is it appropriate?

The *financing out condition* provides that the buyer need not close if it is unable to finance the transaction. It is a very broad exception to the buyer's obligation to close the deal, and the seller must be wary of allowing such a condition. The seller may have kept its company off the market for a long period of time and incurred substantial expenses only to find out that the buyer failed to obtain the necessary financing. For these reasons a seller should resist the use of a financing condition or narrow the risk if there must be one.

The seller's initial position should be that if the buyer is confident of the financing, it should be willing to take the risk that the financing will not be available; that is, there should be no financing out. Next, the seller can attempt to require the buyer to have its financing commitments in place before the contract is signed. This strategy limits the seller's risk to those cases where the lenders refuse to consummate the transaction. In addition, the parties will know in advance that the basic transaction is acceptable to the lenders who propose to finance the transaction. Another alternative is to require the buyer to provide financing commitments (or executed loan agreements) within a specified number of days after the contract is signed. After that period, the financing condition falls away. This approach may be preferable to a buyer that doesn't want to incur what can be very costly commitment fees to lenders before it has a contract signed. In addition, the seller should attempt to require the buyer to pay the seller's expenses if the transaction is abandoned because the commitments could not be obtained.

At the very least, the seller should know what the proposed financing structure will be. For example, how much equity will be invested? How much mezzanine and senior debt will be necessary? What are the buyer's assumptions about the lender's interest rates and equity demands? With this information, the seller's financial advisors can assist in evaluating the feasibility of the proposed financing. It should go without saying that the buyer should be required in a covenant to use its best efforts to obtain the necessary financing.

Many contracts do not contain a financing out because the buyer is a shell company with no assets. Even if the buyer breaches the contract, a lawsuit by the seller will not yield significant damages. For this reason, a seller should investigate the buyer's financial strength and inquire who will stand behind the buyer's contract obligations.

All this being said, the buyer has a strong interest in obtaining a financing out. Often, financing can fall through for reasons beyond the control of the buyer, and it needs protection in such a case. Moreover, in an era of extremely volatile interest rates, a transaction that is financeable when the contract is signed may not be when the time for closing arrives because new rates may place too high a financial burden on the buyer. The buyer, forced to put more equity in the transaction, may not have the required funds or may no longer find the deal attractive. When all else fails, the buyer should try to obtain a dollar limit on its exposure, in the form of a liquidated damages clause, in the event it refuses to close a deal in which there is no financing out.

This controversial provision generally should be addressed by the seller as early as possible, usually in the letter of intent. The buyer, on the other hand, is better off letting this issue ride until the seller becomes emotionally committed to the deal by signing the letter of intent. Once the letter of intent is signed, the seller also may be bureaucratically (if not legally) committed to selling and may be more amenable to compromise on the point. The parties must approach this problem by crafting a solution that is carefully tailored to the specific concerns of the parties. Buyers and sellers can often compromise by adjusting (1) the time within which financing commitments must be provided and (2) the consequences of the buyer's failure to finance the transaction.

One of the typical conditions to closing for the buyer is that there has been no material adverse change in the financial condition of the seller. Who bears the risk if there is a general business downturn or a specific problem in the industry of the seller that causes a deterioration in its financial condition—and what if the adverse change will clearly occur, but only after the closing?

The buyer's right to abandon the deal usually depends on the condition of the company it is buying—not the reason for the condition. Some sellers try to shift to the buyer the risk of general or industry-specific economic reversals, but buyers are usually successful in resisting the attempt. The seller's argument is not fatuous, however. The buyer clearly gets the benefit of unanticipated improvements in the financial condition due to such factors because the seller still must close; why shouldn't the buyer absorb the downside as well as the upside?

This issue stems from the signing of a contract binding the parties to close the transaction before they are ready to close. The seller benefits because the buyer is legally obligated to close unless material seller's problems surface. The buyer, on the other hand, has the deal locked up; yet if significant problems arise, the buyer can terminate or renegotiate the acquisition. But from the seller's perspective, it has given up the upside (which should be reflected in the purchase price) but still retains the economic downside until the deal closes. Thus, if the parties' expectations prove untrue—for example, because oil is discovered on the property—the buyer gets the benefit. But if a new material lawsuit arises, the buyer can walk. In other words, once the contract is signed, the buyer is the owner, but only if things continue to look good.

It is for this reason that many sellers try to shift the date of the transfer of risk from the seller to the buyer to the date the contract is signed. Their theory is that the buyer has to accept a balanced economic deal—it gets both the good and the bad occurring after the signing. The buyer is getting what it bargained for so long as the representations and warranties as of the signing date are accurate on the closing date and the seller doesn't breach its covenants concerning the conduct of the business pending closing.

The argument has logical appeal, particularly if there will be a great deal of time between the signing and closing, say, on account of the need for regulatory approvals. If the seller is going to push this point, it must also be willing to give up any earnings during the interim period.

Logic notwithstanding, the seller has an uphill battle. This is one of those situations where one custom is worth a thousand arguments. A buyer can be expected to resist strenuously: "Deals just aren't done this way," "Hey, you still control the operation of the business," or "My price doesn't take into account this type of risk." Because tradition is on the buyer's side, the seller can expect to have to give up something significant to win this point. Where the time span between signing and closing is customarily 30 to 60 days, it may not be worth the fight.

The seller's argument may prove too much. The buyer rarely is expected to assume the risk of other post-signing adverse changes, such as new lawsuits, major undisclosed liabilities, or major uninsured casualty losses. There is no logical basis for distinguishing financial deterioration resulting from a general recession from other types of risks. In any event, the buyer must resist this attempt by the seller, because the buyer may not be able to close its financing in the face of negative events. It does not seem fair to tag the buyer with damages for failing to close in this situation, particularly if the seller knows it is selling in a highly leveraged transaction and if the buyer has obtained financing commitments in advance.

In order to govern events that occur before closing that will harm the financial condition of the company afterward, the conditions to closing should require that there be no material adverse change in the company's "prospects." In the absence of such a provision, the buyer would be obligated to close under these circumstances. The seller often argues that the word *prospects* is too vague. The buyer can respond by being more specific, without agreeing to shift the risk to itself.

What happens if the buyer is aware of a material breach in a representation or warranty and nevertheless proceeds to close?

The buyer would be stopped from asserting a claim for damages based on the material breach because it had notice. Most likely the buyer has negotiated the price accordingly or does not consider the breach of the representation or warranty as substantially altering the basic terms or desirability of the transaction.

THE INDEMNITY SECTION

Why is there an indemnity section?

The purpose of the indemnification section is to set forth the circumstances under which either party can claim damages or take other remedial action in the event the other party to the agreement has breached a representation or warranty or failed to abide by its covenants. This section usually includes provisions concerning the procedural aspects of indemnity claims and the rights of the parties to take part in any legal proceedings that could give rise to an indemnity claim.

Why is there a need for an indemnity section? Can't the parties simply rely on their general legal rights?

The parties would have the right to collect damages or take other legal action in the event of a breach of a representation or warranty or a specific legal covenant. However, those rights are often vague and do not always include the kinds of recovery to which the parties may feel entitled. For example, it is typical for the indemnity provision to provide specifically that all losses, including reasonable attorney fees and out-of-pocket expenses, will be recovered by the indemnified party. This is often not the result under general case law. In addition, the indemnification provisions contain specific rules governing the involvement of the indemnifying party in proceedings that could give rise to indemnification claims, as well as specific provisions governing the length of time that the representations and warranties will survive the closing.

The indemnity section also governs items that do not constitute a breach of a representation or warranty because they were specifically disclosed to the buyer at the time of the signing or closing but in respect of which the buyer nevertheless wishes protection. As mentioned earlier, because the seller disclosed this fact to the buyer, there is no breach of a representation or warranty in connection with these items. However, the indemnification provisions may allocate to the seller the risks associated with disclosed items.

For what period of time is the buyer protected under the indemnity?

This issue is generally expressed in a different way: How long do the representations and warranties "survive" after the closing? Without a specific provision to the contrary, it is not clear that the representations and warranties survive at all. Consequently, the duration of the indemnity term is often the subject of substantial negotiation. Theoretically, the statute of limitations applicable to actions for breach of contract could govern the claims under the contract, but in most cases the sellers feel that the statutory period is too long.

The buyer should request at least a two-year indemnity period. As a fallback position if the seller resists (and it will), the buyer can suggest that the indemnity continue until the buyer receives audited financial statements of the company for a full fiscal year of operations after the acquisition. Because of the time necessary to prepare the company's financials for its first full fiscal year, the buyer may obtain an indemnity period as long as 15 months after the acquisition closes.

One further point: It is important to provide that each party will be indemnified for all breaches discovered during the indemnity period, not merely for losses actually realized during that period. For example, a lawsuit brought by a third party during the period might not be finally resolved by the end of the period. The indemnified party should nevertheless be entitled to recover so long as the claim arose during the survival period.

Should the time limitation for recovering under the agreement apply to all claims under the contract?

The time limitation should not apply to breaches of covenants, which involve a willful act, or to willful breaches of representations or warranties. The seller shouldn't be offered reduced exposure for purposeful breaches. Representations and warranties about taxes customarily survive for the full period of limitation under applicable federal, state, or local law.

What is a basket, and how does it work?

A *basket* is the dollar amount set forth in the indemnification provision as the loss that must be suffered by the buyer before it can recover damages under the indemnity provisions. In a transaction involving a purchase price of $100 million it would not be uncommon for the basket amount to be $1 million or even higher. The buyer is often successful in arguing that the seller should indemnify losses resulting from breaches of covenants or willful breaches of representations and warranties without regard to the basket amount.

The basket closes the gap between the buyer and seller and permits reasonable negotiation of the post-closing liability issue. The typical argument that the seller will make is, "You're buying my business, warts and all." The standard buyer's response to this is, "We understand that we are accepting the risks of operating the business on a going forward basis, but we fully expect to get what we paid for without any significant deviation from the company described in the representations and warranties."

Both parties must assume that there will be problems with the business and realize that dollar-for-dollar compensation for imperfections is not realistic. The purchase price should take into account material deviations from the expectations of the parties about the company. However, as noted more than once earlier, significant damages flowing from the breach of the representations or warranties may cause the buyer to overpay for the company. The happenstance that the problem arises after the signing or the closing rather than before should not put the buyer in a substantially worse position than if both parties knew of the problem in advance of the closing.

The dollar amount of the basket and the exact mechanics of its operation are often the subject of a great deal of negotiation between the buyer and the seller. It is unwise for the parties, particularly the buyer, to commit to an exact amount early in the negotiation process, since basket flexibility can become a negotiating tool. Seemingly intractable issues can often be resolved by adjusting one feature or another of the basket, including the dollar amount, even when the problematic issue is unrelated to the basket. For example, differences over the representations and warranties can be resolved if the parties negotiate the minimum amount of the claims, the basket amount, how claims are aggregated, or the length of the survival period. Common sense and negotiations experience dictate that the buyer should start lower than where it wants to end up.

What are the kinds of issues that most frequently arise in connection with a basket?

The first question is the size of the basket. Basket amounts in the range of 1 to 2 percent of the purchase price are most common, but much larger baskets (in the 4 to 5 percent range) are not unheard of.

The next question about the basket is whether the buyer or the seller should absorb the amount of the basket once the threshold is crossed. For example, if the basket is $1 million and the buyer suffers $1.5 million in damages, is the seller liable for the $500,000 over the basket amount, the full $1.5 million, or the $500,000 excess plus half of the $1 million? Most often the buyer absorbs the entire amount of the basket (so that in the example the seller would be liable for only $500,000).

There is a cogent argument that buyer and seller ought to split the losses up to the basket amount. The basket is an incentive for the buyer to be thorough in its due diligence, since the basket provision requires the buyer to absorb a significant part of any losses due to breaches of representations and warranties. Splitting liability for the basket amount has the same due diligence incentive for the seller, because if the basket threshold is passed, the seller will be required to pay some part of the initial basket amount. If the basket amount is not split, the buyer may have a legitimate concern that the seller will not be diligent in unearthing problems because it is protected by the basket, especially if the basket amount is large.

Another issue relates to minimum claims. Because the seller does not want to be bothered with small claims—however many of them there might be—the seller often asks for the following additional protection: No claim can be brought if the claim is for less than a specified amount (the *minimum amount*). The seller may insist that such claims not even count toward meeting the basket amount. Of course, the buyer should be expected to resist this approach, particularly if the minimum amount is significant in light of the size of the business being acquired. In addition, the buyer will likely request that these smaller claims be subject to the indemnity if in the aggregate they are a significant amount.

What is the relationship between the basket amount, the minimum amount, and the word *material* when used in connection with representations and warranties?

As discussed above, in order to limit the exposure of the seller to frivolous claims or claims that are normal to the business being acquired, many of the representations and warranties require disclosure only of material items, or items that are material to the business of the target and its subsidiaries taken as a whole. In the absence of a specific dollar threshold to define what is material, it is unclear exactly how much damage the buyer must incur before it can claim that there has been a breach of a representation containing a materiality limitation. These materiality limitations can create an unfair result for the buyer if there are several legal problems for the company that cause a significant aggregate loss for the buyer but there is no single breach that has a material adverse effect on the business.

The precise effect of the basket amount on all this is uncertain. It might be argued that the basket amount is a numerical definition of the word *material*. Thus, if the basket amount is $1 million, a loss of less than $1 million arising from a breach of a single warranty might not be viewed by a court interpreting the agreement as material to the business as a whole. But what if there are claims in five areas covered by representations and warranties, averaging $750,000 each? If the agreement is construed to mean that only a loss of more than $1 million is "material," the buyer will suffer $3.75 million of damage and will have no recourse against the seller. The result may not be sensible, but in the absence of any other guidance it is, unfortunately, plausible. If the parties do not wish the basket amount to be used as a definition of *material,* they should state so in the agreement.

Can use of a basket and a minimum amount provision eliminate the need for including materiality limitations in the representations and warranties?

It is possible to resolve the ambiguity of using the term *material* by using the concepts of the *basket amount* and *minimum amount* in the following manner. A representation or warranty would not be breached unless the resulting loss exceeded the minimum claim amount (say $50,000), and there would be no recovery by the buyer until all the potential claims add up to the basket amount. This way the seller is assured that relatively minor imperfections in the business will not result either singly or in the aggregate in exposure for indemnity claims, and both parties will have a much better idea of what the expectations surrounding the indemnity provisions are.

The seller must exercise care here. The materiality limitations in the representations and warranties serve another function: They limit the ability of the buyer to terminate the transaction without penalty between the time of signing and closing. If the materiality limitations are eliminated altogether, the buyer could point to a minor legal defect in the business causing a loss equal to the minimum amount and say that the representations and warranties were not "true as of the closing date." This problem can be remedied either (1) by leaving the materiality limitations in the agreement solely for this purpose, as is often the case, or (2) by leaving them out and requiring that potential losses equal the basket amount or some other agreed-upon figure before the buyer would be permitted to terminate the transaction.

The latter solution can be very risky for the buyer. The basket amount is frequently the subject of negotiation and manipulation having little or nothing to do with the concept of materiality as incorporated into individual representations or warranties. The buyer may assess the risk of an unknown or undisclosed problem arising after the closing as small because it knows the company being acquired or the industry extremely well, or because it has tremendous faith in the management coparticipants in the acquisition. The buyer may also feel that it is getting a bargain. In this situation, and because of the speculative nature of the losses, the buyer may be willing to agree to a very large basket amount.

On the other hand, the buyer might well feel that if problems actually arise before the closing, it should be free to reevaluate the wisdom of its decision to buy the target long before its losses reach the basket amount. To meet this concern, either a different threshold amount should be established for the conditions to closing section or, as is most often the case, the materiality caveats should remain in place in the representations and warranties for purposes of the conditions to closing section.

Is the indemnity sufficient protection for the parties, or are other protections necessary?

The indemnity alone is meaningless unless the indemnifying party is creditworthy. The parties should take care to satisfy themselves about the financial strength of indemnifying parties. This is achieved, in part, by the representations and warranties made by the buyer and its owners about its and their respective financial condition. Where there are doubts about the ability of the seller to meet its obligations, or where the company has many stockholders, it may be advisable to place a portion of the purchase price in escrow to serve as security for the seller's obligations under the indemnity. Under a typical escrow, which often (but not always) lasts as long as the survival period, the buyer has access to the escrowed funds after it is finally determined that the seller is liable under the indemnity portion of the contract.

Another device that is useful when the seller has a right to receive deferred payments is to give the buyer a right to set off any damages it suffers for breach of the contract against payments due the seller. It is legally acceptable and preferable for the parties to define such *setoff rights* in the agreement. Agreements may permit a setoff either after a final determination of liability or when a loss is suffered despite the fact that the buyer has not yet established the seller's liability. The latter arrangement reverses the normal posture of the parties negotiating a claim for indemnification—normally the indemnifying party has control of the money, and the party who has suffered damages must sue to get it. For this reason, an immediate setoff right is fiercely, and usually successfully, fought off by the seller.

In the absence of a specific setoff provision, in most jurisdictions it does not appear that a buyer has the legal right to withhold payments from the seller until there is a final determination of liability under the indemnity. If note payments to the seller are withheld before such a determination, it is probable that a court would grant a summary judgment to the seller and force the buyer to pay principal and interest on the note in accordance with the terms even if the buyer has a separate claim under the contract.

Are there any special concerns of the seller in connection with the indemnity?

Most of the issues for the seller are covered in the preceding text since the basket amounts, survival period, and minimum amount are all issues of great concern to both parties. Obviously, the seller will try to avoid all indemnity completely.

In the case of a privately held company, the major thrust of the seller's argument is often to reinforce the basic argument outlined above about who assumes the risk of owning a business, with the additional argument that if the company were a public company, the representations and warranties would not survive the closing. This argument is more persuasive if there are public securities issued by the company, so that it has been regularly filing public reports with the SEC and has a relatively long history of audited financial statements. One major reason for the different treatment of public companies is the impracticality of bringing suits against hundreds or even thousands of stockholders. This burden is not usually present in the sale of a closely held private company. Nevertheless, the apparent willingness of buyers in the public arena to live without indemnities, together with the sale of companies through auction procedures (discussed below), has allowed sellers to avoid indemnities in an increasing number of situations.

When there are several selling stockholders, the sellers ought to (1) try to limit each stockholder's liability to "several" liability, meaning that one stockholder is not liable if another is unable to satisfy its liabilities under the indemnity, and (2) be certain that breaches of representations and warranties that are specific to a stockholder, such as a stockholder's failure to have or convey good title to its shares being sold, will not create liability for other stockholders.

The sellers also should argue that there should be a limit on liability. Most buyers will agree to limit liability to the purchase price paid, and some sellers have been successful in arguing for a lower cap on liability, although a lower cap doesn't make much sense.

Finally, the sellers ought to pay close attention to the terms of notes they accept as part of the payment. In order to placate senior lenders, seller notes are often deeply subordinated (see the discussion in Chapter 4) and contain provisions that limit the ability of the seller to sue if there is a payment default. A buyer should not be permitted to take advantage of this provision to hold back payments (that is, create a payment default) when there is a potential claim under the indemnity. The subordination provisions are for the benefit of the senior lenders and are not designed to allow the buyer to use the seller's funds to finance indemnity claims; the limitation on the seller's remedies under the note ought not to apply to a constructive setoff by the buyer because of potential indemnity liabilities.

Are there any special items that a buyer is indemnified for even if they are disclosed, such as litigation?

Yes. In the course of due diligence the buyer will often uncover items for which it will either seek a price adjustment or request specific indemnification. Typical examples are unusual litigation that is not insured or reserved for on the balance sheet and major environmental problems.

What about litigation arising after the closing based on business conducted before the acquisition?

In an asset transaction, the buyer usually does not assume the risk of such litigation and will obtain a specific indemnity against any losses from the seller.

In the case of a merger or stock acquisition, many contracts contain indemnities specifically protecting the buyer against this type of loss. Even in the absence of specific protection, it is at least arguable that such litigation is an unmatured and contingent undisclosed liability that constitutes a breach of the warranty, or an undisclosed liability to which the general indemnity applies.

Before engaging in lengthy negotiation about this issue, the parties should focus on insurance coverage for this type of loss. In this area, the availability of insurance coverage may render the parties' exposure immaterial. In most cases, insurance is on a "claims made" basis; that is, the insured is protected against losses from claims made during the insurance period. If so, the company's insurance policy will provide protection, and it would be unfair to expect the seller to cover such losses. It is critical to avoid an insurance coverage gap during which neither the old policy (because it is a "claims made" policy) nor the company's new policy (because it only insures claims based on events occurring during the insurance period) will make good on a legitimate claim. A gap is more likely to arise when the company is part of a conglomerate and coinsured under a single umbrella policy covering all members of the seller's corporate group. In this situation, the company must take out separate policies effective as of the closing date.

TERMINATION PROCEDURES

What is the purpose of the termination section of the agreement?

The termination section of the agreement sets forth the circumstances under which the transactions can be terminated by either party and the consequences of the termination. This section normally includes a date by which the closing must occur. If the closing fails to occur by that date as a result of the action or inaction of one party, the party that was capable of closing typically can elect to terminate the contract and sue the other party for breach of contract.

The section also allows a party to terminate if it discovers a material breach by the other of a representation, warranty, or covenant that would cause the bring-down condition to be unsatisfied. A party should not have to wait until the termination date to terminate if it is clear that it won't be obligated to close in any event.

This section will also set forth any limitation on damages that can be collected in a breach of the contract, special remedies that a nonbreaching party may seek, and conditions for arbitration (unless set forth in the last class for legal miscellany).

What are the advantages and disadvantages of arbitration provisions in the agreement?

The oft-stated benefits of arbitration—such as quick and inexpensive resolution of disputes—may make arbitration a satisfactory mechanism by which parties to an acquisition agreement can enforce their rights. As discussed earlier in Chapter 6, alternative dispute resolution (ADR) is gaining acceptance by courts as well as by companies. It should be noted, however, that the benefits of arbitration can be offset by its risks.

Arbitration is best suited for resolution of disputes of little economic consequence or of technical issues, such as valuation of inventory, not readily within the ken of a trial judge. Even in the latter situation, the parties should consider whether the savings in time and money by arbitration are outweighed by the protections of judicial resolution, particularly where the amounts involved potentially constitute a significant multiple of litigation costs. Where the benefits of arbitration outweigh its disadvantages, the arbitration clause should be drafted to minimize the negative aspects of arbitration.

One factor that contributes to prompt resolution by arbitration is the use of a nonjudicial or extrajudicial decision maker. An arbitrator's schedule will usually be more open and flexible than that of a court. However, an arbitrator may have biases or lack sufficient knowledge of the law or subject area to reach a proper decision. This disadvantage can be minimized by careful drafting. For example, if the agreement designates arbitration under the rules of the American Arbitration Association (AAA), the parties will have to choose an arbitrator from one or more lists of names provided to them. These arbitrators may be unsatisfactory. To avoid this situation, the acquisition agreement can designate another means of choosing an arbitrator, such as having each party choose its own arbitrator and then having these select a third arbitrator.

A second factor that contributes to the speed of arbitration, as well as its lower costs, is the absence of discovery. In certain situations, the lack of discovery may not be a serious disadvantage. For example, if each party has sufficient familiarity with, or access to, the company's books and records, discovery may not be necessary to resolve a dispute concerning those documents. Even if discovery is necessary with regard to a particular issue, arbitration may still be a viable alternative to court proceedings. The parties can draft the agreement to allow some discovery but not so much as to make the arbitration process comparable to a judicial one. Furthermore, the extent of discovery can be made subject to decision of the arbitrators.

In drafting an arbitration agreement, the parties should attempt to anticipate all future disputes. If arbitration is broadly required for all disagreements, the parties may be barred from seeking emergency injunctive relief from a court. A narrow arbitration clause, however, may result in requiring counterclaims to be filed in court, thereby compounding, rather than simplifying, resolution of disagreements.

The parties should also draft the arbitration agreement with the controlling law of the relevant jurisdiction in mind. In many jurisdictions, for example, absent the parties' agreement to the contrary, only the arbitrators have the power to subpoena witnesses. However, in New York State, the parties themselves have the power to issue subpoenas. Certain jurisdictions, such as California, are less likely than others to limit the scope of the arbitration clause. In those jurisdictions, courts tend to interpret narrow arbitration provisions to require arbitration of issues that the parties neither mentioned nor intended to be arbitrated.

One caveat: In the M&A area, arbitration proceedings, even before an AAA tribunal, can be very expensive if they are pursued by lawyers normally involved in litigative court proceedings. Both sides should recognize that the services of law firms specializing in ADR are now widely available and resolution of disputes using their services is highly efficient.

AUCTIONS

Do auction procedures for selling companies have any effect on the contract negotiation process?

Yes, a significant effect. In the auction process, a seller hires an investment banker to sell the company on a bid basis. The investment banker prepares a "book" describing the company and solicits bids from potential buyers. The buyers receive a form contract and are told that the bid should be accompanied by the form contract together with any changes to it required by the buyer. The buyer is expressly warned that extensive changes will be considered negatively in evaluating the competitive nature of the bid. Often the buyer is offered limited access to the company's management and carefully controlled opportunities for due diligence before the initial bid must be made. Needless to say, the form contract typically provides the buyer no indemnities and only limited representations and warranties. Typically, extensive changes are required to make the contract similar to a typical and reasonable buyer's contract.

After the investment banker winnows out unacceptable bids, the seller will deal with only a few serious bidders who are given the chance for more thorough due diligence, often including full, rather than limited, access to management. The seller's representatives will often negotiate the contracts submitted by those bidders in order to finalize the contract before a decision is made. Nevertheless, contract negotiations often continue even after the deal has been awarded to a specific bidder.

The bid process often has an intended psychological effect on many buyers, who get spooked by contractual overkill and don't want the lawyers to lose the deal. The buyer's lawyer is likely to hear: "Don't give me the world's most perfect contract. I want the absolute minimum protection I need. Don't overlawyer and get me knocked out in the first round." If the deal is priced on an as-is basis, and the buyer is fully informed of the risks, then the buyer would be wise to accept the seller's wording without protest.

The simplicity of the buyer's response will depend entirely upon the strength of its desire to buy the company and its confidence that it knows the company well enough to take the risk of an as-is transaction.

Nonetheless, even if the buyer is willing to take such risks, certain points should be addressed in the contract, and the buyer must insist upon the opportunity to do thorough due diligence:

- First, the buyer should get representations and warranties ensuring that if the company is not up to legal snuff, the buyer may terminate the contract without penalty.

- Second, the seller should be willing to provide the buyer with indemnity for matters of which it has knowledge.

- Third, the same arguments about the unfairness of the buyer's "overpaying" apply here. The question is how far to carry the comments provided above.

If additional protection is desired, the buyer might require indemnification for breaches of representations and warranties made regarding the financial statements, undisclosed liabilities, taxes, and litigation. The pill can be made easier for the seller to swallow with generous minimum amount and basket provisions.

As a final word, the buyer should not be fooled by the putative formality of the bid procedures and the investment banker's stern admonitions. Most buyers do submit changes to the contract along the lines described above, and in the end the insiders will tell you that the price and a credible ability to close, and not the contract terms (provided they are reasonable), will dictate the results in most cases. A buyer that has concerns about the legal aspects of the target or its business should not hesitate to say that it reserves the right to submit further changes after it has been given complete access to management and an opportunity for full due diligence. It is not unusual for the buyer to submit a solid bid and indicate that it would like the opportunity to negotiate the terms of the contract with the seller face-to-face. Typically the buyer would also indicate the several areas where it would require changes.

Another favored approach is to do a relatively extensive markup and suggest that the contract can be watered down in face-to-face negotiations after due diligence is completed. This approach is constructive because the seller will usually negotiate the contract with the two or three top bidders. Whatever the buyer sends in will be the starting point for negotiation. Even if the buyer is willing to accept only minimum protection, it is important to start ahead of where the buyer wants to end up.

Why have auction procedures become so popular?

Although not as popular in the 1990s as they were in the 1980s, auctions are still generally believed to be the best way of ensuring that the highest possible price is obtained. The same sentiment probably drives the seller to use auction methods for sales of divisions or subsidiaries of companies. Also, who can fault a corporate executive for the price he or she agrees to if it was the result of a competitive bid procedure?

The auction process also saves the seller the time and effort of dealing with dozens of potential buyers, many of whom may be "shoppers" that never buy anything, and bringing it down to serious negotiations with two or three serious potential buyers. Sellers must be very careful to supervise the way the investment bankers deal with the bidders. The seller, and not the investment banker, should be negotiating the deal because most serious buyers are justifiably put off by having to negotiate substantive points through an intermediary who rarely has the authority to cut a deal.

ACQUISITIONS FROM AN AFFILIATED GROUP

Are there any special aspects to be negotiated when the buyer is acquiring the assets of a division or the stock of a subsidiary that is a part of a larger corporate group?

There are numerous issues that arise under such circumstances that should be addressed:

1. Is the buyer getting all the assets needed to operate the company as a separate business, or are some critical assets located elsewhere in the group?

2. Are there any special, advantageous contractual or administrative relationships with the seller that must be continued (for example, supply or purchase contracts), or are there unfavorable ones that must be terminated? This can be a very useful aspect of a transaction for the buyer or the seller. As part of the pricing and as an inducement to complete the transaction, one party can offer a favorable long-term contract to the other.

3. Are there administrative services provided to the company by the group that should be continued for a period of time? In many cases

the seller's group provides legal, accounting, billing, and other administrative support as well as shared office and warehouse space. Unless replacements will be available at closing, the agreement should contain provisions to continue those services at an agreed-upon cost for a specified period of time (ranging from 30 days to as many as 360 days).

4. Finally, is it clear that the company's financial information upon which the deal is based takes into account the need to provide for the services or other arrangements described in issues 2 and 3 above?

TRANSACTIONS INVOLVING PUBLIC COMPANIES

Are acquisition agreements different when the company being acquired is a public company?

Yes. The acquisition agreement in a public company transaction is very different from the type of agreement used for a privately held firm. The differences may be divided into two categories: (1) provisions that are present in agreements involving private companies but are typically absent from agreements involving public companies and (2) provisions that are typically absent from private company agreements but are present in public company agreements.

What provisions common to private company agreements will be missing from agreements involving public companies?

In agreements involving public companies, the representations and warranties do not survive the closing of the transaction, so that the buyer is given no protection in the event breaches are discovered afterward. In short, there is no indemnity provision, mainly because an indemnity against hundreds or thousands of shareholders is considered impractical. The buyer therefore must rely on the substantial disclosures required under federal securities laws as the basis for evaluating the legal and financial risks of ownership. These disclosures, if materially inaccurate or misleading, can give rise to criminal and civil liability on the part of the officers and directors, so they tend to be truthful and complete. Together with a history of audited financial statements that are also required under the securities laws, they provide a reliable rendition of the legal and financial history of the company.

Because the representations and warranties don't survive anyway, and because there are extensive public disclosures, the representations and warranties tend to be far briefer in a public company deal. They serve more as a means of organizing due diligence. The buyer shouldn't get too carried away, however, with agreeing to gut the representations and warranties. As repeated so often in this chapter, these provisions serve another function—they give the buyer a way to terminate the transaction if the representations, warranties, and covenants are breached in a material way. Therefore, although many of the detailed disclosures are eliminated, the key concepts must be retained. The key sections that would be retained in a public deal agreement are discussed in the introduction to the form agreement at the end of this chapter.

What are some of the provisions that appear only in the public deal acquisition agreement?

First, the agreement will contain specific representations and warranties to the effect that the parties have complied with all applicable securities laws and, specifically, that the disclosures made pursuant to those laws are all materially accurate.

Second, the agreement will set forth the specific form of the transaction, for example, a merger or a tender offer or a combination of the two, and what the responsibilities of the various parties will be for preparing, reviewing, and filing the documents that must be filed with the SEC.

NEGOTIATING AND DOCUMENTING AN MBO

How do negotiations generally go between a management group and an outside financial or investor group?

The typical MBO involving an outside financial partner requires at least three separate but coordinated negotiations: (1) the negotiation between management and the financial partner as to the nature of their relationship, (2) the acquisition negotiation between a team consisting of management and the financial partner on the one side and the seller on the other, and (3) the negotiation with lenders, in which the financial partner usually plays the lead role but management participates because of its knowledge of the business and its financing needs, and the lenders' desire to keep management involved.

Because both the second and third negotiations demand close coordination between management and the financial partner and a considerable amount of mutual trust, the first negotiation should, to the extent possible, be completed at the earliest possible stage but is often delayed. MBOs, like most LBOs, normally take place under acute time pressure, and management and the financial partner may have met for the first time and for the sole purpose of doing the acquisition. The issues between them are difficult and go to basic questions of allocation of benefits and burdens and management self-esteem.

It is often difficult for management to accept how much equity the financiers want to receive when they don't even know how to run the company. Therefore, it is likely that management and the financial partner are working out their relationship at the same time that they are negotiating with the seller and the lenders. To some extent, this is unavoidable, even with ample time and advance contact, because the terms negotiated with the seller or the obligations imposed by a lender cannot be entirely foreseen and will involve changes in the allocations of responsibilities or benefits between the acquirers. It may even be beneficial, as during the course of negotiations both management and the financial partner begin to appreciate how essential each is to the other in bringing the deal to a proper closing.

The first step is reaching an understanding of the terms of management and the financial partner's relationship. Although this is often an oral agreement, occasionally management and its financial partner may enter into a written *pre-incorporation agreement*—a document that lenders may ask to see part of their due diligence.

What issues should the pre-incorporation agreement address?

The four main issues are as follows:

1. The terms on which the acquisition will be conducted: that each party will bear its own expenses or how they will be shared; that neither will be liable to the other if the transaction is not consummated; that neither will negotiate with another party; that information about the other will be kept confidential; that each will use its reasonable efforts to accomplish the acquisition; and that each party will have specific responsibilities in negotiating the acquisition (that is, the financial party will probably commit to obtain financing on a best-efforts or reasonable-efforts basis)

2. The share each party will have in the ownership of the acquired company

3. The voting power or veto power each party will have over the business operations of the acquired company and over sale or refinancing of the company

4. The makeup of the board of directors

Are there any provisions a pre-incorporation agreement should not contain?

Some attorneys will say that the written agreement should not contain any details that might dilute the parties' position with lenders—such as contingency plans specifying which of the parties will provide personal guarantees for the loan. These provisions may be based on handshakes rather than memorialized in the written agreement.

How is a manager-investor understanding expressed if there is no pre-incorporation agreement?

These arrangements are then handled as a matter of oral understanding and custom that ultimately, after the acquisition, may be reduced to writing in various agreements such as employment, consulting, and stockholder agreements, and in articles of incorporation and bylaws. Informal agreements are often indicators of a more healthy and successful relationship between the management and the investor group, since the key element in most MBOs is trust and cooperation. Getting everything in writing at an early stage is nearly impossible anyway since the parties are dealing, in part, with ephemera, and attempts to reduce verbal agreements to precise language can lead to arguments, delays, mistrust, and perhaps the breakup of the deal before it's had a chance to get going.

In a typical LBO, what levels of equity does management hold?

Management may own all the equity, if it has no partner, but most MBOs do involve an outside backer. In an MBO a CEO who controls the deal can sometimes achieve a 50-50 or even a 60-40 deal or better for management. More typically, key management will often receive between 10 and 25 percent of the equity. Equity percentages reflect the relative negotiating strength of the parties, often determined by which of the two parties brought the deal to the other. Such stakes will be reduced or diluted by equity, or equity equivalents such as warrants or convertible securities, issued to a seller or to a financial institution and sometimes to a finder.

What are typical allocations of control over corporate decisions?

Again, allocations vary greatly according to which party controls the deal, how badly they need each other, and how much they trust each other. Discussions tend to reflect a basic division of interest: Management tends to think in operating and strategic terms (how to meet the operating needs of the company while expanding it), whereas the financial partner tends to think in financial terms how to get a lender to commit funds, and, after that, how to realize value by paying dividends, selling stock, or divesting units.

Management will presumably make "ordinary course of business" decisions, subject to the board of directors, which may be equally divided between the parties at first but will swing one way or the other depending on events. Sometimes board membership is divided proportionate to stock holdings. If management has less than 50 percent of the stock, it may have the protection of a supermajority provision for stockholder votes affecting major transactions, such as sale of the company, public issuances of stock, or refinancings. If the financial partner does not have a majority of the stock, it may insist on the ability to sell its interest or to take the company public after a certain period of time if certain conditions are met.

How many members of management are typically included in an MBO?

Key management can range from as few as one or two managers to over twenty people. The numbers may be limited because of securities law limitations on purchasers in a Regulation D private offering (35 unaccredited investors) or tax limitations on the number of shareholders in an S corporation (75 individuals, no corporations).

How can the value of management be locked in—for example, if key people leave or die?

Two very important factors in an MBO are:

- Employment contracts with key personnel for three-year or five-year terms
- Key-executive life insurance

Compensation and equity participations can be structured through employment and stockholder agreements so that key managers have everything to gain and nothing to lose by staying; therefore, the risk of voluntary departure can be minimized.

Key-executive life insurance should always be part of any MBO planning. No group of financial wizards will substitute for a strong CEO who knows the business, particularly if the plan is to place the company deeply into debt to finance the acquisition. Lenders will frequently require life insurance on the chief executive and perhaps one or two others. Even if they don't require it, any financial group working with management probably will. The principal author of this book was advising a seller some years ago and noticed at the closing that the buyer-CEO was smoking and coughing very heavily. The author insisted successfully that the closing not occur without obtaining a key-executive (then called "key-man") life insurance binder in the amount of the acquisition loan. The closing was delayed until the binder was obtained. Two weeks later the buyer-CEO died.

EMPLOYMENT AGREEMENTS

In addition to equity, what other benefits are typically made available to management?

Prior to trying to sell a division or subsidiary to a third party or to managers, a seller must be sure that its managers have signed employment agreements and they conform with what is actually happening and adequately cover bonuses, vacations, stock options, and so on. Such agreements keep managers with the company while the business is being offered for sale.

Should an MBO manager enter into an employment agreement?

Generally, managers should accept such agreements, as they often offer protection against precipitous termination by a new owner. Further, those financing the deal including lenders may insist on it. On the other hand, managers should be wary of signing off on broad "covenants not to compete" that will prevent them from working for competitors for long periods of time. If an employee must agree to such provisions, which is likely given the strong interest the company will have in protecting its business, he or she will want to be compensated during the noncompete period if it results in hardship and will want to limit the period, for example, to one year, and perhaps limit the territory affected.

After purchasing the business, key members of management will want to have new employment agreements replacing those entered into before the sale of the business. Such an agreement will at the least provide a term, a specified salary, and noncompetition provisions. Management's partner or its bank lenders will usually also want key management to have such agreements.

What provisions relating to noncompetition normally appear in employment agreements?

Such agreements prohibit an employee from doing any of the following:

- Competing with the employer by participating in a competing business or aiding a competitor
- Disclosing confidential information
- Owning equity in a competitor (other than insubstantial interests—less than 5 to 10 percent) of publicly held companies

Will courts enforce covenants not to compete?

Courts will enforce the restrictions of covenants not to compete that are reasonable in duration and territory. In general, however, courts are reluctant to prevent employees from earning their livelihood in their chosen profession and so tend to favor employees in their decisions.

What are the typical terms of a post-buyout employment agreement with managers involved in an MBO?

An employment agreement should specify the term of employment, the amount of compensation and bonuses, and the conditions under which an executive can be terminated.

Employment agreements can be for a fixed term of years or can be extended from year to year under an "evergreen" provision unless one party gives notice to the contrary to the other within a limited period before the start of each year.

The agreement will specify a base salary. The agreement can provide that the salary can be increased by specified increments or by an adjustment such as a rise in the consumer price index. The agreement may also require that the executive receive a percentage of the excess of the company's pretax earnings or net income over projected levels of earnings or income. The agreement might also incorporate an existing bonus plan, as well as special pensions or stock plans, and might guarantee specific benefit levels.

The employer will have the right to terminate the employee for just cause, which usually includes at minimum willful misconduct or gross negligence in the course of employment, fraud in the course of employment, or the conviction for a crime. Just cause may include other matters, but the employee's interest is in limiting the bases for termination for just cause. If the employer has the right to terminate an employee without just cause, the employee is usually compensated by receiving his or her base salary through the end of the term in a lump sum or periodic payments, or by receiving payments in addition to his or her base salary. In any event, the basis for the terms of the severance agreement should be anticipated in the employment agreement. For instance, if the employee gets a new job, his or her salary may or may not reduce the amount that must be paid under these provisions by the terminating employer.

The agreement protects the employer and the employee if the employee is disabled for a continuous period of time. If an employee is disabled or dies, the employee or his or her estate may be entitled to receive benefits after disability or death.

What other provisions may be included in an employment agreement?

Other employment agreement provisions may stipulate that:

- The executive work in a specified city and not be required to relocate
- The executive receive a company car
- The company pay for country club memberships and other expenses
- Other special benefits be provided, such as guaranteed vacation leave policies or the right to run for public office

An employee may also negotiate for a deferred compensation agreement. Deferring income can have financial and tax benefits to individuals. The employee may be able to negotiate funded deferred compensation, with amounts payable out of insurance or a special trust.

What are the benefits and detriments of a deal-induced severance agreement?

Occasionally, an employee who is not offered an employment agreement or is resistant to entering into an employment agreement will enter into a severance agreement instead. The severance agreement, sometimes called a *golden parachute,* will provide that the employee receive two or three times his or her annual salary if he or she is terminated as the result of a change in control of the company. The employee may also be entitled to receive substantial severance benefits if he or she chooses to leave under such circumstances. Such agreements are more prevalent in public companies than the private companies that emerge from an MBO and management is often asked to give up or scale back its golden parachute protections as part of the price for participating in an MBO.

Such agreements can harm the employer by giving the employee a strong incentive to become uncooperative and even disruptive in order to cause termination and trigger the severance payment.

Golden parachutes can also have significant negative tax consequences to the employer.

What are the tax penalties for golden parachute payments?

In 1984, concerned about certain tactics utilized by companies to fight hostile takeovers, Congress enacted the golden parachute rules taxing excess parachute payments. Under the legislation, as amended in 1986, if a corporation makes an "excess parachute payment" to an employee, the payment may not be deducted by the corporation (per Code Section 280G), and the employee will be subject to a 20 percent nondeductible excise tax on the excess parachute payment (per Code Section 4999).

The definition of an excess parachute payment is complex. Generally an excess parachute payment is made to a high-level management employee, is exceptional in relation to the employee's previous compensation, and is contingent upon a change of control of the company. The definition of change of control is broad enough to include circumstances in which a friendly buyer enters into a compensation arrangement with the employee. Management equity participation that results in taxable compensation under Code Section 83 (discussed in Chapter 5) will be taken into account along with all other compensation under the golden parachute rules and thus may be subject to additional tax as an excess parachute payment.

STOCKHOLDERS' AGREEMENTS

At or shortly following the acquisition closing, it is usually advisable for the acquirers to enter into a stockholders' agreement. If the post-acquisition entity is a partnership, the partnership agreement will contain comparable provisions.

What are the main reasons for the buyers of a business to enter into a stockholders' agreement?

To the extent that they have not already done so in a pre-incorporation agreement, a stockholders' agreement will allow the buyers to do the following:

- Obtain advance commitments for additional equity or debt.
- Exercise control over who the owners of the business will be.
- Specify their respective legal rights over the governance of the business.

Why might the buyers want to exercise control over who the owners of the business will be?

Presumably, one of the main reasons the buyers completed the transaction was their particular individual and collective strengths. They wanted to be in business together rather than with other persons or entities. In an MBO (with or without an outside investor group), equity ownership by the persons who will be running the business is a key ingredient of the future success of the enterprise. Therefore, especially in the early period following the acquisition closing, the buyers will want to limit the ownership of the business to those who are active employees or members of the initial investor group. Moreover, the acquisition lenders will have similar concerns and usually will require that the equity ownership of management and the initial investor group be maintained at certain levels for as long as their loans are outstanding.

What are some of the typical ways to limit the equity ownership of the company?

The stockholders' agreement will contain so-called restrictions on transferability, which are limitations on the persons or entities to whom the stockholders may transfer their stock, the time periods during which the stock may be transferred, or the manner in which the stock may be transferred. For example, the stockholders may agree that, in order to give themselves an opportunity to put the business on a solid footing, for a specified period of time, usually from one to five years after the closing, no stockholder will be allowed to transfer stock to anyone other than to an affiliate in the case of a corporate stockholder or to a spouse or child in the case of a stockholder who is a natural person. Management stockholders may even be locked in for a longer period, perhaps as long as they continue to be employed by the corporation.

Conversely, in the case of a management stockholder, the stockholders' agreement may also provide that upon termination of his or her employment, the corporation or the other stockholders will have the option to purchase the terminated employee's stock. One benefit of a provision like this is that the purchased stock could then be sold to another employee of the corporation, including the terminated employee's replacement, enhancing his or her incentive to perform well. Another benefit is that the stock need not remain in the hands of a fired or otherwise disgruntled former employee.

Are such restrictions on transferability legally enforceable?

Generally speaking, yes, assuming that there is a valid business purpose for the restriction, the restriction is reasonably related to a business purpose, and no stockholder has been induced by deception or forced into agreeing to the restriction. However, the more expansive the restriction, the greater the risk that a court will find the restriction to be an "unlawful restraint on the alienation of property." In addition, under the laws of most states, the existence of transfer restrictions must be noted in the form of a legend on the stock certificate in order for those restrictions to be enforceable against third-party transferees who have no knowledge of their existence.

Are there any other ownership restrictions that management may want to have in a stockholders' agreement?

Where management is in a minority position vis-à-vis the other stockholders, it may want some protection against dilution of its interest or some influence over when, and to whom, additional stock may be issued.

Through the stockholders' agreement, management could be given an option to purchase such additional stock, or a proportion thereof, for the same price and terms on which the stock would otherwise be sold to a third person or entity. Management could also be given certain consensual rights over the issuance of such additional stock (see the discussion below).

How may a stockholders' agreement create the framework by which the corporation will be governed?

The stockholders' agreement may contain provisions (1) that require the stockholders to commit themselves in advance to vote their shares to maintain a certain governing structure, (2) that require that certain matters normally within the province of the board of directors or the president shall be regulated by the stockholders, or (3) that require that, under certain circumstances, normal majority rule by the board or the stockholders, as applicable, will not be sufficient.

An example of the first type of provision is where the stockholders agree that they will exercise their power to adopt and amend the corporation's by-laws to maintain a board of directors of a particular number and that they will vote to elect as directors representatives nominated by various groups of stockholders. In the case of a typical MBO in which the majority of stock is held by an investor group, the stockholders' agreement would provide that the stockholders will at all times vote their shares so as to maintain a board of directors of, say, five members, three of whom shall be nominated by the investor group and two of whom shall be nominated by the management group.

An example of the second type of provision is where the parties agree that the stockholders must approve the dismissal of certain executive officers, or any contracts with affiliates of the corporation, or the issuance of stock—activities that are usually handled by the board of directors.

An example of the third type of provision is where the stockholders agree that the corporation cannot engage in certain major transactions, such as a merger or a sale of substantially all the assets of the corporation, without the approval of all the stockholders or some greater proportion of the stockholders than the proportion required under the applicable state corporation statute.

In most, if not all, states it will also be necessary for the second and third types of provisions to be stated in the certificate of incorporation or bylaws of the corporation. For example, Delaware Code Sections 141 and 216 provide, respectively, (1) that the business and affairs of every Delaware corporation shall be managed by its board of directors unless the corporation's certificate of incorporation provides otherwise, and (2) that unless the corporation's certificate of incorporation or bylaws provide otherwise, all matters, other than election of directors, subject to stockholder approval shall be approved by majority vote, and by plurality vote in the case of the election of directors. In this case the stockholders' agreement should also provide that the stockholders will vote their shares to adopt and maintain these types of provisions as part of the company's certificate of incorporation or bylaws, as applicable.

How long are voting agreements enforceable?

This matter is governed by the corporation statutes of the state in which the company is incorporated. In Delaware, for example, such agreements are valid for only 10 years, but at any time within 2 years prior to expiration of a voting agreement, the stockholders may extend such agreement for as many additional periods, each not exceeding 10 years, as they desire. It is possible, however, through the use of devices such as irrevocable proxies, to lock in stockholder votes for a longer period than that permitted for voting agreements.

What kinds of additional financial commitments are usually found in stockholders' agreements?

Because in most cases, especially LBOs, the buyers do not intend to make further equity contributions to the corporation, the stockholders' agreement usually does not contain any provision for additional capital calls. However, where the corporation is in a volatile industry, or where the acquisition is highly leveraged, serious consideration should be given to requiring the stockholders to commit themselves to contributing additional equity to, making loans to, or extending personal guarantees on behalf of the corporation. In addition to the conditions under which such a commitment will be triggered, the extent to which any group of stockholders, such as the investor group, will assist the other stockholders in obtaining the funds to meet their commitment should also be incorporated in the stockholders' agreement.

What are some of the exit strategies typically embodied in a stockholders' agreement?

There are several provisions that give stockholders opportunities to liquidate their investment. Such provisions might give stockholders the right to:

1. Vote their shares in favor of any arm's-length merger or asset sale recommended by a certain group of stockholders (such as the investor stockholder group) or a certain percentage of all the stockholders.
2. Sell stock to any third-party person or entity, subject to the right of the corporation or the other stockholders to purchase the stock for the same terms offered by the third party (a "right of first refusal").
3. Sell stock to any other stockholder.
4. "Tag along" with other stockholders, that is, require a third-party offeror to purchase a pro rata portion of each stockholder's stock rather than purchase the same number of shares from the original offeree.
5. "Force along" the other stockholders, that is, sell their shares to a third-party offeror.
6. Sell (either directly or through heirs) stock to the corporation in the event of death, disability, or termination of employment.
7. Require the corporation to register its shares in a public offering.

From management's point of view, what are the important negotiation points of a "buy/sell" arrangement upon termination of employment?

The following are crucial:

1. *Mandatory versus optional requirement.* Management wants a mandatory obligation or, preferably, a put, particularly in the case of death or disability.
2. *Price.* Management wants fair market value, preferably at all times, but at least in the case of death, disability, retirement, or termination without cause.
3. *Determination of price.* Management at least wants an opportunity to get an independent appraisal at the time a buyback is triggered.

4. *Payment terms.* Management wants the payout period to be as short as possible, preferably in cash at the closing (particularly in case of death or disability).

5. *Security for payment.* Unless premium payments would cripple the company, where the buyout price is significant or where acquisition loan agreements have low caps on the amount of noninsured buy-backs the corporation can make, management wants the corporation to purchase life insurance and, if possible, disability insurance, to fund the buyback. In other cases involving deferred payments, management wants protections such as an opportunity to get the stock back free of transfer restrictions in the event of uncured payment defaults and prepayments out of the proceeds of public offerings.

As in the case with every contractual arrangement, each party must carefully consider the tax consequences associated with the various provisions under negotiation.

CONCLUDING COMMENTS

Every deal is unique, and every written agreement must reflect the one-of-a-kind transaction it describes. But dealmakers don't have to reinvent the wheel with every document. Instead, they can start by using standard models and restructure them according to their needs. In the process of restructuring, buyers and sellers will disagree on many points. In working out disagreements, each party needs to focus on the most important points and let the others go. By being true to themselves yet flexible, buyer and seller alike can meet with success—not only in closing the deal, but also in building a rewarding long-term future for all stakeholders.

ABOUT THE APPENDICES

Appendices 8A and 8B are written in typical "legalistic" language. That is, these documents are not written in the "plain language" recommended by a growing number of state legislatures in the United States (nearly half at this writing) and by the SEC. Plain language movements in other countries, such as Norway, have advanced similar standards. New SEC rules effective October 1, 1998, make "plain English" mandatory for certain parts of company prospectuses. The SEC defines plain English as writing with:

- Short sentences
- Definite, concrete, everyday language
- Active voice
- No legal or business jargon
- No multiple negatives
- Graphic presentation (including bullet lists) of complex material

As public companies begin conforming to these new rules, we expect that plain English style will become more common in all m/a/b documents, including letters of intent and acquisition agreements. As soon as we learn of an actual example, we will ask permission to reprint it in the next edition. In this current edition, however, we are staying with the deal-tested models, boilerplate and all (including use of the word *target*). Readers who have used plain language documents in their transactions are invited to contact the coauthor, Alexandra Reed Lajoux, at her e-mail address arlajoux@aol.com.

APPENDIX 8A

Sample Letter of Intent

STRICTLY PRIVATE AND CONFIDENTIAL
[Date]

Target Corporation
Corporate Office Park
New York, New York

To the Board of Directors:

This letter of intent sets forth the basic terms and conditions under which Acquisition, Inc. (the "Purchaser") will enter into a definitive merger agreement (the "Merger Agreement") with Target Corporation (the "Company") for the merger of the Purchaser with and into the Company (the "Merger"). It is anticipated that the consummation of the Merger will occur on or before _____, or on such other date to which the parties may agree.

Purchase Price

Pursuant to the Merger Agreement, upon consummation of the Merger, the selling stockholders of the Company will receive in exchange for each share of the Company's common stock and preferred stock (the "Stock") outstanding as of the date of this letter:

_____ Dollars ($_____) in cash; and

One share of preferred stock ("Preferred Stock") of the surviving corporation of the Merger with a liquidation preference in the amount of _____ Dollars ($_____) and containing the terms set forth on Exhibit A hereto.

Conditions to Closing

The consummation of the Merger shall be subject to the satisfaction of the following conditions:

(a) the parties shall have received all required approvals and consents from governmental authorities and agencies and third parties;

(b) the Purchaser and the Company shall have executed on or prior to _____, a definitive Merger Agreement containing mutually acceptable provisions relating to, among other things, representations, warranties, conditions and indemnification;

(c) the truth and accuracy of all representations and warranties and the satisfaction of all conditions;

(d) the consummation of the Merger on or prior to _____;

(e) Purchaser and certain members of management of the Company designated by Purchaser having entered into mutually satisfactory employment contracts simultaneously with the execution of the Merger Agreement;

(f) since _____, [date of last audited balance sheet] the business of the Company and its subsidiary shall have been conducted in the ordinary course, and there shall have been no material adverse change in the business, prospects, operations, earnings, assets or financial condition of the Company and its subsidiaries;

(g) Purchaser shall have obtained financing in an amount and upon terms satisfactory to it to consummate the Merger; [and]

(h) there shall have been no dividend, redemption or similar distribution, or any stock split, recapitalization or stock issuance of any kind, by the Company since _____, [date of last audited balance sheet] other than regularly scheduled dividends on the preferred stock.

General

After executing this letter and until _____, the Company agrees, and shall use its best efforts to cause its officers, directors, employees, agents and stockholders, not to solicit or encourage, directly or indirectly, in any manner any discussion with, or furnish or cause to be furnished any information to, any person other than Purchaser in connection with, or negotiate for or otherwise pursue, the sale of the Stock of the Company or the capital stock of its subsidiaries, all or substantially all of the assets of the Company or its subsidiaries or any portion or all of its business or that of its subsidiaries, or any business combination or merger of the Company or its subsidiaries with any other party. You will promptly inform Purchaser of any inquiries or proposals with respect to the foregoing. [In the event that the agreements in this paragraph are violated by the Company or its officers, directors, employees, agents or stockholders, and Purchaser does not consummate the Merger, then, in addition to other remedies available to Purchaser, Purchaser shall be entitled to receive from the Company all out-of-pocket expenses (including reasonable attorneys' fees and expenses relating to the financing), which Purchaser has incurred.]

Neither of the parties to this letter shall disclose to the public or to any third party the existence of this letter or the proposed sale described herein other than with the express prior written consent of the other party, except as may be required by law.

From and after the date hereof, upon reasonable prior notice and during normal business hours, the Company will grant to each of Purchaser and its agents, employees and designees full and complete access to the books and records and personnel of the Company and its subsidiaries. Except as may be required by law or court order, all information so obtained, not otherwise already public, will be held in confidence.

[Except as provided herein,] each party will be responsible for its own expenses in connection with all matters relating to the transaction herein proposed. If this proposed transaction shall not be consummated for any reason other than a violation of the agreement not to solicit other offers or negotiate with other purchasers, neither party will be responsible for any of the other's expenses.

Each party will indemnify, defend and hold harmless the other against the claims of any brokers or finders claiming by, through or under the indemnifying party.

Except for matters relating to (i) the confidentiality of this proposal and the business operations of the Company and its subsidiary, (ii) the agreement not to negotiate with others for or otherwise pursue the sale of the Company or its subsidiary, and (iii) the agreement that each party will bear its own expenses in connection herewith, this letter does not create a binding, legal obligation on any party but merely represents the present intentions of the parties.

In the event that for any reason the definitive Merger Agreement is not executed by _____, any party may discontinue negotiations and terminate this letter without liability to any other party.

Your signature below shall indicate your agreement with the foregoing letter of intent. We look forward to working with you on this transaction.

Very truly yours,

Acquisition, Inc.

By: _____
Its: Vice President—Strategic Planning

Agreed to and Accepted this _____ day of _____,

Target Corporation

By:_____
Its:_____

A P P E N D I X   8B

Typical Merger Agreement and Commentary

The following articles and sections typify the content of an acquisition agreement used in a merger.

RECITALS

ARTICLE I   THE BUSINESS COMBINATION

Section 1.1   The Merger
Section 1.2   Stockholders' Meeting
Section 1.3   Filing of Articles of Merger; Effective Time
Section 1.4   Effect of Merger
Section 1.5   Certificate of Incorporation and Bylaws
Section 1.6   Directors
Section 1.7   Officers
Section 1.8   Alternate Structure of Merger
Section 1.9   Taking of Necessary Action

ARTICLE II   CONVERSION AND EXCHANGE OF SHARES

Section 2.1   Conversion of Shares
Section 2.2   Dissenting Stockholders
Section 2.3   Stock Transfer Books
Section 2.4   Surrender and Exchange of Stock Certificates
Section 2.5   Determination and Payment of Merger Payment

ARTICLE III   CLOSING

ARTICLE IV   REPRESENTATIONS AND WARRANTIES OF SELLER AND TARGET

Section 4.1	Organization; Subsidiaries and Other Ownership Interests
Section 4.2	Authorization
Section 4.3	Capitalization of Target and Subsidiaries
Section 4.4	Title to Securities of Target and Subsidiaries
Section 4.5	Financial Statements and Projections
Section 4.6	Absence of Undisclosed Liabilities
Section 4.7	Accounts Receivable
Section 4.8	Most Recent Inventory
Section 4.9	Solvency
Section 4.10	Debt
Section 4.11	Fairness Opinion
Section 4.12	Product and Service Warranties and Reserves
Section 4.13	Reserve for Public Liability and Property Damage Claims
Section 4.14	Insurance
Section 4.15	Real Property Owned or Leased
Section 4.16	Fixed Assets; Leased Assets
Section 4.17	Title and Related Matters
Section 4.18	Intellectual Property
Section 4.19	Assets Necessary to the Business
Section 4.20	Additional Contracts
Section 4.21	Customers and Suppliers
Section 4.22	Competing Lines of Business
Section 4.23	Restrictive Covenants
Section 4.24	Books and Records
Section 4.25	Bank Accounts

Section 4.26   Employee Benefit Plans; Labor
                          Relations

Section 4.27   Litigation

Section 4.28   Compliance with Laws

Section 4.29   Non-Contravention; Consents

Section 4.30   Unlawful Payments

Section 4.31   Brokers and Finders

Section 4.32   Absence of Certain Changes
                          or Events

Section 4.33   Accuracy of Information Furnished

Section 4.34   Reports Filed with the Securities
                          and Exchange Commission

Section 4.35   Investment Purpose

Section 4.36   Dealership and Franchises

ARTICLE V   **REPRESENTATIONS AND
                          WARRANTIES OF THE BUYER**

Section 5.1   Organization

Section 5.2   Authorization

Section 5.3   Non-Contravention; Consents

Section 5.4   Litigation

Section 5.5   Brokers and Finders

Section 5.6   Business

Section 5.7   Accuracy of Information Furnished

ARTICLE VI   **COVENANTS OF SELLER AND
                          TARGET**

Section 6.1   Conduct of Business

Section 6.2   Pre-Closing Activities

Section 6.3   Proposals; Disclosure

Section 6.4   Additional Financial Statements

Section 6.5   Additional Summaries of Accounts Receivable

Section 6.6   Investigation by Buyer
Section 6.7   Notification
Section 6.8   Access to Records
Section 6.9   Stockholders' Meeting
Section 6.10   Dissenting Stockholders; Notice

ARTICLE VII   COVENANTS OF THE BUYER

**ARTICLE VIII COVENANTS OF BUYER, SELLER
               AND TARGET**
Section 8.1   Governmental Filings
Section 8.2   Publicity

**ARTICLE IX   CONDITIONS TO OBLIGATIONS
               OF BUYER**

Section 9.1   Compliance with Agreement
Section 9.2   Representations and Warranties
                            True as of Closing Date
Section 9.3   Third Party Orders and Consents
Section 9.4   Corporate Action
Section 9.5   Opinion of the Seller's and Target's Counsel
Section 9.6   No Material Adverse Change
Section 9.7   Litigation
Section 9.8   Financing
Section 9.9   Title Insurance
Section 9.10   Dissenting Stockholders

**ARTICLE X   CONDITIONS TO OBLIGATIONS OF
               SELLER AND TARGET**

Section 10.1   Compliance with Agreement

Section 10.2   Representations and Warranties True
                          as of Closing Date
Section 10.3   Third Party Orders and Consents
Section 10.4   Corporate Action
Section 10.5   Opinion of the Buyer's Counsel
Section 10.6   Litigation

ARTICLE XI   TAX MATTERS

Section 11.1   Representations, Warranties
                          and Covenants
Section 11.2   Payment of Tax Liabilities
Section 11.3   Indemnification
Section 11.4   Post-Closing Obligations
Section 11.5   Further Assurances and
                          Assistance
Section 11.6   Audit Matters
Section 11.7   Certain Tax Claims for Which
                          Seller May Be Liable

**ARTICLE XII SURVIVAL OF REPRESENTATIONS;
               INDEMNIFICATION**

Section 12.1   Indemnification by Seller
Section 12.2   Indemnification by the
                          Surviving Corporation
Section 12.3   Materiality
Section 12.4   Survival of Indemnification
Section 12.5   Limitation on Claims
                          and Damages
Section 12.6   Claims by Third Parties
Section 12.7   Indemnity for Taxes of
                          Indemnified Party
Section 12.8   Right of Offset

ARTICLE XIII NON-COMPETE

ARTICLE XIV TERMINATION

Section 14.1   Termination for Failure to Close on Time
Section 14.2   Default; Remedies
Section 14.3   Specific Performance

ARTICLE XV MISCELLANEOUS

Section 15.1   Definitions
Section 15.2   Payment of Expenses
Section 15.3   Modifications or Waivers to
                the Agreement
Section 15.4   Assignment
Section 15.5   Burden and Benefit
Section 15.6   Brokers
Section 15.7   Entire Agreement
Section 15.8   Governing Law
Section 15.9   Notices
Section 15.10   Counterparts
Section 15.11   Rights Cumulative
Section 15.12   Severability of Provisions
Section 15.13   Further Assurance
Section 15.14   Confidential Information
Section 15.15   Writings and Disclosures

ARTICLE I: THE BUSINESS COMBINATION

The following is a discussion of the material items that are usually included in Article I of a merger agreement (the "Agreement"). The section headings listed below provide the topics frequently covered in this article.

Section 1.1   The Merger

Section 1.2   Stockholders' Meeting

Section 1.3   Filing of Articles of Merger; Effective Time

Section 1.4   Effect of Merger

Section 1.5   Certificate of Incorporation and Bylaws

Section 1.6   Directors

Section 1.7   Officers

Section 1.8   Alternate Structure of Merger

Section 1.9   Taking of Necessary Action

Article I of the Agreement typically (a) describes how the merger will be accomplished (the "merger"), (b) identifies which corporation's legal existence will cease and which corporation will be the "surviving corporation" in the merger, and (c) identifies the state laws that will govern the surviving corporation's legal existence. This section also contains the agreement of the parties to meet the corporate legal requirements of the states of incorporation of the respective parties in order to obtain approval of the Merger.

The disappearing corporation frequently commits itself to call a special meeting of stockholders and to use its best efforts to obtain stockholder approval of the merger. These undertakings tend to be more elaborate where the disappearing corporation is a publicly held corporation and therefore must provide a proxy statement or information statement to its stockholders.

Once the stockholders of the disappearing corporation have approved the merger and the additional corporate actions and the conditions contained in Articles IX and X of the Agreement are satisfied, the Agreement provides that the articles of merger will be filed in the respective offices of the secretary of state (or comparable authority) of the states in which each corporation is incorporated. The merger will become effective upon such filing. The effect of the merger is described by reference to a section of the business corporation laws governing the corporate existence of each corporation involved in the transaction. Some states require the surviving corporation to appoint an agent for service of process if the surviving corporation will no longer be present or resident within the state following consummation of the merger. This requirement is intended to enable creditors in the state to continue to have recourse against the disappearing corporation. The merger will have no effect on the rights of creditors or on any liens on the property of either company; liens and debts of the disappearing corporation will become the obligations of the surviving corporation.

The parties stipulate in this article which corporation's articles and bylaws will apply to the surviving corporation and whether any changes or amendments to these documents will be made upon the consummation of the merger. The officers and directors of the surviving corporation may also be identified.

In order to preserve structural flexibility, the buyer can suggest the inclusion of language that gives the buyer the right to restructure the transaction for tax, financial, or other reasons. Because a change in the structure of the transaction could have a significant adverse impact on the seller if, for example, the direction of the merger were to be changed from downstream to upstream, the buyer and seller must reach a resolution that satisfies each of their concerns.

ARTICLE II: CONVERSION AND EXCHANGE OF SHARES

The following discussion pertains to the mechanics of the conversion of shares of the merging corporations and the transfer of the purchase price. The section headings listed below provide the topics generally covered in this article.

Section 2.1	Conversion of Shares
Section 2.2	Dissenting Stockholders
Section 2.3	Stock Transfer Books
Section 2.4	Surrender and Exchange of Stock Certificates
Section 2.5	Determination and Payment of Merger Payment

This article describes the manner in which shares in each of the merging corporations will be converted or, in the case of the surviving corporation, the number of shares that remain outstanding upon consummation of the merger. It also describes the nature of the cash or securities consideration to be received by each holder of stock of the nonsurviving corporation.

Where the disappearing corporation has a diverse group of stockholders, the buyer may wish to consider the potential effects of stockholders' exercise of their dissenters' or appraisal rights under the laws of a particular jurisdiction. In transactions where exercise of dissenters' rights may occur, the buyer should include a provision that describes the effect of the merger on such stockholders' rights and imposes an obligation upon the seller and target to give the buyer notice of any communications by stockholders with respect to their dissenters' or appraisal rights. The notice obligation is frequently included in the covenant section. The buyer should also attempt to procure for itself the opportunity to direct all negotiations and proceedings concerning these rights.

Also included in this article is the method of surrender and exchange of stock certificates that enables the stockholders of the disappearing corporation to receive the merger payment. For a closely held target this may simply involve the seller's surrender of the certificates to the buyer and the buyer's payment to the seller of the agreed-upon merger consideration. However, in the case of a public target or where the target has a significant number of stockholders, the method for surrender of certificates is somewhat more complicated. The buyer and target will agree that the stock transfer books of the target will be closed as of a particular time, usually the time of the filing of the certificate of merger with the secretary of state, and that stockholders must surrender their certificates to a paying agent that will be responsible for the disbursement of the merger payment. Typically, the buyer will agree that simultaneously with the consummation of the merger it will transfer the entire amount of the merger consideration to an account that will be administered by a paying agent. Funds in the account are then disbursed to the target's stockholders upon the surrender of their stock certificates. See Chapter 5 for a discussion concerning the timing of the payment of the merger consideration and the filing of the certificate of merger.

In the event that the target has outstanding preferred stock, options, warrants, or securities convertible into common stock, the buyer should make provision in this article for the effect that the merger will have on such securities. The buyer's preeminent concern in dealing with these securities is to extinguish through the merger, to the extent possible, any right that a third party may have to receive common stock of the surviving corporation and not be subject to any dilution as a result of the exercise or conversion of any such securities. This assures the buyer that it will hold 100 percent of the common stock of the surviving corporation immediately after the merger. In certain cases the terms of such securities require the surviving corporation to honor the holder's right to receive common stock; other securities merely fail to provide for their termination in the event of a merger. The buyer should always attempt to include, as a condition to the buyer's obligation to close the transaction, the agreement of all holders of such securities to surrender their securities for cancellation at the closing.

ARTICLE III: CLOSING

This article provides the date, time, and place for the closing of the transaction (the "Closing"). Typically, the parties agree to close the transaction at the offices of the legal counsel for the buyer. Closings generally commence early in the morning so that wire transfers of funds can be accomplished prior to the afternoon close of the federal wire. The parties further agree that at the closing the parties will deliver all the documents and instruments required to be delivered by the acquisition agreement. (The date that the certificate of merger is filed with the appropriate officials governing the merger is referred to as the "Closing Date.") For a more detailed discussion of the closing procedures, see Chapter 9.

ARTICLE IV: REPRESENTATIONS AND WARRANTIES OF SELLER AND TARGET

The representations and warranties included in this article are extremely comprehensive and may, in some instances, be inappropriate in light of the size of the transaction or the nature of the target's business.

In an acquisition of a publicly traded target, it would not be customary to include all these representations and warranties. As we previously mentioned, the reason for fewer representations and warranties in a public context is that there is usually no one to sue after closing for a misrepresentation or breach of warranty. It is unrealistic for the buyer to expect to recover from thousands of public stockholders. Accordingly, some of the representations and warranties, which are of less importance to the buyer or not directly related to the buyer's ability to terminate the acquisition agreement because of certain adverse changes in the target, are frequently omitted. For example, the following seller/target representations and warranties are typically omitted in the acquisition of a publicly traded target:

Section 4.4   Title to Securities of Target and Subsidiaries

Section 4.9   Solvency

Section 4.10   Debt

Section 4.12   Product and Service Warranties and Reserves

Section 4.13   Reserve for Public Liability and Property Damage Claims

Section 4.18   Intellectual Property

Section 4.19   Assets Necessary to the Business

Section 4.21   Customers and Suppliers

Section 4.22   Competing Lines of Business

Section 4.23   Restrictive Covenants

Section 4.24   Books and Records

Section 4.25   Bank Accounts

Section 4.35   Investment Purpose

Section 4.36   Dealership and Franchises

The following language is typical of the seller/target representations and warranties sections in a merger agreement.

The Seller and the Target represent and warrant to Buyer as follows:

Section 4.1. Organization; Subsidiaries and Other Ownership Interests. The Target and the Seller are each corporations duly organized, validly existing and in good standing under the laws of the jurisdiction of their incorporation. Section 4.1 of the disclosure statement of even date herewith delivered to Buyer by Seller (the "Disclosure Statement") sets forth the name of each Person (as defined in Article XII) in which the Target or any other Subsidiary (on a combined basis) owns or has the right to acquire, directly or indirectly, an equity interest or investment of ten percent (10) or more of the equity capital thereof or having a book value of more than _____ Dollars ($_____) (a "Subsidiary"). Each Subsidiary is duly organized, validly existing and in good standing under the laws of its jurisdiction of incorporation or organization. Each of the Target and the Subsidiaries has the corporate or other necessary power and authority to own and lease its properties and assets and to carry on its business as now being conducted and is duly qualified or licensed to do business as a foreign corporation or other entity and is in good standing in each jurisdiction in which the properties owned or leased by it or the nature of the business conducted by it makes such qualification or licensure necessary except where the failure to be so qualified or licensed and in good standing would not have a Material Adverse Effect. For purposes of this Agreement, the term Material Adverse Effect shall refer to any event which would have a material adverse effect on the financial condition, business, earnings, assets, prospects or condition of the Target and its Subsidiaries taken as a whole. Section 4.1 of the Disclosure Statement sets forth the name of each jurisdiction in which the Target and each Subsidiary are incorporated and is qualified to do business. The Target has delivered to the Buyer true and correct copies of its Certificate of Incorporation and Bylaws and true and correct copies of the certificate of incorporation or comparable charter documents and bylaws of each of the Subsidiaries. Except as set forth in Section 4.1 of the Disclosure Statement, neither the Target nor any Subsidiary owns any equity investment or other interest in any Person other than the equity capital of the Subsidiaries which are owned by the Target or a Subsidiary.

It is customary in acquisition agreements to have the seller and target warrant that the seller, the target, and its subsidiaries are duly organized, and that each is qualified to do business in every jurisdiction in which each is required to qualify. If the seller or the target is not duly organized, the acquisition agreement may not be binding against it since it will not have the authority to execute the document in a corporate capacity. The utility of this representation is often debated in a theoretical context but is rarely heavily negotiated. Underlying the debate is the following question: If the agreement is not binding on the seller or the target, whom do you sue and for what? The answer is not carved in stone; the buyer could probably sue the person who signed the document in an individual capacity for misrepresentation, although a sizable recovery is unlikely. More importantly, the buyer would certainly have the right to walk from the deal, and that right is the primary reason the buyer should require this representation.

It is also prudent for the buyer to know that the subsidiaries are duly organized and qualified to do business in order to be assured of the subsidiaries' ability to conduct business or maintain a suit in a particular jurisdiction.

The definition of subsidiaries in this provision is extremely broad as it includes entities in which the target may only have a small equity interest. Depending upon the particular situation, the seller may want to increase the 10 percent ownership requirement in order to avoid making representations and warranties about entities with which it may not be overly familiar. In addition, the seller may wish to specifically exclude from this definition entities that are not material to the target.

Section 4.2. Authorization. The execution, delivery and performance of this Agreement and any instruments or agreements contemplated herein to be executed, delivered and performed by Target or Seller (including without limitation [list important agreements to be executed on or before the Closing]) (the Related Instruments), and the consummation of the transactions contemplated hereby and thereby, have been duly adopted and approved by the Board of Directors and the Stockholders of the Target and the Board of Directors of the Seller, as the case may be. The Target and the Seller have all requisite power and authority to execute, deliver and perform this Agreement and the Related Instruments, as applicable, and to consummate the transactions contemplated hereby and in the Related Instruments. This Agreement has been and as of the Closing Date, and each of the Related Instruments will be, duly and validly authorized, executed and delivered on behalf of the Seller and the Target. This Agreement is and the Related Instruments will be as of the Closing Date, the valid and binding obligation of the Target and Seller, as applicable, enforceable against the Target or Seller, as the case may be, in accordance with their respective terms.

It is customary for the seller and target to represent to the buyer that the Agreement is properly authorized and enforceable. Certainly, the buyer is entitled to know that the seller and target have taken all the steps that are necessary to authorize the agreement and any documents that are material to the consummation of the transaction (referred to above as the "Related Instruments") in order to ensure that such documents are binding. The related instruments might include a noncompete agreement, a separate purchase agreement relating to certain other assets, and other documents containing agreements between the parties that are special to the transaction and therefore are not specifically covered by a stock purchase, asset purchase, or merger agreement.

The most important aspect of this representation relates to enforceability of the agreement and related instruments, as this will directly affect the buyer's rights under these documents.

A similar issue arises here as was discussed in connection with Section 4.1. What damages would be recoverable by the buyer if the seller breached this representation? If the breach arises because the signatory to the document on behalf of the seller or the target did not have authority to bind that party, the buyer may have a cause of action against the signatory (if the signatory misrepresented his or her authority) or against the party on whose behalf the signatory executed the document (if such party knew of the misrepresentation, or if the acts of such party created the appearance of authority on the part of the signatory). In addition, the buyer faced with a seller or target who refuses to close the deal because the agreement was not signed by an authorized agent may be able to force the seller or target to close the transaction if its acts created an appearance of authority, or if it ratified the agreement after it was signed. Partial performance of the terms of the deal—applying for regulatory approval, permitting continued due diligence investigation, or complying with representations requiring the consent of the buyer to certain actions by the target, for example—may provide convincing evidence of such ratification. In any event, the buyer would definitely have the right to refuse to close the transaction.

In a representation by the seller that an agreement is enforceable, the seller may request the inclusion of an exception for certain future events that are beyond its control. For example, a court applying bankruptcy laws or equitable principles may not honor the express terms of the documents if such terms are not in accordance with the principles of bankruptcy or equity. Although the seller may have a basis for arguing for the inclusion of this exception, it seems unfair for the buyer to bear this risk. If the documents prove to be unenforceable in some respect against the seller, the buyer should be able, at least, to attempt to recover damages for this misrepresentation, rather than be forced to waive rights in the case of bankruptcy.

Section 4.3. Capitalization of Target and Subsidiaries.

(i) The authorized, issued and outstanding shares of the Target's capital stock consist of _____ shares of common stock, $ _____ par value per share, of which _____ shares are issued and outstanding [and any other shares, such as preferred stock] (the "Company Capital Stock"). The issued and outstanding shares of the Company Capital Stock are duly authorized, validly issued and fully paid and nonassessable and were not issued in violation of the preemptive rights of any person or of any agreement, law or regulation by which the issuer of such shares at the time of issuance was bound. The authorized, issued and outstanding equity capital of each Subsidiary is listed in Section 4.3(i) of the Disclosure Statement. The outstanding shares of, and the outstanding units of equity capital of, the Subsidiaries have been duly authorized, validly issued and are fully paid and non-assessable. Neither the Target nor any Subsidiary has issued any securities, or taken any action or omitted to take any action, giving rise to claims for violation of federal or state securities laws or the securities laws of any other jurisdiction.

(ii) Except as set forth in Section 4.3(ii) of the Disclosure Statement, at the date hereof there is no option, warrant, call, convertible security, arrangement, agreement or commitment of any character, whether oral or written, relating to any security of, or phantom security interest in, the Target or any Subsidiary, and there are no voting trusts or other agreements or understandings with respect to the voting of the capital stock of the Target or the equity capital of any Subsidiary.

A representation that requires that a seller set forth the capitalization of the target and its subsidiaries is rarely negotiated. Rather, discussions between the buyer and seller generally involve the factual circumstances surrounding the matter being represented. In order for a buyer to understand the effect of its purchase of the capital stock of the target (including the capital stock of the subsidiaries), it must be aware of the capital structure of the target and its subsidiaries.

Section 4.4. Title to Securities of Target and Subsidiaries.

(i) Except as set forth in Section 4.4(i) of the Disclosure Statement, the Seller has good and valid title to all of the issued and outstanding shares of the Company Capital Stock free and clear of all claims, liens, mortgages, charges, security interests, encumbrances and other restrictions or limitations of any kind whatsoever (other than pursuant to this Agreement). The Seller is not party to, or bound by, any other agreement, instrument or understanding restricting the transfer of such shares.

(ii) Except as set forth in Section 4.4(ii) of the Disclosure Statement and other than pursuant to this Agreement, the issued and outstanding units of equity capital of each of the Subsidiaries are owned by the Persons listed as owner on Section 4.4(ii) of the Disclosure Statement, in each case free of preemptive rights and free and clear of all claims, liens, mortgages, charges, security interests, encumbrances and other restrictions or limitations of any kind whatsoever.

Generally, a buyer entering into an acquisition agreement is acquiring the entire company. Therefore, it is essential that the buyer know that it is purchasing all the outstanding capital securities of the target, and that no one can challenge its ownership thereof after closing.

Section 4.5. Financial Statements and Projections.

(i) Seller has furnished to Buyer true and complete copies of the audited consolidated financial statements (including balance sheets, statements of income, statements of changes in stockholder's equity and statements of changes in financial position) of the Target and its Subsidiaries as of and for the years ended [fill in fiscal year-end for last five years] accompanied by the related opinions of the Target's official independent auditors as of such dates and for such periods (collectively, the "Financial Statements"). The Financial Statements, together with the notes thereto, fairly present the consolidated financial position of the Target and its Subsidiaries at the dates of, and the combined results of the operations and the changes in stockholders' equity and financial position for each of the Target and its Subsidiaries for the periods covered by, such Financial Statements in accordance with generally accepted accounting principles ("GAAP") consistently applied with prior periods except as indicated in the accompanying opinion of the official independent auditors. Seller has furnished to Buyer true and complete copies of the unaudited consolidated and consolidating balance sheets of the Target and its Subsidiaries as at [fill in the date of the most recent quarterly or fiscal period then ended] (the "Most Recent Balance Sheet") and the related consolidated and consolidating statements of income, statements of changes in stockholders' equity and statements of changes in financial position of the Target and its Subsidiaries as of and for the period then ended (collectively, the "Unaudited Financial Statements"). The Unaudited Financial Statements fairly present the financial position of the Target and its Subsidiaries at the date of, and the consolidated results of the operations and the changes in stockholders' equity and financial position for the Target and of its Subsidiaries for the period then ended. Such Unaudited Financial Statements have been prepared in accordance with GAAP consistently applied with prior periods, except that the Unaudited Financial Statements do not contain any or all of the footnotes required by GAAP, are condensed and are subject to year-end adjustments consistent with prior practice.

(ii) Seller has delivered to Buyer true and correct copies of the projected balance sheets of the Target for the fiscal years ending [fill in appropriate information], and the related statements of projected earnings and projected cash flow for the periods then ended (the "Projected Financial Statements"). The Projected Financial Statements are reasonable and mathematically accurate, and the assumptions underlying such projections provide a reasonable basis for such projections. The factual data used to prepare the Projected Financial Statements are true and correct in all material respects.

Generally, the most important representation that a buyer must require of the seller is that the consolidated financial statements of the target fairly present the financial condition of the target in accordance with GAAP. Almost every other representation in an acquisition agreement is in some way related to the financial statements of the target. For example, representations relating to receivables, inventory, real property, and tangible and intangible assets and liabilities concern items that are included on the balance sheet of the target to the extent required by GAAP. Accordingly, although the financial statement representations are somewhat standard in their format, they are vital to the buyer because the buyer has based its entire investment decision on either the overall financial condition of the target or certain financial characteristics of the target such as operating performance or net assets. As a result, the financial statements are usually the basis for fixing the purchase price of the target. Although situations exist where financial statements are less vital to the buyer's investment decision (for example, in the purchase of a start-up company), such statements are usually of critical importance.

The financial statement representation is usually not the subject of intense negotiation. The most frequently negotiated aspects of this representation relate to the kind of financial statements to be included in this representation and the periods to be covered by such financial statements. For example, will the financial statements that are the subject of the representation include balance sheets, operating statements, statements of changes in financial position, and stockholders' equity? Will the seller warrant the accuracy of historical financial statements covering a five-year period? Another area of discussion may relate to specific problems in preparing the financial statements that require the buyer to grant certain exceptions from GAAP. This problem usually arises when the buyer is already aware of the target's accounting problems. However, exceptions from GAAP can have the effect of diminishing the reliability of the financial statements. The determination whether the buyer is entitled to certain financial statements or should accept statements not prepared in accordance with GAAP depends on what information about the target was provided to the buyer prior to striking a deal with the seller, and what the buyer honestly relied on when it made its decision to purchase the target.

In many circumstances, the seller has provided the buyer with projected financial statements of the target. In such cases, if the buyer has relied on them, it is prudent for the buyer to have the seller warrant the reasonableness of the assumptions used in the preparation of the projected financial statements and the accuracy of the financial data underlying such projections. This representation is frequently negotiated and will certainly be more difficult to obtain from the seller than representations regarding the historical financial statements of the target. The reason for this is that projections, no matter how reasonable the assumptions that underlie them, are always the subject of hindsight. For example, a buyer might claim a breach of this representation if, one year after closing, the target fails to meet its projections. The buyer would argue that the projections were obviously based upon unreasonable assumptions given the post-closing performance of the target. The decision whether or not this representation should be pursued is, like decisions related to historical financials, largely dependent on the degree of the buyer's reliance on these projections in its decision to buy the target. If the buyer is heavily relying on the projections, which may very well be the case if the target is a company that does not have a long operating history, then this representation should be vigorously pursued. In addition, this representation will commonly be found in loan agreements, and lenders will be able to gain some additional comfort from the buyer's right of action back to the seller on this representation.

> ***Section 4.6. Absence of Undisclosed Liabilities.*** As of the date hereof and as of the Closing Date, except as and to the extent reflected, reserved against or otherwise disclosed on the Most Recent Balance Sheet or the notes thereto, or set forth in Section 4.6 of the Disclosure Statement, or otherwise properly disclosed in any other Section of the Disclosure Statement and except for those incurred in the ordinary course of business, the Target and its Subsidiaries did not have and do not have, any indebtedness or liability of any nature, whether accrued, absolute, contingent or otherwise, whether due or to become due, which is in excess of _____ Dollars ($_____).

The absence of undisclosed liabilities is by and large a representation that serves as a catch-all for any and all liabilities of the target and its subsidiaries that were not reflected on the most recent balance sheet of the target or the notes thereto, or were not otherwise disclosed pursuant to any of the other representations in the acquisition agreement. A smart seller should never agree to this representation without some resistance. To begin with, why should the seller (after having made numerous representations about the target) now be asked to warrant something the buyer may have failed to ask the seller to disclose? The answer is one that relates to a shifting of risk. Who should bear the risk of the buyer's omission? There is no clear answer, except that if the seller has agreed to the concept that it will generally warrant that the most recent balance sheet includes all liabilities of any kind or nature, then this representation does little more than provide additional comfort for the buyer.

If the seller had not made that general warranty, the buyer should be aware that many liabilities need not be disclosed on a balance sheet of the target prepared in accordance with GAAP. For example, when the amount of a liability cannot be determined because of its nature, such as a lawsuit the outcome of which is uncertain, GAAP would not require its disclosure. (See Financial Accounting Standards Board Statement No. 5.) If the target is subject to off-balance-sheet liabilities, this representation provides the buyer with much more than an additional assurance.

Another aspect of this representation that may be difficult to negotiate with the seller is the period of time to be covered by the representation. A buyer often wants protection against material liabilities beyond the date of the most recent balance sheet. This may be a problem for the seller since it has no financial statements to rely on for that period. The seller may be able to supply a balance sheet that is current as of the closing. If this is not possible, and if the buyer fails to persuade the seller to warrant the period after the date of the most recent balance sheet, the buyer must rely on the covenants (operation of the business in the ordinary course; see Section 6.1 below) or the conditions (material adverse change; see Section 9.6 below) as its way of addressing undisclosed liabilities.

In light of the nature of this representation it would be overreaching not to incorporate an exclusion for minimal undisclosed liabilities. Accordingly, the form of representation set forth above contains a blank amount for such an exclusion. The dollar amount of this exclusion is negotiable and usually depends upon the size of the target and its subsidiaries. For example, in an acquisition of an extremely large company, the buyer would find it extremely difficult to justify an exclusion of only $1,000 for undisclosed liabilities.

> *Section 4.7. Accounts Receivable.* Seller has delivered, or shall deliver at Closing, to Buyer a list of all accounts receivable of the Target and its Subsidiaries as at [fill in appropriate date] (the "Accounts Receivable") which list is true, correct and complete in all material respects and sets forth the aging of such Accounts Receivable. All Accounts Receivable of the Target and its Subsidiaries represent sales actually made or services actually performed in the ordinary and usual course of their business consistent with past practice. Since the date of the Most Recent Balance Sheet, (A) no event has occurred that would, under the practices of the Target or the Subsidiary in effect when the Most Recent Balance Sheet was prepared, require a material increase in the ratio of (I) the reserve for uncollectible accounts receivable to (II) the accounts receivable of the Target or the Subsidiary, and (B) there has been no material adverse change in the composition of such Accounts Receivable in terms of aging. There is no contest, claim or right of set-off contained in any written agreement with any account debtor relating to the amount or validity of any Account Receivable, or any other account receivable created after the date of the Most Recent Balance Sheet, other than accounts receivable which do not exceed, in the aggregate, the reserve for uncollected accounts. At the date of the Most Recent Balance Sheet, as of the date hereof and as of the Effective Time of the Merger, all accounts receivable of the Target and the Subsidiary, if any, were, are and will be, respectively, unless previously collected, valid and collectible and there is no contest, claim or right of set-off contained in any written agreement with any maker of an account receivable relating to the amount or validity of such account or any note evidencing the same.

In instances where the most recent balance sheet reflects a significant amount of receivables, the buyer should require this representation in order to get specific protection that the receivables of the target and its subsidiaries are collectible. A representation with respect to the receivables of the target is sometimes unnecessary depending upon the type of company that is being acquired. For example, if the company that is being acquired entered into a factoring arrangement with respect to all its receivables, then this representation may be altogether unnecessary or to a great degree simplified. Conversely, the buyer purchasing assets may, in circumstances where the collectibility of the accounts is in doubt, require the seller to guarantee the buyer's ability to collect the receivables.

Section 4.8. Most Recent Inventory. The inventories of the Target and the Subsidiaries on a consolidated basis as reflected on the Most Recent Balance Sheet consist only of items in good condition and salable or usable in the ordinary course of business, except to the extent of the inventory reserve included on the Most Recent Balance Sheet, which reserve is adequate for such purpose. Such inventories are valued on the Most Recent Balance Sheet at the lower of cost or market in accordance with GAAP.

In the event that the company to be acquired is engaged in manufacturing or is otherwise involved in the distribution of goods whether retail or wholesale, it is extremely important for the buyer to have the seller make a specific representation with respect to the inventory of the target and its subsidiaries. A buyer needs to understand the relationship between the value of the inventory reflected on the most recent balance sheet and the condition of the inventory. Items that are or may become obsolete should be reserved against on the most recent balance sheet. In addition, it is important for the buyer to know whether the valuation of inventory on the financial statements reflects its actual value. Accordingly, the seller's representation that inventories are valued at the lower of cost or market in accordance with GAAP will assure the buyer that the inventories are valued in the most conservative fashion. In some cases, the buyer may include a representation that a particular dollar amount is the minimum value of the target's inventories. That type of representation is more common in an asset purchase.

Section 4.9. Solvency. The Seller and each of the Target and its Subsidiaries is on the date hereof, and immediately prior to the Closing Date will be, Solvent. "Solvent" shall mean, in respect of an entity, that (i) the fair value of its property is in excess of the total amount of its debts and (ii) it is able to pay its debts as they mature.

Aside from the obvious pricing implications of acquiring an insolvent corporation, one of the primary purposes of obtaining a solvency representation from a seller regarding the target and its subsidiaries is that lenders providing acquisition debt often require such a representation from the buyer. Especially in leveraged buyouts, one of the principal concerns of lenders is the solvency of the leveraged company because transfers (for example, security interests granted to lenders) from insolvent companies are voidable as fraudulent conveyances. Although the leveraged surviving corporation may certainly be in a more precarious position than the target, this representation provides the initial base from which the buyer will attempt to satisfy its lenders on the solvency issue.

The solvency representation regarding the seller is intended to protect the buyer against the risk of acquiring the target and its subsidiaries in a transaction that could be characterized as a fraudulent conveyance by the seller. A buyer's decision to include the seller in the solvency representation must be based upon the financial condition of the seller, the extent to which the target and its subsidiaries constitute a substantial portion of the seller's assets, and the seller's ability to pay its debts as they mature after the sale of the target and its subsidiaries.

> *Section 4.10. Debt.* Set forth in Section 4.10 of the Disclosure Statement is a list of all agreements for incurring of indebtedness for borrowed money and all agreements relating to industrial development bonds to which the Target is a party or grantor, which list is true and correct in all material respects. Except as set forth in Section 4.10 of the Disclosure Statement, none of the obligations pursuant to such agreements are subject to acceleration by reason of the consummation of the transactions contemplated hereby, nor would the execution of this Agreement or the consummation of the transactions contemplated hereby result in any default under such agreements.

This representation serves to break down the debt components of the most recent balance sheet that relate to debt for money borrowed. It also requires the seller to identify debt items that may be accelerated by reason of the consummation of the transactions contemplated by the agreement. Because this representation has an information-gathering purpose, it is not usually negotiable.

> *Section 4.11. Fairness Opinion.* The Target has received an opinion of [name of independent and nationally recognized investment banker], dated the date hereof, addressed to the Target and has delivered a copy of such opinion to Buyer to the effect that, as of the date of the Agreement, the consideration per share to be received by the holders of the Target's Common Stock in the Merger is fair to the holders of the Target's Common Stock from a financial point of view. The Target believes that it is justified in relying upon such opinion.

The buyer should attempt to include this representation where the target has a significant number of stockholders or is a publicly traded company. The buyer should require the target to obtain a fairness opinion because, after consummation of the merger, the buyer will succeed to the target's liabilities, including liabilities that may result from stockholder suits against the target or its officers and directors alleging that the merger price was inadequate. Liabilities could result where stockholders have exercised dissenter's or appraisal rights and sued the target directly or have instituted a derivative suit against officers or directors who are indemnified by the target.

The last sentence of the representation regarding reliance is intended to elicit from the target any facts that might undermine the validity of the opinion, such as facts not disclosed to the investment bankers or knowledge of conflicts of interest that might tend to bias the opinion. Several factors make this reliance representation important. First, investment bankers typically require indemnification in connection with rendering fairness opinions, and the buyer will succeed to any liability of the target to its investment bankers after the merger. Second, although a target might argue that the buyer is in a position to evaluate the reasonableness of the opinion based on the representations of the target in the Agreement and on its own financial investigation of the target, the buyer is not privy to all the circumstances involving the preparation and delivery of the fairness opinion. Consequently, the buyer should not be reticent about making inquiries into the fairness opinion process and the manner in which the target has attempted to satisfy itself that the opinion rendered is reasonable.

> *Section 4.12. Product and Service Warranties and Reserves.* Except as disclosed in Section 4.12 of the Disclosure Statement, the amount of any and all product warranty claims relating to sales occurring on or prior to the Most Recent Balance Sheet Date shall not exceed the amount of the product warranty reserve included on the Most Recent Balance Sheet which reserve was prepared in accordance with GAAP consistently applied and which the Target believes is adequate in light of any and all circumstances relating to its warranties of which it was aware and the amounts actually paid by it for product warranty claims. The only express warranties, written or oral, including without limitation, [insert warranty], with respect to the products or services sold by the Target and its Subsidiaries are as set forth in Section 4.12 of the Disclosure Statement.

One area that may expose a buyer to tremendous liability is product and service warranties made by the target or any subsidiary. A seller is required under GAAP to have "adequate" reserves on its balance sheet to cover such liabilities, but this standard is a very subjective one. Accordingly, a prudent buyer should have the seller specifically warrant the accuracy of this element of the most recent balance sheet. In addition, the buyer should be apprised of any and all of the warranties made and reserves held by the target so that the buyer can make its own determination of the adequacy of the target's reserves. In certain situations, a buyer may require specific representations setting forth the annual amount paid in satisfaction of claims under a particular product warranty. Gambling on the law of averages, the buyer may derive some degree of comfort.

> *Section 4.13. Reserve for Public Liability and Property Damage Claims.* The amount of the public liability, property damage and personal injury reserve included on the Most Recent Balance Sheet was prepared in accordance with GAAP consistently applied and the Target reasonably believes such reserve is adequate.

A buyer may be concerned about this type of liability if it is foreseeable that the target or a subsidiary could have exposure above and beyond the limits of its insurance policies. Similar to the product warranty reserve discussed in Section 4.12 above, the adequacy of this reserve is a subjective judgment.

> *Section 4.14. Insurance.* Set forth in Section 4.14 of the Disclosure Statement is a complete and correct schedule of all currently effective insurance policies or binders of insurance or programs of self-insurance which relate to the Target and its Subsidiaries, which insurance is with financially sound and reputable insurance companies, against such casualties, risks and contingencies, and in such types and amounts, as are consistent with customary practices and standards of companies engaged in businesses similar to the Target and its Subsidiaries. The coverage under each such policy and binder is in full force and effect, and no notice of cancellation or nonrenewal with respect to, or disallowance of any claim under, or material increase of premium for, any such policy or binder has been received by the Target or its Subsidiaries, nor to the Seller. Neither the Target, the Seller nor the Subsidiaries has knowledge of any facts or the occurrence of any event which (i) reasonably might form the basis of any claim against the Target or the Subsidiaries relating to the conduct or operations of the business of the Target or the Subsidiaries or any of the assets or properties covered by any of the policies or binders set forth in Section

4.14 of the Disclosure Statement and which will materially increase the insurance premiums payable under any such policy or binder, or (ii) otherwise will materially increase the insurance premiums payable under such policy or binder.

A representation with respect to the insurance policies of the target is important to the buyer in order to safeguard the assets it is buying against a variety of damage claims. Since the buyer may be unaware of what type of insurance should be carried by the target, the seller should warrant that the target has all the insurance that is customary for the business of the target and its subsidiaries. The seller will not usually quarrel about this part of the representation; what troubles the seller most is the buyer's desire for assurances that the premiums for such insurance will not increase dramatically because of an event or claim that the seller may be aware of. How can the seller be certain what events will increase the premiums? In a clear case—where the seller has recently become aware that its product is carcinogenic, for example—the seller should be aware that its insurance premiums will obviously increase dramatically when this fact comes to the attention of its insurance companies. The buyer should also investigate whether such policies will survive after the acquisition since many policies lapse on a change of control of the target or, in some cases, a buyer may be prudent to include a representation by the seller stating that such policies will survive after the acquisition.

A second important consideration is whether the insurance policies are "claims made" or "claims incurred" policies. The difference between these types of policies is that a "claims made" policy covers only those claims that are made to the insurance company while the policy was in full force and effect, whereas a "claims incurred" policy covers all claims made at any time, provided that the events giving rise to a liability occurred during the time the policy was in full force and effect.

Lastly, if insurance is an important aspect of the business and a certain portion of the insurance consists of self-insurance, the buyer should factor this in when analyzing the cost of running the business. In the event the buyer wishes to continue to self-insure, the buyer should require the seller's cooperation in obtaining any regulatory approvals necessary to continue to self-insure the operations of the target.

Section 4.15. Real Property Owned or Leased. Section 4.15 of the Disclosure Statement sets forth a complete and accurate list or description of all real property (including a general description of fixtures located at such property and specific identification of any such fixtures not owned by the Target or any Subsidiary) which the Target or any Subsidiary owns or leases, has agreed (or has an option) to purchase, sell or lease, or may be obligated to purchase, sell or lease and any title insurance or guarantee policies with respect thereto, specifying in the case of leases, the name of the lessor, licensor or other grantor, the approximate square footage covered thereunder, the basic annual rental and other amounts paid or payable with respect thereto and a summary of the other terms thereof. True copies of all such leases for real property with aggregate annual rental payments (excluding payments to third parties on account of real estate taxes (or increases therein), insurance, operating costs, or common area expenses), individually in excess of _____ Dollars ($_____) (including all amendments thereof and modifications thereto) have been delivered to Buyer prior to the date hereof. Except as set forth in Section 4.15 of the Disclosure Statement, no consent to the consummation of the transactions contemplated by this Agreement is required from the lessor of any such real property.

The scheduling of real property serves to support the buyer's due diligence efforts by identifying each property owned or leased by the target or any subsidiary. In requesting disclosure of leases, consideration should be given to the dollar threshold in annual rental payments that identifies a lease that the target must disclose. For smaller targets, it may be appropriate to include no threshold at all, requiring the disclosure of all leases of real property.

This representation is also designed to elicit disclosure of both (i) obligations for periodic payments or capital commitments that have been incurred by the target or any subsidiary, and (ii) those leases where landlord consents may be required to avoid lease terminations by virtue of the acquisition. Rental commitments and agreements to purchase will have an impact on the cash flow requirements of the target but may not have been apparent to the buyer from a review of the target's financial statements.

The buyer should require the annual lease payment information in order to prepare a cash flow analysis. In addition, this disclosure will aid a buyer who is trying to determine the financeability of the target's and subsidiaries' real estate and the necessity of obtaining appraisals of the real estate to assist its financing efforts.

Section 4.16 Fixed Assets; Leased Assets.

(i) Section 4.16(i) of the Disclosure Statement sets forth a complete and accurate list or description of all equipment, machinery and other items of tangible personal property which the Target or any Subsidiary owns or leases, has agreed (or has an option) to purchase, sell or lease, or may be obligated to purchase, sell or lease having a book value of _____ Dollars ($_____) or more or requiring annual rental payments in excess of _____ Dollars ($ _____), specifying in the case of leases, the name of the lessor, licensor or other grantor, the description of the property covered thereby, the basic annual rental and other amounts paid or payable with respect thereto and a summary of the other terms thereof. True copies of all leases for such assets with aggregate rental payments individually in excess of _____ Dollars ($ _____) (including all amendments thereto and modifications thereof) have been delivered to Buyer prior to the date hereof. The book value of all such assets owned or leased by the Target and its Subsidiaries not included on such list does not, in the aggregate, exceed _____ Dollars ($ _____) at the date hereof.

(ii) Except as set forth in Section 4.16(ii) of the Disclosure Statement, no consent to the consummation of the transactions contemplated by this Agreement is required from the lessor, licensor or other grantor of any such tangible personal property.

As with the representation relating to real estate in Section 4.15, this representation elicits disclosure of each item of tangible personal property owned or leased by the target or any subsidiary that has a value or annual cost in excess of a given dollar threshold. Unlike the real property representation, where the buyer may reasonably request and be interested in information on each piece of real property owned by the target or any subsidiary, requesting disclosure of every item of tangible personal property absent a dollar threshold would impose an unreasonable burden on the seller and would subject the seller to the risk of misrepresentation in the event an asset were inadvertently omitted.

This risk will motivate the seller to negotiate for a higher dollar threshold. A buyer may determine that it can live with a dollar threshold on the book value of owned assets but must require a lower amount in respect of lease obligations since the latter will have a direct impact on cash flow projections. The buyer, in any event, should base its threshold on the individual value of assets that it deems relevant to any financing that may be necessary for it to finance the purchase price.

Section 4.17. Title and Related Matters.

(i) Subject to the exceptions contained in the second sentence of this Section 4.17, the Target or a Subsidiary has, and immediately after giving effect to the transactions contemplated hereby will have, good and marketable title (or, in jurisdictions where title insurance policies insuring good and marketable title are not available, good and indefeasible title, or good and merchantable title or some quality of title substantially equivalent thereto) to or a valid leasehold interest in (a) all of the properties and assets reflected in the Most Recent Balance Sheet or acquired after the date of the appropriate Most Recent Balance Sheet by the Target or a Subsidiary, (b) all properties or assets which are subject to operating leases as defined in Financial Accounting Standards Board Statement No. 13 and are not reflected in the Most Recent Balance Sheet, and (c) all other properties and assets owned or utilized by the Target or any Subsidiary in the conduct of their respective businesses. All properties and assets referred to in the preceding sentence are presently owned or held by the Target or a Subsidiary, and at and immediately after the Closing Date, will be held by the Target or a Subsidiary, free and clear of all title defects or objections, mortgages, liens, pledges, charges, security interests, options to purchase or other encumbrances of any kind or character, except: (v) liens for current taxes not yet due and payable; (w) liens, imperfections of title and easements which do not, either individually or in the aggregate, materially detract from the value of, or interfere with the present use of, the properties subject thereto or affected thereby, or otherwise materially impair the operations of the entity which owns, leases or utilizes such property or materially impair the use of such property by such entity; (x) mortgages and liens securing debt which is reflected as a liability on the Most Recent Balance Sheet; (y) mechanics', carriers', workmen's, repairmen's and other similar liens arising or incurred in the ordinary course of business; and (z) as set forth in Section 4.17(i) of the Disclosure Statement.

(ii) All the plants, structures, facilities, machinery, equipment, automobiles, trucks, tools and other properties and assets owned or leased by the Target and the Subsidiaries, including but not limited to such as are reflected in the Most Recent Balance Sheet or acquired after the respective dates of the Most Recent Balance Sheet by the Target or a Subsidiary are structurally sound with no defects known to Seller and in good operating condition and repair (except for routine immaterial maintenance in the ordinary course of business) and usable in a manner consistent with their current use.

(iii) All leases pursuant to which the Target and the Subsidiaries lease (as lessee) real and/or personal property are valid and enforceable by the

Target or a Subsidiary in accordance with their respective terms; other than with respect to property which has been sublet by the Target or the Subsidiaries as noted on Section 4.17(iii) of the Disclosure Statement, the Target or a Subsidiary has been in peaceable possession since the commencement of the original term of each such lease; except for the tenancies in respect of property being sublet, as specified in the second clause of this sentence, there are no tenancies or other possessory interests with respect to any real or personal property owned by the Target or any Subsidiary; all rents due under, or other amounts required to be paid by the terms of, each such lease have been paid; and there is not under any of such leases, to Seller's knowledge, any default (or event which, with the giving of notice, the passage of time or both, would constitute a default), waiver or postponement of any of the Target's or any Subsidiary's obligations thereunder.

(iv) Except as stated in Section 4.17(iv) of the Disclosure Statement, none of the real property owned or leased by the Target or any Subsidiary is subject to any governmental decree or order to be sold and there is no condemnation or eminent domain proceeding pending, or, to the best of Seller's knowledge, threatened, against any real property owned or leased by the Target or any Subsidiary or any part thereof, and neither Target nor any Subsidiary has made a commitment or received any notice, oral or written, of the desire of any public authority or any entity to take or use the real property owned or leased by the Target or any Subsidiary or any part thereof, whether temporarily or permanently, for easements, rights-of-way, or other public or quasi-public purposes, or for any other purpose whatsoever, nor is there any proceeding pending, or threatened in writing or by publication, or, to the best knowledge of the Seller, threatened, which could adversely affect, as to any portion of any parcel of the real property owned or leased by the Target or any Subsidiary, the zoning classification in effect on the date hereof. On the Closing Date, the real property owned or leased by the Target and its Subsidiaries shall be free and clear of any management, leasing, maintenance, security or service obligations other than utilities and except those incurred in the ordinary course of business.

(v) All rights-of-way, easements, licenses, permits and authorizations in any manner related to the location or operation of the business of the Target and the Subsidiaries are in good standing, valid and enforceable in all material respects in accordance with their respective terms. Except as stated in Section 4.17(v) of the Disclosure Statement, neither the Target nor any Subsidiary is in violation of any, and each has complied with all, applicable zoning, building or other codes, statutes, regulations, ordinances, notices and orders of any governmental agency with respect to the occupancy, use, maintenance, condition and operation of the real property owned or leased by the Target and its Subsidiaries or any material portion of any parcel thereof, and the use of any improvements for all purposes for which the real property owned or leased by the Target and its Subsidiaries is being used on the date hereof will not violate any such code, statute, regulation, ordinance, notice or order. The Target and the Subsidiaries possess and shall maintain in effect all licenses, certificates of occupancy, permits and authorizations required to operate and maintain the real property owned or leased by the Target and its Subsidiaries for all uses for which the real property owned or leased by the Target and its Subsidiaries is operated on the date hereof. Except as stated in Section 4.17(v) of the Disclosure Statement, no equipment installed or located in any part of the real property owned or leased by the Target and its Subsidiaries violates any law, ordinance, order, regulation or requirement of any governmental authority which violation would have an adverse effect on the real property owned or leased by the Target or any Subsidiary or any portion of any parcel thereof.

Title to the property owned by the target and its subsidiaries is important for the purpose of verifying the value and financeability of the assets acquired. It is useful to include within the scope of the title representations assets leased under operating leases as these assets will generally not be disclosed on a balance sheet and may represent significant value if the target's rental payments are below market rates, especially if the target's leasehold interest is mortgageable.

An acquisition lender advancing funds on a secured basis will require the buyer to make extensive representations regarding the quality of its title to the assets securing the loan. The buyer should therefore attempt to obtain as much comfort on the existence of liens and encumbrances from the seller as possible. Not only is it important to elicit in the disclosure statement all liens that might have an impact on the buyer's ability to obtain sufficient financing, but the buyer must also carefully review the liens disclosed and assess the degree to which the liens impair financeability of the assets of the target and its subsidiaries. Close scrutiny may reveal the existence of liens that limit marketability and prevent the buyer from providing its lender with a first-priority security interest. Once these liens have been identified, the buyer may wish to require as its condition to closing that certain liens be discharged.

As an alternative to having the seller schedule existing liens [as is the approach in the second sentence of paragraph (i)], the buyer could permit an exception for "liens, imperfections of title and easements which do not, either individually or in the aggregate, materially detract from the value of, or interfere with the present value of, the properties subject thereto or affected thereby, or otherwise materially impair the operations of the entity which owns, leases or utilizes such property or materially impair the use of such property by such entity." In addition, the materiality standard might be made more definite by referring to a lien or imposition in excess of a specified dollar amount. However, although a materiality exception may provide sufficient protection to the buyer vis-à-vis the seller, a lender may find it unacceptable. The buyer employing the exception must be willing to take on the risk that a lender may, through certain loan representations and covenants, require the discharge of liens that are not material to either the seller or the buyer.

The representations in paragraphs (ii) and (iii) are intended to assure the buyer that the assets to be acquired are in good operating condition and that the target's and subsidiaries' leases are enforceable and not in default.

Paragraphs (iv) and (v) attempt to verify that no violations or proceedings exist that might prevent the buyer from using the real estate acquired as it had been used in the past by the target and the subsidiaries. The seller may seek to limit the statement about existing violations by imposing a materiality standard. A buyer might well concede this point; a useful compromise position might be to require the representation that any violation would not result in an award of damages, or require expenditures to remedy the violation, in excess of a specified dollar amount.

Section 4.18. Intellectual Property.

(i) Section 4.18(i) of the Disclosure Statement sets forth a complete and accurate list, including, where applicable, the date of registration or expiration, serial or registration number or patent number, of all United States (including the individual states and territories of the United States) and foreign registered trademarks, service marks and trade names; unregistered trademarks, service marks and trade names; trademark, service mark and trade name applications; product designations; designs; unexpired patents; pending and filed patent applications; current and active invention disclosures; inventions on which disclosures are to be prepared; trade secrets; registered copyrights; and unregistered copyrights (collectively, the "Intellectual Property"), which the Target or any Subsidiary owns or licenses, has agreed (or has an option) to purchase, sell or license, or may be obligated to purchase, sell or license. With respect to each of the foregoing items, there is listed on Section 4.18(i) of the Disclosure Statement (a) the extent of the interest of the Target and its Subsidiaries therein; (b) the jurisdictions in or by which each such patent, trademark, service mark, trade name, copyright and license has been registered, filed or issued; (c) each agreement and all other documents evidencing the interest of the Target and its Subsidiaries therein, including, but not limited to, license agreements; (d) the extent of the interest of any third party therein, including, but not limited to, any security interest or licenses; and (e) each agreement and all other documents evidencing the interest of any third party therein.

(ii) Except as set forth in Section 4.18(ii) of the Disclosure Statement, the right, title or interest of the Target and its Subsidiaries in each item of Intellectual Property is free and clear of material adverse Liens.

(iii) Except as set forth in Section 4.18(iii) of the Disclosure Statement, the Target and its Subsidiaries have all right, title and interest in all inventions, trade secrets and proprietary information, and have all other intellectual property rights necessary in any material respect for the non-infringing manufacture, use or sale, as the case may be, of all of the products, components of products and services which the Target or any Subsidiary manufactures, uses or sells in their business as currently conducted or which the Target or any Subsidiary contemplated manufacturing, using or selling in connection with the preparation of the Projected Financial Statements.

(iv) Except as set forth in Section 4.18(iv) of the Disclosure Statement, the Target and its Subsidiaries have all right, title and interest in all trademarks, service marks, trade names and product designations necessary for the non-infringing use of all such marks and trade names which the Target or any Subsidiary uses in their business as currently conducted or which the Target or any Subsidiary contemplated using in connection with the preparation of the Projected Financial Statements.

(v) Except as set forth in Section 4.18(v) of the Disclosure Statement, the Target and its Subsidiaries have all right, title and interest in all material copyrights necessary for the non-infringing publication, reproduction, preparation of derivative works, distribution, public performance, public display and importation of all copyrighted works of the Target. This includes works which the Target or any Subsidiary—in business as currently conducted or as contemplated in connection with the preparation of the Projected Financial Statements—publishes, reproduces, prepares or has prepared a derivative of, distributes, publicly performs, publicly displays or imports.

(vi) Except as set forth in Section 4.18(vi) of the Disclosure Statement, neither the Target nor any of the Subsidiaries has, whether directly, contributorily or by inducement, within any time period as to which liability of the Target or the Subsidiaries is not barred by statute, infringed any patent, trademark, service mark, trade name or copyright or misappropriated any intellectual property of another, or received from another any notice, charge, claim or other assertion in respect thereto or committed any actions of unfair competition.

(vii) Except as set forth in Section 4.18(vii) of the Disclosure Statement, neither the Target nor any of the Subsidiaries has sent or otherwise communicated to another person any notice, charge, claim or other assertion of, or has any knowledge of, present, impending or threatened patent, trademark, service mark, trade name or copyright infringement by such other person, or misappropriation of any intellectual property of the Target or any of the Subsidiaries by such other person or any acts of unfair competition by such other person.

(viii) The Target warrants that (a) no product, license, patent, process, method, substance, design, part or other material presently being sold or contemplated to be sold or employed by the Target or any Subsidiary infringes on any rights owned or held by any other person; (b) no claim, litigation or other proceeding is pending or threatened against the Target or any Subsidiary contesting the right of such entity to sell or use any such product, license, patent, process, method, substance, design, part or other material and no such claim is impliedly threatened by an offer to license from a third party under a claim of use; and (c) no patent, formulation, invention, device, application or principle nor any statute, law, rule, regulation, standard or code, exists or is pending or proposed that would have a Material Adverse Effect.

(ix) No filing or recording fees, stamp or transfer taxes or other fees, costs or taxes of any kind are payable by the Target or any Subsidiary in respect of the Intellectual Property and no such filing or recording fees, stamp taxes or other fees, costs or taxes of any kind will be payable by the Target, any Subsidiary or Buyer in connection with the Merger except as set forth in Section 4.18(ix) of the Disclosure Statement.

The intellectual property representation requires the disclosure of all intellectual property that the target or any subsidiary uses in its business and is designed to assure the buyer that the intellectual property, or the target's or its subsidiaries use thereof, does not infringe upon the rights of third parties. The representation has been drafted to cover any intellectual property rights that may exist or are pending that would adversely affect the target or its subsidiaries. This representation may be extremely important if, for example, the value of the target's business is largely dependent upon its possession of a particular patent or its ability to market its product under a particular trademark.

Subparagraph (ix) is intended to elicit information about filing or transfer fees that might be incurred in connection with the transaction. Where the target and its subsidiaries have extensive foreign intellectual property holdings, these fees can be so big that the buyer may try to obligate the seller to pay a portion of these costs.

> ***Section 4.19. Assets Necessary to the Business.*** Except as set forth in Section 4.19 of the Disclosure Statement, the Target and the Subsidiaries collectively own or lease, directly or indirectly, all of the assets and properties, and are parties to all licenses and other agreements, in each case which are presently being used or are reasonably necessary to carry on the businesses and operations of the Target and the Subsidiaries as presently conducted, and none of the stockholders of the Target, the Seller nor any of their affiliates (other than any of the Target and the Subsidiary) owns any assets or properties which are being used to carry on the business or operations of the Target and the Subsidiaries as presently conducted.

Notwithstanding all the other representations made by the seller about the specific assets, liabilities, and other agreements, rights, and obligations that the target and its subsidiaries may have, a buyer has no way of knowing that it is getting everything that it needs to operate the business of the target and its subsidiaries as presently conducted without this broad representation.

This type of representation is critical if the buyer is purchasing a company by means of an asset acquisition or a business that has been operated as a division of another company. If, for example, certain equipment or services necessary to the business of the target or its subsidiaries were provided by the seller or its affiliates, the buyer would be unable to operate the business without replacing such equipment or services, most likely at a cost that far exceeds the cost at which they were provided by the seller or its affiliates.

> ***Section 4.20. Additional Contracts.*** In addition to the other items set forth in the Disclosure Statement attached hereto pursuant to the other provisions of this Agreement, Section 4.20 of the Disclosure Statement identifies as of the date hereof the following:

(i) each agreement to which the Target or any Subsidiary is a party which involves or may involve aggregate annual future payments (whether in payment of a debt, as a result of a guarantee or indemnification, for goods or services, or otherwise) by the Target or any Subsidiary of _____ Dollars ($ _____) or more;

(ii) each outstanding commitment of the Target or any Subsidiary to make capital expenditures, capital additions or capital improvements in excess of _____ Dollars ($ _____);

(iii) any contract for the employment of any officer or employee or former officer or employee of the Target or any Subsidiary (other than, with respect to any employee, contracts which are terminable without liability upon notice of 30 days or less and do not provide for any further payments following such termination) pursuant to which payments in excess of _____ Dollars ($ _____) may be required to be made at any time following the date hereof;

(iv) any stock option or stock appreciation rights plan or arrangement of the Target or any Subsidiary;

(v) any mortgage or other form of secured indebtedness of the Target or any Subsidiary;

(vi) any unsecured debentures, notes or installment obligations of the Target or any Subsidiary, the unpaid balance of which exceeds _____ Dollars ($ _____) in the aggregate except trade payables incurred in the ordinary course of business;

(vii) any guaranty of any obligation of the Target or any Subsidiary for borrowings or otherwise, excluding endorsements made for collection, guaranties made or letters of credit given in the ordinary course of business, and other guaranties which in the aggregate do not exceed _____ Dollars ($ _____);

(viii) any agreement of the Target or any Subsidiary, including options, for the purchase, sale, disposition or lease of any of its assets (other than inventory) having a book value of more than _____ Dollars ($ _____) for any single asset or _____ Dollars ($ _____) in the aggregate or for the sale of inventory other than in the ordinary course of business;

(ix) any contract to which the Target or any Subsidiary is a party pursuant to which the Target or any Subsidiary is or may be obligated to make payments, contingent or otherwise, exceeding _____ Dollars ($_____) in the aggregate, on account of or arising out of the prior acquisition of businesses, or all or substantially all of the assets or stock, of other companies or any division thereof;

(x) any contract with any labor union of which the Target or any Subsidiary is a party;

(xi) any contract or proposed contract, including but not limited to assignments, licenses, transfers of exclusive rights, "work for hire" agreements, special commissions, employment contracts, purchase orders, sales orders, mortgages and security agreements, to which the Target or any Subsidiary is a party and which (A) contains a grant or other transfer, whether present, retroactive, prospective or contingent, by the Target or any Subsidiary, of any rights in any invention, trade secret, proprietary information, trademark, service mark, trade name, copyright or other intellectual property by whatever name designated, without regard to whether such invention, trade secret, proprietary information, trademark, service mark, trade name, copyright, material object or other intellectual property was in existence at the time such contract was made, or (B) contains a promise made by the Target or by any Subsidiary to pay any lump sum or royalty or other payment or consideration in respect to the acquisition, practice or use of any rights in any invention, trade secret, proprietary information, trademark, service mark, trade name, copyright, material object in which an original work of authorship was first fixed or other intellectual property by whatever name designated and without regard to whether such lump sum, royalty payment or other consideration was ever made or received;

(xii) any contract with the Seller or any officer, director or employee of the Target or any Subsidiary of the Seller (A) involving at least _____ Dollars ($ _____) in aggregate payments over the entire term thereof or more than $_____ Dollars in any 12-month period or (B) the terms of which are not arms-length; or

(xiii) any other contract, agreement or other instrument which the Target or any Subsidiary is a party not entered into in the ordinary course of business which is material to the financial, business, earnings, prospects or condition of the Target or the Subsidiaries and not excluded by reason of the provisions of clauses (i) through (xii), inclusive, of this subsection.

Except as otherwise agreed to by the parties as set forth in Section 4.20 of the Disclosure Statement, true and complete copies of all contracts, agreements and other instruments referred to in Section 4.20 of the Disclosure Statement have heretofore been delivered, or will be delivered at least ten business days prior to Closing, to Buyer by the Seller. All such contracts, agreements and other instruments are enforceable by the Target or the Subsidiaries which is (are) a party thereto in accordance with their terms except as to enforceability thereof may be affected by applicable bankruptcy, reorganization, insolvency, moratorium or other similar laws now or hereafter in effect, or by general equity principles.

This is an information-gathering representation that is designed to identify all the important contractual relationships of the target and its subsidiaries. Depending upon the type of deal being negotiated, a seller may be reluctant to make this representation because of the inordinate amount of work required to satisfy the disclosure obligation. The seller may instead tell the buyer that it is welcome to review all the contracts and other agreements at the offices of the seller. However, like any other representation that is founded on access as opposed to identification, the buyer takes responsibility at its own peril. Therefore, a prudent buyer will demand that the seller identify all such documents and, if need be, offer to assist in the seller's preparation of the disclosure statement.

The amount of the dollar thresholds in this representation are deal-specific, and the same considerations previously discussed are appropriate here.

Section 4.21. Customers and Suppliers. Section 4.21 of the Disclosure Statement sets forth (i) a true and correct list of (A) the ten largest customers of the Target and each of the Subsidiaries in terms of sales during the fiscal year ended [fill in date of most recent fiscal year end] and (B) the ten largest customers of the Target and each of the Subsidiaries in terms of sales during the three (3) months ended [fill in the most recent quarter end], showing the approximate total sales to each such customer during the fiscal year ended [fill in date of most recent fiscal year end] and the three (3) months ended [fill in most recent quarter end]; (ii) a true and correct list of (A) the ten largest suppliers of the Target and each of the Subsidiaries in terms of purchases during the fiscal year ended [fill in date of most recent fiscal year end], and (B) the ten largest suppliers of the Target and each of the Subsidiaries on a consolidated basis in terms of purchases during the three (3) months ended [fill in most recent quarter end], showing the approximate total purchases from each such supplier during the fiscal year ended [fill in date of most recent fiscal year end], and the three (3) months ended [fill in most recent quarter end], respectively. Except to the extent set forth in Section 4.21 of the Disclosure Statement, there has not been any material adverse change in the business relationship of the Target or any Subsidiary with any customer or supplier named in the Disclosure Statement. Except for the customers and suppliers named in Section 4.21 of the Disclosure Statement, neither the Target nor any Subsidiary had any customer who accounted for more than 5 of its sales during the period from [insert appropriate period of 12 to 18 months prior to date of Agreement], or any supplier from whom it purchased more than 5 of the goods or services purchased by it during such period.

Depending upon the nature of the target's and the subsidiaries' businesses, the buyer may agree to require disclosure of the largest customers and suppliers on "a consolidated basis." The principal reason for this representation is to identify the dependence of the business on a single or small group of customers or suppliers.

Section 4.22. Competing Lines of Business. Except as set forth on Section 4.22 of the Disclosure Statement, no affiliate of the Seller owns, directly or indirectly, any interest in (excepting not more than 5 stockholdings for investment purposes in securities of publicly held and traded companies), or is an officer, director, employee or consultant of, or otherwise receives remuneration from, any person which is, or is engaged in business as, a competitor, lessor, lessee, customer or supplier of the Target or any Subsidiary.

In certain situations, it may appear unnecessary to require a seller to enter into some sort of noncompete agreement because of the nature of the seller's business. However, it still may be useful for the buyer to assure itself that there are no hidden companies that the seller operates or controls that compete with the target or a subsidiary. The protection afforded by this representation is limited; the seller may be able to adversely affect the business of the target or a subsidiary in light of the seller's inside knowledge or simply because it has greater resources. The buyer should be forewarned that, despite its receipt of this representation, a seller may remain a competitor given the practicalities of a particular situation.

Section 4.23. Restrictive Covenants. Except as set forth in Section 4.23 of the Disclosure Statement, neither Target nor any Subsidiary is a party to any agreement, contract or covenant limiting the freedom of the Target or any Subsidiary from competing in any line of business or with any person or other entity in any geographic area.

A buyer must be aware of agreements that constrain the operation of the target and its subsidiaries. Many buyers purchase targets with the expectation that the business of the target can be expanded geographically. In some cases, the buyer may be relying on this expectation to the point of including such expansion in its projections. Therefore, the buyer should carefully review any agreements that are disclosed as a result of this representation.

Section 4.24. Books and Records.
(i) The books of account and other financial records of the Target and its Subsidiaries are in all material respects complete and correct, and have been maintained in accordance with good business practices.

(ii) The minute books of the Target and its Subsidiaries, as previously made available to the Buyer and its counsel, contain accurate records of all meetings and accurately reflect all other material corporate action of the stockholders and directors and any committees of the Board of Directors of the Target and its Subsidiaries.

(iii) The Buyer has been or will be prior to the Closing Date, afforded access to all such records referred to in subparagraphs (i) and (ii) above.

Section 4.25. Bank Accounts.
Section 4.25 of the Disclosure Statement contains a true and correct list of the names of each bank, savings and loan or other financial institution, in which the Target or its Subsidiaries has an account, including cash contribution accounts, or safe deposit boxes, and the names of all persons authorized to draw thereon or to have access thereto.

Sections 4.24 and 4.25 above are representations that confirm the accuracy of information usually furnished to the buyer in connection with its due diligence efforts.

Section 4.26. Employee Benefit Plans; Labor Relations.
(i) The term "Employee Plan" shall mean any pension, retirement, profit-sharing, deferred compensation, bonus or other incentive plan, any medical, vision, dental or other health plan, any life insurance plan, or any other employee benefit plan, including, without limitation, any "employee benefit plan" as defined in Section 3(3) of the Employee Retirement Income Security Act of 1974, as amended ("ERISA") and any employee benefit plan covering any employees of the Target or any Controlled Entity in any foreign country or territory (a "Foreign Plan"), to which the Target or any Controlled Entity contributes or is a party or is bound and under which employees of the Target or any Controlled Entity are eligible to participate or derive a benefit, except any government-sponsored program or government-required benefit. Section 4.26(i) of the Disclosure Statement lists each Employee Plan and identifies each

Employee Plan (other than a Foreign Plan) which, as of the date hereof, is a defined benefit plan as defined in Section 3(35) of ERISA (a "Defined Benefit Plan") or is a multi-employer plan within the meaning of Section 3(37) of ERISA (a "Multi-Employer Plan"). In the case of each Defined Benefit Plan, the unfunded accrued liabilities of such plan as of [insert date], determined on an ongoing plan basis by the actuaries for such plan using the actuarial methods and assumptions used in the latest actuarial valuation of the plan, do not exceed the assets of the plan. Section 4.26(i) of the Disclosure Statement identifies each of the Employee Plans which purports to be a qualified plan under Section 401(a) of the Code (as defined below). In the case of each Multi-Employer Plan, Section 4.26(i) of the Disclosure Statement sets forth the Target or Controlled Entity contributions made to such Plan for the 12 months ended on the last day of its most recent fiscal year. In the case of each Foreign Plan, Section 4.26(i) of the Disclosure Statement sets forth the Target or Controlled Entity contributions made to such Plan for the last plan year ending prior to the date of this Agreement. The Target has delivered, or will deliver prior to the Closing, to Buyer the following documents as in effect on the date hereof: (a) true, correct and complete copies of any Employee Plan, other than a Foreign Plan, including all amendments thereto, which is an employee pension benefit or welfare benefit plan (within the meaning of Sections 3(1) or 3(2) of ERISA), and, in the case of any unwritten Employee Plans, descriptions thereof, (b) with respect to any plans or plan amendments described in the foregoing clause (a), (1) the most recent determination letter issued by the Internal Revenue Service (the "IRS") after September 1, 1974, if any, (2) all trust agreements or other funding agreements, including insurance contracts, (3) with respect to each Defined Benefit Plan, all notices of intent to terminate any such Employee Plan and all notices of reportable events with respect to any such Employee Plan as to which the PBGC has not waived the thirty (30) day notice requirement, (4) the most recent actuarial valuations, annual reports, summary plan descriptions, summaries of material modifications and summary annual reports, if any, and (5) a true, correct and complete summary of the benefits provided under each Foreign Plan, together with the most recent actuarial valuation of financial information relative thereto.

(ii) As of the date hereof:

(a) Each of the Employee Plans that purports to be qualified under Section 401(a) of the Internal Revenue Code, as amended (the "Code") is qualified as of the Closing Date and any trusts under such plans are exempt from income tax under Section 501(a) of the Code. The retroactive cure period with respect to any plan amendments not yet submitted to the

IRS has not expired. The Employee Plans each comply in all material respects with all other applicable laws (including, without limitation, ERISA, the Age Discrimination in Employment Act, the Americans with Disabilities Act, the Family Leave Act, and the Taxpayer Relief Act of 1997) of the United States and any applicable collective bargaining agreement. Other than claims for benefits submitted by participants or beneficiaries or appeals from denial thereof, there is no litigation, legal action, suit, investigation, claim, counterclaim or proceeding pending or threatened against any Employee Plan.

(b) With respect to any Employee Plan, no prohibited transaction (within the meaning of Section 406 of ERISA and/or Section 4975 of the Code) exists which could subject the Target or any Controlled Entity to any material liability or civil penalty assessed pursuant to Section 502(i) of ERISA or a material tax imposed by Section 4975 of the Code. Neither the Seller nor the Target, nor any Controlled Entity, nor any administrator or fiduciary of any Employee Plan (or agent of any of the foregoing) has engaged in any transaction or acted or failed to act in a manner which is likely to subject the Target or any Controlled Entity to any liability for a breach of fiduciary or other duty under ERISA or any other applicable United States law. The transactions contemplated by this Agreement and the Related Instruments will not be, or cause any, prohibited action.

(c) No Defined Benefit Plan has been terminated or partially terminated after September 1, 1974.

(d) No plan termination liability to the Pension Benefit Guaranty Corporation ("PBGC") or withdrawal liability to any Multi-Employer Plan that is material in the aggregate has been or is expected to be incurred with respect to any Employee Plan or with respect to any employee benefit plan sponsored by any entity under common control (within the meaning of Section 414 of the Code) with the Target or a Controlled Entity by reason of any action taken by the Seller, the Target or any Controlled Entity prior to the Closing Date. The PBGC has not instituted, and is not expected to institute, any proceedings to terminate any Employee Plan. Except as described in Section 4.26(ii)(d) of the Disclosure Statement, there has been no reportable event since [insert date] (within the meaning of Section 4043(b) of ERISA and the regulations thereunder) with respect to any Employee Plan, and there exists no condition or set of circumstances which makes the termination of any Employee Plan by the PBGC likely.

(e) As of the date hereof, as to each Employee Benefit Plan, all filings required by ERISA and the Code have been timely filed and all notices and disclosures to participants required by ERISA or the Code have been timely provided.

(iii) Except as indicated in Section 4.26(iii) of the Disclosure Statement, the Target and each Controlled Entity has made full and timely payment of all amounts required under the terms of each of the Employee Plans that are employee pension benefit plans, including the Multi-Employer Plans, to have been paid as contributions to such plans for the last plan year ended prior to the date of this Agreement and all prior plan years. No accumulated funding deficiency (as defined in Section 302 of ERISA and Section 412 of the Code), whether or not waived, exists with respect to any Employee Plan (other than a Foreign Plan) as of the end of such plan year, provided contributions owed with respect to such plan year are timely paid. Further, the Target and each Controlled Entity has made or shall make full and timely payment of or has accrued or shall accrue all amounts which are required under the terms of the Employee Plans to be paid as a contribution to each such Employee Plan that is an employee pension benefit plan with respect to the period from the end of the last plan year ending before the date of this Agreement to the Closing Date in accordance with [insert covenant cross reference] hereof.

(iv) No state of facts exists with respect to a Foreign Plan, the effect of which would have a material adverse effect on the business, assets, earnings, financial condition or prospects of the Target and the Controlled Entities taken as a whole.

(v) All contributions made to, or accrued with respect to, all Employee Plans are deductible under Section 404 or 162 of the Code. No amounts, nor any assets of any Employee Plan are subject to tax as unrelated business taxable income under Sections 511, 512 or 419A of the Code.

(vi) No facts exist which will result in a material increase in premium costs of Employee Plans for which benefits are insured or a material increase in benefit costs of Employee Plans which provide self-insured benefits.

(vii) No Employee Plan provides medical, disability, life or other benefits to retired former employees.

(viii) Except as described in Section 4.26(v) of the Disclosure Statement, no union has been recognized as a representative of any or all of the Target's or any Subsidiary's employees. There are no agreements with, or pending petitions for recognition of, a labor union or association as the exclusive bargaining agent for any or all of the Target's or any Subsidiary's employees; no such petitions have been pending at any time within two (2) years of the date of this Agreement and, to the best of the Seller's knowledge, there has not been any organizing effort by any union or other group seeking to represent any employees of the Target or any Subsidiary as their exclusive bargaining agent at any time within two (2) years of the date of this Agreement; and there are no labor strikes, work stoppages or other troubles, other than routine grievance matters, now pending, or, to the best of Seller's knowledge, threatened, against the Target or any Subsidiary, nor have there been any such labor strikes, work stoppages or other labor troubles, other than routine grievance matters, at any time within two (2) years of the date of this Agreement.

This particular representation is extremely important in situations in which the target or any subsidiary has a substantial number of employees. Over the past few years, potential liability with respect to employee benefits and related plans has increased dramatically. Therefore, it is important for the buyer to know that the employee plans maintained by the target or any subsidiary are in compliance with existing regulations and are adequately funded. (For further discussion of employee benefits, see Chapter 7.)

> *Section 4.27. Litigation.* Except as set forth in Section 4.27 of the Disclosure Statement, there is no action, suit, proceeding or investigation pending or, to the best knowledge after due inquiry of Seller and the Target, threatened, which would be likely to have a Material Adverse Effect; there is no reasonable basis known to the Seller or the Target for any such action that may result in any such effect and that is probable of assertion; and the Target, or any Subsidiary, is not in default in respect of any judgment, order, writ, injunction or decree of any court or any federal, state, local or other governmental department, commission, board, bureau, agency or instrumentality which would be likely to have a Material Adverse Effect.

Generally, a seller will have no problem disclosing to the buyer the existence of any pending or threatened action against the target or a subsidiary that would have material adverse effect. The part of this representation that is more difficult for the seller to make relates to whether the seller has a reasonable basis to know of any action that may result in a material adverse effect. Although there may be no claim pending or action threatened, the buyer wants to know whether the seller, target, or subsidiary has taken any action that would result in a material adverse effect. For example, if immediately prior to the signing of the acquisition agreement the target were to willfully breach a contract essential to its business, the other party to the contract, unaware of the breach, would not yet have filed a claim. Without this particular representation, the seller would not have to disclose this event. Not surprisingly, the seller is often unwilling to evaluate which of its actions may result in a claim that would have a material adverse effect, or make warranties based on its evaluation. The seller may argue that routine corporate actions could result in a material adverse effect, or the seller may express unwillingness to take on liability for the knowledge of each of its directors, officers, and employees. As with other representations, the issue is risk allocation. A smart buyer will soften this representation to appease the seller but will nonetheless seek disclosure, since the seller should be aware of an action taken that would or may constitute a material adverse effect and can always choose to disclose it rather than guess as to its outcome.

Section 4.28. Compliance with Laws.

(i) The Target and the Subsidiaries comply with, and have made all filings required pursuant to, all federal, state, municipal or local constitutional provisions, laws, ordinances, rules, regulations and orders in connection with the conduct of their businesses as now conducted.

(ii) The Target and the Subsidiaries have all governmental licenses, permits and authorizations necessary for the conduct of their respective businesses as currently conducted (the "Permits"), and all such Permits are in full force and effect, and no violations exist in respect of any such Permits, and no proceeding is pending or, to the knowledge of the Seller, threatened, to revoke or limit any thereof. Except as otherwise disclosed in Section 4.28(ii) of the Disclosure Statement, all such Permits are set forth on the Disclosure Statement.

(iii) Except as set forth in Section 4.28(iii) of the Disclosure Statement, neither the Target nor any Subsidiary has received notice of violation or of any alleged or potential violation of any such constitutional provisions, laws, ordinances, rules, regulations or orders, cured or not, within the last five years or any injunction or governmental order or decree.

(iv) Except as set forth in Section 4.28(iv) of the Disclosure Statement, there are no present or past Environmental Conditions in any way relating to the business of the Target or any Subsidiary. For purposes of this Agreement, "Environmental Condition" means (a) the introduction into the environment of any pollution, including without limitation any contaminant, irritant, or pollutant or other toxic or hazardous substance (whether or not such pollution constituted at the time thereof a violation of any federal, state or local law, ordinance or governmental rule or regulation) as a result of any spill, discharge, leak, emission, escape, injection, dumping or release of any kind whatsoever of any substance or exposure of any type in any work places or to any medium, including without limitation air, land, surface waters or ground waters, or from any generation, transportation, treatment, discharge, storage or disposal of waste materials, raw materials, hazardous materials, toxic materials or products of any kind or from the storage, use or handling of any hazardous or toxic materials or other substances, as a result of which the Target or any Subsidiary has or may become liable to any person or by reason of which any of the assets of the Target or any Subsidiary may suffer or be subjected to any Lien, or (b) any noncompliance with any federal, state or local environmental law, rule, regulation or order as a result of or in connection with any of the foregoing.

The buyer might limit the representation contained in paragraph (ii) by excepting "any such licenses, permits and authorizations the failure to obtain which will not have a Material Adverse Effect."

Similarly the buyer might agree to limit the scope of paragraph (iii) by adding to the five-year limitation the phrase "which would be reasonably likely to result in any liability for penalties or damages exceeding _____ Dollars ($ _____) in the aggregate."

The environmental representation in paragraph (iv) is extremely important in light of the tremendous cost that can be incurred in correcting environmental problems. As a result of significant legislative and judicial developments over the past two decades, unwary buyers may find themselves saddled with obligations to clean up environmental problems caused by their predecessors. Such problems can range from removing asbestos in buildings to installing expensive groundwater purification systems made necessary by leaks from underground storage tanks.

Section 4.29. Non-Contravention; Consents. Except as set forth in Section 4.29 of the Disclosure Statement, the execution, delivery and performance of this Agreement and the Related Instruments and the consummation of any of the transactions contemplated hereby and thereby by the Seller and the Target do not and will not:

(i) violate any provisions of Seller's or Target's certificate of incorporation or bylaws;

(ii) violate, or result with the passage of time in the violation of, any provision of, or result in the acceleration of or entitle any party to accelerate (whether after the giving of notice or lapse of time or both) any obligation under, or result in the creation or imposition of any lien, charge, pledge, security interest or other encumbrance upon any of the properties of Target or any Subsidiary pursuant to any provision of, any mortgage, lien, lease, agreement, permit, indenture, license, instrument, law, order, arbitration award, judgment or decree to which the Seller, Target or any Subsidiary is a party or by which it or any of its properties are bound, the effect of all of which violations, accelerations, creations and impositions would result, in the aggregate, in subjecting the Target or the Subsidiaries to liabilities in excess of _____Dollars ($ _____);

(iii) violate any law, order, judgment or decree to which the Target or any Subsidiary is subject;

(iv) violate or conflict with any other restriction of any kind or character to which Target or any Subsidiary is subject, or by which any of their assets may be bound, the effect of all of which violations or conflicts would result, in the aggregate, in subjecting Target or the Subsidiaries to aggregate liabilities in excess of _____Dollars ($ _____);

(v) constitute an event permitting termination of an agreement to which Target or any Subsidiary is subject, if in any such circumstance, individually or in the aggregate with all other such events, could have a Material Adverse Effect; or

(vi) require a consent, license, permit, notice, application, qualification, waiver or other action of any kind, authorization, order or approval of, or filing or registration with, any governmental commission, board, regulatory, or administrative agencies or authorities or other regulatory body.

This representation is quite useful in that it clearly lays out the various items that should be of concern to the buyer in its operation of the business after the consummation of the transactions contemplated by the acquisition agreement. The utility of the representation lies in the ability it gives the buyer to address each adverse consequence of the transaction before the deal is closed. For example, many agreements provide for their termination in the event that there is a change of control of the target or a subsidiary, as the case may be. Advance notice of the number and nature of these agreements gives the buyer the opportunity to put replacement contracts in place. In addition, the disclosure of certain consents may prompt the buyer to condition its obligation to close upon the success of the seller in obtaining such consents.

The buyer should give careful consideration to the amount of the dollar thresholds, as items beneath the threshold will not be disclosed and may result in dollar-for-dollar liability to the surviving corporation.

Section 4.30. Unlawful Payments. Neither the Target nor any Subsidiary, nor to the best of the Target's knowledge any officer or director of the Target nor any officer or director of any Subsidiary, nor any employee, agent or representative, of the Target or any Subsidiary has made, directly or indirectly, with respect to the business of the Target or such Subsidiary, any illegal political contributions, payments from corporate funds not recorded on the books and records of the Target or such Subsidiary, payments from corporate funds that were falsely recorded on the books and records of the Target or such Subsidiary, payments from corporate funds to governmental officials in their individual capacities for the purpose of affecting their action or the action of the government they represent to obtain favorable treatment in securing business or licenses or to obtain special concessions or illegal payments from corporate funds to obtain or retain business.

The purpose of this representation is to identify whether the target or any subsidiary has made any payments that violate laws, such as the Foreign Corrupt Practices Act, or any payments that are not accurately reflected on the targets or subsidiaries books and records. In addition, disclosure of these payments might reveal the tenuous nature of certain aspects of the target's or its subsidiaries' business, or the necessity for continuing such payments in order to obtain favorable treatment.

Section 4.31. Brokers and Finders. Neither the Seller, Target or any Subsidiary nor any stockholder, officer, director or agent of the Seller, the Target or any Subsidiary has incurred on behalf of Seller, the Target or any Subsidiary any liability to any broker, finder or agent for any brokerage fees, finders' fees or commissions with respect to the transactions contemplated by this Agreement, except to [name of broker or finder]. Such fees and commissions will be paid by Seller.

This representation protects the buyer against obligations of the target or any subsidiary to pay certain fees in connection with the acquisition. Buyer and seller may agree to share some of these fees, but the buyer certainly doesn't want to be obligated to pay any fees of which it is not aware or that are not included in its calculation of the purchase price. As discussed in Chapter 2, these liabilities can be incurred even though no formal written agreement has been executed.

Section 4.32. Absence of Certain Changes or Events. Except as reflected in Section 4.32 of the Disclosure Statement or as specifically set forth herein, since the date of the Most Recent Balance Sheet neither Target nor any Subsidiary has

(i) conducted its business other than in the ordinary course of business;

(ii) issued or sold, or contracted to sell, any of its stock, notes, bonds or other securities, or any option to purchase the same, or entered into any agreement with respect thereto;

(iii) amended its certificate of incorporation or bylaws;

(iv) had or made any capital expenditures or commitments for the acquisition or construction of any property, plant or equipment in excess of _____Dollars ($_____) individually and _____Dollars ($ _____) in the aggregate;

(v) entered into any transaction inconsistent in any material respect with the past practices of its business or has conducted its business in any manner materially inconsistent with its past practices;

(vi) incurred (A) any damage, destruction or similar loss in an aggregate amount exceeding _____ Dollars ($_____) and which is covered by insurance or (B) any damage, destruction or loss in an aggregate amount exceeding _____Dollars ($ _____) and which is not covered by insurance;

(vii) suffered any loss or, to the best knowledge of the Seller, Target and the Subsidiaries, any prospective loss, of any dealer, customer or supplier or altered any contractual arrangement with any dealer or supplier, the loss or alteration of which would (or would, when added to all other such losses or alterations) have a Material Adverse Effect;

(viii) incurred any material liability or obligation (absolute or contingent) or made any material expenditure, other than such as may have been incurred or made in the ordinary course of business and other than capital expenditures described in clause (iv) of this subsection;

(ix) suffered any material adverse change in the business, operations, earnings, properties, liabilities, prospects, assets or financial condition or otherwise of the Target or any Subsidiary and no event which would have Material Adverse Effect has occurred;

(x) declared, set aside or paid any dividend or other distribution (whether in cash, shares, property or any combination thereof) in respect of the capital stock of the Target or any Subsidiary;

(xi) redeemed, repurchased, or otherwise acquired any of its capital stock or securities convertible into or exchangeable for its capital stock or entered into any agreement to do so;

(xii) except as reflected on the Most Recent Balance Sheet and covered by an adequate reserve therefor, made any sale of accounts receivable or any accrual of liabilities not in the ordinary course of business or written off any notes or accounts receivable or portions thereof as uncollectible;

(xiii) purchased or disposed of, or contracted to purchase or dispose of, or granted or received an option to purchase or sell, any properties or assets having a value greater than _____ Dollars ($ _____) for any single asset, or greater than _____Dollars ($ _____) in the aggregate;

(xiv) except for normal annual increases or increases resulting from the application of existing formulas under existing plans, agreements or policies relating to employee compensation, made any increase in the rate of compensation payable or to become payable to the Target's or any Subsidiary's officers or employees or any increase in the amounts paid or payable to such officers or employees under any bonus, insurance, pension or other benefit plan, or any arrangements therefor made for or with any of said officers or employees;

(xv) adopted, or amended, any collective bargaining, bonus, profit-sharing, compensation, stock option, pension, retirement, deferred compensation or other plan, agreement, trust, fund or arrangement for the benefit of employees;

(xvi) made any change in any material accounting principle, material accounting procedure or material accounting practice, if any, followed by the Target or any Subsidiary or in the method of applying such principle, procedure or practice [except as required by a change in generally accepted accounting principles in the country of domicile];

(xvii) made any provision for markdowns or shrinkage with respect to inventories other than in the ordinary course of business and consistent with past practices or any write-down of the value of inventory by the Target or any Subsidiary of more than _____Dollars ($ _____) in the aggregate;

(xviii) discharged any lien or paid any obligation or liability (whether absolute, accrued, contingent or otherwise) other than current liabilities shown on the Most Recent Balance Sheet, and current liabilities incurred thereafter;

(xix) mortgaged, pledged or subjected to any lien, except liens specifically excepted from the provisions of Section 4.17 hereof, any properties or assets, real, personal or mixed, tangible or intangible, of Target or any Subsidiary;

(xx) experienced any material shortage of raw materials or supplies;

(xxi) made any gifts or sold, transferred or exchanged any property for less than the fair value thereof; or

(xxii) made or entered into any agreement or understanding to do any of the foregoing.

In order to bring down the financial condition of the target and its subsidiaries from the date of the most recent balance sheet, the buyer should have the seller represent the lack of certain events since such date. Because there are no financial statements covering the period between the date of the most recent balance sheet and the closing date, it is important for the buyer to understand the operation of the business during this period. In addition, the buyer should require the seller to covenant that it will not breach this representation on or prior to the closing date (see Section 6.1). Included in Section 4.32 are representations regarding matters which, although not specifically related to the financial statements, provide vital information about the ongoing business of the target. For example, the representation requires the disclosure of any material shortage of raw materials or supplies. A buyer must, of course, tailor this representation to the business of its target.

> ***Section 4.33. Accuracy of Information Furnished.*** No representation or warranty by the Seller or Target contained in this Agreement, the Disclosure Statement or in respect of the exhibits, schedules, lists or other documents delivered to Buyer by the Seller and referred to herein, and no statement contained in any certificate furnished or to be furnished by or on behalf of the Seller or Target pursuant hereto, or in connection with the transactions contemplated hereby, contains, or will contain as of the date such representation or warranty is made or such certificate is or will be furnished, any untrue statement of a material fact, or omits, or will omit to state as of the date such representation or warranty is made or such certificate is or will be furnished, any material fact which is necessary to make the statements contained herein or therein not misleading. To the best knowledge of the Seller, the Target and the Subsidiaries, there is no fact which could have a Material Adverse Effect on the Target or any Subsidiary which the Seller has not prior to or on the date hereof disclosed to Buyer in writing.

The buyer will request this representation to provide assurance that the information upon which the buyer has based its evaluation of the target and its subsidiaries is accurate and complete. This representation is typically referred to as a "10b-5 representation" because the language closely parallels Rule 10b-5 promulgated by the Securities and Exchange Commission (SEC).

Similar to the representation made in Section 4.6 with respect to undisclosed liabilities, the last sentence in this representation shifts to the seller the responsibility of providing any information of which the buyer should be aware. The seller, although typically reluctant to make this representation, may derive some comfort from the fact that it has already told the buyer everything it could possibly know about the target and the subsidiaries in the preceding representations.

> *Section 4.34. Reports Filed with the Securities and Exchange Commission.* Buyer has been furnished with accurate and complete copies of each annual report on Form 10-K that Target has filed with the Securities and Exchange Commission, all other reports or documents, including all amendments and supplements thereto, required to be filed by the Seller pursuant to Section 13(a) or 15(d) of the Securities Exchange Act since the filing of the most recent annual report on Form 10-K and its most recent annual report to its stockholders. Such reports do not contain any material false statements or any misstatements of any material fact and do not omit to state any fact necessary to make the statements set forth therein not misleading in any material respect.

This representation is applicable only to targets that are publicly traded corporations required to file reports with the SEC. The buyer must assure itself that the target has discharged its obligations to file reports with the SEC, and that the statements contained in the target's filings are true and are not misleading. Failure to obtain this representation may expose the buyer to significant post-closing liabilities, as the target may be the object of stockholders' suits or SEC enforcement actions.

> *Section 4.35. Investment Purpose.* The Seller's acquisition of the [describe securities of Buyer to be purchased by Seller] is made for its own account for investment purposes only and not with a view to the resale or distribution thereof. The Seller agrees that it will not sell, assign or otherwise transfer or pledge the [describe securities of Buyer to be purchased by Seller] or any interest therein except in compliance with the transfer restrictions set forth on such securities.

When the seller has agreed to accept securities of the buyer in partial payment of the purchase price for the acquisition, the buyer should require certain investment representations from the seller. The representations of the seller are intended to provide the basis for characterizing the sale of securities to the seller as a private placement, thereby exempting the securities from registration under the Securities Act of 1933 and applicable state securities laws. However, this representation is not meant to satisfy all the requirements for exemption under the securities laws, especially in cases where there are more than a handful of persons receiving these securities.

Section 4.36. Dealership and Franchises.

(i) Section 4.36(i) of the Disclosure Statement contains a list of (a) those franchisees or dealers who or which, as of the date of this Agreement, were authorized by the Seller to operate stores under the name "_____," or other similar name associating such franchisee or dealer with the Seller (the "Franchisees"), (b) those Franchisees whose relationship with the Seller, the Target or any Subsidiary has been terminated within one year prior to the date hereof and (c) those persons who have become Franchisees within one year prior to the date hereof. Such list is true, correct and complete and includes the expiration date of each existing Franchise Agreement. The Seller has given Buyer an opportunity to review true and correct copies of each of the agreements between it, the Target or any Subsidiary and each Franchisee. Except as stated in Section 4.36(i) of the Disclosure Statement, each agreement between the Seller, the Target or any Subsidiary and each Franchisee (A) has been duly and validly authorized, executed and delivered by, and is the valid and binding obligation of, such Franchisee, enforceable against such Franchisee in accordance with its terms, except as may be limited by applicable bankruptcy, reorganization, insolvency, moratorium or other similar laws or by legal or equitable principles relating to or limiting creditors' rights generally, and (B) does not violate any law or regulation applicable thereto, and (C) does not conflict with the provisions of any other agreement.

(ii) Except as set forth in Section 4.36(ii) of the Disclosure Statement, there is not, under any agreement between the Seller, the Target or any Subsidiary and any Franchisee, any existing default or event which with notice or lapse of time, or both, would constitute an event of default and which has or would be reasonably likely to have a Material Adverse Effect. The execution and delivery of this Agreement and the performance of the transactions contemplated hereby will not result in any event of default under any agreement between the Seller, the Target or any Subsidiary and any Franchisee.

(iii) Except as set forth in Section 4.36(iii) of the Disclosure Statement, each Franchisee was offered his, her or its franchise in accordance with all applicable laws and regulations, including, without limitation, the regulations of the Federal Trade Commission, and any state and/or local agencies regulating the sale of franchised businesses. The Seller has not offered any person or entity a franchise since [insert a date 18 months prior to date of Agreement].

Where the target has entered into franchise or distributorship arrangements in the conduct of its business, the buyer will want to obtain specific disclosures about the terms of these arrangements. This representation is designed to require the seller to disclose the health of its contractual relations with its franchisees and distributors. A statement certifying compliance with Federal Trade Commission (FTC) regulations is important, as the target may be liable for any failure to comply with FTC disclosure requirements.

ARTICLE V: REPRESENTATIONS AND WARRANTIES OF THE BUYER

The Buyer represents and warrants to the Seller and the Target as follows:

Section 5.1. Organization. The Buyer is a corporation duly organized, validly existing and in good standing under the laws of the jurisdiction of its incorporation. The Buyer has delivered to the Seller true and correct copies of its Certificate of Incorporation and Bylaws.

Section 5.2. Authorization. The execution, delivery and performance of this Agreement and any instruments or agreements contemplated herein to be executed, delivered and performed by the Buyer (including without limitation, [list important agreements to be executed by Buyer on or before Closing]) (the "Buyer's Related Instruments"), and the consummation of the transactions contemplated hereby and thereby, have been duly adopted and approved by the Board of Directors and the stockholders, of the Buyer. The Buyer has all requisite power and authority to execute, deliver and perform this Agreement and the Buyer's Related Instruments and to consummate the transactions contemplated hereby and in the Buyer's Related Instruments. This Agreement has been and as of the Closing Date, each of the Buyer's Related Instruments will be, duly and validly authorized, executed and delivered by the Buyer. This Agreement is and the Buyer's Related Agreements are or will be, as of the Closing Date, the valid and binding obligation of the Buyer, enforceable against the Buyer in accordance with their respective terms.

Section 5.3. Non-Contravention; Consents. Except as set forth in Section 5.3 of the Disclosure Statement, the execution and delivery of this Agreement and the Related Instruments and the consummation of any of the transactions contemplated hereby and thereby by the Buyer do not and will not:

(i) violate any provisions of the Buyer's certificate of incorporation or bylaws;

(ii) violate, or result with the passage of time in the violation of, any provision of, or result in the acceleration of or entitle any party to accelerate (whether after the giving of notice or lapse of time or both) any obligation under, or result in the creation or imposition of any lien, charge, pledge, security interest or other encumbrance upon any of the properties of the Buyer pursuant to any provision of, any mortgage, lien, lease, agreement, permit, indenture, license, instrument, law, order, arbitration award, judgment or decree to which the Buyer is a party or by which it or any of its properties are bound, the effect of all of which violations, accelerations, creations and impositions would result, in the aggregate, in subjecting the Buyer to liabilities in excess of _____Dollars ($_____);

(iii) violate any law, order, judgment or decree to which the Buyer is subject;

(iv) violate or conflict with any other restriction of any kind or character to which the Buyer is subject, or by which any of their assets may be bound, the effect of all of which violations or conflicts would result, in the aggregate, in subjecting the Buyer to aggregate liabilities in excess of _____Dollars ($ _____); or

(v) require any consent, license, permit, notice, application, qualification, waiver or other action of any kind, authorization, order or approval of, or filing or registration with, any governmental commission, board, regulatory, or administrative agencies or authorities or other regulatory body.

Section 5.4. Litigation. There is no action, suit, proceeding or investigation pending, or, to the best of the Buyer's knowledge, threatened, against or related to the Buyer or its respective properties or business which would be reasonably likely to adversely affect or restrict the Buyer's ability to consummate the transactions contemplated hereby or in the Related Instruments; and there is no reasonable basis known to the Buyer for any such action that may result in such effect and is probable of assertion.

Section 5.5. Brokers and Finders. Neither the Buyer nor any stockholder, officer, director or agent of the Buyer has incurred on behalf of the Buyer any liability to any broker, finder or agent for any brokerage fees, finders' fees or commissions with respect to the transactions contemplated by this

Agreement, except to [name of broker or finder], whose fees will be paid by the Buyer.

Section 5.6. Business. The Buyer has not engaged in any activities other than those incident to its organization or as contemplated by the terms of this Agreement.

Section 5.7. Accuracy of Information Furnished. No representation or warranty by the Buyer contained in this Agreement, the Disclosure Statement or in respect of the exhibits, schedules, lists or other documents delivered to the Seller by the Buyer and referred to herein, and no statement contained in any certificate furnished or to be furnished by or on behalf of the Buyer pursuant hereto, or in connection with the transactions contemplated hereby, contains, or will contain as of the date such representation or warranty is made or such certificate is or will be furnished, any untrue statement of a material fact, or omits, or will omit to state as of the date such representation or warranty is made or such certificate is or will be furnished, any material fact which is necessary to make the statements contained herein or therein not misleading.

The representations and warranties of the buyer generally parallel the representations made by the seller and target in Article IV. However, there is no need for the buyer, as the acquirer, to make the vast number of representations and warranties required of the seller and target, because it is the businesses and assets of the seller that are being purchased and in respect of which most representations and warranties therefore apply.

In some instances, the buyer may accomplish its acquisition of the target by utilizing a shell company as the acquirer. If properly structured, this strategy may permit the parties to avoid filing a premerger notification under the Hart-Scott-Rodino Antitrust Improvements Act of 1974. The representation made in Section 5.6 above regarding the scope of the business of the buyer is useful to the seller in that it assures the seller that there should be few contractual constraints on the shell company to consummate the acquisition.

In circumstances where the buyer is not a shell company, it may be appropriate for the seller to include additional representations about the buyer. For example, a representation relating to the buyer's financial statements and the absence of certain changes or events since the date of such financial statements might assure the seller of the buyer's ability to consummate the transaction.

ARTICLE VI: COVENANTS OF SELLER AND TARGET

Section 6.1. Conduct of Business. Except as set forth on Section 6.1 of the Disclosure Statement or required to consummate the transactions contemplated hereby, from and after the execution and delivery of this Agreement and until the Closing Date, the Seller shall cause the Target and each of the Subsidiaries (a) to use its best efforts to preserve the respective present business organizations of the Target and the Subsidiaries substantially intact; (b) to maintain in effect all foreign, federal, state and local approvals, permits, licenses, qualifications and authorizations which are required to carry on their respective businesses as now being conducted; (c) to use their best efforts to maintain their respective relationships with and preserve the goodwill of, employees, agents, distributors, franchisees, licensees, customers, suppliers and others having business dealings with them; and (d) without the prior written consent of the Buyer, to take any action which would result in a breach of any of the representations set forth in Section 4.32 hereof.

The "conduct of business" covenant is used by a buyer to ensure that the seller will not do, or cause to be done, anything that would (a) alter the business being purchased, (b) diminish the value of such business to the buyer, or (c) create for the buyer an unanticipated liability or problem with respect to the business it is acquiring. This is important because the buyer has presumably negotiated an acceptable purchase price for the target based on the operations and performance of the business as it presently exists. If the seller were to allow necessary permits or licenses, or business relationships with distributors, employees, or franchisees to lapse, the value of the business could be diminished. If not restricted by such a covenant, the seller could render the buyer's valuation meaningless by taking some action outside of the ordinary course of business that impairs the financial position of the target or the value of the target to the buyer. One issue that often arises is how to define the actions that are in the ordinary course of business. Since most agreements fail to include a definition of this phrase, the buyer should acquaint itself with applicable case law in order to be aware of its usage in the jurisdiction governing the acquisition agreement.

In negotiating this representation, the seller should be certain that, between the signing of the agreement and the closing date, it need not obtain the buyer's consent for anything other than items that would not normally occur in the ordinary course of business of the target or its subsidiaries. Subsection (d) incorporates all the items represented in Section 4.32 and consequently may require the seller to obtain the buyer's consent for actions to be taken by the target or any subsidiary that are extremely important to the continued operation of the business. A seller would likely request that the buyer agree not to unreasonably withhold its consent in order for the seller to take such actions. Although this language may seem innocuous, it can in certain circumstances have consequences that the buyer did not intend at the time. As state courts have not consistently interpreted the standard of reasonableness, the buyer may be unable to reconcile its business judgments with local case precedent. A common strategy is for a buyer to require unmodified consent in its first draft, and then, if the seller requests it, add the reasonableness standard as a bargaining point or show of good faith.

> *Section 6.2. Pre-Closing Activities.* Prior to the Closing Date, the Seller shall cause the Target, with the cooperation of the Buyer where appropriate, and the Target shall and shall cause each Subsidiary to use their best efforts to obtain any consent, authorization or approval of, or exemption by, any governmental authority or agency or other third party, including without limitation, their landlords and lenders and those persons (other than the Target or a Subsidiary) who are parties to the agreements described in Section 4.29 of the Disclosure Statement required to be obtained or made by them in connection with the transactions contemplated by this Agreement and the Related Instruments or the taking of any action in connection with the consummation thereof, including without limitation, any consent, authorization or approval necessary to waive any default under any of the agreements described in Section 4.29 of the Disclosure Statement.

Once the buyer is made aware of the various consents necessary to consummate the acquisition by means of the seller's disclosure in Section 4.29, the buyer typically will attempt to require the seller to use its best efforts to obtain such consents. The seller, who has an interest in getting the deal done, should agree to accommodate the buyer, but only to the extent it is reasonable for the seller to do so under the circumstances. It should make clear that "best efforts" do not extend to spending money.

> *Section 6.3. Proposals; Disclosure.* Prior to the Closing Date, the Target and the Seller (i) will not, directly or indirectly, whether through any of their officers, employees, representatives or otherwise, solicit or encourage any written inquiries or proposals for the acquisition of stock, or all or substantially all of the assets or the business or any portion thereof of the

Target or any Subsidiary and (ii) will promptly advise the Buyer orally and in writing of any inquiry or proposal for the acquisition of any stock, or all or substantially all of the assets or business or any portion thereof of the Target or any Subsidiary occurring on or after the date hereof.

This covenant is designed (a) to prevent the seller from shopping for a better deal during the period between the signing of the acquisition agreement and the Closing Date and (b) to keep the buyer apprised of any unsolicited inquiries. From the buyer's point of view, the seller has made a commitment to sell to the buyer and should be concentrating all its efforts toward a closing with the buyer rather than continuing to court other would-be suitors. In addition, the acquisition agreement represents a binding contract, and the buyer has made a commitment to purchase provided that all conditions to closing are satisfied. The buyer should have the benefit of having made such a commitment as well as the risk of a deterioration in the target's business in the ordinary course of events. One benefit of ownership is the opportunity to sell at a profit. The *Pennzoil v. Texaco* case has highly publicized the fact that this benefit belongs to a potential buyer once a contractual commitment between the seller and buyer has been put in place.

Section 6.4. Additional Financial Statements. Prior to the Closing Date, the Target shall furnish to the Buyer as soon as practicable but in no event later than _____ days after the close of each quarterly period or _____ days after the close of each monthly period (i) for each successive quarterly period ending after the date of the Most Recent Balance Sheet, an unaudited consolidated quarterly balance sheet and related statements of income, stockholders' equity and changes in financial position of the Target and its Subsidiaries and (ii) for each successive monthly period ending after the date of the Most Recent Balance Sheet, an unaudited consolidated monthly balance sheet and related monthly statements of income, stockholders' equity and changes in financial position of the Target and its Subsidiaries. Such financial statements shall be complete, accurate and correct and present fairly the financial condition of the Target and the Subsidiaries, both individually and taken as a whole, as of the end of each such quarterly or monthly period, as the case may be, and shall present fairly the results of operations for each of the quarterly or monthly periods then ended, in accordance with generally accepted accounting principles consistently applied except for the footnotes thereto, normal year-end adjustments consistent with past practices or as contemplated by this Agreement.

Section 6.5. Additional Summaries of Accounts Receivable. Prior to the Closing Date, the Target will deliver to the Buyer, as soon as practicable but in no event later than _____ days after the close of the appropriate monthly period hereinafter referred to, for each successive monthly period after the date of the Most Recent Balance Sheet a true and correct summary of all accounts receivable of the Target and the Subsidiaries as at the end of each such monthly period.

Sections 6.4 and 6.5 permit the buyer to monitor the operations of the business after the execution of the acquisition agreement by reviewing monthly and quarterly financial statements furnished by the seller. This can be extremely important to the buyer, especially if the financial statements reveal a material adverse change in the business. In this event, the buyer would not be obligated to close, since a customary condition to its obligation to close is the absence of any material adverse changes in the business. For a further discussion of material adverse change, see Section 9.6.

Section 6.6. Investigation by Buyer. The Seller and Target shall, and the Target shall cause its Subsidiaries to, afford to the officers and authorized representatives of the Buyer free and full access, during normal business hours and upon reasonable prior notice, to the offices, plants, properties, books and records of the Target and its Subsidiaries in order that the Buyer may have full opportunity to make such investigations of the business, operations, assets, properties and legal and financial condition of the Target and its Subsidiaries as the Buyer deems reasonably necessary or desirable and the officers of the Seller, the Target and its Subsidiaries shall furnish the Buyer with such additional financial and operating data and other information relating to the business operations, assets, properties and legal and financial condition of the Target and its Subsidiaries as the Buyer shall from time to time reasonably request. Prior to the Closing Date, or at all times if this Agreement shall be terminated, the Buyer shall, except as may be otherwise required by applicable law, hold confidential all information obtained pursuant to this Section 6.6 with respect to the Target and its Subsidiaries and, if this Agreement shall be terminated, shall return to the Target and its Subsidiaries all such information as shall be in documentary form and shall not use any information obtained pursuant to this Section 6.6 in any manner that would have a material adverse consequence to the Target or its Subsidiaries.

The representations, warranties and agreements of the Seller, the Target and its Subsidiaries set forth in this Agreement shall be effective regardless of any investigation that the Buyer has undertaken or failed to undertake.

The "investigation" covenant ensures that the seller will cooperate with the buyer by granting access and logistical support for the buyer's due diligence review of the target and its subsidiaries. It is important for the buyer to include the last paragraph of this covenant so that the seller cannot attempt to prevent the buyer from taking action against the seller as a result of a material breach of the seller's or target's representations by alleging that, since the buyer discovered or could have discovered the breach during its investigation of the target and its subsidiaries, the seller should be relieved of any responsibility for such misrepresentations.

> **Section 6.7. Notification.** The Seller shall give prompt notice to the Buyer of (i) any notice of, or other communication received by the Seller, the Target or any Subsidiary subsequent to the date of this Agreement and prior to the Closing Date, relating to a default or event which with notice or lapse of time or both would become a default, or which would cause any warranty or representation of the Seller or the Target to be untrue or misleading in any material respect, under this Agreement, or any other material contract, agreement or instrument to which the Target or any Subsidiary is a party, by which it or any of its property is bound or to which it or any of its property is subject, (ii) any notice or other communication from any third party alleging that the consent of such third party is or may be required in connection with the transactions contemplated by this Agreement, (iii) any material adverse change in the business, operations, earnings, prospects, assets or financial condition of the Target or its Subsidiaries, or (iv) any information received by the Seller or Target prior to the Closing Date relating to the operations of the Buyer which, to the best knowledge of the Seller or Target, constitutes (or would be reasonably likely to constitute) or indicates (or would be reasonably likely to indicate) a breach of any representation, warranty or covenant made by the Buyer herein or in any other document relating to the transactions contemplated hereby.

The "notice" covenant places on the seller the onus of notifying the buyer of any potential material breaches of the seller's representations and warranties. Upon such notification, the buyer has the option of asserting a breach and abandoning the deal on the grounds that the conditions to closing are not met. However, a buyer does not have a right to walk from the deal if the breach can be cured by the seller prior to the closing.

> **Section 6.8. Access to Records.** After the Closing, the Buyer shall be entitled to reasonable access to the business and tax records of the Seller relating to the Target and its Subsidiaries for proper business purposes, includ-

ing the preparation of tax returns. In connection with any such purpose, the Seller agrees to cooperate with the Buyer in the communication of information contained in such records and the handling of examinations, appeals and litigations.

This covenant may be important where many of the records of the target and its subsidiaries are consolidated with those of the seller. It is impossible in such circumstances for the seller to turn over to the buyer such records, since they may also relate to other companies owned by the seller.

Section 6.9. Stockholders Meeting. The Target, acting through its Board of Directors shall, as soon as practicable and in accordance with its Articles of Incorporation and By-Laws and applicable law:

(1) prepare and distribute proxy materials (the "Proxy Statement") in compliance with applicable law for, and duly call, give notice of, convene and hold, a special meeting (the "Special Meeting") of its stockholders as soon as practicable after the date hereof but not later than [insert the date] for the purposes of considering and voting upon this Agreement in accordance with the [name of business code for Target's state of incorporation] Code;

(2) include in the Proxy Statement (as hereinafter defined) the recommendation of the Board that stockholders of the Target vote in favor of the approval and adoption of this Agreement; and

(3) use its best efforts (a) to obtain and furnish the information required to be included by it in the Proxy Statement, (b) to file a preliminary version of the Proxy Statement with the Securities and Exchange Commission ("SEC") not later than [insert number of days] after the receipt by the Target of its audited financial statement for the year ended [insert year], furnish copies thereof to the Buyer and, after consultation with the Buyer, respond promptly to any comments made by the SEC with respect to the Proxy Statement and any preliminary version thereof, (c) to cause the Proxy Statement to be mailed to its stockholders as early as practicable after the date hereof but no later than [insert number of days], and (d) to obtain the necessary approval of this Agreement by its stockholders. Notwithstanding any consultation with the Buyer in connection with the Proxy Statement, neither the Buyer nor any of its officers, directors, employees or affiliates shall incur any liability to the Target or its stockholders with respect thereto, except with respect to any information contained in the Proxy Statement which any of them has furnished, or confirmed the accuracy of, in writing to the Target.

(4) amend, supplement or revise the Proxy Statement as may from time to time be necessary in order to insure that the Proxy Statement does not

contain any statement which, at the time and in the light of the circumstances under which it is made, is false or misleading with respect to any material fact, or omits to state any material fact necessary in order to make the statements therein not false or misleading. Prior to submitting any such amendment, supplement or revision of the Proxy Statement to the stockholders of the Target, such amendment, supplement or revision shall be submitted to the Buyer for its approval. Notwithstanding such approval, neither the Buyer nor any of its officers, directors, employees or affiliates shall incur any liability to the Target or its stockholders with respect thereto, except with respect to any information contained in such amendment, supplement or revision which any of them has furnished, or confirmed the accuracy of, in writing to the Target.

In an acquisition of a target whose equity securities are publicly traded, it is essential that the target comply with all relevant regulations, especially those promulgated by the Securities and Exchange Commission dealing with proxies and required stockholders' meetings. Failure to comply with these regulations can expose the target to stockholder suits or regulatory enforcement actions. The buyer is also desirous of placing an affirmative obligation on the target to solicit proxies and to obtain stockholder approval.

In some circumstances, the buyer may require the seller to deliver a cold comfort letter from the seller's or target's accountants at closing confirming the financial information in the proxy statement. The purpose of this requirement is to reduce the potential for error in the financial information presented in the proxy statement and thereby reduce the chance that a stockholder may prevail in a suit against the surviving corporation.

Section 6.10. Dissenting Stockholders; Notice. The Target will promptly advise the Buyer of each notice given or demand made by a dissenting Target stockholder pursuant to [cite relevant section of business law in state where Target is incorporated].

No buyer wants to close a transaction in which a large percentage of the target's stockholders are seeking appraisal rights. If such stockholders were to be awarded a price per share in excess of the price paid by the buyer, it could expose the surviving corporation to an inordinate amount of liability. Therefore, as covered in Section 9.10 and the discussion that follows, in order for a buyer to exercise its right not to consummate the transaction pursuant to Section 9.10, it must be aware of any dissenting stockholders of the target.

ARTICLE VII: COVENANTS OF THE BUYER

The Buyer shall give prompt notice to the Seller of (i) any notice of, or other communication received by the Buyer subsequent to the date of this Agreement and prior to the Closing Date, relating to a default or event which with notice or lapse of time or both would become a default, or which would cause any warranty, or representation of the Buyer to be untrue or misleading in any material respect, under this Agreement, or any other material contract, agreement or instrument to which the Buyer is a party, by which it or any of its property is bound or to which it or any of its property is subject, (ii) any notice or other communication from any third party alleging that the consent of such third party is or may be required in connection with the transactions contemplated by this Agreement, or (iii) any information received by the Buyer prior to the Closing Date relating to the operations of the Seller, the Target or its Subsidiaries which, to the best knowledge of the Buyer, constitutes (or would constitute) or indicates (or would indicate) a breach of any representation, warranty or covenant made by the Seller or Target herein or in any other document relating to the transactions contemplated hereby.

Similar to the representations, the seller's covenants usually far outnumber the covenants of the buyer. Typically, a seller would at a minimum require a buyer to give the same "notice" that it is required to give. One useful device (which is advantageous to both buyer and seller) is the requirement that each notify the other in the event that the first party is aware of the other's breach of a particular representation, warranty, or covenant. The utility of this obligation, especially for the seller, is that neither side has a distinct advantage over the other post-closing by reason of a breach that was known about prior to the closing.

ARTICLE VIII: COVENANTS OF BUYER, TARGET AND SELLER

Section 8.1. Governmental Filings. The Buyer, the Target and the Seller shall cooperate with each other in filing any necessary applications, reports or other documents with any federal or state agencies, authorities or bodies (domestic and foreign) having jurisdiction with respect to the Merger, and in seeking necessary consultation with and prompt favorable action by any such agencies, authorities or bodies. Without limiting the generality of the foregoing, the Buyer, the Target and the Seller shall as soon as practicable, and in any event within fifteen (15) days, after the date hereof, make the necessary filings under the Hart-Scott-Rodino Antitrust Improvements Act of 1976 (the "Hart-Scott-Rodino Act") and shall cooperate in attempting to secure early termination of the applicable waiting period.

This covenant requires the buyer, target, and seller to work together in making any governmental filing or application. The buyer and the seller should use a general covenant of this type and then specify the particular filings that must be made (Hart-Scott-Rodino Act filings with respect to a merger, SEC filings, state government filings, and so on).

> ***Section 8.2. Publicity.*** The Buyer, the Target and the Seller will consult with each other before making any public announcements with respect to the Merger or the Related Instruments or the transactions contemplated hereby or thereby, and any public announcements shall be made only at such time and in such manner as the Seller and the Buyer shall mutually agree, except that either party shall be free to make such public announcements as it shall reasonably deem necessary to comply with foreign, federal or state laws.

The buyer and the seller must be aware of each other's plans with respect to publicity surrounding the acquisition of a target so as to be able to coordinate their efforts. It can be extremely harmful to the transaction or one of the parties to the transaction if there are conflicting reports or misleading statements. For example, conflicting reports in the press can disrupt management of the target or may even damage the ongoing business. More importantly, where one or both of the entities involved are public companies, liability can arise from premature press reports that might be alleged to have been made to manipulate the market or mislead stockholders and investors. When possible, the buyer and seller should issue joint press releases or, at least, carefully review releases before they are distributed.

ARTICLE IX: CONDITIONS TO OBLIGATIONS OF THE BUYER

> The obligations of the Buyer to consummate this Agreement, and the transactions to be consummated by the Buyer hereunder on the Closing Date, shall be subject to the satisfaction, prior to or concurrently with the Closing, of each of the conditions set forth in this Article IX; such conditions may be waived in writing in whole or in part by the Buyer to the extent permitted by applicable law.

Section 9.1. Compliance with Agreement. The Seller and the Target shall have complied with and performed the terms, conditions, acts, undertakings, covenants and obligations required by this Agreement to be complied with and performed by each of them on or before the Closing Date; and the Buyer shall have received from the Seller at the Closing a certificate, dated the Closing Date and signed by the President or a Vice President of the Seller to such effect.

This condition gives the buyer the opportunity to abandon the acquisition if the seller or the target has failed to perform its obligations under the acquisition agreement. Although this condition is less critical than the bring-down of representations and warranties to the closing date that appears in Section 9.2, it provides the buyer a valuable "out" if the seller or the target has breached a covenant that is essential to the buyer's valuation of the target. For example, the duty of the target to endeavor to obtain all regulatory approvals necessary for the transaction would usually arise from a covenant made to the buyer in the acquisition agreement, as would the obligation of the target to conduct business only in the ordinary and usual course. Because failure to perform under these covenants may compromise the value of the target, the buyer must ensure its right to abandon the transaction in these circumstances.

The requirement for an officer's certificate is based upon the belief that prior to any officer's execution of such a certificate, the officer will investigate to ascertain its accuracy, and the certificate can be drafted to include a representation to that effect.

This condition can be drafted without a materiality standard. However, sellers typically demand that the materiality qualifier be incorporated. This position is a reasonable one given the broad language of both the condition itself and the covenants and other agreements to which it refers. Consequently, the buyer should be prepared to accept "performance in all material respects of the terms" of the agreement as adequate protection of its interests. A similar qualifier appears in the condition set forth in Section 9.2 below.

Section 9.2. Representations and Warranties True as of Closing Date. All representations and warranties of the Seller and the Target set forth in this Agreement shall be true and correct in all material respects on and as of the Closing Date with the same force and effect as though such representations and warranties had been made on and as of the Closing Date and the Buyer shall have received from the Seller at the Closing a certificate, dated the Closing Date and signed by the President or a Vice President of the Seller to such effect.

The importance of this bring-down condition was discussed in detail in this chapter. A bring-down of the representations and warranties to the closing date is, from the buyer's perspective, insurance that the target it acquires is the target for which it bid and upon which it conducted due diligence.

Section 9.3. Third Party Orders and Consents.

(i) The Seller and the Buyer shall have fully complied with the applicable provisions of the Hart-Scott-Rodino Act and any and all applicable waiting periods thereunder shall have expired, or an opinion, reasonably acceptable to the Buyer, that no such filing is required shall have been delivered to the Buyer.

(ii) All consents and approvals listed in Section 4.29 of the Disclosure Statement hereto shall have been obtained, and the Seller and the Buyer shall have been furnished with appropriate evidence, reasonably satisfactory to them and their respective counsel, of the granting of such consents and approvals.

This condition enables the buyer to abandon a transaction if all necessary consents are not obtained before closing. Failure to obtain the consent of the target's lenders, for example, may prejudice the pricing of the acquisition or its financeability because consummation of the transaction may entitle the lenders to accelerate their debts or impose a lien on the property of the target. Failure to obtain necessary governmental consent to an acquisition may preclude the buyer from operating the business of the target as previously operated.

The seller should attempt to limit this condition to governmental consents necessary in order to consummate the transactions contemplated by the acquisition agreement. The seller could reasonably maintain that any debt instruments that are accelerated by their terms should be refinanced by the buyer. If this limitation is accepted, the obligation of the buyer to close the deal should not be conditioned upon the consent of the holders of such debt. Clearly, the buyer and the seller must agree on exactly what consents must be obtained prior to the closing.

Section 9.4. Corporate Action. The Buyer shall have received:

(i) a copy of the resolution or resolutions duly adopted by the Board of Directors of the Seller and the Target and by the stockholders of the Target authorizing the execution, delivery and performance of this Agreement and the Related Instruments by the Seller and the Target, and authorizing all other necessary or proper corporate action to enable the Seller and the Target to comply with the terms of this Agreement, certified in each case by the Secretary or an Assistant Secretary of the Seller or the Target as the case may be; and

(ii) a certificate of the Secretary or an Assistant Secretary of each of the Seller and the Target, dated the Closing Date, as to the incumbency and signatures of the officers of the Seller and the Target, respectively, executing this Agreement and the Related Instruments and any other documents in connection with the transactions contemplated by this Agreement or the Related Instruments.

A further protection for the buyer that the acquisition agreement and related documents are properly authorized and delivered is a review of the resolutions authorizing such documents.

Section 9.5. Opinion of the Sellers and Targets Counsel. At the Closing, the Seller shall furnish the Buyer and the banks and/or other financial institutions providing financing for the Merger (the "Acquisition Lenders") with an opinion, dated the Closing Date, of [name of Seller's counsel], in form and substance satisfactory to the Buyer and its counsel and the Acquisition Lenders and counsel to the Acquisition Lenders, to the effect that:

(i) Target (a) is a corporation duly organized, validly existing and in good standing under the laws of its state of incorporation, (b) is duly qualified or licensed to transact business as a foreign corporation and is in good standing in each jurisdiction in which the properties owned or leased by it or the nature of the business conducted by it makes such qualification or licensing necessary, except in those jurisdictions where the failure to be so qualified or licensed and in good standing will not, individually or in the aggregate, have a Material Adverse Effect, and (c) has full power and authority to carry on its business as it is now being conducted and to own the properties and assets it now owns;

(ii) Target has full power and authority to execute, deliver and perform the Agreement and the Related Instruments and to consummate the transactions contemplated hereby and by the Related Instruments; and the execution, delivery and performance of the Agreement and the Related Instruments and the consummation of the transactions contemplated by the Agreement and the Related Instruments have been duly authorized by all requisite action on the part of the Target;

(iii) the Seller is a corporation duly organized, validly existing and in good standing under the laws of its state of incorporation and has full power and authority to execute, deliver and perform the Agreement and the Related Instruments and to consummate the transactions contemplated by the Agreement and the Related Instruments; and the execution, delivery and performance of the Agreement and the Related Instruments and the consummation of the transactions contemplated by the Agreement and the Related Instruments have been duly authorized by all requisite action on the part of the Seller;

(iv) each of the Subsidiaries (a) is a corporation duly organized, validly existing and in good standing under the laws of its jurisdiction of organization, (b) is duly qualified or licensed to transact business and is in good standing in each jurisdiction in which the properties owned or leased by it or the nature of the business conducted by it makes such qualification or licensing necessary, except in those jurisdictions where the failure to be so qualified or licensed and in good standing will not, individually or in the aggregate, have a Material Adverse Effect and (c) has full power and authority to carry on its business as it is now being conducted and to own the properties and assets it now owns;

(v) the authorized, issued and outstanding equity capital of the Target and each Subsidiary consists solely of (a) in the case of the Target, _____shares of Common Stock, of which _____shares are issued and outstanding and _____shares of Preferred Stock, of which _____shares are issued and outstanding and (b) in the case of each Subsidiary, as set forth in Section 4.3 of the Disclosure Statement (the "Subsidiary Stock"). All outstanding shares of the Target Common Stock and the Subsidiary Stock have been duly and validly authorized and issued and are fully paid, nonassessable and free of preemptive rights and based upon an examination of the organizational documents, minute books, stock registers and other similar records of the Target, all of such shares are owned of record and beneficially by (a) the Seller, in the case of the Target and (b) as set forth in Section 4.1 of the Disclosure Statement, in the case of each Subsidiary, in each case free and clear of all claims, liens, mortgages, charges, security interests, encumbrances and other restrictions or limitations of any kind whatsoever, and there are no outstanding options, warrants, calls, convertible securities or other rights relating to unissued shares of capital stock of Target or any Subsidiary;

(vi) the Agreement and the Related Instruments have been executed and delivered by each of the Seller and the Target and constitutes the legal, valid and binding obligations of each of the Seller and the Target, enforceable against each in accordance with their respective terms, except (a) as such enforcement may be subject to fraudulent conveyance, bankruptcy, insolvency, reorganization, moratorium or other similar laws now or hereafter in effect, or by legal or equitable principles, relating to or limiting creditors' rights generally and (b) that the remedy of specific performance and injunctive and other forms of equitable relief are subject to certain equitable defenses and to the discretion of the court before which any proceeding therefor may be brought;

(vii) neither the execution, delivery and performance of the Agreement or the Related Instruments by the Seller or the Target, nor the consummation of the transactions contemplated hereby or thereby will violate any provision of the Certificate of Incorporation or Bylaws of the Seller or the Target or of any of the Subsidiaries or, to the best knowledge of such counsel after due inquiry, will violate, conflict with, or constitute a default under, or cause the acceleration of maturity of any debt or obligation pursuant to, or result in the creation or imposition of any security interest, lien or other encumbrance upon any property or assets of the Target or any of the Subsidiaries under, any contract, commitment, agreement, trust, understanding, arrangement or restriction of any kind to which the Target or any of the Subsidiaries is a party or by which the Target or any of the Subsidiaries is bound or violate any statute or law, or any judgment, decree, order, regulation or rule of any court or governmental authority;

(viii) to the best knowledge of such counsel, none of the Target, the Seller nor any Subsidiary is engaged in or threatened with any legal action or other proceeding or has incurred or been charged with or is under investigation with respect to any violation of any law or administrative regulation which if adversely determined might, in such counsel's opinion, materially adversely affect or impair (a) the business or condition, financial or otherwise, of the Target or any of the Subsidiaries except as specifically disclosed in the Agreement or the Disclosure Statement or (b) the ability of the Target and/or the Seller to consummate the transactions contemplated by the Agreement or the Related Instruments;

(ix) no filing, declaration or registration with, or any permit, authorization, license, consent or approval of, any governmental or regulatory authority is required in connection with the execution, delivery and performance of the Agreement or the Related Instruments by the Seller and the Target or the consummation of the transactions contemplated by the Agreement or the Related Instruments, except as expressly disclosed in this Agreement, all of which have been duly and validly obtained;

(x) no facts have come to the attention of such counsel that cause such counsel to believe that any information provided to the Buyer in writing by or on behalf of the Seller or the Target contained any untrue statement of a material fact or omitted to state any material fact necessary to make the statements therein, in light of the circumstances under which they were made, not misleading, except that counsel may also state that it has not independently verified the accuracy, completeness or fairness of such information, and the limitations inherent in the examination made by it and the knowledge available to it are such that it is unable to assume, and does not assume, any responsibility for the accuracy, completeness or fairness of such information.

As to any matter contained in such opinion which involves the laws of a jurisdiction other than the United States or the State of [state in which such counsel is licensed to practice], such counsel may rely upon opinions of local counsel of established reputation reasonably satisfactory to the Buyer, which opinions shall expressly state that they may be relied upon by the Buyer and the Acquisition Lenders. Such counsel may also expressly rely as to matters of fact upon certificates furnished by appropriate officers of the Seller, the Target and any Subsidiary, or appropriate governmental officials.

Typically, the seller and the target will require an opinion from the buyer's counsel (see Section 10.6) that mirrors many of the provisions included in the opinion given by the seller's counsel. Although these opinions may be heavily negotiated by the counsel who must render them, they are useful for a variety of reasons. First, legal opinions serve as a due diligence device and force counsel to closely examine the important aspects of the transaction. Second, counsel's reluctance to deliver an opinion regarding a particular issue raises a red flag, permitting the parties to reexamine that aspect of the transaction. Third, the opinion gives the party to which it is addressed legal recourse against counsel delivering the opinion. In this regard, the buyer may be asked to accept the opinion of general counsel to the seller or target. The buyer should resist this request since the buyer's recourse against the general counsel of the target may be tantamount to recourse against the surviving corporation. In contrast, outside counsel's opinion provides recourse against an independent source, one that may be more diligent in its efforts and less biased in its evaluation as a result of its potential liability and relative "distance" from seller's management.

In some circumstances, the buyer may be required to accept the opinion of general counsel with respect to certain matters relating to the law of a jurisdiction where it would be impractical or inordinately expensive to retain outside counsel. In addition, outside counsel frequently relies on a backup opinion from the general counsel of the target with respect to matters that pertain to the business of the target in general. For example, general counsel would probably provide a backup opinion with respect to whether the target is qualified as a foreign corporation in each jurisdiction in which the properties owned or leased by it or the nature of the business conducted by it makes such qualification or licensure necessary.

The opinion also may be used as a negotiating tool in the earlier phases of the transaction; counsel's unwillingness to opine that no governmental consent is required in connection with the contemplated transactions or to the enforceability of particular documents may cause the parties to revamp the structure of the transaction.

One opinion that counsel is often reluctant to deliver is expressed in clause (x) above. Only rarely will counsel accept such a high level of responsibility. If the acquisition involves a public company, counsel may agree to opine to the accuracy of the proxy statement if counsel oversaw its preparation. Otherwise, despite the buyer's legitimate concern with the accuracy of information provided by the seller, the target, and the subsidiaries, it will not have the comfort of counsel's opinion on the matter. If a party is extremely concerned about the withholding of information or the accuracy thereof, it may be able to persuade the seller's counsel to include clause (x) at the end of its opinion letter without giving it the benefit of being a legal opinion.

> **Section 9.6. No Material Adverse Change.** No material adverse change in the business, operations, earnings, prospects, assets or financial condition of the Target or any Subsidiary and no event which would have such an effect shall have occurred.

As discussed, a customary condition to the buyer's obligation to close the transaction is that the target has not suffered any adverse change prior to the closing. The seller should attempt to limit this condition to the target and its subsidiaries taken as a whole since the buyer is not buying the target and its subsidiaries piecemeal. The seller should also focus on the phrase "business, operations, earnings, prospects, assets or financial condition" because, in some instances, the buyer may not have bargained for a certain earnings stream or the prospects of the target. For example, in a transaction based on the net assets of the target, a seller who has not made any projections as to the growth of the business of the target could argue that the target's "earnings" and "prospects" are irrelevant and should be deleted from this condition since the deal was not priced on a multiple of earnings or discounted cash flow. This appears plausible, since the buyer has based its investment decision only on the value of the net assets. However, most buyers will resist this approach, alleging that future earnings were an important factor in the investment decision.

Conversely, where the buyer has relied on projections, it should specifically include the projections in this condition as a yardstick for measuring the prospects of the target.

What constitutes a material adverse change is unclear and varies from circumstance to circumstance. It's easy to identify an obvious one, such as the single line target that has lost the only supplier of raw materials for the manufacture of its product. But the loss of a customer whose purchase of goods from the target constitutes 5 percent of the target's overall revenues is a less clear-cut situation. The usual vagueness of this condition gives the buyer the opportunity to get out of the deal, even in circumstances where the change is of uncertain harm to the target, because the seller is usually disinclined to bring suit on the basis that no material adverse change has occurred. Of course, the buyer must have some real basis for its belief that a material adverse change has occurred. Usually, the seller and buyer attempt to restructure the transaction in light of any material adverse change.

> *Section 9.7. Litigation.* At the Closing, there shall be no effective injunction, writ or preliminary restraining order or any order of any nature issued by a court or governmental agency of competent jurisdiction restraining or prohibiting the consummation of the transactions provided for herein or any of them or limiting in any manner the Buyer's right to control the Target and the Subsidiaries or any aspect of their businesses or requiring the sale or other disposition of any of the operations of the Target or any Subsidiary or making the consummation of the Merger or the transactions contemplated by this Agreement and the Related Instruments unduly burdensome to the Target or any Subsidiary, and immediately prior to the Closing Date no proceeding or lawsuit shall have been commenced and be pending or be threatened by any governmental or regulatory agency or any other person with respect to the transactions contemplated by this Agreement or the Related Instruments which the Buyer, in good faith and with the advice of counsel, believes is likely to result in any of the foregoing or which seeks the payment of substantial damages by the Target, any Subsidiary or the Buyer.

The utility of this condition is self-explanatory. It is usually triggered in circumstances in which the acquisition is either unfriendly and a potential suitor has brought suit to enjoin the consummation of the transaction contemplated by the acquisition agreement, or a governmental agency has attempted to enjoin the transaction because of antitrust or other governmental concerns.

Section 9.8. Financing.

(i) The Buyer shall have received the financing proceeds pursuant to, and on substantially the same terms and conditions as those contained in, the commitment letter from [name of Acquisition Lender].

(ii) The final documentation of such financing arrangements referred to in the commitment letter from [name of Acquisition Lender] shall in all respects be reasonably satisfactory in form and substance to the Buyer.

This "financing out" is discussed earlier in this chapter. The version included here is appropriate if the buyer has obtained financing commitments before signing the acquisition agreement. Another method, which is appropriate if the parties have agreed that the buyer must finance the transaction within a certain period of time, is to build in a provision enabling the parties to terminate the acquisition agreement if commitment letters are not obtained or the deal is not closed by a specific date.

Section 9.9. Title Insurance.
[Insert name of title company], or any other reputable title company reasonably satisfactory to the Buyer (the "Title Company") shall have issued owners', lessees' and mortgagees' title insurance policies (or unconditional commitments therefor) with respect to, and in the amount of the fair market value of, the real property and the leased real property listed in Section 4.15 of the Disclosure Statement and located in the United States, the United States territories and possessions and Canada, on the current edition of the A.L.T.A. Form B, Rev. 1970 (or Loan Policy Form, in the case of mortgagees' title insurance) insuring title, with all standard and general exceptions deleted or endorsed over so as to afford full "extended form coverage," except for the lien of taxes not yet due and payable, and with no further exceptions not reasonably satisfactory to the Buyer. It is hereby agreed that if, in order to delete, or endorse over, standard form or general exceptions so as to afford to owners, lessees or lenders "extended form coverage," the Title Company requires standard form seller's affidavits, the conditions set forth in this Section 9.10 shall be satisfied by an authorized officer of the Seller giving such affidavit. The Buyer

shall have received unconditional title insurance commitments reflecting the foregoing matters at least ten (10) days prior to Closing.

This condition provides the buyer comfort that the real property owned or leased by the target is free from defects in title and, consequently, may be used to secure acquisition financing. The seller may demand that this condition be effective only to the extent that acquisition lenders require title insurance. On the other hand, the buyer may strengthen the condition to make the existence of a title defect that compromises the business of the target a sufficient basis for abandoning the transaction. To the extent that title insurance is unavailable and the real property is an integral part of the business of the target, this condition gives the buyer the opportunity to renegotiate the price of the acquisition or to walk away from the deal.

Section 9.10. Dissenting Stockholders. Holders of not more than [insert percentage] of the Target's Common Stock shall have elected dissenter's rights as provided in Section [ ] of the [business code of Target's state of incorporation] Code, and the Target shall have taken all action with respect to the rights of dissenting stockholders required of it pursuant to such Code.

In an acquisition of a target with numerous stockholders, a buyer should attempt to limit its exposure to liability in the event that the stockholders of the target achieve a higher price for the value of their shares than that paid by the buyer through an appraisal proceeding brought by such stockholders post-closing. The seller should obviously negotiate a percentage high enough to prevent the buyer from abandoning the deal without good cause, and the buyer should be willing to accept some level of risk. The exact percentage of holders seeking appraisal rights in this condition depends on the circumstances.

ARTICLE X: CONDITIONS TO OBLIGATIONS OF SELLER AND TARGET

The obligations of the Seller and the Target to consummate this Agreement, and the transactions to be consummated by the Seller hereunder on the Closing Date, shall be subject to the satisfaction, with the Closing, of each of the conditions set forth in this Article X; which conditions may be waived in writing in whole or in part by the Seller to the extent permitted by applicable law.

Section 10.1. Compliance with Agreement. The Buyer shall have complied with and performed in all material respects the terms, conditions, acts, undertakings, covenants and obligations required by this Agreement to be complied with and performed by it on or before the Closing Date; and the Seller shall have received from the Buyer at the Closing a certificate, dated the Closing Date and signed by the President or a Vice President of the Buyer to such effect.

Section 10.2. Representations and Warranties True as of Closing Date. All representations and warranties of the Buyer set forth in this Agreement shall be true and correct in all material respects on and as of the Closing Date with the same force and effect as though such representations and warranties had been made on and as of the Closing Date and the Seller shall have received from the Buyer at the Closing a certificate, dated the Closing Date and signed by the President or a Vice President of the Buyer to such effect.

Section 10.3. Third Party Orders and Consents.

(i) The Seller and the Buyer shall have fully complied with the applicable provisions of the Hart-Scott-Rodino Act and any and all applicable waiting periods thereunder shall have expired, or an opinion, reasonably acceptable to the Seller, that no such filing is required shall have been delivered to the Seller.

(ii) All consents and approvals listed in Section 4.29 of the Disclosure Statement shall have been obtained, and the Seller and the Buyer shall have been furnished with appropriate evidence, reasonably satisfactory to them and their respective counsel, of the granting of such consents and approvals, and such consents and approvals remain in full force and effect on the Closing Date.

Section 10.4. Corporate Action. The Seller shall have received:

(i) a copy of the resolution or resolutions duly adopted by the Board of Directors of the Buyer and by the stockholders of the Buyer authorizing the execution, delivery and performance of this Agreement and the Related Instruments by the Buyer, and authorizing all other necessary or proper corporate action to enable the Buyer to comply with the terms of this Agreement and the Related Instruments, certified in each case by the Secretary or an Assistant Secretary of the Buyer; and

(ii) a certificate of the Secretary or an Assistant Secretary of the Buyer, dated the Closing Date, as to the incumbency and signatures of the officers of the Buyer executing this Agreement and the Related Instruments and any other documents in connection with the transactions contemplated by this Agreement and the Related Instruments.

Section 10.5. Opinion of the Buyer's Counsel. At the Closing, the Buyer shall furnish the Seller with an opinion, dated the Closing Date, of [name of Buyer's outside counsel], in form and substance reasonably satisfactory to the Seller and its counsel, to the effect that:

(i) the Buyer is a corporation duly organized, validly existing and in good standing under the laws of the state of its incorporation;

(ii) the Buyer has the power and authority to execute, deliver and perform the Agreement and the Related Instruments and to consummate the transactions contemplated by the Agreement and the Related Instruments; and the execution, delivery and performance of the Agreement and the Related Instruments and the consummation of the transactions contemplated by the Agreement and the Related Instruments have been duly authorized by all requisite action on the part of the Buyer;

(iii) this Agreement and the Related Instruments have been executed and delivered by the Buyer and is the legal, valid and binding obligation of the Buyer, enforceable against the Buyer in accordance with their respective terms, except (a) as such enforcement may be subject to fraudulent conveyance, bankruptcy, insolvency, reorganization, moratorium or other similar laws now or hereafter in effect, or by legal or equitable principles, relating to or limiting creditors' rights and (b) that the remedy of specific performance and injunctive and other forms of equitable relief are subject to certain equitable defenses and to the discretion of the court before which any proceeding therefor may be brought;

(iv) neither the execution, delivery and performance of the Agreement and the Related Instruments by the Buyer, nor the consummation of the transactions contemplated by the Agreement and the Related Instruments will violate any provision of the Certificate of Incorporation or Bylaws of the Buyer, or to the best knowledge of such counsel, will violate, conflict with, or constitute a default under, or cause the acceleration of maturity of any debt or obligation pursuant to, or result in the creation or imposition of any security interest, lien or other encumbrance upon any property or assets of the Buyer, any contract, commitment, agreement, trust, understanding, arrangement or restriction of any kind to which the Buyer is a party or by which the Buyer is bound or violate any statute or law, or any judgment, decree, order, regulation or rule of any court or governmental authority;

(v) to the best knowledge of such counsel, the Buyer is not engaged in or threatened with any legal action or other proceeding nor has it incurred or been charged with, nor is it under investigation with respect to, any violation of any law or administrative regulation which if adversely determined might, in such counsel's opinion, materially adversely affect or impair the ability of the Buyer to consummate the transactions contemplated hereby;

(vi) no filing, declaration or registration with, or any permit, authorization, license, consent or approval of, any governmental or regulatory authority is required in connection with the execution, delivery and performance of the Agreement and the Related Instruments by the Buyer or the consummation of the transactions contemplated by the Agreement and the Related Instruments, except as expressly disclosed in the Agreement or the Disclosure Statement, all of which have been duly and validly obtained;

(vii) no facts have come to the attention of such counsel that cause such counsel to believe that any information provided to the Seller in writing by or on behalf of the Buyer contained any untrue statement of a material fact or omitted to state any material fact necessary to make the statements therein, in light of the circumstances under which they were made, not misleading, except that counsel may also state that it has not independently verified the accuracy, completeness or fairness of such information, and the limitations inherent in the examination made by it and the knowledge available to it are such that it is unable to assume, and does not assume, any responsibility for the accuracy, completeness or fairness of such information.

As to any matter contained in such opinion which involves the laws of a jurisdiction other than the United States or the State of [state in which Buyer's counsel is licensed to practice], Buyer's counsel may rely upon opinions of local counsel of established reputation reasonably satisfactory to the Seller, which opinions shall expressly state that they may be relied upon by the Seller. Such counsel may also expressly rely as to matters of fact upon certificates furnished by appropriate officers of the Buyer, or appropriate governmental officials.

Section 10.6. Litigation. At the Closing, there shall be no effective injunction, writ or preliminary restraining order or any order of any nature issued by a court or governmental agency of competent jurisdiction restraining or prohibiting the consummation of the transactions provided for herein or any of them or limiting in any manner the Buyer's right to control the Target and the Subsidiaries or any aspect of their businesses or requiring the sale or other disposition of any of the operations of the Target or any Subsidiary or making the consummation of the Merger or the transaction contemplated by this Agreement and the Related Instruments unduly burdensome to the Target or any Subsidiary, and immediately prior to the Closing Date no proceeding or lawsuit shall have been commenced and be pending or be threatened by any governmental or regulatory agency or any other person with respect to the transactions contemplated by this Agreement or the Related Instruments which the Buyer, in good faith and with the advice of counsel, believes is likely to result in any of the foregoing or which seeks the payment of substantial damages by the Target, any Subsidiary or the Buyer.

Sections 10.1 and 10.2 afford the seller the same right to abandon the transaction as the buyer has under Sections 9.1 and 9.2. However, since the buyer enters into fewer and less expansive representations and covenants than the seller, this right is typically less valuable to the seller than it is to the buyer.

Sections 10.3, 10.4, 10.5, and 10.6 are the seller's equivalent of the bring-down, consent, and corporate action legal opinions and litigation conditions given the buyer in Sections 9.3, 9.4, 9.5, and 9.7, respectively.

ARTICLE XI: TAX MATTERS

Section 11.1. Representations, Warranties and Covenants.
The Seller and the Target each represents and warrants to the Buyer that:

(i) The Seller, the Target, and each of the Subsidiaries have filed or will file when due all federal, foreign, state and local tax returns, tax information returns, reports and estimates for all years and periods (and portions thereof) for which the due date (with extensions) is on or before the Closing Date. All such returns, reports and estimates were or will be prepared in the manner required by applicable law, and reflect or will reflect the liability for taxes of the Target or the Subsidiary filing same in all material respects and all Taxes (as defined in paragraph (v) of this Section 11.1 hereof) shown thereby to be payable and all assessments received by the Target and any Subsidiary have been paid or will be paid when due.

(ii) Section 11.1(ii) of the Disclosure Statement sets forth all jurisdictions in which the Target and the Subsidiaries have filed or will file income or franchise tax returns for each taxable period, or portion thereof, beginning on [insert date] and ending on or before the Closing Date.

(iii) The Target and each Subsidiary have withheld or will withhold amounts from their respective employees and have filed or will file all federal, foreign, state and local returns and reports with respect to employee income tax withholding and social security and unemployment Taxes for all periods (or portions thereof) ending on or before the Closing Date, in compliance with the provisions of the Internal Revenue Code, as amended and currently in effect (the "Code"), and other applicable federal, foreign, state and local laws.

(iv) The Target and the Subsidiaries have paid, or have provided a sufficient reserve on the Most Recent Balance Sheet for the payment of, all federal, state, local, and foreign Taxes with respect to all periods, or portions thereof, ending on or before the date of the Most Recent Balance Sheet.

(v) "Taxes" or "Tax" means all net income, capital gains, gross income, gross receipts, sales, use, ad valorem, franchise, profits, license, withholding, payroll, employment, excise, severance, stamp, occupation, premium, property, or windfall profit taxes, customs duties, or other taxes, fees, assessments, or charges of any kind whatsoever, together with any interest and any penalties, additions to tax, or additional amounts imposed by any taxing authority ("Taxing Authority") upon the Target or any Subsidiary.

(vi) The consolidated federal income tax returns of the Target through the taxable year ended _____, have been examined by the United States Internal Revenue Service (the "IRS") or closed by applicable statutes of limitations, and any deficiencies or assessments, including interest and penalties thereon, claimed or made as a result of such examinations in respect of the Target and any of the Subsidiaries whose results of operations are includible for such years in the consolidated federal income tax returns of the Target have been paid or provided for.

(vii) Except as set forth in Section 11.1(vii) of the Disclosure Statement, there are no material claims or investigations by any Taxing Authority pending or to the best of the knowledge of Seller threatened against the Target or any Subsidiary for any past due Taxes; and there has been no waiver of any applicable statute of limitations or extension of the time for the assessment of any Tax against the Target or any Subsidiary except as set forth on Section 11.1(vii) of the Disclosure Statement.

(viii) Neither the Target nor any Subsidiary has made, signed or filed, nor will it make, sign or file any consent under Section 341(f) of the Code with respect to any taxable period ending on or before the Closing Date.

(ix) No event has occurred or will occur on or prior to the Closing Date that would require indemnification by the Target or any Subsidiary of any tax lessor under any agreements relating to tax leases executed under Section 168(f)(8) of the Internal Revenue Code or by Seller as to assets of the Target or any Subsidiary.

(x) Any and all consolidated federal income tax (or similar) agreements executed between the Target or a Subsidiary and the Seller, or any other member of the Seller's consolidated group that relate to any payments or liability therefor by or to the Target or a Subsidiary with respect to its federal income and other Taxes and that are continuing in effect will terminate as of the Closing Date, and notwithstanding any provisions contained in such agreements, and on the Closing Date, the Target and the Subsidiaries shall be relieved of all liability and obligation thereunder.

Section 11.2. Payment of Tax Liabilities.

(i) Subject to indemnification by the Seller under Section 11.3(i) hereof, the Target shall pay or cause to be paid at the times required by the relevant Taxing Authority all unpaid separate (unconsolidated) state, local or foreign Tax liabilities, including interest and any penalties thereon, of the Target and any Subsidiary for all periods, or portions thereof, ended on or before the Closing Date.

(ii) The Seller shall pay at the times required by the relevant Taxing Authority all unpaid federal or combined foreign, state or local Tax liabilities, including interest and any penalties thereon, attributable to the Target and the Subsidiaries for all periods, or portions thereof, with respect to which the Target and the Subsidiaries are included in a combined return.

Section 11.3. Indemnification.

(i) The Seller agrees to indemnify, defend and hold the Buyer, the Target and the Subsidiaries harmless against and from (a) all unpaid federal or combined foreign, state or local Tax liabilities of the Target and any Subsidiary for all periods, or portions thereof, ended on or before the Closing Date, together with any penalties and interest attributable to such liabilities, and (b) all unpaid separate (unconsolidated) state, local or foreign Tax liabilities of the Target and any Subsidiary for all periods, or portions thereof, ended on or before the Closing Date, together with any penalties and interest attributable to such liabilities. The amount of the Seller's obligation under this Section 11.3 shall be reduced by the value of any net Tax benefit ("Net Tax Benefit") realized by the Target and/or any Subsidiary by reason of a Tax deduction or loss, basis adjustment, and/or shifting of income, deductions, gains, losses and/or credits. For this purpose, the value of a Net Tax Benefit shall be determined by the accountant of the Target, using reasonable assumptions and methods of valuation.

(ii) The Seller shall indemnify and hold the Buyer, the Target, the Surviving Corporation and each Subsidiary harmless against any loss, liability, damage or expense (including reasonable attorneys' fees) arising out of or resulting from any inaccuracy or misrepresentation in or breach of any of the warranties, representations, covenants or agreements made by the Seller or the Target in this Article XI.

(iii) The Buyer, the Target, the Surviving Corporation and the Subsidiaries shall indemnify and hold the Seller harmless against any loss, liability, damage or expense (including reasonable attorneys' fees) arising out of or resulting from any inaccuracy or misrepresentation in or breach of any of the warranties, representations, covenants or agreements made by the Buyer in this Article XI.

(iv) The Seller and the Buyer shall satisfy their obligations to each other for indemnification hereunder by check or cash within sixty (60) days after written notice thereof from the other respective party.

(v) The Buyer, the Target and each Subsidiary, on the one hand, and the Seller, on the other hand, hereby agree that in the event a claim is made by one party to this Agreement against the other party, the party making the claim shall furnish to the other party all books, records and other information reasonably requested by such other party that relate to such claims.

Section 11.4. Post-Closing Obligations.

(i) The Seller shall include the results of operations of the Target and the Subsidiaries for the period ending on the Closing Date in its consolidated federal income tax return and in any consolidated or combined foreign, state or local income Tax return required to be filed by Seller after the Closing Date; and Seller will pay all federal, state, local and foreign income Taxes (including interest and penalties relating thereto) due for the periods covered by such returns with respect to the Target and each Subsidiary.

(ii) The Buyer shall cause the Target and the Subsidiaries to include the results of their respective operations in any separate (unconsolidated) state, foreign or local income Tax return for any taxable year beginning before and ending on or after the Closing Date. Subject to indemnification by the Seller under Section 11.3 hereof, the Buyer shall pay, or cause to be paid, all state, foreign or local income Taxes (including interest and penalties relating thereto) shown as due on any such return with respect to the Target or any Subsidiary.

(iii) All refunds or credits of Taxes paid by the Seller with respect to the Target or the Subsidiaries for periods ending on or prior to the Closing Date shall be the property of the Seller (except for refunds attributable to the carryback of any credits, losses or deductions arising out of the operation of the Target or the Subsidiaries after the Closing Date), and the Buyer shall forward to or reimburse the Seller for such refunds or credits (except as aforesaid) as soon as practicable after receipt thereof. Any refunds or credits of foreign, federal, state or local income Taxes, paid by the Buyer, the Target, the Surviving Corporation or any Subsidiary in accordance with the provisions of Section 11.4(ii) hereof with respect to the Target or any Subsidiary shall be the property of Buyer, the Target or the Subsidiary, as the case may be, and the Seller shall forward or reimburse the Buyer, the Target, or the Subsidiary for any such refunds or credits as soon as practicable after receipt thereof.

(iv) Any losses, credits or other Tax items of the Target or a Subsidiary, including, but not limited to, net operating losses, capital losses, business, foreign and other tax credits (the "Tax Attributes"), which may be attributable to the operation of the business of the Target or a Subsidiary after the Closing Date, including any carrybacks of such Tax Attributes to any period ending on or before the Closing Date, and any refunds of Taxes attributable thereto, shall belong to the Target. To the extent the Tax Attributes are carried back to the Seller's returns under applicable Treasury Regulations, the Seller will file appropriate refund claims upon receipt from the Target of information to be included in such claims. Any refunds attributable to such refund claims received by the Seller shall be received by the Seller solely as agent for the Target and the Seller shall pay over such refunds to the Target immediately upon receipt thereof. The out-of-pocket expenses incurred by the Seller in filing any such refund claim shall be borne by the Target.

(v) To the extent that any election or other action by the Seller or an audit by the IRS or relevant state revenue agency for taxable years ending on or before the Closing Date results in an increase in the federal, state or foreign income Tax liability of the Target or any Subsidiary for a taxable year ending after the Closing Date, the Seller shall promptly pay the amount of such increase to the Buyer, provided, however, that the Seller shall not be required to make such payment until it receives from the Target reasonable evidence that the increased liability of the Target (or a Subsidiary, as the case may be) is due and payable and provided further that in the event that a subsequent audit by the IRS or relevant state revenue agency of the Buyer, the Target or any Subsidiary results in a reduction or elimination of such increase that resulted in any payment made under this paragraph, the Buyer shall promptly refund such payment or portion thereof, as the case may be, together with interest thereon at the prime rate from the date of such payment through the date of such refund.

(vi) If requested by the Buyer, the Seller shall make or cause the Target, with respect to the Subsidiaries, to make a deemed dividend election as of [_____], the first day of the Target's most recent taxable year, pursuant to consolidated return Treas. Regs. 1.1502-32(f)(2) and, with respect to such Subsidiaries, a consent dividend with respect to the period commencing on [_____], the first day of the Target's most recent taxable year, through the Closing Date pursuant to Section 565 of the Code. The Seller shall also cause the Target and any Subsidiary, to the extent not inconsistent with the requirements of the preceding sentence, to not have an excess loss account, as defined in Treas. Regs. 1.1502-32(e)(1), in the stock of any domestic subsidiary at the Closing Date.

(vii) At the reasonable request of the Buyer, the Seller will furnish to the Buyer, to the extent prepared or available and without representation or warranty, copies of (i) studies on the earnings and profits of the Target and each Subsidiary made pursuant to Treas. Regs. 1.1502-33 and (ii) computations pursuant to Treas. Regs. 1.1502-32 of actual investment adjustments with respect to the stock of, or any ownership interest in, the Target and each Subsidiary through the Closing Date.

(viii) Subsequent to the filing of the Seller's consolidated federal income tax return which includes the taxable period ending on the Closing Date, the Seller shall determine, under the Seller's policy, consistently applied, and pursuant to Treas. Reg. 1.1502-79, the portion of any net operating loss or capital loss carryover, charitable contribution carryover, or business and other credit carryovers, not availed of in the Seller's consolidated federal income tax returns that are allocable to the Target and each domestic subsidiary of the Target when each such corporation ceased to be a member of the Seller's consolidated group.

(ix) In the event that (a) the Target or a Subsidiary pays any separate (unconsolidated) state, local or foreign tax liability, including interest and penalty thereon, pursuant to Section 11.2(i) hereof and (b) the Target is indemnified against such payment by the Seller under Section 11.3(i), then the Seller shall reimburse the Target or the Subsidiary in the following manner: Any reimbursement payment required to be made by Seller to the Target or a Subsidiary pursuant to this Section 11.4(ix) shall be made no later than thirty (30) days after receipt by the Seller of a notice or demand for payments, a copy of the complete return or report to be filed with the Taxing Authority, and copies of all supporting workpapers or other appropriate assurances showing that the Tax liability less the value of any Net Tax Benefit, as provided in Section 11.3(i), has been correctly computed and apportioned to the Seller.

Section 11.5. Further Assurances and Assistance. From time to time prior to and after the Closing, the Seller and the Buyer will, without further consideration, (i) execute and deliver such documents as the other may reasonably request in order to consummate more effectively the transactions contemplated by this Agreement and (ii) provide such assistance and records as the other may reasonably request in connection with any tax return, tax investigation or audit, judicial or administrative proceeding or other similar matter relating to the Target or any of its Subsidiaries.

There are at least two approaches for dealing with the concerns of the seller and the buyer as to who should control the tax audit. Sections 11.6 and 11.7 are examples of each approach. The first approach is quite straightforward and eliminates any involvement by the buyer provided that the seller completely indemnifies the target from any tax liability relating thereto. The second approach gives the buyer the right to control the tax contest in situations in which the buyer has greater exposure than the seller. The advantages of each of these approaches are discussed in connection with the control of proceedings in the indemnity provisions in Article XII.

Section 11.6. Audit Matters. The Seller will be responsible for and have the right to control, at the Seller's expense, the audit of any Tax return relating to periods ended on or prior to the day of Closing. The Buyer will have the right, directly or through its designated representatives, to approve any settlement, provided, however, that the Seller may settle an audit on any terms by providing the Target with full indemnification against any Tax liability as a result thereof, in form and substance satisfactory to the Buyer.

Section 11.7. Certain Tax Claims for Which Seller May Be Liable.

(i) If a claim is made by any Taxing Authority or, if during the course of an examination by a Taxing Authority, it appears that the examining agent will propose adjustments that will result in a claim (a "Proposed Claim") with respect to the Target or a Subsidiary (the "Target Group"), the party to this Agreement that has the legal right to settle or compromise such Proposed Claim under applicable law (the "Controlling Party") shall notify in writing ("Notice") the other party to this Agreement that may incur any liability in respect of such Proposed Claim under this Article XI (the "Noncontrolling Party") within ten (10) business days of the date of such Proposed Claim. If the Controlling Party is a member of the Target Group, Notice shall be given to the Seller; if the Seller is the Controlling Party, Notice shall be given only to the Target. In the case of any such Proposed Claim, the Controlling Party shall not agree to such Proposed Claim or make payment thereof for at least sixty (60) days (or such shorter period as may be required by applicable law) after the giving of Notice with respect thereto. The Controlling Party need not give Notice of a Proposed Claim if the Controlling Party assumes liability for it. The failure to give Notice as provided hereunder shall not affect a Noncontrolling Party's liabilities under this Article XI unless such failure materially prejudices the ability of the Noncontrolling Party to defend against such Proposed Claim or to seek a refund of amounts paid in regard of such Proposed Claim.

(ii) As to a Tax that would result from a Proposed Claim for which the Controlling Party or the Noncontrolling Party would be solely liable under this Article XI hereof, the party that would be solely liable shall have the right, at its sole cost, to resist the Proposed Claim and if any Tax is paid, to seek the recovery of any such tax ("Tax Contest"). Such party may contest such Tax Contest by any and all appropriate proceedings, whether involving amended tax returns, claims for refund, administrative proceedings, litigation, appeals or otherwise, and in connection therewith, the other party will execute and deliver, or cause to be executed and delivered, to the party conducting the Tax Contest or its designees all instruments (including without limitation powers of attorney) reasonably requested by the party conducting the Tax Contest in order to implement the provisions of this paragraph.

(iii) As to a Tax for which the Noncontrolling Party is liable for a portion hereunder ("Joint Tax"), either the Controlling Party or the Noncontrolling Party shall have the right to institute or maintain a Tax Contest with respect thereto, subject to the provisions of Section 11.7(ii) hereof, as further modified by the following:

(a) If the asserted liability of the Controlling Party hereunder is equal to fifty percent (50) or more of the Proposed Claim, the Controlling Party may elect to conduct all proceedings of the Tax Contest as to such Joint Tax or to tender the conduct of all proceedings to the Noncontrolling Party.

(b) If the asserted liability of the Controlling Party hereunder is less than fifty percent (50) of the Proposed Claim, the Controlling Party shall tender the conduct of all proceedings of the Tax Contest to the Noncontrolling Party.

(c) If the conduct of all proceedings of the Tax Contest is tendered to the Noncontrolling Party and it declines to conduct such proceedings, then the Controlling Party (unless it elects to settle or not to contest as provided below) will conduct such proceedings. All costs of the Tax Contest will be shared as between the Controlling Party and the Noncontrolling Party in the ratio in which the Joint Tax is ultimately assessed.

(d) If the party conducting the Tax Contest (the "Manager") wishes to concede a Joint Tax or wishes and is able to compromise a Joint Tax and so notifies the other, the other party must either concede or agree to such compromise, as appropriate, or else agree to bear any portion of the Manager's tax liability in excess of the conceded or compromised amount. The party not wishing to concede or compromise will then assume responsibility for the conduct of the proceedings relating to the Tax Contest, and shall bear all costs of the Tax Contest thereafter incurred.

(iv) The "costs" of a Tax Contest means all out-of-pocket costs incurred by the Manager during the period it is acting as the Manager and any reasonable costs incurred by the other party for other than routine services or materials requested by the Manager in connection with such Tax Contest.

(v) The Target and the Seller will cooperate fully with each other in connection with any audit examinations of the Target by any Taxing Authority or any Tax Contests, including, without limitation, the furnishing or making available of records, books of account, or other materials necessary or helpful for the defense against the assertions of any Taxing Authority as to any income tax returns (consolidated or otherwise) of the Target and the Subsidiaries.

(vi) The Seller shall not agree to a settlement of any such Tax liabilities which would adversely affect any member of the Target Group in any taxable period ending after the Closing Date to any material extent (including, without limitation, the imposition of income tax deficiencies or the reduction of asset basis or cost adjustments) without the Target's prior written consent, which consent shall not be unreasonably withheld, unless the Seller indemnifies the Target Group against the effects of any such settlement. The Target shall not resolve, settle or contest any tax issue with respect to the Target which would have an adverse material effect on the Seller without the Seller's prior written consent, which consent shall not be unreasonably withheld, unless the Target indemnifies the Seller against the effects of any such settlement.

Many nontax lawyers merely skim the tax section of an acquisition agreement, since they find it extremely esoteric. Although this may be unavoidable, the importance of tax provisions should not be minimized or overlooked. Article XI is used in connection with the acquisition of a target whose federal income tax returns are filed as part of the consolidated tax return of the seller. Although pre-closing federal tax liabilities of the target will be automatically included in the seller's consolidated return, the target will itself have liability to various other taxing authorities for periods prior to the closing. Therefore, since the target will file a tax return after closing that covers a portion of the period prior to closing, the agreement should require the seller to pay any taxes for periods prior to the closing that may be due to various taxing authorities. This is logical, as the seller reaped the benefits of the target's income during this period. It is also necessary for the seller and the buyer to coordinate the filing of tax returns post-closing as well as the handling of tax refunds or credits.

When agreeing to indemnify the target for the target's tax liability covering periods prior to the closing, the seller should require its indemnity obligation to be reduced by the amount of any offsetting tax benefits realized by the target by reason of pre-closing tax liability. [See Section 11.3(i).] This is at least theoretically a fair result, since the buyer should not be expected to get a windfall from the indemnity provisions. The principal, and fairly valid, argument against such a provision is that the actual determination of an offsetting tax benefit can be quite difficult in practice.

The representations and warranties set forth in Section 11.1 assure the buyer that it should not be faced with unanticipated tax liabilities of any kind.

In situations in which the target is not a member of the seller's consolidated group, much of Article XI may be unnecessary, and the buyer should instead require a representation by the seller in Article IV as follows:

> *Tax Matters.* For purposes of this Agreement "Taxes" or "Tax" means all net income, capital gains, gross income, gross receipts, sales, use, ad valorem, franchise, profits, license, withholding, payroll, employment, excise, severance, stamp, occupation, premium, property, or windfall profit taxes, customs duties, or other taxes, fees, assessments, or charges of any kind whatsoever, together with any interest and any penalties, additions to tax, or additional amounts imposed by any taxing authority ("Taxing Authority") upon the Target or the Subsidiary.
>
> (i) Except as set forth in Section _____ of the Disclosure Statement, the Target and the Subsidiary have filed or will file when due all federal, foreign, state, and local tax returns, tax information returns, reports, and estimates for all years and periods (and portions thereof) ending on or before the Closing Date for which any such returns, reports or estimates were due. All such returns, reports and estimates were prepared in

the manner required by applicable law, and all Taxes shown thereby to be payable have been paid when due.

(ii) Section _____ of the Disclosure Statement sets forth all jurisdictions in which the Target and the Subsidiaries have filed or will file income or franchise tax returns for each taxable period, or portion thereof, ending on or before the Closing Date.

(iii) The Target and the Subsidiaries each has withheld or will withhold amounts from its respective employees and has filed or will file all federal, foreign, state and local returns and reports with respect to employee income tax withholding and social security and unemployment Taxes for all periods (or portions thereof) ending on or before the Closing Date, in compliance with the provisions of the Internal Revenue Code, as amended and currently in effect (the "Code"), and other applicable federal, foreign, state and local laws.

(iv) The Target and the Subsidiaries each has paid, or provided a sufficient reserve on the Balance Sheet for the payment of, all federal, state, local and foreign Taxes with respect to all periods, or portions thereof, ending on or before _____. The amount of any net operating loss for federal income tax purposes shown on the Target's federal income tax returns has been accurately and properly determined in accordance with the Code and other applicable law without giving effect to the transactions contemplated hereby.

(v) The separate and consolidated federal income tax returns of the Target and its Subsidiaries, through the taxable year ended [insert date], have been examined by the United States Internal Revenue Service (the "IRS") or closed by applicable statute of limitations, and any deficiencies or assessments, including interest and penalties thereon, claimed or made as a result of such examinations in respect of the target and any of its Subsidiaries.

(vi) Except as set forth in Section _____ of the Disclosure Statement there are no material claims or investigations by any Taxing Authority pending or, to the best knowledge of the Seller and the Target, threatened, against the Target or the Subsidiaries for any past due Taxes; and there has been no waiver of any applicable statute of limitations or extension of the time for the assessment of any Tax against the Target or the Subsidiaries, except as set forth in Section _____ of the Disclosure Statement.

(vii) Neither the Target nor any Subsidiary has made, signed or filed, nor will it make, sign or file any consent under Section 341(f) of the Code with respect to any taxable period ending on or before the Closing Date.

(viii) Except as set forth in Section _____ of the Disclosure Statement, no event has occurred or will occur on or prior to the Closing

Date that would require indemnification by the Target or the Subsidiaries of any tax lessor under any agreements relating to tax leases executed under Section 168(f)(8) of the Internal Revenue Code as to assets of the Target or its Subsidiaries.

(ix) Neither the Target nor any Subsidiary has ever been, nor is the Target or any Subsidiary currently, a party to any agreement relating to the sharing of any liability for, or payment of, Taxes with any other person or entity.

ARTICLE XII: SURVIVAL OF REPRESENTATIONS; INDEMNIFICATION

Section 12.1. Indemnification by Seller. Notwithstanding any other provision of this Agreement and subject to the terms and conditions of this Article XII, the Seller hereby agrees to indemnify, defend and hold harmless the Buyer, any subsidiary or affiliate thereof (including the Target, the Surviving Corporation and the Subsidiaries) and their respective successors, if any, and their officers, directors and controlling persons (the "Buyer Group"), at any time after the Closing Date, from and against all demands, claims, actions or causes of action, assessments, losses, damages, liabilities, costs and expenses, including without limitation, interest, penalties and attorneys' fees and expenses, which were reasonably incurred by or imposed upon the Buyer Group or any member thereof, net of any insurance proceeds received by any member of the Buyer Group with respect thereto (all such amounts, net of insurance proceeds being hereafter referred to collectively as "Buyer Group Damages"), asserted against, resulting to, imposed upon or incurred by the Buyer Group or any member thereof, directly or indirectly, by reason of or resulting from any misrepresentation, breach of any warranty or nonperformance or breach of any covenant, obligation or agreement of the Seller or the Target or its Subsidiaries contained in or made pursuant to this Agreement, the Disclosure Statement, the Related Instruments or pursuant to any statement, certificate or other document furnished pursuant to this Agreement or the Related Instruments (collectively referred to as the "Indemnity Documents") or any facts or circumstances constituting such a breach. (A claim for indemnification under this Section 12.1 shall be referred to as the "Buyer Group Claims.")

Section 12.2. Indemnification by the Surviving Corporation. Notwithstanding any other provision of this Agreement and subject to the terms and conditions of this Article XII, the Surviving Corporation hereby agrees to indemnify, defend and hold harmless the Seller and their respective successors, if any, and their officers, directors and controlling persons (the "Seller Group"), at any time after the Closing Date, from and against all demands, claims, actions, or causes of action, assessments, losses, damages, liabilities, costs and expenses, including, without limitation, interest, penalties and attorneys' fees and expenses, which were reasonably incurred by or imposed upon the Seller Group or any member thereof, net of any insurance proceeds received by any member of the Seller Group with respect thereto (all such amounts, net of insurance proceeds being hereafter referred to collectively as "Seller Group Damages"), asserted against, resulting to, imposed upon or incurred by the Seller Group or any member thereof, directly or indirectly, by reason of or resulting from any misrepresentation, breach of any warranty, or nonperformance or breach of any covenant, obligation or agreement of the Buyer contained in or made pursuant to any Indemnity Document or any facts or circumstances constituting such a breach. (A claim for indemnification under this Section 12.2 shall be referred to as the "Seller Group Claims.")

The buyer group damages and seller group damages take into account any insurance proceeds that are received by the indemnified party in order to reduce the amount of damages that can be recovered by the indemnified party. Another item that arguably should offset the amount of damages that an indemnified party can claim is the amount of any tax benefits that the surviving corporation has enjoyed as a result of such damages. The difficulty of determining the exact amount of the tax benefit that directly resulted from the damages almost always causes the buyer and seller to overlook this potential windfall.

Section 12.3. Materiality. For purposes of determining whether an event described in Section 12.1 or 12.2 has occurred, any requirement in any representation, warranty, covenant or agreement contained in any Indemnity Document that an event or fact be material, meet a certain minimum dollar threshold or have a Material Adverse Effect, which is a condition to such event or fact constituting a misrepresentation or a breach of such warranty, covenant or agreement (a "Materiality Condition"), shall be ignored, if the aggregate Buyer Group Damages or Seller Group Damages, as the case may be, resulting from all such breaches and misrepresentations (determined by ignoring all Materiality Conditions) exceeds the amount of the Basket (as defined in Section 12.5). Notwithstanding the foregoing, an event described in Section 12.1 or 12.2 (other than a claim for indemnification under Article XI) that would otherwise give rise to a claim for Buyer Group Damages or Seller Group Damages, as the case may be, shall not be deemed to have occurred unless the Buyer Group Damages or Seller Group Damages, as the case may be, resulting from the single misrepresentation or breach of warranty, covenant or agreement that constitute such event exceeds Dollars, provided that for the purposes of this sentence, all claims for Buyer Group Damages or Seller Group Damages, as the case may be, arising out of the same facts or events causing any such breach shall be treated as a single claim.

Section 12.4. Survival of Indemnification. The right to make a claim for indemnification under this Agreement shall survive the Closing Date for a period of twenty-four (24) months except that a claim for indemnification under (a) Section 4.4 of this Agreement or based upon any misrepresentation or breach of a warranty which was actually known to be untrue by the indemnifying party when made or asserted or to any willful breach of a covenant, shall continue to survive indefinitely, (b) Article XI shall continue to survive until the latest to occur of (i) the date twenty-four (24) months after the Closing Date, (ii) the expiration date of the statute of limitations applicable to any indemnified liability for Taxes, and extensions or waivers thereof and (iii) ninety (90) days after the final determination of any such Tax liability, including the final administrative and/or judicial determination thereof, and thereafter no party shall have a right to seek indemnification under this Agreement unless a notice of claim setting forth the facts upon which the claim for indemnification is based, and if possible, a reasonable estimate of the amount of the claim, is delivered to the indemnifying party prior to the expiration of the right to make a claim as provided in this Section 12.4. This Section 12.4 shall have no effect upon any other obligation of the parties hereto, whether to be performed before or after the Closing Date. It shall not be a condition to the indemnification with respect to such claim that the loss or liability upon which the claim would be based actually be realized or incurred prior to the date that the indemnifying party is no longer obligated to indemnify the indemnified party pursuant to this Article XII.

The length of time that the seller's indemnification obligations survive the closing date is often heavily negotiated, and its outcome is largely dependent upon the nature of the transaction and the strength of the parties' respective bargaining positions. The buyer should require the seller to indemnify the title to the securities to be purchased by it for an indefinite period of time. For indemnification relating to tax liability, the buyer should require the seller to indemnify the surviving corporation until the target can no longer suffer any loss. In some cases, the buyer may require the seller to indemnify certain items, such as an environmental or product liability concern, beyond the general indemnification period.

Section 12.5. Limitation on Claims and Damages.

(i) No amount shall be payable in indemnification under this Article XII, unless (a) in the case of the Seller, the aggregate amount of Buyer Group Damages in respect of which the Seller would be liable under this Article XII, or (b) in the case of the Surviving Corporation, the aggregate amount of Seller Group Damages in respect of which the Surviving Corporation would be liable under this Article XII, exceeds in the aggregate _____ Dollars ($ _____) (the "Basket"); provided, however, the Basket shall not apply to (a) any Buyer Group Claim or Seller Group Claim, as the case may be, based upon any misrepresentation or breach of a warranty which was actually known to be untrue by the indemnifying party when made or asserted or to any willful breach of a covenant or (b) any claim for indemnity under Article XI. In the event that the Buyer Group Damages or Seller Group Damages exceeds the Basket, the indemnified party shall be entitled to seek indemnification for the full amount of the Buyer Group Damages or Seller Group Damages, as the case may be.

(ii) The maximum amount of Buyer Group Damages for which the Seller may be liable under this Article XII shall be an amount equal to _____ Dollars ($ _____).

(iii) A party shall not be liable for Buyer Group Damages or Seller Group Damages, as the case may be, under this Article XII resulting from an event relating to a misrepresentation, breach of any warranty or nonperformance or breach of any covenant by the indemnifying party if the indemnifying party can establish that the party seeking indemnification had actual knowledge on or before the Closing Date of such event.

(iv) In any case where an indemnified party recovers from third parties all or any part of any amount paid to it by an indemnifying party pursuant to this Article XII, such indemnified party shall promptly pay over to the indemnifying party the amount so recovered (after deducting therefrom the full amount of the expenses incurred by it in procuring such recovery and any additional amounts owed to the indemnified party by the indemnifying party under this Agreement), but not in excess of any amount previously so paid by the indemnifying party.

(v) The indemnified party shall be obligated to prosecute diligently and in good faith any claim for Buyer Group Damages or Seller Group Damages, as the case may be, with any applicable insurer prior to collecting or indemnification payment under this Article XII. However, an indemnified party shall be entitled to collect an indemnification payment under this Article XII if such indemnified party has not received reimbursement from an applicable insurer within one year after it has given such insurer written notice of its claim. In such event, the indemnified party shall assign to the indemnifying party its rights against such insurer.

(vi) Except in the case of fraud and other than as set forth in Article XI or Section 12.5(vii) hereof, the indemnification and terms thereof provided for in this Article XII shall be the exclusive remedy available to any indemnified party against any indemnifying party for any damages arising directly or indirectly from any misrepresentation, breach of any warranty or nonperformance or breach of any covenant, obligation or agreement pursuant to the Indemnity Documents.

(vii) Nothing in this Article XII or in Article XI shall be construed to limit the non-monetary equitable remedies of any party hereto in respect of any breach by any other party of any covenant or other agreement of such other party contained in or made pursuant to the Indemnity Documents required to be performed after the Closing Date.

The seller, who usually has the most at stake under the indemnification provisions, should require the surviving corporation to pursue collection from an insurance company for the redress of buyer group damages if the insurance policy arguably covers the buyer group damages. In addition, with respect to the covenants in Section 6.7 and Article VII, the seller should not be liable for any buyer group damages if the buyer was aware of the seller's misrepresentation or breach prior to the closing date.

A seller should always attempt to limit its exposure for indemnification. As a practical matter, the seller should not be liable for any amount in excess of the purchase price paid for the target. During negotiations of this ceiling, every argument conceivable is put on the table for consideration. However, its outcome, like that of any other highly controversial provision, rests with the party holding the trump card.

Section 12.6. Claims by Third Parties. The obligations and liabilities of an indemnifying party under any provision of this Agreement with respect to claims relating to third parties shall be subject to the following terms and conditions:

(i) Whenever any indemnified party shall have received notice that a Buyer Group Claim or a Seller Group Claim, as the case may be, has been asserted or threatened against such indemnified party, which, if valid, would subject the indemnifying party to an indemnity obligation under this Agreement, the indemnified party shall promptly notify the indemnifying party of such claim in the manner described in Section 12.4; provided, however, that the failure of the indemnified party to give timely notice hereunder shall not relieve the indemnifying party of its indemnification obligations under this Agreement unless, and only to the extent that, such failure caused the Buyer Group Damages or the Seller Group Damages, as the case may be, for which the indemnifying party is obligated to be greater than they would have been had the indemnified party given timely notice.

(ii) The indemnifying party or its designee will have the right, but not the obligation, to assume the defense of any claim described in Section 12.6(i); provided, however, if there is a reasonable probability that a Buyer Group Claim may materially and adversely affect the Surviving Corporation or any other member of the Buyer Group despite the indemnity of the Seller, the Surviving Corporation or such member of the Buyer Group shall have the right at its option to defend, at its own cost and expense, and to compromise or settle such Buyer Group Claim which compromise or settlement shall be made only with the written consent of the Seller, such consent not to be unreasonably withheld. If the indemnifying party fails to assume the defense of such claim within 15 days after receipt of notice of a claim pursuant to Section 12.6(i), the indemnified party against which such claim has been asserted will (upon delivering notice to such effect to the indemnifying party) have the right to undertake, at the indemnifying party's cost and expense, the defense, compromise or settlement of such claim on behalf of and for the account and risk of the indemnifying party, subject to the right of the indemnifying party to assume the defense of such claim at any time prior to settlement, compromise or final determination thereof and provided, however, that the indemnified party shall not enter into any such compromise or settlement without the written consent of the indemnifying party. In the event the indemnified party assumes defense of the claim, the indemnified party will keep the indemnifying party reasonably informed of the progress of any such defense, compromise or settlement. The indemnifying party shall not be liable for any settlement of any action effected without its consent, but if settled with the consent of the indemnifying party or if there be a final judgment beyond review or appeal, for the plaintiff in any such action, the indemnifying party agrees to indemnify and hold harmless an indemnified party from and against any loss or liability by reason of such settlement or judgment. Any party who does not undertake the defense of a claim may, at its own expense, retain such additional attorneys and other advisors as it shall deem necessary, which attorneys and advisors will be permitted by the party undertaking such defense, and its attorneys, to observe the defense of such claim.

(iii) Any member of the Buyer Group shall give the Seller at least thirty (30) days prior written notice before such member shall waive the provisions of any statute of limitations as such provisions may apply to the assessment of taxes payable by the Surviving Corporation or any Subsidiary for any taxable year or period (or portion thereof) ending on or prior to the Closing Date.

An area that can be extremely sensitive is control of a proceeding relating to a claim that is the subject of indemnification. If the indemnifying party refuses to acknowledge its obligation to indemnify a claim, then it should certainly have no right to control the proceeding. However, where the indemnifying party has accepted its obligation to indemnify for a claim, the indemnifying party will probably want to control the proceeding in order to be in command of its own destiny. If the buyer is comfortable with the creditworthiness of the seller, this should not pose a serious threat to the buyer. There are, of course, circumstances in which the buyer may want to control the proceedings notwithstanding the creditworthiness of the seller. For example, if the surviving corporation is temporarily enjoined from conducting its business as a result of the action of a third party, the buyer may feel that the seller will not move quickly enough to resolve the matter.

In some cases, the buyer and seller may have a joint interest in the outcome of a certain proceeding. For example, the proceeding may involve numerous claims against the surviving corporation, only one of which relates to a buyer group claim. One approach that may appease both the seller and buyer in this circumstance is to let the party that has the most to lose control the proceeding.

Section 12.7. Indemnity for Taxes of Indemnified Party. Each party hereto further agrees that, with respect to payment or indemnity under this Article XII, such payment or indemnity shall include any amount necessary to hold the indemnified party harmless on an after-tax basis from all taxes required to be paid with respect to the receipt of such payment or indemnity under the laws of any Federal, state or local government or taxing authority in the United States, or under the laws of any foreign government or taxing authority or governmental subdivision of a foreign country.

In circumstances in which the indemnification payment is taxable to the indemnified party, it is common for the seller and buyer to negotiate the inclusion of a tax gross-up provision. One difficulty with this concept is that the indemnifying party may be grossing up the indemnified party for taxes that it would have been responsible for had no indemnity been necessary.

> *Section 12.8. Right of Offset.* In the event the Seller should be required to pay monies to the Surviving Corporation pursuant to Section 12.1 or any other indemnification provision of this Agreement, the Surviving Corporation may offset the amount the Seller owes in indemnification against any outstanding principal balance of the [insert title of instrument under which the surviving corporation has continuing payment obligations].

In an acquisition in which the seller has agreed to accept, as part of the purchase price of the target, a note or other instrument that represents a payment obligation of the surviving corporation, the buyer may attempt to satisfy its right to indemnification by the seller by canceling a portion or all of such payment obligations. A creditworthy seller should resist this provision on several grounds. First, the surviving corporation should have a setoff right only after it has demonstrated, through a final determination from which no appeal can be taken, that the seller is obligated to indemnify the surviving corporation for the buyer group claim. Second, if the seller has sufficient resources, it should be able to choose whether it wants to forgive a portion of the payment obligation or simply pay cash. It is conceivable that the payment obligation may bear an interest rate well in excess of the prevailing market rate. A creditworthy seller should not lose this benefit through an offset provision.

ARTICLE XIII: NON-COMPETE

> The Seller agrees that for the period of three years following the Closing Date (the "Non-Compete Period"), the Seller shall not, without the prior written consent of the Buyer, either directly or indirectly, engage in business of the type presently conducted by the Target or any Subsidiary in the

United States or any other jurisdiction in which the Target or any Subsidiary currently conducts business (the "Business"). The Seller may acquire any entity which, directly or indirectly, engages in the Business or any portion thereof (the "Acquired Entity"), if (i) the total assets and gross revenues attributable to or derived from such Business do not exceed [insert percentage] of the total assets and gross revenues of the Acquired Entity and its subsidiaries in the fiscal year immediately preceding the date of acquisition, or (ii) the Seller uses its reasonable efforts to divest itself of the Acquired Entity within a reasonable time (not to exceed six months), subject to receipt of all regulatory approvals. The Seller also agrees that, after the Closing Date, the Seller will not disclose or reveal to any person or an Acquired Entity any trade secret or other confidential or proprietary information relating to the Business, including, without limitation, any financial information relating to the Target or any Subsidiary, or any customer lists, unless readily ascertainable from public information, and the Seller confirms that after the Closing Date, such information will constitute the exclusive property of the Target and its Subsidiaries. During the Non-Compete Period, the Seller agrees not to, and to cause its affiliates not to, recruit, directly or indirectly, employees of the Target or any Subsidiary for employment with or as a consultant to the Seller or its affiliates. The Buyer and the Seller hereby agree that of the total cash consideration to be paid to the Seller at Closing, $_____ represents the consideration for the covenants of the Seller contained in this Article XIII.

Covenants not to compete can be difficult to enforce if not structured properly. The difficulty arises from a court's reluctance on public policy grounds to give force to a contractual provision restricting the ability of one of the parties to work freely in any way it chooses, even if the party being restricted has voluntarily agreed and has received consideration to be so bound. Courts have invalidated noncompetition provisions (a) that continue for too long a period of time, (b) that are too broad geographically, or (c) that are too indefinite or broad with respect to the restricted activity. Consequently, the buyer must ensure that its noncompetition clause is specific with respect to the term (typically one to five years), extends to a limited geographical area, and restricts a specific activity in the industry. For example, a court would probably accept a provision restricting the seller from selling or distributing aluminum baseball bats in the state of California for a period of two years, but would probably not accept a provision restricting the seller from selling or distributing sports equipment anywhere in the world for a period of 25 years. It is, of course, within these extremes that the enforceability of a covenant not to compete is less clear. The buyer must be cognizant of courts' rulings under the state laws that govern the acquisition agreement and must balance the case law against its need to acquire the target without fear that the seller will acquire or establish a similar business in the same territory and attempt to lure away existing customers of the target.

The seller may also desire to modify clause (ii) above, which requires the seller's divestiture of the acquired entity within a reasonable period of time by providing that the seller is only obligated to divest the acquired entity "at a price which is economically reasonable in light of the circumstances."

ARTICLE XIV: TERMINATION

Section 14.1. Termination for Failure to Close on Time. This Agreement may be terminated upon two (2) days' written notice (i) by Buyer, on the one hand, or the Seller, on the other hand, at any time after [insert date], or (ii) by the mutual agreement of all parties at any time. In the event of such termination, this Agreement shall be abandoned without any liability or further obligation to any other party to this Agreement unless otherwise stated expressly herein. This Section 14.1 shall not apply in the event of the failure of the transactions contemplated by this Agreement to be consummated as a result of a breach by the Seller, Target or Buyer of a representation, warranty or covenant contained in this Agreement. In such event, the provisions of Section 14.2 hereof shall apply.

Section 14.2. Default; Remedies. This Section shall apply in the event that a party refuses to consummate the transactions contemplated by this Agreement or if any default under, or breach of any representation, warranty or covenant of, this Agreement on the part of a party (the "Defaulting Party") shall have occurred that results in the failure to consummate the transactions contemplated hereby. In such event, the non-Defaulting Party shall be entitled to seek and obtain specific performance pursuant to Section 14.3 or to seek and obtain money damages from the Defaulting Party plus its court costs and reasonable attorneys' fees in connection with the pursuit of its remedies hereunder.

Section 14.3. Specific Performance. In the event that any party shall fail or refuse to consummate the transactions contemplated by this Agreement or if any default under, or breach of, any representation, warranty or covenant of this Agreement on the part of any party (the "Defaulting Party") shall have occurred that results in the failure to consummate the transactions contemplated hereby, then in addition to the other remedies provided in this Article XIV, the non-Defaulting Party may seek to obtain an order of specific performance thereof against the Defaulting Party from a court of competent jurisdiction, provided that it files its request with such court within forty-five (45) days after it became aware of such failure, refusal, default or breach. In addition, the non-Defaulting Party shall be entitled to obtain from the Defaulting Party court costs and reasonable attorneys' fees incurred by it in enforcing its rights hereunder. As a condition to seeking specific performance hereunder, Buyer shall not be required to have tendered the [insert defined term for the total purchase price] but shall be ready, willing and able to do so.

The termination section provides both the mechanism for the termination of, and the remedies available against a nonperforming or defaulting party to, the acquisition agreement. In some cases, a seller may want to modify this section to limit liability for a willful failure to perform. Obviously, there are situations in which the buyer may be disadvantaged by the inclusion of this modifier. Therefore, like other disputed provisions, the outcome rests on the balance of power between seller and buyer. In an acquisition requiring regulatory approval, the buyer and seller should consider extending the term of the acquisition agreement in Section 14.1 for a certain period of time in case the approval process takes longer than anticipated. The relief of specific performance afforded the nondefaulting party in Section 14.3 is extremely difficult to enforce in a court of law. If a court can ascertain the amount of monetary damages to award the nondefaulting party, it will not generally grant specific performance.

Special consideration should be given to the termination section in connection with the acquisition of a publicly traded target. For example, an independent committee of the board of directors of the target may determine in light of the circumstances to include a fiduciary out for the target. A *fiduciary out* is a unilateral right of the target to terminate the acquisition agreement in the event a more favorable offer for the target is received prior to closing. The buyer should in this situation, and possibly others, require a "breakup" or "topping" fee to compensate the buyer for its damages and out-of-pocket expenses. The following is an example of a "bustup" fee that covers both buyer and seller:

Damages upon Default. In the event that either Target or Buyer shall fail to refuse to consummate the transactions contemplated by this Agreement or if any default under, or breach of any representation (other than those contained in Section 3.5 hereof), warranty, covenant (other than those contained in hereof) or conditions of, this Agreement on the part of the Target or Buyer shall have occurred that results in the failure to consummate the transactions contemplated hereby, then (i) if Target shall be the defaulting party, Target shall pay to the Buyer Dollars ($), or (ii) if the Buyer shall be the defaulting party, then the Buyer shall pay to Target Dollars ($). In each case such payment shall be in consideration of the expenses incurred by and efforts expended by and opportunities lost by the nondefaulting party. The parties agree that in such circumstances it would be impossible to determine the actual damages which any party may suffer and that therefore such payments shall be in lieu of any such actual damages and shall be full and complete liquidated damages and shall constitute the sole remedy in the event of such default.

ARTICLE XV: MISCELLANEOUS

Article XV contains provisions that define the key terms of the agreement and set forth rules of conduct related to the agreement. Although the bulk of these provisions are generally not negotiated by the parties to the agreement, several sections provide valuable rights to both buyer and seller and may be subject to closer scrutiny by the parties.

Section 15.1. Definitions.
Agreement. See Article I.
Buyer. See Article I.
Closing. See Article III.
Closing Date. See Article III.
Company Capital Stock. See Section 4.3(i).
Disclosure Statement. See Section 4.1.
Financial Statements. See Section 4.5(i).
GAAP. See Section 4.5(i).
Material Adverse Effect. See Section 4.1(i).
Merger. See Article I.
Most Recent Balance Sheet. See Section 4.5(i).

Persons. First used in Section 4.5(ii) but not defined.

*Related Instruments. **See Section 4.2.***

SEC. Defined in paragraph describing Section 4.33.

*Seller. **See Article I.***

*Subsidiary. **See Article I.***

*Target. **See Article I.***

Section 15.2. Payment of Expenses. Buyer shall pay its own expenses and the Seller and Target shall pay their own expenses incident to preparing for, entering into and carrying out this Agreement and the Related Instruments, except as otherwise provided in this Agreement and the Related Instruments.

Section 15.3. Modifications or Waivers to the Agreement. The parties may, by mutual written agreement, make any modification or amendment of this Agreement.

Section 15.4. Assignment. Neither the Buyer, Seller nor Target shall have the authority to assign its rights or obligations under this Agreement without the prior written consent of the other party, except that the Buyer may assign all or any portion of its respective rights hereunder without the prior written consent of the Seller or Target to an entity controlled by, controlling or under common control with it or to any Acquisition Lender, and the Seller, Target and the Buyer shall execute such documents as are necessary in order to effect such assignments.

Section 15.5. Burden and Benefit.
(i) This Agreement shall be binding upon and, to the extent permitted in this Agreement, shall inure to the benefit of, the parties hereto and their respective successors and assigns.

(ii) In the event of a default by the Seller or Target of any of its or their obligations hereunder, the sole and exclusive recourse and remedy of the Buyer shall be against the Seller or Target and its assets and under no circumstances shall any officer, director, stockholder or affiliate of the Seller or Target be liable in law or equity for any obligations of the Seller or Target hereunder.

(iii) In the event of a default by the Buyer of any of its obligations hereunder, the sole and exclusive recourse and remedy of the Seller or Target hereunder shall be against the Buyer and its assets, and under no circumstances shall any officer, director, stockholder or affiliate of the Buyer be liable in law or equity for any obligations of the Buyer hereunder.

(iv) It is the intent of the parties hereto that no third-party beneficiary rights be created or deemed to exist in favor of any person not a party to this Agreement, unless otherwise expressly agreed in writing by the parties.

The buyer and seller may seek to include a provision, often entitled "Burden and Benefit," limiting the rights of the seller in the event of a breach of the agreement to an action against the buyer and not against any officer, director, or controlling stockholder of the buyer. This provision, assuming the entity purchasing the target has elected to do so through a shell or thinly capitalized corporation, generally should insulate the acquiring entity from liability to the seller in the event the deal goes sour.

Section 15.6. Brokers.
(i) Each of the Seller and Target represents and warrants to the Buyer that there are no brokers or finders entitled to any brokerage or finder's fee or other commission or fee based upon arrangements made by or on behalf of the Seller or Target in connection with this Agreement or any of the transactions contemplated hereby other than the fee due [insert name of any such entity].

(ii) The Buyer represents and warrants to the Seller and the Target that no broker or finder is entitled to any brokerage or finder's fee or other commission or fee based upon arrangements made by or on behalf of the Buyer in connection with this Agreement or any of the transactions contemplated hereby other than fees payable by it in connection with the financing of this transaction.

Section 15.7. Entire Agreement. This Agreement and the exhibits, lists and other documents referred to herein contain the entire agreement among the parties hereto with respect to the transactions contemplated hereby and supersede all prior agreements with respect thereto, whether written or oral.

Section 15.8. Governing Law. This Agreement shall be governed by and construed in accordance with the laws of the State of [insert name of state].

Section 15.9. Notices. Any notice, request, instruction or other document to be given hereunder by a party shall be in writing and delivered personally or by facsimile transmission, or by telex, or sent by registered or certified mail, postage prepaid, return receipt requested, addressed as follows:

If to the Seller: [insert name and address of Seller]

with a copy to: [insert name and address of Seller's counsel]

If to Target: [insert name and address of Target]

If to Buyer: [insert name and address of Buyer]

with a copy to: [insert name and address of Buyer's counsel]

If to the Surviving Corporation: [insert name and address of Target post-Closing]

with a copy to: [insert any other desired parties]

or to such other persons or addresses as may be designated in writing by the party to receive such notice. If mailed as aforesaid, ten days after the date of mailing shall be the date notice shall be deemed to have been received.

Section 15.10. Counterparts. This Agreement may be executed in two or more counterparts, each of which shall be an original, but all of which shall constitute but one agreement.

Section 15.11. Rights Cumulative. All rights, powers and privileges conferred hereunder upon the parties, unless otherwise provided, shall be cumulative and shall not be restricted to those given by law. Failure to exercise any power given any party hereunder or to insist upon strict compliance by any other party shall not constitute a waiver of any party's right to demand exact compliance with the terms hereof.

Section 15.12. Severability of Provisions. The parties agree that (i) the provisions of this Agreement shall be severable in the event that any of the provisions hereof are held by a court of competent jurisdiction to be invalid, void or otherwise unenforceable, (ii) such invalid, void or otherwise unenforceable provisions shall be automatically replaced by other provisions which are as similar as possible in terms to such invalid, void or otherwise unenforceable provisions but are valid and enforceable and (iii) the remaining provisions shall remain enforceable to the fullest extent permitted by law.

Section 15.12, "Severability of Provisions," while addressing a purely legal issue, may have great practical impact. The section provides that, in the event particular portions of the document are found invalid, void, or otherwise unenforceable by a court interpreting the agreement, the remaining provisions shall be considered severable from the invalid provisions and shall therefore remain enforceable. This result is of particular concern when the agreement contains ancillary agreements, such as a covenant by the seller not to compete with the buyer after the acquisition. The enforceability of the agreement should not depend on the enforceability of a noncompetition agreement, and the severability provision serves to accomplish this end.

Section 15.13. Further Assurance. The Seller, the Target and the Buyer agree that at any time and from time to time after the Closing Date they will execute and deliver to any other party such further instruments or documents as may reasonably be required to give effect to the transactions contemplated hereunder.

Section 15.14. Confidential Information. The Seller, the Target and the Buyer for themselves, their directors, officers, employees, agents, representatives and partners, if any, covenant with each other that they will use all information relating to any other party, the Target or any Subsidiary acquired by any of them pursuant to the provisions of this Agreement or in the course of negotiations with or examinations of any other party only in connection with the transactions contemplated hereby and shall cause all information obtained by them pursuant to this Agreement and such negotiations and examinations, which is not publicly available, to be treated as confidential except as may otherwise be required by law or as may be necessary or appropriate in connection with the enforcement of this Agreement or any instrument or document referred to herein or contemplated hereby. In the event of termination of this Agreement, each party will cause to be delivered to the other all documents, work papers and other material obtained by it from the others, whether so obtained by it from the others, whether so obtained before or after the execution of this Agreement, and each party agrees that it shall not itself use or disclose, directly or indirectly, any information so obtained, or otherwise obtained from the other hereunder or in connection therewith, and will have all such information kept confidential and will not use such information in any way which is detrimental to any other party, provided that (i) any party may use and disclose any such information which has been disclosed publicly (other than by such party or any affiliate of such party in breach of its obligations under this Section 15.14) and (ii) to the extent that any party or any affiliate of a party may become legally compelled to disclose any such information if it shall have used its best efforts, and shall have afforded the other parties the opportunity, to obtain an appropriate protective order, or other satisfactory assurance of confidential treatment, for the information required to be disclosed.

The confidential information section typically requires each party to keep confidential all information obtained in the course of the transaction. Because the target has already been or will shortly thereafter be the object of an intensive due diligence review when the agreement is signed, the seller is initially more concerned with disclosure issues than the buyer. The seller may take the position that all materials provided to the buyer relating to the target should be returned or destroyed in the event the parties fail to close the transaction.

Section 15.15. Writings and Disclosures. Except as otherwise provided or contemplated herein, each exhibit, schedule, writing or other disclosure described in this Agreement as having been delivered or to be delivered by one party to the other shall be identified by reference to the section of this Agreement to which it relates and shall be signed or initialed on the first page by an officer or legal counsel of the Seller and by an officer or legal counsel of the Buyer and unless so identified and signed or initialed, the party receiving the same shall not be chargeable with notice of its content.

CHAPTER 9

Closing

INTRODUCTION

For the most part, the M&A journey unfolds as a gradual, interconnected process. A plan may bring to light an opportunity, or an opportunity may inspire a plan. Price may depend on financing, and financing may depend on price. Structuring may be a consideration from the beginning of a CEO's acquisition quest, or may be a last-minute job for attorneys. The paperwork of due diligence, compensation planning, and the acquisition agreement occur simultaneously, each impacting the others. As this process unfolds, days and months go by, and deadlines may be extended. Trivial matters can take months, and destinies can be determined in minutes. In these respects, the M&A process can be likened to the ancient Greek concept of *keiros*—time that knows no limits.

The closing, however, stands apart from this living drama. The timing here is strictly *kronos*—and measured by the stop watch. The date is fixed, the timing limited—typically to 48 hours or less. If dealmakers master nothing else, they need a good sense of this very important occasion—hence this chapter.

THE BASICS OF CLOSING

What is a closing?

A *closing* is the event through which the parties to a transaction consummate that transaction by the execution and delivery of documentation, and if applicable, the transfer of funds. Unless funded from internal sources by the buyer, the typical acquisition closing has two major elements: the *acquisition,* or *corporate,* closing, in which the seller and the buyer effect the merger or the transfer and delivery of the stock or assets pursuant to the acquisition agreement, and the *financial* closing, pursuant to which one or more lenders or other funding parties provide funding for the acquisition to the buyer, as borrower, pursuant to a specific loan agreement or other financing documentation, a portion of which is remitted to the seller in payment of the purchase price.

When is the acquisition agreement usually executed— at the closing or before it?

Sometimes the parties will want to sign and close the corporate side of the transaction simultaneously. This most often occurs when the buyer is financing the transaction internally, when no governmental approvals are required to consummate the transaction, or when the deal must close very quickly after the parties have reached their initial meeting of the minds—for example, to take advantage of the provisions of a soon-to-expire tax law or to enable a seller to obtain the sales proceeds in time to meet a debt retirement obligation. In some instances, the parties do not intend to sign and close simultaneously but end up doing so because it takes them right up to the closing date to reach basic agreement.

If the transaction is at all complex and requires governmental approval or third-party financing, the parties will most likely sign a letter of intent, negotiate and execute the acquisition agreement, and then proceed to close when the "conditions precedent to closing" (often a formally drawn document) have been met and when the financing has been made available. Government agencies may require that the parties execute the acquisition agreement prior to consideration of an application for governmental approval of the transaction. Similarly, lenders may require that the terms of a transaction be established before they commit their resources to evaluating the transaction; in particular, they will want to know what representations and warranties are being made by the seller and the remedies available to the buyer if the seller breaches them.

What about financing agreements? When are they typically signed?

Most financing agreements are not signed until the closing. Before this time, however, the borrower and the lenders will have executed a commitment letter, or reached agreement on a term sheet, setting forth the basic terms of the lending arrangements.

How long does a closing take?

The closing process may last for a few hours or for days or weeks, depending on how much negotiation is left for the finale and on how well and how quickly the parties can satisfy the conditions precedent to closing. The period immediately prior to the closing is often consumed by final negotiation of the terms and conditions of the operative documents, but this is not always the case. Closings on transactions for which the terms have been negotiated and finalized prior to the closing involve review of documents and confirmation that the conditions precedent to closing have been met, followed by the execution and delivery of documents and, when appropriate, the actual receipt of funding. The simplest of closings may be effected by an exchange of documents signed in counterpart without convening the parties at a single location.

Can a closing be held if either of the parties has not yet met all the conditions to closing?

Yes. An escrow closing may occur when one or more of the necessary conditions to closing have not been met but the parties wish to go forward subject to satisfaction of the remaining conditions. In this case, transaction documentation can be executed and entrusted to a designated escrow agent, chosen by the parties, who will break escrow and deliver the documents to the parties upon fulfillment of the outstanding conditions. An arrangement of this nature will require the negotiation and drafting of an escrow agreement among the parties; the agent must clearly set forth the terms upon which the breaking of escrow may occur, and the actions to be taken if those conditions are not fulfilled.

Alternatively, the parties may close the transaction if the party for whose benefit the unsatisfied condition was negotiated decides to waive the condition and proceed. In some cases it may be possible for the waiving party to exact some additional concession, such as an increase in the purchase price, or a pledge from the other party that it will satisfy the condition after the closing. If the unsatisfied condition is so critical that the deal would unwind were it not to be fulfilled, the prudent path is not to close, since the cost of unwinding a closed transaction or resolving the unsatisfied condition may be much higher than the cost of failing to close.

Who should attend a closing?

Each person responsible for executing a document at the closing should expect to be present at the closing offices, or to be otherwise available, from the time that the closing is scheduled to the time of actual signing. If the signatory officer is also the businessperson responsible for the transaction, he or she is likely to be engaged throughout the pre-closing and closing process. If, on the other hand, the individual with signing authority is not otherwise involved in the transaction, he or she should be willing and able to remain available in the event that there is a delay in the closing process. Each individual sharing responsibility for the transaction should be on hand to review documents and participate in the negotiation of any final changes.

Attorneys for each of the parties to the transaction will typically be required to participate in final negotiations and preparation and review of the closing documents, including, if required, opinions of counsel. The participation of parties at other locations may also be required, depending on the nature of the transaction. For example, a transaction involving the transfer of assets (rather than stock) will typically require that certain conveyance documents be recorded at the time of closing at the appropriate federal, state, or local recordation offices in the jurisdiction within which that property is located. For multistate acquisitions involving real and personal property, this may require filings in numerous locations. Further, counsel from each of those jurisdictions may have to render an opinion on the effectiveness of the conveyances as a condition to closing. If the transaction involves one or more mergers, attorneys or other appropriate persons will have to file merger certificates and other documents at the offices of the secretary of state of each jurisdiction where filing is required to effectuate such mergers. Finally, if the conveyed assets secure the financing of the transaction, then the parties will need to record documentation such as mortgages, and UCC-1 forms [required under the Uniform Commercial Code (UCC)] along with opinions of local counsel. The effective coordination of all these off-site parties is one of the more significant organizational challenges of a transactional closing.

Where should the closing take place?

The closing should be planned for the location most convenient to all parties involved. In the event that a financing is involved, this is almost always the city in which the principal lender is located. The offices in which the closing takes place should offer adequate services, space, communications, word processing, and photocopying, together with sufficient secretarial (and notarial) staff, to complete the transaction documentation and otherwise consummate the deal. These facilities and services are typically found at transactional law firms that maintain offices for these specific purposes. However, the closing is often scheduled to take place at the offices of counsel to one of the parties. In the event that a major financing is involved, it is usually held in the offices of the lender's attorneys.

The buyer should seriously consider having the corporate closing and the financing closing in separate offices, within the same city, if possible. Having two locations (or possibly more, if several pieces of large, complex financings are involved) serves the practical purpose of reducing the confusion and tension generated when many people are confined to the same quarters under stressful conditions. It also has tactical significance to the buyer. The most difficult aspect of any closing is last-minute negotiation (and renegotiation) of deal points, major and minor. Most often, it is in the buyer's best interest to keep the seller and the various lenders physically apart from each other so that the buyer can control the flow of information that each group receives and can broker a consensus on open points of common concern to its best advantage.

Having separate closings for each major financing agreement can help the buyer avoid a "me too" syndrome among lenders. This can be particularly important in the area of intercreditor relationships. As closing approaches, lenders get increasingly nervous about the risks they are about to take, particularly in a highly leveraged deal, and seek to improve their position by getting more collateral to secure their loans or a piece of the equity, or by imposing tighter post-acquisition covenants. Whatever concession one lender wins, the others will demand for themselves. The buyer has a better chance of neutralizing this syndrome if it can keep the lenders from talking to each other.

How many people should be involved in a closing?

Each party should plan to have staffing adequate to cover all aspects of the transaction, from negotiating issues that exist or may arise, to performing all the mechanical tasks required to complete the transaction. Most of the tasks will be performed by attorneys and other law firm employees. The parties' accountants and various people from the business entities involved in the transaction, particularly the finance department, will also need to be on hand, or be easily reachable.

If the transaction will be financed by third parties, it is advisable that the attorneys for the buyer have separate closing teams for the corporate side of the transaction and each major piece of financing. This will be necessary if the closing is split among several physical locations. Each team should consist of the attorneys who have been primarily responsible for that aspect of the transaction since its inception and other attorneys and legal assistants as required. With adequately staffed teams in place to handle the details, the attorney in charge of the entire matter will be freed up to advise his or her client about the "big picture" and to troubleshoot different aspects of the transaction where necessary. It is critical, however, that all attorneys and legal assistants involved in the closing be kept informed of changes in the big picture that affect them. Periodic "all-hands" briefings are a good way to keep everyone abreast of changing events.

What are the phases of a closing?

The typical complex closing has three distinct phases: (1) the pre-closing process, (2) the closing itself, and (3) post-closing matters.

PRE-CLOSING

What happens during the pre-closing process?

During the pre-closing process, (1) the parties and their counsel distribute closing documents, including drafts of execution documents, for final review and approval prior to the scheduled date of execution and funding; (2) each party satisfies itself that all conditions to closing have been either satisfied or waived; and (3) the parties negotiate and resolve any open deal points. The size and complexity of the transaction and the number of open points, including new issues that may arise during this final phase, will determine the length of the pre-closing phase. A typical complex transaction, that is, one with one or two layers of financing, multistate collateral, and several third-party or governmental consents, can easily involve one or two weeks of pre-closing activities.

How do the parties satisfy themselves that the conditions precedent to closing have been satisfied or waived?

Some closing conditions are satisfied through the delivery of documents such as regulatory approvals, landlord waivers, estoppel certificates, and management employment agreements. In these cases, the parties and their counsel will examine the pertinent documentation and determine whether it comports with the requirements of the acquisition agreement or the relevant financing agreement, as applicable.

In other cases, more work is required. Consider, for example, legal opinions and officers' certifications as to the accuracy of all representations and warranties as of the closing date. The parties delivering these documents and/or their counsel will have the additional burden of satisfying themselves prior to delivery that the legal and factual matters set forth in the documents are, in fact, true. For example, prior to delivering a legal opinion, counsel will review documents such as UCC lien searches, corporate resolutions, good-standing certificates, and officers' certificates as to factual matters. Through this review, counsel will try to verify that certain actions such as the filing of merger documents and the recording of mortgages and UCC financing statements have been completed. The results of this review will form the necessary foundation for issuing the legal opinion.

What are some examples of closing conditions that are not satisfied through the delivery of documents?

One is the condition that there be no pending litigation that threatens to enjoin the consummation of the transaction. Another is that the company being acquired shall not have suffered a material adverse change in its business. In these cases, the parties must resort to a combination of examination and analysis of documents, such as the company's most recently available financial statements and the other due diligence investigation techniques they employed from the outset of the transaction to satisfy themselves that these conditions have been met.

To assist in the foregoing process, well in advance of the closing, the parties should have prepared one or more closing checklists (see below) that set forth the steps and documentation required for closing. Buyers and sellers who comply with the checklist and with the conditions precedent to closing set forth in the basic loan or acquisition documents will increase their chances of a successful closing.

How can a buyer or seller ensure that its representations and warranties are true as of the closing date?

Counsel for each party should periodically confirm with the client that nothing has occurred that makes a representation or warranty of the client untrue. Generally speaking, as soon as any significant event occurs that will make a representation or warranty untrue, such as a loss of a major customer of the seller or the filing of a lawsuit, the warranting party should inform the other parties of such occurrence so that appropriate waivers or modifications of terms can be negotiated and resolved in advance of the closing.

In addition, at least two or three days prior to the closing, counsel should review the client's representations and warranties line by line with appropriate employees and representatives of the client. Any facts that deviate from these representations and warranties should be incorporated as exceptions to the client's closing certificate regarding the accuracy of the representations and warranties and be immediately presented to the other relevant parties for their review. If they agree to accept the certificate with such exceptions, they shall be deemed to have waived the condition to closing (although, as discussed in Chapter 8, they may not have waived their claims to indemnification for breach of the representation or warranty).

What other forms do waivers take?

Waivers of conditions to closing may also be made through the acceptance of documents containing terms that differ from the previously negotiated terms, such as legal opinions that take exceptions, make assumptions, or exclude matters not originally contemplated by the parties. Where there is no previously contemplated document into which a waiver may be incorporated, the best course is to create a written waiver for the waiving party to execute.

How much renegotiation of the deal really takes place during the pre-closing phase?

A considerable amount! Therefore, the parties should be prepared for anything and everything, including the following:

- The filing of a lawsuit against the seller
- The assessment of a tax deficiency against the seller
- A change in the financial condition of the seller
- An unresolved personality conflict between principals in the buying and selling companies
- A demand by lenders that:
  - the transaction between the buyer and seller be modified

- additional security be provided
- the buyers raise additional equity
- the lenders be given an equity kicker

These "unthinkable" events can and do happen and may require the parties to renegotiate fundamental business issues. As a result, the buyer and seller should come to the pre-closing phase prepared to compromise where appropriate and to identify what items are nonnegotiable for them.

Who has the most leverage in closing-week negotiations?

First of all, the convergence of the parties at the various appointed closing offices, added to the resources they have already expended in getting to this phase of the transaction, creates tremendous momentum and incentives for everyone to close. Therefore, there will be some room for compromise by each party. Nevertheless, the parties will not necessarily have equal bargaining strength simply because both of them are fast approaching the finish line. Differences in leverage that developed through the course of prior negotiations are likely to persist during the closing week. However, there are no hard and fast rules about the degree to which the power relationships among the parties will, or will not, change.

For example, it would be logical for the buyer to assume that the sweet image of sales proceeds is dancing in the seller's head and, as a result, the seller will bend easily to any changes requested by the lenders. But the seller, in fact, may be having second thoughts about its bargain and resist any modifications of the acquisition agreement as a way of trying to force the buyer into a position where it cannot close. Conversely, the buyer may think (or know) that it is buying the target cheaply and may therefore do whatever it takes to achieve a quick closing.

What is a pre-closing drill?

The *pre-closing drill* is a dress rehearsal for the closing, preferably held no earlier than three days prior to closing and no later than the night prior to closing. Counsel for the parties conduct the drill; their clients and other persons will be present as needed. Each party puts all its closing documents out on the closing room table so that the other appropriate parties can satisfy themselves that the conditions to closing embodied in those documents have been met.

To the extent feasible, the parties will execute as many documents as possible in order to save time on the closing day and thereby ensure that all conditions to closing will be satisfied early enough in the day to allow any wire transfer of funds or investment of sale proceeds to be completed on the closing day. After review of the closing documents and the closing checklist, the parties will identify tasks that must be completed before, legally and logistically, closing can be effected. However, it is not unusual to generate a schedule of minor uncompleted items and agree that they will be resolved post-closing.

In transactions involving third-party financing, lenders and lenders' counsel may require two or more pre-closing drills—that is, one involving their own financing, one involving review of the corporate side of the transaction, and, if applicable, others involving the other financing pieces of the transaction.

CLOSING

What happens on the closing day itself?

Assuming the parties have conducted a pre-closing drill, three things will happen.

- First, the parties and their counsel will review any documents that were revised or newly generated, the parties will execute any previously unexecuted documents, all undated documents will be dated, any required meetings of the board of directors that have not previously been held will be held, and any changed documents or signature pages that must be submitted to local counsel prior to release of their opinions will be transmitted to them.

- Second, the parties will recheck all the documents lined up on the closing table against the closing checklists.

- Third, when all counsel are satisfied that all conditions to closing have been satisfied or waived, they will instruct their clients' respective agents to wire funds or file or record documents (simultaneously or in the sequence set forth in the closing checklist and other governing agreements). Once the agents have been instructed, then the parties may consider all the documentation on the closing table to have been delivered.

In the case of a transaction involving third-party financing, what part of the deal closes first?

Typically, all transactions are deemed to take place simultaneously. Practically speaking, the lenders usually will not release the loan proceeds until they receive confirmation that the corporate portion of the transaction has been completed—that is, stock certificates or bills of sale have been delivered or merger certificates have been filed, and security and title documents have been properly recorded.

How long does it actually take to close a transaction?

Depending on the complexity of the transaction, the number of things that do not go according to plan or schedule, and the goodwill, patience, and ingenuity of the parties and their counsel in devising acceptable bridge arrangements, substitutes, or accommodations, the closing phase may be effected within a matter of an hour or two, or it may stretch over several days.

On what day should the closing take place?

Preferably any day but a Friday or a day before a holiday. The failure to achieve the closing on the scheduled day prior to a weekend or holiday puts the parties in the awkward position of having to work into or through the nonbusiness day, without the ability to transfer or invest funds prior to the next business day, and with the attendant disruption in the personal lives of all concerned (which can be particularly troublesome for nonprofessional staff). Depending on the point at which the transaction slipped off schedule, any number of complications may have occurred. Title may have been transferred without funding. Issues of who owns what or who bears the risk of loss may arise. Interest may be claimed on the "lost" or withheld funding by the lender or the seller. Finally, the documents, especially exhibits thereto, even if prepared in an "as-of" form, may contain material inaccuracies caused by the passage of time that will require redating, amendment, or waiver in order to close the transaction.

What are some of the most common logistical snafus that can derail a closing?

Some of the biggest headaches result from the following:

- Unavailability of key businesspeople
- Failure to have local counsel on standby to review last-minute document changes
- Failure to provide local counsel with copies of requested documents
- Failure to have precleared articles of merger with appropriate jurisdictions
- Failure to have persons on standby to file or record documents, including merger documents, UCC-1 forms, mortgages, and terminations of UCCIs required to be removed off-record
- Failure to have adequate support staff to make last-minute revisions in documents
- Failure to have conducted the pre-closing drill, including execution of all documents not subject to change
- Failure to have adequate legal staff at closing headquarters to negotiate final documents, including local counsel legal opinions
- Failure to obtain proper wiring instructions for funds transfers
- Failure to ascertain time periods by which wires must be sent or to make arrangements to have banks hold their wires open past normal hours
- Failure to consummate any pre-closing corporate reorganizations (such as mergers of subsidiaries into parent companies, dissolution of defunct subsidiaries, or filing of charter amendments) in a timely fashion
- Failure to have tax counsel review the final terms and documentation to ensure that tax planning objectives have not been adversely affected by last-minute restructuring or drafting
- Failure to obtain required bring-down good-standing certificates or other certified documents from appropriate jurisdictions

Proper advance planning can prevent most if not all of these failures.

WIRE TRANSFERS

What is a wire transfer of funds?

A *wire transfer of funds* is payment through a series of debits and credits transmitted via computers. A domestic wire transfer is made through the Federal

Reserve System, which is divided into 12 districts throughout the United States, with each district having one main Federal Reserve Bank and a myriad of branch banks. The actual physical transfer of funds takes place on the books of the Federal Reserve Banks and branches. An international wire transfer of funds is payment through a series of debits and credits transmitted directly via telex among correspondent banks.

How is a domestic wire transfer made?

To make a wire transfer, both the buyer's and seller's banks must be members of the Federal Reserve System and maintain accounts with a Reserve Bank, or have an account with a member bank. The buyer or lender remitting funds by wire must provide to its bank the name of the seller, the name of the seller's bank and the identity of the account to be credited, and the American Banking Association number that identifies the seller's bank in the Federal Reserve System.

Upon the confirmation of customer funds, the originating member bank, or transferor, will notify its Reserve Bank to debit the transferor's account for credit to the member bank transferee. If the transferor and transferee maintain accounts at two separate Reserve Banks, the request for credit will be sent by the transferor's Reserve Bank to the transferee's Reserve Bank for credit to the latter. The transferee's Reserve Bank will then credit the transferee's account.

How does the originating bank confirm customer funds?

All funds to be remitted must be collected. Thus, a check deposit covering the wire transfer that has not yet cleared will delay or prevent the transfer. Essentially, the remitting bank is protecting itself from exposure on items subject to stop payment orders until final payment is effectuated. This includes certified checks and bank checks. Often, reference is made to "immediately available funds" or "federal funds," which signifies that the funds for remittance have been collected.

When is the wire transfer actually completed?

As soon as the transferee receives notice of the credit—the "Fedwire transfer" from its Federal Reserve Bank—payment is considered final, and except as described below, the seller has the right to the use of such funds.

Can a transferor revoke the request for a wire transfer of funds once the transferor has notified its Reserve Bank to debit its account?

The Reserve Bank may cease acting on the wire transfer if the transferor's request for revocation allows the Reserve Bank a reasonable opportunity to comply with the requested revocation. If the request is received too late, the Reserve Bank may ask the transferee's Reserve Bank to ask the transferee to return the funds, if the transferor so desires. However, the Reserve Bank will only be liable for lack of good faith or failure to exercise ordinary care. Therefore, it is not responsible if the transferee refuses to return the funds.

What is the deadline for placing a wire transfer order for funds intended to be received by the seller on the same day?

Although no Reserve Bank will guarantee that it will complete a transfer of funds on the day requested, generally speaking, 3:00 P.M. is the originating banks deadline. Moreover, the Reserve Bank may, at its discretion, process a wire transfer after its closing hour. This will usually occur when there is an emergency or when large sums of money are being transferred. The deadline for placing an international wire transfer order is generally 12:30 P.M.

What are the differences between the domestic and international wire transfer of funds?

With an international wire transfer, the ease and security of the Federal Reserve are not available. Hence, the transfer generally takes longer. In addition, with international wire there is a problem of provisional payment. Specifically, the bank that debits the customer's account usually reserves the right to withdraw the credit extended to the corresponding bank, if the customer's account is overdrawn in the process. This may create problems in determining when final payment is made.

What are the advantages and disadvantages to a seller in requiring payment through a wire transfer of funds?

Next to actual cash in hand, this is the best way for a seller to assure itself that it will have use of the sale proceeds on the closing day, because the Federal Reserve Bank assumes the risk of final payment once the transferor's request is accepted by its Reserve Bank.

One potential disadvantage associated with a wire transfer concerns the nature of the account agreement the seller has with its bank. The seller's bank may not be required to credit the seller's account immediately upon receiving Federal Reserve credit because of the account agreement. Federal law requires that the transferee "promptly" credit the beneficiary's account. However, what "promptly" means is not clearly specified. The seller would be best advised to be familiar with the terms of its bank account agreement. Moreover, the seller could specify in the acquisition agreement that the buyer's duty to deliver funds is completed only when the seller's individual account has been credited.

Are there methods of payment, other than cash or wire transfer, that would be acceptable to sellers at a closing?

There are three types of bank-issued checks that are virtually risk-free to a seller who accepts them: (1) the certified check, (2) the cashier's check, and (3) the bank check. Each of these checks has some distinguishing feature that differentiates it from the others, but all of them are designed to offer comfort to the recipient that payment will definitely be made by the designated payor bank.

Certified checks are instruments that, upon certification by the payor bank, are not subject to an order to stop payment. Under the UCC, the certifying bank becomes personally liable for failure to honor the check, and the customer is secondarily liable thereon.

When a bank issues a cashier's check, the bank acts as both the payor and the payee for the amount of the check. As with the certified check, a bank is deemed to have accepted a cashier's check for payment at the moment it is issued. The customer cannot stop payment on it. The seller's only risk of nonpayment is if the issuing bank becomes insolvent before payment can be made. Even in that event, if the bank is a member of the Federal Deposit Insurance Corporation (FDIC), the check will be insured up to $100,000, including accrued interest.

A bank check does not give a seller the same degree of comfort as either a certified or cashier's check, because, unlike the certified and cashier's check, the issuing bank of a bank check has not accepted the check for payment (that is, committed to pay the stated amount upon demand) at the moment of issuance. Rather, presentment of the check is required for payment. Despite this difference, the UCC treats bank checks as cash equivalents, and the only instance in which the issuing bank can stop payment is if it is a direct party to the transaction. The only time a customer ordering a bank check can request that payment be stopped is in the case of fraud or a theft of the instrument.

POST-CLOSING

What are typical post-closing activities?

Post-closing tasks typically fall into one of two categories: document distribution and cleanup.

Document distribution requires planning. Although each of the parties to a closing generally wants to depart from the closing table with a complete stack of original closing documents for its file, this is not frequently practical. First, each of the parties has different requirements for closing documents. Some parties should not receive documents that other parties will receive, and some parties need original documents whereas others need only photocopies.

Further, some documents held or executed at other locations may be available at the time and place of closing only by telecopy, or not at all. Finally, the sheer number and volume of documents may preclude sorting and photocopying of the executed papers swiftly enough to be delivered to the parties prior to their departure from the premises.

At some point, however, each of the participants should receive a complete set of the transaction documents to which it is entitled. In some transactions, the initial distribution of originals and, as available, copies is followed by the production of a closing binder containing a complete indexed set of documents in one or more volumes. These binders may be velobound or, if the expense is approved by the clients, permanently bound in stitched covers with stamped lettering on the spine. The acquisition documents often are bound separately from the financing documents.

The final document assembly and distribution effort will be much easier if a good closing document checklist was utilized prior to closing. When completed and updated, the checklist may be turned into a closing memorandum (which may double as an index to the closing document binders), with the addition of a brief narrative chronology of the transactions taken prior to, at, and following the closing to complete the transaction. A common closing memorandum can be used even if the acquisition and financing closings occurred at different offices.

The second principal post-closing effort is the cleanup process, which involves the finalization or completion of tasks and documents that were not or could not have been completed at or prior to closing. This may include corrections or amendments to ancillary documents, the termination of pension plans, the receipt of consents and approvals not obtainable by closing, the completion and documentation of a closing date audit for balance sheet pricing adjustment purposes, or the receipt of title insurance commitments or policies as of the closing date from jurisdictions with filing delays. In addition, where many real estate parcels in multiple jurisdictions are required to be mortgaged, or collateral is located in foreign countries, completion of recordation of mortgages and perfection of security interests are commonly put aside as post-closing matters, with a deadline for completion of several months after the closing date.

In both cases, individuals responsible for post-closing efforts should strive to complete their tasks as soon as possible before the pressure of other matters and the passage of time make the wrapping up of these loose ends more difficult than would otherwise have been the case. A post-closing checklist similar in design to the closing checklist described below should be prepared, and adhered to, by the parties responsible for these activities.

PLANNING AIDS

What's the best way to prepare for a closing?

Have your attorney prepare a comprehensive closing checklist well in advance of the closing, in fact, as soon as the deal begins to jell. This checklist should:

- Set forth each and every task that must be completed in order for the parties to be legally and logistically ready to consummate the transaction and the date by which such task must be completed.
- State, where applicable, the document in which the completion of the task will be embodied.
- Set forth the name of one or more persons responsible for the task.
- Contain a space for status notes.

The closing checklist is both a road map and a progress report of the transaction. It can also be a source of embarrassment and a goad to those responsible for producing or reviewing documents whose failure to meet deadlines is documented in the status notes. Finally, it is the basis for the preparation of a closing memorandum for the transaction.

How should one schedule pre-closing tasks?

The first concern should be to deal with documents and actions of parties who either will not be at the closing, will have a limited role in the closing, or are beyond the control of the parties to the transaction. These persons include directors and shareholders whose authorizations are required; governmental agencies without any incentive to expedite review of applications for regulatory approvals; third parties to critical agreements who may prove recalcitrant when asked for consents, estoppel letters, solvency letters, or legal opinions; actuaries who must give up-to-date valuations of pension assets; and persons who are committed to other tasks but need to be on call to file or record mortgages, UCC financing statements, or merger certificates upon a moment's notice. The persons responsible for ensuring that the closing takes place on the appointed day must make an accurate assessment of how long it is likely to take to obtain a required document or to accomplish a necessary task, and, working backward from the expected closing date, attempt to develop a realistic schedule for reaching closing.

Should all the parties use the same closing checklist?

At the very least, by the time the parties arrive for the pre-closing phase, they should be working from the same closing checklist, with the following exceptions. The seller does not need those portions of the checklist dedicated to the financing of the transaction other than items related to the financing in which the seller has a role (such as delivery of reliance letters from the seller's counsel to lenders allowing them to rely on such counsel's legal opinion, and delivery of the seller's consent to assignments by the buyer to the lenders of the buyer's rights under the acquisition agreement).

The seller and the lenders do not need an expansive checklist relating to the tasks associated with the formation and capitalization of the buying group. Moreover, there may be certain tasks or documents, including side letters, that each party wishes to keep confidential within its own group. As a result of the foregoing, each party may have more than one closing checklist, that is, an expansive one setting forth everything about which it is concerned, and other lists that are abridged versions of the global checklist and are to be shared with one or more of the other parties. These short lists must be developed along with the other parties so that all agree about what activities will make everyone ready, legally and logistically, to consummate the transaction.

CLOSING MEMORANDUM

Is there one document that sums up the transaction?

Yes. The closing memorandum memorializes the significant activities that constituted the transaction. The sample closing memorandum in Appendix 9A, which is from a very complex transaction, shows how much craft it takes to master "the art of M&A."

CONCLUDING COMMENTS

As the culmination of a deal, the closing calls for focus and agility. Details abound, and coordination counts. This process may seem overwhelming to executives. Concerned with the big picture, they may wish to delegate the process entirely to advisors. But executives need to pay attention to the closing, too. For the closing may be the end of the deal, but it is the beginning of something even more important—the creation of a new company.

A P P E N D I X 9A

Merger of Target Acquisition Corp. into Target Co. Inc. Closing Memorandum

DECEMBER 31, 1998
9:00 A.M. Eastern Standard Time

I. GENERAL

This memorandum describes the principal transactions that have occurred in connection with the acquisition (the "Acquisition") of Target Co. Inc., a Delaware corporation ("Target"), by Purchaser Holdings, Inc., a Delaware corporation ("Holdings"). Holdings; Target Acquisition Corp., a Delaware corporation and a wholly owned subsidiary of Holdings ("TAC"); and Target and Seller Holdings, Ltd., a Delaware corporation which owns all of the issued and outstanding Stock of Target ("Seller"), have entered into an Agreement of Merger, dated as of October 1, 1998 (the "Agreement"), pursuant to which TAC will be merged into Target pursuant to the Certificate of Merger.

In connection with the capitalization of Holdings to accomplish the Acquisition on the Effective Date, affiliates (the "Investor Shareholders") of Investor Corporation, a Delaware corporation ("IC"), purchased 800,000 shares of the common stock of Holdings for an aggregate amount of $4,000,000. Concurrently, IC loaned $1,000,000 on a recourse basis to certain management personnel at Target (the "Management Shareholders"). The Management Shareholders purchased 200,000 shares of the common stock of Holdings for $1,000,000 and pledged such stock to IC to secure repayment of the loan. TAC then merged into Target.

On the Effective Date, Holdings entered into a Credit Agreement with Lender Bank ("Bank") pursuant to which Holdings obtained a term loan of $40,000,000 and revolving credit loans of up to $10,000,000 (the "Credit Agreement"). Concurrently therewith, Holdings entered into a Bridge Funding Agreement with The Investment Bank Group Inc. ("Investment Bank Group") pursuant to which Holdings obtained a bridge loan of $60,000,000 (the "Bridge Agreement"). Holdings sold warrants for 200,000 shares of its Common Stock (the "Investment Banker Warrants") to Lead Investment Banker Incorporated ("Lead Investment Banker") and its designees for $20,000.

After the Effective Date it is anticipated that Holdings and Lead Investment Banker will enter into a Securities Purchase Agreement (the "Securities Purchase Agreement") pursuant to which Holdings will return the $20,000 to Lead Investment Banker and Lead Investment Banker will return the Investment Banker Warrants to Holdings. Holdings will then sell Warrants for 200,000 shares of its Common Stock to the Purchasers named in the Securities Purchase Agreement (the "Purchasers") for $20,000 (the "Note Purchase Warrants") and deliver to the Purchasers Notes due December 31, 2003, in an aggregate principal amount of $60,000,000 and bearing interest at approximately 14 percent per annum (the "Note") for which Holdings will receive $60,000,000 cash which it will use to pay off the $60,000,000 bridge loan under the Bridge Agreement.

After the Effective Time and concurrently with the funding of the term loan, the initial revolving loans and the bridge loan, Holdings contributed to TAC the amount of $100,000,000 as a capital contribution. Seller received $100,000,000 cash less the amount of the intercompany loan to be paid after Closing, Series A Preferred Stock of Holdings having a redemption value of $10,000,000 and a Warrant entitling it to purchase 40,000 shares of the common stock of Holdings (the "Seller Warrant").

The Closing occurred on December 31, 1998 (the "Effective Date"), at 9:00 A.M. Eastern Standard Time. The merger was effective on the Effective Date at the time the Certificate of Merger was filed with the Secretary of State of Delaware (the "Effective Time").

All capitalized terms used herein which are not defined herein and which are defined in the Agreement, the Credit Agreement, the Bridge Funding Agreement or the Securities Purchase Agreement have the respective meanings attributed to them in the Agreement, the Credit Agreement, the Bridge Funding Agreement or the Securities Purchase Agreement.

II. TRANSACTIONS PRIOR TO THE CLOSING

The following actions were taken prior to the Closing.

1. On October 1, 1998, the Agreement among Holdings, Target, TAC and Seller was executed and delivered.

2. On October 1, 1998, TAC, Seller and Agent Bank (the "Escrow Agent") entered into an Escrow Agreement pursuant to which TAC deposited with the Escrow Agent One Million Dollars ($1,000,000) pursuant to Section 3.3 of the Agreement.

3. On October 1, 1998, the Board of Directors of each of Holdings and TAC approved the terms of the Merger and the Agreement and the Board of Directors of TAC approved the Escrow Agreement.

4. On October 1, 1998, the Board of Directors of each of Target and Seller approved the terms of the Merger and the Agreement and the Board of Directors of Seller approved the Escrow Agreement.

5. On October 2, 1998, Seller issued a press release announcing the Holdings, Target, Seller and TAC agreement to the terms of the Merger and announcing the execution of the Agreement.

6. On November 16, 1998, Bank delivered to Holdings a commitment letter pursuant to which Bank agreed to provide a $40,000,000 term loan and a $10,000,000 revolving line of credit to facilitate the Acquisition and to provide working capital thereafter.

7. On November 24, 1998, Lead Investment Banker delivered to Holdings a commitment letter pursuant to which Lead Investment Banker undertook to provide a bridge loan for an aggregate amount of $60,000,000.

8. On November 24, 1998, Holdings delivered to Lead Investment Banker a retention letter pursuant to which Holdings retained Lead Investment Banker to sell the Notes and Note Purchaser Warrants.

9. On December 24, 1998, a date at least three business days before the Closing, Seller delivered to TAC pursuant to Section 4.3 of the Agreement a notice setting forth the amount of the Intercompany Loan to be paid immediately after Closing.

10. On December 28, 1998, the Board of Directors and shareholders of Holdings adopted an amendment of the certificate of incorporation of Holdings to authorize the Series A Preferred Stock.

11. On December 28, 1998, Holdings caused to be filed an Amended and Restated Certificate of Incorporation providing for 1,500 shares of Series A Preferred Stock par value $1.00 per share.

12. As of December 30, 1998, the Certificate of Merger was executed by the President of TAC and attested by the Secretary of such corporation and was executed by the President of Target and sealed and attested by the Secretary of such corporation.

13. On December 30, 1998, the Board of Directors of Holding authorized the issuance of 1,000 shares of Series A Preferred Stock to Seller with the rights designated in the Amended and Restated Certificate of Incorporation of Holdings.

14. On December 30, 1998, Seller, as sole stockholder of Target, consented to the Agreement and Certificate of Merger.

15. On December 30, 1998, Holdings, as sole stockholder of TAC, consented to the Agreement and Certificate of Merger.

III. CLOSING DOCUMENTS AND TRANSACTIONS

The following documents were delivered at or prior to the Effective Date, but all such documents are deemed delivered at the Effective Date. All documents are dated as of the Effective Date and delivered in New York, New York, unless otherwise indicated. All transactions in connection with the Closing shall be considered as accomplished concurrently, so that none shall be effective until all are effective. Executed copies (or photocopies, or conformed copies where necessary) of each document will be delivered after the Closing as follows:

one to IC
one to Holdings
one to Seller
one to Target
one to Bank
one to Lead Investment Banker

with photocopies to be distributed as follows:

one to Investment Banker Counsel (IBC)
one to Seller Counsel (SC)
one to Bank Counsel (BC)
one to Investor Corporation Counsel (ICC)

IV. SCHEDULE OF CLOSING DOCUMENTS

1. Corporate Good Standing, Articles, Bylaws and Incumbency of Target, Its Subsidiaries and Seller

1.01. Certificate of Incorporation and all amendments to date of Target certified by the Secretary of State of Delaware on December 3, 1998.

1.02. Certificate of the Secretary of State of Delaware, dated December 3, 1998, certifying that Target is an existing corporation and in good standing under the laws of the State of Delaware.

1.03. Telex from the Secretary of State of Delaware, dated the Effective Date, updating the information described in item 1.02 above.

1.04. Certificates of the Secretaries of State of California and New York dated December 1 and 2, 1998, respectively, certifying that Target is qualified to conduct business and in good standing in such states.

1.05. Telexes or verbal consents from the Secretaries of State of California and New York, dated the Effective Date, updating the information described in item 1.04 above.

1.06. (a)–(b) Articles or Certificates of Incorporation or other organization documents and all amendments to date of the following Subsidiaries of Target ("Subsidiaries") certified by the appropriate authority of the governing jurisdiction:

(a) New York Target Subsidiary Ltd. (N.Y.)

(b) Delaware Target Subsidiary, Inc. (Del.)

1.07. (a)–(b) Certificates of the authorities described in item 1.06, certifying that each of the Subsidiaries is an existing corporation and in good standing.

1.08. (a)–(b) Telexes or verbal consents of the authorities described in item 1.06, dated the Effective Date, updating the information set forth in item 1.07 above.

1.09. Certificate of Incorporation and all amendments to date of Seller certified by the Secretary of State of Delaware, dated December 3, 1998.

1.10. Certificate of the Secretary of State of Delaware, dated December 3, 1998, certifying that Seller is an existing corporation and in good standing under the laws of Delaware.

1.11. Telex from the Secretary of State of Delaware, dated the Effective Date, updating the information described in item 1.10 above.

1.12. Certificate of Secretary of Target, dated the Effective Date, as to the Certificates of Incorporation and Bylaws of such corporation, the election, incumbency and signatures of officers of such corporation, and certifying as to the resolutions of the Board of Directors and stockholders of such corporation relating to the transaction pursuant to Section 8.4 of the Agreement.

1.13. Certificate of Secretary of Seller, dated the Effective Date, as to the Certificate of Incorporation and Bylaws of such corporation, the election, incumbency and signatures of officers of such corporation, and certifying as to the resolutions of the Board of Directors of such corporation relating to the transaction pursuant to Section 8.4 of the Agreement.

2.   Good Standing, Articles, Bylaws and Incumbency of Holdings and TAC

2.01. Certificate of Incorporation and all amendments to date of Holdings certified by the Secretary of State of Delaware on December 21, 1998.

2.02. Certificate of the Secretary of State of Delaware, dated December 21, 1998, certifying that Holdings is an existing corporation and in good standing under the laws of the State of Delaware.

2.03. Telex of the Secretary of State of Delaware, dated the Effective Date, updating the information set forth in item 2.02 above.

2.04. Certificate of the Secretary of State of each of California and New York, dated December 22, 1998, certifying that Holdings is qualified to conduct business and in good standing in such states.

2.05. Certificate of Incorporation and all amendments to date of TAC certified by the Secretary of State of Delaware on December 10, 1998.

2.06. Certificate of the Secretary of State of Delaware, dated December 21, 1998, certifying that TAC is an existing corporation and in good standing under the laws of the State of Delaware.

2.07. Telex of the Secretary of State of Delaware, dated the Effective Date, updating the information set forth in item 2.06 above.

2.08. Certificate of the Secretary of Holdings, dated the Effective Date, as to the Certificate of Incorporation and Bylaws of such corporation, the election, incumbency and signatures of officers of such corporation and certifying as to the resolutions of the Board of Directors of such corporation relating to the transaction pursuant to Section 9.4 of the Agreement, Sections 5.01(e), (f) and (h) of the Credit Agreement and the Bridge Agreement.

2.09. Certificate of the Secretary of TAC, dated the Effective Date, as to the Certificate of Incorporation and Bylaws of such corporation, the election, incumbency and signatures of officers of such corporation, and certifying as to the resolutions of the Board of Directors and stockholders of such corporation relating to the transaction pursuant to Section 9.4 of the Agreement, Sections 5.01(e), (f) and (h) of the Credit Agreement and the Bridge Agreement.

2.10. Certificate of the Secretary of Target (the Surviving Corporation), dated the Effective Date, certifying as to the resolutions of the Board of Directors of such corporation relating to Sections 5.01(e), (f) and (h) of the Credit Agreement and the Bridge Agreement.

2.11. (a)–(b) Certificates of the Secretaries of the Subsidiaries listed in (a)–(b) of item 1.06 as to the Certificate of Incorporation and By-laws, the election, incumbency and signatures of officers and certifying as to resolutions of the Board of Directors of such corporations relating to Sections 5.01(e), (f) and (h) of the Credit Agreement.

3. Principal Documents

3.01. Agreement of Merger, dated as of October 1, 1998.

3.02. Certificate of Merger.

3.03. Escrow Agreement, dated October 1, 1998.

3.04. Certificate No. PA-1-1 evidencing 1,000 shares of Series A Preferred Stock of Holdings.

3.05. Seller Registration Rights Agreement.

3.06. Seller Warrant.

3.07. Credit Agreement, together with Schedules and Exhibits thereto.

3.08. Target Security Agreement, between Bank as Agent and for the Ratable Benefit of Lenders and Target.

3.09. (a)–(b) Subsidiary Security Agreement between Bank as Agent and for the Ratable Benefit of Lenders and each of the Subsidiaries listed in (a)–(b) of item 1.06.

3.10. Holdings Pledge Agreement.

3.11. Certificate No. 8 evidencing 100 shares, constituting all of the issued and outstanding shares of Target together with a stock power duly endorsed.

3.12. Target Pledge Agreement.

3.13. (a)–(b) Certificates evidencing all of the issued and outstanding shares of each of the Subsidiaries listed in item 1.06, together with stock powers or other instruments of transfer duly endorsed.

3.14. Individual Stock Pledge Agreements, executed by each of the Investor Shareholders and Management Shareholders in favor of the Bank.

3.15. Certificates evidencing all of the issued and outstanding common shares of Holdings, together with stock powers from each shareholder duly endorsed.

3.16. Mortgage.

3.17. Joinder Agreement executed by Target.

3.18. Private Placement Memorandum of December 27, 1998.

3.19. Supplement to the Private Placement Memorandum dated December 30, 1998.

3.20. Bridge Agreement.

3.21. Bridge Notes Indenture.

3.22. Senior Subordinated Bridge Note.

3.23. Bridge Note Registration Rights Agreement.

3.24. Warrants issued by Holdings to Lead Investment Banker.

3.25. Subordinated Pledge Agreement between Holdings and Investment Bank Group.

3.26. Intercreditor Agreement between Bank and Investment Bank Group.

4. Documents Relating to the Escrow Agent

4.01. Joint Written Notice executed by Seller and TAC pursuant to Section 4(a) of the Escrow Agreement to the effect that the Merger has been effected and instructing the Escrow Agent to pay the Escrow Deposit and interest accrued thereon to Target.

4.02. Receipt of Target, dated the Effective Date, for funds received from the Escrow Agent in the amount of $1,025,000.

5. Documents Relating to Compliance with Agreement of Merger

5.01. Certificate of the President of Seller, dated the Effective Date, pursuant to Sections 8.1 and 8.2 of the Agreement and as to compliance with and performance of the Agreement and as to the representations and warranties set forth in the Agreement.

5.02. Certificate of the Vice President of TAC dated the Effective Date, pursuant to Sections 9.1, 9.2 and 9.7 of the Agreement as to compliance and performance of the Agreement; the representations and warranties set forth in the Agreement; and its business, financial conditions and operations.

5.03. Releases executed by each person holding an option to purchase common stock of Target under the Target Stock Option Plan pursuant to Section 8.9 of the Agreement.

5.04. Certificate No. 7 of Target evidencing 1,000 shares of common stock of Target issued to Seller together with such stock transfer tax stamps as may be required.

6. Documents Relating to Compliance with Credit Agreement

6.01. Certificate executed by CEO and CFO of Holdings as to representations and warranties and no event of default pursuant to Section 5.01(d) of the Credit Agreement.

6.02. (a)–(d) UCC-1 Financing Statements covering personal property and appropriate documents for perfecting security interest in U.S. intellectual property as follows:

(a) Holdings—California Secretary of State; Clerk of Los Angeles County, California; New York Department of State; and City Register of New York City;

(b) Target—California Secretary of State; Clerk of Los Angeles County, California; New York Department of State; and City Register of New York City;

(c) New York Target Subsidiary Ltd.—New York Department of State; and City Register of New York City; and

(d) Delaware Target Subsidiary Inc.—Delaware Secretary of State; Clerk of New Castle County, Delaware.

6.03. Certificate of President of Target to the effect that all indebtedness of Target has been paid or refinanced pursuant to Section 5.01(o) of the Credit Agreement.

6.04. Appointments of CT Corporation System in State of California as agent for service of process executed by CT Corporation, Holdings, Target and the Subsidiaries pursuant to Section 5.01(s) of the Credit Agreement.

6.05. Pro Forma Closing Date Balance Sheet for Holdings and its consolidated Subsidiaries pursuant to Section 5.01(t) of the Credit Agreement.

6.06. Borrowing Base Report, dated not more than two (2) days prior to the Effective Date pursuant to Section 5.01(y) of the Credit Agreement.

6.07. Appraisal of Appraisal Co. as to fair market value and orderly liquidation value of the real and personal property of Target pursuant to Section 5.01(b) of the Credit Agreement.

6.08. Written undertakings, executed by each of Target and the Subsidiaries pursuant to Section 5.01(d) of the Credit Agreement.

6.09. Solvency letters from CFOs and accountants for Holdings and Target pursuant to Section 5.01(k) of the Credit Agreement.

6.10. Bank Credit Audit pursuant to Section 5.01(p) of the Credit Agreement.

6.11. Certificate of Borrower as to consents pursuant to Section 6.03 of the Credit Agreement.

6.12. Evidence of payment of or indemnification against tax liens: City of New York—$10,000,000, State of New York—$500.

7. Consents, Waivers and Estoppel Certificates of Landlords of Target and Real Estate Matters

7.01. Consent of Lessor Ltd., lessor to New York Target Subsidiary, Ltd. with respect to the facility located at One Main Street, New York, New York.

7.02. Owners' title insurance policy with respect to the California property, dated the Effective Date, pursuant to Section 8.8 of the Agreement.

7.03. Lenders' title insurance policy with respect to the California property.

7.04. Title Insurance Questionnaire.

7.05. Estoppel Certificate.

7.06. Survey.

7.07. Indemnities of Seller to the Title Insurance Company.

7.08. Discharges of Trust Company Mortgages.

7.09. Seller Agreement regarding effluent discharge.

8. Insurance

8.01. Insurance endorsements naming Agent as additional insured or loss payee pursuant to Section 5.01(x) of the Credit Agreement.

9. Documents Relating to Compliance with Bridge Agreement

9.01. Certificate of Vice President of Holdings pursuant to Section 3.1.4 of the Bridge Agreement as to the satisfaction of certain conditions of the Bridge Agreement.

9.02. Warrant Repurchase Letter Agreement, dated the Effective Date, between Holdings and Investment Bank Group.

10. Opinions of Counsel

10.01. Opinion of SC, dated the Effective Date, addressed to Holdings, the Agent, Lead Investment Banker and the Indenture Trustee pursuant to Section 8.5 of the Agreement, Section 5.01(mm) of the Credit Agreement and Section 3.1.8 of the Bridge Agreement.

10.02. Opinion of ICC, dated the Effective Date, pursuant to Section 9.5 of the Agreement.

10.03. Opinion of ICC, dated the Effective Date, addressed to the Agent pursuant to Section 5.01(c) of the Credit Agreement.

10.04. Opinion of ICC, dated the Effective Date, addressed to Lead Investment Banker and the Indenture Trustee pursuant to Section 3.1.7 of the Bridge Agreement.

10.05. Opinion of California Counsel, dated the Effective Date, addressed to the Agent pursuant to Section 5.01(v) of the Credit Agreement.

10.06. Opinion of Copyright Counsel, dated the Effective Date, addressed to the Agent and Holdings as to the trademark and copyright registrations in the United States pursuant to Section 5.01(w) of the Credit Agreement.

10.07. Opinion of BC dated the Effective Date, addressed to the Lenders pursuant to Section 5.01(u) of the Credit Agreement.

11. Documents Relating to IC and Management Shareholders

11.01. Employment Agreement between Target and John Smith, President of Target.

11.02. Powers of Attorney from each Management Shareholder appointing John Smith Attorney-in-fact.

11.03. Recourse Notes in the aggregate of $1,000,000 executed by each of the Management Shareholders (originals delivered to IC).

11.04. Pledge Agreement executed by Management Shareholders in favor of IC.

11.05. Cross Receipt of IC acknowledging receipt of the notes described in 11.03 and by John Smith as Attorney-in-fact for each of the Management Shareholders acknowledging receipt of an aggregate amount of $1,000,000.

11.06. Stockholders Agreement among Holdings, Investor Shareholders and Management Shareholders.

11.07. Agreement for Management Consulting Services between IC and Target.

11.08. IC Intercreditor Agreement by and between IC and Bank.

11.09. Letter as to Recourse Promissory Notes in favor of IC, dated the Effective Date, from IC to counsel for the Management Shareholders.

12. Funding of Holdings and TAC and Merger Payment

12.01. Cross Receipt executed by Holdings acknowledging receipt of $4,000,000, and by the Investor Shareholders acknowledging receipt of Certificate Nos. 1-4 evidencing 800,000 shares of the common stock of Holdings.

12.02. Cross Receipt executed by Holdings acknowledging receipt of $1,000,000, and by the Management Shareholders acknowledging receipt of Certificate Nos. 5-8 evidencing 200,000 shares of the common stock of Holdings.

12.03. Cross Receipt executed by Seller, dated the Effective Date, acknowledging receipt of (a) the Cash Portion of the Merger Payment in the amount of $100,000,000 determined pursuant to Section 3.2(b) of the Merger Agreement; (b) the Warrant; and (c) Certificate No. PA-1 evidencing 1,000 shares of Series A Preferred Stock, and by Holdings acknowledging receipt of (i) $10,000,000 as consideration for the issuance of the Series A Preferred Stock and (ii) a certificate evidencing 1,000 shares of Common Stock of Target.

12.04. Receipt executed by IC acknowledging receipt of $3,000,000 as a structuring fee.

13. Funding of Loan and Sale of Warrants

13.01. Term Note in the amount of $40,000,000 (original delivered to Lender).

13.02. Revolving Note in the amount of $10,000,000 (original delivered to Lender) (only $1,000,000 borrowed at Closing).

13.03. Cross Receipt of Lender acknowledging receipt of the Term Note and the Revolving Note and of Holdings acknowledging receipt of $41,000,000.

13.04. Cross Receipt of Investment Bank Group and Lead Investment Banker acknowledging receipt of the Investment Banker Warrants and Bridge Note and of Holdings acknowledging receipt of $60,000,000.

V. FILING OF CERTIFICATE OF MERGER

When all parties and their counsel were satisfied that the documents described in Section IV above were complete and in order, the Certificate of Merger was filed in the office of the Secretary of State of Delaware, in accordance with the General Corporation Law of the State of Delaware.

CHAPTER 10

Postmerger Integration

INTRODUCTION

It takes conscientious effort to combine two or more companies after they have come under common ownership. As experienced acquirer Milton L. Rock has noted, "After the honeymoon, the real job begins. To live happily ever after requires planning and commitment."[1] Dealmakers may be good at combining them on paper—but what about in reality? This is the flesh-and-blood-and-widgets stuff of true *postmerger integration,* the subject of this chapter. *Postmerger,* of course, means after the merger (or other transaction) that leads to the combination of two companies. *Integration* refers to a combination of elements resulting in wholeness.

Not all deals result in postmerger integration. As mentioned earlier (in the introduction to Chapter 2), there are two basic types of acquirers: strategic and financial. Only the strategic acquirer is likely to integrate acquired companies into an existing entity. The financial acquirer, by contrast, is likely to leave the acquired entity alone, providing only capital and guidance.

The path toward postmerger integration is a series of decisions. It begins with the choice *to grow or to shrink.* Assuming growth, the choice becomes *to buy or to build,* and then, if buying, *to keep or to sell*—and if keep, to integrate or to "ignore." This chapter is dedicated to companies that choose to grow through acquisition, to keep what they buy, and to integrate what they keep. We will begin by offering preliminary data and checklists for postmerger success, and then guide acquirers in integrating specific resources, processes, and responsibilities.

POSTMERGER PERFORMANCE: THE BASICS

How successful are most mergers generally? Isn't it true that most of them turn out to be failures?

It depends on how you define *failure*. If you are not sure of your definition, you are not alone. In the past 30 years, scholars have published hundreds of studies of postmerger financial performance, and few have defined failure—or, conversely, success—in exactly the same way.

When failure is defined in extreme terms, such as the eventual liquidation or sale of the unit, failure rates are low—under 20 percent. When failure is defined as an inability to reach certain financial norms, such as significant growth in net income or return on equity, reported failure rates can be high—up to 80 percent.

Comparing results from 17 major studies of long-term postmerger performance conducted between 1965 and 1997, the coauthor of this book found that the postmerger cup is only a little more than "half empty"—and thus almost "half full." Of the 10 studies reporting failure, the average result was a 55 percent failure rate (or, conversely, a 45 percent success rate). Assuming a 5 percent margin of error, this result is consistent with the old cliché that "half of all mergers fail," but it is also consistent with the notion that half of all mergers succeed.

What are the critical failure or success factors here? What makes some mergers fail while others succeed?

The research published on this subject over the past 30 years yields a checklist of 15 points.

- Does the buyer have *experience* making acquisitions?
- Does the buyer bring something unique to the deal, so that competitive bids by other companies cannot push the purchase *price* too high?
- Is the merger or acquisition consistent with sound *strategy* with respect to diversification and other key issues?
- Has the acquirer attempted to make accurate *forecasts* of the seller's business? For example, if appropriate, has the buyer assessed the seller's *technology?*
- Can the acquirer handle an acquisition of the target's *size?*

- Is there good *operating and market synergy* between buyer and seller?
- Is the new parent committed to *sharing capital, markets, and technology* with the acquired company?
- Are there plans to boost combined *asset productivity?*
- Do the buyer and seller have reasonably compatible *cultures?*
- Do the buyer and seller share a clear *vision* of the newly combined organization?
- Is this vision based in *reality?*
- Are the newly combined organizations able to achieve postmerger *alignment* of capabilities?
- Can senior managers subordinate their egos for the *common good* of the new organization?
- Do buyer and seller have an effective *communications program* in place to help the integration process?
- Will the acquirer strive for a *rapid pace of implementation* for the new company's integration plan?

Integration is obviously an important part of merger success. What elements should be integrated following a merger?

Everything that can be usefully combined. The very term *merger* as it is used by most businesspeople implies no less an effort. It is useful to think of a merger as combining all *resources, processes,* and *responsibilities* of the buying and selling company, both domestically and globally.

As far as resources go, there are human resources at the board, management, and support levels. Beyond this, acquirers will need to consider integration of financial, tangible, and intangible resources—notably reputational resources such as the company name and brand names of the seller. As for processes, acquirers and sellers should consider how they might integrate their processes, including management systems, their compensation plans, and their incentives for innovation. Finally, when it comes to responsibilities, it is useful to think of these in terms of commitments—binding by law or ethics—to various stakeholder groups, including customers, suppliers, shareholders, bondholders, employees, and communities.

Beyond this, there is the ultimate integration: combining the newly integrated resources, processes, and responsibilities into a single successful whole.

Why is it important to integrate these matters? Isn't it sometimes best to leave matters alone?

Organizationwide integration can leverage the value of resources by reinforcing strengths and offsetting weaknesses, improving the efficiency of processes by reducing redundancy, and ensuring fulfillment of responsibilities through continuity of commitments to stakeholders. More generally, integration can create a sense of shared purpose for everyone in the newly combined company. This sense of shared purpose can help employees embrace rather than resist the fact that after a merger, the new organization must change. Common sense and research alike prove that for any organizational change to be successful, change cannot be limited to one unit or one level of the organization. The entire organization must be involved in the change.[2]

Integrating various resources, processes, and responsibilities is obviously a massive undertaking. When and how should companies begin?

Prior to closing, the buyer should engage in a thorough due diligence review of the seller's business. The purpose of this review will be to detect any legal, financial, and business risks that the buyer might inherit from the seller. If the risk is too great, the buyer may walk away. Usually, however, buyers simply use the results of their due diligence investigations to extract price concessions and/or warranties and representations in the acquisition agreement.

At the same time as the due diligence review, however, there should be a strategic review in which the acquirer determines what synergies there are and how it will take advantage of them.

The most important aspects of both the due diligence and strategic reviews will appear in the *acquisition agreement*—the legal "DNA" of the merger covered extensively in Chapter 8. In addition, the senior management of the acquiring company (often in consultation with the acquired firm) will create an *integration plan*.

INTEGRATION ELEMENTS IN THE ACQUISITION AGREEMENT

What impact does an acquisition agreement have on the future life of the new company?

Quite often, the most important impact that the acquisition agreement has on the successor entity comes from the styles of due diligence and negotiation adopted by the parties as they work out the terms of the agreement. A distrustful, hostile negotiating process will result in deep-seated suspicions and antagonism between the management teams of the two previously separate companies. Often, these are exacerbated by post-closing litigation over alleged inaccuracies in the acquisition agreement.

The analogy of a prenuptial agreement is most apt: It can strengthen a marriage by eliminating potential future controversies and establishing useful guidelines for future behavior, or it can weaken it by creating more problems than it solves. For this reason, the personalities of lawyers and other professionals involved in the due diligence and negotiating process should be carefully evaluated.

Does the acquisition agreement between the buyer and seller usually set conditions for postmerger integration?

It can—if either party insists on it and the other party is agreeable. The acquired company may insist on a certain level of job security for its employees or on continuing authority for its CEO. Such matters were covered, for example, in the 1996 agreement struck between Lockheed Martin and Loral.[3] Conversely, the acquiring company may set forth some postmerger ground rules. In acquiring Miracle-Gro in 1995, Scott Co. gave a very big role to the Miracle-Gro senior management team but restricted Miracle-Gro's ability to influence the composition of the Scotts board.[4]

Even the bare-bones acquisition agreement will contain some basic assurances about postmerger life beyond the seller's financial projections. Instead, an average agreement will establish the ground rules for the agreement and a few basic facts about the parties to the agreement: that the selling company is what it claims to be, that the seller has a right to sell it, and that the buyer has the right (and the ability) to buy it.

Of the dozen or so sections in a typical acquisition agreement, the most forward-looking section is the one containing the representations and warranties of the seller.

What postmerger matters might be covered under the section on representations and warranties of the seller?

This section, as its title suggests, will typically have all the representations and warranties (that is, assertions and promises) that the seller is making to the buyer concerning the seller's company. Most of these refer only to the past and present state of the company, not to its future state. For example, as mentioned in Chapter 8, this section of the acquisition agreement will typically cover the seller's organization, capitalization, ownership of securities and property (real and intellectual), current levels of inventory and debt, exposure to lawsuits, and so forth. It is, in essence, the buyer's "due diligence" checklist. The more detail it has, the better the chances for smooth postmerger integration.

There is one type of representation, however, that explicitly refers to postmerger performance. This is the part of the agreement where the seller has provided financial projections, and the buyer will ask the seller to *assert the reasonableness of the assumptions and accuracy of the data used to make the projections.* Lenders may also insist on such representations in the loan agreement. Wise sellers will resist providing these unless absolutely necessary to the sale because if the company performs poorly in the future, the buyer or lender may sue the seller, claiming breach of representation.

While the representations may relate to current and past events, they have numerous forward-looking consequences. For example, a seller's representation that it has committed no employment law violations may be challenged later in the event of a suit alleging a pattern of discriminatory employment practices.

Beyond the obligations spelled out in the acquisition agreement, what other postmerger obligations might there be going forward for the acquirer?

These are myriad, limited only by the imagination of federal and state regulators and the plaintiff's bar. Based on the yearly surveys of Watson Wyatt Worldwide in Chicago, directors and officers of companies involved in mergers are twice as likely to be sued as their peers who are not involved in M&A activity. Many of these lawsuits involve postmerger matters. Indeed, a company involved in mergers is twice as likely to be sued as the average company, says Watson Wyatt.

It is important also to respect not only the letter but the spirit of the law. Ethicist George Sammet, former vice president of International Ethics and Business Conduct at Lockheed Martin, tells the story of an employee who retired just a few days short of 20 years. The human resources manager who presided over the retirement never told the employee that if he waited just a few more days, he would receive a much better retirement package. Senior management agreed with Sammet that the HR manager should have followed the spirit—not just the letter—of company policy, and the employee was accorded benefits for 20 full years of service.[5]

THE INTEGRATION PLAN

What exactly is an integration plan?

A postmerger plan is a document outlining exactly when and how the major resources, processes, and commitments of the acquiring and acquired company will be combined in order to achieve the strategic goals of the newly combined company. Ultimately, this outline will be distributed to key employees and (in modified form) to other interested parties. Like any corporate document, it should be reviewed by counsel.

What should be in a postmerger plan?

This varies greatly by industry and by situation. Clearly, however, there should be three elements in the postmerger plan: the goals of the new company; the way the integration of resources, systems, and responsibilities will support those goals; and the timetable for the integration.

For example, a postmerger plan for two hospitals might include a description of the primary goals for the new alliance along with details of when and how these goals will be accomplished. Details might include how the board, management, and staff will be organized; how the staff will be credentialed; who will be responsible for clinical policy making; how budgeting, accounting, accounts receivable, and bond covenants will be handled; what clinical services will be changed, expanded, or cut back; and what nursing models will be used. The thorough integration plan might also include how the mission, values, and vision of the two hospitals will be merged.

Some plans never get implemented. How can postmerger planners avoid this problem?

The following checklist (based with permission on the well-known work of George Steiner) can help integration planners see if they are on the right track:

1. Are the plans consistent with the intrinsic logic of the deal?
2. Do the plans specify how the company will pay for the deal?
3. Are there written plans to cover both the short term (less than five years) and the long term (five years or more)?
4. Do short- and long-term plans mesh?
5. Has the planning process involved both senior managers and employees most affected by the plans?
6. Do the plans take into account the operational and cultural realities of the two companies involved?
7. Have senior managers and the board of directors reviewed the plan documents?
8. Are senior managers and the board using the plans to make their decisions?
9. Are the plans supported by appropriate policies?
10. Are the plans supported by adequate resources?
11. Do the plans specify measures and milestones of progress?
12. Who will be held accountable for achieving the plans?
13. Have the plans been distributed to all appropriate parties?
14. Is there a program for communicating the plans internally?
15. Is there a program for communicating the plans externally?

The answer to each question should be yes!

Should someone be designated as chief planner of the integration?

No. True, the acquiring and selling CEOs may be the first and final architects of the merger itself (including, of course, their own leadership roles),[6] and the acquiring CEO may appoint an individual to make sure that a detailed plan gets created and respected. Nonetheless, the best postmerger plans are ultimately created by *groups*. Obviously, in the earliest "search and screen" stages, everyone in the planning group or "team" will be from the acquiring company, but once the acquiring company has entered negotiations with a specific merger partner, an equal number of representatives of the target company should join the team or teams. If this makes the planning group/s too large—more than 12 per group is probably too many[7]—each side can drop members.

How many groups should be formed to plan postmerger integration?

The larger the company, the greater the number of planning groups that may be involved. In the early stages of preparing for their planned merger, Bell Atlantic Corp. and NYNEX Corp. had 25 joint planning groups working together at one time.[8]

Who should be on the postmerger planning teams?

Team members should be those with a stake in the long-term success of the merger, such as CEOs, senior managers, and key employees, including any interim executives that may be hired to guide and/or implement the emerging plan.

There may also be seats at the table for advisors—such as investment bankers, accountants, attorneys, or consultants—or for professional decision-making facilitators, but these outsiders should not have a vote on the outcome.

In the end, it is up to the board of directors of the newly combined company to approve the plan. Directors should not merely rubber-stamp the plan but should question it thoroughly. The board of directors is often a secret weapon in postmerger planning. In most public companies, the board as a whole is independent—and thus has the objectivity of outside consultants. Furthermore, most boards—whether for public or private companies—will include people who are chosen for their relevant expertise. Finally, an increasing number of directors today own stock in the companies they serve, making them long-term stakeholders in the future of the company.

Any postmerger plan that is created by stakeholders, advised by qualified experts, and approved by a well-structured board of directors is bound to serve the future company well.

THE ROLE OF OUTSIDERS IN PLANNING M&A INTEGRATION

What are the benefits of using outsiders in planning integration?

Ideally, the benefits are experience, expertise, and objectivity. Managers should consider using the services of outsiders to compensate for their deficiencies in one or more of these regards. Recent research by Mercer Management Consulting shows that experienced acquirers tend to achieve better postmerger returns because they are more likely than inexperienced companies to have the right vision and to implement it effectively and quickly. If an inexperienced acquirer wants to achieve these things, it may hire one or more outside parties who can help it form, implement, and accelerate a postmerger strategy.

What are the drawbacks of using outsiders to help in M&A integration planning?

It depends in part on how the advisors are paid. If advisors are paid on a contingency basis (a common practice when it comes to investment bankers), they may be overly optimistic about how much synergy a deal contains and how easy it will be to achieve. Such advisors may have much valuable expertise to impart when it comes to financing, marketing, and structuring a transaction, but their enthusiasm should be taken with more than one grain of salt. This is especially true if the fee is paid on the basis of the size of the transaction (as in the traditional "Lehman's formula" fee: 5 percent of the first million, 4 percent of the next million, and so forth).

Conversely, if advisors are paid on a sliding scale depending on the amount of time a transaction takes (a common practice when it comes to lawyers, who typically bill by the hour), whether or not the transaction ever closes successfully, such advisors might be tempted to take an overly pessimistic view about the transaction, finding liability exposure under every hubcap. These advisors may have invaluable advice when it comes to the tax and legal implications of a transaction, but like their opposite numbers, the investment bankers, their voice should never predominate at the postmerger planning table.

Consultants are immune to these pressures, as they are paid a flat fee or on a retainer basis (not a contingency fee or an hourly fee). The temptation faced by consultants is the temptation to take over the decision-making role from managers, which is never good. Managers should use consultants and others to help them make decisions, not to make their decisions for them.

These warnings are not meant to impugn the integrity of M&A transaction advisors, who as a group are worthy of their hire. The moral is twofold. First, when it comes to postmerger advice, clients get what they pay for and how they pay for it. Second, the best choices in any endeavor will come from those who have a vested interest in it.

In the case of postmerger integration, the best decision makers will be those whose destinies are linked to the long-term success of the merger—that is, stakeholders such as customers, suppliers, stockholders, bondholders, lenders, employees, and communities. Of course, a company's "suppliers" do include long-term advisors—but the point is that their perspective, however qualified, should never predominate in the planning process.

If an acquirer decides to engage a third party to help its postmerger integration effort, how should it begin?

First, the acquirer (or, more accurately, potential acquirer, since planning for integration should start early) should determine who is working in this field. Sources of advisors include the following:

- The acquirer's current advisors
- Advisors recommended by trusted sources
- Advisors listed in books about postmerger integration (including this one)
- Trade and professional associations
- Professional reference books

On this last point, you should never choose an advisor "straight out of a book." For one thing, not all qualified advisors are listed in reference books for their profession. Moreover, just because someone is listed in a reference book does not mean that he or she is superior to those who are not listed. Nonetheless, seekers can derive some comfort from the professional and editorial control that goes into the publication of professional reference books. Furthermore, they contain valuable background information.

For background information on an attorney, one might consult the *Martindale-Hubbell Law Directory,* an encyclopedic reference source based in Providence, New Jersey, and published annually for well over a century. This reference lists law firms by state and city. Each law firm describes the firm's practice and the expertise of each lawyer.

To learn more about a recommended consultant, a good place to begin is with the comprehensive source *Directory of Management Consultants,* published every other year by Kennedy Publications in Fitzwilliam, New Hampshire.[9] This directory lists people by up to four areas of expertise. Over 300 consultants listed themselves as specialists in the M&A area (defined by the directory as "mergers and acquisitions, divestments, joint ventures, buy/sell agreements"). There is also *Management Consultants Resource Guide,* published biannually by the Institute of Management Consultants in New York. The IMC, established in 1968, awards a CMC (certified management consultant) title to members who pass its certification requirements. IMC members must adhere to a code of conduct that includes provisions for confidentiality, independence, fee disclosure, and so forth. These are real directories, not glorified yellow pages: No fee is required for listing.

If an advisor is hired to help with senior management integration, who should pay for these services?

Ideally, the advisor's payment should come from both entities. Payment can be made by the new entity in the event of a successful merger or by both entities if the merger never takes place. Alternatively, each company can retain its own advisor, each one acceptable to the other. If only one advisor is retained, and if only one party retains that advisor (for example, the acquirer), it is imperative that the advisor gain acceptance from the other company (the acquired firm) before beginning work.

What are interim executives, and how can they help in planning M&A integration?

Interim executives, also called *project executives,* are qualified line managers who are hired on a temporary basis for a specific assignment, such as the integration of two companies. Such managers—usually employees of a temporary personnel agency specializing in interim management—are hired to assist in planning the more technical aspects of postmerger integration. Such aspects include the following:

- Information systems (particularly for financial management and re-porting)
- Process engineering in the manufacturing function
- Various "logistics" functions, such as purchasing, transportation, and order fulfillment

What is a facilitator, and how can a facilitator's services help a group form its postmerger integration plan?

A *group facilitator* is an independent third party who helps a group identify problems, find solutions, and make decisions. *Independent* means that the person should be neutral with respect to the matters being decided and should have no decision-making authority within the group. Obviously, to be effective, the facilitator should be someone who is acceptable to all members of the group. Also, the facilitation process requires accurate information from the group and free choices by the group. Although some group members may resent the presence of an "outsider," facilitators can be helpful to many groups, particularly those that are susceptible to dominance or deadlocking.

Facilitation can be *basic* or *developmental.* Basic facilitation focuses primarily on a given problem (for example, achieving a better pay system), using a predetermined methodology for group decision making provided by the facilitator (for example, the Delphi method of decision making discussed in Chapter 2). By contrast, developmental facilitation focuses on developing a useful process to solve the problem. Basic facilitation is good enough (and most cost-effective) for groups that will exist only for a short period of time; developmental facilitation is recommended for groups that will last over time (for example, six months or more).

In both types of facilitation, the group, not the facilitator, is solely responsible for the quality of its decisions: The facilitator facilitates; he or she does not advise. In developmental facilitation, however, the facilitator guides group members in using their faculties of reason and fairness to make the best possible decisions.

A common term of art to describe developmental facilitation is *participative-process consulting.* An area of expertise first developed in the 1960s, process consultation is a branch of consulting officially recognized by the aforementioned IMC. Over 200 consultants in the United States offer such services, and of these, 25 also have special expertise in mergers and acquisitions.[10]

COMMUNICATING THE INTEGRATION PLAN

When should companies first announce their merger plans?

The earlier the better, unless making the announcement would cause harm to one or both of the parties. Privately held companies can make their own determinations of the trade-offs inherent in this timing decision. Publicly held companies must adhere to federal disclosure laws in this regard and should consult with counsel from the earliest stages.

The most important federal disclosure law in this area is Rule 10b-5, which forbids "any person, directly or indirectly . . . to make any untrue statement of a material fact or to omit to state a material fact necessary in order to make the statement made, in the light of circumstances under which they were made, not misleading."

The classic case here is *Basic, Inc. v. Levinson* (1988). In this case, a group of shareholders sued Basic, Inc., for denying that it was engaged in merger talks when it was so engaged. The Supreme Court held that Basic should not have made the denial but should have either confirmed that it was engaged in talks or stated that it had no comment.

The general consensus is that it is better to make merger announcements as far along in the process as possible. The simple reason is that many seemingly successful merger negotiations break down even after the price and key terms are agreed upon in a "handshake" deal. Whether in a private or a public company, aborted merger talks that have previously been announced can cause ill will with the stakeholders of the two companies.

Pushing in the other direction are concerns about leaks and rumors, with the resulting uncertainty and erosion of confidence. The challenge is to do everything possible to avoid such leaks as long as possible and to be ready to make a carefully planned and well-staged public announcement if rumors cannot be suppressed.

What guidelines would you give for the announcement of merger plans?

At the stage when a letter of intent containing all key terms of the acquisition is signed, public companies are required to make a disclosure to all their stockholders. This announcement must describe all the salient terms of the transaction. Obviously, a simultaneous announcement should be made to the other stakeholders of the company. There is nothing worse than having them learn about the deal from reading the newspaper.

Unfortunately, at the time of the initial announcement of a planned merger, there are no plans to announce. In many mergers between public companies, in-depth due diligence only begins after the public announcement. In other circumstances, integration plans can only be developed after the negotiation of the merger agreement—a process that should yield useful information about resources, processes, and responsibilities, as well as critical insights into culture.

Yet, for many constituencies, it is not enough to simply talk about the basic deal terms. Questions will arise from customers, suppliers, shareholders, lenders, employees, and others: What will happen to prices? Will the new company still buy from us? What will happen to share prices after the deal? Will the new company remain solvent? Will my job be eliminated? Will our local plant be closed?

Yet, at this early stage, there are no answers to most or all of these questions. In announcing their deal, companies should acknowledge that these questions exist and should explain how and when they will be answered. Any commitment to address such questions within a specified time frame must be honored, as a breach in this regard will cause even more consternation and insecurity.

Assuming that at the time of the merger announcement, companies do have detailed plans, how much of these plans should they disclose?

In general, acquirers should communicate as much about the deal's logic and plans as they can without compromising their competitive position. In public companies, such disclosures will help the market appreciate the value-creation potential of the deal and to manage shareholder expectations of timing and results.

In the case of postmerger divestiture plans, companies will want to balance the positive impact an announcement may have on share price against the negative impact the announcement may have on productivity. In most cases, companies can and should opt for early and complete disclosure. For example, at the same time that Revlon, Inc., announced its plans to merge its cosmetics stores with Cosmetic Center Inc., it stated that the merger would probably lead to a spin-off of the unit.

It should be noted, though, that public companies must conform to various legal requirements outlining what they may and may not say (in public announcements and in filings with regulators) about their postmerger plans.

What must public companies say about their postmerger integration plans?

Acquirers making a tender offer bid for a U.S. public company must follow the disclosure laws for their states. They must also follow federal laws. Two Securities and Exchange Commission (SEC) filings are relevant here: a Schedule 13D form, disclosing acquisition of 5 percent or more of company stock, and a Schedule 14D1 form, disclosing intention to make a tender offer bid. These two forms will be discussed more fully in Chapter 12, but here are a few aspects of special postmerger relevance.

In addition to asking for basic information (name, address, and so on) the forms query the bidder's long-term intentions.

Schedule 13D in Item 4 asks acquirers to describe the "Purpose of [the] Transaction," as follows:

> State the purpose or purposes of the acquisition of securities of the issuer. Describe any plans or proposals which the reporting persons may have which relate to or would result in:
>
> (a) The acquisition by any person of additional securities of the issuer, or the disposition of securities of the issuer;
>
> (b) An extraordinary corporate transaction, such as a merger, reorganization, or liquidation, involving the issuer or any of its subsidiaries;
>
> (c) A sale or transfer of a material amount of assets of the issuer or any of its subsidiaries;
>
> (d) Any change in the present board of directors or management of the issuer. . . . [11]

In a similar vein, Schedule 14D1 in Item 5 asks acquirers to disclose the "Purpose of the Tender Offer and Plans or Proposals of the Bidder," as follows:

> State the purpose or purposes of the tender offer. . . . Describe any plans or proposals which relate to or would result in:
>
> (a) An extraordinary corporate transaction, such as a merger, reorganization, or liquidation involving the subject company or any of its subsidiaries;
>
> (b) A sale or transfer of a material amount of assets of the subject company or any of its subsidiaries;
>
> (c) Any change in the present board of directors or management of the subject company . . .;
>
> (d) Any material change in the present capitalization or dividend policy of the subject company;

(e) Any other material change in the subject company's corporate structure or business. . . .[12]

Although only acquirers of public companies have to make and update these disclosures, this regulation makes a sensible "short list" of what any stakeholder in any company—public or private—would want to know about postmerger plans.

Bidders must send a copy of their SEC filings to the stock exchange where their companies' shares are listed. They should also make an announcement to the public via press releases. Finally, as mentioned in Chapter 1, the Federal Trade Commission and the Department of Justice must be notified of merger plans involving one or more large U.S. companies.

In addition to reviewing filings, these agencies may request copies of various acquisition documents such as the postmerger plan or the acquisition agreement. Although these documents are treated confidentially, they may be used against the companies in a finding of undue market concentration—one good reason to ask counsel to review all merger documents, including the integration plan.[13]

Some companies must notify the regulatory agencies overseeing their industries. For example, U.S. banks must disclose their merger plans to the Federal Reserve Banking System (the Fed).

How long does the regulatory approval process usually take?

Anywhere from several months to several *years* in a contested case. R. R. Donnelly & Sons Co. had to wait nearly four years before receiving FTC approval to merge with Meredith/Burda Co. Fortunately, though, the period of regulatory review is shrinking. The SEC has offered quick review to companies that write their filings (and related communications to shareholders) in plain English.[14] Also, the FTC has adopted rules (effective January 1, 1997) that guarantee a "fast track" of no more than 13 months for a decision, and the Fed is working to speed up its bank merger reviews.[15]

Suppose disclosing certain plans for postmerger change would be harmful to a company's business? Does it have to disclose them?

It does have to disclose them to the SEC, but it may request an "order of confidential treatment" from the SEC for a limited amount of time.

As a practical matter, companies cannot hide behind the SEC's confidential disclosure policy—largely because the SEC is unwilling to allow confidentiality in circumstances where a proposed change in the merged entity would have a substantial impact on the capital markets. Additionally, while merger candidates sometimes believe that certain announcements might be harmful to their business, often the opposite is true, as shareholders and other stakeholders are far happier dealing with the certainty of announced intentions than the risk and unpredictability of unannounced intentions. At the same time, many companies do not have definite postmerger plans at this stage, and conclude, both for securities law and for business purposes, that an announcement of potential changes would be premature.

What may publicly held acquirers *not* tell the public about their integration plans?

In announcing postmerger plans, the parties to the transaction can say anything, but they must be cautious about making any "forward-looking statements" about the results they anticipate of the merger to come. Although forward-looking statements are protected under the safe harbor provisions of the Securities Litigation Reform Act of 1995, this protection has limits.

To conform to federal securities law (specifically new Section 27 of the Securities Act of 1933 and new Section 21D of the Securities Exchange Act of 1934), forward-looking statements must be accompanied by meaningful "cautionary statements" identifying "important factors" that could cause actual results to differ "materially" from results projected in the statement. The law does not impose a duty to update, but it is generally considered a good idea when there are material postmerger changes to report.

Could you give an example of a cautionary statement that a company has made when announcing details of a postmerger integration plan?

Consider the last paragraph of a press release sent September 3, 1997, announcing Aspect Telecommunication Corporation's acquisition of Commerce Soft. In the press release, Commerce Soft founder and president, Dilip Venkatachari, expressed his belief that together the two companies could deliver "Web-based, Java-enabled customer interaction technology to a broad array of customers," and Tom McCalmont, a vice president of Aspect, welcomed the Commerce Soft's "talented team" to his company.

These statements may seem perfectly prudent, but to ensure a safe harbor under federal securities laws, the companies added the following cautionary statement:

> Except for historical information contained herein, the matters discussed in this news release are forward-looking statements that are subject to certain risks and uncertainties that could cause actual results to differ materially from those projected, including: Aspect's ability to retain key Commerce Soft employees, Aspect's ability to integrate the personnel and operations of Commerce Soft efficiently, and Aspect's ability to build a successful internet interactive call center business. Other risks that could cause actual results to differ materially from those projected are discussed in Aspect's Form 10-K for the fiscal year ended December 31, 1996, and in Aspect's Form 10-Q for the quarters ended March 31 and June 30, respectively. Readers are cautioned not to place undue reliance on these forward-looking statements, which reflect management's analysis only as of the date hereof. Aspect undertakes no obligation to publicly release the results of any revision to these forward-looking statements which may be made to reflect events or circumstances after the date hereof or to reflect the occurrence of unanticipated events.[16]

A disclaimer like this takes all the romance out of the merger announcement. Is it really necessary?

Your legal counsel will be the best judge of such matters on a case-by-case basis. As a general rule, though, any forward-looking statement should be accompanied by such a "meaningful cautionary statement." And even if it were not required, this disclaimer would be a good idea because of the litigious environment for corporate directors and officers. Year after year, Watson Wyatt Worldwide's Chicago office reaffirms the same sad truth in its annual D&O liability survey: About half of all lawsuits against corporate directors are filed by stockholders, and of these, about one-fourth allege inaccurate or inadequate disclosure.[17] These disclosure-based lawsuits are typically filed retroactively: After a stock loses value, attorneys specializing in so-called strike suits immediately go to work, poring over past statements for those vulnerable to the dreaded label of "misrepresentations and omissions." Forward-looking statements issued in the M&A context are a magnet for such suits, so companies should do whatever they can to adhere to the letter of disclosure law in this area—as unromantic as it may be.

What about communications between the merging companies? Are there any restrictions here?

Unfortunately, yes if the companies are considered competitors subject to federal antitrust law (that is, anticompetitive according to the HHI). Under Section 1 of the Sherman Act, competitors may not "conspire" to lessen competition in their markets—a restriction that, incredibly enough, can apply to competitors that are in the process of planning to merge.

Premerger discussions of postmerger plans may be considered a conspiracy to restrain trade if the discussions do the following:

- Depart from the normal routine of merger activity
- Significantly affect customers' purchasing choices
- Occur well in advance of the closing date[18]

As mentioned in the beginning of this section on communications, companies should check with counsel very early on in the communications process.

How can buyers and sellers stem the tide of rumors from various stakeholders before, during, and immediately after the deal?

Bear in mind that rumors are a symptom of a more pernicious problem: lack of information. The responsibility for the latter rests squarely with senior management.

In general, companies that plan to merge should say so publicly as soon as they have reached an agreement to combine. This announcement should go out to all the companies' stakeholders and to the general public.

This initial announcement should be the beginning of a series of regular communications through letters, memos, meetings, and any other available media about each phase of the transaction. Once the transaction is close to completion or completed and a plan is in place, both the acquirer and the acquired firm should disseminate the plan (in brief format) to all stakeholder groups, developing a special *position statement* for *each* group.[19]

The communications process must continue for the entire period of active integration—generally up to 12 months. The best strategy is to establish, at the front end, a regular process of communications, both formal and informal. In the case of employees, for example, these would include monthly updates on the merged business. Communications should include not only a description of postmerger plans but also an explanation of how and why they were made and how they will be carried out. Ideally, the affected parties will have participated in forming the plans, so the announcements will not come as great surprises.

To build stakeholder ownership of the plans, announcements should contain financial details, which ultimately measure the success or failure of new policies.[20] The goal is to have different stakeholders "buy into" postmerger plans by following the transformation process, understanding its components, and checking its success.

Meanwhile, at every stage of postmerger integration, management of the new company should communicate to all stakeholders in all appropriate media, as shown in Figure 10-1.

INTEGRATING HUMAN RESOURCES

Employees are clearly an important resource in any company. Isn't it true that most acquirers tend to lose employees following an acquisition—through either layoffs or through attrition?

No. The real trend is volatility, not decline. In the years following an acquisition, acquirers are more likely to either lose or gain employees when compared with nonacquirers. That is the main finding of a comprehensive 1996 study by David Birch of Cognetics, Inc., in Cambridge, Massachusetts.[21]

The Cognetics study of companies acquired between 1992 and 1995 showed that 24 percent experienced significant declines in employment in the period studied, 36 percent showed significant growth in employment, and 40 percent showed no significant change. ("Significant" was defined as a change of 10 percent or more in either direction.) By contrast, the same study showed that during the same period, only 9 percent of nonacquirers lost employees, and only 10 percent gained employees. In other words, only 40 percent of companies showed employment stability in the three years following their purchase, whereas over 80 percent of nonacquirers showed stable employment patterns.

What are some examples of companies that gained employees after a merger?

Consider the BMW purchase of the Rover Group in 1994. By the end of 1995, the new company, BMW Group, had increased by 6,400 to 115,763 employ-

F I G U R E 10-1

Audience-Media Communications Matrix

Audiences	Letter	Capabilities Brochure	Special Brochure/Flyer	News Releases	Special Press Kit	Quarterly Report	Annual Report	Special Newsletter	Regular Newsletter	Promotional Item	Magazines/Bulletins	Personal Meetings	Special Event	Advertisement—Financial	Advertisement—General	Advertisement—Trade	Internal Meeting	External Group Meeting	Internet Home Page	Other	Other
Employees																					
Salespeople																					
Vendors																					
Retail Customers																					
Commercial Customers																					
Community Businesspeople																					
Bank(s)																					
Telephone Listings																					
General Public (National)																					
General Public (Regional)																					
Special-Interest Groups																					
Elected Officials																					
Local Press																					
Opinion Leaders																					
Securities Analysts																					
Brokers																					
Shareholders																					
Institutional Shareholders																					
Key Investors																					
Board of Directors																					
Advisory Directors																					
Senior Management																					
Subsidiary Officers																					
Subsidiary Nonofficials																					
Retired Employees																					
Financial Media																					
General Business Media																					
Directories																					
Rating Agencies																					
Peer Groups																					
Prospective Acquirees																					
State Regulators																					
Government Agencies																					

Courtesy of Gene Grossman, Anspach Grossman Enterprise

Source: Alexandra Reed Lajoux, *The Art of M&A Integration* (New York: McGraw-Hill, 1998), p. 64.

ees. The Rover Group workforce numbered 36,238 in 1994 but rose to 40,137 in 1995. Most of the increases were in plant jobs, but some were in technical planning and development.[22]

Another example *could* have been offered by the planned merger of Boeing Co. with McDonnell Douglas Corp., which was called off in 1998 under regulatory pressure. At the time of the $13.3 billion merger announcement (in December 1996), the two companies had a combined backlog of $92 billion—more than enough to keep their future workforce of 200,000 fully occupied. In fact, executives from the two companies told *The Wall Street Journal* that despite an anticipated $1 billion in savings per year, they did not anticipate significant layoffs.[23]

Why are acquired companies more likely to lose or gain employees than other companies?

First, let's look at the macroeconomic reasons—that is, reasons stemming from collective industry trends. Recent research by Mark Mitchell of the University of Chicago shows that mergers and acquisitions tend to cluster in industries that are already going through fundamental change and therefore are more susceptible to large gains or losses in employment. As for the microeconomic reasons—that is, reasons stemming from conditions in individual companies—these vary according to the company's situation. Mergers tend to magnify what is already going on—making well-managed companies do better and making poorly managed companies do worse.

What are the main reasons an acquired company would lose employees following an acquisition?

First of all, some employees quit. One classic study of 200 acquisitions made by *Fortune* 500 firms found that 6 out of 10 key managers left within five years of the closing date.[24] This is not surprising considering the difficulty some firms have in combining (or even coexisting) following some mergers, as detailed earlier.

Second, sometimes employees are laid off. The main reason for this is postmerger redundancy—or more precisely, the elimination of operational redundancies created when two similar companies merge. This reason is commonly cited as the driving strategic force in mergers of equals (that is, mergers between competitors), where many operations are duplicated almost exactly.

Another reason for postmerger layoffs may be very simply a need to cut costs irrespective of operational needs. These cash flow–driven layoffs often result from transactions financed through a large amount of debt (or what bank regulators term "highly leveraged transactions").

And what about gaining employees after an acquisition? Under what circumstances does this happen?

Again, the answer can be traced to the strategic rationale for the merger. When the rationale is to reduce costs by eliminating redundancies, layoffs automatically ensue. But cost reduction is not the only good reason for a merger. Another good reason (and some believe, a superior reason) is revenue growth. In this case, a newly merged company is more likely to hire than to fire.

Sage observers have coined two very simple equations that illustrate this contrast in strategies:

- The equation for synergy through cost cutting is $-2 - 2 = -3$. (The merger will reduce costs, which otherwise would be -4.)
- The equation for synergy through revenue growth is $2 + 2 = 5$. (The merger will increase revenues, which otherwise would be 4).[25]

Why is retaining employees so important?

At the most basic level, businesses cannot run without people. Beyond that, qualified, experienced people add value to any business. Indeed, professional appraisers can and do put numbers on this value—at both the senior management and employee levels.

How do appraisers value human resources in the merger context?

For tax accounting purposes, companies have to record the difference between what they paid for a company and the as-booked value of all the assets (financial, tangible, and intangible) that they purchased. This difference is called *goodwill.*

Most of the goodwill recorded in the purchase of very small personal services businesses stems from personal goodwill: the value of the implicit and explicit employment and noncompetition agreements the business has with its key employees. As a company grows, this personal goodwill diminishes in favor of business goodwill, as the contacts, skills, and knowledge of key people become infused into the value of the firm. This process takes time, however. Letting people leave an enterprise before they have made their full contribution can harm postmerger value.

Consider the case of IBM and Lotus Development Corp. After IBM bought Lotus in 1995, six senior executives left, including the CEO of Lotus. (The exodus stopped after that, perhaps in part because of IBM's aggressive postmerger efforts to create an integrated management team.) Talent-drain rumors also dogged the early departure of a key Chase Manhattan Corp. executive following his bank's 1996 merger with Chemical Banking Corp. Although the Chase name prevailed, Chemical executives won most top jobs, prompting one analyst to opine, "This is not a merger, this is an acquisition."[26] A late 1997 management restructuring created a better balance, helping the new company to retain executives from both sides.

These worries are not unreasonable, considering that most senior executives in U.S. companies today are being wooed by competitors and are actively seeking to change employers.[27]

How can an acquirer prevent the loss of key employees?

The acquirers' strongest defense against employee defections is a good reputation as an employer, substantiated by actions consistent with that reputation. The new owner must demonstrate immediately and clearly to all the new company's employees at all levels that their future is bright individually and collectively. This means attending to all the critical success factors listed above. It also means following the accepted norms for ethical treatment of employees, as explained in the conclusion to this chapter.

Are there legal means to increase the chances of employee retention? What about a noncompete agreement?

Good point. At the time it invites each key employee to stay (ideally with a raise or promotion), the acquirer can ask the employee to sign an agreement that would restrict the employee's ability to work for a competitor if he or she breaks the contract. The contract may set forth specific restrictions—for example, banning the solicitation of former customers or the use of company trade secrets. Or it may be extremely broad, prohibiting any and all competition with the former employer. In either case, the agreement must be considered "reasonable" in a court of law.

Why is it ideal to offer employees a raise or promotion before they sign a noncompete agreement? If employees really want to keep their jobs, won't they sign the agreement anyway?

They may, but if they change their minds, they may be able to challenge the contract in court. Courts do not view the offer of continued employment as adequate reward (or "consideration") for the restriction. The legal concept of consideration means that the employee should receive something of value in exchange for promising not to compete. If an agreement does not pass the consideration test, it may be unenforceable.

How would a court define a "reasonable" noncompete agreement?

The agreement should satisfy four tests. It must be necessary to protect the employer's legitimate interests, reasonable in duration and scope, not unreasonably burdensome to the employee, and not harmful to the general public.[28]

INTEGRATING ASSETS (ON PAPER AND IN REALITY)

What are the main types of tangible assets that might be combined following a merger or acquisition?

The standard balance sheet provides a good checklist of assets that may be combined. First and foremost, financial assets may be combined. These include cash, marketable securities, and accounts receivable. Second, a company may wish to consolidate plants, equipment,[29] and inventories, and leases for land. On paper, this is done through a consolidated balance sheet.[30]

How can balance sheets be consolidated?

To consolidate multiple balance sheets under U.S. GAAP, one must combine into one statement all the assets, liabilities, and equity of the parent and the corporations owned by the parent. This consolidation is not merely a matter of addition, however. If there are duplications among the statements, these must be eliminated.

What are some examples of duplications that must be eliminated in the consolidated balance sheet?

One duplication is the parent's investment in the shares of a subsidiary's stock. On the parent company's balance sheet prior to consolidation, this would show up as an asset of the parent. On the subsidiary's balance sheet prior to consolidation, it would show up as equity. If both these line items appeared in the consolidated balance sheet, there would be duplication. In the consolidated balance sheet, both these items are offset and eliminated.

Another duplication is any debt the subsidiary may owe to the parent. Obviously, a single enterprise cannot owe a debt to itself. For example, suppose that the parent company has loaned $10,000 to the subsidiary. The parent's accounts would reflect a $10,000 receivable, while the subsidiary would reflect a $10,000 payable. From the consolidated point of view, however, there is no receivable and no payable. Therefore, receivables and payables between the parent and the subsidiary are eliminated in preparing a consolidated balance sheet.

In addition to their combination on a balance sheet, are these tangible assets ever actually combined from an operational standpoint?

Plants, equipment, and *inventories* may be combined in whole or in part when two companies integrate their operations. *Land* and *real estate,* of course, cannot be combined physically, but the leasing or ownership terms for use of the land may be consolidated.

What are the main valuation issues to consider when combining tangible assets on a consolidated balance sheet?

It depends on the type of transaction involved. As explained earlier, if a transaction is structured as a purchase (rather than as a pooling), the buyer may step plant, equipment, and inventory values up to their current market value. This step-up may be considerable. Due to accelerated tax depreciation methods, most acquired assets are already heavily depreciated for tax purposes and carried on the seller's books for less than their fair market value. Restating the value of depreciable acquired assets at a higher, market value increases the tax benefits available to the acquirer by increasing the value of depreciable assets with shorter lives relative to longer-lived or nonamortizable intangible assets. As mentioned earlier, for tax accounting purposes, acquirers often want to step up the basis of the tangible assets to fair market value in order to realize a greater tax benefit from depreciation. Prior to 1993, in the United States, goodwill was not amortizable for tax purposes, and acquirers sought to maximize the values of depreciable assets as much as possible to increase their future tax savings.

How can plants be combined "operationally" (as opposed to merely on the balance sheet)?

First, let's define our key term. A *plant* is a production operation at a defined physical location. It is usually envisioned in a manufacturing context. A plant's major assets include real estate, structures (foundations, buildings, framework, and related improvements), equipment (for production, communication, control, and administration), distribution assets (such as piping, conveyers, and docks), wiring and instrumentation (for electrical supply, communications, and control of operations), and software. In a service context, a plant may be a physical location in which services are performed. Examples of service plants include a computer processing facility, a branch bank facility, and a phone operation.

In both the manufacturing and service sections, plants can be consolidated in many different ways, ranging from plant closings to integration of plant operations through common, integrated systems.

What are the main costs associated with plant consolidation?

In consolidating plants, employers may incur costs associated with disposal of assets (including environmental aspects); relocation, termination, and/or recruitment of employees; investments in physical assets or software to support consolidation; and redesign of products and/or services to accommodate integration. In addition, acquirers may have to spend money on new marketing efforts to preserve goodwill if plant consolidation has involved layoffs. Finally, closing or relocating plant operations may cause the loss of a group of customers or increase transportation and distribution costs to a set of customers.

How can equipment be combined "operationally"?

Physically combining equipment is uncommon unless the equipment is mobile or unattached, such as forklifts, trucks, office equipment, and furniture. Combining companies are often at distant locations. Even when operations are consolidated, it is often preferable (if money permits) to purchase and install new equipment, rather than remove, transport, and install older equipment from a discontinued operation. Furthermore, in addition to equipment purchased for replacement, some equipment may be purchased for enhancement—for example, to facilitate the integration of systems and operations.

Note also that the shareholders of the acquired business may retain some equipment, either to keep or to sell separately. The owners of closely held companies may wish to retain personal property (including equipment) for their own use, and such property will not convey with the sale.

What are the main valuation issues associated with the combination of equipment in a purchase transaction?

All the equipment that will continue to remain in use after the acquisition should be restated at *fair market value in use* and integrated into the balance sheet accordingly. *Fair market value in use* means that certain delivery, installation, and setup costs should be included in the valuation of the equipment since an acquirer of the equipment would have to bear those costs if each unit were acquired separately. Appraisers may consider replacement or reproduction cost as if new (including installation and freight), less economic and physical obsolescence, as an appropriate measure of value.

Most other equipment (especially any equipment being moved or relocated, typically that of the acquired entity) should be valued at fair market value in exchange or, alternatively, stated to reflect the expected value to be realized (possibly negative) upon sale or disposal. The buyer can then expense or capitalize the costs associated with moving and reinstalling the equipment at the new location. The equipment's fair market value in exchange, plus the cost of bringing it into use in a newly consolidated operation, should equal the fair market value in use of the equipment once it is fully integrated into the new operations. The difference between the fair market value of the sum of the financial and tangible assets should be recorded as *goodwill* or allocated to identified intangible assets. The allocation of value to identified intangible assets should be based upon the application of valuation methods appropriate for each asset. For more on this subject, see the section below on combining intellectual property.

What are the cost implications of combining equipment?

Some equipment held by the acquired entity and/or the acquirer may be written off in value because of costs associated with disposing of it or transferring it (the aforementioned cost of transportation, installation, and setup that is part of fair market value in use).

What tips do you have on valuing and combining inventories on a consolidated balance sheet and in reality?

Inventories of the acquirer are stated, as always, at the lower of "cost or market" value. If certain units in inventory become obsolete, are likely to be sold at a discount, or will require more time to sell, then some downward adjustment in the value of these items in inventory may be appropriate. If significant, the inventories of the acquired entity should be audited during the due diligence process and appraised at the current fair market value in exchange. For large inventories—even with heterogeneous units—it is possible to use sampling techniques to value the inventories with reasonable precision by comparing the market value of a set of units sampled with the current book value for those same units. For example, an acquired salvage operation reports $2,560.35 on its balance sheet as the cost basis of its inventory of used parts. A sample of 5,000 items out of 100,000 items (representing $245,199.10 of inventory at original cost) reveals that the current cost (in wholesale auction) of these items would be $250,619.50. This yields a value-to-book ratio of 1.022106. Thus the overall inventory can be valued based on this cost-to-book ratio at $2,616,751.50. This is especially true if the acquirer and acquired entities are using different accounting assumptions [that is, last-in-first-out (LIFO), first-in-first-out (FIFO), or weighted average].

At a minimum, the inventory of the acquired company should be adjusted to an accounting basis consistent with the acquiring firm's inventory accounting if there is any consolidation of operations expected in the future. Often, acquired inventories are merely carried on the books of the acquirer at their original book basis because of regular adjustments and the close approximation to fair market value.

Inventory valuation adjustments are much more likely if there is some consolidation of the inventory of the acquirer and of the acquired entity. If this consolidation renders some units obsolete or discontinued, these will be sold at a discount or discarded. Consolidation of distribution or retail operations will typically involve some such consolidation and/or repositioning of inventory. Inventory consolidation can lead to cost savings. For example, one recently active acquirer—U.S. Office Products (mentioned in Chapter 1)—achieves its economies of scale in part through consolidation of the warehousing function.[31]

How can land and/or real estate from two different companies be valued and "combined" on a consolidated balance sheet?

The real estate of the acquired entity should be valued at fair market value in purchase accounting and at historical cost in a pooling-of-interests, whereas in both cases the real estate of the acquirer is recorded at historical cost. Each tract of real estate is typically valued separately but in connection with any surrounding tracts commonly owned by the same entity.

What are some valuation issues to consider when combining the land and/or real estate of two companies?

It is possible for the value of two adjoining properties to increase as a result of having common ownership. A change in the expected use of a specific piece of real estate may impair the value of that real estate, especially if the property is to be sold after being acquired and the future use of the property would require some modification or remedial efforts.

How often are terms of land ownership or leasing consolidated, and why?

In a purchase of assets, there is typically a transfer of title to land and/or a transfer or renegotiation of leases. In a purchase of stock, by contrast, title may be retained by the acquired corporation, especially when the acquired entity retains its original identity. Leases in purchase accounting may give rise to a capitalized asset or liability associated with the leasehold interest (the contractual right of the tenant to occupy the leased property). If the acquired lease is favorable (a below-market lease rate), then a leasehold interest has value as an asset and is amortizable over the remaining term of the lease. If the acquired lease is unfavorable, then a leasehold interest liability may be recorded and amortized over the term of the lease.

As mentioned earlier, if a company acquires or is acquired by another company to which it was leasing property, the merger eliminates the lease on a consolidated basis, even though the individual entities may continue to account for the lease as lessor and lessee on an operational basis.

So much for tangible assets. What about intangibles—for example, the acquired company's name?

First and foremost, acquirers must resolve a basic question. Will the company be named after the acquirer (which happens in about 85 percent of cases) or the target (which happens in about 1 percent of cases)? Or will there be a new name (which happens less than 15 percent of the time)? If so, will it be a blend of the old names, or will it mark a brand-new start? The decision will depend in part on the market strength of the effective names and on the nature of the new organization.

How might a newly merged company create a new name for itself?

In selecting a new name, companies should consider the following checklist (provided courtesy of Anspach Grossman Enterprise, New York):

1. Compare present names with future of company.
2. Determine the needs and expectations of stakeholders.
3. Develop criteria for a new name.
4. Develop a long list of names.
5. Review/screen names, making a short list.
6. Conduct a preliminary legal search.
7. Select final candidates.
8. Evaluate graphic and phonetic attributes.
9. Obtain final legal clearance.
10. Seek approval from board and/or stockholders.
11. Create a graphic system.
12. Develop a communications plan.

What about other acquired intangibles? How can these be integrated into the new business?

The value of the acquired company's name may be closely linked to one or more *trademarks* or *service marks.* A *trademark* is the right to use a name associated with a company, product, or concept, whereas a *service mark* is the right to use an image associated with these elements. Other intangibles may include *patents* and *trade secrets.* A *patent,* according to *Black's Legal Dictionary,* is "a grant to exclude others from making, using, or selling one's invention" and "includes the right to license others to make, use, or sell it." A *trade secret* is defined by the U.S. Uniform Trade Secrets Act as "information, including a formula, pattern, compilation, program, device, method, technique, or process" that is kept a secret and that derives value from being kept secret.[32]

INTEGRATING COMMITMENTS TO EMPLOYEES

Why is it important to make and keep commitments to employees in the postmerger period?

Not only is breaking a promise wrong (and sometimes illegal), but it is likely to have negative economic consequences. For example, key employees may leave because they lose trust in the new organization.

If employees leave after a merger, can't the new company just hire new people to replace them?

Yes, but this can be costly. Existing employees have already been recruited and trained. Replacing them with equally qualified employees is not economically neutral because it usually means that a company must pay for recruitment and training a *second time* for the same positions. Outsourcing is not always an easy solution. In fact, sometimes it can be more expensive.

In addition, there are the negative "multiplier" effects of employee departures, whether voluntary or involuntary. For example, remaining employees may feel guilt with respect to the employees who lose their jobs—either personal guilt because they (as managers) axed jobs or survivor guilt because their own jobs were spared.

When firms eliminate large numbers of jobs, the negative impact shows up in their number of disability claims—salary-replacement benefits paid to employees. Recent research by the American Management Association and Cigna shows that after a downsizing, employees—whether they go or stay—file more disability claims for longer periods of time.[33] In some cases, the expense of disability payments cancels out any savings from job cuts.

Another negative impact can be seen in lower productivity. This is particularly evident in the acute health-care field, where one measure of productivity is a low rate of death and dying. One mid-1995 study showed that job cuts in acute care hospitals were correlated with a rise in mortality and morbidity. For example, job cuts of 4 percent led to a 200 percent increase. By contrast, hospitals that *redesigned* work instead of eliminating jobs experienced no increase in these indicators.[34]

In recent years, many large companies have undergone massive layoffs. What are some examples, and what connection, if any, did they have to mergers?

The largest layoffs in this decade have *not* been associated with mergers. Whether considering numbers (such as 70,000 layoffs from General Motors, announced in 1991) or percentages (such as 50 percent from Sunbeam announced, in 1996 or 55 percent at Northwest Airlines, announced in 1998), the biggest downsizings are caused by economic conditions—or in the case of Northwest, troubled labor relations—not M&A transactions. Nor did big mergers precede the rest of the decade's largest layoffs: 63,000 from International Business Machines in 1996, 50,000 from Sears, Roebuck & Company in 1993, and 40,000 from AT&T's split-up in 1996. Note, though, that AT&T's woes can be traced to inept downsizing following its 1991 merger with NCR.

Nonetheless, it is fair to say that large-scale layoffs do often result from large mergers of equals. Consider Lockheed Martin (15,000 in 1995) and Chemical/Chase Manhattan (12,000 as we go to press in 1998). Moreover, in such mergers, layoffs may be more devastating because they are often concentrated in a single area. When Wells Fargo took over First Interstate in 1996, it announced plans to lay off 85 percent of the bank's 6,000 California employees.

Media accounts tend to tar all layoffs with the same brush, but aren't some worse than others?

Yes. Media accounts tend to make all layoffs look bad. (Remember *Newsweek*'s "Corporate Killers" cover?)[35] But it is not just a question of *how many*—that is, the number of employees and the percentage of a company's workforce to be affected. It's also a question of *why* and *how*. By communicating legitimate *reasons* for the layoffs, and by offering humane *policies* for notice, compensation, and outplacement, managers can reduce the personal trauma of the event.

In general, don't job cuts usually lead to savings?

Yes, but so what? It is true that job cuts reduce the outflow of compensation payments to employees over the long term, but they also can reduce the inflow of revenue over the long term and may lead to a decrease in profitability and long-term shareholder value for reasons mentioned above.

And remember, savings from job cuts only count if they are *net* savings, after payment of termination benefits. These payments often lead to large one-time charges immediately after a merger, depressing financial performance in the short term (a single quarter).

Most investors recognize this charge as an accounting phenomenon and do not penalize companies for it per se, so stock prices may rise temporarily at downsizing announcements. In the longer run, however, as mentioned earlier in this chapter, investors gain more from profitable growth companies than from cost-cutting downsizers. In other words, the stock price of extreme downsizers *eventually suffers.*

Suppose an acquired company is not generating enough revenue to cover compensation costs? What choice does an acquirer have but to downsize?

In many industries in Japan and in the automotive industry in the United States, companies take a four-step approach.

1. Guarantee 50 percent of pay as base salary; link the rest to profit or productivity.
2. Cut the number of hours.
3. Cut salaries.
4. If all else fails, these companies make arrangements with other employers to take the displaced workers.

This four-step approach is good, but there are other things companies can do to avoid downsizing, including the following:

- Redeployment within the organization[36]
- Leaves of absence
- Shared ownership
- Employee buyouts, both external and internal

An external employee buyout is a sale of a company or a company unit to employees. An internal buyout is the formation of a new profit center by employees. 3M is a leader in this kind of intrapreneurship.

Do employee-friendly policies lead to better financial performance?

Ample research suggests they do. For example, in a recent study of total shareholder return, Linda Bilmes (currently an official with the U.S. Department of Labor) and members of the Boston Consulting Group found that the more strongly a company focused on its employees, the better it did for its shareholders.

The Bilmes study, which covered 100 German companies from 1987 to 1994, measured employee focus both in terms of traditional human resources policies and in terms of opportunities for "intrapreneurship" within the company.

Traditional measures were as follows:

- The extent to which the corporate philosophy recognizes the contribution of employees as reflected in mission statements and publications
- The number of layoffs relative to the industry average and efforts to help relocate redundant employees
- The general human resources policies, including recruitment, performance evaluation and feedback, and promotion opportunities
- The expenditures per employee on training and on continuing levels of training

"Intrapreneurship" measures were as follows:

- The flexibility of work hours
- Project organization, including the prevalence of teams, number of levels of hierarchy (the fewer the better), and independence of working units

- The opportunities for employees to learn skills in new areas and the speed with which a firm can transfer staff to new fields
- The extent to which employees share in company performance through profit sharing, performance pay, and bonuses[37]

Postmerger integration teams responsible for employees might consider creating a master "checklist" consolidating all the points of the Caux Round Table with all the points listed here—plus any issues important to their particular industry or company.

Critics of postmerger downsizing say companies should do more to preserve jobs. Isn't the idea of job security passé—and uneconomical?

No. It is true that the notion of job security weakened during the 1980s takeover movement and nearly died altogether during the 1990s downsizing era in the United States. Now, however, it is experiencing a revival for several reasons. A growing number of unions have job security built into their contracts, and an increasing number of companies have promised postmerger job security in the form of both "golden" and "tin" parachutes, as mentioned earlier. The famous "pattern contract" that the UAW used in negotiations with Chrysler, Ford, and GM guaranteed 95 percent of the union members' jobs for the duration of the agreement. Thanks to escape clauses, the contracts allow for significant layoffs in the future, but guarantee jobs for senior members of the UAW union; if a plant closes, they can be relocated to work at a different plant. Furthermore, changes in national labor and pension laws have made it more cumbersome and costly to lay people off. Meanwhile, recent research (such as the Bilmes study) shows a correlation between job retention and shareholder value.

In response to such findings, some pension funds have begun to espouse job retention over and above short-term profits to beneficiaries. The $98 billion California Public Employees' Retirement System (CalPERS) takes "workplace practices" into consideration when investing in companies. In a recent proxy season, CalPERS submitted a resolution at several companies that would require that boards approve layoffs only if they are necessary to meet long-term strategic goals.

You say pension funds are "reviving" the value of job retention in mergers. Since pension funds represent workers, haven't they always considered job security when voting for or against mergers?

The short answer is no. Explaining this point requires a little historical background. Under ERISA, which covers private (nongovernment) companies, fund fiduciaries have an affirmative duty to vote in the interests of beneficiaries. For many years, most funds ignored this duty and voted instead with management.

In 1988, however, the Department of Labor (DOL) sent a letter to the Avon Company pension fund that articulated this duty. The letter was widely influential. Many fiduciaries interpreted it to mean that they should in most cases vote for a high-premium bidder, even if it was a known liquidator that would lay off union members.

In subsequent communications, the DOL has clarified this "Avon letter duty," letting pension funds consider long-term returns to beneficiaries. Fund fiduciaries can vote against a tender offer with a high premium, said the DOL, if they have reason to believe that resisting the takeover would bring larger gains to beneficiaries over time.

For pension funds, the proxy voting decision in a hostile deal is not always simple: not always the story of the rich bad guy versus the poor good guy, not always a choice between new life with a raider offering high returns and a small workforce versus continued life with a target offering low returns and a large workforce. Companies resisting takeovers can do so through defensive restructurings that are in essence preemptive liquidations,[38] and not every hostile acquirer downsizes. Over time, though, funds have developed confidence in their ability to distinguish unnecessary layoffs from necessary ones, as witnessed by the recent CalPERS initiatives.

How often do employees sue companies, what do they sue for, and how much do they sue for?

In 1996, 25 percent of all claims filed to director and officer liability insurers were from employees. Over half of these suits (103 out of 199 claims) were for wrongful termination. Other issues, in order of frequency, were discrimination, breach of employment contract (not termination), harassment or humiliation, employee benefits, defamation, and workplace safety.[39] The average size of a claim paid to employees was $3,160,459.[40] This may seem high, but it is low compared with the $176.1 million settlement amount approved for Texaco in a racial discrimination suit settled March 1997. This was the largest amount ever paid in a discrimination suit. This total does not include suits filed on behalf of employees by regulators.

What commitments does a company typically have to fulfill for its employees after a merger?

The primary commitments will be in writing. Managers should review all outstanding contractual commitments with employees. Ideally, this will be a second review, benefiting from good due diligence.

The Caux Round Table's *Principles for Business,* reprinted as Appendix 10A, provides a useful overview. Here is the "Employees" section of the stakeholder list, with our postmerger checkpoints.

Employees
We believe in the dignity of every employee and in taking employee interests seriously. We therefore have a responsibility to:

■ provide jobs and compensation that improve workers' living conditions

CHECKPOINTS: Are there plans to eliminate locations and/or jobs as a result of this merger? Are these plans iron-clad, or can the company consider alternatives such as divisional sales? If layoffs are unavoidable, has the company given adequate notice and compensation? For those who stay, will work and pay improve?

■ provide working conditions that respect each employee's health and dignity

CHECKPOINTS: How do the two merging companies compare with respect to working conditions? If one company is clearly superior to the other, will its policies take precedence?

■ be honest in communications with employees and open in sharing information, limited only by legal and competitive complaints

CHECKPOINTS: What is the communications style of the leading postmerger management team? What about the rest of the company? What can be done to improve the communications environment postmerger?

■ engage in good-faith negotiations when conflict arises

CHECKPOINTS: What potential conflicts concern management of the newly merged concern? Who should address these when and how? What procedures will the new company have for resolving grievances?

- avoid discriminatory practices and guarantee equal treatment of opportunity in areas such as gender, age, race, and religion

   CHECKPOINTS: Does the newly merged company have a clear, consistent plan for equal opportunity? What is the level of diversity/"proversity"[41] in each of the two merging companies? Is there a plan to improve these?

- promote in the business itself the employment of differently abled people in places of work where they can be genuinely useful

   CHECKPOINTS: With respect to the differently abled, do the hiring, training, and promotion practices and policies of the newly merged company engage and reward the best in people, making reasonable accommodations for their differences?

- protect employees from avoidable injury and illness in the workplace

   CHECKPOINTS: What safety and health policies do each of the merging companies have? How will these be combined?

- encourage and assist employees in developing relevant and transferable skills and knowledge

   CHECKPOINTS: What training and retraining will the combination require? To what extent will the new company consider these as alternatives to employee replacements?

- be sensitive to the serious unemployment problems frequently associated with business decisions, and work with governments, employees groups, other agencies, and each other in addressing these dislocations.

   CHECKPOINTS: Is management of the newly merged company engaged in a dialogue with various stakeholders about the long-term employment outlook? What hope can this dialogue offer? What outplacement programs does the new company offer?

This comprehensive list presents positive values for nine distinct values: job creation, working conditions, communications, negotiations, equal opportunity, accommodation of differences, safety/wellness, training/retraining, and outplacement. If the merging companies have made commitments in these areas, the new company must honor them. If the new company has not made commitments in these areas, it should consider doing so. Other stakeholders can benefit from a similar consideration. For the complete Caux document, see Appendix 10A, which follows.

CONCLUDING COMMENTS

In concluding this chapter, we offer one word: *integrity.* It is no coincidence that *integration* and *integrity* share a common root, traceable to the mathematical term *integer,* or whole number—derived in turn from the Latin verb *tangere,* to touch. An integrated company is one that owners, employees, and other stakeholders can both admire and understand, can "wrap their arms around." If your experience with a merger has been otherwise, the fault may lie not in differences but in disconnection—a failure to knit the myriad resources, processes, and responsibilities that define the essence of a company as it changes and grows.

APPENDIX 10A

Principles for Business:

The Caux Round Table

GENERAL PRINCIPLES

Principle 1. The Responsibilities of Businesses: Beyond Shareholders toward Stakeholders

The value of a business to society is the wealth and employment it creates and the marketable products and services it provides to consumers at a reasonable price commensurate with quality. To create such value, a business must maintain its own economic health and viability, but survival is not a sufficient goal.

Businesses have a role to play in improving the lives of all their customers, employees, and shareholders by sharing with them the wealth they have created. Suppliers and competitors as well should expect businesses to honor their obligations in a spirit of honesty and fairness. As responsible citizens of the local, national, regional, and global communities in which they operate, businesses share a part in shaping the future of those communities.

Principle 2. The Economic and Social Impact of Business: Toward Innovation, Justice, and World Community

Businesses established in foreign countries to develop, produce, or sell should also contribute to the social advancement of those countries by creating productive employment and helping to raise the purchasing power of their citizens. Businesses also should contribute to human rights, education, welfare, and vitalization of the countries in which they operate.

Businesses should contribute to economic and social development not only in the countries in which they operate, but also in the world community at large, through effective and prudent use of resources, free and fair competition, and emphasis upon innovation in technology, production methods, marketing, and communications.

Principle 3. Business Behavior: Beyond the Letter of Law toward a Spirit of Trust

While accepting the legitimacy of trade secrets, businesses should recognize that sincerity, candor, truthfulness, the keeping of promises, and transparency contribute not only to their own credibility and stability but also to the smoothness and efficiency of business transactions, particularly on the international level.

Principle 4. Respect for Rules

To avoid trade frictions and to promote freer trade, equal conditions for competition, and fair and equitable treatment for all participants, businesses should respect international and domestic rules. In addition, they should recognize that some behavior, although legal, may still have adverse consequences.

Principle 5. Support for Multilateral Trade

Businesses should support the multilateral trade systems of the GATT [General Agreement on Tariffs and Trade] / World Trade Organization and similar international agreements. They should cooperate in efforts to promote the progressive and judicious liberalization of trade and to relax those domestic measures that unreasonably hinder global commerce, while giving due respect to national policy objectives.

Principle 6. Respect for the Environment

A business should protect (and, where possible, improve) the environment, promote sustainable development, and prevent the wasteful use of natural resources.

Principle 7. Avoidance of Illicit Operations

A business should not participate in or condone bribery, money laundering, or other corrupt practices: indeed, it should seek cooperation with others to eliminate them. It should not trade in arms or other materials used for terrorist activities, drug traffic, or other organized crime.

STAKEHOLDER PRINCIPLES

Customers

We believe in treating all customers with dignity, irrespective of whether they purchase our products and services directly from us or otherwise acquire them in the market. We therefore have a responsibility to:

- provide our customers with the highest quality products and services consistent with their requirements
- treat our customers fairly in all aspects of our business transactions, including a high level of service and remedies for their dissatisfaction
- make every effort to ensure that the health and safety of our customers, as well as the quality of their environment, will be sustained or enhanced by our products and services
- assure respect for human dignity in products offered, marketing, and advertising, and
- respect the integrity of the culture of our customers.

Employees

We believe in the dignity of every employee and in taking employee interests seriously. We therefore have a responsibility to:

- provide jobs and compensation that improve workers' living conditions
- provide working conditions that respect each employee's health and dignity
- be honest in communications with employees and open in sharing information, limited only by legal and competitive complaints
- engage in good-faith negotiations when conflict arises
- avoid discriminatory practices and guarantee equal treatment of opportunity in areas such as gender, age, race, and religion
- promote in the business itself the employment of differently abled people in places of work there they can be genuinely useful
- protect employees from avoidable injury and illness in the workplace
- encourage and assist employees in developing relevant and transferable skills and knowledge, and
- be sensitive to the serious unemployment problems frequently associated with business decisions, and work with governments, employees groups, other agencies, and each other in addressing these dislocations.

Owners/Investors

We believe in honoring the trust our investors place in us. We therefore have a responsibility to:

- apply professional and diligent management in order to secure a fair and competitive return on our owners' investment
- disclose relevant information to owners/investors subject only to legal requirements and competitive constraints
- conserve, protect, and increase the owners'/investors' assets, and
- respect owners'/investors' requests, suggestions, complaints, and formal resolutions.

Suppliers

Our relationship with suppliers and subcontractors must be based on a mutual respect. We therefore have a responsibility to:

- seek fairness and truthfulness in all our activities, including pricing, licensing, and rights to sell
- ensure that our business activities are free from coercion and unnecessary litigation
- foster long-term stability in the supplier relationship in return for value, quality, competitiveness, and reliability
- share information with suppliers and integrate them into our planning processes
- pay suppliers on time and in accordance with agreed terms of trade, and
- seek, encourage, and prefer suppliers and subcontractors whose employment practices respect human dignity.

Competitors

We believe that fair economic competition is one of the basic requirements for increasing the wealth of nations and ultimately for making possible the just distribution of goods and services. We therefore have a responsibility to:

- foster open markets for trade and investment
- promote competitive behavior that is socially and environmentally beneficial and demonstrates mutual respect among competitors
- refrain from either seeking or participating in questionable payments or favors to secure competitive advantages
- respect both tangible and intellectual property rights, and
- refuse to acquire commercial information by dishonest or unethical means, such as industrial espionage.

Communities

We believe that as global corporate citizens we can contribute to such forces of reform and human rights as are at work in the communities in which we operate. We therefore have responsibility in those communities to:

- recognize government's legitimate obligation to the society at large and support public policies and practices that promote human development through harmonious relations between business and other segments of society

- collaborate with those forces in the community dedicated to raising standards of health, education, workplace safety, and economic well-being
- promote and stimulate sustainable development and play a leading role in preserving and enhancing the physical environment and conserving the earth's resources
- support peace, security, diversity, and social integration
- respect the integrity of local cultures, and
- be a good corporate citizen through charitable donations, educational and cultural contributions, and employee participation in community and civic affairs.

The Caux Round Table
Caux, Switzerland
©1994

The Caux Round Table consists of senior business leaders from Europe, Japan, and the United States. The Round Table was founded in 1986 by Frederick Philips, the former president of Philips Electronics, and Olivier Giscard d'Estaing, vice chairman of INSEAD. It has offices in The Hague, Netherlands; Tokyo, Japan; and Washington, D.C. Many of the group's principles are based on values championed by the Minnesota Center for Corporate Responsibility, based in Minneapolis, Minnesota, and headed by Robert McGregor, a U.S. member of the Caux Round Table.

A Master Checklist
for Postmerger Integration

Companies wishing to integrate their resources, processes, and responsibilities may find helpful guidance in this checklist. Although it cannot claim to be comprehensive (no such list can), it does cover many important postmerger issues faced by merging companies—the collective "you" addressed in the list. Areas detailed in the previous chapter are marked with an asterisk. For detailed coverage of other areas, please consult *The Art of M&A Integration,* cited below.

PLANNING AND COMMUNICATING INTEGRATION

Have you formed an integration plan?*

Have you taken advantage of outside consultants, setting appropriate limits on their involvement in planning?*

Have you included integration elements in your acquisition agreement?*

Have you set forth a timetable to communicate with all stakeholders?*

INTEGRATING HUMAN RESOURCES

Have you used all available means (such as noncompete agreements) to retain human resources?*

Have you set forth specific plans for integrating the following key human resources?

– Board of directors

– Office of the CEO and/or chairman

– Senior management teams

– Sales, merchandising, and distribution forces

– Other key employees

INTEGRATING FINANCIAL AND TANGIBLE RESOURCES

Have you anticipated the potential financial impact of the type of transaction chosen (purchase versus pooling)?*

Have you prepared consolidated financial statements?*

Have you valued and combined the following tangible resources (on paper and in reality)?*

– Plants

– Equipment

– Land/real estate

INTEGRATING REPUTATIONAL AND OTHER INTANGIBLE RESOURCES

Have you considered all your options for renaming the combined company?*

Have you taken the necessary steps to ensure preservation of brand identity?

Have you integrated your mission statements?

Have you valued and combined your other intangible assets?*

– Trademarks

– Service marks

– Patents

– Trade secrets

INTEGRATING MANAGEMENT SYSTEMS

Have you taken a "big picture view" of the combined company's organizational structure?

Have you done the necessary planning for integration of major processes?

– Design

– Production

– Supply

– Internal financial controls

– Compensation*

INTEGRATING TECHNOLOGY AND INNOVATION

Have you planned the integration of your information technologies?
Have you planned the integration of your systems of innovation?

INTEGRATING CORPORATE RESPONSIBILITIES

Have you taken a broad look at who your stakeholders are?
Have you considered in detail how to meet your responsibilities to:
Customers?
- Legal and regulatory issues
- Pricing and quality issues
- Technological issues
- Continuity

Suppliers?
- Legal and regulatory issues
- Outsourcing issues
- Technological issues
- Continuity

Shareholders?
- Legal and regulatory issues
- Building shareholder value

Bondholders?
- Legal and regulatory issues
- Building bondholder value

Lenders?
- Legal and regulatory issues
- Repayment issues

Employees* and communities?
- Legal and regulatory issues
- Job retention and relocation

Source: This checklist was adapted from the table of contents to *The Art of M&A Integration: A Guide to Merging Resources, Processes, and Responsibilities,* by Alexandra Reed Lajoux (New York: McGraw-Hill, 1998).

E N D N O T E S

1. These words are quoted from Milton Rock's endorsement of Alexandra Reed Lajoux's book, *The Art of M&A Integration: A Guide to Merging Resources, Processes, and Responsibilities* (New York: McGraw-Hill, 1998), the main source for this chapter. When Dr. Rock was General Partner of The Hay Group, he acquired *Mergers & Acquisitions* magazine from its founder, Stanley Foster Reed, in 1980 as one of several Hay acquisitions of that era. After the sale of Hay to Saatchi & Saatchi (which later sold Hay back to its partners), Dr. Rock joined with his son, Dr. Robert H. Rock, with Charles E. Fiero, both former Hay Group partners, to form MLR Holdings LLC, which has made numerous acquisitions in the information and publishing fields.

2. This was the conclusion of a fairly recent (1996) study of senior managers of 50 multinational companies in the United States, Europe, and the Asian Pacific. The study, conducted by the Economist Intelligence Unit in cooperation with London-based Gemini Consulting, found seven additional imperatives. Change management, say EIU and Gemini, should create great expectations, state objectives simply, set a fast pace, encourage change-oriented culture, earn trust, develop inspirational leadership, and "communicate, communicate, communicate." In its Human Capital Services practice, Arthur Andersen LLP has reached similar conclusions, expressed in its *HR Director* series, published annually in New York and semiannually in London by Profile Pursuit, Inc., in the United States and Europe.

3. Quoted in "The Latest Chapter," an interview with Norman Augustine in *Across the Board,* June 1996, pp. 21ff.

4. *Source:* "Turning the Tables: Miracle-Gro Family Seeds Ranks of Firm That Bought It Out," *The Wall Street Journal,* July 23, 1996, pp. A-1ff.

5. Based on remarks at the annual meeting of the National Association of Corporate Directors, in Washington, DC, November 11, 1996.

6. Diane C. Harris, president of the Chicago-based Association for Corporate Growth, has written an excellent checklist for "Pre-Deal Communications for Post-Deal Success: Four Aspects to Communications between CEOs," first presented at the Conference on Post-Acquisition Consolidation Strategies, held by the American Society for Quality and Productivity on September 15, 1997. Ms. Harris, former vice president of corporate development for Bausch & Lomb, now heads her own corporate development consulting firm. For a copy of the list, readers may contact Harris at Hypotenuse Enterprises, Inc., 1545 East Avenue, Rochester, NY 14610.

7. Most corporate boards (three out of four) have twelve members or fewer, according to the *1997 Corporate Governance Survey* (Washington, DC: The

National Association of Corporate Directors, 1997), p. 7. Also, one-third of boards surveyed by NACD said they had downsized their board within the past two years, continuing a trend that has been noted for two decades by Korn/Ferry International and others.

8. Unfortunately, these groups had to halt their work for arcane antitrust reasons. The Department of Justice expressed concerns that this *planning* of integration, which is allowed by law, could cross the line into *actual integration,* which would not be allowed for the two companies prior to regulatory approval of their combination. See "Bell Atlantic, NYNEX to Alter Merger Pact," *The Wall Street Journal,* June 26, 1996, pp. A-3ff.

9. See, for example, *The Directory of Management Consultants 1997–1998* (Fitzwilliam, NH: Kennedy Publications, 1998).

10. Each of the 1,639 firms listed in *The Directory of Management Consultants 1997–1998,* ibid., were allowed to list up to four specialties. Of these firms, 324 are listed the M&A area (defined as including mergers, acquisitions, divestitures, joint ventures, and buy/sell agreements), and 228 listed participative process consulting. The overlap between these two areas is about 10 percent—that is, only 25 consulting firms offer participative-process consulting services in the M&A arena.

11. Quoted in part from Schedule 13D (Rule 13d-101) under the Securities Exchange Act of 1934. For a sample form with instructions, see *Exchange Act Rules, Volume II, Rules 13a-1 through 15b9-1: General Rules and Regulations under the Securities Exchange Act of 1934* (New York: Bowne & Co., Inc., 1997), printed March 16, 1998.

12. Quoted in part from Schedule 14D-1 (Rule 14d-100) under the Securities Exchange Act of 1934. For a sample form with instructions, see *Regulations 14D and 14E: Tender Offers under the Securities Exchange Act of 1934* (New York: Bowne & Co., Inc., 1997), printed November 7, 1997.

13. See Ilene Knable Gotts and Martin D. Mann, "Ten Don'ts for Acquisition Documents," *The Practical Lawyer* 41, no. 2, pp. 15ff.

14. *Source:* "At Last, a Proxy in Plain English: To SEC's Chairman, Bell Atlantic-NYNEX Filing May Be a Model," *The Washington Post,* September 22, 1996, p. H-4. As mentioned earlier (in the introduction to Appendices 8A and 8B), the SEC has issued final rules on plain English in prospectuses.

15. See "FTC, Heeding Companies' Complaints, Moves to Speed Its Challenges to Mergers," *The Wall Street Journal,* September 18, 1996, p. B-1, and "Fed Plans to Ease Many Banking Rules, Speed Up Process of Approving Mergers," *The Wall Street Journal,* August 26, 1996, p. C-1.

16. *Source:* Joint press release from Commerce Soft and Aspect Telecommunications dated September 3, 1997.

17. *Source: 1998 Watson Wyatt D&O Liability Report* (Chicago: Watson Wyatt Worldwide, 1998) and previous years.

18. For more on this topic, see William Blumenthal, "The Scope of Permissible Coordination between Merging Entities prior to Consumption," *Antitrust Law Journal,* vol, 63, no. 1, pp. 1–58.

19. For more on this subject, see Mark Feldman, "Disaster Prevention Plans after a Merger," *Mergers & Acquisitions,* July/August 1995, pp. 31–36.

20. For an excellent model plan including financial details, see Mark L. Feldman et al., "Maximizing Shareholder Value in Acquisitions and Mergers," in the *Handbook of Business Strategy* (New York: Warren Gorham & Lamont, 1992), pp. 10ff.

21. The Cognetics study is cited in "Entrepreneurs and a Clash with Corporate Cultures," *The Washington Post,* July 31, 1996, pp. C-1ff.

22. *Source: BMW Annual Report,* 1995, pp. 13 and 85.

23. *Source:* "Boeing Plan to Acquire McDonnell Douglas Bolsters Consolidation," *The Wall Street Journal,* December 16, 1996, pp. A-1ff.

24. Robert H. Hayes, "The Human Side of Acquisitions," *Management Review,* November 1979, pp. 41ff.

25. The formula "2 + 2 = 5" has been around for decades as an expression of synergistic growth, but its corollary in synergistic shrinkage ("2 + 2 = 3") is new. It was originated by Mark N. Clemente and David S. Greenspan, principals of Clemente, Greenspan & Co, Inc., Glen Rock, New Jersey.

26. *Source:* "Top Chase Executive Abruptly Resigns, Stirring Speculation of More Departures," *The Wall Street Journal,* July 17, 1996, p. B-12. For a different view, see the case history of the Chase-Chemical merger that appears in Lajoux, op. cit., note 1, pp. 106–110.

27. A survey of 1,885 executives of U.S. companies showed that in any given year, each executive was contacted six times, and each one contacted an average of 29 organizations for opportunities. The survey also showed that 69 percent had sent resumes to prospective employers, and 64 percent had gone to a job interview. *Source:* Ray Berndtson, an international executive recruiting firm based in Fort Worth, Texas, in a press release dated June 17, 1996.

28. For more details, see Lajoux, op. cit., note 1, pp. 86–88.

29. Plants and equipment may also be referred to as plants, property, and equipment (PP&E, sometimes also classified as furniture, fixtures, and equipment, or FF&E, in a retail or office-type business).

30. After a merger, only one corporation continues to exist, and consolidated financial statements are not necessary. After an acquisition, all the primary

financial statements generally must be consolidated, including balance sheets, income statements, and cash flow statements.

31. *Source:* "U.S. Office Products Buys 48 More Firms," *The Washington Post,* June 7, 1997, p. F-2.

32. The exact wording is as follows: "information, including a formula, pattern, compilation, program, device, method, technique, or process, that: i. derives independent value from not being generally known to, and not being readily ascertainable by proper means by, other persons who can obtain economic value from its disclosure or use, and ii. Is the subject of efforts that are reasonable under the circumstances to maintain its secrecy." Uniform Trade Secrets Act, Section 1ff., 14 U.S.A. 541. This definition was provided by Business Valuation Services, Dallas, Texas.

33. "Disability Claims Mirror Rising Job Cuts," *The Wall Street Journal,* November 21, 1996, p. A-2. The 1996 survey of 292 companies with 100 or more employees (half manufacturing, half service) showed a general trend toward increasing disability claims—with a higher rate for companies that have eliminated jobs since 1990. Most employers (70 percent) reported a rise in disability claims, with physical injuries such as repetitive motion and back injuries taking a lead. The frequency of other types of claims was higher for downsizers. A high 38 percent of companies cutting jobs since 1990 reported an increase in psychiatric and substance abuse claims, versus 29 percent of those that did not. There was also a rise in stress-related claims, with 19 percent of downsizers reporting such claims, versus 13 percent of others.

34. This study, conducted by E. C. Murphy, Ltd., in cooperation with the American Society for Work Design, is cited in "Exploring Alternatives to Downsizing: Options in Workforce Planning," an unpublished white paper by Rick Maurer, Maurer & Associates, Arlington, Virginia.

35. The cover, which appeared on February 26, 1996, featured the title words in large red letters, and showed four CEO faces that looked less than kind. Consultant Rick Maurer, cited in note 34, notes that in addition to *Newsweek,* six national publications ran major articles on downsizing in early 1996, including a seven-part series by the *New York Times.* "Most of the articles were not favorable," says Maurer.

36. For example, in anticipation of its merger with Time Warner, Turner Broadcasting System announced a hiring freeze, to ensure that people whose jobs were threatened by the merger would get the first option on any vacancies. *Source:* "Turner Executive Falls Foul of Merger," *Financial Times,* September 18, 1997, p. 17.

37. Linda Bilmes, Konrad Wetzker, and Pascal Xhonneux, "Value in Human Resources," *Financial Times,* February 10, 1997, p. 10. Ms. Bilmes is currently (1998) serving as Deputy Secretary of Commerce at the U.S. Department of Commerce. Mssrs. Wetzker and Xhonneux are with the Boston Consulting Group in Dusseldorf, Germany. For more details on this research and similar research on the value of "human capital," see Brian Friedman, James Hatch, and David M. Walker, *Delivering on the Promise: How to Attract, Manage, and Retain Human Capital* (New York: Simon & Schuster, 1998, pp. 13ff). Friedman and Hatch are partners in the Human Capital Services practice of Arthur Andersen LLP. David Walker recently resigned as an Arthur Andersen partner to serve as the Comptroller General of the United States, heading the General Accounting Office.

38. *Corporate Restructuring,* a newsletter published from January 1988 to June 1990 by MLR Publishing Company, then the publisher of *Mergers & Acquisitions,* contained many case studies (including 25 based on research by the coauthor) that proved this sad point.

39. Watson Wyatt, op. cit., note 17.

40. Ibid., p. 47.

41. *Proversity* is a term coined by Lawrence Otis Graham, who wrote about it in his book *Proversity* (New York: John Wiley, 1997).

CHAPTER 11

Workouts and Bankruptcies

INTRODUCTION

Recovery from business failure is a basic right guaranteed by the U.S. Constitution. This right stems from Article I, Section 8, Clause 4, which in 1787 gave Congress the power to establish *"Uniform Laws on the subject of Bankruptcies throughout the United States."* In granting this power, the new government took a huge step forward, for at the time debtors were subject more to retribution than to rehabilitation. The new nation's founders felt that the insolvent should have a second chance, and they wanted the process to be controlled at the federal level.

Today, the founders' vision is enshrined in the U.S. Bankruptcy Code. Although the Code undergoes revision in almost every generation, its fundamental principles remain the same. In this chapter, we will show buyers and sellers of businesses how the Code can be used to best advantage in practicing the "art of M&A." (While bankruptcy law covers all kinds of bankruptcies—those of individuals and families, farmers, fishermen, as well as corporations and political bodies—the thrust of this chapter will be on business bankruptcies.[1])

As long as we have competitive enterprise, we will have business failure, particularly in the United States. Here it is possible to have an idea one day and a going business the next. The same personal characteristics that drive entrepreneurs into the competitive marketplace in the first place can lead them to take unreasonable chances and ignore oncoming disaster. But it is inherent in the American entrepreneurial psyche that these risk-takers should be given that second chance, and even a third.

It is estimated that some 20,000 professionals in the United States are directly involved in the "business of bankruptcy," ranging from lawyers and accountants with a bankruptcy shingle to judges and law clerks serving bankruptcy courts. The American Bankruptcy Institute (ABI) has about 5,200 dues-paying members who refer to themselves as "insolvency professionals." As such, they are heavily involved with the ongoing activities of the National Bankruptcy Review Commission that is seeking to discover how efficiently the nation's bankruptcy processes are working. One of the Commission's major projects for the past few years has been the preparation of a massive (1,200-page) report called "Report of the National Bankruptcy Review Commission."[2]

This report contains hundreds of recommendations to Congress to repair the wording of various parts of the U.S. Bankruptcy Code. Most of these will probably be enacted in some form either in the current Congress or in the next. Some of the changes will be retroactive; others will not. But whatever changes may occur, one fundamental fact remains: Business is risky, and any buyer using debt to buy a company, or buying a company with preexisting debt, may eventually run into financial trouble.

Any buyer contemplating M&A activity in an industry it is not intimately familiar with creditwise should be extremely cautious in taking on any obligations where debt is a major portion of assets or liabilities.

Even if a company's management and its advisors have meticulously prepared financial projections and have successfully implemented strategies to reach profitability, sometimes these projections and strategies fall short of their intended outcomes. In the case of many management buyouts, managers are too eager to be owners and make overly optimistic projections of the time it will take for cash flows to reach the break-even point. If a company does not have enough free cash flow to meet its debt obligations as they are due, the company is considered to be "in default," and unless new financing can be found, the result is some form of bankruptcy.

In this chapter, we will explain the fundamentals of workouts and bankruptcies, and give guidance for current and prospective owners of companies that are experiencing financial distress.

WORKOUTS

What occurs first after an entity fails either to make a scheduled debt payment or to pay its bills as they become due?

Generally, one or two or sometimes even three missed scheduled debt payments will not trigger a response from a creditor if there is no history of financial difficulty or mismanagement. However, a reoccurring pattern of missed payments will eventually trigger some type of action. If the debt is a bank loan, a loan officer will call and point out that the loan agreement has been violated and ask for an immediate meeting, which usually includes someone from the bank's workout department. If the debt is a commercial bill for merchandise, usually someone from the accounts receivable department will telephone and will follow up by letter to inquire about the missed payment or payments.

What should be done to rectify this situation?

Quite frankly, if the defaulting party has the funds to pay such debts, then it should cut a check immediately and apologize for the delay in payment. If it does not have the funds, then it must address the situation head-on. The worst thing a delinquent party can do is to ignore the problem. Some managers go on vacation and hope that others in the company will be able to explain the problem away. Others simply do nothing but pace back and forth in their office or on the front porch at home.

It seems that just about every company at one time or another experiences cash flow problems. If the cash shortage is chronic, however, there may be an underlying problem.

Earl Bunting, an engineer, management consultant, and longtime executive director of the National Association of Manufacturers, always said that "a company that is short of cash is usually short of something else." That "something else" is usually lack of budgeting and planning and good cash controls, failure to assess risk properly, and a fear of facing up to creditors and obtaining extended terms when the going gets tough.

The executives who fail to anticipate cash shortages and who don't immediately contact the creditors are the ones who convert what should be only a temporary problem into a chronic and perhaps catastrophic one.

What are the various alternatives available to an entity that cannot meet its current debt structure with its current cash flow?

Several alternatives are available to a defaulting entity, including but not limited to an out-of-court workout, a turnaround, filing for bankruptcy protection, and—the least desirable alternative—liquidation.

What is an out-of-court workout?

A *workout* is a procedure by which a defaulting entity negotiates a payment schedule or plan with its creditors.[3] In a workout, one or more creditors refrain from forcing immediate payment from a defaulting entity, and instead agree to an organized payment schedule. A workout can be either formal or informal. A formal workout generally involves more than one creditor and a creditors' committee. A workout is strictly a voluntary process that is controlled by the parties involved.

What are the advantages of a workout?

The major advantages of a workout as compared with the other alternatives include greater control over the business entity by the participants, more rapid solutions to problems as they arise, and substantially reduced administrative costs as compared with formal bankruptcy filings. But perhaps the most important advantage of a workout is its confidentiality. Since there are no public hearings and no public records, the company's public reputation is preserved.

How does an out-of-court workout operate?

Typically, a business burdened with heavy debt or bad revenues halts all payments to its creditors and suppliers and asks to meet with them in private. (Secured creditors usually are not invited to meetings that distressed entities have with unsecured creditors.) At the meeting, the company presents the current status of its operations and details of its financial condition. In addition, it distributes at the meeting a plan detailing how it is intending to meet its current and future financial obligations. The plan often includes a capital restructuring, and sometimes a drastic operating restructuring as well.

An important part of the presentation is a realistic estimate of the recovery the creditors—both secured and unsecured—can expect if the company is forced into liquidation and must bear the cash costs of administration of the bankruptcy filing. The lower the estimate of recovery is, the more motivated creditors will be to agree to a workout plan. If the defaulting entity files for bankruptcy protection, there is no guarantee that the creditors will receive *any* moneys whatsoever because the costs of administration, including fees for legal and accounting services, may eat up what little equity might remain. By contrast, the workout allows the defaulting entity to remain an ongoing business concern and may continue to be a source of future business and profits for them. Be careful, though! If the bankruptcy recovery estimate is too low, creditors may lose confidence in the potential solvency of the entity altogether, and opt for the cash-and-carry benefits of liquidation, however meager, rather than the less tangible benefits of a business plan. The watchword then is *realistic, not drastic.*

The company then makes a formal request to the creditors to hold off any court action and participate in the out-of-court workout.

What are some of the types of concessions that defaulting entities are requesting that their creditors accept?

The predominant concession seems to be debt restructuring, such as acceptance of stock—either common or preferred—for debt, lower coupon rates, and, most importantly, debt stretchouts. Most of the time the largest concessions are taken by either a bank or a lead lender, who usually is asked for partial forgiveness of the debt along with a reduced interest rate as well as a request to lend the defaulting entity additional money.

If the defaulting entity's plan satisfies the creditors that they might eventually be paid in full, then the creditors will generally accept the plan as proposed.

From an operations point of view, what must a distressed entity do in order to orchestrate a workout successfully?

A distressed entity must, above all, control its accounts receivable. Cash is king when the chips are down. The distressed entity must also devise a realistic budget that will support the concessions the creditors have made. Even more important, the distressed entity must control its accounts payable and prove to the creditors that it has the will and the way to reduce expenses and to bring cash expenses into line with cash receipts. Communication is the key. During any period of company change, creditors like to be dealt into the information flow and will, as a result, be more cooperative. Otherwise, they inject themselves into management decision making, which can mean the kiss of death for both creditors and management.

What are some examples of successful workouts?

Baldwin United Inc., Chrysler Corp., Penn Central Corp., Revlon, Inc., and *The Ladies Home Journal* all successfully restructured themselves with the cooperation of their creditors short of formal bankruptcy proceedings.

What happens when the creditors do not go along with a workout proposal and either call in the loan or commence collection proceedings?

The distressed entity has three choices outside of finding the money to satisfy the creditors:

- It can file for bankruptcy protection under federal law.
- It can liquidate itself.
- It can start insolvency proceedings under state law.

BANKRUPTCIES

What is Chapter 11 bankruptcy?

Chapter 11 bankruptcy, in its most general terms, is an administrative process by which an entity that is unable to meet its financial obligations or pay its debts as they become due is allowed to reorganize its financial condition. Bankruptcy is designed to facilitate the successful reorganization of a temporarily distressed entity that is otherwise economically viable. If the entity is not economically viable, then it is liquidated under Chapter 7 of the United States Bankruptcy Code.

What is the main purpose of Chapter 11 bankruptcy?

The main purpose of bankruptcy is not to punish a defaulted debtor but to relieve an entity of immediate payment of its debts and afford it the opportunity for a fresh start. Chapter 11 bankruptcy is meant to prevent the premature liquidation of an entity after it has defaulted on its debts and to provide an orderly environment to enforce creditors' claims. Giving failed businesses and, of course, businesspeople a second chance is unique to the United States. In Europe and elsewhere, businesses traditionally have had two choices: life or death.

Who can file for bankruptcy?

Under the United States Bankruptcy Code, any individual, corporation, partnership, or other entity may file for bankruptcy or have a bankruptcy case filed against it. Under Section 101(12) of the Bankruptcy Code,[4] these parties are called "debtors," or in a Chapter 11 case, the debtor is called a "debtor in possessions."

What are the main parts of the Bankruptcy Code?

The current Bankruptcy Code contains eight operating chapters. Chapters 1, 3, and 5 contain general rules, definitions, and provisions for the commencement and administration of cases as well as the protections for debtors. Chapter 7 provides for the liquidation or the orderly sale of the assets of a debtor. Chapter 10 corporate reorganizations are reserved for large corporations with secured creditors and publicly held debt. Chapter 11 is designated as the *rehabilitation* or *reorganization* chapter, and here we must differentiate between a *corporate* reorganization, which infers the creation of new *legal* entities, and an *administrative* reorganization, which simply moves people and property around. Chapter 12 provides for relief for family farmers with regular annual income. Finally, Chapter 13 provides a process by which an individual with regular income may repay all or a portion of his or her indebtedness. Our discussion here will center on Chapter 11.[5]

What are the current trends with regard to entities filing for Chapter 11 reorganizations?

The number of companies filing for bankruptcy has been declining in recent years, but their post-bankruptcy failure rates remain high. According to the

Annual Report to the Director of the Administrative Office of the United States Courts, there were 11,231 Chapter 11 filings in 1997, as compared with 11,911 in 1996, 12,904 in 1995, and 14,733 in 1994.[6] Less than 18 percent of the companies that file for Chapter 11 successfully reorganize and exit Chapter 11 as going concerns, of which approximately half fail within the following 12 months. The other 82 percent either are liquidated in some form or are sold to third parties. In 1998, there has been a slight decline in bankruptcy filings—to 11,552, according to The American Bankruptcy Institute (at abiworld.org).

Where should a multinational entity file for bankruptcy?

If the entity is a multinational with assets all over the world, it would probably be in its best interest to file in the United States rather than in one of the other industrialized countries. The United States bankruptcy system is unique compared with the other industrialized nations, which are creditor-oriented rather than debtor-oriented. In other countries, almost all bankruptcies result in liquidation, though this is changing. Today Russia is struggling with codification of bankruptcy law, as are all the former Communist bloc countries.

Does a U.S. entity have a choice of where to file for bankruptcy?

Under Section 1408 of the U.S. Bankruptcy Code, an entity must file its bankruptcy petition in the federal district court either where the entity is domiciled, where it has its principal place of business, or where its principal assets are located. The broad language of Section 1408, however, has resulted in extensive forum shopping on the part of many defaulting entities.

What is forum shopping?

In its purest form, *forum shopping* is the process by which a defaulting entity searches for a jurisdiction where the judges grant debtors more favorable treatment than they do creditors in their interpretation of the Bankruptcy Code. For instance, the United States Bankruptcy Court for the Southern District of New York is much friendlier to debtors than are other districts. Over one-third of the largest bankruptcies filed have been filed in that district.

Why is it important for an entity seeking bankruptcy protection to seek a court that is sympathetic to its cause?

An insolvent entity can continue its unprofitable operations if a judge determines, within his or her discretionary powers, that the entity is worth more to its creditors as an ongoing concern than as one whose corporate life is to be extinguished. Through the judge's discretionary powers, the court can award rights to the debtor that in another jurisdiction might belong to the creditors. An example of such powers is the extension of the 120-day exclusive time period for a debtor to file its plan of reorganization. These extensions can and have been extended from 120 days after the filing of the bankruptcy petition to three and four years. The 120-day exclusive period allows only the debtor to file a plan of reorganization, and once the exclusive period terminates, any party in interest may file a competing plan. One of the objectives of forum shopping is to forestall creditors from filing competing plans of reorganization.

What is the typical profile of an entity conducting a Chapter 11 reorganization?

The typical entity has taken on a highly leveraged transaction funded with large amounts of senior and subordinated debt secured by its equity and assets. Obligations to make scheduled payments of the debt could not be met because they were predicated either on planned sales of major assets that never took place or on predictions of future revenues and profits that were unrealistic. These entities never learned the lessons of the leveraged buyout binge of the 1980s. The LBO era produced thousands of over-leveraged deals that resulted in defaults, expensive refinancings, and, in some cases, dissolution.

What are some examples of larger companies fitting the above profile that have filed for Chapter 11 reorganization?

In recent years, major companies that have filed include Barney's Inc.; Bradlees Inc.; Buster Brown Apparel, Inc.; The Caldor Corp.; Farm Fresh, Inc.; Healthco Int'l., Inc; Kiwi International Air Lines, Inc.; Maidenform Worldwide, Inc.; Van Camp Seafood Co., Inc.; Western Pacific Airlines, Inc.; and Wiz, Inc.[7] These companies were unable to service their excessive debt load and either defaulted on the interest payments or, in anticipation of such default, sought protection through filing for bankruptcy reorganization. The Healthco case has attracted considerable attention.

What is the chief advantage of bankruptcy?

The "automatic stay" provision of the Bankruptcy Code provides the entity in bankruptcy an opportunity to resolve its problems and concentrate on reorganizing its business without pressure from creditors and any other legal actions that its creditors might bring. This provision is a statutory injunction that takes immediate effect when an entity files its Chapter 11 petition, and it protects the entity and its property from most actions by creditors. The automatic stay ensures a fair distribution of the debtor's nonexempt, unencumbered assets among creditors. The debtor retains possession of these assets and continues to operate its business protected by the automatic stay.

What, if any, are the disadvantages of filing for bankruptcy reorganization?

There are several disadvantages to filing for bankruptcy reorganization, and most of these center on money. First of all, it costs money to go bankrupt, and many an owner/manager, whose company experiences temporary shortages in the cash department and wants to file under Chapter 11 to gain some breathing time, discovers that it costs a minimum of $50,000 in up-front legal, accounting, and management fees. For larger companies, the up-front amounts can run well into seven figures.

The sheer complexity of bankruptcy makes the assistance of professionals a necessity, yet the cost of their expertise can sometimes be the precipitating cause of the company's ultimate collapse. And it's not only legal fees that do it. Court-approved appraisers' fees and financial advisors' fees charged by investment banking firms can also run into the millions of dollars. Many people feel that something must be done to cut the number of committees and the number of professionals feeding at the bankruptcy trough. It must be noted that sometimes there are *thousands* of creditors involved. The extent of legal and advisory services (and size of fees) merely parallels the complexity of the reorganization process.

Another disadvantage that the distressed entity must consider prior to filing for Chapter 11 is that if it cannot get the court and/or the creditors to confirm a plan of reorganization, the creditors can demand liquidation and the court will usually grant it.

Does a bankruptcy usually require a change in leadership?

Sadly, yes. Go-go executives whose reach exceeds their grasp can bring a company to the edge of bankruptcy, but only rarely can they pull it back from that brink. Managers consumed by the "growth imperative" will not do well in the necessary downsizing, cost-cutting, and general operating restructurings—including the very delicate negotiations with creditors and the courts that are part and parcel of the turnaround process.

It takes a special kind of executive to run a company that is involved in bankruptcy—a conservative planner rather than an optimistic promoter. Fortunately, there are many such executives and they are easy to find. In recent years in the United States the specialty of "turnaround executive" has come into its own. Today the Turnaround Management Association, headquartered in Chicago, boasts over 3,000 members who specialize in downsizing and turnarounds.

Their job is not an easy one. Managers acting as debtors in possession not only must solve day-to-day operating problems but must bear the constant scrutiny of creditor committees and their representatives. And the added administrative burden of continuous (at least monthly) reporting of financial condition is costly and wearing. It takes a special kind of person to handle such challenges.

Is any attempt being made currently to simplify the bankruptcy process?

On October 22, 1994, the Bankruptcy Reform Act of 1994 was signed by President Clinton. With this new legislation, the National Bankruptcy Review Commission was established to study the Bankruptcy Code and to prepare a report on recommendations to improve and update current law. The work of this Commission has not been to completely overhaul the current law, but with the rising tide of consumer and business bankruptcies, to make the process more efficient and reduce the costs in both time and money. The Commission has also tried to take into account the many economic changes that have occurred since the last major reconstruction of bankruptcy law in 1978. The National Bankruptcy Review Commission's final report lists some of the changes.

Some factors taken into consideration are the rise in international business with little or no laws protecting American creditors; the steady increase in consumer bankruptcy filings; the introduction of legalized gambling in many states that has become the "single, fastest-growing" cause of consumer bankruptcy; the rising number of credit card solicitations (approximately 25 to every household a year); and the corruption of the bankruptcy process by some companies to "force consumers to repay discharged or dischargeable debts."[8] The Commission has sent 170 recommendations to Congress on improving the bankruptcy laws in areas of consumer bankruptcy, business bankruptcy, jurisdiction, procedure and administration, and other issues. For more information, read the Commission's report (see note 2).

PREPACKAGED BANKRUPTCIES

What is a prepackaged bankruptcy?

A *prepackaged bankruptcy,* also called a *prepack,* is one in which a distressed entity enters Chapter 11 bankruptcy with its restructuring plan already approved by the requisite number of its creditors. A prepackaged bankruptcy is usually filed after a distressed entity does not receive the required number of votes to orchestrate an out-of-court workout. The terms of the prepackaged plan are then imposed on all the creditors, including those who opposed the out-of-court workout. In a sense, a prepackaged bankruptcy is an administrative extension of an informal reorganization. A prepackaged bankruptcy is most effective when the distressed entity's principal problem is servicing heavy subordinated debt.

What is the legal basis for prepackaged bankruptcies?

The legal right to do a "prepack" has been part of the United States Bankruptcy Code since 1978. Section 1126(b) authorizes that all solicited out-of-court votes be effective in the bankruptcy proceeding as long as the solicitation of the votes is conducted in accordance with all applicable disclosure rules under the Code as well as federal and state securities laws and regulations.[9] The out-of-court votes are then counted toward the confirmation of the plan of reorganization.

How long have prepackaged bankruptcies been around?

Prepacks have been around since the 1978 overhaul of the Bankruptcy Code. The first major company to utilize a prepackaged bankruptcy successfully was Crystal Oil Co., a Louisiana company that had absorbed a large number of family-owned oil producers, paying for them with borrowed money it couldn't pay back. The use of prepacks has accelerated in recent years in direct response to the LBO/MBO movement of the 1980s, which created thousands of over-leveraged companies that have been struggling in the 1990s.

What effect does a prepackaged bankruptcy have on the distressed entity?

A prepack gives a distressed entity a fast, clean, and inexpensive vehicle to deleverage itself. Compared with an out-of-court workout, a prepack is faster, less costly, and much easier to get approved. A prepack allows a company in trouble to enter Chapter 11 in pre-agreement about the terms of its reorganization and to use the bankruptcy process to overhaul its debt structure quickly. The process often allows a distressed entity to emerge from Chapter 11 in a matter of weeks or months rather than the typical time of two to five years.

What effect does a prepackaged bankruptcy have on the creditors?

Unlike a normal Chapter 11 process, in which creditors may act separately to accept or reject the terms of a reorganization plan, a prepack forces all creditors to go along with the restructuring plan proposed in the out-of-court workout. A prepack turns up the pressure on reluctant and recalcitrant creditors who can effectively block a reasoned out-of-court workout but who can't torpedo a prepack. Unlike most bond indenture agreements, where a significant majority of the holders (usually 90 percent) must approve any change, a prepack requires a much smaller fraction of holders to approve a reorganization plan.

How are prepackaged bankruptcies structured?

Each case differs according to the circumstances surrounding the default, but, generally, old debt is exchanged for a package that includes new debt instruments, equity, and sometimes cash. Heavily leveraged companies persuade their bondholders and other creditors to exchange high-yield bonds for a package of lower-yielding debt and equity.

What are the advantages of doing prepackaged bankruptcies?

First of all, in the usual prepack, management is allowed to retain an equity stake even though it usually has had to give up a large chunk of its equity to make the prepack work. This is certainly better than a liquidation for all parties. Second, there are significant cost savings because the negotiations are conducted out of court and professional fees are considerably reduced. Third, a prepack is fast; the company hardly loses a beat in its operations. Fourth, creditors' claims are preserved rather than washed out, as they may be in various court proceedings. Finally, there may be tax benefits available in a prepack that would not be available in an out-of-court workout.

What are the disadvantages of a prepackaged bankruptcy?

As with any reorganization process, a prepack cannot be forced on a significant number of creditors. And there is always the risk that dissident creditors will challenge the legitimacy of the solicitation and voting process.

How does a distressed entity initiate a prepackaged bankruptcy?

Once an entity has defaulted on its scheduled obligations, it must solicit its creditors for forbearance or for a change in the structure of the debt. Where there are bondholders that are governed by a bond indenture agreement, a plan to reorganize must receive approval of over 90 percent of the bondholders. If the bondholders do not approve the plan, then the defaulting company can file for a prepackaged bankruptcy, where it is required to have received only the approval of a minimum of 51 percent of the creditors holding at least 66 percent of the debt.

What are some of the companies that have successfully gone through a prepackaged bankruptcy?

Notable cases include Crystal Oil Co. (which in 1986 was the first prepack); E-11 Holdings; Farley, Inc.; Gaylord Container Corp.; LTV; Memorex; Merv Griffin's Resorts International; Republic Health Corporation; Riviera Inc.; Southland Corp. (7-11 Stores); and Trans World Airlines.

The LTV case created a powerful disincentive for bondholders to participate in out-of-court workouts rather than court-involved plans. Judge Burton R. Lifland of the U.S. Bankruptcy Court for the Southern District of New York held in the LTV case that bondholders who participated in an out-of-court workout—swapping or purchasing of bonds below par (face value)—could value the bonds only at the discounted purchase price and not their face value. That decision has made prepackaged bankruptcies a more attractive alternative than an out-of-court workout as a reorganizing vehicle. Judge Lifland was also involved in supervising what worked out to be a kind of Dutch auction of LTV's assets, with competing groups continuing to up their offers for large chunks of LTV under his prodding.

STATE INSOLVENCY PROCEDURES

Are any other alternatives available to a distressed entity if it does not want to go through an out-of-court workout or a bankruptcy reorganization?

Yes. It can opt for state insolvency procedures as an alternative. The state insolvency process is considerably limited by the supremacy clause of the U.S. Constitution. The supremacy clause states that where the U.S. Constitution has preempted an area, the states cannot act in conflict with the federal jurisdiction. Since the Article 1, Section 8, clause empowers Congress to enact bankruptcy laws, the states are left to abide by such laws.

How does a state insolvency proceeding work?

Generally, a distressed entity voluntarily commences an action whereby it assigns its property to its creditors for liquidation. The process allows for a granting of a discharge of the debts in that state; however, the discharge is not binding on creditors located in other states. This can be a major disadvantage to a distressed entity with creditors in several states, as their claims will not be discharged, whereas in a Chapter 7 bankruptcy proceeding under federal law all claims will be discharged regardless of location in the United States.

Are there any advantages to a state insolvency proceeding?

To a distressed entity whose only concern is to liquidate its assets and disperse the proceeds to its creditors, the state insolvency proceeding is less expensive, less complex, and more expedient than bankruptcy.

INVESTMENT OPPORTUNITIES

What does an astute investor look for when investing in a distressed entity?

The investor takes a pragmatic, realistic look at the company's basic viability to see if enough of the distressed entity's operation is left to reorganize and operate successfully. Telltale signs of successful recovery are its short-term financial continuity and asset stabilization along with solutions to general creditor problems. The successful formula, as with any investment, continues to be a blend of fundamental asset management, proper evaluation of the problems that got the company in trouble in the first place, and the management skills to make the plan of reorganization work.

Are there opportunities for astute investors to benefit from the reorganization process?

Investing in distressed companies has become a cottage industry. Billions of dollars have been raised by workout funds, vulture funds, turnaround funds, and reorganization funds, as well as sophisticated limited partnerships formed for the express purpose of cashing in on specific opportunities for refinancings of distressed entities—over-leveraged LBOs in particular.

Is there a preferred time when an investor should get involved?

As with other investments, timing is everything. However, there are a dozen successful examples of astute investments in the early, middle, and late stages of a reorganization. The timing depends on not only the type of investment being contemplated, but also on the size of investment and who the co-investors (if any) might be. Also, if the contemplated investment is promoted by an investment bank, the bank's general standing and success/failure record in this type of investment is important. Further, it is important to know whether or not bankers are putting their own funds at risk along with yours. Investors should stay away from anything that looks like a bailout of an investment banker.

Is investing in a distressed entity prior to the actual reorganization process advisable?

Generally, purchasing stock in a distressed entity prior to the filing for bankruptcy is not advisable, because pre-petition shareholders are quite low on the priority payment scale. Purchasing equity or lending money to a distressed entity prior to its filing for Chapter 11 is generally a bad idea.

If investing in a distressed entity prior to its reorganization process is not recommended, when is a good time to invest?

Most fund managers who invest in distressed entities invest either at the time of the filing or just after an entity exits Chapter 11.

Several successful fund managers have purchased the bonds of a distressed entity at the time of its bankruptcy filing. The theory behind such purchases is that the distressed entity's plan of reorganization will swap the interest-bearing bonds for a package of new equity or cash. These investors create a second investment vehicle at the time of the Chapter 11 filing to purchase the claims of creditors who just want to take their losses and avoid the complexities of the bankruptcy process. Sam Zell's purchase of Carter Hawley Hale Stores bonds and MFS Fund's purchase of Maxicare's junk bonds are two examples of this.

Are there investment opportunities at or near the end of the process?

Investing after a company emerges from bankruptcy can also bring rewards. At the time of its plan of reorganization, a distressed entity will usually issue new shares of stock—often at bargain prices. Once it is evident that the company has survived the bankruptcy process, the price of these shares often rises. The key to success during this period is assessing the likelihood that the plan of reorganization will be accepted by the creditors.

Are there investment opportunities in distressed entities once they have completed the reorganization process?

In many situations, the court-approved plan will include a provision for the exchange of old bonds or old preferred stock for new shares of common stock. The best time to purchase these post-petition shares is before the plan of reorganization is confirmed. However, because of the headaches caused by the bankruptcy, many creditors will want to sell off the shares received. Some investors recognize the possibility for quick gains and buy up these new issues when they are offered, even contacting the company's creditors to ask if their shares are for sale. Investors interested in the company long-term, however, should wait a few months until the trading flurry has died down in order to get a clearer picture of how the reorganized company and its securities are being treated in the marketplace.

What types of securities will have the greatest protections during the reorganization process?

Debt instruments are more secure than equity instruments in any bankruptcy process. After all, it is the creditors that have control over the process. During the formative stages of the bankruptcy plan, the creditors have reasoned out, and negotiated out, a deal that will give them not only protection but a share in the future potential if the debtor's problems are successfully resolved. If the distressed entity cannot resolve its problems with creditors, the creditors will still have a first call on the proceeds from the sale of the assets in a liquidation. In that case, equity and nonsecured bondholders are often left with nothing as the senior creditors stand at the head of the line and collect the cash from the sale of the assets.

What kind of senior debt instruments might an investor want to purchase?

The most senior debt, usually bank debt, has the most clout in a reorganization because it usually already has control of the equity in the assets of the distressed entity. Most often, commercial and industrial loans are secured by the accounts receivable, machinery and equipment, inventory, or real estate. The collateral securing the loans will determine outcomes if the company is liquidated.

Are there opportunities for investors to purchase the bank debt in a bankruptcy?

Yes. Banks want to sell off their nonperforming loans in order to get them off their books and out of the bank examiners' reports. In contrast to earlier times, banks want to get out of bad loans as fast as possible and have learned that they must "merchandise" their bad loans: to sell them off to those who are more experienced at doing workouts and have a better chance of collecting.

How does a holder of bank debt exert its influence over other creditors?

A holder of bank debt can usually exchange it for a controlling equity stake in the company and force the other creditors to accept a plan of reorganization. The holder can also swap debt for cash and a majority share of newly minted bonds or common stock. But a promise or even the prospect of new financing can also be a major factor in getting the other creditors to go along with the plan of reorganization.

In addition to senior and/or bank debt, are there other classes of debt securities that an investor might consider as an investment in a distressed entity?

The average non-financial company currently requires 50 cents on every pretax dollar to meet its interest payments. Therefore, acquiring any debt position—either secondary or in subordinated bonds—can be a worthwhile investment. However, sometimes in a Chapter 11 reorganization, principal and interest payments are suspended while the distressed entity renegotiates the terms of its debt instruments.

Note that as with most other unsecured issues of junk or high-yielding bonds, bonds issued through a plan of reorganization are extremely risky if they are not secured by any of the assets, and investors must look to the quality of the ongoing management and the extent of their own personal financial exposure before joining management in making such high-risk investments. Naturally, any collateral that can be added changes the picture and can lower the risk, perhaps disproportionately to the yield.

What about the equity side of distressed entities? Are there investment opportunities there?

The success or failure of a long-term investor in the equities of a distressed entity rests squarely on the future price movement of the stock. No one has a weaker voice in the bankruptcy process than the common shareholder. On the other hand, newly issued common stock in a reorganization is considerably cheaper than senior or subordinated debt securities. The cost of these new shares is generally lower because, unlike initial public offerings (IPOs) that reach the market through investment bankers and the fee-burdened underwriting process, these new shares are not underwritten and there is no firm guarantee issued by an investment banker underwriter. Most fund managers who invest in such new shares of distressed entities wait until the equities are offered as an integral part of the reorganization. It is wise to wait until the lawyers get through with the "carcass" (as the saying goes) and then buy the newly issued shares when the company leaves bankruptcy.

Finally, is there a type of equity investment in a distressed entity that offers both a high comfort level and a decent return on investment?

Yes. Investing in the bonds of distressed utilities can be very rewarding. Utilities are regulated monopolies that provide essential services and through legislative action are not allowed to fail. Most states have agencies set up that guarantee payments. When utilities file for bankruptcy protection, the price of their bonds usually goes down. That is a good time to buy as long as the distressed utility continues paying the interest on its bonds.

Is it true that bankrupt companies can be "bargain" purchases?

Yes. One of the most compelling reasons to acquire a business in bankruptcy, say experts, is to obtain assets which are undervalued.[10] Bankruptcies operate in an efficient market where trading values are very difficult to establish. Very often, creditors are at a disadvantage in this market. Even secured creditors suffer from "lenders' fatigue" and may settle for less than the face amount of their debt. And trade creditors, realizing that a tough stance may get them little or nothing, often agree to compromise an old debt and to continue to do business with the old company under new management.

This is not to say that creditors in a bankruptcy can or should be "duped." All formal financial reporting in bankruptcy cases is done under oath. And there are criminal penalties for falsification of records and statements. Further, by law, the debtor must file detailed reports on its finances, which are a matter of public record. Also, debtors may be compelled to testify in more detailed examinations dictated by Bankrupcy Rule 2004 examinations. Thus, if debtors (or buyers that inherit their debt) have an advantage, it is or should be through negotiation, not fraud.

How can I as an individual investor go about acquiring a business in bankruptcy?

While the best route to go is with a prepack, this requires foreknowledge of the situation and is often met with unrealistic hopes of the "debtor-in-possession." A debtor that has trouble in operating profitably after taking advantage of the protections afforded by Chapter 11 may be more amenable to a sale on the buyer's terms.

From there on out one of the best methods is to effect a "purchase of assets" pursuant to Section 363 of the Bankruptcy Code. Although this kind of deal is not a substitute for an "otherwise feasible plan" according to the bankruptcy court, as long as a proper effort has been made to market the assets, the deal will go through.

There is more to the process than this. The services of a knowledgeable bankruptcy attorney are a must. Even so, the onus is on the buyer to perform the maximum of due diligence in discovering how and why the company got into trouble in the first place. But acquiring a bankrupt business can be a way to get rich quick. Further, it has been possible for some companies to "go public by the back door," as securities issued to creditors in federal bankruptcy actions in some circumstances are tradable without incurring the normal expense of registration.

BANKRUPTCY INFORMATION SOURCES

What resources are there for learning more about the bankruptcy process?

A variety of publishers are producing guides to bankruptcy law and strategy. As of October 1998, Amazon.com lists 630 books—many of them on business bankruptcy. But books alone will not suffice.

Today, everything is on the Internet. Information on bankruptcies is no exception. Among the millions of citations available (well over 8 million on Excite! as of October 1998), there are some truly outstanding sources for information on bankruptcy law, personal and consumer bankruptcy, companies currently in Chapter 11 and their status, and much more. Here are some of the sites we recommend and a description of the type of information available.

The American Bankruptcy Institute   www.abiworld.org This site provides a comprehensive look at what is going on in bankruptcy today. There is a section for today's headlines that focuses on the latest-breaking news in the bankruptcy field. ABI has also compiled quarterly statistics on both consumer and business bankruptcies. The Bankruptcy Library section covers law review, recent court opinions, and other resources for bankruptcy information. ABI also publishes a journal. Sample articles and table of contents for the journal can also be found.

Internet Bankruptcy Library   http://bankrupt.com The Bankruptcy Creditor's Service, Inc., sponsors this informative site on the web. It is here that one can find in-depth data on companies under Chapter 11 reorganization. Check out the Hot News section for lists of companies currently under Chapter 11. This section includes articles about their status under bankruptcy and are indexed under corporation name. Points of interest include recent headlines and articles on bankruptcy, discussion groups, and a host of links to other helpful sites.

Federal Filings, Inc. Bankruptcy Online   www.fedfil.com/bankruptcy/ This is a great source of information on distressed companies and companies under Chapter 11 reorganization. An important highlight is the updated listing of the status of major cases. Don't miss the latest news on their business news wire. Document retrieval services are available where reorganization plans, financial reports and documents, and Chapter 11 filings can be obtained for particular companies.

New Generation Research   www.turnarounds.com Although most of this web site is dedicated to promoting the company's various publications such as *The Turnaround Letter* and *Bankruptcy Yearbook & Almanac,* there is still a lot of good information available. Some sample articles are available as well as a list of companies New Generation is currently following.

Law Journal Extra Bankruptcy News   www.ljx.com This site has many articles and case studies available on bankruptcy.

Other Sites   For information concerning bankruptcy case law, the following sites are available:

www.law.cornell.edu

www.agin.com

www.hg.org/bankrpt.html (also highlights international law)

www.findlaw.com/01topics/03bankruptcy/index.html

gopher://hamilton1.house.gov/11d:/uscode/title11a/sect01

Documents and court filings from many of the current bankruptcy cases can be found at the following sites:

www.legalink.com/Query/notice.cfm

www.bkauthority.com

www.sec.gov/edgarhp.htm

www.uscourts.gov/bankruptcy

There are also many Internet newspapers and news agencies that provide current financial information, and many have sections highlighting the latest news in bankruptcy. Some of our favorites include:

www.cnnfn.com

www.trib.com (excellent financial news coverage and links)

www.tfc.com

www.wsj.com (*The Wall Street Journal*)

Many of these web pages also have links to other web sites that can provide more information. Several of the more popular search engines such as Yahoo! and Infoseek list numerous other references. Search under keywords such as *bankruptcy, Chapter 11, distressed companies, insolvency, reorganization,* and *turnarounds.* Add particular company names, industries, and/or locations (for example, "turnarounds AND California") to narrow your search. There is sure to be no end to the amount of useful information you will find.

CONCLUDING COMMENTS

The power of the Chapter 11 bankruptcy processes can be seen in the Toys "Я" Us story. Toys "Я" Us was too successful! It expanded too rapidly in the early 1970s and, as a result of the rapid expansion, could not meet its obligations as they came due. Toys "Я" Us filed for Chapter 11 bankruptcy in 1974, but with hard work and the cooperation of its creditors it soon emerged from bankruptcy. Today Toys "Я" Us is one of the most profitable companies in the world. Those creditors and investors who backed Toys "Я" Us, and hundreds of companies in similar straits, have made many millions of dollars as the bankrupt companies' problems have been solved under the provisions of Chapter 11.

Today there are investment opportunities in hundreds, if not thousands, of companies in the United States that are in default on debt or that cannot pay their bills as they come due. Many are basically good, sound companies in temporary trouble. This chapter has offered guidance for dealmakers aspiring to succeed as managers and owners of such entities. Who knows? The troubled business you buy today may become the Toys "Я" Us of tomorrow.

E N D N O T E S

1. Sometimes the line between business and personal bankruptcy can be thin, as entrepreneurs often use credit cards—sometimes dozens of them—to start up businesses. As noted in Chapter 4, credit cards are a common source of small business capital. The focus in this chapter will be the *business entity* that files for bankruptcy, whatever its source of capital.

2. National Bankruptcy Review Commission, *Bankruptcy: The Next Twenty Years* (Washington, DC: Government Printing Office, October 20, 1997).

3. The most comprehensive guides to workouts are several years old, but still useful. See Silver, David A., *The Turnaround Survival Guide* (Chicago: Dearborn Financial Publishers, Inc., 1992), and Stephen R. Gross, Deborah F. Stiles, and Richard F. Hahn, *The Collier Business Workout Guide* (New York: Matthew Bender/Times Mirror, 1992). For additional classic references, see the previous (1995) edition of *The Art of M&A* (this book).

4. 11 U.S.C. 101(12).

5. See *Bankruptcy Code, Rules and Forms,* published periodically by West/Wadsworth. The 1999 edition is posted on amazon.com.

6. Christopher M. McHugh, *The 1998 Bankruptcy Yearbook & Almanac* (New York: New Generation Research, Inc., 1998). For online statistics, see abiworld.org.

7. A listing of companies currently in bankruptcy can be found at http://www.fedfil.com/bankruptcy/statustable.htm. For details on Healthco, See Robert Stobaugh and Mark W. Parry, Esq., "Life after Healthco: Directors' Duties in Leveraged Transactions," slated for publication in *Director's Monthly,* February 1999.

8. See Preface of *Bankruptcy: The Next Twenty Years,* op. cit (note 2).

9. 11 U.S.C. 1126(b). See, generally, Grant W. Newton and Gilbert D. Bloom, *Bankruptcy and Insolvency Taxation, 1998 Cumulative Supplement* (New York: John Wiley, 1998).

10. See Leonard P. Goldberger and Harvey L. Tepner, "A Guide for Acquiring Business in Bankruptcy." *Internet Bankruptcy Library,* http://bankrupt.com/about.nor.usa.guidelg.htm.

CHAPTER 12

Special Issues for M&A
in Public Companies

INTRODUCTION

Virtually every public company listed or quoted on a major stock exchange—over half of the nearly 15,000 now reporting to the Securities and Exchange Commission (SEC)—is vulnerable to an unwanted change of control, whether through tender offers or through the proxy process.

These pages should serve as a guide through the maze of state and federal laws and unique business considerations that so greatly affect a public acquisition. Although the bulk of this chapter will focus on "friendly," negotiated transactions, most of the rules and regulations cited here, unless otherwise noted, apply as well to "hostile" acquisitions. By *hostile* we mean an acquisition pursued directly with shareholders via the tender offer or proxy process rather than negotiated with the board of directors of the "target" company.[1] The last part of the chapter discusses briefly some of the major issues involved in making or defending against a hostile acquisition.

LEGAL AND BUSINESS CONSIDERATIONS

What are the most important laws to consider when engaging in a public acquisition?

At the state level, state corporate statutes govern corporate charters and by-laws. These vary from state to state, although there is some uniformity thanks to the influence of Delaware, which is often used as a prototype for state corporate statutes, and the guidance of the Model Business Corporation Act, which is continually updated under the auspices of a committee of the American Law Institute–American Bar Association (ALI–ABA).

At the federal level, securities laws are encompassed in two main laws: the Securities Act of 1933 (commonly referred to as the Securities Act), which sets forth registration requirements for public companies, and the much more extensive Securities Exchange Act of 1934 (commonly called the Exchange Act), which sets the disclosure and filing requirements. The basic text of these laws has been amended and expanded over time. In M&A terms, the most significant expansion was the Tender Offer Act of 1968, known as the Williams Act, after its original Senate sponsor. For over three decades, legislative amendments have come through new laws such as the Insider Trading and Securities Fraud Enforcement Act of 1988, the Penny Stock Reform Act of 1990, and the National Capital Markets Efficiency Act of 1996.

In addition to such legislative changes, federal securities laws are expanded under the aegis of the SEC, the independent federal agency created to promulgate and administer rules and regulations under the Securities Act and Exchange Act.

Are all securities laws cases brought under the Securities Act and Exchange Act?

No. Other laws may be applied in securities cases. For example, in the late 1980s, RICO was often applied.

What is RICO?

The Racketeer Influenced and Corrupt Organizations Act was passed as part of broad anticrime legislation in 1970. RICO sets steep penalties, which include asset freezes, treble damages, and up to 20 years in jail, for those who engage in a "pattern" of crime. It was first applied in "white-collar" (securities fraud) cases in 1987. Under then U.S. Attorney Rudolph Giuliani in the late 1980s, RICO indictments in the Southern District of New York averaged about 90 per year; some 20 percent of these were white-collar cases.[2] Since then the pace of RICO convictions has slowed but has not stopped.[3] Judicial application of the statute has been moderate in recent cases. For example, in March 1992 the U.S. Supreme Court ruled in *Holmes v. Securities Corp.* that plaintiffs must prove that the alleged wrongdoing did *direct* harm to the plaintiffs.

Has RICO been used in M&A cases?

Yes. For example, in December 1991 Carl Lindner, an 8.4 percent holder in Pennsylvania Enterprises, accused that utility's directors of violating RICO by making only "sham" attempts to sell the concern. His suit called for the court to force the company to seek a buyer and to appoint an "independent oversight committee."

What are the major differences between the Securities Act and the Exchange Act?

As mentioned, the Securities Act covers *registration* of securities, whereas the Exchange Act covers *disclosure and filings.* To reduce the chance of confusion between the two, Securities Act rules are numbered from 100 to 236 and on up (to 903 now, if you count shell-type rules "reserved" under Regulation ST for electronic filers), and Exchange Act rules from 01 on up (to 31 now). Conveniently, Exchange Act rules are named after sections. Thus, for example, under Section 10(b) there are rules 10b-1 on up (to 10b-21 now). Regulations and forms are also named in accordance with sections.

What are the major differences between negotiations for buying a publicly held company and a privately held company?

First, the negotiation of a public deal involves fiduciary and disclosure considerations that are inapplicable to a private setting. The board of directors of the selling company must be ever mindful of its fiduciary responsibilities under state corporate law. Traditionally under state law, as represented by Delaware law and the Model Business Corporation Act, the directors' chief fiduciary duty is to shareholders. In the landmark case of *Revlon Inc. v. MacAndrews & Forbes Holdings* (discussed below), the court described the role of the board of directors as that of a price-oriented "neutral auctioneer" once a decision has been made to sell the company. Obviously, this would apply constraints to a board's ability to favor one buyer over another that don't apply to most sales of private companies. (As discussed below, however, state "constituency" statutes and shifting interrelations of the so-called business judgment rule can give boards more decision-making discretion.)

Second, unlike the sale of a private company, the structure, timing, financing, and negotiation of this type of sale is greatly affected by the federal and state securities laws discussed in detail later in this chapter. Because of these laws, the transaction is conducted in a fishbowl, as most material aspects of the transaction quickly become public knowledge.

For example, the existence of an agreement in principle as to price and structure with a successful bidder is most often publicly announced. Moreover, there are always statutory and practical delays in closing the transaction that provide ample opportunity for a new bidder to arrive on the scene. In fact, the board of directors may be required under state law to provide information to a competing bidder and may no longer be able or required to recommend the agreed-upon transaction once a better, credible offer is on the table. In any event, the stockholders will be free either to vote against the proposed merger with the buyer or to tender their shares into a more desirable tender offer. Thus, an agreement by the board on behalf of the company has only limited value when another bidder appears on the scene with a more favorable bid.

As a result of the publicity surrounding its offer, the buyer becomes a stalking horse to attract other bidders. It will have incurred substantial transaction expenses such as legal and accounting fees, and it may have laid out significant sums as commitment fees to lenders to arrange for financing. It may have also passed up other investment opportunities while pursuing the acquisition of the target. These considerations cause the buyer to focus particularly on two aspects of the transaction: (1) timing and (2) protections, such as lockup arrangements, "bustup" or "topping" fees, and "no-shop" agreements with the target and/or its shareholders, designed to decrease the risk of a successful competing bid and to compensate the potential buyer if it loses to one.

What form will the acquisition of a public company take?

A public company acquisition can be accomplished through either a one-step or a two-step transaction. In the one-step acquisition the buyer organizes an acquisition subsidiary that will merge into the target. Upon consummation of the merger, the stockholders of the target receive cash and, perhaps, other property such as notes, and the stockholders of the acquisition subsidiary receive all the stock of the target. The merger will require the approval of the stockholders of the target; the exact percentage of stockholder approval required will depend upon the articles of incorporation of the target and could be as low as a majority of the voting power of the common stock. To effect the approval, the target will be required to solicit proxies from the stockholders and to vote the proxies at a stockholders' meeting called for the purpose of voting on the transaction. The proxy solicitation must comply with the federal securities laws.

What is a two-step acquisition?

A *two-step acquisition* involves a tender offer followed by a merger. In the first step, the buyer organizes an acquisition subsidiary that makes a tender offer for the shares of the target. The acquisition subsidiary may or may not be recognizable as the buyer.[4] Usually, the offer is conditioned upon enough shares being tendered to give the buyer sufficient voting power to ensure that the second-step merger will be approved. For example, if approval by a majority of the voting stock of the target is required, the offer is conditioned on the buyer obtaining at least a majority of the target stock in the tender offer. In the second step, the buyer obtains stockholder approval, the acquisition subsidiary is merged into the target, the stockholders of the acquisition subsidiary become stockholders of the target, and the original stockholders of the target who did not tender their shares receive cash. If the buyer obtains sufficient stock of the target (90 percent in Delaware), the merger will not require approval of the target's remaining stockholders (a so-called short-form merger).

Is the two-step approach the same as the so-called two-tier tender offer?

No. A two-tier offer is one in which the bidder, generally a hostile one, sets a deadline for an initial, high price. Those who sell their stock to the bidder after the deadline get a second, lower price. This was a popular technique in the 1980s, but it has met with legal challenges (for example, the 1991 decision in *USX v. Marathon,* a case that originated in 1982) and has become relatively rare.[5]

What are the major advantages and disadvantages of the tender offer approach?

Timing is the major advantage. The tender offer can close as early as 20 business days from the date of commencement, and there is no requirement that the tender offer documents be filed with the SEC prior to commencement. At the conclusion of the tender offer, the buyer will have control of the target.

This contrasts sharply with a proxy solicitation. Proxy materials must be submitted for review by the SEC; the review takes from 10 to 30 days. The materials are rarely sent to shareholders before completion of the SEC review. The shareholders' meeting usually won't occur until at least 20 days (depending upon state law and the bylaws of the target) after the proxy materials are sent out. Twenty days is usually a minimum to ensure that the shareholders get the material and have a chance to review it and to submit their proxy. Generally, the time to gain control is 45 to 60 days after the proxy materials are initially submitted to the SEC.

Timing is of great importance to a buyer that wants to minimize the risk that a competing bidder will make an attempt to acquire the company. Timing is also important to the target stockholders—those who tender will be paid sooner in a two-step transaction.

The major disadvantage of the two-step approach relates to financing. As discussed later in this chapter, it is somewhat more difficult to finance a tender offer than a one-step merger.

In a public transaction, must the stock be acquired only through a tender offer or a merger?

No. The buyer may precede its tender offer or the merger with ordinary purchases through the stock market (open market purchases) or may acquire, or enter into arrangements to acquire, stock from the target or from some of its major stockholders (lockup arrangements). The timing and method of such purchases, however, must respect federal securities laws, which preclude certain transactions after a tender offer begins and also may characterize certain open market purchases as tender offers.

In the friendly two-step transaction, at what point do the parties enter into the merger agreement?

The merger agreement is entered into before the tender offer is commenced. There are several reasons for this. First, if the merger agreement is entered into before commencement of the tender offer, the acquisition subsidiary will be able to utilize certain types of unsecured loans to finance the transaction that would otherwise be unavailable. Second, the buyer often wants to finalize agreements relating to expense reimbursement, bustup fees, lockup arrangements, and so on, before incurring the expense of a tender offer. Also, under the target's articles of incorporation the percentage of stockholder votes required for approval of the second-step merger may depend upon board approval prior to the tender offer. The board approval, in turn, may hinge upon the buyer's agreeing to make the same payments to all stockholders in the tender offer and the second-step merger. Third, the target board would like to ensure fair treatment for all stockholders by binding the buyer to accomplish the merger promptly after the tender offer.

Generally, how long after the closing of the tender offer will the second-step merger occur?

If the parties are Delaware corporations, and the buyer acquires at least 90 percent of the stock of the target, the merger usually can be accomplished shortly after the tender offer closes. If less stock is acquired, the buyer must cause a stockholders' vote to be taken to approve the merger. In almost every case, the buyer will not require any favorable votes from the other stockholders because it will own enough stock to ensure stockholder approval after the tender offer, so no proxies will be solicited. Nevertheless, the buyer must submit an "information statement" to the SEC and cause it to be distributed to the stockholders. The distribution cannot occur until 10 days after the information statement is sent to the SEC. The stockholders must receive the information statement at least 20 calendar days before the corporate action approving the merger. The result is that the minimum waiting period for a merger following a tender offer is 30 days.

Generally speaking, what are the special considerations applicable to a friendly acquisition of a public company?

To understand and negotiate a public company acquisition, the first step is to gain a working understanding of the basic securities laws that govern the transaction. As noted earlier, these are the Securities Act of 1933 and the Securities Exchange Act of 1934, as amended. These include not only the rules on tender offers and mergers but also rules on disclosure of negotiations, insider trading, and certain filings upon the acquisition of a 5 percent or more holding of common equity in the target.

Next, it is critical for buyer and seller to understand the state corporate laws that regulate the behavior of the board of directors of the target. These rules are significant in connection with the agreements that the buyer will seek to negotiate to (1) reduce the flexibility of the board in dealing with other bidders and (2) make a competing bid less attractive (as mentioned, so-called lockup arrangements, bustup or topping fees, no-shop provisions, and so on).

Finally, participants in a public company transaction should realize that the financing of tender offers is subject to certain unique rules that make its financing somewhat more difficult than the normal financing.

TENDER OFFER BASICS

What is a tender offer?

A typical or conventional *tender offer* has been defined as a general, publicized bid by an individual or group to buy shares of a publicly owned company at a price significantly above the current market price per *Hanson Trust PLC v. ML SCM Corp.* (1985).

One problem for a company seeking to gain control of a public company through open market purchases of stock is that such purchases may, under certain circumstances, be deemed to constitute a tender offer.

Although the SEC has never formally adopted a rule defining a tender offer, on November 29, 1979, the SEC proposed the following definition of a tender offer:

> The term "tender offer" includes a "request or invitation for tenders" and means one or more offers to purchase or solicitations of offers to sell securities of a single class, whether or not all or any portion of the securities sought are purchased, which (i) during any 45-day period are directed to more than 10 persons and seek the acquisition of more than 5 percent of the class of securities, except that offers by a broker (and its customer) or by a dealer made on a national securities exchange at the then current market or made in the over-the-counter market at the then current market shall be excluded if in connection with such offers neither the person making the offers nor such broker or dealer solicits or arranges for the solicitation of any order to sell such securities and such broker or dealer performs only the customary functions of a broker or dealer and receives no more than the broker's usual and customary commission or the dealer's usual and customary mark-up; or (ii) are not otherwise a tender offer under [clause (i)] of this section, but which (A) are disseminated in a widespread manner, (B) provide for a price which represents a premium in excess of the greater of 5 percent of or $2 above the current market price and (C) do not provide for a meaningful opportunity to negotiate the price and terms.

This proposed rule has been neither adopted nor withdrawn.[6]

What are tender offer premiums, and how are they measured?

A tender offer premium is the "plus factor" in an offer—it is the incremental amount paid for securities in excess of an established market price as of a stated date. Traditionally in academic practice, premiums were measured five days before announcement.[7] This was to prevent distortions based on trading in the stock based on rumors, guesses, or nonpublished inside information (that is, illegal insider trading).[8] Such trading tends to boost the target's stock price prior to a merger, so premiums—unless measured well in advance—can appear to be smaller than they really are.[9]

What is considered to be an acceptable premium for a company?

In a "perfect market," an acceptable premium would be whatever the market will bear. More reasonably, it would be one that exceeds the target management's own projections for share price appreciation in the reasonably near term.

Why would a shareholder care about promises later when he or she could get cash now?

Whereas short-term, speculative holders and some individual investors might not have the patience to wait a year or more for such appreciation, institutional investors prefer to hold on to stocks.[10] Since they own over half of all publicly traded equities, this means that strategically minded managements have less to fear from raiders than in the past.

But aren't most institutional investors indexed?

Good point. Many are indexed, buying and selling according to a preset computer program based on an index such as the S&P 500. But there is a strong trend away from this and toward holding higher percentages of fewer stocks and selecting them carefully.[11]

So much for premiums paid for target company stock—what about the acquirer's stock?

Sad to say, this typically declines in price following a tender offer, especially if the offeror has taken on too much debt or incurred other obligations.[12]

What are some of the practical considerations in commencing a tender offer?

The first steps in commencing a tender offer are the formation of a team and the creation of a timetable indicating each planned activity and the person responsible for it.

The formation of the team should begin with the retention of a dealer-manager/investment banker and an independent accountant. Initially, the dealer-manager and accountant will assist in the review of the target company's financials and business and advise as to the desirability/feasibility of the proposed transaction. The dealer-manager will also be responsible for the solicitation of large stockholders and for the communications with the financial community and may also assist the buyer in the accumulation of a significant stock position prior to the commencement of the actual tender offer.

Experienced lawyers who will prepare the many legal documents required in conjunction with the tender offer are essential members of the team. The lawyers should be familiar with federal and state securities laws, antitrust laws, and numerous other areas of the law that may apply to a specific transaction.

Additionally, as litigation is often a by-product of tender offers, the lawyers on a tender offer team should come from a law firm with a strong and experienced litigation department.

Other members of the team will generally include a shareholder solicitation firm that will arrange for delivery of tender offer materials and will contact shareholders to solicit their shares, and a depository bank that will receive and pay for tendered securities.

Tender offer teams also usually include a forwarding agent that will receive shares as an agent for tendering stockholders and a financial printer with the ability to prepare tender offer documents quickly and provide the confidential treatment necessary to avoid premature disclosure of the proposed transaction.

Must the bidder contact the target company's management prior to commencement of a tender offer?

Not necessarily—although failure to do so moves a transaction out of the "friendly" or "neutral" category and into the "hostile" camp. Although a tender offer can be commenced with no prior disclosure to the target company's management, this approach puts significant pressure on the target by allowing it the least amount of time to respond to the offer or to develop a workable defense strategy. A tender offeror may also choose to contact the target's management and request a meeting at the same time it makes a public announcement of its intention to commence a tender offer. At this meeting, the tender offeror may attempt to obtain the approval and cooperation of the target company's management for the proposed transaction and may also apply additional pressure by indicating that, unless the management of the target company approves the transaction, the tender offer will be made at a lower price. In any event, making a public announcement that a tender offer will be made requires the offeror to proceed with or abandon the offer within five days of such announcement.

When does a tender offer begin?

A tender offer commences at 12:01 A.M. on the date when the bidder does one of the following:

- Publishes a long-form notice of the tender offer, containing required information, in a newspaper or newspapers.
- Publishes a summary advertisement of the tender offer, disclosing certain information, in a newspaper or newspapers.
- Publishes, or provides to shareholders of the target, definitive copies of tender offer materials.
- Publicly announces certain information: the identity of the bidder, the identity of the target, the amount and class of securities sought, and the price or range of prices being offered. An offer, however, will not be deemed to be given to the shareholders on such date if, within five business days of the public announcement, the bidder does one of the following:
  - Publicly announces its decision not to proceed with the tender offer.
  - Files a required disclosure form, in which event the commencement date will be deemed to be the date on which the required disclosures are first published, sent, or given to shareholders.

In almost all cases, the tender offer is commenced by the use of the summary advertisement, the type so often seen in the financial pages of *The Wall*

Street Journal. Copies of the pertinent tender offer materials are sent to the shareholders on the date that the advertisement is published. The date of the commencement is important because it begins the 20 business days that the tender offer must remain open and because certain activities, particularly purchases of shares by the acquirer other than through the offer, are prohibited after the offer is commenced.

What disclosure form must the bidder file?

With the exception of those claiming that they are exempt from a filing obligation, bidders must file a Form 13D, which discloses a control intent or reserves the right to engage in a control transaction.

When must an acquirer file a Schedule 13D?

The Exchange Act provides for disclosure concerning the accumulation of blocks of voting equity securities if that accumulation might represent a potential change in corporate control regardless of how such securities are accumulated. Any person who is the "beneficial owner" of 5 percent or more of the shares of a class of voting equity securities registered under Section 12 of the Exchange Act is required to file a Schedule 13D with the SEC (and each securities exchange on which the securities are traded) containing specified information concerning the filing person. Schedule 13D must be filed with the SEC and sent to the issuer and to each exchange where the security is traded within 10 days after a person acquires 5 percent or more of an outstanding voting equity security.

This requirement is somewhat relaxed for certain institutional investors whose purchases are made in the ordinary course of their business without the purpose or effect of changing or influencing the control of the issuer, and for investors that owned their shares prior to the time the company became subject to the Exchange Act. Such investors need only file a Schedule 13G, which is a substantially shorter form than Schedule 13D, 45 days after the end of the calendar year in which the threshold ownership interest was acquired. If, however, such an institutional securityholder changes its intention and decides to influence control of the company, it must file a Schedule 13D within 10 days of making that decision. During the 10-day period, the shares already owned may not be voted, and the owner may not buy any additional shares of the target company.

What is a beneficial owner?

A beneficial owner of equity is a person or group of persons possessing "voting power" or "investment power" over a security as defined in Rule 13d-3 of the Exchange Act. Thus shares beneficially owned include not only shares directly owned but all shares with respect to which a person has (or shares) direct (or indirect) power to vote or sell. For instance, all shares subject to a shareholders' voting agreement become beneficially owned by each person who is a party to the agreement. The concept of beneficial ownership is especially important in view of the 5 percent threshold to the filing requirements. Thus, if each member of a group of five persons owns 1 percent of the shares of a class of a company, that group must file a Schedule 13D or 13G if the group has agreed to vote or dispose of those securities as a block. Also, a person is deemed to own beneficially any security that he or she, directly or indirectly, has the right to acquire within 60 days, whether such acquisition is pursuant to a purchase contract, exercise of a warrant or option, or conversion of a convertible security (Rule 13d-3).

Is a written agreement necessary for a group to exist?

No. The existence of a written agreement is not required; circumstantial evidence of an agreement in itself may be enough. Section 13(d) states, in part, that "when two or more persons act as a partnership, limited partnership, syndicate, or group acquiring or disposing of securities of an issuer, such syndicate or group shall be deemed a person for the purposes of this subsection" [Section 13(d)-1(E)3].

At what stage of an acquisition is a group formed?

It can be formed as soon as the members of the group reach an agreement, even if the agreement is merely preliminary. In at least one case the court compared an agreement in principle to act in concert with the final agreement and, finding the two agreements substantially similar, declared that a group had been formed as of the first agreement.

Is an agreement to acquire additional shares necessary to form a group?

No. As long as the members of the group (shareholders who together hold a total of 5 percent or more of a class of voting stock) agree to act together to further the group's purposes, they don't have to buy more stock after the agreement—or even vote the stock they have.

Does the management of the company to be acquired constitute a group subject to Section 13(d)?

Yes. The target's management could be considered a group if it acts as such to acquire shares and if its members own more than 5 percent of the company. A management group would have to comply with all reporting requirements.

Must members of a group file jointly, or may individual members file separately?

A group may file one joint Schedule 13D, or each member may file individually. An individual filing jointly is not responsible for the information concerning other members of the group unless the individual knows or has reason to know that the information pertaining to another group member is inaccurate [Rule 13d-1(f)(1)].

What information is required to be disclosed in a Schedule 13D?

A Schedule 13D filed by an individual must disclose information about the filing person's identity and background. A Schedule 13D filed by a group must disclose the identities and employment of each group member. The filing person or group must disclose the number of shares of the company to be acquired that it beneficially owns; its purpose in acquiring those shares; any plans or proposals to acquire or dispose of shares of the target company; any plans for an extraordinary corporate transaction (such as a merger, reorganization, or liquidation) affecting the target company or any of its subsidiaries; any proposed change in the target's directors or management, in the target's capitalization or dividend policy, or in its business or corporate structure; any past involvement of the individual or group members in violation of state or federal securities laws; the source and amount of funds or other considerations for the acquisition; and any contracts, arrangements, understandings, or relationships that it has with any other person concerning the shares of the company to be acquired.

When must a Schedule 13D be amended?

A Schedule 13D must be amended "promptly" upon the occurrence of any "material change" in the information contained in the original Schedule 13D. Although the SEC has not officially defined the terms *promptly* and *material change,* Rule 13d-2 provides that the acquisition or disposition of beneficial ownership of 1 percent of a class of securities is material and requires the amendment of a previously filed Schedule 13D. Furthermore, the acquisition or disposition of a smaller amount may also require an amendment depending on the surrounding facts and circumstances. Changes in intention regarding the acquisition or disposition of securities also must be disclosed promptly.

The SEC has indicated that *promptly* means immediately when the facts requiring the amendment are important to the market. In a 1985 release the SEC stated the following:

> Whether an amendment to a Schedule 13D is "prompt" must be judged, at least in part, by the market's sensitivity to the particular change of fact triggering the obligation to amend, and the effect on the market of the filing person's previous disclosures. Although the promptness of an amendment to a Schedule 13D must be judged in light of all the facts and circumstances of a particular situation, [any] delay beyond the time the amendment reasonably could have been filed may not be deemed to be [prompt].

Six years later, in an April 1991 enforcement action the SEC charged Data Point chairman Asher Edelman with concealing takeover plans because he made stock purchases without updating his 13D filing until afterward. (He bought on the 11th and 12th of September and filed on the 13th.)

What are the remedies for failure to comply with Section 13(d)?

In most cases, both shareholders and target companies may sue for damages for violations of Section 13(d). However, some district court decisions hold that a target does not have an implied right of action under Section 13(d) because the target's shareholders, not the target, were the intended beneficiaries of that section of the statute. The relief given for violations of Section 13(d) generally is equitable rather than compensatory and involves curative disclosure or other injunctive relief rather than damages. This is because the purpose of the law is to provide disclosure, not to prevent takeovers, and once full disclosure is made, prior misleading statements or omissions of material facts usually will not even result in an injunction. Other remedies for Section 13(d) violations include injunctions designed to prevent voting or further purchases of an issuer's securities until the filer has amended his or her Schedule 13D to correct any false statements or omissions. Some courts also require a "cooling-off" period to provide adequate time for the newly disclosed information to reach the public.

Finally, the SEC may bring an enforcement action that may lead to a rescission or a divestiture order; however, the SEC usually will not take such action while corporate control is being contested.

What materials are sent to shareholders?

The shareholders receive an "offer to purchase" that sets forth the material terms of the offer, and a "letter of transmittal" that the shareholder sends back to accept the offer. The contents of the offer to purchase must reflect the requirements of Rule 14d-6. The bidder is also required to publish, send, or give to shareholders notice of any material change in the tender offer materials.

What filings are acquirers of a public company to make?

On the day that the tender offer commences, the buyer must file a Tender Offer Statement on Schedule 14D-1 with the SEC and hand-deliver copies of the statement to the target and other bidders. It must also mail a copy of the statement to stock exchanges on which the target's stock is traded (or the NASD if the securities are traded over the counter) after giving them telephonic notice of the information required by Rule 14d-2(i) and (ii).

What information must be included in Schedule 14D-1?

The 14D-1 filing usually includes the offer to purchase, which contains most of the information required in the schedule. This includes the following:

- The name of the target and the address of its principal executive offices; the title and exact amount of the securities being sought; the consideration being offered for the securities; and certain information about the market for such securities, including the stock's current market value

- The identity and background of the buyer
- A description (including the appropriate dollar amount) of any contracts, transactions, or negotiations between the buyer and the target and its affiliates that occurred during the three fiscal years of the target preceding the date of filing of the Schedule 14D-1
- The source and amount of funds or other consideration for the offer and, if any part of such funds will be borrowed, a summary of the loan arrangements
- The purpose of the tender offer and any plans or proposals that the buyer has to sell or trade assets of the target or change the target's corporate structure, board of directors, management, or operations
- The number and percentage of shares of the target held by the buyer and a description of any transactions by the buyer involving the target's securities during the 60 days preceding the filing of the Schedule 14D-1
- Any contracts, arrangements, understandings, or relationships that the buyer has with any person concerning any shares of the target
- The identities of persons retained, employed, or to be compensated by or on behalf of the buyer to make solicitations or recommendations in connection with the tender offer, and the terms of compensation for such persons
- The buyer's compliance with regulatory requirements, including antitrust laws and margin requirements, and any material legal proceedings relating to the tender offer

Finally, the following are included if they are material to a decision by a securityholder whether to sell, tender, or hold its securities:

- The financial statements of the buyer [or its parent(s)]
- Information concerning arrangements between the buyer and the target company not otherwise disclosed in the Schedule 14D

Do the tender offer materials need to disclose any projections that may have been provided by the target to the acquirer?

The courts that have considered this question have taken different approaches, but generally they have held either that there is no duty to disclose projections in tender offer documents or that there is a duty to disclose only when the projections are substantially certain. Because projections are inherently uncertain, this latter test may in practice result in no duty to disclose financial projections. However, the current SEC staff takes the position that the purchaser must disclose any financial projections it receives from the seller in its tender offer documents. As a result, most buyers make some disclosure of projections furnished by the target in the offering materials.

What are the requirements for updating a Schedule 14D-1?

If a material change occurs in the information contained in a Schedule 14D-1, the buyer must file an amendment with the SEC disclosing the change, hand-deliver it to the target and other bidders, and mail it to the National Association of Securities Dealers (NASD) or the stock exchange on which the target's shares are traded promptly after the material is first published or sent or given to securityholders [Rule 14d-3(b)]. Each material amendment should also be the subject of a press release to be issued promptly.

Is there a way to avoid filing certain documents with the SEC?

No. However, it is possible to avoid the public disclosure of certain material if it can be demonstrated that the disclosure of such material would be detrimental to the operations of the company and that the disclosure of the material is unnecessary for the protection of investors. A company seeking to avoid the public disclosure of such information must seek an Order of Confidential Treatment from the SEC. Generally, if appropriate grounds for relief are asserted, the SEC will grant confidential treatment of such information for a limited period of time.

What kind of disclaimers should an offeror run in announcing its offer?

A typical disclaimer, often appearing in italics at the top of a tender offer announcement, reads as follows:

> *This announcement is neither an offer to purchase nor a solicitation of an offer to sell Shares. The Offer is made solely by the Offer to Purchase dated _____*

and the related Letter of Transmittal, and any amendments and supplements thereto, and is being made to all holders of Shares. Purchaser is not aware of any jurisdiction where the making of the Offer is prohibited by administrative or judicial action pursuant to any valid statute. If Purchaser becomes aware of any valid statute prohibiting the making of the Offer or the acceptance of Shares pursuant thereto, Purchaser will make a reasonable good faith effort to comply with such statute. If, after such reasonable good faith effort, Purchaser cannot comply with such statute, the Offer will not be made to nor will tenders be accepted from or on behalf of the holders of the Shares in such jurisdiction. In any jurisdiction where the securities, blue sky or other laws require the Offer to be made by a licensed broker or dealer, the Offer shall be deemed to be made on behalf of Purchaser by one or more registered brokers or dealers licensed under the laws of such jurisdiction.[13]

How long must a tender offer remain open?

A tender offer must remain open continuously for at least 20 business days. This 20-day period commences upon the date the tender offer is first published, sent, or given to the target company's shareholders [Rule 14e-1(a)]. Once an offeror has made a public announcement that it intends to commence a tender offer, the tender offer must commence or be abandoned within five days.

Additionally, a tender offer must remain open for a least 10 business days following an announced increase or decrease in the tender offer price or in the percentage of securities to be bought [Rule 14e-1(b)].

If any other change in the tender offer terms is made, the offeror should keep the offer open for five business days to allow dissemination of the new information in a manner reasonably designed to inform shareholders of such changes. If there are fewer than five days left before the scheduled expiration of the 20-day period, this will cause the tender offer period to be open longer than 20 business days.

May the offering period be extended?

Yes, but the buyer must announce the extension not later than 9:00 a.m. on the business day following the day on which the tender offer expires, and the announcement must state the approximate amount of securities already purchased [Rule 14e-1(d)].

Once a shareholder tenders his or her shares, may the shareholder withdraw them?

Shareholders who tender shares may withdraw them at any time during the tender offer period unless the shares are actually purchased [Rule 14d-7(a)].

Tendered shares may also be withdrawn at any time after 60 days from the date of the original tender offer if those shares have not yet been purchased by the bidder (Section 14d-5).

When must payment for tendered securities be made?

An offeror must either "promptly" pay the consideration offered or return the tendered securities [Rule 14e-1(c)].

May a bidder make an offer for less than all of the outstanding shares of a target company?

Yes. However, if more shares are tendered than the offeror wishes to purchase, the offeror must purchase the desired amount of shares on a pro rata basis from among those shares tendered.

May an offeror quickly acquire control of the target's board of directors after purchasing shares in the tender offer?

Yes. The tender offeror and the target frequently agree that, after a successful tender offer, the offeror may elect a majority of directors to the board of the target. Such an agreement permits the offeror to obtain control of the target's board of directors without holding a meeting of shareholders. In accordance with Rule 14f-1, 10 days before the newly elected directors are permitted to take office, the target company must file with the SEC and transmit to the holders of its voting securities information about such directors that would be required to be provided to shareholders if such persons were nominees for election as directors at a meeting of the target's shareholders.

Must all shareholders in a tender offer be treated equally?

Yes. The same consideration must be paid to all tendering shareholders. The offer must be open to all shareholders of the class of securities subject to the offer. However, while the bidder does not need to pay the same type of consideration to each shareholder, it must afford each the opportunity to elect among the types offered. In addition, each shareholder must receive the highest consideration paid to any other shareholder receiving the same type of consideration. Therefore, if the tender price is increased at any time during the period, the increased amount must be paid to all tendering shareholders, including those who tendered before the price increase and those whose shares have already been purchased.

If a shareholder has won a settlement as part of a class-action suit, seeking injunctive relief against a merger or similar transaction, can he or she "opt out" and pursue private action?

No, said the Supreme Court of Delaware, writing *In re Mobile Communications Corporation of America, Inc.,* a February 1992 decision.

What is "short tendering" during a tender?

"Short tendering" occurs when a shareholder in a partial tender offer tenders more shares than he or she actually owns, a practice banned by the SEC, but still attractive to some.[14] A person is prohibited from tendering a security unless that person, or the person on whose behalf he or she is tendering, owns the security (or an equivalent security) at the time of the tender and at the end of the probation period. A person is deemed to own a security only to the extent that he or she has a net long position in such security. SEC rules also prohibit "hedged tendering." Hedged tendering occurs when a shareholder tenders securities in response to more than one offer or tenders some securities while selling others in the open market.

How do risk arbitrageurs work, then?

Risk arbitrageurs buy, sell, borrow, or tender shares or options on shares in the hope that a change in their price, typically through an offer or a rumor of an offer, will yield a profit. They must work within securities laws. Some, however—notably Ivan Boesky—have gained and used (to their woe) an unfair and illegal advantage from receipt of inside information concerning specific offers. Boesky and others have served prison sentences because of such insider trading, as discussed below.

May an offeror purchase shares during a tender offer other than pursuant to the tender offer?

No. During a tender offer, the offeror may not directly or indirectly purchase or arrange to purchase, other than pursuant to the tender offer, securities that are the subject of that offer (Rule 10b-13). This prohibition also includes privately negotiated purchases until the tender offer is concluded or withdrawn.

Purchases made before a public announcement are generally permissible, even if a decision has been made by the purchaser to make the tender offer, but purchase agreements scheduled to close during the offering period are illegal no matter when they were or are made.

PROXY SOLICITATION DISCLOSURES

What information must be disclosed to stockholders if the form of the acquisition is a merger?

Regulation 14A under the Exchange Act requires that stockholders be provided with a proxy statement that includes the information set forth in Schedule 14A.

Although information is specifically required to be included in the proxy statement if the shareholder meeting to which the proxy statement relates is being held in connection with any merger, consolidation, acquisition, or similar matter, and the manner of disclosure thereof varies depending on the level of information available about the parties, such information generally includes the following:

1. The mailing address and telephone number of the principal executive offices of each party
2. A brief discussion of the general nature of the business conducted by each party
3. A summary of the material features of the proposed transaction, including (i) a brief summary of the transaction agreement; (ii) the reason for engaging in the transaction; (iii) an explanation of any material differences in the rights of securityholders as a result of the transaction; (iv) a brief statement about accounting treatment; and (v) federal income tax consequences

4. A statement on the effect of the transaction on dividends in arrears or defaults in the payment of the principal or interest on the securities of any party

5. Selected financial data relating to the target company and the acquirer

6. If material, such financial information in Item 5 above on a pro forma basis

7. Certain historical and pro forma per share data of the target company and the acquirer

8. Detailed pro forma financial information as required by Article 11 of Regulation S-X

9. A statement on the status of any federal or state regulatory approval that must be obtained in connection with the transaction

10. Detailed information concerning any report, opinion, or appraisal materially relating to the transaction

11. A description of any past, present, or proposed material contracts, arrangements, understandings, relationships, negotiations, or transactions between the target company and other persons and any of their affiliates

12. The high and low sale prices of the relevant securities as of the date immediately prior to the public announcement of the transaction

13. A statement about whether representatives of the principal accountants for the current year and for the most recently completed fiscal year are expected to be at the meeting and will have the opportunity to make a statement if they desire to do so and are expected to be available to respond to questions

Schedule 14A also requires detailed information relating to material changes in the affairs of the company being acquired that have occurred since the end of the latest year for which audited financial statements were included in the latest annual report to securityholders.

Any action to be taken with respect to any amendment of the registrant's charter, bylaws, or other documents must be described and the reasons for and general effect of such amendment must be disclosed.

The vote required for approval must be described.

What about groups seeking control through a proxy fight?

They must adhere to the proxy rules promulgated under Section 14 of the Exchange Act, with certain exemptions. Traditionally, such exemptions were rare, but in October 1992, after nearly two years of proposals and comments, the SEC published new proxy rules that expanded these exemptions.

What are the current SEC rules on shareholder communications?

Recent rules on shareholder communications enable more types of shareholders to communicate more effectively and more broadly. These rules—which we passed in 1992 and amended later, most recently in May 1998—also strengthen investors' chances to gain control of a public company through a proxy contest. The rules:

- Narrowed the definition of "solicitation"
- Expanded exemptions for certain categories of shareholders previously not covered
- Added exemptions for mass media communications
- Enabled shareholders to start a solicitation more easily
- Unbundled voting items for shareholders
- Unbundled nominees for board positions
- Forced companies to give copies of their shareholders' lists to dissidents
- Rescinded the requirement to file 14B (see below)
- Changed proxy forms to require greater disclosure of voting results and of the vote needed for passage of resolutions

How did the rules narrow the definition of solicitation?

Rule 14a-1 has a new, narrower definition of solicitation that excludes many forms of communication. The new rule says that a shareholder can publicly announce how he or she intends to vote and why, without necessarily having to comply with proxy rules. Major institutional investors, such as the California Public Employees' Retirement System (CalPERS), have used this technique to encourage other shareholders to follow their lead. Prior to this new exemption, critics complained that even signing an op-ed in a newspaper could trigger proxy rules.

What shareholders are exempt from the new rules?

Rule 14a-2(b)[15] offers a broad exemption from the proxy statement "delivery and disclosure" requirements for shareholder communications unless the person soliciting is seeking proxy authority and has a substantial interest in the matter subject to a vote or is otherwise ineligible for the exemption. On the other hand, public notice—through publication, broadcast, or submission of written materials to the SEC—of soliciting activity will still be required of all beneficial owners of more than $5 million worth of stock. For example, the exemption applies to proxy advisors such as Institutional Shareholder Services, a Bethesda, Maryland–based group that advises institutional shareholders on proxy voting matters.

Under the rules, may shareholders solicit proxies via the mass media? May they bypass the SEC altogether?

Yes to the first question; no to the second. Rule 14a-3 has been amended to add a new paragraph (f), exempting solicitations communicated by public broadcast, speech, or publication, provided a definitive proxy statement is on file with the SEC. In other words, a person who has a proxy statement on file with the SEC would be permitted to solicit votes without delivering a copy of the proxy statement to all shareholders in the audience. This could facilitate insurgent campaigns by increasing the solicitation techniques that can be used without mailing the proxy statement to all shareholders. This issue arose during the 1991 proxy contest at Sears, where shareholder activist Robert A. G. Monks, seeking a seat on the board, distributed his proxy statement only to institutional investors and other selected shareholders but made widespread use of the media.

How do the new proxy rules enable a faster start for a proxy fight?

Rules 14a-3(a) and 14a-4 have been eased to allow registrants and other soliciting parties to commence a solicitation on the basis of a preliminary proxy statement publicly filed with the SEC, so long as no form of proxy is provided to the solicited shareholders until the dissemination of a definitive proxy statement.

How do the new proxy rules unbundle voting issues?

Rules 14a-4(a) and (b)1 have been amended to require that the form of proxy separately list each matter to be voted on in order to allow shareholders to vote individually on each matter.

How did the new proxy rules unbundle board nominees?

Rule 14a-4(d) has been amended to enable shareholders voting for dissident candidates for minority representation on the board of directors to also vote for one or more of management's nominees. The dissident's proxy form and proxy statement may not include the names of management's nonconsenting nominees.

Under what circumstances must companies give dissidents their shareholder lists?

Rule 14a-7 has been amended to require registered companies engaged in rollups or going private transactions to provide shareholders, under certain conditions and upon written request, with a list of shareholder names, addresses, and positions, including names of consenting beneficial owners, if known. In all other cases registrants can either give such a list to the requesting shareholders or mail materials for them.

What about filing a 14B?

This is no longer required. Rule 14a-11(c), which mandated the filing of Schedule 14B by all proxy fight participants (other than the registrant), has been rescinded.[16]

How has proxy voting disclosure changed under the new rules?

Several forms—including 10-K, 10-Q, and Schedule 14A—have been revised to require improved disclosure of voting results and of the vote needed for passage of resolutions presented to shareholders. This disclosure must now include the number of abstentions on resolutions and on votes for director elections, and a statement of how exemptions are treated under applicable state law charter and bylaw provisions.

Did the new rules contain requirements for clearer disclosure of top executive compensation?

No. These were issued in a separate document revising both the Securities Act and the Exchange Act.[17] Since these new disclosure rules do not directly affect tender offers or proxy fights, they will not be discussed here except to note that if they expose excessive compensation, they could stimulate bids for corporate control, while if they help curb overcompensation, they could avert such bids.

Don't all of the above changes tilt the "control panel" of the playing field to the advantage of dissident investors rather than incumbent managements?

Many in the corporate community certainly think so. In response to corporate concerns about secrecy, the SEC stipulated that, with certain exceptions, a new form must be furnished or mailed to the SEC (but not formally filed) by those claiming exemptions from the filing requirements under Section 14. The new form requires disclosure of the person's name and address, with any written solicitation materials attached. The form must be mailed within three days of the first use of such materials.

Note, however, that no notice is required if the solicitation is only made by radio or television broadcast; by publication, such as in a newspaper interview or advertisement; or in "speeches in a public forum."

Most significantly, no notice is required for solicitations made solely by oral means, such as those made at meetings or in telephone conversations.

MERGER DISCLOSURE ISSUES

Under what circumstances may a public company deny that it is engaged in merger negotiations?

Only if it is not so engaged. That was the gist of the Supreme Court's 1988 decision in *Basic, Inc., v. Levinson.* In this landmark case, the Court said that outright denial of negotiations is improper even if the negotiations in question are discussions that have not yet resulted in an agreement on the price and structure of a transaction. The appropriate response to inquiries about such a matter is either "no comment" or a disclosure that negotiations are, in fact, taking place.

Prior to the *Basic* decision, the Court of Appeals for the Third Circuit had held that merger proposals and negotiations were not "material" until the parties had reached agreement in principle on the price and structure of a transaction. In *Basic,* the Supreme Court rejected this so-called bright line test and held that the materiality of merger negotiations must be evaluated on a case-by-case basis after considering all relevant facts and circumstances.

Since *Basic,* courts seem to have backed down on this issue, but the SEC has been active. In appealing a dismissal of its case against Amster & Co. in mid-1991, the SEC applied the *Basic* doctrine to preliminary plans to wage a proxy contest. But it admitted in its filing that it was not trying to "suggest that every consideration or thought given to a plan must be disclosed; at an early enough stage, possible plans or proposals may simply be too ephemeral to require disclosure."

When does a company have a duty to disclose merger negotiations?

Generally, the timing of disclosure of material information is at the discretion of the company and will be protected by the business judgment rule. Nevertheless, a company that is the subject of takeover speculation or whose stock is trading erratically typically finds itself under disclosure pressure by brokers, news services, securities analysts, and officials of stock exchanges, including the NASD's Nasdaq exchange, recently merged with the American Stock Exchange. The *Basic* decision has accelerated the trend toward voluntary disclosures in these circumstances, although it is still acceptable under certain circumstances for a company to adopt a policy of silence or state that "no comment" will be made with respect to merger proposals or rumors.

However, a company may not remain silent where (1) there is an affirmative disclosure rule (such as the tender offer regulations), (2) the company is about to purchase its own shares in the public market, (3) a prior public disclosure made by the company is no longer accurate (such as when a company has publicly denied that merger negotiations with a party were occurring), or (4) rumors that have been circulating concerning the proposed transactions are attributable to a leak from the company.[18]

Disclosure may also be appropriate when it is apparent that a leak has occurred, even if the leak is not from the company. In such a situation, consideration should be given to a variety of factors, including the requirements of any agreement with a stock exchange or Nasdaq, the effect of wide price fluctuations on shareholders generally, and the benefits to the market provided by broad dissemination of accurate information. If the company does elect to disclose either the existence or the substance of negotiations, it must take care that its disclosures are neither false nor materially misleading.

It should be noted that if the company refuses to respond to a stock exchange's request for disclosure or issues a "no comment," it may be subject to disciplinary action by the exchange. This disciplinary action may include public notice of a violation, temporary suspension of trading in the corporation's stock, or delisting. However, the exchanges have a reputation for being "paper tigers" in this area because of their reluctance to enforce these rules. This reluctance is attributed to the competition of "third-market" securities firms that trade listed securities off the exchanges. Moreover, courts have not found a private right of action for violation of exchange rules.

Is management required to disclose inquiries about a possible merger or acquisition?

There is no specific obligation to disclose mere inquiries or contacts made by those interested in acquiring the corporation or its stock. If they are pursued, however, the above complexities apply.

What if an advisor recommends a disclosure stance that comes under challenge?

Then not only will the issuing company be exposed to liability, but so will the advisor. This was the case with George C. Kern, Jr., an attorney subjected to over four years of harrowing SEC administrative proceedings after advising his client, Allied Stores Corporation, to delay disclosure of pending negotiations to sell its shopping center holdings. In June 1991, the SEC dropped the matter.[19]

DIRECTOR RESPONSIBILITIES IN RESPONDING TO UNSOLICITED BIDS

What are the primary responsibilities of a corporate board of directors upon receipt of a takeover bid?

The director's primary responsibility is to evaluate and recommend what action a company should take in the event of an offer to acquire the company.

The director's conduct in this and other contexts is evaluated under the business judgment rule.

What is the business judgment rule?

The *business judgment rule* is a judicial doctrine applied by courts in cases where shareholders have sued directors for violating their fiduciary duties to the corporation. The rule is that the board of directors will be protected unless the shareholders can prove that in making a business decision a director did not act with due care, good faith, and loyalty to the corporation. The business judgment rule protects directors from liability if they act in a manner consistent with their duties of due care and loyalty.

What is a director's duty of due care?

For a director, *exercising due care* means acting on behalf of the company's stockholders by making informed decisions after obtaining all reasonably available information required to make an intelligent decision and after evaluating all relevant circumstances. Under this standard, the directors' duty is not merely to make the best possible decision for the corporation but to make their decision only after careful, informed deliberation. Both the process of decision making and the substantive decisions themselves are taken into consideration by courts in evaluating whether directors acted with due care.

The 1985 Delaware case of *Smith v. Van Gorkom* dealt a blow to the business judgment rule when the Delaware court found that the board of directors of Trans Union and, in particular, Trans Union's chief executive officer, Jerome Van Gorkom, were personally liable for actions taken in connection with approving and recommending to shareholders a cash-out merger proposal. The court held that they were not entitled to the protection of the business judgment rule even though Van Gorkom and the other board members may well have been highly qualified to make the decisions they did and had obtained a substantial premium over the market price for the shares of Trans Union.

Nevertheless, the court found that the following actions by the Trans Union board and Van Gorkom evidenced a lack of due care:

- The CEO did not establish a "fair price" for the company's stock.
- The CEO met with the offeror without consulting his directors or any senior management personnel.

- The CEO did not seek the advice of investment bankers or ensure adequate legal counsel.
- Copies of the proposed merger agreement were not available for review by the board of directors at the meeting convened to discuss the merger.
- The CEO did not tell the directors that it was he who had valued the company's stock and suggested the purchase price to the offeror, together with suggestions on how to finance the purchase.
- The directors did not study the merger agreement before voting on it.
- The directors approved the merger agreement based on representations of several members of the management team.
- Neither the CEO nor the other directors read the merger agreement before signing and delivering it to the offeror.
- The directors approved amendments to the merger agreement in a meeting convened by the CEO without reviewing the documents or attempting to understand the implications of the amendments.
- The directors did not request that any valuation report or study be prepared to evaluate the value placed on the company's stock.
- The directors decided to approve the merger without allowing adequate time to consider its adequacy or its repercussions.
- The company's stockholders were not fully informed of all material facts when the merger was put to a vote.

The unusual element in *Van Gorkom* is that the court did not concern itself primarily with the ultimate decision (which was arguably a very good one for the shareholders of Trans Union) but instead emphasized the importance of the correct decision-making process. Directors must make informed decisions and take careful steps to ensure that they are acting responsibly.

Since *Van Gorkom*, the business judgment rule has gone through considerable refinement in a series of landmark cases, notably *Time* (1990), *Paramount* (1994), and *Caremark* (1997). (See the Table of Cases in the back of the book.)

What is a director's duty of loyalty?

A director of a corporation owes a *duty of loyalty* to act in the best interests of the corporation and its shareholders, for which he or she is a fiduciary. As such, the director is prohibited from entering into a transaction that is tainted by fraud or bad faith, or in which the director has a personal interest. If it appears that a director has a personal interest in a particular corporate transaction, a court often will shift the burden of proof to the director to show that the transaction is fair and that it serves the best interests of the corporation and its shareholders.

Why are these duties concerning the board's responsibilities so important?

First, these rules affect timing—the need for the board to act with due care will restrict the board's ability to act quickly on a friendly offer. It will have to appoint a special committee if the transaction involves a management buyout (MBO). At the very least, a fairness opinion must be obtained, and the investment banker will need several days, at a minimum, to complete the task.

Second, the rules restrict the ability of the board to take action that either eliminates the possibility of a competing bid—so-called lockups or other arrangements (bustup and topping fees and no-shop clauses) that are designed (in part) to frustrate the efforts of other bidders. These arrangements are among the most negotiated provisions of the public deal.

For reasons outlined above, the buyer will seek to minimize the risk of a successful competing bid and will seek to ensure that it is compensated if it loses to another bidder. The next several questions deal with these issues in the context of the board's fiduciary responsibilities to the shareholders.

When is it appropriate for a selling company to appoint a special committee of its board of directors to review a proposed transaction?

If there is any question that a majority of the members of the board of directors may have a personal interest in the proposed merger (where the management directors predominate and will obtain benefits from the merger), an independent special committee of the board should be appointed to handle the negotiation and recommendation of any proposed transaction. A special committee is also appropriate where a proposed transaction is complex enough to require careful study for the board to act responsibly. Having a special committee with adequate authority over the transaction will tend to shift to a plaintiff the burden of showing that the transaction is unfair. This shift will generally preclude the issuance of injunctive relief against a proposed merger.

What is the role of counsel to the special committee?

Counsel should advise the members of the special committee about the interpretation of the business judgment rule in the company's jurisdiction of incorporation. In addition, counsel should advise the committee of any potential liability for its actions and the extent to which it may be indemnified or otherwise protected under the company's charter and bylaws and directors' and officers' liability insurance. Counsel should attend each meeting of the special committee and should prepare or review minutes of each meeting. These minutes should be reviewed for accuracy by each member of the committee. In the event that the proposed transaction may attract other offers, counsel to the special committee should be prepared to advise the committee about the duty of the directors to obtain the best possible price for all shareholders. Counsel should also advise the committee of the extent of its obligations to consider such offers, and of the techniques that it may and may not employ to enhance or limit bidding opportunities.

Which directors are appropriate members of a special committee?

A special committee should consist of independent or disinterested directors. Such directors must not have any financial or personal interest in the proposed transaction that would inhibit their ability to act in an unbiased manner.

What are the benefits of a special committee?

Although there is no guarantee that a special committee will legitimate board action, such a committee may be extremely helpful in, and perhaps essential to, providing directors with the protection of the business judgment rule. It should be noted, however, that courts will closely scrutinize the facts surrounding the actions of the board, and that the mere formation of a special committee will not protect the directors from liability for careless actions.

What steps should a special committee take to ensure that it is acting responsibly?

The special committee should examine all information about the proposed transaction. This examination must be thorough, and members of the special committee should question carefully the persons supplying such information to be sure the information is complete and accurate. The committee should also

take care not to act hastily and should make sure that it documents its deliberations. Recent judicial decisions have indicated that directors who make decisions without adequate deliberation may have difficulty in establishing that
they acted with the care necessary to provide the protection of the business
judgment rule.

Should a special committee retain independent advisors?

In the context of mergers and acquisitions, the special committee of a board of
directors should retain independent legal counsel and financial advisors.

Should a special committee obtain a fairness opinion?

Yes, but the opinion must be from a qualified, independent source (such as an
investment banking firm, a commercial bank, or an appraiser) and must be
supplemented by board deliberations. Although the fairness opinion can be a
useful tool both in determining whether to accept an offer and in obtaining the
protection of the business judgment rule, when there is a potential or actual
conflict of interest in a transaction, courts will also examine the transaction to
determine its "intrinsic fairness." Because fairness generally depends on the
price to be received by the target company's shareholders, the investment
bankers' financial expertise, as reflected in a fairness opinion, can be invaluable to the board. It is, however, necessary for a board of directors to question
the investment bankers to determine that they have a reasonable basis for their
opinion and that they are free from conflicts of interests, as reliance on a fairness opinion alone may not suffice as proof of the exercise of due care.

What should a fairness opinion say?

A fairness opinion should describe the process the source used in making its
determination that a proposed transaction is fair and should indicate what matters have been investigated and independently verified and what matters the
source has not verified independently. The opinion should also describe the
fee or fees being paid and all possible conflicts of interest. The firm offering
the opinion should not accept contingent compensation for the fairness opinion because doing so suggests a lack of independence.

What is a lockup option?

One mechanism employed by companies to give the favored bidder an edge is a *lockup option.* The lockup agreement may be granted with respect to stock or assets.

In the *stock lockup,* the bidder receives an option to purchase authorized but unissued shares. This option favors the bidder in two ways: If the option is exercised, either the bidder may vote the shares in favor of the transaction or, if another bidder wins the contract for the company, the favored bidder may realize a profit by tendering the stock to the higher bidder. A variation on the lockup is the reverse lockup, where stockholders or management agree not to tender their shares to a rival bidder. For the same reason, a buyer will attempt to obtain options to acquire the stock of stockholders, typically those that have significant holdings. Such options are not subject to scrutiny under the business judgment rule because they are not acts of the board of directors. (See below for a discussion of lockup arrangements with stockholders.)

Stock lockup agreements with the target have received mixed results from courts applying the business judgment doctrine. The courts' main concern is that the lockup may prevent competitive bidding and thereby limit the premiums stockholders would otherwise receive from buyers. Courts are most likely to approve lockups granted at the end of the bidding process rather than at the beginning, particularly if there are no other bidders contending for the company.

In the *asset lockup* (or "crown jewel" lockup), the company grants the bidder the option to acquire a particularly attractive asset at a price that may or may not be commensurate with its full market value. Such an option may discourage other bidders if they were also interested in the crown jewel or if the loss of the asset would considerably change the financial position or prospects of the company.

Asset lockup agreements have received generally negative treatments from courts, as discussed below.

Can directors adopt a lockup agreement without violating their fiduciary duties?

Yes. A lockup agreement is not illegal per se. However, court decisions hold that a lockup arrangement generally must advance or stimulate the bidding process, not retard it or cut it off. That is, a board can tilt the playing field toward a bidder if the purpose is to elicit a higher bid from that bidder or to otherwise stimulate the competition.

If the purpose of the lockup agreement is to completely stifle competitive bidding by definitively preferring one bidder over another, however, the board will likely be found to have breached its duty of loyalty to the shareholders. In *Revlon, Inc. v. MacAndrews & Forbes Holdings* (1986), Revlon was faced with a hostile tender offer from Pantry Pride. Having determined that Pantry Pride's initial bid was inadequate, the board advised the shareholders to reject the bid and began the search for a white knight, which it found in the LBO firm of Forstmann Little and Co.

Revlon then began negotiating with Forstmann Little to the exclusion of Pantry Pride. It did not invite Pantry Pride to participate in any negotiations, nor did Revlon share financial data with Pantry Pride as it did with Forstmann Little. Eventually, an increased bid from Pantry Pride prompted an increased bid from Forstmann Little that was conditioned upon, among other things, the receipt by Forstmann Little of a lockup option to purchase two Revlon divisions at a price substantially lower than the lowest estimate of value established by Revlon's investment banker, plus a no-shop provision that prevented Revlon from considering bids from any third party. The board immediately accepted the Forstmann Little offer, even though Pantry Pride had increased its bid.

The court held that when the focus of the directors changed from keeping the company intact to maximizing the return from a sale of assets, the board assumed the role of auctioneer obligated to obtain the best price for the shareholders. The court then determined that by stifling competitive bidding through the lockup agreement with Forstmann Little, the Revlon board had violated its duty of loyalty to the company and its shareholders. Cases subsequent to *Revlon* have indicated clearly that a court will not permit a board to grant a crown jewel lockup option to one bidder that would have the effect of cutting other bidders out of the process while bidding is still active.

Is a lockup that shuts off the process never permissible?

Case law has yet to present the best case for upholding a lockup. In certain cases, where lockup options were defeated, the lockups favored an insider group or were designed to favor a friendly bidder—even one bidding at the low end—instead of one that was hostile to the board. The courts, however, have not addressed a case where the board acts in a truly disinterested manner, granting the lockup to secure the highest bid.

In such a case, the business judgment of the board logically should be respected, particularly if the company has been shopped to other bidders who have had a chance to evaluate the company. Even in the absence of a shopping expedition, a strong argument can be advanced under the business judgment rule that the judgment of a well-advised and disinterested board should be respected. The practical problem is that the case probably won't arise unless another higher bid surfaces after the lockup is granted. If such a bid does arise, it will usually be conditioned on the court's invalidating the lockup, so a court will be hard pressed to find a reason to deny the shareholders the chance of getting the highest possible bid.

Will a lockup agreement subject the bidders to liability for short-swing profits?

A bidder will not be subject to short-swing profits under Section 16(b) of the Exchange Act unless the bidder beneficially owned more than 10 percent of the target's stock prior to the purchase of the stock pursuant to the lockup agreement. Once a bidder achieves insider status as a beneficial owner of more than 10 percent of the stock, all subsequent transactions will be subject to Section 16(b).

What should be considered when selling a large block of stock?

One of the most important considerations to a selling stockholder when selling a large block of stock is the duty of due care that such stockholder must exercise, which includes reasonable investigation of the potential purchaser. The courts have imposed liability on a controlling stockholder in circumstances in which such stockholder could reasonably foresee that the person acquiring the shares would engage in activities that would clearly be damaging to the corporation, such as looting, fraud, or gross mismanagement of the corporation. In planning a sale, a potential seller should fully investigate the potential purchaser's motive, resources, reputation, track record, conflicts of interest, and any other material items relevant to the transaction and the corporation.

A second consideration is the duty of loyalty that a controlling stockholder owes to the minority stockholders. This duty generally arises when a controlling stockholder is selling shares at a premium. For example, if a corporation owns a large quantity of a product that is in short supply and could be sold at above-market rates, a controlling stockholder may have a fiduciary obligation to refrain from selling shares at a premium on the theory that the shareholder's receipt of the premium would constitute a misappropriation of a corporate opportunity (that is, the stockholder would be appropriating a certain amount of the corporate goodwill). In addition, a few courts have imposed a requirement of "equal opportunity" on a controlling stockholder. This requires a controlling stockholder to offer all the other stockholders an opportunity to sell the same proportion of their shares as the controlling stockholder. Most courts have refused to apply this unwieldy principle.

Accordingly, if a block purchase is challenged, the courts will review the particular facts surrounding the purchase to determine its fairness.

If a merger or acquisition involves the issuance of securities to the target's shareholders, may such securities be resold freely, or are sales restricted?

Generally, such securities are similar to restricted securities in that Rule 145 under the Securities Act states that any party to a merger or acquisition transaction receiving securities is deemed to be engaged in a distribution and therefore to be an underwriter.

Because of this "underwriter" status it is necessary to use a Form S-4 registration statement to register securities issued to the target's security shareholders. This form is basically a wraparound of the proxy statement and permits the shareholders of the target who are noncontrol persons to sell without restriction. Control persons or "affiliates" must sell, however, either under the registration statement or in accordance with restrictions in Rule 144 under the Securities Act.

What are topping and bustup fees?

Although these terms are used interchangeably, they each have a special meaning. *Topping fees,* which were very common in the mid-to-late 1980s, are agreements with the target to compensate the buyer for potential losses if a new bidder usurps the deal. Because these fees are liabilities of the target, the winning bidder will have to bear their economic burden. This burden has the effect of increasing the cost of, and thus discouraging, other bids. Another arrangement is for the payment of *bustup* or *breakup* fees if the transaction is terminated by the target (other than for cause).

The fees are designed, at the very least, to reimburse the buyer for all its out-of-pocket expenses. More often, the arrangements include an additional payment for lost time and opportunity. The fees can be quite high—in the $20 million to $30 million range. In a large transaction (over $1 billion), usually they are in the range of 1 to 5 percent of the purchase price. The higher percentages apply to smaller and medium-sized public transactions ($50 million to $500 million).

Aren't bustup fees subject to legal challenge?

Yes. The size of the fee must not be so large that it substantially discourages other bidders or it may be struck down by a court as a disguised lockup arrangement. Provided that the fee is not excessive, under current case law it is very likely to withstand judicial scrutiny if the agreement to pay the fee is viewed as reasonably necessary to attract the bidder or keep it interested in the target in the face of competition. The defensibility of the fee will be enhanced if it is granted by the target in exchange for a "fiduciary out" clause (discussed below) or if the buyer permits the board to "shop" the company for a period of time, that is, to try and find other bidders. Note also that creditors—particularly in the case of companies that are in bankruptcy proceedings—may challenge such fees in court.[20]

What is a no-shop agreement, and when can it be used?

A *no-shop agreement* is a provision either in the acquisition contract or in a letter of intent that prohibits the board of directors from soliciting or encouraging other bids. It is always found in private company acquisition agreements and, far more often than not, in the acquisition agreement for public company transactions.

The buyer should always be expected to request such an agreement at the letter of intent stage, and the seller will usually agree to it if it has chosen the bidder as the result of either an auction process or a completed bidding war. Under certain circumstances, however—such as when the buyer is the first on the scene or is a member of management or a white knight (see below) whose bid was solicited to fend off a hostile takeover—such an agreement should be avoided or at least mitigated by adding a fiduciary out clause (see below) in the agreement.

Although there is no legal requirement that a company be shopped before a definitive agreement to sell is executed, the courts do not look kindly on no-shop provisions, alone or as part of a package (such as with lockups), when the effect of such provisions is to frustrate the role of the board as a neutral auctioneer or where they may result in a bargain price to corporate insiders, such as management. (See the discussion of MBOs above.) The absence of shopping, coupled with the existence of such provisions, may provide the basis for an argument that the price was not determined fairly, with the result that the transaction could be enjoined by a court at the behest of a competitor or an aggrieved stockholder.

In especially egregious situations, members of the board of directors can be subject to personal liability if the price is too low or the board has not performed its duties. (See *Van Gorkom* in the landmark legal case summaries in the back of the book.) When a board is required to defend the process and result as fair to the stockholders, the fact that it has unsuccessfully solicited better offers is telling evidence of the fairness of the transaction.

The buyer, of course, will argue that it needs the no-shop provision to avoid incurring expenses for a deal that doesn't succeed because the board attracts a higher bidder. The response: Give the buyer a bustup fee.

Finally, the board must determine whether the bidder will refuse to enter into the transaction without the no-shop clause. If so, and if the board is comfortable with the fairness of the price, the no-shop agreement may be advisable to secure for the shareholders the benefit of a good sale price.

Once the letter of intent stage is passed, the buyer certainly should expect a no-shop clause in the definitive agreement. Otherwise, why sign an agreement? Notwithstanding the clause in the agreement, because of its fiduciary responsibilities the board should avoid agreeing that it may not provide a competing bidder with the same information given to the buyer.

It is worth reiterating that the decision about whether to grant a no-shop agreement falls within the purview of the business judgment of the board of directors. Thus, the timing of the offer, the surrounding circumstances (hostile bidders, management buyers, and the like), other evidence of fairness, and the necessity of the clause to get the best deal for the stockholders all must be considered. There is no hard and fast rule.

What is a fiduciary out clause?

A *fiduciary out clause* is a provision in an acquisition agreement that enables the target to terminate the agreement in the event that a more favorable offer is made. The clause typically allows the board to back out of its obligation to recommend the agreement if the target company has received a more favorable offer. The clause gives comfort to the target without unduly binding the acquirer. Indeed, such a clause may be unnecessary because the board may have a fiduciary duty to refuse to continue its recommendation if a more favorable offer has been made. Furthermore, from a buyer's perspective, the insertion of a fiduciary out clause in an agreement may not matter, because if a clearly more favorable bid is made, the chances are great that the stockholders won't approve the buyer's offer or will refuse to tender their shares to the buyer in its tender offer.

INSIDER TRADING

Who or what is an insider?

An *insider* is an officer, a director, or a principal shareholder (generally, any beneficial owner of more than 10 percent of the company's equity securities).

An insider may also include any employee who, in the course of his or her employment, acquires material nonpublic information about a publicly traded corporation. These individuals owe a fiduciary duty to the employer and its securityholders not to trade on this information prior to its release and absorption by the market. The importance of this distinction became clear in June 1991, when the SEC extended its definition of insider to any "corporate employee performing important executive duties."

In addition, "outsiders" may become "temporary insiders" if they are given information in confidence solely for a corporate purpose. Attorneys, accountants, consultants, investment bankers, financial printers, and underwriters are examples of "temporary insiders" who are involved in a merger or acquisition.

Trading on inside information concerning mergers and acquisitions may be closely scrutinized by the SEC and may result in criminal prosecutions and very substantial civil penalties.

What laws prohibit insider trading?

Most insider trading cases are covered by one well-known rule promulgated by the SEC under authority of the Exchange Act, Rule 10b-5, which prohibits fraudulent or manipulative conduct in connection with the purchase or sale of securities. Holders of promissory notes may also sue under 10b-5, as the Supreme Court held in a case involving note holders in the Farmer's Corporation, an Arkansas company. The reach of 10b-5 on "Employment of Manipulative and Deceptive Devices" is very broad, but its text is extremely short. In its entirety it reads as follows:

> It shall be unlawful for any person, directly or indirectly, by the use of any means or instrumentality of interstate commerce, or of the mails, or of any facility of any national securities exchange:
> (a) To employ any device, scheme, or artifice to defraud,
> (b) To make any untrue statement of a material fact or to omit to state a material fact necessary in order to make the statements made, in the light of the circumstances under which they were made, not misleading, or
> (c) To engage in any act, practice, or course of business which operates or would operate as a fraud or deceit upon any person, in connection with the purchase or sale of any security.[21]

What other laws prohibit insider trading in a tender offer?

Rule 14e-3 prohibits trading on the basis of inside information in the context of a tender offer, whether as an insider or as the "tippee" of an insider. The Insider Trading Sanctions Act of 1984 sets penalties for these violations. Subsequent legislation has built on this bill, notably the International Securities Enforcement Cooperation Act of 1989, which became law in November 1990.

Also, Section 16(b) of the Exchange Act prohibits any officer or director, or any shareholder owning more than 10 percent of the issuer's stock, from profiting from a purchase and sale or a sale and purchase (a short sale) of securities of the issuer within a six-month period.[22] This is known as the short-swing profit rule. Any profits from such a purchase and sale or sale and purchase must be paid to the issuer. The short-swing profit rule applies whether or not that person was in possession of material inside information.

Can a shareholder who has exchanged his or her stock in a company for the stock of the company's acquirer sue for Section 16(b) violations?

Yes. In the 1991 case of *Gollust v. Mendell*,[23] the U.S. Supreme Court affirmed the legal standing of the plaintiff, a shareholder of Viacom International, Inc., to sue Coniston Partners for alleged 16(b) violations in connection with its 10 percent holding in the company, which was later merged into Viacom, Inc. (today part of Paramount, Inc.).

The Court ruled that the plaintiff's ownership of stock in the parent corporation, whose only asset was the stock of the issuer, gave it standing to sue. Securities tax specialists have noted, however, that "the Court's reasoning could result in the opposite outcome if a merger were solely for cash."

Isn't there a statute of limitations on suits like this?

Yes, but it's not necessarily retroactive for cases filed prior to June 1991. That is the date of the U.S. Supreme Court decision in *Lampf et alia v. Gilbertson* (1991).[24] This decision federalized statutes of limitation on securities fraud suits, which had ranged widely. It set a limit of three years after occurrence and one year after discovery. An amendment to the banking bill passed in December 1991, the so-called Bryan amendment, named after Senator Richard Bryan (Democrat, Nevada), denied retroactivity for this decision. The Bryan amendment preserved many of the securities lawsuits filed against bankrupt savings and loan officers and directors. Some courts have declared the Bryan amendment unconstitutional: They have applied and cited *Lampf* guidelines in dismissing some older cases filed before June 1991. Other courts have agreed to hear such cases, citing the Bryan amendment.

Must a tender offeror file under Section 16 of the Exchange Act?

Yes. Once a tender offeror becomes a beneficial owner of 10 percent of the target's securities, it is an insider for purposes of Section 16 and must file a Form 3 with the SEC within 10 days of becoming an insider. The amount and type of ownership interest of the offeror must be disclosed on Form 3. An offeror must file a Form 4 upon any subsequent change in its beneficial ownership of the target's securities. Form 4 must be filed within 10 days after the end of any month in which change in beneficial ownership occurred. Forms 3 and 4 must be filed with the SEC and the exchange on which the target securities are traded.

Are tender offerors subject to the requirement to disgorge short-swing profits established by Section 16(b) of the Exchange Act?

Yes. All persons required to file Forms 3 and 4 are subject to Section 16(b).

Are there any exemptions from Section 16(b) liability that apply to mergers and acquisitions?

Yes. Under Rule 16b-7 an insider is exempt from liability under Section 16(b) if it acquires or disposes of shares pursuant to a merger or consolidation of companies and one of the companies owns 85 percent or more of the combined assets of the other. Rule 16b-7 usually applies to second-stage mergers after completion of a partial tender offer. Also, a transaction that does not follow a typical sale-purchase or purchase-sale sequence may be exempt from the automatic liability provisions of Section 16(b).

"Unorthodox" transactions, such as option transactions, stock conversions and reclassifications, and mergers of a target into a white knight and other corporate reorganizations are frequently judged by a pragmatic or subjective test that may enable an insider to avoid liability when the automatic rules of Section 16(b) might otherwise apply. Under this alternative test, liability may be avoided if the insider did not have access to inside information or if the insider did not have a control relationship with the issuer of the securities.

Private actions are far more common in cases of Section 16(b) violations than Rule 10b-5 violations. The SEC does not enforce Section 16(b); rather, the statute gives the issuing corporation or a shareholder suing derivatively on behalf of the corporation the right to recover any profit made by an insider from purchases and sales, or sales and purchases, made within six months of each other. Section 16(b) provides for strict liability; that is, it requires that profits be disgorged without regard to whether the insider possesses any material nonpublic information.

What is the "disclose or abstain" rule, and how is it applied?

The "disclose or abstain" theory applies when an individual possesses material nonpublic information about a corporation and he or she owes a fiduciary duty to the corporation. The individual must either disclose the information to the market or abstain from trading in securities of the affected company. In the *Texas Gulf Sulfur* case of 1968, the Second Circuit Court in New York ruled that anyone who possesses material inside information must either strive to tell all (and trade if they wish) or tell nobody and refrain from trading. The precedent for these cases was a 1909 decision in *Strong v. Rapid.*

In practical terms, the disclose or abstain rule means *abstain*. To be effective, disclosure of a material development affecting a security must result in dissemination broad enough to inform the entire public trading in that security. Most individuals cannot adequately disseminate such information themselves, and disclosure itself may constitute a breach of fiduciary duty. If the inside information is incomplete or inaccurate, disclosure could be misleading to other investors and result in separate liability under other SEC disclosure rules.

What is the misappropriation theory, and how is it applied?

The *misappropriation theory* of liability holds that an individual violates the securities laws when he or she secretly converts information given to him or her for legitimate business or commercial purposes by trading on the information for personal benefit.

For example, in one highly publicized case, Dennis Levine, an investment banker who received material information concerning a client and traded in securities of that client on the basis of that information, was found to have violated a duty to his employer and to the client not to use that information for his personal benefit. Under the misappropriation theory, Mr. Levine traded illegally on insider information.

The Supreme Court upheld the misappropriation theory of liability in a case involving *Wall Street Journal* reporter R. Foster Winans. Winans was charged with, among other offenses, violating the securities laws by misappropriating information from his employer, even though the information was not about his employer and was not used to trade in his employer's securities. In the Winans case, the misappropriated information was the content and timing of publication of Winans's influential "Heard on the Street" column in *The Wall Street Journal* about market information. The High Court's decision was hailed by then–SEC enforcement chief Gary Lynch as "an affirmation of our insider trading program."

How do Rule 10b-5 and Rule 14e-3 relate?

Rule 10b-5 has been used alone or with other rules such as Rule 14e-3 to prosecute insider trading cases. Until recently Rule 14e-3 was never used alone. In September 1992, however, the SEC filed 14e-3 charges against seven people who allegedly traded in Pillsbury Co. stock during a bid by Grand Metropolitan in 1988. This was the first case in which 14e-3 was used apart from 10b-5.

What if a tippee has no fiduciary relationship to the source of confidential information—does this mean that he or she can still be charged with insider trading?

That is correct. Traditionally, the more distant tipping was, the harder it was to prosecute, in part because of the lack of an implied fiduciary duty. Two landmark cases exemplified this principle. In the 1980 case of *Chiarella v. The United States,* the Supreme Court reversed the insider trading conviction of Vincent L. Chiarella, a financial printer who construed target names from confidential documents and traded on that information. The Supreme Court cleared Chiarella because, it said, there must be a confidential relationship, or fiduciary duty, between a defendant and another person, and Chiarella had no duty to the sellers of the stock he had bought.

The development of the misappropriation theory (discussed above) strengthened this theme of fiduciary duty. The Insider Trading and Securities Fraud Reform Act of 1988 affirmed this theory, "but only in 10b-5 cases."[25]

In a 1983 decision, the Supreme Court ruled that financial analyst Raymond Dirks did not commit illegal insider trading by advising clients to take actions based on inside information. The Court said that the duty of a tippee depends on whether the source of the tip has breached a legal duty to the shareholders in communicating the information. Both of these decisions have helped defense attorneys to protect fourth- and fifth-level tippees.

But these two cases were decided for the defendant in part because they were brought under Rule 10b-5. New use of 14e-3 as a threatened tool of prosecution could change this.[26] Another factor is passage of the Securities Law Enforcement Remedies Act of 1990, which strengthened the SEC's power to exact civil penalties in insider trading cases. The 1998 case of *SEC v. Warde* shows the long arm of the law in this respect.[27]

Can an insider be convicted of insider trading if the insider is unaware that information he or she is trading on is material and confidential?

Traditionally, the answer has been no. Section 10(b) has a *scienter* requirement. This means that to be found liable for violating Rule 10b-5, an insider must have either "actual knowledge" of the fraud or omission or have acted with "recklessness and disregard of the truth." Furthermore, judicial interpretation of 10b-5 has often centered on the issue of fiduciary duty of the tipper to the issuer of the securities or some other party. But another key insider trading rule, Rule 14e-3, does not contain such a requirement.

How does Rule 14e-3 operate?

Rule 14e-3(a) prohibits an individual from trading while he or she possesses material nonpublic information concerning a tender offer if the individual knows or has reason to know that such information is nonpublic and has been obtained, directly or indirectly, from any of the following: the entity making the tender offer, the corporation that is the subject of the tender offer, any persons affiliated with these entities, or any person acting on behalf of either entity. The transfer of such information from a tipper to a tippee violates laws against tipping.

What is tipping?

Tipping is the selective disclosure of material nonpublic information for trading or other personal purposes.

What is a tipper?

A *tipper* is a person who, in return for some direct or indirect benefit, provides material nonpublic information to another person who then trades in that security.

What is a tippee?

A *tippee* is a person who receives material nonpublic information about a security and then trades in that security. Note that a tippee may also become a tipper if he or she then divulges the information to another person (who becomes a second- or third-level tippee). This area of law is still evolving.

What about a fourth-level tippee?

In general, the more distant the tipping is, the harder it is to prosecute, as seen in the continuing saga of fourth-level tippee Robert Chestman. In May 1990 a three-judge appellate panel in Manhattan threw out a previous conviction, finding no violation of Rule 14e-3. In October 1991, however, a judge reinstated the conviction, ruling that insider trading can occur even when the defendant hasn't been explicitly informed that the information was confidential.[28]

What laws prohibit tipping?

Courts have interpreted Rule 10b-5 to prohibit tipping, although the rule does not address the issue directly. Rule 14e-3, which supplements Rule 10b-5, does contain an antitipping provision that applies in the context of a takeover. However, neither of these rules contains the term *tipping*. The Insider Trading Sanctions Act of 1984 also imposes civil penalties for tipping.

How does Rule 10b-5 treat tipping?

Tipping is only prohibited by Rule 10b-5 if two tests are met: (1) The tipper has breached a duty that he or she owed to the corporation or its shareholders (for example, a fiduciary duty to a company and its shareholders as an officer and director); and (2) the insider will receive a personal benefit, directly or indirectly, from the disclosure.

If the tipper gains no personal benefit, can he or she still be accused of tipping?

No. But the interpretation of "benefit" is very broad. Obvious examples of personal benefit include not only monetary gain but also any enhancement of the tipper's reputation that might translate into increased future earnings. However, the Supreme Court has stated that divulging inside information to a relative or friend who then trades and returns a gift or a portion of the proceeds resembles trading by the tipper himself.

Under Rule 10b-5, must a tippee have such a fiduciary relationship with the tipper?

No, the typical tippee has no such relationship. However, if the tippee knows or should have known of the tipper's breach of duty and participates in the violation through silence or inaction, the tippee becomes liable as an aider and abettor if he or she then trades or divulges the information to one who trades.

How does Rule 14e-3 treat tipping?

In contrast to Rule 10b-5, Rule 14e-3(d) contains clear antitipping provisions in the context of tender offers (although even in Rule 14e-3, the word *tipping* is not used). Rule 14e-3(d) makes it unlawful for certain persons to "communicate material, non-public information relating to a tender offer . . . under circumstances in which it is reasonably foreseeable that such communication is likely to result in [improper trading or tipping]." This portion of the rule expressly excludes communications "made in good faith to certain individuals."

When are the antitipping provisions of Rule 14e-3 triggered?

Rule 14e-3 is triggered when any person has taken a "substantial step" to commence a tender offer, even if the offer never actually begins. A "substantial step" includes the offeror's directors voting on a resolution with respect to the tender offer; the offeror's formulation of a plan to make an offer; arranging financing for a tender offer; authorizing negotiations for a tender offer; and directing that tender offer materials be prepared.

What penalties may be imposed for insider trading?

Damages for violation of Rule 10b-5 are limited to actual damages. However, additional charges are usually made in insider trading cases. In general, insider trading may result in criminal penalties of up to $100,000 and five years in jail, or both, if the trading is found to be a willful violation of the Exchange Act or of SEC rules and regulations promulgated under the act. In addition, the Insider Trading Sanctions Act of 1984 gives the SEC the authority to seek a civil money penalty of up to three times the amount of profit gained or loss avoided by insider trading on a national securities exchange or through a broker or dealer in violation of federal securities laws. Damages are limited to actual damages.

In addition to the civil penalty for insider trading, the SEC may seek ancillary relief, including a court order enjoining the violator from future violations, plus disgorgement of profits resulting from the illegal trading. The disgorged funds may be paid into an escrow account so that private parties damaged by the insider trading can be compensated for their losses.

Suppose a tipper or tippee doesn't make money?

This can make a court more lenient, since the amount earned is one factor that courts, particularly appellate courts, weigh in rendering decisions.

Who typically engages in illegal insider trading?

In the late 1980s, the chief culprits appeared to be investment bankers, which is not surprising given their constant exposure to inside information and many opportunities to trade. A *New York Times* article summarizing government cases against inside traders as of November 30, 1987, names a preponderance of investment bankers in a mix of professions: one takeover lawyer (Ivan K. Reich), one securities analyst (Randell D. Cecola of Lazard Frères), one stockbroker (Boyd L. Jefferies of Jefferies & Co.), two arbitrageurs (Ivan F. Boesky and his associate, Michael Davidoff), and five investment bankers (Dennis B. Levine and Martin A. Siegel of Drexel Burnham Lambert, Robert M. Wilkes of Lazard Frères, Ira B. Sokolow of Shearson Lehman Brothers, and David S. Brown of Goldman Sachs). This tally does not include the "Yuppy Five" ring that involved a mix of young law firm and investment banking associates, or junk bond developer Michael Milken, who was formally charged with insider trading in January 1988 but was never convicted of it.[29] But not all those accused of insider trading are investment bankers, and not all accusations stick.

"Insider traders"—both tippers and tippees—come from all walks of life. Anyone with access to confidential inside information can tip, be tipped, or act alone. Insider trading case defendants indicted in recent years include not only control participants in the M&A process, such as investment bankers, arbitrageurs, consultants, and attorneys, but also their assistants, such as secretaries and paralegals. Corporate chief executives and their outside directors are also occasionally found guilty of this practice, along with their "tippee" relatives and in-laws. In one case, men installing a security system to protect confidential files used such confidential information to trade. Financial printers are another susceptible group.

Perhaps the most unusual—and egregious—case of insider trading was that of a psychiatrist who enriched himself through information provided unwillingly by an executive's wife under his "care."[30]

FINANCING THE PUBLIC TRANSACTION

Is the financing of a public company acquisition very different from the financing of the acquisition of a private company?

The financing of a one-step transaction, involving the merger of an acquiring company into the target, is essentially the same as the financing of any other acquisition (see Chapter 4). The financing of a two-step acquisition (a tender offer followed by a merger of the acquiring company into the target) is somewhat different.

How is the financing of a two-step transaction different?

The financing of the first step, the tender offer, is subject to Federal Reserve margin rules. These rules generally prohibit lenders, including banks, brokers, and others, from making loans secured directly or indirectly by "margin" stock (most publicly traded stock) if the loan exceeds a specified percentage of the value of the collateral (generally, 50 percent).

For example, if the acquisition subsidiary intends to acquire stock of a target worth $100 million in a tender offer, the maximum secured loan that can be made would be $50 million. This means that the other $50 million has to be financed by other than secured loans, such as unsecured debt or equity investments. The unsecured loans may be, for example, "bridge loans" from investment bankers or privately placed debt. Assets of the target are, of course, not available to secure the financing until after the merger.

It is important to know that the margin rules apply even to indirectly secured debt; the substance, not the form, of the transaction will govern the application of the rules. Therefore, if the borrower has no assets other than the target stock and has agreed with the lender not to pledge the stock to any other lender, the loan may be deemed to be indirectly secured by the stock.

If the acquisition subsidiary is a shell corporation, can it freely incur unsecured debt and not violate the margin rules?

No. The position of the Federal Reserve is that if lenders make unsecured loans to a shell subsidiary for purposes of a tender offer, the loan will be presumed to be secured by margin stock subject to the 50 percent of value limitation. There is an important exception to this rule: The presumption does not apply if a merger agreement with the target is signed prior to the closing of the tender offer. Thus, in the case of a friendly two-step transaction, it is important that a merger agreement be signed before the tender offer in order to facilitate the financing of the tender offer. If there is no merger agreement, the amount that can't be financed under the margin rules may have to be financed by preferred or common equity or by loans guaranteed by other entities that have substantial assets.

What is "going private"?

Going private means getting out of public equity markets. More technically, it is a Rule 13e-3 transaction in which certain of the existing stockholders or affiliates of a public target become stockholders of the entity surviving the acquisition of the target and the target is no longer subject to Section 12(g) or Section 15(d) of the Exchange Act. Because certain stockholders may be on both sides of the transaction, Rule 13e-3 attempts to provide additional disclosures to the public stockholders in order to demonstrate the overall fairness of the transaction. Such disclosures include full-blown discussions of any fairness opinions and appraisals obtained in connection with the transaction and statements by the target as to the fairness of the transaction.

Determining whether a particular transaction may constitute a 13e-3 transaction largely depends upon the percentage of stock that the existing stockholders own in the target or the relationship of such affiliates to the target and the percentage ownership that such persons may have in the surviving entity. If a public company goes private and then goes public again, this is called a "reverse leveraged buyout." Reverse LBOs are discussed in Chapter 4.

CONSIDERATIONS APPLICABLE TO HOSTILE ACQUISITIONS

What does the directors' duty of loyalty require when responding to an unsolicited tender offer?

When considering the response to an unsolicited tender offer, the board of directors of a target corporation owes a duty of loyalty to the corporation's shareholders to adopt defensive measures to defeat a takeover attempt that is contrary to the best interests of the corporation and its shareholders. However, the board must be careful to adopt defensive measures only when motivated by a good-faith concern for the welfare of the corporation and its shareholders.

Does it violate the duty of loyalty if a board adopts a defensive tactic in part to retain management control?

No. Defending a corporation against hostile takeovers to maintain control, among other motives, does not violate the duty of loyalty. However, it is improper if a director's sole or primary motive for implementing a defensive tactic is to retain control of the company.

What steps should a board of directors consider after it decides to reject a tender offer?

If the directors determine that it is in the company's best interests to reject a tender offer or defend against a potential tender offer, the directors' duties of due care and loyalty would require that they have taken into account the following kinds of considerations:

- The present and future impact of defenses on the value of the company's stock
- The ability of the company to pursue a negotiated transaction with friendly bidders (white knights) if the defensive measures are implemented
- The reasonableness of the defenses in relation to the threat posed

It is very important to document the decision-making process in this regard. As the Wyatt Company of Chicago noted in its 1998 survey of director and officer liability, companies with a history of merger, acquisition or divestiture activity are more likely to experience a claim against their directors and officers than were companies that have not had such activity.[31]

On what basis can directors reject an acquisition offer?

There are generally three reasons why an offer can be rejected and defenses implemented: (1) The offer is inadequate (that is, the target company's directors have information that enables them to make a reasonable judgment that the company's outstanding capital stock is worth more than what is being offered)[32]; (2) the offer is unfair in that those stockholders not tendering their shares will receive less consideration at a later date (such as in the case of a front-end-loaded, two-tier offer); or (3) the company determines that it is better served by remaining independent.

Can directors sell their shares of the target company to an acquirer without violating their duty of loyalty?

Directors have the right to deal freely with their shares of stock and to sell them at the best price they can, as long as they act in good faith. "Good faith" means that the director does not misuse confidential information or usurp any corporate opportunity. A director has no duty to disclose his or her stock dealings to the corporation (except in certain required public filings), nor does he or she have a duty (outside of an agreement to this effect) to offer the shares to the corporation before selling them.

This relative freedom to trade in company stock, as long as it is traded in good faith, applies even when a director of a target corporation decides to sell his or her shares of stock of the target corporation to a hostile acquiring company. A director of a corporation also has the right to use his or her company stock to effectuate and promote a third-party takeover of the company.

In *Treadway Companies, Inc. v. Care Corp.* (1980), a director of the target corporation failed to disclose to management that he had sold his stock and had subsequently advised a third party of the suitability of making a tender offer. The court held that he breached no duty to the corporation or its shareholders. Moreover, since he was not a controlling shareholder, he had no duty to account for any premium received from the sale of his stock.

The court also found that the director breached no duty by failing to disclose his contacts with the third party and his knowledge of the third party's intention to seek control. Even if he betrayed the trust placed in him by incumbent management, this was of no legal significance. Management—as distinct from the corporation and its stockholders—had no legitimate claim to a director's allegiance.

The plaintiff in this case also claimed that two other directors breached their duty of loyalty by placing the third party's interest in obtaining control above any interest of the corporation. However, the court held that a director does not necessarily breach any duty owed to the corporation by promoting an offer that is likely to result in a change of management, as long as a takeover is not in any way adverse to the best interests of the shareholders. Even if the target company's board of directors, as a whole, determines that the takeover would not be in the best interests of the corporation, each director is "under no duty to follow management blindly." Instead, each director is under a duty to exercise his or her own best judgment on the corporation's behalf. Therefore, a director may, in certain circumstances, oppose the majority of the board and support a hostile tender offeror's efforts to win control.

What defenses are commonly adopted against hostile takeovers?

Takeover defenses can be classified generally as antitrust defenses, restructuring defenses, "poison pills," charter and bylaw amendments, defensive sales or acquisitions, and defensive payments. State antitakeover statutes can also play an important role in defending against a hostile takeover.

ANTITRUST DEFENSES

What is an antitrust defense?

In a typical *antitrust defense,* the target accuses a bidder of violating antitrust rules by tendering for it. For example, target Square D Company obtained a delay in a takeover bid by Schneider S. A. of France by claiming the two companies were in the same market segment—electrical products.[33]

Can bidders for a public company be sued under antitrust laws because of their relationship?

No. In April 1991 the Supreme Court let stand a ruling that federal antitrust laws do not apply to alleged agreement between bidders of a company up for sale. The case involved two bidders—R. H. Macy & Co. and Campeau Corp.—for Federated Department Stores Inc. The plaintiffs argued that the two bidders had in effect divided the company between them. Even though Campeau "won," Macy also got what it had sought.

RESTRUCTURING DEFENSES

What are the main types of restructuring defenses?

Common restructuring defenses include recapitalizations, self-tenders, and master limited partnerships.

How do recapitalizations work?

A recapitalization substitutes portions of the outstanding capital stock held by the public with cash, debt instruments or securities, or preferred stock. These transactions may increase the percentage of voting stock held by management and employee benefit plans. They may also increase ownership levels of individual stockholders who retain their stock instead of selling into the company buyback. (Indeed, a recapitalization has been likened to a public LBO because the number of outstanding shares decreases as they are purchased by the company, thereby increasing the percentage holdings of remaining stockholders.)

There are basically three ways to accomplish a recapitalization:

- Through a tender offer for the company's own stock.

- Through a transaction such as a merger, where a subsidiary merges into the company when the plan becomes effective.
- Through a reclassification amendment of the company's charter. (This requires shareholder approval and may involve the issuance of options to shareholders to purchase shares of the recapitalized company upon the occurrence of certain events.)

It is also sometimes possible to issue massive dividends to stockholders, financing such a transaction through debt. Any one of these actions can cool off even the most ardent of pursuers.

Each type of recapitalization has its advantages and disadvantages. In a tender offer situation, speed is the primary advantage because no stockholder vote or proxy statement is required. The company may also issue securities without filing a registration statement with the SEC because Section 3(a)(9) of the Securities Act permits the exchange of securities without registration if it only affects existing securityholders, and no remuneration is paid for soliciting the exchange.

Recapitalizations have generally withstood court challenges. However, courts will not uphold recapitalizations that appear coercive, that is, leave the stockholders without a real option to decline participation.

How can a company recapitalize using an employee stock ownership plan (ESOP)?

An ESOP may be used as a tool in a recapitalization (see Chapter 7). An ESOP purchases stock in the open market or from the company, allowing its employees and management to own part of the company. By borrowing to acquire the shares, an ESOP can help finance a recapitalization; it can also purchase shares directly from unrelated parties at a premium, which allows it to purchase shares from a hostile bidder. The disadvantage of ESOP participation is this: It can dilute the public's percentage of ownership in the company if the company issues new shares to the ESOP.

An ESOP is managed by trustees who have the duty to act in the best interests of its beneficiaries. If the trustees are also the company's directors, a hostile bidder may assert a conflict of interest by the directors and question their motives for initiating an ESOP during a takeover attempt. The suggestion would be that the directors, as trustees, implemented the ESOP not to further the interest of the beneficiaries, but to fend off the bidder and preserve management.

There may also be a conflict of interest issue when the ESOP is in place before a hostile bid, if the trustees decide to purchase more of the company's stock immediately preceding or during such a bid. However, if the trustees can justify their decisions on the basis of acting in the best interests of all the ESOP's participants and demonstrate the requisite detached judgment, legal challenges can be overcome.

What are some of the concerns involved in a recapitalization?

A company that has undertaken a recapitalization that has caused it to become highly leveraged or cash-poor may no longer have the financial resources to weather unexpected economic conditions or even to carry on its intended business. The recapitalization plan that engenders such consequences is subject to not only state laws but also the federal fraudulent conveyance and transfer laws and the Federal Bankruptcy Code (see Chapters 4 and 11). Creditors and stockholders alike may contend that the company has become insolvent or is no longer able to function with the remaining working capital, or that the company has incurred debts that are beyond its capacity to repay. Many fraudulent conveyance suits have been filed as a result of the overleveraging of the 1980s and are still being filed in the 1990s.

Most states impose limitations upon a company's ability to make dividend distributions and to repurchase or redeem its own stock if such transactions would impair the company's capital. These corporation statutes may affect the kind of recapitalization a company might initiate.

How do self-tenders work?

A self-tender is a defensive measure implemented to defeat an unsolicited tender offer or at least to obtain a higher price. The company announces its intentions to repurchase its own outstanding stock, or a portion thereof, to prevent the offeror from acquiring a controlling interest in the company. Stock repurchases are seldom effective as a defensive tactic if not combined with other techniques, such as stock purchases by management, by ESOPs, or by other major stockholders, which tend to lock up substantial blocks of stock in friendly hands.

Self-tenders, like other tender offers, are regulated by the federal securities laws. In 1986 the SEC adopted an amendment to the tender offer rules to prohibit discriminatory self-tenders. Rule 141-10 requires that all holders of the same class of stock be treated in the same way; that is, the same offer must be made to all stockholders, whether they are hostile bidders or not. The company is also required to accept all shares tendered to it, including a hostile bidder's shares.

How can open market repurchases dissuade hostile takeovers?

By repurchasing its own shares on the open market without making a formal tender offer, not only can a company boost its level of ownership, crowding hostile acquirers, but it can also maintain or increase its stock prices and thereby make itself less attractive to a bidder. Such purchases, whether financed by cash flow, asset sales, or borrowing, tend to reduce the benefits of a potential buyer while increasing the burdens.

What legal considerations are there in a repurchase?

In implementing a repurchase plan, directors must satisfy the business judgment rule and comply with various other state and federal laws, including, in particular, Rule 10b-18, which regulates the purchase of registered equity securities by an issuer.

How can a master limited partnership be used as a takeover defense?

A company may preserve stockholder values, and even increase stockholder values, by placing crown jewels in a master limited partnership and distributing limited partnership interests to all shareholders. This would make it more difficult for an acquirer to obtain the long-term benefits of such assets. Such a distribution requires substantial disclosures under the federal securities laws. Also note that ongoing state and federal reforms to limited partnership laws have weakened the value of this defensive strategy.

POISON PILLS

How do poison pills work?

A poison pill, the nickname for what is technically called a shareholders' rights plan, involves the issuance to stockholders of rights to acquire securities.

These rights can be exercised only under certain circumstances (such as a take-over attempt) and may be redeemed by the company at a nominal price until the occurrence of such events. Poison pills is to give management in tender offers negotiating leverage, which they can use to avoid unfair treatment of stockholders (in coercive two-tier takeovers or partial tenders) by ensuring a minimum price in any takeover.

Although poison pills normally do not require stockholder approval, shareholders at some companies have put forth successful proxy resolutions recommending a change in company bylaws to require shareholder approval of their company's shareholders' rights plan, or redemptions in full. Such shareholder proposals are by no means rare, but they rarely succeed.[34]

There are two common kinds of poison pills: flip-over and back-end. These may be combined in one defensive plan. Less frequently seen, and not described here, are chewable, convertible preferred stock, dead hand, flip-in, and voting rights poison pills.

The use of poison pills as a defensive measure has generally been upheld by courts, but some plans have been enjoined because of their specific provisions and purposes. In implementing these plans, directors must be able to prove that the measure was adopted in good faith after reasonable investigation and is reasonably related to the threat posed.

What is a flip-over plan?

In this plan, each common stockholder receives for each share owned a right to purchase shares of the surviving corporation upon the occurrence of a triggering event. Triggering events are typically the acquisition by a single purchaser or group of a specified amount of stock or the commencement of a tender offer for a specified percentage of the company's stock. Following the occurrence of a triggering event, the company issues certificates to stockholders that allow them to exercise and trade their rights. Because the rights issuance is in the nature of a dividend, it does not generally require shareholder approval, although company bylaws may mandate this.

The rights usually allow the certificate holder to purchase stock of the surviving entity for half price after the merger has been consummated, so the effect of the flip-over is to reduce the acquirer's equity. There is a plus and minus here. Because the rights usually may be redeemed for a nominal amount before the triggering event (and often within a short period of time thereafter), a bidder has an incentive to negotiate with management before the actual takeover attempt. But there is a catch: Once the takeover bid has occurred and the rights become redeemable, they may adversely affect the company's ability to negotiate with a white knight, as they would dilute the white knight's future potential equity.

Thus a flip-over plan should also include a provision that a transaction approved by the directors will not result in the stockholders' rights becoming exercisable even though the triggering events have occurred. Such a provision allows the company to seek a white knight.

What is a back-end plan?

A back-end plan is similar to a flip-over plan, although its objectives differ. Holders of the company's common stock receive a right for each share owned that entitles them, upon the occurrence of certain triggering events (for example, a 20 percent acquisition by a bidder), to exchange each share for a note that matures typically within a short period of time (such as one year). Alternatively, the right may be exchanged for cash or preferred stock, or a combination of the three. The value of the right may be fixed at the outset or may be calculated from a formula based on the highest price per share paid or offered by a bidder during the takeover attempt.

The purpose of the plan is to maximize stockholder value in the event of a merger or business combination by ensuring a minimum acceptable price and to protect stockholders from the adverse effects a significant minority interest can have on other bidders even if no merger results. A back-end plan is not designed to prevent a takeover but to ensure a proper negotiated value for the company and its stockholders.

The plan will usually provide that the rights will not be exercisable if the acquirer, upon reaching a certain level of ownership, offers to purchase the remainder of the outstanding shares at the price set by the plan. The rights are usually redeemable for a specified period of time (for example, 120 days) to allow a bidder to express its intentions to complete the transaction as specified.

Such a plan will likely be upheld by the courts if (1) it is not designed to prevent all takeovers, (2) the back-end price is reached with the advice of investment bankers and reflects the realizable value over the plan's life (for example, one year), (3) the plan is a reasonable response to the threat perceived by the directors (for example, a possible second-step merger), and (4) the plan is "plausibly related to the goal of shareholder wealth maximization."

CHARTER AND BYLAW AMENDMENTS

How do charter and bylaw amendments help companies deter takeovers?

Charter and bylaw amendments will generally not prevent takeover attempts, but they do provide protection from coercive and abusive acquisition tactics. These amendments may also slow down the acquisition process, giving the company's directors more time to react and negotiate. Proposed amendments must be approved by stockholders, and they almost always are. In recent years, however, shareholders of several companies have denied management the support required to initiate or maintain such defensive measures.[35]

Any amendments adopted by the stockholders will apply equally to the company's management and any bidder who acquires shares. There is another important consideration in adopting amendments: If the stockholders reject the proposals, the company may seem—and indeed may be—more vulnerable to takeovers by bidders.

What kinds of defensive charter and bylaw amendments are there?

The most widely used charter and bylaw amendments include supermajority provisions, fair price provisions, contingent cumulative voting provisions, staggered board provisions, defensive consent requirements/notice of business and special meetings provisions, and special classes of stock.

What are supermajority provisions?

A company may adopt a charter amendment to require more than a simple majority (a supermajority) of its stockholders to approve certain matters, such as any merger or business combination. There are several effective variations of this defense, one of which is a requirement that a majority of the disinterested stockholders—a majority of the minority—approve the transaction. To protect the supermajority provisions, there should be a provision that would require a supermajority to modify the supermajority provisions of the charter.

What are the drawbacks of supermajority provisions?

One of the disadvantages of supermajority provisions is that they apply to friendly as well as hostile takeovers. Therefore, to the extent such provisions may deter hostile bidders, they may also make it more difficult to negotiate a friendly takeover. As a partial cure, such a provision may be coupled with one specifying that a simple majority is sufficient if the directors approve the merger.

Some companies can find themselves stuck with supermajority provisions that are unnecessarily broad. Sometimes managements have tried to eliminate supermajority vote requirements but have failed to get the two-thirds vote that was required to do so.[36]

What are fair price provisions?

A *fair price provision* is a variation of a supermajority requirement that would require a specified supermajority to approve a proposed merger unless the bidder pays the minority stockholders a fair price. Usually a fair price means a price that equals or exceeds the highest price paid by the bidder in acquiring shares of the company before the merger. The purpose of this provision is to ensure fairness to stockholders in a two-tier acquisition.

How does contingent cumulative voting work as a defense?

Cumulative voting permits a stockholder to vote the number of shares owned by him or her multiplied by the number of directors being elected; all of a stockholder's potential votes may be added together and cast for a specific director.

Contingent cumulative voting, if coupled with a staggered board of directors (see below), may provide the minority stockholders who disfavor the merger with a tool to block or delay the election of a slate of the bidder's directors. For example, a charter amendment may provide that when and if a bidder acquires a certain specified percentage of the company's stock (for example, 35 percent or more), cumulative voting goes into effect. In this case, the minority stockholders may be able to elect or retain more directors than if the charter amendment were not in place.

What effect does a staggered board have on a target company?

The election of directors on a staggered basis—usually one-third of the directors are elected each year for a three-year term—prevents a bidder from electing a new slate of directors in a single meeting of stockholders and thereby gaining immediate control of management.

By itself, the staggered board (or "classified board") provision would not deter a takeover, but in conjunction with contingent cumulative voting, staggered elections may give a company more flexibility in dealing with unwanted bidders.

Unfortunately for some managements, stockholders are not always willing to approve staggered board provisions.[37]

How do "consent requirements" provisions work?

Many states' corporation laws provide that a majority of stockholders may, without calling a meeting, act by written consent. A company that does not amend its charter to provide otherwise may be susceptible to a bidder acquiring a majority interest and then immediately amending its charter to remove other impediments to control.

To combat this possibility, the company may, by charter amendment, eliminate the written consent provisions entirely or require that all stockholders consent before actions can be approved without a meeting unless state law prohibits the elimination of the consent procedure. If the consent procedure cannot be eliminated, the company may consider amending its charter or by-laws to require stockholders wishing to take action by written consent to notify the board of directors and request that it establish a record date to determine which stockholders are entitled to sign a consent. The passage of such an amendment would also permit the directors a reasonable opportunity to prepare a response and oppose the proposed action, by soliciting proxies, if necessary. Such an amendment might also contain specified periods for consent revocation and consent validity.

What about special classes of stock?

Until 1988 many corporations defending against takeovers created special classes of stock that gave superior voting rights to management. In that year the SEC approved Rule 19c-4, the so-called one-share, one-vote rule banning such a technique, and some exchanges—the New York Stock Exchange and NASDAQ—have similar rules. In 1990 in *Business Round Table v. SEC,* the U.S. Court of Appeals for the Second Circuit overturned Rule 19c-4, and companies have now returned to this practice.

How does confidential voting fit in all of this?

Confidential voting is one of several causes célèbres for many shareholders, especially these who want to vote against management without detection. Some 160 companies now have confidential voting policies—often because of pressure from shareholders.[38]

Another popular type of shareholder resolution is the rescission of the antitakeover devices listed above. Note, however, that larger institutional investors are moving away from piecemeal confrontation and toward unseating entire boards—or working behind the scenes for voluntary changes.[39]

DEFENSIVE SALES OR ACQUISITIONS

What kinds of defensive sales are there?

A company may radically downsize a crown jewel to avoid being taken over, or sell its stock to a white squire or white knight.

What is radical downsizing?

Radical downsizing occurs when a company virtually liquidates itself through massive sell-offs.[40]

What is the crown jewel defense?

The *crown jewel defense* is the sale of particularly attractive assets by the target company to dissuade a bidder from pursuing its takeover attempt. Such sales may also give the company flexibility and resources to fend off a bidder by generating capital and/or reducing costs. On the other hand, if a bidder is interested in a specific asset, such as a subsidiary, and is willing to acquire the entire company for it, the asset may be very valuable to the company as well, and its sale may be detrimental over the long term.

As discussed earlier, courts will generally view with disfavor an asset or crown jewel sale or lockup that has the effect of stopping or discouraging the bidding process.[41]

What is a white squire?

To remain independent, the company may determine that its best course of action is to sell a large block of its stock to a friendly investor, a *white squire*, that the company does not believe is a threat. The more well-known white squires are investment vehicles such as Warren Buffet's Berkshire Partners or Goldman Sachs's GS Capital Partners L.P., but white squires can also be operating companies. The obvious danger here is that relations between the white squire and company may take a turn for the worse, and the white squire may decide to acquire control of the company at a later date.

To prevent the white squire from becoming a hostile bidder, companies typically use standstill agreements. A standstill agreement imposes certain limitations on the investor that assure the company that the stock will not find its way to a hostile bidder. Typically, the stock purchase agreement will limit the percentage of stock the white squire may acquire in addition to the shares in question for a specific period of time. It will also contain restrictions on the resale of the minority interest to third parties, which is usually coupled with a right of first refusal by the company. The voting rights relating to the block of shares sold also may be limited.

The directors' decision to enter into such an arrangement and the provisions of the standstill agreement will be evaluated under the business judgment doctrine. These arrangements are generally upheld if the court finds that entrenchment is not the directors' sole or primary purpose.

What is a white knight?

A *white knight* is a friendly acquirer sought by the target as a positive alternative to a hostile acquirer. Unless the friendly acquirer pays as much as or more than a hostile acquirer, however, this kind of defensive sale is vulnerable to legal challenge.

What is in it for the white knight?

White knights can make money in the right deal. A. Alfred Taubman, for example, made an estimated profit of $275 million on his gallant purchase of Sotheby's Holdings, Inc., the auction house.[42]

May a company make an acquisition or agree to a merger to avoid being acquired?

Yes. A company may combat an unwanted bidder by acquiring other companies or divisions that make it less attractive to the bidder. The company may also acquire assets that may precipitate an antitrust problem for the bidder if the transaction is completed. The effectiveness of antitrust barriers is mitigated by the fact that government agencies are generally willing to consider proposed curative measures by the bidder [that is, a promise to sell the unit(s) in question] before rejecting a merger.

This same defense can be used in merger form. When Paramount wanted Time, Time merged with Warner Corporation in a successful attempt to flee its suitor. In the landmark case of *Paramount, Inc. v. Time, Inc.* (1990), the court used the business judgment rule to uphold this merger.

What is the Pac-Man strategy of defense?

When a company learns it is the object of a tender offer, it may respond by tender-offering for the stock of the hostile bidder. In this eat-or-be-eaten strategy, named after a video game popular in the early 1980s, the company undertaking the counter tender offer thereby concedes that the business combination is desirable but indicates that it should control the resulting entity. It also forgoes certain defenses it might otherwise bring, such as antitrust and other regulatory barriers that concern the legality of the combination.

The disadvantages of the Pac-Man defense are that the original target company's stockholders will not receive any premium (the original target company may actually give the other company's stockholders a premium), it is very costly, and it may damage the company, even if successful.

When considering the legality of this defense, courts will apply the business judgment rule. In *Bendix Corp.*, Martin Marietta countered Bendix's tender offer by tendering for shares of Bendix. As Martin Marietta's majority stockholder, Bendix contended that the company's directors breached their fiduciary duty by disregarding the wishes of their majority stockholder (that is, Bendix) in purchasing Bendix stock. The court decided that Martin Marietta's directors owed a fiduciary duty to Bendix stockholders, not to Bendix as a corporate entity, and that Martin Marietta's directors had fulfilled their fiduciary duties because the business rationale spurring them to acquire Bendix was in the best interests of the Bendix stockholders.

An interesting legal question not answered by this case is whether this co-ownership situation would be prohibited by state subsidiary voting provisions. For example, the Delaware statute provides that a subsidiary may not vote the stock of its parent. Therefore, if both companies were deemed to be subsidiaries (and parents) of one another, the majority of each company's stock would be nonvoting.

DEFENSIVE PAYMENTS

What kinds of defensive payments may a target make?

Two ways to spend a company out of immediate danger are greenmail and golden parachutes. Both, however, entail risks.

What are the potential risks of greenmail as a takeover defense?

Bidders sometimes accumulate stock and threaten to initiate a tender offer with the ultimate purpose of reselling those shares to the company at a premium rather than obtaining control of the company. Greenmail is a payment to purchase such stock at a premium.

Paying greenmail is largely ineffective in protecting the interests of the target (other greenmailers may surface once the company has succumbed the first time), it is discriminatory (other holders of the same class of stock may not share in the premium), and it is legally questionable: There have been stockholder lawsuits with various degrees of success to recover greenmail payments as corporate assets. Furthermore, greenmail is relatively unpopular with stockholders. So-called antigreenmail provisions were very popular in the late 1980s. Although few succeeded, they did send a message.

Finally, greenmail payments are expensive. Not only are the premiums high, but they may be taxable. Section 5881 of the Internal Revenue Code imposes a 50 percent excise tax on greenmail payments, payable by the recipient. The tax is imposed not only upon cash payments by the target to purchase the greenmailer's stock, but also on other, more disguised payments constituting consideration for the stock, such as reimbursement of the greenmailer's related transaction expenses or purchases of other assets of the greenmailer. It can also be imposed on payments made by related parties, such as a white knight, and thus tends to compel a defeated raider to sell out to an independent holder, such as an arbitrageur, rather than to a party controlled by or acting under agreement with the target.

The effect of all these developments has been to decrease greatly the incidence of greenmail in recent years.[43]

What are golden, lead, and tin parachute payments?

These are the nicknames given to severance payments promised to top management, middle management, and workers, respectively, in the event of their dismissal during or immediately subsequent to a change of control.

Aren't these parachute payments also unpopular with stockholders?

Yes, and increasingly more so, because stockholders, who often oppose such payments, get advance warning of them through compensation disclosures in the proxy statement. In recent years, the percentage of shareholders voting against parachutes has been rising.[44]

RELATED STATE LAWS

What provisions of state law limit director and officer liability for defensive measures?

Charter opt-in provisions authorize corporations to pass a charter or bylaw provision eliminating or reducing the personal liability of directors for money damages. This provision is particularly significant in takeovers, since many shareholder suits against defensive target boards do request money damages.

Several states have raised the threshold of liability to require more than proof of simple negligence by board members. Gross negligence, or recklessness, generally must be proved by the plaintiff for personal liability to attach.

One state (Virginia) has established a money damage "cap" (except in cases of willful misconduct or knowing violation of criminal law or state securities laws), which is the lesser of:

- The monetary limit approved by the stockholders in either the charter or bylaws

■ The greater of (1) the amount of compensation received by the individual from the corporation during the 12 preceding months or (2) $100,000

This provision has been challenged as unconstitutional and is unlikely to be adopted by other states.

Other provisions protecting directors include expanded indemnification for derivative suits against the board, expanded provisions permitting corporations to provide benefits other than indemnification, and provisions that permit directors to base their decision to reject an offer on considerations other than price, for example, the effect of the transaction on the community and other corporate constituencies.

How many states have passed antitakeover statutes, and what kind of statutes are they?

As of mid-1998, over 40 states had passed antitakeover statutes.[45]

State antitakeover statutes may offer one or more of several protections. In order of popularity, these are control-share requirements, nonstockholder/nonmonetary considerations, business combination freeze-outs, fair price provisions, poison pills, antigreenmail provisions, labor contract or severance pay requirements, cash-out requirements, recapture of profits, and, most rarely, classified board mandates for staggered terms of board service.

Aren't antitakeover statutes usually overturned?

Court decisions for or against state antitakeover statutes seem to go in cycles. Prior to the 1982 decision of *Edgar v. MITE,* 37 states had antitakeover statutes, all of which were overturned by the decision. Then, in 1987, the *CTS* v. *Dynamics Corporation of America* case reversed the *MITE* decision. In this landmark decision, the court upheld states' "authority to regulate domestic corporations, including the authority to define the voting rights of shareholders."[46]

What is a control share statute?

Most recent statutes are patterned after the Indiana Control Share Acquisition Act of 1986. In this and many other statutes—totaling 28 now—acquirers of over a specified percent (for example, 20) of the outstanding stock will have voting rights only if a majority of disinterested shareholders so vote.

Pursuant to the Delaware statute, Section 203 of the Delaware General Corporation Law, no acquirer owning more than 15 percent of a publicly held company's stock can commence any business combination within three years of the stock acquisition unless (1) the directors approve the proposed business combination; (2) the acquirer owned 85 percent of the stock before the combination was proposed; or (3) the directors approve the combination on or after the date of the combination, and it is authorized at an annual or special stockholders' meeting (but not through written consents) by a vote of at least 66 percent of the disinterested shareholders.

Antitakeover statutes apply generally to corporations organized within the state. However, some states (for example, Massachusetts) have statutes that say companies not incorporated in the state will still be subjected to the statute's provisions under certain circumstances. In the case of Massachusetts, companies qualify for protection if they have substantial operations there (such as executive offices), if the bulk of their workforces or assets are in the state, if at least 10 percent of the shares are owned by state residents (excluding brokers or nominees), or if 10 percent of the shareholders reside in the state.

What about nonstockholder/nonmonetary considerations?

Statutes in 30 states impose a different standard of care on directors in evaluating any business combination. Directors must examine and consider the long-term effects of an offer on the company, its stockholders, the affected community, and other corporate constituencies.[47]

What about freeze-out provisions?

At least 28 states have enacted statutes for business combination freeze-outs. These statutes state that acquirers must wait a certain period—from two to five years—before completing the second step of their desired merger with resistant targets, under a defined supermajority vote for the merger initially. Delaware's freeze-out law suspends any merger for three years unless the board approves it or the acquirer obtains 85 percent of the stock in its initial tender offer.

What is a fair price statute?

At least 27 states have approved fair price statutes or fair price provisions within freeze-out statutes. These require any bidder who is rebuffed by a board to pay a defined fair price to all shareholders unless a supermajority approves the bid.

How do poison pill and antigreenmail provisions work? Aren't these areas usually covered through the proxy process?

Poison pill provisions, offered in 23 states, authorize corporate boards to enact shareholders' rights plans. Without such authorization, poison pills may not be instituted or may be more vulnerable to legal attack by regulators and/or shareholders.

Conversely, antigreenmail provisions, adopted in seven states, effectively ban, rather than protect, another popular antitakeover measure. These bar the repurchase of a specified percentage of shares at a premium from an investor who has held the shares for less than a specified amount of time, unless the same premium is offered to all shareholders, or all shareholders approve it.

How common are the other types of antitakeover statutes, such as provisions governing labor contracts?

The remaining types of antitakeover statutes or provisions are relatively rare, with five or fewer states having them. Five states—Delaware, Illinois, Massachusetts, Pennsylvania, and Rhode Island—have adopted statutes or provisions forcing acquirers to honor labor contracts, the last three providing severance pay for employees who lose their jobs as a result of a takeover. Three states—Maine, Pennsylvania, and South Dakota—have adopted cash-out provisions requiring the acquirer of a certain percentage of a company's shares to buy the shares of remaining shareholders at a statutorily defined fair price.

Two states—Ohio and Pennsylvania—have statutes allowing companies to recapture the profits of bidders who put them "into play" by buying their shares and reselling them within 18 months. Finally, one state—Massachusetts—requires all companies incorporated in that state to have staggered terms for their boards of directors.

Do any states ban specific antitakeover practices?

At least two states—Arizona and Minnesota—have enacted statutes prohibit-ing companies from granting nonroutine increases in compensation such as golden parachutes or special bonuses while a tender offer is open.

CONCLUDING COMMENTS

With so many rules, regulations, and risks, public company acquisitions are not for the novice. Fortunately, however, the reasons underlying securities laws are basically sound, and studying this area can be rewarding profession-ally as well as financially to advisors and dealmakers alike. Knowing the tech-nicalities of public company M&A adds perspective and color to the work of those who wish to master the art of M&A.

E N D N O T E S

1. In previous chapters, we have, for the most part, avoided using the term *target* because of its unflattering connotations for sellers. In this chapter, however, we bow to overwhelming usage of this term in the public company arena.
2. For example, in June 1996, homeowners in the Valley of Lakes Development were granted class action status to sue PNC Bank Corp., NA, in a RICO suit. PNC inherited the problem when it acquired another bank (First Eastern Corp. of Scranton).
3. RICO is used in some 2,000 cases against accountants and lawyers annually. Defendants almost always challenge RICO charges, however, and convictions are rare.
4. In late 1991, when Eastman Kodak Co. organized an acquisition subsidiary to acquire Image Bank, its target negotiated for weeks without knowing who was behind "JS Acquisition Corp."
5. In November 1991 U.S. magistrate Leonard A. Berkinow in New York said USX improperly accepted shares tendered after its announced deadline in a battle for control of Marathon Oil Company in 1981.
6. As there is no clear definition of the term *tender offer,* practitioners are well advised to assume that if securityholders need the protection of the securities laws and the transaction would constitute a tender offer under the SEC's proposed definition, a court would find the rules governing tender offers applicable.

7. For example, by longtime *Mergers & Acquisitions* magazine contributor Dr. Douglas Austin of the University of Toledo in Toledo, Ohio.

8. The power of rumor accounts for the short-term run-up in target company stocks, before a bid announcement, but even if the bid does not materialize, the speculation may be just the motivation target company management needs to improve its performance. For a discussion of the "kick in the pants" hypothesis, see J. Fred Weston, Kwang S. Chung, and Juan A. Siu, *Takeovers, Restructuring, and Corporate Governance* (Upper Saddle River, NJ: Prentice Hall, 1998) p. 79.

9. Indeed, according to a May 1991 study by Goldman Sachs limited partner Barrie A. Wigmore entitled "How Can We Explain the Growth of the S&P 500 in the 1980s?" at least 12 percent of the 226 percent jump in growth stock prices during the 1980s could be attributed to tender offer premiums.

10. Edward V. "Ned" Regan, then-Controller, State of New York, "Institutional Investors: Are Their Demands Justified?" Speech given at the Annual Corporate Governance Review of the National Association of Corporate Directors, October 12, 1992.

11. Ibid.

12. This is especially true if the takeover aggressor fails to achieve control. For example, the stock of Pirelli S.P.A. of Italy lost one-quarter of its value in one day when it decided not to acquire Continental AG of Germany. This was partly due to the indemnities against loss that Pirelli promised allies. Sometimes the acquirer's stock goes up, but not by very much. When Hanson P.L.C. announced plans in 1991 to buy Beazer P.L.C., Hanson's stock went up by 37.5 cents, Beazer's by $2.25.

13. "Notice of Offer to Purchase for Cash All Outstanding Shares of Common Stock of Bohemia Inc. at $24 Net per Share by B Acquisition Corp," *The Wall Street Journal,* Wednesday, August 28, 1991, p. C-15.

14. As *Business Week* has noted (in a June 10, 1991, article), "the technique of betting on stock market declines by selling borrowed stock, with the idea of replacing it later at a cheaper price, is the traditional preserve of 'smart money.'"

15. *Regulation of Communication among Shareholders,* Securities and Exchange Commission, October 16, 1992 17 CFR Parts 240 and 249. Release Nos. 34-31326; 1C-19031; File No. S7-15-92. RIN: 3235-AE12. Our description of the 1992 rules draws on an October 20, 1992, client memorandum by Robert Rosenbaum, Partner, Arnold & Porter, Washington, D.C. Updated material is based on *Regulations 14A and 14C: Solicitation of Proxies Under the Securities Exchange Act of 1934* (New York: Bowne & Co., Inc., 1998, published July 9, 1998).

16. Items 4(c) of Forms 14-K, 10-Q, , and 10-QSB, and Item 21 of Schedule 14A.

17. "Executive Compensation Disclosure," SEC, October 16, 1992 17 CFR Parts 228, 229, and 249. Release Nos. 33-6962; 34-31327; 1C-19032. RIN: 3235-AF34.

18. No doubt because of the wide judicial interpretation of such principles, in February 1992 RJR Nabisco Inc. agreed to pay $72.5 million to former shareholders and employee stock option holders in connection with its alleged failure to disclose a takeover bid in the months before its October 1988 leveraged buyout (at $25 billion, the world's largest). Note also that in April 1991 the SEC instituted an enforcement action—*SEC v. Paul Borman*—against Borman Inc.'s CEO for denying the existence of merger talks during a rise in its stock two weeks before the company's merger with Atlantic & Pacific Tea Company. Borman consented to the entry of a court order barring "further violation of securities laws."

19. *In re George C. Kern, Jr.,* Exchange Act Rel. No. 29, 356 (June 21, 1991). A discussion of this "Kern Commission Opinion" appears in a client memo dated July 1, 1991, by Harvey L. Pitt and Dixie L. Johnson of Fried, Frank, Harris, Shriver & Jacobson, Washington, D.C.

20. For example, in late 1991, creditors of Integrated Resources Inc. announced plans to appeal a bankruptcy court ruling that granted a breakup fee to suitor Bankers Trust New York Corp. ($1.25 million to $6 million).

21. *Exchange Act Rules, Vol. IV: Rules 16a-1 Through 31-1: General Rules and Regulations Under the Securities Exchange Act of 1934* (New York: Bowne & Co., Inc.: 1998, published September 15, 1998).

22. Note that this rule applies only to insiders. It is not to be confused with short selling.

23. *Gollust v. Mendell,* No. 90-659 (June 10, 1991), as described in a June 11, 1991, client memo from D. A. Neff and D. M. Silk of Wachtell, Lipton, Rosen & Katz.

24. For the full citation to *Lampf,* see the table of cases at the back of the book. See also *First Republicbank Corp. v. Pacific Mutual Life Insurance Co.* (1994).

25. Harvey L. Pitt and Karl Groskaufmanis, *An Analysis of the Insider Trading and Securities Fraud Enforcement Act of 1988,* November 1, 1988.

26. In February 1992, the SEC exacted the promise of a settlement from Peter D. Garvy, a tippee of B. F. Saul III, son of B. F. Saul II, head of Chevy Chase Savings Bank. In September 1992 the SEC filed a civil lawsuit against 18 people who traded in the securities of Motel Co., including defendants who were even five levels removed from the original source of the information.

27. *S.E.C. v. Warde* appears in the Table of Cases.

28. For an early discussion of the case and others, see "Prosecutorial Indiscretions and Reversals of Fortune," by Harvey L. Pitt, Dixie L Johnson, and Anthony J. Renzi of Fried, Frank, Harris, Shriver & Jacobson, New York, July 19, 1991. See also the "Rule of Law" column by L. Gorden Crovitz, *The Wall Street Journal,* July 24, 1991; Paul Vizcarrondo, Jr., and Theodore N. Mirvis, "The 'Chestman' En Banc Decision," *New York Law Journal,* October 24, 1991.

29. Insider trading was alleged in at least 30 cases filed against Milken prior to his April 1990 guilty plea and was mentioned in his indictment, but Milken never admitted to this practice. Ellen Joan Pollack and Ann Hagedorn, "Milken Faces Myriad Suits," *The Wall Street Journal,* April 26, 1990, p. A-2.

30. Whatever your profession, please note: Engaging in insider trading can cost you hundreds of thousands of dollars in law fees, loss of income, huge fines, jail time, and loss of professional reputation and even practice. Modern computer trading makes detection and proof much easier for enforcement authorities.

31. See the *1998 Watson Wyatt Worldwide Directors and Officers Liability Survey* (Chicago: Watson Wyatt Worldwide, 1998).

32. Indeed, directors have been sued—but not always successfully—for accepting an inadequate offer. In mid-1991, two shareholders of Intermec Corp. filed a motion for a preliminary injunction against the completion of a $24-a-share tender offer for the company by Litton Industries. The shareholders claimed that Intermec directors breached their fiduciary duty in agreeing to the offer at a price below Intermec's true value.

33. For more about the antitrust defense, see the antitrust section of Chapter 1.

34. For a thorough discussion of acquisition techniques (and, by extension, defensive techniques) using a partnership or limited liability company, see Martin D. Ginsberg and Jack S. Levin, *Mergers, Acquisitions, and Buyouts: A Analysis of the Governing Tax, Legal and Accounting Considerations* (New York: Aspen Law and Business, 1998), Section 1401, p. 14-1ff.

35. See current issues of *IRRC Corporate Governance Bulletin.* The bulletin is published by the Investor Responsibility Research Center, Washington, DC.

36. Ibid.

37. Ibid.

38. Ibid.

39. For example, the California Public Employees Retirement System (CalPERS) has reduced its practice of targeting firms for proxy action in favor of negotiating.

40. One controversial (and fortunately unusual) example of this was the case of DeSoto, Inc., a print manufacturer that liquidated 80 percent of itself and paid its key managers huge severance agreements while maintaining control of the company.

41. One of the impediments to full competition for Harcourt Brace Jovanovich was the publishing firm's inclusion of a crown jewel clause in its merger agreement with General Cinema. The clause promised that if Harcourt sold itself to another buyer within four months after terminating the merger agreement, it would sell its Academic Press Division to General Cinema for a set price ($390 million).

42. Floyd Norris, "'White Knight' at Sotheby's Cashes in Part of His Stake," *New York Times,* June 12, 1992.

43. Note, however, that in February 1996 directors of Chrysler Corporation, under proxy-fight pressure from Kirk Kerkorian, found it necessary to pass a provision forbidding payment of greenmail.

44. *IRRC Corporate Governance Bulletin,* op. cit., note 35.

45. "From the Hustings: The Roll of States with Takeover Control Laws," *Mergers & Acquisitions,* September/October 1998, pp. 44ff. The ultimate source of information on state antitakeover law, and the primary source for the *M&A* article, is the Investor Responsibility Research Center, Washington, D.C.

46. For an insightful contemporaneous account of this decision, see A. A. Sommer, Jr., "One Share, One Vote: the SEC Stumbles," *Director's Monthly,* October 1988, pp. 1ff.

47. Interestingly, these considerations may also be cited to defend—rather than resist—a merger. In public announcements of its mergers, NationsBank (recently merged with BankAmerica) typically states that the mergers will benefit bank "customers" and "communities," not just stockholders.

CHAPTER 13

M&A in Family Businesses, Partnerships, Franchises, and Nonprofits

INTRODUCTION

In the minds of many, the art of M&A is practiced primarily by investment bankers serving multibillion dollar companies traded on public stock exchanges. In fact, the vast majority of M&A transactions involve smaller entities, many of them privately held. The typical U.S. deal is worth not billions of dollars, but less than $40 million.[1] Moreover, most deals involve private companies, which are by far the most common type of company (often estimated at 98 percent of all businesses). Buyers looking to acquire a company will have a far wider field of choice if they include nonpublic entities.

Simple mathematics makes the point. Every year, the U.S. Internal Revenue Service receives tax returns from four basic categories: individuals, sole proprietorships, partnerships, and corporations. Adding together every category except individuals (in other words, all the business entities, however defined) gives us approximately *20 million entities* generating business income. The most dominant type of company is the sole proprietorship, followed by corporations (of which only 15,000 are publicly traded) and partnerships. Even if we subtract half the sole proprietorships to exclude the smallest tier—self-employed individuals and the like—we still have a good *15 million* to consider. And among these 15 million are 300,000 private American businesses with revenues over $5 million—including more than 45,000 private American businesses with revenues over $25 million.[2] Add to that the *millions* of entities (charities, churches, foundations, and so forth) that have succeeded in obtaining nonprofit status, and the size of our nonpublic M&A universe quickly becomes apparent.

The lesson is clear: Any executive or professional hoping to master "the art of M&A" must be acquainted with the fundamentals of not only public companies, but the legions of other entities that form our national and world economy—including family businesses, partnerships, franchises, and nonprofits.

FAMILY BUSINESSES

What are family businesses, and how common are they?

There are two common definitions of *family businesses*—one based on ownership, the other based on management:

- The ownership definition says that a family business is a pool of capital owned or controlled by a family. This broad definition includes not only businesses commonly thought of as family businesses (the mom-and-pop or parent-and-child small businesses owned by families) but also widely held public companies that have significant family ownership (e.g., Campbell Soup, Ford Motor Company, and Marriott International)—a large minority of all public companies. It also includes nonoperating pools of capital controlled by family offices, family limited partnerships, and grant-making family foundations.[3]
- The management-based definition says that a family business is any business in which two or more officers are related by blood or marriage. This universe is smaller than the ownership universe, but in some senses it is more meaningful to a merger-minded buyer looking for operating companies to acquire.

The two definitions overlap in many cases: Family-managed companies are usually family-owned, and family-owned or -controlled companies are often family-managed. Thus in our view, the most practical definition mentions both aspects. We would define a family business as an operating company *managed, owned,* or *controlled by members of an extended family.*

What is the most common problem in the M&A area faced by owners of family businesses?

The most common problem is whether to grow the company or to sell it. And the decision depends very much on the answers to the following questions:

- Is the family name of value in doing business?
- Do we have a business plan?
- Do we have a plan of succession—especially who will be the next CEO?
- If yes, has he or she been trained for the job?
- Will the family agree to let a non-family "outsider" come in as CEO?
- Will we give the outsider an equity position?

If the predominate answer is no, then the company probably should be sold.

How does one go about selling a family-owned company?

Very carefully! Remember that most buyers have heavy experience in buying companies, while most sellers of family businesses have little or none.

What are the most important steps?

Remember the Boy Scouts' motto: "Be prepared." That preparation is generally called "due diligence." Here are the most important steps:

- *First,* obtain the services of a qualified appraiser. Although appraisers are not certified by local or national governments the way accountants, doctors, engineers, and lawyers are, they can be certified by professional associations, as explained in Chapter 2.
- If you are incorporated, make sure that you have a good set of corporate books. (Or if you are not incorporated, *do* incorporate and create such a set.) Many businesspeople do not know that this does not refer to the books of account, but to the key legal documents such as the articles of incorporation, the minute books, stock transfer sheets, and by-laws, which, in the case of many incorporated family businesses, are either incomplete, missing in whole or in part,

or badly out of date. Sellers should know that when tax time comes, the first books the IRS wants to see after a sale are the corporate books. They want to know who owned what, and when and why the company was sold. So put your corporate books in order and make sure that the state franchise taxes have been paid.

- Make sure the books of account are up to date and accurate and that someone internal to the company understands them and can answer questions about them. For instance, the way that many family businesses have handled inventory suddenly becomes important after a sale. It will be one of the first things that the IRS will look at. It is also one of the first things that a buyer wants to know about, because where there is undervalued inventory, much of the negotiation revolves around who will take the tax hit, buyer or seller.

- Make sure that no one lies. Not about anything: not about numbers of customers, returned merchandise, or lawsuits. Sellers have a tendency to minimize the negatives and magnify the positives. Then, when the buyer's due diligence kicks in and the seller's misrepresentations are discovered, it makes further bargaining more difficult, delays the deal, and, in some cases, kills it outright. Remember, failure to state a material fact in a securities transaction is considered to be fraud—not only civil fraud, but in some cases, criminal. So it's really best to lay out all the bad things right up front. If the buyer is still there when you're finished, you'll probably have a deal. Besides, if you point out what's wrong and the buyer says he or she can fix it, it raises the value of the company! This is even more true when a buyer, seeking to knock down the value of the company, points out things that are bad: "At my company we never do things like that." The seller should immediately tell the buyer that the price is going to be raised because the company is worth more to a buyer who can run it (or believes he or she can run it) more efficiently than the seller can.

- Be sure that you have a business plan including projections of sales, profits, and cash flows. But watch out for the "hockey sticks"—those graphic projections of sales and profits that suddenly turn up a few years out. Only in turnaround situations should this be allowed, and the seller had better have solid support for the numbers.

- Finally, make sure that just one person is authorized to negotiate the sale—not necessarily to close it, but to negotiate it. There really is no such thing as an effective "negotiating team." Why? Because an experienced buyer will zero in on the least knowledgeable or weakest member of such a team and will win concessions that get impounded in the final price.

Should sellers of family businesses use a professional intermediary to negotiate the deal?

Yes. Anyone can act legally as an M&A advisor—even your next-door neighbor or your brother-in-law—both of them, incidentally, bad choices. The real problem is this: Just because you built the business, you think you know how to sell it. And this is a dangerous assumption.

But if I need help, where do I go?

The best negotiators are those who understand the industry in general and the company in particular and have experience in negotiating deals. These negotiators may be accountants, attorneys, consultants—or almost anybody (except a friend or relative—that's almost always a bad idea). Here are some rules to help you in your selection.

- Make sure that the intermediary is licensed if he or she is to act as a "business opportunity broker" rather than as a consultant or "finder."
- Be sure to have him or her sign a confidential disclosure agreement before disclosing anything about the company—including the fact that it might be for sale.
- Make sure the intermediary is experienced and insist on getting the names of firms and principals that the intermediary has helped. And check them all out. Many marginal deal-doer wannabes will tell you that secrecy restricts them from giving references. This is rarely true. Many deal-doers specialize in M&A activity by industry. Some specialize in drug stores; others, printing plants; others, publishers; others, radio and television stations; and so forth. If you don't already know, discover who they are in your industry. One of them can usually get you the best price.

- Make sure there are no conflicts of interest, actual or potential. An expert in radio stations might be on retainer to find good deals for a longtime buyer and might sell you out.

- Make sure he or she has an office and a staff, is familiar with books about M&A like the one you are reading, and subscribes to various M&A-involved periodicals. Beware of "investment bankers" with only a desk and a telephone answering service. And if the person you are considering wants real money up front, be especially careful. (This latter caveat does not apply where it is necessary to get appraisals of real estate, machinery, etc.)

- Be sure that any fee agreement is carefully drawn and unambiguous as to how the amount of the fee is to be calculated, who pays it—the buyer or the seller—and when and where it is to be paid.

- Be aware that while many sellers want to stick the buyer with the fee, it's usually the seller that needs the advice. With the buyer paying the fee, your intermediary may be more interested in the buyer's welfare than yours. And the courts will back the intermediary because he or she may owe a fiduciary duty to the fee-payer to negotiate in the buyer's interest rather than in yours. The accounting rules might come into play, for that fee may not be deductible as an expense to a seller but may be for a buyer. That could affect the price.

- Finally, make sure that before you cut a deal with an intermediary, he or she agrees to have any prospective purchaser sign a nondisclosure agreement before the prospect is given any information—especially the name of the company for sale. And make sure that you are copied for each and any of those agreements.

What are some typical underutilized assets of family businesses?

- Established product or service lines that give them steady cash flows well in excess of those needed to support their continued existence or growth

- Excess production capacity

- Surplus of management coming from either shutdown or soon-to-be-shutdown operations

- A distribution/customer universe eager and able to take on new products or service lines
- Trademarks that can be transferred to new product or service lines
- Underused or unused bank lines
- An installed base of equipment that can be mined for peripheral and add-on sales
- Good supplier relations
- New, protected technology that can be broadly applied

What are some typical lacks that family business can cure by M&A?

- Weak or ineffective marketing and distribution systems—they need partners. (This is typical of high-tech companies.)
- A shrinking market for their core products—they need to grow.
- High seasonality, with capital, warehouses, and plants used only part of the year—they need to find their "other half."
- High cyclicality—they need a defensive entry.
- Heavy union presence—they need a nonunion entry.
- Domestic markets only—they need to go international.
- Single industry—they need to diversify.
- Weather-dependency—they need to diversify geographically.

Please refer to Chapter 2 for a further explanation of the strength/weakness problem and the Wheel of Opportunity and the Fit Chart constructs.

PARTNERSHIPS

Are the answers to the above questions any different for partnerships than they are for family businesses?

The answer is a qualified no. Why qualified? First, because many family businesses are organized in simple partnership form where each of the partners, regardless of his or her share of benefits in the enterprise, has the same exposure to the liabilities as the other partners. This is very unfair to non-family members, because the risk/return ratio is out of balance. This is why many old-style partnerships have been converted to some form of limited liability partnership[4] or to a limited liability corporation. The risk/reward ratio should be in proportion to ownership.

How do I sell my shares in a limited liability partnership?

With great difficulty! Trading in the shares of limited liability partnership interests has been difficult because there is no auction market. Estates and trusts that need to sell their LP shares must rely on one-on-one negotiations—always a difficult proposition.

In order to solve this problem, the Chicago Partnership Board (CPB) was formed in February 1988 and started operations that June. In February 1992, open-bid outcry auction processes were formalized and the number of transactions effected rose to nearly 10,000 in 1996, with dollar volume reaching $35 million. Unfortunately, CPB filed for the equivalent of Chapter 7 bankruptcy with the Securities Investor Protective Corporation in December 1997. The creation of a "secondary market" for such securities is very badly needed. It is hoped that something like CPB will reemerge soon in some form or other.

Also, many major partnership-interest holders (some deals had tens of thousands of partners) have converted their holdings to equity in a phenomenon called a "rollup" where the partnership interest is traded in for common, preferred, or other equities—usually at a substantial discount over the cost of their original investment. Often the rollup is created and run by the investment bankers who sold the partnership securities in the first place. These bankers have been criticized for extracting exorbitant fees in the process. (Partnership rollups are not to be confused with strategic rollups—the current very popular serial consolidation movement where a large number of independent operations such as funeral homes, real estate agencies, and other stand-alone units in highly fractionated industries are brought together under common ownership.)

In view of the troubles with the CPB, what is the future for LLPs?

According to a piece in *Business Week* (July 8, 1997) entitled "Back from the Dead: Limited Partnerships," the market for the sale of limited liability partnership units (LLPs) has good, long-term prospects. The article lists some 16 firms that trade in such securities—though none appear to offer open-outcry auctioneer services, as did the Chicago Partnership Board.

FRANCHISES

What exactly is a franchise?

The phenomenon of franchising is a U.S. invention. A franchise is a company that shares products or services—usually protected by trademarks, service marks, trade dress, or other indications of exclusivity—with franchisees by giving them the right to exploit those protected products or processes for a period of time in accordance with a well-defined format, all as outlined in a franchise agreement, in return for a franchise fee and a royalty stream.

Franchising is not an industry. It is a business relationship and had its beginnings in the automobile manufacturer/dealer relationship. Later, petroleum refiners established similar relationships with gasoline retailers. According to the authoritative web site www.franchise.org, there are some 3,000 franchiser companies and some 500,000 outlets in the U.S. today.

There are three forms of franchise ownership:

- First is the standard franchiser/franchisee relationship.
- Second is the franchiser/franchiser relationship, where the franchiser owns its own franchisees.
- Finally, there's what is called *conversion franchising,* where existing businesses such as real estate brokers become franchised outlets of some central organization.

The standard form of franchising is seen in the fast-food business, which has many "single-unit" franchisees, which might have as many as three outlets. Many of these grow to be multi-units—sometimes with dozens and even hundreds of units. Some of these may even have started off as multi-unit franchisees because they bought up rights to large geographical areas and then subfranchised individual units—either self-owned or independent.

The franchiser/franchisee financial relationship is multifaceted. Some franchisers are heavily involved in financing their outlets. It is simply more efficient for a franchiser organization to raise money from the public and lend it to potential franchisees than it is for myriad franchisees to borrow from banks. The problem is this: Franchisers are not bankers. And the criteria for credit approval are diluted by the prospect of franchise fee and royalty cash flows. Further, the usual "discipline of debt" element that brings a modicum of rationality to day-to-day entrepreneurial decision making may be lost when the lender is a kind of parent.

Some franchisers profit by selling their franchisees parts or raw materials, avoiding anti-trust problems by claiming (and rightly) that they need to control "quality." Further, most franchisers, at the risk of stifling the entrepreneurial imperative to be "different," or the need to respond to local preferences, run smack up against the franchiser imperative to impose uniformity to preserve the franchise's "image." However, the thrust of most franchiser/franchisee relationships is to produce a true "partnership" where there is a considerable amount of give and take and mutual sharing of ideas and innovations so that all can share in their joint success.

What kinds of products or services do the fastest-growing franchises sell, and how much do these franchises cost to start up?

As mentioned earlier, fast food tops the list. Of the 20 highest-growth franchises cited annually by *Entrepreneur Magazine,* typically half are in the fast-food arena. The fastest-growing franchise (and a prototype for many) is McDonald's, which has a start-up fee of over $360,000. Most other franchises cost far less, except for KFC, which asks for nearly $1 million up front from franchisees.

But fast food is by no means the only high-growth franchise. Almost any type of product or service can be franchised. Here is a list of popular franchised industries, in order of growth rates: commercial cleaning (Jani-King), professional tools and equipment (Snap-On Tools), windshield repair (Novus Windshield Repair), commercial office cleaning (Coverall Cleaning Concepts), residential real estate brokerage (Coldwell Banker Residential Affiliates), and postal services (Mail Boxes, Etc.). Entry prices here, not counting franchising fees, which vary widely, range from a low of about $200 (for Coverall Cleaning Concepts) to a high of nearly $70,000 (for Mail Boxes, Etc.). For more on the strategic aspects of franchising, see *Franchise Your Business,* available on-line at www.franchise.org. (Click on resources/business.)

How does one go about selling or buying existing franchised operations?

With great difficulty. The franchiser/franchisee agreement has very strict rules about the transfer of ownership. The most restrictive of these is the clause that says that the franchisee can sell out only to the franchiser. Next is the "first re-fusal" option where the franchiser has the right to match any bona fide offer. Further, the rules barring hypothecation, partnership survivor, advertising units for sale, and so forth, are particularly restrictive. For more information, see "Buying or Selling an Existing Franchise Outlet" (salesdoctors.com/franch/fran12).

What other M&A worries are there in franchising?

Mostly franchiser hype. Get a copy of *Beyond Franchising Hype* by Ann Dugan of the University of Pittsburgh *and read it!* (smallbiz.sunycentral.edu/faq/franchising/hype).

Can franchisees expand by the M&A route?

Most franchise agreements ban the merger or consolidation of franchised units without franchiser permission. Franchisers worry that a strategic "buildup" or "rollup" by franchisers will result in a franchisee group powerful enough to challenge the franchiser in court, alleging that the basic contract is unfair. Many highly successful franchisees have historically been allowed to buy out the weaker sisters. Obviously, it is in the interests of both the franchiser and the franchisee to consider M&A. If the best franchisees operate as many units as they can, this yields economies of scale and increased profits for the franchisee and decreased supervisory costs for the franchiser.[5] However, only certain kinds of franchised operations lend themselves to cashing these bene-fits—namely, those that require high levels of financing, inventory, and/or skill levels.

How would a franchisee go about a consolidation program?

Assuming that there are benefits to be extracted by consolidation—or a rollup of a number of multi-unit franchisees into one larger whole—a business plan should be developed and financing sought—not only for the financing itself, but for the discipline that the financing source will bring to the operation. However, if making money depends on a high level of entrepreneurial ef-fort—including long hours—the merger route may not be the way to go.

Do franchisees ever take over franchisers?

Yes. While rare, it is often successful. One example is Relax the Back. Dairi M. Johnson, a former IBM executive with back problems, bought four franchises and soon had $5 million in annual sales. He thought the basic idea had more merit than the founders did. So he found two institutional investors who agreed with him and together they bought out the franchiser for $6 million.

What about those "bundling" deals where two or more franchisees join together?

It looks as though such "co-branded" outlets will be a permanent feature of some of the larger chains. One reason is this: The growing popularity of drive-through eating has left extra dining space, and franchisees need to pay the rent. *Co-branding,* where franchisees share a "store," may be the answer. Here are some examples: White Castle (hamburgers) and Church's Chicken; Taco Bell and KFC; Wendy's and Tim Horton's (baked goods). This last joining worked so well that Wendy's soon bought out Horton's.

A similar phenomenon has yet to be proved out as McDonald's opens hamburger stands in Amoco and Chevron gas stations. And now that Pepsico has spun off all its restaurant operations—Taco Bell, KFC, and Pizza Hut—into a new company with $30 billion in sales, we can look for more co-branded outlets.

Merger mavens should know that one way to make money from the franchise phenomenon will be to anticipate changing national tastes and their effect on operations. Then, figure out what kinds of franchised operations should share space, staff, advertising, training, etc., and bring them together in co-brand or multibrand combinations. With half a million franchised outlets out there, the prospects for deal-doing by the M&A route, or other forms of strategic co-venturing, are certainly inviting.

NONPROFITS

What is a nonprofit organization, and how is it different from a for-profit one?

A simple answer to this question is that a *nonprofit organization* exists in order to accomplish a mission with redeeming social value. By contrast, a for-profit organization exists primarily in order to produce business profits for the benefit of its owners.[6] Because of this distinction, most nonprofit organizations do not have to pay taxes on their income, whereas most for-profit organizations must pay taxes.

Also, there are many more restrictions on nonprofit operations. For example, a nonprofit may pay people, but the total compensation package has to be reasonable. Paying excessive compensation is like distributing profits to individuals—it is considered *private inurement*—illegal distribution of the assets or profits of a nonprofit organization to individuals for their personal purposes. By contrast, if there is excessive compensation in a corporation, shareholders may have grounds for suit on the basis of waste of corporate assets, but such suits are relatively rare, and they are usually only filed when the company is suffering from poor financial performance.

In addition to restrictions on how much they can pay their officers, nonprofits also operate under restrictions on how much cash and other valuable assets they can accumulate. In some states there are laws governing what are called "excess holdings."

This said, however, it is worth noting that nonprofits can operate pretty close to the edge of these restrictions, and can appear very much like for-profit organizations. For example, in order to survive and thrive, nonprofits must take in more money than they spend, just as for-profit organizations do. Sometimes they take in a lot more. True, the money these organizations take in may come from grants and donations rather than sales, and true, the difference is called "surplus," rather than "profit," but there is still very much a "bottom line" involved in the operation of all nonprofits.[7] Conversely, for-profit organizations do not always succeed in taking in more money than they spend, and despite this fact they continue to operate—often with a high value in the marketplace, which is capable of looking beyond short-term profits in valuing a company. Furthermore, many for-profit organizations generate and follow missions that go far beyond mere profit making—and may not even rank profits high among its goals.[8]

What kinds of missions can a nonprofit have?

This varies by state, but if a nonprofit wants to be exempt from federal taxes, as described under 501-c-3 of the Internal Revenue Code, then it must state in its founding document (charter or deed) that it exists exclusively to pursue charitable, religious, educational, scientific, or literary goals, to engage in testing for public safety, to foster amateur sports, or to prevent cruelty to children or animals. Organizations may adopt no more than three of these goals as their founding mission.

Who owns a nonprofit organization?

Usually, no one owns a nonprofit organization in the way shareholders own a for-profit organization. The nonprofit organization's assets must be used to accomplish its mission; they cannot be distributed to individuals except as reasonable compensation for services rendered in service of the nonprofit's mission. This obviously precludes the traditional role of the investor.

Then who is in control?

The typical nonprofit organization is controlled by a board of directors. Some organizations have members who elect the board of directors. Other boards are self-perpetuating; that is, the board elects its own successors. As a practical matter, officers or key volunteers or employees are often in control.

Can a for-profit company convert to a nonprofit? If so, what does it have to do?

The for-profit can change its articles of incorporation to indicate that it will be henceforth a nonprofit entity. It can then change its stock from transferable, proprietary business corporation stock to restricted, nontransferable stock. This means that it must change its stock from one entitling holders to dividends and a share of assets upon dissolution, to restricted, nontransferable stock that does not entitle the holder to either dividends or a share of the assets upon dissolution. During the conversion, none of the assets of the entity may be distributed to shareholders because of or in conjunction with the conversion. On the other hand, the new nonprofit entity may collect the accounts receivable earned by the old for-profit entity, on the grounds that this is a necessary administrative function and not an unrelated business. It is somewhat easier to convert a nonprofit company into a for-profit, since fewer restrictions apply to the latter.

The ability to convert from a nonprofit to a for-profit and vice versa gives a great deal of flexibility to companies operating in both realms, or in the borderline between them. It also can help nonprofits and for-profits have more flexibility to engage in M&A activity.

In what ways might nonprofits get involved in M&A activity?

Nonprofits, like for-profits, can engage in mergers and acquisitions—not to mention other activities "beyond M&A" (to quote the title of our next chapter) such as divestitures and strategic alliances. It can also choose from among several types of reorganization.[9] The following examples are pure versions of their type. (Hybrid transactions are also possible.)

- *Merger.* A nonprofit may acquire one or more nonprofits for the purpose of merging all of them into a single company with one set of assets, liabilities, operations, and employees. The surviving nonprofit will contain the other, merged nonprofits—typically under its own name.
- *Acquisition.* A nonprofit may acquire another nonprofit or a for-profit and run the new unit separately. Sometimes this is done through a holding company structure and interlocking directorships.
- *Divestiture.* A nonprofit may sell or transfer a unit to another entity—either nonprofit or for-profit. Divestiture is sometimes required by law when a nonprofit has excess holdings.
- *Strategic alliance.* Like their for-profit peers, nonprofits may enter into agreements to share their activities, expenses, and/or resources (including managers and board of directors) in whole or in part—while at the same time maintaining separate legal and public identities. This type of strategic alliance is often referred to as an *affiliation.*
- *Reorganization.* As seen above, multiple nonprofits (and even for-profits as well) can coexist within the same structure—often via a holding company. Such complex organizations may be reorganized in many possible ways.

What are the main benefits and disbenefits of merging nonprofits?

Every case is different, but some generalities apply.
    Possible benefits include:

- *More efficient use of resources.* Nonprofits may be integrated into fewer, stronger, more flexible, and more effective organizations. Investment decision making in many of the smaller nonprofits is inefficient because managers have been hired for their social awareness rather than their financial skills.

- *More efficient operations.* The merging of back-office operations will result in greater efficiency. Further, in this computer age, larger firms can often use computers more efficiently than can smaller companies.

- *More public clout.* The larger you are, the more clout you will have at the local, state, and federal level to accomplish your objectives. It also works to preserve the nonprofit sector from attack. It takes major PR skills to build the public image needed to raise funds.

- *Better controls.* The chances of uncovering bad accounting and major fraud are increased in larger organizations.

- *Better leadership.* The larger the operation, the better chance to get more highly skilled people in management and to serve at the board level. This is becoming of increasing importance in community-involved operations where the devolution of social responsibility is moving from the federal government to the local community.

- *Stronger grant generation.* Grant-approval processes are, unfortunately, too informal in the smaller nonprofits. Larger operations can afford to formalize the process.

- *Improved service to community.* There will be better anticipation of future needs and wants and continuous redefinition of the purpose and mission of the nonprofit.

Possible disbenefits include:

- *Dehumanization.* A merger may deaden the "personal touch" between contributors, managers, and grantees.

- *Problems with "turf."* As larger, more efficient organizations enter the historical domain of longtime operators, resentments may flare.

- *Loss of managerial autonomy.* Changing the lines of reporting (giving people new bosses) may provoke anxiety in key personnel.

- *Culture shock.* The new organization's creation may disturb the dedication of management, staff, and donors to the long-established purpose and mission of the nonprofit entity.

- *Mission amnesia.* The personal survival instinct of stewards of the nonprofit organization may take precedence over the advancement of mission.

CONCLUDING COMMENTS

The art of M&A can be practiced in all types of entities—not just large, widely held public companies, but also family businesses, franchises, and nonprofits. Executives and advisors involved in transactions outside the public company domain need to take special care in respecting the nuances of different types of entities. This chapter has explored these nuances only superficially. We encourage readers to do much more exploration on their own.

E N D N O T E S

1. The average dollar value of the 7,834 deals involving U.S. companies in 1997 (not counting deals not disclosing prices and deals worth less than $5 million) was $213.5 million, but the *median* price was $36 million. Source: *Mergers & Acquisitions* (March/April 1998), p. 46. Then, if we factor in the thousands of transactions that occur every year with a purchase price of *under* $5 million, the true M&A deal average is bound to be much lower.

2. *Source of this sentence:* Richard L. Narva, "Creating Effective Corporate Governance in Family Businesses," *Director's Monthly,* June 1998, pp. 6ff.

3. Ibid.

4. Space does not allow a complete exposition on the complexities of this phenomenon, but the sale of equities in limited partnership form by investment banking firms has facilitated the defrauding (often as a result of deceptive sales practices) of hundreds of thousands of investors of billions of dollars.

5. *Source:* David J. Kaufman, a New York-based franchising lawyer.

6. This is the definition given by Pamela McAllister, an attorney based in Seattle, Washington. She has posted it on her Internet site, www.exemptlaw.com, where she can be reached at pmcallister@exemptlaw.com.

7. This is the central message of Herrington Bryce, *Financial and Strategic Management for Nonprofit Organizations,* 2d ed. (Englewood Cliffs, NJ: Prentice-Hall, 1992), which includes an entire section on "the suitability of business income."

8. A good example of this type of for-profit organization is AES Corporation, an international power company based in Arlington, Virginia, which places a very high priority on its values, which include stewardship of the environment and fairness to all constituencies. In its original filing with the SEC in 1991, AES stated that "If the Company perceives a conflict between [its] values and profits, it will try to adhere to its values—even though doing so might result in diminished profits or forgone opportunities." Cited in Alex Markels, "Power to the People," *Fast Company,* February–March 1998 (reprint). In an interview

with Alexandra Lajoux in May 1998, Dennis Bakke, cofounder and CEO of AES, said that he did not believe owners were his company's primary constituency. AES considers the needs of all constituencies jointly—a position acceptable under federal and state law, Bakke noted. See Dennis Bakke, "An Alternative View of Corporate Governance," *Director's Monthly,* September 1998, pp. 1ff.

9. This discussion is based in part on Chapter 13 of Bryce, op. cit., note 7. Bryce gives details of real examples based on IRS letter rulings. *Note:* The use of the term *merger* here does not necessarily imply that the transaction was structured as a statutory merger. As explained in Chapter 1 and 5, that use of the term *merger* has very specific implications that do not apply to all consolidating acquisitions.

CHAPTER 14

Beyond M&A: Spin-Offs and Strategic Alliances

INTRODUCTION

Welcome to a new world "beyond M&A"—one that uses all the tricks of the M&A trade, but with very different results. In previous chapters, we have seen how to plan, value, finance, structure, refine, and close transactions that put two companies under common ownership for good—or at least for a long time. Whether the buyer was a small leveraged buyout (LBO) group offering know-how and financing or a large operating company offering strategic synergies, the deals discussed so far have been based on the values of unity, growth, and permanence. In this chapter, we will look at some very different types of transactions. We will begin by looking at *spin-offs* and other transactions that (in direct contrast to mergers) turn one company into two or more. Then we will consider *strategic alliances,* transactions that enable multiple companies to accomplish a single goal for a temporary period without ever fully uniting.

Spin-offs and strategic alliances require many of the same techniques that mergers, acquisitions, and buyouts do—from planning to closing. Nonetheless, because these transactions have outcomes so different from the traditional merger/acquisition/buyout deal, this chapter may seem like alien territory to M&A die-hards.

The "strangeness" of this world beyond M&A is particularly acute with respect to its lack of emphasis on growth. The M&A field has traditionally emphasized the growth factor, with companies merging or acquiring in order to increase market share, revenues, and ultimately profits. Yes, the M&A pros talk about building a company's "core business," a strategy that often requires selling as well as buying, but most M&A pros prefer to buy.

The growth concept, indeed, is virtually inseparable from M&A culture. We hear that companies must "grow or go"—even "grow or die." It is no coincidence that the leading association for M&A professionals is the Association for Corporate *Growth* (emphasis added). The typical member of this Chicago-based group is called a director of corporate development—again, a growth concept. Yes, M&A dealmakers know better than anybody else that unless growth increases shareholder value, it will eventually trigger its opposite—downsizing through cost-cutting and layoffs. But to the inveterate merger master, periods of shrinkage can seem like only a temporary setback on the road to grandeur.

The worlds of spin-offs and strategic alliances, by contrast, emphasize focus rather than growth. For the die-hard M&A and buyout pro, these cautious machinations may seem inferior to the real thing. But in this chapter we hope to show that there is life—and dealmaking—"beyond M&A."

SPIN-OFFS

What is a spin-off, and how is it different from an ordinary divestiture (or "sell-off")?

A spin-off is a wholly or partly tax-free division of a single corporation into two or more corporations.[1] The division typically involves converting a preexisting company division into a wholly owned subsidiary, and distributing the stock in the subsidiary pro rata to all shareholders in the original company. For a diagram of this transaction, see Figure 14-2 in Appendix 14C at the end of this chapter. By contrast, the ordinary divestiture or sell-off is the sale (often taxable) of the stock or assets of a business unit to another company or to an investment group.[2]

How common are spin-offs?

Not very. In the two years between January 1, 1996, and December 1, 1997, there were only 150 spin-offs from U.S. public companies, and that was a spin-off boom![3] During the same period, there were almost 10 times as many mergers, based on data from Securities Data Company in Newark, New Jersey. On the other hand, interest in spin-offs is keen. A recent (May 21, 1998) search on the "NetFind" search engine found nearly *3 million* web sites containing this term.[4]

What are some recent examples of spin-offs?

In December 1997, nursing-home operator Beverly Enterprises transferred the stock of its Pharmacy Corporation of America unit to Capstone Pharmacy Services. Beverly shareholders now own 57 percent of Capstone. Another late 1997 spin-off announcement was the creation of Meritor Automotive, Inc. (formerly Rockwell Automotive), spun off from Rockwell International. In that transaction, Rockwell International shareholders received one share of Meritor stock for each three Rockwell shares held on September 17, 1997. Also of note: In early 1997, Pepsico spun off its fast-food companies into a unit now called Tricon Global Restaurants, Inc.

In 1996, there were spin-offs of Lucent and NCR (from AT&T), Electronic Data Systems (from General Motors), Imation (from Minnesota Mining and Manufacturing, also known as 3M), and the Westinghouse industrial operations (from its old parent, Westinghouse, which was renamed CBS in December 1997). Sometimes spin-offs precede mergers. For example, in Switzerland, Sandoz and Ciba spun off their chemicals business units—one as a taxable initial public offering, one as a tax-free "demerger"—before merging their pharmaceutical cores into Novartis.[5]

The units may be sold separately in separate spin-offs or may be combined into a single spin-off. This process usually begins with a pro rata distribution of stock to shareholders in the form of a special dividend, followed by (or combined with) an initial public offering of the unit's shares.[6] A common type of spin-off is the *IPO carveout* in which the company goes straight to the initial public offering (IPO) without the distributions to stockholders. If the parent retains interest in an IPO carveout, this may be termed a *divestiture IPO.*[7]

Could you give an example of timing issues in a particular spin-off?

The AT&T spin-off of NCR had two separate time tables—one for AT&T and one for NCR.[8]

The AT&T sequence was as follows:

- At the time of the spin-off, the value of holdings in a single stock—AT&T—were spread across two stocks—AT&T and NCR. Both stocks were traded on the New York Stock Exchange.
- On December 31, 1996, AT&T began trading under two stock symbols. Trading under ticker symbol T were AT&T shares including the value of NCR and the right to NCR shares at the time of the spin-off. Trading under the ticker symbol TWD (for "AT&T when distributed") were AT&T shares without the value of NCR or the right to NCR shares.
- After the December 31 spin-off, AT&T again traded under one symbol: T. This symbol reflected the value of AT&T without NCR.

The NCR sequence was as follows:

- NCR stock began trading on December 31, 1996, under the ticker symbol NCR WI (for NCR when issued).
- After the December 31 spin-off, NCR traded under the ticker symbol NCR.

Since spin-offs are generally tax-free and sell-offs are taxable, why do companies even bother with sell-offs—why don't they just do spin-offs?

First of all, it is not easy to qualify a transaction as a spin-off. The transaction must meet all the requirements of Internal Revenue Code Section 355 (as well as Code Section 367 for transactions involving foreign corporations and/or shareholders). In fact, the technical term for spin-off is a "Code Section 355 divisive transaction." The requirements of Code Section 355 are many and complex. One leading guide to the subject devotes 118 pages to the topic![9]

Second, even if a transaction qualifies as a tax-free spin-off, it may not make strategic sense for the spun-off unit. If the unit has a track record of managing itself, a spin-off can work. But if the unit is poorly managed to begin with, it hardly helps to cut it loose to a faceless group of stockholders. It would be better to sell it to a company or group that can manage it well.[10]

Finally, remember the old adage (mentioned way back in Chapter 4) that there are no free mergers? The same rule applies here: There are no free spin-offs—tax-free or not. Just as parents expect to be paid for units they sell, parents expect to be paid for units they spin off. For example, in spinning itself off from Rockwell, Meritor had to pay a $456 million "dividend" to the parent company—and the spin-off could require another $500 million to finance. (That is why Meritor has sought $1 billion in a line of credit from a consortium of 19 banks.)

How secure is the tax-free status of spin-offs?

The years have chipped away at the tax-free status of spin-offs—most recently with the 1997 tax bill. The bill narrowed the tax-free zone demarcated in the so-called Morris Trust transaction. It also changed the tax treatment of nonqualified preferred stock received in spin-offs. Instead of being considered nontaxable stock, such securities are now considered to be taxable "boot."

What is a Morris Trust transaction, and how was it affected by the 1997 tax law?

A Morris Trust transaction is a tax-free or partly tax-free spin-off modeled after the deal featured in the *Morris Trust* legal case over 30 years ago. In the classic Morris Trust spin-off, a company could distribute the shares of some parts of its business to shareholders, and then merge the remaining part(s) into another company—all without incurring any taxable gains for itself, for the selling company, or for the selling company's shareholders. The 1997 tax act raised the bar for nontaxable treatments of spin-offs. Since April 16, 1997, spin-offs have been taxable to the selling company (but not to its shareholders) unless the transaction enables shareholders to maintain ownership of more than 50 percent of the vote and value of the stock involved. (In effect, the buyer has to give the divesting company's shareholders so much stock that they end up controlling more than half of the acquiring company.)

What is "boot," and how did the 1997 tax law apply it to spin-offs?

Boot is taxable consideration received in a nontaxable transaction. Receipt of boot does not disqualify a transaction from being taxable. Prior to the 1997 tax law, a shareholder could receive preferred stock in a spin-off tax-free. The 1997 tax law changed this. In a provision effective June 8, 1997, the new law said that certain kind of debt-like preferred stock would now be considered taxable to the recipient. In other words, the new law changed preferred stock from nontaxable stock to taxable boot.

Given these changes, did the 1997 tax act put the kaibash on spin-offs?

No. The new ownership requirements of the 1997 tax bill have not prevented companies from pursuing spin-offs since April 16, 1997, the law's effective date. Consider the recent spin-offs mentioned earlier in this chapter.

Do shareholders in the newly spun-off company generally do well?

Eventually, yes. As one observer has noted, spin-offs have a "life cycle."[11] With some notable exceptions,[12] they tend to be undervalued in the early stages and then gain value as shareholders appreciate them. A good example is Lucent Technologies, whose share price has more than doubled since being spun off from AT&T in 1995. By contrast, the AT&T spin-off of NCR has been less successful. The shares started at $34 in January 1997, went up to a high of $43 in 1997, but then settled back to their original levels in early 1998.[13]

What impact does a spin-off have on dividends paid by the parent (who did the spin-off and is now smaller)?

Overall, a spin-off need not change the dividend rate paid by the parent. For example, at the time of the NCR spin-off (December 1996), AT&T announced that it *"intends to continue* its $.33 per share quarterly cash dividend rate"—and it has. For example, on December 17, 1997, the company declared a quarterly dividend of 33 cents per share (payable February 2, 1998, to some 3.3 million shareowners of record December 31, 1997).

On the other hand, a spin-off can have a very different effect for different shareholders, depending on what shares they buy or sell when. For example, in AT&T's NCR spin-off, shares purchased in December 1996 under the ticker symbol TWD did not settle until January 1997, so buyers of those shares were not entitled to the AT&T fourth-quarter 1996 dividend; only *sellers* of those transitional shares received that dividend. Conversely, buyers of T shares during that same time period did receive the fourth-quarter dividend, while sellers of T shares did not. NCR did not declare any dividend during this time period.

AT&T avoided shareholder confusion by publishing the details of this "dividend impact" in advance of the spin-off. It also published a disclaimer stating, "As with any company, of course, the declaration and payment of future dividends are subject to the discretion of the respective boards of directors of AT&T and NCR, and will depend on various factors."[14]

What, if any, are the emotional issues involved in spin-offs, and how can these be resolved?

Anecdotal evidence suggests that a spin-off, if not handled with sensitivity from the beginning, can leave the managers of the spun-off company feeling abandoned by their parent company and bereft of the benefits that the company had provided. Managers involved in a spin-off need to be aware of this "orphan" syndrome and become their own "parents" by following the same basic management principles used by any independent company.[15]

Do spin-offs always involve a complete separation of the selling parent and the spun-off unit?

No. In the early 1990s, executives from the LBO firm Clayton, Dubelier & Rice, Inc., coined the term *satellite* to describe a divested unit that maintains continuing links between the divested unit and the selling parent. The first known example of such a transaction is IBM Corporation's satellite Lexmark International, created when IBM sold its information products division (which makes printers, keyboards, and typewriters for computer workstations) to Clayton-Dubelier, but retained ties to the unit.

What is the difference between a spin-off and other divisive transactions such as split-offs and split-ups?

A *split-off* is the same as a spin-off except that instead of simply receiving stock in the new subsidiary pro rata, the original shareholders (or some portion of them) must redeem their old shares (or some portion of them). A *split-up* is the breakup of a company into two or more separate companies. It is different from a spin-off or a split-off because it involves the entire company, not just a unit or two, and it causes the original company to disappear. For examples of a split-off and a spin-off, see Figures 14-3 and 14-4 in Appendix 14C at the end of this chapter.

What are some examples of big split-ups?

The most famous split-ups have involved AT&T. In 1984, AT&T broke up under order from the Department of Justice Antitrust Division, dividing into a telecommunications company (today's AT&T) and regional Bell companies (a.k.a. "baby Bells") to handle local calls. Then in 1996, having grown through acquisition, AT&T divided itself again—this time voluntarily. Citing business complexities that outweighed the benefits of integration,[16] it split into three companies: AT&T, NCR, and Lucent Technologies. Following the split-up, it spun off parts of the new companies. For details on this combination split-up/spin-off, see Appendix 14A.

What usually motivates postmerger divestitures?

One common reason is a poor fit between the parent and the subsidiary. This is true whether the divestitures are structured as sell-offs, spin-offs, split-offs, or split-ups. There may be a bad match between the parent's and the subsidiary's *businesses*—a problem financial economists have recognized for decades.[17] Or there may be a bad match between the parent's and the sub's *management needs*—a problem that has gained attention only recently.[18]

Parental fit aside, a unit may be divested because it is performing poorly and the seller wants to stem its tide of losses. Conversely, it may be sold as a "crown jewel" because it can fetch a good price. Finally, and least appealingly, it may be tagged for sale to appease regulators—for example, the Antitrust Division of the Department of Justice—who may set this as a condition for regulatory approval of a merger. (For example, in 1996, West Publishing, a leading U.S. publishing firm, had to sell 50 properties in order to merge with Thomson Corp. of Toronto, Canada).

How can an acquirer decide what to divest when?

Companies often purchase other firms with the intent of selling off some units eventually, holding this divestiture "option" open until the businesses in question develop further or until the industry consolidates to the point that it becomes a seller's market. Assigning a quantitative value to each divestiture option can help acquirers make the decision of keeping versus selling. It can also help set an appropriate price for the purchased company.[19]

STRATEGIC ALLIANCES

What are strategic alliances?

A *strategic alliance* is a substitute for a merger or acquisition and in U.S. law is treated as such for antitrust and other legal purposes. The most common strategic alliance is the *joint venture* (JV), in which two different corporations set up a third, jointly owned enterprise in corporate form. If more than two corporations are involved in a venture, it is called a *consortium* rather than a joint venture. Consortia are quite common in Europe, with as many as five and six corporations combining to set up new permanent corporations. Other forms of strategic alliances are joint *marketing agreements, technology exchanges,* and so-called *cooperative agreements,* in which two companies swap products and/or services. For example, a U.S. manufacturer might cut a deal to sell and service, say, a Swedish manufacturer's line of tractors, while the Swedish manufacturer might agree to sell and service the U.S. manufacturer's line of corn planters.

How common are strategic alliances?

The number of new joint venture announcements has risen dramatically to rival the number of merger completions—a correlation of nearly 100 percent.[20] Based on this ratio, we can estimate that in 1998, there have been 8,000 joint ventures—about the same number as completed mergers anticipated for the year. Just two decades ago, the ratio of joint ventures and mergers was only about 1 to 4, and overall JV and merger activity was lower. For example, in 1978 (shortly before *Mergers & Acquisitions* stopped tallying JVs), only about 500 JVs were announced, compared to 2,000 mergers.

What are some examples of successful joint ventures?

Successes abound, and have been well documented by scholars—notably J. Fred Weston of the University of California-Los Angeles.[21] Texas Instruments and Hitachi have engaged in joint efforts since 1988 to develop new memory chips. In 1995 they jointly founded a $500 million plant near Dallas to produce memory chips. Another example is joint activity between Compaq Computer Corp. and Intel Corp., a major supplier of microprocessors. The two companies have worked together to develop new products. Compaq also has a joint venture with Digital Equipment Corp. to handle service and support for Compaq customers.

The value of combining different skills is demonstrated by the relationship between USX Corp., a large integrated steel producer, and Nucor Corp., the leading minimill steel producer, notes Weston. USX researchers developed a theory for a new process of making steel from iron carbide, eliminating blast furnaces and supporting coke batteries. If successful, the new process would cut steel-producing costs by as much as one-fourth. The two companies entered into an agreement to study the feasibility of the process. Nucor possessed considerable experience and expertise on constructing the types of plants that would be required. The Nucor group planned to work closely with the engineers at USX, who had formulated the new concepts.

Additional examples encompass several different industries. Since 1984 Hewlett Packard has sold more than 15 million laser printers that use an engine by Canon. These machines compete with Canon's own laser printers. In telecommunications, we see companies competing in the United States but participating in international joint ventures. U S West Inc. competes with Tele-Communications Inc. (TCI), a leader in cable in the U.S. market. The two have formed a joint venture in Great Britain to sell phone and cable services on one network. But in the U.S. market, U S West has had a relationship with Time Warner to offer local service in the New York market of NYNEX Corp. (now merging with Bell Atlantic). U S West and NYNEX have formed a four-company enterprise to sell wireless personal communications/cellular phones. TCI is also engaged in a joint venture with Sprint Corp., a competitor to U S West and other telephone operating companies that were spun off from AT&T in 1984. Chrysler Corp. had a joint venture with Mitsubishi Motors Corp. for the purchase of as many as 200,000 vehicles a year. Chrysler, now merging with Daimler-Benz, no longer needs the alliance. It has announced plans to discontinue purchases from Mitsubishi by the year 2000.

What is a JV?

A *joint venture* is a type of strategic alliance in which two companies form a third entity to accomplish a goal. The entity may be a partnership, a corporation, or any other type of business. Joint ventures are usually set forth in a contract, which usually specifies the following contributions by the participants:

- Contribution of money, property, effort, knowledge, skill, or other asset to a common undertaking
- Joint property interest in the subject matter of the venture
- Right of mutual control or management of the enterprise
- Expectation of profit and the right to share in it
- Single, specified objective[22]

Why do companies engage in JVs?

A joint venture can enable its participants to accomplish a specific goal that it could not as easily achieve alone. For example, through a JV, a company can:

- Enter a new line of business using another company's financial or technical means.
- Obtain a new distribution channel or a new source of raw materials via another company.
- Share technology and/or skills in organization, planning, and control with another company.

In pursuing these strategic ends, a company can use a joint venture to:

- Share cost.
- Diversify risk.
- Take advantage of favorable tax or regulatory treatment.

Each of these benefits can bring the companies a kind of "synergy"—the much-discredited term of merger art that describes how firms can benefit one another through sharing.

Can't the same benefits come from a merger or acquisition? Why a JV?

All these transaction types can foster synergies. The difference is that a JV typically involves a single activity for a defined period of time, whereas a merger typically involves many activities for an indefinite period of time. If two firms have only one area of potential synergy that takes up only a small part of their business, then they would be better off with a JV. Conversely, if they have many areas of synergy, or an area that is dominant, then a merger or acquisiton would be more appropriate. And finally, sometimes companies don't have a full range of choices. In some cases, antitrust regulators would forbid a merger, but would allow a JV (or series of JVs).

How successful are JVs generally?

Most studies conclude that JVs have a high failure rate.

Why are joint ventures relatively unsucessful?

Reasons for JV failure vary. A study conducted by researchers with the International Finance Corporation of the World Bank found that international JVs had a high failure rate because managements often fail to remember that JVs are "dynamic relationships where the basis for the intercorporate marriage can change considerably over time." The study concludes that both sides need to sustain comparative advantages in the relationship. The absence of comparative advantages can cause the JV to be less successful or, at the extreme, to fail. The study also found that while cultural and personal factors can clearly be important to success as well, they are less critical than the maintenance of organizational complementarities between the two or more corporate partners.[23]

A study by J. Fred Weston, Kwang S. Chung, and Juan A. Siu showed five reasons for JV failure:

- The hoped-for technology never developed.
- Preplanning for the joint venture was inadequate.
- Agreements could not be reached on alternative approaches to solving the basic objectives of the joint venture.
- Managers with expertise in one company refused to share knowledge with their counterparts in the joint venture.
- Management difficulties were sometimes compounded because parent companies could not share control or compromise on difficult issues.[24]

Could you give some examples of recent joint ventures?

Lucent Technologies' JV with Finolex Cables began operations in January 1997 to provide international-grade dielectric and armored fiber optic cables to the telecommunications market in India. The JV has won an $11.1 million order from a local Indian phone company (Bharati Telnet) to manufacture and supply the optical fiber cable needed for Bharati's basic telecom services project in the

Indian state of Madhya Pradesh. (Bharati Telnet is itself a joint venture between an Indian company, Bharatic Enterprises, and an Italian Company, Telecom Italia.) Under the terms of the agreement, the Lucent-Finolex joint venture will supply armored cable as well as nonarmored cable to Bharati.

Any parting thoughts on JVs?

Like all forms of organization, JVs defy easy definition.[25] To be sure, the classic JV is short term, single purpose, just as the classic "acquisition" is long term, multipurpose. (See Figure 14-1.) But some transactions could be called hybrids. For example, some transactions are JVs in legal form, but they are really preludes to merger. And some acquisitions lead to a very limited degree of integration—and could almost be called functional JVs.

F I G U R E 14-1

The JV/Merger Quadrant

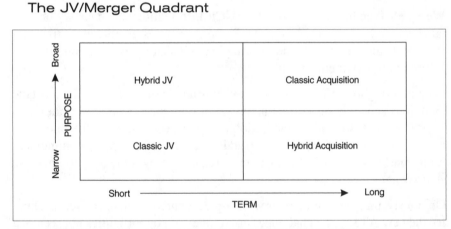

The classic JV is short in term and narrow in purpose, while the classic acquisition is long in term and broad in purpose. But there are hybrids. Some JVs (such as those that are merely preludes to mergers) serve a broad purpose. And some acquisitions (such as financial ones that involve little or no integration) have only a narrow purpose.

CONCLUDING COMMENTS

The current boom in spin-offs and strategic alliances shows a strong creative streak on the part of companies worldwide. Rather than pursuing business as usual, many firms are reinventing themselves through these increasingly popular strategies. Like any bold strategies, spin-offs and strategic alliances are risky, but those who learn from history are likely to beat the odds building a better world "beyond M&A."

The AT&T Spin-Offs

In April 1996, following the creation of Lucent as a separate company, AT&T sold 20 percent of Lucent's stock for $3 billion—the biggest initial public offering in history. The following text appeared on AT&T's Internet site att.com, signed by then-chairman Robert E. Allen.

A MESSAGE FROM THE CHAIRMAN

We expect the spin-off of NCR, the final phase in one of the largest corporate restructurings in history, to be completed by year's end. In the following pages, we've tried to answer questions you may have about how that spin-off affects your investment in AT&T.

We are also sending you a copy of the NCR Information Statement which contains detailed information about NCR and its businesses, including financial statements and other financial information. All shareowners should read this Information Statement carefully.

People throughout AT&T have worked long and hard to successfully meet the ambitious schedule of our restructuring. In little more than a year, they will have launched two independent global corporations—Lucent Technologies and NCR—and redefined AT&T to address a dynamic, growing communications marketplace. We believe this creates strong potential to increase shareowner value.

Obviously, this presents all of us with unprecedented challenges. But speaking for the new AT&T, the challenges also come with opportunities not seen in a century. In short, the business has been and will be tested as never before. With focus and determination we believe we can meet the challenges and achieve new rewards.

Sincerely,

Robert E. Allen

November 1996

The Joint Venture Agreement: A Checklist from the Regional and Economic Development Services of Saskatchewan, Canada

SUMMARY

Repeated reference has been made to the importance Joint Venture Agreements play in the formation and implementation of the joint venture.

The Joint Venture Agreement legally creates the joint venture through the process of contract, and identifies the major rights, duties and obligations of the participants of the joint venture.

The Joint Agreement identifies:

the project or object of the joint venture;

the contribution, role and involvement of each co-venturer;

the terms or duration for which the joint venture will exist;

the provisions for management and performance of joint venture obligations;

and

allocation of revenues and expenses from the project.

The Joint Agreement checklist:

1. The date on which the agreement is established and executed.
2. The names, addresses and identification of the parties, including the type of business of each member of the joint venture.
3. The name under which the joint venture will do business.
4. The principal place of business of the joint venture.
5. The purpose of the joint venture. If the purpose is to access a specific project, a full description of that project is required.
6. The terms of the joint venture: when and how the joint venture is terminated; and how such items as guarantees, defects, and insurance will be handled after termination.

7. A statement that the parties are actually co-venturers for the project whether or not the contract is in the name of all members.

8. A declaration that the organization is a joint venture, not a partnership.

9. The establishment of a fund by the parties to finance the work, together with the amounts to be contributed by each party, with the fund being deposited in a special bank account under dual control and all progress payments and other revenues being deposited in such account.

10. A clause providing that, if additional working capital is required, the parties will proportionally contribute additional funds, as needed, and naming the penalty for failure to contribute.

11. A declaration of the participation of the parties and percentage in which profits and losses are shared. Usually these percentages are proportional to the contributions to the working fund, but the amount of contribution of funds by parties can be increased or decreased depending on the contributions of equipment or expertise which also must be considered.

12. Payment of any fee to the controlling co-venturer or sponsor should be specified; whether a share of the profits in excess of that contemplated is given to the controlling manager or a flat dollar sum is paid.

13. If equipment is involved, a specific clause should be inserted especially where the parties contribute varying amounts of equipment.

14. The parties to the joint venture should agree to sign all necessary documents relating to the contract, bank loans, bonds, indemnity agreements, and the like.

15. Control management committee may be determined. A management committee may be established with provision for remuneration. Alternatively, one of the co-venturers should be designated as general manager of the project, with authority to bind the joint venture. A provision clearly defines not only the management duties, but all other duties of the co-venturers and procedures to be followed in dealing with unusual situations or problems that may develop.

16. A regular meeting schedule should be considered.

17. A financial and periodic joint venture and progress reporting procedure should be implemented.

18. Establishment of a joint venture bank account, and the appointment of a chartered accountant and lawyer.

19. The possibility of the death, bankruptcy, or insolvency of a member must be handled.

20. The acquisition of equipment and materials by the joint venture and the disposal of such equipment and material either by sale with the proceeds treated as ordinary revenues, or by distributing the funds to the co-venturers on a pro-rata basis.

21. Provide for the acquisition of licences in the name of the joint venture or each co-venturer as required.

22. Specify the type of insurance carried by the joint venture and clearly define the liabilities that are to be insured against by each participant.

23. Define items which are to be considered as costs to the joint venture for the purpose of determining profit or loss and describe those items which are not reimbursable to members of the joint venture.

24. A clause should be included respecting the confidentiality of trade information passed between the co-venturers.

25. Ownership or retention of patents, technology, and consultant reports should be addressed.

26. Establish the performance security requirements of the project and the bonding obligations of the co-venturers.

27. State that undivided pro-rata interests are held by the co-venturers on all assets of the joint venture.

28. Restriction should be considered regarding assignment of co-venturers undivided pro-rata interests in assets of the joint venture.

29. Indemnification.

30. Substitution or addition of co-venturers.

31. Payout of funds.

32. Disputes arbitration clause.

33. Winding up, final performance and financial statements for the joint venture.

34. Notice clause.

35. The applicable jurisdiction of the Agreement should be stated.

The nature, size and complexity of the project together with the sophistication of the parties will determine the detail in which the Joint Venture Agreement is prepared and aforementioned topics dealt with. This checklist is meant only as a guide to putting a Joint Venture Agreement together. The appropriate professional services, such as legal counsel, should be sought and utilized.

Source: Thomas Pavlovsky, B. Adim., C.A., and Ted C. Zarzeczny, Jr., B.A., LL.B, *How to Use Joint Ventures—A Handbook for Firms Bidding on Major Projects,* Regina; Saskatchewan: Saskatchewan Economic and Co-operative Development, Regional Economic Development Services, 1997.

A P P E N D I X 14C

Diagrams

F I G U R E 14-2

Spin-Offs

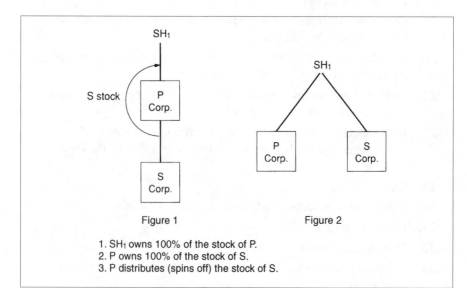

Figure 1   Figure 2

1. SH₁ owns 100% of the stock of P.
2. P owns 100% of the stock of S.
3. P distributes (spins off) the stock of S.

F I G U R E   14-3

Split-Offs

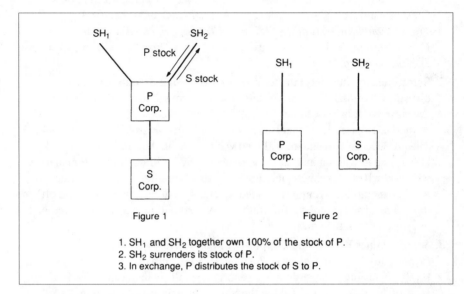

Figure 1   Figure 2

1. SH_1 and SH_2 together own 100% of the stock of P.
2. SH_2 surrenders its stock of P.
3. In exchange, P distributes the stock of S to P.

F I G U R E   14-4

Split-Ups

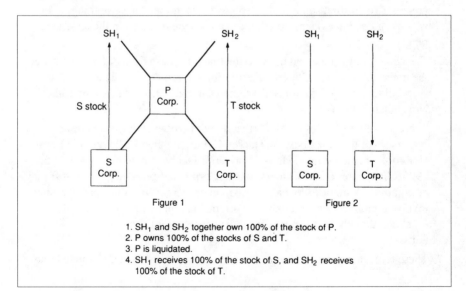

Figure 1   Figure 2

1. SH_1 and SH_2 together own 100% of the stock of P.
2. P owns 100% of the stocks of S and T.
3. P is liquidated.
4. SH_1 receives 100% of the stock of S, and SH_2 receives 100% of the stock of T.

E N D N O T E S

1. This definition is a summary of a longer one that appears in Martin D. Ginsburg and Jack S. Levin, *Mergers, Acquisitions, and Buyouts: A Transactional Analysis of the Governing Tax, Legal, and Accounting Considerations,* Vol. 1 (New York: Aspen Law & Business, March 1998), Section 1001, pp. 10–3ff.

2. Sometimes (confusingly) the term *spin-off* is used to describe ordinary divestitures or MBOs. Consider this passage from the international edition of *Business Week* on November 24, 1997. "Take Nutreco Holding, a Netherlands-based LBO that was *spun off* of British Petroleum Co. in 1994. The producer of fish and animal feed went public in Amsterdam on June 3 [1997] and now has a market value of about $575 million. Some 70 managers still own a 10% stake, with about 6%, worth $34 million, held by Nutreco's top 10 executives." (Emphasis added.) Actually, Nutreco was not "spun off" in the technical sense of the term. Rather, it was sold to managers in a leveraged buyout that took the unit private.

3. *Source:* James K. Glassman, "Spin-Off Main Provides Wealth of Opportunity," *The Washington Post,* pp. H-5ff. Compared with previous levels, this is high. According to a report on spin-offs in the June 30, 1997, issue of *Business Week* ("Taking the Shine Off Spin-offs," edited by Larry Light), there were only 30 spin-offs for all of 1995.

4. The exact count of Internet sites using the term "spin-off" was 2,815,175, to be precise. (To be sure, some of the "spin-offs" mentioned have nothing to do with business, but even more refined searches yield counts in the six-figure range.)

5. The Ciba spin-off received tax-free treatment because Ciba did not structure the transactions as an initial public offering but rather as a sale to existing stockholders. See "Ciba Wins Tax-Free Demerger Deal," *Financial Times,* November 4, 1996, p. 19.

6. There are other types of spin-offs that do not involve widespread public ownership of the unit stock. As Harvey L. Pitt, Stephen I. Glover, and Lanae Holbrook of Fried, Frank, Harris, Shriver & Jacobson note in a January 25, 1996, client letter on "Considerations in Corporate Spin-Offs," a spin-off may be combined with or follow an acquisition or merger by a third party or may involve continued ownership by the original parent company. Generally speaking, though, the term implies independence for the previously owned units.

7. These terms are used by *Mergers & Acquisitions* in its annual almanac issue.

8. This sequence is adapted from an AT&T web site description of the NCR spin-off, accessed via America OnLine's NetFind, December 28, 1997.

9. Ginsberg and Levin, op. cit., note 1, pp. 10-1–10-118.

10. This is Roger Lowenstein's basic point in "Corporate Breakups Are No Panacea," *The Wall Street Journal,* June 5, 1997, p. B-1.

11. Glassman, op. cit., note 3.

12. Waban Inc., a Nasdaq company, offers a case of shareholders giving an early positive response to a spin-off announcement. After Waban announced its intention to split its BJ's Wholesale chain from its Home-Base unit, Waban's stock rose from $3.75 to $27.25 in a single day. On the other hand, Moody's Investors Service Inc. placed the company under review for a possible downgrade from its Ba3 debt rating. *Source:* "Waban Plans to Split Company in Bid to Raise Shareholder Value," *The Wall Street Journal,* October 24, 1996, p. A-6.

13. For a negative view of spin-offs, see Lowenstein, op. cit., note 10.

14. AT&T web site.

15. Kevin Ryan, CEO of Wesley Jessen Visioncare, Inc. For views on "parenting" in corporate life, see Andrew Campbell and Michael Gould, *Synergy: Why Links between Business Units Fail and How to Make Them Work* (Oxford: Capstone, 1998). Some links cannot be made successfully, the authors argue, in which case a spin-off or similar action is called for.

16. "The complexity of trying to manage these different businesses began to overwhelm the advantages of our integration," AT&T CEO Robert Allen told the *Wall Street Journal* the day after AT&T announced its decision to break up. (John J. Keller, "Defying Merger Trend, AT&T Plans to Split into Three Companies," *The Wall Street Journal,* September 21, 1996, p. A-1.)

17. This was a key notion in the wheel of opportunity/fit chart approach to acquisitions first proposed in 1977 by the principal author of this book (as explained in Chapter 2). This idea was generated from experience and intuition, but it can easily be supported by scholarly financial analysis. Two decades ago, Malcolm S. Salter and Wolf A. Weinhold, in *Diversification through Acquisition: Strategies for Creating Economic Value* (New York: The Free Press, 1979), identified this Achilles heel of diversification and showed how to conquer it through good strategic planning.

18. See Marcus Alexander, Andrew Campbell, and Michael Goold, "Parenting Advantage," *Prism,* Second Quarter 1995, pp. 22–33. (*Prism* is a quarterly journal published by Arthur D. Little, an international consulting firm based in Cambridge, Massachusetts.) Good and bad parenting is also the subject of

Breakup! When Companies Are Worth More Dead Than Alive (Oxford/New York: Capstone/Free Press, 1997), which Campbell coauthored with David Sadtler and Richard Koch. *Breakup* authors argue that half of U.S. and U.K. firms with more than one product line should consider coming asunder.

19. See Kenneth W. Smith and Alexander Triantis, "Untapped Options for Creating Value in Acquisitions," *Mergers & Acquisitions,* November/December, 1994 pp. 22ff.

20. The source of the 0.95 percent correlation is J. Fred Weston, Kwang S. Chung, and Juan A. Siu, *Takeovers, Restructuring, and Corporate Governance,* 2d ed. (Upper Saddle River, NJ: Prentice Hall, 1998), p. 278.

21. This answer is excerpted almost verbatim from Weston, et al., ibid.

22. This list and many of the basic concepts in this section were provided by J. Fred Weston. For a more in-depth scholarly treatment of this subject, see Weston, et al., op. cit., note 20.

23. This discussion is based on a research project by the International Finance Corporation's Economics Department. The research involved detailed interviews carried out by IFC economists with 75 companies in six developing countries. IFC is a member of the World Bank Group and is the largest multilateral source of equity and loan financing for private-sector projects in developing countries.

24. Weston et al., op. cit., note 20.

25. As Armen Alchian and S. Woodward have noted, "The form of organization—franchises, mutuals, partnerships, joint ventures, and so on—is determined by a *nexus of contracts* governing the special relations among people and physical assets," paraphrased in Weston et al., op. cit., note 20. As such, organizational forms are difficult to define precisely.

CHAPTER 15

Special Issues for Transactions with International Aspects

INTRODUCTION

Today, business buyers and sellers operate in a truly global economy. The plans they make, the financing they find, the tax and accounting laws they study, and the due diligence they conduct are all likely to have an international dimension even if their deals are entirely domestic. The purely domestic deal—involving two companies located entirely in the same country—is becoming an anachronism in a world that sets no firm national boundaries for corporate and financial growth.

Trade liberalization has continued on track in the years that have passed since the August 1992 signing of the North American Free Trade Agreement involving Canada, Mexico, and the United States, and the December 1993 signing of the General Agreement on Tariffs and Trade among 117 nations. With every passing year, key provisions take effect, stimulating trade and investment in new arenas. And in some industries, the biggest changes are yet to come. For example, by the year 2004, Mexico will lift all restrictions on U.S. and Canadian ownership of its banks.

Meanwhile, the fall of old currency barriers is speeding the pace of mergers and other alliances—notably in Europe, where a looming deadline (January 1, 2002) for the euro, a common currency in a new European Monetary Union is already changing business conduct in that region. On the global scene, coordinated intervention into currency exchanges continues through the work of the renamed "G8" nations—Canada, France, Germany, Italy, the United Kingdom, Japan, the United States, and, as of 1998, Russia. Meanwhile, continued deregulation in debt and equity financing, enhanced by the development and dissemination of global accounting standards by the London-based International Accounting Standards Committee, continues to generate opportunities for cross-border expansion. Foreign companies long content to sell their equities through American depository receipts (ADRs) are considering full-fledged listing on national stock exchanges such as the New York Stock Exchange.

In these multinational times, institutions and individuals are more willing than ever before to invest their funds overseas. U.S. direct investment abroad currently stands at nearly $800 billion, significantly up from previous years. Conversely, foreign investors are placing more of their money here; direct investment in the United States is just over $600 billion, also up from the recent past. Adding the two flows together, we see that the total volume of cross-border investment is now $1.4 trillion—an all-time record.[1]

Moreover, a significant portion of this international flow of capital involves actual purchases of controlling interests in companies, not merely purchases of shares. In 1997, U.S. companies closed 1,804 cross-border deals valued at $5 million or more, as either buyer or seller, for a total value of $164.9 billion. In terms of both deal volume and dollar volume, this cross-border merger movement is the largest ever recorded—and it represents a particularly dynamic rebound from the low activity recorded in the early 1990s.[2] In early 1998, the heavy cross-border traffic slowed somewhat, with only 70 inbound and 115 outbound transactions closing in the first two months. But a May 1998 announcement of a planned merger between automakers Daimler-Benz and Chrysler revived global growth strategies everywhere, prompting a new wave of cross-border deal announcements and closings.

As traditional boundaries fall, it seems almost archaic to talk about "outbound" versus "inbound" investment. Yet despite our global economy, we still have nations. Moreover, most readers of this book are based in the United States. Therefore, throughout this chapter, we make a distinction in each of those areas between issues relating to foreign investment in the United States (inbound) and issues relating to U.S. investment overseas (outbound). Although this chapter does not cover every issue that one might encounter in embarking on an inbound or outbound transaction, it does highlight information useful to foreign companies acquiring U.S. companies, to U.S. companies acquiring foreign companies or other U.S. companies with international components, and to U.S. companies wishing to finance their domestic or foreign activities through international techniques and sources.

Buyers and sellers should consult legal counsel familiar with the U.S. laws that apply, as well as special counsel located in the foreign country or countries involved. Each of the Big Five accounting firms has issued booklets—usually by country—on how to do business abroad, with special attention usually paid to M&A-related problems. A collection of such booklets, usually available without cost, is a precondition to doing M&A business in those countries. Some major international law firms have similar publications, though they tend to be more regionalized and are more specialized.

NONTAX ISSUES REGARDING FOREIGN INVESTMENT IN THE UNITED STATES (INBOUND)

Are there any limitations under U.S. law on the form of business association in which a foreign person can participate?

Generally, U.S. laws impose no limitations on the form of business association a foreign person can use to create or conduct a business or own business interests. The type of business association a foreign person decides to use is often dictated by the particular needs of the enterprise and the impact upon that enterprise of federal and state laws—particularly tax laws, which can be an incentive to use one particular structure and a disincentive to use another. Any foreign person would be well advised to check with local counsel on the impact of all relevant tax, business, securities, and related laws prior to deciding on the most favorable form of business association to achieve his or her specific goals.

Must the parties forming a new corporation be citizens of the United States and residents of the state of incorporation?

Not necessarily. A corporation formed under the laws of any state is simply a corporation of that state. The ease and simplicity of corporate formation in the United States may come as a surprise to those accustomed to the formality of certain foreign systems of incorporation. In the absence of express requirements in state corporation statutes, these parties, called "incorporators" (not synonymous with stockholders), are merely legal instruments used to organize a corporation. They need not be citizens or residents of the state under whose laws the formation of the corporation will be formed. For example, Delaware corporation law, Section 101(a), states the following: "Any person, partnership, association, or corporation, singly or jointly with others, and without regard to his or their residence, domicile, or state of incorporation, may incorporate or organize a corporation under this chapter by filing with the Secretary of State a certificate of incorporation which shall be executed, acknowledged, filed, and recorded in accordance with Section 103 of this title."

Note however, that the business activities of that corporation may be restricted because its owners are not U.S. citizens. Also a corporation's owners may have to pay additional taxes because of their foreign citizenship (see International Tax and Disclosure Considerations, below).[3]

What type of federal restrictions apply to foreign ownership of U.S. businesses?

There are no blanket restrictions on the ownership of U.S. businesses by foreign persons. However, certain federal regulations restrict or limit foreign ownership in particular industries or in certain circumstances. In 1975, the Committee on Foreign Investment in the United States (CFIUS) was formed by executive order to review investments by foreign governments in the United States that may have an effect on the national interests of the United States. Although the committee has no power to block or modify investments by foreign governments, its recommendations are taken seriously by agencies that do have such power. The following laws control foreign investment and activity in specific industries or circumstances:

- *The Edge Act* limits foreign ownership of corporations chartered by the Federal Reserve Board to engage in international banking and finance.[4]

- *The Federal Aviation Act* prohibits any foreign air carrier, or person controlling such an entity, from acquiring "control in any manner whatsoever" of any U.S. entity or enterprise substantially engaged in the aeronautics business.

- *The Federal Communications Act* bars aliens, foreign governments, certain U.S. corporations controlled by foreign interests, and corporations organized outside the United States from possessing a broadcast or common carrier license.

- *The Merchant Marine Act* restricts the registration and licensing of vessels to those vessels owned, chartered, or leased from the Secretary of Commerce by a U.S. citizen, or a corporation, partnership, or association which is organized in the United States and controlled by U.S. citizens.

- *The Mineral Lands Leasing Act* requires that any corporation applying to the Secretary of the Interior for a federal lease to develop certain natural resources of the United States disclose the identity and citizenship of shareholders owning more than 10 percent of its stock, in which case the lease will be granted only if U.S. persons can obtain reciprocal licenses or leases from the home governments of such foreign shareholders.

- *The Omnibus Trade and Competitiveness Act,* passed in 1988, authorizes the U.S. President to suspend or prohibit mergers, acquisitions, and takeovers of U.S. entities by "foreign persons" if it is determined that "the foreign interest exercising control might take action that threatens to impair the national security." The President's determination is not subject to judicial review. In making the determination, the President may take into account domestic capacity to meet national defense requirements, among other factors.[5] The President must commence any investigation within 30 days after notice of the merger, acquisition, or takeover and complete the investigation within 45 days. Any decision to take action must be announced no later than 15 days after the investigation is completed.

- *The Shelflands Act* stipulates that offshore leases for the development of energy resources be held only by citizens, nationals, and permanent resident aliens of the United States, and business associations thereof. However, because the Department of the Interior considers any corporation organized in the United States an entity suitable for an award of a lease, foreign possession of leases is possible through incorporation of a U.S. subsidiary.

Are there any special federal requirements that apply to U.S. businesses owned or controlled by foreign persons?

Yes—primarily disclosure requirements. First, disclosure requirements generally applicable to acquisitions, such as requirements under the Hart-Scott-

Rodino Act and the Williams Act (see Chapters 2 and 12), apply to foreign, as well as U.S., investors. Second, the following federal laws establish specific disclosure requirements for foreign investors:

- *The International Investment and Trade in Services Survey Act* requires U.S. business enterprises to report to the Department of Commerce, within 45 days, the acquisition of a voting interest of 10 percent or more in such enterprise by one or more foreign persons if the interest was acquired for a price exceeding U.S.$1 million. Under this law, passed in 1976, if the enterprise has annual sales, assets, or net income of greater than $10 million, annual and quarterly financial reporting are also required. In addition to the reporting requirements of foreign investors, the act also requires reporting by any citizen of the United States who assists or intervenes in the acquisition of a voting interest of at least 10 percent by a foreign person or who enters into a joint venture with a foreign person to create a U.S. business enterprise.

- *The Foreign Investment in Real Property Tax Act,* passed in 1986, granted the Secretary of the Treasury the authority to require reporting by foreign persons holding direct investments in U.S. real property interests having an aggregate fair market value of $450,000 or more.

- *The Agricultural Foreign Investment Disclosure Act* requires a foreign person or entity to file a report within 90 days following the acquisition or transfer of any interest, other than a lien or security interest, in U.S. farming, ranching, or timberland.

- *The Tax Equity and Fiscal Responsibility Act,* passed in 1982, requires domestic and foreign corporations that (1) are controlled by a foreign person and (2) engage in a trade or business in the United States to file annual information returns.

- *The Tax Reform Act of 1986,* the *Revenue Reconciliation Act of 1990,* the *Omnibus Budget Reconciliation Act of 1993,* and the *Taxpayer Relief Act of 1997* have preserved or expanded foreign reporting requirements. The 1997 tax law contained several technical provisions relating to the taxation of controlled foreign corporations. Readers should note Section 1131 regarding transfers to foreign entities, Section 1144 regarding earnings invested in excess passive assets, and Section 13232, which modifies taxation of investment in U.S. property.

Must foreign investors be concerned about specific state regulations as well as U.S. federal law when acquiring a U.S. business interest?

In general, states do not restrict foreign investment, except with respect to specific industries, such as banking and insurance. Most states have passed antitakeover laws (see Chapter 12), but these apply equally to U.S. and foreign acquirers. Some states, such as California, Iowa, New Mexico, and Pennsylvania, restrict land ownership with respect to certain types of property, and the exploitation or development of natural resources by foreign investors. A foreign person desiring to acquire a business interest in the United States should seek legal counsel to ensure that there are no special restrictions imposed by the state in which the target business is domiciled, or by federal law.

Do any of the foregoing restrictions apply to U.S. businesses in which foreign persons hold debt rather than equity?

No. In the United States the percentage of equity owned is the exclusive means of measuring the extent of a foreign investor's control of a U.S. corporation. Debt holdings are not considered.

Does federal or state law limit the ability of a U.S. company to guarantee the indebtedness of a foreign affiliate?

There are no federal limitations on the ability of a U.S. company to guarantee foreign indebtedness. Any state limitations on a corporation's ability to guarantee indebtedness would be set forth in the state's corporation statutes, but such limitations are relatively rare. Where limitations do exist under state law, these limitations apply regardless of the nationality of the person on whose behalf the guarantee is given.

Are there legal limitations under U.S. law on the ability of a U.S. company to pledge its assets to a foreign lender?

The power of a corporation to acquire, utilize, and dispose of assets arises from state corporation statutes and is not dependent upon the identity of other parties to the transaction. For example, Section 122 of the Delaware general corporation law empowers any Delaware corporation to "sell, convey, lease, exchange, transfer, or otherwise dispose of, or mortgage or pledge, all or any of its property and assets, or any interest therein, wherever situated." U.S. federal law imposes no restriction on the pledge of assets by U.S. individuals or entities.

Does the United States impose any restrictions on the amount of dollars that can be paid by a U.S. business to a foreign investor?

There is no limit, under current U.S. law, to the amount of money that can be taken out of the United States by either U.S. or foreign investors. In fact, it is the lack of such restrictions that has led to the rapid development of large offshore currency markets.

Do most countries have laws that affect their citizens' acquisitions in other countries?

Many industrialized nations impose certain domestic laws and/or additional external investment laws on foreign companies acquired by their citizens. The acquirer must be aware of how these domestic and external investment laws might affect its investment.

An example of one area of concern is trade policy. In a merger between two companies, one company's country may want to increase exports, while the other company's country may wish to restrict imports. Acquirers should also consider trade policy issues such as quotas, tariffs, and licensing requirements for imports and exports

Trade restrictions are not the only ones that should concern acquirers. In any given country, the potential restraints on economic activity are legion. The Heritage Foundation of Washington, D.C., along with the *Wall Street Journal,* annually measure the extent of freedom in the economies of most of the world's countries. Their *1998 Index of Economic Freedom* scores 156 countries, considering 50 economic variables organized into 10 economic factors, namely trade, taxation, government intervention into the economy, monetary policy, capital flows and foreign investment, banking, wage and price controls, property rights, regulation, and the presence or absence of a black market. Acquirers would be wise to consider all these factors, and to consult the *Index* to see how particular countries or regions rate.

NONTAX ISSUES REGARDING U.S. INVESTMENT ABROAD (OUTBOUND)

What are the main differences between acquisitions that are confined geographically to the United States and those that are international in whole or in part?

One of the advantages that the United States offers dealmakers is that it is a large, homogeneous area that runs on the same basic accounting, legal, and cultural principles. A buyer from Washington State making an acquisition in Florida, or a company in Arizona selling to a firm in Vermont, negotiates from a great deal of shared knowledge, shared perceptions, and shared business practices.

This is not true when a buyer goes abroad, even if only part of a transaction is international. It may seek to find the foreign equivalent of a particular transactional structure in a particular jurisdiction, only to find that there is no such equivalent. For example, a buyer of a Japanese corporation may assume it can offer its lenders warrants as part of its financing package. However, warrants are not contractual obligations enforceable against a Japanese corporation. Therefore, the buyer would have to find other devices to give its lender economic and legal rights that were the same as or similar to those embodied in a warrant.

In the United States a CEO might say, "I'll strike my deal, and then I'll call in the accountants and lawyers." However, that executive is basing his transaction on a great deal of law, tax, and accounting he or she already knows. When dealing in the international arena, managers will need a background on the meaning and reliability of information about the target and country in which it is located.

International dealmaking often forces buyers or sellers to learn an entirely different conceptual vocabulary or framework. At a very basic level, they will find that the same words have different meanings in different countries. For example, the British title *director* and the French title *directeur* do not mean the same thing as the U.S. title *director,* as in board member, but instead refer more generally to an executive.

Similarly, the American concept of antitrust takes on a different meaning in Europe. Whereas the primary aim of U.S. antitrust law has been to maintain market efficiency and to protect consumers by preventing undue market concentration, antitrust law in the European Union (EU) has been to foster market integration by pulling down barriers. In both Europe and Japan, strong cross-shareholdings render the terms *shareholders' rights* and *investor activism* virtually untranslatable.[6]

On the tax and regulatory front, in some countries an acquirer may find that the seller has government as a silent partner. Many foreign countries will reserve the right to review and amend the contracts between a domestic seller and a foreign buyer, in some cases to protect their citizens against overreaching by more sophisticated foreign businessmen, and in others to ensure that the transaction promotes economic development or other governmental policies.

Furthermore, U.S. accounting standards are not universal. In fact, due to generally higher corporate taxes, among other things, Europeans have been accused of playing with reserves in ways to reduce profits (and taxes) in good years. As a result, an income statement of a European company might be substantially misleading to analysts in the United States and must be reinterpreted (and usually recast) by local counsel. Despite the issuance of numerous "accounting directives" for the EU (for example, the Fourth Council Directive on annual accounts and the Seventh Council Directive on consolidated accounts), European accounting remains a patchwork of differing practices:

- Many European companies do not report earnings per share.
- Companies in Europe have different definitions of net profit, shareholders' equity, and extraordinary items. For example, German companies usually don't recognize profit from a project until it is completed and they have been paid, whereas U.K. companies report such profit as soon as they believe they will be paid.
- Until very recently, European treatment of goodwill differed dramatically from U.S. treatment.

These differences may fade now that the aforementioned International Accounting Standards Committee has begun publishing a set of unified global accounting rules for possible adoption by all the world's stock exchanges. The standards are likely to be adopted in most developed countries, with the United States as a last, lone holdout.[7] Some influential voices argue that because U.S. accounting standards are the most stringent in the world, U.S. companies and their investors have little to gain and much to lose by allowing stock exchange listings by companies that do not conform to those standards.

Finally, an American firm acquiring abroad will encounter a new cultural and ethical framework. Differences in forms of government, legal systems, language, and economic approaches must be considered and generally understood by potential cross-border investors. Furthermore, a country's identity is a product of its historical, religious, and social underpinnings, all of which have played a role in the development of that nation's business culture.

U.S. AND FOREIGN LAWS AFFECTING U.S. ACQUISITIONS OF FOREIGN COMPANIES AND ASSETS

What are some of the principal issues a U.S. company should know about in connection with the acquisition of a non-U.S. business or a U.S. business with significant foreign assets?

Some of the key areas to focus on are as follows:

- Differences in rights accorded to employees
- Sources of overseas financing
- The ability to use foreign assets to support financing from lenders
- Regulatory requirements and limitations with respect to the acquisition itself and with post-acquisition operations

In Italy, for example, limitations on foreign purchasers include the following:

- A prohibition preventing foreign entities from purchasing, directly or indirectly, a controlling interest in newspaper publishing companies and television broadcasting companies
- A ban on foreign ownership of ships and aircraft registered in the Italian naval or aircraft registry
- Various restrictions and prohibitions contained in articles and by-laws of Italian corporations (especially banks) as to the ownership of securities by foreigners
- Disclosure rules pertaining to filing obligations applicable to anyone purchasing interests above certain financial thresholds

What types of regulatory requirements affect the pre-acquisition stage of a transaction?

The actual purchase of stock or assets and/or any other contractual arrangements between the parties, such as licenses of intellectual property, may require prior foreign government approval or, at minimum, pre-closing, or immediate post-closing, notification. Under the Australian Foreign Takeovers Act, for example, foreign investors acquiring over 15 percent of an Australian company must notify the Australian Treasury Department for approval, and the Treasury can prohibit any such acquisition it deems would not be in the national interest.

Do many countries have local (or state or private) ownership requirements for businesses operating within their borders?

Yes, it is common for a government to restrict the percentage of ownership that a foreign investor may hold in a local business. For example, in nations belonging to the Andean Pact (a regional organization in Latin America), no more than 20 percent of the capital stock of a company engaged in domestic distribution may be acquired by foreigners. Mexico and Canada have similar restrictions in certain industry sectors.

Weren't restrictions like these lifted under the North American Free Trade Agreement?

The North American Free Trade Agreement (NAFTA) has reduced restrictions but has not eliminated them. Canada has retained its investment screening provisions for investments of more than $150 million and will continue to restrict investments in cultural enterprises (broadcasting, cable, television, film, music, publishing, and recording). Mexico is allowed to screen acquisitions involving more than $25 million—a threshold that will rise to $150 million by 2004, with exceptions in certain sectors (cultural enterprises, financial services, transportation, oil and gas, and uranium production). In these sectors, the Mexican government reserves the right to review smaller transactions.

Are there many restrictions on the form in which one can do business outside the United States?

Generally speaking, one has the same options as those available in the United States. That is, foreign companies may operate through a branch or division located in a foreign country, a subsidiary corporation, or a partnership, although it may be necessary to form the corporation or partnership within the foreign country in accordance with local laws. The joint venture—covered in Chapter 14—is another common form of business association. In fact, in some countries, such as most nonmarket economies, it is the only investment vehicle available to foreigners.

What is the current stance of U.S. antitrust law with regard to U.S. outbound acquisitions?

Unless the product manufactured or distributed by the foreign entity enters into the stream of commerce in, or causes a direct anticompetitive effect inside, the United States, U.S. antitrust laws will not apply to the acquisition or to the operations of the entity thereafter. This is true whether the manufacturing or distributing entity is a wholly owned foreign concern or a foreign subsidiary of a U.S. corporation. If, however, the product does enter the stream of commerce or cause an anticompetitive effect in the United States, then U.S. antitrust laws will apply in the same manner as if the foreign entity were located in the United States, although enforcement is difficult. Even where U.S. courts might find that an act overseas is causing an anticompetitive effect within the United States, the jurisdiction of U.S. courts will usually not reach within the boundaries of another sovereign nation. The Department of Justice has issued guidelines that deal with these kinds of international antitrust concerns.

What do the Department of Justice guidelines concerning international antitrust say about U.S. acquisitions of foreign entities?

A decade ago, the Department of Justice issued Antitrust Guidelines for International Operations, which say that the Department's Antitrust Division will seek to prohibit mergers that would create, enhance, or facilitate the exercise of market power. The guidelines also define what would constitute foreign competition, and give four examples of the competitive analysis that the Department would use in mergers involving foreign competitors:

- The first case describes an acquisition of a foreign competitor by a U.S. firm. The guidelines discuss the difficulty in measuring the market power of foreign competitors. Allocating all a foreign firm's capacity to the U.S. market may be inappropriate if the firm would have difficulty establishing a reputation for quality or a service and/or distribution network, or if exchange rates are unfavorable. If market share data alone give a distorted view of the market, the Department will consider qualitative evidence regarding the competitive significance of foreign competitors (for example, the existence of significant worldwide excess capacity).

- The second case discusses how trade restraints such as voluntary export restraints (VERs), import quotas, and tariffs affect competitive analysis in a merger. Foreign competitors will not be excluded from the relevant market solely because their sales into the United States are subject to quotas or VERs; it is difficult to assess the effectiveness and longevity of such restraints and to measure the likely supply responses of competitors not subject to the restraints. However, the competitive significance of a foreign competitor will be discounted in the case of an "effective binding" percentage quota because a reduction in domestic production would lead to a reduction in imports by foreign firms subject to the quota, making collusion among domestic firms more likely. The guidelines define an "effective" trade restraint as one that cannot be substantially avoided through diversion and arbitrage. A trade restraint is "binding" if firms would sell more than the restraint ceiling if the restraint did not exist. A tariff will be given little significance unless its price level is so prohibitive that imports into the United States would be unprofitable. An example of a significant tariff would be the 25 percent tariff now levied against imported trucks, and the proposed extension of this tariff to minivans and sport/utility vehicles.

- The third case involves the acquisition of a foreign potential competitor. The guidelines note that the merger of a potential competitor will have a significant anticompetitive effect only if (a) the competitor would enter the market independently in the near future, (b) the market is very highly concentrated, and (c) the foreign competitor is one of only a few firms capable of entering into the U.S. market. Even if the U.S. market is very highly concentrated, eliminating only one of several potential entrants would not have any significant anticompetitive effect. If there are few potential competitors, the Department says it will consider whether the foreign competitor actually intended to enter the market, what attempts the competitor made in the past to enter the market, and whether independent entry would be profitable.

- Finally, the fourth case involves the merger of two foreign firms. The guidelines note that in evaluating the merger of two foreign firms, the Department would consider the legitimate interest of other nations in determining whether to challenge the transaction. The Department will be more likely to challenge a transaction if the production facilities of the foreign firms are in the United States. If U.S. production facilities constitute a viable business standing alone, the merger might be permitted to go through conditioned on the divestiture of all or a portion of those assets. In addition, the Department may seek the views of the foreign government concerning the impact of various remedies on its national interests.

What are some other examples of U.S. laws that can affect foreign acquisitions?

Of particular concern to an American owner are laws such as the U.S. Foreign Corrupt Practices Act of 1977 (FCPA), the Anti-Boycott Regulations of the Export Administration Act administered by the U.S. Commerce Department, the Trading with the Enemy Act, and the International Investment and Trade in Services Survey Act of 1976 (IITSSA).

- The FCPA requires all U.S. companies to "devise and maintain a system of internal accounting controls sufficient to provide reasonable assurances" that its bookkeeping will adhere to GAAP. It also makes it unlawful for any company "to make use of the mails or any means or instrumentality of interstate commerce corruptly in furtherance of [a payment] . . . while knowing or having reason to know" that the payment will be used to influence a foreign official to assist the company in obtaining or retaining business. The U.S. parent will be responsible for a failure of a foreign subsidiary to comply with these requirements.

- The Anti-Boycott Regulations empower the President to issue regulations to prevent U.S. companies engaged in interstate or foreign commerce and their subsidiaries from taking any action intending to comply with a boycott by a foreign country against another country with which the United States maintains friendly relations, as long as the company engages in activities in interstate or foreign commerce.[8]

- The Trading with the Enemy Act prohibits unlicensed trade between U.S. persons and any individual, partnership, or other body of individuals that is (1) resident within the territory of any nation with which the United States is at war or (2) engaged in business within such territory. Unlicensed trade with corporations incorporated under the laws of an enemy nation is also prohibited, as is unlicensed trade with any party determined to be an ally of a nation with which the United States is at war.

- The IITSSA requires U.S. companies investing overseas to file certain reports with the Department of Commerce. The filing of reports is mandatory if a U.S. person, including a U.S. corporation, has more than a 10 percent ownership interest in a foreign business enterprise and such enterprise has significant assets, sales, or after-tax income. Moreover, there is a proposal that, if adopted, would require a U.S. company that sells services to or purchases services from an unaffiliated foreign person, including legal and accounting services, to file reports.

What regulations beyond national securities commissions govern international equity investment?

The central organization for equity involvement regulation is the International Organization of Securities Commissions (IOSCO). Headquartered in Montreal, Canada, it is composed of 80 regulatory agencies from around the world. Although stock market rules vary considerably from country to country,[9] the very existence of IOSCO points to a core of values. Moreover, the group and its individual members could gain more importance as the definition of what constitutes a "security" is brought into focus.[10] And securities commissions are working together more often. For example, in October 1991 regulators in the United States and the United Kingdom approved the first single-offer document for a takeover affecting investors in both countries.

What about the merger regulations of the European Union?

Each member has its own comprehensive merger laws, but these are superseded by any directives intended for the EU. For example, the EU's European Commission issued a proposed regulation on merger control in 1973 and subsequently amended it in 1982 and 1984; this was proposed to member states in 1989, but withdrawn in 1992 after strong resistance from several EU members.

In 1996, the European Commission issued a new policy with five guiding principles:

- All securities holders should be treated equally.
- All those to whom an offer is addressed must have enough time and receive enough information to make a properly informed decision.
- The board of an offeree company must act in the best interests of the company as a whole.
- An offer must not create false markets in the securities of the offeree company, the offeror company, or any other company concerned by the offer.
- The business of an offeree company should not be hindered beyond a reasonable time by an offer for its securities.[11]

Has the EU been tough on mergers?

Yes. The EU's antitrust staff has been rigorous in enforcing the new merger laws, and the European Court of Justice has been tough in its rulings,[12] despite concerns expressed by the American Bar Association and others.[13]

What are foreign exchange control laws, and how can they affect post-acquisition operations?

Foreign exchange control laws restrict the amount of a country's local currency that can be converted into foreign currencies. These laws can operate either to completely restrict, or partially limit, the ability of a foreign investor to remove any funds from the target's country to the foreign investor's home country ("repatriation") or, if it can withdraw funds, to take its profits in its own currency.

Do foreign exchange control laws include restrictions on repayments of loans to nonlocal parent companies?

Yes, in some cases. For example, Japan's foreign exchange control law imposes such restrictions for loans above a certain amount. Above this threshold, the loan transaction will require prior Japanese government approval.

In Taiwan, if a subsidiary needs to obtain foreign currency to repay a loan from its foreign parent, the loan agreement itself must be submitted for approval to the Central Bank of China, and only then may the foreign currency be bought.

French regulations require approval from the French exchange control authorities prior to each advance by a foreign company to its French subsidiary or, conversely, for any setoff or voluntary prepayment of such loan by the French subsidiary.

What is the role of groups such as the European Union's Exchange Rate Mechanism (ERM)?

The ERM functions somewhat like the Organization of Petroleum Exporting Countries (OPEC). It is a group of integrated parties (in the case of ERM, European national governments and central banks) that agree to buy and sell a commodity within a certain price range. The ERM is structured more loosely, however, and allows for market forces—including speculators—to play a role in price setting.

Are there any risks involved in doing business in a foreign country because of currency differences between the parent and a foreign subsidiary or affiliate?

Yes, fluctuating exchange rates pose two types of risk to the investor. First, there is the purely economic risk of an unfavorable change in currency rates. A deteriorating exchange rate will require domestic parent companies to pay more for foreign currency–denominated obligations than was originally anticipated when the obligations were approved, and a relative increase in the value of a foreign currency will cause domestic creditors to be repaid a lesser amount in satisfaction of domestic currency–denominated obligations to them. Second, there is an accounting risk that the balance sheet, which in some countries must express the value of assets and liabilities denominated in a domestic currency at the exchange rate in place on the balance sheet date, will lose value in the translation from the local foreign currency to domestic dollars.

The accounting risk was reduced by Statement No. 52 of the Financial Accounting Standards Board (FASB). This altered the U.S. rule that foreign currency translation gains and losses had to be immediately reported as income. Now gains or losses resulting from the translation of foreign-denominated income statements are only reported as an adjustment to stockholders' equity. This allows a company's lenders or investors to analyze its income statements much more consistently, without worrying as much about the impact of a volatile currency exchange.

How can U.S. owners mitigate the risk inherent in fluctuating exchange rates?

In order to alleviate the risk of economic losses due to exchange rate volatility, two forms of hedging contracts have been developed: the forward purchase contract and the forward sales contract—in essence, a "put" and a "call." Both are derivative instruments that can be risky.[14] Forward purchase contracts are used to protect a U.S. debtor who is obligated to repay a certain amount in a foreign currency at a future date. When the value of the foreign currency rises relative to the U.S. dollar, the debtor will have to spend more dollars to obtain the necessary amount of foreign currency to repay its debt. The forward purchase contract locks up the price at which the debtor may acquire the needed amount of currency at the necessary time for a fixed price determined at the time the forward purchase contract is entered into. It is, in effect, a "call" on foreign currency.

Similarly, a U.S. creditor who is afraid that rising exchange rates may cause it to lose the value of its foreign-denominated receivables may hedge against such loss through a forward sales contract. In this case, the creditor contracts to sell the foreign currency to be received at a future date for U.S. dollars at a fixed rate determined at the time the forward contract is entered into. This is a "put" equivalent. Both kinds of swap are discussed in more detail later in this chapter.

In addition to currency swaps, owners can use currency options. Options to purchase various currencies at a fixed price are available on many foreign and domestic securities exchanges. Currency options are listed on the exchanges at a particular fixed price (the *strike price*) in accordance with the length of the option period, which is generally 30, 60, or 90 days. The hedging party pays a premium for the ability to purchase the optioned currency at the relevant strike price at any time up to the termination date of the option. If the actual price for one unit of foreign currency exceeds the strike price, the hedging party can exercise its option and receive the currency at a cheaper price per unit. If the actual price never exceeds the strike price for the currency during the option period, the hedging party loses its premium paid for the option but is not required to take delivery of (or pay for) the actual currency.

This feature is the distinguishing factor between forward contracts and options, because forward contracts obligate one to take physical delivery of the currency at an agreed-upon date in the future. The degree of certainty of a hedger's need for a specific amount of foreign currency, plus the difference in the fixed price per unit of foreign currency between forward contracts and options at any given time, will dictate which form of hedging technique will be used.

In addition to currency hedging through swaps or options, companies can consider shifting production and/or fulfillment to countries where currencies are weakening.[15]

The foregoing arrangements add to the cost of the overseas investment, and both legal and accounting experts should be consulted with respect to the tax and financial reporting consequences of such hedging methods.

After a foreign acquisition, can the investor repatriate profits or investment capital from its business interests located in a foreign country without limitations or restrictions?

As a general proposition, most developing and newly industrialized countries have some form of repatriation restrictions, and some other nations that impose exchange controls also regulate repatriation.

Repatriation restrictions or requirements are usually imposed for the same purposes as exchange controls, that is, to acquire or retain foreign currency in a country, to monitor foreign investment, and to police potential tax evasion. Many countries regulating repatriations also provide tax incentives for investors to reinvest profits.

Repatriation restrictions are generally accompanied by some form of additional restriction or reporting requirements, such as (1) registration of foreign capital with corresponding restrictions on withdrawal of such capital from the host country and (2) notification of amounts of foreign capital invested in the host country.

For instance, under Brazil's profit remittance law, registration of foreign investments is required if capital or profit repatriation, royalties, or technical assistance fee remittances are desired. The Central Bank issues a certificate of registration stating the amount of capital brought in, which is called the *registered foreign capital base*. This number will limit the total amount to be subsequently repatriated without penalty. Beyond the permitted amounts, a supplementary tax will be imposed. The greater the registered foreign capital base, the higher the remittances and repatriations can be in the foreign currency. If not registered, the investment will remain in the local currency, and no repatriation will be permitted.

For years, foreign-owned Brazilian firms were allowed to repatriate at the rate of 12 percent per annum of their registered capital base. The money to be repatriated had to be deposited in a government bank. In recent years many such deposits have had to wait for a sufficient quantity of the desired repatriation currency to be accumulated by the government before the repatriation could take place and was prioritized based on reciprocal currency movements. The effect of this has been to discourage repatriation and to help conserve Brazil's slim foreign exchange reserves—especially of the world's hard currencies. (Brazil continues to have major problems with its currencies and has had several different currencies within the past decade.)

Under Argentina's foreign investments law, even when foreign exchange controls are in force, there is no cap on the amount of profits that may be repatriated by foreign investors, provided the investment has been duly registered at the Foreign Investments Registry. During a foreign exchange crisis, however, the government is empowered to curtail the ability of foreign investors to repatriate profits freely upon proper notification.

What are some other regulatory concerns involved in a foreign acquisition?

Most other regulations concerning overseas investments can be classified into the following categories: performance requirements, local content regulations, labor requirements, and technology transfer restrictions.

Performance requirements include setting minimum export levels on the one hand and maximum import levels (such as quotas) on the other. Export-level requirements are designed to promote the flow of foreign currency into a country by permitting a foreign person to invest in a particular local enterprise provided a minimum percentage of its finished product will be exported rather than distributed locally. Countries may also impose import restrictions, usually expressed as a maximum percentage of the cost of goods produced locally that can be imported, to encourage use of local products and industries.

Local content regulations specify minimum levels of domestic raw materials or component parts to be utilized in manufacturing, limitations on the type of products that can be manufactured, and restrictions on product distribution within the country and in the world market. Such limitations are often tied to economic incentives such as government subsidies or tax breaks and, if not imposed by statute, can be negotiated with the host country. Various countries relate local content requirements to specific industries to ensure that local companies do not suffer from the foreign presence.

Countries concerned with unemployment will usually require foreign companies to employ a certain percentage of local labor in both unskilled and managerial jobs. Failure by the investor to accede to such demands can cause the host country government to withhold required approval of the acquisition itself.

Restrictions on technology transfers usually take the form of limitations on royalty or profit remittances, technical assistance, and payments for transfers of technology, especially between related entities. These regulations are encountered most frequently in the less-developed and newly industrialized nations, although they also exist in any country that desires to promote a particular high-technology domestic industry. Technical assistance and royalty payments are frequently subjected to restrictions because they could potentially be used to circumvent dividend remittance regulations, especially to foreign parent companies.

One example of such restrictions can be found in Argentina, where a license agreement between a foreign parent company and the local subsidiary requires prior government approval. The approval will be granted if the agreement exhibits the characteristics of an arm's-length transaction. By contrast, in Brazil, royalty payments between related entities are entirely prohibited when the royalty recipient exercises voting control over the Brazilian subsidiary. Assuming the contract for royalties has received government approval, the subsidiary may only make such payments to the parent's account in Brazil and must make such payments in Brazilian currency.

What issues concerning employees should the acquirer be on the lookout for?

First of all, the acquirer should ascertain whether the employees have any rights to approve the proposed acquisition. For example, most workers in Europe have the right to information and consultation when management contemplates major changes or plans. This right emanates from national industry sector collective bargaining agreements that set minimum standards and specific company agreements with employee representatives or trade unions.

Second, the acquirer should familiarize itself with the rights of employees with respect to the governance of the enterprise. For example, Europeans have had decades of experience with various forms of so-called co-determination, imposed by law or won through collective bargaining. Worker participation in management ranges from the right to information, to obligatory consultations, and even to a veto in decision making. The most well-known example of co-determination is found in Germany, where, by law, each company must have two boards, one concerned with operations and the other with more strategic issues. Both boards have employee representatives. In the Netherlands, any company of medium size or larger must consult with its Works Council before implementing any decision affecting investments, dismissals, and pensions. The Works Council also has the power to challenge corporate decisions in court if its advice is not followed.

Third, the acquirer should understand the nature of employee benefits afforded in a particular country and take the cost of such benefits into account in evaluating the merits of a potential acquisition. For example, the majority of European workers have, under certain conditions, the right not to be unfairly dismissed. In most European countries, an employee is entitled to redundancy compensation—that is, continued payment even though there may no longer be work for him or her. Moreover, unemployment compensation rights in the EC generally are more substantial than in the United States. Aside from these legislated rights, an employee can also avail himself or herself of the usual breach of contract remedies, which may include damages and specific performance—forcing the employer to perform on the written contract that is required between the two parties outlining employment terms covering pay scales, work hours, pensions, holidays, and so on. Finally, in several European countries unfair or "abusive" dismissal is actionable, giving affected employees a claim for damages against the companies that dismissed them.

CROSS-BORDER DEAL FINANCING

Once a suitable acquisition of a foreign concern has been identified, how can an acquirer obtain financing for it?

For the most part, the methods of financing an international acquisition will not be very different from those used in a purely domestic deal. Various types of debt, ranging from standard commercial bank debt to subordinated debt (junior/senior/mezzanine), to debt secured by a variety of assets, can be used in the international context. This debt financing can be obtained from both public and private sources. Equity financing through the sale and issuance of new securities is also possible in the global deal. But whatever sources of financing an acquirer uses, they will have a global dimension.

In considering an international transaction, the potential acquirer may find it necessary to call on a variety of different currencies and to operate within several international jurisdictions. The acquirer must learn how such financial transactions can be affected by regulations imposed by its own government, as well as the governments of the target country, the countries in which investors and lenders reside, and the countries in which banks and securities exchanges may be located. Areas of concern will include tax consequences, the ability of investors to repatriate profits, perfecting of the lenders' security interests, and the like. Similarly, the rules of certain supranational or regional institutions, such as the United Nations, the EU, or the Organization of American States, or agreements, such as GATT and NAFTA, may apply.

What special public sources of financing are available to the transnational acquirer?

Many countries have loan programs for businesses that wish to expand into overseas markets. Although most of these programs focus on export, they are not limited to this realm. In the United States, the Overseas Private Investment Corp. (OPIC) provides hundreds of millions of dollars in yearly loans and loan guarantees to companies—including small companies—that do business abroad. In some cases, the borrowers have used their funds to invest in foreign concerns.

Suppose a seller demands to be paid in a currency that is different from the operating currency of the entity making the payments. How can the acquirer accomplish this?

The incompatibility of differing currencies has always ranked high among the classic dilemmas buyers and sellers face when structuring an international transaction.

At the end of World War II, many American corporations decided to apply some of their newfound wealth to direct investment in foreign companies, particularly in Europe. To finance these investments, they found it necessary to come up with large amounts of the functional currency used by the companies they were acquiring. To do this, the U.S. firms either had to borrow from unfamiliar banking institutions in the acquirees' home country, which did not always have sufficient funds to meet the purchase price, or had to go through the cumbersome process of obtaining the necessary funds in U.S. dollars and converting them into the needed currency, incurring the added expense of an intermediary broker. Since the downfall of the Bretton Woods system in 1971, when the U.S. dollar was taken off the gold standard, potential acquirers have inherited the further difficulty of predicting the rise and fall of fluctuating exchange rates of individual currencies.

It is within this framework that the concept of large offshore international banking markets has developed as an alternative to currency conversion. An example of such a system is the Eurodollar market, that is, the deposit or redeposit of U.S. dollars into a large pool on foreign territory without the conversion of the funds into the local currency. The transaction is recorded by book entry, and there is no physical importation of the dollars into the foreign country. The pooling entity into which dollars are deposited may be either a foreign branch of a U.S. banking institution or an independent foreign bank, both of which have become known as "Eurobanks." The Eurobanks can make short-, medium-, or long-term loans for acquisitions or working capital and participate in a wide variety of interbank lending activities. Eurobank deposits also exist for offshore deposits of Japanese yen, British sterling, and other currencies in demand.[16]

Because offshore banking in different currencies has not been heavily regulated by any jurisdiction (for example, Eurobanks are not subject to the same reserve requirements as domestic banks), offshore banks are able to commit a much higher percentage of bank funds to corporate and other loans.

The Eurodollar market and the new European Monetary Union help foster investment in Europe, but how can investors in other parts of the world use offshore markets to finance their acquisitions?

The Eurocurrency market is not the only site of offshore currency deposits. Another major example of U.S. dollar deposits used for foreign corporate investments is the Asian international currency market, principally located in Singapore and Hong Kong. In Singapore the government and banking authorities have invented special units of money called Asian currency units (ACUs). Banks authorized by the government of Singapore to handle ACUs accept deposits in all foreign currencies to accommodate corporate financing throughout the Pacific Rim.

How are interest rates on funds borrowed in the offshore market calculated?

Generally, interest in the Eurocurrency market is tied to the London interbank offered rate (LIBOR), and ACUs are tied to the Singapore interbank offered rate (SIBOR). The interbank offered rate is the interest charged by an offshore depository of a particular currency for funds lent in that currency to another offshore banking facility. This rate is used in international finance in the same way the prime rate is used in the United States, that is, as a reference rate from which the individual interest rate of a particular loan is created. LIBOR, SIBOR, and other interbank rates are listed in many of the world's financial newspapers.

What happens when one bank, whether an onshore or an offshore facility, does not have adequate funds to meet an acquirer's lending needs?

This is the function of the international syndicated loan market, which is particularly useful for onshore banks that must maintain a high ratio of capital reserves to borrowed funds, or banks that do not want to bear the entire risk of a large international loan by themselves.

How do international syndicated loans work?

The principles behind international syndication are generally the same as in a purely domestic syndicated loan, with the added considerations of differing currencies, interest and exchange rates, tax and other government regulatory schemes, supranational currency controls, and the like.

In an international syndication, a group of lenders will pool its funds via a network of selling participations and other agreements until the required borrowing amount is obtained. There is only one loan agreement between the borrower and the syndication, which is negotiated among the parties to fit the particular needs of the transaction. Funds can flow from either onshore or offshore currency markets.

Typically, the funds borrowed under an international syndicated loan agreement will be subject to five charges to the borrower: (1) interest (which can be tied to an international reference rate such as LIBOR or SIBOR, plus a spread); (2) a management fee, which is paid to the lead bank for arranging and managing the syndication; (3) a commitment fee; (4) an agent's fee, which is usually paid to the lead bank for negotiating the loan and acting as agent on behalf of the other members of the syndicate; and (5) any expenses associated with putting together the loan, which can include legal and accounting fees, travel costs, and the like.

There are generally two forms of international syndication. In one, the lenders who are party to the loan agreement commit to lend a stated amount directly to the borrower. The lenders are severally, but not jointly, liable on their lending obligations. Every member of the syndication receives a pro rata portion of the overall receipts from the loan based on its individual commitment of funds.

In the other form of syndication, the lead bank is the only bank bound by a loan agreement to the borrower, and it is solely responsible for the commitment to fund the loan. The lead bank then signs participation or subscription agreements with other lenders who want to participate in the loan as it was negotiated by the lead bank (although, in some cases, it may be necessary for the lead bank to come back to the borrower and ask for amendments that will facilitate the lead bank's finding willing participants). Again, the lead bank will pay the participants their pro rata share of the loan receipts, after deducting whatever management, agent, or subscription fees it may have negotiated.

A very typical situation is where a U.S. company wants to finance the acquisition of another U.S. company that has significant overseas operations. In this case, the lead bank will usually be the primary domestic lender, which may use syndication as a means of bringing in foreign lenders familiar with the business and economic climates of the countries where the company's overseas operations are concentrated. Such syndication will reduce the risk of a U.S. lender that otherwise may be reluctant to lend overseas, but lenders will need to work out a variety of intercreditor issues, including the priority of assets securing the acquisition funding.

Are banks the only institutions that can participate in an international loan syndication?

No. Recently, international syndications have included large-scale investors willing to take the risk of lending for corporate acquisitions or refinancings. Such entities could include insurance companies, pension funds, government-sponsored investment pools, mutual funds, or large corporations. Whether or not a particular entity can participate in a syndicated loan may be governed by national regulations in force in the country where the potential participant is domiciled.

What types of assurances will the syndicating lenders generally require from the borrower?

The covenants and representations required by the lenders in an international syndication today are generally not much different from a domestic U.S. syndicator's requirements, although historically international loans have tended to be unsecured. Today more and more foreign lenders are looking to corporate fixed assets, inventories, and accounts receivable as security for international syndicated loans. Most syndication agreements include, at minimum, a negative pledge clause (where the borrower promises not to encumber any future assets) and a *pari passu* clause stating that the priority of the lending banks' rights will be equivalent compared with those of any other creditor of the same class. The loan agreement may also contain financial covenants and other restrictions upon the borrower typically found in domestic loans.

Are traditional loans the only kind of financing that can be syndicated?

No; lenders may also wish to use syndication to spread the risk of large letters of credit or guarantees backed by offshore currency deposits, or international commercial paper programs such as a Euro-CD or Asian dollar-CD.[17]

Can an acquirer's international merger and acquisition activities be funded by issuing private or public debt securities?

Yes. Private or public placements of debt can be effectively utilized by issuers who feel they can attract investors at lower rates than the interbank offered rates, or who desire long-term, fixed-interest debt.

The offshore currency markets have funded individual corporate debt issues in a multitude of currencies, facilitating investment in corporations located all over the world. The best example of this has been the Eurobond market, which has been expanding rapidly over the past two decades.

Eurobonds can be denominated in any currency but are issued offshore and are usually structured to be sold outside the jurisdiction of the nation whose currency is used or where the issuer resides. For example, in the United States the present policy seems to be that unregistered debt securities may be issued overseas by U.S. issuers but must not be sold or offered for sale to any U.S. person, or anywhere within the United States, until the passage of a 90-day "rest abroad" period. The SEC imposes certain requirements on U.S. issuers designed to ensure that no such sales are made during the rest abroad period, including the placement of a restrictive legend on the bond itself.

Offshore bonds are generally issued in bearer form, and many can have provisions that exclude the interest paid thereon from withholding taxes imposed by countries where the bonds are distributed. They may be privately or publicly traded and often appear on the stock exchanges of the major financial centers from London to Tokyo. Again, the use of international syndicates of underwriters and lending institutions will be instrumental in issuing offshore corporate bonds.

What other types of debt financing are available?

The list is long, thanks to two factors: borrowers' and lenders' needs for greater liquidity. These twin needs have led to the development of a whole spectrum of international negotiable instruments, the utility of which depends upon the needs and repayment abilities of borrowers.

Negotiable medium-term or long-term fixed-rate notes (FRNs) are bearer notes evidencing the obligation of the maker of the notes to pay a stated principal amount upon maturity of the note, with periodic payments of interest at a fixed rate. This type of note may be more convenient than conventional bank notes, which usually require the principal to be amortized over the life of the note, rather than deferring payment until maturity. Sale of the FRNs is accomplished through subscription agreements, which provide for investors to buy a note or notes worth a certain stated amount upon fulfillment of various conditions or the making of certain representations and warranties by the issuer. Terms and conditions appear on the reverse of the notes.

Another innovation in the Eurocurrency market is the Euronote, a short-term bearer note evidencing the obligation of the maker to pay the stated principal amount at maturity (generally three to six months). Because of the short term of the notes, Euronote makers can take advantage of lower interest rates in the Eurocurrency markets. The terms and conditions of short-term notes will generally be much less rigorous than those found on FRNs or in bond underwriting agreements.

Suppose an acquirer encounters a group of multinational investors, all of which want to lend, and be repaid, in their own currencies rather than in offshore funds?

One fairly recent innovation in promissory notes is the medium-term note (MTN), in which the maker offers a program of notes through one or more agents that place the notes for a commission on a best-efforts basis. Initial holders can negotiate the terms of their individual notes to suit such holders' specific repayment requirements with respect to currencies, payment structures, or rates of interest. Therefore, using an MTN program a maker may have a series of notes outstanding, each one with a different currency, interest rate calculation, or term. This kind of note program allows an issuer to attract a larger pool of investors by catering to their specific needs at a cost that is often less than a comparable underwriter's fee would be for an underwritten offering.

How can an acquirer obtain the different currencies it needs to meet its obligations to its investors?

It could simply convert the currency generated by the acquired company through a foreign exchange broker for a fee, or through the use of a swap.

Swaps, a forward contract type of derivative instrument (see note 14), may be used to exchange currencies or to exchange interest rates, or they may combine the two. A currency swap agreement is a contract calling for the parties to supply each other with a stated amount of currency at specific intervals. For example, one party might agree to pay the other in euros in exchange for an equivalent amount of U.S. dollars and British pounds.

In such a case an interest rate swap agreement is negotiated in which the borrower corporation and another party with access to various currencies, perhaps through its own subsidiaries, agree to pay each other a sum equal to the interest that would have accrued on a specific amount over a specific period of time at the desired rate. The exchanging party may be a bank or a large corporation with access to various currencies, perhaps through its own subsidiaries. This corporation may have a Eurobond issue outstanding on which it is obligated to pay a fixed rate of interest. In this case an interest rate swap agreement may be in order, in which the corporation and another party agree to pay to each other a sum equal to the interest that would have accrued on a specific amount over a specific period of time at a negotiated rate.

For example, take a company with outstanding loans bearing interest at LIBOR plus 0.25 percent, payable to one investor in euros and another investor in pounds, and another company that pays interest in U.S. dollars at a fixed rate (say, 8.5 percent) to its Eurobondholders. A swap could be structured so that the first company receives from the second company a payment in euros and pounds equal to the interest it must pay its investors in exchange for payments to the second company of the interest that would accrue on the same principal amount at the fixed rate of 8.5 percent. This is a combined interest rate and currency swap, which meets the first company's requirements for repayment to its investors. So long as the floating rate does not fall significantly below the fixed rate, the foregoing is a good business transaction for the first company.

Swap agreements should generally be for shorter terms to protect against significant fluctuations in interest rates or currency exchange rates, which can throw off the economics of a swap transaction, with periodic rollover provisions allowing for the continuation of the agreement on the same or renegotiated terms of exchange. From a legal point of view, swap agreements are nothing more than international contracts that will be governed under the contract law of whichever country the parties choose to govern interpretation of contract terms. Swaps are complicated, and, some might argue, risky, but as international currency markets have grown, swaps have become more and more important in structuring transnational deals.

Another financing technique is the conversion of debt for equity, or a debt-equity swap. How does it work, and when is its use appropriate?

Debt-for-equity conversions evolved as one solution to the paucity of hard currency foreign exchange available to a debtor country for external debt payments. The conversion allows the debtor country to discharge foreign hard currency-denominated debt through payments in soft local currency. Some countries that have such formal debt-for-equity conversion programs are Argentina, Brazil, Chile, Costa Rica, Ecuador, Mexico, and the Philippines. There are commercial firms that specialize in arranging such swap programs, which tend to get rather complicated. Further, more and more negotiated and even some limited auction markets are opening up for the purchase and sale of debt instruments payable in many different currencies but taking advantage of the growth and sophistication of the currency swap markets.

The basic steps in a debt-equity swap are as follows: (1) The foreign commercial bank creditor will decide either to invest in a local business located in the debtor country or to sell its loan asset to a third-party investor at a discount; (2) the bank or the investor then redeems the credit for its designated value in the debtor's local currency; and (3) the bank or the investor subsequently invests the proceeds in a local enterprise.

The investor generally has one of two reasons for engaging in a swap transaction: the desire to make a new investment in the debtor country or the desire to recapitalize an existing subsidiary or affiliate in the debtor country. In both cases, the highly favorable discount rate will substantially reduce the cost of equity to the investor. On the converse side, the debtor country wishes to reduce its external debt and to encourage or maintain investment interest in its economy. Moreover, the debtor country can create value for itself if it can retire its debt at a price below its face value.

Resources derived from such transactions are intended to enhance the debtor country's economy. As a result, certain types of investments—such as those that increase exports of the debtor country, bring new technology into the country, or finance industry expansion or new product development—are given preferential consideration.

Can acquirers obtain security interests on the assets of foreign companies to finance acquisitions?

Yes. Today, most foreign countries have concepts that are the same as or analogous to those of the United States regarding security interests in assets to serve as collateral for borrowing.

There are many differences, however, in the types of assets that can be secured, the methods of accomplishing such a transaction, the type of notice required, if any, and the authority to whom notice must be given. Thus, it is imperative that local counsel be enlisted to complete these transactions. In the United Kingdom, the method of securitization is similar to that employed in the United States. A fixed charge (or mortgage interest) is granted over specific real or leasehold property interests, fixed assets, and goodwill, and a floating charge (or after-acquired property security interest) is granted on accounts receivable and inventory.

France is an example of a country in which securitization becomes more problematic. A *contract hypothecaire* is used to grant a mortgage on real property, whereas a *nantissement de fonds de commerce* is the French document granting a security interest in tangible or intangible fixed assets. It becomes effective upon the occurrence of a default by the borrower. The *nantissement de fonds de commerce,* however, does not include accounts receivable or inventory, and although it may be legally possible to include such assets in the agreement, perfecting it may not be a practical expedient. In the case of accounts receivable, perfection requires that notice of the security interest be sent to each account party by a French process server upon establishment of the account. In the case of inventory, the only method of perfecting such an interest is by possession, that is, a field warehousing arrangement whereby a third party is hired to keep custody of the inventory on behalf of the secured party.

In Japan, civil liens (*sakidori tokken*) and possessory liens (*riyachiken*) are given only by law and cannot be established by contract or by judicial decree. A Japanese entity may assign rights it has in real property or movable chattels (including inventory) by contract, but in the case of chattels, in order for such an assignment to be valid against third parties the secured party must be in possession, and the consent of the assignor must be certified by a notary public or post office. Accounts receivable may be pledged as security in Japan, provided that there is nothing to the contrary contained in the agreement between the original parties establishing the account.

What happens if a country does not permit a floating security interest on after-acquired property?

As previously discussed, in contrast to the customary U.S. practice of obtaining "floating" liens on assets not as yet acquired, many countries do not permit this type of security interest. To include new assets as collateral, the parties must enter into additional security agreements and comply with all formalities imposed by the governing law of the country every time a newly acquired asset is to be included in the lender's security.

Can the concept of an LBO be applied in the international context?

Yes. The leveraged LBO has become an accepted acquisition structure in several European nations, particularly in the United Kingdom, France, and Germany. It is a useful tool for large family-owned enterprises established after

World War II by owners now reaching retirement age, and for large state-owned conglomerates now in the process of privatizing. In the latter case, new owners are selling off unrelated businesses, a practice not permitted under state ownership.

What would the structure of a management LBO look like, for example, in France?

The structure employed in France would not be vastly different from the structure one would use in the United States, with certain exceptions resulting from the corporate and business laws of France. The financing will usually entail a tripartite structure comprising (1) senior debt from a traditional lending institution, which may or may not be collateralized; (2) middle-tier financing, including subordinated or convertible debt at a higher fixed rate of interest; and (3) straight equity investment by the managers and other investors. Applicable laws in France and other EU countries are, for the most part, liberal enough to allow creativity in structuring an LBO.

Other than the perfection of security interests, which has already been discussed, are there any other problems a senior lender might face in a French LBO?

If shares of the foreign parent company's stock are pledged to a French lender, the lender may not be able to foreclose upon such shares in the event of a default without the prior approval of the French government. In practice this risk has not been an impediment to accepting such pledges of foreign stock.

Can an acquired company in France guarantee the debt of the foreign parent for acquisition funding?

This sort of upstream guarantee is a problem, because the 1981 French Company Law prohibits a French corporation from advancing moneys, making loans, or facilitating security interests with the intent of aiding a third party to purchase such French corporation's own stock. There is an exemption, however, for loans to employees of the French company. This problem goes away if the LBO is structured as an asset deal, but there are significant tax consequences in the event of an asset transaction, so the potential investor should be very careful in his or her analysis of which structure to use. In the case of an international LBO, as with all international transactions, it is important to consult with local counsel in the country where the acquired company is located.

INTERNATIONAL TAX AND DISCLOSURE CONSIDERATIONS

What are the fundamental tax considerations for an acquirer that apply specifically to international acquisitions?

Generally, when a transaction involves multiple jurisdictions, the rules of all the jurisdictions apply. In other words, an international transaction, whether outbound or inbound, is rarely exempt from domestic rules. As a result of these rules, tax planning in the international context will inevitably become more complex.[18]

The most important thing that a buyer or a seller of a business with international components must bear in mind is that at every stage of planning, consideration must be given to the tax rules of each of the countries involved, as well as to the manner in which their tax systems overlap and interact. It is not uncommon to have three or four different tax systems governing parts or all of a single transaction, and this may present both opportunities and traps. Because of the disparities in the tax laws, and because of the existence in many cases of income tax treaties between the countries, it may be possible to structure a transaction so that it results in less overall tax cost than would be the case if the transaction were undertaken in a single country. On the other hand, because there is often overlapping taxing jurisdiction, it is possible, in the absence of careful planning, that the overall tax cost may be greater than if only a single country were involved. In focusing on the U.S. tax aspects of a transaction, several principles must be borne in mind. First, the United States imposes different tax rules on individuals and corporations depending upon whether they are classified as "U.S. persons" or "foreign persons" for U.S. tax purposes. For this reason, a determination should be made early in the planning process as to the classification of each of the parties and entities involved in a transaction.

Second, generally speaking, the United States imposes an overall income tax on the worldwide income of individuals who are citizens or residents of the United States and on corporations that are formed in the United States. In contrast, nonresident alien individuals and foreign corporations are not subject to U.S. taxation except on income that is "sourced" in the United States. Therefore, once it is determined whether a party is a U.S. person or a foreign person, each item of income must be analyzed to determine whether it has its source in the United States or outside the United States, that is, whether it is domestic source income or foreign source income.

Third, foreign persons generally are subject to a gross percentage withholding tax on certain kinds of domestic source passive income. The chief exception to this is the tax upon income that is effectively connected with a U.S. trade or business or permanent establishment in the case of foreign persons that are engaged in a U.S. trade or business (or maintain a U.S. permanent establishment). In such a case, the foreign person will pay a net income tax on this trade or business income in much the same way that a U.S. person would on his or her overall income. Additionally, for U.S. nontrade or business income, the taxation will depend on the precise class or category of such income (for example, dividends, interests, or royalties). Therefore, determinations will have to be made about the characterization of any U.S. source income on a fairly specific basis.

As we will see, numerous other significant issues of U.S. international taxation will have to be understood and taken into account in undertaking any inbound or outbound acquisition.

What are some of the primary reporting obligations of U.S. companies investing abroad and of foreign companies investing in the United States?

Detailed disclosures are required of both U.S. investors in foreign companies and foreign investors in U.S. companies. Here are some highlights:

- U.S. investors owning 5 percent or more of a foreign company stock must file Form 5471 with the IRS. Conversely, every domestic or foreign company that is "engaged in a trade or business in the U.S." and "controlled" by a "foreign person" must file an information return to the IRS on Form 5472. "Control" for the purposes of this reporting requirement is deemed to occur in a tax year if at any time in the year a foreign person owns at least 25 percent of the value or voting power of a corporation's stock.[19]
- In particular, a new rule requires that both outbound and inbound owners provide more information about transfer pricing. Companies

must demonstrate that they used the "best method" of pricing to ensure that the prices they charge their foreign subsidiaries are not artificially low or high. The rules were intended primarily to obtain more tax revenues from foreign multinationals with subsidiaries in the United States, but as one source notes, they also apply to U.S. firms that might shift profits to subsidiaries in low-tax countries.[20]

- Also, Code Section 6038c requires foreign corporations doing business in the United States to maintain certain records (for example, allocations of U.S. versus foreign income).

- Foreign corporations registering securities in the United States may have to fill out one or more of a series of forms with the SEC called "Foreign Forms," including Form 4 pertaining to mergers. In general, these forms require U.S. standards of disclosure.[21]

What is the role of income tax treaties in the acquisition process?

Income tax treaties play a major role in structuring international transactions, generally by minimizing the overall tax costs that may be imposed. When a tax treaty is applicable to a particular transaction, it is often useful to review the transaction in light of the treaty before focusing on the laws of the particular countries. In many cases, the treaty becomes the "tax law of the transaction." Treaty-related tax planning consists of analyzing the alternative structures for the chain of entities, selecting the tax jurisdictions, and defining the sources and classes of income. At each stage, tax treaties may be utilized to avoid double taxation or, in certain circumstances, triple taxation.

Most tax treaties provide for the reduction or elimination of withholding taxes on portfolio income, such as interest, dividends, and royalties, by the country from which such income is derived (the so-called country of source) and prohibit the country of source from taxing the business income of an enterprise resident in the other country, unless the enterprise has a "permanent establishment" in the source country. For example, if a foreign entity is likely to be engaged in business activities in the United States, consideration should be given to placing those activities in an entity that is a resident of a country that has a tax treaty with the United States, in order to avoid the U.S. taxation of the activity. Furthermore, because most tax treaties provide that capital gains derived by a resident of one country from sources in another contracting country will be exempt from tax by such other country, such a strategy makes even more sense.

What are income tax treaties?

Income tax treaties, or *income tax conventions,* are international agreements entered into between two or more sovereign nations (and sometimes extended to dependent territories) for the purpose of reducing double taxation on income generated by residents of one of these countries from sources located in the other contracting country. In the United States, an income tax treaty is signed by the executive branch (usually by the Secretary of State) and becomes effective, unless modified, after the U.S. Senate ratifies the treaty. The United States currently has 40 income tax treaties in force.

Under the U.S. Constitution, treaties are the supreme law of the land and rank equally with any federal statute. If the terms of a treaty conflict with a federal statute, whichever was most recently adopted will generally control. Case law holds, however, that Congress must clearly specify an intent to override a tax treaty for a later-enacted statute to prevail over the treaty.[22]

In addition to their role in reducing double taxation, income tax treaties provide, through the "competent authority" mechanism, a means to resolve disputes between two tax jurisdictions that claim the right to tax income that arises in one or both of these countries. Treaties may assist in the prevention of fiscal evasion, for instance, by allowing tax information exchanges between the tax authorities of the contracting countries. Sometimes income tax treaties are used to advance foreign or economic policies of one or both of the countries, for instance, when one of the countries is committed to allow tax breaks for capital investments in preferred industries in the other country.

Can a taxpayer avail itself of a particular tax treaty by incorporating a subsidiary in the treaty country?

Tax treaties ordinarily apply to, and can be invoked by, persons who are residents of the respective treaty countries. Although the definition of a "person" may vary from treaty to treaty, it usually includes individuals, corporations, partnerships, estates, and trusts.

A corporation incorporated in a treaty jurisdiction will in most circumstances be considered a resident of such jurisdiction. Generally speaking, by establishing a corporation resident in a treaty country, investors from another country can subject their investments to the benefits available under that country's tax treaties. However, such so-called treaty shopping has in recent years been the subject of increasing scrutiny, and restrictions have been imposed by the U.S. Department of the Treasury and Congress. Specific actions taken have included (1) the termination of existing treaties with tax haven jurisdictions, (2) the renegotiation of existing treaties, (3) the ratification of new treaties that contain "limitation of benefits" provisions, and (4) the amendment of the U.S. Tax Code to allow treaty benefits only to bona fide residents of a treaty country.

How important is the issue of entity classification in the international context?

The question of whether a particular entity should be classified as a corporation or a pass-through entity (that is, a partnership or trust) for U.S. income tax purposes is of crucial importance in the international context. For inbound transactions, if a pass-through entity is operating a U.S. business, the foreign owner will be subject to regular U.S. income tax at graduated rates. In contrast, if the entity is classified as a corporation, the foreign owner will be subject to a withholding tax on dividend income at a flat rate (30 percent or reduced treaty rate). Depending upon the application of the branch profits tax, to be discussed later, the overall treatment in these two cases may be quite different. In outbound transactions, if a foreign entity is characterized as a corporation, its U.S. owners may be able to avoid being taxed currently on the income being earned abroad. If, instead, the entity is a pass-through entity, the U.S. owners will be taxed currently under any circumstances. In addition to the above, there are numerous other consequences of the classification of domestic and foreign entities as corporations, trusts, or partnerships.

How does the United States classify an entity that is formed under foreign law?

The IRS has published a list of certain foreign entities and their classification for U.S. tax purposes. With respect to entities not named on this list, the proper classification of a foreign enterprise under U.S. law may occasionally be a difficult task because foreign countries have forms of business entities that do not have U.S. equivalents.

The U.S. classification principles applicable to foreign entities provide that, as a starting point, local law (that is, foreign law) will determine the legal relationships among the entity and its members, and among the entity, its members, and the public at large. When these legal relationships are ascertained, U.S.

tax principles will classify an entity as a corporation, a partnership, or a trust. It is generally perceived that the IRS does not apply classification principles to foreign entities in the same manner as it does to U.S. entities. Therefore, caution must be used before assuming that the foreign entity would be treated for U.S. tax purposes in a similar manner to its foreign treatment. In addition, one should consider whether a tax treaty prohibits the United States from reclassifying the entity for federal tax purposes because of a specific definition in the treaty.

For classification purposes, when is a person considered foreign?

A U.S. person is either an individual who is a citizen or resident of the United States, a domestic corporation, a domestic partnership, or a domestic trust or estate. A foreign person is a person who is not a U.S. person. Under the above definition, a resident alien individual can be a U.S. person. Tax treaties may provide different rules.

When does an alien individual become a U.S. resident?

An alien individual is treated as a resident of the United States for a calendar year if such individual satisfies either of the following two tests: (1) The alien is a lawful permanent resident of the United States; or (2) subject to certain exceptions, the alien is physically present in the United States for a specified period of time (as of this writing, under U.S immigration law, 183 days or more during the calendar year).

An individual who is a U.S. resident is taxed on his or her worldwide income regardless of its source, and is entitled to claim deductions and credits against his or her worldwide income. If a resident alien is subject to foreign taxes on his or her foreign source income, he or she will be able to claim a foreign tax credit or deduction against his or her U.S. tax liability. Tax treaties may provide "tiebreaker" rules in situations in which an individual is treated as a resident by more than one country.

What is a U.S., or domestic, corporation?

Under U.S. principles, all organizations incorporated under the laws of the United States or of any state (including the District of Columbia) are treated as domestic corporations for federal tax purposes. For certain purposes, corporations organized in or under the laws of Guam, American Samoa, Northern Mariana Islands, or the Virgin Islands will not be treated as foreign corporations.[23]

What is a dual resident company?

As far as the United States is concerned, a corporation incorporated in the United States is a U.S. corporation. This corporation, however, could at the same time be treated by Country X as a Country X corporation, if Country X employed different criteria to determine whether corporations are resident for its tax purposes. In particular, some countries, including the United Kingdom and Australia, treat corporations as domestic corporations if they are managed and controlled therein. Thus, a U.S. corporation that is managed and controlled in one of these jurisdictions can also be a resident of the United Kingdom or Australia under their respective rules. Such companies are referred to as "dual resident companies." Although at one time there could be certain tax advantages in using such dual resident companies in lieu of corporations subject to "domestic" tax in only one country (such as the deduction of financing costs on the same loan in two jurisdictions), these advantages were substantially eliminated in 1986.

Can a foreign corporation be treated as a domestic corporation for U.S. tax purposes?

Yes. Code Section 269B provides that if a domestic corporation and a foreign corporation are "stapled entities," the foreign corporation will be treated as a domestic corporation. The term *stapled entities* means any group of two or more entities if more than 50 percent in value of the beneficial ownership in each such entity consists of stapled interests (that is, if by reason of form of ownership, restrictions on transfer, or other terms or conditions in connection with the transfer of one of such interests the other such interests are also transferred or required to be transferred).

More importantly, there are two situations in which an election may be made to treat a foreign corporation as if it were a domestic corporation. One involves an election under Section 1504(d) of the Code to treat certain Canadian or Mexican subsidiaries of a U.S. parent as domestic corporations eligible to be included in the parent's consolidated return. The other involves an election under FIRPTA (Foreign Investment in Real Property Tax Act, explained later in this chapter). FIRPTA provides that a foreign corporation holding a U.S. real property interest may elect to be treated as a domestic corporation.

Are U.S. persons and foreign persons treated alike under U.S. tax rules?

U.S. taxation of U.S. persons and foreign persons differs in a number of significant ways. The most noticeable difference concerns the scope of taxation: Whereas a U.S. person is subject to U.S. taxation on its worldwide income regardless of where it was derived (or sourced) and the class of income, a foreign person is subject to tax only on the income that has a substantial nexus to the United States. The nexus is generally defined with reference to a U.S. source or business. Often, the United States will not exercise its taxing jurisdiction over certain kinds of U.S.-related income that are generated by foreign persons, because of administrative difficulties concerning collection of the tax from foreign investors.

Would U.S. acquirers of foreign targets be indifferent about whether they receive foreign or domestic source income?

Source of income (and loss), whether U.S. or foreign, can be a critical factor in determining the U.S. income tax liability of both U.S. and foreign persons. In the case of U.S. taxpayers, foreign source income is often desirable because it increases their ability to offset foreign taxes against U.S. taxes under the foreign tax credit mechanism. On the other hand, if a loss can be sourced in the United States, the U.S. tax liability on domestic source income can be reduced and more foreign tax credits can be claimed against U.S. tax liability on foreign sources. In the case of a foreign taxpayer over whom the United States asserts only a limited taxing authority, foreign source income would likely escape U.S. taxation altogether. Accordingly, in general, there is a strong incentive to convert U.S. source income into foreign source income.

How is the source of most investment income determined?

Generally, interest or dividends paid by a U.S. person will be U.S. source income and therefore subject to the current rate (or any lower treaty rate) of withholding tax. Exceptions are provided where the U.S. payor meets certain foreign income tests. Rentals or royalties are generally sourced in the United States if they are paid for the use of tangible or intangible property that is located in the United States.

Note that U.S. source interest income of a foreign person is not subject to a U.S. withholding tax if it qualifies as "portfolio interest." Generally, among the other requirements for interest to qualify as portfolio interest, the foreign lender must be neither a bank extending an ordinary loan nor a party that is related to the U.S. borrower.

How do you determine the source of gain derived from the sale of stock of a foreign or a U.S. entity?

Income derived by a U.S. resident from the sale of personal property, tangible or intangible, is generally sourced in the United States. Similarly, income derived by a nonresident from the sale of personal property, tangible or intangible, is generally treated as foreign source income. This is called the *residence-of-the-seller rule.*

Under the residence-of-the-seller rule, when an individual nonresident who does not have a U.S. office to which the sale is attributed disposes of stock of a domestic corporation, the sale will generate foreign source income, gain, or loss. Similarly, when a U.S. resident individual sells stock in a foreign corporation and the sale is not attributable to a foreign office of the seller, the income, gain, or loss generated by the sale will be U.S. sourced.[24]

Note that for individuals, the definition of the term *U.S. resident* for sourcing purposes does not equal the definition of a U.S. resident for other tax purposes. The Code contains an antiabuse rule that is intended to prevent a U.S. person from claiming to be a nonresident of the United States for income that is sourced in a tax haven country. A tax haven is a sovereign tax jurisdiction that generally imposes only minimal or no tax on income, capital, or estates of nonresidents of such jurisdiction (for example, the Cayman Islands, the Bahamas, and the Channel Islands). Note also that since December 1991 investment of $1 million or more in a business employing 10 people or more qualifies foreigners for permanent residency ("green card") status in the United States, and eventual citizenship.[25]

TAX CONSIDERATIONS IN INBOUND ACQUISITIONS

Why are tax considerations important in an inbound U.S. transaction?

First, let us review some fundamentals. An inbound acquisition is an acquisition of a U.S. enterprise by a non-U.S. person. This acquisition may involve financing from the acquirer's country, from the United States, or from a third country. In debt-financed acquisitions, revenues received from the U.S. enterprise will likely be used to pay off acquisition indebtedness. The acquirers may wish at some point in the future to dispose of the entity or parts thereof in a transaction that will generate a profit over the acquisition price. For these and other reasons, U.S. tax considerations may be important in every stage of the acquisition and disposition process.

This section will discuss the basic U.S. tax consequences applicable to a foreign corporation or a nonresident alien engaged in M&A activities in the United States; particular attention will be given to financing the acquisition and planning for eventual disposition.

What are the basic U.S. income tax principles that determine the overall tax burden on U.S. income and repatriated funds of a foreign investor?

A foreign corporation not engaged in a U.S. trade or business is taxable at a flat rate determined by current tax law (or reduced treaty rate), collected by withholding at source, on its U.S. source passive income (such as interest, rents, royalties, dividends, and premiums). A foreign corporation engaged in a U.S. trade or business, even if it does not maintain an office within the United States, is subject to a U.S. net income tax at graduated rates on its U.S. source income that is effectively connected with its conduct of the trade or business in the United States. The latter tax may be referred to as the regular income tax. In addition, a foreign corporation is subject to the branch profits tax (BPT) rules on its "effectively connected earnings and profits," subject to certain adjustments. (The BPT will be discussed later in this chapter.) If a foreign corporation owns an interest in a partnership (domestic or foreign) engaged in a trade or business in the United States, withholding under the Code may be required on distributions to the corporation. Capital gains, whether short term or long term, are not subject to U.S. tax if the foreign corporation is not engaged in a U.S. trade or business, or if the interest disposed of is not a real estate asset subject to FIRPTA.

A nonresident alien individual who is not engaged in a U.S. trade or business will be subject to U.S. tax at the standard rate (or reduced treaty rate) on his or her U.S. source passive income and will pay the going rate on net capital gains derived from U.S. sources provided that the individual spent 183 days or more in the United States within the taxable year of sale. In addition, if a nonresident alien is engaged in a U.S. trade or business within a taxable year but does not maintain an office in the United States, then any U.S. source income effectively connected with that trade or business will be subject to U.S. tax at graduated rates. Withholding rules may apply to distributions with respect to partnership interests held by such individual. Like a foreign corporation, if the nonresident alien is careful enough not to fall within the above restrictions, no U.S. tax will be imposed on his or her U.S. source capital gains.

If a nonresident alien or a foreign corporation engaged in a U.S. trade or business maintains an office in the United States, specified categories of such person's foreign source income are also treated as income effectively connected with a U.S. trade or business.

Tax treaties generally modify the rules described above as they apply to treaty country residents. In particular, tax treaties reduce withholding tax rates and limit taxation of business income to income attributable to a permanent establishment.

Thus, in summary, income from operations of the acquired U.S. target will ordinarily be subject to U.S. taxation, even if carried on directly by the foreign acquirer. On the other hand, with proper planning of their U.S. activities, foreign investors may find it relatively easy to avoid U.S. tax on capital gains (other than from the disposition of United States real property interests) derived from the sale of their interest in the U.S. activity.

When is a foreign person treated as engaged in a U.S. trade or business?

Neither the Code nor the regulations thereunder define when a foreign person is engaged in a U.S. trade or business. The determination is generally based on the facts and circumstances of each case and, in particular, on the level of the taxpayer's activities in the United States. If the U.S. activities of the foreign person are not considerable, continuous, and regular, the person will probably be considered as not engaged in a U.S. trade or business. Business activities of an agent in the United States will be attributed to its principal. U.S. real estate gains received by a foreign person will be deemed to be income effectively connected with a U.S. trade or business. Gains from U.S. securities trading activities for the taxpayer's own account are generally not trade or business income.

What issues should an investor consider when undertaking foreign debt financing to acquire a U.S. business?

Foreign financing to acquire U.S. business operations can take many forms. It may take the form of an investment of equity or debt, and it may involve only one foreign lender in a single-lender transaction or many lenders in an offshore public debt offering. Single-lender loans can be made from foreign banks acting in the ordinary course of their business or from foreign nonbanking institutions. In addition, loans can be made by foreign shareholders of the corporation. Publicly offered debt obligations may be in bearer form to protect investor anonymity but can also take place in registered form. Among these alternatives one may find various forms of syndicated loans and private debt placements to various investors. In addition, foreign financing may be in the form of short-term obligations, such as a Eurocommercial paper, and long-term debt. Finally, the debt issued may be in the form of straight debt or in the form of convertible debt or debt with equity features.

An entire chapter could be written on the tax treatment of transnational financing. Very broadly, when a foreign acquirer wishes to raise debt capital outside the United States, it should consider the following issues:

1. Whether the acquisition indebtedness should be incurred by the U.S. target corporation or by the foreign acquirer. In this regard, the acquirer should weigh the relative values of the interest deductions in the United States and in the foreign jurisdiction.

2. Whether the interest paid to the foreign lender will be free of U.S. withholding tax by virtue of a treaty exemption or a statutory provision (such as the portfolio interest exemption), or whether it will be subject to a reduced withholding rate. Note that investors in the Eurobond market generally require that interest payments be free of U.S. withholding tax. Furthermore, consideration should be given to the risk of change of law or treaty termination with respect to U.S. withholding tax liability.

3. Whether a back-to-back loan structure to a U.S. corporation to take advantage of a tax treaty or statutory tax exemption will be respected by the IRS.

4. Whether debt with equity features will be respected as debt for U.S. tax purposes.

What is the branch profits tax (BPT), and why should an acquirer be concerned about it?

The issue of whether to hold the acquired U.S. business through a U.S. or foreign corporation is often a major consideration in the acquisition process. If a U.S. business is held through a foreign corporation, the foreign corporation may be subject to a second layer of tax in the form of the branch profits tax. If the U.S. business is held through a U.S. corporation, the tax cost may in certain circumstances be substantially reduced.

The BPT imposes a second layer of tax on profits of U.S. branches or other U.S. operations of a foreign corporation. The BPT was introduced in 1986 principally to duplicate, in the case of U.S. branches of foreign corporations, the second level of tax on dividends and interest paid by U.S. subsidiaries of foreign corporations.

If one is concerned about whether the BPT applies to certain U.S. operations, one should focus on these two rules: First, the BPT does not apply to foreign individuals engaged directly or indirectly through foreign partnerships in a trade or business in the United States; second, foreign corporations whose U.S. investments or contacts do not amount to a trade or business (or, in the case of a treaty-protected corporation, to a U.S. permanent establishment) are not subject to the BPT. Nonetheless, the BPT provisions contain certain antitreaty shopping rules that will affect even foreign corporations that are not engaged in a trade or business in the United States to the extent that they receive dividends or interest from a foreign corporation that is engaged in a trade or business in the United States. Thus, if an entity is neither a foreign corporation nor engaged (or deemed to be engaged) in a U.S. trade or business, and it does not receive dividends or interest from the U.S. operations of such a corporation, the following discussion will not pertain to its operations.

On the other hand, if one's U.S. operations might be subject to the BPT, the next two questions will provide a short road map on the effects of the BPT on the regular operations of a U.S. branch of a foreign corporation and on the financing of a branch of a foreign corporation.

What are the BPT rules concerning the U.S. operations of a foreign corporation?

Whenever a foreign corporation operates or acquires an unincorporated business (including a partnership interest) in the United States, consideration should be given to the BPT consequences of such operation. Remember that under the regular rules, the foreign corporation pays one income tax on its "effectively connected" U.S. trade or business income. The BPT is an additional tax equal to the standard rate (or a reduced treaty rate) of any foreign corporation's "dividend equivalent amount" for any taxable year in which such corporation is engaged, or deemed to be engaged, in a trade or business in the United States. A foreign corporation that is subject to the full regular tax rate and the BPT may pay an effective U.S. tax rate in excess of 50 percent.

The dividend equivalent amount includes the "effectively connected earnings and profits" (E&P) of such corporation for the taxable year, as adjusted downward or upward to reflect certain increases or decreases in the "U.S. net equity" for the year. In effect, the statute treats a decrease in U.S. net equity as a withdrawal of earnings by the foreign parent, and an increase in U.S. net equity as a contribution of capital to the U.S. branch. The use of the E&P account as the tax base was designed to approximate dividend treatment.

U.S. net equity is any money and the aggregate adjusted bases of the foreign corporation's property treated as connected with the conduct of a trade or business in the United States, less the foreign corporation's liabilities connected with such operation. Investments in business assets will increase the net equity amount and repatriations will decrease such amount, but only to include previous increases of net equity that reduced earnings and profits.

For the BPT to apply to a particular branch of a foreign corporation, such branch must generate "effectively connected" income. Generally, income will be treated as effectively connected if the corporation is engaged in an active business, if the corporation is a partner in a partnership engaged in a U.S. trade or business, or if the corporation invests in U.S. real property with respect to which the foreign corporation has elected under Section 897(d) to be taxed on a net basis, or with respect to a gain from a disposition of a U.S. real property interest (other than interest in a U.S. real property holding corporation). E&P includes certain items not subject to the regular corporate tax, such as tax-exempt income. Distributions by the foreign corporation within the taxable year will not reduce E&P for the purposes of the BPT.

If a treaty country corporation earns effectively connected income that is exempt from U.S. tax because such foreign corporation does not maintain a permanent establishment in the United States, such earnings will not be subject to the BPT, provided that the foreign corporation is a "qualified resident" of the treaty country, as defined above. In addition, BPT rules may be modified in other ways by an applicable tax treaty (see discussion above).

How do the BPT rules affect the financing for a U.S. branch of a foreign corporation?

Generally, if a U.S. branch of a foreign corporation borrows money from a foreign lender, the branch (but in practice, the foreign corporation) will be required to withhold the standard rate (or reduced treaty rate) of the gross interest paid to the foreign lender. Certain Code provisions, such as the portfolio interest exemption and the bank deposit exemption, may apply to eliminate the withholding requirement. The tax treaties that will determine the lower rate of withholding on interest paid by the U.S. branch will be the treaty between the United States and the country of the foreign lender and the treaty between the United States and the country of the foreign corporation that maintains the U.S. branch. Section 884, however, curtails treaty benefits to discourage treaty shopping. The effect of the withholding requirement can be to increase the cost of borrowing from foreign lenders that do not qualify for an exemption from U.S. taxation and cannot obtain complete foreign tax credit benefits in their own country.

Interest expense incurred by the foreign corporation on its worldwide borrowings may be allocated, under a formula, to the U.S. branch beyond the amount of interest actually paid or accrued directly by the branch ("excess interest"). Such excess interest will be deductible by the foreign corporation in computing its U.S. net taxable income for the U.S. branch but will be treated as paid by the U.S. branch to the foreign owner as if it were a separate lender. As such, unless a specific Code exemption applies, the excess interest will be subject to a withholding tax at the going rate or any lower treaty rate imposed on the foreign corporation.

In determining the applicability of a treaty, the excess interest is deemed paid by the branch to the foreign corporation as lender. If the foreign corporation is a "qualified resident" of the treaty country, the excess amount may be subject to lower treaty rates. It is noteworthy that the tax imposed on excess interest allocable to the U.S. branch is levied regardless of whether the excess interest actually resulted in a tax benefit to the U.S. branch. Thus, it is possible that the tax on excess interest will exceed the foreign corporation's U.S. tax benefit from the deduction of excess interest, for instance, in situations where the U.S. branch has net operating losses.

Does the BPT override tax treaties?

Congress intended that the BPT not apply where its application would be inconsistent with an existing U.S. income tax treaty obligation; however, this principle is modified in cases of "treaty shopping." When treaty shopping is not involved, (1) a foreign corporation and its shareholders may continue to rely on any benefits provided by an income tax treaty with respect to BPT on earnings, and (2) a foreign corporation and a third-party foreign lender may continue to rely on benefits provided by applicable income tax treaties. When treaty shopping is involved, treaty benefits are generally overridden. For instance, unless the actual or deemed creditor or dividend recipient, as the case may be, is a "qualified resident" of a treaty country, the creditor or the dividend recipient cannot claim treaty benefits to reduce the standard withholding obligation.

It is noteworthy that U.S. shareholders of a treaty shopping corporation or of a nontreaty country corporation may be subject to triple taxation. Several proposals are currently under consideration to eliminate this additional layer of tax on U.S. shareholders.

How can a taxpayer determine whether the foreign corporation in which it holds stock will be treated as engaging in treaty shopping?

A foreign corporation will not be considered to be treaty shopping if it is a "qualified resident" of the treaty country at issue. A foreign corporation that is resident in a foreign country will be a qualified resident, unless either (1) more than 50 percent in value of the foreign corporation's stock is owned by individuals who are neither residents of such country (regardless of whether they are bona fide residents of another treaty country) nor U.S. citizens or resident aliens, or (2) 50 percent or more of the foreign corporation's gross income is used (directly or indirectly) to meet liabilities to persons who are neither residents of that country nor residents of the United States. Note that these rules still allow treaty benefits to inure to nontreaty country shareholders, as long as they hold less than 50 percent of the corporation's stock.

If the foreign corporation fails to qualify under these tests, it will nevertheless be treated as a qualified resident if either (1) the foreign corporation's stock is primarily and regularly traded on an established securities exchange in the country in question or (2) the foreign corporation is wholly owned (either directly or indirectly) by another corporation organized in the country in which such stock is traded. This may provide an advantage to foreign shareholders of publicly traded treaty country corporations over shareholders of nontreaty or U.S. publicly traded corporations.

What would be the best way to avoid the BPT?

Nontreaty investors and often residents in certain treaty countries will find that operating in the United States through a U.S. corporation is the most attractive way to avoid the BPT. In other words, in an asset acquisition, a foreign corporation will avoid the BPT if it incorporates the branch into a U.S. corporation. The rate of tax on dividends and interest required to be withheld at source by a U.S. subsidiary may be reduced if a treaty country parent corporation is used. If dividends are to be distributed, at least a 5 percent treaty rate withholding tax will apply. In addition, if the investor is a treaty country resident, he or she can capitalize the U.S. corporation with indebtedness and receive interest income, sometimes free of U.S. tax, contemporaneously with interest deductions at the corporate level.

What is FIRPTA?

As discussed briefly earlier, the Foreign Investment in Real Property Tax Act of 1980, as amended, also known as FIRPTA, was enacted to close a number of perceived loopholes that enabled foreign investors to own and dispose of U.S. real properties without incurring U.S. tax on the appreciation of the property or on the cash flow from the property. Since 1985 FIRPTA has overridden all income tax treaties.

FIRPTA applies to dispositions of U.S. real property interests (USRPIs). A USRPI generally includes (1) an interest in real estate located in the United States or the United States Virgin Islands or (2) any interest (other than an interest solely as a creditor) in a domestic corporation, unless it can be established that such corporation was at no time a U.S. real property holding corporation (USRPHC).

A domestic corporation is a USRPHC if the fair market value of its USRPIs equals or exceeds 50 percent of its worldwide real estate plus any other trade or business assets. Thus, if the assets disposed of are clearly not USRPIs or interests in certain pass-through entities that own USRPIs, neither the seller nor the buyer of the assets ought to be concerned about FIRPTA. FIRPTA regulations provide elaborate rules concerning the definition of a USRPI. Because many U.S. corporations own significant amounts of real estate, it will often be difficult to conclude at an early planning stage that a given target is not a USRPHC.

What are the general rules regarding FIRPTA, and how are they enforced?

FIRPTA provides that gain or loss of a nonresident alien individual or a foreign corporation from the disposition of a USRPI will be treated as if the gain or loss was effectively connected with a U.S. trade or business of such person. As such, the gain will be taxed at the regular rates applicable to U.S. citizens and residents, or domestic corporations, as the case may be. Unlike other passive investments, gain recognized in a transaction subject to FIRPTA ought to be reported on a U.S. income tax return. Nonresident alien individuals are also subject to FIRPTA's minimum tax.

FIRPTA compliance is enforced through a withholding system. The Code generally provides that a transferee of a USRPI is required to withhold and pay over to the IRS 10 percent of the amount realized (that is, the consideration) on the disposition by the foreign transferor. Partnerships and trusts disposing of real estate are required to withhold 34 percent of the amount allocable to their foreign partners or foreign beneficiaries. There are several exceptions to the withholding rules, but these are beyond the scope of this discussion.

FIRPTA applies to dispositions of interests in partnerships holding real estate and to dispositions of USRPIs by partnerships held by foreigners. Moreover, FIRPTA applies to distributions of USRPIs by foreign corporations to their shareholders, and to capital contributions to foreign corporations. In addition, FIRPTA provisions can override the nonrecognition treatment provided by various other sections of the Code, where necessary to ensure that the gain subject to taxation under FIRPTA is not diminished through transactions such as reorganizations and tax-free liquidations.

Who should be concerned about FIRPTA?

Although the FIRPTA provisions may seem to be of little importance in a merger or acquisition that does not involve real estate holding corporations or direct acquisitions of real estate assets, its application is far-reaching. First, as mentioned earlier, the definition of a USRPHC is broad enough to include even a manufacturing company that owns a large plant. A foreign acquirer should take future FIRPTA taxes into account in evaluating a potential acquisition. A domestic as well as a foreign acquirer from a foreign holder is liable as transferee-payor to withhold tax on the consideration paid for the stock if the corporation is a USRPHC and the payee is subject to FIRPTA. Failure to withhold may result in civil and criminal penalties. On the other hand, the foreign transferor (seller) is required to file a U.S. tax return to report his or her gain from the sale. Finally, if a public offering to refinance a portion of the acquisition indebtedness is contemplated, certain foreign holders (5 percent or more) will be subject to U.S. tax on the disposition of their holdings if the corporation is a USRPHC; under certain circumstances, the buyer of publicly traded stock from a 5 percent or more shareholder will be required to withhold FIRPTA tax.

Consequently, in any stock acquisition, consideration should be given to the value of the U.S. realty owned by the acquired entity, vis-à-vis its other assets, and to the tax status of the seller. If the seller provides a certificate that it is not a foreign person, no withholding will be required. In addition, no withholding is required if a domestic corporation furnishes to the transferee an affidavit stating that it is not and has not been a USRPHC during a certain test period.

TAX CONSIDERATIONS IN OUTBOUND ACQUISITIONS

Do foreign owners have to pay U.S. taxes?

In theory, no. In practice, yes—a thousand times yes! As explained earlier in this chapter, the United States asserts taxing jurisdiction over the worldwide income of its citizens, residents, and corporations. As a general rule, the United States taxes only income received or accrued by U.S. taxpayers. In the domestic context, with the exception of a group filing a consolidated return or an S corporation, income earned by a U.S. taxpayer from a controlled corporation is not taxed to the U.S. owner except and to the extent that such earnings are actually distributed to the owner. As we will soon see, the exceptions to the above rules in the international context are so voluminous and complex in U.S. tax law as to suggest that the general rules do not apply at all. As a result of long-standing concerns about the avoidance of U.S. taxes through the expatriation of assets and earnings, there is now an extensive patchwork of rules under which the United States seeks to tax, or at least take into account, income generated in foreign subsidiaries of U.S. persons.

Needless to say, in any transaction involving an acquisition of a foreign business, the primary focus of the tax planner's attention must be the tax laws of the country or countries in which the target does business and holds assets and the country or countries in which its shareholders are located. This is all the more true at a time when income tax rates of most industrialized countries significantly exceed those in the United States. There may in fact be significant opportunities to reduce the impact of foreign taxes through the use of tax treaties and the United States foreign tax credit system. These mechanisms are inherently imperfect, however, and a great deal of attention must be paid to the rules of United States taxation of the international activities of its taxpayers in order to minimize the overall tax costs of U.S. persons engaging in a variety of multinational operations.

When planning an outbound acquisition, what information should the purchaser solicit from the seller in order to minimize foreign and domestic tax liabilities?

Today, where an auction process is commonly used to obtain the highest bid for a group of corporations that is for sale, the buyer cannot ignore the tax consequences to the seller resulting from the sale. To obtain a competitive edge over other bidders, the buyer should strive to maximize its own tax benefits without raising the seller's tax costs above its expectations. Alternatively, without sacrificing the purchaser's own goals, it may be possible to structure the offer in a way that reduces the seller's tax costs. With these goals in mind, the purchaser should solicit from the seller the following information:

- A precise organization chart. The chart should describe the holding company (assuming that the target is a parent of a group of corporations) and the stock ownership in all the various tiers of the domestic corporations, if any, and of the foreign corporations or entities (the "group").
- The estimated U.S. and foreign tax bases as of the projected acquisition date that the holding company is expected to have in the various domestic and foreign corporations.
- To the extent feasible, a description of the overall income tax position of the target group and the seller.
- For each of the foreign companies:
  - The taxable year(s) used by the company, whether calendar or fiscal, in any tax jurisdictions where the company does business.
  - The actual and projected earnings and profits by taxable period of such corporation as of the acquisition date computed by the rules set forth in Sections 902 and 964 of the Code.

- The creditable foreign income taxes paid or accrued during each taxable period ending on or before the acquisition date.
- The earnings and profits and creditable foreign taxes set forth in Subparagraphs B and C accumulated prior to the seller's ownership of the company.
- All other information—foreign currency gains and losses, tax accounting elections, distributions, utilization of foreign tax credits, and so on—necessary to determine the tax consequences of a later sale of each corporation.
- The estimated net book value, or pro forma balance sheet, of each foreign company as of the acquisition date.
- A listing of the intercompany receivables and payables, if any.

Why would one need an organization chart of the structure of the target?

An organization chart will describe the precise ownership of the group and will inform one of the different tax jurisdictions (and income tax treaties) that may affect the acquisition process and the subsequent disposition of the group or several of its members. One may be aiming to buy a Greek company but may find out that the Greek company is owned by a Spanish holding company, which is in turn owned by a U.S. subsidiary of the holding company. Therefore, in this scenario the prospective buyer will be required to evaluate the possible tax consequences of the acquisition in Greece, Spain, and the United States.

The organization chart will also provide information about whether any of the foreign subsidiaries is, or would be in the purchaser's hands, a "controlled foreign corporation" (CFC). As will be explained below, CFC status may have significant U.S. tax consequences to a U.S. shareholder.

What is a CFC?

A *controlled foreign corporation,* or CFC, is any foreign corporation of which more than 50 percent of the total combined voting power, or the total value of its stock, is owned directly or indirectly by "United States shareholders" on any day during the taxable year of the foreign corporation. A United States shareholder, in turn, is a U.S. person who owns, or is considered to own under attribution rules, 10 percent or more of the foreign corporation's voting power.

Note that in the definition of U.S. shareholder, voting power and not stock value is the sole criterion.

In considering the application of Subpart F, it is important to keep in mind the separate status and consequences of the CFC and the U.S. shareholder. For example, because of the 10 percent voting power test, it is possible to have U.S. persons owning stock in a CFC who are not "United States shareholders" and thus not subject to Subpart F. Additionally, there is much room for structuring flexibility so as to have substantial U.S. ownership of a foreign corporation without causing it to be characterized as a CFC. One thing to bear in mind in this area is that there may be circumstances in which it will be beneficial for a foreign subsidiary of a U.S. parent to be characterized as a CFC.

What is Subpart F of the Code?

Subpart F (Sections 951–964 of the Code) requires U.S. shareholders of a CFC to include in their U.S. gross income as constructive dividends certain amounts earned by the CFC, regardless of whether such earnings were actually repatriated to the U.S. shareholder. In addition to the CFC and U.S. shareholder requirements, Subpart F treatment will generally only apply to certain types of income earned by the CFC, which may be broadly termed Subpart F income. Note that a U.S. tax is not imposed on the CFC itself; in fact, if the foreign corporation were itself subject to U.S. taxation, an entirely different set of rules would apply.

How does Subpart F operate?

Subpart F provides that a U.S. shareholder must include in gross income certain classes of the CFC's income as a constructive dividend. Following such an imputation, the basis of the U.S. shareholder's stock in the CFC is increased in order to avoid double taxation when the U.S. shareholder later disposes of the stock of the CFC. An actual distribution of the CFC's earnings subsequent to Subpart F treatment will not be taxable to the U.S. shareholder if it pertains to the previously taxed earnings and profits, and a corresponding reduction in the basis of the stock will take place. Under certain circumstances, the U.S. shareholder may be eligible for the foreign tax credit with respect to foreign taxes paid by the CFC.

As explained in greater detail below, a U.S. shareholder of a CFC is also required to include in gross income its pro rata share of the foreign corporation's increase in earnings invested in certain U.S. properties.

What classes of CFC income are subject to Subpart F?

Subpart F income includes "insurance income," "foreign base company income," and certain other classes of income subject to specific limited rules (such as international boycott-related income and illegal bribes). If more than 70 percent of the CFC's gross income is Subpart F income, the full amount of the CFC's gross income will be treated as Subpart F income.

Insurance income means income attributable to the issuance of any insurance, reinsurance, or annuity contract in connection with property in, with liability arising out of activity in, or with the lives or health of residents of a country other than the country under the laws of which the CFC is created or organized. *Foreign base company income* includes "foreign personal holding company income," "foreign base company sales income," "foreign base company services income," "foreign base company shipping income," and "foreign base company oil-related income" for the taxable year.

- Foreign personal holding company income consists of interest, dividends, rents, royalties, and other kinds of passive income.
- Foreign base company sales income generally includes various forms of income derived by the CFC in connection with the sale or purchase of property involving a related party, where the property originated in a country other than that of the CFC and is sold or purchased for use or disposition outside of the country of the CFC.
- Foreign base company services income generally includes income derived in connection with the performance of various services on behalf of a related person where the services are performed outside the country of the CFC.
- Foreign base company shipping income includes income from a variety of activities involving the use of aircraft or vessels in foreign commerce.
- Foreign base company oil-related income generally includes income from oil and gas products except where the income is derived in the country from which the oil or gas product was extracted.

What are the rules concerning a CFC's increase in earnings invested in U.S. property?

As a general rule, each U.S. shareholder is required to take into gross income his or her pro rata share of the CFC's increase in earnings invested in U.S.

property for the taxable year. This rule is applicable to all CFCs whether or not they have earned Subpart F income, but to avoid double counting this rule applies only after Subpart F income, if any, has been imputed to the shareholder.

Indirect investments in U.S. property are also subject to these rules. Under Treasury regulations, any obligation of a U.S. person for which a CFC is a pledgor or guarantor will be considered U.S. property held by the CFC. If the assets of a CFC serve at any time, even indirectly, as a security for the performance of an obligation of a U.S. person, then the CFC will be considered a pledgor or guarantor of that obligation. Consequently, if an acquirer plans to use the stock or assets of foreign subsidiaries as collateral for acquisition indebtedness, it may risk receiving a deemed distribution or "constructive dividend" from the CFCs to the extent of the earnings and profits of the foreign subsidiaries that are used as collateral.

What is a foreign tax credit?

A common theme throughout the tax system is that a person should be relieved of the burden resulting from the imposition of tax by more than one jurisdiction on the same income. One example of this principle is the deduction for income taxes paid to states, localities, and foreign governments contained in Section 164 of the Code. In the case of income taxes paid to foreign governments, the Internal Revenue Code provides an alternative to the deduction of the foreign tax from gross income by way of a unilateral tax credit against U.S. tax for the foreign taxes. When the credit works properly, it generally provides a more complete relief from double taxation of income than the deduction. The goal of the foreign tax credit system is to limit the overall rate of tax on foreign source income to the greater of the foreign rate or the U.S. rate. The foreign tax credit is elected by a taxpayer on an annual basis and is not binding for future years. Because of the various limitations under the foreign tax credit rules, in certain circumstances it may, in fact, be more advantageous for a taxpayer to claim the deduction instead of the credit.

How is the amount of allowable foreign tax credit determined?

The amount of foreign tax credit that may be claimed as a direct credit against U.S. income tax liability is generally determined by applying a fraction to the tentative U.S. tax liability for the year. The numerator of the fraction is the taxable income from foreign sources, and the denominator is worldwide taxable income. Foreign income and related foreign taxes are divided into several new categories, or "baskets," described in Section 904d of the Code. These are passive income, shipping income, high withholding tax interest, dividends from certain noncontrolled foreign corporations, financial services income, certain dividends from domestic international sales corporations (DISCs), certain distributions from present or former foreign sales corporations (FSCs), and certain taxable income attributable to foreign trade income.

Can a U.S. person obtain a foreign tax credit for foreign taxes paid by a foreign subsidiary?

Under Section 902 of the Code, a U.S. corporation owning 10 percent or more of the voting stock of a foreign corporation may be entitled to a "deemed paid credit," or indirect credit, for foreign taxes paid by the subsidiary. The deemed paid credit is only available against dividend income received (or deemed received under Subpart F or other provisions) from the foreign subsidiary. The principle underlying this indirect credit is that a U.S. corporation receiving a dividend from a foreign corporation is deemed to have paid the foreign taxes paid or accrued by the foreign corporation on the earnings from which the dividend is distributed.

The deemed paid credit generally works as follows. First, under Section 78 of the Code, a domestic corporation must include in income not only the amount of dividends actually or constructively received, but also an amount equal to the foreign taxes attributable to such dividend income. This is the so-called gross-up provision. Under Section 902, the U.S. corporation is deemed to have paid the same proportion of the income taxes paid by the subsidiary as the dividends received bear to the foreign subsidiary's total earnings. Additionally, if the foreign corporation owns 10 percent or more of the voting stock of a second foreign corporation, it is deemed to have paid foreign taxes of the subsidiary on the same basis. The same rule goes for a third tier of the subsidiary as well.

Under Section 960 of the Code, similar rules are provided for an indirect foreign tax credit with respect to deemed dividend income from the foreign corporation to the domestic corporate shareholder as a result of Subpart F. Under Section 962, an individual may take advantage of this indirect foreign tax credit by electing to be taxed on Subpart F income as if he or she were a domestic corporation.

How is a U.S. person treated upon the sale of stock in a foreign corporation?

For the application of Section 1248 of the Code, a U.S. person will generally recognize capital gain or loss on the sale of stock in a foreign corporation just as it would on the sale of stock in a domestic corporation. Recognizing that this provided an opportunity for the repatriation of foreign earnings at favorable capital gains rates, the United States enacted Section 1248 of the Code in 1962. The main purpose and effect of Section 1248 is to recharacterize the gain realized on the sale of stock in the foreign corporation from capital gain to ordinary dividend income to the extent of the selling stockholder's ratable share of the earnings of the foreign corporation accumulated during the period that the stock was owned by the U.S. person. If the selling shareholder is a domestic corporation, then it may claim the benefit of the indirect foreign tax credit with respect to the deemed dividends under Section 902. Where the selling shareholder is an individual, Section 1248 includes a mechanism that indirectly reduces his or her U.S. tax liability on account of foreign taxes paid by the foreign corporation.

CONCLUDING COMMENTS

To be successful in the new global economy, dealmakers must remain open to the international dimensions at every phase of their deals. In formulating plans, obtaining financing, structuring transactions, and conducting due diligence, M&A movers and shakers need to look beyond national boundaries to focus on emerging global markets. That far horizon will seem much nearer as they step away from the closing table and into the future: They will be part of a world-class company that has grown through the increasingly international "art of M&A."

ENDNOTES

1. *Source: The World Almanac and Book of Facts 1998* (Mahwah, NJ: World Almanac Books, 1997), p. 123.
2. *Source: Mergers & Acquisitions,* May/June 1998, p. 57.
3. Ownership of a U.S. corporation by a foreign citizen, that is, a "controlled foreign corporation," should not be confused with the term *foreign corporation,* which has a narrower meaning. Unlike many countries, the

United States has allocated to its 50 states the act of incorporation. For
instance, a Delaware corporation—that is, a company incorporated in the state
of Delaware—doing business in Virginia is known in Virginia as a foreign
corporation.

4. The most famous case in the banking arena was, of course, the scandal
   involving the Bank of Credit and Commerce controlled by BCCI Holdings
   (Luxembourg) SA (BCCI). The U.S. Federal Reserve Board brought civil
   charges against two principals of a U.S. BCCI subsidiary (the former First
   American Bankshares, Inc.), Clark Clifford and Robert Altman, for allegedly
   lying to the Fed when they said that BCCI would have no involvement in First
   American's operations. Regulators also charged the two with making false
   statements in connection with BCCI's purchase of the National Bank of
   Georgia. The charges against Altman resulted in acquittal, and those levied
   against Clifford were dropped, clearing his name before his death in October
   1998. In Europe, the scandal led to EU-wide reform in banking rules.

5. In June 1990, a blue-ribbon panel appointed by the Defense Department
   concluded that restrictions on defense-related acquisitions may harm U.S.
   security interests.

6. Traditionally, Japan has been leery of free markets for changes in corporate
   control. See, for example, Howard D. Sherman and Bruce A. Babcock,
   Redressing Structural Imbalances in Japanese Corporate Governance
   (Washington, DC: Institutional Shareholder Services, Inc., 1993). This attitude
   may be changing, however. The coauthor of this book, Alexandra Reed
   Lajoux, was invited to speak at an August 1998 conference on mergers and
   acquisitions hosted by Capital Management, a joint venture of IntellAsset and
   Deloitte & Touche Tohmatsu. She found the 200 executives assembled there
   well-informed and open-minded.

7. "Fixing the Tower of Babel in Global Accounting," *The Wall Street Journal,*
   May 11, 1998, p. A-1.

8. Perhaps the most well-known example is the long-standing U.S. law against
   collusion with the Arab boycott against trade with Israel.

9. For example, in 20 major equity markets around the world, the stake of equity
   ownership that must be disclosed ranges from 2 percent (in Italy) to 25 percent
   (in Germany). For a complete guide to international stock exchange
   requirements, see *International Securities Laws Handbook* (New York: Bowne
   Publishing Division, 1998) (updated quarterly).

10. In 1991, for example, the government of Yugoslavia sued Drexel Burnham
    Lambert, Inc., in the United States, claiming that what the investment bank had
    sold as a short-term note was in fact a security.

11. For background on this directive, which is still under consideration by member states, see Alistair Bird and Penny Bryce, "The Proposed European Directive on Takeovers," *Corporate Governance Advisor,* November–December 1996, pp. 18ff.

12. For further discussion see M. H. Byowitz, "Overview of the European Economic Community's Merger Regulation," Wachtell, Lipton, Rosen & Katz (New York), November 9, 1990, and subsequent updates.

13. "European Court Is Advised to Overturn Antitrust Ruling," *The Wall Street Journal,* June 9, 1994. See also "European Antitrust Officials Earning Tough Reputation," *The Washington Post,* May 11, 1991.

14. Derivative instruments can be very risky. In the early 1990s, several major companies including Procter & Gamble in the United States, Metallgesellschaft in Germany, and Allied Lyons in the United Kingdom, endured heavy losses from trading in derivatives, prompting regulatory scrutiny in all three countries. Fortunately, guidance is available. Multinational accounting firms have issued guidelines, as have smaller risk management boutiques. The Group of Thirty, a Washington, D.C.-based think tank of international bankers and former government officials, has published 20 recommendations for banks to use as guidelines in managing and disclosing investments in domestic and international "derivatives" based on such instruments as forward contracts and options.

15. "U.S. Companies Move to Limit Currency Risk," *The Wall Street Journal,* August 3, 1993.

16. All this will change, at least in the EU countries, when the Maastricht Treaty becomes a reality—targeted for 1999. For an excellent discussion of the European Monetary Union, see Mike Battles and Mike Thompson, "Issues Related to the Adoption of the Euro," *Director's Monthly,* March 1998, p. 12. Further details can be found in *Questions at Stockholders Meetings 1998,* available free from any office of Deloitte & Touche LLP.

17. Bridge loans can also be syndicated. For example, Citibank, Swiss Bank, and Banco Santandes joined to provide a bridge loan to Astra/Argentina in the early 1990s.

18. This section will not discuss U.S. tax consequences to foreign investors of owning U.S. portfolio investments or U.S. properties unless such holdings are directly related to acquisition of operating businesses. It is assumed that the reader is generally familiar with the basic U.S. federal income tax principles that apply to acquisitions in the domestic context. (See Chapter 5.) The purpose of this segment is not to advise readers of specific, current tax rules; readers are urged to consult specialized tax guides such as those published by Matthew Bender or other legal publishers. Rather, our goal is to give a broad

overview of the tax issues buyers and sellers should consider when structuring an international transaction.

19. Under Internal Revenue Code Section 6038A a corporation subject to IRS reporting requirements must report its transactions with all "related persons" as defined under IRC Section 267 (b) 482 or 707, not merely its transactions with corporations in its controlled group.

20. For an excellent guide to transfer pricing, see Ernst & Young LLP's *Transfer Pricing: 1997 Global Survey,* available through any E&Y office.

21. Under General Instructions for the use of Form 20F, for example, which can be used as a registration statement or annual report, Item 12 reads in part that "financial statements may be prepared according to United States generally accepted accounting principles [or] according to a comprehensive body of accounting principles" as long as certain conditions are met, including a disclosure of cash flow information "substantially similar to the requirements under U.S. generally accepted accounting principles." *Foreign Forms 1: Under the Securities Act of 1933 and the Securities Exchange Act of 1934.* (New York: Browne & Co., Inc., 1998), published September 15, 1998, pp. 20ff.

22. A notable example is a provision enacted in the Foreign Investment in Real Property Tax Act of 1980 (FIRPTA), as amended, which provided that foreign investors will be subject to U.S. taxation upon the disposition of a U.S. real property interest (which includes equity interests in U.S. real property holding corporations), regardless of any tax treaty that provides to the contrary.

23. Puerto Rico has its own tax law. For Puerto Rican residents, the U.S. income tax law is applied to income only from sources within Puerto Rico.

24. A sale by a U.S. corporation of stock in a foreign-owned subsidiary that is engaged in the active conduct of a trade or business whose conduct takes place in the foreign country from which the affiliate has derived more than a certain percentage of its gross income for its last three taxable years will be sourced in that foreign country. The practical result of this exception to the residence-of-seller rule is that in such case, this income will be treated for U.S. tax purposes as foreign source income, and the seller will be able to credit foreign taxes against his or her U.S. tax liability. If this income were treated as U.S. source income, foreign taxes could not be credited against the U.S. tax liability.

25. Interestingly, the investor-visa program has not attracted many takers because of the tax burdens that go with U.S. citizenship, which subject investors' world income to U.S. taxes. Canada, which has a similar program, has had more applicants, but there the investment is only $250,000 and with fewer tax strings attached.

M&A in the New Millennium

INTRODUCTION

Right now, in mid-1998, here in the United States, by any measure—be it number of transactions announced or closed, prices paid, equities exchanged, assets acquired, sales consolidated, purchase debt created or absorbed—we are in the midst of the largest merger wave in our history. In 1997, U.S. companies closed 7,834 deals worth $791.3 billion. Worldwide, the deal and dollar volume was double that amount.

It is said that we are in the midst of the "Fifth Merger Wave," which implies not only that there were four earlier waves, but that there will be a sixth—with more to come.[1]

THE MEGAMERGER WAVE

In actuality, the Sixth Merger Wave—the Megamerger Wave—may already have begun.

This new era began with a bang with the announcement of the biggest deal of all time—the merger of Travelers and Citibank to form CitiGroup, a $80+ billion deal that created a financial giant with combined assets just under $700 billion. It was followed by NationsBank/BankAmerica, a $570 billion assets deal and First-Chicago/BancOne, a $300+ billion assets deal.

In response to just these three deals, the press fired off a barrage of articles with titles such as "Is Big Back?" And the rhetoric was equally flashy: "In an age of consolidation, are sleek, entrepreneurial companies being overtaken by gas-guzzling corporate Cadillacs" (from *Inc.*). And this: "The Trillion-Dollar Bank: Once Unimaginable—Now Inevitable?" (from *Business Week*).

And before any of us here at M&A Central could catch our breath from these finance-related deals, we were hit with the news of the biggest *industrial* merger of all time, the cross-border merger of Chrysler and Daimler-Benz—not as big a deal in dollars or assets as CitiGroup, but far more significant as a harbinger of the megamergers and megacompanies to come.

These megamergers have attracted megamedia coverage—as print, electronic, and live media buzz with M&A bywords. Meanwhile, thousands of investment institutions are trying to figure out where the next megadeal will come from and how they can profit from it, as millions of individual investors pound on the doors of their stockbrokers, demanding to be let in on the action—before, not after, the deals are spun. Amazingly, few seem worried by market dynamics, even though they saw the $13 billion of public value created in one day by the announcement of the Travelers-Citibank deal—from $60 billion to $73 billion—vanish the next. Poof!

And "poof" is the latest M&A buzzword as *Inc.* magazine talks about the "poof-company," one created practically overnight by the "rollup" of a series of stand-alone companies into brand-new companies in industries such as printing, video rental, waste hauling, storage, and so on. Roll them up into a new company and "poof," you suddenly have a major new publicly traded company!

In light of all this activity, would-be trustbusters are trying to figure out what is and is not pro-competition, and what they can, should, or may do about it. And like the rest of us, they are asking the ultimate question: What's *really* going on?

THE "MERGER WAVE" CONCEPT

So what *is* going on? Most of the investing public believe that corporate-growth-by-merger is a recent phenomenon, when, to the contrary, it has been an important and even an integral part of our business life for the past two centuries. However, serious note of the phenomenon did not take place until 1965 with the founding of the magazine *Mergers & Acquisitions* by the senior author of this book.[2]

Many analysts of the merger scene have broken the M&A "movement" down into "waves," but where did the analysts get their numbers from? Since 1966, when the senior author added "rosters" to his newly founded *Mergers & Acquisitions* magazine, we reported on every major merger that could be confirmed by the acquiring corporation. But prior to that, reporting was hit-or-miss.

(Please note that, in this chapter, following both academic and press practice, we are using the words *merger, acquisition,* and *consolidation* as generic descriptors of the process of effecting a legal conjoining of two or more corporations or other kinds of business entities, even though the unit or units might never be integrated operationally or corporately into the buyer. For a true understanding of the real meaning of the words *merger* and *acquisition,* read the first few pages of Chapter 1.)

We had to be very careful in our reporting. We discovered that many announced deals never actually closed, even after the exchanges—mainly the New York Stock Exchange and the American Stock Exchange—had reported them to us as completed deals by mailing us copies of the listing applications for the stock to be issued in the deal. Further, no law required that all mergers and acquisitions be reported to any single regulatory body, and thousands of deals went down that *M&A* knew about but could not report on for lack of corporate or regulatory agency confirmation.

The Federal Trade Commission also gathered statistics in those days. At the end of each year we would compare. We found that our totals rarely matched. For every 85 we counted, the FTC counted 100. Year after year, we found that the FTC had listed many deals that never took place, and we had missed some that did take place and were reported to the FTC but were unreported in the press.

The seminal studies of Northwestern University's Ralph Nelson on the first three "merger waves" carried numerous footnotes correcting the numbers of previous investigators.[3] Over the past 33 years, we or our successors have kept the *M&A* magazine's Roster series going, and have reported on some 50,000 mergers.

Generally, here in the United States, the amount of cash or securities that passes across the table at a closing in effecting the deal is the controlling figure and the number used in publicity. If a $100 million company (public value) acquires another $100 million company (public value) for $100 million, it is entered at the acquisition price, $100 million. And that number goes into the statistical base.

However, in some countries in Europe, this same deal may be reported as a $200 million deal because when you put two $100 million (equity) companies together you get a $200 million (equity) company.

In other cases, revenue figures are reported. When there is a merger of two companies whose annual sales add up to $5 billion, it might be headlined as a "$5 Billion Merger."

Bank mergers, on the other hand, historically have been reported based on the total of the merged companies' *assets,* as *Business Week* did in the above reference in talking about the "Trillion-Dollar Bank" to come.

PROBLEMS WITH THE MERGER WAVE CONCEPT

Another problem with breaking the "merger movement" down into waves is this: Successive acquisitions—especially when followed by a statutory merger—mean that the same numbers are reported over and over. Say that in 1998, Steel Processors, Inc., itself the result of the consolidation over the past three years of five mid-sized steel processors, pays $10 billion for Midwestern Steel, which in turn had been the result of the consolidation of five mid-sized steel processors over its past three years. Each time one of them absorbed another steel processor it sent out a press release and notified the NYSE and the FTC. All of those same equities, revenues, and assets were reported over and over as pristine elements, and each transaction found its way into the statistical base of "completed mergers." Chroniclers of the merger wave phenomenon totaled up the revenues, assets, and equities of each deal even though they were the same numbers reported consolidated just a few months earlier. And those totals found their way into the yearly totals reported by various services. It can be proved that the totals of such numbers—say, for equities—over time can add up to more than the entire industry is worth!

And investigators like Ralph Nelson and others have used those numbers to trace the peaks and troughs of the "waves." Some would consider this double-counting, others would not, depending on what they were in the process of discovering. However, now that we have better data about the M&A phenomenon, it would be interesting to deconstruct the numbers and discover what pristine—that is, first-time—equities, revenues, and assets were consolidated. Only thus will we be able to assess the true impact of the so-called merger movement on local or national economies.

Without this deconstruction of the numbers, and with the merger movement so all-pervasive worldwide, it would not surprise us to see M&A annual deals reported to total $5 and $6 trillion in equities, $10 to $15 trillion in revenues, and $20 trillion and up in assets. They'll be the same equities, revenues, and assets reported consolidated a few years previously—perhaps several times each—yet all those numbers will be impounded in "wave" totals.

Whatever the true size of the merger wave that is now upon us, we know that it is tidal in its force. As suppliers, customers, and competitors continue to grow and shrink in a continuum of combinatory and decombinatory activity, the merger phenomenon has become an integral—and even crucial—part of business planning and operating worldwide.

THE FIRST WAVE (CREST: 1890s)

When was the first U.S. merger wave? Early researchers of the merger phenomenon had few formal records to go by, and press reports were often biased and inaccurate. So most merger activity was misreported. Investigators of the phenomenon had to guess a lot and tabulated only numbers of "corporate disappearances" with very little if any supporting data. Nelson's data reported on many misstatements of earlier investigators and corrected them. Nelson also reported that most of the merger activity took place after the Panic of 1893 and that the peak of the First Merger Wave was reached in 1898 when there were 401 "disappearances."

The first merger wave was driven by the following forces:

- The ability to eliminate competition, and so control production, and so control supply—to create monopoly conditions in order to set prices independent of competition
- The ability to use predatory pricing to drive a competitor out of business so that it could be acquired at a low price
- The ability to control not only the transport of goods from one place to another, but also the price of the transport, again to drive a competitor into a monopolist's arms
- The ability to acquire the means of production at or near zero cost—land grants, for instance
- The ability to control the courts and so operate without legal constraints
- The ability to control financial resources

The problems were these:

- Merger activity was often halted and frustrated by financial "panics."
- Price-fixing by the trusts and monopoly pricing by merged entities raised the ire of poor and rich alike. Their voices were eventually heard in the country's state and national legislatures, and regulation resulted.
- Labor unrest caused major problems in steel production and coal mining.

In 1832 the Hartford and New Haven Railroad began a 40-year program of consolidation of some 125 smaller railroads. This effort culminated in 1872 when it joined with the New York and New Haven Railroad to form the New York, New Haven and Hartford, which in turn was absorbed by the Pennsylvania Railroad in 1969 after it had merged with the New York Central. Their assets in turn were broken up in 1976, with the passenger business going to Amtrak and the freight business to Conrail.

In 1837 William Procter and James Gamble merged their candle and soap companies to form Procter & Gamble. Today, through dozens and dozens of mergers and acquisitions and internal growth, Procter & Gamble is one of the world's most successful companies. Under its umbrella are hundreds of familiar branded products, including Aunt Jemima, Olestra, and one of its latest and most successful acquisitions, Cover Girl.

The P&G deal was followed in that First Wave by many thousands of mergers, creating hundreds of companies with names and products that are now household words. For example, American Express, with a worldwide presence today, was created by the merger in 1850 of three companies, two of which were Livingston Fargo and Wells & Company. Today, it, in turn, is a candidate for a megamerger.

In 1863 the Singer Manufacturing Company "took over" the sewing industry. Isaac M. Singer had built his business based on the patents of Elias Howe, inventor of the sewing machine. But Singer made many, many improvements to the Howe machine, patented them, and wound up dominating the industry worldwide.

General Mills was formed in 1866 by the consolidation of a dozen independent milling companies and now gives us Wheaties, Cheerios, and Bisquick—and hundreds of other products. It is the world's largest marketer of paint-by-number art kits.

During this era, railroad deals were probably the most frequent. Many rail companies were given huge land grants by state and federal governments. Railroads were started by the thousands and were later merged in hundreds of deals into larger and larger companies—most of them holding companies. In the mid-to-late 19th century, bribery of state and national legislators to approve consolidations was common and there were continual scandals. But running all those thousands of separate railroads was as inefficient then as it is today (which is why consolidation is still going on).

In 1872, Aaron Montgomery Ward with two partners began the world's first mail-order company. The next year saw the Panic of 1873, his partners got scared, and he bought them out. In 1881 the Quaker Oats company joined with seven other oat millers to form the American Cereal Company, which, in 1901, reverted to the Quaker Oats name. National Cash Register began in 1879, but did poorly until it was bought by John H. Patterson in 1884, who built a terrific sales organization by giving his salesmen exclusive territories—a first. And Pillsbury Mills, now part of Britain's Grand Metropolitan, was created in 1889 by the merger of a large number of competing milling companies.

Richard W. Sears hired Alvah C. Roebuck to work for his watch company, and in 1887 they formed Sears Roebuck and Company and launched their first mail-order catalogue. In 1885 the founders were in turn bought out by one Julius Rosenwald, who sold his clothing manufactory and used the cash and his formidable marketing talent to build Sears into a merchandising powerhouse.

In 1892, not only was General Electric formed out of the merger of the Edison General Electric Company and the Thomson-Houston Electric Company, but the National Biscuit company, a.k.a. "Nabisco," came out of the conjoining of the American Biscuit Company and the New York Biscuit Company.

The list of mergers, buyouts, and so on, goes on and on. In 1900, W. K. Kellogg and his brother, Dr. John H. Kellogg, founded the Sanitas Food Company to make a new product called "corn flakes." W. K. soon bought his brother out and in 1906 established the Kellogg Toasted Corn Flakes Company.

While corporate takeovers, buyouts, acquisitions, and mergers were quite common in the late 19th century, far more frequent was the creation of "trusts," where the owners of competing companies put their stock in a voting trust and agreed not to compete with each other. (Many investigators did not and still do not differentiate between corporate mergers and trust agreements.) As Adam Smith had written many years before, "People of the same trade seldom meet together, even for merriment or diversion, but the conversation ends in a conspiracy against the public, or in some contrivance to raise prices."[4] And the ability to raise prices was the driving force behind most merger/acquisition and trust activity in the "age of the robber barons."

In a typical trust, equity holders placed the voting rights to their shares in the hands of trustees to be administered for their common benefit. Many were the arguments advanced in favor of such trusts. Not only would they be "benignly administered" so as not to exploit the public, but they would eliminate "disastrous competition," which, according to Yale Professor William Graham Sumner, newly caught up in the Darwinian revolution and pounding the lectern for his "social survival" theories, "threatened the very existence of the species"!

"Soon there were 440 large trusts, some created by 'mergers' of as many as 200 once-independent competitors. There was the shipping trust, the copper trust, the tobacco trust, the steel trust, the sugar trust, [the bread trust], and of course the Standard Oil trust controlled by John D. Rockefeller."[5] And that trust was far, far from benign. Once, with tears in his eyes, John D. promised "A certain widow, a Mrs. Backus of Cleveland, who had inherited an oil refinery, that he would 'stand by her.' But the Standard Oil trust squeezed that 'mother of fatherless children' out of most of her inheritance." His Standard Oil controlled the railroads, legislatures, local, state, and federal courts, and the Congress itself.

At the same time, Jay Gould and Jim Fisk, two other robber barons, joined with another famous crook, William "Boss" Tweed of Tamany Hall fame, in bribing the New York State legislators to approve his fraudulent railroad stock deals. Gould even got control of Western Union, and when criticized in the press, he bought the city's leading newspaper, the *New York World*.

The continuum of predatory acts in restraint of trade by the robber barons of the late 19th century brought on the Sherman Antitrust Act. Proposed by a Republican Senator from Ohio, it passed with only one negative vote in the U.S. House of Representatives and unanimously in the U.S. Senate. Incredible! However, the next three Presidents—Harrison, a Republican; Cleveland, a Democrat; and McKinley, another Republican—never enforced it and the trusts, helped by some very trust-friendly U.S. Supreme Court decisions, operated virtually unchanged as prices rose 50 percent between 1897 and 1913.

Then along came Teddy Roosevelt the trustbuster, who, as President, initiated many court assaults on the robber barons. However, he lost in the courts—especially the U.S. Supreme Court. A particularly vicious trust then was the Sugar Trust in the person of the American Sugar Refining Company. But the Supreme Court ruled in 1895 that the Sugar Trust was "not a monopoly in restraint of trade." It took Roosevelt's successor, William Howard Taft, to push the Supreme Court to break up the trusts. In 1911 the Court finally broke up Standard Oil into 30 smaller companies which today are household names—Amoco, Chevron, Exxon, Arco, and Mobile Oil (which used to be Socony—Standard Oil Company of New York).

But barons in other fields found a way around the Sherman Antitrust Act by merging corporately rather than by trust agreements. In 1913 regulators caught up to the robber barons with passage of the Clayton Act and the creation of the Federal Trade Commission. Its mission: to regulate U.S. corporations' predatory pricing tactics. After a long series of adverse court decisions, it was finally allowed to do just that. World War I brought an end to the First Wave.

THE SECOND WAVE (CREST: 1920s)

The principal driver for the Second Merger Wave was "vertical integration" combined with the benefits of mass production. The advantages were:

- Better quality control based on immediate feedback from the assembly line
- Better inventory control—scheduling deliveries as they were needed
- Freedom from extortionate pricing[6]
- Access to capital to pay for the costs of automatic assembly lines and production facilities
- Access to protected technology through patents and trademarks to allow *legal* monopoly pricing

The disbenefits were:

- Being a captive of your own suppliers
- Lack of competition to keep costs and prices down

The Second Merger Wave lasted until the Great Depression. It was primarily driven by the economics of vertical rather than horizontal integration. (Remember that Sherman and Clayton were targeted in Smithian terms at firms operating in the same trade or business—that is, direct competitors. Neither Sherman nor Clayton said anything to prevent the pulling together of all or most of the firms making parts for, say, automobiles, as General Motors did in acquiring and merging 80 manufacturers of different automobile parts into one giant whole, buying only from them and squeezing everybody else out.)

Ford wound up with the most fully integrated operation ever seen, even making its own tires from rubber from its own plantations in Brazil. Car bodies were made from Ford's own steel produced at its own River Rouge plant from iron ore shipped on its own railroad from its own mines.

The Second Wave ended with the 1929 Crash and the advent of the Great Depression.

THE THIRD WAVE (CREST: 1960s)

The Third Wave, which arose after World War II, had all the same causes as the first two waves, plus the following additional drivers:

- Acquisitions took advantage of the fact that the book values of hundreds of old-line companies did not reflect current market value. In general, the public did not know this, and performance measures such as "return on assets" were computed at book rather than at market or replacement value. The companies were sitting ducks for takeovers of various kinds.

- Many deals were driven by tax considerations—especially the cashing of the tax losses of acquired companies. Using debt to buy companies was the way to go because the interest was deductible. (With the tax rate at 50 percent, government was picking up half the cost of carrying the debt—provided the operation was profitable, which was not always the case.)

- Market extension continued in fragmented industies. A good example was the buildup of Detroit-based Avis Car Rental by Warren Avis who merged a large group of independent car-rental agencies into one large company. He then cut deals with the automobile manufacturers to buy cars at a substantial discount using cash borrowed at preferred rates to pay for them or getting the automobile manufacturers themselves to carry the paper.

- Spinning off as little as 20 percent of an acquired company to the public gave acquirers enormous leverage as they hocked their 80 percent to raise cash to buy more companies or to swap stock for stock, a.k.a. "Jimmy-Linging it."

- Berle and Means's 1930s admonition that eventually managers and not owners would be the decisionmakers came true in the age of the conglomerates as many managements spent corporate funds freely—without any stockholder say.[7]
- "Portfolio theory," invented to lower risk and even out returns for securities investment purposes, was now to be applied to groupings of acquisitions—that's the "swimming-pool/Christmas-tree syndrome."
- Next was the belief that good managers could manage anything. A typical example was International Telephone and Telegraph (ITT). It was one of the earliest to build a diversified empire through acquisitions, notably under Harold Geneen.
- Finally was an accounting trick created by the "pooling" phenomenon. Here's how it worked. A conglomerate with a high P/E, or higher P/E than a seller, could pay a premium in stock or in "funny money" and get an "earnings kicker" when the two companies were merged and the reported earnings were pooled. This resulted in "phantom earnings."[8]

Companies generated a series of "phantom earnings" kickers by making a series of acquisitions at discounted prices and pooling the numbers. This led to increased earnings, which soon pushed up the stock price. It was a formula for disaster: The worse the company, the higher the discount, and the bigger the earnings kicker.

All the conglomerates would—and did—buy just about anything, provided that the deal resulted in a boost in the conglomerate's earnings per share (EPS). Even with a long series of such boosts, ITT's Geneen complained bitterly that his stock never attained the price/earnings multiples given to the stock of rival conglomerators with near-identical earnings growth records.

Other notorious mass conglomerators were J.P. Fuqua and Fuqua Industries; Tex Thornton and his Litton Industries; Jimmy Ling's Ling Temco Vought (LTV); the Tisch brothers (Larry and Preston's Loew's Theatres/Hotels); and conglomerates such as U.S. Industries, National Student Marketing, American Standard, and several hundred more.

Why were such deals so easy to do? Why would companies sell out?

- First, it was an easy way for a privately owned company to "go public." It avoided the formidable time and expense of doing an initial public offering (IPO).
- Second, many old-line companies had millions of dollars of assets on their books carried at a fraction of their current market value. Due diligence required that they pursue a program to unlock those values. Merger was a convenient avenue.
- Third, many of the deals were made using stock swaps. A company that was worth, say, $100 million cash, could be bought for $125 million of common stock whose price had been pumped up by a series of earnings kickers. In many cases the stock a few months later might not be worth the cash in the selling company's bank at the time of the sale. This was the case with the acquisition of the publisher of *Psychology Today,* which had $12 million in cash in the bank from an IPO when it sold out to Ebasco Services for $23 million in stock. Ebasco, the detritus of the company known in 1923 as Electric Bond and Share and broken up back then by antitrust action, had a residual portfolio of some $300 million in stocks and never did anything with it until the Age of the Conglomerate. It then leveraged this portfolio into a buy-anything-as-long-as-it's-wood conglomerate. Well, *Psychology Today* was printed on paper which came from wood! But everything Ebasco touched turned back to dirt, the stock price got depressed, and the prodigies who founded *Psychology Today* got very little return for their genius.
- Fourth, many deals were tax-effect driven. To avoid taxation, many transactions were structured as stock swaps. Most of these deals were tax-free exchanges, and this was a big incentive for sellers. Further, a 1935 Supreme Court decision upholding the treatment of gains from the sale of assets of a corporation as exempt from the double-taxation rule and known as the General Utilities rule, allowed huge gains on the post-acquisition sale of assets to be passed on to stockholders with little or no tax consequences.
- Further, many conglomerates were built by cashing tax losses of various kinds. A company with a large net operating loss (NOL) could be acquired and its losses carried over to apply to the earnings of a series of acquired companies' earnings streams. Using NOL carryovers, with the then-current tax rate of about 50 percent, a con-

glomerate could pay up to twice as much as an ordinary buyer for the same earnings stream—or pay the going rate and get almost "instant" return on the investment.[9]

One of the earliest conglomerators was Charlie Bluhdorn, who started off by taking over moribund National Lead and then getting control of an obscure Texas automobile parts company called Gulf and Western. Using it as a base, Bluhdorn went on to make acquisitions in a wide variety of industries—racetracks, cigars, mining, panty hose, etc., and a prize publisher Simon & Schuster. But its crowning achievement was the takeover of Paramount Pictures—after which G+W dropped its name and called itself Paramount Communications. And it in turn became a takeover target in a hot battle between Barry Diller and Sumner Redstone, with Redstone, the eventual winner.

Another major conglomerator was Royal Little, who built up Textron Corporation beginning with near-dead American Woolen Mills. He used it as a base to build up a multibillion dollar manufacturer of everything from aircraft to zirconium.

Jimmy Ling took over Braniff Airlines and painted its planes mauve. But the color should have been red. He bought Jones and Laughlin Steel—the first billion dollar deal—and borrowed most of the money. To swing the deal, he issued debentures (sometimes convertible into common stock) and other kinds of exotic instruments like preferred stock carrying high dividends. People called them "funny money," but in spite of this opprobrium, like the term *junk bonds* later on, they were easily marketable. The peak (or is it the trough?) of the Third Wave came when Jimmy Ling bought Wilson Sporting Goods using funny money, and leveraged the transaction at an incredible 14.2 times equity.

Complicating it all was the financial structure of most conglomerates. Where sellers insisted on cash rather than stock, acquirers had to hock the company's assets or issue high-interest debt. Only the fact that the interest was deductible made the deals go. The beginning of the end for the Third Wave came in 1970, when the American Institute of Certified Public Accountants (AICPA), pushed by old-line companies afraid of being taken over by funny-money offers, pressured their accountants to promulgate their antipooling rules in the form of APB 16—called "Accounting for Business Combinations." This was a move that was good politics, but bad accountancy. (See box on the next page.) The General Utilities rule (discussed in Chapter 5) offered a solution, but it was progressively narrowed and finally repealed with the passage of the Tax Reform Act of 1986.

AN OPINION ON APB 16

APB 16 was "bad accountancy" because the rule forced the capitalization and the subsequent write-off *without tax credit* of amounts paid for equity interests that were in excess of book value. This was a very common occurrence, as in a typical transaction the purchase price represented the capitalization of a future earnings stream.

The rule insisted that securities—and especially common stock—used to effect a transaction be considered the equivalent of cash, which it nearly never is as cash is a most fungible commodity and stock is certainly not. The stock could be worth $100 one day, $80 the next, $60 the next, and so on. But APB 16 said that once issued, any premium over book paid for in common stock was to be valued at the market price for that day and written off at that value over the next 40 years or earlier—and the rules for "earlier" were never spelled out.

It was bad accountancy because it violated accounting mantras which insist that accounts be "consistent," "uniform" and "comparable." And APB 16 did violence to all three: It forcibly injected a huge inconsistency—one-time stock market prices—into the books of the acquirer; it violated the uniformity requirement if, by any one of twelve everyday acts involving capital stock transactions had been taken, pooling treatment was denied; and finally, it made comparability of one year's results with another an impossibility without a highly sophisticated deconstruction of the accounts growing out of not only one M&A transaction, but perhaps a hundred—and in a worst-case scenario, for every M&A future transaction for the next 40 years.

Today, a variety of regulators are reexamining APB 16 with an eye toward reform. It is high time!

SFR

The controversy surrounding APB 16 was one of the driving forces behind the creation of the Financial Accounting Standards Board (FASB), which was created to act as a Chinese Wall between the investing public and the accounting professionals. But it has never corrected the antipooling distortion.

The conglomerates were playing with fire. Knowing how to cash tax credits is not the equivalent of knowing how to manage an agglomeration of highly diverse enterprises. And for those who did know how to operate at a profit, like the famous marine artist who painted boats for a living answering his girlfriend's demand that he paint her portrait, "OK, I'll do it. But you're going to look like a boat," many acquirers, in search of diversification, got into big trouble by buying businesses that they knew little or nothing about and running them in the same way as their core business.

So many really bad deals came out of the Third Wave because of operating uncertainties, that it could not last. But in its death throes it gave life to the Fourth Wave, which had its work cut out for it: reconstructing American industry by deconstructing the conglomerates through, literally, 10,000 M&A deals.

THE FOURTH WAVE (CREST: 1980s)

The Fourth Wave was characterized by the following trends:

- Many companies that had acquired diversifying operations during the Third Wave found them too hard to run because they didn't fit and divested them.
- Many companies acquired—often at bargain prices—these sell-offs, seeking to build up strategically and to "go with the flow" and accommodate downturns in the economy by downsizing plant and personnel.
- Nonstrategic buyers increased acquisition activity.
- Tight money near the end of the cycle coupled with the high carrying cost for acquisition-based debt made the divestment of operations for cash a near necessity.
- Many companies realized that some bankers were more interested in cashing fees than they were in finding something that would fit long-time criteria for growth and profits. They set up their own internal M&A banking operations.
- Some investment bankers got greedy and not only wanted their fees for initiation, valuation, and negotiation of M&A deals, but wanted a piece of the equity action and actually financed some deals with bridge loans. When the market plunged in the late 1980s and early 1990s, they were stuck.
- Many unsound deals went insolvent as promoters like Robert Campeau, with no retail operating experience, overborrowed at high rates to take over famous department store chains like Federated and Allied, which wound up bankrupt. Later, even august Macy's went into the tank in 1992, growing out of an incredibly naïve LBO

forced on it by its long-time CEO Edward Finkelstein, who knew a lot about retail but little about finance.[10]

- The IRS's insistence that the costs of doing a deal must be capitalized helped bring the Fourth Wave to an end in the late 1980s.

The Fourth Wave was powered not only by the need to restructure present businesses—including those of the conglomerators, most of which had gotten into serious trouble from both operating and financing deficiencies—but by disgust with overregulation by government in a dozen industries.

Pinpointing the start of the Fourth Wave is a problem. However, we already have seen how the AICPA issued its restrictive pooling rules in 1970, which threw cold water on many a hot deal. And the oil embargo of 1973 was another major deal-damper for a time until its full impact on domestic oil companies was fully understood. It then created thousands of deals.

Deregulation was one of the major driving forces of the Fourth Wave. For a really well-done account of this phenomenon—particularly as it applies to the telecommunications industry—read Chapter 11 of Bruce Wasserstein's *Big Deal: The Battle for Control of America's Leading Corporations* (New York: Time Warner, 1998), entitled "The Telco Revolution."[11]

But as Wasserstein notes in his book, M&A history is also made by individuals. In 1970, a young man by the name of Michael Milken emerged from Wharton's Graduate School of Business and joined the relatively obscure third-level investment banking firm called Drexel Harriman-Ripley for which he had worked part-time during his days at Wharton. Together, they made M&A history.

Milken brought to the financial markets of the time a level of sophistication unseen in previous ages. He had studied the research of an obscure academician, W. Braddock Hickman, and his multivolume tome *Corporate Bond Quality and Investor Experience.* Hickman argued that investors could get high yields from portfolios of high-risk bonds if they bought them at the right time. As a potential default date approachs, said Hickman, prices are heavily discounted, so investors can get bargain rates. Milken extended Hickman's work, and in 1973, he and a professor from Wharton published their own analysis of the phenomenon.

Milken's thesis was simple: If you could buy at deeply discounted prices and diversify by cutting across several industries, the yields would be much higher than would be expected. Some issues would surely go into default. But so what? The chances that *all* or a major portion of them would go in the tank were, in the language of the statistician, "vanishingly small."

In the early 1970s, and later, when the oil prices threw the economy into endless turmoil, the junk bonds of the conglomerates were selling for as low as 10 cents on the dollar—far too low a price for the risk involved. With his theory working well, it was nothing but up from there for Milken and Drexel as they bought and traded and made money, money, and more money, cashing in on the overblown fears of conglomerate-generated securities.

Milken got 35 percent of the profits to be distributed any way he wanted. That deal was good for the next 20 years according to Connie Bruck's account in *The Predators' Ball.*[12] Milken and Drexel, later Drexel-Burnham and later still Drexel Burnham Lambert, both made billions of dollars trading bonds not only for their own account, but for clients like Saul Steinberg of Reliance Insurance, Meshulam Riklis of Rapid American, Carl Lindner of American Financial, and the Tisch brothers, Larry and Preston, of C.N.A. Later Milken sold junk bonds to raise the money to finance MCI, Ted Turner's takeover of MGM-UA, and hundreds of other deals. Milken was seen as a hero by many, but was successfully charged as a felon by federal regulators. Milken went to jail for it, and Drexel filed for bankruptcy.

The Fourth Wave lasted through the 1970s and 1980s and included the biggest LBO of all time, the $25 billion leveraged buyout of RJR Nabisco, Inc., after a three-month battle with a bid by the buyout firm of KKR at a nearly 100 percent premium over the previous market price. But that deal was such a messy affair that it turned many potential LBO investors off. Treating the RJR deal more as a farce than merger history, two *Wall Street Journal* reporters wrote it up in a best-selling book with the dramatic title *Barbarians at the Gate.*[13] And while many more deals in process were completed, the RJR deal really marked the beginning of the end of the Fourth Wave, which broke helplessly on the shore of the late 1980s recession.

THE FIFTH WAVE (CREST: 1990s)

Recovery of the M&A movement from the excesses of the 1980s was not long in coming. This time the push was toward strategic extension—building up in the lines that the owners and managers knew produced profits.

The Fifth Wave was characterized by the following:

- Tight money and huge carrying costs from the M&A excesses of the 1980s continued to force many former acquirers to sell off operations and delayed the start of the Fifth Wave until the third quarter of 1992.

- With the victory in Desert Storm, there was a general feeling that world tensions were subsiding. This feeling, coupled with the poor state of the national economy causing budget problems, led to defense cuts. As a result, the defense industry was in need of consolidation.
- Deregulation in telecommunications and in electric power generation and distribution created hundreds of potential deals—billion dollar deals.
- Junk-bond financing which had gotten so many companies and people in trouble was coming back in style—especially for financial buyers.
- Real estate was still in trouble, but there were bargains galore just waiting for the right deals to come along—and they did.
- The government and the insurance industry came down hard on the health-care industry and forced it to become more efficient. And that meant mergers to extract the benefits of scale.
- What was true of health care was also true of biotech, pharmaceuticals, and cable TV, where loans no longer had to be booked as HLTs.
- Corporate directors were losing their fears of personal liability from bad M&A deals.
- The new rules for the write-off of goodwill generated in an M&A transaction made U.S. companies more competitive against Canadian, British, German, Japanese, and other bidders.
- A recovering—even "booming"—stock market gave buyers a "new currency" to effect deals.
- The unofficial ban against "hostile" bids was relaxed.
- Huge buyout funds were generated which were bidding for companies and raising prices of companies for sale to unheard-of values.

All of the above led to the creation of CitiGroup, at a value of $80+ billion, the biggest merger of all time, and the herald of a new era in M&A.

THE SIXTH WAVE

In the first half of 1998, over $1 trillion in acquisitions were announced—equal to the dollar amount of all closed deals for 1997. The boost in dollars came from a growth in size of the largest companies involved. Although as always, small deals (especially very new Internet-related firms) remain the true fuel of M&A activity, the fact is that very large companies are combining as never before. Here are a few predictions on the shape of the Sixth Wave.

- World monetary stability will increase as financial markets (for example, the European Monetary Union) consolidate by region, boosting the confidence of megamerger deal-doers.
- Increasing efficiency of communications will allow the administration of increasingly larger and larger organizations to be managed from central locations.
- Language barriers inhibiting cross-border communications necessary to deal-doing and the daily transaction of business will be reduced and will eventually be eliminated as English becomes the accepted *lingua franca* of finance and business.
- Economy of scale will continue to be the driving force behind most deals; very large mergers of equals will yield new experiments for sharing top power, as at Citigroup.
- There will be continuing experimentation with near mergers—mostly joint ventures—where subsidiaries of megacompanies join up to explore "activity-sharing," high-risk entries which will eventually be absorbed by the parent with the best fit.
- National sovereignties will be downplayed by governments, which will be increasingly driven by economic reality rather than political ideology.
- The increasingly militant role of institutional investors will act as a bar to any entrenched management's merger mania.
- Competitive intelligence—especially technology tracking—will become the major driving force behind M&A activity.
- Antitrust activity will continue to be frustrated by national protectionism and the difficulty of defining true competition. Intimate knowledge of GAAP will be a prime requisite for executives in international affairs.
- À la Daimler/Chrysler, more and more deals and postmerger integration planning will be done by principals' CEOs using unit executives and without early advice from investment bankers.

When will the current wave end? As we stated earlier, the Sixth Wave, the Age of the Megamerger, may have already begun with the $80 billion

Travelers/Citibank deal. In proof that it was not a fluke transaction, note that it was followed by the almost $60 billion NationsBank/BankAmerica deal. And that, in turn, was followed by the $30 billion BancOne/First Chicago deal. The value of all three deals, measured by stock price paid to assume control, was boosted by a bull market. Nonetheless, the real operational sizes were and are big.

We believe that these deals mark only the beginning of the Age of the Megamerger. Certainly there will be a host of bank mergers as the United States' highly fractionated banking establishment, with its 9,000-odd banking corporations (down from 12,900 only a few years ago), begins the consolidation down to 300 or 400—probably including 5 to 10 megabanks. And while the rest of the banking world has never permitted the bank fractionation that has taken place in the United States, still, there will be more and more megabanks created as in the recently announced merger of Canada's number two and number five banks—Canadian Imperial and Toronto Dominion.

All this activity in the financial sector shouts that "bigger is better." We believe that these mergers in the financial sector will serve to goad tens of thousands of companies in all fields to merge into larger—and what they believe will be more viable—entities. These in turn will consolidate themselves into even bigger megacompanies, of which Daimler/Chrysler is only the beginning.

In 1908 there were 253 automobile manufacturers in the United States. Now there are three. Other industries may not see consolidation on this scale, but surely there will be more concentration in many sectors. The consolidation trend is certainly evident in the automobile parts industry.[14]

The merger phenomenon is now so all-pervasive of business worldwide—even including the once-off-limits domain of the public utilities—that breaking present and future merger activity down into waves may be as important as breaking down the basic functions of business such as research and development or capital spending, into "waves"!

We must assume that as more mergers "go international," the deals will become more complex as cross-border cultural, financial, and monetary effects are factored in. Increasingly, sophisticated information systems are generating increasing amounts of useful information that can be converted to real numbers, as computer-driven analytical methods are used to extract M&A meaning from those numbers. Cross-impact analysis, for instance, will become routine, and the quantified results will be fed into series of what-if scenarios for various potential merger candidates, with the best of them (the risk-optimized favorites) chosen for investment. But if there are major post-merger troubles in the future, most likely they will arise from failure to anticipate natural cultural differences and cultural sovereignties that cannot be easily factored into the modeling or into the cross-impact analyses.

We are also beginning to be aware that combinatory and decombinatory activity waxes and wanes with the national, and lately, the world economy. However, we are less sure about the lag and lead effects. Most important, we are learning that the M&A phenomenon is intimately related to entrepreneurship.

M&A: THE ULTIMATE ENTREPRENEURSHIP

The term *entrepreneur* and its numerous cognates such as *entrepreneurial* and *entrepreneurship* are usually associated by the public with the acts of an individual leading to a business start-up. As such, people think of M&A as "entrepreneurial" only when it involves small, new companies. In fact, *all* merger/acquisition/buyout activity should be considered as a special class of entrepreneurial activity.

According to classical economics, an entrepreneur is a person who brings together the elements of enterprise—capital, property, and labor—into a new combination so as to produce return on the capital, rent for the property, and wages for the labor. To the extent that entrepreneurs provide capital, they are paid a return. To the extent that they contribute property, they are paid a rent. To the extent that they labor (including labor as managers), they are paid a wage. And all these payments are made at market rates to reward the entrepreneurs as capital providers, property owners, or employees. But they are not paid as entrepreneurs!

How do entrepreneurs get paid?

Only if entrepreneurs bring the elements of enterprise into a *new* combination—so as to produce *above-market rates* of return for capital, or rents, or wages—are they compensated as entrepreneurs. And that is what the merger/acquisition/buyout process is all about—creating new combinations of the elements of enterprise which will result in above-market returns for capital, property, and labor. In fact, an entrepreneur does not need to supply any of the capital, property, or labor. All that must be done is to bring those elements of enterprise together in the new combination to be paid as an entrepreneur.

This, then, is the most enduring aspect of the forces at work behind M&A waves—the *ever-renewing corporate society,* today and in the future.

E N D N O T E S

1. One problem with statistical reporting on the merger phenomenon is that three numbers are involved. The first is the price paid to effect the transaction, in cash or securities. The second is the postmerger public equity value or "market cap" of the merged entity. Third is the total revenues or assets (for financial institutions) of the merged parties.

2. "New Journal Keeps Firm Eye on Busy World of Mergers," *The Washington Post,* April 4, 1967.

3. Ralph Nelson, *Merger Movements in American Industry 1895–1956* (Princeton, NJ: Princeton University Press, 1959).

4. "An Inquiry into the Nature and Causes of the Wealth of Nations," 1776, V1, Bk. 1, Ch. 2.

5. James Harwood, "The Mystique of Antitrust," *Mergers & Acquisitions,* September 1965.

6. It should be noted that at that time many American courts were venal: Contracts were hard to enforce, and favorable verdicts could be bought. In this environment, suppliers grew extortionate, so many companies solved the problem by buying them.

7. Adolph A. Berle and Gardiner C. Means, *The Modern Corporation and Private Property* (New York: Legal Classics Library Edition, 1933).

8.

	Buyer	Seller	Together
P/E	20	10	20
Earnings	$1 million	$1 million	$2 million
Shares out	1 million	1 million	2 million
EPS	$1	$1	$1.33
Market per share	$20	$10	$26.67

Source: Bruce Wasserstein, *Big Deal: The Battle for Control of America's Leading Corporations* (New York: Warner Books, 1991).

9. That's how Nick Salgo built his Punta Alegra Corporation (later Bangor Punta). He acquired control of Punta Alegra Sugar, which had some $100+ millions of losses from Castro's expropriation of the corporation's Cuban sugar cane properties, which Salgo cashed against the earnings of a series of acquisitions. When he used those gains up, he acquired control of the Bangor & Aroostock Railroad, whose stock, selling for $27 per share, had a reported $70 per share of fixed assets that could be abandoned for dollar-for-dollar tax credits against current earnings of acquired companies. In effect, by using tax

laws to his advantage, Salgo got these companies for free—and it was all perfectly legal.

10. Jeffrey A. Trachtenberg, *The Rain on Macy's Parade: How Greed, Ambition, and Folly Ruined America's Greatest Store* (New York: Random House, 1996).

11. Bruce Wasserstein, op. cit., note 8.

12. Connie Bruck, *The Predators' Ball: The Inside Story of Drexel Burnham and the Rise of the Junk Bond Raiders* (New York: Penguin Books, 1989).

13. Bryan Burroughs and John Helyar, *Barbarians at the Gate: The Fall of RJR Nabisco* (New York: Harper & Row, 1990).

14. "Maximum Merger," *U.S. News & World Report,* May 18, 1998.

A WOFC CASE STUDY: J. T. Smith Consultants

This case study is designed to demonstrate the wheel of opportunity and fit chart (WOFC) method of growth planning. The WOFC system has been used in hundreds of different companies in a wide range of industries and countries. The author has applied the WOFC method productively to companies as diverse as a major insurance company with 12 "product lines" and a pecan packager with only one. A multibillion-dollar publisher with eight profit centers used it to target and make a $300 million acquisition. An electrical transmission manufacturer used it to aid negotiations in selling itself off at a premium, as did a major U.S. manufacturer of automobile window lifts and door, hood, and trunk latches.

Successful WOFCers include two major cosmetics companies, three auto parts manufacturers in Brazil and Japan, a major U.S. aerospace manufacturer, a chain of supermarkets, a multilocation structural steel fabricator, and farm machinery manufacturers in the United States and Brazil. WOFC can be used anywhere there is business—in Italy, for instance, the WOFC method was used to plan the consolidation of some 30 knitting mills that had been taken over by the government because it was thought to be cheaper than paying unemployment; WOFC was also used after the consolidation. In Brazil it was used to outline an economic development program to discover how to best utilize an entire region's resources—human, educational, agricultural, geophysical, infrastructural, and financial.

A caveat: Do not make the mistake of applying to your own case the particular set of variables that survived the Instant Delphi in the following J.T. Smith case. Every company, like every person, is different. Each has its own persona. Every business entity has its own special strengths/weaknesses/opportunities universe. Never borrow plans from another; develop your own.

The authors believe that the relative importance of any of the hundreds of things that can be said about a company—its management, its workers, its markets, or its operations—can be quantified using the Instant Delphi process as described in this case and in the main text. Those numbers can and should be used to rate internal or external entry opportunities against each other so that those that fit can be differentiated from those that don't before resources are committed to any acquisition or de novo entry.

THE CASE

J.T. Smith Consultants is a firm of consulting mechanical engineers (ME) in corporate form based in Detroit, Michigan. It was founded in 1970 and specializes in the layout and design of automobile parts manufacturing and automobile assembly facilities. J.T. Smith is a so-called close corporation with only a few stockholders. Stock is issued only to department heads and changes hands infrequently.

During the good years, rather than reinvesting earnings in growing the company, the founding principals had habitually drawn out the company's earnings in salaries and bonuses and reinvested them in Detroit real estate.

After seven fat years (1980–1986) and seven *very* lean years (1987–1993), the automobile boom of 1994–1998 had made J.T. Smith's operations extremely profitable.

By 1998 J.T. Smith's billings were in the low nine figures and the backlog was substantial. Sales had been helped by the automobile industry's long years of downsizing, which had forced the Big Three (GM, Ford, and Chrysler) and many of their parts suppliers to contract out, or "outsource," engineering work normally performed in-house. Smith had exploited this phenomenon to the full, and in 1998 billings were running some 35 percent ahead of 1993. In addition, J.T. Smith had used its computer expertise to develop quick-response capabilities (QRC) by establishing in-plant "virtual engineering" centers hooked up to its Detroit headquarters' computers, library, and staff by broadband communications.

The centers were ideal for situations such as Ford's $95 million rush-rush reengineering of its Sharonville, Ohio, truck transmissions plant. Many at J.T. Smith believed that outsourcing of normally in-house engineering was a sea-change in the industry, effective not only in the United States but in all of North America and perhaps the world.

Cofounder Jackson Tecumseh Smith was such a believer. At age 59 he was very much involved in the day-to-day affairs of his company. He had been through good times and bad, and he did not want to repeat those last seven difficult years ever again. "This time, we're going to reinvest in ourselves rather than in real estate," he vowed at a crucial board meeting. "We simply must get bigger: The big firms survive in good times and bad. However, we've finally learned that automobile manufacturing is a cyclical industry, so while we're growing, we're also going to diversify."

Smith decided that he needed a 10-year strategic plan and began by creating a planning committee. Committee members included Smith; cofounder Tom Jones, chief operating officer; Hal Miller, executive vice president; Harry Teets, vice president for marketing; Wilber Clarke, vice president for finance; Jasper Walsh, vice president for engineering; and Carole Henry, comptroller. Each of them was a stockholder and had been with the firm for many years. All except Carole Henry, a CPA, were registered professional engineers.

Alfred Klinger, vice president of planning (a recent hire), was made secretary of the committee. He was a registered professional engineer (mechanical) and had his MBA as well.

The first meeting of the committee was held in early March of 1997. Very little happened—everyone had been too busy with the crush of new business to think about planning. Besides, they expected Klinger to come up with a plan. Smith pointed out that the job of a planner was not to plan, but to see that those responsible for the operations of the firm made a plan to which they could commit. Klinger was therefore directed to come up with a "plan to plan."

In early April of 1998 Klinger recommended the wheel of opportunity and fit chart (WOFC) method of strategic planning and took the following steps:

1. He scheduled an off-site, three-day WOFC session for June 5, 6, and 7—a Sunday-afternoon-through-Tuesday-afternoon series of sessions (see Exhibit Case-1) to be held at a local country club.

2. He devised Strength (Supplement) and Weakness (Complement) sheets and filled them in with sample supplements and complements (see Exhibit Case-2 and Case-3).

3. He prepared a description of potential variables (see Exhibit Case-4).

4. He devised an Opportunity Description sheet and filled it in with a sample opportunity (Exhibit Case-5).

5. He devised a flow chart to depict the entire WOFC process (Exhibit Case-6).

6. He held a series of six one-hour WOFC "orientation" sessions to ensure that everyone understood his or her responsibilities to the plan and to discuss sample Strength and Weakness sheets.

7. During the orientation sessions each of the participants pledged to consult with his or her subordinates to discover their ideas of strengths and weaknesses, to abstract them, to add their own, and to enter them each on separate Strength and Weakness sheets.

8. All attendees promised to look through their own files for opportunities and to hold meetings with their subordinates to develop more ideas and write them up on the opportunity sheets.

9. Klinger appointed himself facilitator and in turn appointed the assistant comptroller as monitor. The monitor in turn selected an assistant monitor.

10. He set up on a projecting computer the Instant Delphi Tally Input sheet to be used in the Delphi sessions (see Exhibit Case-7) and to follow the scoring in the Fit Chart itself (Exhibit Case-8).

11. He devised a wheel of opportunity for J.T. Smith to be filled in with the most logical opportunities as determined at the scheduled planning meeting (see Exhibit Case-9).

THE WOFC SESSIONS

Session 1—Orientation

The first session was held as planned on-site at the country club. Attendees were the seven participants, the facilitator, the monitor, and the assistant monitor. The reception, strictly a social affair, was followed by a dinner. Promptly at 8:00 P.M. the orientation session began.

Using a projector, the facilitator outlined the rules for running the sessions and led the ensuing discussion:

1. The fit chart was developed first so as not to be unduly influenced by the opportunities universe.

2. Only the seven participants were to vote in the Delphi. The facilitator and monitor were cautioned that they were to be careful not to influence the votes or distort the tallies.

3. Although observers were permitted to attend, they were not to interrupt the meetings (though they were encouraged to discuss the variables during the breaks). They were there to serve as support

personnel only—to supply factual information when it was called for. (There were no observers present during the first session.)

4. Only those scoring high or low in the Delphi were allowed to express an opinion without the special permission of the facilitator.

5. There were to be no phone calls made by or to any of the participants, the facilitator, or the monitor during the sessions. However, the assistant monitor was assigned the responsibility of screening any emergency calls for any of the participants, who were allowed to respond during the breaks. The sessions were to be suspended if any of the participants left the meeting for any reason. Any significant time lost was to be made up by extending the session into extra days.

6. The monitor was to ensure that the site and the sessions and records were secure and that nondisclosure agreements had been signed with all participants, as well as the facilitator, the monitor, and the assistant monitor. (If any observers attended later, they were also to sign nondisclosure agreements.)

7. The assistant monitor was to arrange for the taping and transcription of the sessions and to ensure that the taping process, the tapes, and the transcriptions were secure.

Immediately after dinner, each participant received sample Strength and Weakness sheets and a flow chart with a sample fit chart and a wheel of opportunity left blank.

Using transparencies and a projector, Klinger, the facilitator, took the group through the WOFC process beginning with the sample Strength and Weakness sheets (Exhibits Case-2 and Case-3) and answering questions as they arose. The rationale of the Delphi process was explained in detail. Klinger then took the group through the entire WOFC process using the flow chart (Exhibit Case-6).

At the end of the first session, participants received the actual Strength and Weaknesses sheets that were to be considered in the morning sessions along with summary descriptions contained in the Descriptions of Potential Variables (Exhibit Case-4). The participants were urged to discuss the strengths and weaknesses with the preparers and each other, and to make notes where clarification might be needed so that each of the participants would be voting on the same thing.

Session 2

Session 2 began with requests for clarification of several key strengths and weaknesses followed by general discussion led by the facilitator. Agreed-upon corrections were made by the assistant monitor, and new Strength and Weakness sheets were created, copied, and distributed to the participants in time for the beginning of Session 3.

Session 3

By discussion and voice vote, eight weaknesses were isolated and entered as complements and seven strengths were isolated and entered as supplements. The assistant monitor entered these selected variables on the master transparency of the Instant Delphi Tally Sheet, which was projected for all to see, with blank copies distributed to each of the participants to be filled in by hand as the Delphi proceeded in Sessions 4 and 5 and the relative ratings of the strength and weaknesses were developed. (See Exhibit Case-8 for the *completed* Tally Sheet. The blank tally sheet is not shown in any exhibit.) During the lunch break the monitor revised the early draft of the Description of Potential Variables prepared by the facilitator (Exhibit Case-4), edited it in accordance with the discussion, duplicated it, and passed it out to the participants.

Session 4

Following the lunch break, Rounds 1 and 2 of the Delphi were completed.

Session 5

Rounds 3 and 4 of the Delphi were completed by the end of the day.

DISCUSSION AND OBSERVATIONS

Complements (Weaknesses)

Cyclical Complements, Client Dependency, and Entry/Exit Threats.
The seasonal and product life-cycle variables were dismissed with very little discussion. They also felt they were not affected by random forces such as

weather, fads, and fashions. They knew very well that they were super-dependent on the Big Three, and only geographic dispersion could help them there. As for entry threats, there had not been a major ME engineering startup in 15 years and no sign—in spite of the current good times—that there would be one. The group felt that, in general, they were not sensitive to entry threat and, except for Ford, there was little exit threat. Only Long-Term Cyclical Resistance survived the discussion and became the first Complement.

Long-Term Cyclical Resistance. During Round 1, the CEO and the COO were at odds on this variable. The CEO gave it zero points and the COO a high score of 200. In view of Mr. Smith's pre-session statements as to the cyclicality of the automobile business and the desirability of "diversifying," his entry of zero was hard for the group to understand. But, backed by Clarke and Walsh, who also entered zeroes for the variable, he explained that by "diversification" he meant to get away from dependence on mechanical engineering alone and envisioned the building of a full-line professional engineering services company.

In opposition, the COO argued that even if they added electrical and civil engineering, their principal client would still be the highly cyclical automobile industry. Furthermore, mechanical engineering work both led and lagged the automobile cycle, whereas electrical and civil seemed to be tied more tightly to it. He suggested that the firm's sensitivity to cyclicality might be exacerbated if they diversified into those areas. Further, he said that his research had shown that many firms in cyclical industries were very profitable because there was very little threat of competitive entry, pricing was generally inelastic, and margins were high. Further, once numbers were developed to define the cycle—exactly how their sales were affected by the cycle and whether they led it or lagged it or both—they then anticipated its effects and compensated for the cycle.

This variable commanded increased attention during subsequent rounds and wound up with solid support from six of the seven participants, eventually becoming the third-ranking complementary variable with 100 points.

GROWTH VARIABLES

Billings Growth. In the first round, Smith gave Billings Growth zero points, saying that he was "saving his points for the full-lining Complement." Jones responded by saying that while they were very busy today, the Big Three supplied 70 percent of the firm's total billings and the firm had become increasingly dependent on one of the Big Three, Chrysler. He felt that they should develop more clients—perhaps 50 rather than their present 25 (they considered profit centers at the Big Three, especially geographically dispersed operations, as separate clients). He was supported by Teets, who said it took a year's effort to develop one new client and they had to get going now if they were to keep their present increased billing rate through the year 2000 and beyond.

Teets also observed that they had only a 12 percent penetration in the mechanical engineering market anyway, although their penetration in the ME subspecialty of automation was considerably higher. Teets believed that investing in more sales help could bump their share of the Detroit-sourced ME market to 18 percent. "We keep our clients, once we've got 'em," said Teets. "Let's invest where we know we're good."

In spite of two stubborn holdouts, Walsh and Henry, the cyclical resistance variable was awarded increasing points in subsequent rounds and finished up as the second-ranking complement at 120 points.

Profit Improvement.   Surprisingly, each participant had allocated 100 points to this variable in the first round. Why? Because none of them could believe that anyone would want *not* to make more money—that is, increase their margins.

Clarke pointed out that profits in most businesses are either margin-driven or capital-turns driven, and profits at J.T. Smith, as at most service companies, were margin-driven. "Pricing in the engineering field is important but is seldom cutthroat in competitive situations except in hard times, and much of our work is awarded in noncompetitive, negotiated contracts. Further, many jobs are split between competing firms. Hourly billing rates tend to be the same for comparable skills. Improving profits by bumping margins is risky. If we want to make more money, we should increase volume and turn our capital faster. Right now we have substantial amounts of cash available to finance it."

Following Clarke's lead, the discussion centered on the relationship between sales (billings) and profits as impounded in the classic equation, $S/C \times P/S = ROC$, where S is sales, C is capital and P is profit.

As the discussion progressed, however, the big question remained unanswered: Could they charge more for the same old service? Teets suggested that perhaps they were all leaving something on the table—especially during the current boomlet. He noted that the legal and accounting professions had accelerated billing rates far faster than the consumer price index (CPI), which engineers had generally tracked. Smith agreed. Henry thought they should at least try to raise prices. But Clarke asked, "When was the last time we lost a job on price alone?" The answer was, "In 1990." Clarke also noted that some 50 percent of the firm's billings were on task orders on master contracts that had been negotiated years before with annual reviews and adjustments on hourly rates tied to the CPI.

By Round 3, the variable had been dropped. Why? They made good profits on their work, they seldom took a loss on a job, and the participants needed the points to support other Complements and Supplements.

MARKETING-RELATED VARIABLES

The group reviewed the variables outlined in the Review of Potential Variables. Of particular concern was the effect on QRC (which kept margins up) if they got bigger. Teets said he was just as concerned with survival as he was with growth. The last seven years had been tough. He wanted to make sure that they knew the dollar volume of billings to be reached in any one field of endeavor (such as CAD services) to ensure its survival *and* growth.

The group did not believe that the PIMS data, developed for industry in general, applied to them. If J.T. Smith became a market leader with a 35 percent share of market, their annual billings would be over a billion dollars, which would give them impossible administrative problems; thus the Attain Maximum Market Penetration variable was not included. The Attain Pricing Independence variable was also passed over for consideration as they did not have much proprietary software and had little hope of developing more.

They did want to broaden their client base but were not sure how they could do it while being based in Detroit. Their "virtual engineering centers" concept might lend itself to that broadening, but it was too new for them to know. As the automobile market was the largest market in the world, the Enter Larger Markets variable was passed over. So was the Increase Clients by Number variable, since the automobile industry itself, with decentralization, was now effectively a highly fractionated industry and not the purchasing monolith it had been. The full-lining variable was selected with little discussion.

There was nearly unanimous agreement that they wanted nothing to do with a "slave-labor" entry as a "second-line" entry. As for buying up one of the new CAD-CAM companies, they wanted to wait and see how their own CAD-CAM program developed. As for improving their "social image," they were highly critical of the person who suggested the variable.

Effect Minimum Market Penetration.   This B-school variable got attention only from Teets, who had picked up the concept at a marketing seminar and had difficulty explaining it in defending his point allocation. He tried to explain that there was a "share-of-market penetration point" that had to be reached before a firm's size affected its QRC abilities, which would affect margins. But most needed the points elsewhere. The variable was dropped after the second round.

Exploit Full-Lining Potential.   This was what they were all waiting for. Adding products and services that could be sold to their present customers had helped firms like Hewlett-Packard to grow year after year. The fabulous success of superstores such as Sam Walton's WalMart and Sam's, with their one-stop shopping, could perhaps be applied in the engineering services business. They could add not only civil and electrical power engineering (which included cogeneration, in which they had already had a good start) but architectural services, land planning, city planning, landscape architecture and environmental engineering services—perhaps even management consulting!

"The list is nearly endless," said Smith in defending his position and his allocation of a humongous 300 points. In the final tally it led all the other complements with 130 points.

OPERATIONS

The supplier clout variable was rejected because the relationship with some of their suppliers was important in securing work, and they had long-standing relationships with them. Although everyone wanted to reduce direct costs, the only way suggested was to convert more paper-and-pencil work to CAD-CAM. The variable was not included because the group was waiting to see how their in-house CAD-CAM group performed. Overhead reduction was a natural, and so was the reduction of downtime. Here again the participants did not have direct knowledge of the possible effects of the CAD-CAM revolution and the actual effect on capital requirements, so reduction of capital costs was not selected as a salient variable.

Customer (Client) Clout.   Only Walsh and Henry gave points to this variable, and it was soon dropped from consideration because the other participants did not like the sound of it.

Reduce Overhead. This began as another motherhood-and-apple-pie variable. Who could challenge it? J.T. Smith could and did. Here again, Smith, the CEO, and Jones, the COO, were on opposite sides in the first round. The CEO held that increased billings would automatically reduce overhead. But the COO and VPF said that it was the *kind* of business that was important. Adding a low volume of electrical engineering (EE) sales, for instance, might not reduce overhead but instead increase it if the company had to absorb the costs of EE marketing, estimating, software, library, and downtime. In contrast, a horizontal acquisition—buying a head-to-head competitor mechanical engineering firm, for example—would probably reduce overhead substantially.

The point score jumped around and the discussion at times was quite heated. In the end, however, the variable lost most of its support as the participants reallocated their point to other, more important variables. It barely survived with 30 points.

Reduce Downtime. This was the only area on which the CEO and COO saw eye-to-eye. Carrying unbillable bodies on the payroll is always a problem for a consulting firm and gets worse as the firms specializes.

There was considerable discussion of why there were two overhead variables. Why was the Reduce Downtime variable not included in Reduce Overhead? The argument was made that it was by far the biggest part of the overhead variable and was very difficult to control; it *had* to be broken out separately.

It was pointed out that careful selection of employees and in some cases cross-training could reduce the downtime problem. Also, salesmen should be told well in advance about the holes in the billable bodies schedule. The variable survived with 70 points as the result of Walsh's application of a massive 300 points in the last round. Downtime was his biggest headache and he didn't need any acquisitions that would give him roomfuls of unbillable bodies.

Overall, the Complements wound up with a score of 450 points out of 1000, leaving 550 for the Supplements, which meant that J.T. Smith probably had more things right with it than wrong.

Strengths (Supplements)

People Variables. All of the people variables made it into the fit chart. Also included was the client fit variable, which was also at least partially people related.

Top Management Fit. This variable gave the CEO and VPE fits. Smith said "I don't care how we make money. It's the bottom line that should matter to all of us."

Walsh responded, "But J.T., that's what you said about the last acquisition that we made. You never even had any of them to dinner!" (The discussion was of a "draftsperson" training school that J.T. Smith had purchased 10 years before and closed down 2 years later with substantial losses and some damage to their reputation.)

Smith answered, "Well, why should I have had them to dinner? Their head guy wore white socks with a business suit and had a *black* handkerchief in the breast pocket of a *black* suit! And they wore pointy-toed shoes and said 'between you and I'! I couldn't take them to the country club looking and talking like that. I still think it was a good fit. It could have made money. The management was bad, that was all."

But Walsh persisted and was strongly supported by the ExVP and the COO. They asserted that the comfort factor was important in making acquisitions in engineering-related fields. Top management of any potential entry for J.T. Smith should be of a "professional" character in order to communicate and to build teams. In the school acquisition they never met to determine what should be taught, how to teach it, and how to market the graduates. "It was a poor acquisition because the kind of people who run vocational schools are promoters first and instructors second or they don't survive, much less grow," one participant said.

In sum, there was poor *social* fit between J.T. Smith's registered professional engineers and the vocational school managers. This would probably be a problem with any acquisition that J.T. Smith made. The variable drew increasing support in subsequent rounds and wound up in the fourth round as the leading variable with 160 points.

Middle Management Fit. In the opening round, the VPE stated that, in his opinion, J.T. Smith's greatest asset was its carefully built middle management staff. Most of the department heads, like Smith, were in their mid-to-late fifties. Management had made a careful effort to staff up with younger engineers with good academic backgrounds, most of whom had been sent back to school for graduate training in engineering administration. Not only where they working, billable professionals, they doubled as supervisors and expediters and had frequent client contact. He felt that their low client turnover was a result of the careful buildup of middle management. Further, they were a source for low-risk manager succession.

In opposition, both Smith and Jones held that it was the department heads who did most of the client contact and project management; middle management simply followed orders and could easily be replaced. They pointed out that the downsizing movement in the automobile industry had concentrated on reductions in middle management and had proved very successful in cutting overhead by getting rid of a lot of deadwood—especially at General Motors.

The EVP and VPF strongly disagreed. It was the corps of competent middle managers that allowed the principals the time to play golf and bring in the business. It was the middle managers that got the jobs out the door. Gradually their view was adopted in subsequent rounds and the Middle Management Fit variable wound up with 140 points.

Staff Skills Fit. There was considerable discussion on where the "profit power" rested at J.T. Smith. At the beginning, all except the COO believed that their greatest strength was in the 400-odd, longtime engineers and draftspersons that had been tried and tested. Jones did not agree. He took the position that present staff skills were unimportant in rating any potential entry. He pointed out that the purpose of the planning meeting was to plan for an expansion. Present staff people and their skills were not important in rating any potential entry or managing it afterward. His argument went as follows:

1. In any horizontal merger (acquiring a competitor), J.T. Smith would also absorb the *target's* staff.

2. In any vertical acquisition (buying a customer such as an architectural design firm), J.T. Smith's staff, in general, would not be useable.

3. In any service extension (a new service sold to their present customers), staff skills would, most likely, be inapplicable.

4. In any geographic market expansion, J.T. Smith would use the target's staff. In addition, if more bodies were needed, they would probably recruit and hire there rather than move people from Detroit, which was expensive. Further, many of their staff in the past had proved highly resistant to relocating.

5. In any free-form extension, the risks were too high to depend on home-office personnel for the success of any entry. It would have to stand on its own.

In opposition, the other participants, each of whom had spent considerable points on the variable, stated that not only was it important to provide second-line engineering managers with opportunities for advancement, but seeding an acquisition with trusted home-office people could also be important. Why? Here is what they said in favor of placing a high value on this variable:

1. It would ensure the quality of engineering work performed.
2. It would ensure truthful reporting of job status.
3. It would yield reliable information on the technical competency of individuals in the acquired organization.
4. It would strengthen the relationship between J.T. Smith's career people and the target's principal customers, preventing the target's key people from splitting off to compete.
5. It would ensure competent succession management in the event of mass defections of the target's staff.

Marketing Fit. There are usually no "salespeople" per se in professional engineering organizations. As at J.T. Smith, the principals do most of the marketing—much of it on the golf course. (Teets' title for many years, rather than VP Marketing, was the euphemistic title "VP for Project Development.") The thrust of the discussion of the variable led to the conclusion that the variable was not important as long as the principals of the target were locked into staying with the new merged entity for sufficient time for J.T. Smith Consultants to develop marketing skills; the variable was dropped.

Customer (Client) Fit. Except for Teets, the VP for Marketing, and Walsh, VP for Engineering, all of the participants spent points on this variable, with Smith leading the pack. Teets, who scored the variable zero in the opening round, came to see what the others saw—that J.T. Smith Consultants should discover what engineering and consulting services other than ME that its current clients bought or might buy in the future. He then scored it 300 points and, along with Walsh, who also went from zero to 300, brought it in at 150 and made it the highest-ranking variable.

Physical Resources. There was very little discussion of the lone variable in this category. Most agreed with the late R. Buckminister Fuller, who had held that *physical* problems were easily solved as compared with the *metaphysical*. Machinery, furniture, and buildings were not important. People were important.

Operations

Only EDP Fit and Synergy survived. Vertical Integration Fit was thrown out; the participants were turned off by the vertical integration mode.

EDP Fit. From Round 1 to Round 4 the point score for this variable doubled. The high score was largely the result of Clarke's 300-point allocation in the final round—up from zero in the first round. Here Clarke was using information from one of his assistants who had hooked up his laptop to the company's mainframe; he had discovered that their CAD and computer-aided manufacture (CAM) jobs were very profitable and had very low personnel turnover. He said, "When you combine these numbers with the prospects for the on-site virtual engineering centers, we must conclude that our EDP capability is one of our prime assets."

There was some good-humored comment that there was collusion between J.T. Smith and Clarke, because even though J.T. had scored the variable zero, he did not take issue with Clarke's 300 points because he was "out of points" by the time he got to that variable. (That is not a valid argument; the monitor should have objected, as this defeats the purpose of the fit chart, which is to weigh one potential entry or field against another. If a participant votes zero points it means that he or she is against it.) As for the variable, the participants felt that they were leaders in the field and had invested substantial funds in both equipment and software, including some developments of their own. They felt that it was one of their top assets, if not their primary one. Although the CAD-CAM skills of top management, middle management, staff, and marketing management had been impounded in those ratings, J.T. Smith's library of proprietary software programs and the very considerable specialized hardware to run it had not.

Synergy. Synergy was a difficult item to handle. The old "two-plus-two equals five" equation was not enough for engineers. The CEO had allocated 200 points to it. He argued that they should not make any entry unless they got some extra benefits from it. His first example was that of merging with another ME firm so that downtime would be reduced, but that was redundant with the downtime reduction variable already treated as a complement. (Double-counting is rate in the WOFC process, but it *can* happen.) The CEO mentioned software utilization, but again, that had already been impounded in the EDP fit variable. Finally, in the last round Synergy was eliminated.

Summary

Based on the Fit Chart Tally sheet alone, it was possible to make a Strategic Statement as follows:

J.T. Smith is looking to complement its weaknesses, first by making an entry that is countercyclical to the automobile industry cycle—a so-called defensive entry. It wants to maintain its present increased billings rate and wishes to enter new, high-growth areas. Further, it wishes to diversify by adding new lines of services that could be marketed to its present customers with the expectation that any such entry would lower overhead and reduce downtime.

J.T. Smith is looking to exploit its strengths by utilizing its top managers who are experts in automation engineering and production planning. They are backed by a highly skilled staff of middle managers seeking opportunities for advancement. J.T. Smith principals believe they have very low client turnover because of their long-tenured staff and believe that they can expand sales to their client base by offering additional engineering-related lines such as electrical engineering (EE) and civil engineering (CE). Finally, their recently developed high-level skills in computer-aided design (including their development of proprietary software and related hardware systems) should result in more business if properly exploited.

Session Five—The Wheel of Opportunity

Each of the participants had submitted candidate opportunity areas for consideration—in some cases they had isolated specific companies as targets. This was particularly true in the area of their specialty, mechanical engineering services provided to automobile manufacturers and their high-volume parts suppliers.

THE MARKET INTENSIFICATION MODE

Horizontal Integration

J.T. Smith's principal competitor, Coleman Engineering, was "available." Its three founder/owners were in their late sixties and early seventies—on average some 14 years older than J.T. Smith's top management. They were looking forward to retirement. Like J.T. Smith, Coleman also was very busy and currently was making good money. Their principals had explored selling the firm to the employees using an employee stock ownership plan (ESOP) but no one came forward to "honcho" the plan, as most of Coleman's top men were also senior people—about the same age as the principals, and also looking forward to retirement.

Some 50 percent of the target's work was heating, ventilating, and air conditioning (HVAC); it was only 10 percent of Smith's. Coleman had developed one specialty: the design of clean rooms where electronic subassemblies were made in a dust-free atmosphere—this was a growing business, as more and more electronics were added to automobiles. The target's current billings included some "slave labor" contracts where they "rented out" engineers and draftspersons to manufacturers, which provided supervision. Many of those employees were located in cities other than Detroit. The firm was available for a reasonable price with a buyout on the installment plan.

Smith disliked the idea of expanding in the ME area because it wasn't "diversification." However, he acknowledged that Coleman's clean room specialty had worldwide potential and met the diversification criterion. He also observed that "slave labor contracting is unprofessional." But after some discussion, he came to believe that it might be a continuing trend that followed naturally from the downsizing movement and also was a kind of diversification. He also began to give more credence to the rumor that a hotshot West Coast firm was looking at the target in order to expand its own slave labor business. This could threaten Smith's continuum of work if the Big Three went that way and Smith refused to go along.

Market Extension. Automobile manufacture—both parts manufacture and assembly—had been moving out of the Detroit area for many years. New plants, many foreign-owned, were being built on the West Coast and in the Southeast. Smith felt that J.T. Smith should "diversify away from Detroit," which he considered to be a "dead city" in spite of the recent boom, and effect an entry or entries in either the Southeast, in sunny California, or even in South Africa, which he felt, with the death of apartheid, could become a boom area. An entry in China, which is just getting started in the mass production of automobiles, should also be considered. Furthermore, the resurgence of U.S. domestic automobile manufacturing had come as the result of hundreds of innovations that were well-known to J.T. Smith's people. They had eclipsed Japanese and German methodologies. Those skills might be highly marketable in the rest of the world.

Market Intensification Mode (Summary)

Building up billings in the ME field by horizontal integration could be highly profitable. However, as its name implied, it was certainly not "diversification" but its opposite. Although a market extension entry would dilute their tie to the Detroit economy with all of its social problems and was a kind of diversification in that sense, they would still be tied, even with a South African entry, to the automobile cycle, which seemed to run worldwide. However, all recognized that it was by far the least riskiest area of entry for expansion.

THE VERTICAL INTEGRATION MODE

Vertical Backward Integration.   J.T. Smith bought the services of other specialized engineering companies, including environmental planning, urban planning, geophysical consulting, surveying, community planning, and architectural design. Of those, environmental planning was tops. It took up to half of J.T. Smith's purchasing dollar, was the company's fastest-growing supplier industry at 20 percent per year, had a large quotient of mechanical engineering in it, and seemed relatively independent of the automobile cycle.

Vertical Forward Integration.   J.T. Smith's primary clients were the automobile and automobile parts manufacturers, which absorbed 60 percent of their sales. After that came developers of shopping centers and industrial parks—mostly low-margin HVAC work. Next came turnkey contractors building or modifying plant buildings for automobile parts production and assembly—again, mostly HVAC work. Architectural design firms were the last.
   The first three were arbitrarily eliminated. Only moving into architectural services was to be considered.

Vertical Integration Mode (Summary)

While some diversification could result from targeting this mode—for instance, architectural work leads rather than lags the economic cycle—except for environmental planning, growth rates were low, and competition limited profit. Most of the firms were small and they were either very busy or very dead. Further, it was not "diversification" but "intensification." Moving vertically would bind J.T. Smith even more tightly to the automobile industry and its cyclicality and tie the company too closely to the local economy.

THE DIVERSIFICATION MODE

Product (Service) Extension. Adding new services that could be sold to their present clients appealed very much to everyone at J.T. Smith—especially adding electrical engineering (EE). (In most areas of the United States, ME/EE firms were very common, some were very large, and they were consistently profitable.)

In most of the service extension fields shown on the Wheel of Opportunity, J.T. Smith's software could be used or adapted. Exploiting the deterioration of the nation's infrastructure (some estimates of the cost of rebuilding were in the $200-$300 billion range) inferred the addition of civil and sanitary engineering to the company's skills spectrum. However, many believed that the firm's ME skills could be utilized to develop superior road and bridge maintenance and rebuilding methods and equipments. The participants all believed that their skills in project planning and control could be well utilized in highway and bridge rebuilding, although there might be a price to pay in having to deal with government rather than private industry, and J.T. Smith had little experience in marketing to government.

Free-Form Diversification

This was by far the riskiest area of entry. Entering a new geographical territory with a new service had only one benefit: If it failed, the news might not get back to Detroit. Only two entries were proposed: road and bridge engineering in South Africa, which had massive infrastructure problems, and power engineering in China, which had huge and ongoing requirements for electricity. Making a seed entry in these areas was risky, but if a firm could be purchased, they could expand later into automobile-related areas. (Preliminary inquiries had indicated that there were firms for sale in South Africa and in Hong Kong in those selected fields.)

Diversification Mode (Summary)

This area provided the highest change to meet Smith's "diversification" requirement—the concept that got him started on making a long-term strategic plan in the first place. Although expanding in the Detroit area did not appeal to anyone at J.T. Smith, most recognized that it would be relatively easy to add an

EE firm in the Detroit area and *then* go after new geographic markets by acquiring other ME/EE firms by a series of LBOs.

There had been considerable discussion of the difference between a "strategic" entry and an "investment" entry, and the participants agreed that a free-form entry would probably be priced as a stand-alone investment rather than as a strategic entry.

E X H I B I T CASE-1

Schedule for J.T. Smith Strategic Planning Meeting— June 7–9, 1998

Note: Breakfast is at 0700. Sessions start at 0800. Morning and afternoon breaks are at 1000 and 1500, respectively. Lunch breaks are at 1230 each day.

First Day

1800	Reception.
1900	Dinner.
2000	First Session—Orientation.
	Review of Strength and Weakness (S&W) sheets and walkthrough of Flow Chart.
2030	Q&A and discussion of S&W sheets and Flow Chart.
2200	Individual study of S&W sheets and Flow Chart.

Second Day

0800	Second Session—Review of S&W sheets.
1015	Third Session—Review of S&Ws continued.
1400	Fourth Session—Conversion of S&Ws to complements and supplements and differential ratings.
1500	Fifth Session—S&W Ratings continued.
1700	Discussion of results of Fit Chart Tally sheet.
1800	Reception.
1900	Dinner.
2000	Individual and group study of Opportunity sheets.

Third Day

0800	Sixth Session—Selection of opportunities.
1015	Seventh Session—Rating opportunities.
1400	Eighth Session—Continue rating opportunities.
1330	Ninth Session—Continue rating. Final totals.

E X H I B I T   CASE-2

Company Confidential   Author and date <u>JTS 5/20/98</u>

STRENGTH ANALYSIS (FIT CHART SUPPLEMENT)

Every enterprise has its own special strengths—those things that set it apart from others and cause it to remain in business and grow. J.T. Smith is a successful enterprise. However, the industry is changing rapidly. Please describe (using separate sheets) those special strengths that you believe can be exploited for growth and profit in the coming years, breaking it down into short-term—next few years; medium term—next 2–4 years; long-term—next 6–10 years.

Description of strength:
One of our greatest strengths is our client list. We have been doing business with Ford Motor for the past 30 years. We know they are dissatisfied with some of their engineering service vendors—that's the reason they pulled a lot of their work in-house. But now they want to outsource everything they can. (They have hinted that they would like to see us buy out their principal EE services contractor, which is always late and has excessive turnover.) We should use our "installed base" of clients to lead us in the right direction.

Why do you believe this?
I just can't believe that Ford would suggest a buyout of one of their long-term suppliers if we weren't held in high regard there. This would give us a solid EE entry that we could use as a base to expand in other geographical areas and thus get some diversification away from Detroit.

Who are the competitors (if any)?
There are many EE companies, but most of them are small and can't gear up for the big jobs. Further, they don't seem too aggressive as far as technology is concerned. One of our top MEs worked for that Ford supplier and says that their top people are very hide-bound and don't want to change. This is probably the same with the other four EE firms in our immediate market area—they're all running scared and don't want to risk anything on innovation. Even if we did an EE startup without an acquisition, I think we'd prevail.

Give a specific example.
On the Porto job, the EE people were always late. They refused to deal themselves into the PERT program even though it was in their contract that they have to. I believe that if we had our own EE department we could get jobs done faster, cheaper, and better. My perspective is long-term—we should become an ME/EE firm permanently.

How should this be marketed?
All of our top ME people know *something* about EE work, since we have to subcontract a lot of it ourselves—small jobs, admittedly, but remember, we bid them.

Where can J.T. Smith principals read about this? (List and attach any literature, memoranda, news stories, etc.)
We subscribe to most of the EE journals—they're in our library.

Session Comments:
That our clients were our greatest asset was generally agreed to. The only
trouble was that it tied us more tightly to Detroit and the automobile
business. This was of considerable concern.

E X H I B I T CASE-3

Company Confidential   Author and date JTS 5/25/98
WEAKNESS ANALYSIS (FIT CHART COMPLEMENT)

**Every enterprise has its own special problems—those things that hold it back from profit-
able growth. Reality escapes the best of us at times and the recognition of inherent weaknesses is a precondition to profitable growth.**

Description of Weakness:
Our greatest weakness is our time to the automobile cycle. We have just
been through five good years after seven very bad years. It's not going to
change. It seems to be a worldwide phenomenon. It may get worse as the
world's economies become more dependent on each other and share the same
information.

Why do you believe this?
I've seen it in my paycheck. I've seen our billings at times drop by half.
Although the automobile cycle tends to follow the world economic cycle, it
usually leads it and lags it and is always higher in amplitude than the
economy itself.

Is this weakness industry, company, or management related?
It is industry related. However, management is much to blame, as it spends
its good-time profits on management bonuses and finances losers pushed by
Wall Street brokers. It seems that the kind of people who can produce good
automobiles are the kind of people who have very little long-term trend
sensitivity. It's a curse.

Give a specific example.
When, in the mid 1980s, the Japanese voluntarily restricted imports,
Chrysler made all kinds of money, which it promptly spent on bonuses and
some crazy acquisitions. They should have invested in something
countercyclical *or* simply anticipated the downturn, conserved their cash,
and spent money on technical innovation or made capital investments that
would allow them to compete with the Japanese and Germans.

How can this weakness be compensated for?
J.T. Smith has to diversify away from automobiles and the Detroit economy.
When Times are bad governments spend money on infrastructure improvements. For instance, we should look overseas for growing economies such as
those of China, Indonesia, and perhaps even South Africa, now that their
apartheid problems have been solved.

Session Comments:
There was general agreement that they all should look for opportunities to
diversify at least 50 percent of their billings to nonautomotive work.

E X H I B I T CASE-4

Description of Potential Variables

Following is a list of variables abstracted from the Strength and Weakness Analysis sheets and converted to Complements and Supplements, along with suggested legends to be sued on the Fit Chart to identify the variable if and when selected.

COMPLEMENTS

A complement, according to *Webster's New Collegiate Dictionary,* is "the quantity or number required to make a thing complete." Inherent in the WOFC process is the targeting of industries and their component companies, with products or services that will offset or "complement" the weaknesses of the acquiring company.

Cyclical Complements

Weakness: The automobile industry, which supplies 70 percent of our billings, is *cyclical*. It follows the capital spending cycle very closely.
Complement: Enter a countercyclical industry—sometimes called a "defensive" industry—that is drive by the entertainment, retail food, fast food, automobile parts rebuilding, government-stimulated social programs, defense spending industries, etc.
Fit Chart Legend: Countercyclical Entry.

Weakness: Our industry is *seasonal*. The winter months are especially difficult; J.T. Smith must lay off people just as Christmas approaches.
Complement: Enter an industry—that has peak activity in the winter.
Fit Chart Legend: Opposite Season Entry

Weakness: The "product life" of our services seems to be short and we are constantly required to update our in-house knowledge about environmental concerns, new physiological constraints in the workplace, restrictive economic constraints on costs, and new OSHA and local fire and underwriters codes for hundreds of new materials; all these, and many more, are complicating our operations.
Complement: Find an entry in a "commodity-type" or "assembly-line" operation where we can institutionalize design processes.
Fit Chart Legend: Commodity-Type Entry

Weakness: Sales and backlog seem affected by random factors such as weather, political happenings, fads, and fashions in design.
Complement: Increase our involvement with industries affected by random forces and thus decease the net randomness. This is why insurance companies exist. Do this both by extending our geographic base and by dispersing our services over more industries.
Fit Chart Legend: Effective Dispersive Entries

(continued)

E X H I B I T CASE-4 *(continued)*

Weakness: We are too dependent on three long-time customers—20 percent of our customer base provides 80 percent of our work. Although the jobs are bigger and longer-running, like garbage-raised seagulls who die when the town dump is replaced by an incinerator, we have grown too dependent on our larger clients. Some of our best client-executives are retiring. There is no way we're going to keep those accounts when J.T. retires—and maybe before: We could have serious problems in a year or two. Remember that switching costs for our clients are quite low.

Complement: Make an entry where the average order is smaller and more frequent and can be sold by junior people.

Fit Chart Legend: Reduce Customer Clout or Broaden Client Base.

Entry and Exit Threats

Weakness: We have no major proprietary items. Except for some of our software and a few matching pieces of hardware, J.T. Smith's plans and drawings belong, in general, to the client. While competing defections have been few, we must develop more specialties that defy casual transfer. We must also fear vertical backward competitive entry by our three prime types of customer. ADP, CAD, and other high-tech, computer-aided processes, which can be proprietary, may help us to avoid this threat.

Complement: Raise entry barriers by raising the level of technology and service and continuously lower costs to us and clients.

Fit Chart Legend: Create Entry Barriers

Weakness: We have high barriers to exit. Many of our jobs run over years. Our ongoing task-order contract with Ford Motor Company has low margins and would be hard to end. If we wanted to build up business in the Southeast, for instance, and shut down the Ford contract, which may become only marginally profitable in a year or two, we would have a hell of a time doing it unless we could sell it off to our principal competitor. (The engineering consulting services industry is characterized by noneconomic exit barriers—sons carrying on the family name, the panache of being a *registered* Professional Engineer, and so on.)

Complement: Effect an entry where exit problems are not so pronounced.

Fit Chart Entry: Lower Exit Barriers

Growth Variables

Weakness: We are in a mature industry. This is giving us problems in attracting new employees and keeping the old. While J.T. Smith's profits, according to trade industry figures, have been above average lately, we are investing excess cash flows in things that are foreign to our base business. This has diverted top management's attention away from building our basic business.

Complement: Enter either high-growth (or at least higher-growth) areas: either industries or geographic areas.

Fit Chart Legend: Effect Billings Growth Entry

Weakness: While our profits have been above the norm for our industry, it stems from our long-term relationship with Ford and Chrysler. Further, some areas of professional practice have higher net profit margins than ours, for instance, computer-aided-design (CAD). The higher profit may come because of higher risk. Maintaining our CAD proficiency means substantial continual investment not only in maintaining our equipment but in training. And due to the specialized nature of the personnel, much higher-than-normal downtime *may* result. Both of these factors may affect our profit stream in the future, but the upside potential, long-term, does appear to be great.

Complement: Enter higher-margin, higher-markup, higher-profit areas—either geographic or skill-wise.

Fit Chart Legend: Profit Improvement

Marketing

Weakness: We are in a fragmented industry with low overall entry barriers and very little potential economies of scale. The learning curve has very little slope. Our clients have special industry/area specific needs with only limited transferability to other industries and geographies, and there are few benefits that increases in size alone can wring from our suppliers. And there are some diseconomies of scale; for instance, quick reaction capability (QRC) keeps our clients happy and the net margins up. But, the larger we get, the less quickly we can respond. What we don't know is what the optimum market share should be. (We should not call it the "optimum" market share, but the "minimum" market share to ensure survival and continued growth.)

Complement: Maintain Minimum Market Share. In the J.T. Smith case, it means having at least 400 billable bodies at work that at $110,000 average yields $44 million minimum. We are currently billing about three times that in total. We have about 12 percent of the Detroit market.

Fit Chart Legend: Attain Minimum Market Share or Attain Critical Billing Mass

Weakness: In accordance with classic PIMS (profit impact of marketing strategy) theory, in neither of our markets have we attained sufficient market share to ensure our long-term survival. In other industries, that seems to be at the 35 percent market penetration figure. We don't know whether that statistic applies to us in our industry in the particular geographical areas we serve; we have the additional problems of defining the relevant market and getting usable numbers.

Complement: Attain that market share that will allow us to give our customers maximum service, that will optimize our overhead spreads, and that will not trigger large capital expenditures for either special buildings or equipment or, for that matter, will cause us to move from our present locations.

Fit Chart Legend: Attain Maximum Market Penetration

(continued)

E X H I B I T CASE-4 *(continued)*

Weakness: Although we have some clients that give us work on a noncompetitive basis, we cannot get a premium for it. In other words, we have no "pricing independence" except that our overheads are lower, and thus our net margins higher than the norm for the industry because of a flow of work that we do not have to prepare bids for. Only one or two firms competing in the mechanical engineering field have this advantage. But it may hold true in other fields that we are considering entering due to the nature of the work, the growth rate, the inexperience of the competition, and so on. We should either merge with them and thus compound the advantage or make sure in the event that we make a diversifying entry that either the sector or the target company has a large proportion of such work.

Complement: We should attain a higher percentage of noncompetitive work by differentiating ourselves from the competition, by upping the level of QRC, or by other means yet to be discovered.

Fit Chart Legend: Attain Pricing Independence

Weakness: We are entirely dependent on three classes of clients, generally in the heavy industry area, except for the developers who are mostly in mall development. We need to serve other than such architects, developers, and turnkey contractors. We need more *kinds* of clients. For instance, we have no historical restoration work at all, no alteration work, no modernization work, no plant rebuild work, no bridge rebuild work, no cogeneration work, no playground or recreation work, no golf courses or country clubs, and so on. We need to broaden our client base. (This may imply the opposite of specialization with its supposedly higher net margins.)

Complement: We should try to broaden our client base by entering de novo or by acquiring firms that serve different clients in different markets than we now serve.

Fit Chart Legend: Broaden Client Base

Weakness: The dollar amount of all mechanical engineering consulting work for developers, turnkey contractors, and architectural design firms that we are contracting with is probably not more than $100 million in each area. If we got it all, we would still not be a BIG company. If we could establish ourself in, say, the bridge rehabilitation business, where the market is in the *billions,* we would not suffer this restriction. We could go national or international and have some chance of attaining gross revenues in the $500 million to $1 billion level. In other words, while we're scheming and dreaming, let's dream and scheme BIG.

Complement: We should enter only those markets (either by industry or geography) that are truly big and bigger in absolute size than our present markets.

Fit Chart Legend: Enter Larger Markets

Weakness: Although we have "salespeople" in our offices, they are really only office workers scanning industry reports and building permit applications and feeding the results to the middle managers, who figure the job and then pass the results to the principals of the firm, who then do the real selling. All of our *real* marketing is personal and done on golf courses and in the better clubs in the city. We do not advertise and we have never laid out a nickel for a public relations campaign. Being tied to such a restricted marketing methodology, although it has been successful so far, may not allow us to survive the retirement or death of our principal partners. If we are to expand by the acquisition route, we should look for firms that get either leads or work by some method other than one-on-one personal contact. (Note that some of our competition have hired public relations firms, have developed traveling exhibits, are writing articles for trade journals, and have junior partners serving on hospital boards and in other public-sector activities. And some are beginning to advertise now that the stigma has gone from this one-time nonprofessional approach to marketing.)

Complement: We must develop marketing methodologies that do not depend on personal social contact and explore entries into sectors that market by methods other than those we presently employ.

Fit Chart Legend: Add Marketing Method

Weakness: In addition to the Big Three, there are only a limited number of developers, architectural design firms, and turnkey contractors in our present market area. We have a very limited client universe and have developed great dependence on those clients. We should try, in our diversification program, to enter activities where the *number* of potential clients is larger.

Complement: Enter industries with a large potential client base.

Fit Chart Legend: Increase Clients by Number

Weakness: Our services are too narrow. Confining ourselves to mechanical engineering services only has some advantages in that, as a "boutique," our clients can more easily focus on our abilities; however, in their attempts to lower their costs of contract negotiation and administration, clients are leaning toward broadening their subcontractors' responsibilities. That this has not yet been sensed by our competition should not deter us from becoming an "engineering conglomerate" or at least a major assembler of engineering services, as there are substantial savings to be realized in marketing, administration, and recruitment.

Complement: Develop a full line of engineering services probably beginning with the addition of electrical engineering services, which in much of the country are combined with mechanical engineering services. Next add civil engineering, foundation engineering, sanitary engineering, and so on. (In the alternative, in the event that such full-lining is too expensive to build due to high prices of target acquisitions, we should consider becoming an assembler or a "bundler" of engineering services—an engineering general contractor.)

Fit Chart Legend: Develop Full-Lining Potential

(continued)

Weakness: There are some areas of activity that will not support our overhead structure and that will dilute our image as a top-of-the-line mechanical engineering design outfit. However, other people are making money at it. "Slave-labor" contracting, where design bodies are supplied like Kelly Temporary Services workers on a daily, weekly, or monthly basis, is an example. Although we would not like the name of J.T. Smith to be associated with this kind of activity, we should consider this as a so-called second line. We could start such an outfit de novo or enter by acquisition and not integrate it into our operations, but operate it as a stand-alone. We continuously run into situations where we are asked to supply such services. We can supply these leads to such a service, and from time to time we ourselves need such services but have refrained from using them due to cultural, noneconomic, arbitrary decisions of the firms' founder-owners.

Complement: Create or acquire a "slave-labor" operation and operate it as a stand-alone.

Fit Chart Legend: Make Second-Line Entry

Weakness: The advent of CAD (computer-aided design) might give us some problems. Although we have successfully entered the field, we are encountering some resistance from some of our old-line employees. For many jobs it is much faster and thus bills out at lower cost to the client. This is, in a very real sense, a "functional competitor" to our standard methods of pencil-on-paper design. With new equipment and new software coming out daily we must face up to the fact that some of the smaller firms that compete with us don't have any pencil-on-paper work at all. It could be that they will eventually cut prices and do us in. Rather than sit back and wait for that guillotine, let us target one of the better shops and again, as in the preceding entry on "slave-labor," operate it separately as a stand-alone and feed it some of our leads and even some of our regular work that might better be done by CAD.

Complement: Meet potential CAD competition by entering the CAD market with a full-scale entry exclusively engaged in CAD services.

Fit Chart Legend: Effect CAD Entry

Weakness: Due to our association with the automobile companies in Detroit with their years-long resistance to safety, fuel economy, comfort, repairability, and beauty; with the increasing advent of smog-filled cities, ozone problems, the greenhouse effect, acid rain, and other pollution problems; with long lines at the gas pump at times, and huge trade deficits caused by petroleum imports; and with our work for the oil and petrochemical companies in the Gulf, our image as a benefactor of humanity is deteriorating and we are finding it increasingly difficult to recruit the better engineers. We do know that this was a major reason that the second generation of Smiths refused to join our firm. We should enter—or accelerate or expand our activity if we are presently involved—areas of social responsibility such as retirement housing, environmental engineering, recreation facilities, and so on—doing more that is identified with the public rather than with the private benefit.

Complement: Make an entry that will enhance our image as a community benefactor.

Fit Chart Legend: Improve Social Image

Regulatory Legal Aspects

Weakness: Our industry, with the exception of the licensing requirements for professional engineer status, is relatively unregulated and has no government subsidy and no government-sanctioned monopolistic benefits such as are granted to public utilities. However, one of the most exciting things to come along in many years was the U.S. government's PURPA regulation (Public Utilities Regulation Policies Act) that forced local public utilities to take power generated by industry in so-called cogeneration projects, usually using waste heat from the process industries. We have had only a peripheral acquaintance with this growing field—generally in the design of heating and air conditioning systems.

Complement: Exploit cogeneration potential.

Fit Chart Legend: Exploit Cogeneration Potential

Weakness: Ours is a fractionated industry with thousands of small shops nationwide. Most are poorly managed. Some are heavily niched, either serving special geographic-dependent needs or having a lock on some very large accounts. But this may be changing. Two forces at work are the advent of CAD and broadband communications that will allow us to transmit designs quickly and inexpensively. With a central storage system that can store millions of proprietary design details that can be recalled any place in the world in minutes, the design of a maharaja's palace can be assembled in Detroit and sent to New Delhi by satellite. CAD is going to allow the concentration of the industry.

Complement: Exploit the concentration potential of our industry.

Fit Chart Legend: Exploit Concentration Potential

Weakness: Unfortunately, we have very little tax shelter available to us out of our operations. But when we are involved in a merger, acquisition, or buyout—especially a highly leveraged buyout—there are a number of ways to shelter income that should be explored. For instance, the very generous tax shelter provisions of the ESOP programs should be explored. And in some cases acquired assets can be "stepped up" and amortized at rates higher than their true economic rate. It should also be noted that the tax attributes of the generation of intellectual properties including Research and Development Partnerships (RDLPs) and tax credits for research have not been explored.

Complement: Exploit tax shelter potential.

Fit Chart Legend: Exploit MAB Tax Shelter Potential

(continued)

E X H I B I T CASE-4 *(continued)*

Weakness: We have only one patent, no technology that can be transferred for money, no trademarks or copyrights, and very little proprietary technology. We should, if we can, target an entry where we can pick up some protections on our potential income streams.

Complement: Target industries that are characterized by the generation of intellectual property rights (IPR).

Fit Chart Legend: Exploit IPR Potential

Weakness: Our headquarters are in heavily unionized Detroit. We have not completely escaped the long arm of the union and came near losing the election last year, thus escaping ongoing problems in recruitment, training, and so on. Today, Chrysler and GM are having major problems in their design groups with contract workers side-by-side with UAW members. We have some people on-site in our virtual engineering centers. We don't want them to be unionized.

Complement: Explore only those entries in those geographic areas where there is no strong tendency to unionize professionals.

Fit Chart Legend: Nonunion Entry

Operations

Weakness: Only 20 percent of our sales are from the resale of subcontracted services. Some services such as environmental planning, our largest purchase sector, are in short supply and jobs and billings have been held up because of it. *Percentage-wise* they make more money than we do. If we grow by horizontal acquisition, say double our present sales, we will probably double our purchases. We have the problems as to whether that will give us more clout on our suppliers because we're buying more, or less clout because their services are in more demand than ever. The other factor is that in some cases, where we must bid on a job, the premiums that we must pay because of high subcontractor costs have lost us the job.

Complement: We must lower our price dependence on our subcontractors.

Fit Chart Legend: Develop Supplier Clout

Weakness: We have very little clout with our customers except that we are the archivists for their designs, but they may call for them at will. The fact that we are local and they are, in general, multiplant, multinational, or multiarea operators gives us very little clout—only the social clout of the principal partners is important. With the present movement in the world, and especially in the United States in this deconglomerating age, toward decentralization, we still have trouble in getting a job in Winston-Salem, North Carolina, to be run out of Detroit—the Winston-Salem operators want local talent on the job. But that talent is often expensive because it is inexperienced and does not have the CAD-supported data bank that we believe will be important in the future. Further, we should gain clout by emphasizing our skills in what used to be called "supervision" but that is now, because of liability, called "inspection." Such services not only tie the clients to us by making them more dependent on us, but are also very profitable, and we should be able to cash in on industry's movement toward the reduction of in-house supervisory services and the purchase of "inspection" services.

Complement: Develop more services that will cause our clients to increasingly depend on us.

Fit Chart Legend: Develop Client Clout

Weakness: We seem to be locked into an invariate operating cost structure because draftspersons are hard to find and get increasing rates of pay. Scale economies are hard to develop and the slope of our learning curve is not very steep. However, CAD may change all that. The ratio of one professional to five draftspersons is reduced to one to three where CAD had been introduced, and is heading downward. Today, CAD content can run from 20 percent to 80 percent, averages about 40 percent, but has been growing about 10 percent per year. In five years it will *average* 80 percent. Thus we will unlock the structure and will substantially reduce our costs and get the job out the door faster.

Complement: Develop our CAD skills and resources to reduce operating costs.

Fit Chart Legend: Reduce Direct Costs

Weakness: Reduction of direct costs is important, but it is overhead—usually in the form of fixed costs such as rent—that affects the bottom line and that, in hard times, is the primary reason for engineering business failures. We must learn to operate lean and mean *and* learn how to reduce our indirect costs by expansion of our present activities. One of the best ways of doing this is vertical and horizontal integration and full-lining. That is the way the competition is going not only in Detroit but all over the country.

Complement: Use the merger/acquisition process to reduce overhead.

Fit Chart Legend: Reduce Overhead

Weakness: Downtime (that is, unbilled bodies) is the curse of the consulting business. Although such charges usually go directly to overhead accounts, because they are so important in our business they are listed separately. (The participants are warned not to double-count.) Downtime seems to decrease as the number of billable bodies goes up, so the reductions in staff that we anticipate from CAD may exacerbate the problem. Probably horizontal merger is the best way to go to reduce downtime. Market extension entries, although not as sensitive to downtime reduction as are pure horizontal mergers, still can be effective absorbers of downtime bodies provided that the job is sufficiently priced to pay for the transportation and maintenance. We should also have a carefully contrived program to absorb downtime in our CAD training program.

(continued)

E X H I B I T CASE-4 *(continued)*

Complement: Reduce downtime by emphasizing the Market Intensification Mode.

Fit Chart Legend: Reduce Downtime

Weakness: One of the problems in any program of expansion is the capital it takes to finance it. In our business, the marginal, incremental capital cost to add one more dollar of sales is about 11 percent for working capital and 13 percent for fixed capital. (The working capital number has been constant for many years but the fixed capital number is double the historical number because of the CAD revolution, which requires very expensive machinery and training that has to be capitalized.) Although the numbers are hard to come by, some of our newer personnel claim that our numbers are higher than the competition. Others are not so sure. An educated guess says that the incremental capital cost is a function of size and that the bigger the operation the lower the incremental capital cost due to more rigid billing and collection procedures and more economical purchasing.

Complement: Reduce the marginal, incremental capital costs to add sales dollars.

Fit Chart Legend: Reduce Capital Costs

SUPPLEMENTS*

Strength: We have highly skilled people at the top, both at board level and as managers. Six have taken advanced degrees in "engineering management" with a heavy accent on human relations—rare in this industry. With the exception of the comptroller, all are registered professional engineers. Their experience, without exception, is in engineering-related enterprise. It is a general feeling that our top management is underutilized, that these managers can do considerably more with their talents.

Supplement: We should learn how to exploit our top management skills. But we should ensure that the deal involves something our managers *want* to do and are good at.

Fit Chart Legend: Top Management Fit

---

* A supplement is, according to *Webster's New Collegiate Dictionary*'s first definition, "something that completes or makes an addition [to]." In the WOFC process, this word describes the action that must be taken to exploit basic strengths. Just as a "dietary supplement" adds to the strength and well-being of a person, so, in the merger/acquisition area, any entry move must supplement the basic strengths of the organization. As might be expected, people-strengths are by far the most important, and they are treated first. (Please note that excess resources or underutilized resources fit better into the *complement* side of the fit chart because there is something wrong with an operation that has excess machinery, equipment, property, and so on. However, experience has shown a very strong tendency to classify as a strength or *supplement* any underutilized resource. In the long run, it does not matter which side it is entered in so long as the participants understand the variable for what it is.)

Strength: We have a highly skilled, dependable group of middle managers who double as both line (billable bodies) and staff (administrators). Some have spent their entire working lives here. We must ask and answer this question: How important is it that we enter a field of endeavor where their skills and knowledges can be utilized?

Supplement: Learn to exploit our middle management skills.

Fit Chart Legend: Middle Management Fit

Strength: We have a large staff of draftspersons who are, in general, familiar with our work. Some are in school getting their engineering degrees. We must ask and answer the question: How important is it that we enter a field where their skills can be utilized?

Supplement: Learn to exploit our staff skills.

Fit Chart Legend: Staff Skills Fit

Strength: We have a small staff of white-collar people including librarians, bookkeepers, secretaries, and typists, and some blue-collar janitorial and service people. We must ask and answer the question: How important is it that we enter a field of endeavor where their skill can be utilized?

Supplement: Learn to exploit our white-collar and blue-collar skills.

Fit Chart Legend: Staff Skills Fit

Strength: We have an experienced group of "project development" people who really function as "salespeople," although that word is taboo in the solicitation of professional engineering services. They scan Dodge Reports, building permits, and the like for leads, write them up, and then point the partner principals toward the power that will award the job. The partners do the closing. We must ask the question: How important is it to utilize our present staff of "project development" people in any expansion move?

Supplement: Utilize project development staff.

Fit Chart Legend: Salespeople Fit

Strength: Our customers made us what we are; they pay out rent, educate our children, and put food on our table. To ignore their wants and needs is to ignore our very existence. Friction and a modicum of stress are natural components of an economic relationship that has profit as its goal. Old friends are the best because they have learned to cross-nurture and to communicate. And good communications are the stuff of which profitable relationships are made. One of our greatest strengths is our client lists. It seems logical that we would first find out what services our present customers are buying or want to buy before chasing rainbows looking for the legendary pot of gold at the end.

Supplement: Exploit our present client relationships by entering those areas that synchronize with their needs.

Fit Chart Legend: Customer (Client) Fit

(continued)

E X H I B I T CASE-4 *(concluded)*

Physical Resources Fit

Strength: We have excellent facilities in Detroit (we own our Detroit head-quarters). With the contemplated reduction in staff brought about by CAD, we should have ample room to expand in additional areas of engineering activities at minimal expense. How important is it that we enter a field where we can utilize this resource?

Supplement: Utilize our present physical plant.

Fit Chart Legend: Workplace Fit

Operations Fit

Strength: We are constantly doing work for some of our subcontractors and some of our clients become subcontractors from time to time. We "borrow" people from each other as we "assemble" a job. So we have a kind of de facto vertical integration. The first question to be asked is this: Can we wring more profit out of the marketplace if we actually merged operations—or at least the major ones? And the second question is: Where is the profit vertically in our industry?

Supplement: Will our operations improve if we integrate vertically?

Fit Chart Legend: Vertical Integration Fit

Strength: Our computer installation is becoming more important each day as our electronic data processing system is expanded to interface and interact with our CAD system. We must answer the question: How important is it that we utilize the machinery, equipment, personnel, software, and communications links that we have developed in any entry?

Supplement: Utilize our present EDP complex.

Fit Chart Legend: EDP Fit

Strength: We have a high level of intelligence in the organization and have been exposed to hundreds of different environments all over the world, even though we are based in Detroit. This exposure and experience has to be of some value. We must look for synergistic situations where $2 + 2 = 5$.

Supplement: Exploit synergistic potential.

Fit Chart Legend: Synergy

Many more variables were written up in the laundry list of fit chart variables that appeared in the Fall 1977 issue of *Mergers and Acquisitions*. They include factors such as scale, industrial relations, financing considerations, budgeting, and many different kinds of information flows. However, these concerns have been distributed out to the variables discussed above or have been arbitrarily dismissed as inapplicable or only remotely applicable to this J.T. Smith case study.

E X H I B I T CASE-5

Company Confidential   Author and date T.J. 6/1/98
OPPORTUNITY DESCRIPTION

Description

Coleman Engineers, Ltd., might be for sale at a reasonable price. I spoke
to Steve Coleman and he said that their attempt at an ESOP had failed.
Their backlog is way up and they're billing about $12 billion a month.
Their clean room work is up a good 100 percent and their "slave labor" work
has about doubled. He thinks that kind of outsourcing is a permanent
change in the way the Big Three do business. There are a few problems, however—the unions. Wants a long-term payout. Will stay one year.

Customers

Their clients are the same as ours with a heavier emphasis on services sold
to foreign companies establishing plants in the United States. They tried
to establish in-plant service centers but their computer expertise is much
lower than ours and they had communications problems. He hinted that they
were talking to a West Coast outfit. It's probably true.

Suppliers

He buys the same kind of services that we do and uses the same sources. Does
not want to "diversify"; just wants to retire and play golf. Believes that
buying suppliers is a bad idea. "They don't make any money because their
backlog is so spotty."

Competitors

We're their biggest competitor for ME work. He feels that our growing sophistication in CAD could be a threat to their future. He feels that a
merger of the two firms would be welcomed by everyone at Coleman and won-
dered if "Coleman-Smith Engineering" would be a good trade name. I told
him I thought it sounded great.

What are the principal technical journals?

The same as ours. However, many more HVAC materials and few automation materials.

Why do you believe this is a good fit?

HVAC will always be good. If we can go in-plant with virtual engineering
centers in HVAC we should be able to work anywhere in the world. The clean
room business is high-tech and bound to grow. Again, this movement is
worldwide. It does bind us more tightly to the Detroit economy, but it may
help us move out globally. I just think that we can double our billing base
and increase profits because of less downtime and overhead.

Candidates

N.A.

Sessions comments

A good move if the price is right and the potential for world business is
there.

E X H I B I T CASE-6

Stanley Foster Reed's Systems Approach to Corporate Growth

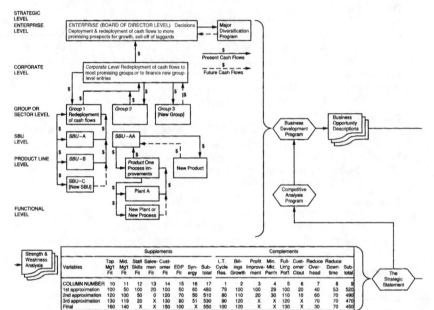

DEPLOYMENT & REDEPLOYMENT of CASH FLOWS

INSTANT DELPHI VARIABLES RATINGS PROCESS

		Supplements								Complements							
Variables	Top Mg't Fit	Mid. Mg't Fit	Staff Skills Fit	Sales men Fit	Cust- omer Fit	EDP Fit	Syn- ergy	Sub- total	L.T. Cycle Res.	Bill- ings Growth	Profit Improve- ment	Min. Mkt. Pen'n	Full- Lin'g Pot'l	Cust- omer Clout	Reduce Over- head	Reduce Down- time	Sub- total
COLUMN NUMBER	10	11	12	13	14	15	16	17	1	2	3	4	5	6	7	8	9
1st approximation	100	50	100	20	100	50	60	480	79	100	100	29	100	20	40	53	520
2nd approximation	120	100	50	0	120	70	50	510	80	110	20	30	110	10	60	70	490
3rd approximation	130	119	20	X	130	80	51	530	90	120	X	X	120	X	70	70	470
Final	160	140	X	X	150	100	X	550	100	120	X	X	130	X	30	70	450

STRATEGIC SKILLS & BEHAVIORS

	ENTERPRISE	CORPORATE	SECTOR	BUSINESS	PRODUCT	FUNCTION
STRATEGIC FOCUS	Discontinuous	Adaptive	Adaptive	Creative	Creative	Adaptive
COGNITIVE PROCESS	Intuitive	Deductive/ Analytical	Analytical	Analytical	Intuitive	Deductive/ Observational
PATTERNS OF DECISION	Autocratic	Small Group	Large Group	Small Group	Individualistic	Individualistic
PROBLEM SOLVING	Creative	Extrapolative	Extrapolative	Extrapolative	Creative Extrapolative	Creative
MANAGEMENT	Entrepreneur	Administrator	Administrator	Cooperator	Innovator/ Adaptor	Innovator
RISK- TAKING	High-Risk, High-Gain	Familiar Risk	Familiar Risk	Minimum Risk	Limit Risk	Limit Risk
TIME FRAME	Forever	Next Ten Years	Next Five Years	Next Year	Tomorrow	Today
PERFORMANCE MEASURES	Stock Market Price	Return on Capital	Return on Capital	Sales Growth Return on Sales	Quality Improvement	Cost- Reduction
REWARD SYSTEM	Stock Appreciation	Stock Appreciation + Cash	Stock/Cash	Cash/ Advancement	Cash/ Advancement	Recognition Spot Cash
ACCOUNTABILITY	Stockholders	Board	Corporate Executives	Senior Chiefs	Business Unit Managers	Engineering
FUNCTIONAL GOALS	Position for Change	Achieve "All- Weather" Performance	Strengthen Competitive Position	Build Solid Customer Base	Keep Up with Market Forces	Lower Costs

NOTE: Use this chart to classify opportunities by strategic levels

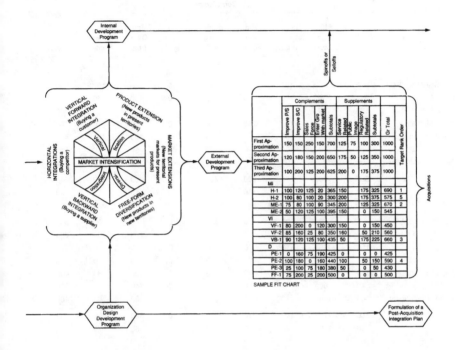

SAMPLE FIT CHART

How to use this Flow Diagram

Most development programs are structurally dependent. Planners should have a general Business Development Plan (BDP) that is broken down by the level of entry—Enterprise, Corporate, Sector or Group, Strategic Business Unit (SBU), product line, or plant or process.

1. From the table above labeled "Strategic Skills & Behaviors," select the level that you wish to plan for.

2. Tie plan into chart labeled "Deployment & Redeployment of Cash Flows."

3. Tie plan into a "Competitive Analysis Program" (see "Competitive Strategy" by Michael Porter for guidance).

4. Perform Strength and Weakness Analysis using instant Delphi technique described in text.

5. Write out the "Strategic Statement"

6. Enter Business Opportunities on sample Wheel of Opportunity.

7. Code each target entry by mode and manner–for instance, "MI" for Market Intensification." and "HI" for Horizontal Integration."

8. Develop "Organization Design & Development Program" to prepare company for future strategic involvements.

9. Shunt opportunities that are to be pursued in-house into the "Internal Development Program."

10. All other opportunities will be pursued under the "External Development Program" by acquisition, joint venture or similar means.

E X H I B I T   CASE-7

Instant Delphi Tally Sheet for Fit Chart

				Complements				
	Cycle Res.	Bill-ings Growth	Profit Improve-ment	Min. Mkt. Share	Full-Lin'g Pot'l	Cust-omer Clout	Reduce Over-head	Reduce Down-time	Sub-total
ROUND 1:									
J.T. Smith, CHRM & CEO	0	0	100	0	300	0	0	100	500
Tom Jones, Pres. & COO	200	200	100	0	0	0	100	100	700
H. Miller, Ex. VP	150	150	100	0	0	0	0	0	400
H. Teets, VP Marketing	100	100	100	200	200	0	0	0	700
W. Clarke, VP Finance	0	100	100	0	0	0	100	100	400
J. Walsh, VP Eng'g	0	50	100	0	0	50	80	70	350
Carole Henry, Comptroller	100	100	100	0	200	90	0	0	590
Total	550	700	700	200	700	140	280	370	3640
Average	79	100	100	100	100	29	40	53	520
ROUND 2:									
Bill Smith, CHRM & CEO	0	70	30	0	300	0	0	100	500
Tom Jones, Pres. & CEO	200	200	0	0	0	0	100	100	600
H. Miller, Ex. VP	150	150	0	0	100	0	0	0	400
H. Teets, VP Marketing	100	100	0	200	300	0	0	0	700
W. Clarke, VP Finance	0	100	110	10	0	0	100	80	400
J. Walsh, VP Eng'g	10	50	0	0	0	0	140	150	350
Carole Henry, Comptroller	100	100	0	0	70	70	80	60	480
Total	560	770	140	210	770	70	420	490	3430
Average	80	110	20	30	110	10	60	70	490
ROUND 3:									
Bill Smith, CHRM & CEO	80	100	X	X	300	X	0	0	480
Tom Jones, Pres. & COO	200	240	X	X	100	X	100	0	640
H. Miller, Ex. VP	150	200	X	X	100	X	100	0	550
H. Teets, VP Marketing	100	100	X	X	300	X	0	0	500
W. Clarke, VP Finance	0	200	X	X	40	X	200	100	540
J. Walsh, VP Eng'g	0	0	X	X	0	X	90	200	290
Carole Henry, Comptroller	100	0	X	X	0	X	0	190	290
Total	630	840	X	X	840	X	490	490	3290
Average	90	120	X	X	120	X	70	70	470
ROUND 4:									
Bill Smith, CHRM & CEO	100	200	X	X	300	X	0	0	600
Tom Jones, Pres. & COO	200	200	X	X	100	X	0	0	500
H. Miller, Ex. VP	150	200	X	X	100	X	10	40	500
H. Teets, VP Marketing	100	40	X	X	300	X	0	0	440
W. Clarke, VP Finance	50	200	X	X	0	X	200	100	550
J. Walsh, VP Eng'g	0	0	X	X	10	X	0	300	310
Carole Henry, Comptroller	100	0	X	X	100	X	0	50	250
Total	700	840	X	X	910	X	210	490	3150
Average	100	120	X	X	130	X	30	70	450

						Supplements			
Top Mg't Fit	Mid. Mg't Fit	Staff Skills Fit	Market- ing Fit	Client Fit	EDP Fit	Syn- ergy	Sub- total	Effic- iency	Rank Order
0	0	100	0	200	0	200	500	1000	—
100	0	0	0	100	100	0	300	1000	—
200	100	100	0	50	50	0	600	1000	—
0	0	110	90	0	0	100	300	1000	—
0	100	180	0	200	0	120	600	1000	—
300	150	100	50	0	50	0	650	1000	—
100	0	110	0	150	50	0	410	1000	—
700	350	700	140	700	350	420	3360	7000	—
100	50	100	20	100	50	60	480	1000	—
0	0	100	X	200	0	200	500	1000	—
300	100	0	X	0	0	0	400	1000	—
200	150	100	X	100	50	0	600	1000	—
0	0	0	X	300	0	0	300	1000	—
0	0	110	X	40	300	150	600	1000	—
300	200	0	X	100	50	0	650	1000	—
40	250	40	X	100	90	0	520	1000	—
840	700	350	X	840	490	350	3570	7000	
120	100	50	X	120	70	50	510	1000	—
100	0	0	X	200	20	200	520	1000	—
300	60	0	X	0	0	0	360	1000	—
200	200	40	X	10	0	0	450	1000	—
0	200	0	X	300	0	0	500	1000	—
10	0	0	X	0	300	150	460	1000	—
200	10	100	X	300	100	0	710	1000	—
100	360	0	X	100	140	10	710	1000	—
910	830	140	X	910	560	360	3710	7000	—
130	119	20	X	130	80	51	530	1000	—
300	30	X	X	70	0	X	400	1000	—
300	200	X	X	0	0	X	500	1000	—
200	210	X	X	0	90	X	500	1000	—
0	200	X	X	300	60	X	560	1000	—
20	0	X	X	130	300	X	450	1000	—
200	40	X	X	300	150	X	690	1000	—
100	300	X	X	250	100	X	750	1000	—
1120	980	X	X	1050	700	X	3850	7000	—
160	140	X	X	150	100	X	550	1000	—

E X H I B I T CASE-8

Fit Chart: J.T. Smith Consultants

	Complements								
[Growth Rates in Brackets]	Cycle Res.	Bill- ings Growth	Profit Improve- ment	Min. Mkt. Share	Full- Lin'g Pot'l	Cust- omer Clout	Reduce Over- head	Reduce Down- time	Sub- total
COLUMN NUMBER	1	2	4	5	6	7	8	9	
1st approximation	79	100	100	29	100	20	40	53	520
2nd approximation	80	110	20	30	110	10	60	70	490
3rd approximation	90	120	X	X	120	X	70	70	470
Final (4th approximation)	100	120	X	X	130	X	30	70	450
HORIZONTAL INTEGRATION									
Coleman, Detroit	60	120	X	X	40	X	30	70	320
MARKET EXTENSION									
West Coast [8%]	0	40	X	X	30	X	10	30	110
Southeast [8%]	80	80	X	X	30	X	10	30	230
South Africa	80	120	X	X	0	X	0	0	200
China [20%]	100	120	X	X	0	X	0	0	220
SUBTOTAL MARKET INTENSIFICATION MODE									
VERTICAL BACKWARD INTEGRATION									
Environmental planning [15%]	40	40	X	X	0	X	10	10	100
Urban planning [10%]	40	40	X	X	0	X	10	10	100
Geophysical consulting [0%]	0	0	X	X	0	X	0	0	0
Surveying [0%]	0	0	X	X	30	X	20	0	50
Community planning [5%]	40	40	X	X	0	X	10	20	110
Architectural design [10%]	0	0	X	X	130	X	30	70	230
VERTICAL FORWARD INTEGRATION									
Auto and Auto Parts Mfg. [5%]	0	0	X	X	0	X	0	0	0
Architectural design svcs [8%]	0	0	X	X	130	X	30	70	230
Turnkey contractors [5%]	0	0	X	X	0	X	0	0	0
Developers [0%]	0	0	X	X	0	X	0	0	0
SUBTOTAL VERTICAL INTEGRATION MODE									
PRODUCT OR SERVICE EXTENSION									
Electrical engineering [5%]	0	0	X	X	130	X	30	70	230
Docks, harbors, and airports [5%]	60	0	X	X	60	X	20	60	200
Recreation/leisure [10%]	40	40	X	X	0	X	20	40	140
Industrial plant redesign [15%]	40	30	X	X	60	X	30	70	230
Power engineering [20%]	40	60	X	X	130	X	10	50	350
Bridge/Reconstruction [30%]	100	120	X	X	60	X	20	40	300
FREE-FORM EXTENSION									
Power engineering—China	50	120	X	X	60	X	0	0	230
Road/bridge engineering—South Africa	100	120	X	X	60	X	0	0	280
SUBTOTAL DIVERSIFICATION MODE									

				Supplements					
Top Mg't Fit	Mid. Mg't Fit	Staff Skills Fit	Market- ing Fit	Client Fit	EDP Fit	Syn- ergy	Sub- total	Effic- iency	Rank Order
10	11	12	13	14	15	16	17	18	19
100	50	100	20	100	50	60	480	1000	—
120	100	50	0	120	70	50	510	1000	—
130	119	20	X	130	80	51	530	1000	—
160	140	X	X	150	100	X	550	1000	—
160	140	X	X	150	100	X	550	870	1
160	70	X	X	0	50	X	280	390	
100	70	X	X	0	50	X	220	450	
40	0	X	X	0	50	X	90	290	
40	0	X	X	0	50	X	90	310	
								Average: 480	
40	35	X	X	50	50	X	175	275	
40	35	X	X	50	50	X	175	275	
0	0	X	X	0	50	X	50	50	
80	35	X	X	100	50	X	265	315	
40	35	X	X	50	50	X	175	285	
120	70	X	X	100	100	X	390	620	3
0	0	X	X	0	0	X	0	0	
120	35	X	X	100	100	X	355	585	4
100	70	X	X	50	100	X	320	320	
100	35	X	X	50	100	X	285	285	
								Average: 334	
100	70	X	X	150	100	X	420	650	2
150	70	X	X	25	100	X	345	545	
100	70	X	X	50	100	X	320	460	
50	105	X	X	50	100	X	305	535	
50	70	X	X	0	100	X	220	570	5
50	70	X	X	0	100	X	220	520	
80	70	X	X	0	100	X	250	530	
80	70	X	X	0	50	X	200	480	

E X H I B I T CASE-9

A Wheel of Opportunity for J. T. Smith Consultants

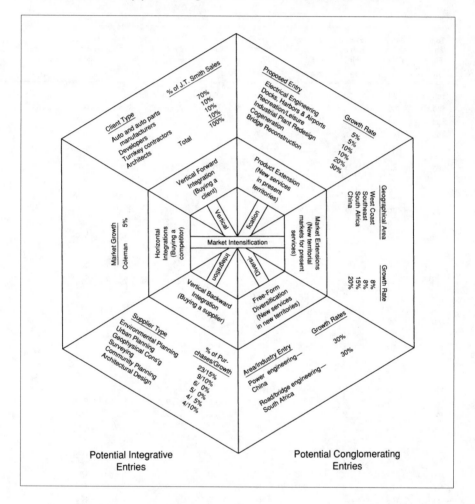

Potential Integrative
Entries

Potential Conglomerating
Entries

TABLE OF CASES

In describing legal cases in this book, we have used short form legal citations—and sometimes (for example in Chapter 11) only the names of the companies involved. The following Table of Cases provides full legal citations for the reader's reference. An asterisk means that we provide more information in the next section, "Landmark Cases."

Accardi*	*Accardi v. Control Data*, 658 F. Supp. 881 (S.D.N.Y. 1987), *rev'd and rem'd,* 836 Fed. 2d 126 (2d Cir. 1987)
Adcock*	*Adcock v. Firestone Tire & Rubber Co.*, 616 F. Supp. 409 (D.C. Tenn. 1985), *aff'd in part and vacated in part,* 822 F.2d 623 (6th Cir. 1987)
Allied Stores*	*Federated Dept. Stores, Inc.*, 1991 WL 79143 (Bankr. S.D. Ohio 1991)
Basic*	*Levinson v. Basic, Inc.*, 786 F.2d 741 (6th Cir. 1986), *vacated* 485 U.S. 224
Beazer*	*Koppers Co., Inc. v. American Express Co.*, 689 F. Supp. 1371 (W. D. Pa. 1988)
Bendix*	*Martin Marietta Corp. v. Bendix Corp.*, 549 F.Supp. 623 (D. Md. 1982)
Bestfoods*	*United States v. Bestfoods, et al.,* No. 97-454, 1998 WL 292076 (1998)
Blau*	*Blau v. Del Monte Corp.*, 748 F.2d 1348 (9th Cir. 1984)
Blessitt*	*Blessitt v. Retirement Plan for Employees of Dixie Engin. Co.*, 817 F. 2d 1528 (11th Cir. 1987) *rev'd in part and rem'd* 836 F 2d 1571 *vacated* (11th Cir. 1988) 848 F.2d 1164 (11th Cir. 1988)

Business Roundtable	*The Business Roundtable v. S.E.C.*, 905 F.2d (D.C. Cir. 1990) 406
Caremark	*In re Caremark International Inc. Derivative Litigation,* 698 A-2D 959 (1996)
Carter Hawley	Carter Hawley Hales Stores, Inc., No. LA 91-64140-JD (Bankr. C.D. Cal)
Chiarella	*Chiarella v. U.S.,* 588 F.2d 1358 (2nd Cir. 1978) *cert granted* 445 U.S. 222, 100 S. Ct. 1108, 63 L. Ed. 2d 348 (1980), (U.S.N.Y. 1980) (No. 78-1202)
Credit Managers*	*Credit Managers Ass'n of Southern Cal. v. Federal Co.,* 629 F. Supp. 175 (C.D. Cal. 1985)
Crowthers	*Crowthers McCall Pattern Inc. v. Lewis et al.,* 129 B.R. 992, (S.D.N.Y. 1991)
Crystal Oil	*In re Crystal Oil Co.,* 854 F.2d 79 (5th Cir. 1988)
CTS*	*CTS Corp. v. Dynamics Corp. of America,* 481 U.S. 69, 107 S. Ct. 1637, 95 L. Ed.2d 67 (1987)
Dunn	*Dunn v. Hovic,* 1 F.3d 1362 (3rd. Cir. [Virgin Islands] 1993)
Edelman*	*Edelman v. Fruehauf Corp.,* 798 F.2d 882 (6th Cir. 1986)
Edgar*	*Edgar v. MITE Corp.,* 457 U.S. 624, 102 S. Ct. 2629, 73 L. Ed. 2d 269 (1982)
Fall River Dyeing*	*Fall River Dyeing and Finishing Corp. v. NLRB,* 482 U.S. 27, 107 S. Ct. 2225, 96 L. Ed. 2d 22 (1987)
Federated	*Federated Dept. Stores, Inc.,* 132 B. R. 572 (Bankr. S.D. Ohio 1991)
Gaylord Container	*Gaylord Container Corp.,* 130 Bankr 304 (Bankr. E.D. Mo (1991)
General Utilities*	*General Utilities & Operating Co. v. Helvering,* 296 U.S. 200 (1936)
Gleneagles*	*United States v. Gleneagles Inv. Co.,* 565 F. Supp. 556 (M.D. Pa. 1983), 571 F. Supp. 935 (1983), 584 F. Supp. 671 (1984), *aff'd sub nom. United States v. Tabor Court Realty Corp.,* 803 F.2d 1288 (3d Cir. 1986)
Gollust*	*Gollust v. Mendell,* 498 U.S. 1023, 112 L. Ed. 2d 662, 111 S. Ct. 669 (1991)
Hanson Trust*	*Hanson Trust PLC v. SCM Corp.,* 774 F. 2d 47 (2d Cir. 1985)
Healthco*	*In re Healthco International, Inc., Securities Litigation* 208 B.R. 288, 300 (Bankr. D. Mass, 1997).
Holmes	*Holmes v. Securities Investor Protection Corp.,* 112 S. Ct. 1311, 117 L. Ed. 2d 532 (U.S. Cal. 1992)

Irving Trust* | *K.M.C. Co., Inc. v. Irving Trust Co.*, 757 F. 2d 752 (6th Cir. 1985)

Kaiser Steel | *Kaiser Steel Resources, Inc. v. Pearl Brewing Co., In Re Kaiser Steel Corp.*, 952 F.2d 1230 (10th Cir. 1991), *cert. den'd*, 112 S. Ct. 3015, 120 L. Ed 2d 887 (U.S. Colo. 1992)

Kupetz* | *Kupetz v. Wolf*, 845 F.2d 842 (9th Cir. 1988)

Lampf | *Lampf, Pleva, Lipkind, Prupis & Petigrow v. Gilbertson*, 111 S. Ct. 2773, 115 L. Ed. 2d 321 (U.S. Or. 1991)

Litton Industries* | *Litton Industries, Inc. v. Lehman Brothers Kuhn Loeb Inc.*, 967 F.2d 742 (2nd. Cir. 1992)

LTV | *Chateaugay Corp.*, 115 B.R. 760 (Bankr. S.D.N.Y. 1990)

Maxicare | *In re Family Health Services, Inc.*, 104 BR 279. *See In re Family Health Services, Inc.* (Bankr. C. D. Cal. 1989)

Mobile Communications | *In re Mobile Communications Corp. of America, Inc. Consol. Litigation*, 1992 WI 53379, 608 A. 2d 729 (Del. Supr. 1992)

Moran* | *Moran v. Household International Inc.*, 500 A 2d 1346 (Del. 1985)

Morris Trust | *Commissioner v. Morris Trust*, 367 F2d 794 (4th Cir. 1966).

National Starch* | *Indopco, Inc. v. C.I.R.*, 112 S. Ct. 1039 (1992)

Newark Morning Ledger* | *Newark Morning Ledger Co. v. United States*, 113 S. Ct. 1670 (1993)

Northeast Bank* | *Northeast Bancorp. Inc. v. Board of Governors* 472 U.S. 159 (1985)

O'Day | *In re O'Day Corp.*, 126 B.R. 370 (Bankr. D. Mass. 1991)

Olin* | *Olin Corporation v. Federal Trade Commission*, 986 F.2d. 1295 (9th Cir. 1993)

Paramount* | *QVC Network Inc. v. Paramount Inc., Viacom Inc., et al.*, 637 A-2d 34 (Del. 1994) aff'ing 635 2d 1245 (Del. Ch. 1993)

Pennzoil* | *Texaco Inc. v. Pennzoil Co.*, 729 S. W. 2d 768 (Tex. App. 1987), cert. dism'd, 485 U.S. 994, 108 S. Ct. 1305, 99 L. Ed. 2d 686 (1988)

Philadelphia National Bank* | *United States vs. Philadelphia National Bank et al.*, Bank 374 U.S. 321, 83 S. Ct. 1715, 10 L. Ed. 2d 915 (1963).

Revlon* | *Revlon, Inc. v. MacAndrews & Forbes Holdings, Inc.*, Del. Supr., 506 A.2d 173 (1986)

Riviera Inc. | *Riviera Club, Inc.*, 280 F. Supp. 741 (W.D. Mo 1967)

Southland Corp. | Southland Corp., 124 B.R. 211 (Bankr. N.D. Tex. 1991)

Square D | *Square D Co. v. Schneider S.A. SQD.*, 760 F. Supp. 362 (S.D.N.Y. 1991)

Strong	*Strong v. Rapid*, 213 U.S. 419, 29 S. Ct. 521, 53 L. Ed. 853 (U.S. Phil. Islands 1909)
Texas Gulf Sulphur*	*SEC vs. Texas Gulf Sulphur*, 401 F. 2d 833 (2d Cir. 1968)
Tilley*	*B. E. Tilley v. Mead Corp.*, 927 F.2d 756 (4th Cir. 1991)
Time*	*Paramount Communications Inc. v. Time Inc.*, 517 A. 2d 1140 (Del. 1990)
Treadway*	*Treadway Companies, Inc. v. Care Corp.*, 638 F.2d 357 (2d Cir. 1980)
TWA	*Trans World Airlines*, 22 Bankr. Ct. Dec 1236 (Bankr. D. Del. 1992)
Unocal*	*Unocal Corp. v. Mesa Petroleum Co.*, 493 A. 2d 946 (Del. 1985)
USX	*Pryor v. USX*, 806 F. Supp. 460 (S.D.N.Y. 1992)
Van Gorkom*	*Smith v. Van Gorkom*, Del. Supr., 488 A.2d 858 (1985)
Virginia Bankshares*	*Virginia Bankshares, Inc. v. Sandberg*, 501 U.S. 1083 (1991)
Warde	*S.E.C. v. Warde*, 97-6190 (2d Cir. 1998).

LANDMARK CASES

ACCARDI (1987)

The plaintiffs were former employees of International Business Machines (IBM) who worked for the BTSI division. In accord with the Employee Retirement Income Security Act of 1974 (ERISA), they received certain benefits. When IBM sold BTSI to Control Data Corporation (CDC), they entered into a "benefits agreement" under which CDC agreed to continue making benefits payments to the former employees of the division. On June 30, 1985, CDC sold BTSI to Automatic Data Processing (ADP) and the benefits payments stopped. The former BTSI employees requested continuation of their benefits.

The question before the court was whether the plaintiffs were entitled to continued overall benefits under the IBM/CDC benefits agreement, and whether the denial of the plaintiff's request for continued benefits was arbitrary and capricious. The U.S. Court of Appeals of the Second Circuit affirmed a decision by the U.S. District Court in the Southern District of New York stating that the plaintiffs were no longer eligible employees according to the terms of the benefits agreement, and that therefore denial of continued benefits was not arbitrary and capricious.

ADCOCK (1987)

The plaintiffs were nonunion salaried employees of Bridgestone Tire and Rubber Co. On January 1, 1983, Firestone Tire & Rubber Co. sold its

Lavergne plant to Bridgestone for $55 million. The 75-page sales agreement included an "employee termination pay plan" stating that Firestone would not terminate the employment of any employee prior to the sale. It also stated that if Bridgestone reduced its workforce, any employee who lost his or her job would receive termination pay. At the time of the suit, Bridgestone had not reduced its workforce, so the plaintiffs remained employed. Nonetheless, they sought to receive termination pay.

The question before the court was whether the termination pay plan was arbitrary and capricious. The Court of Appeals in the Sixth Circuit, affirming the District Court of Tennessee's interpretation of the federal common law, stated that Bridgestone's application of the termination pay plan was consistent with a fair reading of the plan, and that Firestone's interpretation and application of the termination pay plan was not arbitrary and capricious.

ALLIED STORES (1991)

On September 12, 1986, a subsidiary of Campeau Corporation commenced a hostile takeover of Allied Stores. Allied turned to DeBartolo Corporation as a "white knight," promising to pay DeBartolo a breakup fee if its rescue effort failed, which it did. After the merger with Campeau was completed, Allied paid DeBartolo approximately $116.3 million in breakup fees. Allied deducted those fees on its federal income tax return.

Less than two years later, a subsidiary of Campeau attempted a hostile takeover of Federated Department Stores, then the largest store chain in the United States. On February 29, 1988, R. H. Macy & Co. stepped in and offered to purchase Federated. Macy's proposal included a request to be paid a breakup fee in the event the attempted merger failed, which it did. Federated paid Macy a breakup fee of $60 million.

The question before the court was whether the breakup fees paid were deductible as ordinary and necessary business expenses. The Bankruptcy Court for the District of Ohio said yes, citing 26 U.S.C. Sections 162(a) and 165(a). Section 162(a) permits deduction for all ordinary and necessary expenses paid in carrying on any trade or business. Section 165(a) permits the current deduction of any loss sustained during the taxable year and not compensated for by insurance.

BASIC (1986)

The plaintiff was a group of Basic, Inc., shareholders who sold stock in Basic, Inc., prior to formal announcement of a merger that caused Basic stock to rise. Basic spokespersons had denied that the merger was under consideration. The stockholders brought an action under Rule 10b-5 alleging material misrepresentation.

The question before the U.S. Supreme Court was whether the public statements denying merger talks constituted material misrepresentation. The court ruled that it is not proper to deny that a company is engaged in merger talks when, in fact, it is so engaged. In handing down its ruling, the U.S. Supreme Court rejected the "bright line" test for materiality offered in an earlier Sixth Circuit Appeals Court decision. Materiality must be decided on a case-by-case basis, opined the court. In this instance, negotiations were material—even though the talks had not yet resulted in any agreement on the price and structure of the transaction. The court said that the appropriate response to an inquiry about undisclosed merger talks is either "no comment" or disclosure that the talks are taking place.

BEAZER (1988)

Koppers Co., Inc., brought an action against American Express, Shearson Lehman Brothers, and others seeking to enjoin the parties' hostile tender offer based upon Koppers's allegations that the tender offer violated federal securities laws (more specifically, certain disclosure requirements). American Express and the other defendants requested a preliminary injunction ordering Koppers to correct allegedly misleading statements regarding the tender offer.

The U.S. District Court in the Western District of Pennsylvania stated that it will not hesitate to enjoin a tender offer until compliance with securities laws can be determined. The Williams Act does not require that a tender offer disclose all information that it possesses about itself or the target company, but only those material objective factual matters that a reasonable stockholder would consider important in deciding whether to tender his, her, or its shares.

BENDIX (1982)

In August 1982 the Bendix Corp. announced a tender offer for approximately 45 percent of Martin Marietta Corp.'s common stock. On August 30, 1982, as a direct response to Bendix's tender offer, Martin Marietta announced its tender offer for approximately 51 percent of Bendix's common stock. In September 1982 United Technologies Corp. announced its own tender offer for approximately 51 percent of Bendix's common stock. All three tender offers were considered hostile, and all three corporations brought actions in federal court to enjoin each others' tender offers. In this case, Martin Marietta sought an injunction against the Bendix tender offer on the grounds that Bendix made misrepresentations and omissions in its disclosures.

The question before the court was whether Bendix's disclosures violated the Williams Act. The U.S. District Court of Maryland said they did not, exonerating Bendix.

BESTFOODS (1998)

This U.S. Supreme Court case dealt with responsibility and payment for cleaning up industrial waste generated by a chemical plant. The U.S. government brought an environmental enforcement action against both the subsidiary company, which operated the polluting facility, and its parent company, which actively participated in, and exercised control over, the operations of its subsidiary.

The question before the court was whether a parent corporation is responsible under federal Superfund laws for the pollution caused by a subsidiary. In a unanimous ruling, the court said that to be held liable, a parent must have been directly involved in the relevant operations or compliance activity of the subsidiary. The court found Bestfoods not liable in this case.

BLAU (1984)

In 1966 Del Monte Corp. purchased Granny Good, which became a wholly owned subsidiary of Del Monte. The employees of Granny Good became eligible for coverage under various Del Monte pension and benefit plans. In December 1980 Del Monte sold Granny Good to a group of investors. The new owners kept all but four employees. The four severed employees sued Del Monte for their severance benefits.

The question before the court was whether the denial of the severance benefits violated ERISA and whether the denial was arbitrary and capricious. The Ninth Circuit Court of Appeals held that the actions by Del Monte were arbitrary and capricious, and that ERISA preempted state common law theories of breach of contract.

BLESSITT (1988)

The plaintiffs were employees of Dixie Engine Co. when it established an ERISA plan in 1972. Dixie Engine Co. was sold in 1982 and the ERISA plan was terminated. Employees brought action against their employer for violation of ERISA, claiming that upon termination of a defined benefits plan they were entitled to receive the full, unreduced pension benefits they would have received had they continued to work until normal retirement age.

The question before the court was whether ERISA requires the defined benefits plan to pay an employee the full, unreduced benefits the employee would have received had he or she continued to work until normal retirement age. The Court of Appeals in the Eleventh Circuit held that when a plan terminates, ERISA does not require that employees receive full benefits, only the benefits provided for under the plan (that is, the benefits calculated on the basis of their actual years of service as of the termination date).

CREDIT MANAGERS (1985)

In 1980 Cresent Food Co., a cheese importation and distribution entity wholly owned by Federal Company, entered into a management-led leveraged buyout. The stock purchase price was over $1.4 million. Cresent received an additional loan from new management of $189,000, as well as approximately $10 million from General Electric Credit Corp. Cresent's debt service increased significantly because of the buyout. Finding itself with insufficient cash to continue operations, Cresent eventually shut down and executed an assignment of its assets for the benefit of creditors. The plaintiff brought action against Federal, alleging that the buyout was a fraudulent conveyance.

The question before the court was whether or not the transaction was a fraudulent conveyance. The U.S. District Court in California held that the law does not require that companies be sufficiently well capitalized to withstand any and all setbacks to their business; it requires only that the companies not be left with unreasonably small capital at the time of conveyance.

CTS (1987)

Dynamics Corp. of America announced a tender offer for CTS Corp., an Indiana corporation. Six days before the tender offer, the state of Indiana revised its business corporation law to include a provision affecting control via acquisition. The revised law allows companies in the state of Indiana to condition acquisition of control of the corporation on the approval of the majority of the preexisting disinterested shareholders. Dynamics brought suit to enjoin the forcement of this statute, citing *Edgar v. MITE.*

The question before the court was whether the Indiana Act was preempted by the federal securities laws as amended by the Williams Act or by the commerce clause of the U.S. Constitution. The Supreme Court stated that the Indiana Act would be preempted by federal securities laws only if it frustrated the purposes of those laws. In overturning *MITE,* the *CTS* case enabled states to reenact the antitakeover laws that *MITE* had struck down.

EDELMAN (1986)

In February 1986 the Edelman Group began acquiring Fruehauf stock on the open market. Edelman attempted a friendly acquisition, which Fruehauf's board of directors rejected. Subsequently, members of Fruehauf's management negotiated a two-tier leveraged buyout along with Merrill Lynch. A special committee of Fruehauf's outside directors approved the management-led buyout. Edelman sought a preliminary injunction restraining Fruehauf from completing the buyout.

The question before the court was whether the outside directors breached its fiduciary duty to the company. The Sixth Circuit Appeals Court held that Fruehauf's board of directors, in using corporate funds to finance the buyer, did not act in good faith to negotiate the best deal for shareholders and thus breached their fiduciary duty to the shareholders. Moreover, the court stated that once it becomes apparent that a takeover target will be acquired by new owners, it becomes the duty of the directors to see that the shareholders obtain the best possible price.

EDGAR (1982)

In January 1979 Mite Corp. initiated a tender offer for all the outstanding shares of Chicago Rivet & Machine Co., an Illinois company. The state of Illinois passed an act that required that all tender offers for shares of any company organized under the laws of Illinois or having at least 10 percent of its stated capital within the state must be registered with the Secretary of State. Mite did not comply with the state requirement and filed for a preliminary injunction and declaratory relief.

The question before the court was whether the Illinois Act was preempted by the Williams Act and violated the commerce clause of the U.S. Constitution. The Supreme Court held that the Illinois Act was in conflict with the Williams Act because it would unreasonably delay a takeover offer. The Illinois Act, said the court, was void to the extent that it conflicts with the accomplishment and execution of the full purposes and objectives of Congress in passing the Williams Act and in ratifying the U.S. Constitution. This case was rendered moot by the finding of the Court in *CTS*.

FALL RIVER DYEING (1987)

In 1952 Sterlingwale began operating a textile dyeing plant; the plant continued to run for the next 30 years. For nearly its entire existence, the production and maintenance personnel of Sterlingwale were members of a union. Sterlingwale, along with the entire textile dyeing industry, began to suffer adverse economic conditions in late 1979. In February 1982 Sterlingwale laid off its employees and made an assignment for the benefit of its creditors.

In the fall of 1982 a former officer of Sterlingwale, together with the president of a creditor, formed an entity that purchased the assets of Sterlingwale from the auctioneer. Over time, the entity employed many former employees of Sterlingwale. The union requested that the entity recognize it as the bargaining agent for the employees, and the entity refused. The union then filed unfair labor practice charges with the National Labor Relations Board.

The question before the court was whether a successor employer is obligated to bargain with a union representing its predecessor's employees. The U.S. Supreme Court held that the successor employer's obligation to bargain with the union representing its predecessor's employees is contingent not only upon certification of the union but also on whether a majority of its employees were employed by its predecessor.

GENERAL UTILITIES (1936)

General Utilities purchased 20,000 shares of Island Edison Co. The remainder of the stock was owned by Gillett & Co. Southern Cities Utilities Co. agreed to purchase all of the shares of Utilities. Utilities, however, did not desire a taxable transaction. It therefore declared a dividend that was to be paid by delivering shares of Island Edison Co. to its shareholders, who then in turn agreed to sell the shares to Southern Cities Utilities Co. The IRS declared a taxable gain upon the distribution of the stock in payment of the General Utilities dividend.

The question before the court was whether a corporation distributing among its stockholders shares of another corporation as a dividend derived a taxable gain. The U.S. Supreme Court held that a corporation distributing among its stockholders shares of another corporation as a dividend derived no taxable gain since distribution was not a sale and assets were not used to discharge indebtedness.

[As noted in the main text of this book, the rule was later codified to include both liquidating and nonliquidating distributions of appreciated property by a corporation to its shareholders, as well as liquidating sales (certain sales of appreciated property made during the course of a complete liquidation). Over time, application of the rule was narrowed, and finally the rule was repealed with the passage of the Tax Reform Act of 1986, with some temporary exceptions for small businesses.]

GLENEAGLES (1986)

This lawsuit had been the subject of two earlier opinions by the U.S. District Court for M.D. Pennsylvania. In the first opinion, the court concluded that certain mortgages granted by Institutional Investors Trust were fraudulent conveyances within the meaning of 354, 355, 356, and 357 of the Pennsylvania Uniform Fraudulent Conveyance Act, 39 Pa. Stat. 351, *et seq* (*United States v. Gleneagles Inv. Co., Inc.,* hereinafter *Gleneagles I*). In the second opinion, the court concluded that Gleneagles' subsidiary, Pagnotti Enterprises, which purchased the IIT mortgages and caused the assignment thereof to its subsidiary, McClelland Realty, was not a purchaser of the IIT mortgages for fair consideration without knowledge that they were fraudulent conveyances (*United States v. Gleneagles Inv. Co., Inc.,* hereinafter *Gleneagles II*). The court also concluded in *Gleneagles II* that the Lackawanna County tax sales of the lands of Raymond Colliery in 1976 and 1980 and the consequent tax deed were void and ineffective to transfer title to the purchasers at those tax sales.

The United States had sought the third litigation to set aside as fraudulent conveyances mortgages held by IIT on the lands of Raymond Colliery and to foreclose on tax liens against Raymond Colliery and its parent, Great American Coal Company, free and clear of the IIT mortgages. Those mortgages were delivered by Raymond Colliery on November 26, 1973, to IIT and assigned by IIT to defendant McClelland Realty.

The court held that (1) payment of $6.1 million would not place creditors of the mortgagor in the same or similar position that they held prior to the fraudulent transaction; (2) settlement moneys paid to the mortgagor's creditors by former shareholders of the mortgagor would not be deducted from recovery to which creditors were entitled from the mortgage assignee; and (3) assigned mortgages were not entitled to protection under the Fraudulent Conveyances Act.

GOLLUST (1991)

Mendell filed a 16b (insider trading) complaint against a collection of limited partnerships, general partnerships, individual partners, and corporations alleging that these entities, acting as one, were liable for 16b violations with regard to trading activities of Viacom stock. Six months after the complaint was filed, Viacom was acquired by another company, and Mendell exchanged his Viacom stock for the new stock.

The question before the court was whether a 16b action can be pursued by any party other than an issuer or holder of a security. The U.S. Supreme Court held that it was not necessary for a plaintiff to continue to hold stock of the issuer in order to maintain a 16b action where the plaintiff has a financial stake in the parent corporation of the issuer. The court stated that the plaintiff who seeks to recover insider profits must own a security of the issuer whose stock is traded by the 16b defendant.

HANSON TRUST (1985)

Hanson Trust PLC tendered a $60 per share offer for any and all shares of SCM Corp., which was followed by a counteroffer by the SCM board and their white knight, Merrill Lynch Capital Markets. Hanson then increased its offer to $72 each, contingent upon SCM's agreement not to enter into a lockup agreement. The SCM Merrill counteroffer was revised to $74 along with a lockup option for an SCM "crown jewel." Hanson terminated its offer as a direct result of the lockup option.

The question before the court was whether the members of SCM's board of directors could be protected under the business judgment rule when they approved of the lockup option. The business judgment rule is a judicial doctrine under which reasonable decisions by directors are insulated from second-guessing by the courts. The Second Circuit Court of Appeals denied protection under the business judgment rule on the grounds that SCM directors' "paucity of information" and the swiftness of their decision making strongly suggested a breach of the duty of care.

HEALTHCO (1997)

In June 1990, a minority shareholder of Healthco, alleging that the price of Healthco's stock was undervalued, began a proxy contest to remove the incumbent board. The proxy contest was resolved after Hicks Muse, a major leveraged buyout firm, entered the picture as a white knight and helped the minority shareholders replace the incumbent directors. In March 1991, the new Healthco board, which included directors who were Healthco stockholders, agreed to sell the company to a subsidiary of Hicks Muse. The new company experienced operating problems. In June 1993, Healthco filed for relief under Chapter 11 of the U.S. Bankruptcy Code. Then, in September of that year, the case was converted to Chapter 7 and the company was liquidated, causing severe losses to the company's creditors.

In June 1995, the bankruptcy trustee for the creditors began legal action in U.S. Bankruptcy Court against virtually all the participants in the company—65 defendants in all, including the company's directors, who were accused of violating their duty of loyalty. The plaintiffs alleged that the directors' ownership of stock in Healthco rendered them "interested" in its sale. The directors, citing legal precedent and documenting their decisionmaking process, argued that they had fulfilled their duties of loyalty and care. They asked the Bankruptcy Court for a summary judgment dismissal, but the court refused, holding that the directors were indeed "interested" parties by law.

Two years later, the case came to trial again in U.S. District Court in Worcester, Massachusetts, where the court declined to adopt the Bankruptcy Court's ruling, and ordered a jury trial. The directors repeated their defense, this time bringing in an expert witness on behalf of the directors—Dr. Robert Stobaugh, an Emeritus Professor at the Harvard Business School and a member of the board of directors of the National Association of Corporate Directors. Dr. Stobaugh testified that Healthco directors had met generally accepted practice with respect to both their duty of loyalty and their duty of care. After a seven-week trial, the jury returned a verdict in favor of all the defendants on all of the claims.

IRVING TRUST (1985)

In 1979 KMC entered into a financing agreement with Irving Trust Co., whereby Irving Trust would provide KMC with a line of credit to a maximum amount of $3.0 million in exchange for Irving Trust's holding a security interest in KMC's assets. The line of credit was increased a year later to $3.5 million. In March 1982, without notice to KMC, Irving Trust refused to advance $800,000, which would have placed the loan value at just under $3.5 million. KMC suffered a collapse and sued Irving for breach of the financing agreement.

The question before the court was whether Irving had breached its contract with KMC. The Sixth Circuit Court of Appeals affirmed the decision and stated that there is "implied in every contract an obligation of good faith." The court further stated that unless Irving's decision to refuse to advance funds without prior notice was made in good faith and in the reasonable exercise of its discretion, the good-faith obligation imposed on Irving a duty to give notice.

KUPETZ (1988)

In July 1988 the owners of Wolf & Vine decided to sell their company to David Adashek. Adeshek formed Little Red Riding Hood to purchase Wolf & Vine from its owners with financing from Continental Illinois National Bank. Little Red Riding Hood then merged into Wolf & Vine. Subsequently Wolf & Vine could not meet its debt obligations and filed for Chapter 11 protection and later changed its petition to Chapter 7.

The bankruptcy trustee filed a complaint alleging that the original sale of Wolf & Vine to Little Red Riding Hood was a fraudulent conveyance. The previous owners sought summary judgment based on the argument that the business was sold in good faith for fair consideration. The U.S. District Court granted the summary judgment and the trustee appealed to the Ninth Circuit Court of Appeals.

The question before the court was whether or not the sale was a "fraudulent conveyance" within the meaning of the bankruptcy statute or California's fraudulent conveyance law. Because no evidence was presented of actual intent to defraud creditors and the claims of existing creditors arose after the sale, the petition was denied.

LITTON INDUSTRIES (1992)

In 1982 Litton Industries, Inc., decided to expand its business through an acquisition. Litton retained Lehman Brothers to assist in its search for a suitable target. After Litton had decided upon Itek Corporation as its target, Litton acted upon Lehman Brothers's acquisition strategy.

Information regarding Litton's plans to acquire Itek was passed from Ira Sokolow, a member of the Lehman Brothers team working on the acquisition, to Dennis Levine, who began purchasing large blocks of Itek stock through offshore banks. Litton brought an action against Lehman Brothers, Sokolow, Levine, and the offshore banks, alleging that if they had not engaged in insider trading, Litton could have acquired Itek at a lower purchase price.

The question before the court was whether the insider trading, aside from its illegality, caused Litton harm with respect to its merger with Itek. More specifically, was the purchase price artificially inflated as a result of the insider trading? The Second Circuit Court of Appeals denied the allegations and held that even absent insider trading in the target corporation's stock, the acquiring corporation would not necessarily have acquired Itek at a lower price.

MORAN (1985)

Household was a diversified holding company with securities approaching $2 billion in value. In the early 1980s, the board began to grow apprehensive over the company's vulnerability to hostile takeover attempts. Household's long-time attorney Martin ("Marty") Lipton of Wachtell, Lipton, Rosen and Katz suggested a "preferred share purchase rights plan" that was later nicknamed the "poison pill" by investment banker Martin ("Marty") Siegel of Kidder Peabody. The board adopted the plan on August 14, 1984.

Basically, the plan provided that upon certain triggering events, owners of Household common stock would be issued one "right" per share owned. Two triggering events would activate the plan: announcement of a tender offer for 30 percent or more of Household's shares, or acquisition by an entity of 20 percent or more of the company's shares.

The Chancery Court of Delaware found that at the time of the board's August 1984 meeting, that directors "had an informed basis for believing that Householder was vulnerable to a two-tier takeover and that the adoption of a defensive plan was required." The court warned, however, that its opinion "does not end the matter," because the "ultimate response to an actual takeover bid must be judgment by the directors' actions at that time, and nothing we say here relieves them of their basic fundamental duties to the corporation and its stockholders."

NATIONAL STARCH (1992)

In 1977 Indopco, formerly named National Starch and Chemical Corporation, and Unilever United States, Inc., entered into a "reverse subsidiary cash merger" specifically designed to be a tax-free transaction for National Starch's largest shareholders.

In its 1978 federal income tax return, National Starch claimed a deduction for the approximately $2.3 million in investment banking fees it paid to Morgan Stanley & Co. as ordinary and necessary expenses under Section 162(a) of the U.S. Tax Code. The IRS disallowed the deduction, and National Starch sought a redetermination including the $490,000 legal fees it paid its attorney as well.

The question before the court was whether National Starch could deduct its expenses as ordinary and necessary business expenses. The Tax Court and the Third Circuit Court of Appeals denied the deduction, saying that the expenses did not "create or enhance . . . a separate or distinct additional asset." The Supreme Court granted *certiorari* and held that investment banking, legal, and other costs incurred by the target corporation were not deductible as ordinary and necessary business expenses but instead should be capitalized as long-term benefits to the corporation.

The court also held that future benefit may help distinguish an ordinary business expense from a capital expenditure. That is, a taxpayer's realization of benefits beyond the year in which the expenditure is incurred can help determine whether the appropriate tax treatment is immediate deduction or capitalization. Indopco's postmerger record, said the court, supported the lower courts' findings that the transaction produced significant benefits to petitioner beyond the tax year in question.

NEWARK MORNING LEDGER (1993)

In 1976 the Herald company purchased substantially all of the outstanding shares of Booth Newspapers, Inc. The Herald company, which was succeeded by the Newark Morning Ledger, claimed depreciation in the amount of $67.8 million, which represented the depreciable value of the future income stream from the newspaper's current subscribers.

The question before the court was whether an intangible asset such as a subscriber list can be depreciated. The Federal District Court for the District of New Jersey entered a judgment in favor of Newark Morning Ledger Co., and the Court of Appeals for the Third District reversed. The Supreme Court reversed the Court of Appeals, stating that an asset is depreciable if it is capable of being valued and if the asset's value diminishes over time. The Court went on to state that a taxpayer able to prove that a particular asset can be valued and that the asset has a limited useful life may depreciate the asset's value over its useful life regardless of how much the asset appears to reflect the expectancy of continued patronage.

NORTHEAST BANK (1985)

The Bank Holding Company Act of 1956 requires a bank holding company to obtain the approval of the Federal Reserve Board (Fed) before it may acquire a bank. Section 3(d) of the act (known as the Douglas Amendment) prohibits the Board from approving an application of a bank holding company located in one state to acquire a bank located in another state unless the acquisition "is specifically authorized by the statute laws of the State in which such bank is located, by language to that effect and not merely by implication." Substantially similar Connecticut and Massachusetts statutes provide that an out-of-state bank holding company with its principal place of business in one of the other New England states may acquire an in-state bank, provided that the other state accords equivalent reciprocal privileges to the enacting state's banking organizations.

Certain bank holding companies (respondents in this case) had applied to the Fed as out-of-state companies for purposes of either the Connecticut or Massachusetts statute, seeking approval for acquisitions of banks located in one or the other of those states. Northeast Bancorp. and the other petitioners, prospective competitors, opposed the proposed acquisitions in proceedings before the Fed based on two main arguments. First, they contended that the acquisitions were not authorized by the Douglas Amendment. Second, they argued that the Connecticut and Massachusetts bank merger statutes, by discriminating against non–New England out-of-state bank holding companies, violated the commerce, compact, and equal protection clauses of the Constitution. This line of argument met with defeat all the way up the line. The Fed had approved the applications, the U.S. Court of Appeals affirmed the approval, and the Supreme Court affirmed the lower court's decision. This landmark case opened the way to a wave of banking mergers in the late 1980s and throughout the following decade.

OLIN (1993)

In 1985 the Olin corporation entered into an agreement with the FMC corporation to purchase FMC's swimming pool chemicals business. Since the late 1970s Olin had been experiencing considerable difficulties in the manufacture of certain swimming pool sanitizing chemicals. The FMC assets that Olin was purchasing included the manufacturing plant for sanitizers.

The Federal Trade Commission challenged the acquisition on the grounds that it would violate federal antitrust laws. The FTC ordered Olin to divest itself of the assets it had acquired from FMC. An administrative law judge agreed with the FTC and concluded that the acquisition would likely result in a substantial lessening of competition in the sanitizers' marketplace. Olin appealed the FTC's divestiture order.

The issue before the Court of Appeals for the Ninth Circuit was whether the FTC had the right to order Olin to divest itself of assets acquired through a merger and whether the acquisition would likely result in substantial lessening of competition. The Court of Appeals affirmed the FTC's ruling that Olin's acquisition of the assets would result in a substantial lessening of competition in the relevant markets in violation of Section 7 of the Clayton Act, 15 U.S.C. 18, and Section 5 of the Federal Trade Commission Act, 15 U.S.C. 45. The court went on to state that the FTC's order to Olin to divest itself of the assets was a remedy within the FTC's realm of discretion.

PARAMOUNT (1994)

On September 12, 1993, the board of Paramount Communications Inc. announced a proposed merger with Viacom Inc. Viacom was offering $69.14 per share in cash for controlling interests, with the remainder of the purchase price to be paid in stock. On September 27 Paramount directors rebuffed a comparably structured $80 per share bid from QVC Network Inc., saying they would not talk unless QVC could show evidence of financing. On November 15 Paramount directors refused a revised $90 per share offer on the grounds that it was too conditional.

Meanwhile, Paramount and Viacom continued to plan their merger. As Viacom's offer rose to the $85 per share level, Paramount granted Viacom an option to buy Paramount stock and promised to pay a termination fee in the event Paramount rejected Viacom for bidder. Paramount also made plans to redeem a shareholder rights ("poison pill") plan.

QVC sued Paramount and Viacom in the Chancery Court of Delaware, seeking to prevent these actions. The court upheld the termination fee, which it found a "fair liquidated amount to cover Viacom's expenses," but it handed QVC a victory on the other two points. The Chancery Court decision was upheld by the Delaware Supreme Court in a December 9 order, which was followed by a formal opinion on February 4, 1994.

In its opinion, the Delaware Supreme Court, concurring with the Chancery Court, stated repeatedly that directors in a "sale or change of control" must seek to obtain "the best value reasonably available to the stockholders."

In cases that do not involve a sale or change of control, the court recognized "the prerogative of a board of directors to resist a third party's acquisition proposal or offer."

(The *Paramount* decision spurred Paramount directors to set forth bidding rules in a contest to be decided by shareholders by a certain date. Viacom offered shareholders $105 per share, with certain protections against loss in share value. QVC offered $107 per share, but without such protections. The market chose Viacom, and the rest is history.)

PENNZOIL (1988)

In December 1983 Pennzoil announced a tender offer for 16 million shares of Getty Oil common stock at $100 per share. Subsequently, Pennzoil met with Getty Oil representatives to discuss the tender offer and possible sale of Getty Oil to Pennzoil. Then, over a period of several days, the following occurred:

- On January 2, 1984, as a result of the meetings, Pennzoil and Getty Oil representatives signed a memorandum of agreement for the sale of Getty Oil to Pennzoil, subject to approval by the board of directors of Getty Oil.

- On January 3 Pennzoil revised its offer to $110 per share, plus a $3 stub. Getty Oil's board of directors rejected the offer but made a counterproposal for a $5 stub. Pennzoil agreed, and a memorandum of agreement was executed.

- On January 4 both parties issued a press release.

- On January 5 Texaco contacted Getty Oil representatives to inquire about a possible sale to Texaco for $125 per share.

- On January 6 Getty Oil's board of directors voted to withdraw its Pennzoil offer and accept Texaco's offer. Texaco purchased Getty Oil stock, and Pennzoil brought an action for tortious interference.

The question before the court was whether Pennzoil and Getty Oil had a binding agreement absent a definitive purchase agreement. On approval, the Court of Appeals for Texas, citing the language in the prospective stock buyer's draft and the term "agreement in principle" in the press release, found that there was a binding agreement.

PHILADELPHIA NATIONAL BANK (1963)

In November 1960 the Philadelphia National Bank and the Girard Trust Corn Exchange Bank were the second and third largest commercial banks in the city of Philadelphia. The boards of directors for the two banks approved a merger of Girard into Philadelphia. The Department of Justice enjoined the merger, alleging that the consolidation violated the Sherman Antitrust Act and the Clayton Act. The District Court for the Eastern District of Pennsylvania ruled in favor of the banks, and the United States appealed.

The question before the U.S. Supreme Court was whether a merger that created anticompetitiveness and a monopoly violated the Clayton Act. The Supreme Court, speaking through Justice Brennan, rejected the banks' arguments on the basis of the social good. A merger the effect of which is to substantially lessen competition is not saved from violation of the Clayton Act because, on some ultimate reckoning of social or economic debits and credits, it may be deemed beneficial. The court also stated that growth by internal expansion is socially preferable to growth by acquisition.

REVLON (1986)

In June 1985 Pantry Pride approached Revlon to propose a friendly acquisition. Revlon declined the offer. In August 1985 Revlon's board recommended that shareholders reject the offer. Revlon then initiated certain defensive tactics. It sought other bidders. Pantry Pride raised its bid again. Revlon negotiated a deal with Forstmann Little, which included a lockup provision and relief from cumulative convertible exchangeable preferred stock. Revlon also provided Forstmann additional financial information that it did not provide to Pantry Pride.

The questions before the court were (1) whether the lockup agreements were permitted under Delaware law and (2) whether the Revlon board acted prudently. The Delaware Supreme Court held the following:

- Lockups and related agreements are permitted under Delaware law where their adoption is untainted by director interest or other breaches of fiduciary duties.
- Actions taken by directors in this case did not meet that standard.
- Concern for various corporate constituencies is proper when addressing a takeover threat.
- Proper concern for multiple constituencies is limited by the requirement that there be some rationally related benefits accruing to the stockholders.
- There were no such benefits in this case.
- When sale of a company becomes inevitable, the duty of a board of directors changes from preservation of the corporate entity to maximization of the company's value at a sale for the stockholders' benefit. This final point has come to be called the Revlon doctrine.

TEXAS GULF SULPHUR (1968)

The SEC brought suit against Texas Gulf Sulphur and 13 of its insiders for trading in the company's stock while possessing material inside information. The insiders in this case were officers, directors, and employees of the company, and the material information was knowledge of an oil strike in eastern Canada.

The U.S. Court of Appeals of the Second Circuit held that Section 10(b) and Rule 10(b) of the Securities Exchange Act of 1934 apply not only to such insiders as directors or officers, but also to anyone possessing inside information about a company's securities. The rule, said the court, requires anyone possessing material inside information to disclose it to the public or abstain from trading in the securities. An insider is not barred from investing in a company merely because he or she may be more familiar with its operations than other investors. Rather, the "basic test of materiality . . . is whether a reasonable man would attach importance [to the information] in determining his choice of action in the transaction in question." The court also held that insiders may act on material inside information only after such information has been "effectively disclosed in a manner sufficient to insure its availability to the investing public."

TILLEY (1991)

The plaintiffs were employed by Lynchburg Foundry Company prior to its buyout by Mead Corporation. The employees then fell under the Mead retirement plan, which provided for early retirement benefits commencing at age 55. Subsequently, Mead sold off the foundry and terminated the plan. The plaintiffs received a sum of money equal to their portion of the present value of the plan reduced by 5 percent for each year the participant was under the age of 65. Plaintiffs sued Mead in Virginia state court alleging that Mead's failure to pay the present value of the unreduced early retirement benefits violated ERISA.

Mead removed the case to the U.S. District Court for the Western District of Virginia where the court granted Mead summary disposition, holding that the plaintiffs were not entitled to the unreduced early retirement benefits. The Court of Appeals for the Fourth Circuit reversed the U.S. District Court, and the Supreme Court reversed and remanded to the Court of Appeals. On renewal, the Court of Appeals held that the lawsuit had been the subject of two earlier opinions by the court.

The court held that, under the terms of ERISA, unreduced early retirement benefits that employees would have been eligible for upon reaching age 62 were "contingent liabilities" that had to be satisfied prior to reversion of the plan's surplus assets to the employer upon termination of the plan. Unreduced early retirement benefits for which employees would have become eligible upon reaching age 62 were not "accrued benefits," which employees had a vested right to receive upon plan termination, for purposes of determining whether the employer's recoupment of plan assets without paying such benefits violated ERISA.

TIME (1990)

In July 1989 the Delaware Chancery Court ruled that Time Inc. should be allowed to proceed with its planned $14 billion acquisition of Warner Communications, Inc., despite protest from would-be hostile acquirer Paramount. In a landmark 79-page decision affirmed later by the Delaware Supreme Court, Chancellor William T. Allen declared that "corporation law does not operate on the theory that directors, in exercising their powers to manage the firm, are obligated to follow the wishes of a majority of shares. In fact, directors, not shareholders, are charged with the duty to manage the firm."

This decision was widely considered to be an affirmation of the so-called business judgment rule, a judicial doctrine that protects decisions of directors, in their exercise of discretion based on informed judgment, from second-guessing by plaintiffs and judges.

On the other hand, several legal commentators noted at the time of the decision that it did not necessarily cover instances of a sale or change of control, as in the classic case of *Revlon* (1985).

[Sure enough, five years later, in Paramount (1994)—a case ironically involving Paramount again—the court drew this change-of-control distinction, denying the protections of the business judgment rule to Paramount directors because the transaction they were considering did involve a change of control.]

TREADWAY (1980)

In 1978 Care Corp. started acquiring shares of stock in Treadway Co., leading Treadway to believe that Care was mounting a hostile takeover. In response to this action, Treadway put certain officers of Care on its board. Then, without fully informing the Care representatives, the Treadway board sought other merger candidates and struck a deal with Fair Lanes. Care filed an action alleging violations of Section 13(d) of the 1934 Securities Exchange Act, breach of fiduciary duties, and misuse of confidential information.

The question before the U. S. District Court for the Southern District of New York was whether the directors had acted improperly in their actions arising out of a struggle for control of their company. The U.S. District Court entered a judgment in favor of Care Corp., two of its directors, and Cowin. The U.S. Court of Appeals for the Second Circuit held that a director does not breach his or her fiduciary duty merely by supporting an effort or promoting a change of management. Moreover, a director does not owe his or her fiduciary duty directly to shareholders with respect to shares of stock they own and has no obligation to afford other shareholders an opportunity to participate in sale of stock.

UNOCAL (1985)

T. Boone Pickens's Mesa II Partners offered $54 dollars per share for 64 million shares of Unocal. Moran countered it with an exchange offer for up to 87.2 million of its own shares (just under 50 percent) in return for a series of secured notes of Unocal in an aggregate principal amount of $72 per share. The added twist in this offer was a condition that no shares tendered by or on behalf of Mesa or its affiliates would be accepted for exchange.

The Central District Court of California disagreed with Mesa's charge that the exclusion of Mesa from the exchange offer violated Sections 13(e) and 14(e) of the Securities Exchange Act of 1934, as amended in the famed Tender Offer Act of 1968, known as the Williams Act. The preliminary injunction against the Unocal exchange was denied. The court found nothing in the legislative history of the Williams Act to support the claim that Sections 13(e) and 14(e) required an all-holders rule for tender offers. Indeed, the court declared that "Congress never intended to substantially regulate tender offers," adding that courts could judge the fairness of a corporation's treatment of shareholders on a case-by-case basis. Unocal eventually succeeded in its attempt to employ a discriminatory self-tender offer to shield itself from the Mesa bid.

According to the Delaware Supreme Court, the action was reasonable in light of the threat Unocal directors saw in Mesa. This decision foreshadowed Moran, in which the court upheld Household International's pioneering use of a poison pill defense. In the end, though, Unocal won the battle but lost the war. The SEC eventually amended Rule 13(e) and passed a new Rule 14(d)10 that bars discriminatory offers like Unocal's.

VAN GORKOM (1985)

Shareholders brought a class action against the board of directors of Trans-Union Corporation alleging that the board was grossly negligent in its duty of care to the shareholders for recommending that the shareholders approve a merger agreement at $55 per share. Although the price per share was well above current market values, shareholders alleged that it was inadequate. The Delaware Court of Chancery granted the directors summary judgment, and the shareholders appealed. The Delaware Supreme Court indicated that it would closely scrutinize the process by which the board's decision was made.

Historically, courts would not substitute their judgment for that of a corporate board; however, this case eroded that principle and the court embarked down a road of increasing judicial scrutiny of business decisions. The court refused to afford corporate directors the usual presumption that, in making business decisions, they acted on an informed basis, in good faith, and in the best interests of the company and shareholders.

The court held that the determination of whether the business judgment of a board of directors is informed turns on whether directors have informed themselves, prior to making business decisions, of all material information reasonably available to them. The court went on to say that, under the business judgment rule, there is no protection for directors who have made uninformed or unadvised judgments.

VIRGINIA BANKSHARES (1991)

This case involved a proposed "freeze-out" merger, in which First American Bank of Virginia (Bank) would be merged into petitioner Virginia Bankshares, Inc. (VBI), a wholly owned subsidiary of petitioner First American Bankshares, Inc. (FABI). In this proposal, the bank's executive committee and board approved a price of $42 a share for the minority stockholders, who would lose their interests in the Bank after the merger. Although Virginia law required only that the merger proposal be submitted to a vote at a shareholders' meeting, preceded by a circulation of an informational statement to the shareholders, petitioner bank directors nevertheless solicited proxies for voting on the proposal. In their solicitation the directors urged the proposal's adoption and stated that the plan had been approved because of its opportunity for the minority shareholders to receive a "high" value for their stock.

Respondent Sandberg did not give her proxy and filed suit in U.S. District Court after the merger was approved, seeking damages from petitioners for, among other things, soliciting proxies by means of materially false or misleading statements in violation of 14(a) of the Securities Exchange Act of 1934 and the Security and Exchange Commission's Rule 14a-9. Sandberg alleged that the directors believed they had no alternative but to recommend the merger if they wished to remain on the board. At trial, she obtained a jury instruction that she could prevail without showing her own reliance on the alleged misstatements, so long as they were material and the proxy solicitation was an "essential link" in the merger process. Sandberg was awarded an amount equal to the difference between the offered price and her stock's true value. The remaining respondents prevailed in a separate action raising similar claims.

The Court of Appeals affirmed, holding that certain statements in the proxy solicitation, including the one regarding the stock's value, were materially misleading, and that respondents could maintain the action even though their votes had not been needed to effectuate the merger.

INDEX

A reorganization, 287, 340
ABC accounting, 88
Absolute priority rule, 174
Acceleration of loan, 181
Accord, 412
Accounting treatment, 317–337
    consolidated balance sheet, 652, 654
    employee stock ownership plans, 430
    pooling of interests (*see* Pooling of interests
      accounting)
    preferred stock, carrying amount, 336
    purchase method (*see* Purchase accounting)
    pushdown accounting, 336, 337
Acquisition agreements:
    acquisition of part of company/corporate group,
      486, 487
    acquisition of public company, 487, 488
    conditions to closing, 468–473
    covenants, 467, 468
    deposit, 457
    indemnity section, 474–482
    integration elements, 647–649
    introductory material, 456, 457
    overview, 454–456
    parties' concerns, 451, 452
    pricing clauses, 112–121
    purpose, 450, 451
    representations and warranties, 458–467 (*See
      also* Representations and warranties)
    risk allocation, 452–454
    sample agreement, 506–610
    termination section, 482–484
    two-part negotiation process, 456
    when signed, 612
    who drafts it, 449, 450
Acquisition, 6
Acquisition closing, 612
Acquisition structuring (*see* Structuring issues)
Activity-based costing (ABC), 88
ACUs, 864

Adcock v. Firestone Tire – Rubber Co., 360, 973
Adjusted basis, 275
Administrative-services-only (ASO) plan, 389
ADR process, 356, 482–484
ADRs, 840
Advance rate, 164
AES Corporation, 815n
Affiliated group of corporations, 271
Agee, William, 396
Agricultural Foreign Investment Disclosure Act,
    844
Alco Standard, 18, 19
Alien individuals, 878
Allied Stores, 317, 974
Allocation of purchase price, 297
Alpha, 85
Alphabet stock, 303
Alternate investment decision, 88
Alternative dispute resolution (ADR), 356,
    482–484
Alternative minimum tax (AMT), 274
Amalgamation, 6
American Bankruptcy Institute (ABI), 698, 718
American Can Company, 15
American depository receipts (ADRs), 840
Amortization of intangibles, 297, 298
Amortization payments, 176
AMT, 274
Announcement of merger plans, 656–664
Anti-Boycott Regulations, 853
Antigreenmail provisions, 793
Antitakeover statutes, 791–794
Antitrust defenses, 777
Appraisal of assets, 348, 349
Arbitrageur, 54, 55
Arbitration, 482–484
Articles of incorporation, 349
Asian currency units (ACUs), 864
ASO plan, 389
Asset-based loan, 103

Asset lockup agreements, 757
Asset purchase, 256–260, 338
Association for Corporate Growth, 36, 38, 818
AT&T spin-offs, 819, 820, 822, 830
Auction, 54
Auctions, 484–486
Audience-media communications matrix, 664
Auditor's opinions, 179
Automatic stay provisions, 706
Availability, 164
Average rate of return method, 92, 93
Avis, Warren, 23, 912
Avis Rent-A-Car, 23
Avon letter duty, 680

B reorganization, 288, 341
Back-end plan, 782
Back-end provision, 396
Balance sheet problems, 361
Bank book, 162
Bank check, 625, 626
Banking syndicates, 173, 174
Bankruptcies, 702–711
 automatic stay provision, 706
 Bankruptcy Code, 704
 change of leadership, 707
 Commission recommendations, 707, 708
 disadvantages, 706, 707
 filing procedure, 704
 forum shopping, 704, 705
 information/Internet sources, 717–719
 investment opportunities, 712–717
 prepacks, 708–711
 profile of typical company, 705
Barbarians at the Gate, 919
Base case, 112
Base pay, 388
Basic facilitation, 655
Basic, Inc. v. Levinson, 656, 749, 974
Basis, 275, 277
Basket amount, 475–478
Beazer, 71, 975
Bendix, 788, 975
Beneficial owner of equity, 735
Benefit plans (*see* Employee benefit plans)
Bestfoods, 976
Best of knowledge representations, 464–466
Beta, 85, 86

Beyond Franchising Hype, 809
*Big Deal: The Battle for Control of America's
 Leading Corporations*, 918
Bilmes, Linda, 678
Birch, David, 663
Blau v. Del Monte Corp., 391, 976
Blessitt, 421, 976
Blockage, 225, 226
Bluhdorn, Charlie, 915
Boesky, Ivan F., 55, 743, 772
Bond indenture, 195
Bond rating services, 194
Bonus pay, 388
Book, organization, 8, 9
Book value formula price, 113
Boot, 821
Borrowed cash (*see* Financing and refinancing)
Borrowing base, 164
Branch profits tax (BPT), 885–889
Breached representation, 181
Bridge loans, 104, 105, 200–202
Bring-down clause, 469, 470
Bring-down list, 369
Brokers and finders:
 brokers/finders, distinguished, 49
 commercial banks, 59, 60
 fees, 52–58
 investment bankers, 54, 55, 58–60
 negotiation, 49
 regulation, 50, 51
Brown, David S., 772
Bryan amendment, 765
Buffet, Warren, 392
Bulk sales law, 259, 260
Bundling, 18
Bunting, Earl, 699
Business development program, 19, 20
Business judgment rule, 752, 753
Business Periodicals Index (BPI), 42
Business Reference Guide, 51
Business Round Table v. SEC, 786
Business unit strategy, 16
Bustup fees, 760, 761
Buy/sell arrangement, 500, 501

C corporation, 291
C reorganization, 288, 342
Campeau, Robert, 3, 917

Candidates, 32
Cap, 163
Capital rationing, 88
Carryover basis transactions, 275–280
Cases, 9
    landmark, 973–994 (*See also* Landmark cases)
    table of, 969–971
Cash flow loan, 103, 104
Cash flow projections, 102, 103
Cashier's check, 625
Cautionary statements, 660, 661
Caux Round Table, 688
Caveat emptor, 48
Cecola, Randell, 772
Certified checks, 625
CFCs, 893–896
Chapter 11 bankruptcy, 702
    (*See also* Bankruptcies)
Charter/bylaw amendments, 783–786
Charter opt-in provisions, 790
Chestman, Robert, 769
Chiarella v. The United States, 768
Chinese walls, 59
Choice of entity, 290–299
Chung, Kwang S., 828
Classified board provisions, 785
Cleanup process, 626
Closing, 611–642
    cleanup process, 627
    closing checklist, 627, 628
    closing memorandum, 629–642
    day of, 620–622
    document distribution, 626
    length, 613
    location, 614, 615
    logistical snafus, 621, 622
    major elements, 612
    methods of payment, 622–626
    planning aids, 627
    post-closing activities, 626, 627
    pre-closing drill, 619, 620
    pre-closing process, 616–620
    staffing requirements, 615, 616
    unsatisfied conditions, 613
    what day of week, 621
    who should attend, 614
    wire transfers, 622–625
Closing checklist, 627, 628
Closing fee, 171

Closing memorandum, 629–642
Co-branding, 810
Collar, 116
Comfort letters, 121
Commercial bank loans, 171–189
Commercial banks, 59, 60
Commercial paper, 155
Commercial reasonableness, 159
Commitment letter, 163–165
Commitment letter fee, 171
Commitments to employees, 675–682
Commodity theory of M&A pricing, 90, 91
Common-size financial statements, 47
Company reports, 40, 41
Comparable net worth to market value method, 95, 96
Compensation:
    benefit plans (*See also* employee benefit plans)
    bridging strategy, 398–399
    design considerations, 391, 392
    different plans for different units, 392–394
    emotional viability of new plan, 400, 401
    ESOPs (*See also* Employee stock ownership plans (ESOPs))
    financial viability of new plan, 398–400
    golden handcuffs, 397
    golden handshakes, 396
    golden parachutes, 395–397
    pay elements, 388
    postmerger pay inflation, 395
    principles (do's/don'ts), 394, 395
    severance agreements, 390, 391
    special pay arrangements, 388, 389
    technical viability of new plan, 401, 402
Complements, 27, 28
Comprehensive Environmental Response, Compensation, and Liability Act (CERCLA), 361, 363
Concentration levels, 67–69
Conditions to closing, 178, 179, 468–473
Confidential voting, 786
Confidentiality agreement, 352, 382–385
Consent requirement provisions, 785
Consolidated balance sheet, 652, 654
Consolidated tax returns, 271, 272, 292
Consolidation, 5, 18
Consortium, 825
Consultants/outside advisors, 652–655
Contingency, 330

Contingent cumulative voting, 784
Continuity of interest, 288
Control share statute, 791, 792
Controlled foreign corporations (CFCs), 893–896
Conversion franchising, 807
Cooperative agreements, 825
Corporate acquisition, 5
Corporate closing, 612
Corporate consolidation, 5, 18
Corporate distribution, 269
Corporate liquidation, 269
Corporate name, 674
Corporate strategy, 16
Corporate strategy procedures guide, 17
Corporate tax rates, 272
Cost basis transactions, 275–280
Cost of capital, 123
Counsel opinions, 178
Covenants:
    acquisition agreements, and, 467, 468,
        561–569
    compliance with business plan, 182, 183
    early warning of economic trouble, 183
    financial, 184–187
    financial leakage, 184
    junk bonds, 195–198
    negative pledge, 175
    protection of collateral, 183
Cramdown, 117
Credit Managers, 168, 977
Cross-default, 187
Cross-streaming, 169, 170
Crown jewel defense, 786
Crown jewel lockup, 757
Crowthers McCall Pattern Inc. v. Lewis et al., 169
CTS v. Dynamics Corporation of America, 791,
    977
Cumulative voting, 784
Cure periods, 188
Currency hedging, 857, 858
Currency options, 857
Currency swap agreement, 868

D reorganization, 288, 342
Data structuring (*see* Structuring issues)
Davidoff, Michael, 772
DCF method, 96–98
De facto merger doctrine, 258

Deal disasters, 3
Debt-equity ratio, 110, 111
Debt-equity swap, 870
Debt-for-equity conversions, 869
Default events, 187, 188
Default rates, 176
Default softeners, 188
Defensive payments, 789, 790
Defensive sales/acquisitions, 786–788
Deferred compensation, 388
Defined benefit plan, 402, 407
Defined contribution plan, 402, 407, 408, 415
Definitions, 4–8
Delphi process, 30, 31
Demand lending, 158
Deposit, 457
Derivative instruments, 857, 868, 869
Developmental facilitation, 655
Diagrams (*see* Transaction diagrams)
Differential diagnosis, 88
Dilution, 235
Director's duty of due care, 752, 753
Director's duty of loyalty, 753, 754, 774–776
Directory of Management Consultants, 654
Dirks, Raymond, 768
Disasters, 3
Disclose or abstain rule, 766, 767
Disclosure-based lawsuits, 661
Disclosure schedules, 458–460
Discounted cash flow (DCF) method, 96–98
Discounting, 86
Distressed entities, 697–721
    bankruptcies (*see* Bankruptcies)
    investment opportunities, 712–717
    prepacks, 708–711
    state insolvency procedures, 711, 712
    workouts, 699–702
Diversification mode, 25
Divestiture IPO, 819
Divestitures (*see* Postmerger divestitures)
Document distribution, 626
Documenting the transaction (*see* Negotiation
    issues)
Double taxation, 273, 283, 284
Dual resident company, 879
Due diligence, 347–386
    appraisal of assets, 348, 349
    bring-down list, 369
    checklist, 352, 353, 370–381

Due diligence—*Cont.*
  confidentiality agreement, 352, 382–385
  do-it-yourself, 365, 366
  duration of process, 368, 369
  emerging legal issues, 364, 365
  environmental exposure analysis, 360–364
  ground rules, 352
  insurance policies, 355
  intracompany transactions, 351
  litigation analysis, 353–360
  off-site investigations, 367
  on-site inquiries, 366, 367
  post-closing significance, 369
  search of public records, 349, 350
  subsidiary/divisional performance, 367, 368
  thoroughness, 351, 352
  when to begin, 348
  wrongful termination/severance agreements,
    360
Dunn v. Hovic, 365

Earnings and profits, 269
Earnouts, 117–119
Edelman, Asher, 737
Edgar v. MITE, 791, 978
Edge Act, 842
80/20 law, 71
Eligible receivables, 164
Emerging legal issues, 364, 365
Employee benefit plans:
  basic concerns, 405–407
  defined benefit plan, 402, 407
  defined contribution plan, 402, 407, 408, 415
  effect on company books, 408–412
  effect on corporate structure, 434, 435
  fiduciary concerns, 416
  health plans, 403–405
  medical plans, 389, 390
  multiemployer plan, 407
  pension plans, 402, 403
  plan split-ups/partial terminations, 412
  reporting obligations, 416, 417
  surplus, 419, 420
  transfer of plan assets, 414
  types of, 402
  underfunding/overfunding, 417
Employee buyouts (EBOs), 7
Employee lawsuits, 680, 681

Employee retention/layoffs, 663–668, 675–682
Employee stock ownership plans (ESOPs), 304,
  421
  accounting treatment, 430
  companies best suited for ESOPs, 426, 428,
    429
  drawbacks, 426, 427
  insider trading, 431
  number of ESOPs, 423
  recapitalization, as, 778
  recent amendments (Taxpayer Relief Act of
    1997), 435
  regulatory background, 423, 426
  repurchase obligations, 429
  required stock holding, 424
  sale of employer stock, 433
  securities issues, 430, 431
  tax benefit to lender, 425
  tax benefit to selling company, 425, 426
  tax benefit to selling stockholder, 424, 425
  tax benefits, 422
  trustee voting, 428
  uses, 421, 422
  voting control (management), 427
  when ESOP in sold, 428
Employment agreements, 492–496
Enterprise strategy, 15
Entity, choice of, 290–299
Environmental concerns, 62
Environmental exposure analysis, 360–364
Equity investment funds, 202–206
ERM, 856
Escrow agreement, 479, 613
ESOPs (*see* Employee stock ownership plans
  (ESOPs))
Eurobanks, 863
Eurodollar rate, 173
Euronote, 867
European Union, 854–856
Examples (*see* Sample documents)
Exchange rate mechanism (ERM), 856
Exchange rate volatility, 857, 858
Exhibits, 458–460

Facilitators, 655
Failure rates, 644
Fair market value, 81
Fair market value in use, 671

Fair price provisions, 784
Fair price statute, 793
Fairness opinion, 54, 756
Fall River Dyeing, 436, 979
Family businesses, 800–805
FAS No. 87, 410, 419
FAS No. 88, 410
FAS No. 109, 281, 282
FCPA, 853
Federal Aviation Act, 842
Federal Communications Act, 842
Federal Filings, Inc. Bankruptcy Online, 718
Federal funds effective rate, 173
Fedwire transfer, 623
Fees:
    brokers and finders, 52–58
    bustup, 760, 761
    commercial banks, 171, 172
    outsider advisors/consultants, 652, 654
    topping, 760
    volunteers, 55
Fiduciary out clause, 762, 763
Filing schedules, 178
Financial acquirer, 4, 11, 12
Financial covenants, 184–187
Financing agreements, 612
Financing and refinancing, 139–253
    absolute priority rule, 174
    bank book/commitment letter, 162–165
    banking syndicates, 173, 174
    bridge loans, 200–202
    commercial bank loans, 171–189
    conditions to closing, 178, 179
    covenants, 182–187 (*See also* Covenants)
    default events, 187, 188
    default rates, 176
    default softeners, 188
    equity investment funds, 202–206
    existing debt, 147, 148, 152, 153
    fees (commercial banks), 171, 172
    financing structure, 154–157
    fraudulent conveyances, 166–171
    highly leveraged transactions, 140–144
    how much is needed, 144
    insurance company financing, 189–193
    intercreditor agreements, 231, 232
    intercreditor issues, 219–222
    interest rates, 173, 200
    international acquisitions, 861–873

Financing and refinancing—*Cont.*
    junk bonds, 193–199 (*See also* Junk bonds)
    layers of debt, 155, 156
    leases, 148–154
    letters of credit, 177–180
    liens, 175, 176
    mandatory prepayment requirements, 176, 177
    minimizing borrowing, 144–147
    negative pledge, 175
    partial divestments, 146
    prepayments, 176, 177
    preserving debt/lease obligations,
      147–154
    public company acquisitions, 772–774
    refinancing issues, 232–236
    registration rights, 211–218
    representations/warranties, 180–182
    sale-leasebacks, 159–162
    seller takeback financing, 206–211
    senior debt, 157–159
    spin-offs, 146
    subordination provisions (*see* Subordination
      provisions)
    tax-exempt industrial development bonds, 152,
      153
    360-day year, 176
    working capital debt, 151, 152
Financing out condition, 470–472
Finders, 49
    (*See also* Brokers and finders)
Findex, 40
Finding (*see* Planning and finding)
Finkelstein, Ed, 3
Fire walls, 59
FIRPTA, 889–891
Fisk, Jim, 910
Fit chart, 27, 28
    (*See also* WOFC process)
Fixed-rate notes (FRNs), 867
Flip-over plan, 781, 782
Focus companies, 32
Focus company files, 44
Focus industry, 31, 32
Focus industry surveys, 43, 44
Ford, Henry, 23
Forecast period, 89
Foreign base company income, 895
Foreign Corrupt Practices Act (FCPA), 853
Foreign exchange control laws, 855

Foreign Investment in Real Property Tax Act (FIRPTA), 844, 889–891
Foreign tax credit, 896, 897
Form S-4 registration statement, 760
Forms of acquisition (*see* Structuring issues)
Forum shopping, 704
Forward-looking statements, 660, 661
Forward merger, 262, 339
Forward purchase contracts, 857
Forward sales contracts, 857
Fourth-level tippee, 769
Franchise Your Business, 808
Franchises, 807–810
Fraudulent conveyances, 166–171, 258
Free cash flow ratio, 107–110
Free-form diversification, 25
Freeze-out provisions, 792, 793
Friendly acquisitions (*see* Public company acquisitions)
Friendly transactions, 8
FRNs, 867
Functional strategy, 16
Fuqua, J.P., 913

Gamble, James, 908
, Harold, 913
General Utilities rule, 274
Giscard d'Estaing, Olivier, 688
Glass-Steagall Act, 59
Gleneagles, 168, 980
Going private, 774
Golden handcuffs, 308, 397
Golden handshakes, 396
Golden parachutes, 395–397, 495, 790
Gollust v. Mendell, 764, 981
Good bank, bad bank technique, 235
Goodwill, 297, 298, 666
Gould, Jay, 910
Grace, Peter, 15
Grace Lines, 15
Grace period, 188
Greenmail, 789
Group facilitator, 655
Group strategy, 16

Hanson Trust PLC v. SCM Corp., 728, 753, 981
Hart-Scott-Rodino Antitrust Improvements Act, 65–71

Health maintenance organizations (HMOs), 404
Health plans, 403–405
Hedged tendering, 743
Henderson, Bruce, 13
Herfindahl-Hirschmann Index (HHI), 67, 68
Herlihy, Edward D., 18
Hewlett-Packard Company, 25
HHI, 67, 68
Hickman, W. Braddock, 918
High-yield securities, 194
   (*See also* Junk bonds)
Highly concentrated industries, 68, 69
Highly leveraged transactions (HLTs), 140–144, 400
Historical cost of capital, 123
HLTs, 140–144, 400
HMOs, 404
Holding company structure, 265
Holmes v. Securities Corp., 724
Hoover's Handbook of Private Companies, 41
Horizontal integration, 22, 23
Horizontal Merger guidelines, 67, 75–78
Hostile acquisitions (*see* Takeover bids)
Human resource issues, 663–668, 675–682
Hurdle rate, 86, 87, 92
Hybrid A reorganization, 341

IITSSA, 844, 854
Ikon Office Solutions, 19
Illustrative documents (*see* Sample documents)
In re Mobile Communications Corporation of America, Inc., 743
In re O'Day Corporation, 169
In-house search (*see* Search-and-screen process)
Incentive pay, 388
Income tax treaties, 875–877
Indemnity plan, 403
Indemnity section (acquisition agreement), 474–482
   basket amount, 475–478
   materiality, 477–479
   minimum amount, 477, 478
   purpose, 474
   sample provisions, 594–601
   seller's concerns, 480
   subsequent litigation claims, 481
   survival period, 474, 475
Index, Herfindahl-Hirschmann, 9

Industrial organization, 22
Industry and deal data, 36, 37
Industry concerns, 62
Industry consolidation, 18
Industry gurus, 36, 42, 43
Industry players, 36, 39–41
Industry research reports, 40
Industry situation analysis, 36
Initial basis, 275
Insider trading, 763–772
    disclose or abstain rule, 766, 767
    employee stock ownership plans, 431
    insider, defined, 763
    junk bonds, 199
    legislative provisions, 763, 764
    misappropriation theory, 767
    section 16(b) violations, 764–766
    temporary insiders, 763
    tipping, 769–771
    typical insiders, 772
Installment sale, 285
Instant Delphi process, 30, 31
Insurance company financing, 189–193
Insurance policies, 355
Intangibles, 674, 675
Integration plan, 649–651
    (*See also* Postmerger integration)
Intercreditor agreements, 231, 232
Intercreditor issues, 219–222
Interest rate swap, 868
Interest rates:
    bridge loans, 200
    commercial bank loans, 173
    international loans, 864
Interim executives, 654
Interim loan, 104, 105
Interim period, 114
Intermediaries, 50
Internal rate of return (IRR) method, 93, 94
International dimensions, 839–901
    alien individuals, 878
    branch profit tax (BPT), 885–889
    classification principles, 877, 878
    controlled foreign corporations (CFCs),
      893–896
    currency hedging, 857, 858
    debt-equity swaps, 870
    debt financing, 866
    debt-for-equity conversions, 869

International dimensions—*Cont.*
    derivative instruments, 857, 868, 869
    disclosure requirements, 874, 875
    domestic corporations (tax purposes), 878, 879
    dual resident companies, 879
    employee rights, 860, 861
    ERM, 856
    European Union, 854–856
    exchange rate volatility, 857, 858
    financing, 861–873
    FIRPTA, 889–891
    fixed-rate notes (FRNs), 867
    foreign exchange control laws, 855
    foreign tax credit, 896, 897
    inbound investments (nontax issues), 841–846
    inbound investments (tax issues), 881–891
    interest rates, 864
    investor-visa program, 901
    IOSCO, 854
    LBOs, 871–873
    medium-term notes (MTNs), 868
    NAFTA, 850
    outbound investments (nontax issues), 847–849
    outbound investments (tax issues), 891–898
    repatriation restrictions, 858, 859
    residence-of-the-seller rule, 881
    securitization, 870, 871
    swap agreements, 857, 868, 869
    syndicated loans, 864–866
    tax considerations, 873–898
    tax treaties, 875–877
    treaty shopping, 876, 888
    U.S. acquisitions of foreign companies/assets,
      849–861
International Investment and Trade in Services
    Survey Act (IITSSA), 844, 854
International Organization of Securities
    Commissions (IOSCO), 854
Internet Bankruptcy Library, 718
Internet search, 37–39
Interstate Banking and Efficiency Act, 18
Intracompany transactions, 351
Intrapreneurship, 678
Inventory consolidation, 672, 673
Inventory sublimit, 164
Investment bankers:
    M&A services, 58–60
    payment of fees to brokers, 55
    what they do, 54

Investment banking fees, 54
Investment Company Act, 205
Investment method, 92, 93
Investor-buyer, 4, 11, 12
Investor-visa program, 901n
IOSCO, 854
IPO carveout, 819
IRR method, 93, 94

Jefferies, Boyd L., 772
Johnson, Dairi M., 810
Joint ventures, 825–829, 831–834
Junk bonds, 193–199
    bond indenture, 195
    bridge loans, as, 200–202
    covenants, 195–198
    default rates, 199
    insider trading, 199
    leverage buyouts, and, 105, 106
    past performance, 198, 199
    quasi-junk bonds, 199
    to who/how sold, 194
    warrants, 194

Kaiser Steel Corporation v. Pearl Brewing Co.,
    169
Kellogg, W. K., 909
Kelly, Donald P., 142
Kern, George C., Jr., 751
Key-executive life insurance, 492
Kupetz, 168, 983

Labor issues, 436–438
Lampf et alia v. Gilbertson, 765
Land/real estate consolidation, 673
Landmark cases:
    Accardi, 973
    Adcock, 973
    Allied Stores, 974
    Basic, 974
    Beazer, 975
    Bendix, 975
    Bestfoods, 976
    Blau, 976
    Blessitt, 976
    Credit Managers, 977

Landmark cases—*Cont.*
    CTS, 977
    Edelman, 978
    Edgar, 978
    Fall River Dyeing, 979
    General Utilities, 979
    Gleneagles, 980
    Gollust, 981
    Hanson Trust, 981
    Healthco, 982
    Irving Trust, 982
    Kupetz, 983
    Litton Industries, 983
    Moran, 984
    National Starch, 985
    Newark Morning Ledger, 985
    Northeast Bank, 986
    Olin, 987
    Paramount, 987
    Pennzoil, 988
    Philadelphia National Bank, 989
    Revlon, 989
    table of cases, 969–971
    Texas Gulf Sulphur, 990
    Tilley, 991
    Time, 991
    Treadway, 992
    Unocal, 992
    Van Gorkom, 993
    Virginia Bankshares, 994
Law Journal Extra Bankruptcy News, 719
Layers of debt, 155, 156
LBOs (*see* Leverage buyouts (LBOs))
Lease consolidation, 673
Leases, 148–154
Legal cases (*see* Cases)
Lehman scale, 52
Letter of credit, 177–180
Letter of intent, 352, 446–449, 502–505
Leveraged buildup, 18
Leveraged buyouts (LBOs):
    amount of equity, 106
    cash flow projections, 103, 104
    DCF concepts, 107
    debt-equity ratio, 110, 111
    defined, 7
    determining advisability of deal, 100
    equity holders, 101
    financial plan, 106, 107

Leveraged buyouts (LBOs)—*Cont.*
  free cash flow ratio, 107–110
  international acquisitions, 871–873
  junk bonds, 105, 106
  length of loan, 109
  management projections, 111, 112
  payment terms, 105
  pricing issues, 99–112
  senior loans, 103, 104
  types, 7
Leveraged ESOP, 423
  (*See also* Employee stock ownership plans
    (ESOPs))
Levine, Dennis B., 767, 772
Lewis, John J., 91
Lexis/Nexis, 42
LIBOR, 173, 864
Liens, 175, 176
Limited liability company (LLC), 290, 292
Limited liability partnership, 806
Limited-service bank, 189
Lindner, Carl, 725, 919
Ling, Jimmy, 913, 915
Liquidating distribution, 269
Liquidation, 269
Literature search, 36, 37
Litigation analysis, 353–360
LLC, 290, 292
Lock boxing, 181
Lockup agreements/arrangements, 324, 757–759
London InterBank Offered Rate (LIBOR), 173, 864
Loss carrybacks/carryforwards, 280–282
Lynch, Gary, 767

M&A formula, 52
M&A investment risk, 86
M&A leverage, 89
Make-whole arrangement, 192
Managed care plan, 403
Management buyout (MBO), 305–314
  conflicts of interest, 346n
  employment agreements, 492–496
  ESOP, as, 306
  key-executive life insurance, 492
  negotiation, 488–492
  non recourse note, 311, 312
  recourse loan, 312
  stockholders' agreements, 496–501

Management buyout (MBO)—*Cont.*
  tax considerations, 306–311
  tax-free rollovers, 313
  typical structure, 305
Management Consultants Resource Guide, 654
Management projections, 111, 112
Mandatory prepayment requirements, 176, 177
Margin-driven operations, 29
Marginal cost of capital, 123
Market extension, 23
Market intensification strategy, 22, 23
Market outs, 116
Market value method, 94, 95
Marketing agreements, 825
Martindale-Hubbell Law Directory, 653
Master limited partnership, 780
Materiality:
  basket amount, and, 477–479
  default provisions, and, 188
  representations and warranties, and, 461
MBO transaction (*see* Management buyout
  (MBO))
McCalmont, Tom, 661
McGregor, Robert, 688
Medical plans, 389, 390
Medium-term note (MTN), 868
Mendoza, Roberto, 83
Merchant banking, 60
Merchant Marine Act, 843
Mere volunteer, 55
Merger:
  acquisition, contrasted, 6
  defined, 4, 5
  forward, 262, 339
  reverse, 262, 339
  short-form, 6, 727
  subsidiary, 262–265, 340
Merger agreement (*see* Acquisition agreements)
Merger mania, 903–925
  fifth wave, 919, 920
  first wave, 907–911
  fourth wave, 917–919
  second wave, 911, 912
  sixth wave, 903, 904, 920–923
  third wave, 912–917
Merger transactions, 262, 263, 339, 340
Mergers & Acquisitions magazine, 1, 2
Mezzanine debt, 155
Milken, Michael, 194, 772, 918, 919

Million Dollar Directory, 41
Mineral Lands Leasing Act, 843
Minimizing borrowing, 144–147
Minimum amount, 477, 478
Misappropriation theory, 767
Mitchell, Mark, 665
Monks, Robert A. G., 747
Morris Trust transaction, 821
MTN, 868
Multiemployer plan, 407
Multiple employer plan, 414

NAFTA, 850
Names, 674
National Starch, 317, 985
National Starch transaction, 289, 343
Negative goodwill, 330
Negative pledge, 175
Negotiating intermediary, 50
Negotiation issues:
    acquisition agreement (*see* Acquisition
      agreements)
    letter of intent, 446–449, 502–505
    management buyouts (*see* Management buyout
      (MBO))
    public company acquisitions, 725, 726
Nelson, Ralph, 905–907
Nelson's Directory of Investment Research, 40
New capital exception, 175
New Generation Research, 718
No-shop agreement, 761, 762
NOL carrybacks/carryforwards, 280–282
Nonbank bank, 189
Noncompete agreements, 388, 493, 601–603, 668
Nondiversifying growth by acquisition, 17–19
Nonliquidating distribution, 269
Nonprofit organizations, 810–814
Nonqualified pension plans, 402
North American Free Trade Agreement (NAFTA),
    850

Omnibus Trade and Competitiveness Act, 843
One-share, one-vote rule, 786
Operator-buyer, 4, 11, 12
OPIC, 862
Opportunity makers, 12, 34, 35
Opportunity takers, 12, 34, 35

Ordinary course of business, 463, 464
Organization of book, 8, 9
Out-of-court workout, 700, 701
Outside advisors, 652–655
Overseas Private Investment Corp. (OPIC), 862

Pac-Man defense, 788, 789
Paramount, 753, 987
Paramount, Inc v. Time, Inc., 788
Participation agreement, 174
Participative-process consulting, 655
Partnership, 292, 299
Partnerships, 805, 806
Pass-through entities, 290, 291
Patent, 675
Patterson, John H., 909
Payback method, 93
PAYSOPs, 423
Pennzoil, 448, 988
Pension funds, 205, 680
Pension plans, 402, 403
Percs, 236
Permanent establishment, 875
Perquisites, 388
Personal goodwill, 666
Phantom stock grants, 400
Philadelphia National Bank, 69, 989
Philips, Frederick, 688
Piggyback registration rights, 213–215
Planning and finding, 11–77
    brokers and finders, 49–58
    business development program, 19, 20
    80/20 rule, 71
    in-house search (*see* Search-and-screen
      process)
    regulatory considerations (*see* Regulatory
      considerations)
    strategic planning, 13–17
    wheel of opportunity/fit chart (*see* WOFC
      process)
Plant consolidation, 670
Point of service plans (POSs), 404
Poison pill provisions, 793
Poison pills, 780–782
Poof-company, 904
Pooling of interests accounting, 318
    advantages/disadvantages, 319
    disclosure requirements, 334, 335

Pooling of interests accounting—*Cont.*
  expenses, 324, 325
  lockup arrangements, 324
  standstill agreements, 323
  when not used, 322, 323
  when used, 319–322
POSs, 404
Post-acquisition tax issues, 314, 315
Post-closing activities, 626, 627
Postmerger divestitures:
  spin-offs, 818–823, 834
  split-offs, 824, 835
  split-ups, 823, 824, 835
Postmerger integration, 643–696
  acquisition agreement, 647–649
  announcement of merger plans, 656–664
  combining equipment, 671, 672
  commitments to employees, 675–682
  consolidated balance sheet, 668–675
  consultants/outside advisors, 652–655
  due diligence review, 646
  employee retention/layoffs, 663–668, 675–682
  facilitators, 655
  failure/success factors, 644, 645
  intangibles, 674, 675
  integration plan, 649–651
  interim executives, 654
  inventory consolidation, 672, 673
  land/real estate consolidation, 673
  lease consolidation, 673
  master checklist, 689–691
  new corporate name, 674
  planning checklist, 650
  planning teams, 651
  plant consolidation, 670
  regulatory approval, 659
  SEC filings/disclosure, 658–661
  strategic review, 646
PPOs, 404
Pre-acquisition contingency, 331
Pre-closing drill, 619, 620
Pre-closing process, 616–620
Predators' Ball, The, 919
Preferred equity redemption cumulative stock
  (percs), 236
Preferred provider organizations (PPOs), 404
Preferred stock, 229, 336
Premerger notification, 65, 66
Prepackaged bankruptcies (prepacks), 708–711

Prepayments, 176, 177
Pricing:
  acquisition agreement (pricing clauses),
    112–121
  LBOs, 99–112 (*See also* Leveraged buyouts
    (LBOs))
  20-day figure, 79
Pricing clauses (acquisition agreements):
  book value formula price, 113
  contingent consideration, 120
  cramdowns, 117
  earnouts, 117–119
  fixed price provisions, 112–115
  formula price, 113–115
  market value, 116
Principles for Business (Caux Round Table),
  681–688
Private company information, 41, 42
Private placement, 266, 267
Pro forma financial information, 335
Procter, William, 908
Product extension, 25
Product-line strategy, 16
Professional association, 818
Progressive buildup, 18
Project executives, 654
Projection problems, 361
Prospects, 32
Proxy solicitations, 744–749
  (*See also* Public company acquisitions)
Public company acquisitions, 723–798
  block purchase, 759, 760
  bustup fees, 760, 761
  director responsibilities, 751–756
  fiduciary out clause, 762, 763
  financing, 772–774
  hostile acquisitions (*see* Takeover bids)
  insider trading, 763–772 (*See also* Insider
    trading)
  issuance of securities to target shareholders, 760
  legislative provisions, 723–725
  lockup agreements, 757–759
  merger disclosure issues, 749–751
  negotiating techniques, 725, 726
  no-shop agreement, 761, 762
  one-step transaction, 726
  proxy solicitations, 744–749
  special committee of board, 754–756
  tender offer, 730–744 (*See also* Tender offer)

Public company acquisitions—*Cont.*
 topping fees, 760, 761
 two-step transaction, 727–729
Purchase accounting, 318
 advantages/disadvantages, 325
 allocation of purchase price, 326–328
 allocation period, 330
 contingent consideration, 332
 date to report results, 331, 332
 determination of purchase price, 325, 326
 differences between market/appraisal values,
  330
 direct acquisition costs, 333
 disclosure requirements, 333, 334
 negative goodwill, 330
 pre-acquisition contingencies, 330, 331
 when used, 325
Pushdown accounting, 336, 337

Quaker Oats, 3
Qualified pension plans, 402
Quasi-junk bond, 199

Rabbi trust, 402
Racketeer Influenced and Corrupt Organizations
 Act (RICO), 724, 725
Radical downsizing, 786
Real estate consolidation, 673
Reasonable consent, 468, 469
Reasonably worst case, 112
Recapitalization, 7, 289, 777–779
Reference rates, 173
Refinancing, 232–236
 (*See also* Financing and refinancing)
Registered foreign capital base, 858
Registration rights, 211–218
Regulation D, 267
Regulatory approval, 659
Regulatory considerations, 61–71
 antitrust concerns, 64, 65
 areas of concern, 61, 62
 Hart-Scott-Rodino Act, 65–71
 premerger notification, 65, 66
Reich, Ivan K., 772
Related filing schedules, 178
Reorganizations, 286–288, 340–342
Repatriation restrictions, 858, 859

Replacement value method, 92
"Report of the National Bankruptcy Review
 Commission," 698, 708
Representations and warranties, 458–467
 best of knowledge, 464–466
 breached representations, 181, 182
 exhibits/disclosure schedules, 458–460
 materiality, 461
 most important representations, 467
 ordinary course of business, 463, 464
 postmerger matters, and, 648
 pre-closing, and, 617, 618
 purpose, 458
 sample provisions, 515–560
 scope of, 461–463
 typical warranties, 180
Repurchase plan, 780
Reservation of rights, 355
Residence-of-the-seller rule, 881
Restrictions on transferability, 497
Restructuring defenses, 777–780
Restructurings, 7
Retention agreements, 389
Reverse leveraged buyouts, 235, 774
Reverse merger, 262, 339
Reverse subsidiary merger, 262, 263
Revlon, Inc. v. MacAndrews – Forbes Holdings,
 725, 758, 989
Revolver loans, 105
RICO, 724, 725
Right to accelerate, 181
Riklis, Meshulam "Rik," 194, 919
Risk, 83–87
Risk allocation, 452–454
Risk arbitrageurs, 743
Rock, Milton L., 643
Rockefeller, John D., 910
Roebuck, C., 909
Rollup, 18
Rule 10b-5, 763, 764, 767–771
Rule 10e-3, 764, 767–771
Rule 13d-2, 737
Rule 13e-3, 774
Rule 14a-1, 746
Rule 14a-11(c), 747
Rule 14a-2(b), 747
Rule 14a-3, 747
Rule 14a-4(d), 747
Rule 14a-7, 747

Rule 14l-10, 779
Rule 19c-4, 786
Ryder Systems, 23

S corporation, 291, 293, 298, 299
Salary, 388
Sale-leasebacks, 156, 159–162, 234
Sammet, George, 649
Sample documents:
  closing memorandum, 629–642
  confidentiality agreement, 382–385
  joint ventures, 831–834
  letter of intent, 502–505
  merger agreement, 506–610
  subordinate provisions, 236–247
Satellite, 823
SBICs, 206
SBUs, 90, 91
Schedule 13D, 658, 734–737
Schedule 13G, 734
Schedule 14A, 744, 745
Schedule 14D-1, 658, 738–740
Search-and-screen process, 32–48
  contacting the focus company, 45–48
  duration of program, 33
  focus company files, 44
  focus industry surveys, 43, 44
  industry gurus, 42, 43
  industry players, 39–41
  Internet search, 37–39
  literature search, 36, 37
  private company information, 41, 42
  ranking candidates, 45
  steps in process, 33, 34
Sears, Richard W., 909
SEC filings/disclosure, 658–661
  (*See also* Public company acquisitions)
SEC v. Warde, 768
Section 16(b) violations, 764–766
Section 83, 307–311, 314
Section 83(b) election, 309, 310, 314
Section 125 plan, 408
Section 197 intangibles, 297, 298
Section 279, 302, 303
Section 304 transactions, 294, 295
Section 338 election, 294, 296
Section 351 transaction, 289, 296
Section 382 limitation, 281

Sector strategy, 16
Securities Act of 1933, 724, 725
Securities Exchange Act of 1934, 724, 725
Securitization, 236
Self-tender, 779
Seller takeback financing, 206–211
Senior debt, 157–159
Senior loans, 103, 104
Senior revolving debt, 155
Senior subordinated debt, 155
Senior term debt, 155
Serial consolidation, 18
Service extension, 25
Service mark, 675
Setoff provision, 479
Severance agreements/plans, 360, 389–391,
  495
Shelf registration, 212, 214
Shelflands Act, 843
Shell transactions, 110
Sherwin-Williams, 24, 25
Shoemaker strategy, 22
Short-form merger, 6, 727
Short-swing profit rule, 764–766
Short tendering, 743
SIBOR, 864
Siegel, Martin A., 772
Signing bonuses, 389, 396
Singapore interbank offered rate (SIBOR), 864
Singer, Isaac M., 908
Siu, Juan A., 828
Small business investment companies (SBICs),
  206
Smith v. Van Gorkom, 752, 993
Smith, Gregory, 141
Sokolow, Ira B., 772
Solvency opinions, 120, 171
Special-class stock, 303
Special pay arrangement, 388, 389
Specific risk, 84
Spin-offs, 289, 290, 818–823, 834
Split-offs, 824, 835
Split-ups, 823, 824, 835
Sponsor, 101
Squeeze-outs, 95
Staggered board provisions, 785
Standstill agreements, 323, 787
Stapled entities, 879
State antitakeover statutes, 791–794

State insolvency procedures, 711, 712
State pension funds, 205
Steinberg, Saul, 919
Step-up amount, 279
Step-up transaction, 278
Stock consistency rule, 294
Stock lockup agreements, 757
Stock plans, 431–434
    (*See also* Employee stock ownership plans
        (ESOPs))
Stock purchase, 260, 261, 284, 338
Stockholders' agreements, 496–501
Stocking, 236
Straight debt, 299
Strategic alliances, 825–829
Strategic business units (SBUs), 90, 91
Strategic buyer, 4, 11, 12, 99
Strategic planning, 13–17
Strike suits, 661
Strong v. Rapid, 766
Structuring issues, 255–346
    accounting considerations, 317–337
    asset purchase, 256–260, 338
    carryover basis transactions, 275–280
    choice of entity, 290–299
    consolidated tax returns, 271, 272, 292
    cost basis transactions, 275–280
    diagrams, 338–343 (*See also* Transaction
        diagrams)
    double taxation, 273, 283, 284
    holding company structure, 265
    installment sale, 285
    loss carryovers/carrybacks, 280–282
    management buyout, 305–314 (*See also*
        Management buyout (MBO))
    merger transactions, 262, 263, 339, 340
    National Starch transaction, 289, 343
    pooling of interests (*see* Pooling of interests)
        accounting
    post-acquisition tax issues, 314, 315
    private placement, 266, 267
    purchase accounting (*see* Purchase accounting)
    section 304 transactions, 294, 295
    section 338 election, 294, 296
    section 351 transactions, 289, 296
    securities laws, 266
    special-class (alphabet) stock, 303
    step-up transaction, 278
    stock purchase, 260, 261, 284, 338

Structuring issues—*Cont.*
    tax concepts/definitions, 269–275
    tax considerations, 267–269, 299–304, 316,
        317
    tax-free reorganizations, 286–288, 340–342
    transaction diagrams, 338–343 (*See also*
        Transaction diagrams)
    two-step transactions, 264
Stuart, John E., 19
Stub period, 114
Subordination provisions, 222–231
    corporate structure, and, 229–231
    major provisions, 223
    negotiating procedural provisions, 225, 226
    negotiating substantive provisions, 223–225
    preferred stock, 229
    public debt provisions, 228
    substantive/procedural provisions,
        distinguished, 222, 223
    typical provisions (privately placed
        institutional notes), 240–245
    typical provisions (publicly issued notes),
        236–240
    typical provisions (seller notes), 245–247
    what are they, 222
    where do they appear, 229
Subpart F, 894, 895
Subsequent draws (revolving letter of credit), 179,
    180
Subsidiary merger, 262–265, 340
Success factors, 644, 645
Successor plan rule, 403
Superfund, 361, 363
Supermajority provisions, 783, 784
Supplements, 28
Survival period, 474, 475
Suspension provisions, 226
Swap agreements, 857, 868–870
Synergy, 27
Systematic risk, 84

Table of cases, 969–971
Tail, 355
Takeback financing, 206–211
Takeback provision, 396
Takeover bids
    antitrust defenses, 777
    charter/bylaw amendments, 783–786

Takeover bids—*Cont.*
  defensive payments, 789, 790
  defensive sales/acquisitions, 786–788
  director responsibilities, 774–776
  master limited partnership, 780
  Pac-Man defense, 788
  poison pills, 780–782
  recapitalization, 777–779
  repurchase plans, 780
  restructuring defenses, 777–780
  self-tender, 779, 780
  state laws, 790–794
Target, 7, 8
Target ownership plan (TOP), 391
Taubman, A. Alfred, 787
Tax concepts/definitions, 269–275
Tax considerations, 267–269, 299–304, 316, 317
Tax Equity and Fiscal Responsibility Act, 844
Tax-exempt industrial development bonds, 152, 153
Tax-free forward merger, 287, 340
Tax-free forward triangular merger, 341
Tax-free reorganizations, 286–288, 340–342
Tax-free spin-offs, 289, 290, 818–823, 834
Tax rates, 272, 273
Tax treaties, 875–877
Tax year, 272
Taxpayer Relief Act of 1997, 435, 844
Technology exchanges, 825
Telephone book finder, 55
Tender offer:
  acquirer's stock price, 731
  advantages, 727
  commencement date/time, 733, 734
  contacting target's management, 732, 733
  disclaimers, 740, 741
  disclosure requirements, 734–737
  filings, 738–740
  groups, 735, 736
  hedge tendering, 743
  insider trading, 764
  length of offering period, 741
  practical considerations, 732
  premiums, 730, 731
  privately negotiated purchases, 744
  risk arbitrageurs, 743
  SEC definition, 730
  short tendering, 743
  treatment of shareholders, 742, 743
  withdrawal of tender shares, 742

Term loans, 105
Termination section (acquisition agreement),
    482–484, 603–605
Texaco v. Pennzoil, 448, 988
Texas Gulf Sulfur, 766, 990
Thomas Register, 40
Thornton, Tex, 913
360-day year, 176
Tie-in deals, 60
Tilley, 421, 991
Time horizon, 89
Time, 753, 991
Tin parachutes, 389
Tippee, 769
Tipper, 769
Tipping, 769–771
TOP, 391
Topping fees, 760, 761
Total compensation, 389
Toys "R" Us, 720
Trade associations, 39, 40
Trade secret, 675
Trademark, 675
Trading with the Enemy Act, 854
Tranches, 236
Transaction diagrams
  acquisition of property for voting stock (C
      reorganization), 342
  acquisition of property for voting stock (D
      reorganization), 342
  asset purchase, 338
  National Starch transaction, 343
  spin-offs, 834
  split-offs, 835
  split-ups, 835
  stock purchase, 338
  tax-free acquisition of stock for voting stock
      (B reorganization), 341
  tax-free forward merger (A reorganization),
      340
  tax-free forward triangular merger, 341
  taxable forward merger, 339
  taxable forward subsidiary merger, 340
  taxable reverse merger, 339
TRASOPs, 423
Treadway Companies, Inc. v. Care Corp., 776,
    971, 992
Treaty shopping, 876, 888
Trended analyses, 47

Tsai, Jerry, 15
Turner, Ted, 919
Turns-driven operations, 29
Tweed, William "Boss," 910
20-day figure, 79
Two-step transactions, 264, 727–729
Two-tier offer, 727
Tyco Industries, 394

U.S. net equity, 886
Unionized companies, 436–438
Unsolicited bid (*see* Takeover bids)
Upstreaming, 169, 170
USRPHC, 889–891
USRPIs, 889, 890
USX v. Marathon, 727
Utility function, 83, 84

Valuation, 79–98
    comparable net worth to market value method,
      95, 96
    discounted cash flow (DCF) method, 96–98
    example, 123–135
    historical figures, 87
    internal rate of return (IRR) method, 93, 94
    investment (average rate of return) method, 92,
      93
    market value method, 94, 95
    payback method, 93
    replacement value method, 92
    risk, 83–87
    rules of thumb, 83
Van Gorkom, 752, 993
Variant method, 115
Venkatachari, Dilip, 660
Vertical backward integration, 23–25
Vertical forward integration, 24
Vertical integration, 23, 24
Vertical ROI analysis, 24
Volunteers, 55

Voting agreements, 499

Wall Street rule, 52
Wall Street Transcript, 40
Ward, Aaron Montgomery, 909
Warranties (*see* Representations and warranties)
Warrants:
    junk bonds, 194
    seller takeback financing, 210
Weill, Sandford, 15
Weiser-Pratt, Guy, 55
Weston, J. Fred, 828
Wheel of opportunity/fit chart (*see* WOFC
    process)
Whistle-blowers, 438
White knight, 787
White squires, 787
Whyncha processes, 14
Wilkes, Robert M., 772
Williams Act, 724
Winans, R. Foster, 767
Wire transfers, 622–625
WOFC process, 20–32
    basic strategic modes, 22–25
    case study, 927–968
    Delphi process, 30, 31
    discovery process, 26
    final output, 32
    fit chart, 27, 28
    fit chart variables, 28–30
    general phases, 20–22
    how it works, 22
    identifying sell-offs, 32
    ranking of opportunities, 31, 32
    supplements/complements, 27, 28
Working capital debt, 151, 152
Workouts, 699–702
Wrongful termination, 360, 680

Yuppy Five, 772

Stanley Foster Reed teaches advanced management courses as Entrepreneur in Residence at the College of Charleston. An accomplished author, Mr. Reed has been a merger consultant to numerous global businesses, including Allied Chemical, Gillette, Schering Plough, and Seiko Watch. He is the founder of a number of successful businesses in publishing, high-tech research, and consulting, and is founding editor and publisher of *Mergers & Acquisitions* and *Directors & Boards* magazines.

    Alexandra Reed Lajoux is president of Alexis & Company, a research and communications firm. She is editor of *Director's Monthly*, the official newsletter of the National Association of Corporate directors, and is author of *The Art Of M&A Integration*. Her work has appeared in *International Business, Los Angeles Times, M&A Today, Mergers & Acquisitions, Trustee,* and numerous other publications. The former editor of *Mergers & Acquisitions*, Dr. Lajoux has two decades of experience speaking and writing about M&A.